MANAGERIAL ACCOUNTING
Concepts for Planning, Control, Decision Making

FIFTH CANADIAN EDITION

RAY H. GARRISON, D.B.A., CPA
Professor Emeritus
Brigham Young University

ERIC W. NOREEN, PH.D., CMA
University of Washington
and
INSEAD

G. R. (DICK) CHESLEY, PH.D.
Saint Mary's University

RAYMOND F. CARROLL, PH.D., FCGA
Dalhousie University

McGraw-Hill Ryerson

Toronto   Montréal   Boston   Burr Ridge, IL   Dubuque, IA   Madison, WI   New York
San Francisco   St. Louis   Bangkok   Bogotá   Caracas   Kuala Lumpur   Lisbon
London   Madrid   Mexico City   Milan   New Delhi   Santiago   Seoul   Singapore
Sydney   Taipei

McGraw-Hill
Ryerson Limited

*A Subsidiary of The **McGraw-Hill** Companies*

MANAGERIAL ACCOUNTING
Concepts for Planning, Control, Decision Making
Fifth Canadian Edition

Copyright © 2001, 1999 by McGraw-Hill Ryerson Limited, a Subsidiary of The McGraw-Hill Companies. Copyright © 2000, 1997, 1994, 1988, 1985, 1982, 1979, 1976, by The McGraw-Hill Companies, Inc. All rights reserved. No part of this publication may be reproduced or transmitted in any form or by any means, or stored in a data base or retrieval system, without the prior written permission of McGraw-Hill Ryerson Limited, or in the case of photocopying or other reprographic copying, a licence from CANCOPY (the Canadian Copyright Licensing Agency), 6 Adelaide Street East, Suite 900, Toronto, Ontario, M5C 1H6

ISBN: 0-07-087111-6

1 2 3 4 5 6 7 8 9 10 TCP 0 9 8 7 6 5 4 3 2 1

Printed and bound in Canada.

Care has been taken to trace ownership of copyright material contained in this text; however, the publisher will welcome any information that enables them to rectify any reference or credit for subsequent editions.

Vice President and Editorial Director: *Pat Ferrier*
Senior Sponsoring Editor: *Nicole Lukach*
Developmental Editor: *Katherine Goodes*
Copy Editor: *Shirley Corriveau*
Production Coordinator: *Madeleine Harrington*
Senior Marketing Manager: *Jeff MacLean*
Page Layout: *GAC/Indy*
Cover Design: *Dianna Little*
Cover Image Credit: *Dave Madison/Stone*
Printer: *Transcontinental Printing*

Canadian Cataloguing in Publication Data

Managerial accounting: concepts for planning, control, decision making

Includes index

ISBN 0-07-087111-6

Managerial accounting.   I. Garrison, Ray H.

HF5657.4.M382000   658.15′11   C00-931962-X

Photo credits: page 160, © Greenlar/The Image Works; page 173, © Jeff Greenberg/ PhotoEdit; page 769, Jim Pickerell/Stone; page 776, © Joan Baron/The Stock Market; page 842, © Sylvain Coffie/Tony Stone Images

My efforts in this book are dedicated to the late Dr. Brian Emerson, a long time colleague, whose devotion to his students and his colleagues is a continuing inspiration.
GRC

To my wife, Carole for her continued support throughout this project.
RFC

RAY H. GARRISON is *emeritus* Professor of Accounting at Brigham Young University, Provo, Utah. He received his B.S. and M.S. degrees from Brigham Young University and his D.B.A. degree from Indiana University.

As a certified public accountant, Professor Garrison has been involved in management consulting work with both national and regional accounting firms. He has published articles in *The Accounting Review, Management Accounting,* and other professional journals. Innovation in the classroom has earned Professor Garrison the Karl G. Maeser Distinguished Teaching Award from Brigham Young University.

ERIC W. NOREEN is a globe-trotting academic who has held appointments at institutions in the United States, Europe, and Asia. He is currently Professor of Accounting at the University of Washington and Visiting Price Waterhouse Professor of Management Information & Control at INSEAD, an international graduate school of business located in France.

He received his B.A. degree from the University of Washington and MBA and Ph.D. degrees from Stanford University. A Certified Management Accountant, he was awarded a Certificate of Distinguished Performance by the Institute of Certified Management Accountants.

Professor Noreen has served as Associate Editor of *The Accounting Review* and the *Journal of Accounting and Economics.* He has numerous articles in academic journals including: the *Journal of Accounting Research; The Accounting Review;* the *Journal of Accounting and Economics; Accounting Horizons; Accounting, Organizations and Society; Contemporary Accounting Research;* the *Journal of Management Accounting Research;* and the *Review of Accounting Studies.* He is a frequent presenter at workshops and conferences throughout the world.

Professor Noreen teaches management accounting at the undergraduate, masters, and doctoral levels and has won a number of awards from students for his teaching.

G.R. (DICK) CHESLEY is Professor of Accounting at Saint Mary's University in Halifax, Nova Scotia. He is a graduate of Mount Allison University and the Ohio State University with B. Comm., M.A., and Ph.D. degrees. He has served appointments at Dalhousie University, the University of Pennsylvania, Lingnam University, Hong Kong Baptist University, and the University of Iowa. His publication credits include articles in the *Accounting Review,* the *Journal of Accounting Research,* the *CA Magazine,* and numerous proceedings and books. In 1996, he was recognized by his peers as Outstanding Accounting Educator Canada. His research interests include probability theory and management accounting practices.

RAYMOND F. CARROLL is currently at Hong Kong Baptist University on leave from Dalhousie University. He teaches a variety of subjects in both financial and managerial accounting at undergraduate and graduate levels. Dr. Carroll has lectured at Xiamen University in China through the CIDA/Dalhousie University linkage program. He has had extensive experience in the community college system and has taught professional accounting and MBA subjects for programs based in Canada, Australia, and the UK. Dr. Carroll is a fellow of the Certified General Accountants' Association of Canada where he has held a variety of posts including chairman of the National Education program, president of CGA-Nova Scotia, and member of the CGA National Executive Committee. He has also served on the Global Initiative Committee of the American Accounting Association and on the Canadian Advisory Committee for international accounting standards.

Brief Contents

Contents

Managerial Accounting provides a foundation for a one-term course in managerial accounting for students who have one or two terms of financial accounting. The book also serves as a reference source for students who wish to be aware of how managers use accounting information within an organization. The focus of the book is on the information needs for three essential management functions: (1) planning operations, (2) controlling activities, and (3) making decisions. The contents of *Managerial Accounting* address how the information can be used to assist managers in these three functions.

This edition of *Managerial Accounting* provides *relevance*, *balance* and a continued tradition of *clarity* of the subject, with coverage of current topics such as the balanced scorecard, activity-based costing and management, and the theory of constraints. The topics present the varied applications of managerial accounting in not-for-profit, retail and wholesale organizations in addition to the traditional manufacturing units both large and small. In addition, the international presentations, both in the text and the problems, provide the type of geographic balance that students need in Canada's global environment.

Organization and Content

New in This Edition

The fifth Canadian edition builds on successes of four previous Canadian editions and the award-winning ninth US edition. Changes reflect the continuing desire for currency, clarity, and educational relevance. While many possible sequences of chapters and topics are possible, the choice presented in the fifth edition represents a sound and effective flow of materials.

The sections on Managerial Accounting in Action and Focus on Current Practice provide realistic contexts for the chapter presentations without cluttering the reading. Maintaining a balance between comprehension and real world relevance is the objective. Colour is used to help make the text more readable and appealing to students.

There are evident changes to content, such as a brief discussion of strategic planning in Chapter 2 which serves as a base for the decision emphasis in subsequent chapters, alterations to activity-based costing in Chapter 8 which better focus on decision information, and further development of the balanced scorecard in Chapter 10. Shareholder value added and emphasis on marketing analysis in Chapter 12 reflect the increasing focus of business practice on these tools. Chapter 17 was altered to reflect the need by management for benchmarking. Material on quality was moved to an appendix to improve the readability of management control in Chapters 8 and 12. Pricing analysis was also placed in an appendix to permit more discussion and to enable a more complete presentation while retaining the typical decision focus of Chapter 13.

Careful reading of the text will find extensions and improvements to nearly every chapter. In addition, problem material and open-ended research questions were revised and altered to reflect both the new materials and the needs of a new edition. Web (WWW) based research questions were extended to conform to new uses for this medium.

Beneficial changes to the text are in response to the analysis of reviewers. Their comments reflect the diversity of Canadian managerial accounting education and the need for flexibility in our presentations. We could not accommodate all of their suggestions because of our overriding needs for clarity, balance, and relevance. Our choices satisfy our perceptions of the needs of all users while retaining the successful traditions and integrity of the text.

Specific Chapter Enhancements

All the chapters have been improved and updated in various ways in this edition. The following table summarizes the most significant of these changes:

Chapter	Major Content Changes in This Edition
Chapter 1	A readable presentation is provided of the forces of change in managerial accounting.
Chapter 2	Exhibits were redesigned to enhance readability. More emphasis has been placed on service companies. A brief discussion of strategic planning was added along with a major case.
Chapter 3	The schedule of cost of goods manufactured has been simplified to make it easier to understand and to construct. Under- or overapplied overhead is allocated among ending inventories and Cost of Goods Sold on the basis of the amount of overhead applied during the period and in terms of the ending balances of the accounts. A new appendix covers the controversy over the choice of the level of activity in the denominator of the predetermined overhead rate.
Chapter 5	This was Chapter 6 in the fourth edition and has been revised and updated.
Chapter 6	This was Chapter 7 in the fourth edition and has been revised and updated.
Chapter 7	This was Chapter 8 in the fourth edition and has been revised and updated.
Chapter 8	This new chapter covers activity-based costing. The ABC material in the text has been completely rewritten to emphasize decision making in both service and manufacturing companies. Spreadsheet templates are presented to illustrate computations. Cost flows are presented in an appendix. A major case was added.
Chapter 9	Technical and behavioural materials were retained with extensions included on business intelligence and modern management changes in budgeting practices. Spreadsheet illustrations are incorporated. Strategic planning, business plans and activity budgeting have been integrated with the traditional material.
Chapter 10	The balanced scorecard has been added to the chapter and integrated with the material on operating performance measures.
Chapter 11	Much greater emphasis has been given to the control of overhead costs in service companies.
Chapter 12	The chapter has been reorganized. The discussion of decentralization now comes first, followed by the segment margin. Life cycle and activity costing have been integrated into the discussion along with customer analysis and activity analysis. RI and EVA have received extended discussion. The transfer pricing appendix has been completely rewritten with a new approach based on the economics of negotiated transfer prices.
Chapter 13	Included is a discussion of the managing of constraints while deemphasizing the technical aspects of linear programming.
Chapter 14	The preference ranking material that was previously in Chapter 15 has been brought forward to Chapter 14.
Chapter 17	Trend analysis now includes time-series plots of data. Benchmarking and extended references are included along with a discussion of productivity.

| Pricing Appendix | A new section stresses the role of the price elasticity of demand in setting prices. The contribution approach to cost-plus pricing has been dropped. The drawbacks of using the absorption costing approach to cost-plus pricing are given more coverage. |
| Quality Appendix | This cost of quality material has been extracted and presented here to streamline other chapters. |

Features

"Focus on Current Practice" boxes contain glimpses of how actual companies use or are affected by concepts discussed in the chapter. Each chapter has a number of boxes, helping a student understand the uses of managerial accounting in actual business practice.

Vignettes known as "Managerial Accounting in Action," involve businesspeople in lifelike settings. They are frequently used to introduce core concepts and stimulate interest. They are essential to, and an integral part of, reading and understanding the text. Real products and services that students can relate to are used as much as possible.

International aspects of management have become increasingly important in recent years due to the emergence of regional and global markets. Discussion and examples that have an international dimension are identified by the icon shown in the margin.

The integration of Microsoft® Excel spreadsheet screen captures help students recognize the importance of spreadsheets as an ABC and budgeting tool.

More than 100 exercises, problems, and cases requiring written solutions (identified by the logo shown in the margin) improve students' written communication skills and address educational concerns.

Ethical issues are included both in assignment material and in the text (and identified by the icon shown in the margin). End-of-chapter assignments allow students an opportunity to consider ethical issues in making managerial decisions.

Clear presentation is always important, and the fifth edition does not ignore function for the sake of aesthetics. A contemporary design offers new real-world chapter openers, redesigned logos in the margins, as well as other engaging features—like boxed material that is integrated within the text and colour-coded chapter openers that reflect the division of chapters into parts. Discussions and examples ranging from ethics to the real world are identified in the margin of the text by an appropriate icon:

World Wide Web
Indicates an end-of-chapter
exercise requiring research on
the Internet.

International
Represents discussions with an
international dimension.

Writing
Represents an exercise that offers
a chance for students to hone
their written communication skills.

**Spreadsheet Application
Template Software (SPATS)**
Identifies selected end-of-chapter
material that may be solved using
these spreadsheet templates.

Ethics
Found in margin whenever ethical
issues are discussed.

Real World
Appears in margin when an actual
company is discussed in the text.

Supplements for the Instructor

The supplements listed here may accompany *Managerial Accounting*. Please contact
your local McGraw-Hill Ryerson representative for details concerning policies, prices
and availability as some restrictions may apply.

SOLUTIONS MANUAL. Prepared by the textbook authors, the Solutions
Manual was also carefully reviewed for accuracy. This supplement contains completely worked-out solutions to all assignment material and a general discussion of the
use of group exercises. In addition, the manual contains suggested course outlines and
a listing of exercises, problems and cases scaled as to difficulty. ISBN 0870985

SOLUTIONS TRANSPARENCIES. These transparencies feature completely worked-out solutions to all assignment material. ISBN 0870977

READY SHOWS (PowerPoint Slides). These slides offer a great visual compli-
ment for your lectures. A complete set of slides, available as a password-protected
downloadable from the Online Learning Centre, covers each objective and key topic
of the text.

INSTRUCTOR'S RESOURCE MANUAL. The Instructor's Resource
Manual contains fairly extensive chapter-by-chapter lecture notes, including learning
objectives, that can serve as a basis for classroom presentations. The lecture notes also
have suggestions for ways of presenting key concepts and ideas. Also included are an
assignment grid, indicating the topics covered by each exercise, problem and case, and
teaching transparency masters. ISBN 0870993

TEST BANK/COMPUTERIZED TEST BANK. The newly revised test
bank contains over 1,200 true/false and multiple-choice questions, computational
problems and essay questions, organized by chapter. ISBN 0870403/ISBN 087039X

Supplements for the Student

STUDY GUIDE.   This study aid provides suggestions for studying chapter material, summarizes the essential points in each chapter, and tests students' knowledge using self-test questions and exercises. The Workbook/Study Guide can be used as an efficient and effective way to prepare for exams. ISBN 0871132

STUDENT CD-ROM.   (Shrink-wrapped free with Managerial Accounting, 5/E) Students can use this software's tutorial feature for added learning opportunities. ISBN 0-07-088032-X

E-SOURCE.   This interactive electronic book offers advance searching, links to supplements, hyperlinks to the world wide web, and much more. Available in the spring of 2001, more information about this product will be posted on the book's web site.

ONLINE LEARNING CENTRE.   The Online Learning Centre offers students such aids as flashcards, online quizzes, internet exercises, key terms, spreadsheet application templates, ready shows, and plant tours. See the text immediately following the preface for details.

ALSO AVAILABLE

VIDEO LIBRARY.   Designed to strengthen your classroom presentations, grab student interest and add variety to your students' learning process, these six volumes of videos include international and service examples to go along with numerous manufacturing examples.

MANAGERIAL ACCOUNTING USING EXCEL 97.   This product incorporates spreadsheets into a managerial accounting course with a four-step process:

- provides students with a brief introduction to the computer;
- introduces students to an Excel spreadsheet and its functions;
- asks students to solve managerial accounting problems using Excel templates; and
- requires students to solve managerial accounting problems by creating a spreadsheet from scratch.

ISBN 0072296291

KJC MANUFACTURERS, INC.   This manual practice set contains a narrative of transactions for a manufacturing company. KJC is a small corporation that manufactures patio furniture. Its records include Sales Journal, a Cash Receipts Journal, a Voucher System, General Ledger and Accounts Receivable Ledger. Estimated completion time is 15 to 20 hours. ISBN 007030744X

RAMBLEWOOD MANUFACTURING, INC.   This computerized practice set simulates the operations of a company that manufactures customized fencing. It can be used to illustrate job-order costing systems with JIT inventory in a realistic setting. The entire simulation requires 10 to 14 hours to complete. Available on 3.5" disk and CD-ROM, Windows platform. ISBN 0072348151

COMMUNICATION FOR ACCOUNTANTS: EFFECTIVE STRATEGIES FOR STUDENTS AND PROFESSIONAL. This brief and inexpensive handbook addresses the need for accountants to communicate effectively through both writing and speaking. ISBN 0070383901

Acknowledgements

Suggestions have been received from many of our colleagues throughout the country who have used previous editions of *Managerial Accounting*. This is vital feedback that we rely on in revising each edition. Each of those who have offered comments and suggestions has our thanks.

The efforts of many people are needed to develop a book and improve it from edition to edition. Among these people are the reviewers who point out areas of concern, cite areas of strength and make recommendations for change. In this regard, the following professors provided in-depth reviews that were enormously helpful in preparing the fifth Canadian edition of *Managerial Accounting*: Robert Harvey, Algonquin University; R.B. Schenk, Bishop's University; Raafat Roubi, Brock University; Hilary Becker, Carleton University; Claudia Parker, Northern Alberta Institute of Technology; Robert F. Madden, St. Francis Xavier University; Carole Bowman, Sheridan College; Anne MacDonald, Simon Fraser University; and Mary Heisz, University of Western Ontario.

We acknowledge the Canadian Institute of Chartered Accountants (CICA), the Certified General Accountants Association of Canada (CGA-Canada) and the Society of Management Accountants (SMA) for permitting us to use questions and solutions from their past years' examinations. Also appreciation is extended to the Institute of Management Accountants for the use of questions and unofficial answers from past Certified Management Accounting (CMA) examinations. Similarly, our appreciation is extended to the American Institute of Certified Public Accountants (CPA) for permission to use selected problems from its examinations. These problems bear the notations CICA, CGA-Canada, SMAC, CMA and CPA, respectively.

Finally, we would like to thank Shirley Corriveau and the McGraw-Hill Ryerson editorial and production staff for their excellent technical support.

G. R. (Dick) Chesley
Raymond F. Carroll

McGraw-Hill Ryerson offers you an online resource that combines the best content with the flexibility and power of the Internet. Organized by chapter, the GARRISON Online Learning Centre (OLC) offers the following features to enhance your learning and understanding of Managerial Accounting.

- Online Quizzing
- Web Links
- Microsoft® PowerPoint® Presentations
- Internet Application Questions

By connecting to the "real world" through the OLC, you will enjoy a dynamic and rich source of current information that will help you get more from your course and improve your chances for success, both in managerial accounting and in the future.

For the Instructor

DOWNLOADABLE SUPPLEMENTS

All key supplements are available, password-protected for instant access!

WEB COMMUNITY

Access to a dynamic brain trust of resources, information, ideas and opportunities coming from faculty! Content includes such topics as current events, Web links, lecture suggestions and more, all discipline-specific! Visit www.communities.mcgrawhill.ca

PAGEOUT

Create your own course Web page for free, quickly and easily. Your professionally designed Web site links directly to OLC material, allows you to post a class syllabus, offers an online gradebook, and much more! Visit www.pageout.net

A New Way to Deliver

For the Student

ONLINE QUIZZING

Do you understand the material? You'll know after taking an Online Quiz! Try the Multiple Choice and True/False questions for each chapter. They're auto-graded with feedback and the option to send results directly to faculty.

WEB LINKS

This section references various Web sites including all company Web sites linked from the text.

MICROSOFT® POWERPOINT® PRESENTATIONS

View and download presentations created for each text. Great for pre-class preparation and post-class review.

INTERNET APPLICATION QUESTIONS

Go online to learn how companies use the Internet in their day-to-day activities. Answer questions based on current organization Web sites and strategies.

Your Internet companion to the most exciting educational tools on the Web!

The Online Learning Centre can be found at:
www.mcgrawhill.ca/college/garrison

EDUCATIONAL CONTENT

Chapter One

Managerial Accounting and the Business Environment

Business Focus

"When Wendelin Wiedeking became chief of Porsche in 1992, the marque seemed destined for the junkyard. Sales that year plunged to 14,362 cars, one-fourth their 1986 peak. Losses mounted to $133 million. Most industry insiders believed that the company couldn't survive on its own . . .

"Change didn't come easily. But Wiedeking's determination overcame Porsche's stubborn traditionalism. He hired two Japanese efficiency experts . . . They immediately tackled a wasteful inventory of parts stacked on shelves all over the three-story Stuttgart factory. One of the experts handed Wiedeking a circular saw. While astounded assembly workers watched, he moved down an aisle and chopped the top half off a row of shelves.

"That was only the start . . . A revamped assembly process will turn out the new 911 [Carrera model] in just 60 hours, vs. 120 for its predecessor. Developing a new model, a process that used to drag on for seven years, now takes just three. Porsche uses 300 parts suppliers, down from nearly 1,000. And a quality-control program has helped reduce the number of defective parts by a factor of 10." As a consequence of these, and other actions, the company's sales have more than doubled to about 34,000 cars, and earnings were about $55 million in the latest fiscal year.

Source: David Woodruff, "Porsche Is Back—And Then Some," Business Week, *September 15, 1997, p. 57. Reprinted with permission of the McGraw-Hill Companies.*

Learning Objectives

After studying Chapter 1, you should be able to:

1 Describe what managers do and why they need accounting information.

2 Identify the major differences and similarities between financial and managerial accounting.

3 Explain the basic characteristics of just-in-time (JIT).

Managerial accounting
The phase of accounting concerned with providing information to managers for use in planning and controlling operations and in decision making.

Financial accounting
The phase of accounting concerned with providing information to shareholders, creditors, and others outside the organization.

Managerial accounting is concerned with providing information to managers—that is, people *inside* an organization who direct and control its operations. In contrast, **financial accounting** is concerned with providing information to shareholders, creditors, and others who are *outside* an organization. Managerial accounting provides the essential data with which organizations are actually run. Financial accounting provides the scorecard by which a company's past performance is judged.

Because it is manager oriented, any study of managerial accounting must be preceded by some understanding of what managers do, the information managers need, and the general business environment. Accordingly, the purpose of this chapter is to briefly examine these subjects.

The Work of Management and the Need for Managerial Accounting Information

Objective 1

Describe what managers do and why they need accounting information.

Planning Selecting a course of action and specifying how the action will be implemented.

Every organization—large and small—has managers. Someone must be responsible for making plans, organizing resources, directing personnel, and controlling operations. This is true of the Canadian Imperial Bank of Commerce, the Canadian Cancer Society, the University of Toronto, the Catholic Church, and the Nova Corporation, as well as the local Green Gables convenience store. In this chapter, we will use a particular organization—Good Vibrations, Inc.—to illustrate the work of management. What we have to say about the management of Good Vibrations, Inc., however, is very general and can be applied to virtually any organization.

Good Vibrations, Inc., runs a chain of retail outlets that sell a full range of music CDs. The chain's stores are concentrated in Pacific Rim cities such as Sydney, Singapore, Hong Kong, Beijing, Tokyo, and Vancouver. The company has found that the best way to generate sales, and income, is to create an exciting shopping environment. Consequently, the company puts a great deal of effort into planning the layout and decor of its stores—which are often quite large and extend over several floors in key downtown locations. Management knows that different types of clientele are attracted to different kinds of music. The international rock section is generally decorated with bold, brightly coloured graphics, and the aisles are purposely narrow to create a crowded feeling much like one would experience at a popular nightclub on Friday night. In contrast, the classical music section is wood-panelled and fully sound insulated, with the rich, spacious feeling of a country club meeting room.

Managers at Good Vibrations, Inc., like managers everywhere, carry out three major activities—*planning, directing and motivating,* and *controlling.* **Planning** involves selecting a course of action and specifying how the action will be imple-

Directing and motivating　Mobilizing people to carry out plans and run routine operations.

Controlling　Ensuring that the plan is actually carried out and is appropriately modified as circumstances change.

mented. **Directing and motivating** involves mobilizing people to carry out plans and run routine operations. **Controlling** involves ensuring that the plan is actually carried out and is appropriately modified as circumstances change. Management accounting information plays a vital role in these basic management activities—but most particularly in the planning and control functions.

Planning

The first step in planning is to identify alternatives and then to select from among the alternatives the one that does the best job of furthering the organization's objectives. The basic objective of Good Vibrations, Inc., is to earn profits for the owners of the company by providing superior service at competitive prices in as many markets as possible. To further this objective, every year top management carefully considers a range of options, or alternatives, for expanding into new geographic markets. This year management is considering opening new stores in Shanghai, Jakarta, and Auckland.

When making this and other choices, management must balance the opportunities against the demands made on the company's resources. Management knows from bitter experience that opening a store in a major new market is a big step that cannot be taken lightly. It requires enormous amounts of time and energy from the company's most experienced, talented, and busy professionals. When the company attempted to open stores in both Beijing and Vancouver in the same year, resources were stretched too thinly. The result was that neither store opened on schedule, and operations in the rest of the company suffered. Therefore, entering new markets is planned very, very carefully.

Among other data, top management looks at the sales volumes, profit margins, and costs of the company's established stores in similar markets. These data, supplied by the management accountant, are combined with projected sales volume data at the proposed new locations to estimate the profits that would be generated by the new stores. In general, virtually all important alternatives considered by management in the planning process have some effect on revenues or costs, and management accounting data are essential in estimating those effects.

After considering all of the alternatives, Good Vibrations, Inc.'s top management decided to open a store in the burgeoning Shanghai market in the third quarter of the year, but to defer opening any other new stores to another year. As soon as this decision was made, detailed plans were drawn up for all parts of the company that would be involved in the Shanghai opening. For example, the Personnel Department's travel budget was increased, since it would be providing extensive on-the-site training to the new personnel hired in Shanghai.

Budget　A detailed plan for the future, usually expressed in formal quantitative terms.

Controller　The manager in charge of the accounting department in an organization.

As in the Personnel Department example, the plans of management are often expressed formally in **budgets,** and the term *budgeting* is applied to generally describe this part of the planning process. Budgets are usually prepared under the direction of the **controller,** who is the manager in charge of the Accounting Department. Typically, budgets are prepared annually and represent management's plans in specific, quantitative terms. In addition to a travel budget, the Personnel Department will be given goals in terms of new hires, courses taught, and detailed breakdowns of expected expenses. Similarly, the manager of each store will be given a target for sales volume, income, expenses, pilferage losses, and employee training. These data will be collected, analyzed, and summarized for management use in the form of budgets prepared by management accountants.

Directing and Motivating

In addition to planning for the future, managers must oversee day-to-day activities and keep the organization functioning smoothly. This requires the ability to motivate and effectively direct people. Managers assign tasks to employees, arbitrate disputes, answer questions, solve on-the-spot problems, and make many small decisions that affect customers and employees. In effect, directing is that part of the managers' work that deals with the routine and the here and now. Managerial accounting data, such as daily sales reports, are often used in this type of day-to-day decision making.

Controlling

Control The process of instituting procedures and then obtaining feedback to ensure that all parts of the organization are functioning effectively and moving toward overall company goals.

In carrying out the **control** function, managers seek to ensure that the plan is being followed. **Feedback,** which signals whether operations are on track, is the key to effective control. In sophisticated organizations this feedback is provided by detailed reports of various types. One of these reports, which compares budgeted to actual results, is called a **performance report.** Performance reports suggest where operations are not proceeding as planned and where some parts of the organization may require additional attention. For example, before the opening of the new Shanghai store in the third quarter of the year, the store's manager will be given sales volume, income, and expense targets for the fourth quarter of the year. As the fourth quarter progresses, periodic reports will be made in which the actual sales volume, income, and expenses are compared to the targets. If the actual results fall below the targets, top management is alerted that the Shanghai store requires more attention. Experienced personnel can be flown in to help the new manager, or top management may come to the conclusion that plans will have to be revised. As we shall see in following chapters, providing this kind of feedback to managers is one of the central purposes of managerial accounting.

Feedback Accounting and other reports that help managers monitor performance and focus on problems and/or opportunities that might otherwise go unnoticed.

Performance report A detailed report comparing budgeted data to actual data.

The End Results of Managers' Activities

As a customer enters one of the Good Vibrations stores, the results of management's planning, directing and motivating, and control activities will be evident in the many details that make the difference between a pleasant and an irritating shopping experience. The store will be clean, fashionably decorated, and logically laid out. Featured artists' videos will be displayed on TV monitors throughout the store, and the background rock music will be loud enough to send older patrons scurrying for the classical music section. Popular CDs will be in stock, and the latest hits will be available for private listening on earphones. Specific titles will be easy to find. Regional music, such as CantoPop in Hong Kong, will be prominently featured. Checkout clerks will be alert, friendly, and efficient. In short, what the customer experiences doesn't simply happen; it is the result of the efforts of managers who must visualize and fit together the processes that are needed to get the job done.

Planning and control cycle The flow of management activities through planning, directing and motivating, and controlling, and then back to planning again.

The Planning and Control Cycle

The work of management can be summarized in a model such as the one shown in Exhibit 1–1. The model, which depicts the **planning and control cycle,** illustrates the

Exhibit 1–1   The Planning and Control Cycle

smooth flow of management activities from planning through directing and motivating, controlling, and then back to planning again. All of these activities involve decision making, so it is depicted as the hub around which the other activities revolve.

Comparison of Financial and Managerial Accounting

Objective 2

Identify the major differences and similarities between financial and managerial accounting.

Financial accounting reports are prepared for the use of external parties such as shareholders and creditors, whereas managerial accounting reports are prepared for managers inside the organization. This contrast in basic orientation results in a number of major differences between financial and managerial accounting, even though both financial and managerial accounting rely on the same underlying financial data. These differences are summarized in Exhibit 1–2.

As shown in Exhibit 1–2, in addition to the difference in who the reports are prepared for, financial and managerial accounting also differ in their emphasis between the past and the future, in the type of data provided to users, and in several other ways. These differences are discussed in the following paragraphs.

Exhibit 1–2   Comparison of Financial and Managerial Accounting

Financial Accounting	Managerial Accounting
• Reports to those outside the organization: Owners, Lenders, Tax authorities, Regulators	• Reports to those inside the organization for: Planning, Directing and motivating, Controlling, Performance evaluation
• Emphasis is on summaries of financial consequences of past activities.	• Emphasis is on decisions affecting the future.
• Objectivity and verifiability of data are emphasized.	• Relevance and flexibility of data are emphasized.
• Precision of information is required.	• Timeliness of information is required.
• Only summarized data for the entire organization are prepared.	• Detailed segment reports about departments, products, customers, and employees are prepared.
• Must follow GAAP.	• Need not follow GAAP.
• Mandatory for external reports.	• Not mandatory.

Accounting
• Recording
• Estimating
• Organizing
• Summarizing
Financial Data

Emphasis on the Future

Since *planning* is such an important part of the manager's job, managerial accounting has a strong future orientation. In contrast, financial accounting primarily provides summaries of past financial transactions. These summaries may be useful in planning, but only to a point. The difficulty with summaries of the past is that the future is not simply a reflection of what has happened in the past. Changes are constantly taking place in economic conditions, customer needs and desires, competitive conditions, and so on. All of these changes demand that the manager's planning be based in large part on estimates of what will happen rather than on summaries of what has already happened.

Relevance and Flexibility of Data

Financial accounting data are expected to be objective and verifiable. However, for internal uses the manager wants information that is relevant even if it is not completely objective or verifiable. By relevant, we mean *appropriate for the problem at hand.* For example, it is difficult to verify estimated sales volumes for a proposed new store at Good Vibrations, Inc., but this is exactly the type of information that is most useful to managers in their decision making. The managerial accounting information system should be flexible enough to provide whatever data are relevant for a particular decision.

Less Emphasis on Precision

Timeliness is often more important than precision to managers. If a decision must be made, a manager would much rather have a good estimate now than wait a week for a more precise answer. A decision involving tens of millions of dollars does not have to be based on estimates that are precise down to the penny, or even to the dollar. Estimates that are accurate to the nearest million dollars may be precise enough to make a good decision. Since precision is costly in terms of both time and resources, managerial accounting places less emphasis on precision than does financial accounting. In addition, managerial accounting places considerable weight on nonmonetary data. For example, information about customer satisfaction is of tremendous importance even though it would be difficult to express such data in a monetary form.

Segments of an Organization

Segment Any part of an organization that can be evaluated independently of other parts and about which the manager seeks financial data. Examples include a product line, a sales territory, a division, or a department.

Financial accounting is primarily concerned with reporting for the company as a whole. By contrast, managerial accounting focuses much more on the parts, or **segments,** of a company. These segments may be product lines, sales territories, divisions, departments, or any other categorization of the company's activities that management finds useful. Financial accounting does require some breakdowns of revenues and costs by major segments in external reports, but this is a secondary emphasis. In managerial accounting, segment reporting is the primary emphasis.

Generally Accepted Accounting Principles (GAAP)

Financial accounting statements prepared for external users must be prepared in accordance with generally accepted accounting principles (GAAP). External users must have some assurance that the reports have been prepared in accordance with some common set of ground rules. These common ground rules enhance comparability and help reduce fraud and misrepresentation, but they do not necessarily lead to the type of reports that would be most useful in internal decision making. For example, GAAP requires that land be stated at its historical cost on financial reports. However, if management is considering moving a store to a new location and then selling the land the store currently sits on, management would like to know the current market value of the land—a vital piece of information that is ignored under GAAP.

Managerial accounting is not bound by generally accepted accounting principles. Managers set their own ground rules concerning the content and form of internal reports. The only constraint is that the expected benefits from using the information should outweigh the costs of collecting, analyzing, and summarizing the data. Nevertheless, as we shall see in subsequent chapters, it is undeniably true that financial reporting requirements have heavily influenced management accounting practice.

Managerial Accounting—Not Mandatory

Financial accounting is mandatory; that is, it must be done. Various outside parties such as the provincial securities commissions and the tax authorities require periodic financial statements. Managerial accounting, on the other hand, is not mandatory. A company is completely free to do as much or as little as it wishes. There are no regulatory bodies or other outside agencies that specify what is to be done, or, for that matter, whether anything is to be done at all. Since managerial accounting is completely optional, the important question is always, "Is the information useful?" rather than, "Is the information required?"

Expanding Role of Managerial Accounting

Managerial accounting has its roots in the industrial revolution of the nineteenth century. During this early period, most firms were tightly controlled by a few owner-managers who borrowed based on personal relationships and their personal assets. Since there were no external shareholders and little unsecured debt, there was little need for elaborate financial reports. In contrast, managerial accounting was relatively sophisticated and provided the essential information needed to manage the early large-scale production of textiles, steel, and other products.[1]

After the turn of the century, financial accounting requirements burgeoned because of new pressures placed on companies by capital markets, creditors, regulatory bodies, and taxation of income. Johnson and Kaplan state that "many firms needed to raise funds from increasingly widespread and detached suppliers of capital. To tap these vast reservoirs of outside capital, firms' managers had to supply audited financial reports. And because outside suppliers of capital relied on audited financial statements, independent accountants had a keen interest in establishing well-defined procedures for corporate financial reporting. The inventory costing procedures adopted by public accountants after the turn of the century had a profound effect on management accounting."[2]

As a consequence, management accountants focused their efforts on ensuring that financial accounting requirements were met and financial reports were released on time. The practice of management accounting stagnated because of this focus until the early part of the century. As product lines expanded and operations became more complex, forward-looking companies such as Du Pont, General Motors, and General Electric saw a renewed need for management-oriented reports that was separate from financial reports.[3] But in most companies, management accounting practices up through the mid-1980s were largely indistinguishable from practices that were common prior to World War I. In recent years, however, new economic forces have led to many important innovations in management accounting. These new practices will be discussed in later chapters.

---

1. A. D. Chandler, *The Visible Hand: The Managerial Revolution in American Business* (Cambridge, MA: Harvard University Press, 1977).
2. H. Thomas Johnson and Robert S. Kaplan, *Relevance Lost: The Rise and Fall of Management Accounting* (Boston, MA: Harvard Business School Press, 1987), pp. 129–30.
3. H. Thomas Johnson, "Management Accounting in an Early Integrated Industrial: E. I. du Pont de Nemours Powder Company, 1903–1912," *Business History Review* (Summer 1975), pp. 186–87.

The Changing Business Environment

The last two decades have been a period of tremendous foment and change in the business environment. Competition in many industries has become worldwide in scope, and the pace of innovation in products and services has accelerated. This has been good news for consumers, since intensified competition has generally led to lower prices, higher quality, and more choices. However, the last two decades have been a period of wrenching change for many businesses and their employees. Many managers have learned that cherished ways of doing business do not work anymore and that major changes must be made in how organizations are managed and in how work gets done. These changes are so great that some observers view them as a second industrial revolution.

This revolution is having a profound effect on the practice of managerial accounting—as we will see throughout the rest of the text. First, however, it is necessary to have an appreciation of the ways in which organizations are transforming themselves to become more competitive. Since the early 1980s, many companies have gone through several waves of improvement programs, starting with just-in-time (JIT) and passing on to total quality management (TQM), process reengineering, and various other management programs—including in some companies the theory of constraints (TOC). When properly implemented, these improvement programs can enhance quality, reduce cost, increase output, eliminate delays in responding to customers, and ultimately increase profits. They have not, however, always been wisely implemented, and there is considerable controversy concerning the ultimate value of each of these programs. Nevertheless, the current business environment cannot be properly understood without an appreciation of what each of these approaches attempts to accomplish. Each is worthy of extended study, but we will discuss them only in the broadest terms. The details are best handled in operations management courses.

Just-in-Time (JIT)

Objective 3

Explain the basic characteristics of just-in-time (JIT).

Just-in-time (JIT)   A production and inventory control system in which materials are purchased and units are produced only as needed to meet actual customer demand.

Raw materials   Materials that are used to make a product.

When companies use the **just-in-time (JIT)** production and inventory control system, they purchase materials and produce units only as needed to meet actual customer demand. In a JIT system, inventories are reduced to the minimum and in some cases are zero. For example, firms such as Maax Inc., a Quebec maker of bathtubs and showers, have been able to reduce costs significantly by reducing inventory levels, and Canadian manufacturers have reduced their level of raw materials, goods in process and finished goods from $2.20 to $1.30 for every dollar of shipments.[4]

The JIT approach can be used in both merchandising and manufacturing companies. It has the most profound effects, however, on the operations of manufacturing companies, which maintain three classes of inventories—*raw materials, work (goods) in process,* and *finished goods*. **Raw materials** are the materials that are used to make a product. **Work in process** inventories consist of units of product that are only partially complete and will require further work before they are ready for sale to a customer. **Finished goods** inventories consist of units of product that have been completed but have not yet been sold to customers.

Traditionally, manufacturing companies have maintained large amounts of all three kinds of inventories to act as *buffers* so that operations can proceed smoothly even if there are unanticipated disruptions. Raw materials inventories provide insurance in case suppliers are late with deliveries. Work in process inventories are maintained in case a workstation is unable to operate due to a breakdown or other reason. Finished goods inventories are maintained to accommodate unanticipated fluctuations in demand.

While these inventories provide buffers against unforeseen events, they have a cost. In addition to the money tied up in the inventory, experts argue that the presence

---

4. Allan Freeman, "Why Firms Avoid Taking Inventory," *The Globe and Mail*, December 12, 1994, p. B1.

Work in process Units of product that are only partially complete and will require further work before they are ready for sale to a customer.

Finished goods Units of product that have been completed but have not yet been sold to customers.

of inventories encourages inefficient and sloppy work, results in too many defects, and dramatically increases the amount of time required to complete a product. None of this is obvious—if it were, companies would have long ago reduced their inventories. Managers at Toyota are credited with the insight that large inventories often create more problems than they solve, and Toyota pioneered the JIT approach.

THE JIT CONCEPT   Under ideal conditions, a company operating a just-in-time system would purchase *only* enough materials each day to meet that day's needs. Moreover, the company would have no goods still in process at the end of the day, and all goods completed during the day would have been shipped immediately to customers. As this sequence suggests, "just-in-time" means that raw materials are received *just in time* to go into production, manufactured parts are completed *just in time* to be assembled into products, and products are completed *just in time* to be shipped to customers.

Although few companies have been able to reach this ideal, many companies have been able to reduce inventories to only a fraction of their previous levels. The result has been a substantial reduction in ordering and warehousing costs, and much more effective operations.

How does a company avoid a buildup of parts and materials at various workstations and still ensure a smooth flow of goods when JIT is in use? In a JIT environment, the flow of goods is controlled by a *pull* approach. The pull approach can be explained as follows: At the final assembly stage, a signal is sent to the preceding workstation as to the exact amount of parts and materials that will be needed *over the next few hours* to assemble products to fill customer orders, and *only* that amount of parts and materials is provided. The same signal is sent back through each preceding workstation so that a smooth flow of parts and materials is maintained with no appreciable inventory buildup at any point. Thus, all workstations respond to the pull exerted by the final assembly stage, which in turn responds to customer orders. As one worker explained, "Under a JIT system you don't produce anything, anywhere, for anybody unless they *ask* for it somewhere *down*stream. Inventories are an evil that we're taught to avoid." The pull approach is illustrated in Exhibit 1–3.

The pull approach described above can be contrasted to the *push* approach used in conventional manufacturing systems. In conventional systems, when a workstation completes its work, the partially completed goods are "pushed" forward to the next workstation regardless of whether that workstation is ready to receive them. The result is an unintentional stockpiling of partially completed goods that may not be completed for days or even weeks. This ties up funds and also results in operating inefficiencies. For one thing, it becomes very difficult to keep track of where everything is when so much is scattered all over the factory floor.

Another characteristic of conventional manufacturing systems is an emphasis on "keeping everyone busy" as an end in itself. This inevitably leads to excess inventories—particularly work in process inventories—for reasons that will be more fully

Exhibit 1–3   JIT Pull Approach to the Flow of Goods

explored in a later section on the theory of constraints. In JIT, the traditional emphasis on keeping everyone busy is abandoned in favour of producing only what customers actually want—even if that means some workers are idle.

Focus on Current Practice

McDonald's new just-in-time (JIT) system called "Made for You" is "plainly an answer to the charge that made-to-order food from rivals such as Burger King and Wendy's tastes fresher." McDonald's franchisees often cook burgers and other food in batches which then sit around, losing flavour and freshness. The objective of the new system, which costs about $25,000 to install in a restaurant, is to serve each customer with the freshest food possible within 90 seconds of ordering. To design the new "Made for You" system, McDonald's carefully studied JIT manufacturing systems like Toyota's.

"The moment a Big Mac is ordered, a computer screen in the kitchen tells one of the workers to start assembling it. Meanwhile, by monitoring the flow of orders, the computer also estimates future demand, indicating when to start cooking things (like fries) that cannot be squeezed into the 90-second slot.

" 'Made for You' should help cut stock costs, and there may be some staff savings. But the proof of the pudding will, so to speak, be in the burgers."[5] ■

JIT Purchasing　　Any organization with inventories—retail, wholesale, distribution, service, or manufacturing—can use *JIT purchasing*. Under JIT purchasing:

1. *A company relies on a few ultrareliable suppliers.* IBM, for example, eliminated 95% of the suppliers from one of its plants, reducing the number from 640 to only 32. Rather than soliciting bids from suppliers each year and going with the low bidder, the dependable suppliers are rewarded with long-term contracts.
2. *Suppliers make frequent deliveries in small lots just before the goods are needed.* Rather than deliver a week's (or a month's) supply of an item at one time, suppliers must be willing to make deliveries as often as several times a day, and in the exact quantities specified by the buyer. Undependable suppliers who do not meet delivery schedules are weeded out. Dependability is essential, since a JIT system is highly vulnerable to any interruption in supply. If a single part is unavailable, the entire assembly operation may have to be shut down. Or, in the case of a merchandising company, if the supplier allows inventories to get down to zero, customers may be turned away unsatisfied.
3. *Suppliers must deliver defect-free goods.* Because of the vulnerability of a JIT system to disruptions, defects cannot be tolerated. Indeed, suppliers must become so reliable that incoming goods do not have to be inspected.

Companies that adopt JIT purchasing often realize substantial savings from streamlined operations. Note that a company does not have to eliminate all inventories to use the JIT approach. Indeed, retail organizations must maintain some inventories or they could not operate. But the amount of time a product spends on a shelf or in a warehouse can be greatly reduced.

KEY ELEMENTS IN A JIT SYSTEM　　In addition to JIT purchasing, four key elements are usually required for the successful operation of a JIT manufacturing system. These elements include improving the plant layout, reducing the setup time needed for production runs, striving for zero defects, and developing a flexible workforce.

---

5. "McJITers," *The Economist*, April 4, 1998, p. 70.

Improving Plant Layout   To properly implement JIT, a company typically must improve the manufacturing flow lines in its plant. A *flow line* is the physical path taken by a product as it moves through the manufacturing process as it is transformed from raw materials to completed goods.

Traditionally, companies have designed their plant floors so that similar machines are grouped together. Such a functional layout results in all drill presses in one place, all lathes in another place, and so forth. This approach to plant layout requires that work in process be moved from one group of machines to another—frequently across the plant or even to another building. The result is extensive material-handling costs, large work in process inventories, and unnecessary delays.

In a JIT system, all machines needed to make a particular product are often brought together in one location. This approach to plant layout creates an individual "mini" factory for each separate product, frequently referred to as a *focused factory* or as a "factory within a factory." The flow line for a product can be straight, as shown earlier in Exhibit 1–3, or it can be in a U-shaped configuration as shown in Exhibit 1–4. The key point is that all machines in a product flow line are tightly grouped together so that partially completed units are not shifted from place to place all over the factory. *Manufacturing cells* are also often part of a JIT product flow line. In a *cell,* a single worker operates several machines. An example of a cell is illustrated in Exhibit 1–5.

The focused factory approach allows workers to focus all of their efforts on a product from start to finish and minimizes handling and moving. After one large manufacturing company rearranged its plant layout and organized its products into individual flow lines, the company determined that the distance travelled by one product had been decreased from 3 kilometres to just 300 metres. Apart from reductions in handling, this more compact layout makes it much easier to keep track of where a particular job is in the production process.

As the above discussion illustrates, an improved plant layout can dramatically increase *throughput,* which is the total volume of production through a facility during a period, and it can dramatically reduce **throughput time** (also known as **cycle time**), which is the time required to make a product.

Reduced Setup Time   **Setups** involve activities—such as moving materials, changing machine settings, setting up equipment, and running tests—that must be performed whenever production is switched over from making one type of item to

---

Throughput time   The time required to make a completed unit of product starting with raw materials. Throughput time is also known as cycle time.

Cycle time   Same as *Throughput time.*

Setup   Activities that must be performed whenever production is switched over from making one type of item to another.

Exhibit 1–4   Plant Layout in a JIT System

Exhibit 1–5   Example
of a Manufacturing Cell

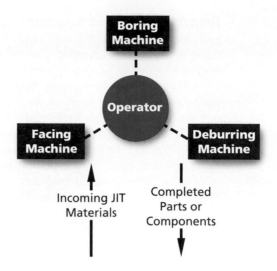

another. For example, it may not be a simple matter to switch over from making one size of brass screws to making another size of brass screws on a manually controlled milling machine. Many preparatory steps must be performed, and these steps can take hours. Because of the time and expense involved in such setups, many managers believe setups should be avoided and therefore items should be produced in large batches. For example, one batch of 400 units requires only one setup, whereas four batches of 100 units each would require four setups. The problem with big batches is that they create large amounts of inventory that must wait for days, weeks, or even months before further processing at the next workstation or before they are sold. The importance of setups is evident to every reader who must travel to attend classes. The issue of scheduling classes to minimize the travel (setup) for these classes is a common consideration.

One advantage of a dedicated flow line, such as the one illustrated in Exhibit 1–4, is that it requires fewer setups. If equipment is dedicated to a single product, setups are largely eliminated and the product can be produced in any batch size desired. Even when dedicated flow lines are not used, it is often possible to slash setup time by using techniques such as *single-minute-exchange-of-dies*. A die is a device used for cutting out, forming, or stamping material. For example, a die is used to produce the stamped metal door panels on an automobile. A die must be changed when it wears out or when production is switched to a different product. This changeover can be time-consuming. The goal with *single-minute-exchange-of-dies* is to reduce the amount of time required to change a die to a minute or less. This can be done by simple techniques such as doing as much of the changeover work in advance as possible rather than waiting until production is shut down.[6] When such techniques are followed, batch sizes can be very small.

Smaller batches reduce the level of inventories, make it easier to respond quickly to the market, reduce cycle times, and generally make it much easier to spot manufacturing problems before they result in a large number of defective units.

Zero Defects and JIT   Defective units create big problems in a JIT environment. If a completed order contains a defective unit, the company must ship the order with less than the promised quantity or it must restart the whole production process to make just one unit. At minimum, this creates a delay in shipping the order and may generate a ripple effect that delays other orders. For this and other reasons, defects

6. Shigeo Shingo and Alan Robinson, *Modern Approaches to Manufacturing Improvement: The Shingo System* (Cambridge, MA: Productivity Press, 1990).

cannot be tolerated in a JIT system. Companies that are deeply involved in JIT tend to become zealously committed to a goal of *zero defects*. Even though it may be next to impossible to attain the zero defect goal, companies have found that they can come very close. For example, many companies now measure defects in terms of the number of defects per *million* units of product.

In a traditional company, parts and materials are inspected for defects when they are received from suppliers, and quality inspectors inspect units as they progress along the production line. In a JIT system, the company's suppliers are responsible for the quality of incoming parts and materials. And instead of using quality inspectors, the company's production workers are directly responsible for spotting defective units. A worker who discovers a defect is supposed to punch an alarm button that stops the production flow line and sets off flashing lights. Supervisors and other workers then descend on the workstation to determine the cause of the defect and correct it before any further defective units are produced. This procedure ensures that problems are quickly identified and corrected, but it does require that defects are rare—otherwise there would be constant disruptions to the production process.

Flexible Workforce Workers on a JIT line must be multiskilled and flexible. Workers are often expected to operate all of the equipment on a JIT product flow line. Moreover, workers are expected to perform minor repairs and do maintenance work when they would otherwise be idle. In contrast, on a conventional assembly line a worker performs a single task all the time every day and all maintenance work is done by a specialized maintenance crew.

BENEFITS OF A JIT SYSTEM Many companies—large and small—have employed JIT with great success. Among the major companies using JIT are Ford, Magna, and Nortel. The main benefits of JIT are the following:

1. Working capital is bolstered by the recovery of funds that were tied up in inventories.
2. Areas previously used to store inventories are made available for other, more productive uses.
3. Throughput time is reduced, resulting in greater potential output and quicker response to customers.
4. Defect rates are reduced, resulting in less waste and greater customer satisfaction.

As a result of benefits such as those cited above, more companies are embracing JIT each year. Most companies find, however, that simply reducing inventories is not enough. To remain competitive in an ever changing and ever more competitive business environment, companies must strive for *continuous improvement*.

Total Quality Management (TQM)

The most popular approach to continuous improvement is known as *total quality management*. There are two major characteristics of **total quality management (TQM):** (1) a focus on serving customers and (2) systematic problem solving using teams made up of front-line workers. A variety of specific tools are available to aid teams in their problem solving. One of these tools, **benchmarking,** involves studying organizations that are among the best in the world at performing a particular task. For example, when Xerox wanted to improve its procedures for filling customer orders, it studied how the mail-order company L. L. Bean processes its customer orders.

THE PLAN-DO-CHECK-ACT CYCLE Perhaps the most important and pervasive TQM problem-solving tool is the *plan-do-check-act (PDCA) cycle*, which is

---

Objective 4

Describe the total quality management (TQM) approach to continuous improvement.

Total quality management (TQM) An approach to continuous improvement that focuses on customers and using teams of front-line workers to systematically identify and solve problems.

Benchmarking A study of organizations that are among the best in the world at performing a particular task.

Exhibit 1–6   The Plan-Do-Check-Act Cycle

Plan-do-check-act (PDCA) cycle   A systematic approach to continuous improvement that applies the scientific method to problem solving.

also referred to as the Deming Wheel.[7] The **plan-do-check-act cycle** is a systematic, fact-based approach to continuous improvement. The basic elements of the PDCA cycle are illustrated in Exhibit 1–6. The PDCA cycle applies the scientific method to problem solving. In the Plan phase, the problem-solving team analyzes data to identify possible causes for the problem and then proposes a solution. In the Do phase, an experiment is conducted. In the Check phase, the results of the experiment are analyzed. And in the Act phase, if the results of the experiment are favourable, the plan is implemented. If the results of the experiment are not favourable, the team goes back to the original data and starts all over again.

AN EXAMPLE OF TQM IN PRACTICE   Sterling Chemicals, Inc., a producer of basic industrial chemicals, provides a good example of the use of TQM.[8] Among many other problems, the company had been plagued by pump failures. In one year, a particular type of pump had failed 22 times at an average cost of about $10,000 per failure. The company first tried to solve the problem using a traditional, non-TQM approach. A committee of "experts"—in this case engineers and manufacturing supervisors—was appointed to solve the problem. A manager at Sterling Chemicals describes the results:

> This team immediately concluded that each of the 22 pump failures . . . was due to a special or one-of-a-kind cause. There was some finger pointing by team members trying to assign blame. Maintenance engineers claimed that production personnel didn't know how to operate the pumps, and production supervisors blamed maintenance people for poor repair work.

---

7. Dr. W. Edwards Deming, a pioneer in TQM, introduced many of the elements of TQM to Japanese industry after World War II. TQM was further refined and developed at Japanese companies such as Toyota.

8. The information about Sterling Chemicals in this section was taken from Karen Hopper Wruck and Michael C. Jensen, "Science, Specific Knowledge, and Total Quality Management," *Journal of Accounting and Economics* 18 (1994), pp. 247–87. The quotations are from pages 260 and 261 of this article and are used with permission from Elsevier Science.

One year later, a TQM team was formed to tackle the same pump failure problem. The team consisted primarily of hourly workers with hands-on experience working with the pumps. A Sterling Chemicals manager describes what happened:

> Based on their knowledge and the data they had collected, the team brainstormed and listed 57 theories that potentially explained the high pump failure rates. The team reviewed and edited the brainstorming list, testing each theory against the data. Through this process, they reduced the brainstorming list to four potential causes of failure: i) the pump seal installation procedure, ii) pump suction pressure, iii) excessive pump vibration, and iv) missing or broken equipment upstream from the pump.
>
> They then experimented to determine which of these causes were important determinants of pump failure. Testing the pump suction theory rejected it as a cause of failure. The broken or missing equipment theory was eliminated through inspection. Since testing the two remaining theories required making changes and observing the results of those changes over time, the team developed recommendations to address [them] both . . . The recommendations were implemented . . . Since then we have had no pump failures.

Notice how the plan-do-check-act cycle was used to solve this pump failure problem. Instead of bickering over who was responsible for the problem, the team began by collecting data. They then hypothesized a number of possible causes for the problem, and these hypotheses were checked against the data. Perhaps the most important feature of TQM is that "it improves productivity by encouraging the use of science in decision-making and discouraging counter-productive defensive behavior."[9]

TQM IS WIDELY USED Thousands of organizations have been involved in TQM and similar programs. Some of the more well-known companies are American Express, Corning, Dun & Bradstreet, Ericsson of Sweden, Federal Express, General Electric, Hydro Quebec, IBM, Johnson & Johnson, KLM Royal Dutch Airlines, 3M, Milliken & Company, Motorola, Nortel, Phillips of the Netherlands, Ritz Carlton Hotel, and Xerox. As this list illustrates, TQM is international in scope and is not confined to manufacturing. Indeed, a survey by the American Hospital Association of 3,300 hospitals found that 69% have launched quality-improvement programs. For example, Intermountain Healthcare's LDS Hospital in Salt Lake City is using total quality management techniques to reduce infection rates among surgery patients and the toxic side effects of chemotherapy.[10]

An important element of TQM is its focus on the customer. The accounting and consulting firm KPMG Peat Marwick periodically surveys its customers' satisfaction with its services. The firm's CEO points out that it costs four times as much to gain a new customer as to keep an old customer, and the most satisfied customers are generally the most profitable customers for the firm. "For each complaint that you hear, there are fifty you don't hear. If you don't monitor clients' satisfaction, you may find out about their dissatisfaction as they walk out the door."[11]

In summary, TQM provides tools and techniques for continuous improvement based on facts and analysis; and if properly implemented, it avoids counterproductive organizational infighting.

Process Reengineering

Objective 5

Explain the basic ideas underlying process reengineering.

Process reengineering is a more radical approach to improvement than TQM. Instead of tweaking the existing system in a series of incremental improvements, in **process reengineering** a *business process* is diagrammed in detail, questioned, and then completely redesigned in order to eliminate unnecessary steps, to reduce opportunities for

Process reengineering
An approach to improvement that involves completely redesigning business processes in order to eliminate unnecessary steps, reduce errors, and reduce costs.

---

9. Ibid., p. 247.
10. Ron Wilson, "Excising Waste: Health-Care Providers Try Industrial Tactics in U.S. to Cut Costs," *The Wall Street Journal Europe,* November 10, 1993, p. 1, 8.
11. Jon C. Madonna, "A Service Company Measures, Monitors and Improves Quality," *Leadership and Empowerment for Total Quality,* The Conference Board Report No. 992 (New York, 1992), pp. 9–11.

Business process A series of steps that are followed in order to carry out some task in a business.

Non-value-added activity An activity that consumes resources or takes time but that does not add value for which customers are willing to pay.

errors, and to reduce costs. A **business process** is any series of steps that are followed in order to carry out some task in a business. For example, the steps followed to make a large pineapple and Canadian bacon pizza at Godfather's Pizza are a business process. The steps followed by your bank when you deposit a cheque are a business process. While process reengineering is similar in some respects to TQM, its proponents view it as a more sweeping approach to change. One difference is that while TQM emphasizes a team approach involving people who work directly in the processes, process reengineering is more likely to be imposed from above and to use outside consultants.

Process reengineering focuses on *simplification* and *elimination of wasted effort*. A central idea of process reengineering is that *all activities that do not add value to a product or service should be eliminated*. Activities that do not add value to a product or service that customers are willing to pay for are known as **non-value-added activities.** For example, moving large batches of work in process from one workstation to another is a non-value-added activity that can be eliminated by redesigning the factory layout as discussed earlier in the section on JIT. To some degree, JIT involves process reengineering as does TQM. These management approaches often overlap.[12]

Process reengineering has been used by many companies to deal with a wide variety of problems. For example, the EMI Records Group was having difficulty filling orders for its most popular CDs. Retailers and recording stars were rebelling—it took the company as much as 20 days to deliver a big order for a hit CD, and then nearly 20% of the order would be missing. Small, incremental improvements would not have been adequate, so the company reengineered its entire distribution process with dramatic effects on on-time delivery and order fill rates.[13] Another example of reengineering is provided by Petro-Canada which is continually improving its refining operations, maintenance procedures, and management of supply in its strategy to be a low-cost producer of quality refined petroleum products and services. Petro-Canada's 1996 annual report reveals that the refining segment garnered the full benefit of a reengineering initiative, resulting in estimated annual before-tax expense and cost of sale savings of $58 million.

AN EXAMPLE OF PROCESS REENGINEERING Racing Strollers, Inc., of Yakima, Washington, provides an interesting illustration of process reengineering at work. The company originated the three-wheeled stroller for joggers in 1984.[14] While the company was still the market leader, there was growing concern about losing ground to competitors—some of whom were selling strollers for half the price charged by Racing Strollers. Mary Baechler, the president of Racing Strollers, felt that a radical approach such as process reengineering was required to keep Racing Strollers competitive.

Mary Baechler describes the results of using process reengineering on a very simple task—receiving orders over the fax machine:

> Take faxes. Pretty simple, right? Not at our place! We had 15 steps just to get a fax from the fax machine to the computers, where an order would be entered into our accounting program. (Laugh all you want, but you probably do something similar at your place.) A fax would come in. We'd log it into a fax book. (Someone once told us to do that for legal reasons.) A copy of each fax would be saved for me. (Someone once told me I should glance at all faxes.) It all added up to those 15 steps. Only after a lot of work did we reduce the number to 4.

---

12. Activity-based costing and activity-based management, both of which are discussed in Chapter 8, can be helpful in identifying areas in the company that could benefit from process reengineering.
13. Glenn Rifkin, "EMI: Technology Brings the Music Giant a Whole New Spin," *Forbes ASAP,* February 27, 1995, pp. 32–38.
14. The information in this section about Racing Strollers, Inc., was taken from an article by Mary Baechler. Reprinted with permission of *Inc.* magazine, Goldhirsh Group, Inc., 38 Commercial Wharf, Boston, MA, "First Steps," Mary Baechler, May 1995. Reproduced by permission of the publisher via Copyright Clearance Center, Inc.

> That was just one area, and it's typical of what we found throughout the company. If you were to look at all those steps for a fax, every one originally had a purpose. The process was very much like a tribal superstition, though, since the original reason for each step had disappeared long ago. What was even worse was that no one could remember who started many of the steps. I had no idea why we were doing them, and everybody else thought they were what I wanted done!

Note that Racing Strollers is a comparatively young company. The situation is typically much worse at older companies—a step may have been introduced into a process many years ago to handle a problem that has long since disappeared and no one can remember.

THE PROBLEM OF EMPLOYEE MORALE A recurrent problem in process reengineering is employee resistance. The cause of much of this resistance is the fear that people may lose their jobs. Workers reason that if process reengineering succeeds in eliminating non-value-added activities, there will be less work to do and management may be tempted to reduce the payroll. Process reengineering, if carried out insensitively and without regard to such fears, can undermine morale and will ultimately fail to improve the bottom line (i.e., income). As with other improvement projects, employees must be convinced that the end result of the improvement will be more secure, rather than less secure, jobs. Real improvement can have this effect if management uses the improvement to generate more business rather than to cut the workforce. If by improving processes the company is able to produce a better product at lower cost, the company will have the competitive strength to prosper. And a prosperous company is a much more secure employer than a company that is in trouble.

The Theory of Constraints (TOC)

Objective 6

Describe how the theory of constraints (TOC) can be used to focus improvement efforts.

Constraint Anything that prevents an organization or individual from getting more of what it wants.

Theory of constraints (TOC) A management approach that emphasizes the importance of managing constraints.

A **constraint** is anything that prevents you from getting more of what you want. Every individual and every organization faces at least one constraint, so it is not difficult to find examples of constraints. You may not have enough time to study thoroughly for every subject *and* to go out with your friends on the weekend, so time is your constraint. Air Canada has only a limited number of loading gates available at its busy Toronto hub, so its constraint is loading gates. Banff Resorts has only a limited amount of land to develop as homesites and commercial lots at its ski areas, so its constraint is land.

Since a constraint prevents you from getting more of what you want, the **theory of constraints (TOC)** maintains that effectively managing the constraint is a key to success. For example, Air Canada should concentrate on quickly turning around its aircraft on the ground so they do not tie up precious gates. Delays on the ground decrease the number of flights that can be flown out of Toronto and therefore result in lost business.

AN EXAMPLE OF TOC A simple example will be used to illustrate the role of a constraint. ProSport Equipment, Inc., manufactures aluminum tennis rackets on the production flow line that is sketched in Exhibit 1–7. Each workstation has a particular capacity that, in this case, may be stated in terms of the maximum number of rackets processed in a week. For example, the aluminum extruding workstation can extrude enough aluminum each week to build as many as 2,500 tennis rackets.

Suppose the company could sell as many as 2,100 rackets each week. All of the workstations except frame assembly and stringing are capable of producing this many rackets in a week. The capacity in stringing is 2,000 rackets per week, but since the capacity in frame assembly is only 1,800 rackets per week, no more than 1,800 complete tennis rackets can be processed per week. The capacity of frame assembly is the constraint, or *bottleneck*. The capacity (and rate of output) of the entire operation can be no more than the capacity of the bottleneck, which is 1,800 rackets per week.

Exhibit 1–7   A Flowchart of an Aluminum Tennis Racket Production Line

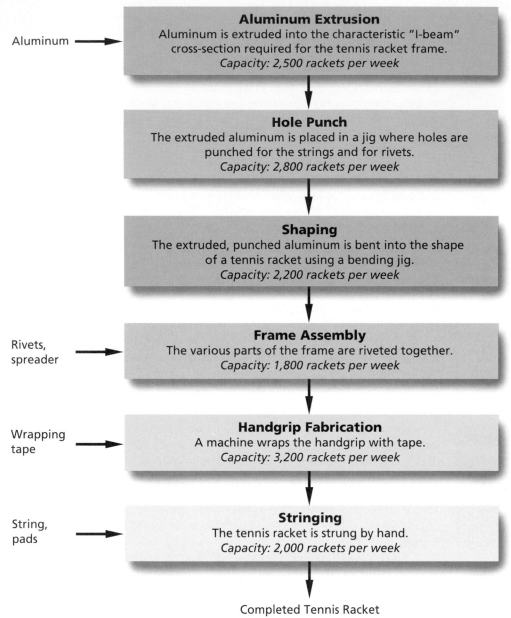

Aluminum →

Aluminum Extrusion
Aluminum is extruded into the characteristic "I-beam"
cross-section required for the tennis racket frame.
Capacity: 2,500 rackets per week

Hole Punch
The extruded aluminum is placed in a jig where holes are
punched for the strings and for rivets.
Capacity: 2,800 rackets per week

Shaping
The extruded, punched aluminum is bent into the shape
of a tennis racket using a bending jig.
Capacity: 2,200 rackets per week

Rivets,
spreader →

Frame Assembly
The various parts of the frame are riveted together.
Capacity: 1,800 rackets per week

Wrapping
tape →

Handgrip Fabrication
A machine wraps the handgrip with tape.
Capacity: 3,200 rackets per week

String,
pads →

Stringing
The tennis racket is strung by hand.
Capacity: 2,000 rackets per week

Completed Tennis Racket

Therefore, if the company wants to increase its output, it must increase the capacity of this particular workstation.[15]

There are several ways the capacity of the constraint can be increased. These will be discussed in detail in Chapter 13. As one example, the capacity of the frame assembly can be increased by improving the frame assembly process so that it requires less time. Thus, TQM and process reengineering efforts can be leveraged by targeting the constraint.

---

15. If demand was less than 1,800 tennis rackets per week, there would not be a production constraint. However, there would still be a constraint of some type. For example, the company's constraint might be a poor logistical system that limits how many tennis rackets can be distributed in a timely fashion to retailers. All businesses that are organized to make a profit face at least one constraint.

Consider what would happen if process reengineering were used to improve one of the *nonconstraints*. Suppose, for example, that the handgrip fabrication process is improved so that it requires only half as much time. Will this increase profits? The answer is "Probably not." Handgrip fabrication already has plenty of excess capacity—it is capable of processing 3,200 rackets per week, but demand is only 2,100 rackets. Speeding up this process will simply create more excess capacity. Unless resources can now be shifted from handgrip fabrication to the constraint area (frame assembly) or unless spending can be cut in the handgrip fabrication work centre, there will be no increase in profits. In contrast, if the processing time were cut in half in frame assembly, which is the constraint, the company could produce and sell more tennis rackets. The margins on the additional tennis rackets would go straight to the bottom line as additional income.

Bottlenecks may occur in any business sector. For Western Canadian farmers, for example, the bottleneck has been in the transportation part of their operations, costing farmers millions of dollars of lost revenue plus penalties for shipping delays. The Canadian Wheat Board blames the railways, saying they do not give wheat a high priority while the railways say severe winter weather and other factors have been the problem.[16] In the pulp and paper industry the bottlenecks are usually in the drying operations and the industry is currently researching new drying methods for their production facilities.[17]

TOC AND CONTINUOUS IMPROVEMENT   In TOC, an analogy is often drawn between a business process—such as the tennis racket production line—and a chain. If you want to increase the strength of a chain, what is the most effective way to do this? Should you concentrate your efforts on strengthening the strongest link, the largest link, all the links, or the weakest link? Clearly, focusing effort on the weakest link will bring the biggest benefit.

Continuing with this analogy, the procedure to follow in strengthening the chain is straightforward. First, identify the weakest link, which is the constraint. Second, do not place a greater strain on the system than the weakest link can handle. Third, concentrate improvement efforts on strengthening the weakest link. Fourth, if the improvement efforts are successful, eventually the weakest link will improve to the point where it is no longer the weakest link. At this point, the new weakest link (i.e., the new constraint) must be identified, and improvement efforts must be shifted over to that link. This simple sequential process provides a powerful strategy for continuous improvement. The TOC approach is a perfect complement to TQM and process reengineering—it focuses improvement efforts where they are likely to be most effective.

International Competition

<table>
<tr><td>

Objective 7

Discuss the impact of international competition on businesses and on managerial accounting.

</td><td>

Over the last several decades, competition has become worldwide in many industries. This has been caused by reductions in tariffs, quotas, and other barriers to free trade; improvements in global transportation systems; and increasing sophistication in international markets. These factors work together to reduce the costs of conducting international trade and make it possible for foreign companies to compete on a more equal footing with local firms.

The movement toward freer trade has been most dramatic in the European Union (EU). The EU has grown from a very small free-trade zone involving a few basic commodities such as coal and steel in the late 1950s to a free-trade zone of over a dozen European nations involving almost unlimited movement of goods and services across

</td></tr>
</table>

---

16. "Deregulation Answer to Grain Shipment Woes: CPR's Ritchie," *The Financial Post*, February 22/24, 1997.
17. J. F. Bond, V. G. Gomes, and W. J. Douglas, "Computer Simulation of Drying Paper by Multiple Techniques," *Pulp & Paper Canada* (December 1996) pp. 110–12.

national borders. This vast, largely unified market has a population of over 375 million, as compared with over 268 million in the United States and about 125 million in Japan. Many of the countries in the EU are adopting a common currency called the euro, which should make trading within the EU even easier. The euro will fully replace traditional currencies such as the French franc, the German mark, and the Italian lira in July 2002. The relatively new North American Free Trade Association (NAFTA) trading block, which consists of Canada, the United States, and Mexico, has a combined population in excess of 395 million.

Such reductions in trade barriers have made it easier for agile and aggressive companies to expand outside of their home markets. As a result, very few firms can afford to be complacent. A company may be very successful today in its local market relative to its local competitors, but tomorrow the competition may come from halfway around the globe. As a matter of survival, even firms that are presently doing very well in their home markets must become world-class competitors. On the bright side, the freer international movement of goods and services presents tremendous export opportunities for those companies that can transform themselves into world-class competitors. And, from the standpoint of consumers, heightened competition promises an even greater variety of goods, at higher quality and lower prices.

What are the implications for managerial accounting of increased global competition? It would be very difficult for a firm to become world-class if it plans, directs, and controls its operations and makes decisions using a second-class management accounting system. An excellent management accounting system will not by itself guarantee success, but a poor management accounting system can stymie the best efforts of people in an organization to make the firm truly competitive.

Throughout this text we will highlight the differences between obsolete management accounting systems that get in the way of success and well-designed management accounting systems that can enhance a firm's performance. It is noteworthy that elements of well-designed management accounting systems have originated in many countries. More and more, managerial accounting has become a discipline that is worldwide in scope.

Focus on Current Practice

Global competition sometimes comes from unexpected sources. Companies in the former Soviet bloc in Central and Eastern Europe are rapidly raising the quality of their products to Western standards and are beginning to provide stiff competition. The Hungarian company Petofi Printing & Packaging Co., a maker of cardboard boxes, wrappers, and other containers, provides a good example. "Only a few years ago, Petofi's employees drank beer at work. Flies buzzing in open windows got stuck in the paint and pressed into the paperboard. Containers were delivered in the wrong colors and sizes." Under the Communist system, the company's customers didn't dare complain, since there was no other source for their packaging needs.

The company was privatized after the fall of the Soviet system, and the company "began overhauling itself, leapfrogging Western companies with state-of-the-art machinery. It whipped its workforce into shape with a combination of inducements and threats." Now, most of its products are exported. PepsiCo, for example, buys Petofi wrappers for Cheetos and Ruffles snacks and claims that Petofi's quality compares very favorably with Western suppliers. PepsiCo's buyer states, "They have filled the gap between competitive quality and best cost."[18] ■

---

18. Dana Milbank, "New Competitor: East Europe's Industry Is Raising Its Quality and Taking on West," *The Wall Street Journal*, September 21, 1994, pp. A1, A7.

Organizational Structure

Since organizations are made up of people, management must accomplish its objectives by working *through* people. Presidents of companies like Good Vibrations, Inc., could not possibly execute all of their company's strategies alone; they must rely on other people. This is done by creating an organizational structure that permits *decentralization* of management responsibilities.

Decentralization

Decentralization   The delegation of decision-making authority throughout an organization by providing managers at various operating levels with the authority to make key decisions relating to their area of responsibility.

Decentralization is the delegation of decision-making authority throughout an organization by providing managers at various operating levels with the authority to make decisions relating to their area of responsibility. Some organizations are more decentralized than others. Because of Good Vibrations, Inc.'s geographic dispersion and the peculiarities of local markets, the company is highly decentralized.

Good Vibrations, Inc.'s president (also called chief executive officer or CEO) sets the broad strategy for the company and makes major strategic decisions such as opening stores in new markets, but much of the remaining decision-making authority is delegated to managers on various levels throughout the organization. These levels are as follows: The company has a number of retail stores, each of which has a store manager as well as a separate manager for each section such as international rock and classical/jazz. In addition, the company has support departments such as a central Purchasing Department and a Personnel Department. The organizational structure of the company is depicted in Exhibit 1–8.

Organization chart   A visual diagram of a firm's organizational structure that depicts formal lines of reporting, communication, and responsibility between managers.

The arrangement of boxes shown in Exhibit 1–8 is called an **organization chart.** The purpose of an organization chart is to show how responsibility has been divided among managers and to show formal lines of reporting and communication, or *chain of command.* Each box depicts an area of management responsibility, and the lines between the boxes show the lines of formal authority between managers. The chart tells us, for example, that the store managers are responsible to the operations vice president. In turn, the latter is responsible to the company president, who in turn is responsible to the board of directors. Following the lines of authority and communication on the organization chart, we can see that the manager of the Hong Kong store would ordinarily report to the operations vice president rather than directly to the president of the company.

Informal relationships and channels of communication often develop outside the formal reporting relationships on the organization chart as a result of personal contacts between managers. The informal structure does not appear on the organization chart, but it is often vital to effective operations.

Line and Staff Relationships

Line   A position in an organization that is directly related to the achievement of the organization's basic objectives.

Staff   A position in an organization that is only indirectly related to the achievement of the organization's basic objectives. Such positions are supportive in nature in that they provide service or assistance to line positions or to other staff positions.

An organization chart also depicts *line* and *staff* positions in an organization. A person in a **line** position is *directly* involved in achieving the basic objectives of the organization. A person in a **staff** position, by contrast, is only *indirectly* involved in achieving those basic objectives. Staff positions *support* or provide assistance to line positions or other parts of the organization, but they do not have direct authority over line positions. Refer again to the organization chart in Exhibit 1–8. Since the basic objective of Good Vibrations, Inc., is to sell recorded music at a profit, those managers whose areas of responsibility are directly related to the sales effort occupy line positions. These positions, which are shown in a darker colour in the exhibit, include the managers of the various music departments in each store, the store managers, the operations vice president, and members of top management.

Exhibit 1–8   Organization Chart, Good Vibrations, Inc.

By contrast, the manager of the central Purchasing Department occupies a staff position, since the only function of the Purchasing Department is to support and serve the line departments by doing their purchasing for them.

The Controller

As previously mentioned, in Canada the manager in charge of the accounting department is usually known as the *controller*. The controller is the member of the top-management team who is given the responsibility of providing relevant and timely data to support planning and control activities and of preparing financial statements for external users.

The organization of a typical controller's office is shown in Exhibit 1–9. From that organization chart we see that the controller's office combines a number of important functions including, quite often, management of the company's computer services. Because the controller becomes familiar with all parts of a company's operations by working with managers throughout the company, it is not unusual for the controller's office to be a stepping-stone to the top position in a company.

The Professional Management Accountant

Three professional accounting groups in Canada have members who make up the ranks of management accountants. CGAs, CAs, and CMAs represent designations used by professional accountants who belong to provincial societies or associations

Exhibit 1–9 Organization of the Controller's Office

known as *Certified General Accountants Associations, Institutes (Ordré) of Chartered Accountants*, and *Societies of Management Accountants*. Members of these three associations work in various fields—industry, commerce, government, education, and public practice—after completing their particular programs of study and passing their professional certification examinations.[19] In the United States, both CPAs and CMAs make up the professional management accountants. The CPA designation is used by members of the American Institute of Certified Public Accountants or various state CPA associations. The CMAs are members of the *Institute of Management Accountants*.

Management accounting is not subject to the type of regulation that is evident for financial accounting. However, the Society of Management Accountants of Canada issues *management accounting guidelines* on fundamental areas of practice. Adherence to the guidelines is voluntary, but wide acceptance is expected because of the relevance and expertise used in their preparation. Currently nearly 50 guidelines have been issued on such topics as capital expenditures, internal control, cash management, foreign currency risk management, the annual financial statement audit, managing quality improvements, benchmarking, activity-based costing, incentive plans, value chain analysis, and just-in-time production systems. New topics are continually being presented to the accounting community.

---

19. Web sites for these three groups contain background information. See http://www.cga-canada.org/, http://www.cica.ca/, and http://www.cma-canada.org/.

Professional Ethics

In recent years, many concerns have been raised regarding ethical behaviour in business and in public life. These concerns have resulted from insider trading scandals, violations of environmental standards by manufacturers, fraudulent billing by defence contractors, scandal in government departments, and management fraud in the financial institutions. Indeed, allegations of unethical conduct have been directed toward managers in virtually all segments of society, including government, business, charitable organizations, and even religion.

Although these scandals have received a lot of attention, it is doubtful that they represent a wholesale breakdown of the moral fibre of the nation. After all, hundreds of millions of transactions are conducted every day untainted by any scandal. Nevertheless, it is important to have an appreciation of what is and is not acceptable behaviour in business and why. Fortunately, the major accounting bodies in Canada and the United States have developed useful codes of ethics and professional conduct.

Code of Conduct for Management Accountants

In a nutshell, the management accountant has ethical responsibilities in four broad areas: first, to maintain a high level of professional competence; second, to treat sensitive matters with confidentiality; third, to maintain personal integrity; and fourth, to be objective in all disclosures. Professional accounting bodies around the globe incorporate these general guidelines into their codes of professional conduct. For example, Exhibit 1–10 illustrates the Standards of Ethical Conduct of the Institute of Management Accountants. Note that this exhibit provides examples of competence, confidentiality, integrity, and objectivity and also provides steps to be taken in the case of ethical conflict.

Ethical standards provide sound, practical advice for the management accountant (or manager for that matter). Most of the rules in the ethical standards are motivated by a very practical consideration—if these rules were not generally followed in business, then the economy would come to a screeching halt. Consider the following specific examples of the consequences of not abiding by the standards:

- Suppose employees could not be trusted with confidential information. Then top managers would be reluctant to distribute confidential information within the company. As a result, operations would deteriorate, since they would be based on incomplete information.
- Suppose employees accepted bribes from suppliers. Then contracts would tend to go to suppliers who pay the highest bribes rather than to the most competent suppliers. Would you like to fly in an aircraft whose wings were made by the subcontractor who was willing to pay the highest bribe to a purchasing agent? What would happen to the airline industry if its safety record deteriorated due to shoddy workmanship on contracted parts and assemblies?
- Suppose the presidents of companies routinely lied in their annual reports to shareholders and grossly distorted financial statements. If the basic integrity of a company's financial statements could not be relied on, investors and creditors would have little basis for making informed decisions. Suspecting the worst, rational investors would pay less for securities issued by companies. As a consequence, less funds would be available for productive investments and many firms might be unable to raise any funds at all. Ultimately, this would lead to slower economic growth, fewer goods and services, and higher prices.

As these examples suggest, if ethical standards were not generally adhered to, there would be undesirable consequences for everyone. Essentially, abandoning ethical standards would lead to a lower standard of living with lower-quality goods and services, less to choose from, and higher prices. In short, following ethical rules is not just a matter of being "nice"; it is absolutely essential for the smooth functioning of an advanced market economy.

Exhibit 1–10

Standards of Ethical Conduct for Management Accountants

Management accountants have an obligation to the organizations they serve, their profession, the public, and themselves to maintain the highest standards of ethical conduct. In recognition of this obligation, the Institute of Management Accountants, formerly the National Association of Accountants, has promulgated the following standards of ethical conduct for management accountants. Adherence to these standards is integral to achieving the *Objectives of Management Accounting.** Management accountants shall not commit acts contrary to these standards nor shall they condone the commission of such acts by others within their organization.

Competence   Management accountants have a responsibility to:

• Maintain an appropriate level of professional competence by ongoing development of their knowledge and skills.

• Perform their professional duties in accordance with relevant laws, regulations, and technical standards.

• Prepare complete and clear reports and recommendations after appropriate analyses of relevant and reliable information.

Confidentiality   Management accountants have a responsibility to:

• Refrain from disclosing confidential information acquired in the course of their work except when authorized, unless legally obligated to do so.

• Inform subordinates as appropriate regarding the confidentiality of information acquired in the course of their work and monitor their activities to assure the maintenance of that confidentiality.

• Refrain from using or appearing to use confidential information acquired in the course of their work for unethical or illegal advantage either personally or through third parties.

Integrity   Management accountants have a responsibility to:

• Avoid actual or apparent conflicts of interest and advise all appropriate parties of any potential conflict.

• Refrain from engaging in any activity that would prejudice their ability to carry out their duties ethically.

• Refuse any gift, favor, or hospitality that would influence or would appear to influence their actions.

• Refrain from either actively or passively subverting the attainment of the organization's legitimate and ethical objectives.

• Recognize and communicate professional limitations or other constraints that would preclude responsible judgment or successful performance of an activity.

• Communicate unfavorable as well as favorable information and professional judgments or opinions.

• Refrain from engaging in or supporting any activity that would discredit the profession.

Objectivity   Management accountants have a responsibility to:

• Communicate information fairly and objectively.

• Disclose fully all relevant information that could reasonably be expected to influence an intended user's understanding of the reports, comments, and recommendations presented.

RESOLUTION OF ETHICAL CONFLICT

In applying the standards of ethical conduct, management accountants may encounter problems in identifying unethical behavior or in resolving an ethical conflict. When faced with significant ethical issues, management accountants should follow the established policies of the organization bearing on the resolution of such conflict. If these policies do not resolve the ethical conflict, management accountants should consider the following course of action:

• Discuss such problems with the immediate superior except when it appears that the superior is involved, in which case the problem should be presented initially to the next

Exhibit 1–10
Standards of Ethical
Management Accountants
(continued)

higher managerial level. If satisfactory resolution cannot be achieved when the problem is initially presented, submit the issues to the next higher managerial level.

   If the immediate superior is the chief executive officer, or equivalent, the acceptable reviewing authority may be a group such as the audit committee, executive committee, board of directors, board of trustees, or owners. Contact with levels above the immediate superior should be initiated only with the superior's knowledge, assuming the superior is not involved.

- Clarify relevant concepts by confidential discussion with an objective advisor to obtain an understanding of possible courses of action.

- If the ethical conflict still exists after exhausting all levels of internal review, the management accountant may have no other recourse on significant matters than to resign from the organization and to submit an informative memorandum to an appropriate representative of the organization.

Except where legally prescribed, communication of such problems to authorities or individuals not employed or engaged by the organization is not considered appropriate.

*Institute of Management Accountants, formerly National Association of Accountants, *Statements on Management Accounting: Objectives of Management Accounting*, Statement No. 1B, New York, N.Y., June 17, 1982.

Company Codes of Conduct

"Those who engage in unethical behaviour often justify their actions with one or more of the following reasons: (1) the organization expects unethical behaviour, (2) everyone else is unethical, and/or (3) behaving unethically is the only way to get ahead."[20]

   To counter the first justification for unethical behaviour, many companies have adopted formal ethical codes of conduct. These codes are generally broad-based statements of a company's responsibilities to its employees, its customers, its suppliers, and the communities in which the company operates. Codes rarely spell out specific do's and don'ts or suggest proper behaviour in a specific situation. Instead, they give broad guidelines. An ethical code can never serve as the final moral authority. Accountants have an obligation to develop moral competence in addition to technical competence. Society should expect accountants to act with the highest standards of integrity and not just conform to written codes of professional conduct.

   According to Leonard Brooks of the University of Toronto the majority of large companies in Canada and abroad have issued codes of conduct. Professor Brooks surveyed chief executive officers of many of these companies and found CEOs to be relatively satisfied with their codes of conduct. CEOs did indicate, however, that improvements can and need to be made to improve code effectiveness and compliance. Areas singled out as needing code content improvement include environmental and community responsibilities and training, compliance, evaluation and reporting ethical performance.[21] An example of a corporate code of conduct is illustrated in Exhibit 1–11.

   Unfortunately, the single-minded emphasis placed on short-term profits in some companies may make it seem like the only way to get ahead is to act unethically. When top managers say, in effect, that they will only be satisfied with bottom-line results and will accept no excuses, they are asking for trouble.

---

20. Michael K. McCuddy, Karl E. Reichardt, and David Schroeder, "Ethical Pressures: Fact or Fiction?" *Management Accounting* (April 1993), pp. 57–61.
21. L. Brooks. "A Survey on the Effectiveness/Compliance of Corporate Codes of Conduct in Canada," in *Professional Ethics for Accountants* (New York: West Publishing Company, 1995).

Exhibit 1–11 Ethical
Guidelines Summary

Many companies have their own codes of business conduct such as the following summarization provided by Petro-Canada

• **Integrity**

In all our business affairs, the Corporation and each of us individually must behave with integrity; our success and reputation depend on it.

• **Trust**

Petro-Canada places the highest trust in the honesty, integrity and dedication of its employees; in turn, employees have the right to be treated with honesty, respect and fairness.

• **Customers**

We will provide value for money and deal fairly and honestly with our customers.

• **Social Responsibility**

Petro-Canada is committed to workplace safety, valuing workforce diversity, and employee freedom from discrimination and harassment. We will strive to be a positive force in the social and environmental welfare of the communities in which we operate.

• **Illegal or Unethical Actions**

Petro-Canada does not condone nor permit any employee, partner or supplier to commit an illegal or unethical act on behalf of the Corporation nor to instruct any other person or company to do so.

• **Conflict of Interest**

There can be no situations where our personal or personal business arrangements conflict with the interests of the Company. Using our position with the Company in an unsanctioned manner for personal gain is unacceptable.

• **Confidential Information**

We will safeguard competitive and confidential information from disclosure. Information about our competitors will be acquired only through legal means.

• **Insider Trading**

It is illegal to use knowledge gained through our position with Petro-Canada, that is not public information, to trade in securities of Petro-Canada or another company.

• **Secret Commissions**

Bribes, payoffs, or kickbacks to business representatives, suppliers, or public officials as payments to obtain business are prohibited both domestically and internationally.

Source: *Code of Business Conduct*, Petro-Canada, p. 3.

Codes of Conduct on the International Level

The *Guideline on Ethics for Professional Accountants*, revised January 1998 by the International Federation of Accountants (IFAC), governs the activities of *all* professional accountants throughout the world, regardless of whether they are practising as independent public accountants, employed in government service, or employed as internal accountants.[22] In addition to outlining ethical requirements in matters dealing with competence, objectivity, independence, and confidentiality, the IFAC's code also outlines the accountant's ethical responsibilities in matters relating to taxes, fees and commissions, advertising and solicitation, the handling of monies, and cross-border activities. Where cross-border activities are involved, the IFAC ethical requirements must be followed if these requirements are stricter than the ethical requirements of the country in which the work is being performed.[23]

---

22. A copy of this code can be obtained from http://www.IFAC.org/.

23. *Guideline on Ethics for Professional Accountants* (New York: International Federation of Accountants, January 1998), section 6.

Summary

Managerial accounting assists managers in carrying out their responsibilities, which include planning, directing and motivating, and controlling.

Since managerial accounting is geared to the needs of the manager rather than to the needs of outsiders, it differs substantially from financial accounting. Managerial accounting is oriented more toward the future, places less emphasis on precision, emphasizes segments of an organization (rather than the organization as a whole), is not governed by generally accepted accounting principles, and is not mandatory.

The business environment in recent years has been characterized by increasing competition and a relentless drive for continuous improvement. Several approaches have been developed to assist organizations in meeting these challenges—including just-in-time (JIT), total quality management (TQM), process reengineering, and the theory of constraints (TOC).

JIT emphasizes the importance of reducing inventories to the barest minimum possible. This reduces working capital requirements, frees up space, reduces through-put time, reduces defects, and eliminates waste.

TQM involves focusing on the customer, and it employs systematic problem solving using teams made up of front-line workers. Specific TQM tools include benchmarking and the plan-do-check-act (PDCA) cycle. By emphasizing teamwork, a focus on the customer, and facts, TQM can avoid the organizational infighting that might otherwise block improvement.

Process reengineering involves completely redesigning a business process in order to eliminate non-value-added activities and to reduce opportunities for errors. Process reengineering relies more on outside specialists than TQM and is more likely to be imposed by top management.

The theory of constraints emphasizes the importance of managing the organization's constraints. Since the constraint is whatever is holding back the organization, improvement efforts usually must be focused on the constraint in order to be really effective.

Most organizations are decentralized to some degree. The organization chart depicts who works for whom in the organization and which units perform staff functions rather than line functions. Accountants perform a staff function—they support and provide assistance to others inside the organization.

Ethical standards serve a very important practical function in an advanced market economy. Without widespread adherence to ethical standards, the economy would slow down dramatically. Ethics are the lubrication that keep a market economy functioning smoothly. The Standards of Ethical Conduct for Practitioners of Management Accounting and Financial Management provide sound, practical guidelines for resolving ethical problems that might arise in an organization.

Questions

1–1   What is the basic difference in orientation between financial and managerial accounting?

1–2   What are the three major activities of a manager?

1–3   Describe the four steps in the planning and control cycle.

1–4   What function does feedback play in the work of the manager?

1–5　Distinguish between line and staff positions in an organization.

1–6　What are the major differences between financial and managerial accounting?

1–7　In a just-in-time (JIT) system, what is meant by the pull approach to the flow of goods, as compared to the push approach used in conventional systems?

1–8　How does the plant layout differ in a company using JIT as compared to a company that uses a more conventional approach to manufacturing? What benefits accrue from a JIT layout?

1–9　Identify the benefits that can result from reducing the setup time for a product.

1–10　How does a workforce in a JIT facility differ from the workforce in a conventional facility?

1–11　What are the major benefits of a JIT system?

1–12　Explain how the plan-do-check-act cycle applies the scientific method to problem solving.

1–13　Why is process reengineering a more radical approach to improvement than total quality management?

1–14　How can process reengineering undermine employee morale?

1–15　Why does the theory of constraints emphasize managing constraints?

1–16　Why is adherence to ethical standards important for the smooth functioning of an advanced market economy?

Exercises

E1–1　Listed below are a number of terms that relate to organizations, the work of management, and the role of managerial accounting:

Budgets	Controller
Decentralization	Directing and motivating
Feedback	Financial accounting
Line	Managerial accounting
Nonmonetary data	Performance report
Planning	Precision
Staff	

Choose the term or terms above that most appropriately complete the following statements:

1. A position on the organization chart that is directly related to achieving the basic objectives of an organization is called a _____ position.
2. When _____ , managers oversee day-to-day activities and keep the organization functioning smoothly.
3. The plans of management are expressed formally in _____ .
4. _____ consists of identifying alternatives, selecting from among the alternatives the one that is best for the organization, and specifying what actions will be taken to implement the chosen alternative.
5. A _____ position provides service or assistance to other parts of the organization and does not directly achieve the basic objectives of the organization.
6. The delegation of decision-making authority throughout an organization by allowing managers at various operating levels to make key decisions relating to their area of responsibility is called _____ .

7. Managerial accounting places less emphasis on _____ and more emphasis on _____ than financial accounting.

8. _____ is concerned with providing information for the use of those who are inside the organization, whereas _____ is concerned with providing information for the use of those who are outside the organization.

9. The accounting and other reports coming to management that are used in controlling the organization are called _____ .

10. The manager in charge of the accounting department is generally known as the _____ .

11. A detailed report to management comparing budgeted data against actual data for a specific time period is called a _____ .

E1–2   Listed below are a number of terms that relate to just-in-time, total quality management, process reengineering, and theory of constraints:

Benchmarking	Business process
Constraint	Frequent
Just-in-time	Nonconstraint
Non-value-added activities	Plan-do-check-act cycle
Process reengineering	Pull
Setup	Total quality management

Choose the term or terms above that most appropriately complete the following statements:

1. To successfully operate a JIT system, a company must learn to rely on a few suppliers who are willing to make _____ deliveries.

2. _____ is an incremental approach to improvement, whereas _____ tends to be a much more radical approach that involves completely redesigning business processes.

3. A production system in which units are produced and materials are purchased only as needed to meet actual customer demand is called _____ .

4. In just-in-time, the flow of goods is controlled by what is described as a _____ approach to manufacturing.

5. Increasing the rate of output of a _____ as the result of an improvement effort is unlikely to have much effect on profits.

6. _____ involves studying the business processes of companies that are considered among the best in the world at performing a particular task.

7. The activities involved in getting equipment ready to produce a different product are called a _____ .

8. The theory of constraints suggests that improvement efforts should be focused on the company's _____ .

9. The _____ is a systematic, fact-based approach to continuous improvement that resembles the scientific method.

10. In process reengineering, two objectives are to simplify and to eliminate _____.

11. A _____ is any series of steps that are followed in order to carry out some task in a business.

E1–3   The management at Megafilters, Inc., has been discussing the possible implementation of a just-in-time (JIT) production system at its Quebec plant, where oil and air filters are manufactured. The Metal Stamping Department at the Quebec plant has already instituted a JIT system for controlling raw materials inventory, but the remainder of the plant is still discussing how to proceed with the implementation of this concept. The Metal Stamping Department implemented JIT with no advance planning, and some of the other department managers have become uneasy about adopting JIT after hearing about the problems that have arisen.

Robert Richard, manager of the Quebec plant, is a strong proponent of the JIT approach. He recently made the following statement at a meeting of all departmental managers:

> We will all have to make many changes in the way we think about our employees, our suppliers, and our customers if we are going to be successful in using JIT procedures. Rather than dwelling on some of the negative things you have heard from the Metal Stamping Department, I want each of you to prepare a list of things we can do to make a smooth transition to the JIT approach for the rest of the plant.

Required
1. The JIT approach has several characteristics that distinguish it from conventional production systems. Describe these characteristics.
2. For the JIT approach to be successful, Megafilters, Inc., must establish appropriate relationships with its suppliers. Describe these relationships under JIT.

(CMA, adapted)

E1–4   Mary Karston was hired by a popular fast-food restaurant as an order-taker and cashier. Shortly after taking the job, she was shocked to overhear an employee bragging to a friend about shortchanging customers. She confronted the employee who then snapped back: "Mind your own business. Besides, everyone does it and the customers never miss the money." Mary didn't know how to respond to this aggressive stance.

Required   What would be the practical consequences on the fast-food industry and on consumers if cashiers generally shortchanged customers at every opportunity?

Problems

P1–5 Preparing an Organization Chart   Bristow University is a large private school located in the Manitoba. The university is headed by a president who has five vice presidents reporting to him. These vice presidents are responsible for, respectively, auxiliary services, admissions and records, academics, financial services (controller), and physical plant.

In addition, the university has managers over several areas who report to these vice presidents. These include managers over central purchasing, the university press, and the university bookstore, all of whom report to the vice president for auxiliary services; managers over computer services and over accounting and finance, who report to the vice president for financial services; and managers over grounds and custodial services and over plant and maintenance, who report to the vice president for physical plant.

The university has four faculties—business, humanities, fine arts, and engineering and quantitative methods—and a law school. Each of these units has a dean who is responsible to the academic vice president. Each college has faculty departments.

Required
1. Prepare an organization chart for Bristow University.
2. Which of the positions on your chart would be line positions? Why would they be line positions? Which would be staff positions? Why?
3. Which of the positions on your chart would have need for accounting information? Explain.

P1–6   Ethics and the Manager   Richmond, Inc., operates a chain of department stores located in Alberta. The first store began operations in 1965, and the company has steadily grown to its present size of four stores. Two years ago, the board of directors of Richmond approved a large-scale remodelling of its stores to attract a more upscale clientele.

Before finalizing these plans, two stores were remodelled as a test. Linda Perlman, assistant controller, was asked to oversee the financial reporting for these test stores, and she and other management personnel were offered bonuses based on the sales growth and profitability of these stores. While completing the financial reports, Perlman discovered a sizable inventory of outdated goods that should have been discounted for sale or returned to the manufacturer. She discussed the situation with her management colleagues; the consensus was to ignore reporting this inventory as obsolete, since reporting it would diminish the financial results and their bonuses.

Required
1. According to the Standards of Ethical Conduct for Practitioners of Management Accounting and Financial Management, would it be ethical for Perlman *not* to report the inventory as obsolete?
2. Would it be easy for Perlman to take the ethical action in this situation?

(CMA, adapted)

P1–7 JIT; Process Reengineering Snedden Products manufactures athletic equipment, including footballs. The footballs are manufactured in several steps, which are listed below:

a. Leather and other materials are received at a centrally located dock where the materials are checked to be sure they conform to exacting company standards. Rejected materials are returned to the supplier.
b. Acceptable materials are transported to a stores warehouse pending use in production.
c. A materials requisition form is issued, and materials are transferred from the stores warehouse to the Cutting Department where all cutting equipment is located.
d. Since the Cutting Department cuts materials for a variety of products, the leather is placed on large pallets and stationed by the appropriate machines.
e. The leather and other materials are cut to proper shape, with the operator taking care to cut all sections of a football from a single piece of leather. Waste materials are placed in a bin, and at the end of each day the materials are sorted to reclaim the items that can be used in manufacturing other products.
f. Each cut item of material is examined by one of three checkers to ensure uniformity of cut, thickness of the leather, and direction of the grain. Rejected pieces are tossed in the scrap bin.
g. Cut materials are placed on pallets and transferred to the Centralized Sewing Department, where the pallets are placed in a staging area.
h. Materials are taken from the pallets, the company's name and logo are stamped into one section of each set of cut pieces, and the pieces are then sewed together.
i. The sewn pieces are placed in bins, which are then transferred to the staging area of the Assembly Department.
j. An operator in the Assembly Department installs a lining in the football, stitches the ball closed with a stitching machine, and then inflates it.
k. The completed footballs are placed on a conveyor belt that passes by another set of checkers. Each ball is checked for uniformity of shape and for other potential defects.
l. Completed footballs are boxed and transferred to the finished goods warehouse.

Required Assume that the company adopts JIT inventory practices and establishes individual product flow lines. Explain what changes would have to be made in manufacturing procedures and prepare a sketch of how the football product flow line would be arranged.

P1–8 Line and Staff Positions Special Alloys Corporation manufactures a variety of specialized metal products for industrial use. Most of the revenues are generated by large contracts with companies that have government defence contracts. The company also develops and markets parts to the major automobile companies. It employs many metallurgists and skilled technicians because most of its products are made from highly sophisticated alloys.

The company recently signed two large contracts; as a result, the workload of Wayne Washburn, the general manager, has become overwhelming. To relieve some of this overload, Mark Johnson was transferred from the Research Planning Department to the general manager's office. Johnson, who has been a senior metallurgist and supervisor in the Research Planning Department, was given the title "assistant to the general manager."

Washburn assigned several responsibilities to Johnson in their first meeting. Johnson will oversee the testing of new alloys in the Product Planning Department and be given the authority to make decisions as to the use of these alloys in product development; he will also be responsible for maintaining the production schedules for one of the new contracts. In addition to these duties, he will be required to meet with the supervisors of the production departments regularly to consult with them about production problems they may be experiencing. Washburn is expecting that he will be able to manage the company much more efficiently with Johnson's help.

Required 1. Positions within organizations are often described as having (a) line authority or (b) staff authority. Describe what is meant by these two terms.
2. Of the responsibilities assigned to Mark Johnson as assistant to the general manager, which tasks have line authority and which have staff authority?

3. Identify and discuss the conflicts Mark Johnson may experience in the production departments as a result of his new responsibilities.

(CMA, adapted)

P1–9 Ethics; Just-in-Time (JIT) Purchasing (The situation described below was adapted from a case published by the Institute of Management Accountants' Committee on Ethics.[24])

WIW is a publicly owned corporation that makes various control devices used in the manufacture of mechanical equipment. J.B. is the president of WIW, Tony is the purchasing agent, and Diane is J.B.'s executive assistant. All three have been with WIW for about five years. Charlie is WIW's controller and has been with the company for two years.

J.B.: Hi, Charlie, come on in. Diane said you had a confidential matter to discuss. What's on your mind?

Charlie: J.B., I was reviewing our increased purchases from A-1 Warehouse Sales last week and wondered why our volume has tripled in the past year. When I discussed this with Tony he seemed a bit evasive and tried to dismiss the issue by stating that A-1 can give us one-day delivery on our orders.

J.B.: Well, Tony is right. You know we have been trying to implement just-in-time and have been trying to get our inventory down.

Charlie: We still have to look at the overall cost. A-1 is more of a jobber than a warehouse. After investigating orders placed with them, I found that only 10% are delivered from their warehouse and the other 90% are drop-shipped from the manufacturers. The average markup by A-1 is 30%, which amounted to about $600,000 on our orders for the past year. If we had ordered directly from the manufacturers when A-1 didn't have an item in stock, we could have saved about $540,000 ($600,000 × 90%). In addition, some of the orders were late and not complete.

J.B.: Now look, Charlie, we get quick delivery on most items, and who knows how much we are saving by not having to stock this stuff in advance or worry about it becoming obsolete. Is there anything else on your mind?

Charlie: Well, J.B., as a matter of fact, there is. I ordered a Dun & Bradstreet credit report on A-1 and discovered that Mike Bell is the principal owner. Isn't he your brother-in-law?

J.B.: Sure he is. But don't worry about Mike. He understands this JIT approach. Besides, he's looking out for our interests.

Charlie (to himself): This conversation has been enlightening, but it doesn't really respond to my concerns. Can I legally or ethically ignore this apparent conflict of interests?

Required
1. Would Charlie be justified in ignoring this situation, particularly since he is not the purchasing agent? In preparing your answer, consider the IMA's Standards of Ethical Conduct in Exhibit 1–10.
2. State the specific steps Charlie should follow to resolve this matter.

P1–10 Ethics Refer to Exhibit 1–11 concerning Petro-Canada. Suppose all automotive service businesses routinely followed the practice of attempting to sell customers unnecessary parts and services.

Required
1. How would this unethical behaviour affect customers? How might customers attempt to protect themselves against this unethical behaviour?
2. How would this unethical behaviour probably affect profits and employment in Petro-Canada?

---

24. Neil Holmes, ed., "Ethics," *Management Accounting* 73, no. 8 (February 1992), p. 16. Used (and adapted) by permission.

P1–11   Managerial Accounting Information   Business Duplicating Ltd. has a managerial accounting system that generated the following financial statements:

BUSINESS DUPLICATING LTD.

Income Statement
For the Year Ended December 31, 2000

Revenues:

Stenographic revenue	$30,000	
Printing revenue	25,000	
Mailing revenue	13,000	
Total revenues		$68,000

Expenses:

Salary expense	30,750	
Employee benefits expense	1,100	
Rent expense for office space	2,400	
Rental payments for copiers	6,600	
Utilities expense	400	
Advertising expense	960	
Supplies expense	90	
Interest expense	70	
Depreciation expense on office equipment	1,200	
Total expenses (excluding income tax)		43,570
Pretax income		24,430
Income tax expense ($24,430 × 17%)		4,153
Net income		**$20,277**
Earnings per share (EPS) ($20,277 ÷ 3,000 shares)		$6.76

BUSINESS DUPLICATING LTD.

Balance Sheet
At December 31, 2000

Assets			Liabilities		
Cash		$12,877	Accounts payable		$900
Accounts receivable		18,000	Income taxes payable		500
Land		20,000	Note payable, short term, 7%		1,000
Office equipment	$6,000				
Less: Accumulated depreciation	1,200	4,800	Total liabilities		$2,400
			Shareholders' Equity		
			Contributed capital:		
			Capital stock (3,000 shares, no par)	$33,000	
			Retained earnings	20,277	
			Total shareholders' equity		53,277
			Total liabilities and shareholders' equity		
Total assets		$55,677	equity		$55,677

BUSINESS DUPLICATING LTD.

Statement of Changes in Financial Position, Cash Basis
For the Year Ended December 31, 2000

Sources of cash (inflows):		
From operations:		
From cash revenues	$50,000	
Less: Cash used for expenses	45,123	
Cash inflow from operations		$4,877
Financing:		
Investment by owners		
(shares issued for cash)	33,000	
Loan—note payable	1,000	
Cash inflow from financing		34,000
Total cash inflow during the year . . .		38,877
Uses of cash (outflows):		
Investing:		
To purchase office equipment	6,000	
To purchase land	20,000	
Total cash used for investing purposes .		26,000
Change—increase in cash during the year . .		**$12,877**

Required You have been employed to refine the managerial accounting system for Business Duplicating. Speculate on the additional information a managerial accounting system should develop that would be beneficial to the manager of Business Duplicating.

Group Exercises

GE1–11 Ethics on the Job Ethical standards are very important in business, but they are not always followed. If you have ever held a job—even a summer job—describe the ethical climate in the organization where you worked. Did employees work a full day or did they arrive late and leave early? Did employees honestly report the hours they worked? Did employees use their employer's resources for their own purposes? Did managers set a good example? Did the organization have a code of ethics and were employees made aware of its existence? If the ethical climate in the organization you worked for was poor, what problems, if any, did it create?

IE1–12 Management Accounting Profession The CMA-Canada web site contains a significant amount of information about the society and its members. Answer the following questions by accessing data on the web site.

Required
1. How do you become a CMA?
2. What is the difference between the entrance examination and the professional program?
3. What practical experience is required to become a CMA?
4. What are the salary ranges for a senior accountant and a junior accounting clerk?
5. What is the suggested role for a CMA?

IE1–13 Malcolm Baldrige National Quality Award The National Quality Program maintains a web site at www.quality.nist.gov that provides information about the prestigious Malcolm Baldrige National Quality Award.

Required
1. What is the Malcolm Baldrige National Quality Award?
2. What organizations are recent winners of the award? What industries are they from?
3. Is any evidence presented on the web site that winners of the award are more successful than other organizations?

4. Awards are currently given in three categories: business, education, and health care. Briefly describe the criteria that are used for awarding the education award. Do the criteria require that specific goals be met in terms of achievement on standardized tests or other measures of performance?

IE1–14   Business Process Reengineering   ProSci, a business process reengineering publishing and research organization, has its web home page at www.prosci.com. Among other things, this web site contains a tutorial concerning business process reengineering and a yellow pages directory of consultants and other specialists in the field. Use information gleaned from this web site to answer the following questions:

Required 1. Were most early attempts at business process reengineering successful?
2. Who should be on a business process reengineering team?
3. Why is top-management support necessary for a successful implementation of business process reengineering?
4. How can consultants sometimes unintentionally create barriers to successful implementation of business process reengineering?

IE1–15   Just-in-Time (JIT) Suppliers   JIT Manufacturing Incorporated is a just-in-time supplier of medical and industrial products to other companies. The company maintains a web site at www.jitmfg.com where the company's products and services are described.

Required 1. How often can customers pull items from JIT Manufacturing Incorporated's inventories?
2. How does JIT Manufacturing Incorporated ensure that it is able to fill customer orders? What information does JIT Manufacturing require from its customers?
3. In return for its services, what does JIT Manufacturing Incorporated ask of its customers?

Chapter Two

Cost Terms, Concepts, and Classifications

Business Focus

Terri, the owner of a retail florist shop, has been trying to decide for some time whether she should continue to use a local courier service to deliver flowers to customers or buy a delivery truck and use one of her employees to make the deliveries. At a recent family Thanksgiving dinner, she brought up the subject of the delivery truck with her brother-in-law, who fancies himself as an expert on all management subjects. He grabbed this opportunity to impress on Terri his understanding of costs.

In rapid-fire succession, Terri's brother-in-law told her that the fees paid to the courier to deliver flowers are a variable cost and a period cost, but the costs of the flowers are product costs rather than period costs, even though the flower costs are also variable costs. On the other hand, the depreciation of the delivery truck would be a fixed cost and a period cost. And while the fuel for the truck would be a variable cost and a differential cost, the wages of the person making the deliveries would be

a fixed cost, not a differential cost, and would involve an opportunity cost. At this point, Terri excused herself—pleading that she had to help in the kitchen.

Terri felt that her brother-in-law's comments were more confusing than helpful, but she knew that she could no longer put off the decision about the delivery truck. She would have to think carefully about her costs and determine what costs should be considered in this decision.

Learning Objectives

After studying Chapter 2, you should be able to:

1 Identify and give examples of each of the three basic cost elements involved in the manufacture of a product.

2 Distinguish between product costs and period costs and give examples of each.

3 Prepare a schedule of cost of goods manufactured in good form.

4 Explain the flow of direct materials cost, direct labour cost, and manufacturing overhead cost from the point of incurrence to sale of the completed product.

5 Identify and give examples of variable costs and fixed costs, and explain the difference in their behaviour.

6 Define and give examples of direct and indirect costs.

7 Define and give examples of cost classifications used in making decisions: differential costs, opportunity costs, and sunk costs.

8 Explain what an organization is and the importance of strategic planning.

9 (Appendix 2A) Properly classify labour costs associated with idle time, overtime, and fringe benefits.

As explained in Chapter 1, the work of management focuses on (1) planning, which includes setting objectives and outlining how to attain these objectives; and (2) control, which includes the steps to take to ensure that objectives are realized. To carry out these planning and control responsibilities, managers need *information* about the organization. From an accounting point of view, this information often relates to the *costs* of the organization.

In managerial accounting, the term *cost* is used in many different ways. The reason is that there are many types of costs, and these costs are classified differently according to the immediate needs of management. For example, managers may want cost data to prepare external financial reports, to prepare planning budgets, or to make decisions. Each different use of cost data demands a different classification and definition of costs. For example, the preparation of external financial reports requires the use of historical cost data, whereas decision making may require current cost data.

In this chapter, we discuss many of the possible uses of cost data and how costs are defined and classified for each use. Our first task is to explain how costs are classified for the purpose of preparing external financial reports—particularly in manufacturing companies. To set the stage for this discussion, we begin the chapter by defining some terms commonly used in manufacturing.

General Cost Classifications

Costs are associated with all types of organizations—business, nonbusiness, manufacturing, retail, and service. Generally, the kinds of costs that are incurred and the way in which these costs are classified depends on the type of organization involved. Managerial accounting is as applicable to one type of organization as to another. For this reason, we will consider in our discussion the cost characteristics of a variety of organizations—manufacturing, merchandising, and service.

Our initial focus in this chapter is on manufacturing companies, since their basic activities include most of the activities found in other types of business organizations. Manufacturing companies such as Magna, Ford, and Molson are involved in acquiring raw materials, producing finished goods, marketing, distributing, billing, and almost every other business activity. Therefore, an understanding of costs in a manufacturing company can be very helpful in understanding costs in other types of organizations.

In this chapter, we develop cost concepts that apply to diverse organizations. For example, these cost concepts apply to fast-food outlets such as Kentucky Fried Chicken, Pizza Hut, and Taco Bell; movie studios such as Disney, Paramount, and United Artists; consulting firms such as Andersen Consulting and KPMG; and your local hospital. The exact terms used in these industries may not be the same as those used in manufacturing, but the same basic concepts apply. With some slight modifications, these basic concepts also apply to merchandising companies such as Wal-Mart, Canadian Tire, Zellers, and The Bay that resell finished goods acquired from manufacturers and other sources. With that in mind, let us begin our discussion of manufacturing costs.

Manufacturing Costs

Most manufacturing companies divide manufacturing costs into three broad categories: direct materials, direct labour, and manufacturing overhead. A discussion of each of these categories follows.

Raw materials Any materials that go into the final product.

Direct materials Those materials that become an integral part of a finished product and can be conveniently traced into it.

Indirect materials Small items of material such as glue and nails. These items may become an integral part of a finished product but are traceable to the product only at great cost or inconvenience.

Direct labour Those factory labour costs that can be easily traced to individual units of product. Also called *touch labour.*

Indirect labour The labour costs of janitors, supervisors, materials handlers, and other factory workers that cannot be conveniently traced directly to particular products.

DIRECT MATERIALS The materials that go into the final product are called **raw materials.** This term is somewhat misleading, since it seems to imply unprocessed natural resources like wood pulp or iron ore. Actually, raw materials refer to any materials that are used in the final product; and the finished product of one company can become the raw materials of another company. For example, the plastics produced by Du Pont are a raw material used by Compaq Computer in its personal computers.

Direct materials are those materials that become an integral part of the finished product and that can be physically and conveniently traced to it. This would include, for example, the seats Bombardier purchases from subcontractors to install in its commercial aircraft. Also included is the tiny electric motor Panasonic uses in its CD players to make the CD spin.

Sometimes it is not worth the effort to trace the costs of relatively insignificant materials to the end products. Such minor items would include the solder used to make electrical connections in a Sony TV or the glue used to assemble an Ethan Allen chair. Materials such as solder and glue are called **indirect materials** and are included as part of manufacturing overhead, which is discussed later in this section.

DIRECT LABOUR The term **direct labour** is reserved for those labour costs that can be easily (i.e., physically and conveniently) traced to individual units of product. Direct labour is sometimes called *touch labour,* since direct labour workers typically touch the product while it is being made. The labour costs of assembly-line workers, for example, would be direct labour costs, as would the labour costs of carpenters, bricklayers, and machine operators.

Labour costs that cannot be physically traced to the creation of products, or that can be traced only at great cost and inconvenience, are termed **indirect labour** and treated as part of manufacturing overhead, along with indirect materials. Indirect labour includes the labour costs of janitors, supervisors, materials handlers, and night security guards. Although the efforts of these workers are essential to production, it would be either impractical or impossible to accurately trace their costs to specific units of product. Hence, such labour costs are treated as indirect labour.

In some industries, major shifts are taking place in the structure of labour costs. Sophisticated automated equipment, run and maintained by skilled indirect workers, is increasingly replacing direct labour. In a few companies, direct labour has become such a minor element of cost that it has disappeared altogether as a separate cost category. More is said in later chapters about this trend and about the impact it is having on cost systems. However, the vast majority of manufacturing and service companies throughout the world continue to recognize direct labour as a separate cost category.

Focus on Current Practice

Inco is reported to use a load-haul-dump machine and drills that are run from a control room above ground using a tele-remote system in Sudbury.

One significant saving results from avoiding the setup costs associated with the travel time of miners to and from the face of the mine.[1] ∎

Manufacturing overhead All costs associated with manufacturing except direct materials and direct labour.

MANUFACTURING OVERHEAD **Manufacturing overhead,** the third element of manufacturing cost, includes all costs of manufacturing except direct materials and direct labour. Manufacturing overhead includes items such as indirect materials; indirect labour; maintenance and repairs on production equipment; and heat and light, property taxes, depreciation, and insurance on manufacturing facilities. A company also incurs costs for heat and light, property taxes, insurance, depreciation, and so forth, associated with its selling and administrative functions, but these costs are not included as part of manufacturing overhead. Only those costs associated with *operating the factory* are included in the manufacturing overhead category.

Various names are used for manufacturing overhead, such as *indirect manufacturing cost, factory overhead,* and *factory burden.* All of these terms are synonymous with *manufacturing overhead.*

Conversion cost Direct labour cost plus manufacturing overhead cost.

Prime cost Direct materials cost plus direct labour cost.

Manufacturing overhead combined with direct labour is called **conversion cost.** This term stems from the fact that direct labour costs and overhead costs are incurred in the conversion of materials into finished products. Direct labour combined with direct materials is called **prime cost.**

The proportion of labour to overhead varies from company to company and even within companies within the same industry. Some automated companies have a large proportion of overhead compared to direct labour costs. A number even classify all labour as overhead. Others, such as those engaged in meat packing, have a large proportion of direct labour. There are those production companies that buy materials partially assembled while others manufacture their subassembled parts to be used by other departments in the manufacturing process. How organizations determine their proportions of materials, labour and overhead is a significant part of their strategic planning.

Nonmanufacturing Costs

Generally, nonmanufacturing costs are subclassified into two categories:

1. Marketing or selling costs.
2. Administrative costs.

Marketing or selling costs All costs necessary to secure customer orders and get the finished product or service into the hands of the customer.

Marketing or selling costs include all costs necessary to secure customer orders and get the finished product or service into the hands of the customer. These costs are often called *order-getting and order-filling costs.* Examples of marketing costs include advertising, shipping, sales travel, sales commissions, sales salaries, and costs of finished goods warehouses.

Administrative costs All executive, organizational, and clerical costs associated with the general management of an organization rather than with manufacturing, marketing, or selling.

Administrative costs include all executive, organizational, and clerical costs associated with the *general management* of an organization rather than with manufacturing, marketing, or selling. Examples of administrative costs include executive compensation, general accounting, secretarial, public relations, and similar costs involved in the overall, general administration of the organization *as a whole.*

Managerial accounting concepts and techniques apply just as much to nonmanufacturing activities as they do to manufacturing activities, although in the past the central focus has been on the manufacturing environment. Service organizations in

1. Paul Bagnell, "Robo Miners," *The Financial Post,* May 23, 1998, p. R20.

particular are making increased use of cost concepts in analyzing and costing their services. For example, banks now use cost analysis in determining the cost of offering such services as chequing accounts, consumer loans, and credit cards; and insurance companies determine costs of servicing customers by geographic location, age, marital status, and occupation. Cost breakdowns of these types provide data for control over selling and administrative functions in the same way that manufacturing cost breakdowns provide data for control over manufacturing functions.

Product Costs versus Period Costs

Objective 2

Distinguish between product costs and period costs and give examples of each.

In addition to the distinction between manufacturing and nonmanufacturing costs, there are other ways to look at costs. For instance, they can also be classified as either *product costs* or *period costs*. To understand the difference between product costs and period costs, we must first refresh our understanding of the matching principle from financial accounting.

Generally, costs are recognized as expenses on the income statement in the period that benefits from the cost. For example, if a company pays for liability insurance in advance for two years, the entire amount is not considered an expense of the year in which the payment is made. Instead, one-half of the cost would be recognized as an expense each year. The reason is that both years—not just the first year—benefit from the insurance payment. The unexpensed portion of the insurance payment is carried on the balance sheet as an asset called prepaid insurance. You should be familiar with this type of *accrual* from your financial accounting coursework.

The *matching principle* is based on the accrual concept and states that *costs incurred to generate a particular revenue should be recognized as expenses in the same period that the revenue is recognized.* This means that if a cost is incurred to acquire or make something that will eventually be sold, then the cost should be recognized as an expense only when the sale takes place—that is, when the benefit occurs. Such costs are called *product costs.*

Product Costs

Product costs All costs that are involved in the purchase or manufacture of goods. In the case of manufactured goods, these costs consist of direct materials, direct labour, and manufacturing overhead. Also see Inventoriable costs.

Inventoriable costs Same as *product costs.*

For financial accounting purposes, **product costs** include all the costs that are involved in acquiring or making a product. In the case of manufactured goods, these costs consist of direct materials, direct labour, and manufacturing overhead. Product costs are viewed as "attaching" to units of product as the goods are purchased or manufactured, and they remain attached as the goods go into inventory awaiting sale. So initially, product costs are assigned to an inventory account on the balance sheet. When the goods are sold, the costs are released from inventory as expenses (typically called cost of goods sold) and matched against sales revenue. Since product costs are initially assigned to inventories, they are also known as **inventoriable costs.**

We want to emphasize that product costs are not necessarily treated as expenses in the period in which they are incurred. Rather, as explained above, they are treated as expenses in the period in which the related products *are sold.* This means that a product cost such as direct materials or direct labour might be incurred during one period but not treated as an expense until a following period when the completed product is sold.

Period Costs

Period costs Those costs that are taken directly to the income statement as expenses in the period in which they are incurred or accrued; such costs consist of selling (marketing) and administrative expenses.

Period costs are all the costs that are not included in product costs. These costs are expensed on the income statement in the period in which they are incurred, using the usual rules of accrual accounting you have already learned in financial accounting. Period costs are not included as part of the cost of either purchased or manufactured goods. Sales commissions and office rent are good examples of the kind of costs we are talking about. Neither commissions nor office rent are included as part of the cost of purchased or manufactured goods. Rather, both items are treated as expenses on the income statement in the period in which they are incurred. Thus, they are said to be period costs.

As suggested above, *all selling and administrative expenses are considered to be period costs.* Therefore, advertising, executive salaries, sales commissions, public relations, and other nonmanufacturing costs discussed earlier would all be period costs. They will appear on the income statement as expenses in the period in which they are incurred.

Exhibit 2–1 contains a summary of the cost terms that we have introduced so far.

Cost Classifications on Financial Statements

In your prior accounting training, you learned that firms prepare periodic financial reports for creditors, shareholders, and others to show the financial condition of the firm and the firm's earnings performance over some specified interval. The reports you

Exhibit 2–1 Summary of Cost Terms

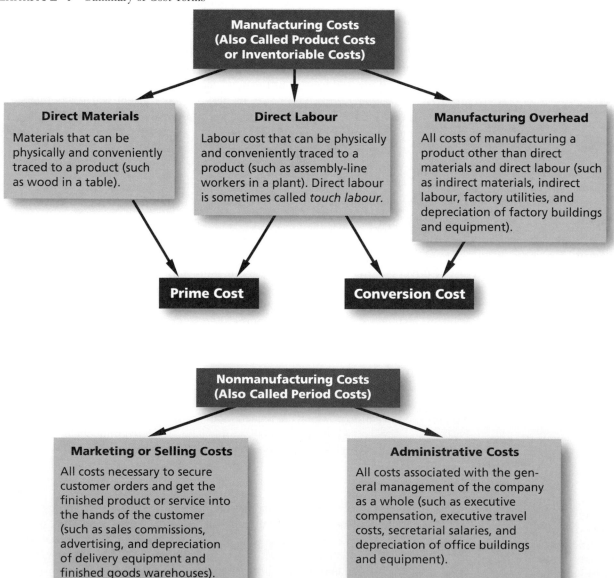

studied were probably those of merchandising companies, such as retail stores, which simply purchase goods from suppliers for resale to customers.

The financial statements prepared by a *manufacturing* company are more complex than the statements prepared by a merchandising company. Manufacturing companies are more complex organizations than merchandising companies because the manufacturing company must produce its goods as well as market them. The production process gives rise to many costs that do not exist in a merchandising company, and somehow these costs must be accounted for on the manufacturing company's financial statements. In this section, we focus our attention on how this accounting is carried out in the balance sheet and income statement.

The Balance Sheet

The balance sheet, or statement of financial position, of a manufacturing company is similar to that of a merchandising company. However, there are differences in the inventory accounts. A merchandising company has only one class of inventory—goods purchased from suppliers that are awaiting resale to customers. By contrast, manufacturing companies have three classes of inventories—*raw materials, work in process,* and *finished goods*. As discussed in Chapter 1, *work in process* consists of goods that are only partially completed, and *finished goods* consist of goods that are ready to be sold. The breakdown of the overall inventory figure into these three classes of inventories is usually provided in a footnote to the financial statements.

We will use two companies—Graham Manufacturing and Reston Bookstore—to illustrate the concepts discussed in this section. Graham Manufacturing is located in Victoria, British Columbia, and makes precision brass fittings for yachts. Reston Bookstore is a small bookstore in Moncton, New Brunswick, specializing in selling books about Maritime Canada.

The footnotes to Graham Manufacturing's Annual Report reveal the following information concerning its inventories:

Graham Manufacturing Corporation
Inventory Accounts

	Beginning Balance	Ending Balance
Raw Materials	$ 60,000	$ 50,000
Work in Process	90,000	60,000
Finished Goods	125,000	175,000
Total inventory accounts	$275,000	$285,000

Graham Manufacturing's raw materials inventory consists largely of brass rods and brass blocks. The work in process inventory consists of partially completed brass fittings. The finished goods inventory consists of brass fittings that are ready to be sold to customers.

In contrast, the inventory account at Reston Bookstore consists entirely of the costs of books the company has purchased from publishers for resale to the public. In merchandising companies like Reston, these inventories may be called *merchandise inventory*. The beginning and ending balances in this account appear as follows:

Reston Bookstore
Inventory Account

	Beginning Balance	Ending Balance
Merchandise Inventory	$100,000	$150,000

Exhibit 2–2   Comparative Income Statements: Merchandising and Manufacturing Companies

MERCHANDISING COMPANY
Reston Bookstore

Sales		$1,000,000
Cost of goods sold:		
Beginning merchandise inventory	$100,000	
Add: Purchases	650,000	
Goods available for sale	750,000	
Deduct: Ending merchandise inventory	150,000	600,000
Gross margin		400,000
Less operating expenses:		
Selling expense	100,000	
Administrative expense	200,000	300,000
Net income		$ 100,000

The cost of merchandise inventory purchased from outside suppliers during the period. → (brace pointing to Add: Purchases)

MANUFACTURING COMPANY
Graham Manufacturing

Sales		$1,500,000
Cost of goods sold:		
Beginning finished goods inventory	$125,000	
Add: Cost of goods manufactured	850,000	
Goods available for sale	975,000	
Deduct: Ending finished goods inventory	175,000	800,000
Gross margin		700,000
Less operating expenses:		
Selling expense	250,000	
Administrative expense	300,000	550,000
Net income		$ 150,000

The manufacturing costs associated with the goods that were finished during the period. (See Exhibits 2–4 and 2–5 for details.) → (brace pointing to Add: Cost of goods manufactured)

The Income Statement

Exhibit 2–2 compares the income statements of Reston Bookstore and Graham Manufacturing. For purposes of illustration, these statements contain more detail about cost of goods sold than you will generally find in published financial statements.

At first glance, the income statements of merchandising and manufacturing firms like Reston Bookstore and Graham Manufacturing are very similar. The only apparent difference is in the labels of some of the entries that go into the computation of the cost of goods sold figure. In the exhibit, the computation of cost of goods sold relies on the following basic equation for inventory accounts:

Basic Equation for Inventory Accounts

$$\text{Beginning balance} + \text{Additions to inventory} = \text{Ending balance} + \text{Withdrawals from inventory}$$

The logic underlying this equation, which applies to any inventory account, is illustrated in Exhibit 2–3. During a period, there are additions to the inventory account through purchases or other means. The sum of the additions to the account and the beginning balance represents the total amount of inventory that is available for use during the period. At the end of the period, all of the inventory that was available must either be in ending inventory or must have been withdrawn from the inventory account.

Exhibit 2–3   Inventory Flows

These concepts are applied to determine the cost of goods sold for a merchandising company like Reston Bookstore as follows:

Cost of Goods Sold in a Merchandising Company

$$\begin{array}{c}\text{Beginning}\\\text{merchandise}\\\text{inventory}\end{array} + \text{Purchases} = \begin{array}{c}\text{Ending}\\\text{merchandise}\\\text{inventory}\end{array} + \begin{array}{c}\text{Cost of}\\\text{goods sold}\end{array}$$

or

$$\begin{array}{c}\text{Cost of}\\\text{goods sold}\end{array} = \begin{array}{c}\text{Beginning}\\\text{merchandise}\\\text{inventory}\end{array} + \text{Purchases} - \begin{array}{c}\text{Ending}\\\text{merchandise}\\\text{inventory}\end{array}$$

The cost of goods sold for a manufacturing company like Graham Manufacturing is determined as follows:

Cost of Goods Sold in a Manufacturing Company

$$\begin{array}{c}\text{Beginning finished}\\\text{goods inventory}\end{array} + \begin{array}{c}\text{Cost of goods}\\\text{manufactured}\end{array} = \begin{array}{c}\text{Ending finished}\\\text{goods inventory}\end{array} + \begin{array}{c}\text{Cost of}\\\text{goods sold}\end{array}$$

or

$$\begin{array}{c}\text{Cost of}\\\text{goods sold}\end{array} = \begin{array}{c}\text{Beginning finished}\\\text{goods inventory}\end{array} + \begin{array}{c}\text{Cost of goods}\\\text{manufactured}\end{array} - \begin{array}{c}\text{Ending finished}\\\text{goods inventory}\end{array}$$

To determine the cost of goods sold in a merchandising company like Reston Bookstore, we only need to know the beginning and ending balances in the Merchandise Inventory account and the purchases. Total purchases can be easily determined in a merchandising company by simply adding together all purchases from suppliers.

To determine the cost of goods sold in a manufacturing company like Graham Manufacturing, we need to know the *cost of goods manufactured* and the beginning and ending balances in the Finished Goods inventory account. The **cost of goods manufactured** consists of the manufacturing costs associated with goods that were *finished* during the period. The cost of goods manufactured figure for Graham Manufacturing is derived in Exhibit 2–4, which contains a *schedule of cost of goods manufactured.*

Schedule of Cost of Goods Manufactured

At first glance, the **schedule of cost of goods manufactured** in Exhibit 2–4 appears complex and perhaps even intimidating. However, it is all quite logical. Notice that the schedule of cost of goods manufactured contains the three elements of product costs that we discussed earlier—direct materials, direct labour, and manufacturing overhead.

Cost of goods manufactured   The manufacturing costs associated with the goods that were finished during the period.

Schedule of cost of goods manufactured   A schedule showing the direct materials, direct labour, and manufacturing overhead costs incurred for a period and assigned to Work in Process and completed goods.

Exhibit 2–4   Schedule of Cost of Goods Manufactured

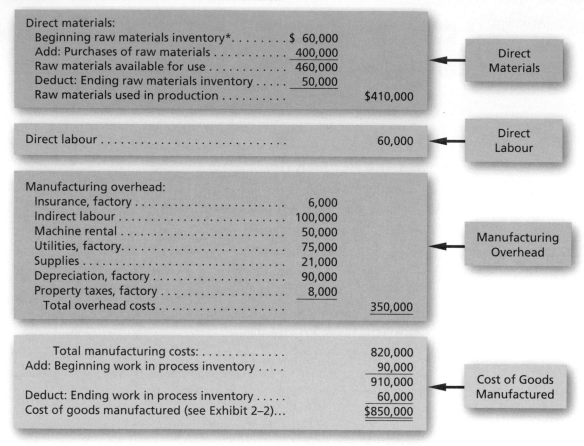

Direct materials:
Beginning raw materials inventory*. . . . . $ 60,000	
Add: Purchases of raw materials 400,000	
Raw materials available for use 460,000	
Deduct: Ending raw materials inventory 50,000	
Raw materials used in production	$410,000

→ Direct Materials

Direct labour   60,000

→ Direct Labour

Manufacturing overhead:
Insurance, factory 6,000	
Indirect labour 100,000	
Machine rental 50,000	
Utilities, factory. 75,000	
Supplies 21,000	
Depreciation, factory 90,000	
Property taxes, factory 8,000	
Total overhead costs	350,000

→ Manufacturing Overhead

Total manufacturing costs:	820,000
Add: Beginning work in process inventory	90,000
	910,000
Deduct: Ending work in process inventory	60,000
Cost of goods manufactured (see Exhibit 2–2)...	$850,000

→ Cost of Goods Manufactured

*We assume in this example that the Raw Materials inventory account contains only direct materials and that indirect materials are carried in a separate Supplies account. Using a Supplies account for indirect materials is a common practice among companies. In Chapter 3, we discuss the procedure to be followed if *both* direct and indirect materials are carried in a single account.

Objective 3

Prepare a schedule of cost of goods manufactured in good form.

The total of these three cost elements is *not* the cost of goods manufactured, however. The reason is that some of the materials, labour, and overhead costs incurred during the period relate to goods that are not yet completed. The costs that relate to goods that are not yet completed are shown in the work in process inventory figures at the bottom of the schedule. Note that the beginning work in process inventory must be added to the manufacturing costs of the period, and the ending work in process inventory must be deducted, to arrive at the cost of goods manufactured.

The logic underlying the schedule of cost of goods manufactured and the computation of cost of goods sold is laid out in a different format in Exhibit 2–5. To compute the cost of goods sold, go to the top of the exhibit and work your way down using the following steps:

1. Compute the raw materials used in production in the top section of the exhibit.
2. Insert the total raw materials used in production ($410,000) into the second section of the exhibit, and compute the total manufacturing cost.
3. Insert the total manufacturing cost ($820,000) into the third section of the exhibit, and compute the cost of goods manufactured.
4. Insert the cost of goods manufactured ($850,000) into the bottom section of the exhibit, and compute the cost of goods sold.

Exhibit 2–5 An Alternative Approach to Computation of Cost of Goods Sold

Computation of Raw Materials Used in Production

Beginning raw materials inventory	$ 60,000
+Purchases of raw materials	400,000
–Ending raw materials inventory	50,000
=Raw materials used in production	$410,000

Computation of Total Manufacturing Cost

Raw materials used in production	$410,000
+Direct Labour	60,000
+Total manufacturing overhead costs	350,000
=Total manufacturing cost	$820,000

Computation of Cost of Goods Manufactured

Beginning work in process inventory	$ 90,000
+Total manufacturing cost	820,000
–Ending work in process inventory	60,000
=Cost of goods manufactured	$850,000

Computation of Cost of Goods Sold

Beginning finished goods inventory	$125,000
+Cost of goods manufactured	850,000
–Ending finished goods inventory	175,000
=Cost of goods sold	$800,000

Product Costs—A Closer Look

Objective 4

Explain the flow of direct materials cost, direct labour cost, and manufacturing overhead cost from the point of incurrence to sale of the completed product.

Earlier in the chapter, we defined product costs as consisting of those costs that are involved in either the purchase or the manufacture of goods. For manufactured goods, we stated that these costs consist of direct materials, direct labour, and manufacturing overhead. To understand product costs more fully, it will be helpful at this point to look briefly at the flow of costs in a manufacturing company. By doing so, we will be able to see how product costs move through the various accounts and affect the balance sheet and the income statement in the course of producing and selling products.

Exhibit 2–6 illustrates the flow of costs in a manufacturing company. Raw materials purchases are recorded in the Raw Materials inventory account. When raw materials are used in production, their costs are transferred to the Work in Process inventory account as direct materials. Notice that direct labour cost and manufacturing overhead cost are added directly to Work in Process. Work in Process can be viewed most simply as an assembly line where workers are stationed and where products slowly take shape as they move from one end of the assembly line to the other. The direct materials, direct labour, and manufacturing overhead costs added to Work in Process in Exhibit 2–6 are the costs needed to complete these products as they move along this assembly line.

Notice from the exhibit that as goods are completed, their cost is transferred from Work in Process into Finished Goods. Here the goods await sale to a customer. As goods are sold, their cost is then transferred from Finished Goods into Cost of Goods Sold. It is at this point that the various material, labour, and overhead costs that are required to make the product are finally treated as expenses.

Exhibit 2–6   Cost Flows and Classifications in a Manufacturing Company

Inventoriable Costs

As stated earlier, product costs are often called inventoriable costs. The reason is that these costs go directly into inventory accounts as they are incurred (first into Work in Process and then into Finished Goods), rather than going into expense accounts. Thus, they are termed *inventoriable costs. This is a key concept in managerial accounting, since such costs can end up on the balance sheet as assets if goods are only partially completed or are unsold at the end of a period.* To illustrate this point, refer again to the data in Exhibit 2–6. At the end of the period, the materials, labour, and overhead costs that are associated with the units in the Work in Process and Finished Goods inventory accounts will appear on the balance sheet as part of the company's assets. As explained earlier, these costs will not become expenses until later when the goods are completed and sold.

As shown in Exhibit 2–6, selling and administrative expenses are not involved in the manufacture of a product. For this reason, they are not treated as product costs but rather as period costs that go directly into expense accounts as they are incurred.

An Example of Cost Flows

To provide a numerical example of cost flows in a manufacturing company, assume that a company's annual insurance cost is $2,000. Three-fourths of this amount ($1,500) applies to factory operations, and one-fourth ($500) applies to selling and administrative activities. Therefore, $1,500 of the $2,000 insurance cost would be a product (inventoriable) cost and would be added to the cost of the goods produced during the year. This concept is illustrated in Exhibit 2–7, where $1,500 of insurance cost is added into Work in Process. As shown in the exhibit, this portion of the year's insurance cost will not become an expense until the goods that are produced during the year are sold—which may not happen until the following year or even later. Until the goods are sold, the $1,500 will remain as part of the asset, inventory (either as part of Work in Process or as part of Finished Goods), along with the other costs of producing the goods.

Exhibit 2–7 An Example of Cost Flows in a Manufacturing Company

$1,500 of the insurance goes to support factory operations

(Manufacturing overhead)

Total insurance cost is $2,000

$500 of the insurance goes to support selling and administration

(Selling and administrative)

Balance Sheet

Work in Process inventory

The $1,500 moves slowly into finished goods inventory as units of the product are completed.

Finished Goods inventory

The $1,500 moves slowly into cost of goods sold as finished goods are sold.

Income Statement

Cost of goods sold

Selling and administrative expenses

By contrast, the $500 of insurance cost that applies to the company's selling and administrative activities will go into an expense account immediately as a charge against the period's revenue.

Thus far, we have been mainly concerned with classifications of manufacturing costs for the purpose of determining inventory valuations on the balance sheet and cost of goods sold on the income statement of external financial reports. There are, however, many other purposes for which costs are used, and each purpose requires a different classification of costs. We will consider several different purposes for cost classifications in the remaining sections of this chapter. These purposes and the corresponding cost classifications are summarized in Exhibit 2–8. To maintain focus, we suggest that you refer back to this exhibit frequently as you progress through the rest of this chapter.

Cost Classifications for Predicting Cost Behaviour

Cost behaviour The way in which a cost reacts or responds to changes in the level of business activity.

Quite frequently, it is necessary to predict how a certain cost will behave in response to a change in activity. For example, a manager at MT&T may want to estimate the impact a 5% increase in long-distance calls would have on the company's total electric bill or on the total wages the company pays its long-distance operators. **Cost behaviour** means how a cost will react or respond to changes in the level of business activity. As the activity level rises and falls, a particular cost may rise and fall as well—or it may remain constant. For planning purposes, a manager must be able to anticipate which of these will happen; and if a cost can be expected to change, the manager must know by how much it will change. To help make such distinctions, costs are often categorized as variable or fixed.

Exhibit 2–8 Summary of Cost Classifications

Purpose of Cost Classification	Cost Classifications

Preparing external financial statements	• Product costs (inventoriable)
	  • Direct materials
	  • Direct labour
	  • Manufacturing overhead
	• Period costs (expensed)
	  • Nonmanufacturing costs
	    • Marketing or selling costs
	    • Administrative costs

Predicting cost behaviour in response to changes in activity	• Variable cost (proportional to activity) • Fixed cost (constant in total)
Assigning costs to cost objects such as departments or products	• Direct cost (can be easily traced) • Indirect cost (cannot be easily traced; must be allocated)
Making decisions	• Differential cost (differs between alternatives) • Sunk cost (past cost not affected by a decision) • Opportunity cost (forgone benefit)

Variable Cost

Objective 5

Identify and give examples of variable costs and fixed costs, and explain the difference in their behaviour.

Variable cost A cost that varies, in total, in direct proportion to changes in the level of activity. A variable cost is constant per unit.

A **variable cost** is a cost that varies, in total, in direct proportion to changes in the level of activity. The activity can be expressed in many ways, such as units produced, units sold, kilometres driven, beds occupied, lines of print, hours worked, and so forth. A good example of a variable cost is direct materials. The cost of direct materials used during a period will vary, in total, in direct proportion to the number of units that are produced. To illustrate this idea, consider the Nova Bus Corporation. Each bus requires one battery. As the output of buses increases and decreases, the number of batteries used will increase and decrease proportionately. If bus production goes up 10%, then the number of batteries used will also go up 10%. The concept of a variable cost is shown in graphic form in Exhibit 2–9.

It is important to note that when we speak of a cost as being variable, we mean the *total* cost rises and falls as the activity level rises and falls. This idea is presented below, assuming that a battery costs $24:

Number of Buses Produced	Cost per Battery	Total Variable Cost— Batteries
1	$24	$ 24
500	24	12,000
1,000	24	24,000

One interesting aspect of variable cost behaviour is that a variable cost is constant if expressed on a *per unit* basis. Observe from the tabulation above that the per unit cost of batteries remains constant at $24 even though the total amount of cost involved increases and decreases with activity.

Exhibit 2–9 Variable and Fixed Cost Behaviour

There are many examples of costs that are variable with respect to the products and services provided by a company. In a manufacturing company, variable costs include items such as direct materials and some elements of manufacturing overhead such as lubricants, and period costs such as shipping, and sales commissions. For the present we will also assume that direct labour is a variable cost, although as we shall see in Chapter 6, direct labour may act more like a fixed cost in many situations. In a merchandising company, variable costs include items such as cost of goods sold, commissions to salespersons, and billing costs. In a hospital, the variable costs of providing health care services to patients would include the costs of the supplies, drugs, meals, and perhaps nursing services.

The activity causing changes in a variable cost need not be how much output is produced or sold. For example, the wages paid to employees at a Blockbuster Video outlet will depend on the number of hours the store is open and not strictly on the number of videos rented. In this case, we would say that wage costs are variable with respect to the hours of operation. Nevertheless, when we say that a cost is variable, we ordinarily mean it is variable with respect to the volume of revenue-generating output—in other words, how many units are produced and sold, how many videos are rented, how many patients are treated, and so on.

Fixed Cost

Fixed cost A cost that remains constant, in total, regardless of changes in the level of activity within the relevant range. If a fixed cost is expressed on a per unit basis, it varies inversely with the level of activity.

Relevant range The range of activity within which assumptions about variable and fixed cost behaviour are valid.

A **fixed cost** is a cost that remains constant, in total, regardless of changes in the level of activity. Unlike variable costs, fixed costs are not affected by changes in activity. Consequently, as the activity level rises and falls, the fixed costs remain constant in total amount unless influenced by some outside force, such as price changes. Rent is a good example of a fixed cost. Suppose the PEI Clinic rents a machine for $8,000 per month that tests blood samples for the presence of leukemia cells. The $8,000 monthly rental cost will be sustained regardless of the number of tests that may be performed during the month. The concept of a fixed cost is shown in graphic form in Exhibit 2–9.

Very few costs are completely fixed. Most will change if there is a large enough change in activity. For example, suppose that the capacity of the leukemia diagnostic machine at the PEI Clinic is 2,000 tests per month. If the clinic wishes to perform more than 2,000 tests in a month, it would be necessary to rent an additional machine, which would cause a jump in the fixed costs. When we say a cost is fixed, we mean it is fixed within some *relevant range*. The **relevant range** is the range of activity within which the assumptions about variable and fixed costs are valid. For example, the assumption

Exhibit 2–10
Summary of Variable and
Fixed Cost Behaviour

Cost	Behaviour of the Cost (within the relevant range)	
	In Total	**Per Unit**
Variable cost	Total variable cost increases and decreases in proportion to changes in the activity level.	Variable costs remain constant per unit.
Fixed cost	Total fixed cost is not affected by changes in the activity level within the relevant range.	Fixed costs decrease per unit as the activity level rises and increase per unit as the activity level falls.

that the rent for diagnostic machines is $8,000 per month is valid within the relevant range of 0 to 2,000 tests per month.

Fixed costs can create difficulties if it becomes necessary to express the costs on a per unit basis. This is because if fixed costs are expressed on a per unit basis, they will react *inversely* with changes in activity. In the PEI Clinic, for example, the average cost per test will fall as the number of tests performed increases. This is because the $8,000 rental cost will be spread over more tests. Conversely, as the number of tests performed in the clinic declines, the average cost per test will rise as the $8,000 rental cost is spread over fewer tests. This concept is illustrated in the table below:

Monthly Rental Cost	Number of Tests Performed	Average Cost per Test
$8,000	10	$800
8,000	500	16
8,000	2,000	4

Note that if the PEI Clinic performs only 10 tests each month, the rental cost of the equipment will average $800 per test. But if 2,000 tests are performed each month, the average cost will drop to only $4 per test. More will be said later about the problems created for both the accountant and the manager by this variation in unit costs.

Examples of fixed costs include straight-line depreciation, insurance, property taxes, rent, supervisory salaries, administrative salaries, and advertising.

A summary of both variable and fixed cost behaviour is presented in Exhibit 2–10.

Cost Classifications for Assigning Costs to Cost Objects

Objective 6

Define and give examples of direct and indirect costs.

Costs are assigned to objects for a variety of purposes including pricing, profitability studies, and control of spending. A **cost object** is anything for which cost data are desired—including products, product lines, customers, jobs, and organizational sub-units. For purposes of assigning costs to cost objects, costs are classified as either *direct* or *indirect*.

Cost object Anything for which cost data are desired.

Direct Cost

A **direct cost** is a cost that can be easily and conveniently traced to the particular cost object under consideration. The concept of direct cost extends beyond just direct materials and direct labour. For example, if Reebok is assigning costs to its various regional and national sales offices, then the salary of the sales manager in its Tokyo office would be a direct cost of that office.

Direct cost   A cost that can be easily and conveniently traced to the particular cost object under consideration.

Indirect cost   A cost that cannot be easily and conveniently traced to the particular cost object under consideration.

Common costs   A common cost is a cost that is common to a number of costing objects but cannot be traced to them individually.

Indirect Cost

An **indirect cost** is a cost that cannot be easily and conveniently traced to the particular cost object under consideration. For example, a Moosehead Breweries factory may produce many varieties of beer. The factory manager's salary would be an indirect cost of a particular variety such as Dry. The reason is that the factory manager's salary is not caused by any one variety of beer but rather is incurred as a consequence of running the entire factory. *To be traced to a cost object such as a particular product, the cost must be caused by the cost object.* The factory manager's salary is called a *common cost* of producing the various products of the factory. A **common cost** is a cost that is common to a number of costing objects but cannot be traced to them individually. A common cost is a particular type of indirect cost.

A particular cost may be direct or indirect, depending on the cost object. While the Moosehead Breweries factory manager's salary is an *indirect* cost of manufacturing Dry beer, it is a *direct* cost of the manufacturing division. In the first case, the cost object is the brand of beer. In the second case, the cost object is the entire manufacturing division.

Cost Classifications for Decision Making

Costs are an important feature of many business decisions. In making decisions, it is essential to have a firm grasp of the concepts *differential cost, opportunity cost,* and *sunk cost.*

Differential Cost and Revenue

Differential cost   A difference in cost between any two alternatives.

Differential revenue   The difference in revenue between any two alternatives.

Incremental cost   An increase in cost between two alternatives.

Decisions involve choosing between alternatives. In business decisions, each alternative will have certain costs and benefits that must be compared to the costs and benefits of the other available alternatives. A difference in costs between any two alternatives is known as a **differential cost.** A difference in revenues between any two alternatives is known as **differential revenue.**

A differential cost is also known as an **incremental cost,** although technically an incremental cost should refer only to an increase in cost from one alternative to another; decreases in cost should be referred to as *decremental costs.* Differential cost is a broader term, encompassing both cost increases (incremental costs) and cost decreases (decremental costs) between alternatives.

The accountant's differential cost concept can be compared to the economist's marginal cost concept. In speaking of changes in cost and revenue, the economist employs the terms *marginal cost* and *marginal revenue.* The revenue that can be obtained from selling one more unit of product is called marginal revenue, and the cost involved in producing one more unit of product is called marginal cost. The economist's marginal concept is basically the same as the accountant's differential concept applied to a single unit of output.

Differential costs can be either fixed or variable. To illustrate, assume that Nature Way Cosmetics, Inc., is thinking about changing its marketing method from distribution through retailers to distribution by door-to-door direct sale. Present costs and revenues are compared to projected costs and revenues in the following table:

	Retailer Distribution (present)	Direct Sale Distribution (proposed)	Differential Costs and Revenues
Revenues (V)	$700,000	$800,000	$100,000
Cost of goods sold (V)	350,000	400,000	50,000
Advertising (F)	80,000	45,000	(35,000)
Commissions (V)	–0–	40,000	40,000
Warehouse depreciation (F)	50,000	80,000	30,000
Other expenses (F)	60,000	60,000	–0–
Total	540,000	625,000	85,000
Net income	$160,000	$175,000	$ 15,000

V = Variable; F = Fixed.

According to the above analysis, the differential revenue is $100,000 and the differential costs total $85,000, leaving a positive differential net income of $15,000 under the proposed marketing plan.

    The decision of whether Nature Way Cosmetics should stay with the present retail distribution or switch to door-to-door direct selling could be made on the basis of the net incomes of the two alternatives. As we see in the above analysis, the net income under the present distribution method is $160,000, whereas the net income under door-to-door direct selling is estimated to be $175,000. Therefore, the door-to-door direct distribution method is preferred, since it would result in $15,000 higher net income. Note that we would have arrived at exactly the same conclusion by simply focusing on the differential revenues, differential costs, and differential net income, which also show a $15,000 advantage for the direct selling method.

    In general, only the differences between alternatives are relevant in decisions. Those items that are the same under all alternatives and that are not affected by the decision can be ignored. For example, in the Nature Way Cosmetics example above, the "Other expenses" category, which is $60,000 under both alternatives, can be ignored, since it has no effect on the decision. If it were removed from the calculations, the door-to-door direct selling method would still be preferred by $15,000. This is an extremely important principle in management accounting that we will return to in later chapters.

Focus on Current Practice

The annual report of the Bank of Montreal Group of Companies for 1998 announced the strategic emphasis on improving technology and access channels to enter new markets. To accomplish this, the Bank announced agreements with The Great Atlantic and Pacific Company of Canada and Canada Safeway Limited to open instore branches. In addition, the Bank installed 560 new InstaBank Extra printers for ABMs. These activities result in minor incremental costs and provide improved technology and new markets without the cost of new full-service branches. ■

Opportunity Cost

Opportunity cost The potential benefit that is given up when one alternative is selected over another.

Opportunity cost is the potential benefit that is given up when one alternative is selected over another. To illustrate this important concept, consider the following examples:

Example 1

Vicki has a part-time job that pays her $100 per week while attending college. She would like to spend a week at the beach during spring break, and her employer has agreed to give her the time off, but without pay. The $100 in lost wages would be an opportunity cost of taking the week off to be at the beach.

Example 2

Suppose that The Bay is considering investing a large sum of money in land that may be a site for a future store. Rather than invest the funds in land, the company could invest the funds in high-grade securities. If the land is acquired, the opportunity cost will be the investment income that could have been realized if the securities had been purchased instead.

Example 3

Steve is employed with a company that pays him a salary of $20,000 per year. He is thinking about leaving the company and returning to school. Since returning to school would require that he give up his $20,000 salary, the forgone salary would be an opportunity cost of seeking further education.

Opportunity cost is not usually entered in the accounting records of an organization, but it is a cost that must be explicitly considered in every decision a manager makes. Virtually every alternative has some opportunity cost attached to it. In example 3 above, for instance, if Steve decides to stay at his job, there still is an opportunity cost involved: it is the greater income that could be realized in future years as a result of returning to school.

Sunk Cost

Sunk cost   Any cost that has already been incurred and that cannot be changed by any decision made now or in the future.

A **sunk cost** is a cost *that has already been incurred* and that cannot be changed by any decision made now or in the future. Since sunk costs cannot be changed by any decision, they are not differential costs. Therefore, they can and should be ignored when making a decision.

To illustrate a sunk cost, assume that a company paid $50,000 several years ago for a special-purpose machine. The machine was used to make a product that is now obsolete and is no longer being sold. Even though in hindsight the purchase of the machine may have been unwise, no amount of regret can undo that decision. And it would be folly to continue making the obsolete product in a misguided attempt to "recover" the original cost of the machine. In short, the $50,000 originally paid for the machine has already been incurred and cannot be a differential cost in any future decision. For this reason, such costs are said to be sunk and should be ignored in decisions.

Organizations and Their Objectives

Objective 8

Explain what an organization is, and the importance of strategic planning.

An organization can be defined as a group of people united for some common purpose. A bank providing financial services is an organization; so is a university or community college providing educational services and a manufacturing firm providing appliances or other products for consumers. An organization consists of *people,* not physical assets. Thus, a bank building is not an organization; rather, the organization consists of the people who work in the bank and who are bound together for the common purpose of providing financial services to a community.

The common purpose toward which an organization works is called its *objective*.[2] Not all organizations have the same objective. For some organizations the objective is to produce a product and to earn a return on investment. For other organizations the objective may be to render humanitarian service (the Red Cross), to provide aesthetic enrichment (a symphony orchestra), or to provide government services (a water utility).

Objectives and the planning that goes toward achieving these objectives provides the basics for determining the structure, marketing emphasis, production, inventory practices and the financing. Planning and business practices selected will necessitate

---

2. The term objective, used here to mean a common purpose, is also described as a mission or goal. The technical distinctions among these terms are left to a more advanced discussion where the refinements of terminology are needed.

information. The types of information, the types of costs and the systems used to provide information will result from the objectives and planning decisions the organization selects.

To focus the discussion to follow, we present a single organization, the Bestway Furniture Company, and look closely at this organization's objectives, structure, and management, and at how these factors influence its need for managerial accounting data.

Setting Objectives

The Bestway Furniture Company is a corporation, and its owners have placed their money in the organization to earn a return on their investment. Thus, the first objective of the company is to earn a return on the money committed to it. This so-called profit objective is tempered by other objectives, however. The company is anxious to acquire and maintain a reputation for integrity, fairness, and dependability. It also wants to be a positive force in the social and ecological environment in which it carries out its activities.

The owners (shareholders) of the Bestway Furniture Company prefer not to be involved in the day-to-day operation of the company. Instead, they have outlined the broad objectives of the organization and have selected a president and other officers, collectively termed management, to oversee the implementation of these objectives. Although management should pursue the central objective of earning a return on the owners' investment, this must be done with a sensitivity to the other objectives that the organization desires to achieve.

Strategic Planning

Strategic planning The planning that leads to the implementation of an organization's objectives. Such planning occurs in two phases: (1) deciding on the products to produce and/or the services to render, and (2) deciding on the marketing and/or manufacturing methods to employ in getting the intended products or services to the proper audience.

The selection and implementation of an organization's long-term objectives is known as **strategic planning.** The strategic planning process as it is described here represents how the operations will be conducted to achieve the return on investment, the integrity, and the fairness and dependability desired by its owners. In many organizations, strategic planning occurs in two phases:

1. Deciding on the products to produce and/or the services to render.
2. Deciding on the marketing and/or manufacturing strategy to employ in getting the intended products or services to the proper audience.

The set of strategies emerging from strategic planning is often referred to as an organization's *policies,* and strategic planning itself is often referred to as *setting policy.*[3]

PHASE 1: PRODUCT STRATEGY   In deciding on the products to produce or the services to render, there are several strategies that Bestway Furniture Company could follow. The company could specialize in office furniture, it could specialize in appliances, it could be a broad supermarket furniture outlet, or it could employ any one of a number of other product and/or service strategies.

After careful consideration of the various strategies available, Bestway's management has decided to sell only home furnishings, including appliances. For one reason or another, several other possible strategies were rejected. For example, management has decided not to service appliances and not to sell office furniture or to deal in institutional furnishings.

---

3. For an expanded discussion of strategic planning and its relation to cost management, see Robert N. Anthony and Vijay Govindarajan, *Management Control Systems,* 9th ed. (Irwin McGraw-Hill, 1998), chapters 2, 8, and 13; and John K. Shank and Vijay Govindarajan, *Strategic Cost Analysis: The Evolution from Managerial to Strategic Accounting* (Homewood, IL: Richard D. Irwin, 1989).

PHASE 2: MARKETING STRATEGY   Having made the decision to concentrate on home furnishings, the management of the Bestway Furniture Company is now faced with a second strategy decision. Some furniture dealers handle only the highest-quality home furnishings, thereby striving to maintain the image of a quality dealer. The markups of these dealers are usually quite high, their volume is quite low, and their promotional efforts are directed toward a relatively small segment of the public. Other furniture dealers operate volume outlets. They try to keep markups relatively low, with the thought that overall returns will be augmented by a larger number of units sold. Still other dealers may follow different strategies. The selection of a particular strategy is a matter of managerial judgment; some companies make a return by following one strategy, while other companies are equally rewarded by following another. Decisions are needed on the products, their price, their place, and their promotion. The words *products, price,* and *promotion* signify the product selection, their pricing rules, and the promotion strategy of the organization. The word *place* denotes quality, delivery, and service. The decision characteristics represent the "four p's" of marketing strategy selection and implementation. The Bestway Furniture Company has decided to operate volume outlets and to maintain a discount image.

Every organization must make other strategic plans. The set of strategies may not be written down, but they exist nonetheless and they are a central guiding force in the organization's activities and in its need for accounting information. A full discussion of the strategic planning process involves numerous considerations such as the assessment of strengths, weaknesses, opportunities, and threats. Part of this process involves the consideration of five competitive forces: the power of their suppliers in negotiations, the power of their customers, the possible effects of substitutes, the entry of new competitors, and the threat of existing competitors. Each of the factors can impact on prices, costs, and investments made. Competitive advantages resulting from lower costs or product differentiation are combined with questions of how businesses are structured and conducted to provide an overall strategic plan.

Information is being used as a means of achieving success. Information can be restricted so that it hinders competitors from entering the business. Information can be used to gain an advantage in many of the negotiations that must be conducted with customers and suppliers. Reservation systems used by the transportation or hospitality industries and purchasing systems employed in industries such as motor vehicle manufacture create dependencies among organizations that will assist business. Thus, information not only serves in developing and selecting strategies but it serves as a means of achieving the results desired.

Two directions that constitute the advantage organizations attempt to achieve are low cost and differentiation. Low cost provides the advantage in a competitive environment whereby the organization can underprice its competition. Differentiation involves, as the term suggests, a means of distinguishing the output of the organization in terms of function, service or quality. Number of products, product complexity, service levels and associated costs and cost classifications will be determined by the strategic directions set by the management of the organization. For example, what is direct labour and its behaviour depends on the employment practices which in turn result from the competitive direction of the organization. Organizational structures depend on business location, size, and management practices which result from the strategic planning.

In summary, strategic planning to achieve the objectives of the organization set the decision framework for managers and in turn these decisions provide the direction for the information providers and analysts.

One attempt at providing a link from the performance measurement system to the strategy has been termed *balanced scorecard*. One approach to implementing this scorecard is to report results from four perspectives, the customer, learning and innovation, internal processes, and financial. The connection of these perspectives to strategic areas such as TQM, JIT, and process reengineering is obvious as is the connection to financial statements. More details about this approach to reporting on strategic performance will be provided in Chapter 10. For now it is important to be aware that such an approach is available for use by management accountants.[4]

Summary

In this chapter, we have looked at some of the ways in which managers classify costs. How the costs will be used—for preparing external reports, predicting cost behaviour, assigning costs to cost objects, or decision making—will dictate how the costs will be classified.

For purposes of valuing inventories and determining expenses for the balance sheet and income statement, costs are classified as either product costs or period costs. Product costs are assigned to inventories and are considered assets until the products are sold. At the point of sale, product costs become cost of goods sold on the income statement. In contrast, following the usual accrual practices, period costs are taken directly to the income statement as expenses in the period in which they are incurred.

In a merchandising company, product cost is whatever the company paid for its merchandise. For external financial reports in a manufacturing company, product costs consist of all manufacturing costs. In both kinds of companies, selling and administrative costs are considered to be period costs and are expensed as incurred.

For purposes of predicting cost behaviour—how costs will react to changes in activity—managers commonly classify costs into two categories—variable and fixed. Variable costs, in total, are strictly proportional to activity. Thus, the variable cost per unit is constant. Fixed costs, in total, remain at the same level for changes in activity that occur within the relevant range. Thus, the average fixed cost per unit decreases as the number of units increases.

For purposes of assigning costs to cost objects such as products or departments, costs are classified as direct or indirect. Direct costs can be conveniently traced to the cost objects. Indirect costs cannot be conveniently traced to cost objects.

For purposes of making decisions, the concepts of differential costs and revenue, opportunity cost, and sunk cost are of vital importance. Differential cost and revenue are the cost and revenue items that differ between alternatives. Opportunity cost is the benefit that is forgone when one alternative is selected over another. Sunk cost is a cost that occurred in the past and cannot be altered. Differential cost and opportunity cost should be carefully considered in decisions. Sunk cost is always irrelevant in decisions and should be ignored.

These various cost classifications are *different* ways of looking at costs. A particular cost, such as the cost of cheese in a taco served at Taco Bell, could be a manufacturing cost, a product cost, a variable cost, a direct cost, and a differential cost—all at the same time.

All organizations have basic objectives and a set of strategies for achieving those objectives. Both determining objectives and the setting of strategy, termed *strategic planning,* are key functions for managers and also set the framework for much of what managerial accounting needs to carry out.

---

4. Micheal Senyshen, "Keeping Score," *CGA Magazine* (June 1998), pp. 24–31.

Review Problem 1: Cost Terms

Many new cost terms have been introduced in this chapter. It will take you some time to learn what each term means and how to properly classify costs in an organization. To assist in this learning process, consider the following example: Porter Company manufactures furniture, including tables. Selected costs associated with the manufacture of the tables and the general operation of the company are given below:

1. The tables are made of wood that costs $100 per table.
2. The tables are assembled by workers, at a wage cost of $40 per table.
3. Workers assembling the tables are supervised by a factory supervisor who is paid $25,000 per year.
4. Electrical costs are $2 per machine-hour. Four machine-hours are required to produce a table.
5. The depreciation cost of the machines used to make the tables totals $10,000 per year.
6. The salary of the president of Porter Company is $100,000 per year.
7. Porter Company spends $250,000 per year to advertise its products.
8. Salespersons are paid a commission of $30 for each table sold.
9. Instead of producing the tables, Porter Company could rent its factory space out at a rental income of $50,000 per year.

In the following tabulation, these costs are classified according to various cost terms used in the chapter. *Carefully study the classification of each cost.* If you don't understand why a particular cost is classified the way it is, reread the section of the chapter discussing the particular cost term. The terms *variable cost* and *fixed cost* refer to how costs behave with respect to the number of tables produced in a year.

Solution to Review Problem 1

	Variable Cost	Fixed Cost	Period (selling and adminis- trative) Cost	Product Cost — Direct Materials	Product Cost — Direct Labour	Product Cost — Manufacturing Overhead	To Units of Product — Direct	To Units of Product — Indirect	Sunk Cost	Oppor- tunity Cost
1. Wood used in a table ($100 per table)	X			X			X			
2. Labour cost to assemble a table ($40 per table) ...	X				X		X			
3. Salary of the factory supervisor ($25,000 per year)		X				X		X		
4. Cost of electricity to produce tables ($2 per machine- hour)	X					X		X		
5. Depreciation of machines used to produce tables ($10,000 per year)		X				X		X	X*	

Solution to Review Problem 1 (cont.)

	Variable Cost	Fixed Cost	Period (selling and adminis-trative) Cost	Direct Materials	Direct Labour	Manufacturing Overhead	Direct	Indirect	Sunk Cost	Oppor-tunity Cost
6. Salary of the company president ($100,000 per year)		X	X							
7. Advertising expense ($250,000 per year)		X	X							
8. Commissions paid to salespersons ($30 per table sold)	X		X							
9. Rental income forgone on factory space										X†

*This is a sunk cost, since the outlay for the equipment was made in a previous period.

†This is an opportunity cost, since it represents the potential benefit that is lost or sacrificed as a result of using the factory space to produce tables. Opportunity cost is a special category of cost that is not ordinarily recorded in an organization's accounting books. To avoid possible confusion with other costs, we will not attempt to classify this cost in any other way except as an opportunity cost.

Review Problem 2: Schedule of Cost of Goods Manufactured and Income Statement

The following information has been taken from the accounting records of Klear-Seal Company for last year:

Selling expenses	$ 140,000
Raw materials inventory, January 1	90,000
Raw materials inventory, December 31	60,000
Utilities, factory	36,000
Direct labour cost	150,000
Depreciation, factory	162,000
Purchases of raw materials	750,000
Sales	2,500,000
Insurance, factory	40,000
Supplies, factory	15,000
Administrative expenses	270,000
Indirect labour	300,000
Maintenance, factory	87,000
Work in process inventory, January 1	180,000
Work in process inventory, December 31	100,000
Finished goods inventory, January 1	260,000
Finished goods inventory, December 31	210,000

Management wants to organize these data into a better format so that financial statements can be prepared for the year.

Required
1. Prepare a schedule of cost of goods manufactured as in Exhibit 2–4.
2. Compute the cost of goods sold.
3. Using data as needed from (1) and (2) above, prepare an income statement.

Solution to Review Problem 2

1.

KLEAR-SEAL COMPANY
Schedule of Cost of Goods Manufactured
For the Year Ended December 31

Direct materials:

Raw materials inventory, January 1	$ 90,000	
Add: Purchases of raw materials	750,000	
Raw materials available for use	840,000	
Deduct: Raw materials inventory, December 31	60,000	
Raw materials used in production		$ 780,000
Direct labour		150,000

Manufacturing overhead:

Utilities, factory	36,000	
Depreciation, factory	162,000	
Insurance, factory	40,000	
Supplies, factory	15,000	
Indirect labour	300,000	
Maintenance, factory	87,000	
Total overhead costs		640,000
Total manufacturing costs		1,570,000
Add: Work in process inventory, January 1		180,000
		1,750,000
Deduct: Work in process inventory, December 31		100,000
Cost of goods manufactured		$1,650,000

2. The cost of goods sold would be computed as follows:

Finished goods inventory, January 1	$ 260,000
Add: Cost of goods manufactured	1,650,000
Goods available for sale	1,910,000
Deduct: Finished goods inventory, December 31	210,000
Cost of goods sold	$1,700,000

3.

KLEAR-SEAL COMPANY
Income Statement
For the Year Ended December 31

Sales		$2,500,000
Less cost of goods sold (above)		1,700,000
Gross margin		800,000
Less selling and administrative expenses:		
Selling expenses	$ 140,000	
Administrative expenses	270,000	
Total expenses		410,000
Net income		$ 390,000

Appendix 2A: Further Classification of Labour Costs

Objective 9

Properly classify labour costs associated with idle time, overtime, and fringe benefits.

Labour costs often present difficult problems of segregation and classification. Although companies vary considerably in how they break down labour costs, the following subdivisions represent the most common approach:

Direct Labour	Indirect Labour (part of manufacturing overhead)	Other Labour Costs
(Discussed earlier)	Janitors	Idle time
	Supervisors	Overtime premium
	Materials handlers	Labour fringe benefits
	Night security guards	
	Maintenance workers	

The costs listed in the Indirect Labour and Other Labour Costs columns are representative of the kinds of costs that one might expect to find under these classifications. The costs in the Other Labour Costs column require further comment.

Idle Time

Idle time represents the costs of direct labour workers who are unable to perform their assignments due to machine breakdowns, materials shortages, power failures, and the like. Although direct labour workers are involved, the costs of idle time are treated as part of manufacturing overhead cost rather than as part of direct labour cost. The reason is that managers feel that such costs should be spread over *all* the production of a period rather than just over the jobs that happen to be in process when breakdowns and the like occur.

To give an example of how the cost of idle time is computed, assume that a press operator earns $12 per hour. If the press operator is paid for a normal 40-hour workweek but is idle for 3 hours during a given week due to breakdowns, labour cost would be allocated as follows:

Direct labour ($12 × 37 hours)	$444
Manufacturing overhead (idle time: $12 × 3 hours)	36
Total cost for the week	$480

Overtime Premium

The overtime premium paid to *all* factory workers (direct labour as well as indirect labour) is usually considered to be part of manufacturing overhead and is not assigned to any particular order. At first glance this may seem strange, since overtime is always spent working on some particular order. Why not charge that order for the overtime cost? The reason is that it would be considered unfair to charge an overtime premium against a particular order simply because the order *happened* to fall on the tail end of the daily scheduling sheet.

To illustrate, assume that two batches of goods, order A and order B, each takes three hours to complete. The production run on order A is scheduled early in the day, but the production run on order B isn't scheduled until late in the afternoon. By the time the run on order B is completed, two hours of overtime have been logged in. The necessity to work overtime was a result of the fact that total production exceeded the regular time available. Order B was no more responsible for the overtime than was order A. Therefore, managers feel that all production should share in the premium charge that resulted. This is considered a more equitable way of handling overtime premium in that it doesn't penalize one run simply because it happens to occur late in the day.

Let us again assume that a press operator in a plant earns $12 per hour. She is paid time and a half for overtime (time in excess of 40 hours a week). During a given week, she works 45 hours and has no idle time. Her labour cost for the week would be allocated as follows:

Direct labour ($12 × 45 hours)	$540
Manufacturing overhead (overtime premium: $6 × 5 hours)	30
Total cost for the week	$570

Observe from this computation that only the overtime premium of $6 per hour is charged to the overhead account—*not* the entire $18 earned for each hour of overtime work ($12 regular rate × 1.5 = $18).

Labour Fringe Benefits

Labour fringe benefits are made up of employment-related costs paid by the employer and include the costs of insurance programs, retirement plans, various supplemental unemployment benefits, and hospitalization plans. The employer also pays the employer's share of Canada Pension, Blue Cross, workers' compensation, and employment tax. These costs often add up to as much as 30% to 40% of base pay.

Many firms treat all such costs as indirect labour by adding them in total to manufacturing overhead. Other firms treat the portion of fringe benefits that relates to direct labour as additional direct labour cost. This approach is conceptually superior, since the fringe benefits provided to direct labour workers clearly represent an added cost of their services.

Questions

2–1 What are the three major elements of product costs in a manufacturing company?

2–2 Distinguish between the following: (a) direct materials, (b) indirect materials, (c) direct labour, (d) indirect labour, and (e) manufacturing overhead.

2–3 Explain the difference between a product cost and a period cost.

2–4 Describe how the income statement of a manufacturing company differs from the income statement of a merchandising company.

2–5 Of what value is the schedule of cost of goods manufactured? How does it tie into the income statement?

2–6 Describe how the inventory accounts of a manufacturing company differ from the inventory account of a merchandising company.

2–7 Why are product costs sometimes called inventoriable costs? Describe the flow of such costs in a manufacturing company from the point of incurrence until they finally become expenses on the income statement.

2–8 Is it possible for costs such as salaries or depreciation to end up as assets on the balance sheet? Explain.

2–9 What is meant by the term *cost behaviour?*

2–10 "A variable cost is a cost that varies per unit of product, whereas a fixed cost is constant per unit of product." Do you agree? Explain.

2–11 How do fixed costs create difficulties in costing units of product?

2–12 Why is manufacturing overhead considered an indirect cost of a unit of product?

2–13 Define the following terms: differential cost, opportunity cost, and sunk cost.

2–14 Only variable costs can be differential costs. Do you agree? Explain.

2–15 Some persons consider strategic planning to be the most important work that a manager does. In what ways might this be true? In what ways might this be false?

2–16 Describe "the four P's" of strategic planning.

2–17 Outline the basis for deciding strategic decisions, in other words, the areas where the business can be challenged.

2–18 Besides using information to make strategic decisions, information can serve a strategic purpose. Describe how information can serve a strategic objective.

2–19 (Appendix 2A) Mary Adams is employed by Acme Company. Last week she worked 34 hours assembling one of the company's products and was idle 6 hours due to material shortages. Acme's employees are engaged at their workstations for a normal 40-hour week. Ms. Adams is paid $8 per hour. Allocate her earnings between direct labour cost and manufacturing overhead cost.

2–20 (Appendix 2A) John Olsen operates a stamping machine on the assembly line of Drake Manufacturing Company. Last week Mr. Olsen worked 45 hours. His basic wage rate is $10 per hour, with time and a half for overtime (time worked in excess of 40 hours per week). Allocate Mr. Olsen's wages for the week between direct labour cost and manufacturing overhead cost.

Exercises

E2–1 Following are a number of cost terms introduced in the chapter:

Variable cost	Product cost
Fixed cost	Sunk cost
Prime cost	Conversion cost
Opportunity cost	Period cost

Choose the term or terms above that most appropriately describe the cost identified in each of the following situations. A cost term can be used more than once.

1. Lake Company produces a tote bag that is very popular with university students. The cloth going into the manufacture of the tote bag would be called direct materials and classified as a __product__ cost. In terms of cost behaviour, the cloth could also be described as a __variable__ cost.
2. The direct labour cost required to produce the tote bags, combined with the manufacturing overhead cost involved, would be known as __conversion__ cost.
3. The company could have taken the funds that it has invested in production equipment and invested them in interest-bearing securities instead. The interest forgone on the securities would be called __opportunity__ cost.
4. Taken together, the direct materials cost and the direct labour cost required to produce tote bags would be called __prime__ cost.
5. The company used to produce a smaller tote bag that was not very popular. Some three hundred of these smaller bags are stored in one of the company's warehouses. The amount invested in these bags would be called a __sunk__ cost.

6. The tote bags are sold through agents who are paid a commission on each bag sold. These commissions would be classified by Lake Company as a ~~period~~ cost. In terms of cost behaviour, commissions would be classified as a ~~variable~~ cost.

7. Depreciation on the equipment used to produce tote bags would be classified by Lake Company as a ~~product~~ cost. However, depreciation on any equipment used by the company in selling and administrative activities would be classified as a ~~period~~ cost. In terms of cost behaviour, depreciation would probably be classified as a ~~fixed~~ cost.

8. A ~~product~~ cost is also known as an inventoriable cost, since such costs go into the Work in Process inventory account and then into the Finished Goods inventory account before appearing on the income statement as part of cost of goods sold.

9. The salary of Lake Company's president would be classified as a ~~period~~ cost, since the salary will appear on the income statement as an expense in the time period in which it is incurred.

10. Costs can often be classified in several ways. For example, Lake Company pays $5,000 rent each month on its factory building. The rent would be part of manufacturing overhead. In terms of cost behaviour, it would be classified as a ~~fixed~~ cost. The rent can also be classified as a ~~product~~ cost and as part of ~~sunk~~ cost.
or conversion.

E2–2   A product cost is also known as an inventoriable cost. Classify the following costs as either product (inventoriable) costs or period (noninventoriable) costs in a manufacturing company:

1. Depreciation on salespersons' cars.
2. Rent on equipment used in the factory.
3. Lubricants used for maintenance of machines.
4. Salaries of finished goods warehouse personnel.
5. Soap and paper towels used by factory workers at the end of a shift.
6. Factory supervisors' salaries.
7. Heat, water, and power consumed in the factory.
8. Materials used in boxing units of finished product for shipment overseas. (Units are not normally boxed.)
9. Advertising outlays.
10. Workers' compensation insurance on factory employees.
11. Depreciation on chairs and tables in the factory lunchroom.
12. The salary of the switchboard operator for the company.
13. Depreciation on a Lear Jet used by the company's executives.
14. Rent on rooms at a Florida resort for holding of the annual sales conference.
15. Attractively designed box for packaging breakfast cereal.

E2–3   The Devon Motor Company produces automobiles. During April, the company purchased 8,000 batteries at a cost of $10 per battery. Devon withdrew 7,600 batteries from the storeroom during the month. Of these, 100 were used to replace batteries in autos being used by the company's travelling sales staff. The remaining 7,500 batteries withdrawn from the storeroom were placed in autos being produced by the company. Of the autos in production during April, 90% were completed and transferred from work in process to finished goods. Of the cars completed during the month, 30% were unsold at April 30.

There were no inventories of any type on April 1.

Required
1. Determine the cost of batteries that would appear in each of the following accounts at April 30:
   a. Raw Materials.
   b. Work in Process.
   c. Finished Goods.
   d. Cost of Goods Sold.
   e. Selling Expense.
2. Specify whether each of the above accounts would appear on the balance sheet or on the income statement at April 30.

E2–4 Below are a number of costs that are incurred in a variety of organizations.

Required Classify each cost as being variable or fixed with respect to the number of units of product or services sold by the organization.

	Cost Behaviour	
Cost Item	**Variable**	**Fixed**

Place an *X* in the appropriate column for each cost to indicate whether the cost involved would be variable or fixed with respect to the number of units of products or services sold by the organization.

1. X-ray film used in the radiology lab at Saint Martha's Hospital in Sydney.
2. The costs of advertising a Madonna rock concert in Toronto.
3. Depreciation on the Planet Hollywood restaurant building in Hong Kong.
4. The electrical costs of running a roller coaster at Magic Mountain.
5. Property taxes on your local cinema.
6. Commissions paid to salespersons at Nortel.
7. Property insurance on a Coca-Cola bottling plant.
8. The costs of synthetic materials used to make Nike running shoes.
9. The costs of shipping Panasonic televisions to retail stores.
10. The cost of leasing an ultra-scan diagnostic machine at the American Hospital in Paris.

E2–5 The following cost and inventory data are taken from the accounting records of Mason Company for the year just completed:

Costs incurred:

Direct labour cost	$ 70,000
Purchases of raw materials	118,000
Indirect labour	30,000
Maintenance, factory equipment	6,000
Advertising expense	90,000
Insurance, factory equipment	800
Sales salaries	50,000
Rent, factory facilities	20,000
Supplies	4,200
Depreciation, office equipment	3,000
Depreciation, factory equipment	19,000

	Beginning of the Year	End of the Year
Inventories:		
Raw materials	$ 7,000	$15,000
Work in process	10,000	5,000
Finished goods	20,000	35,000

Required
1. Prepare a schedule of cost of goods manufactured in good form.
2. Prepare the cost of goods sold section of Mason Company's income statement for the year.

E2–6 Below are listed various costs that are found in organizations.

1. Hamburger buns in a McDonald's outlet. *product → variable*
2. Advertising by a dental office. *selling cost, fixed*
3. Apples processed and canned by Del Monte Corporation. *product, variable*
4. Shipping canned apples from a Del Monte plant to customers. *period, selling + admin cost*
5. Insurance on a Bausch & Lomb factory producing contact lenses. *product, fixed*
6. Insurance on IBM's corporate headquarters. *period, fixed*
7. Salary of a supervisor overseeing production of circuit boards at Hewlett-Packard. *product, fixed*
8. Commissions paid to Encyclopedia Britannica salespersons. *period, variable*

9. Depreciation of factory lunchroom facilities at a General Electric plant. *product, fixed*
10. Steering wheels installed in BMWs. *product variable*

Required Classify each cost as being either variable or fixed with respect to the number of units sold. Also classify each cost as either a selling and administrative cost or a product cost. Prepare your answer sheet as shown below.

Cost Item	Cost Behaviour		Selling and Administrative Cost	Product Cost
	Variable	Fixed		

Place an *X* in the appropriate columns to show the proper classification of each cost.

E2–7 (Appendix 2A) Paul Clark is employed by Aerotech Products and assembles a component part for one of the company's product lines. He is paid $10 per hour for regular time and time and a half (i.e., $15 per hour) for all work in excess of 40 hours per week.

Required

1. Assume that during a given week Paul is idle for five hours due to machine breakdowns and that he is idle for four more hours due to material shortages. No overtime is recorded for the week. Allocate Paul's wages for the week between direct labour cost and manufacturing overhead cost.
2. Assume that during the following week Paul works a total of 48 hours. He has no idle time for the week. Allocate Paul's wages for the week between direct labour cost and manufacturing overhead cost.
3. Paul's company provides an attractive package of fringe benefits for its employees. This package includes a retirement program and a health insurance program. So far as direct labour workers are concerned, explain two ways that the company could handle the costs of fringe benefits in its cost records.

E2–8 (Appendix 2A) Several days ago you took your TV set into a shop to have some repair work done. When you later picked up the set, the bill showed a $75 charge for labour. This charge represented two hours of service time—$30 for the first hour and $45 for the second.

   When questioned about the difference in hourly rates, the shop manager explained that work on your set was started at 4 o'clock in the afternoon. By the time work was completed two hours later at 6 o'clock, an hour of overtime had been put in by the repair technician. The second hour therefore contained a charge for an "overtime premium," since the company had to pay the repair technician time and a half for any work in excess of eight hours per day. The shop manager further explained that the shop was working overtime to "catch up a little" on its backlog of repairs, but it still needed to maintain a "decent" profit margin on the technician's time.

Required

1. Do you agree with the shop's computation of the service charge on your job?
2. Assume that the shop pays its technicians $14 per hour for the first eight hours worked in a day and $21 per hour for any additional time worked in a day. Prepare computations to show how the cost of the repair technician's time for the day (nine hours) should be allocated between direct labour cost and general overhead cost on the shop's books.
3. Under what circumstances might the shop be justified in charging an overtime premium for repair work on your set?

Problems

P2–9 Cost Identification   Wollogong Group Ltd. of New South Wales, Australia, acquired its factory building about 10 years ago. For several years the company has rented out a small annex attached to the rear of the building. The company has received a rental income of $30,000 per year on this space. The renter's lease will expire soon, and rather than renewing the lease, the company has decided to use the space itself to manufacture a new product.

Direct materials cost for the new product will total $80 per unit. To have a place to store finished units of product, the company will rent a small warehouse nearby. The rental cost will be $500 per month. In addition, the company must rent equipment for use in producing the new product; the rental cost will be $4,000 per month. Workers will be hired to manufacture the new product, with direct labour cost amounting to $60 per unit. The space in the annex will continue to be depreciated on a straight-line basis, as in prior years. This depreciation is $8,000 per year.

Advertising costs for the new product will total $50,000 per year. A supervisor will be hired to oversee production; her salary will be $1,500 per month. Electricity for operating machines will be $1.20 per unit. Costs of shipping the new product to customers will be $9 per unit.

To provide funds to purchase materials, meet payrolls, and so forth, the company will have to liquidate some temporary investments. These investments are presently yielding a return of about $3,000 per year.

Required 1. Prepare an answer sheet with the following column headings:

Name of the Cost	Variable Cost	Fixed Cost	Direct Materials	Direct Labour	Manufacturing Overhead	Period (selling and administrative) Cost	Opportunity Cost	Sunk Cost
			Product Cost					

List the different costs associated with the new product decision down the extreme left column (under Name of the Cost). Then place an X under each heading that helps to describe the type of cost involved. There may be X's under several column headings for a single cost. (For example, a cost may be a fixed cost, a period cost, and a sunk cost; you would place an X under each of these column headings opposite the cost.)

2. Why is cost identification by cost behaviour important for strategic planning purposes?

P2–10 Supply Missing Production and Cost Data Supply the missing data in the following cases. Each case is independent of the others.

	Case 1	Case 2	Case 3	Case 4
Direct materials	$ 4,500	$ 6,000	$ 5,000	$ 3,000
Direct labour	?	3,000	7,000	4,000
Manufacturing overhead	5,000	4,000	?	9,000
Total manufacturing costs	18,500	13000	$20,000	?
Beginning work in process inventory	2,500	?	3,000	?
Ending work in process inventory . . .	?	1,000	4,000	3,000
Cost of goods manufactured	$18,000	$14,000	$?	$?
Sales	$30,000	$21,000	$36,000	$40,000
Beginning finished goods inventory . .	1,000	2,500	?	2,000
Cost of goods manufactured	?	?	?	17,500
Goods available for sale	?	?	?	?
Ending finished goods inventory	?	1,500	4,000	3,500
Cost of goods sold	17,000	?	18,500	?
Gross margin	13,000	?	17,500	?
Operating expenses	?	3,500	?	?
Net income	$ 4,000	$?	$ 5,000	$ 9,000

P2–11 Allocating Labour Costs (Appendix 2A) Mark Hansen is employed by Eastern Products, Inc., and works on the company's assembly line. Mark's basic wage rate is $10 per hour. The company's union contract states that employees are to be paid time and a half (i.e., $15 per hour) for any work in excess of 40 hours per week.

Required
1. Suppose that in a given week Mark works 46 hours. Compute Mark's total wages for the week. How much of this amount would be allocated to direct labour cost? To manufacturing overhead cost?
2. Suppose in another week that Mark works 48 hours but is idle for 3 hours during the week due to machine breakdowns. Compute Mark's total wages for the week. How much of this amount would be allocated to direct labour cost? To manufacturing overhead cost?
3. Eastern Products, Inc., has an attractive package of fringe benefits that costs the company $3 for each hour of employee time (either regular time or overtime). During a particular week, Mark works 50 hours but is idle for 2 hours due to material shortages. Compute Mark's total wages and fringe benefits for the week. If the company treats all fringe benefits as part of manufacturing overhead cost, how much of Mark's wages and fringe benefits for the week would be allocated to direct labour cost? To manufacturing overhead cost?
4. Refer to the data in (3) above. If the company treats that part of fringe benefits relating to direct labour as added direct labour cost, how much of Mark's wages and fringe benefits for the week will be allocated to direct labour cost? To manufacturing overhead cost?

P2–12 Cost Classification   Various costs associated with the operation of a factory are given below:

1. Electricity used in operating machines.
2. Rent on a factory building.
3. Cloth used in drapery production.
4. Production superintendent's salary.
5. Cost of labourers assembling a product.
6. Depreciation of air purification equipment used in furniture production.
7. Janitorial salaries.
8. Peaches used in canning fruit.
9. Lubricants needed for machines.
10. Sugar used in soft-drink production.
11. Property taxes on the factory.
12. Cost of workers painting a product.
13. Depreciation on cafeteria equipment.
14. Insurance on a building used in producing TV sets.
15. Picture tubes used in TV sets.

Required   Classify each cost as being either variable or fixed with respect to the number of units produced and sold. Also indicate whether each cost would typically be treated as a direct cost or an indirect cost with respect to units of product. Prepare your answer sheet as shown below:

	Cost Behaviour		To Units of Product	
Cost Item	Variable	Fixed	Direct	Indirect
Example: Factory insurance		X		X

P2–13 Cost Identification   The Dorilane Company specializes in producing a set of wood patio furniture consisting of a table and four chairs. The set enjoys great popularity, and the company has ample orders to keep production going at its full capacity of 2,000 sets per year. Annual cost data at full capacity follow:

Factory labour, direct	$118,000
Advertising	50,000
Factory supervision	40,000
Property taxes, factory building	3,500
Sales commissions	80,000
Insurance, factory	2,500

Depreciation, office equipment	4,000
Lease cost, factory equipment	12,000
Indirect materials, factory	6,000
Depreciation, factory building	10,000
General office supplies (billing)	3,000
General office salaries	60,000
Direct materials used (wood, bolts, etc.)	94,000
Utilities, factory	20,000

Required

1. Prepare an answer sheet with the column headings shown below. Enter each cost item on your answer sheet, placing the dollar amount under the appropriate headings. As examples, this has been done already for the first two items in the list above. Note that each cost item is classified in two ways: first, as variable or fixed, with respect to the number of units produced and sold; and second, as a selling and administrative cost or a product cost. (If the item is a product cost, it should be classified as being either direct or indirect as shown.)

	Cost Behaviour		Selling or Administrative	Product Cost	
Cost Item	**Variable**	**Fixed**	**Cost**	**Direct**	**Indirect***
Factory labour, direct	$118,000			$118,000	
Advertising		$50,000	$50,000		

*To units of product.

2. Total the dollar amounts in each of the columns in (1) above. Compute the cost to produce one patio set.
3. Assume that production drops to only 1,000 sets annually. Would you expect the cost per set to increase, decrease, or remain unchanged? Explain. No computations are necessary.
4. Refer to the original data. The president's brother-in-law has considered making himself a patio set and has priced the necessary materials at a building supply store. The brother-in-law has asked the president if he could purchase a patio set from the Dorilane Company "at cost," and the president agreed to let him do so.
   a. Would you expect any disagreement between the two men over the price the brother-in-law should pay? Explain. What price does the president probably have in mind? The brother-in-law?
   b. Since the company is operating at full capacity, what cost term used in the chapter might be justification for the president to charge the full, regular price to the brother-in-law and still be selling "at cost"?
5. How does knowledge of cost behaviour help managers with strategic planning decisions?

P2–14 Cost Classification   Listed below are a number of costs typically found in organizations.

1. Property taxes, factory.
2. Boxes used for packaging detergent.
3. Salespersons' commissions.
4. Supervisor's salary, factory.
5. Depreciation, executive automobiles.
6. Workers assembling computers.
7. Packing supplies for out-of-province shipments.
8. Insurance, finished goods warehouses.
9. Lubricants for machines.
10. Advertising costs.
11. "Chips" used in producing calculators.
12. Shipping costs on merchandise sold.
13. Magazine subscriptions, factory lunchroom.

14. Thread in a garment factory.
15. Billing costs.
16. Executive life insurance.
17. Ink used in textbook production.
18. Fringe benefits, assembly-line workers.
19. Yarn used in sweater production.
20. Receptionist, executive offices.

Required   Prepare an answer sheet with column headings as shown below. For each cost item, indicate whether it would be variable or fixed with respect to the number of units produced and sold; and then whether it would be a selling cost, an administrative cost, or a manufacturing cost. If it is a manufacturing cost, indicate whether it would typically be treated as a direct cost or an indirect cost with respect to units of product. Three sample answers are provided for illustration.

Cost Item	Variable or Fixed	Selling Cost	Administrative Cost	Manufacturing (product) Cost	
				Direct	Indirect
Direct labour	V			X	
Executive salaries	F		X		
Factory rent	F				X

P2–15   Cost Identification   Staci Valek began dabbling in pottery several years ago as a hobby. Her work is quite creative, and it has been so popular with friends and others that she has decided to quit her job with an aerospace firm and manufacture pottery full time. The salary from Stacy's aerospace job is $2,500 per month.

Staci will rent a small building near her home to use as a place for manufacturing the pottery. The rent will be $500 per month. She estimates that the cost of clay and glaze will be $2 for each finished piece of pottery. She will hire workers to produce the pottery at a labour rate of $8 per pot. To sell her pots, Staci feels that she must advertise heavily in the local area. An advertising agency states that it will handle all advertising for a fee of $600 per month. Staci's brother will sell the pots; he will be paid a commission of $4 for each pot sold. Equipment needed to manufacture the pots will be rented at a cost of $300 per month.

Staci has already paid the legal and filing fees associated with incorporating her business in the province. These fees amounted to $500. A small room has been located in a tourist area that Staci will use as a sales office. The rent will be $250 per month. A phone installed in the room for taking orders will cost $40 per month. In addition, a recording device will be attached to the phone for taking after-hours messages.

Staci has some money in savings that is earning interest of $1,200 per year. These savings will be withdrawn and used to get the business going. For the time being, Staci does not intend to draw any salary from the new company.

Required   1. Prepare an answer sheet with the following column headings:

Name of the Cost	Variable Cost	Fixed Cost	Product Cost			Period (selling and administrative) Cost	Opportunity Cost	Sunk Cost
			Direct Materials	Direct Labour	Manufacturing Overhead			

List the different costs associated with the new company down the extreme left column (under Name of Cost). Then place an *X* under each heading that helps to describe the type of cost involved. There may be *X*'s under several column headings for a single cost. (That is, a cost may be a fixed cost, a period cost, and a sunk cost; you would place an *X* under each of these column headings opposite the cost.)

Under the Variable Cost column, list only those costs that would be variable with respect to the number of units of pottery that are produced and sold.

2. All of the costs you have listed above, except one, would be differential costs between the alternatives of Staci producing pottery or staying with the aerospace firm. Which cost is *not* differential? Explain.

P2–16 Schedule of Cost of Goods Manufactured; Cost Behaviour
Various cost and sales data for Meriwell Company for the just completed year follow:

Finished goods inventory, beginning	$ 20,000
Finished goods inventory, ending	40,000
Depreciation, factory	27,000
Administrative expenses	110,000
Utilities, factory	8,000
Maintenance, factory	40,000
Supplies, factory	11,000
Insurance, factory	4,000
Purchases of raw materials	125,000
Raw materials inventory, beginning	9,000
Raw materials inventory, ending	6,000
Direct labour	70,000
Indirect labour	15,000
Work in process inventory, beginning	17,000
Work in process inventory, ending	30,000
Sales	500,000
Selling expenses	80,000

Required
1. Prepare a schedule of cost of goods manufactured.
2. Prepare an income statement.
3. Assume that the company produced the equivalent of 10,000 units of product during the year just completed. What was the unit cost for direct materials? What was the unit cost for factory depreciation?
4. Assume that the company expects to produce 15,000 units of product during the coming year. What per unit cost and what total cost would you expect the company to incur for direct materials at this level of activity? For factory depreciation? (In preparing your answer, assume that direct materials is a variable cost and that depreciation is a fixed cost; also assume that depreciation is computed on a straight-line basis.)
5. As the manager responsible for production costs, explain to the president any difference in unit costs between (3) and (4) above.

P2–17 Preparing Manufacturing Statements   Swift Company was organized on March 1 of the current year. After five months of start-up losses, management had expected to earn a profit during August, the most recent month. Management was disappointed, however, when the income statement for August also showed a loss. August's income statement follows:

SWIFT COMPANY
Income Statement
For the Month Ended August 31

Sales		$ 450,000
Less operating expenses:		
Indirect labour cost	$ 12,000	
Utilities	15,000	
Direct labour cost	70,000	
Depreciation, factory equipment	21,000	
Raw materials purchased	165,000	
Depreciation, sales equipment	18,000	
Insurance	4,000	
Rent on facilities	50,000	
Selling and administrative salaries	32,000	
Advertising	75,000	462,000
Net loss		$ (12,000)

After seeing the $12,000 loss for August, Swift's president stated, "I was sure we'd be profitable within six months, but our six months are up and this loss for August is even worse than July's. I think it's time to start looking for someone to buy out the company's assets—if we don't, within a few months there won't be any assets to sell. By the way, I don't see any reason to look for a new controller. We'll just limp along with Sam for the time being."

The company's controller resigned a month ago. Sam, a new assistant in the controller's office, prepared the income statement above. Sam has had little experience in manufacturing operations. Additional information about the company follows:

    a. Some 60% of the utilities cost and 75% of the insurance apply to factory operations. The remaining amounts apply to selling and administrative activities.

    b. Inventory balances at the beginning and end of August were:

	August 1	August 31
Raw materials	$ 8,000	$13,000
Work in process	16,000	21,000
Finished goods	40,000	60,000

    c. Only 80% of the rent on facilities applies to factory operations; the remainder applies to selling and administrative activities.

The president has asked you to check over the income statement and make a recommendation as to whether the company should look for a buyer for its assets.

Required

1. As one step in gathering data for a recommendation to the president, prepare a schedule of cost of goods manufactured in good form for August.
2. As a second step, prepare a new income statement for August.
3. Based on your statements prepared in (1) and (2) above, would you recommend that the company look for a buyer?

P2–18 Schedule of Cost of Goods Manufactured; Cost Behaviour

Selected account balances for the year ended December 31 are provided below for Superior Company:

Selling and Administrative Salaries	$110,000
Insurance, Factory	8,000
Utilities, Factory	45,000
Purchases of Raw Materials	290,000
Indirect Labour	60,000
Direct Labour	?
Advertising Expense	80,000
Cleaning Supplies, Factory	7,000
Sales Commissions	50,000
Rent, Factory Building	120,000
Maintenance, Factory	30,000

Inventory balances at the beginning and end of the year were as follows:

	Beginning of the Year	End of the Year
Raw materials	$40,000	$10,000
Work in process	?	35,000
Finished goods	50,000	?

The total manufacturing costs for the year were $683,000; the goods available for sale totalled $740,000; and the cost of goods sold totalled $660,000.

Required

1. Prepare a schedule of cost of goods manufactured in good form and the cost of goods sold section of the company's income statement for the year.
2. Assume that the dollar amounts given above are for the equivalent of 40,000 units produced during the year. Compute the unit cost for direct materials used and the unit cost for rent on the factory building.

3. Assume that in the following year the company expects to produce 50,000 units. What per unit and total cost would you expect to be incurred for direct materials? For rent on the factory building? (In preparing your answer, you may assume that direct materials is a variable cost and that rent is a fixed cost.)
4. As the manager in charge of production costs, explain to the president the reason for any difference in unit costs between (2) and (3) above.

P2–19 **Classification of Salary Cost**

You have just been hired by Ogden Company to fill a new position that was created in response to rapid growth in sales. It is your responsibility to coordinate shipments of finished goods from the factory to distribution warehouses located in various parts of the United States so that goods will be available as orders are received from customers.

The company is unsure how to classify your annual salary in its cost records. The company's cost analyst says that your salary should be classified as a manufacturing (product) cost; the controller says that it should be classified as a selling expense; and the president says that it doesn't matter which way your salary cost is classified.

Required
1. Which viewpoint is correct? Why?
2. From the point of view of the reported net income for the year, is the president correct in his statement that it doesn't matter which way your salary cost is classified? Explain.

P2–20 **Ethics and the Manager**

M. K. Gallant is president of Kranbrack Corporation, a company whose stock is traded on a national exchange. In a meeting with investment analysts at the beginning of the year, Gallant had predicted that the company's earnings would grow by 20% this year. Unfortunately, sales have been less than expected for the year, and Gallant concluded within two weeks of the end of the fiscal year that it would be impossible to ultimately report an increase in earnings as large as predicted unless some drastic action was taken. Accordingly, Gallant has ordered that wherever possible, expenditures should be postponed to the new year—including cancelling or postponing orders with suppliers, delaying planned maintenance and training, and cutting back on end-of-year advertising and travel. Additionally, Gallant ordered the company's controller to carefully scrutinize all costs that are currently classified as period costs and reclassify as many as possible as product costs. The company is expected to have substantial inventories of work in process and finished goods at the end of the year.

Required
1. Why would reclassifying period costs as product costs increase this period's reported earnings?
2. Do you believe Gallant's actions are ethical? Why or why not?

P2–21 **Cost Behaviour; Manufacturing Statement; Unit Costs**

Visic Company, a manufacturing firm, produces a single product. The following information has been taken from the company's production, sales, and cost records for the just completed year.

Production in units	29,000
Sales in units	? 26,000
Ending finished goods inventory in units	? 3,000
Sales in dollars	$1,300,000
Costs:	
Advertising	105,000
Entertainment and travel	40,000
Direct labour	90,000
✗ Indirect labour	85,000
Raw materials purchased	480,000
Building rent (production uses 80% of the space; administrative and sales offices use the rest)	40,000 / 32000 – 8%*
✗ Utilities, factory	108,000
Royalty paid for use of production patent, $1.50 per unit produced	? 43500

continued

✗ Maintenance, factory		9,000
✗ Rent for special production equipment, $7,000 per year plus $0.30 per unit produced		? 15700
Selling and administrative salaries		210,000
✗ Other factory overhead costs		6,800
Other selling and administrative expenses		17,000

	Beginning of the Year	End of the Year
Inventories:		
Raw materials	$20,000	$30,000
Work in process	50,000	40,000
Finished goods	–0–	? ~~3000~~ 150000

The finished goods inventory is being carried at the average unit production cost for the year. The selling price of the product is $50 per unit.

Required
1. Prepare a schedule of goods manufactured for the year. ✓
2. Compute the following:
   a. The number of units in the finished goods inventory at the end of the year.
   b. The cost of the units in the finished goods inventory at the end of the year.
3. Prepare an income statement for the year.

$4485

Cases

C2–22 Missing Data; Statements; Inventory Computation "I was sure that when our battery hit the market it would be an instant success," said Roger Strong, founder and president of Solar Technology, Inc. "But just look at the gusher of red ink for the first quarter. It's obvious that we're better scientists than we are businesspeople." The data to which Roger was referring follow:

SOLAR TECHNOLOGY, INC.
Income Statement
For the Quarter Ended March 31

Sales (32,000 batteries)		$ 960,000
Less operating expenses:		
Selling and administrative salaries . . .	$110,000	
Advertising	90,000	
Maintenance, production	43,000	
Indirect labour cost	120,000	
Cleaning supplies, production	7,000	
Purchases of raw materials	360,000	
Rental cost, facilities	75,000	
Insurance, production	8,000	
Depreciation, office equipment	27,000	
Utilities	80,000	
Depreciation, production equipment . .	100,000	
Direct labour cost	70,000	
Travel, salespersons	40,000	
Total operating expenses		1,130,000
Net loss		$ (170,000)

"At this rate we'll be out of business within a year," said Cindy Zhang, the company's accountant. "But I've double-checked these figures, so I know they're right."

Solar Technology was organized at the beginning of the current year to produce and market a revolutionary new solar battery. The company's accounting system was set up by

Margie Wallace, an experienced accountant who recently left the company to do independent consulting work. The statement above was prepared by Zhang, her assistant.

"We may not last a year if the insurance company doesn't pay the $226,000 it owes us for the 8,000 batteries lost in the warehouse fire last week," said Roger. "The insurance adjuster says our claim is inflated, but he's just trying to pressure us into a lower figure. We have the data to back up our claim, and it will stand up in any court."

On April 3, just after the end of the first quarter, the company's finished goods storage area was swept by fire and all 8,000 unsold batteries were destroyed. (These batteries were part of the 40,000 units completed during the first quarter.) The company's insurance policy states that the company will be reimbursed for the "cost" of any finished batteries destroyed or stolen. Zhang has determined this cost as follows:

$$\frac{\text{Total costs for the quarter, \$1,130,000}}{\text{Batteries produced during the quarter, 40,000}} = \$28.25 \text{ per unit}$$

$$8,000 \text{ batteries} \times \$28.25 = \$226,000$$

The following additional information is available on the company's activities during the quarter ended March 31:

a. Inventories at the beginning and end of the quarter were as follows:

	Beginning of the Quarter	End of the Quarter
Raw materials	–0–	$10,000
Work in process	–0–	50,000
Finished goods	–0–	?

b. Eighty percent of the rental cost for facilities and 90% of the utilities cost relate to manufacturing operations. The remaining amounts relate to selling and administrative activities.

Required

1. What conceptual errors, if any, were made in preparing the income statement above?
2. Prepare a schedule of cost of goods manufactured for the first quarter.
3. Prepare a corrected income statement for the first quarter. Your statement should show in detail how the cost of goods sold is computed.
4. Do you agree that the insurance company owes Solar Technology, Inc., $226,000? Explain your answer.

C2–23 Inventory Computations from Incomplete Data

Hector P. Wastrel, a careless employee, left some combustible materials near an open flame in Salter Company's plant. The resulting explosion and fire destroyed the entire plant and administrative offices. Justin Quick, the company's controller, and Constance Trueheart, the operations manager, were able to save only a few bits of information as they escaped from the roaring blaze.

"What a disaster," cried Justin. "And the worst part is that we have no records to use in filing an insurance claim."

"I know," replied Constance. "I was in the plant when the explosion occurred, and I managed to grab only this brief summary sheet that contains information on one or two of our costs. It says that our direct labour cost this year has totalled $180,000 and that we have purchased $290,000 in raw materials. But I'm afraid that doesn't help much; the rest of our records are just ashes."

"Well, not completely," said Justin. "I was working on the year-to-date income statement when the explosion knocked me out off my chair. I instinctively held onto the page I was working on, and from what I can make out our sales to date this year have totalled $1,200,000 and our gross margin rate has been 40% of sales. Also, I can see that our goods available for sale to customers has totalled $810,000 at cost."

"Maybe we're not so bad off after all," exclaimed Constance. "My sheet says that prime cost has totalled $410,000 so far this year and that manufacturing overhead is 70% of conversion cost. Now if we just had some information on our beginning inventories."

"Hey, look at this," cried Justin. "It's a copy of last year's annual report, and it shows what our inventories were when this year started. Let's see, raw materials was $18,000, work in process was $65,000, and finished goods was $45,000.

"Super," yelled Constance. "Let's go to work."

To file an insurance claim, the company must determine the amount of cost in its inventories as of the date of the fire. You may assume that all materials used in production during the year were direct materials.

Required   Determine the amount of cost in the Raw Materials, Work in Process, and Finished Goods inventory accounts as of the date of the fire. (Hint: One way to proceed would be to reconstruct the various schedules and statements that would have been affected by the company's inventory accounts during the period.)

C2–24   Ethical and Economic Strategy   Wedgewood Building Supplies Ltd. is a large building supply producer whose production facility is located in Charlottetown, P.E.I. Wedgewood employs 250 unionized workers in the plant and ships building supplies to all Atlantic Canadian provinces.

Wedgewood has been engaged in negotiations with its plant workers for six months. Negotiations have recently broken down and the workers are currently on strike. As a result numerous contracts for building materials are on hold and its stores are running low of inventory at a time when the building season is about to commence.

Wedgewood's personnel manager, Ms. Gale Snow, suggested at a recent meeting of senior executives that operations in Charlottetown could be moved to a mothballed plant in Saint John with very little start-up time. Ms. Snow suggested that she checked labour availability is Saint John and that she could hire a fully capable workforce within a week. In addition, Ms. Snow stated that because labour laws are provincially administered, few repercussions would be felt from the P.E.I. government if the move were made.

Required   1.   What ethical considerations should the management of Wedgewood consider as part of their decision?
2.   Would you expect some economic implications from the move?

C2–25   Cost Estimation and Rules of Conduct   Supply Managers Incorporated is an association of 40 managers who sell their managerial skills to organizations on a fee-for-service basis. Each associate bills the client $10,000 per month for services rendered. A minimum of one month's charge is required for each assignment.

The cost structure for Supply Managers is kept very lean. Ten percent of billings is returned to the company to cover various overhead charges such as rent, utilities, secretarial services, research time, and so forth.

Required   1.   If each associate charges an average of eight months, how much overhead can the company afford?
2.   What rules of conduct would you expect Supply Managers Incorporated to need to be effective in its operations?

C2–26   Cost Behaviour   Dyna Tek Inc. is a high-tech company recently relocated to Bedford, Nova Scotia. Dyna Tek specializes in making a technologically advanced line of computer data storage devices, which it markets worldwide.

As part of its start-up in Bedford, Mr. Key, the production supervisor for the A33 hard-drive line, has to decide the level of mechanization he should implement for the A33 line.

A33 sells about 100,000 units per year at $260 per unit. An employee production line of two workers can be paid $30 per unit each to assemble the materials (cost $50) for each unit. Alternatively, one worker using a specialized machine costing $500,000 can do the assembly for a $50 fee. The expected life of the machine is four years.

Required   1.   Determine the cost structure for the two alternatives.
2.   If the demand for the A33 units is erratic and the capacity of the machine is 100,000 units, which cost structure would you suggest?

C2–27   Costing and Cost Behaviour   Joe Peak is about to graduate from SMU University's accounting program. Given his employment prospects, he is seriously considering the purchase of a new automobile. Since he expects to charge 90% of his transport costs to his new employer, he is concerned about how much the auto will cost him per kilometre.

Some careful library work establishes the following estimated costs based on average Canadian statistics:

Operating costs:
Fuel	16.5%
Insurance	15.0
Maintenance	7.0
Tires	3.0
Miscellaneous	3.5
Total cost	45.0

Fixed costs:
Depreciation and financing	55.0
Total	100%

Annual usage	24,000 kilometres
Average charge	$0.30 per kilometre

Required

1. If Joe expects to charge 90% of his travel to his employer at $0.30 per kilometre and he expects to trade in his car in four years, what can Joe pay for the automobile if he charges himself $0.25 per kilometre?
2. What can Joe pay if he charges 27,000 kilometres to his employer? 18,000 kilometres?

C2–28 Strategic Planning Terry Merton, CGA, hardly noticed the bright sunshine as she drove down the freeway in late October, 1999 on her way to her job as controller for a small manufacturing company in her hometown of Brightside, Newfoundland. She was contemplating the prospect of starting one of two types of businesses, either her own (1) tax practice, or (2) tax and accounting practice. Although quite satisfied with her present employment, she was very excited about the possibility of owning her own business. Prior to assuming the controllership, Terry had worked for four years in the small business division of a Big 6 public accounting firm's Brightside office and had dreamed of opening her own practice. Terry has decided that 2000 is the year her dream will become a reality.

Arriving at her office early, Terry began to think about the possible market segments she might serve and the types of tax and accounting problems these potential clients might have. For instance, Terry might simply establish a tax practice which would focus on serving individuals who typically require only simple return preparation. Serving this target market segment would mean preparing simple tax returns.

On the other hand, Terry could establish both a tax and accounting practice. This would mean she would serve both individuals and small businesses, although her primary target market would be small businesses. Pursuing this alternative would mean that she would render tax services for individuals, small businesses, estates, trusts and pension plans. Further, she would provide compilation, review and audit services for small businesses, as well as advice on designing accounting information systems. Terry knew that her first step would be to identify the market segment she wished to serve. To be successful, she would have to serve the selected target market very well.

Once she identified her target market segment, Terry could then make a decision about the three competitive strategies she might implement. These strategies are: (1) cost leadership, (2) differentiation and (3) focus. Terry decided to pursue a focus strategy, which meant that she would focus on a particular buyer group, segment of the product line, or geographic market. Regardless of the target market served, Terry would serve only the geographic area surrounding Brightside; thus, she was sure she would implement a focus strategy. Therefore, the decisions which remained related to (1) the target market to be served, and (2) whether to implement a cost leadership or differentiation strategy. Terry's decision matrix is shown in Exhibit 1, which shows the combinations of market segments and strategies available to Terry.

Pursuing a cost leadership strategy meant that she would attract clients by keeping her prices (and her costs) low. At the same time, Terry would still be attentive to providing quality service on a timely basis. She would compete on the basis of price and monitor costs to be sure they were kept low.

Pursuing the differentiation strategy meant providing services which are considered to be unique. Differentiating her product probably meant that Terry would provide above-average service and develop a more personal relationship with clients. With the

Exhibit 1   Startup Competitive Strategy Considerations

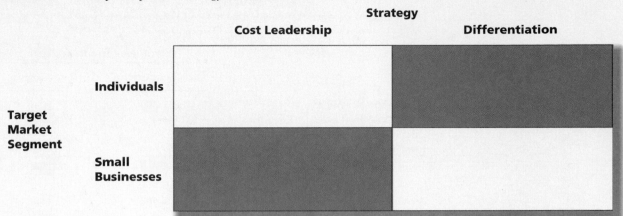

This exhibit shows the possible strategies that Terry Merton might pursue as well as the target market segments she could serve. She could implement a cost leadership strategy focusing on individuals requiring help with simple tax return preparation. Terry's other alternative is to serve small businesses by providing a differentiated product consisting of a variety of tax return and accounting services. Note that the coloured cells represent, strategy-target market segment combinations that Terry will not consider, since competitors are already serving these segments employing the indicated strategies.

differentiation strategy, Terry would be able to charge above-average prices for the services provided to clients and would not have to be as attentive to cost control as she would under the cost leadership strategy.

Terry looked at the sketch she had drawn (Exhibit 1). She noted that theoretically she would be able to implement either the cost leadership or differentiation strategy with either of the two market segments. Thus, she had a total of four alternatives available. However, she immediately eliminated two of the four alternatives: cost leadership-small business and differentiation-individual since there were already other competitors in the Brightside area pursuing these alternatives. Therefore, from a practical standpoint, Terry was left with either selecting the cost leadership-individual tax return combination (hereafter referred to as cost leadership) or the differentiation-small business combination (hereafter referred to as differentiation).

In considering which strategy to pursue, Terry thought about a nationally known provider of tax preparation services which had offices located throughout Canada. This national firm used television, radio and billboard advertising to present 17 reasons why taxpayers should do business with their firm. Terry was certain that the national firm had a costly centralized administrative structure. The firm's tax preparers were typically not professional accountants but were graduates of a training program conducted by the firm. Terry found that this nationally known firm was pursuing a differentiation-individual tax return strategy, since it emphasized the 17 reasons but did not emphasize low price.

If Terry selected the cost leadership strategy, the limited tax expertise required would allow Terry to remain at her present employment. She would hire Jim Wallace, an experienced senior retired preparer of noncomplicated tax returns. Terry would locate her tax practice in a storefront in a nearby shopping mall. Rent was very low there, and there was a high volume of pedestrian traffic past the location. Given this heavy pedestrian traffic, Terry reasoned that she would incur little advertising cost. Terry expected that her costs could be kept low compared with the nationally known firm for two reasons: (1) she would provide minimal training for Jim and (2) she would have minimal administrative and advertising costs.

As already indicated, if she pursued a differentiation strategy, her target market would be small businesses. With the differentiation strategy, the services she would provide would be significantly different from the services provided by competitors. Terry would differentiate herself along a number of dimensions, many of which related to her extensive experience with the Brightside business community. First, from her experience working in a Big 6 firm's small business division, Terry is acquainted with all the bankers in town. She knows how to prepare financial presentations for clients seeking loans in such a way that the loan applications are almost always approved. She also is familiar with virtually all the small business rental

Exhibit 2

STARTUP
Projected Income Statements Under Two Competitive Strategies
For the Twelve Months Ended December 31, 2000

	Strategies for Practice	
	Cost Leadership	**Differentiation**
Revenues (450 clients at $150)	$67,500	
(203 clients at $450)		$91,350
Variable Expenses:		
Supplies ($10 per client)	4,500	2,030
Contribution Margin	63,000	89,320
Fixed Expenses		
Depreciation—Computer	1,600	1,600
Software	500	4,000
Liability Insurance	2,400	11,680
Rental—Furniture	5,660	5,660
Club Membership and Entertainment	—	1,200
Preparer Salary	26,000	31,200
Secretarial Salary	16,000	16,000
Advertising	200	1,180
Rent—Office	8,400	—
Training	—	8,000
Total Fixed Expenses	60,760	80,520
Operating Income*	$ 2,240	$ 8,800

*Assuming that Startup is organized as a proprietorship, operating income and net income are identical. Operating income equals net income because income tax equals zero since Terry Merton, not Startup, is the taxable entity.

property in town, and can direct clients to the most reasonably priced locations. Finally, she is thoroughly familiar with the operation of a small business and can provide extremely useful insights to small business owners. Therefore, like the nationally known firm, Terry would provide small businesses with many reasons to patronize her new firm. If the differentiation-small business strategy is pursued, Terry will leave her $40,000/year controller position to become the principal employee of Startup.

Terry would like to finance her new business start-up costs entirely from her personal savings. This is not possible, however, since she just recently purchased a new automobile for cash, which left her with a savings account balance of only $2,400. She will need a business loan to cover start-up costs including the purchase of a computer and software. Prior to contacting Bill Andersen, the loan officer at a nearby bank, Terry prepares some preliminary profit estimates. Terry's estimates of the revenues and costs associated with each strategy for the first year of operation, 2000, are presented in Exhibit 2. The projected balance sheet of Startup, prior to any bank loans, is presented in Exhibit 3.

Part I: Startup—November 1999   Terry projects revenues of $67,500 (450 clients at $150/client) and $91,350 (203 clients at $450/client) under the cost leadership and differentiation strategies, respectively (see Exhibit 2). Supplies average $10 per client and constitute the only variable costs for Startup. The fixed expenses vary between the strategies in several respects:

1. If she pursues the differentiation strategy, Terry will incur significantly higher liability insurance costs each year than she would under the cost leadership strategy. This is due to the fact that she has much more liability exposure since she will be doing attest work (reviews and audits).
2. Annual computer software costs will be greater under the differentiation strategy. This is because each year Terry will purchase specialized CD-ROM tax preparation disks needed to properly prepare the estate and trust returns. Additional software is also needed if she wishes to advise clients with regard to pensions.

Exhibit 3

STARTUP
Balance Sheet
October 31, 1999

Cash	$2,400
Total Assets	$2,400
Owner's Equity	$2,400
Total Owner's Equity	$2,400

3. If she pursues the differentiation strategy, Terry will incur additional expense for club membership dues and entertainment expenses compared with the cost leadership strategy. This is due to the fact that Terry knows that she can develop the estate and trust work through social contacts with bankers and attorneys.

4. Under the cost leadership provider strategy, Terry will continue in her present employment position. She will hire Jim Wallace for $500/week. Although not a CA or CGA, Jim is approaching retirement at the public accounting firm where Terry had been employed. Jim would be happy to work part-time at Startup. Terry is impressed with Jim's qualifications and is confident he could prepare uncomplicated tax returns. The differentiation strategy, however, will entail more complicated tax return preparations, which are beyond Jim's capabilities. Under the differentiation strategy, Terry would resign from her controller position and work full-time for Startup, drawing a salary of $600 per week.

5. Terry's home has a very large attached apartment which she presently leases to two university students at a rent of $500 per month. The students' lease expires on December 31, 1999. Under the differentiation strategy, she will not renew the lease. Instead, she will set up the offices of Startup in the apartment. Under the cost leadership provider strategy, the students would continue to occupy the apartment, since space in a nearby strip mall will be leased for Startup's offices. The strip mall space would provide needed pedestrian traffic and high visibility for Startup and avoid traffic congestion in Terry's residential neighbourhood.

6. Anticipating the complexity of clients under the differentiation strategy and considering the fact that she has been out of public accounting for three years, Terry estimates $8,000 in annual training costs. Minimal training costs are projected with the cost leadership preparer strategy since Jim Wallace already possesses the necessary experience, and the level of tax expertise required is minimal.

Obtaining a Business Loan   Terry faxed the financial projections in Exhibits 2 and 3 to Bill Andersen in early November 1999. As a loan officer, Bill must follow a set of specific guidelines in making his loan approval decisions. If Bill approves too many loans which ultimately are "bad," he will be dismissed from his job. For all loan applications, he must be able to justify after-the-fact his decision to the bank's board of directors, based largely on the loan applicant's financial statements. In assessing the credit worthiness of Terry's loan application, Bill plans to use operating income before depreciation and working capital as surrogates for cash-paying ability. Terry will offer her nearly new automobile as collateral for the loan. The bank's policy is to approve loans only if the annual payments are less than the beginning working capital balance and the projected before depreciation operating income for the next 12 months. The bank has also instituted a policy to have all loans due and payable on demand at the end of any calendar year if the payee is not in compliance with the original loan requirements.

   Bill's bank has a maximum loan period for startup companies of five years. At an interest rate of 10% per annum, Startup, Inc. qualifies for an $8,000 maximum loan requiring a $2,110 annual payment. Consequently, Startup's December 31 working capital balance and annual operating income (before depreciation expense) must not fall below $2,110, or the bank loan becomes due and payable.

Exhibit 4

STARTUP
***Pro forma* Balance Sheet**
December 31, 2000

Assets
Current Assets:

Cash	$ 3,390	
Accounts Receivable	400	
Supplies	100	
Total Current Assets		$ 3,890

Property, Plant and Equipment:

Computer	8,000	
Less: Accumulated Depreciation	(1,600)	6,400
Total Assets		$10,290

Liabilities and Shareholders' Equity
Current Liabilities:

Accounts Payable	$ 200	
Bank Loan—Current Portion	1,441	
Total Current Liabilities		$ 1,641

Long-Term Liabilities:

Bank Loan (8,000–1,310)	6,690	
Less: Current Portion	(1,441)	5,249
Total Liabilities		6,890

Owner's Equity:

Owner's Equity		3,400
Total Liabilities and Owner's Equity		$10,290

Part II: Startup—November 2000   By November 2000, Startup had completed its first 11 months of operation, and has paid its first annual bank loan payment of $2,110. Startup did not perform up to expectations in 2000. Operating income and depreciation expense for the year ended December 31, 2000 are estimated at $1,000 and $1,600 respectively. The average billings and variable costs per return for 2000 equalled the expected amounts, but client volume was down exactly 2% from the projected volume levels. The *pro forma* balance sheet at December 31, 2000 is presented in Exhibit 4. Although somewhat disappointed with the level of operating profit, Terry is grateful that Startup's projected December 31, 2000 working capital balance and operating income before depreciation exceed the $2,110 minimum loan requirements.

Terry is thinking about how to make Startup more successful in the future. She is contemplating pursuing one of three options to increase the volume of tax preparations. Terry believes that she must select one of these three options by December 31, 2000. After that date, potential clients may already have scheduled appointments with their present accountant. Increased volume of preparations seems appropriate to Terry since, as Exhibit 2 indicates, most of Startup's costs are fixed.

Terry believes that the average revenues and costs per client in 2001 will be the same as experienced in 2000. That is, the billings and cost of supplies per client in 2001 is expected to be the same as predicted for and experienced in 2000. A breakdown of the fees charged clients in 2000 is presented in Exhibit 5. Fifty percent of clients were charged the average billing fee, while 30% were charged less than and 20% greater than the projected average billing fee per return.

Terry would like to pursue one of the following growth options:

Option One   As part of the marketing strategy, Terry would give a coupon to each of the 54 people who had just moved to Brightside. Each coupon would entitle the holder to a free tax return preparation. Any additional tax schedules required will be billed at the standard billing rate of $75 per hour. The coupons would expire on April 15, 2001.

Exhibit 5

STARTUP
Breakdown of Fees Charged
For the Twelve Months Ended December 31, 2000

Exhibit 5 provides a breakdown of the fees charged to clients of Startup during the 12 months ended December 31, 2000. Ten percent of the clients were charged 30% below the average billing fee per client, 5% were charged 20% below the average per client fee, and so forth. The average fee charged to clients was the same as projected in Exhibit 2.

Option Two   In Option Two, Terry would present a coupon to a select group of 40 clients for whom Terry provided services in 2000. The coupons would entitle the holder to a 60% discount off the normal billing rate on services provided during 2001. The coupons will expire on December 31, 2001. The only stipulation is that the user of the coupon must be a new client. That is, 40 individuals who were existing clients of Startup must present the coupons to another 40 individuals. Since Terry believes these 40 first-year clients were pleased with the services provided by Startup, and the coupons would make great stocking stuffers, she fully expects that all 40 coupons will be used by new clients.

Option Three   If Terry pursued Option Three, she would present all clients with an option to currently pay the average 2000 billing per client to purchase a coupon entitling them to an amount of service which they were provided in 2000. That is, if Startup provides a client with the same level of service in 2001 as in 2000, the client would not be billed for the 2001 services since they have already paid the 2000 average billing per client, which was $150 under the cost leadership strategy and $450 with the differentiation strategy. Clients would only be billed for additional services provided by Startup. The coupons would expire on December 31, 2001.

The Strategic Plan and Financial Reporting   Terry realizes that, depending on which option she pursues, a liability and perhaps an expense or an asset will have to be recorded in Startup's accounting records for the year ended December 31, 2000. Terry especially does not want to implement an option that would adversely effect the projected 2000 income of $1,000 and December 31, 2000 working capital balance of $2,249. If anything, Terry would like to shift income into 2000, since the projected 2000 operating income was below expectations. Terry is very concerned about how each option would be reflected in her financial statements for the calendar year ended December 31, 2000. She is concerned because she realizes that those financial reports will be monitored by banker Bill Andersen to determine whether she is complying with the loan agreement terms. Consequently, Terry and Bill are very concerned about how the selected option is reflected in the financial reports. Above all, Terry knows that Bill wants her to use fair and honest accounting. The option selected must not interfere with the loan continuation approval. For without the continuing loan, Terry will not realize her dreams for Startup. Therefore, she must carefully consider the financial reporting implications of each of the three potential growth options. That is, how will each option affect the projected 2000 operating income and working capital balance on December 31, 2000?

Required   1. Terry must select one of two practice strategies: cost leadership or differentiation. Using the profit estimate in Exhibit 2, compute for each strategy a number of clients that must be served to break even. At the projected level of volume, what is the margin of safety for each strategy?
2. From Bill Andersen's perspective, which practice strategy is better? Why?
3. From a managerial and strategic planning perspective, which practice strategy should Terry pursue? Why? (Show computations.)
4. How does GAAP define a liability?

   For Questions 5–9, you must select the practice strategy (cost leadership or differentiation) you believe Terry should pursue and answer the questions accordingly.

5. What is a cost? What was Startup's cost of serving one client during the calendar year ended December 31, 2000?
6. Assume that Terry decides to pursue Growth Option One. She telephoned all 54 new Brightside residents to welcome them to the city and to encourage them to have a free tax return prepared in 2001. From these conversations, 35 new residents indicated positively that they would take advantage of this free offer. The other 19 remained uncommitted. What is the amount of liability to be recorded by Startup related to the coupon offer to the new residents? What is the impact on Startup's projected 2000 operating income and the December 2000 working capital balance?
7. Assume that Terry decides to pursue Growth Option Two. What is the amount of liability to be recorded by Startup as of December 31, 2000 for these discount coupons? What would be the effect on Startup's projected 2000 operating income and December 31, 2000 working capital balance?
8. Assume that Terry decided to pursue Growth Option Three. Suppose that several clients took advantage of the offer by paying $9,000 cash. What is the amount of the liability to be recorded by Startup from these advance payments? What is the effect on the projected 2000 operating income and the December 31, 2000 working capital balance?
9. Refer to your answers to questions 6–8. Does the amount of the liability recognized by Terry have any economic consequences? That is, will Terry refrain from pursuing certain options because those options result in an unfavourable accounting treatment?

Group Exercises

GE2–29   So This Is Why They're Organized This Way   Management accounting systems tend to parallel the manufacturing systems they support and control. Traditional manufacturing systems emphasized productivity (average output per hour or per employee) and cost. This was the result of a competitive philosophy that was based on mass producing a few standard products and "meeting or beating competitors on price." If a firm is going to compete on price, it had better be a low-cost producer.

   Firms achieved low unit cost for a fixed set of resources by maximizing the utilization of those resources. That is, traditional production strategies were based on the economies of mass production and maximizing output for a given productive capacity. North America has experienced over 100 years of unprecedented economic prosperity in large part because innovators like Henry Ford applied these economic principles with a vengeance.

   Competitors, never being completely satisfied with their present condition, were always looking for ways to lower the cost of a product or service even further in order to gain some temporary cost advantage. Additional productivity gains were achieved by standardizing work procedures, specializing work, and using machines to enhance the productivity of individual workers.

Required   1. Henry Ford made a now-famous statement that the Model T "could be had in any colour as long as it was black." Explain what he meant by this statement.
2. How would Henry Ford or any other manufacturer with a narrow product line gain even further efficiencies based on the traditional production model described above?
3. Are there any limits to lowering the cost of black Model Ts, black Bic pens, or any high-volume, commodity product? Explain.

4. Once understood, the economies of mass production were applied to most sectors of the north American economy. Universities, hospitals, and airlines are prime examples. Describe how the concepts of mass production, standardization, and specialization have been applied to lower the costs of a university education. Of a stay in the hospital.
5. As you study additional chapters in this text, refer back to the basic principles described here. An understanding of these concepts will go a long way toward helping you understand why traditional management accounting systems are designed with an emphasis on cost.

GE2–30   If Big Is Good, Bigger Must Be Better   Steel production involves a large amount of fixed costs. Since competition is defined primarily in terms of price, steel manufacturers (and many of their manufacturing and service industry counterparts) try to gain a competitive advantage by using economies of scale and investment in technology to increase productivity and drive unit costs lower. Their substantial fixed costs are the result of their size.

Required
1. How are fixed costs and variable costs normally defined?
2. Give examples of fixed costs and variable costs for a steel company. What is the relevant measure of production activity?
3. Give examples of fixed and variable costs for a hospital, university, and auto manufacturer. What is the relevant measure of production or service activity for each of these organizations?
4. Using the examples of fixed and variable costs for steel companies from (2) above, explain the relationship between production output at a steel company and each of the following: total fixed costs, fixed cost per unit, total variable costs, variable cost per unit, total costs, and average unit cost.
5. With an X axis (horizontal axis) of tonnes produced and a Y axis (vertical axis) of total costs, graph total fixed costs, total variable costs, and total costs against tonnes produced.
6. With an X axis of tonnes produced and a Y axis of unit costs, graph fixed cost per unit, variable cost per unit, and total (or average) cost per unit against tonnes produced.
7. Explain how costs (total and per unit) behave with changes in demand once capacity has been set.

GE2–31   Analysis of Annual Reports   Each member of your group should obtain the annual report of a company. (Your business school's library probably has a file of such annual reports.)

Required
        For each company, compute the following for the two most recent years:

- Cost of sales as a percentage of sales.
- General and administrative expenses as a percentage of sales.
- Net income as a percentage of sales.

If you can, explain why there are differences in these percentages across the companies.

IE2–32   Analysis of SEC Form 10–K   Companies whose shares are publicly traded are required to file financial documents with the Securities and Exchange Commission (SEC in the United States). One of these documents is Form 10–K, which contains the company's annual report along with other information. These and other documents can be viewed and downloaded at the SEC's web site www.sec.gov/edgarhp.htm.

Required   Find Form 10–K for a restaurant chain and a clothing company. Compare the financial data for these two companies. Can you explain any significant differences you observe?

Exhibit 3–3   Employee
Time Ticket

Time Ticket No. 843			Date __March 3__		
Employee __Mary Holden__			Station __4__		
Started	Ended	Time Completed	Rate	Amount	Job Number
7:00	12:00	5.0	$9	$45	2B47
12:30	2:30	2.0	9	18	2B50
2:30	3:30	1.0	9	9	Maintenance
Totals		8.0		$72	

Supervisor __*R.W. Pace*__

termed *indirect labour* and includes tasks such as maintenance, supervision, and cleanup.

Time ticket   A detailed source document that is used to record an employee's hour-by-hour activities during a day.

Workers use *time tickets* to record the time they spend on each job and task. A completed **time ticket** is an hour-by-hour summary of the employee's activities throughout the day. An example of an employee time ticket is shown in Exhibit 3–3. When working on a specific job, the employee enters the job number on the time ticket and notes the amount of time spent on that job. When not assigned to a particular job, the employee records the nature of the indirect labour task (such as cleanup and maintenance) and the amount of time spent on the task.

At the end of the day, the time tickets are gathered and the Accounting Department enters the direct labour-hours and costs on individual job cost sheets. (See Exhibit 3–2 for an example of how direct labour costs are entered on the job cost sheet.) The daily time tickets are source documents that are used as the basis for labour cost entries into the accounting records.

The system we have just described is a manual method for recording and posting labour costs. Many companies now rely on computerized systems and no longer record labour time by hand on sheets of paper. One computerized approach uses bar codes to enter the basic data into the computer. Each employee and each job has a unique bar code. When an employee begins work on a job, he or she scans three bar codes using a handheld device much like the bar code readers at grocery store check-out stands. The first bar code indicates that a job is being started; the second is the unique bar code on his or her identity badge; and the third is the unique bar code of the job itself. This information is fed automatically via an electronic network to a computer that notes the time and then records all of the data. When the employee completes the task, he or she scans a bar code indicating the task is complete, the bar code on his or her identity badge, and the bar code attached to the job. This information is relayed to the computer that again notes the time, and a time ticket is automatically prepared. Since all of the source data is already in computer files, the labour costs can be automatically posted to job cost sheets (or their electronic equivalents). Computers, coupled with technology such as bar codes, can eliminate much of the drudgery involved in routine bookkeeping activities while at the same time increasing timeliness and accuracy.

Objective 3

Compute predetermined overhead rates and explain why estimated overhead costs (rather than actual overhead costs) are used in the costing process.

Application of Manufacturing Overhead

Manufacturing overhead must be included with direct materials and direct labour on the job cost sheet since manufacturing overhead is also a product cost. However, assigning manufacturing overhead to units of product can be a difficult task. There are three reasons for this.

1. Manufacturing overhead is an *indirect cost*. This means that it is either impossible or difficult to trace these costs to a particular product or job.

2. Manufacturing overhead consists of many different items ranging from the grease used in machines to the annual salary of the production manager.
3. Even though output may fluctuate due to seasonal or other factors, manufacturing overhead costs tend to remain relatively constant due to the presence of fixed costs.

Given these problems, about the only way to assign overhead costs to products is to use an allocation process. This allocation of overhead costs is accomplished by selecting an *allocation base* that is common to all of the company's products and services. An **allocation base** is a measure such as direct labour-hours (DLH) or machine-hours (MH) that is used to assign overhead costs to products and services.

The most widely used allocation bases are direct labour-hours and direct labour cost, with machine-hours and even units of product (where a company has only a single product) also used to some extent.

The allocation base is used to compute the **predetermined overhead rate** in the following formula:

Allocation base   A measure of activity such as direct labour-hours or machine-hours that is used to assign costs to cost objects.

Predetermined overhead rate   A rate used to charge overhead cost to jobs in production; the rate is established in advance for each period by use of estimates of total manufacturing overhead cost and of the total allocation base for the period.

Overhead application   The process of charging manufacturing overhead cost to job cost sheets and to the Work in Process account.

$$\text{Predetermined overhead rate} = \frac{\text{Estimated total manufacturing overhead cost}}{\text{Estimated total units in the allocation base}}$$

Note that the predetermined overhead rate is based on *estimated* rather than actual figures. This is because the *predetermined* overhead rate is computed *before* the period begins and is used to *apply* overhead cost to jobs throughout the period. The process of assigning overhead cost to jobs is called **overhead application.** The formula for determining the amount of overhead cost to apply to a particular job is:

$$\begin{array}{c} \text{Overhead applied to} \\ \text{a particular job} \end{array} = \begin{array}{c} \text{Predetermined} \\ \text{overhead rate} \end{array} \times \begin{array}{c} \text{Amount of the allocation} \\ \text{base incurred by the job} \end{array}$$

So, for example, if the predetermined overhead rate is $8 per direct labour-hour, then $8 of overhead cost is *applied* to a job for each direct labour-hour incurred by the job. When the allocation base is direct labour-hours, the formula becomes:

$$\begin{array}{c} \text{Overhead applied to} \\ \text{a particular job} \end{array} = \begin{array}{c} \text{Predetermined} \\ \text{overhead rate} \end{array} \times \begin{array}{c} \text{Actual direct labour-hours} \\ \text{charged to the job} \end{array}$$

USING THE PREDETERMINED OVERHEAD RATE   To illustrate the steps involved in computing and using a predetermined overhead rate, let's return to Yost Precision Machining. The company has estimated its total manufacturing overhead costs to be $320,000 for the year and its total direct labour-hours to be 40,000. Its predetermined overhead rate for the year would be $8 per direct labour-hour, as shown below:

$$\text{Predetermined overhead rate} = \frac{\text{Estimated total manufacturing overhead cost}}{\text{Estimated total units in the allocation base}}$$

$$\frac{\$320,000}{40,000 \text{ direct labour-hours}} = \$8 \text{ per direct labour-hour}$$

The job cost sheet in Exhibit 3–4 indicates that 27 direct labour-hours were charged to job 2B47. Therefore, a total of $216 of overhead cost would be applied to the job:

Exhibit 3–4   A
Completed Job Cost Sheet

JOB COST SHEET

Job Number __2B47__   Date Initiated __March 2__
                                      Date Completed __March 8__

Department __Milling__
Item __Special order coupling__   Units Completed __2__
For Stock _____

Direct Materials		Direct Labour			Manufacturing Overhead		
Req. No.	Amount	Ticket	Hours	Amount	Hours	Rate	Amount
14873	$ 660	843	5	$ 45	27	$8/DLH	$216
14875	506	846	8	60			
14912	238	850	4	21			
	$1,404	851	10	54			
			27	$180			

Cost Summary		Units Shipped		
Direct Materials	$1,404	Date	Number	Balance
Direct Labour	$ 180	March 8	—	2
Manufacturing Overhead	$ 216			
Total Cost	$1,800			
Unit Cost	$ 900*			

*$1,800 ÷ 2 units = $900 per unit.

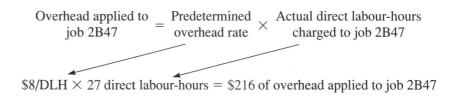

$$\begin{array}{c} \text{Overhead applied to} \\ \text{job 2B47} \end{array} = \begin{array}{c} \text{Predetermined} \\ \text{overhead rate} \end{array} \times \begin{array}{c} \text{Actual direct labour-hours} \\ \text{charged to job 2B47} \end{array}$$

$8/DLH × 27 direct labour-hours = $216 of overhead applied to job 2B47

This amount of overhead has been entered on the job cost sheet in Exhibit 3–4. Note that this is *not* the actual amount of overhead caused by the job. There is no attempt to trace actual overhead costs to jobs—if that could be done, the costs would be direct costs, not overhead. The overhead assigned to the job is simply a share of the total overhead that was estimated at the beginning of the year. When a company applies overhead cost to jobs as we have done—that is, by multiplying actual activity times the predetermined overhead rate—it is called a **normal cost system.**

Normal cost system   A costing system in which overhead costs are applied to jobs by multiplying a predetermined overhead rate by the actual amount of the allocation base incurred by the job.

The overhead may be applied as direct labour-hours are charged to jobs, or all of the overhead can be applied at once when the job is completed. The choice is up to the company. If a job is not completed at year-end, however, overhead should be applied to value the work in process inventory.

THE NEED FOR A PREDETERMINED RATE   Instead of using a predetermined rate, a company could wait until the end of the accounting period to compute an actual overhead rate based on the *actual* total manufacturing costs and the *actual* total units in the allocation base for the period. However, managers cite several reasons for using predetermined overhead rates instead of actual overhead rates:

1. Before the end of the accounting period, managers would like to know the accounting system's valuation of completed jobs. Suppose, for example, that Yost Precision Machining waits until the end of the year to compute its overhead rate. Then there would be no way for managers to know the cost of goods sold for job 2B47 until the close of the year, even though the job was completed and shipped to the customer in March. The seriousness of this problem can be reduced to some extent by computing the actual overhead more frequently, but that immediately leads to another problem as discussed below.
2. If actual overhead rates are computed frequently, seasonal factors in overhead costs or in the allocation base can produce fluctuations in the overhead rates. Managers generally feel that such fluctuations in overhead rates serve no useful purpose and are misleading.
3. The use of a predetermined overhead rate simplifies record-keeping. To determine the overhead cost to apply to a job, the accounting staff at Yost Precision Machining simply multiplies the direct labour-hours recorded for the job by the predetermined overhead rate of $8 per direct labour-hour.

For these reasons, most companies use predetermined overhead rates rather than actual overhead rates in their cost accounting systems.

Choice of an Allocation Base for Overhead Cost

Cost driver A factor, such as machine-hours, beds occupied, computer time, or flight-hours, that causes overhead costs.

An allocation base should be used that is a *cost driver* of overhead cost. A **cost driver** is a factor, such as machine-hours, beds occupied, computer time, or flight-hours, that causes overhead costs. If a base is used to compute overhead rates that does not "drive" overhead costs, then the result will be inaccurate overhead rates and distorted product costs. For example, if direct labour-hours is used to allocate overhead, but in reality overhead has little to do with direct labour-hours, then products with high direct labour-hour requirements will shoulder an unrealistic burden of overhead and will be overcosted.

Most companies use direct labour-hours or direct labour cost as the allocation base for manufacturing overhead. However, as discussed in earlier chapters, major shifts are taking place in the structure of costs in many industries. In the past, direct labour accounted for up to 60% of the cost of many products, with overhead cost making up only a portion of the remainder. This situation has been changing—for two reasons. First, sophisticated automated equipment has taken over functions that used to be performed by direct labour workers. Since the costs of acquiring and maintaining such equipment are classified as overhead, this increases overhead while decreasing direct labour. Second, products are themselves becoming more sophisticated and complex and change more frequently. This increases the need for highly skilled indirect workers such as engineers. As a result of these two trends, direct labour is becoming less of a factor and overhead is becoming more of a factor in the cost of products in many industries.

In companies where direct labour and overhead costs have been moving in opposite directions, it would be difficult to argue that direct labour "drives" overhead costs. Accordingly, in recent years, managers in some companies have used *activity-based costing* principles to redesign their cost accounting systems. Activity-based costing is a costing technique that is designed to more accurately reflect the demands that products, customers, and other cost objects make on overhead resources. The activity-based approach is discussed in more detail in Chapter 8.

We hasten to add that although direct labour may not be an appropriate allocation basis in some industries, in others it continues to be a significant driver of manufacturing overhead.[1] The key point is that the allocation base used by the company should really drive, or cause, overhead costs, and direct labour is not always an appropriate allocation base.

Focus on Current Practice

The most recent surveys of accounting practice indicate that 62% to 74% of manufacturing companies in the United States use direct labour as the primary or secondary allocation base for overhead. Machine-hours are used by another 12% or so of manufacturers, and the remainder of the companies use a variety of different allocation bases.[2] The most recent survey in the United Kingdom reveals a very similar pattern. In the UK, direct labour is used as an allocation base by 68% to 73% of manufacturing companies.[3]

There is some evidence that the proportion of companies that use direct labour-hours as the primary or secondary allocation base has been declining in the United States.[4] Apparently managers believe that direct labour is no longer as significant a cost driver for overhead as it once was. ■

Focus on Current Practice

Japanese companies, like companies in the United States, most frequently use direct labour-hours as a basis for allocating manufacturing overhead. One survey of over 250 manufacturing companies in Japan found the following breakdown:[5]

Basis for Allocation of Manufacturing Overhead	Percent
Direct labour-hours only	41.7%
Machine-hours only	6.4%
Both direct labour-hours and machine-hours	43.6%
Other allocation bases	8.3%
Total	100.0%

Computation of Unit Costs

With the application of Yost Precision Machining's $216 manufacturing overhead to the job cost sheet in Exhibit 3–4, the job cost sheet is almost complete. There are two final steps. First, the totals for direct materials, direct labour, and manufacturing over-

1. George Foster and Mahendra Gupta, "Manufacturing Overhead Cost Driver Analysis," *Journal of Accounting and Economics* (January 1990), pp. 309–37.
2. Jeffrey R. Cohen and Laurence Paquette, "Management Accounting Practices: Perceptions of Controllers," *Journal of Cost Management* 5, no. 3 (Fall 1991), p. 75; and James R. Emore and Joseph A. Ness, "The Slow Pace of Meaningful Change in Cost Systems," *Journal of Cost Management* 4, no. 4 (Winter 1991).
3. Colin Drury and Mike Tayles, "Product Costing in UK Manufacturing Organizations," *The European Accounting Review* 3, no. 3 (1994), pp. 443–69.
4. A 1985 study found that nearly 94% of midwestern manufacturing companies surveyed used direct labour to some extent (either as the primary or secondary base) in overhead costing. Henry R. Schwarzbach, "The Impact of Automation on Accounting for Indirect Costs," *Management Accounting* 67, no. 3 (December 1985).
5. Michiharu Sakurai, "The Influence of Factory Automation on Management Accounting Practices," in Robert Kaplan, ed., *Measures for Manufacturing Excellence* (Cambridge, MA: Harvard Press, 1990), p. 43.

head are transferred to the Cost Summary section of the job cost sheet and added together to obtain the total cost for the job. Then the total cost ($1,800) is divided by the number of units (2) to obtain the unit cost ($900). As indicated earlier, *this unit cost is an average cost and should not be interpreted as the cost that would actually be incurred if another unit were produced.* Much of the actual overhead would not change at all if another unit were produced, so the incremental cost of an additional unit is something less than the average unit cost of $900.

The completed job cost sheet is now ready to be transferred to the Finished Goods inventory account, where it will serve as the basis for valuing unsold units in ending inventory and determining cost of goods sold.

Summary of Document Flows

The sequence of events discussed above is summarized in Exhibit 3–5. A careful study of the flow of documents in this exhibit will provide a good overview of the overall operation of a job-order costing system.

Managerial Accounting in Action

THE WRAP-UP

PRECISION MACHINING

In the 8:00 A.M. daily planning meeting on March 9, Jean Yost, the president of Yost Precision Machining, once again drew attention to job 2B47, the experimental couplings:

Jean: I see job 2B47 is completed. Let's get those couplings shipped immediately to Loops Unlimited so they can get their testing program under way. Marcus, how much are we going to bill Loops for those two units?

Marcus: Just a second, let me check the job cost sheet for that job. Here it is. We agreed to sell the experimental units at cost, so we will be charging Loops Unlimited just $900 a unit.

Jean: Fine. Let's hope the couplings work out and we make some money on the big order later.

Job-Order Costing—The Flow of Costs

Objective 4

Prepare journal entries to record costs in a job-order costing system.

We are now ready to take a more detailed look at the flow of costs through the company's formal accounting system. To illustrate, we shall consider a single month's activity for Rand Company, a producer of gold and silver commemorative medallions. Rand Company has two jobs in process during April, the first month of its fiscal year. Job A, a special minting of 1,000 gold medallions commemorating the 250th anniversary of the founding of Halifax, was started during March and had $30,000 in manufacturing costs already accumulated on April 1. Job B, an order for 10,000 silver medallions commemorating the same event, was started in April.

The Purchase and Issue of Materials

On April 1, Rand Company had $7,000 in raw materials on hand. During the month, the company purchased an additional $60,000 in raw materials. The purchase is recorded in journal entry (1) below:

Exhibit 3–5   The Flow of Documents in a Job-Order Costing System

| Sales order |

A sales order is prepared as a basis for issuing a…

| Production order |

A production order initiates work on a job, whereby costs are charged through…

| Materials requisition form |

| Direct labour time ticket |

| Predetermined overhead rates |

These production costs are accumulated on a form, prepared by the accounting department, known as a…

| Job cost sheet |

The job cost sheet forms the basis for computing product and unit costs that are used to value ending inventories and to determine cost of goods sold for units sold.

Exhibit 3–6 Raw Materials Cost Flows

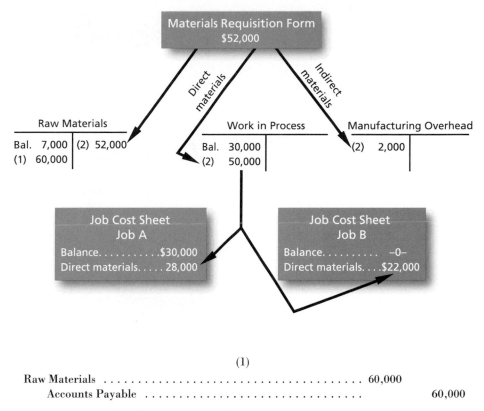

(1)

| Raw Materials | 60,000 | |
| Accounts Payable | | 60,000 |

As explained in Chapter 2, Raw Materials is an asset account. Thus, when raw materials are purchased, they are initially recorded as an asset—not as an expense.

ISSUE OF DIRECT AND INDIRECT MATERIALS   During April, $52,000 in raw materials were requisitioned from the storeroom for use in production. Entry (2) records the issue of the materials to the production departments.

(2)

Work in Process	50,000	
Manufacturing Overhead	2,000	
Raw Materials		52,000

The materials charged to Work in Process represent direct materials for specific jobs. As these materials are entered into the Work in Process account, they are also recorded on the appropriate job cost sheets. This point is illustrated in Exhibit 3–6, where $28,000 of the $50,000 in direct materials is charged to job A's cost sheet and the remaining $22,000 is charged to job B's cost sheet. (In this example, all data are presented in summary form and the job cost sheet is abbreviated.)

The $2,000 charged to Manufacturing Overhead in entry (2) represents indirect materials used in production during April. Observe that the Manufacturing Overhead account is separate from the Work in Process account. The purpose of the Manufacturing Overhead account is to accumulate all manufacturing overhead costs as they are incurred during a period.

Before leaving Exhibit 3–6 we need to point out one additional thing. Notice from the exhibit that the job cost sheet for job A contains a beginning balance of $30,000. We stated earlier that this balance represents the cost of work done during March that has been carried forward to April. Also note that the Work in Process account contains the same $30,000 balance. *The reason the $30,000 appears in both places is that the Work in Process account is a control account and the job cost sheets form a subsidiary ledger. Thus, the Work in Process account contains a summarized total of all costs appearing on the individual job cost sheets for all jobs in process at*

Exhibit 3–7   Labour
Cost Flows

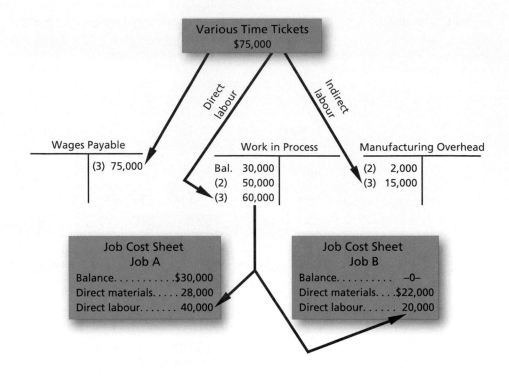

any given point in time. (Since Rand Company had only job A in process at the beginning of April, job A's $30,000 balance on that date is equal to the balance in the Work in Process account.)

ISSUE OF DIRECT MATERIALS ONLY   Sometimes the materials drawn from the Raw Materials inventory account are all direct materials. In this case, the entry to record the issue of the materials into production would be as follows:

Work in Process	XXX	
Raw Materials		XXX

Labour Cost

As work is performed in various departments of Rand Company from day to day, employee time tickets are filled out by workers, collected, and forwarded to the Accounting Department. In the Accounting Department, the tickets are costed according to the various employee wage rates, and the resulting costs are classified as either direct or indirect labour. This costing and classification for April resulted in the following summary entry:

(3)

Work in Process	60,000	
Manufacturing Overhead	15,000	
Salaries and Wages Payable		75,000

Only direct labour is added to the Work in Process account. For Rand Company, this amounted to $60,000 for April.

At the same time that direct labour costs are added to Work in Process, they are also added to the individual job cost sheets, as shown in Exhibit 3–7. During April, $40,000 of direct labour cost was charged to job A and the remaining $20,000 was charged to job B.

The labour costs charged to Manufacturing Overhead represent the indirect labour costs of the period, such as supervision, janitorial work, and maintenance.

Manufacturing Overhead Costs

Recall that all costs of operating the factory other than direct materials and direct labour are classified as manufacturing overhead costs. These costs are entered directly into the Manufacturing Overhead account as they are incurred. To illustrate, assume that Rand Company incurred the following general factory costs during April:

Utilities (heat, water, and power)	$21,000
Rent on factory equipment	16,000
Miscellaneous factory costs	3,000
Total	$40,000

The following entry records the incurrence of these costs:

(4)

Manufacturing Overhead	40,000	
Accounts Payable		40,000

In addition, let us assume that during April, Rand Company recognized $13,000 in accrued property taxes and that $7,000 in prepaid insurance expired on factory buildings and equipment. The following entry records these items:

(5)

Manufacturing Overhead	20,000	
Property Taxes Payable		13,000
Prepaid Insurance		7,000

Finally, let us assume that the company recognized $18,000 in depreciation on factory equipment during April. The following entry records the accrual of this depreciation:

(6)

Manufacturing Overhead	18,000	
Accumulated Depreciation		18,000

In short, *all* manufacturing overhead costs are recorded directly into the Manufacturing Overhead account as they are incurred day by day throughout a period. It is important to understand that Manufacturing Overhead is a control account for many—perhaps thousands—of subsidiary accounts such as Indirect Materials, Indirect Labour, Factory Utilities, and so forth. As the Manufacturing Overhead account is debited for costs during a period, the various subsidiary accounts are also debited. In the example above and also in the assignment material for this chapter, we omit the entries to the subsidiary accounts for the sake of brevity.

The Application of Manufacturing Overhead

Objective 5

Apply overhead cost to Work in Process using a predetermined overhead rate.

Since actual manufacturing costs are charged to the Manufacturing Overhead control account rather than to Work in Process, how are manufacturing overhead costs assigned to Work in Process? The answer is, by means of the predetermined overhead rate. Recall from our discussion earlier in the chapter that a predetermined overhead rate is established at the beginning of each year. The rate is calculated by dividing the estimated total manufacturing overhead cost for the year by the estimated total units in the allocation base (measured in machine-hours, direct labour-hours, or some other base). The predetermined overhead rate is then used to apply overhead costs to jobs. For example, if direct labour-hours is the allocation base, overhead cost is applied to each job by multiplying the number of direct labour-hours charged to the job by the predetermined overhead rate.

To illustrate, assume that Rand Company has used machine-hours in computing its predetermined overhead rate and that this rate is $6 per machine-hour. Also assume that during April, 10,000 machine-hours were worked on job A and 5,000 machine-

Exhibit 3–8   The Flow of Costs in Overhead Application

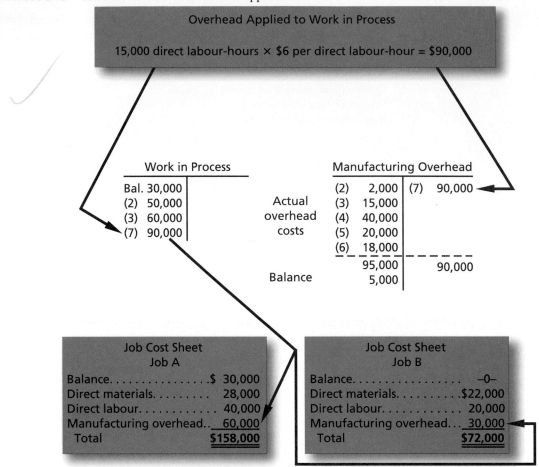

hours were worked on job B (a total of 15,000 machine-hours). Thus, $90,000 in overhead cost (15,000 machine-hours $\times$ $6 = $90,000) would be applied to Work in Process. The following entry records the application of Manufacturing Overhead to Work in Process:

(7)

Work in Process 90,000
    Manufacturing Overhead   90,000

The flow of costs through the Manufacturing Overhead account is shown in Exhibit 3–8.

The "actual overhead costs" in the Manufacturing Overhead account in Exhibit 3–8 are the costs that were added to the account in entries (2)–(6). Observe that the incurrence of these actual overhead costs [entries (2)–(6)] and the application of overhead to Work in Process [entry (7)] represent two separate and entirely distinct processes.

THE CONCEPT OF A CLEARING ACCOUNT   The Manufacturing Overhead account operates as a clearing account. As we have noted, actual factory overhead costs are debited to the accounts as they are incurred day by day throughout the year. At certain intervals during the year, usually when a job is completed, overhead cost is released from the Manufacturing Overhead account and is applied to the Work in Process account by means of the predetermined overhead rate. This sequence of events is illustrated as follows:

Manufacturing Overhead (a clearing account)

Actual overhead costs are charged to the account as these costs are incurred day by day throughout the period. → → Overhead is applied to Work in Process using the predetermined overhead rate.

The actual overhead costs incurred and shown as debits in the manufacturing account are a result of many different types of overhead costs. A brief list of some of the different types is presented in the journal entries, numbers 4, 5 and 6, or in the schedule of cost of goods manufactured, shown in Exhibit 3–11 or previously in Exhibit 2–4. The clearing account concept actually represents a general ledger control account for a subsidiary ledger that contains the detailed information on each type of overhead cost.

As we emphasized earlier, the predetermined overhead rate is based entirely on estimates of what overhead costs are *expected* to be, and it is established before the year begins. As a result, the overhead cost applied during a year will almost certainly turn out to be more or less than the overhead cost that is actually incurred. For example, notice from Exhibit 3–8 that Rand Company's actual overhead costs for the period are $5,000 greater than the overhead cost that has been applied to Work in Process, resulting in a $5,000 debit balance in the Manufacturing Overhead account. We will reserve discussion of what to do with this $5,000 balance until the next section, Problems of Overhead Application.

For the moment, we can conclude by noting from Exhibit 3–8 that the cost of a completed job consists of the actual materials cost of the job, the actual labour cost of the job, and the overhead cost *applied* to the job. Pay particular attention to the following subtle but important point: *Actual overhead costs are not charged to jobs; actual overhead costs do not appear on the job cost sheet nor do they appear in the Work in Process account. Only the applied overhead cost, based on the predetermined overhead rate, appears on the job cost sheet and in the Work in Process account.* Study this point carefully.

Nonmanufacturing Costs

In addition to manufacturing costs, companies also incur marketing and selling costs. As explained in Chapter 2, these costs should be treated as period expenses and charged directly to the income statement. *Nonmanufacturing costs should not go into the Manufacturing Overhead account.* To illustrate the correct treatment of nonmanufacturing costs, assume that Rand Company incurred the following selling and administrative costs during April:

Top-management salaries	$21,000
Other office salaries	9,000
Total salaries	$30,000

The following entry records these salaries:

(8)

Salaries Expense	30,000	
Salaries and Wages Payable		30,000

Assume that depreciation on office equipment during April was $7,000. The entry is as follows:

(9)

Depreciation Expense	7,000	
Accumulated Depreciation		7,000

Pay particular attention to the difference between this entry and entry (6) where we recorded depreciation on factory equipment. In journal entry (6), depreciation on factory equipment was debited to Manufacturing Overhead and is therefore a product cost. In journal entry (9) above, depreciation on office equipment was debited to Depreciation Expense. Depreciation on office equipment is considered to be a period expense rather than a product cost.

Finally, assume that advertising was $42,000 and that other selling and administrative expenses in April totalled $8,000. The following entry records these items:

(10)

Advertising Expense	42,000	
Other Selling and Administrative Expense	8,000	
Accounts Payable		50,000

Because the amounts in entries (8) through (10) all go directly into expense accounts, they will have no effect on the costing of Rand Company's production for April. The same will be true of any other selling and administrative expenses incurred during April, including sales commissions, depreciation on sales equipment, rent on office facilities, insurance on office facilities, and related costs.

The distinction between manufacturing overhead costs and nonmanufacturing costs such as selling and administrative expenses is sometimes difficult because the type of cost, for example depreciation or salaries, is the same but the classification is different. In practice the classification has to be based on what the firm does to incur the costs. If it sells or markets then this is not production and the distinction is clear. If, however, it administers then the distinction depends on what is administered and how important it is to separate production administration from overall administration. For example, if all the company does is produce the Hibernia oil platform, then administration is production (manufacturing) overhead. However, if the company is administering many jobs and marketing new jobs at the same time, it may not be able to distinguish overhead from administrative time on the part of the senior management. Thus unless costs are needed for a cost recovery billing, administration salaries expense may be the expeditious way to treat the salaries.

Cost of Goods Manufactured

When a job has been completed, the finished output is transferred from the production departments to the finished goods warehouse. By this time, the accounting department will have charged the job with direct materials and direct labour cost, and manufacturing overhead will have been applied using the predetermined rate. A transfer of these costs must be made within the costing system that *parallels* the physical transfer of the goods to the finished goods warehouse. The costs of the completed job are transferred out of the Work in Process account and into the Finished Goods account. The sum of all amounts transferred between these two accounts represents the cost of goods manufactured for the period. (This point was illustrated earlier in Exhibit 2–6 in Chapter 2.)

In the case of Rand Company, let us assume that job A was completed during April. The following entry transfers the cost of job A from Work in Process to Finished Goods:

(11)

Finished Goods	158,000	
Work in Process		158,000

The $158,000 represents the completed cost of job A, as shown on the job cost sheet in Exhibit 3–8. Since job A was the only job completed during April, the $158,000 also represents the cost of goods manufactured for the month.

Job B was not completed by month-end, so its cost will remain in the Work in Process account and carry over to the next month. If a balance sheet is prepared at the end of April, the cost accumulated thus far on job B will appear as "Work in process inventory" in the assets section.

Cost of Goods Sold

As units in finished goods are shipped to fill customers' orders, the unit cost appearing on the job cost sheets is used as a basis for transferring the cost of the items sold from the Finished Goods account into the Cost of Goods Sold account. If a complete job is shipped, as in the case where a job has been done to a customer's specifications, then it is a simple matter to transfer the entire cost appearing on the job cost sheet into the Cost of Goods Sold account. In most cases, however, only a portion of the units involved in a particular job will be immediately sold. In these situations, the unit cost must be used to determine how much product cost should be removed from Finished Goods and charged to Cost of Goods Sold.

For Rand Company, we will assume 750 of the 1,000 gold medallions in job A were shipped to customers by the end of the month for total sales revenue of $225,000. Since 1,000 units were produced and the total cost of the job from the job cost sheet was $158,000, the unit product cost was $158. The following journal entries would record the sale (all sales are on account):

(12)

Accounts Receivable	225,000	
Sales		225,000

(13)

Cost of Goods Sold	118,500	
Finished Goods		118,500

($158 per unit × 750 units = $118,500)

With entry (13), the flow of costs through our job-order costing system is completed.

Summary of Cost Flows

Objective 6

Prepare T-accounts to show the flow of costs in a job-order costing system and prepare schedules of cost of goods manufactured and cost of goods sold.

To pull the entire Rand Company example together, journal entries (1) through (13) are summarized in Exhibit 3–9. The flow of costs through the accounts is presented in T-account form in Exhibit 3–10.

Exhibit 3–11 presents a schedule of cost of goods manufactured and a schedule of cost of goods sold for Rand Company. Note particularly from Exhibit 3–11 that the manufacturing overhead cost on the schedule of cost of goods manufactured is the overhead applied to jobs during the month—not the actual manufacturing overhead costs incurred. The reason for this can be traced back to journal entry (7) and the T-account for Work in Process that appears in Exhibit 3–10. Under a normal costing system as illustrated in this chapter, applied—not actual—overhead costs are applied to jobs and thus to Work in Process inventory. Note also the cost of goods manufactured for the month ($158,000) agrees with the amount transferred from Work in Process to Finished Goods for the month as recorded earlier in entry (11). Also note that this $158,000 figure is used in computing the cost of goods sold for the month.

An income statement for April is presented in Exhibit 3–12. Observe that the cost of goods sold figure on this statement ($123,500) is carried down from Exhibit 3–11.

Exhibit 3–9
Summary of
Rand
Company
Journal Entries

(1)

Raw Materials	60,000	
Accounts Payable		60,000

(2)

Work in Process	50,000	
Manufacturing Overhead	2,000	
Raw Materials		52,000

(3)

Work in Process	60,000	
Manufacturing Overhead	15,000	
Salaries and Wages Payable		75,000

(4)

Manufacturing Overhead	40,000	
Accounts Payable		40,000

(5)

Manufacturing Overhead	20,000	
Property Taxes Payable		13,000
Prepaid Insurance		7,000

(6)

Manufacturing Overhead	18,000	
Accumulated Depreciation		18,000

(7)

Work in Process	90,000	
Manufacturing Overhead		90,000

(8)

Salaries Expense	30,000	
Salaries and Wages Payable		30,000

(9)

Depreciation Expense	7,000	
Accumulated Depreciation		7,000

(10)

Advertising Expense	42,000	
Other Selling and Administrative Expense	8,000	
Accounts Payable		50,000

(11)

Finished Goods	158,000	
Work in Process		158,000

(12)

Accounts Receivable	225,000	
Sales		225,000

(13)

Cost of Goods Sold	118,500	
Finished Goods		118,500

Exhibit 3–10   Summary of Cost Flows—Rand Company

Accounts Receivable

	XX*	
(12)	225,000	

Prepaid Insurance

	XX		
		(5)	7,000

Raw Materials

Bal.	7,000	(2)	52,000
(1)	60,000		
Bal.	15,000		

Work in Process

Bal.	30,000	(11)	158,000
(2)	50,000		
(3)	60,000		
(7)	90,000		
Bal.	72,000		

Finished Goods

Bal..	10,000	(13)	118,500
(11)	158,000		
Bal.	49,500		

Accumulated Depreciation

			XX
		(6)	18,000
		(9)	7,000

Manufacturing Overhead

(2)	2,000	(7)	90,000
(3)	15,000		
(4)	40,000		
(5)	20,000		
(6)	18,000		
Bal.	5,000		

Accounts Payable

			XX
		(1)	60,000
		(4)	40,000
		(10)	50,000

Salaries and Wages Payable

			XX
		(3)	75,000
		(8)	30,000

Property Taxes Payable

			XX
		(5)	13,000

Capital Stock

		XX

Retained Earnings

		XX

Sales

		(12)	225,000

Cost of Goods Sold

(13)	118,500	

Salaries Expense

(8)	30,000	

Depreciation Expense

(9)	7,000	

Advertising Expense

(10)	42,000	

Other Selling and Administrative Expense

(10)	8,000	

Explanation of entries:
(1) Raw materials purchased.
(2) Direct and indirect materials issued into production.
(3) Direct and indirect factory labour cost incurred.
(4) Utilities and other factory costs incurred.
(5) Property taxes and insurance incurred on the factory.
(6) Depreciation recorded on factory assets.
(7) Overhead cost applied to Work in Process

(8) Administrative salaries expense incurred.
(9) Depreciation recorded on office equipment.
(10) Advertising and other expense incurred.
(11) Cost of goods manufactured transferred into finished goods.
(12) Sale of job A recorded.
(13) Cost of goods sold recorded for job A.

*XX = Normal balance in the account (for example, Accounts Receivable normally carries a debit balance).

Exhibit 3–11

Schedules of Cost of Goods Manufactured and Cost of Goods Sold

Cost of Goods Manufactured

Direct materials:

Raw materials inventory, beginning	$ 7,000	
Add: Purchases of raw materials	60,000	
Total raw materials available	67,000	
Deduct: Raw materials inventory, ending	15,000	
Raw materials used in production	52,000	
Less indirect materials included in manufacturing overhead	2,000	$ 50,000
Direct labour		60,000
Manufacturing overhead applied to work in process		90,000
Total manufacturing costs		200,000
Add: Beginning work in process inventory		30,000
		230,000
Deduct: Ending work in process inventory		72,000
Cost of goods manufactured		$158,000

Cost of Goods Sold

Finished goods inventory, beginning	$ 10,000
Add: Cost of goods manufactured	158,000
Goods available for sale	168,000
Deduct: Finished goods inventory, ending	49,500
Unadjusted cost of goods sold	118,500
Add: Underapplied overhead	5,000
Adjusted cost of goods sold	$123,500

*Note that the underapplied overhead is added to cost of goods sold. If overhead were overapplied, it would be deducted from costs of goods sold.

Exhibit 3–12

Income Statement

RAND COMPANY
Income Statement
For the Month Ending April 30

Sales		$225,000
Less cost of goods sold ($118,500 + $5,000)		123,500
Gross margin		101,500
Less selling and administrative expenses:		
Salaries expense	$30,000	
Depreciation expense	7,000	
Advertising expense	42,000	
Other expense	8,000	87,000
Net income		$ 14,500

Problems of Overhead Application

We need to consider two complications relating to overhead application. These are (1) the computation of underapplied and overapplied overhead and (2) the disposition of any balance remaining in the Manufacturing Overhead account at the end of a period.

Underapplied and Overapplied Overhead

Underapplied overhead
A debit balance in the Manufacturing Overhead account that arises when the amount of overhead cost actually incurred is greater than the amount of overhead cost applied to Work in Process during a period.

Overapplied overhead
A credit balance in the Manufacturing Overhead account that arises when the amount of overhead cost applied to Work in Process is greater than the amount of overhead cost actually incurred during a period.

Since the predetermined overhead rate is established before a period begins and is based entirely on estimated data, there generally will be a difference between the amount of overhead cost applied to Work in Process and the amount of overhead cost actually incurred during a period. In the case of Rand Company, for example, the predetermined overhead rate of $6 per hour resulted in $90,000 of overhead cost being applied to Work in Process, whereas actual overhead costs for April proved to be $95,000 (see Exhibit 3–8). The difference between the overhead cost applied to Work in Process and the actual overhead costs of a period is termed either **underapplied** or **overapplied overhead.** For Rand Company, overhead was underapplied because the applied cost ($90,000) was $5,000 less than the actual cost ($95,000). If the tables had been reversed and the company had applied $95,000 in overhead cost to Work in Process while incurring actual overhead costs of only $90,000, then the overhead would have been overapplied.

What is the cause of underapplied or overapplied overhead? The causes can be complex, and a full explanation will have to wait for Chapters 10 and 11. Nevertheless, the basic problem is that the method of applying overhead to jobs using a predetermined overhead rate assumes that actual overhead costs will be proportional to the actual amount of the allocation base incurred during the period. If, for example, the predetermined overhead rate is $6 per machine-hour, then it is assumed that actual overhead costs incurred will be $6 for every machine-hour that is actually worked. There are at least two reasons why this may not be true. First, much of the overhead often consists of fixed costs. Since these costs are fixed, they do not grow as the number of machine-hours incurred increases. Second, spending on overhead items may or may not be under control. If individuals who are responsible for overhead costs do a good job, those costs should be less than were expected at the beginning of the period. If they do a poor job, those costs will be more than expected. As we indicated above, however, a fuller explanation of the causes of underapplied and overapplied overhead will have to wait for later chapters.

To illustrate what can happen, suppose that two companies—Turbo Crafters and Black & Howell—have prepared the following estimated data for the coming year:

	Company	
	Turbo Crafters	**Black & Howell**
Predetermined overhead rate based on	Machine-hours	Direct materials cost
Estimated manufacturing overhead	$300,000 (a)	$120,000 (a)
Estimated machine-hours	75,000 (b)	—
Estimated direct materials cost	—	$ 80,000 (b)
Predetermined overhead rate, (a) ÷ (b)	$4 per machine-hour	150% of direct materials cost

Now assume that because of unexpected changes in overhead spending and changes in demand for the companies' products, the *actual* overhead cost and the *actual* activity recorded during the year in each company are as follows:

	Company	
	Turbo Crafters	**Black & Howell**
Actual manufacturing overhead costs	$290,000	$130,000
Actual machine-hours	68,000	—
Actual direct material costs	—	$ 90,000

For each company, note that the actual data for both cost and activity differ from the estimates used in computing the predetermined overhead rate. This results in underapplied and overapplied overhead as follows:

	Company	
	Turbo Crafters	**Black & Howell**
Actual manufacturing overhead costs	$290,000	$130,000
Manufacturing overhead cost applied to		
Work in Process during the year:		
68,000 *actual* machine-hours × $4	272,000	
$90,000 *actual* direct materials cost × 150% . . .		135,000
Underapplied (overapplied) overhead	$ 18,000	$ (5,000)

For Turbo Crafters, notice that the amount of overhead cost that has been applied to Work in Process ($272,000) is less than the actual overhead cost for the year ($290,000). Therefore, overhead is underapplied. Also notice that the original estimate of overhead in Turbo Crafters ($300,000) is not directly involved in this computation. Its impact is felt only through the $4 predetermined overhead rate that is used.

For Black & Howell, the amount of overhead cost that has been applied to Work in Process ($135,000) is greater than the actual overhead cost for the year ($130,000), and so overhead is overapplied.

A summary of the concepts discussed above is presented in Exhibit 3–13.

Disposition of Under- or Overapplied Overhead Balances

What disposition should be made of any under- or overapplied balance remaining in the Manufacturing Overhead account at the end of a period? Generally, any balance in the account is treated in one of two ways:

1. Closed out to Cost of Goods Sold.
2. Allocated between Work in Process, Finished Goods, and Cost of Goods Sold in proportion to the overhead applied during the current period in the ending balances of these accounts.[6]
3. Carried forward to the next period.

The second method, which allocates the under- or overapplied overhead among ending inventories and Cost of Goods Sold, is equivalent to using an "actual" overhead rate and is for that reason considered by many to be more accurate than the first method. Consequently, if the amount of underapplied or overapplied overhead is material, many accountants would insist that the second method be used. In problem assignments we will always indicate which method you are to use for disposing of under- or overapplied overhead.

CLOSED OUT TO COST OF GOODS SOLD   As mentioned above, closing out the balance in Manufacturing Overhead to Cost of Goods Sold is simpler than the allocation method. Returning to the example of Rand Company, the entry to close the $5,000 of underapplied overhead to Cost of Goods Sold would be as follows:

(14)

| Cost of Goods Sold . . . . | 5,000 | |
| Manufacturing Overhead . . . . | | 5,000 |

---

6. Some firms prefer to make the allocation on the basis of the total cost of direct materials, direct labour, and applied manufacturing overhead in each of the accounts at the end of the period. This method is not as accurate as allocating the balance in the Manufacturing Overhead account on the basis of just the overhead applied in each of the accounts during the current period.

Exhibit 3–13

Summary of Overhead
Concepts

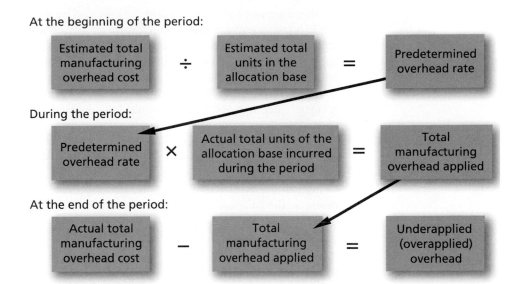

At the beginning of the period:

At the end of the period:

Note that since there is a debit balance in the Manufacturing Overhead account, Manufacturing Overhead must be credited to close out the account. This has the effect of increasing Cost of Goods Sold for April to $123,500:

Unadjusted cost of goods sold [from entry (13)]	$118,500
Add underapplied overhead [entry (14) above]	5,000
Adjusted cost of goods sold	$123,500

After this adjustment has been made, Rand Company's income statement for April will appear as was shown earlier in Exhibit 3–12.

ALLOCATED AMONG ACCOUNTS   Allocation of under- or overapplied overhead among Work in Process, Finished Goods, and Cost of Goods Sold is more accurate than closing the entire balance into Cost of Goods Sold. The reason is that allocation assigns overhead costs to where they would have gone in the first place had it not been for the errors in the estimates going into the predetermined overhead rate.

Had Rand Company chosen to allocate the underapplied overhead among the inventory accounts and Cost of Goods Sold, it would first be necessary to determine the amount of overhead that had been applied during April in each of the accounts. The computations would have been as follows:

Overhead applied in work in process inventory, April 30	$30,000	33.33%
Overhead applied in finished goods inventory, April 30		
($60,000/1,000 units = $60 per unit) × 250 units	15,000	16.67%
Overhead applied in cost of goods sold, April		
($60,000/1,000 units = $60 per unit) × 750 units	45,000	50.00%
Total overhead applied	$90,000	100.00%

Based on the above percentages, the underapplied overhead (i.e., the debit balance in Manufacturing Overhead) would be allocated as in the following journal entry:

Work in Process (33.33% × $5,000)	1,666.50	
Finished Goods (16.67% × $5,000)	833.50	
Cost of Goods Sold (50.00% × $5,000)	2,500.00	
Manufacturing Overhead		5,000.00

Note that the first step in the allocation was to determine the amount of overhead applied in each of the accounts. For Finished Goods, for example, the total amount of overhead applied to job A, $60,000, was divided by the total number of units in job A, 1,000 units, to arrive at the average overhead applied of $60 per unit. Since there were still 250 units from job A in ending finished goods inventory, the amount of overhead applied in the Finished Goods Inventory account was $60 per unit multiplied by 250 units or $15,000 in total.

If overhead had been overapplied, the entry above would have been just the reverse, since a credit balance would have existed in the Manufacturing Overhead account.

An alternative but less accurate way to allocate under- or overapplied overhead among Work in Process, Finished Goods, and Cost of Goods Sold is to use the entire cost of manufacturing in each account.

Had we chosen to allocate the underapplied overhead in the Rand Company example, the computations and entry would have been:

Work in process inventory, April 30		$ 72,000	36.00%
Finished goods inventory, April 30		49,500	24.75
Cost of goods sold	$118,500		
Less: Work in Process inventory, April 1	30,000		
Finished goods inventory, April 1	10,000	78,500	39.25
Total		$200,000	100.00%
Work in Process (36.0% × $5,000)	1,800		
Finished Goods (24.75% × $5,000)	1,237		
Cost of Goods Sold (39.25% × $5,000)	1,963		
Manufacturing Overhead		5,000	

A comparison of the percentages above with those using only overhead suggests that total manufacturing costs and overhead were not in the same proportions in each account. This difference is the inaccuracy in the problem resulting from using total manufacturing costs.

The rationale for deducting the beginning work in process and finished goods inventories from the cost of goods sold is to permit the allocation to be based on costs from the current period. By doing so, the 39.25% in the Rand Company example reflects only costs from April and thus corresponds to the period in which the underapplied overhead occurred. Without this adjustment, cost of goods sold would be assigned the overhead difference based on costs carried over from March and thus bear a disproportionate amount of the under- or overapplied overhead.

CARRY THE BALANCE FORWARD   Recall the section earlier in this chapter entitled "Application of Manufacturing Overhead." Notice that some firms have large seasonal variations in output while being faced with relatively constant overhead costs. Predetermined overhead was used to even out fluctuations in the cost of overhead caused by seasonal variations in output and seasonal variations in costs (e.g., heating costs). The predetermined overhead rate is computed using estimated total manufacturing costs for a year divided by estimated total units in the base. The result is an average rate. When the average predetermined rate is applied to actual production for the period, the applied overhead is determined. The under- or overapplied overhead is a result of two factors, an actual base that is different from one-twelfth of the annual estimated base and actual overhead costs that do not equal one-twelfth of the total estimated overhead costs. Therefore, for any given month, an under- or overapplied overhead amount would be expected. In some months, it would be positive; in other months, it would be negative. Over the year these amounts may largely cancel out. If this is the situation, then significant debits and credits could be carried forward to the year-end so that a final disposition can be made either by adjusting Cost of Goods Sold or allocating (sometimes termed *prorating*) the amount to the inventories and Cost of Goods Sold.

The Rand Company example would be treated as follows:

Underapplied Overhead
 [a deferred debit balance on the balance sheet] 5,000
  Manufacturing Overhead   5,000

A General Model of Product Cost Flows

Plantwide overhead rate
A single predetermined overhead rate that is used throughout a plant.

The flow of costs in a product costing system is presented in the form of a T-account model in Exhibit 3–14. This model applies as much to a process costing system as it does to a job-order costing system. Examination of this model can be very helpful in gaining a perspective as to how costs enter a system, flow through it, and finally end up as Cost of Goods Sold on the income statement.

Multiple Predetermined Overhead Rates

Multiple predetermined overhead rates A costing system in which there are multiple overhead cost pools with a different predetermined rate for each cost pool, rather than a single predetermined overhead rate for the entire company. Frequently, each production department is treated as a separate overhead cost pool.

Our discussion in this chapter has assumed that there is a single predetermined overhead rate for an entire factory called a **plantwide overhead rate.** This is, in fact, a common practice—particularly in smaller companies. But in larger companies, *multiple predetermined overhead rates* are often used. In a **multiple predetermined overhead rate** system there is usually a different overhead rate for each production department. Such a system, while more complex, is considered to be more accurate, since it can reflect differences across departments in how overhead costs are incurred.

Exhibit 3–14 A General Model of Cost Flows

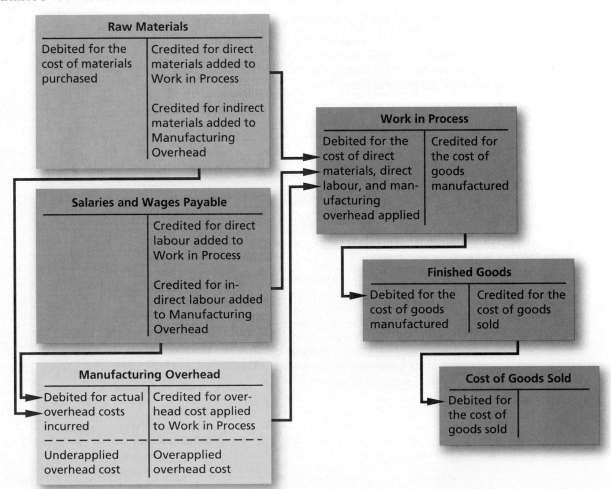

For example, overhead might be allocated based on direct labour-hours in departments that are relatively labour intensive and based on machine-hours in departments that are relatively machine intensive. When multiple predetermined overhead rates are used, overhead is applied in each department according to its own overhead rate as a job proceeds through the department.

Job-Order Costing in Service Companies

We stated earlier in the chapter that job-order costing is also used in service organizations such as law firms, movie studios, hospitals, and repair shops, as well as in manufacturing companies. In a law firm, for example, each client represents a "job," and the costs of that job are accumulated day by day on a job cost sheet as the client's case is handled by the firm. Legal forms and similar inputs represent the direct materials for the job; the time expended by attorneys represents the direct labour; and the costs of secretaries, clerks, rent, depreciation, and so forth, represent the overhead.

In a movie studio, each film produced by the studio is a "job," and costs for direct materials (costumes, props, film, etc.) and direct labour (actors, directors, and extras) are accounted for and charged to each film's job cost sheet. A share of the studio's overhead costs, such as utilities, depreciation of equipment, salaries of maintenance workers, and so forth, is also charged to each film.

In summary, the reader should be aware that job-order costing is a versatile and widely used costing method, and may be encountered in virtually any organization where there are diverse products or services.

Focus on Current Practice

Jobs come in many forms and often from government sources. The list of government contract spending in Ottawa provides examples of many types of job cost situations.

Here are 10 of 20 categories where the largest amount of money was spent in the fiscal year of 1992–1993 with comparable figures for 1984–1985 in parentheses: ■

Unspecified business services:
$498.5 million ($207.3 million)
Unspecified professional services:
$413.4 million ($158.9 million)
Unspecified engineering services:
$248.6 million ($89 million)
Aircraft repair and maintenance:
$332.7 million ($178.9 million)
Purchase of services for development assistance:
$331.4 million ($152.7 million)

Office building repair:
$193.6 million ($89.7 million)
Management consulting:
$181.9 million ($56.4 million)
Computer services:
$151.7 million ($78.9 million)
EDP consultants:
$139.3 million ($40.07 million)
Dental services:
$131.3 million ($38.3 million)[7]

7. Gord McIntosh, "Ottawa Spends $5b on Outsourcing Contracts," *The Mail Star*, May 5, 1994, p. B10. ©
   The Canadian Press.

Use of Bar Code Technology

Earlier in the chapter we discussed the use of bar code technology in recording labour time. Some companies are extending bar code technology to include all steps in the manufacturing process. Bar codes allow people who speak different languages to identify items, amounts, locations, work steps, and so forth, and also to communicate this information to others throughout the world. Thus, bar codes are becoming an international link that allows direct communication between a company, its customers, and its suppliers regardless of where they may be located.

Bar codes are often used in conjunction with electronic data interchange (EDI), which involves a network of computers linking organizations. An EDI network allows companies to electronically exchange business documents and other information that extend into all areas of business activity from ordering raw materials to shipping completed goods.

In a company with a well-developed bar code system, the manufacturing cycle begins with the receipt of a customer's order via ED. The raw materials to produce the goods come from suppliers who have bar coded the materials according to the company's preset specifications. When materials arrive at the company's plant, the bar codes are scanned to update inventory records. The bar codes are scanned again when the materials are requisitioned for use in production. The computer credits the Raw Materials inventory account for the amount and type of goods requisitioned and charges the Work in Process inventory account.

A unique bar code is assigned to each job. This bar code is scanned to update Work in Process records for labour and other costs incurred in the manufacturing process. When goods are completed, another scan is performed that transfers both the cost and quantity of goods from the Work in Process inventory account to the Finished Goods inventory account, or charges Cost of Goods Sold for goods ready to be shipped.

Goods ready to be shipped are packed into containers, which are bar coded with information that includes the customer number, the type and quantity of goods being shipped, and the order number being filled. This bar code is then used for preparing billing information and for tracking the packed goods until placed on a carrier for shipment to the customer. Some customers require that the packed goods be bar coded with point-of-sale labels that can be scanned at retail check-out counters. These scans allow the retailer to update inventory records, verify price, and generate a customer receipt.

In short, bar code technology is being integrated into all areas of business activity. It eliminates a lot of clerical drudgery and allows companies to capture more data and to analyze and report information much more quickly and completely and with less error than with manual systems.

International Job Costing

Studies of the international accounting scene suggest that the general principles of product costing are universally applicable.[8] Nevertheless, differences do exist from country to country in how specific costs are classified. For example, a study of Russian operational accounting and statistical record-keeping, the equivalent of product costing, suggests that the required reporting structure in Russia would assign some cost elements we might classify as selling or administrative to inventory. Other costs such as the rent on plant facilities would be classified outside of the usual overhead

---

8. Dhia D. AlHashin and Jeffrey S. Arpan, *International Dimensions of Accounting*, 2nd ed. (Boston, MA: PWS-Kent, 1988), p. 180.

category.[9] If a company were executing a contract with a foreign government, the differences in what is or is not permitted as contract costs would be particularly important. Similarly, what Supply and Services Canada will allow as contract costs is described by the word "prudent" and elaborated in a specific list of costs excluded from product costs.[10] For example, these requirements would permit certain general and selling costs to be included if a prudent person would incur such costs as part of the contract. Thus, while the general principles may be similar, the specifics can vary as a result of government regulations.

Summary

Job-order costing and process costing are widely used to track costs. Job-order costing is used in situations where the organization offers many different products or services, such as in furniture manufacturing, hospitals, and legal firms. Process costing is used where units of product are homogeneous, such as in flour milling or cement production.

Materials requisition forms and labour time tickets are used to assign direct materials and direct labour costs to jobs in a job-costing system. Manufacturing overhead costs are assigned to jobs through use of a predetermined overhead rate. The predetermined overhead rate is determined before the period begins by dividing the estimated total manufacturing cost for the period by the estimated total allocation base for the period. The most frequently used allocation bases are direct labour-hours and machine-hours. Overhead is applied to jobs by multiplying the predetermined overhead rate by the actual amount of the allocation base used by the job.

Since the predetermined overhead rate is based on estimates, the actual overhead cost incurred during a period may be more or less than the amount of overhead cost applied to production. Such a difference is referred to as under- or overapplied overhead. The under- or overapplied overhead for a period can be (1) closed out to Cost of Goods Sold or (2) allocated between Work in Process, Finished Goods, and Cost of Goods Sold or (3) carried forward to the end of the year. When overhead is underapplied, manufacturing overhead costs have been understated and therefore inventories and/or expenses must be adjusted upwards. When overhead is overapplied, manufacturing overhead costs have been overstated and therefore inventories and/or expenses must be adjusted downwards.

Review Problem: Job-Order Costing

Hogle Company is a manufacturing firm that uses job-order costing. On January 1, the beginning of its fiscal year, the company's inventory balances were as follows:

Raw materials	$20,000
Work in process	15,000
Finished goods	30,000

The company applies overhead cost to jobs on the basis of machine-hours worked. For the current year, the company estimated that it would work 75,000 machine-hours and incur $450,000 in manufacturing overhead cost. The following transactions were recorded for the year:

a. Raw materials were purchased on account, $410,000.

---

9. Adolf J. H. Enthoven, "Accounting in Russia: From Perestroika to Profits," *Management Accounting,* (October 1992), pp. 22–31.

10. Section 3, General Conditions, DSS-MAS 1031-2, "Contract Cost Principles," *Standard Acquisition Clauses and Conditions Manual,* Public Works and Government Services Canada, 1997.

b. Raw materials were requisitioned for use in production, $380,000 ($360,000 direct materials and $20,000 indirect materials).

c. The following costs were incurred for employee services: direct labour, $75,000; indirect labour, $110,000; sales commissions, $90,000; and administrative salaries, $200,000.

d. Sales travel costs were incurred, $17,000.

e. Utility costs were incurred in the factory, $43,000.

f. Advertising costs were incurred, $180,000.

g. Depreciation was recorded for the year, $350,000 (80% relates to factory operations, and 20% relates to selling and administrative activities).

h. Insurance expired during the year, $10,000 (70% relates to factory operations, and the remaining 30% relates to selling and administrative activities).

i. Manufacturing overhead was applied to production. Due to greater than expected demand for its products, the company worked 80,000 machine-hours during the year.

j. Goods costing $900,000 to manufacture according to their job cost sheets were completed during the year.

k. Goods were sold on account to customers during the year at a total selling price of $1,500,000. The goods cost $870,000 to manufacture according to their job cost sheets.

Required

1. Prepare journal entries to record the preceding transactions.
2. Post the entries in (1) above to T-accounts (do not forget to enter the opening balances in the inventory accounts).
3. Is Manufacturing Overhead underapplied or overapplied for the year? Prepare a journal entry to close any balance in the Manufacturing Overhead account to Cost of Goods Sold. Do not allocate the balance between ending inventories and Cost of Goods Sold.
4. Prepare an income statement for the year and a statement of cost of goods manufactured.

Solution to Review Problem

1.
a.	Raw Materials	410,000	
	Accounts Payable		410,000
b.	Work in Process	360,000	
	Manufacturing Overhead	20,000	
	Raw Materials		380,000
c.	Work in Process	75,000	
	Manufacturing Overhead	110,000	
	Sales Commissions Expense	90,000	
	Administrative Salaries Expense	200,000	
	Salaries and Wages Payable		475,000
d.	Sales Travel Expense	17,000	
	Accounts Payable		17,000
e.	Manufacturing Overhead	43,000	
	Accounts Payable		43,000
f.	Advertising Expense	180,000	
	Accounts Payable		180,000
g.	Manufacturing Overhead	280,000	
	Depreciation Expense	70,000	
	Accumulated Depreciation		350,000
h.	Manufacturing Overhead	7,000	
	Insurance Expense	3,000	
	Prepaid Insurance		10,000

i. The predetermined overhead rate for the year would be computed as follows:

$$\frac{\text{Estimated manufacturing overhead, } \$450,000}{\text{Estimated machine-hours, 75,000}} = \$6 \text{ per machine-hour}$$

Based on the 80,000 machine-hours actually worked during the year, the company would have applied $480,000 in overhead cost to production: 80,000 machine-hours $\times$ $6 = $480,000. The following entry records this application of overhead cost:

| Work in Process | 480,000 | |
| Manufacturing Overhead | | 480,000 |

j.	Finished Goods	900,000	
	Work in Process		900,000
k.	Accounts Receivable	1,500,000	
	Sales		1,500,000
	Cost of Goods Sold	870,000	
	Finished Goods		870,000

2.

Accounts Receivable

(k)	1,500,000		

Manufacturing Overhead

(b)	20,000	(i)	480,000
(c)	110,000		
(e)	43,000		
(g)	280,000		
(h)	7,000		
	460,000		480,000
		Bal.	20,000

Sales

		(k)	1,500,000

Cost of Goods Sold

(k)	870,000		

Prepaid Insurance

		(h)	10,000

Accumulated Depreciation

		(g)	350,000

Commissions Expense

(c)	90,000		

Administrative Salary Expense

(c)	200,000		

Raw Materials

Bal.	20,000	(b)	380,000
(a)	410,000		
Bal.	50,000		

Accounts Payable

		(a)	410,000
		(d)	17,000
		(e)	43,000
		(f)	180,000

Sales Travel Expense

(d)	17,000		

Advertising Expense

(f)	180,000		

Work in Process

Bal.	15,000	(j)	900,000
(b)	360,000		
(c)	75,000		
(i)	480,000		
Bal.	30,000		

Salaries and Wages Payable

		(c)	475,000

Depreciation Expense

(g)	70,000		

Insurance Expense

(h)	3,000		

Finished Goods

Bal.	30,000	(k)	870,000
(j)	900,000		
Bal.	60,000		

3. Manufacturing overhead is overapplied for the year. The entry to close it out to Cost of Goods Sold is as follows:

Manufacturing Overhead	....	20,000	
Cost of Goods Sold	....		20,000

4.

HOGLE COMPANY
Income Statement
For the Year Ended December 31

Sales		$1,500,000
Less cost of goods sold ($870,000 − $20,000)		850,000
Gross margin		650,000
Less selling and administrative expenses:		
Commissions expense	$ 90,000	
Administrative salaries expense	200,000	
Sales travel expense	17,000	
Advertising expense	180,000	
Depreciation expense	70,000	
Insurance expense	3,000	560,000
Net income		$ 90,000

HOGLE COMPANY
Schedule of Cost of Goods Manufactured and
Cost of Goods Sold

Direct Materials:		
Raw materials inventory, January 1	$ 20,000	
Add: Purchases of raw materials	410,000	
Total raw materials available	430,000	
Deduct: Raw materials inventory, December 31	50,000	
Raw materials used in production	380,000	
Less: Indirect materials (below)	20,000	
Direct materials used in production		$360,000
Direct Labour		75,000
Manufacturing Overhead:		
Indirect materials	20,000	
Indirect labour	110,000	
Utilities	43,000	
Depreciation	280,000	
Insurance	7,000	
Actual overhead costs	460,000	
Add: Overapplied overhead	20,000	
Overhead applied to work in process		480,000*
Total manufacturing costs		915,000
Add: Beginning work in process inventory		15,000
		930,000
Deduct: Ending work in process inventory		30,000
Cost of goods manufactured		900,000
Add: Finished goods inventory, January 1		30,000
Goods available for sale		930,000
Deduct: Finished goods inventory, December 31 . . .		60,000
Cost of Goods Sold		870,000
Deduct: overapplied overhead		20,000
Adjusted cost of goods sold		$850,000

*The details of manufacturing overhead may be omitted as shown in Exhibit 3–11. If these are not omitted then the overapplied overhead must be added to actual overhead costs and only the total ($480,000) is added to direct materials and direct labour. The reason is that the schedule of cost of goods manufactured represents a summary of costs flowing through the Work in Process account during a period and therefore must exclude any overhead costs that were incurred but never applied to production. If a reverse situation had existed and overhead had been underapplied during the period, then the amount of underapplied overhead would have been deducted from actual overhead costs on the schedule. This would have brought the actual overhead costs up to the amount that had been applied to production.

Appendix 3A: The Predetermined Overhead Rate and Capacity

Objective 8

Explain the implications of basing the predetermined overhead rate on activity at capacity rather than on estimated activity for the period.

Companies typically base their predetermined overhead rates on the estimated, or budgeted, amount of the allocation base for the upcoming period. This is the method that is used in the chapter, but it is a practice that has recently come under severe criticism.[11] An example will be very helpful in understanding why. Prahad Corporation manufactures music CDs for local recording studios. The company has a CD duplicating machine that is capable of producing a new CD every 10 seconds from a master CD. The company leases the CD duplicating machine for $3,600,000 per year, and this is the company's only manufacturing overhead. With allowances for setups and maintenance, the machine is theoretically capable of producing up to 900,000 CDs per year. However, due to weak retail sales of CDs, the company's commercial customers are unlikely to order more than 600,000 CDs next year. The company uses machine time as the allocation base for applying manufacturing overhead. These data are summarized below:

PRAHAD CORPORATION DATA

Total manufacturing overhead cost	$3,600,000 per year
Allocation base: machine time per CD	10 seconds per CD
Capacity	900,000 CDs per year
Budgeted output for next year	600,000 CDs

If Prahad follows common practice and computes its predetermined overhead rate using estimated, or budgeted, figures, then its predetermined overhead rate for next year would be $0.60 per second of machine time computed as follows:

$$\frac{\text{Estimated total manufacturing overhead cost, } \$3,600,000}{\text{Estimated total units in the allocation base, } 600,000 \text{ CDs} \times 10 \text{ seconds per CD}} = \$0.60 \text{ per second}$$

Since each CD requires 10 seconds of machine time, each CD will be charged for $6.00 of overhead cost.

Critics charge that there are two problems with this procedure. First, if predetermined overhead rates are based on budgeted activity, then the unit product costs will fluctuate depending on the budgeted level of activity for the period. For example, if the budgeted output for the year was only 450,000 CDs, the predetermined overhead rate would be $0.80 per second of machine time or $8.00 per CD rather than $6.00 per CD. In general, if budgeted output falls, the overhead cost per unit will increase; it will appear that the CDs cost more to make. Managers may then be tempted to increase prices at the worst possible time—just as demand is falling.

Second, critics charge that under the traditional approach, products are charged for resources that they do not use. When the fixed costs of capacity are spread over estimated activity, the units that are produced must shoulder the costs of unused capacity. That is why the applied overhead cost per unit increases as the level of activity falls. The critics argue that products should be charged only for the capacity that they use; they should not be charged for the capacity they do not use. This can be accomplished by basing the predetermined overhead rate on capacity as follows:

---

11. Institute of Management Accountants, *Measuring the Cost of Capacity: Statements on Management Accounting, Statement Number 4Y,* March 31, 1996, Montvale, NJ; Thomas Klammer, ed., *Capacity Measurement and Improvement: A Manager's Guide to Evaluating and Optimizing Capacity Productivity* (Chicago: CAM-I, Irwin Professional Publishing, 1996); and C. J. McNair, "The Hidden Costs of Capacity," *The Journal of Cost Management* (Spring 1994), pp. 12–24.

$$\frac{\text{Total manufacturing overhead cost at capacity, \$3,600,000}}{\text{Total units in the allocation base at capacity, 900,000 CDs} \times 10 \text{ seconds per CD}} = \$0.40 \text{ per second}$$

Since the predetermined overhead rate is $0.40 per second, the overhead cost applied to each CD would be $4.00. This charge is constant and would not be affected by the level of activity during a period. If output falls, the charge would still be $4.00 per CD.

This method will almost certainly result in underapplied overhead. If actual output at Prahad Corporation is 600,000 CDs, then only $2,400,000 of overhead cost would be applied to products ($4.00 per CD × 600,000 CDs). Since the actual overhead cost is $3,600,000, there would be underapplied overhead of $1,200,000. In another departure from tradition, the critics suggest that the underapplied overhead that results from idle capacity should be separately disclosed on the income statement as the Cost of Unused Capacity—a period expense. Disclosing this cost as a lump sum on the income statement, rather than burying it in Cost of Goods Sold or ending inventories, makes it much more visible to managers.

Official pronouncements do not prohibit basing predetermined overhead rates on capacity for external reports. Nevertheless, basing the predetermined overhead rate on estimated, or budgeted, activity is a long-established practice in industry, and some managers and accountants may object to the large amounts of underapplied overhead that would often result from using capacity to determine predetermined overhead rates. And some may insist that the underapplied overhead be allocated among Cost of Goods Sold and ending inventories—which would defeat the purpose of basing the predetermined overhead rate on capacity.

Appendix 3B: Cost Flows in a JIT System

Objective 9

Prepare journal entries to record the flow of costs in a just-in-time (JIT) inventory system.

When a company utilizes JIT inventory methods, its cost flows are greatly simplified from those we have discussed on preceding pages. Typically, when JIT is in use, only two inventory accounts are utilized. One is a new account, Raw and In-Process Inventory, and the other is the same Finished Goods inventory account with which we are already familiar. Cost flows in a JIT system, as compared to cost flows in a conventional job-order system, are illustrated in Exhibit 3B–1.

In the following paragraphs we discuss Exhibit 3B–1 transaction by transaction as we trace the cost flows under JIT. The numbers below relate to the transaction numbers in the exhibit.

As stated in Chapter 1, the JIT philosophy focuses on simplicity and on the elimination of any activity that does not add value to products. This philosophy is clearly evident in the operation of a JIT system, as described in the preceding paragraphs.

We must emphasize, however, that backflush costing is appropriate *only* in those situations where a *true* JIT system is in operation. If either raw materials or work in process inventories exist at the end of a period, then backflush costing is not appropriate and will be costly to operate. The reason is that when inventories are present, frequent and expensive physical counts of inventory will be necessary to determine the amount of materials and the amount of partially completed goods still on hand. Moreover, with no requisition slips or work orders available, it will be difficult to identify how much cost should be applied to raw materials and work in process inventories and how much should be applied to completed output. Thus, in the absence of a *true* JIT system, backflush costing may result in less timely, less accurate, and more expensive data than a conventional costing system.

Exhibit 3B–1   Cost Flows in a JIT System

Transaction	Entries—Conventional System		Entries—JIT System	

1. Purchase of direct materials on account, $400,000 (of which $50,000 is planned for inventory).	Raw Materials 400,000
	   Accounts Payable ....
		400,000	Raw and In-Process Inventory 350,000
			   Accounts Payable ....
				350,000

2. Issue of direct materials to production, $350,000.	Work in Process ....350,000 Raw Materials	350,000	—	
3. Incurrence of direct labour cost, $40,000.	Work in Process .... 40,000 Factory Wages Payable	40,000	—	

4. Incurrence of manufacturing overhead cost, $160,000.	Manufacturing Overhead 160,000
	   Accounts Payable ....
		160,000	Manufacturing Overhead 200,000
			   Factory Wages Payable ....
			   Accounts Payable ....
				40,000
				160,000

5. Application of manufacturing overhead cost to products, $170,000.	Work in Process ....170,000 Manufacturing Overhead	170,000	—	

6. Completion of products, $560,000 total cost.	Finished Goods 560,000
	   Work in Process ....
		560,000	Finished Goods 560,000
			   Raw and In-Process Inventory ...
			   Manufacturing Overhead ......
				350,000
				210,000*

*Under JIT, the overhead applied consists of:

            Direct labour cost added to overhead ....$ 40,000
            Other overhead costs applied, per transaction 5 170,000
            Total overhead cost applied $210,000

Under both systems, note that overhead costs were overapplied by $10,000 for the period (conventional system: $160,000 incurred − $170,000 applied = $10,000 overapplied; JIT system: $200,000 incurred − $210,000 applied = $10,000 overapplied). This $10,000 would be closed out to Cost of Goods Sold at the end of the period.

Transaction	Comments
1.	Under JIT, materials are purchased only as needed for production. Thus, only $350,000 in materials would be purchased under JIT ($400,000 − $50,000 = $350,000), as compared to the entire $400,000 under a conventional system. (The extra $50,000 under the conventional system would remain in inventory.) The materials purchased under JIT would go directly into a **Raw and In-Process Inventory** account, which is a combination of the Raw Materials and Work in Process inventory accounts found in job-order costing.
2.	Purchase of materials and issue of materials into production occur simultaneously in a JIT environment. Therefore, the entry for transaction 1 under JIT encompasses the entries for both transactions 1 and 2 in a conventional system. This greatly simplifies the record-keeping process, since under JIT there are no inventory records to maintain, no requisition forms, no issue slips, and so forth, to be concerned with. Also note the absence of a separate Work in Process account under JIT.
3.	Direct labour is not treated as a separate cost item in a JIT system. Rather, it is *added to manufacturing overhead* (see the entry for transaction 4 under JIT in the exhibit). There are two reasons for this treatment of direct labour. First, it simplifies the costing process. Second, direct labour cost is too small to be dealt with separately in a highly automated, FMS setting where JIT is typically used. Note particularly from the exhibit how few entries are made in a JIT system. When companies adopt JIT, they typically report that *thousands* of journal entries are eliminated each month.

Raw and In-Process Inventory   An account used in a JIT system that is a combination of the Raw Materials and Work in Process inventory accounts found in a job-order costing system.

4.   Transaction 4, which deals with the incurrence of manufacturing overhead costs, differs in two ways in a JIT system. First, direct labour costs are included, as discussed above. Second, costs are accumulated by *activity* rather than in a single pool for the entire company. The concept of activity-based costing was discussed in the main body of the chapter.

5.   Under JIT, overhead cost is applied to products only at the time of completion.

6.   Material and conversion costs in a JIT system are not added to products until the products are completed and ready for shipment. This eliminates the need to track costs and the need for job cost sheets. When products are completed under JIT, costs are moved from the Raw and In-Process Inventory account and from the Manufacturing Overhead account into Finished Goods. The transfer of costs to Finished Goods under JIT is sometimes referred to as **backflush costing**, since costs are "flushed" out of the system *after* products are completed.

Backflush costing A term used under JIT that refers to flushing costs out of the system after goods are completed and the charging of these costs directly to the Finished Goods inventory account.

Small businesses with a need for job costs but with small amounts of work in process and finished goods could use a variation of the backflush procedures, namely, the periodic inventory system. Such a system is usually described in a merchandising context, but small businesses such as construction contractors could effectively use the periodic approach. Thus, jobs would be costed but inventories would only be costed if and when they are needed. If desired, a perpetual raw materials system could be used with periodic work in process and finished goods systems. Costs and benefits should dictate the approach adopted for accounting purposes, not a rigid adherence to a particular style.

Appendix 3C: Scrap and Rework

Objective 10

Account for scrap and rework of unacceptable production.

Businesses are interested in quality because it tends to enhance profitability. A survey of 340 Canadian businesses reported 80% had a strong commitment to a quality-oriented strategy.[12] Lack of quality costs the company in the form of scrap, rework, delays in production, inventories, warranty cost, and poor customer relations. Estimates of these costs are 25 to 35% of total product cost.[13]

Total quality control systems are being designed to provide organizations with a systematic approach to quality management. Prevention of quality failures by design, material procurement, and conversion procedures represents one aspect. Inspection appraisals to assess production results to ensure they meet the standards desired is another. The costs of prevention and inspection appraisals represent discretionary costs that are based on management policy. Failures both as part of production and while the product is in the hands of the customer are nondiscretionary. A study of Canadian practice suggests a 40/30/30 rule for the causes of quality defects. Design problems account for 40% of the defects. Production errors and defective materials cause the other 60% of quality difficulties.[14]

Prevention costs include training and planning costs. Inspection costs include the salaries and overhead necessary to carry out the quality inspection. Failures occurring as part of production have costs associated with scrap, rework, discounts, inspection, and interruptions. External failures have costs associated with returns and allowances, warranty corrections, and future lost sales.

---

12. Douglas Snetsinger, "Why Quality Must Pay—Or Pay the Price," *The Globe and Mail*, June 23, 1992, p. 322.

13. Robert A. Howell, "World-Class Manufacturing Controls: Management Accounting for the Factory of the Future" in *Cost Accounting, Robotics, and the New Manufacturing Environment*, ed. Robert Cappettini and Donald K. Clancy (Sarasota, FL: American Accounting Association, 1987), p. 2.3.

14. "Implementing Just-in-Time Production Systems," *Management Accounting Guideline* 19 (Hamilton, ON: Society of Management Accountants of Canada, 1993), p. 25.

A total quality control philosophy was articulated to Japanese industry after World War II by the late W. Edwards Deming, a true pioneer in quality control practices.[15] Some of his suggested charting systems and ratios developed to assist management in monitoring quality will be presented in later chapters.

To illustrate the accounting for unacceptable units of production, two alternatives are examined, one where no recovery occurs and one where there is a recovery.

1. No Recovery

Assume a situation where 2,000 units are started but only 1,900 are finished with an acceptable level of quality. The material, labour, and overhead applied to the job totals $4,800. Treatment alternatives:

a. If all good units are charged with the losses, the unit cost of 1,900 units would be $4,800 ÷ 1,900 or $2.53 per unit.
b. If the rejections are charged to overhead so that they can, in turn, be charged to all jobs, the following would occur:

Manufacturing Overhead	240	
Work in Process Inventory		240

Calculations:
$4,800 ÷ 2,000 = $2.40 per unit.
  100 units × $2.40 = $240.
Net cost of 1,900 good units ($4,800 − $240 = $4.560) or $2.40 per unit.

Notice carefully the fact that treatment method *b* has a circular property: $2.40 contains overhead applied to the job. When a total of $240 for the 100 units is charged to manufacturing overhead, part of the amount is overhead applied. Thus, overhead applied becomes manufacturing overhead, which in turn determines overhead applied because it is part of the estimate used in the calculation of the predetermined overhead rate for next year (and probably this year). If the amounts are small, no harm is done. If the amounts are significant, then one should remove only the direct materials and direct labour to avoid the duplication of overhead.

2. A Recovery

Situations:

a. No rework is undertaken; items are sold for scrap. The scrap recovery could be credited to the job or to manufacturing overhead depending on the method of original treatment of the rejects.
b. Rework or repair is undertaken. The materials and labour involved in the rework could be charged to the job. As an alternative, these costs could be charged to manufacturing overhead so they can be spread over all jobs.

A careful reading of the previous procedures points out that a number of the suggested costs of poor quality are not recognized as part of the transactions. Delays in production and poor customer relations are not transactions thus do not trigger entries. Extra inventories would be required to provide the materials for rework, and extra production is necessary to allow for the scrap so that a complete job is accomplished. The cost of delays is an example of an opportunity cost and can be recognized only by special analysis of the situations.

Many industrial processes produce by-products that are environmentally hazardous. Some of these by-products can be recycled, some are sent to a disposal incin-

---

15. An obituary for the late Dr. W. Edwards Deming was reported by Associated Press, "Quality-Control Expert Helped Japan," *The Globe and Mail*, December 21, 1993, p. A 16.

erator, and others are sent to a landfill. New systems for monitoring the disposal costs of these hazardous by-products are needed. Costs of equipment and ongoing accounting for hazardous waste together with the losses from environmental cleanups net of any insurance recoveries represent accounting areas concerned with environmental protection. In turn, these ongoing costs have to be allocated to the products of the production process. Accounting for and costing of waste represents a means of providing management with the economic information associated with scrap and waste from the production process.

Questions

3–1 Why aren't actual overhead costs traced to jobs just as direct materials and direct labour costs are traced to jobs?

3–2 When would job-order costing be used in preference to process costing?

3–3 What is the purpose of the job cost sheet in a job-order costing system?

3–4 What is a predetermined overhead rate, and how is it computed?

3–5 Explain how a sales order, a production order, a materials requisition form, and a labour time ticket are involved in producing and costing products.

3–6 Explain why some production costs must be assigned to products through an allocation process. Name several such costs. Would such costs be classified as *direct* or as *indirect* costs?

3–7 Why do firms use predetermined overhead rates rather than actual manufacturing overhead costs in applying overhead to jobs?

3–8 What factors should be considered in selecting a base to be used in computing the predetermined overhead rate?

3–9 If a company fully allocates all of its overhead costs to jobs, does this guarantee that a profit will be earned for the period?

3–10 What account is credited when overhead cost is applied to Work in Process? Would you expect the amount applied for a period to equal the actual overhead costs of the period? Why or why not?

3–11 What is underapplied overhead? Overapplied overhead? What disposition is made of these amounts at period end?

3–12 Enumerate two reasons why overhead might be underapplied in a given year.

3–13 What adjustment is made for underapplied overhead on the schedule of cost of goods sold? What adjustment is made for overapplied overhead?

3–14 Sigma Company applies overhead cost to jobs on the basis of direct labour cost. Job A, which was started and completed during the current period, shows charges of $5,000 for direct materials, $8,000 for direct labour, and $6,000 for overhead on its job cost sheet. Job B, which is still in process at year-end, shows charges of $2,500 for direct materials and $4,000 for direct labour. Should any overhead cost be added to job B at year-end? Explain.

3–15 A company assigns overhead cost to completed jobs on the basis of 125% of direct labour cost. The job cost sheet for job 313 shows that $10,000 in direct materials has been used on the job and that $12,000 in direct labour cost has been incurred. If 1,000 units were produced in job 313, what is the cost per unit?

3–16   What is a plantwide overhead rate? Why are multiple overhead rates, rather than a plantwide rate, used in some companies?

3–17   What happens to overhead rates based on direct labour when automated equipment replaces direct labour?

3–18   Predetermined overhead rates smooth product costs. Do you agree? Why?

3–19   Explain clearly the rationale for why under- and overapplied overhead for an interim period should be carried to the balance sheet. What conceptual factor is assumed in the argument?

3–20   Why does the calculation of the percentages for prorating the under- or overapplied overhead reduce the costs of goods sold by the opening inventories? What would happen if such a deduction were not made?

3–21   (Appendix 3B) How is the purchase of materials and the issue of materials to production handled in a JIT system? In what way does this approach to the handling of materials save money? What happens to the Work in Process account in a JIT system?

3–22   (Appendix 3B) In what way is direct labour cost handled differently in a JIT system than in a conventional system? What are the reasons for this difference in treatment?

3–23   (Appendix 3B) At what point are materials and overhead costs added to products in a JIT system? Why is this approach to the adding of costs to products sometimes called *backflush costing*?

3–24   (Appendix 3C) Rework and scrap can cause a circular treatment of overhead. Explain how this could happen.

3–25   (Appendix 3C) Why is the cost of customer dissatisfaction with poor quality products not recognized in the accounts? How can the cost be determined?

Exercises

E3–1   Which method of determining product costs, job-order costing or process costing, would be more appropriate in each of the following situations?

a.   An Elmer's glue factory.
b.   A textbook publisher such as McGraw-Hill Ryerson.
c.   An Irving oil refinery.
d.   A facility that makes Minute Maid frozen orange juice.
e.   A Scott paper mill.
f.   A custom home builder.
g.   A shop that customizes vans.
h.   A manufacturer of specialty chemicals.
i.   An auto repair shop.
j.   A Michelin tire manufacturing plant.
k.   An advertising agency.
l.   A law office.

E3–2   Kingsport Containers, Ltd, of the Bahamas experiences wide variation in demand for the 200-litre steel drums it fabricates. The leakproof, rustproof steel drums have a variety of uses from storing liquids and bulk materials to serving as makeshift musical instruments. The drums are made to order and are painted according to the customer's specifications—often in bright patterns and designs. The company is well known for the artwork that appears on its drums. Unit costs are computed on a quarterly basis by dividing each quarter's manufacturing costs (materials, labour, and overhead) by the quarter's production in units. The company's estimated costs, by quarter, for the coming year follow:

	Quarter			
	First	**Second**	**Third**	**Fourth**
Direct materials	$240,000	$120,000	$ 60,000	$180,000
Direct labour	128,000	64,000	32,000	96,000
Manufacturing overhead	300,000	220,000	180,000	260,000
Total manufacturing costs	$668,000	$404,000	$272,000	$536,000
Number of units to be produced	80,000	40,000	20,000	60,000
Estimated cost per unit	$8.35	$10.10	$13.60	$8.93

Management finds the variation in unit costs to be confusing and difficult to work with. It has been suggested that the problem lies with manufacturing overhead, since it is the largest element of cost. Accordingly, you have been asked to find a more appropriate way of assigning manufacturing overhead cost to units of product. After some analysis, you have determined that the company's overhead costs are mostly fixed and therefore show little sensitivity to changes in the level of production.

Required

1. The company uses a job-order costing system. How would you recommend that manufacturing overhead cost be assigned to production? Be specific, and show computations.
2. Recompute the company's unit costs in accordance with your recommendations in (1) above.

E3–3 The Polaris Company uses a job-order costing system. The following data relate to October, the first month of the company's fiscal year.

a. Raw materials purchased on account, $210,000.
b. Raw materials issued to production, $190,000 ($178,000 direct materials and $12,000 indirect materials).
c. Direct labour cost incurred, $90,000; indirect labour cost incurred, $110,000.
d. Depreciation recorded on factory equipment, $40,000.
e. Other manufacturing overhead costs incurred during October, $70,000 (credit Accounts Payable).
f. The company applies manufacturing overhead cost to production on the basis of $8 per machine-hour. There were 30,000 machine-hours recorded for October.
g. Production orders costing $520,000 according to their job cost sheets were completed during October and transferred to Finished Goods.
h. Production orders that had cost $480,000 to complete according to their job cost sheets were shipped to customers during the month. These goods were sold at 25% above cost. The goods were sold on account.

Required

1. Prepare journal entries to record the information given above.
2. Prepare T-accounts for Manufacturing Overhead and Work in Process. Post the relevant information above to each account. Compute the ending balance in each account, assuming that Work in Process has a beginning balance of $42,000.

E3–4 The following cost data relate to the manufacturing activities of Chang Company during the just completed year:

Manufacturing overhead costs incurred:	
Indirect materials	$ 15,000
Indirect labour	130,000
Property taxes, factory	8,000
Utilities, factory	70,000
Depreciation, factory	240,000
Insurance, factory	10,000
Total actual costs incurred	$473,000

Other costs incurred:
Purchases of raw materials (both
direct and indirect) $400,000
Direct labour cost   60,000

Inventories:
Raw materials, beginning   20,000
Raw materials, ending   30,000
Work in process, beginning   40,000
Work in process, ending   70,000

The company uses a predetermined overhead rate to apply overhead cost to production. The rate for the year was $25 per machine-hour. A total of 19,400 machine-hours was recorded for the year. Cost of goods sold for the year amounted to $870,000.

Required
1. Compute the amount of under- or overapplied overhead cost for the year.
2. Prepare a schedule of cost of goods manufactured for the year.
3. Allocate the under- or overapplied overhead cost to the three accounts using the appropriate balances in the three accounts.

E3–5 The following information is taken from the accounts of Latta Company. The entries in the T-accounts are summaries of the transactions that affected those accounts during the year.

	Manufacturing Overhead				**Work in Process**		
(a)	460,000	(b)	390,000	Bal.	5,000	(c)	710,000
Bal.	70,000				260,000		
					85,000		
				(b)	390,000		
				Bal.	30,000		

	Finished Goods				**Cost of Goods Sold**		
Bal.	50,000	(d)	640,000	(d)	640,000		
(c)	710,000						
Bal.	120,000						

The overhead that had been applied to Work in Process during the year is distributed among the ending balances in the accounts as follows:

Work in Process, ending . . . . $ 19,500
Finished Goods, ending   58,500
Cost of Goods Sold   312,000
Overhead applied $390,000

For example, of the $30,000 ending balance in Work in Process, $19,500 was overhead that had been applied during the year.

Required
1. Identify reasons for entries (a) through (d).
2. Assume that the company closes any balance in the Manufacturing Overhead account directly to Cost of Goods Sold. Prepare the necessary journal entry.
3. Assume instead that the company allocates any balance in the Manufacturing Overhead account to the other accounts in proportion to the overhead applied in their ending balances. Prepare the necessary journal entry, with supporting computations.

E3–6 Estimated cost and operating data for three companies for the upcoming year follow:

	Company		
	X	**Y**	**Z**
Direct labour-hours	80,000	45,000	60,000
Machine-hours	30,000	70,000	21,000
Direct materials cost	$400,000	$290,000	$300,000
Manufacturing overhead cost	536,000	315,000	480,000

Predetermined overhead rates are computed using the following bases in the three companies:

Company	Overhead Rate Based on—
X	Direct labour-hours
Y	Machine-hours
Z	Direct materials cost

Required

1. Compute the predetermined overhead rate to be used in each company during the upcoming year.
2. Assume that Company X works on three jobs during the upcoming year. Direct labour-hours recorded by job are: job 418, 12,000 hours; job 419, 36,000 hours; job 420, 30,000 hours. How much overhead cost will the company apply to Work in Process for the year? If actual overhead costs total $530,000 for the year, will overhead be under- or overapplied? By how much?

E3–7 White Company has two departments, Cutting and Finishing. The company uses a job-order cost system and computes a predetermined overhead rate in each department. The Cutting Department bases its rate on machine-hours, and the Finishing Department bases its rate on direct labour cost. At the beginning of the year, the company made the following estimates:

	Department	
	Cutting	**Finishing**
Direct labour-hours	6,000	30,000
Machine-hours	48,000	5,000
Manufacturing overhead cost	$360,000	$486,000
Direct labour cost	50,000	270,000

Required

1. Compute the predetermined overhead rate to be used in each department.
2. Assume that the overhead rates that you computed in (1) above are in effect. The job cost sheet for job 203, which was started and completed during the year, showed the following:

	Department	
	Cutting	**Finishing**
Direct labour-hours	6	20
Machine-hours	80	4
Materials requisitioned	$500	$310
Direct labour cost	70	150

Compute the total overhead cost applied to job 203.

3. Would you expect substantially different amounts of overhead cost to be assigned to some jobs if the company used a plantwide overhead rate based on direct labour cost, rather than using departmental rates? Explain. No computations are necessary.

E3–8 Harwood Company is a manufacturing firm that operates a job-order costing system. Overhead costs are applied to jobs on the basis of machine-hours. At the beginning of the year, management estimated that the company would incur $192,000 in manufacturing overhead costs and work 80,000 machine-hours.

1. Compute the company's predetermined overhead rate.
2. Assume that during the year the company works only 75,000 machine-hours and incurs the following costs in the Manufacturing Overhead and Work in Process accounts:

Manufacturing Overhead			**Work in Process**	
(Maintenance)	21,000	?	(Direct materials)	710,000
(Indirect materials)	8,000		(Direct labour)	90,000
(Indirect labour)	60,000		(Overhead)	?
(Utilities)	32,000			
(Insurance)	7,000			
(Depreciation)	56,000			

    Copy the data in the T-accounts above onto your answer sheet. Compute the amount of overhead cost that would be applied to Work in Process for the year and make the entry in your T-accounts.
3. Compute the amount of under- or overapplied overhead for the year and show the balance in your Manufacturing Overhead T-account. Prepare a general journal entry to close out the balance in this account to Cost of Goods Sold.
4. Explain why the manufacturing overhead was under- or overapplied for the year.

E3–9   Dillon Products manufactures various machined parts to customer specifications. The company uses a job-order costing system and applies overhead cost to jobs on the basis of machine-hours. At the beginning of the year, it was estimated that the company would work 240,000 machine-hours and incur $4,800,000 in manufacturing overhead costs.

    The company spent the entire month of January working on a large order for 16,000 custom-made machined parts. The company had no work in process at the beginning of January. Cost data relating to January follow:

a. Raw materials purchased on account, $325,000.
b. Raw materials requisitioned for production, $290,000 (80% direct materials and 20% indirect materials).
c. Labour cost incurred in the factory, $180,000 (one-third direct labour and two-thirds indirect labour).
d. Depreciation recorded on factory equipment, $75,000.
e. Other manufacturing overhead costs incurred, $62,000 (credit Accounts Payable).
f. Manufacturing overhead cost was applied to production on the basis of 15,000 machine-hours actually worked during the month.
g. The completed job was moved into the finished goods warehouse on January 31 to await delivery to the customer. (In computing the dollar amount for this entry, remember that the cost of a completed job consists of direct materials, direct labour, and *applied* overhead.)

1. Prepare journal entries to record items (a) through (f) above [ignore item (g) for the moment].
2. Prepare T-accounts for Manufacturing Overhead and Work in Process. Post the relevant items from your journal entries to these T-accounts.
3. Prepare a journal entry for item (g) above.
4. Compute the unit cost that will appear on the job cost sheet.

E3–10   Leeds Architectural Consultants began operations on January 2. The following activity was recorded in the company's Work in Process account for the first month of operations:

Work in Process			
Costs of subcontracted work	230,000	To completed projects	390,000
Direct staff costs	75,000		
Studio overhead	120,000		

Leeds Architectural Consultants is a service firm, so the names of the accounts it uses are different from the names used in manufacturing firms. Costs of Subcontracted Work is basically the same thing as Direct Materials; Direct Staff Costs is the same as Direct Labour; Studio Overhead is the same as Manufacturing Overhead; and Completed Projects is the same as Finished Goods. Apart from the difference in terms, the accounting methods used by the company are identical to the methods used by manufacturing companies.

Leeds Architectural Consultants uses a job-order costing system and applies studio overhead to Work in Process on the basis of direct staff costs. At the end of January, only one job was still in process. This job (Lexington Gardens Project) had been charged with $6,500 in direct staff costs.

Required

1. Compute the predetermined overhead rate that was in use during January.
2. Complete the following job cost sheet for the partially completed Lexington Gardens Project.

Job Cost Sheet—Lexington Gardens Project
As of January 31

Costs of subcontracted work	$?
Direct staff costs	?
Studio overhead	?
Total cost to January 31	$?

E3–11 Vista Landscaping uses a job-order costing system to track the costs of its landscaping projects. The company provides garden design services as well as actually carrying out the landscaping for the client. The table below provides data concerning the three landscaping projects that were in progress during April. There was no work in process at the beginning of April.

	Project		
	Harris	**Chan**	**James**
Designer-hours	120	100	90
Direct materials cost	$4,500	$3,700	$1,400
Direct labour cost	9,600	8,000	7,200

Actual overhead costs were $30,000 for April. Overhead costs are applied to projects on the basis of designer-hours since most of the overhead is related to the costs of the garden design studio. The predetermined overhead rate is $90 per designer-hour. The Harris and Chan projects were completed in April; the James project was not completed by the end of the month.

Required

1. Compute the amount of overhead cost that would have been charged to each project during April.
2. Prepare a journal entry showing the completion of the Harris and Chan projects and the transfer of costs to the Completed Projects (i.e., Finished Goods) account.
3. What is the balance in the Work in Process account at the end of the month?
4. What is the balance in the Overhead account at the end of the month? What is this balance called?

E3–12 (Appendix 3A) Security Pension Services helps clients to set up and administer pension plans that are in compliance with tax laws and regulatory requirements. The firm uses a job-costing system in which overhead is applied to clients' accounts on the basis of professional staff hours charged to the accounts. Data concerning two recent years appear below:

	1998	1999
Estimated professional staff hours to be charged to clients' accounts	4,500	4,600
Estimated overhead cost	$310,500	$310,500
Professional staff hours available	6,000	6,000

"Professional staff hours available" is a measure of the capacity of the firm. Any hours available that are not charged to clients' accounts represent unused capacity.

Required
1. Marta Brinksi is an established client whose pension plan was set up many years ago. In both 1998 and 1999, only 2.5 hours of professional staff time were charged to Ms. Brinksi's account. If the company bases its predetermined overhead rate on the estimated overhead cost and the estimated professional staff hours to be charged to clients, how much overhead cost would have been applied to Ms. Brinksi's account in 1998? In 1999?
2. Suppose that the company bases its predetermined overhead rate on the estimated overhead cost and the estimated professional staff hours to be charged to clients as in (1) above. Also suppose that the actual professional staff hours charged to clients' accounts and the actual overhead costs turn out to be exactly as estimated in both years. By how much would the overhead be under- or overapplied in 1998? In 1999?
3. Refer back to the data concerning Ms. Brinksi in (1) above. If the company bases its predetermined overhead rate on the estimated overhead cost and the *professional staff hours available,* how much overhead cost would have been applied to Ms. Brinksi's account in 1998? In 1999?
4. Suppose that the company bases its predetermined overhead rate on the estimated overhead cost and the professional staff hours available as in (3) above. Also suppose that the actual professional staff hours charged to clients' accounts and the actual overhead costs turn out to be exactly as estimated in both years. By how much would the overhead be under- or overapplied in 1998? In 1999?

E3–13   Howard Company uses a job-order costing system. The table below provides selected data on the three jobs worked on during the company's first month of operations:

Job Number

	1010	1020	1030
Units of product in the job	4,000	3,600	3,000
Machine-hours worked	1,200	1,000	900
Direct materials cost	$4,500	$3,700	$1,400
Direct labour cost	9,600	8,000	7,200

Actual overhead costs totalling $30,000 were incurred during the month. Manufacturing overhead cost is applied to production on a basis of machine-hours at a predetermined rate of $9 per hour. Jobs 1010 and 1020 were completed during the month; job 1030 was not completed.

Required
1. Compute the amount of manufacturing overhead cost that would have been charged to each job during the month.
2. Compute the unit cost of jobs 1010 and 1020.
3. Prepare a journal entry showing the transfer of the completed jobs into the finished goods warehouse.
4. What is the balance in the Work in Process account at the end of the month?
5. What is the balance in the Manufacturing Overhead account at the end of the month?
6. Which job was the most costly to undertake? What was the major contributing factor to the cost difference?

E3–14   (Appendix 3C) Home Woodworkers Ltd. was producing 100 birdhouses for export. Costs of production per unit: materials $4, labour $8, and overhead $8.

Twenty of the birdhouses were found to be defective in that the entrance was too large thus permitting predators to enter the nesting area.

Rework costs of replacing the entrance were as follows: materials $1.60, labour $2, and overhead.

Required   Record the cost of reworking the defective products using two alternative treatments.

E3–15   (Appendix 3C) The North Sydney plant of Textiles Ltd. manufactures sail cloth for racing boats. The cloth has a cost per metre of $18 materials, $3 for labour, $5 for overhead. A defective gauge on the knitting machine resulted in the production of 400 metres of sail cloth that are substandard for racing purposes. Spoiled cloth can be sold to pleasure craft owners for 40 percent of its cost.

Required   Prepare the journal entries to record this normal spoilage using two alternative procedures.

E–16   (Appendix 3B) Cottage Products has an FMS in operation and is considering the use of JIT inventory methods. At present, the company is using conventional job-order costing.

Required   1.   For the coming month, the company had planned to purchase $450,000 in raw materials, of which 5% is designated for inventory buildup. The remaining amount will be used in production during the month.
   a. Under conventional job-order costing, what entries would be made to record the purchase of the material and the issue of the material to production?
   b. If the company adopts the JIT inventory approach at the beginning of the month, what entry will be made to record the purchase of the material and the issue of the material to production?
2.   Assume that direct labour cost for the month totals $50,000 and that actual manufacturing overhead costs total $225,000. What entry would be made under a JIT system to record these costs?
3.   Assume that the company does adopt the JIT approach and that $250,000 in overhead cost is applied to the month's production. What entry would be made to record the completed production for the month?

Problems

P3–17   Straightforward Journal Entries; Partial T-Accounts; Income Statement   Almeda Products, Inc., uses a job-order cost system. The company's inventory balances on April 1, the start of its fiscal year, were as follows:

Raw materials	$32,000
Work in process	20,000
Finished goods	48,000

During the year, the following transactions were completed:

a.   Raw materials were purchased on account, $170,000.
b.   Raw materials were issued from the storeroom for use in production, $180,000 (80% direct and 20% indirect).
c.   Employee salaries and wages were accrued as follows: direct labour, $200,000; indirect labour, $82,000; and selling and administrative salaries, $90,000.
d.   Utility costs were incurred in the factory, $65,000.
e.   Advertising costs were incurred, $100,000.
f.   Prepaid insurance expired during the year, $20,000 (90% related to factory operations, and 10% related to selling and administrative activities).
g.   Depreciation was recorded, $180,000 (85% related to factory assets, and 15% related to selling and administrative assets).
h.   Manufacturing overhead was applied to jobs at the rate of 175% of direct labour cost.
i.   Goods that cost $700,000 to manufacture according to their job cost sheets were transferred to the finished goods warehouse.
j.   Sales for the year totalled $1,000,000 and were all on account. The total cost to manufacture these goods according to their job cost sheets was $720,000.

Required   1.   Prepare journal entries to record the transactions for the year.
2.   Prepare T-accounts for Raw Materials, Work in Process, Finished Goods, Manufacturing Overhead, and Cost of Goods Sold. Post the appropriate parts of your journal entries to these T-accounts. Compute the ending balance in each account. (Do not forget to enter the beginning balances in the inventory accounts.)
3.   Is Manufacturing Overhead underapplied or overapplied for the year? Prepare a journal entry to close this balance to Cost of Goods Sold.
4.   Prepare an income statement for the year. (Do not prepare a schedule of cost of goods manufactured; all of the information needed for the income statement is available in the journal entries and T-accounts you have prepared.)

P3–18   Entries Directly into T-Accounts; Income Statement   Hudson
Company's trial balance as of January 1, the beginning of the fiscal year, is given below:

Cash	$ 7,000	
Accounts Receivable	18,000	
Raw Materials	9,000	
Work in Process	20,000	
Finished Goods	32,000	
Prepaid Insurance	4,000	
Plant and Equipment	210,000	
Accumulated Depreciation		$ 53,000
Accounts Payable		38,000
Capital Stock		160,000
Retained Earnings		49,000
Total	$300,000	$300,000

Hudson Company is a manufacturing firm and employs a job-order costing system.
During the year, the following transactions took place:

a. Raw materials purchased on account, $40,000.
b. Raw materials were requisitioned for use in production, $38,000 (85% direct and 15% indirect).
c. Factory utility costs incurred, $19,100.
d. Depreciation was recorded on plant and equipment, $36,000. Three-fourths of the depreciation related to factory equipment, and the remainder related to selling and administrative equipment.
e. Advertising expense incurred, $48,000.
f. Costs for salaries and wages were incurred as follows:

Direct labour	$45,000
Indirect labour	10,000
Administrative salaries	30,000

g. Prepaid insurance expired during the year, $3,000 (80% related to factory operations, and 20% related to selling and administrative activities).
h. Miscellaneous selling and administrative expenses incurred, $9,500.
i. Manufacturing overhead was applied to production. The company applies overhead on the basis of $8 per machine-hour; 7,500 machine-hours were recorded for the year.
j. Goods that cost $140,000 to manufacture according to their job cost sheets were transferred to the finished goods warehouse.
k. Sales for the year totalled $250,000 and were all on account. The total cost to manufacture these goods according to their job cost sheets was $130,000.
l. Collections from customers during the year totalled $245,000.
m. Payments to suppliers on account during the year, $150,000; payments to employees for salaries and wages, $84,000.

Required

1. Prepare a T-account for each account in the company's trial balance and enter the opening balances shown above.
2. Record the transactions above directly into the T-accounts. Prepare new T-accounts as needed. Key your entries to the letters (a) through (m) above. Find the ending balance in each account.
3. Is manufacturing overhead underapplied or overapplied for the year? Make an entry in the T-accounts to close any balance in the Manufacturing Overhead account to Cost of Goods Sold.
4. Prepare an income statement for the year. (Do not prepare a schedule of cost of goods manufactured; all of the information needed for the income statement is available in the T-accounts.)
5. How could the management of Hudson Company utilize the job cost system and the information contained therein in its strategic decision making?

P3–19 Multiple Departments; Overhead Rates; Costing Units of Product High Desert Potteryworks makes a variety of pottery products that it sells to retailers such as Home Depot. The company uses a job-order costing system in which predetermined overhead rates are used to apply manufacturing overhead cost to jobs. The predetermined overhead rate in the Molding Department is based on machine-hours, and the rate in the Painting Department is based on direct labour cost. At the beginning of the year, the company's management made the following estimates:

	Department	
	Molding	**Painting**
Direct labour-hours	12,000	60,000
Machine-hours	70,000	8,000
Direct materials cost	$510,000	$650,000
Direct labour cost	130,000	420,000
Manufacturing overhead cost	602,000	735,000

Job 205 was started on August 1 and completed on August 10. The company's cost records show the following information concerning the job:

	Department	
	Molding	**Painting**
Direct labour-hours	30	85
Machine-hours	110	20
Materials placed into production	$470	$332
Direct labour cost	290	680

Required

1. Compute the predetermined overhead rate used during the year in the Molding Department. Compute the rate used in the Painting Department.
2. Compute the total overhead cost applied to job 205.
3. What would be the total cost recorded for job 205? If the job contained 50 units, what would be the cost per unit?
4. At the end of the year, the records of High Desert Potteryworks revealed the following *actual* cost and operating data for all jobs worked on during the year:

	Department	
	Molding	**Painting**
Direct labour-hours	10,000	62,000
Machine-hours	65,000	9,000
Direct materials cost	$430,000	$680,000
Direct labour cost	108,000	436,000
Manufacturing overhead cost	570,000	750,000

What was the amount of under- or overapplied overhead in each department at the end of the year?

P3–20 Schedule of Cost of Goods Manufactured; Pricing; Work in Process Analysis Gitano Products operates a job-order cost system and applies overhead cost to jobs on the basis of direct materials *used in production* (*not* on the basis of raw materials purchased). In computing a predetermined overhead rate at the beginning of the year, the company's estimates were: manufacturing overhead cost, $800,000; and direct materials to be used in production, $500,000. The company's inventory accounts at the beginning and end of the year were:

	Beginning	Ending
Raw Materials	$ 20,000	$ 80,000
Work in Process	150,000	70,000
Finished Goods	260,000	400,000

The following actual costs were incurred during the year:

Purchase of raw materials (all direct)	$510,000
Direct labour cost	90,000
Manufacturing overhead costs:	
Indirect labour	170,000
Property taxes	48,000
Depreciation of equipment	260,000
Maintenance	95,000
Insurance	7,000
Rent, building	180,000

Required

1. a. Compute the predetermined overhead rate for the year.
   b. Compute the amount of under- or overapplied overhead for the year.
2. Prepare a schedule of cost of goods manufactured for the year.
3. Compute the Cost of Goods Sold for the year. (Do not include any under- or overapplied overhead in your Cost of Goods Sold figure.) What options are available for disposing of under- or overapplied overhead?
4. Job 215 was started and completed during the year. What price would have been charged to the customer if the job required $8,500 in direct materials and $2,700 in direct labour cost and the company priced its jobs at 25% above cost to manufacture?
5. Direct materials made up $24,000 of the $70,000 ending Work in Process inventory balance. Supply the information missing below:

Direct materials	$24,000
Direct labour	?
Manufacturing overhead	?
Work in process inventory	$70,000

P3–21 Job-Order Cost Journal Entries; Complete T-Accounts; Income Statement   Film Specialties, Inc., operates a small production studio in which advertising films are made for TV and other uses. The company uses a job-order costing system to accumulate costs for each film produced. The company's trial balance as of May 1, the start of its fiscal year follows:

Cash	$ 60,000	
Accounts Receivable	210,000	
Materials and Supplies	130,000	
Film in Process	75,000	
Finished Films	860,000	
Prepaid Insurance	90,000	
Studio and Equipment	5,200,000	
Accumulated Depreciation		$1,990,000
Accounts Payable		700,000
Salaries and Wages Payable		35,000
Capital Stock		2,500,000
Retained Earnings		1,400,000
Total	$6,625,000	$6,625,000

Film Specialties, Inc., uses a Production Overhead account to record all transactions relating to overhead costs and applies overhead costs to jobs on the basis of camera-hours. For the current year, the company estimated that it would incur $1,350,000 in production overhead costs, and film 15,000 camera-hours. During the year, the following transactions were completed:

a. Materials and supplies purchased on account, $690,000.
b. Materials and supplies issued from the storeroom for use in production of various films, $700,000 (80% direct to the films and 20% indirect).
c. Utility costs incurred in the production studio, $90,000.
d. Costs for employee salaries and wages were incurred as follows:

> Actors, directors, and camera crew $1,300,000
> Indirect labour costs of support workers . . .   230,000
> Marketing and administrative salaries   650,000

e. Advertising costs incurred, $800,000.
f. Prepaid insurance expired during the year, $70,000. Of this amount, $60,000 related to the operation of the production studio, and the remaining $10,000 related to the company's marketing and administrative activities.
g. Depreciation recorded for the year, $650,000 (80% represented depreciation of the production studio, cameras, and other production equipment; the remaining 20% represented depreciation on facilities and equipment used in marketing and administrative activities).
h. Rental costs incurred on various facilities and equipment used in production of films, $360,000; and rental costs incurred on equipment used in marketing and administrative activities, $40,000.
i. Production overhead was applied to jobs filmed during the year. The company recorded 16,500 camera-hours.
j. Films that cost $3,400,000 to produce according to their job cost sheets were completed during the year. The films were transferred to the finished films storeroom to await delivery to customers.
k. Sales of films for the year (all on account) totalled $6,000,000. The total cost to produce these films was $4,000,000 according to their job cost sheets.
l. Collections on account from customers during the year, $5,400,000.
m. Cash payments made during the year; to creditors on account, $2,500,000; and to employees for salaries and wages, $2,200,000.

Required
1. Prepare journal entries to record the year's transactions.
2. Prepare a T-account for each account in the company's trial balance and enter the opening balances given above. Post your journal entries to the T-accounts. Prepare new T-accounts as needed. Compute the ending balance in each account.
3. Is production overhead underapplied or overapplied for the year? Prepare the necessary journal entry to close the balance in Production Overhead to Cost of Films Sold.
4. Prepare an income statement for the year. (Do not prepare a schedule of cost of goods manufactured; all of the information needed for the income statement is available in the T-accounts.)
5. What role is played by the job cost system and the information contained in it that can assist Film Specialties' management in making future strategic plans?

P3–22 Job Cost Sheets; Overhead Rates; Journal Entries   AOZT

Volzhskije Motory of St. Petersburg, Russia, makes marine motors for vessels ranging in size from harbour tugs to open-water icebreakers. (The Russian currency is the ruble, which is denoted by RUR. All currency amounts below are in thousands of RUR.)

The company uses a job-order costing system. Only three jobs—job 208, job 209, and job 210—were worked on during May and June. Job 208 was completed on June 20; the other two jobs were uncompleted on June 30. Job cost sheets on the three jobs are given below:

	Job Cost Sheet		
	Job 208	**Job 209**	**Job 210**
May costs incurred:*			
Direct materials	RUR 9,500	RUR5,100	RUR —
Direct labour	8,000	3,000	—
Manufacturing overhead	11,200	4,200	—
June costs incurred:			
Direct materials	—	6,000	7,200
Direct labour	4,000	7,500	8,500
Manufacturing overhead	?	?	?

*Jobs 208 and 209 were started during May.

The following additional information is available:

a. Manufacturing overhead is applied to jobs on the basis of direct labour cost.
b. Balances in the inventory accounts at May 31 were:

Raw Materials	RUR30,000
Work in Process	?
Finished Goods	50,000

Required

1. Prepare T-accounts for Raw Materials, Work in Process, Finished Goods, and Manufacturing Overhead. Enter the May 31 balances given above; in the case of Work in Process, compute the May 31 balance and enter it into the Work in Process T-account.
2. Prepare journal entries for *June* as follows:
    a. Prepare an entry to record the issue of materials into production and post the entry to appropriate T-accounts. (In the case of direct materials, it is not necessary to make a separate entry for each job.) Indirect materials used during June totalled RUR3,600.
    b. Prepare an entry to record the incurrence of labour cost and post the entry to appropriate T-accounts. (In the case of direct labour cost, it is not necessary to make a separate entry for each job.) Indirect labour cost totalled RUR7,000 for June.
    c. Prepare an entry to record the incurrence of RUR19,400 in various actual manufacturing overhead costs for June. (Credit Accounts Payable.) Post this entry to the appropriate T-accounts.
3. What apparent predetermined overhead rate does the company use to assign overhead cost to jobs? Using this rate, prepare a journal entry to record the application of overhead cost to jobs for June (it is not necessary to make a separate entry for each job). Post this entry to appropriate T-accounts.
4. As stated earlier, job 208 was completed during June. Prepare a journal entry to show the transfer of this job off of the production line and into the finished goods warehouse. Post the entry to appropriate T-accounts.
5. Determine the balance at June 30 in the Work in Process inventory account. How much of this balance consists of costs charged to job 209? To job 210?

P3–23 Multiple Departments; Overhead Rates Hobart, Evans, and Nix is a small law firm that contains 10 partners and 12 support persons. The firm employs a job-order costing system to accumulate costs chargeable to each client, and it is organized into two departments—the Research and Documents Department and the Litigation Department. The firm uses predetermined overhead rates to charge the costs of these departments to its clients. At the beginning of the year, the firm's management made the following estimates for the year:

	Department	
	Research and Documents	**Litigation**
Research-hours	24,000	—
Direct attorney-hours	9,000	18,000
Legal forms and supplies	$ 16,000	$ 5,000
Direct attorney cost	450,000	900,000
Departmental overhead cost	840,000	360,000

The predetermined overhead rate in the Research and Documents Department is based on research-hours, and the rate in the Litigation Department is based on direct attorney cost.

The costs charged to each client are made up of three elements: legal forms and supplies used, direct attorney costs incurred, and an applied amount of overhead from each department in which work is performed on the case.

Case 418-3 was initiated on February 23 and completed on May 16. During this period, the following costs and time were recorded on the case:

	Department	
	Research and Documents	**Litigation**
Research-hours	26	—
Direct attorney-hours	7	114
Legal forms and supplies	$ 80	$ 40
Direct attorney cost	350	5,700

Required

1. Compute the predetermined overhead rate used during the year in the Research and Documents Department. Compute the rate used in the Litigation Department.
2. Using the rates you computed in (1) above, compute the total overhead cost applied to case 418-3.
3. What would be the total cost charged to case 418-3? Show computations by department and in total for the case.
4. At the end of the year, the firm's records revealed the following *actual* cost and operating data for all cases handled during the year:

	Department	
	Research and Documents	**Litigation**
Research-hours	26,000	—
Direct attorney-hours	8,000	15,000
Legal forms and supplies	$ 19,000	$ 6,000
Direct attorney cost	400,000	750,000
Departmental overhead cost	870,000	315,000

Determine the amount of under- or overapplied overhead cost in each department for the year.

P3–24 Predetermined Overhead Rate and Capacity (Appendix 3A)

Platinum Tracks, Inc., is a small audio recording studio located in Toronto. The company handles work for advertising agencies—primarily for radio ads—and has a few singers and bands as clients. Platinum Tracks handles all aspects of recording from editing to making a digital master from which CDs can be copied. The competition in the audio recording industry in Toronto has always been tough, but it has been getting even tougher over the last several years. The studio has been losing customers to newer studios equipped with more up-to-date equipment that are able to offer very attractive prices and excellent service. Summary data concerning the last two years of operations follow:

	1998	1999
Estimated hours of studio service	1,000	800
Estimated studio overhead cost	$160,000	$160,000
Actual hours of studio service provided	750	500
Actual studio overhead cost incurred	$160,000	$160,000
Hours of studio service at capacity	1,600	1,600

The company applies studio overhead to recording jobs on the basis of the hours of studio service provided. For example, 40 hours of studio time were required to record, edit, and master the *Verde Baja* music CD for a local Latino band. All of the studio overhead is fixed, and the actual overhead cost incurred was exactly as estimated at the beginning of the year in both 1998 and 1999.

Required

1. Platinum Tracks computes the predetermined overhead rate at the beginning of each year based on the estimated studio overhead and the estimated hours of studio service for the year. How much overhead would have been applied to the *Verde Baja* job if it had been done in 1998? In 1999? By how much would overhead have been under- or overapplied in 1998? In 1999?

2. The president of Platinum Tracks has heard that some companies in the industry have changed to a system of computing the predetermined overhead rate at the beginning of each year based on the estimated studio overhead for the year and the hours of studio service that could be provided at capacity. He would like to know what effect this method would have on job costs. How much overhead would have been applied using this method to the *Verde Baja* job if it had been done in 1998? In 1999? By how much would overhead have been under- or overapplied in 1998 using this method? In 1999?

3. How would you interpret the under- or overapplied overhead that results from using studio hours at capacity to compute the predetermined overhead rate?

4. What fundamental business problem is Platinum Tracks facing? Which method of computing the predetermined overhead rate is likely to be more helpful in facing this problem? Explain.

P3–25 Plantwide and Departmental Overhead Rates   "Blast it!" said David Wilson, president of Teledex Company. "We've just lost the bid on the Koopers job by $2,000. It seems we're either too high to get the job or too low to make any money on half the jobs we bid."

Teledex Company manufactures products to customer's specifications and operates a job-order cost system. Manufacturing overhead cost is applied to jobs on the basis of direct labour cost. The following estimates were made at the beginning of the year:

| | Department | | | |
	Fabricating	Machining	Assembly	Total Plant
Direct labour	$200,000	$100,000	$300,000	$600,000
Manufacturing overhead ...	350,000	400,000	90,000	840,000

Jobs require varying amounts of work in the three departments. The Koopers job, for example, would have required manufacturing costs in the three departments as follows:

| | Department | | | |
	Fabricating	Machining	Assembly	Total Plant
Direct materials	$3,000	$200	$1,400	$4,600
Direct labour	2,800	500	6,200	9,500
Manufacturing overhead ...	?	?	?	?

The company uses a plantwide overhead rate to apply manufacturing overhead cost to jobs.

Required

1. Assuming use of a plantwide overhead rate:
   a. Compute the rate for the current year.
   b. Determine the amount of manufacturing overhead cost that would have been applied to the Koopers job.

2. Suppose that instead of using a plantwide overhead rate, the company had used a separate predetermined overhead rate in each department. Under these conditions:
   a. Compute the rate for each department for the current year.
   b. Determine the amount of manufacturing overhead cost that would have been applied to the Koopers job.
3. Explain the difference between the manufacturing overhead that would have been applied using the plantwide rate in question 1 (b) above and using the departmental rates in question 2 (b).
4. Assume that it is customary in the industry to bid jobs at 150% of total manufacturing cost (direct materials, direct labour, and applied overhead). What was the company's bid price on the Koopers job? What would the bid price have been if departmental overhead rates had been used to apply overhead cost?
5. At the end of the year, the company assembled the following *actual* cost data relating to all jobs worked on during the year.

| | Department | | | |
	Fabricating	Machining	Assembly	Total Plant
Direct materials	$190,000	$ 16,000	$114,000	$320,000
Direct labour	210,000	108,000	262,000	580,000
Manufacturing overhead ...	360,000	420,000	84,000	864,000

Compute the under- or overapplied overhead for the year (a) assuming that a plantwide overhead rate is used, and (b) assuming that departmental overhead rates are used.

P3–26 Comprehensive Problem: T-Accounts, Job-Order Cost Flows; Statements; Pricing
Chenko Products, Inc., manufactures goods to customers' orders and uses a job-order costing system. A beginning-of-the-year trial balance for the company is given below:

Cash	$ 35,000	
Accounts Receivable	127,000	
Raw Materials	10,000	
Work in Process	44,000	
Finished Goods	75,000	
Prepaid Insurance	9,000	
Plant and Equipment	400,000	
Accumulated Depreciation		$110,000
Accounts Payable		86,000
Salaries and Wages Payable		9,000
Capital Stock		375,000
Retained Earnings		120,000
Total	$700,000	$700,000

The company applies manufacturing overhead cost to jobs on the basis of direct materials cost. The following estimates were made at the beginning of the year for purposes of computing a predetermined overhead rate: manufacturing overhead cost, $510,000; and direct materials cost, $340,000. Summarized transactions of the company for the year are given below:

a. Raw materials purchased on account, $400,000.
b. Raw materials requisitioned for use in production, $370,000 ($320,000 direct materials and $50,000 indirect materials).
c. Salary and wage costs were incurred as follows:

Direct labour	$ 76,000
Indirect labour	130,000
Selling and administrative salaries	110,000

d. Maintenance costs incurred in the factory, $81,000.
e. Travel costs incurred by salespeople, $43,000.
f. Prepaid insurance on the factory expired during the year, $7,000.

g. Utility costs incurred, $70,000 (90% related to factory operations, and 10% related to selling and administrative activities).

h. Property taxes incurred on the factory building, $9,000.

i. Advertising costs incurred, $200,000.

j. Rental cost incurred on special factory equipment, $120,000.

k. Depreciation recorded for the year, $50,000 (80% related to factory assets, and 20% related to selling and administrative assets).

l. Manufacturing overhead cost applied to jobs, $_____?_____.

m. Cost of goods manufactured for the year, $890,000.

n. Sales for the year totalled $1,400,000 (all on account); the cost of goods sold totalled $930,000.

o. Cash collections from customers during the year totalled $1,350,000.

p. Cash payments during the year: to employees, $300,000; on accounts payable, $970,000.

Required

1. Enter the company's transactions directly into T-accounts. (Do not forget to enter the beginning balances into the T-accounts.) Key your entries to the letters (a) through (p) above. Create new T-accounts as needed. Find the ending balance in each account.

2. Prepare a schedule of cost of goods manufactured.

3. Prepare a journal entry to close any balance in the Manufacturing Overhead account to Cost of Goods Sold. Prepare a schedule of cost of goods sold.

4. Prepare an income statement for the year.

5. Job 412 was one of the many jobs started and completed during the year. The job required $8,000 in direct materials and $1,600 in direct labour cost. If the job contained 400 units and the company billed the job at 175% of the unit cost on the job cost sheet, what price per unit would have been charged to the customer?

P3–27 Journal Entries; T-Accounts; Statements; Pricing

Froya Fabrikker A/S of Bergen, Norway, is a small company that manufactures specialty heavy equipment for use in North Sea oil fields. (The Norwegian currency is the krone, which is denoted by Nkr.) The company uses a job-order costing system and applies manufacturing overhead cost to jobs on the basis of direct labour-hours. At the beginning of the year, the following estimates were made for the purpose of computing the predetermined overhead rate: manufacturing overhead cost, Nkr360,000; and direct labour-hours, 900.

The following transactions took place during the year (all purchases and services were acquired on account):

a. Raw materials were purchased for use in production, Nkr200,000.

b. Raw materials were requisitioned for use in production (all direct materials), Nkr185,000.

c. Utility bills were incurred, Nkr70,000 (90% related to factory operations, and the remainder related to selling and administrative activities).

d. Salary and wage costs were incurred:

Direct labour (975 hours)	Nkr230,000
Indirect labour	90,000
Selling and administrative salaries	110,000

e. Maintenance costs were incurred in the factory, Nkr54,000.

f. Advertising costs were incurred, Nkr136,000.

g. Depreciation was recorded for the year, Nkr95,000 (80% related to factory equipment, and the remainder related to selling and administrative equipment).

h. Rental cost incurred on buildings, Nkr120,000 (85% related to factory operations, and the remainder related to selling and administrative facilities).

i. Manufacturing overhead cost was applied to jobs, Nkr_____?_____.

j. Cost of goods manufactured for the year, Nkr770,000.

k. Sales for the year (all on account) totalled Nkr1,200,000. These goods cost Nkr800,000 to manufacture according to their job cost sheets.

The balances in the inventory accounts at the beginning of the year were:

Raw Materials	Nkr30,000
Work in Process	21,000
Finished Goods	60,000

Required
1. Prepare journal entries to record the preceding data.
2. Post your entries to T-accounts. (Do not forget to enter the beginning inventory balances above.) Determine the ending balances in the inventory accounts and in the Manufacturing Overhead account.
3. Prepare a schedule of cost of goods manufactured.
4. Prepare a journal entry to close any balance in the Manufacturing Overhead account to Cost of Goods Sold. Prepare a schedule of cost of goods sold.
5. Prepare an income statement for the year.
6. Job 412 was one of the many jobs started and completed during the year. The job required Nkr8,000 in direct materials and 39 hours of direct labour time at a total direct labour cost of Nkr9,200. The job contained only four units. If the company bills at a price 60% above the unit cost on the job cost sheet, what price per unit would have been charged to the customer?

P3–28   Disposition of Under- or Overapplied Overhead   Bieler & Cie of Altdorf, Switzerland, makes furniture using the latest automated technology. The company uses a job-order costing system and applies manufacturing overhead cost to products on the basis of machine-hours. The following estimates were used in preparing the predetermined overhead rate at the beginning of the year:

Machine-hours   75,000
Manufacturing overhead cost Sfr900,000

The currency in Switzerland is the Swiss franc, which is denoted by Sfr.

During the year, a glut of furniture on the market resulted in cutting back production and a buildup of furniture in the company's warehouse. The company's cost records revealed the following actual cost and operating data for the year:

Machine-hours	60,000
Manufacturing overhead cost	Sfr850,000
Inventories at year-end:	
Raw materials	30,000
Work in process (includes overhead applied of 36,000)	100,000
Finished goods (includes overhead applied of 180,000)	500,000
Cost of goods sold (includes overhead applied of 504,000)	1,400,000

Required
1. Compute the company's predetermined overhead rate.
2. Compute the under- or overapplied overhead.
3. Assume that the company closes any under- or overapplied overhead directly to Cost of Goods Sold. Prepare the appropriate journal entry.
4. Assume that the company allocates any under- or overapplied overhead to Work in Process, Finished Goods, and Cost of Goods Sold on the basis of the amount of overhead applied in each account. Prepare the journal entry to show the allocation for the year.
5. How much higher or lower will net income be if the under- or overapplied overhead is allocated rather than closed directly to Cost of Goods Sold?

P3–29   Backflush Costing   (Appendix 3B) Norman Company Ltd. is a construction company using two cells, one for new home construction and one for renovations/repairs. In either case, the company buys what it needs for each job and does not keep an inventory of materials. Norman Company implemented backflush costing to simplify its bookkeeping. Labour costs are treated as part of overhead and no finished goods inventory is needed.

Overhead is charged to jobs based on the number of hours worked. Estimates used to set the overhead rates for each cell are as follows:

	Cell C	Cell R
Direct labour	$300,000	$200,000
Direct overhead	90,000	70,000
Total	$390,000	$270,000
Hours available	15,000	10,000

During the current year, Norman had the following activities:

	Cell C	Cell R
Materials purchased	$150,000	$75,000
Direct labour costs	290,000	210,000
Direct overhead	88,000	76,000
Hours worked	14,800	10,900

At the year end, all jobs were finished.

Required   Record the transactions for the year using backflush procedures.

P3–30   Backflush Costing and Periodic Inventory Method   (Appendix 3B)
Able Service Centre Ltd. conducts auto repairs on demand by customers. Because of the cost, Able uses a JIT purchasing system to avoid the need for inventories. Able's accountant, Jane Kosh, is interested in experimenting with the entry process for backflush costing and comparing it to the old periodic system she had studied in university. The following are the costs for May:

Materials purchased	$13,000
Labour—mechanics	3,500
Overhead costs—rent, depreciation, supervision, etc.	18,000
Overhead applied to material costs and labour costs on jobs— (Labour and material costs are charged separately)	20,000

No beginning inventories existed at May 1. One job was unfinished at the end of May because the customer was not anxious for his vehicle. Costs were: Materials, $300: Labour, $180; Overhead applied, $490.

Required
1. Prepare the general ledger entries for the month of May using the perpetual inventory system.
2. Prepare the general ledger entries for the month of May using backflush accounting.
3. Prepare the general ledger entries for the month of May using the periodic inventory system.

P3–31   Job Costing and Rework   (Appendix 3C) Terry Construction Ltd. is a mid-sized contractor engaged in both home renovations and new home construction. It employs a job costing system so it can have a record of costs for various types of jobs and to maintain a test of bidding accuracy.

The following information relates to its activities for the last month of its fiscal year. This month began with the following balances:

Cash	$ 2,000
Accounts receivable	5,000
Inventory—raw materials	1,000
Inventory—work in process	3,000 (job 1107)
Inventory—finished jobs	800 (job 1105)
Prepaid insurance	1,000
Property and equipment	100,000
Accumulated depreciation	(40,000)
Vehicles	30,000
Accumulated depreciation	(7,000)
Total assets	$ 95,800

Accounts payable	$ 6,000
Bank loan	45,000
Common stock	5,000
Retained earnings	39,800
Total liabilities and shareholders' equity .	$ 95,800

The following activities occurred during the current month:

a. Purchased raw materials for $6,000 on credit.
b. Used $6,500 of raw materials for the following jobs: 1201, $800; 1202, $700; 1203, $3,000; and 1204, $2,000.
c. Wages paid to employees: $6,500 for the following jobs: 1107, $300; 1201, $700; 1202, $2,000; 1203, $2,500; 1204, $1,000.
d. Supervision salaries paid in cash $2,000.
e. Depreciation for property and equipment $2,000, vehicles $1,000.
f. Insurance expired, $150.
g. Maintenance for equipment, $500, paid in cash.
h. Overhead applied totalled $5,850: Job 1107, $270; Job 1201, $630; Job 1202, $1,800; Job 1203, $2,250; Job 1204, $900.
i. Bidding expenses paid in cash, $800.
j. Administrative salary, $2,500.
k. Revenues billed: Job 1105, $2,000; Job 1107, $5,000; Job 1201, $2,500; Job 1202, $4,200; Job 1203, $10,000.
l. Cash collected on receivables, $23,000.
m. Cash paid on accounts payable $8,000, interest $500.
n. Job 1204 remained unfinished at the end of the month.

Job 1204 was unfinished at the end of the period in part because of some damage resulting from a late storm that removed some shingles that did not have time to stick. Materials amounting to $200 and labour in the amount of $90 were needed to correct the problem. Terry expects some further work will be needed early in the new year before the contract will be completed.

Required
1. Record the activities for the final month of the current fiscal year.
2. Prepare income results for jobs 1107, 1203, and 1105.
3. Compute the inventory evaluation for Job 1204 at the end of the fiscal year.

Cases

C3–32 Ethics and the Manager   Terri Ronsin had recently been transferred to the Home Security Systems Division of National Home Products. Shortly after taking over her new position as divisional controller, she was asked to develop the division's predetermined overhead rate for the upcoming year. The accuracy of the rate is of some importance, since it is used throughout the year and any overapplied or underapplied overhead is closed out to Cost of Goods Sold only at the end of the year. National Home Products uses direct labour-hours in all of its divisions as the allocation base for manufacturing overhead.

To compute the predetermined overhead rate, Terri divided her estimate of the total manufacturing overhead for the coming year by the production manager's estimate of the total direct labour-hours for the coming year. She took her computations to the division's general manager for approval but was quite surprised when he suggested a modification in the base. Her conversation with the general manager of the Home Security Systems Division, Harry Irving, went like this:

Ronsin: Here are my calculations for next year's predetermined overhead rate. If you approve, we can enter the rate into the computer on January 1 and be up and running in the job-order costing system right away this year.
Irving: Thanks for coming up with the calculations so quickly, and they look just fine. There is, however, one slight modification I would like to see. Your estimate of the total direct labour-hours for the year is 440,000 hours. How about cutting that to about 420,000 hours?

Ronsin: I don't know if I can do that. The production manager says she will need about 440,000 direct labour-hours to meet the sales projections for the year. Besides, there are going to be over 430,000 direct labour-hours during the current year and sales are projected to be higher next year.

Irving: Terri, I know all of that. I would still like to reduce the direct labour-hours in the base to something like 420,000 hours. You probably don't know that I had an agreement with your predecessor as divisional controller to shave 5% or so off the estimated direct labour-hours every year. That way, we kept a reserve that usually resulted in a big boost to net income at the end of the fiscal year in December. We called it our Christmas bonus. Corporate headquarters always seemed as pleased as punch that we could pull off such a miracle at the end of the year. This system has worked well for many years, and I don't want to change it now.

Required

1. Explain how shaving 5% off the estimated direct labour-hours in the base for the predetermined overhead rate usually results in a big boost in net income at the end of the fiscal year.
2. Should Terri Ronsin go along with the general manager's request to reduce the direct labour-hours in the predetermined overhead rate computation to 420,000 direct labour-hours?

C3–33   Incomplete Data; Review of Cost Flows   In an attempt to conceal a theft of funds, Snake N. Grass, controller of Bucolic Products, Inc., placed a bomb in the company's record vault. The ensuing explosion left only fragments of the company's factory ledger, as shown below:

Raw Materials		Manufacturing Overhead	
Bal. 6/1 8,000		Actual costs for June 79,000	
			Overapplied overhead 6,100

Work in Process		Accounts Payable	
Bal. 6/1 7,200			Bal. 6/30 16,000

Finished Goods		Cost of Goods Sold	
Bal. 6/30 21,000			

To bring Mr. Grass to justice, the company must reconstruct its activities for June. You have been assigned to perform the task of reconstruction. After interviewing selected employees and sifting through charred fragments, you have determined the following additional information:

a. According to the company's treasurer, the accounts payable are for purchases of raw materials only. The company's balance sheet, dated May 31, shows that Accounts Payable had a $20,000 balance at the beginning of June. The company's bank has provided photocopies of all cheques that cleared the bank during June. These photocopies show that payments to suppliers during June totalled $119,000. (All materials used during the month were direct materials.)
b. The production superintendent states that manufacturing overhead cost is applied to jobs on the basis of direct labour-hours. However, he does not remember the rate currently being used by the company.

c. Cost sheets kept in the production superintendent's office show that only one job was in process on June 30, at the time of the explosion. The job had been charged with $6,600 in materials, and 500 direct labour-hours at $8 per hour had been worked on the job.

d. A log is kept in the finished goods warehouse showing all goods transferred in from the factory. This log shows that the cost of goods transferred into the finished goods warehouse from the factory during June totalled $280,000.

e. The company's May 31 balance sheet indicates that the finished goods inventory totalled $36,000 at the beginning of June.

f. A charred piece of the payroll ledger, found after sifting through piles of smoking debris, indicates that 11,500 direct labour-hours were recorded for June. The company's Personnel Department has verified that as a result of a union contract, there are no variations in pay rates among factory employees.

g. The production superintendent states that there was no under- or overapplied overhead in the Manufacturing Overhead account at May 31.

Required Determine the following amounts:

1. Predetermined overhead rate being used by the company.
2. Raw materials purchased during June.
3. Work in process inventory, June 30.
4. Overhead applied to work in process during June.
5. Raw materials usage during June.
6. Raw materials inventory, June 30.
7. Cost of goods sold for June.

(Hint: A good way to proceed is to bring the fragmented T-accounts up to date through June 30 by posting whatever entries can be developed from the information given.)

C3–34 Critical Thinking; Interpretation of Manufacturing Overhead Rates Kelvin Aerospace, Inc., manufactures parts such as rudder hinges for the aerospace industry. The company uses a job-order costing system with a plantwide predetermined overhead rate based on direct labour-hours. On December 16, 1999, the company's controller made a preliminary estimate of the predetermined overhead rate for the year 2000. The new rate was based on the estimated total manufacturing overhead cost of $3,402,000 and the estimated 63,000 total direct labour-hours for 2000:

$$\text{Predetermined overhead rate} = \frac{\$3,402,000}{63,000 \text{ hours}}$$

$$= \$54 \text{ per direct labour-hour}$$

This new predetermined overhead rate was communicated to top managers in a meeting on December 19. The rate did not cause any comment because it was within a few pennies of the overhead rate that had been used during 1999. One of the subjects discussed at the meeting was a proposal by the production manager to purchase an automated milling machine built by Sunghi Industries. The president of Kelvin Aerospace, Harry Arcany, agreed to meet with the sales representative from Sunghi Industries to discuss the proposal.

On the day following the meeting, Mr. Arcany met with Jasmine Chang, Sunghi Industries' sales representative. The following discussion took place:

Arcany: Wally, our production manager, asked me to meet with you since he is interested in installing an automated milling machine. Frankly, I'm skeptical. You're going to have to show me this isn't just another expensive toy for Wally's people to play with.

Chang: This is a great machine with direct bottom-line benefits. The automated milling machine has three major advantages. First, it is much faster than the manual methods you are using. It can process about twice as many parts per hour as your present milling machines. Second, it is much more flexible. There are some up-front programming costs, but once those have been incurred, almost no setup is required to run a standard operation. You just punch in the code for the standard operation, load the machine's hopper with raw material, and the machine does the rest.

Arcany: What about cost? Having twice the capacity in the milling machine area won't do us much good. That centre is idle much of the time anyway.

Chang: I was getting there. The third advantage of the automated milling machine is lower cost. Wally and I looked over your present operations, and we estimated that the automated equipment would eliminate the need for about 6,000 direct labour-hours a year. What is your direct labour cost per hour?

Arcany: The wage rate in the milling area averages about $32 per hour. Fringe benefits raise that figure to about $41 per hour.

Chang: Don't forget your overhead.

Arcany: Next year the overhead rate will be $54 per hour.

Chang: So including fringe benefits and overhead, the cost per direct labour-hour is about $95.

Arcany: That's right.

Chang: Since you can save 6,000 direct labour-hours per year, the cost savings would amount to about $570,000 a year. And our 60-month lease plan would require payments of only $348,000 per year.

Arcany: That sounds like a no-brainer. When could you install the equipment?

Shortly after this meeting, Mr. Arcany informed the company's controller of the decision to lease the new equipment, which would be installed over the Christmas vacation period. The controller realized that this decision would require a recomputation of the predetermined overhead rate for the year 2000 since the decision would affect both the manufacturing overhead and the direct labour-hours for the year. After talking with both the production manager and the sales representative from Sunghi Industries, the controller discovered that in addition to the annual lease cost of $348,000, the new machine would also require a skilled technician/programmer who would have to be hired at a cost of $50,000 per year to maintain and program the equipment. Both of these costs would be included in factory overhead. There would be no other changes in total manufacturing overhead cost, which is almost entirely fixed. The controller assumed that the new machine would result in a reduction of 6,000 direct labour-hours for the year from the levels that had initially been planned.

When the revised predetermined overhead rate for the year 2000 was circulated among the company's top managers, there was considerable dismay.

Required

1. Recompute the predetermined rate assuming that the new machine will be installed. Explain why the new predetermined overhead rate is higher (or lower) than the rate that was originally estimated for the year 2000.
2. What effect (if any) would this new rate have on the cost of jobs that do not use the new automated milling machine?
3. Why would managers be concerned about the new overhead rate?
4. After seeing the new predetermined overhead rate, the production manager admitted that he probably would not be able to eliminate all of the 6,000 direct labour-hours. He had been hoping to accomplish the reduction by not replacing workers who retire or quit, but that had not been possible. As a result, the real labour savings would be only about 2,000 hours—one worker. In the light of this additional information, evaluate the original decision to acquire the automated milling machine from Sunghi Industries.

C3–35 Ethics; Predetermined Overhead Rate and Capacity (Appendix 3A) Pat Miranda, the new controller of Vault Hard Drives, Inc., has just returned from a seminar on the choice of the activity level in the predetermined overhead rate. Even though the subject did not sound exciting at first, she found that there were some important ideas presented that should get a hearing at her company. After returning from the seminar, she arranged a meeting with the production manager J. Stevens and the assistant production manager Marvin Washington.

Pat: I ran across an idea that I wanted to check out with both of you. It's about the way we compute predetermined overhead rates.

J.: We're all ears.

Pat: We compute the predetermined overhead rate by dividing the estimated total factory overhead for the coming year by the estimated total units produced for the coming year.

Marvin: We've been doing that as long as I've been with the company.

J.: And it has been done that way at every other company I've worked at, except at most places they divide by direct labour-hours.

Pat: We use units because it is simpler and we basically make one product with minor variations. But, there's another way to do it. Instead of dividing the estimated total factory overhead by the estimated total units produced for the coming year, we could divide by the total units produced at capacity.

Marvin: Oh, the Sales Department will love that. It will drop the costs on all the products. They'll go wild over there cutting prices.

Pat: That *is* a worry, but I wanted to talk to both of you first before going over to Sales.

J.: Aren't you always going to have a lot of underapplied overhead?

Pat: That's correct, but let me show you how we would handle it. Here's an example based on our budget for next year.

Budgeted (estimated) production	160,000	units
Budgeted sales	160,000	units
Capacity	200,000	units
Selling price	$60	per unit
Variable manufacturing cost	$15	per unit
Total manufacturing overhead cost (all fixed)	$4,000,000	
Administrative and selling expenses (all fixed)	$2,700,000	
Beginning inventories	–0–	

Traditional Approach to Computation of the Predetermined Overhead Rate

$$\frac{\text{Estimated total manufacturing overhead cost, \$4,000,000}}{\text{Estimated total units produced, 160,000}} = \$25 \text{ per unit}$$

Budgeted Income Statement

Revenue (160,000 units × $60)		$9,600,000
Cost of goods sold:		
Variable manufacturing (160,000 units × $15)	$2,400,000	
Manufacturing overhead applied (160,000 units × $25)	4,000,000	6,400,000
Gross margin		3,200,000
Administrative and selling expenses		2,700,000
Net income		$ 500,000

New Approach to Computation of the Predetermined Overhead Rate
Using Capacity in the Denominator

$$\frac{\text{Estimated total manufacturing overhead cost, \$4,000,000}}{\text{Total units at capacity, 200,000}} = \$20 \text{ per unit}$$

Budgeted Income Statement

Revenue (160,000 units × $60)		$9,600,000
Cost of goods sold:		
Variable manufacturing (160,000 units × $15)	$2,400,000	
Manufacturing overhead applied (160,000 units × $20)	3,200,000	5,600,000
Gross margin		4,000,000
Cost of unused capacity [(200,000 units − 160,000 units) × $20]		800,000
Administrative and selling expenses		2,700,000
Net income		$ 500,000

J.: Whoa!! I don't think I like the looks of that "Cost of unused capacity." If that thing shows up on the income statement, someone from headquarters is likely to come down here looking for some people to lay off.

Marvin: I'm worried about something else too. What happens when sales are not up to expectations? Can we pull the "hat trick"?

Pat: I'm sorry, I don't understand.

J.: Marvin's talking about something that happens fairly regularly. When sales are down and profits look like they are going to be lower than the president told the owners they were going to be, the president comes down here and asks us to deliver some more profits.

Marvin: And we pull them out of our hat.

J.: Yeah, we just increase production until we get the profits we want.

Pat: I still don't understand. You mean you increase sales?

J.: Nope, we increase production. We're the production managers, not the sales managers.

Pat: I get it. Since you have produced more, the sales force have more units they can sell.

J.: Nope, the marketing people don't do a thing. We just build inventories and that does the trick.

Required   In all of the questions below, assume that the predetermined overhead rate under the traditional method is $25 per unit and under the new method it is $20 per unit. Also assume that under the traditional method any under- or overapplied overhead is taken directly to the income statement as an adjustment to Cost of Goods Sold.

1. Suppose actual production is 160,000 units. Compute the net incomes that would be realized under the traditional and new methods if actual sales are 150,000 units and everything else turns out as expected.
2. How many units would have to be produced under each of the methods in order to realize the budgeted net income of $500,000 if actual sales are 150,000 units and everything else turns out as expected?
3. What effect does the new method based on capacity have on the volatility of net income?
4. Will the "hat trick" be easier or harder to perform if the new method based on capacity is used?
5. Do you think the "hat trick" is ethical?

C3–36 Analysis of Cost Flows and Inventories under Job-Order Costing

Rainmaker Ltd. manufactures lawn equipment. A job-order costing system is used, since the products are manufactured in batches rather than on a continuous basis. The company started operations on January 2, 1999. Operating activities during the first 11 months of the year (through November 30) resulted in the following balances in selected accounts:

Raw Materials		Manufacturing Overhead	
Bal. 36,000		2,260,000*	?
		Bal. ?	

Work in Process		Cost of Goods Sold	
Bal. 1,200,000		Bal. 14,200,000	

Finished Goods	
Bal. 2,785,000	

*This figure represents actual manufacturing overhead costs incurred through November 30, 1999.

The following additional information is available on the company:

a. The work in process inventory at November 30 consisted of two jobs:

Job No.	Units	Item	Total Cost as of November 30
1105	50,000	Estate sprinklers	$ 700,000
1106	40,000	Economy sprinklers	500,000
			$1,200,000

b. The finished goods inventory at November 30 consisted of five separate items in stock:

Items	Quantity and Unit Cost	Total Cost
Estate sprinklers	5,000 units at $22 each	$ 110,000
Deluxe sprinklers	115,000 units at $17 each	1,955,000
Brass nozzles	10,000 gross at $14 per gross	140,000
Rainmaker nozzles	5,000 gross at $16 per gross	80,000
Connectors	100,000 gross at $5 per gross	500,000
		$2,785,000

c. Manufacturing overhead cost is applied to jobs on a basis of direct labour-hours. For 1999, management estimated that the company would work 400,000 direct labour-hours and incur $2,400,000 in manufacturing overhead cost.

d. A total of 367,000 direct labour-hours were worked during the first 11 months of the year (through November 30).

Items (e) through (j) below summarize the activity that took place in the company during December 1999.

e. A total of $708,000 in raw materials was purchased during the month.

f. Raw materials were drawn from inventory and charged as follows:

Job No.	Quantity and Items	Material Charged
1105	See above	$210,000
1106	See above	6,000
1201	30,000 gross rainmaker nozzles	181,000
1202	10,000 deluxe sprinklers	92,000
1203	50,000 ring sprinklers	163,000
—	Indirect materials	20,000
		$672,000

g. The payroll during December was as follows:

Job No.	Hours	Total Cost
1105	6,000	$ 62,000
1106	2,500	26,000
1201	18,000	182,000
1202	500	5,000
1203	5,000	52,000
Indirect labour	8,000	84,000
Sales and administration	—	120,000
		$531,000

h. Other costs incurred in the factory during December were:

Depreciation	$62,500
Utilities	15,000
Insurance	1,000
Property taxes	3,500
Maintenance	5,000
	$87,000

i. Jobs completed during December and the number of good units transferred to the finished goods warehouse were:

Job No.	Quantity	Items
1105	48,000 units	Estate sprinkler
1106	39,000 units	Economy sprinklers
1201	29,500 gross	Rainmaker nozzles
1203	49,000 units	Ring sprinklers

j. Finished products were shipped to customers during December as follows:

Items	Quantity
Estate sprinklers	16,000 units
Deluxe sprinklers	32,000 units
Economy sprinklers	20,000 units
Ring sprinklers	22,000 units
Brass nozzles	5,000 gross
Rainmaker nozzles	10,000 gross
Connectors	26,000 gross

Required

1. Determine the amount of under- or overapplied overhead for the year 1999.
2. What is the appropriate accounting treatment for this under- or overapplied overhead balance? Explain your answer.
3. Determine the dollar balance in the Work in Process inventory account as of December 31, 1999. Show all computations in good form.
4. For the estate sprinklers only, determine the dollar balance in the Finished Goods inventory account as of December 31, 1999. Assume a FIFO flow of units. Show all computations in good form.
5. (Appendix C) How many units of rainmaker nozzles were lost? How should they be treated for costing purposes?

(CMA, heavily adapted)

C3–37 Alternative Inventory Systems   Carl Company Limited is a small construction contractor engaged in home construction and renovations. It employs a job costing system so that it will have a record of costs for various types of jobs for historical purposes and to assess bidding accuracy.

The following information relates to the activities for February of its fiscal year. The month began with the following information:

Cash	$ 1,000	
Accounts receivable	2,500	
Inventory—raw materials	500	(various)
Inventory of work in process	1,500	(job 507)
Inventory of finished product	400	(job 505)
Prepaid insurance	500	
Property and equipment	50,000	
Accumulated depreciation	(20,000)	
Vehicle	15,000	
Accumulated depreciation	(3,500)	
Total assets	$47,900	
Accounts payable	$ 3,000	
Bank loan	22,500	
Common stock	2,500	
Retained earnings	19,900	
	$47,900	

The following entries were used to record the transactions for February:

a.	Inventory—Raw Materials	3,000	
	Accounts Payable		3,000
b.	Cost of Construction Finished	3,250*	
	Inventory—Raw Materials		3,250

	*Jobs:	601	$ 400
		602	350
		603	1,500
		604	1,000

c.	Cost of Construction Finished	3,250*	
	Cash†		3,250

	*Jobs:	507	$ 150
		601	350
		602	1,000
		603	1,250
		604	500

†Note: Deductions and payroll taxes have been omitted for simplicity.

d.	Overhead—Supervision	1,000*	
	Cash		1,000
e.	Overhead—Depreciation on Property and Equipment	1,000	
	Overhead—Depreciation on Vehicle	500	
	Accumulated Depreciation—Property Equipment		1,000
	Accumulated Depreciation—Vehicle		500
f.	Overhead—Insurance	75	
	Prepaid Insurance		75
g.	Overhead—Maintenance	250	
	Accounts Payable		250
h.	Cost of Construction Finished	2,925*	
	Overhead Applied		2,925

	*Jobs:	507	$135
		601	315
		602	900
		603	1,125
		604	450

i.	Bidding Expenses	400	
	Cash		400
j.	Administrative Salary	1,250	
	Cash		1,250
k.	Accounts Receivable	11,850	
	Construction Revenues		11,850*

*Jobs: 505 $1,000
       507   2,500
       601   1,250
       602   2,100
       603   5,000

l.	Cash	11,500	
	Accounts Receivable		11,500
m.	Accounts Payable	4,000	
	Cash		4,000
n.	Interest Expense	250	
	Cash		250
o.	Cost of Construction Finished	1,500*	
	Inventory of Work in Process		1,500

*Job: 507 $1,500

p.	Cost of Construction Finished	400*	
	Inventory of Finished Product		400

*Job: 505 $ 400

q.	Inventory of work in process	1,450*	
	Cost of construction finished		1,450

*Job: 604 $1,450

Required 1. Prepare an income statement and balance sheet for February of the fiscal year. Do not use supporting schedules.
2. Compute the cost and revenue details for jobs 507 and 602.

C3–38 Cost Savings and the Environment
Master Cleaners Ltd. is a custodial service company that has recently received the contract to maintain and clean 42 schools for the Halifax District School Board. The $10.3 million contract is for five years and involves 35 maintenance staff and 104 cleaners.

Max Million is the accountant for Master Cleaners. He is interested in costing the cleaning services for each major school so that a program of continuous cost saving can be implemented in accordance with the overall savings promised in the contract with Halifax District. By comparing costs over time and reviewing costs in terms of custodial activities in each school, the management expects to be able to accomplish the savings promised at contract signing.

The following represent the activities connected with the cleaning of two high schools:

Cleaning Hours	382.5 hours
Cleaning Supplies	$310
Equipment Used	120 hours

The following overhead is assigned to jobs:.

a. Equipment—cost $56,000, life 28,000 hours.
b. Central Administration—$330,000 based on 165,000 labour hours.
c. Warehousing of Supplies—$100,000 assigned based on $90,000 of cleaning supplies.

Required 1. Determine the cost for the first month of cleaning the two high schools assuming custodial staff are paid $13 per hour in wages and benefits.

2. For month two, cleaning hours were 380 hours, supplies $225, and equipment 130 hours. Determine the improvement, if any, in the second month of operations.
3. What environmental concerns would Master Cleaners have to consider as part of its cleaning operations?

C3–39 Costing a New Proposal Anderson Placement Services Ltd. is an employee search and screening company located in Oakville, Ontario. They search out and short-list job candidates for a wide variety of organizations in the Oakville region.

Anderson has recently obtained three screening video tapes from Allu Screen Company of Montreal. Three tapes costing $5,000 each provide a series of scenarios that can be used to test prospective employees for their suitability for certain jobs. Anderson is about to test the cost saving of these videos compared to the interview/testing procedures it had previously employed.

Anderson has a contract to screen 25 candidates for five new teller positions for a local trust company. The following represent the activities associated with the screening:

a. Interview and debriefing, 1.5 hours per candidate.
b. Salary and benefit costs of interviewer, $18.50 per hour.
c. Overhead charge for office, $35 per hour of interview.
d. Life of video, 500 interviews.
e. Screening equipment, $10,000 use life is the life of video.

A comparable project two months earlier had used interviewing and debriefing of 6 hours per candidate.

Required
1. Assess the cost savings, if any, associated with the use of videos.
2. What ethical considerations should Anderson consider when employing videos instead of the personal interviews?
3. What considerations from a business perspective should Anderson take into account before fully employing the videos?

C3–40 Costing and Incentives Ace Auto Shop is a diagnostic and mechanical repair shop located in Sydney, Ontario. Customers bring their automobiles to Ace for diagnostic and repair services. Business has been brisk because Ace has a reputation for quality, efficiency, and customer convenience.

Ace's owner, Ms. Karen Homes, is considering a new job costing system to support her pricing of customer repairs and a new incentive system for her service manager.

Ace has a pricing policy of $50 per service hour plus the cost of parts from a supplier who guarantees immediate response to requests and a large inventory of available items.

Ms. Homes pays her mechanics $16.50 per hour in wages and benefits. Her facility is leased at a cost of $50,000 per year. Her service manager diagnoses each car and assigns the customer to a mechanic in one of five bays available. Equipment for the operation amounts to a depreciation of $30,000 per year.

The service manager is currently paid $40,000 per year. The proposal under consideration is to reduce his salary to $35,000 and give him 2% of the hourly charge to customers.

The following job is used by Ms. Homes to compare alternatives:

a. Parts, $128
b. Hours, 2.5

Overhead costs are assigned to each job based on direct labour-hours. The total estimated labour-hours for the year is 7,800 hours.

Required
1. Compare the cost of the two alternatives.
2. What ethical factors should Ms. Homes consider related to the new proposed method of rewarding her service manager?

Group Exercises

GE3–41   The Plant Layout Case   Read the case by Wayne Morse, "Instructional Case: Rantoul Tool, Inc.," *Issues in Accounting Education,* Spring 1990, pp. 78–83. This case illustrates the impact that different manufacturing environments have on product costing procedures. The case includes a description of three manufacturing processes and diagrams of the plant layout for each process. Answer the questions in the case.

GE3–42   Talk with a Controller   Look in the yellow pages or contact your local chamber of commerce to find the names of manufacturing companies in your area. Make an appointment to meet with the controller or chief financial officer of one of these companies.

Required   Ask the following questions and write a brief report concerning what you found out.

1. Does the company use job-order costing, process costing, or some other method of determining product costs?
2. How is overhead assigned to products? What is the overhead rate? What is the basis of allocation? Is more than one overhead rate used?
3. Are product costs used in making any decisions? If so, what are those decisions and how are product costs used?
4. How are profits affected by changes in production volume? By changes in sales?
5. Has the company recently changed its cost system or is it considering changing its cost system? If so, why? What changes were made or what changes are being considered?

IE3–43   Job-Order versus Process Costing   The chapter mentions that Bechtel International and Bombardier are likely to use job-order costing in most of their lines of business. To help understand the nature of their businesses, access these companies' web sites at www.bechtel.com and www.bombardier.com.

Required
1. Based on the information you found on the companies' web sites, explain why they would be more likely to use job-order costing than process costing in most of their lines of business.
2. Access the web site of KPMG at www.kpmg.com. Is this company more likely to use job-order costing or process costing for its services? Why?
3. Access the web site of Paramount Pictures at www.paramount.com. Is Paramount Pictures more likely to use job-order costing or process costing for keeping track of the costs of its movies? Why?

Chapter Four

Systems Design: Process Costing

Business Focus

Using an old family recipe, Megan started a company that produced cream soda. At first the company struggled, but as sales increased, the company expanded rapidly. Megan soon realized that to expand any further, it would be necessary to borrow money. The investment in additional equipment was too large for her to finance out of the company's current cash flows.

Megan was disappointed to find that few banks were willing to make a loan to such a small company, but she finally found a bank that would con-

sider her loan application. However, Megan was informed that she would have to supply up-to-date financial statements with her loan application.

Megan had never bothered with financial statements before—she felt that as long as the balance in the company's chequebook kept increasing, the company was doing fine. She was puzzled how she was going to determine the value of the cream soda in the work in process and finished goods inventories. The valuation of the cream soda would affect both the cost of goods sold

and the inventory balances of her company. Megan thought of perhaps using job-order costing, but her company produces only one product. Raw ingredients were continually being mixed to make more cream soda, and more bottled cream soda was always coming off the end of the bottling line. Megan didn't see how she could use a job-order costing system since the job never really ended. Perhaps there was another way to account for the costs of producing the cream soda.

Learning Objectives:

After studying Chapter 4, you should be able to:

1 Prepare journal entries to record the flow of materials, labour, and overhead through a process costing system.

2 Compute the equivalent units of production for a period by the weighted-average method.

3 Prepare a quantity schedule for a period by the weighted-average method.

4 Compute the costs per equivalent unit for a period by the weighted-average method.

5 Prepare a cost reconciliation for a period by the weighted-average method.

6 (Appendix 4A) Compute the equivalent units of production for a period by the FIFO method.

7 (Appendix 4A) Prepare a quantity schedule for a period by the FIFO method.

8 (Appendix 4A) Compute the costs per equivalent unit for a period by the FIFO method.

9 (Appendix 4A) Prepare a cost reconciliation for a period by the FIFO method.

10 (Appendix 4B) Compute the cost of lost units or shrinkage.

As explained in the preceding chapter, there are two basic costing systems in use: job-order costing and process costing. A job-order costing system is used in situations where many different jobs or products are worked on each period. Examples of industries that would typically use job-order costing include furniture manufacture, special-order printing, shipbuilding, and many types of service organizations.

By contrast, **process costing** is most commonly used in industries that produce essentially homogenous (i.e., uniform) products on a continuous basis, such as bricks, corn flakes, or paper. Process costing is particularly used in companies that convert basic raw materials into homogenous products, such as Alcan (aluminum ingots), Scott Paper (toilet paper), Dover Mills (flour), Imperial Oil (gasoline and lubricating oils), and Christie's (crackers). In addition, process costing is often employed in companies that use a form of process costing in their assembly operations, such as Panasonic (video monitors), Compaq (personal computers), General Electric (refrigerators), Toyota (automobiles), Maytag (washing machines), and Sony (CD players). A form of process costing may also be used in utilities that produce gas, water, and electricity. As suggested by the length of this list, process costing is in very wide use.

Our purpose in this chapter is to extend the discussion of product costing to include a process costing system.

Process costing A costing method used in situations where essentially homogeneous products are produced on a continuous basis.

Comparison of Job-Order and Process Costing

In some ways process costing is very similar to job-order costing, and in some ways it is very different. In this section, we focus on these similarities and differences in order to provide a foundation for the detailed discussion of process costing that follows.

Similarities between Job-Order and Process Costing

Much of what was learned in the preceding chapter about costing and about cost flows applies equally well to process costing in this chapter. That is, we are not throwing out all that we have learned about costing and starting from "scratch" with a whole new system. The similarities that exist between job-order and process costing can be summarized as follows:

1. The same basic purposes exist in both systems, which are to assign material, labour, and overhead cost to products and to provide a mechanism for computing unit costs.

Exhibit 4–1
Differences between
Job-Order and
Process Costing

Job-Order Costing	Process Costing
1. Many different jobs are worked on during each period, with each job having different production requirements.	1. A single product is produced either on a continuous basis or for long periods of time. All units of product are identical.
2. Costs are accumulated by individual job.	2. Costs are accumulated by department.
3. The *job cost sheet* is the key document controlling the accumulation of costs by a job.	3. The *department production report* is the key document showing the accumulation and disposition of costs by a department.
4. Unit costs are computed *by job* on the job cost sheet.	4. Unit costs are computed *by department* on the department production report.

2. Both systems maintain and use the same basic manufacturing accounts, including Manufacturing Overhead, Raw Materials, Work in Process, and Finished Goods.
3. The flow of costs through the manufacturing accounts is basically the same in both systems.

As can be seen from this comparison, much of the knowledge that we have already acquired about costing is applicable to a process costing system. Our task now is simply to refine and extend this knowledge to process costing.

Differences between Job-Order and Process Costing

The differences between job-order and process costing arise from two factors. The first is that the flow of units in a process costing system is more or less continuous, and the second is that these units are indistinguishable from one another. Under process costing, it makes no sense to try to identify materials, labour, and overhead costs with a particular order from a customer (as we did with job-order costing), since each order is just one of many that are filled from a continuous flow of virtually identical units from the production line. Under process costing, we accumulate costs *by department,* rather than by order, and assign these costs equally to all units that pass through the department during a period.

A further difference between the two costing systems is that the job cost sheet has no use in process costing, since the focal point of that method is on departments. Instead of using job cost sheets, a document known as a **production report** is prepared for each department in which work is done on products. The production report serves several functions. It provides a summary of the number of units moving through a department during a period, and it also provides a computation of unit costs. In addition, it shows what costs were charged to the department and what disposition was made of these costs. The department production report is the key document in a process costing system.

The major differences between job-order and process costing are summarized in Exhibit 4–1.

Production report A report that summarizes all activity in a department's Work in Process account during a period and that contains three parts: a quantity schedule and a computation of equivalent units, a computation of total and unit costs, and a cost reconciliation.

A Perspective of Process Cost Flows

Processing department Any location in an organization where work is performed on a product and where materials, labour, or overhead costs are added to the product.

Before presenting a detailed example of process costing, it will be helpful to see how manufacturing costs flow through a process costing system.

Processing Departments

A **processing department** is any location in an organization where work is performed on a product and where materials, labour, or overhead costs are added to the product.

Exhibit 4–2   Sequential Processing Departments

For example, a potato chip factory operated by Hostess's might have three processing departments—one for preparing potatoes, one for cooking, and one for inspecting and packaging. A brick factory might have two processing departments—one for mixing and molding clay into brick form and one for firing the molded brick. A company can have as many or as few processing departments as are needed to complete a product or service. Some products and services may go through several processing departments, while others may go through only one or two. Regardless of the number of departments involved, all processing departments have two essential features. First, the activity performed in the processing department must be performed uniformly on all of the units passing through it. Second, the output of the processing department must be homogeneous.

The processing departments involved in making a product such as bricks would probably be organized in a *sequential* pattern. By sequential processing, we mean that units flow in sequence from one department to another. An example of processing departments arranged in a sequential pattern is given in Exhibit 4–2, which illustrates a potato chip processing plant.

A different type of processing pattern, known as *parallel processing,* is required to make some products. Parallel processing is used in those situations where after a certain point, some units may go through different processing departments than others. For example, Petro Canada and Shell Canada Limited in their petroleum refining operations input crude oil into one processing department and then use the refined output for further processing into several end products. Each end product may undergo several steps of further processing after the initial refining, some of which may be shared with other end products and some of which may not.

An example of parallel processing is provided in Exhibit 4–3, which shows the process flows in a Coca-Cola™ bottling plant. In the first processing department, raw materials are mixed to make the basic concentrate. This concentrate can be used to make bottled Coke or it may be sold to restaurants and bars for use in soda fountains. Under the first option, the concentrate is sent on to the bottling department where it is mixed with carbonated water and then injected into sterile bottles and capped. In the final processing department, the bottles are inspected, labels are applied, and the bottles are packed in cartons. If the concentrate is to be sold for use in soda fountains, it is injected into large sterile metal cylinders, inspected, and packaged for shipping. This is just an example of one way in which parallel processing can be set up. The number of possible variations in parallel processing is virtually limitless.

Exhibit 4–3 Parallel Processing Departments

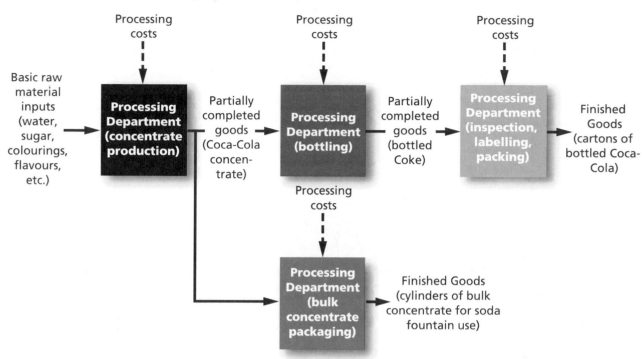

The Flow of Materials, Labour, and Overhead Costs

Cost accumulation is simpler in a process costing system than in a job-order costing system. In a process costing system, instead of having to trace costs to hundreds of different jobs, costs are traced to only a few processing departments. This means that costs can be accumulated for longer periods of time and that just one allocation is needed at the end of a period (week, month, and so forth) to assign the accumulated costs to the period's output.

A T-account model of materials, labour, and overhead cost flows in a process costing system is given in Exhibit 4–4. Several key points should be noted from this exhibit. First, note that a separate Work in Process account is maintained for *each processing department*. In contrast, in a job-order costing system there may be only a single Work in Process account for the entire company. Second, note that the completed production of the first processing department (Department A in the exhibit) is transferred into the Work in Process account of the second processing department (Department B), where it undergoes further work. After this further work, the completed units are then transferred into Finished Goods. (In Exhibit 4–4, we show only two processing departments, but there can be many such departments in a company.)

Finally, note that materials, labour, and overhead costs can be added in *any* processing department—not just the first. Costs in Department B's Work in Process account would therefore consist of the materials, labour, and overhead costs entered directly into the account plus the costs attached to partially completed units transferred in from Department A (called **transferred-in costs**).

Transferred-in cost
The cost attached to products that have been received from a prior processing department.

Materials, Labour, and Overhead Cost Entries

To complete our discussion of cost flows in a process costing system, in the following paragraphs we show journal entries relating to materials, labour, and overhead costs and also make brief, further comments relating to each of these cost categories.

Exhibit 4–4   T-Account Model of Process Costing Flows

<table>
<tr><td>**Objective 1**

Prepare journal entries to record the flow of materials, labour, and overhead through a process costing system.</td><td></td></tr>
</table>

MATERIALS COSTS   As in job-order costing, materials are drawn from the store-room using a materials requisition form. As stated earlier, materials can be added in any processing department, although it is not unusual for materials to be added only in the first processing department, with subsequent departments adding only labour and overhead costs as the partially completed units move along toward completion.

Assuming that the first processing department in a company is Department A, the journal entry for placing materials into process is as follows:

```
Work in Process—Department A . . . . . . . . . . . . . . . . . . . . . . . .   XXX
    Raw Materials . . . . . . . . . . . . . . . . . . . . . . . . . . . . . . . . . .        XXX
```

If other materials are subsequently added in Department B, the entry is the following:

```
Work in Process—Department B . . . . . . . . . . . . . . . . . . . . . . . .   XXX
    Raw Materials . . . . . . . . . . . . . . . . . . . . . . . . . . . . . . . . . .        XXX
```

LABOUR COSTS   Since it is not necessary to identify costs with specific jobs, a time clock is generally adequate for accumulating labour costs and for allocating them to the proper department in a process costing system. Assuming again that a company has two processing departments, Department A and Department B, the following journal entry will record the labour costs for a period:

```
Work in Process—Department A . . . . . . . . . . . . . . . . . . . . . . . .   XXX
Work in Process—Department B . . . . . . . . . . . . . . . . . . . . . . . .   XXX
    Salaries and Wages Payable . . . . . . . . . . . . . . . . . . . . . . . . .        XXX
```

OVERHEAD COSTS   If production is stable from period to period and if overhead costs are incurred uniformly over the year, actual overhead costs can be charged to products. However, if production levels fluctuate or if overhead costs are not incurred uniformly, charging products with actual overhead costs will result in unit product costs that vary randomly from one period to the next. In such a situation, predetermined overhead rates should be used to charge overhead cost to products, the same as in job-order costing. When predetermined overhead rates are used, each department has its own separate rate with the rates being computed in the same way as was discussed in Chapter 3. Overhead cost is then applied to units of product as the units move through the various departments. Since predetermined overhead rates are widely used in process costing, we will assume their use throughout the remainder of this chapter.

If a company has two processing departments, Department A and Department B, the following journal entry is used to apply overhead cost to products:

Work in Process—Department A	XXX	
Work in Process—Department B	XXX	
Manufacturing Overhead		XXX

COMPLETING THE COST FLOWS Once processing has been completed in a department, the units are transferred to the next department for further processing, as illustrated earlier in the T-accounts in Exhibit 4–4. The following journal entry is used to transfer the costs of partially completed units from Department A to Department B:

Work in Process—Department B	XXX	
Work in Process—Department A		XXX

After processing has been completed in Department B, the costs of the completed units are then transferred to the Finished Goods inventory account:

Finished Goods	XXX	
Work in Process—Department B		XXX

Finally, when a customer's order is filled and units are sold, the cost of the units is transferred to Cost of Goods Sold:

Cost of Goods Sold	XXX	
Finished Goods		XXX

To summarize, we stated earlier that the cost flows between accounts are basically the same in a process costing system as they are in a job-order costing system. The only noticeable difference at this point is that in a process costing system there is a separate Work in Process account for each department.

Managerial Accounting in Action
THE ISSUE

Samantha Trivers, president of Double Diamond Skis, was worried about the future of the company. After a rocky start, the company had come out with a completely redesigned ski called The Ultimate. It was made of exotic materials and featured flashy graphics. Exhibit 4–5 illustrates how this ski is manufactured. The ski was a runaway best seller—particularly among younger skiers—and had provided the company with much-needed cash for two years. However, last year a dismal snowfall in the Rocky Mountains had depressed sales, and Double Diamond was once again short of cash. Samantha was worried that another bad ski season would force Double Diamond into bankruptcy.

Just before starting production of next year's model of The Ultimate, Samantha called Jerry Madison, the company controller, into her office to discuss the reports she would need in the coming year.

Samantha: Jerry, I am going to need more frequent cost information this year. I really have to stay on top of things.
Jerry: What do you have in mind?

Samantha: I'd like reports at least once a month that detail our production costs for each department and for each pair of skis.

Jerry: That shouldn't be much of a problem. We already compile almost all of the necessary data for the annual report. The only complication is our work in process inventories. They haven't been a problem in our annual reports, since our fiscal year ends at a time when we have finished producing skis for the last model year and haven't yet started producing for the new model year. Consequently, there aren't any work in process inventories to value for the annual report. But that won't be true for monthly reports.

Samantha: I'm not sure why that is a problem, Jerry. But I'm sure you can figure out how to solve it.

Jerry: You can count on me.

Exhibit 4–5 The Production Process at Double Diamond Skis*

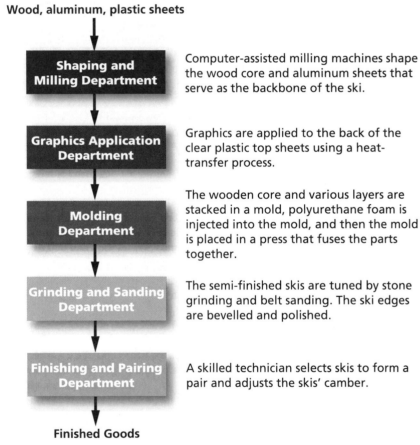

*Adapted from Bill Gout, Jesse James Doquilo, and Studio M D, "Capped Crusaders," *Skiing,* October 1993, pp. 138–44.

Equivalent Units of Production

Jerry, the controller of Double Diamond Skis, was concerned with the following problem: After materials, labour, and overhead costs have been accumulated in a department, the department's output must be determined so that unit costs can be computed. The difficulty is that a department usually has some partially completed units in its ending inventory. It does not seem reasonable to count these partially completed units as equivalent to fully completed units when counting the department's output. Therefore, Jerry will mathematically convert those partially completed units into an *equivalent* number of fully completed units. In process costing, this is done using the following formula:

Equivalent units = Number of partially completed units × Percentage completion

Equivalent units The product of the number of partially completed units and their percentage of completion with respect to a particular cost. Equivalent units are the number of complete whole units one could obtain from the materials and effort contained in partially completed units.

As the formula states, **equivalent units** is defined to be the product of the number of partially completed units and the percentage completion of those units. The equivalent units is the number of complete units that could have been obtained from the materials and effort that went into the partially complete units.

For example, suppose the Molding Department at Double Diamond has 500 units in its ending work in process inventory that are 60% complete. These 500 partially complete units are equivalent to 300 fully complete units (500 × 60% = 300). Therefore, the ending work in process inventory would be said to contain 300 equivalent units. These equivalent units would be added to any fully completed units to determine the period's output for the department—called the *equivalent units of production*.

FIFO method A method of accounting for cost flows in a process costing system in which equivalent units and unit costs relate only to work done during the current period.

There are two different ways of computing the equivalent units of production for a period. In this chapter, we discuss the *weighted-average method*. In Appendix 4A, the *FIFO method* is discussed. The **FIFO method** of process costing is a method in which equivalent units and unit costs relate only to work done during the current period. In contrast, the **weighted-average method** blends together units and costs from the current period with units and costs from the prior period. In the weighted-average method, the **equivalent units of production** for a department are the number of units transferred to the next department (or to finished goods) plus the equivalent units in the department's ending work in process inventory.

Weighted-average method A method of process costing that blends together units and costs from both the current and prior periods.

Weighted-Average Method

Under the weighted-average method, a department's equivalent units are computed as described above:

Equivalent units of production (weighted-average method) The units transferred to the next department (or to finished goods) during the period plus the equivalent units in the department's ending work in process inventory.

Weighted-Average Method
(a separate calculation is made for each cost category in each processing department)

Equivalent units of production = Units transferred to the next department or to finished goods
+ Equivalent units in ending work in process inventory

Objective 2

Compute the equivalent units of production for a period by the weighted-average method.

We do not have to make an equivalent units calculation for units transferred to the next department, since we can assume that they would not have been transferred unless they were 100% complete with respect to the work performed in the transferring department.

Consider the Shaping and Milling Department at Double Diamond. This department uses computerized milling machines to precisely shape the wooden core and metal sheets that will be used to form the backbone of the ski. The following activity took place in the department in May, several months into the production of the new model of The Ultimate ski:

	Units	Percent Completed	
		Materials	**Conversion**
Work in process, May 1	200	50%	30%
Units started into production during May	5,000		
Units completed during May and			
transferred to the next department	4,800	100%*	100%*
Work in process, May 31	400	40%	25%

*It is always assumed that units transferred out of a department are 100% complete with respect to the processing done in that department.

Conversion cost Direct labour cost plus manufacturing overhead cost.

Note the use of the term *conversion* in the table on the previous page. **Conversion cost,** as defined in Chapter 2, is direct labour cost plus manufacturing overhead cost. In process costing, conversion cost is often—but not always—treated as a single element of product cost.

Also note that the May 1 beginning work in process was 50% complete with respect to materials costs and 30% complete with respect to conversion costs. This means that 50% of the materials costs required to complete the units had already been incurred. Likewise, 30% of the conversion costs required to complete the units had already been incurred.

Since Double Diamond's work in process inventories are at different stages of completion in terms of the amounts of materials cost and conversion cost that have been added, two equivalent unit figures must be computed. The equivalent units computations are given in Exhibit 4–6.

Note from the computation in Exhibit 4–6 that units in the beginning work in process inventory are ignored. The weighted-average method is concerned only with the fact that there are 4,900 equivalent units for conversion cost in ending inventories and in units transferred to the next department—the method is not concerned with the additional fact that some of this work was accomplished in prior periods. This is a key point in the weighted-average method that is easy to overlook.

The weighted-average method blends together the work that was accomplished in prior periods with the work that was accomplished in the current period. In the FIFO method, the units and costs of prior periods are cleanly separated from the units and costs of the current period. Some managers believe the FIFO method is more accurate for this reason. However, the FIFO method is more complex than the weighted-average method and for that reason is covered in Appendix 4A.

Averages, in general, hide the details of the elements that make up the average. For example, the average of 2 + 4 is 3. The average of 1 + 5 is 3. If the manager is uninterested in the details of the elements, then the average provides all the information needed. If costs from one period to the next are approximately equal (for example, 3 + 3) the average is also a reasonable representation of the results. A third explanation for the use of the average approach is the relative size of the beginning inventory of work in process compared to the current production. For example, if the beginning inventory is only

Exhibit 4–6
Equivalent Units of Production: Weighted-Average Method

	Materials	**Conversion**
Units transferred to the next department.	4,800	4,800
Work in process, May 31:		
400 units × 40%	160	
400 units × 25%		100
Equivalent units of production.	4,960	4,900

Exhibit 4–7 Visual Perspective of Equivalent Units of Production

DOUBLE DIAMOND SKIS
Shaping and Milling Department
Conversion Costs
(weighted-average method)

Units completed and transferred to next department	4,800	
Work in process, ending:		
400 units × 25%	100	
Equivalent units of production	4,900	

one-tenth the current production, the average (weighted) of ⅒ (1) + ⁹⁄₁₀ (5) = 4.60 is very accurate and very close to a FIFO result. In addition to the advantage of ease of computation another advantage of the weighted-average method is that it generates very accurate results when costs are relatively stable from one period to the next or when the size of current production dwarfs the beginning inventory.

A visual perspective of the computation of equivalent units of production is provided in Exhibit 4–7. The data are for conversion costs in the Shaping and Milling Department of Double Diamond Skis. Study this exhibit carefully before going on.

Production Report—Weighted-Average Method

The production report developed in this section contains the information requested by the president of Double Diamond Skis. The purpose of the production report is to summarize for management all of the activity that takes place in a department's Work in Process account for a period. This activity includes the units and costs that flow through the Work in Process account. As illustrated in Exhibit 4–8, a separate production report is prepared for each department.

Earlier, when we outlined the differences between job-order costing and process costing, we stated that the production report takes the place of a job cost sheet in a process costing system. The production report is a key management document and is vital to the proper operation of the system. The production report has three separate (though highly interrelated) parts:

1. A quantity schedule, which shows the flow of units through the department and a computation of equivalent units.
2. A computation of costs per equivalent unit.
3. A reconciliation of all cost flows into and out of the department during the period.

We will use the data on the next page for the May operations of the Shaping and Milling Department of Double Diamond Skis to illustrate the production report. Keep in mind that this report is only one of the five reports that would be prepared for the company since the company has five processing departments.

Exhibit 4–8   The Position of the Production Report in the Flow of Costs

Shaping and Milling Department
Work in process, beginning:

Units in process		200
Stage of completion with respect to materials	50%	
Stage of completion with respect to conversion	30%	
Costs in the beginning inventory:		
Materials cost	$ 3,000	
Conversion cost	1,000	
Total cost in process	$ 4,000	
Units started into production during May		5,000
Units completed and transferred out		4,800
Costs added to production during May:		
Materials cost	$ 74,000	
Conversion cost	70,000	
Total cost added in the department	$144,000	
Work in process, ending:		
Units in process		400
Stage of completion with respect to materials	40%	
Stage of completion with respect to conversion	25%	

In this section, we show how a production report is prepared when the weighted-average method is used to compute equivalent units and unit costs. The preparation of a production report under the FIFO method is illustrated in Appendix 4A at the end of this chapter.

Step 1: Prepare a Quantity Schedule and Compute the Equivalent Units

The first part of a production report consists of a **quantity schedule,** which shows the flow of units through a department and a computation of equivalent units. To illustrate, a quantity schedule combined with a computation of equivalent units is given below for the Shaping and Milling Department of Double Diamond Skis.

Quantity schedule The part of a production report that shows the flow of units through a department during a period and a computation of equivalent units.

	Quantity Schedule	Materials	Conversion
Units to be accounted for:			
Work in process, May 1 (50% materials; 30% conversion added last month)	200		
Started into production	5,000		
Total units	5,200		
		Equivalent Units	
Units accounted for as follows:			
Transferred to the next department	4,800	4,800	4,800
Work in process, May 31 (40% materials; 25% conversion added this month)	400	160*	100†
Total units and equivalent units of production	5,200	4,960	4,900

*40% × 400 units = 160 equivalent units.
†25% × 400 units = 100 equivalent units.

The quantity schedule permits the manager to see at a glance how many units moved through the department during the period as well as to see the stage of completion of any in-process units. In addition to providing this information, the quantity schedule serves as an essential guide in preparing and tying together the remaining parts of a production report.

Step 2: Compute Costs per Equivalent Unit

As stated earlier, the weighted-average method blends together the work that was accomplished in the prior period with the work that was accomplished in the current period. That is why it is called the weighted-average method; it averages together units and costs from both the prior and current periods by adding the cost in the beginning work in process inventory to the current period costs. These computations are shown below for the Shaping and Milling Department for May:

Shaping and Milling Department

	Total Cost	Materials	Conversion	Whole Unit
Cost to be accounted for:				
Work in process, May 1	$ 4,000	$ 3,000	$ 1,000	
Cost added in the Shaping and Milling Department	144,000	74,000	70,000	
Total cost (a)	$148,000	$77,000	$71,000	

(cont)

Shaping and Milling Department

	Total Cost	Materials		Conversion		Whole Unit
Equivalent units of production (Step 1 above) (b)		4,960		4,900		
Cost per EU, (a) ÷ (b)		$15.524	+	$14.490	=	$30.014

The cost per equivalent unit (EU) that we have computed for the Shaping and Milling Department will be used to apply cost to units that are transferred to the next department, graphics application, and will also be used to compute the cost in the ending work in process inventory. For example, each unit transferred out of the Shaping and Milling Department to the Graphics Application Department will carry with it a cost of $30.014. Since the costs are passed on from department to department, the unit cost of the last department, Finishing and Pairing, will represent the final unit cost of a completed unit of product.

Step 3: Prepare a Cost Reconciliation

Objective 5

Prepare a cost reconciliation for a period by the weighted-average method.

Cost reconciliation The part of a production report that shows what costs a department has to account for during a period and how those costs are accounted for.

The purpose of a **cost reconciliation** is to show how the costs that have been charged to a department during a period are accounted for. Typically, the costs charged to a department will consist of the following:

1. Cost in the beginning work in process inventory.
2. Materials, labour, and overhead costs added during the period.
3. Cost (if any) transferred in from the preceding department.

In a production report, these costs are generally titled "Cost to be accounted for." They are accounted for in a production report by computing the following amounts:

1. Cost transferred out to the next department (or to Finished Goods).
2. Cost remaining in the ending work in process inventory.

In short, when a cost reconciliation is prepared, the "Cost to be accounted for" from step 2 is reconciled with the sum of the cost transferred out during the period plus the cost in the ending work in process inventory. This concept is shown graphically in Exhibit 4–9. Study this exhibit carefully before going on to the cost reconciliation below for the Shaping and Milling Department.

Exhibit 4–9   Graphic Illustration of the Cost Reconciliation Part of a Production Report

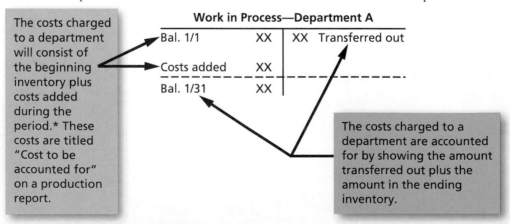

The costs charged to a department will consist of the beginning inventory plus costs added during the period.* These costs are titled "Cost to be accounted for" on a production report.

The costs charged to a department are accounted for by showing the amount transferred out plus the amount in the ending inventory.

*Departments that follow Department A (Department B and so forth) will need to show the amount of cost transferred in from the preceding department.

EXAMPLE OF A COST RECONCILIATION   To prepare a cost reconciliation, *follow the quantity schedule line for line and show the cost associated with each group of units.* This is done in Exhibit 4–10, where we present a completed production report for the Shaping and Milling Department.

The quantity schedule in the exhibit shows that 200 units were in process on May 1 and that an additional 5,000 units were started into production during the month. Looking at the "Cost to be accounted for" in the middle part of the exhibit, notice that the units in process on May 1 had $4,000 in cost attached to them and that the Shaping and Milling Department added another $144,000 in cost to production during the month. Thus, the department has $148,000 ($4,000 + $144,000) in cost to be accounted for.

This cost is accounted for in two ways. As shown on the quantity schedule, 4,800 units were transferred to the Graphics Application Department, the next department in the production process. Another 400 units were still in process in the Shaping and Milling Department at the end of the month. Thus, part of the $148,000 "Cost to be accounted for" goes with the 4,800 units to the Graphics Application Department, and part of it remains with the 400 units in the ending work in process inventory in the Shaping and Milling Department.

Each of the 4,800 units transferred to the Graphics Application Department is assigned $30,014 in cost, for a total $144,067. The 400 units still in process at the end of the month are assigned costs according to their stage of completion. To determine the stage of completion, we refer to the equivalent units computation and bring the equivalent units figures down to the cost reconciliation part of the report. We then assign costs to these units, using the cost per equivalent unit figures already computed.

After cost has been assigned to the ending work in process inventory, the total cost that we have accounted for ($148,000) agrees with the amount that we had to account for ($148,000). Thus, the cost reconciliation is complete.

Managerial Accounting in Action

THE WRAP-UP

Jerry: Here's an example of the kind of report I can put together for you every month. This particular report is for the Shaping and Milling Department. It follows a fairly standard format for industries like ours and is called a production report. I hope this is what you have in mind.

Samantha: The quantity schedule makes sense to me. I can see we had a total of 5,200 units to account for in the department, and 4,800 of those were transferred to the next department while 400 were still in process at the end of the month. What are these "equivalent units"?

Jerry: That's the problem I mentioned earlier. While there are 400 units still in process, they are far from complete. When we compute the unit costs, it wouldn't make sense to count them as whole units.

Samantha: I suppose not. I see what you are driving at. Since those 400 units are only 25% complete with respect to our conversion costs, they should only be counted as 100 units when we compute the unit costs for conversion.

Jerry: That's right. Is the rest of the report clear?

Samantha: Yes, it does seem pretty clear, although I want to work the numbers through on my own to make sure I thoroughly understand the report.

Jerry: Does this report give you the information you wanted?

Samantha: Yes, it does. I can tell how many units are in process, how complete they are, what happened to them, and their costs. While I know the unit costs are averages and are heavily influenced by our volume, they still can give me some idea of how well we are doing on the cost side. Thanks, Jerry.

Exhibit 4–10   Production Report—Weighted-Average Method

DOUBLE DIAMOND SKIS
Shaping and Milling Department Production Report
(weighted-average method)

Quantity Schedule and Equivalent Units

	Quantity Schedule		
Units to be accounted for:			
Work in process, May 1 (50% materials;			
30% conversion added last month)	200		
Started into production	5,000		
Total units	5,200		

	Quantity Schedule	Equivalent Units (EU)	
		Materials	Conversion
Units accounted for as follows:			
Transferred to the next department	4,800	4,800	4,800
Work in process, May 31 (40% materials;			
25% conversion added this month)	400	160*	100†
Total units and equivalent units			
of production	5,200	4,960	4,900

Costs per Equivalent Unit

	Total Cost	Materials	Conversion	Whole Unit
Cost to be accounted for:				
Work in process, May 1	$ 4,000	$ 3,000	$ 1,000	
Cost added in the Shaping and Milling				
Department	144,000	74,000	70,000	
Total cost (a)	$148,000	$77,000	$71,000	
Equivalent units of production (above) (b)		4,960	4,900	
Cost per EU, (a) ÷ (b)		$15.524	+ $14.490	= $30.014

Cost Reconciliation

	Total Cost	Equivalent Units (above)	
		Materials	Conversion
Cost accounted for as follows:			
Transferred to next department:			
4,800 units × $30.014 each	$144,067	4,800	4,800
Work in process, May 31:			
Materials, at $15.524 per EU	2,484	160	
Conversion, at $14.490 per EU	1,449		100
Total work in process, May 31	3,933		
Total cost	$148,000		

*40% × 400 units = 160 equivalent units.

†25% × 400 units = 100 equivalent units.

EU = Equivalent unit.

A Comment about Rounding Errors

If you use a calculator or computer spreadsheet and do not round off the costs per equivalent unit, there shouldn't be any discrepancy between the "Cost to be accounted for" and the "Cost accounted for" in the cost reconciliation. However, if you round off the costs per equivalent unit, the two figures will not always exactly agree. For the report in Exhibit 4–10, the two figures do agree, but this will not always happen. In all of the homework assignments and other materials, we follow two rules: (1) all the costs per equivalent unit are rounded off to three decimal places as in Exhibit 4–10, and (2) any adjustment needed to reconcile the "Cost accounted for" with the "Cost to be accounted for" is made to the cost "transferred" amount rather than to the ending inventory.

Operation Costing

Operation costing   A hybrid costing system used when products are manufactured in batches and when the products have some common characteristics and some individual characteristics. This system handles materials the same as in job-order costing and labour and overhead the same as in process costing.

The costing systems discussed in Chapters 3 and 4 represent the two ends of a continuum. On one end we have job-order costing, which is used by companies that produce many different items—generally to customers' specifications. On the other end we have process costing, which is used by companies that produce basically homogeneous products in large quantities. Between these two extremes there are many hybrid systems that include characteristics of both job-order and process costing. One of these hybrids is called *operation costing.*

Operation costing is used in situations where products have some common characteristics and also some individual characteristics. Shoes, for example, have common characteristics in that all styles involve cutting and sewing that can be done on a repetitive basis, using the same equipment and following the same basic procedures. Shoes also have individual characteristics—some are made of expensive leathers and others may be made using inexpensive synthetic materials. In a situation such as this, where products have some common characteristics but also must be handled individually to some extent, operation costing may be used to determine product costs.

As mentioned above, operation costing is a hybrid system that employs aspects of both job-order and process costing. Products are typically handled in batches when operation costing is in use, with each batch charged for its own specific materials. In this sense, operation costing is similar to job-order costing. However, labour and overhead costs are accumulated by operation or by department, and these costs are assigned to units as in process costing. If shoes are being produced, for example, each shoe is charged the same per unit conversion cost, regardless of the style involved, but it is charged with its specific materials cost. Thus, the company is able to distinguish between styles in terms of materials, but it is able to employ the simplicity of a process costing system for labour and overhead costs.

Examples of other products for which operation costing may be used include electronic equipment (such as semiconductors), textiles, clothing, and jewellery (such as rings, bracelets, and medallions). Products of this type are typically produced in batches, but they can vary considerably from model to model or from style to style in terms of the cost of raw material inputs. Therefore, an operation costing system is well suited for providing cost data.

Flexible Manufacturing Systems

In the two preceding chapters, we discussed the use of the FMS concept, in which plants are heavily automated and the activities are organized around cells, or islands, of automated equipment. The FMS concept is having a major impact on costing in several ways. One of these is through allowing companies to switch their systems from the more costly job-order approach to the less costly process or operation approaches. This switching is made possible through the fact that FMS is proving to be highly efficient in reducing the setup time required between products and jobs. With setup time only a small fraction of previous levels, companies are able to move between products and jobs with about the same speed as if they were working in a continuous, process-type environment. The result is that these companies are able to employ process costing techniques in situations that previously required job-order costing. As the use of FMS grows (and becomes even more efficient), some managers predict that job-order costing will slowly disappear except in a few, selected industries.

A further impact of FMS is through its focus on cells rather than on departments. Although production reports are still prepared in FMS settings, these reports are either much broader to include the entire production process (many cells) or much narrower to include only a single cell or workstation. As stated earlier, if JIT is practised, then the production report becomes greatly simplified, regardless of the level at which it is prepared.

Summary

Process costing is used in situations where homogeneous products or services are produced on a continuous basis. Costs flow through the manufacturing accounts in basically the same way in both job-order and process costing systems. A process costing system differs from a job-order system primarily in that costs are accumulated by department (rather than by job) and the department production report replaces the job cost sheet.

To compute unit costs in a department, the department's output in terms of equivalent units must be determined. In the weighted-average method, the equivalent units for a period are the sum of the units transferred out of the department during the period and the equivalent units in ending work in process inventory at the end of the period.

The activity in a department is summarized on a production report. There are three separate (though highly interrelated) parts to a production report. The first part is a quantity schedule, which includes a computation of equivalent units and shows the flow of units through a department during a period. The second part consists of a computation of costs per equivalent unit, with unit costs being provided individually for materials, labour, and overhead as well as in total for the period. The third part consists of a cost reconciliation, which summarizes all cost flows through a department for a period.

Review Problem: Process Cost Flows and Reports

Luxguard Home Paint Company produces exterior latex paint, which it sells in one-litre containers. The company has two processing departments—Base Fab and Finishing. White paint, which is used as a base for all the company's paints, is mixed from raw ingredients in the Base Fab Department. Pigments are added to the basic white paint, the pigmented paint is squirted under pressure into one-litre containers, and the containers are labelled and packed for shipping in the Finishing Department. Information relating to the company's operations for April is as follows:

a. Raw materials were issued for use in production: Base Fab Department, $851,000; and Finishing Department, $629,000.
b. Direct labour costs were incurred: Base Fab Department, $330,000; and Finishing Department, $270,000.
c. Manufacturing overhead cost was applied: Base Fab Department, $665,000; and Finishing Department, $405,000.
d. Basic white paint was transferred from the Base Fab Department to the Finishing Department, $1,850,000.
e. Paint that had been prepared for shipping was transferred from the Finishing Department to Finished Goods, $3,200,000.

Required

1. Prepare journal entries to record items (a) through (e) above.
2. Post the journal entries from (1) above to T-accounts. The balance in the Base Fab Department's Work in Process account on April 1 was $150,000; the balance in the Finishing Department's Work in Process account was $70,000. After posting entries to the T-accounts, find the ending balance in each department's Work in Process account.
3. Prepare a production report for the Base Fab Department for April. The following additional information is available regarding production in the Base Fab Department during April:

Production data:

Units (litres) in process, April 1: 100% complete as to materials, 60% complete as to labour and overhead	30,000
Units (litres) started into production during April	420,000
Units (litres) completed and transferred to the Finishing Department	370,000
Units (litres) in process, April 30: 50% complete as to materials, 25% complete as to labour and overhead	80,000

Cost data:

Work in process inventory, April 1:	
Materials	$ 92,000
Labour	21,000
Overhead	37,000
Total cost	$150,000

Cost added during April:	
Materials	$851,000
Labour	330,000
Overhead	665,000

Solution to Review Problem

1.
a.	Work in Process—Base Fab Department	851,000	
	Work in Process—Finishing Department	629,000	
	Raw Materials		1,480,000
b.	Work in Process—Base Fab Department	330,000	
	Work in Process—Finishing Department	270,000	
	Salaries and Wages Payable		600,000
c.	Work in Process—Base Fab Department	665,000	
	Work in Process—Finishing Department	405,000	
	Manufacturing Overhead		1,070,000
d.	Work in Process—Finishing Department	1,850,000	
	Work in Process—Base Fab Department		1,850,000
e.	Finished Goods	3,200,000	
	Work in Process—Finishing Department		3,200,000

2.

Raw Materials			
Bal.	XXX	(a)	1,480,000

Salaries and Wages Payable			
		(b)	600,000

Work in Process—
Base Fab Department

Bal.	150,000	(d)	1,850,000
(a)	851,000		
(b)	330,000		
(c)	665,000		
Bal.	146,000		

Manufacturing Overhead

(Various actual costs)		(c)	1,070,000

Work in Process—
Finishing Department

Bal.	70,000	(e)	3,200,000
(a)	629,000		
(b)	270,000		
(c)	405,000		
(d)	1,850,000		
Bal.	24,000		

Finished Goods

Bal.	XXX		
(e)	3,200,000		

LUXGUARD HOME PAINT COMPANY
Production Report—Base Fab Department
For the Month Ended April 30

Quantity Schedule and Equivalent Units

	Quantity Schedule
Units (litres) to be accounted for:	
Work in process, April 1 (all materials, 60% labour and overhead added last month)	30,000
Started into production	420,000
Total units	450,000

		Equivalent Units (EU)		
	Quantity Schedule	Materials	Labour	Overhead
Units (litres) accounted for as follows:				
Transferred to Finishing Department	370,000	370,000	370,000	370,000
Work in process, April 30 (50% materials, 25% labour and overhead added this month) . .	80,000	40,000*	20,000*	20,000*
Total units and equivalent units of production	450,000	410,000	390,000	390,000

Costs per Equivalent Unit

	Total Cost	Materials	Labour	Overhead	Whole Unit
Cost to be accounted for:					
Work in process, April 1	$ 150,000	$ 92,000	$ 21,000	$ 37,000	
Cost added by the Finishing					
Department	1,846,000	851,000	330,000	665,000	
Total cost (a)	$1,996,000	$943,000	$351,000	$702,000	
Equivalent units of production (b) .	—	410,000	390,000	390,000	
Cost per EU, (a) ÷ (b)	—	$2.30 +	$0.90 +	$1.80 =	$5.00

Cost Reconciliation

	Total Cost	Equivalent Units (above)		
		Materials	Labour	Overhead
Cost accounted for as follows:				
Transferred to Finishing Department:				
370,000 units × $5.00 each . . .	$1,850,000	370,000	370,000	370,000
Work in process, April 30:				
Materials, at $2.30 per EU . . .	92,000	40,000		
Labour, at $0.90 per EU	18,000		20,000	
Overhead, at $1.80 per EU . . .	36,000			20,000
Total work in process	146,000			
Total cost	$1,996,000			

* Materials: 80,000 units × 50% = 40,000 equivalent units; labour and overhead: 80,000 units × 25% = 20,000 equivalent units.

EU = Equivalent unit.

Appendix 4A: FIFO Method

The FIFO method of process costing differs from the weighted-average method in two basic ways: (1) the computation of equivalent units, and (2) the way in which costs of beginning inventory are treated in the cost reconciliation report. The FIFO method is generally considered more accurate than the weighted-average method, but it is more complex. The complexity is not a problem for computers, but the FIFO method is a little more difficult to understand and to learn than the weighted-average method.

Objective 6

Compute the equivalent units of production for a period by the FIFO method.

Equivalent Units—FIFO Method

The computation of equivalent units under the FIFO method differs from the computation under the weighted-average method in two ways.

First, the "units transferred out" figure is divided into two parts. One part consists of the units from the beginning inventory that were completed and transferred out, and the other part consists of the units that were both *started* and *completed* during the current period.

Second, full consideration is given to the amount of work expended during the current period on units in the *beginning* work in process inventory as well as on units in the ending inventory. Thus, under the FIFO method, it is necessary to convert both inventories to an equivalent units basis. For the beginning inventory, the equivalent units represent the work done to *complete* the units; for the ending inventory, the equivalent units represent the work done to bring the units to a stage of partial completion at the end of the period (the same as with the weighted-average method):

The formula for computing the equivalent units of production under the FIFO method is more complex than under the weighted-average method:

FIFO Method
(a separate calculation is made for each cost category in each processing department)

Equivalent units of production = Equivalent units to complete beginning inventory*
+ Units started and completed during the period
+ Equivalent units in ending work in process inventory

$$\begin{array}{c}\text{*Equivalent units to complete}\\ \text{beginning inventory}\end{array} = \begin{array}{c}\text{Units in beginning}\\ \text{inventory}\end{array} \times \left(100\% - \begin{array}{c}\text{Percentage completion}\\ \text{of beginning inventory}\end{array}\right)$$

Or, the equivalent units of production can also be determined as follows:

Equivalent units of production = Units transferred out
+ Equivalent units in ending work in process inventory
− Equivalent units in beginning inventory

To illustrate the FIFO method, refer again to the data for the Shaping and Milling Department at Double Diamond Skis. The department completed and transferred 4,800 units to the next department, the Graphics Application Department, during May. Since 200 of these units came from the beginning inventory, the Shaping and Milling Department must have started and completed 4,600 units during May. The 200 units in the beginning inventory were 50% complete with respect to materials and only 30% complete with respect to conversion costs when the month started. Thus, to complete these units the department must have added another 50% of materials costs and another 70% of conversion costs (100% − 30% = 70%). Following this line of reasoning, the equivalent units for the department for May would be computed as shown in Exhibit 4A–1.

Exhibit 4A–1
Equivalent Units of Production: FIFO Method

	Materials	Conversion
Work in process, May 1:		
200 units × (100% − 50%)*	100	
200 units × (100% − 30%)*		140
Units started and completed in May	4,600†	4,600†
Work in process, May 31:		
400 units × 40%	160	
400 units × 25%		100
Equivalent units of production	4,860	4,840

*This is the work needed to complete the units in beginning inventory.

†4,800 units transferred out to the next department − 200 units in beginning inventory. The FIFO method assumes that the units in beginning inventory are finished first.

Exhibit 4A–2 Visual Perspective of Equivalent Units of Production

DOUBLE DIAMOND SKIS
Shaping and Milling Department
Conversion Costs

Weighted-Average Method

Units completed and
 transferred to next department 4,800
Work in process, ending:
 400 units × 25% 100
Equivalent units of production 4,900

FIFO Method

Work in process, beginning:
 200 units × 70%* 140
Units started and completed 4,600
Work in process, ending:
 400 units × 25% 100
Equivalent units of production 4,840

*100% − 30% = 70%. This 70% represents the work needed to complete the units in the beginning inventory.

Comparison of Equivalent Units of Production under the Weighted-Average and FIFO Methods

Stop at this point and compare the data in Exhibit 4A–1 with the data in Exhibit 4–6 in the chapter, which shows the computation of equivalent units under the weighted-average method. Also refer to Exhibit 4A–2, which provides a visual comparison of the two methods.

The essential difference between the two methods is that the weighted-average method blends work and costs from the prior period with work and costs in the current period, whereas the FIFO method cleanly separates the two periods. To see this more clearly, consider the following comparison of the two calculations of equivalent units:

	Materials	Conversion
Equivalent units—weighted-average method	4,960	4,900
Less equivalent units in beginning inventory:		
200 units × 50%	100	
200 units × 30%		60
Equivalent units of production—FIFO method	4,860	4,840

From the previous page, it is evident that the FIFO method removes the equivalent units that were already in beginning inventory from the equivalent units as defined using the weighted-average method. Thus, the FIFO method isolates the equivalent units due to work performed during the current period. The weighted-average method blends together the equivalent units already in beginning inventory with the equivalent units due to work performed in the current period.

Production Report—FIFO Method

The steps followed in preparing a production report under the FIFO method are the same as those discussed earlier for the weighted-average method. However, since the FIFO method makes a distinction between units in the beginning inventory and units started during the year, the cost reconciliation portion of the report is more complex under the FIFO method than it is under the weighted-average method. To illustrate the FIFO method, we will again use the data for Double Diamond Skis on page 168.

Objective 7

Prepare a quantity schedule for a period by the FIFO method.

STEP 1: PREPARE A QUANTITY SCHEDULE AND COMPUTE THE EQUIVALENT UNITS   There is only one difference between a quantity schedule prepared under the FIFO method and one prepared under the weighted-average method. This difference relates to units transferred out. As explained earlier in our discussion of equivalent units, the FIFO method divides units transferred out into two parts. One part consists of the units in the beginning inventory, and the other part consists of the units started and completed during the current period. A quantity schedule showing this format for units transferred out is presented in Exhibit 4A–3, along with a computation of equivalent units for the month.

We explained earlier that in computing equivalent units under the FIFO method, we must first show the amount of work required *to complete* the units in the beginning inventory. We then show the number of units started and completed during the period, and finally we show the amount of work *completed* on the units still in process at the end of the period. Carefully trace through these computations in Exhibit 4A–3.

Objective 8

Compute the costs per equivalent unit for a period by the FIFO method.

STEP 2: COMPUTE THE COSTS PER EQUIVALENT UNIT   In computing unit costs under the FIFO method, we use only those costs that were incurred during the current period, and we ignore any costs in the beginning work in process inventory. Under the FIFO method, *unit costs relate only to work done during the current period.*

The costs per equivalent unit (EU) computed in Exhibit 4A–3 are used to cost units of product transferred to the next department; in addition, they are used to show the cost attached to partially completed units in the ending work in process inventory.

Objective 9

Prepare a cost reconciliation report for a period by the FIFO method.

STEP 3: PREPARE A COST RECONCILIATION   The purpose of cost reconciliation is to show how the costs charged to a department during a period are accounted for. With the FIFO method, two cost elements are associated with the units in the beginning work in process inventory. The first element is the cost carried over from the prior period. The second element is the cost needed *to complete* these units. For the Shaping and Milling Department, $4,000 in cost was carried over from last month. In the cost reconciliation in Exhibit 4A–3, we add to this figure the $1,523 in materials cost and $2,025 in conversion cost needed to complete these units. Note from the exhibit that these materials and conversion cost figures are computed by multiplying the costs per equivalent unit for materials and conversion times the equivalent units of work needed *to complete* the items that were in the beginning inventory. (The equivalent units figures used in this computation are brought down from the "Equivalent units" portion of the production report.)

Exhibit 4A–3
Production Report—FIFO
Method

DOUBLE DIAMOND SKIS
Shaping and Milling Department Production Report
(FIFO method)

Quantity Schedule and Equivalent Units

	Quantity Schedule
Units to be accounted for:	
Work in process, May 1 (50% materials; 30% conversion added last month) . .	200
Started into production	5,000
Total units	5,200

	Quantity Schedule	Equivalent Units (EU)	
		Materials	Conversion
Units accounted for as follows:			
Transferred to next department:			
From the beginning inventory*	200	100	140
Started and completed this month† . . .	4,600	4,600	4,600
Work in process, May 31 (40% materials; 25% conversion added this month)‡ . . .	400	160	100
Total units and equivalent units of production	5,200	4,860	4,840

Costs per Equivalent Unit

	Total Cost	Materials	Conversion	Whole Unit
Cost to be accounted for:				
Work in process, May 1	$ 4,000			
Cost added in the department (a)	144,000	$74,000	$70,000	
Total cost	$148,000			
Equivalent units of production (above) (b)		4,860	4,840	
Costs per EU, (a) ÷ (b)		$15.226 +	$14.463 ×	$29.689

Cost Reconciliation

	Total Cost	Equivalent Units (above)	
		Materials	Conversion
Cost accounted for as follows:			
Transferred to next department:			
From the beginning inventory:			
Cost in the beginning inventory	$ 4,000		
Cost to complete these units:			
Materials, at $15.226 per EU	1,523	100*	
Conversion, at $14.463 per EU	2,025		140*
Total cost	7,548		
Units started and completed this month, at $29.689 per unit	136,570	4,600†	4,600†
Total cost transferred	144,118		
Work in process, May 31:			
Materials, at $15.226 per EU	2,436	160‡	
Conversion, at $14.463 per EU	1,446		100‡
Total work in process, May 31 . . .	3,882		
Total cost	$148,000		

*Materials: 200 × (100% − 50%) = 100 equivalent units. Conversion: 200 × (100% − 30%) = 140 equivalent units.

†5,000 units started − 400 units in ending inventory = 4,600 units started and completed.

‡Materials: 400 × (40%) = 160 equivalent units. Conversion: 400 × (25%) = 100 equivalent units.

EU = Equivalent units.

Exhibit 4A–4   A
Comparison of Production
Report Content

Weighted-Average Method	FIFO Method
Quantity Schedule and Equivalent Units	
1. The quantity schedule includes all units transferred out in a single figure.	1. The quantity schedule divides the units transferred out into two parts. One part consists of units in the beginning inventory, and the other part consists of units started and completed during the current period.
2. In computing equivalent units, the units in the beginning inventory are treated as if they were started and completed during the current period.	2. Only work needed to *complete* units in the beginning inventory is included in the computation of equivalent units. Units started and completed during the current period are shown as a separate figure.
Total and Unit Costs	
1. The "Cost to be accounted for" part of the report is the same for both methods.	1. The "Cost to be accounted for" part of the report is the same for both methods.
2. Costs in the beginning inventory are added in with costs of the current period in computations of costs per equivalent unit.	2. Only costs of the current period are included in computations of costs per equivalent unit.
Cost Reconciliation	
1. All units transferred out are treated the same, regardless of whether they were part of the beginning inventory or started and completed during the period.	1. Units transferred out are divided into two groups: (a) units in the beginning inventory, and (b) units started and completed during the period.
2. Units in the ending inventory have cost applied to them in the same way under both methods.	2. Units in the ending inventory have cost applied to them in the same way under both methods.

For units started and completed during the month, we simply multiply the number of units started and completed by the total cost per unit to determine the amount transferred out. This would be $136,570 (4,600 units × $29.689 = $136,570) for the department.

Finally, the amount of cost attached to the ending work in process inventory is computed by multiplying the cost per equivalent unit figures for the month times the equivalent units for materials and conversion costs in the ending inventory. Once again, the equivalent units needed for this computation are brought down from the "Equivalent units" portion of the production report.

Exhibit 4A–4 summarizes the major similarities and differences between production reports prepared under the weighted-average and FIFO methods.

A Comparison of Costing Methods

In most situations, the weighted-average and FIFO methods will produce very similar unit costs. If there never are any ending inventories, as in an ideal JIT environment, the two methods will produce identical results. The reason for this is that without any ending inventories, no costs can be carried forward into the next period and the weighted-average method will base the unit costs on just the current period's costs—just as in the FIFO method. If there *are* ending inventories, either erratic input prices or erratic production levels would also be required to generate much of a difference in unit costs under the two methods. This is because the weighted-average method will blend the unit costs from the prior period with the unit costs of the current period. Unless these unit costs differ greatly, the blending will not make much difference.

Nevertheless, from the standpoint of cost control, the FIFO method is superior to the weighted-average method. Current performance should be measured in relation to costs of the current period only, and the weighted-average method mixes costs of the current period with costs of the prior period. Thus, under the weighted-average method, the manager's apparent performance is influenced by what happened in the prior period. This problem does not arise under the FIFO method, since it makes a clear distinction between costs of prior periods and costs incurred during the current period. For the same reason, the FIFO method also provides more up-to-date cost data for decision-making purposes.

Some managers prefer the weighted-average method because they feel that the weighted-average method is simpler to apply than the FIFO method. Although this was true in the past when much accounting work was done by hand, computers can handle the additional calculations with ease once they have been appropriately programmed.

Appendix 4B: Shrinkage and Lost Units

Objective 10

Compute the cost of lost units or shrinkage.

The illustrations presented in Chapter 4 assume units that are in process are either completed or still awaiting completion at the end of each period. In reality, units can disappear because of evaporation, losses, or rejection. Such missing units can be considered a normal part of the processing or may be deemed abnormal. Abnormal losses can be thought of as costs akin to unusual losses studied in financial accounting. Normal losses would be normal costs of operating the process department.

Two accounting treatments are prevalent for normal losses. One, the amount of the loss can be charged to a specific loss account which could be charged to manufacturing overhead. Two, the amount of the loss could be spread over all the good units of work done during the period.

If significant in amount and truly abnormal, abnormal losses should always be assigned to the unusual section of the income statement where they can be offset by any recoveries from insurance or other means.

The following illustrates the two alternative treatments of normal losses. The weighted-average method is used for illustration.

Case 1: Normal Loss Charged to Manufacturing Overhead

Assume Stabler Chemical had a machine breakdown causing a loss of 10,000 units that were 100% complete as to materials and 60% complete for labour and overhead. Exhibit 4B–1 presents the cost of production report for Stabler Chemical after the assumption is included in the data for the problem. The lost units are included in the units accounted for and the equivalent units lost become a separate line in the equivalent units calculation. When costs are accounted for, the lost units, whether normal (as they are in this case) or abnormal, are costed according to their equivalent units completed. The journal entry for normal losses would be:

Manufacturing Overhead 11,272
    Work in Process   11,272

The total number of units lost, both normal and abnormal, can be determined from the quantity schedule. Units accounted for have to be transferred out, in Work in Process at the end of the period, or lost. Thus, even when lost units cannot be physically counted, they can be mathematically calculated by knowing the total units to account for. What is more difficult is to distinguish normal from abnormal losses. A common approach is to use a percentage to express what is normal. Usually this percentage is expressed in terms of the number of units that pass a prespecified inspection point. Thus, in Exhibit 4B–1, the inspection point could be at 60% of the total production conversion process. If, for example, 5% of good output is considered to be normal losses, then 8,000 (0.05 × 160,000) units would be normal losses and 2,000 abnormal. Notice the ending Work in Process is only 40% complete so it has not reached the inspection point. Thus, the 5% figure would not be applied to the 30,000 units in the ending Work in Process.

An assumption is needed here to avoid a significant complexity. The preceding entry assumes predetermined overhead is used so that $11,272 is an actual overhead cost that was previously estimated when the overhead rate was calculated. Because the $11,272 includes $4,632 for overhead, overhead is being charged to overhead resulting in some cost duplication, but the amount of error introduced is assumed to be minor.

If the losses were considered to be abnormal, the entry to record the loss would be:

```
Unusual Loss—Machine Breakdown  ......................  11,272
    Work in Process  ...................................              11,272
```

Case 2: Normal Loss Charged to All Good Output

Assume Stabler Chemical had normal evaporation of liquid evenly through the process. The illustrated solution is presented in Exhibit 4B–2. Notice first that the amount of loss is not given in units. The units lost have to be determined from the quantity schedule by computing the difference between the total units to be accounted for and what is known to have been completed or is still in process.

The number of units lost is assigned a 0 equivalent units amount. The resulting smaller number of units is used to determine the unit costs. When costs are accounted for, the unit costs are greater because they include the costs of the evaporation or normal losses. Thus, no entry is required to record the normal loss.

Careful thinking about these two cases presents a number of theoretical issues as to where to charge losses and whether or not it is fair to charge Work in Process with losses if the units in this ending inventory have not been inspected at their stage of completion.

Exhibit 4B–1 provides an opportunity to look at one type of complication. Normal losses have to be calculated and separated from abnormal losses where both types of losses are present. In Exhibit 4B–1, 10,000 units of normal losses represent all of the units lost. In addition, these units were lost at the 60% stage of production. If, however, the ending work in process had reached or passed the 60% stage, then normal losses could be separated from the known total losses by applying the normal loss percentage to both the completed units and the ending work in process.

For example, if 10,000 were the total lost units and the ending work in process was 70% complete instead of the assumed 40%, then a normal loss percentage of, say, 5% would be applied as follows to separate normal and abnormal:

```
5% × 160,000 =   8,000 (from completed items)
5% ×  30,000 =   1,500 (from ending work in process)

Total normal losses   9,500
Abnormal                500 (balance of losses)

Total losses         10,000
```

Exhibit 4B–1   Production Report—Weighted-Average Method

Quantity Schedule and Equivalent Units

	Quantity Schedule
Units to be accounted for:	
Work in process, beginning (all materials, 30% labour and overhead added last month)	20,000
Started into production	180,000
Total units to be accounted for	200,000

	Quantity Schedule	Equivalent Units (EU) Materials	Labour	Overhead
Units accounted for as follows:				
Transferred out	160,000	160,000	160,000	160,000
Units lost, normal (100% of materials, 60% labour and overhead)	10,000	10,000	6,000	6,000
Work in process, ending (all materials, 40% labour and overhead added this month)	30,000	30,000	12,000*	12,000*
Total units accounted for	200,000	200,000	178,000	178,000

Unit Costs	Total	Materials	Labour	Overhead
Work in process, beginning	$ 17,000	$ 8,000	$ 3,600	$ 5,400
Cost added by the department	283,000	63,000	88,000	132,000
Total cost (a)	$300,000	$ 71,000	$ 91,600	$137,400
Equivalent units (b)		200,000	178,000	$178,000
Unit cost, (a) ÷ (b)	$1,642 =	$0.355 +	$0.515 +	$0.772

Cost Reconciliation	Costs
Cost to be accounted for	
Work in process, beginning	$ 17,000
Cost added by the department	283,000
Total cost to be accounted for	$300,000

	Costs	Equivalent Units (EU)		
Cost accounted for as follows:				
Transferred to cooking: 160,000 × $1.642	$262,720	160,000	160,000	160,000
Normal losses				
Materials (at $0.355 × 10,000)	3,550	10,000		
Labour (at $0.515 × 6,000)	3,090		6,000	
Overhead (at $0.772 × 6,000)	4,632			6,000
Total normal losses	11,272			
Work in process, ending:				
Materials (at $0.355 × 30,000)	10,650	30,000		
Labour (at $0.515 × 12,000)	6,180		12,000	
Overhead (at $0.772 × 12,000)	9,264			12,000
Total work in process, ending	26,094			
Total cost accounted for	300,086			
Less: Rounding	86			
Total cost accounted for	$300,000			

*40% × 30,000 units = 12,000 equivalent units.

EU = Equivalent unit.

Exhibit 4B–2   Production Report—Weighted-Average Method

Quantity Schedule

	Quantity Schedule
Units to be accounted for:	
Work in process, beginning (all materials, 30% labour and overhead added last month)	20,000
Started into production	180,000
Total units to be accounted for	200,000

		Equivalent Units (EU)		
		Materials	**Labour**	**Overhead**
Units accounted for as follows:				
Transferred out	160,000	160,000	160,000	160,000
Units lost—normal	10,000*	–0–	–0–	–0–
Work in process, ending (all materials, 40% labour and overhead added this month)	30,000	30,000	12,000†	12,000†
Total units accounted for	200,000	190,000	172,000	172,000

Unit Costs	**Total**	**Materials**	**Labour**	**Overhead**
Work in process, beginning	$ 17,000	$ 8,000	$ 3,600	$ 5,400
Cost added by the department	283,000	63,000	88,000	132,000
Total cost (a)	$300,000	$ 71,000	$ 91,600	$137,400
Equivalent units (b)		190,000	172,000	172,000
Unit cost, (a) ÷ (b)	$1.706 =	$0.374 +	$0.533 +	$0.799

Cost Reconciliation	**Costs**
Cost to be accounted for	
Work in process, beginning	$ 17,000
Cost added by the department	283,000
Total cost to be accounted for	$300,000

		Equivalent Units (EU)		
Cost accounted for as follows:				
Transferred to cooking: (160,000 × $1.706)	$272,960	160,000	160,000	160,000
Work in process, ending:				
Materials (at $0.374 × 30,000)	11,220	30,000		
Labour (at $0.533 × 12,000)	6,396		12,000	
Overhead (at $0.799 × 12,000)	9,588			12,000
Total work in process, ending	27,204			
Total cost accounted for	300,164			
Less: Rounding	164			
Total cost accounted for	$300,000			

*Total units to be accounted for 200,000 − units transferred 160,000 − units in process, ending 30,000 = 10,000 units lost.

†40% × 30,000 units = 12,000 EU.

EU = Equivalent unit.

Questions

4–1 Under what conditions would it be appropriate to use a process costing system?

4–2 What similarities exist between job-order and process costing?

4–3 Costs are accumulated by job in a job-order costing system; how are costs accumulated in a process costing system?

4–4 What two essential features characterize any processing department in a process costing system?

4–5 Distinguish between departments arranged in a sequential pattern and departments arranged in a parallel pattern.

4–6 Why is cost accumulation easier under a process costing system than it is under a job-order costing system?

4–7 How many Work in Process accounts are maintained in a company using process costing?

4–8 Assume that a company has two processing departments, Mixing and Firing. Prepare a journal entry to show a transfer of partially completed units from the Mixing Department to the Firing Department.

4–9 Assume again that a company has two processing departments, Mixing and Firing. Explain what costs might be added to the Firing Department's Work in Process account during a period.

4–10 What is meant by the term *equivalent units of production* when the weighted-average method is used?

4–11 What is a quantity schedule, and what purpose does it serve?

4–12 Under process costing, it is often suggested that a product is like a rolling snowball as it moves from department to department. Why is this an apt comparison?

4–13 Watkins Trophies, Inc., produces thousands of medallions made of bronze, silver, and gold. The medallions are identical except for the materials used in their manufacture. What costing system would you advise the company to use?

4–14 Give examples of companies that might use operation costing.

4–15 (Appendix 4A) How does the computation of equivalent units under the FIFO method differ from the computation of equivalent units under the weighted-average method?

4–16 (Appendix 4A) On the cost reconciliation part of the production report, the weighted-average method treats all units transferred out in the same way. How does this differ from the FIFO method of handling units transferred out?

4–17 (Appendix 4A) From the standpoint of cost control, why is the FIFO method superior to the weighted-average method?

4–18 (Appendix 4B) Describe two methods of dealing with normal losses in a process.

4–19 (Appendix 4A) From the standpoint of cost control, why is the FIFO method superior to the weighted-average method?

4–20 (Appendix 4B) Which of the two methods of dealing with normal losses would you prefer from a management control perspective? Why?

4–21 How does the use of JIT reduce or eliminate the difference in unit costs between FIFO and weighted-average methods of preparing a cost of production report?

Exercises

E4–1   Chocolaterie de Geneve, SA, is located in a French-speaking canton in Switzerland. The company makes chocolate truffles that are sold in popular embossed tins. The company has two processing departments—Cooking and Molding. In the Cooking Department, the raw ingredients for the truffles are mixed and then cooked in special candy-making vats. In the Molding Department, the melted chocolate and other ingredients from the Cooking Department are carefully poured into molds and decorative flourishes are applied by hand. After cooling, the truffles are packed for sale. The company uses a process costing system. The T-accounts below show the flow of costs through the two departments in April (all amounts are in Swiss francs):

Work in Process—Cooking

Bal. 4/1	8,000	Transferred out	160,000
Direct materials	42,000		
Direct labour	50,000		
Overhead	75,000		

Work in Process—Molding

Bal. 4/1	4,000	Transferred out	240,000
Transferred in	160,000		
Direct labour	36,000		
Overhead	45,000		

Required   Prepare journal entries showing the flow of costs through the two processing departments during April.

E4–2   Clonex Labs, Inc., uses a process costing system. The following data are available for one department for October:

		Percent Completed	
	Units	Materials	Conversion
Work in process, October 1	30,000	65%	30%
Work in process, October 31	15,000	80%	40%

The department started 175,000 units into production during the month and transferred 190,000 completed units to the next department.

Required   Compute the equivalent units of production for October assuming that the company uses the weighted-average method of accounting for units and costs.

E4–3   (Appendix 4A) Refer to the data for Clonex Labs, Inc., in E4–2.

Required   Compute the equivalent units of production for October assuming that the company uses the FIFO method of accounting for units and costs.

E4–4   The Labrador Fisheries, Inc., processes salmon for various distributors. Two departments are involved—Department 1 and Department 2. Data relating to kilograms of salmon processed in Department 1 during July are presented below:

	Kilograms of Salmon	Percent Completed*
Work in process, July 1	20,000	30%
Started into processing during July	380,000	—
Work in process, July 31	25,000	60%
*Labour and overhead only.		

All materials are added at the beginning of processing in Department 1. Labour and overhead (conversion) costs are incurred uniformly throughout processing.

Required Prepare a quantity schedule and a computation of equivalent units for July for Department 1 assuming that the company uses the weighted-average method of accounting for units.

E4–5 (Appendix 4A) Refer to the data for The Labrador Fisheries, Inc., in E4–4.

Required Prepare a quantity schedule and a computation of equivalent units for July for Department 1 assuming that the company uses the FIFO method of accounting for units.

E4–6 Hielta Oy, a Finnish company, processes wood pulp for various manufacturers of paper products. Data relating to tonnes of pulp processed during June are provided below:

	Tonnes of Pulp	Percent Completed	
		Materials	Labour and Overhead
Work in process, June 1	20,000	90%	80%
Work in process, June 30	30,000	60%	40%
Started into processing during June	190,000	—	—

Required 1. Compute the number of tonnes of pulp completed and transferred out during June.
2. Prepare a quantity schedule for June assuming that the company uses the weighted-average method.

E4–7 (Appendix 4A) Refer to the data for Hielta Oy in E4–6.

Required 1. Compute the number of tonnes of pulp completed and transferred out during June.
2. Prepare a quantity schedule for June assuming that the company uses the FIFO method.

E4–8 Pureform, Inc., manufactures a product that passes through two departments. Data for a recent month for the first department follow:

	Units	Materials	Labour	Overhead
Work in process, beginning	5,000	$ 4,500	$ 1,250	$ 1,875
Units started in process	45,000			
Units transferred out	42,000			
Work in process, ending	8,000			
Cost added during the month	—	52,800	21,500	32,250

The beginning work in process inventory was 80% complete as to materials and 60% complete as to processing. The ending work in process inventory was 75% complete as to materials and 50% complete as to processing.

Required 1. Assume that the company uses the weighted-average method of accounting for units and costs. Prepare a quantity schedule and a computation of equivalent units for the month.
2. Determine the costs per equivalent unit for the month.

E4–9 (Appendix 4A) Refer to the data for Pureform, Inc., in E4–8.

Required 1. Assume that the company uses the FIFO method of accounting for units and costs. Prepare a quantity schedule and a computation of equivalent units for the month.
2. Determine the costs per equivalent unit for the month.

E4–10 Helox, Inc., manufactures a product that passes through two production processes. A quantity schedule for a recent month for the first process follows:

	Quantity Schedule
Units to be accounted for:	
Work in process, May 1 (all materials, 40% conversion cost added last month)	5,000
Started into production	180,000
Total units	185,000

Units accounted for as follows:		Equivalent Units	
		Materials	Conversion
Transferred to the next process	175,000	?	?
Work in process, May 31 (all materials, 30% conversion cost added this month)	10,000	?	?
Total units	185,000	?	?

Costs in the beginning work in process inventory of the first processing department were: materials, $1,200; and conversion cost, $3,800. Costs added during the month were: materials, $54,000; and conversion cost, $352,000.

Required
1. Assume that the company uses the weighted-average method of accounting for units and costs. Determine the equivalent units for the month for the first process.
2. Compute the costs per equivalent unit for the month for the first process.

E4–11 (This exercise should be assigned only if E4–10 is also assigned.) Refer to the data for Helox, Inc., in E4–10 and to the equivalent units and costs per equivalent unit you have computed there.

Required Complete the following cost reconciliation for the first process:

Cost Reconciliation

	Total Cost	Equivalent Units	
		Materials	Conversion
Cost accounted for as follows:			
Transferred to the next process: (? units × $?)	$?		
Work in process, May 31:			
Materials, at _____ per EU	?	?	
Conversion, at _____ per EU	?		?
Total work in process	?		
Total cost	$?		

E4–12 (Appendix 4A) Refer to the data for Helox, Inc., in E4–10. Assume that the company uses the FIFO cost method.

Required
1. Prepare a quantity schedule and a computation of equivalent units for the month for the first process.
2. Compute the costs per equivalent unit for the month for the first process.

E4–13 (Appendix 4A) (This exercise should be assigned only if E4–12 is also assigned.) Refer to the data for Helox, Inc., in E4–10 and to the equivalent units and costs per equivalent unit that you computed in E4–12.

Required Complete the following cost reconciliation for the first process:

Cost Reconciliation

	Total Cost	Equivalent Units	
		Materials	**Conversion**
Cost accounted for as follows:			
Transferred to the next process:			
From the beginning inventory:			
Cost in the beginning inventory	$?		
Cost to complete these units:			
Materials, at _____ per EU	?	?	
Conversion, at _____ per EU	?		?
Total cost	?		
Units started and completed this			
month: _____ units × _____ each	?	?	?
Total cost transferred	?		
Work in process, May 31:			
Materials, at _____ per EU	?	?	
Conversion, at _____ per EU	?		?
Total work in process	?		
Total cost	$?		

Problems

P4–14 Weighted-Average Method; Step-by-Step Production Report

Builder Products, Inc., manufactures a caulking compound that goes through three processing stages prior to completion. Information on work in the first department, Cooking, is given below for May:

Production data:
Units in process, May 1; 100% complete
as to materials and 80% complete
as to labour and overhead 10,000
Units started into production during May 100,000
Units completed and transferred out 95,000
Units in process, May 31; 60% complete
as to materials and 20% complete
as to labour and overhead .... ?

Cost data:
Work in process inventory, May 1:
Materials cost .... $ 1,500
Labour cost 1,800
Overhead cost 5,400
Cost added during May:
Materials cost 154,500
Labour cost 22,700
Overhead cost 68,100

Materials are added at several stages during the cooking process, whereas labour and overhead costs are incurred uniformly. The company uses the weighted-average method.

Required

Prepare a production report for the Cooking Department for May. Use the following three steps in preparing your report:

1. Prepare a quantity schedule and a computation of equivalent units.
2. Compute the costs per equivalent unit for the month.
3. Using the data from (1) and (2) above, prepare a cost reconciliation.

P4–15 **Weighted-Average Method; Partial Production Report** Martin Company manufactures a single product. The company uses the weighted-average method in its process costing system. Activity for June has just been completed. An incomplete production report for the first processing department follows:

Quantity Schedule and Equivalent Units

	Quantity Schedule
Units to be accounted for:	
Work in process, June 1 (all materials, 75% labour and overhead added last month) ..	8,000
Started into production	45,000
Total units	53,000

	Quantity Schedule	Equivalent Units (EU)		
		Materials	**Labour**	**Overhead**
Units accounted for as follows:				
Transferred to the next department	48,000	?	?	?
Work in process, June 30 (all materials, 40% labour and overhead added this month) ..	5,000	?	?	?
Total units	53,000	?	?	?

Costs per Equivalent Unit

	Total Cost	Materials	Labour	Overhead	Whole Unit
Cost to be accounted for:					
Work in process, June 1	$ 7,130	$ 5,150	$ 660	$ 1,320	
Cost added by the department ..	58,820	29,300	9,840	19,680	
Total cost (a)	$65,950	$34,450	$10,500	$21,000	
Equivalent units (b)	—	53,000	50,000	50,000	
Cost per EU, (a) ÷ (b)	—	$0.65 +	$0.21 +	$0.42 =	$1.28

Cost Reconciliation

	Total Cost
Cost accounted for as follows:	
?	?

Required

1. Prepare a schedule showing how the equivalent units were computed for the first processing department.
2. Complete the "Cost Reconciliation" part of the production report for the first processing department.

P4–16 **FIFO Method; Step-by-Step Production Report** (Appendix 4A)
Selzik Company makes super-premium cake mixes that go through two processes, blending and packaging. The following activity was recorded in the Blending Department during July:

Production data:
Units in process, July 1; 30% complete
    as to conversion costs   10,000
Units started into production   170,000
Units completed and transferred to Packaging   . . . .   ?
Units in process, July 31; 40% complete
    as to conversion costs   20,000

Cost data:
Work in process inventory, July 1:

Materials cost	$ 8,500	
Conversion cost	4,900	$ 13,400
Cost added during the month:		
Materials cost	139,400	
Conversion cost	244,200	383,600
Total cost		$397,000

All materials are added at the beginning of work in the Blending Department. Conversion costs are added uniformly during processing. The company uses the FIFO cost method.

Required Prepare a production report for the Blending Department for July. Use the following three steps as a guide in preparing your report:

1. Prepare a quantity schedule and compute the equivalent units.
2. Compute the costs per equivalent unit for the month.
3. Using the data from (1) and (2) above, prepare a cost reconciliation.

P4–17 Weighted-Average Method; Basic Production Report Sunspot Beverages, Ltd., of Fiji makes blended tropical fruit drinks in two stages. Fruit juices are extracted from fresh fruits and then blended in the Blending Department. The blended juices are then bottled and packed for shipping in the Bottling Department. The following information pertains to the operations of the Blending Department for June. (The currency in Fiji is the Fijian dollar.)

		Percent Completed	
	Units	Materials	Conversion
Work in process, beginning	20,000	100%	75%
Started into production	180,000		
Completed and transferred out	160,000		
Work in process, ending	40,000	100%	25%

Cost in the beginning work in process inventory and cost added during June were as follows for the Blending Department:

	Materials	Conversion
Work in process, beginning	$ 25,200	$ 24,800
Cost added during June	334,800	238,700

Required Prepare a production report for the Blending Department for June assuming that the company uses the weighted-average method.

P4–18 FIFO Method; Basic Production Report (Appendix 4A) Refer to the data for the Blending Department of Sunspot Beverages, Ltd., in P4–17. Assume that the company uses the FIFO method to compute unit costs rather than the weighted-average method.

Required Prepare a production report for the Blending Department for June.

P4–19 Weighted-Average Method; Interpreting a Production Report

Cooperative San José of southern Sonora state in Mexico makes a unique syrup using cane sugar and local herbs. The syrup is sold in small bottles and is prized as a flavouring for drinks and for use in desserts. The bottles are sold for $12 each. (The Mexican currency is the peso and is denoted by $.) The first stage in the production process is carried out in the Mixing Department, which removes foreign matter from the raw materials and mixes them in the proper proportions in large vats. The company uses the weighted-average method in its process costing system.

A hastily prepared report for the Mixing Department for April appears below:

Quantity Schedule
Units to be accounted for:
Work in process, April 1 (90% materials,
80% conversion cost added last month) 30,000
Started into production 200,000
Total units 230,000

Units accounted for as follows:
Transferred to the next department 190,000
Work in process, April 30 (75% materials,
60% conversion cost added this month) 40,000
Total units 230,000

Total Cost
Cost to be accounted for:
Work in process, April 1 .... $ 98,000
Cost added during the month 827,000
Total cost $925,000

Cost Reconciliation
Cost accounted for as follows:
Transferred to the next department $805,600
Work in process, April 30 119,400
Total cost $925,000

Cooperative San José has just been acquired by another company, and the management of the acquiring company wants some additional information about Cooperative San José's operations.

Required
1. What were the equivalent units for the month?
2. What were the costs per equivalent unit for the month? The beginning inventory consisted of the following costs: materials, $67,800; and conversion cost, $30,200. The costs added during the month consisted of: materials, $579,000; and conversion cost, $248,000.
3. How many of the units transferred to the next department were started and completed during the month?
4. The manager of the Mixing Department, anxious to make a good impression on the new owners, stated, "Materials prices jumped from about $2.50 per unit in March to $3 per unit in April, but due to good cost control I was able to hold our materials cost to less than $3 per unit for the month." Should this manager be rewarded for good cost control? Explain.

P4–20 FIFO Method; Analysis of Work in Process T-Account (Appendix 4A)
Superior Brands, Inc., manufactures paint. The paint goes through three processes—cracking, mixing, and cooking. Activity in the Cracking Department during a recent month is summarized in the department's Work in Process account below:

Work in Process—Cracking Department

Inventory, April 1 (10,000 litres, 80% processed)	39,000	Completed and transferred to mixing (__?__ litres)	__?__
April costs added:			
Materials (140,000 litres)	259,000		
Labour and overhead	312,000		
Inventory, April 30 (30,000 litres, 60% processed)	__?__		

The materials are entered into production at the beginning of work in the Cracking Department. Labour and overhead costs are incurred uniformly throughout the cracking process. The company uses the FIFO cost method.

Required   Prepare a production report for the Cracking Department for the month.

P4–21 Weighted-Average Method; Analysis of Work in Process T-Account   Weston Products manufactures an industrial cleaning compound that goes through three processing departments—Grinding, Mixing, and Cooking. All raw materials are introduced at the start of work in the Grinding Department, with conversion costs being incurred evenly throughout the grinding process. The Work in Process T-account for the Grinding Department for a recent month is given below:

Work in Process—Grinding Department

Inventory, May 1 (18,000 kg, 1/3 processed)	21,800	Completed and transferred to mixing (__?__ kg)	__?__
May costs added:			
Raw materials (167,000 kg)	133,400		
Labour and overhead	226,800		
Inventory, May 31 (15,000 kg, 2/3 processed)	__?__		

The May 1 work in process inventory consists of $14,600 in materials cost and $7,200 in labour and overhead cost. The company uses the weighted-average method to account for units and costs.

Required   1. Prepare a production report for the Grinding Department for the month.
2. What criticism can be made of the unit costs that you have computed on your production report?

P4–22 Weighted-Average Method; Journal Entries; T-Accounts; Production Report   Hilox, Inc., produces an antacid product that goes through two departments—Cooking and Bottling. The company has recently hired a new assistant accountant, who has prepared the following summary of production and costs for the Cooking Department for May using the weighted-average method.

Cooking Department costs:

Work in process inventory, May 1: 70,000 quarts, 60% complete as to materials and 30% complete as to labour and overhead	$ 61,000*
Materials added during May	570,000
Labour added during May	100,000
Overhead applied during May	235,000
Total departmental costs	$966,000

Cooking Department costs assigned to:

Litres completed and transferred to the Bottling
Department: 400,000 litres at ___?__ per litre . . . .　　$?

Work in process inventory, May 31: 50,000
litres, 70% complete as to materials and
40% complete as to labour and overhead . . . .　　　?

Total departmental costs assigned . . . .　　$?

*Consists of materials, $39,000; labour, $5,000; and overhead, $17,000.

The new assistant accountant has determined the cost per litre transferred to be $2.415, as follows:

$$\frac{\text{Total departmental costs, \$966,000}}{\text{Litres completed and transferred, 400,000}} = \$2.415$$

However, the assistant accountant is unsure how to use this unit cost figure in assigning cost to the ending work in process inventory. In addition, the company's general ledger shows only $900,000 in cost transferred from the Cooking Department to the Bottling Department, which does not agree with the $966,000 figure above.

The general ledger also shows the following costs incurred in the Bottling Department during May: materials used, $130,000; direct labour cost incurred, $80,000; and overhead cost applied to products, $158,000.

Required　1.　Prepare journal entries as follows to record activity in the company during May. Key your entries to the letters (a) through (g) below.
　　a.　Raw materials were issued to the two departments for use in production.
　　b.　Direct labour costs were incurred in the two departments.
　　c.　Manufacturing overhead costs were incurred, $400,000. (Credit Accounts Payable.) The company maintains a single Manufacturing Overhead account for the entire plant.
　　d.　Manufacturing overhead cost was applied to production in each department using predetermined overhead rates.
　　e.　Units completed as to processing in the Cooking Department were transferred to the Bottling Department, $900,000.
　　f.　Units completed as to processing in the Bottling Department were transferred to Finished Goods, $1,300,000.
　　g.　Units were sold on account, $2,000,000. The Cost of Good Sold was $1,250,000.
　　2.　Post the journal entries from (1) above to T-accounts. Balances in selected accounts on May 1 are given below:

Raw Materials . . . . 　$710,000
Work in Process—Bottling Department . . . . 　　85,000
Finished Goods . . . . 　　45,000

After posting the entries to the T-accounts, find the ending balance in the inventory accounts and the Manufacturing Overhead accounts.

　　3.　Prepare a production report for the Cooking Department for May.

P4–23　Weighted-Average Method; Equivalent Units; Costing of Inventories　You are employed by Spirit Company, a manufacturer of digital watches. The company's chief financial officer is trying to verify the accuracy of the ending work in process and finished goods inventories prior to closing the books for the year. You have been asked to assist in this verification. The year-end balances shown on Spirit Company's books are as follows:

	Units	Costs
Work in process, December 31 (50% complete as to labour and overhead)	300,000	$ 660,960
Finished goods, December 31	200,000	1,009,800

Materials are added to production at the beginning of the manufacturing process, and overhead is applied to each product at the rate of 60% of direct labour cost. There was no finished goods inventory at the beginning of the year. A review of Spirit Company's inventory and cost records has disclosed the following data, all of which are accurate:

	Units	Costs Materials	Labour
Work in process, January 1 (80% complete as to labour and overhead)	200,000	$ 200,000	$ 315,000
Units started into production	1,000,000		
Cost added during the year:			
Materials cost		1,300,000	
Labour cost			1,995,000
Units completed during the year	900,000		

The company uses the weighted-average cost method.

Required

1. Determine the equivalent units and costs per equivalent unit for materials, labour, and overhead for the year.
2. Determine the amount of cost that should be assigned to the ending work in process and finished goods inventories.
3. Prepare the necessary correcting journal entry to adjust the work in process and finished goods inventories to the correct balances as of December 31.
4. Determine the cost of goods sold for the year assuming there is no under- or overapplied overhead.

(CPA, adapted)

P4–24   Weighted-Average Method; Journal Entries; T-Accounts; Production Report   Lubricants, Inc., produces a special kind of grease that is widely used by race car drivers. The grease is produced in two processes: refining and blending.

Raw oil products are introduced at various points in the Refining Department; labour and overhead costs are incurred evenly throughout the refining operation. The refined output is then transferred to the Blending Department.

The following incomplete Work in Process account is available for the Refining Department for March:

Work in Process—Refining Department

March 1 inventory (20,000 litres; 100% complete as to materials; 90% complete as to labour and overhead)	38,000	Completed and transferred to blending (___?___ litres)	___?___
March costs added:			
Raw oil materials (390,000 litres)	495,000		
Direct labour	72,000		
Overhead	181,000		
March 31 inventory (40,000 litres; 75% complete as to materials; 25% complete as to labour and overhead)	___?___		

The March 1 work in process inventory in the Refining Department consists of the following cost elements: raw materials, $25,000; direct labour, $4,000; and overhead, $9,000.

Costs incurred during March in the Blending Department were: materials used, $115,000; direct labour, $18,000; and overhead cost applied to production, $42,000. The company accounts for units and costs by the weighted-average method.

Required
1. Prepare journal entries to record the costs incurred in both the Refining Department and Blending Department during March. Key your entries to the items (a) through (g) below.
   a. Raw materials were issued for use in production.
   b. Direct labour costs were incurred.
   c. Manufacturing overhead costs for the entire factory were incurred, $225,000. (Credit Accounts Payable.)
   d. Manufacturing overhead cost was applied to production using a predetermined overhead rate.
   e. Units that were complete as to processing in the Refining Department were transferred to the Blending Department, $740,000.
   f. Units that were complete as to processing in the Blending Department were transferred to Finished Goods, $950,000.
   g. Completed units were sold on account, $1,500,000. The Cost of Goods Sold was $900,000.

2. Post the journal entries from (1) above to T-accounts. The following account balances existed at the beginning of March. (The beginning balance in the Refining Department's Work in Process account is given above.)

Raw Materials	$618,000
Work in Process—Blending Department	65,000
Finished Goods	20,000

   After posting the entries to the T-accounts, find the ending balance in the inventory accounts and the manufacturing overhead accounts.

3. Prepare a production report for the Refining Department for March.

P4–25 Weighted Average and Analysis ARB Chemicals Ltd. makes a special type of chemical which has a unique 10-day manufacturing process. ARB is open every day of the year.

At the start of the process 10% of the materials is added. When the process is 35% complete, an additional 30% of the materials is added, another 40% is added when the process is 65% complete, and the rest of the material is added when the process is 95% complete.

Conversion costs are added uniformly throughout the process. However, this chemical requires no indirect labour or indirect materials. ARB uses the weighted-average method to cost units of product. The following selected information is available for July 2001:

Work in Process (WIP) inventory, July 31	
(20% complete as to conversion costs)	15,000 units
Units started during July	57,000 units
Units completed during July	54,000 units
Finished goods inventory. July 31	58,000 units
July 1, WIP inventory (70% complete as to conversion costs)	?

The following T-accounts have partial information for the month of July.

Raw Materials				Work in Process		
July 1	20,000			July 1	62,590*	
July 15	74,000					
July 31	35,000			July 31	12,570	

Wages Payable				Manufacturing Overhead		
July 15	48,000	July 1	48,000	July 1	44,000	
				July 15	76,000	
		July 31	40,000	July 31	58,150	

*Of this amount, Raw Materials was $26,400.

1. How many physical units are in the beginning work in process?
2. What was the production for the month of July in equivalent units for materials and conversion costs?
3. What was the unit cost of goods completed and transferred for the month of July? (Show calculation to three decimal places.) Indicate the materials portion and the conversion cost portion separately, as well as the full unit cost.
4. What is the value of the chemical completed and transferred to Finished Goods? What is the value of Ending Inventory for Direct Materials and Conversion Costs?
5. What was the beginning work in process unit costs of materials?
6. A customer has ordered 60,000 units to be delivered by August 10. Will ARB Chemicals Ltd. be able to accept this order? Show all calculations.

(CGA, adapted)

P4–26 Process Cost; Second Department, and Spoilage (Appendix 4B)

The Mosley Co. Ltd. has two departments and uses a weighted-average process costing system. The following information pertains to department 2 for the month of April 2001.

a. At March 31, 2001, the work in process inventory in department 2 consisted of 6,000 units which were 50% complete and had been charged $56,000 for department 1 costs, and $24,000 for conversion costs in department 2.
b. During April, 22,000 units were received from department 1 at a cost of $224,000.
c. Department 2 costs during April were $24,000 for materials and $156,000 for conversion costs.
d. 16,000 units were completed and transferred to finished goods.
e. At the end of April, 10,000 units were still in process in department 2. They were estimated to be 60% complete.

In department 2, it is expected that 5% of good output will be spoiled. Inspection takes place at the end of the process. Materials are added after inspection in department 2.

Required
1. Prepare the cost of production report for the month of April 2001 for department 2.
2. Was the spoilage in department 2 greater or less than normal? What was its cost to Mosley?
3. How much could Mosley save if it could cut its normal spoilage to 2%?

(CGA, adapted)

P4–27 Second Department: Spoilage (Appendix 4B)

The Larado Company uses a process costing system to account for the costs of three production departments (departments I, II, and III). Department II receives units from department I and applies conversion costs evenly throughout the process. When the units are 90% complete, they are inspected and all materials are then added to the good units.

The following is additional information related to department II for the month of November 2001:

a. Two thousand units were in process at the beginning of November 2001. They were estimated to be 40% complete. Costs associated with these units were as follows:

    Department I costs $10,000
    Department II costs . . . . $ 1,800

b. During November 2001, 35,000 units were received from department I at a cost of $205,000.
c. Actual costs incurred by department II during November 2001 were:

    Materials . . . . $ 12,500
    Conversion costs   105,000

d. During November 2001, 32,000 units were completed and transferred to department III.
e. At the end of November 2001, there were 4,000 units in process, which were estimated to be 70% complete.

Required 1. Prepare a cost of production report for department II for November 2001 using the weighted-average method. *Note*: Calculations of unit costs should be rounded to five decimal places.

2. Explain briefly one major difference between the weighted-average method and the FIFO method. No calculations are required.

3. How much could Larado save if it was able to reduce its spoilage to zero? Would society benefit from such an action?

(CGA, adapted)

P4–28 Process Costing—Second Department: Spoilage (Appendix 4B)

The Nieforth Co. Ltd. operates under a weighted-average process cost system. It has two departments, 1 and 2. In department 2, materials are added at the end of the process, following inspection. Normal spoilage is considered to be 9% of good output. Labour and overhead costs are assumed to apply evenly throughout the process.

Inventory at the beginning of the period was one-half complete; ending inventory is two-thirds complete.

Following are the costs and unit production statistics for the period:

Beginning inventory	2,000 units
Received from department 1	8,000 units
Completed and transferred to	
finished goods storeroom	7,000 units
Ending inventory	1,500 units

Costs	Transferred from Department 1	Materials	Labour	Overhead
Beginning inventory	$ 6,100	—	$ 1,400	$ 550
Current costs	23,900	$7,000	12,000	5,050

Required 1. Prepare a cost of production report for department 2, including the amount to be charged to finished goods, the value of the ending inventory, and the disposition of the cost of spoiled units.

2. If Nieforth could improve processing in department 2 and cut spoilage by 50%, what could it save?

(CGA, adapted)

P4–29 Process Cost and Spoilage Milliners Flour Ltd. operates under a process

cost system for one of its products. In the month of June, 5,676 units were put into production and 5,000 units were completed and transferred out. Inspection occurs when the process is 50% complete, and normal spoilage amounts to 10% *of the good units passed*. The ending work-in-process is 75% complete. There were no beginning inventories and during June $56,760 of direct materials were applied at the beginning of the process and conversion costs of $52,820 were applied evenly during the process. There was no abnormal spoilage during June.

Required Compute the cost of goods completed and the cost of the ending inventory of work in process. Charge the costs of all normal spoilage to all good output.

(CGA, adapted)

Cases

C4–30 Ethics and the Manager Gary Stevens and Mary James are production

managers in the Consumer Electronics Division of General Electronics Company, which has several dozen plants scattered in locations throughout the world. Mary manages the plant located in Toronto, while Gary manages the plant in Calgary. Production managers are paid a salary and get an additional bonus equal to 5% of their base salary if the entire division meets or exceeds its target profits for the year. The bonus is determined in March after the company's annual report has been prepared and issued to shareholders.

Shortly after the beginning of the new year, Mary received a phone call from Gary that went like this:

Gary: How's it going, Mary?

Mary: Fine, Gary. How's it going with you?

Gary: Great! I just got the preliminary profit figures for the division for last year and we are within $200,000 of making the year's target profits. All we have to do is to pull a few strings, and we'll be over the top!

Mary: What do you mean?

Gary: Well, one thing that would be easy to change is your estimate of the percentage completion of your ending work in process inventories.

Mary: I don't know if I can do that, Gary. Those percentage completion figures are supplied by Tom Winthrop, my lead supervisor, who I have always trusted to provide us with good estimates. Besides, I have already sent the percentage completion figures to the corporate headquarters.

Gary: You can always tell them there was a mistake. Think about it, Mary. All of us managers are doing as much as we can to pull this bonus out of the hat. You may not want the bonus cheque, but the rest of us sure could use it.

The final processing department in Mary's production facility began the year with no work in process inventories. During the year, 210,000 units were transferred in from the prior processing department and 200,000 units were completed and sold. Costs transferred in from the prior department totalled $39,375,000. No materials are added in the final processing department. A total of $20,807,500 of conversion cost was incurred in the final processing department during the year.

Required

1. Tom Winthrop estimated that the units in ending inventory in the final processing department were 30% complete with respect to the conversion costs of the final processing department. If this estimate of the percentage completion is used, what would be the Cost of Goods Sold for the year?
2. Does Gary Stevens want the estimated percentage completion to be increased or decreased? Explain why.
3. What percentage completion would result in increasing reported net income by $200,000 over the net income that would be reported if the 30% figure were used?
4. Do you think Mary James should go along with the request to alter estimates of the percentage completion?

C4–31 Weighted-Average Method; Production Report: Second Department "I think we goofed when we hired that new assistant controller," said Ruth Scarpino, president of Provost Industries. "Just look at this production report that he prepared for last month for the Finishing Department. I can't make heads or tails out of it."

Finishing Department costs:	
Work in process inventory, April 1, 450 units; 100% complete as to materials; 60% complete as to conversion costs	$ 8,208*
Costs transferred in during the month from the preceding department, 1,950 units	17,940
Materials cost added during the month (materials are added when processing is 50% complete in the Finishing Department)	6,210
Conversion costs incurred during the month	13,920
Total departmental costs	$46,278

Finishing Department costs assigned to:	
Units completed and transferred to finished goods, 1,800 units at $25.71 per unit	$46,278
Work in process inventory, April 30, 600 units; 0% complete as to materials; 35% complete as to processing	–0–
Total departmental costs assigned	$46,278

*Consists of: cost transferred in, $4,068; materials cost, $1,980; and conversion cost, $2,160.

"He's struggling to learn our system," replied Frank Harrop, the operations manager. "The problem is that he's been away from process costing for a long time, and it's coming back slowly."

"It's not just the format of his report that I'm concerned about. Look at that $25.71 unit cost that he's come up with for April. Doesn't that seem high to you?" said Ms. Scarpino.

"Yes, it does seem high; but on the other hand, I know we had an increase in materials prices during April, and that may be the explanation," replied Mr. Harrop. "I'll get someone else to redo this report and then we may be able to see what's going on."

Provost Industries manufactures a ceramic product that goes through two processing departments—Molding and Finishing. The company uses the weighted-average method to account for units and costs.

Required

1. Prepare a revised production report for the Finishing Department.
2. Explain to the president why the unit cost on the new assistant controller's report is so high.

C4–32 FIFO Method; Production Report: Second Department

(Appendix 4A) Refer to the data for Provost Industries in the preceding case. Assume that the company uses the FIFO method to account for units and costs.

Required

1. Prepare a production report for the Finishing Department for April.
2. As stated in the case, the company experienced an increase in materials prices during April. Would the effects of this price increase tend to show up more under the weighted-average method or under the FIFO method? Why?

Group Exercises

GE4–33 Operation Costing
Operation costing combines characteristics of both job-order costing and process costing. It is used in those situations where the products have some common characteristics and also some individual characteristics. Examples of industries where operation costing may be appropriate include shoes, clothing, jewellery, and semiconductors.

Required

Select one of the above products and research how the product is made. Construct a flowchart of the production process. Indicate which steps in the production process would use job-order costing and which steps would use process costing.

IE4–34 Choice of Costing System
The web sites of a number of companies are listed below.

Required

Indicate whether company would be more likely to use job-order costing or process costing. In each case explain why.

1. Alliance Atlantis Commuinications at www.alliance.ca.
2. The Thompson Corporation at www.thomcorp.com.
3. The Seagram Company at www.seagram.com.
4. George Weston Limited at www.weston.ca.
5. Lantic Sugar at www.lantics@nbet.nb.ca.
6. Evian at www.evian.com.

Chapter Five

Cost Behaviour: Analysis and Use

Business Focus

Alicia was recently promoted to be the manager of Cumberland County Prenatal Care Clinic. Although Alicia enjoyed her work, she was frustrated by the fixed budget provided by the county. Alicia was positive that many more low-income expectant mothers could benefit from the clinic's services if a way could be found to provide additional financing.

After contacting a number of philanthropic foundations, Alicia found an interested donor. The donor expressed interest in funding some of the costs of new patients, but he did not want to pay any of the costs of existing patients whose costs were already covered by the county. Also, the donor stipulated that he would only be willing to pay the additional

(i.e., variable) costs that the clinic would incur to serve new patients. He would not pay any additional fixed costs, which he also felt were the responsibility of the county. Alicia immediately agreed to this offer, but as soon as she left the donor's home, she began to wonder how she would determine the fixed and variable costs of the clinic.

Learning Objectives

After studying Chapter 5 you should be able to:

1 Explain the effect of a change in activity on both total variable costs and per unit variable costs.

2 Explain the effect of a change in activity on both total fixed costs and fixed costs expressed on a per unit basis.

3 Use a cost formula to predict costs at a new level of activity.

4 Analyze a mixed cost using the high-low method.

5 Analyze a mixed cost using the scattergraph method.

6 Explain the least-squares regression method of analyzing a mixed cost.

7 Prepare an income statement using the contribution format.

8 (Appendix 5A) Analyze a mixed cost using the least-squares regression method.

In our discussion of cost terms and concepts in Chapter 2, we stated that one way in which costs can be classified is by behaviour. We defined cost behaviour as meaning how a cost will react or change as changes take place in the level of business activity. An understanding of cost behaviour is the key to many decisions in an organization. Managers who understand how costs behave are better able to predict what costs will be under various operating circumstances. Attempts at decision making without a thorough understanding of the costs involved— and how these costs may change with the activity level—can lead to disaster. For example, a decision to drop a particular product line might result in far less cost savings than managers had assumed—leading to a decline in profits. To avoid such problems, a manager must be able to accurately predict what costs will be at various activity levels. In this chapter, we shall find that the key to effective cost prediction lies in understanding cost behaviour patterns.

We briefly review in this chapter the definitions of variable costs and fixed costs and then discuss the behaviour of these costs in greater depth than we were able to do in Chapter 2. After this review and discussion, we turn our attention to the analysis of mixed costs. We conclude the chapter by introducing a new income statement format—called the contribution format—in which costs are organized by behaviour rather than by the traditional functions of production, sales, and administration.

Types of Cost Behaviour Patterns

In our brief discussion of cost behaviour in Chapter 2, we mentioned only variable and fixed costs. There is a third behaviour pattern, generally known as a *mixed* or *semivariable* cost. All three cost behaviour patterns—variable, fixed, and mixed—are found in most organizations. The relative proportion of each type of cost present in a firm is known as the firm's **cost structure.** For example, a firm might have many fixed costs but few variable or mixed costs. Alternatively, it might have many variable costs but few fixed or mixed costs. A firm's cost structure can have a significant impact on decisions. We must reserve a detailed discussion of cost structure until the next chapter, however, and concentrate for the moment on gaining a fuller understanding of the behaviour of each type of cost.

Cost structure The relative proportion of fixed, variable, and mixed costs found within an organization.

Variable Costs

Objective 1

Explain the effect of a change in activity on both total variable costs and per unit variable costs.

We found in Chapter 2 that a variable cost is a cost whose total dollar amount varies in direct proportion to changes in the activity level. If the activity level doubles, the total dollar amount of the variable costs also doubles. If the activity level increases by only 10%, then the total dollar amount of the variable costs increases by 10% as well.

We also found in Chapter 2 that a variable cost remains constant if expressed on a *per unit* basis. To provide an example, consider Nooksack Expeditions, a small company that provides daylong whitewater rafting excursions on rivers in Northern B.C. Mountains. The company provides all of the necessary equipment and experienced guides, and it serves gourmet meals to its guests. The meals are purchased from an exclusive caterer for $30 a person for a daylong excursion. If we look at the cost of the meals on a *per person* basis, the cost remains constant at $30. This $30 cost per person will not change, regardless of how many people participate in a daylong excursion. The behaviour of this variable cost, on both a per unit and a total basis, is tabulated on the next page:

Number of Guests	Cost of Meals per Guest	Total Cost of Meals
250	$30	$ 7,500
500	30	15,000
750	30	22,500
1,000	30	30,000

The idea that a variable cost is constant per unit but varies in total with the activity level is crucial to an understanding of cost behaviour patterns. We shall rely on this concept again and again in this chapter and in chapters ahead.

Exhibit 5–1 provides a graphic illustration of variable cost behaviour. Note that the graph of the total cost of the meals slants upward to the right. This is because the total cost of the meals is directly proportional to the number of guests. In contrast, the graph of the per unit cost of meals is flat. This is because the cost of the meals per guest is constant at $30 per guest.

THE ACTIVITY BASE   For a cost to be variable, it must be variable *with respect to something*. That "something" is its *activity base*. An **activity base** is a measure of whatever causes the incurrence of variable cost. In Chapter 3, we mentioned that an activity base is sometimes referred to as a *cost driver*. Some of the most common activity bases are direct labour-hours, machine-hours, units produced, and units sold. Other activity bases (cost drivers) might include the number of kilometres driven by salespersons, the number of kilograms of laundry processed by a hotel, the number of letters typed by a secretary, and the number of occupied beds in a hospital.

To plan and control variable costs, a manager must be well acquainted with the various activity bases within the firm. People sometimes get the notion that if a cost doesn't vary with production or with sales, then it is not really a variable cost. This is not correct. As suggested by the range of bases listed above, costs are caused by many different activities within an organization. Whether a cost is considered to be variable depends on whether it is caused by the activity under consideration. For example, if a manager is analyzing the cost of service calls under a product warranty, the

Activity base   A measure of whatever causes the incurrence of a variable cost. For example, the total cost of X-ray film in a hospital will increase as the number of X rays taken increases. Therefore, the number of X rays is an activity base for explaining the total cost of X-ray film.

Exhibit 5–1   Variable Cost Behaviour

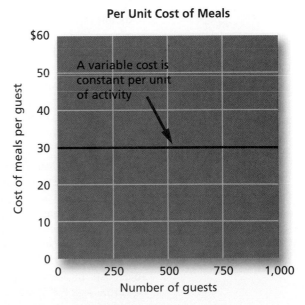

Exhibit 5–2   Examples
of Variable Costs

Type of Organization	Costs That Are Normally Variable With Respect to Volume of Output
Merchandising company	Cost of goods (merchandise) sold

Manufacturing company	Manufacturing costs:
	    Direct materials
	    Direct labour*
	Variable portion of manufacturing overhead:
	    Indirect materials
	    Lubricants
	    Supplies
	    Power

Both merchandising and manufacturing companies	Selling, general, and administrative costs:
	    Commissions
	    Clerical costs, such as invoicing
	    Shipping costs

Service organizations	Supplies, travel clerical

*Direct labour may or may not be variable in practice. See the discussion later in this chapter.

relevant activity measure will be the number of service calls made. Those costs that vary in total with the number of service calls made are the variable costs of making service calls.

Nevertheless, unless stated otherwise, you can assume that the activity base under consideration is the total volume of goods and services provided by the organization. So, for example, if we ask whether direct materials at, Ford Canada is a variable cost, the answer is yes, since the cost of direct materials is variable with respect to Ford's total volume of output. We will specify the activity base only when it is something other than total output.

EXTENT OF VARIABLE COSTS   The number and type of variable costs present in an organization will depend in large part on the organization's structure and purpose. A public utility like Nova Scotia Power, with large investments in equipment, will tend to have few variable costs. Most of the costs are associated with its plant, and these costs tend to be insensitive to changes in levels of service provided. A manufacturing company like Rocky Mountain Bicycle of British Columbia, by contrast, will often have many variable costs; these costs will be associated with both the manufacture and distribution of its products to customers.

A merchandising company like Canadian Tire or Atlantic Superstore will usually have a high proportion of variable costs in its cost structure. In most merchandising companies, the cost of merchandise purchased for resale, a variable cost, constitutes a very large component of total cost. Service companies, by contrast, have diverse cost structures. Some service companies, such as the Tim Hortons Donuts restaurant chain, have fairly large variable costs because of the costs of their raw materials. On the other hand, service companies involved in consulting, auditing, engineering, dental, medical, and architectural activities have very large fixed costs in the form of expensive facilities and highly trained salaried employees.

Some of the more frequently encountered variable costs are listed in Exhibit 5–2. This exhibit is not a complete listing of all costs that can be considered variable. Moreover, some of the costs listed in the exhibit may behave more like fixed than variable costs in some firms. We will see some examples of this later in the chapter. Nevertheless, Exhibit 5–2 provides a useful listing of many of the costs that normally would be considered variable with respect to the volume of output.

Exhibit 5–3 True Variable versus Step-Variable Costs

Direct Materials (true variable)   Maintenance Help (step variable)

Cost / Volume   Cost / Volume

True Variable versus Step-Variable Costs

Not all variable costs have exactly the same behaviour pattern. Some variable costs behave in a *true variable* or *proportionately variable* pattern. Other variable costs behave in a *step-variable* pattern.

TRUE VARIABLE COSTS   Direct materials is a true or proportionately variable cost because the amount used during a period will vary in direct proportion to the level of production activity. Moreover, any amounts purchased but not used can be stored and carried forward to the next period as inventory.

STEP-VARIABLE COSTS   The wages of maintenance workers are often considered to be a variable cost, but this labour cost doesn't behave in quite the same way as the cost of direct materials. Unlike direct materials, the time of maintenance workers is obtainable only in large chunks. Moreover, any maintenance time not utilized cannot be stored as inventory and carried forward to the next period. If the time is not used effectively, it is gone forever. Furthermore, a maintenance crew can work at a fairly leisurely pace if pressures are light but intensify its efforts if pressures build up. For this reason, somewhat small changes in the level of production may have no effect on the number of maintenance people needed to properly carry on maintenance work.

Step-variable cost   A cost (such as the cost of a maintenance worker) that is obtainable only in large chunks and that increases and decreases only in response to fairly wide changes in the activity level.

A cost that is obtainable only in large chunks (such as the labour cost of maintenance workers) and that increases or decreases only in response to fairly wide changes in the activity level is known as a **step-variable cost.** The behaviour of a step-variable cost, contrasted with the behaviour of a true variable cost, is illustrated in Exhibit 5–3.

Notice that the need for maintenance help changes only with fairly wide changes in volume and that when additional maintenance time is obtained, it comes in large, indivisible chunks. The strategy of management in dealing with step-variable costs must be to obtain the fullest use of services possible for each separate step. Great care must be taken in working with these kinds of costs to prevent "fat" from building up in an organization. There may be a tendency to employ additional help more quickly than needed, and there is a natural reluctance to lay people off when volume declines.

The Linearity Assumption and the Relevant Range

Curvilinear costs   A relationship between cost and activity that is a curve rather than a straight line.

In dealing with variable costs, we have assumed a strictly linear relationship between cost and volume, except in the case of step-variable costs. Economists correctly point out that many costs that the accountant classifies as variable actually behave in a *curvilinear* fashion. The behaviour of a **curvilinear cost** is shown in Exhibit 5–4.

Exhibit 5–4
Curvilinear Costs and the
Relevant Range

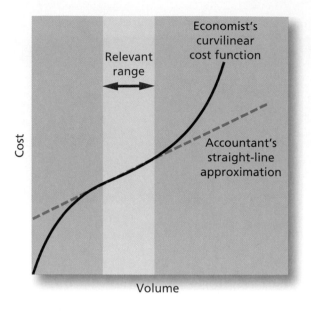

Relevant range   The
range of activity within
which assumptions about
variable and fixed cost
behaviour are valid.

Although many costs are not strictly linear when plotted as a function of volume, a curvilinear cost can be satisfactorily approximated with a straight line within a narrow band of activity known as the *relevant range*. The **relevant range** is that range of activity within which the assumptions made about cost behaviour by the manager are valid. For example, note that the dashed line in Exhibit 5–4 can be used as an approximation to the curvilinear cost with very little loss of accuracy within the shaded relevant range. However, outside of the relevant range this particular straight line is a poor approximation to the curvilinear cost relationship. Managers should always keep in mind that a particular assumption made about cost behaviour may be very inappropriate if activity falls outside of the relevant range.

Fixed Costs

Objective 2

Explain the effect of
a change in activity
on both total fixed
costs and fixed costs
expressed on a per
unit basis.

In our discussion of cost behaviour patterns in Chapter 2, we stated that fixed costs remain constant in total dollar amount within the relevant range of activity. To continue the Nooksack Expeditions example, assume the company decides to rent a building for $500 per month to store its equipment. The *total* amount of rent paid is the same regardless of the number of guests the company takes on its expeditions during any given month. This cost behaviour pattern is shown graphically in Exhibit 5–5.

Since fixed costs remain constant in total, the amount of fixed cost computed on a *per unit* basis becomes progressively smaller as the level of activity increases. If Nooksack Expeditions has only 250 guests in a month, the $500 fixed rental cost would amount to $2 per guest. If there are 1,000 guests, the fixed rental cost would amount to only 50 cents per guest. This aspect of the behaviour of fixed costs is also displayed in Exhibit 5–5. Note that as the number of guests increases, the average unit cost drops, but it drops at a decreasing rate. The first guests have the biggest impact on unit costs.

As we noted in Chapter 2, this aspect of fixed costs can be confusing, although it is necessary in some contexts to express fixed costs on an average per unit basis. We found in Chapter 3, for example, that a broad unit cost figure containing both variable and fixed cost elements is used in *external* financial statements. For *internal* uses, however, fixed costs should not be expressed on a per unit basis because of the potential confusion. Experience has shown that for internal uses, fixed costs are most easily (and most safely) dealt with on a total basis rather than on a per unit basis.

Exhibit 5–5   Fixed Cost Behaviour

Total Fixed Cost of Renting the Building

Fixed costs remain constant in total dollar amount through wide ranges of activity.

Cost of building rental } $500

Number of guests

Per Unit Fixed Cost of Renting the Building

Fixed costs decrease on a per unit basis as the activity level increases.

Number of guests

Focus on Current Practice

Airlines have long recognized that once a flight is scheduled, the variable cost of filling a seat with a passenger is very small. The costs of the cockpit flight crew, fuel, gate rentals, maintenance, aircraft depreciation, and so on, are all basically fixed with respect to the number of passengers who actually take a particular flight. The cost of the cabin flight crew is a step-variable cost—the number of flight attendants assigned to a flight will vary with the number of passengers on the flight. The only true variable costs are the costs of meals and an almost inconsequential increase in fuel consumption. Therefore, adding one passenger to a flight brings in additional revenue but has very little effect on total cost. Consequently, airlines have been stuffing more and more seats into their aircraft. Boeing 747s were configured originally with 9 seats across a row, but now they frequently have 10. One major airline has raised the number of seats in its fleet of DC-10 planes from 232 to nearly 300.[1] ■

Types of Fixed Costs

Fixed costs are sometimes referred to as a capacity costs, since they result from outlays made for buildings, equipment, skilled professional employees, and other items needed to provide the basic capacity for sustained operations. For planning purposes, fixed costs can be viewed as being either *committed* or *discretionary*.

Committed fixed costs
Those fixed costs that are difficult to adjust and that relate to the investment in facilities, equipment, and the basic organizational structure of a firm.

COMMITTED FIXED COSTS   **Committed fixed costs** relate to the investment in facilities, equipment, and the basic organizational structure of a firm. Examples of such costs include depreciation of buildings and equipment, taxes on real estate, insurance, and salaries of top management and operating personnel.

The two key factors about committed fixed costs are that (1) they are long term in nature, and (2) they cannot be reduced to zero even for short periods of time

---

1. Michael J. McCarthy, "Airline Squeeze Play: More Seats, Less Legroom," *The Wall Street Journal*, April 18, 1994, pp. B1 and B6.

without seriously impairing the profitability or long-run goals of the organization. Even if operations are interrupted or cut back, the committed fixed costs will still continue largely unchanged. During a recession, for example, a firm will not usually discharge key executives or sell off key facilities. The basic organizational structure and facilities ordinarily are kept intact. The costs of restoring them later are likely to be far greater than any short-run savings that might be realized.

Since it is difficult to change a committed fixed cost once the commitment has been made, management should approach these decisions with particular care. Decisions to acquire major equipment or to take on other committed fixed costs involve a long planning horizon. Management should make such commitments only after careful analysis of the available alternatives. Once a decision is made to build a certain size facility, a firm becomes locked into that decision for many years to come. Decisions relating to committed fixed costs will be examined in Chapters 14 and 15.

While not much can be done about committed fixed costs in the short run, management is generally very concerned about how these resources are *utilized*. The strategy of management must be to utilize the capacity of the organization as effectively as possible.

Discretionary fixed costs
Those fixed costs that arise from annual decisions by management to spend in certain fixed cost areas, such as advertising and research.

DISCRETIONARY FIXED COSTS   **Discretionary fixed costs** (often referred to as *managed fixed costs*) usually arise from *annual* decisions by management to spend in certain fixed cost areas. Examples of discretionary fixed costs include advertising, research, public relations, management development programs, and internships for students.

Basically, two key differences exist between discretionary fixed costs and committed fixed costs. First, the planning horizon for a discretionary fixed cost is fairly short term—usually a single year. By contrast, as we indicated earlier, committed fixed costs have a planning horizon that encompasses many years. Second, discretionary fixed costs can be cut for short periods of time with minimal damage to the long-run goals of the organization. For example, a firm that has been spending $50,000 annually on management development programs may be forced because of poor economic conditions to reduce its spending in that area during a given year. Although some unfavourable consequences may result from the cutback, it is doubtful that these consequences would be as great as those that would result if the company decided to economize during the year by laying off key personnel.

Whether a particular cost is regarded as committed or discretionary may depend on management's strategy. For example, during recessions when the level of home building is down, many construction companies lay off most of their workers and virtually disband operations. Other construction companies retain large numbers of employees on the payroll, even though the workers have little or no work to do. While these latter companies may be faced with short-term cash flow problems, it will be easier for them to respond quickly when economic conditions improve. And the higher morale and loyalty of their employees may give these companies a significant competitive advantage.

The most important characteristic of discretionary fixed costs is that management is not locked into a decision regarding such costs. They can be adjusted from year to year or even perhaps during the course of a year if circumstances demand such a modification.

THE TREND TOWARD FIXED COSTS   The trend in many companies is toward greater fixed costs relative to variable costs. Chores that used to be performed by hand have been taken over by machines. For example, grocery clerks at Loblaws and

Sobeys used to key in prices by hand on cash registers. Now, most stores are equipped with bar code readers that enter price and other product information automatically. In general, competition has created pressure to give customers more value for their money—a demand that often can only be satisfied by automating business processes. For example, a Collins Barrow employee used to fill out tax returns for customers largely by hand and the advice given to a customer largely depended on the knowledge of that particular employee. Now, sophisticated computer software is used to complete tax returns, and the software provides the customer with tax planning and other advice tailored to the customer's needs based on the accumulated knowledge of many experts.

As machines take over more and more of the tasks that were performed by humans, the overall demand for human workers has not diminished. The demand for "knowledge" workers—those who work primarily with their minds rather than their muscles—has grown tremendously. And knowledge workers tend to be salaried, highly trained, and difficult to replace. As a consequence, the costs of compensating knowledge workers are often relatively fixed and are committed rather than discretionary costs.

IS LABOUR A VARIABLE OR A FIXED COST? As the preceding discussion suggests, wages and salaries may be fixed or variable. The accompanying Focus on Current Practice boxes illustrate that the behaviour of wage and salary costs will differ from one country to another, depending on labour regulations, labour contracts, and custom. In some countries, such as France, Germany, China, and Japan, management has little flexibility in adjusting the labour force to changes in business activity. In countries such as Canada and the United Kingdom, management typically has much greater latitude. However, even in these less restrictive environments, managers may choose to treat employee compensation as a fixed cost for several reasons.

First, companies have become much more reluctant to adjust the workforce in response to short-term fluctuations in sales. Most companies realize that their employees are a very valuable asset. More and more, highly skilled and trained employees are required to run a successful business, and these workers are not easy to replace. Trained workers who are laid off may never return, and layoffs undermine the morale of those workers who remain.

In addition, managers do not want to be caught with a bloated payroll in an economic downturn. Therefore, there is an increased reluctance to add workers when sales activity picks up. Many companies are turning to temporary and part-time workers to take up the slack when their permanent, full-time employees are unable to handle all of the demand for the company's products and services. In such companies, labour costs are a curious mixture of fixed and variable costs.

Many major companies have undergone waves of downsizing in recent years in which large numbers of employees—particularly middle managers—have lost their jobs. It may seem that this downsizing proves that even management salaries should be regarded as variable costs, but this would not be a valid conclusion. Downsizing has been the result of attempts to reengineer business processes and cut costs rather than a response to a decline in sales activity. This underscores an important, but subtle, point. Fixed costs can change—they just do not change in response to small changes in activity.

In sum, we cannot provide a clear-cut answer to the question "Is labour a variable or fixed cost?" It depends on how much flexibility management has and management's strategy. Nevertheless, we will assume in this text that, unless otherwise stated, direct labour is a variable cost. This assumption is more likely to be valid for companies in Canada than in countries where employment laws permit much less flexibility.

Focus on Current Practice

Reducing a company's workforce can be very expensive. In 1993, IBM decided to trim at least 25,000 people from its worldwide workforce of 300,000. To minimize the negative impact on morale of such a reduction, the company provided financial incentives to induce employees to depart voluntarily. The company offered up to half a year of salary and paid medical coverage for departing employees. The cost of the program averaged $120,000 per departing employee and totalled $3 billion.[2] ■

Focus on Current Practice

The labour laws in the country in which the company operates often affect whether employee staff costs are fixed or variable. In Europe, banks have historically had very large numbers of branches, some of which serve very small villages. These branches are expensive to staff and maintain, and banks have argued that they are a drain on profits. In Denmark and the United Kingdom, the number of branches were cut by 34% and 22%, respectively, over a span of 10 years. In both cases, this led to a 15% reduction in staff employees. In contrast, countries with more restrictive labour laws that make it difficult to lay off workers have been unable to reduce staff or the number of branches significantly. For example, in Germany the number of branches was reduced by only 2% and the number of staff by only two-tenths of a percent during the same period.[3] ■

Focus on Current Practice

Japanese law makes it difficult to lay off or fire workers or to hire away employees from competitors. Exemptions may be granted to the no-layoff rule—particularly for small companies—but this rule effectively ties an employee to a single company for life. As a result, labour is commonly regarded as a fixed cost in Japan. This reduces the ability of Japanese companies to adjust costs in response to peaks and valley in the business cycle, but there are advantages to this system. "Since Japanese workers enjoy lifetime job guarantees, they see no downside risk in helping employers improve productivity. In fact, they embrace new technology because they know it will enhance their company's future and their own jobs."[4]

There is another advantage to Japan's lifetime employment system. The really critical business assets are often people. In North America, key employees can easily be hired away by a competitor—taking with them investments in training and their knowledge about the company's innovations and plans. In contrast, the difficulty of hiring a competitor's employees in Japan safeguards those assets and arguably makes Japanese companies more willing to invest in training and in research and development.

2. Laurence Hooper, "IBM Will Cut Back Payments, Benefits for Voluntary Departures and Layoffs," *The Wall Street Journal*, April 5, 1993, p. A3.
3. Charles Fleming, "Kinder Cuts: Continental Banks Seek to Expand Their Way Out of Retail Trouble," *The Wall Street Journal Europe*, March 11, 1997, pp. 1 and 8.
4. Eamonn Fingleton, "Jobs for Life: Why Japan Won't Give Them Up," *Fortune* (March 20, 1995), pp.119–25.

There is an important shock absorber in the Japanese employment system. As much as 40% of workers' compensation is in the form of discre-tionary bonuses. If a company is doing poorly, these bonuses can be reduced or omitted. ■

Fixed Costs and the Relevant Range

The concept of the relevant range, which was introduced in the discussion of variable costs, is also important in understanding fixed costs—particularly discretionary fixed costs. The levels of discretionary fixed costs are typically decided at the beginning of the year and depend on the support needs of the planned programs such as advertising and training. The scope of these programs will depend, in turn, on the overall antici-pated level of activity for the year. At very high levels of activity, programs are usually broadened or expanded. For example, if the company hopes to increase sales by 25%, it would probably plan for much larger advertising costs than if no sales increase was planned. So the *planned* level of activity may affect total discretionary fixed costs. However, once the total discretionary fixed costs have been budgeted, they are unaf-fected by the *actual* level of activity. For example, once the advertising budget has been decided on and has been spent, it will not be affected by how many units are actu-ally sold. Therefore, the cost is fixed with respect to the *actual* number of units sold.

Discretionary fixed costs are easier to adjust than committed fixed costs. They also tend to be less "lumpy." Committed fixed costs tend to consist of costs of buildings, equipment, and the salaries of key personnel. It is difficult to buy half a piece of equip-ment or to hire a quarter of a product-line manager, so the step pattern depicted in Exhibit 5–6 is typical for such costs. The relevant range of activity for a fixed cost is the range of activity over which the graph of the cost is flat as in Exhibit 5–6. As a company expands its level of activity, it may outgrow its present facilities, or the key management team may need to be expanded. The result, of course, will be increased committed fixed costs as larger facilities are built and as new management positions are created.

One reaction to the step pattern depicted in Exhibit 5–6 is to say that discre-tionary and committed fixed costs are really just step-variable costs. To some extent this is true, since almost *all* costs can be adjusted in the long run. There are two major

Exhibit 5–6 Fixed Costs and the Relevant Range

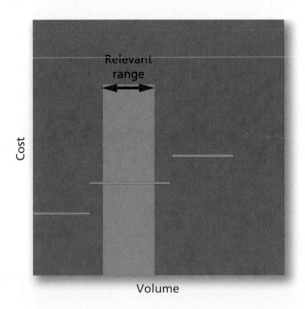

differences, however, between the step-variable costs depicted earlier in Exhibit 5–3 and the fixed costs depicted in Exhibit 5–6.

The first difference is that the step-variable costs can often be adjusted quickly as conditions change, whereas once fixed costs have been set, they often cannot be changed easily. A step-variable cost such as maintenance labour, for example, can be adjusted upward or downward by hiring and laying off maintenance workers. By contrast, once a company has signed a lease for a building, it is locked into that level of lease cost for the life of the contract.

The second difference is that the *width of the steps* depicted for step-variable costs is much narrower than the width of the steps depicted for the fixed costs in Exhibit 5–6. The width of the steps relates to volume or level of activity. For step-variable costs, the width of a step may be 40 hours of activity or less if one is dealing, for example, with maintenance labour cost. For fixed costs, however, the width of a step may be *thousands* or even *tens of thousands* of hours of activity. In essence, the width of the steps for step-variable costs is generally so narrow that these costs can be treated essentially as variable costs for most purposes. The width of the steps for fixed costs, on the other hand, is so wide that these costs must generally be treated as being entirely fixed within the relevant range.

Focus on Current Practice

Superior Quality Workforce
- Canada puts priority on developing knowledge workers—ranked first in G-7, according to the Global Competitiveness Report (1996).
- We have:
  - the highest rate of post-secondary enrollment in the world;
  - highest level of computer literacy among employees in the G-7; and
  - more computers per capita in Canada than in any other G-7 country, except the U.S. ■

Knowledge Workers—World Rank*

*Standing among the 49 countries considered in the Global Competitiveness Report, 1996

Mixed Costs

Mixed cost A cost that contains both variable and fixed cost elements.

A **mixed cost** is one that contains both variable and fixed cost elements. Mixed costs are also known as semivariable costs. To continue the Nooksack Expeditions example, the company must pay a licence fee of $25,000 per year plus $3 per rafting party to the province's Department of Natural Resources. If the company runs 1,000 rafting parties this year, then the total fees paid to the province would be $28,000, made up of

Exhibit 5–7 Mixed
Cost Behaviour

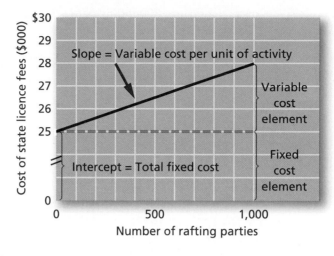

$25,000 in fixed cost plus $3,000 in variable cost. The behaviour of this mixed cost is shown graphically in Exhibit 5–7.

Even if Nooksack fails to attract any customers and there are no rafting parties, the company will still have to pay the licence fee of $25,000. This is why the cost line in Exhibit 5–7 intersects the vertical cost axis at the $25,000 point. For each rafting party the company organizes, the total cost of the state fees will increase by $3. Therefore, the total cost line slopes upward as the variable cost element is added to the fixed cost element.

Since the mixed cost in Exhibit 5–7 is represented by a straight line, the following equation for a straight line can be used to express the relationship between mixed cost and the level of activity:

$$Y = a + bX$$

In this equation,

Y = The total mixed cost
a = The total fixed cost (the vertical intercept of the line)
b = The variable cost per unit of activity (the slope of the line)
X = The level of activity

In the case of the provincial fees paid by Nooksack Expeditions, the equation is written as follows:

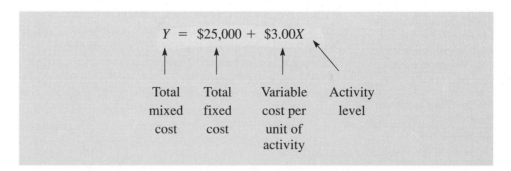

This equation makes it very easy to calculate what the total mixed cost would be for any level of activity within the relevant range. For example, suppose that the company

Objective 3

Use a cost formula to predict costs at a new level of activity.

expects to organize 800 rafting parties in the next year. Then the total provincial fees would be $27,400 calculated as follows:

$$Y = \$25,000 + (\$3.00 \times 800 \text{ rafting parties})$$
$$= \$27,400$$

Focus on Current Practice

A total of 257 American and 40 Japanese manufacturing firms responded to a questionnaire concerning their management accounting practices.[5] Among other things, the firms were asked whether they classified certain costs as variable, semivariable, or fixed. Some of the results are summarized in Exhibit 5–8. Note that firms do not all classify costs in the same way. For example, roughly 45% of the U.S. firms classify materials-handling labour costs as variable, 35% as semivariable, and 20% as fixed. Also note that the Japanese firms are much more likely than U.S. firms to classify labour costs as fixed. ■

The Analysis of Mixed Costs

Account analysis A method for analyzing cost behaviour in which each account under consideration is classified as either variable or fixed based on the analyst's prior knowledge of how the cost in the account behaves.

Engineering approach A detailed analysis of cost behaviour based on an industrial engineer's evaluation of the inputs that are required to carry out a particular activity and of the prices of those inputs.

In practice, mixed costs are very common. For example, the cost of providing X-ray services to patients at the Queen Elizabeth Hospital is a mixed cost. There are substantial fixed costs for equipment depreciation and for salaries for radiologists and technicians, but there are also variable costs for X-ray film, power, and supplies. At Air Canada, maintenance costs are mixed cost. The company must incur fixed costs for renting maintenance facilities and for keeping skilled mechanics on the payroll, but the costs of replacement parts, lubricating oils, tires, and so forth, are variable with respect to how often and how far the company's aircraft are flown.

The fixed portion of a mixed cost represents the basic, minimum cost of just having a service *ready and available* for use. The variable portion represents the cost incurred for *actual consumption* of the service. The variable element varies in proportion to the amount of service that is consumed.

How does management go about actually estimating the fixed and variable components of a mixed cost? The most common methods used in practice are *account analysis* and the *engineering approach*. These methods are used most often in later chapters of this text.

In **account analysis,** each account under consideration is classified as either variable or fixed based on the analyst's prior knowledge of how the cost in the account behaves. For example, direct materials would be classified as variable and a building lease cost would be classified as fixed because of the nature of those costs. The total fixed cost is the sum of the costs for the accounts that have been classified as fixed. The variable cost per unit is estimated by dividing the sum of the costs for the accounts that have been classified as variable by the total activity.

The **engineering approach** to cost analysis involves a detailed analysis of what cost behaviour should be, based on an industrial engineer's evaluation of the production

5. NAA Tokyo Affiliate, "Management Accounting in the Advanced Management Surrounding—Comparative Study on Survey in Japan and U.S.A.," October 1988.

Exhibit 5–8
Percentages of Firms Classifying Specific Costs as Variable, Semivariable, or Fixed

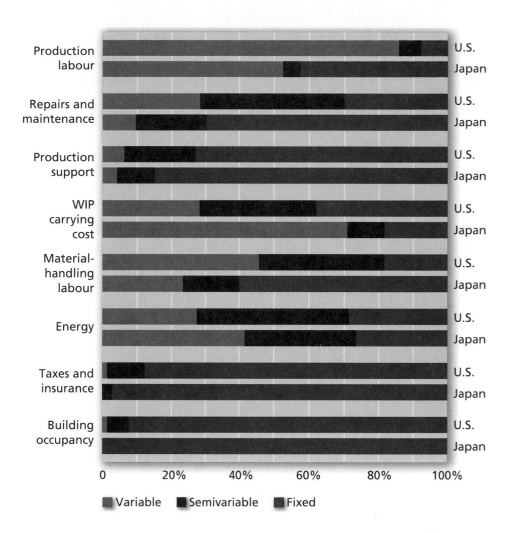

methods to be used, the materials specifications, labour requirements, equipment usage, efficiency of production, power consumption, and so on. For example, Pizza Hut might use the engineering approach to estimate the cost of serving a particular take-out pizza. The cost of the pizza would be estimated by carefully costing the specific ingredients used to make the pizza, the power consumed to cook the pizza, and the cost of the container the pizza is delivered in. The engineering approach must be used in those situations where no past experience is available concerning activity and costs. In addition, it is sometimes used together with other methods to improve the accuracy of cost analysis.

Account analysis works best when analyzing costs at a fairly aggregated level, such as the cost of serving patients in the emergency room (ER) of Victoria General Hospital. The costs of drugs, supplies, forms, wages, equipment, and so on, can be roughly classified as variable or fixed and a mixed cost formula for the overall cost of the emergency room can be estimated fairly quickly. However, this method glosses over the fact that some of the accounts may have elements of both fixed and variable costs. For example, the cost of electricity for the ER is a mixed cost. Most of the electricity is used for heating and lighting and is a fixed cost. However, the consumption of electricity increases with activity in the ER since diagnostic equipment, operating theatre lights, defibrillators, and so on, all consume electricity. The most effective way to estimate the fixed and variable elements of such a mixed cost may be to analyze past records of cost and activity data. These records should reveal whether electrical costs vary significantly with the number of patients and if so, by how much. The remainder of this section will be concerned with how to conduct such an analysis of past cost and activity data.

Managerial Accounting in Action

THE ISSUE

BRENTLINE HOSPITAL

Dr. Derek Chalmers, the chief executive officer of Brentline Hospital, motioned Kinh Nguyen, the chief financial officer of the hospital, into his office.

Derek: Kinh, come on in.

Kinh: What can I do for you?

Derek: Well for one, could you get the government to rescind the bookcase full of regulations against the wall over there?

Kinh: Sorry, that's a bit beyond my authority.

Derek: Just wishing, Kinh. Actually, I wanted to talk to you about our maintenance expenses. I didn't used to have to pay attention to such things, but these expenses seem to be bouncing around a lot. Over the last half year or so they have been as low as $7,400 and as high as $9,800 per month.

Kinh: Actually, that's a pretty normal variation in those expenses.

Derek: Well, we budgeted a constant $8,400 a month. Can't we do a better job of predicting what these costs are going to be? And how do we know when we've spent too much in a month? Shouldn't there be some explanation for these variations?

Kinh: Now that you mention it, we are in the process right now of tightening up our budgeting process. Our first step is to break all of our costs down into fixed and variable components.

Derek: How will that help?

Kinh: Well, that will permit us to predict what the level of costs will be. Some costs are fixed and shouldn't change much. Other costs go up and down as our activity goes up and down. The trick is to figure out what is driving the variable component of the costs.

Derek: What about the maintenance costs?

Kinh: My guess is that the variations in maintenance costs are being driven by our overall level of activity. When we treat more patients, our equipment is used more intensively, which leads to more maintenance expense.

Derek: How would you measure the level of overall activity? Would you use patient-days?

Kinh: I think so. Each day a patient is in the hospital counts as one patient-day. The greater the number of patient-days in a month, the busier we are. Besides, our budgeting is all based on projected patient-days.

Derek: Okay, so suppose you are able to break the maintenance costs down into fixed and variable components. What will that do for us?

Kinh: Basically, I will be able to predict what maintenance costs should be as a function of the number of patient-days.

Derek: I can see where that would be useful. We could use it to predict costs for budgeting purposes.

Kinh: We could also use it as a benchmark. Based on the actual number of patient-days for a period, I can predict what the maintenance costs should have been. We can compare this to the actual spending on maintenance.

Derek: Sounds good to me. Let me know when you get the results. ■

Objective 4

Analyze a mixed cost using the high-low method.

We will examine three methods that Kinh Nguyen might use to break down mixed costs into their fixed and variable elements—the *high-low method,* the *scatter-graph method,* and the *least-squares regression method.* All three methods are based on analyzing cost and activity records from a number of prior periods. In the case of Brentline Hospital, we will use the following records of maintenance costs and patient-days for the first seven months of the year to estimate the fixed and variable elements of maintenance costs:

Month	Activity Level: Patient-Days	Maintenance Cost Incurred
January	5,600	$7,900
February	7,100	8,500
March	5,000	7,400
April	6,500	8,200
May	7,300	9,100
June	8,000	9,800
July	6,200	7,800

The High-Low Method

High-low method　A method of separating a mixed cost into its fixed and variable elements by analyzing the change in cost between the high and low levels of activity.

To analyze mixed costs with the **high-low method,** you begin by identifying the period with the lowest level of activity and the period with the highest level of activity. The difference in cost observed at the two extremes is divided by the change in activity between the extremes in order to estimate the variable cost per unit of activity.

Since total maintenance cost at Brentline Hospital appears to generally increase as the activity level increases, it is likely that some variable cost element is present. Using the high-low method, we first identify the periods with the highest and lowest *activity*—in this case, June and March. We then use the activity and cost data from these two periods to estimate the variable cost component as follows:

	Patient-Days	Maintenance Cost Incurred
High activity level (June)	8,000	$9,800
Low activity level (March)	5,000	7,400
Change	3,000	$2,400

$$\text{Variable cost} = \frac{\text{Change in cost}}{\text{Change in activity}} = \frac{\$2,400}{3,000} = \$0.80 \text{ per patient-day}$$

Having determined that the variable rate for maintenance cost is 80 cents per patient-day, we can now determine the amount of fixed cost. This is done by taking total cost at *either* the high or the low activity level and deducting the variable cost element. In the computation below, total cost at the high activity level is used in computing the fixed cost element:

$$\begin{aligned} \text{Fixed cost element} &= \text{Total cost} - \text{Variable cost element} \\ &= \$9,800 - (\$0.80 \text{ per patient-day} \times 8,000 \text{ patient-days}) \\ &= \$3,400 \end{aligned}$$

Both the variable and fixed cost elements have now been isolated. The cost of maintenance can be expressed as $3,400 per month plus 80 cents per patient-day.

The cost of maintenance can also be expressed in terms of the equation for a straight line as follows:

$$Y = \$3{,}400 + \$0.80X$$

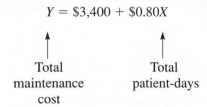

Total maintenance cost

Total patient-days

The data used in this illustration are shown graphically in Exhibit 5–9. Three things should be noted in relation to this exhibit:

Dependent variable
A variable that reacts or responds to some causal factor; total cost is the dependent variable, as represented by the letter Y, in the equation $Y = a + bX$.

Independent variable
A variable that acts as a causal factor; activity is the independent variable, as represented by the letter X, in the equation $Y = a + bX$.

1. Notice that cost, Y, is plotted on the vertical axis. Cost is known as the **dependent variable**, since the amount of cost incurred during a period depends on the level of activity for the period. (That is, as the level of activity increases, total cost will also increase.)
2. Notice that activity, X (patient-days in this case), is plotted on the horizontal axis. Activity is known as the **independent variable**, since it causes variations in the cost.
3. Notice that a straight line has been drawn through the points corresponding to the low and high levels of activity. In essence, that is what the high-low method does—it draws a straight line through those two points. The formula for the

variable cost, $\dfrac{\text{Change in cost (i.e., change in } Y)}{\text{Change in activity (i.e., change in } X)}$, is basically the same as

the formula for the slope of the line, $\dfrac{\text{Rise (i.e., change in } Y)}{\text{Run (i.e., change in } X)}$, that you are familiar

Exhibit 5–9 High-Low Method of Cost Analysis

Activity Level	Patient-Days	Maintenance Cost
High	8,000	$9,800
Low	5,000	$7,400

with from high school algebra. This is because the slope of the l⟨
cost per unit. The higher the variable cost per unit, the steeper t⟨

Sometimes the high and low levels of activity do not coinciae ⟨
low amounts of cost. For example, the period that has the highest level of acu⟨
not have the highest amount of cost. Nevertheless, the highest and lowest levels ɔ⟨
activity are always used to analyze a mixed cost under the high-low method. The reason is that the activity presumably causes costs, so the analyst would like to use data that reflects the greatest possible variation in activity.

The high-low method is very simple to apply, but it suffers from a major (and sometimes critical) defect in that it utilizes only two data points. Generally, two points are not enough to produce accurate results in cost analysis work. Additionally, periods in which the activity level is unusually low or unusually high will tend to produce inaccurate results. A cost formula that is estimated solely using data from these unusual periods may seriously misrepresent the true cost relationship that holds during normal periods. Such a distortion is evident in Exhibit 5–9. The straight line should probably be shifted down somewhat so that it is closer to more of the data points. For these reasons, other methods of cost analysis that utilize a greater number of points will generally be more accurate than the high-low method. If a manager chooses to use the high-low method, he or she should do so with a full awareness of the method's limitations.

The Scattergraph Method

Objective 5

Analyze a mixed cost using the scattergraph method.

Scattergraph method
A method of separating a mixed cost into its fixed and variable elements. Under this method, a regression line is fitted to an array of plotted points by drawing a line with a straight-edge.

Regression line A line fitted to an array of plotted points. The slope of the line, denoted by the letter *b* in the linear equation $Y = a + bX$, represents the average variable cost per unit of activity. The point where the line intersects the cost axis, denoted by the letter *a* in the above equation, represents the average total fixed cost.

A more accurate way of analyzing mixed costs is to use the **scattergraph method,** which takes into account all of the cost data. A graph like the one that we used in Exhibit 5–9 is constructed in which cost is shown on the vertical axis and the level of activity is shown on the horizontal axis. Costs observed at various levels of activity are then plotted on the graph, and a line is fitted to the plotted points. However, rather than just fitting the line to the high and low points, all points are considered when the line is drawn. This is done through simple visual inspection of the data, with the analyst taking care that the placement of the line is representative of all points, not just the high and low ones. Typically, the line is placed so that approximately equal numbers of points fall above and below it.

A graph is this type is known as a *scattergraph,* and the line fitted to the plotted points is known as a **regression line.** The regression line, in effect, is a line of averages, with the average variable cost per unit of activity represented by the slope of the line and the average total fixed cost represented by the point where the regression line intersects the cost axis.

The scattergraph approach using the Brentline Hospital maintenance data is illustrated in Exhibit 5–10. Note that the regression line has been placed in such a way that approximately equal numbers of points fall above and below it. Also note that the line has been drawn so that it goes through one of the points. This is not absolutely necessary, but it makes subsequent calculations a little easier.

Since the regression line strikes the vertical cost axis at $3,300, that amount represents the fixed cost element. The variable cost element can be computed by subtracting the fixed cost of $3,300 from the total cost for any point lying on the regression line. Since the point representing 7,300 patient-days lies on the regression line, we can use it. The variable cost (to the nearest tenth of a cent) would be 79.5 cents per patient-day, computed as follows:

Total cost for 7,300 patient-days (a point falling on the regression line)	$9,100
Less fixed cost element	3,300
Variable cost element	$5,800

$5,800 ÷ 7,300 patient-days = $0.795 per patient-day

Exhibit 5–10

Scattergraph Method of
Cost Analysis

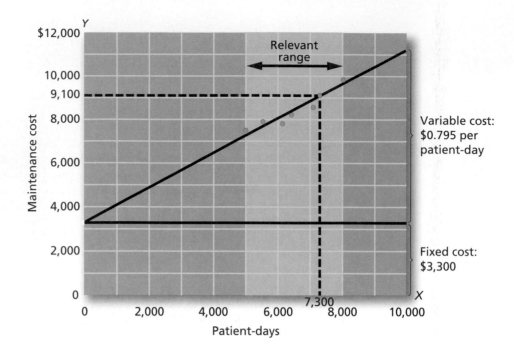

Thus, the cost formula using the regression line in Exhibit 5–10 would be $3,300 per month plus 79.5 cents per patient-day.

In this example, there is not a great deal of difference between the cost formula derived using the high-low method and the cost formula derived using the scattergraph method. However, sometimes there *will* be a big difference. In those situations, more reliance should ordinarily be placed on the results of the scattergraph approach.

Also note that all of the points in Exhibit 5–10 lie reasonably close to the straight line. In other words, the estimates of the fixed and variable costs are reasonably accurate within this range of activity, so the relevant range extends at least from 5,000 to 8,000 patient-days. It may also be accurate below 5,000 patient-days and above 8,000 patient-days—we cannot tell for sure without looking at more data.

A scattergraph can be an extremely useful tool in the hands of an experienced analyst. Quirks in cost behaviour due to strikes, bad weather, breakdowns, and so on, become immediately apparent to the trained observer, who can make appropriate adjustments to the data when fitting the regression line. Some cost analysts would argue that a scattergraph should be the beginning point in all cost analyses, due to the benefits to be gained from having the data visually available in graph form.

There are, however, two major drawbacks to the scattergraph method. First, it is subjective. No two analysts who look at the same scattergraph are likely to draw exactly the same regression line. Second, the estimates of fixed costs are not as precise as they are with other methods, since it is difficult to precisely measure the dollar amount where the regression line intersects the vertical cost axis. Some managers are uncomfortable with these elements of subjectivity and imprecision and desire a method that will yield a precise answer that will be the same no matter who does the analysis. Fortunately, modern computer software makes it very easy to use sophisticated statistical methods, such as *least-squares regression,* that are capable of providing much more information than just the estimates of variable and fixed costs. The details of these statistical methods are beyond the scope of this text, but the basic approach is discussed below. Nevertheless, even if the least-squares regression approach is used, it is always a good idea to plot the data in a scattergraph. By simply looking at the scattergraph, you can quickly verify whether it makes sense to fit a straight line to the data using least-squares regression or some other method.

The Least-Squares Regression Method

Objective 6

Explain the least-squares regression method of analyzing a mixed cost.

Least-squares regression method A method of separating a mixed cost into its fixed and variable elements by fitting a regression line that minimizes the sum of the squared errors.

The **least-square regression method** is a more objective and precise approach to estimating the regression line than the scattergraph method. Rather than fitting a regression line through the scattergraph data by visual inspection, the least-squares regression method uses mathematical formulas to fit the regression line. Also, unlike the high-low method, the least-squares regression method takes all of the data into account when estimating the cost formula.

The basic idea underlying the least-squares regression method is illustrated in Exhibit 5–11 using hypothetical data points. Notice from the exhibit that the deviations from the plotted points to the regression line are measured vertically on the graph. These vertical deviations are called the regression errors and are the key to understanding what least-squares regression does. There is nothing mysterious about the least-squares regression method. It simply computes the regression line that minimizes the sum of these squared errors. The formulas that accomplish this are fairly complex and involve numerous calculations, but the principal is simple.

Fortunately, computers are adept at carrying out the computations required by the least-squares regression formulas. The data—the observed values of X and Y—are entered into the computer, and software does the rest. In the case of the Brentline Hospital maintenance cost data, we used a statistical software package on a personal computer to calculate the following least-squares regression estimates of the total fixed cost *(a)* and the variable cost per unit of activity *(b):*

$$a = \$3{,}431$$
$$b = \$0.759$$

Therefore, using the least-squares regression method, the fixed element of the maintenance cost is \$3,431 per month and the variable portion is 75.9 cents per patient-day.

In terms of the linear equation $Y = a + bX$, the cost formula can be written as

$$Y = \$3{,}431 + \$0.759X$$

where activity *(X)* is expressed in patient-days.

Exhibit 5–11 The Concept of Least-Squares Regression

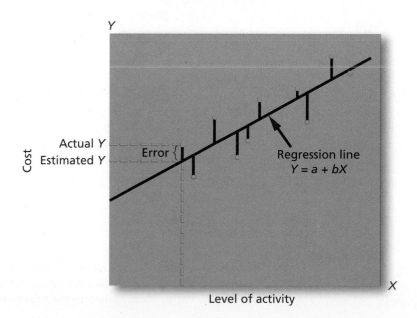

Adjusted R²   A measure of goodness of fit in least-squares regression analysis. It is the percentage of the variation in the dependent variable that is explained by variation in the independent variable.

While we used a personal computer to calculate the values of a and b in this example, they can also be calculated by hand. In Appendix 5A to this chapter, we can show how this can be done.

In addition to estimates of the intercept (fixed cost) and slope (variable cost per unit), least-squares regression software ordinarily provides a number of other very useful statistics. One of these statistics is the *adjusted R²*, which is a measure of "goodness of fit." The **adjusted R²** tells us the percentage of the variation in the dependent variable (cost) that is explained by variation in the independent variable (activity). The adjusted R² varies from 0% to 100%, and the higher the percentage, the better. A regression line that fits the data perfectly would yield an R² of 1. The R² would be 0 in a situation where no fit was achieved by the regression line. In the case of the Brentline Hospital maintenance cost data, the adjusted R² is 88%, which indicates that 88% of the variation in maintenance costs is explained by the variation in patient-days. This is reasonably high and is an indication of a good fit. On the other hand, a low adjusted R² would be an indication that there is a poor fit. You should always plot the data in a scattergraph, but it is particularly important to check the data visually when there is a low adjusted R². A quick look at the scattergraph can reveal that there is little real relation between the cost and the activity or that the relation is something other than a simple straight line. In such cases, additional analysis would be required.

Managerial Accounting in Action

THE WRAP-UP

BRENTLINE HOSPITAL

After completing the analysis of maintenance costs, Kinh Nguyen met with Dr. Derek Chalmers to discuss the results.

Kinh: We used least-squares regression analysis to estimate the fixed and variable components of maintenance costs. According to the results, the fixed cost per month is $3,431 and the variable cost per patient-day is 75.9 cents.

Derek: Okay, so if we plan for 7,800 patient-days next month, what is your estimate of the maintenance costs?

Kinh: That will take just a few seconds to figure out. Here it is. [And Kinh wrote the following calculations on a pad of paper.]

Fixed costs	$3,431
Variable costs:	
7,800 patient-days × $0.759 per patient-day . . .	5,920
Total expected maintenance costs	$9,351

Derek: Nine thousand three hundred and fifty-*one* dollars; isn't that a bit *too* precise?

Kinh: Sure. I don't really believe the maintenance costs will be exactly this figure. However, based on the information we have, this is the best estimate we can come up with.

Derek: Don't let me give you a hard time. Even though it is an estimate, it will be a lot better than just guessing like we have done in the past. Thanks. I hope to see more of this kind of analysis. ∎

Multiple Regression Analysis

In the discussion thus far, we have assumed that a single factor such as patient-days drives the variable cost component of a mixed cost. This assumption is acceptable for many mixed costs, but in some situations there may be more than one causal factor driving the variable cost element. For example, shipping costs may depend on both the number of units shipped *and* the weight of the units. In a situation such as this, *multiple regression* is necessary. **Multiple regression** is an analytical method that is used when the dependent variable (i.e., cost) is caused by more than one factor. Although adding more factors, or variables, makes the computations more complex, the principles involved are the same as in the simple least-squares regressions discussed above. Because of the complexity of the calculations, multiple regression is nearly always done with a computer.

Multiple regression
An analytical method required in those situations where variations in a dependent variable are caused by more than one factor.

The Contribution Format

Objective 7
Prepare an income statement using the contribution format.

Contribution approach
An income statement format that is geared to cost behaviour in that costs are separated into variable and fixed categories rather than being separated according to the functions of production, sales, and administration.

Once the manager has separated costs into fixed and variable elements, what is done with the data? We have already answered this question somewhat by showing how a cost formula can be used to predict costs. To answer this question more fully will require most of the remainder of this text, since much of what the manager does rests in some way on an understanding of cost behaviour. One immediate and very significant application of the ideas we have developed, however, is found in a new income statement format known as the **contribution approach.** The unique thing about the contribution approach is that it provides the manager with an income statement geared directly to cost behaviour.

Why a New Income Statement Format?

The *traditional approach* to the income statement, as illustrated in Chapter 2, is not organized in terms of cost behaviour. Rather, it is organized in a "functional" format— emphasizing the functions of production, administration, and sales in the classification and presentation of cost data. No attempt is made to distinguish between the behaviour of costs included under each functional heading. Under the heading "Administrative expense," for example, one can expect to find both variable and fixed costs lumped together.

Although an income statement prepared in the functional format may be useful for external reporting purposes, it has serious limitations when used for internal purposes. Internally, the manager needs cost data organized in a format that will facilitate planning, control, and decision making. As we shall see in chapters ahead, these tasks are much easier when cost data are available in a fixed and variable format. The contribution approach to the income statement has been developed in response to this need.

The Contribution Approach

Exhibit 5–12 illustrates the contribution approach to the income statement with a simple example, along with the traditional approach discussed in Chapter 2.

Notice that the contribution approach separates costs into fixed and variable categories, first deducting variable expenses from sales to obtain what is known as the *contribution margin.* The **contribution margin** is the amount remaining from sales revenues after variable expenses have been deducted. This amount *contributes* toward covering fixed expenses and then toward profits for the period.

Contribution margin
The amount remaining from sales revenues after all variable expenses have been deducted.

The contribution approach to the income statement is used as an internal planning and decision-making tool. Its emphasis on costs by behaviour facilitates cost-volume-profit analysis, such as we shall be doing in the next chapter. The approach is also very useful in appraising management performance, in segmented reporting of profit data, and in budgeting. Moreover, the contribution approach helps managers organize data pertinent to all kinds of special decisions such as product-line analysis, pricing, use of scarce resources, and make or buy analysis. All of these topics are covered in later chapters.

Exhibit 5–12 Comparison of the Contribution Income Statement with the Traditional Income Statement

Traditional Approach (costs organized by function)		Contribution Approach (costs organized by behaviour)		
Sales	$12,000	Sales		$12,000
Less cost of goods sold	6,000*	Less variable expenses:		
Gross margin	6,000	Variable production	$2,000	
Less operating expenses:		Variable selling	600	
Selling $3,100*		Variable administrative	400	3,000
Administrative 1,900*	5,000	Contribution margin		9,000
Net income	$ 1,000	Less fixed expenses:		
		Fixed production	4,000	
		Fixed selling	2,500	
		Fixed administrative	1,500	8,000
		Net income		$ 1,000

*Contains both variable and fixed expenses. This is the income statement for a manufacturing company; thus, when the income statement is placed in the contribution format, the "cost of goods sold" figure is divided between variable production costs and fixed production costs. If this were the income statement for a *merchandising* company (which simply purchases completed goods from a supplier), then the cost of goods sold would *all* be variable.

Summary

The ability to predict how costs will respond to changes in activity is critical for making decisions and for other major management functions. Three major classifications of costs were discussed—variable, fixed, and mixed. Mixed costs consist of a mixture of variable and fixed elements. There are three major methods of analyzing mixed costs that rely on past records of cost and activity data—the high-low method, the scattergraph approach, and lease-squares regression. The high-low method is the simplest of the three methods and can yield estimates of fixed and variable costs very quickly, but it suffers from relying on just two data points. In most situations, the least-squares regression method should be used to derive a cost formula, although the scattergraph method can also give good results. The least-squares method is objective, and a variety of useful statistics are automatically produced by most software packages along with estimates of the intercept (fixed cost) and slope (variable cost per unit). Nevertheless, even when least-squares regression is used, the data should be plotted to confirm that the relationship is really a straight line.

Managers use costs organized by behaviour as a basis for many decisions. To facilitate this use, the income statement can be prepared in a contribution format. The contribution format classifies costs on the income statement by cost behaviour (i.e., variable versus fixed) rather than by the functions of production, administration, and sales.

Review Problem 1: Cost Behaviour

Neptune Rentals offers a boat rental service. Consider the following costs of the company over the relevant range of 5,000 to 8,000 hours of operating time for its boats:

	Hours of Operating Time			
	5,000	**6,000**	**7,000**	**8,000**
Total costs:				
Variable costs	$ 20,000	$?	$?	$?
Fixed costs	168,000	?	?	?
Total costs	$188,000	$?	$?	$?

Cost per hour:				
Variable cost	$?	$?	$?	$?
Fixed cost	?	?	?	?
Total cost per hour	$?	$?	$?	$?

Required

Compute the missing amounts, assuming that cost behaviour patterns remain unchanged within the relevant range of 5,000 to 8,000 hours.

Solution to Review Problem 1

The variable cost per hour can be computed as follows:

$$\$20{,}000 \div 5{,}000 \text{ hours} = \$4 \text{ per hour}$$

Therefore, in accordance with the behaviour of variable and fixed costs, the missing amounts are as follows:

	Hours of Operating Time			
	5,000	**6,000**	**7,000**	**8,000**
Total costs:				
Variable costs	$ 20,000	$ 24,000	$ 28,000	$ 32,000
Fixed costs	168,000	168,000	168,000	168,000
Total costs	$188,000	$192,000	$196,000	$200,000
Cost per hour:				
Variable cost	$ 4.00	$ 4.00	$ 4.00	$ 4.00
Fixed cost	33.60	28.00	24.00	21.00
Total cost per hour	$ 37.60	$ 32.00	$ 28.00	$ 25.00

Observe that the total variable costs increase in proportion to the number of hours of operating time, but that these costs remain constant at $4 if expressed on a per hour basis.

In contrast, the total fixed costs do not change with changes in the level of activity. They remain constant at $168,000 within the relevant range. With increases in activity, however, the fixed costs decrease on a per hour basis, dropping from $33.60 per hour when the boats are operated 5,000 hours a period to only $21.00 per hour when the boats are operated 8,000 hours a period. *Because of this troublesome aspect of fixed costs, they are most easily (and most safely) dealt with on a total basis, rather than on a unit basis, in cost analysis work.*

Review Problem 2: High-Low Method

The administrator of Azalea Hills Hospital would like a cost formula linking the costs involved in admitting patients to the number of patients admitted during a month. The admitting department's costs and the number of patients admitted during the immediately preceding eight months are given in the following table:

Month	Number of Patients Admitted	Admitting Department Costs
May	1,800	$14,700
June	1,900	15,200
July	1,700	13,700
August	1,600	14,000
September	1,500	14,300
October	1,300	13,100
November	1,100	12,800
December	1,500	14,600

Required

1. Use the high-low method to establish the fixed and variable components of admitting costs.

2. Express the fixed and variable components of admitting costs as a cost formula in the linear equation form $Y = a + bX$.

Solution to Review Problem 2

1. The first step in the high-low method is to identify the periods of the lowest and highest activity. Those periods are November (1,100 patients admitted) and June (1,900 patients admitted).

   The second step is to compute the variable cost per unit using those two points:

Month	Number of Patients Admitted	Admitting Department Costs
High activity level (June)	1,900	$15,200
Low activity level (November)	1,100	12,800
Change	800	$ 2,400

$$\text{Variable cost} = \frac{\text{Change in cost}}{\text{Change in activity}} = \frac{\$2,400}{800} = \$3 \text{ per patient admitted}$$

The third step is to compute the fixed cost element by deducting the variable cost element from the total cost at either the high or low activity. In the computation below, the high point of activity is used:

$$\begin{aligned}\text{Fixed cost element} &= \text{Total cost} - \text{Variable cost element} \\ &= \$15,200 - (\$3 \times 1,900 \text{ patients admitted}) \\ &= \$9,500\end{aligned}$$

2. The cost formula expressed in the linear equation form is $Y = \$9,500 + \$3X$.

Appendix 5A: Least-Squares Regression Calculations

Objective 8

Analyze a mixed cost using the least-squares regression method.

The least-squares regression method for estimating a linear relationship is based on the equation for a straight line:

$$Y = a + bX$$

The following formulas are used to calculate the values of the vertical intercept *(a)* and the slope *(b)* that minimize the sum of the squared errors:[6]

$$b = \frac{n(\Sigma XY) - (\Sigma X)(\Sigma Y)}{n(\Sigma X^2) - (\Sigma X)^2}$$

$$a = \frac{(\Sigma Y) - b(\Sigma X)}{n}$$

where:

X = The level of activity (independent variable)
Y = The total mixed cost (dependent variable)
a = The total fixed cost (the vertical intercept of the line)
b = The variable cost per unit of activity (the slope of the line)
n = Number of observations
Σ = Sum across all n observations

---

6. See calculus or statistics book for details concerning how these forumlas are derived.

To illustrate how these calculations are accomplished, we will use the Brentline Hospital data from page 219.

Step 1. Compute ΣX, ΣY, ΣXY, ΣX^2, and n.

Month	Patient Days X	Maintenance Costs Y	XY	X²
January	5,600	$ 7,900	$ 44,240,000	31,360,000
February	7,100	8,500	60,350,000	50,410,000
March	5,000	7,400	37,000,000	25,000,000
April	6,500	8,200	53,300,000	42,250,000
May	7,300	9,100	66,430,000	53,290,000
June	8,000	9,800	78,400,000	64,000,000
July	6,200	7,800	48,360,000	38,440,000
Total Σ	45,700	$58,700	$388,080,000	304,750,000

From this table:

$$\Sigma X = 45,700$$
$$\Sigma Y = \$58,700$$
$$\Sigma XY = \$388,080,000$$
$$\Sigma X^2 = 304,750,000$$
$$n = 7$$

Step 2. Insert the values computed in step 1 into the formula for the slope (b).

$$b = \frac{n(\Sigma YX) - (\Sigma X)(\Sigma Y)}{n(\Sigma X^2) - (\Sigma X)^2}$$

$$b = \frac{7(\$388,080,000) - (45,700)(\$58,700)}{7(304,750,000) - (45,700)^2}$$

$$b = \$0.759$$

Therefore, the maintenance cost is 75.9 cents per patient-day.

Step 3: Insert the values computed in step 1 and the value of b computed in step 2 into the formula for the intercept (a).

$$a = \frac{(\Sigma Y) - b(\Sigma X)}{n}$$

$$a = \frac{(\$58,700) - \$0.759(45,700)}{7}$$

$$a = \$3,431$$

Therefore, the fixed maintenance cost is $3,431 per month. The cost formula for maintenance cost is as follows:

$$Y = a + bX$$
$$Y = \$3,431 + \$0.759X$$

Questions

5–1   Distinguish between (a) a variable cost, (b) a fixed cost, and (c) a mixed cost.

5–2   What effect does an increase in volume have on—

a.   Unit fixed costs?
b.   Unit variable costs?
c.   Total fixed costs?
d.   Total variable costs?

5–3   Define the following terms: (a) cost behaviour, and (b) relevant range.

5–4   What is meant by an *activity base* when dealing with variable costs? Give several examples of activity bases.

5–5   Distinguish between (a) a variable cost, (b) a mixed cost, and (c) a step-variable cost. Chart the three costs on a graph, with activity plotted horizontally and cost plotted vertically.

5–6   Managers often assume a strictly linear relationship between cost and volume. How can this practice be defended in light of the fact that many costs are curvilinear?

5–7   Distinguish between discretionary fixed costs and committed fixed costs.

5–8   Classify the following fixed costs as normally being either committed or discretionary:
a.   Depreciation on buildings.
b.   Advertising.
c.   Research.
d.   Long-term equipment leases.
e.   Pension payments to the firm's retirees.
f.   Management development and training.

5–9   Does the concept of the relevant range apply to fixed costs? Explain.

5–10   What is the major disadvantage of the high-low method?

5–11   What methods are available for separating a mixed cost into its fixed and variable elements using past records of cost and activity data? Which method is considered to be most accurate? Why?

5–12   What is meant by a regression line? Give the general formula for a regression line. Which term represents the variable cost? The fixed cost?

5–13   Once a regression line has been drawn, how does one determine the fixed cost element? The variable cost element?

5–14   What is meant by the term *least-squares regression?*

5–15   What is the difference between ordinary least-squares regression analysis and multiple regression analysis?

5–16   What is the meaning of R^2?

5–17   What is the difference between the contribution approach to the income statement and the traditional approach to the income statement?

5–18   What is the contribution margin?

5–19   What mathematical model can be used to express net income before income taxes for a contribution-type income statement?

Exercises

E5–1 The Lakeshore Hotel's guest-days of occupancy and custodial supplies expense over the last seven months were:

Month	Guest-Days of Occupancy	Custodial Supplies Expense
March	4,000	$ 7,500
April	6,500	8,250
May	8,000	10,500
June	10,500	12,000
July	12,000	13,500
August	9,000	10,750
September	7,500	9,750

Guest-days is a measure of the overall activity at the hotel. For example, a guest who stays at the hotel for three days is counted as three guest-days.

Required
1. Using the high-low method, estimate a cost formula for custodial supplies expense.
2. Using the cost formula you derived above, what amount of custodial supplies expense would you expect to be incurred at an occupancy level of 11,000 guest-days?

E5–2 Refer to the data in E5–1.

Required
1. Prepare a scattergraph using the data from E5–1. Plot cost on the vertical axis and activity on the horizontal axis. Fit a regression line to your plotted points by visual inspection.
2. What is the approximate monthly fixed cost? The approximate variable cost per guest-day?
3. Scrutinize the points on your graph and explain why the high-low method would or would not yield an accurate cost formula in this situation.

E5–3 The following data relating to units shipped and total shipping expense have been assembled by Archer Company, a manufacturer of large, custom-built air-conditioning units for commercial buildings:

Month	Units Shipped	Total Shipping Expense
January	3	$1,800
February	6	2,300
March	4	1,700
April	5	2,000
May	7	2,300
June	8	2,700
July	2	1,200

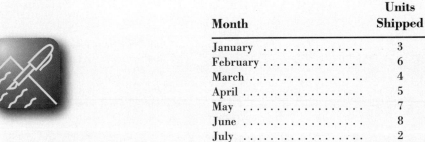

Required
1. Using the high-low method, estimate a cost formula for shipping expense.
2. For the scattergraph method, do the following:
   a. Prepare a scattergraph, using the data given above. Plot cost on the vertical axis and activity on the horizontal axis. Fit a regression line to your plotted points by visual inspection.
   b. Using your scattergraph, estimate the approximate variable cost per unit shipped and the approximate fixed cost per month.
3. What factors, other than the number of units shipped, are likely to affect the company's total shipping expense? Explain.

E5–4 (Appendix 5A) Refer to the data in E5–3.

Required
1. Using the least-squares regression method, estimate a cost formula for shipping expense.
2. If you also completed E5–3, prepare a simple table comparing the variable and fixed cost elements of shipping expense as computed under the high-low method, the scattergraph method, and the least-squares regression method.

E5–5   St. Mark's Hospital contains 450 beds. The average occupancy rate is 80% per month. In other words, on average, 80% of the hospital's beds are occupied by patients. At this level of occupancy, the hospital's operating costs are $32 per occupied bed per day, assuming a 30-day month. This $32 figure contains both variable and fixed cost elements.

      During June, the hospital's occupancy rate was only 60%. A total of $326,700 in operating cost was incurred during the month.

Required
1. Using the high-low method, estimate:
   a. The variable cost per occupied bed on a daily basis.
   b. The total fixed operating costs per month.
2. Assume an occupancy rate of 70% per month. What amount of total operating cost would you expect the hospital to incur?

E5–6   Hoi Chong Transport, Ltd., operates a fleet of delivery trucks in Singapore. The company has determined that if a truck is driven 105,000 kilometres during a year, the average operating cost is 11.4 cents per kilometre. If a truck is driven only 70,000 kilometres during a year, the average operating cost increases to 13.4 cents per kilometre. (The Singapore dollar is the currency used in Singapore.)

Required
1. Using the high-low method, estimate the variable and fixed cost elements of the annual cost of truck operation.
2. Express the variable and fixed costs in the form $Y = a + bX$.
3. If a truck were driven 80,000 kilometres during a year, what total cost would you expect to be incurred?

E5–7   Oki Products, Ltd., has observed the following processing costs at various levels of activity over the last 15 months:

Month	Units Produced	Processing Cost
1	4,500	$38,000
2	11,000	52,000
3	12,000	56,000
4	5,500	40,000
5	9,000	47,000
6	10,500	52,000
7	7,500	44,000
8	5,000	41,000
9	11,500	52,000
10	6,000	43,000
11	8,500	48,000
12	10,000	50,000
13	6,500	44,000
14	9,500	48,000
15	8,000	46,000

Required
1. Prepare a scattergraph by plotting the above data on a graph. Plot cost on the vertical axis and activity on the horizontal axis. Fit a line to your plotted points by visual inspection.
2. What is the approximate monthly fixed cost? The approximate variable cost per unit processed? Show your computations.

E5–8   (Appendix 5A) George Caloz & Frères, located in Grenchen, Switzerland, makes prestige high-end custom watches in small lots. The company has been in operation since 1856. One of the company's products, a platinum diving watch, goes through an etching process. The company has observed etching costs as follows over the last six weeks:

Week	Units	Total Etching Cost
1	4	SFr18
2	3	17
3	8	25
4	6	20
5	7	24
6	2	16
	30	SFr120

The Swiss currency is the Swiss Franc, which is denoted by SFr.

For planning purposes, management would like to know the amount of variable etching cost per unit and the total fixed etching cost per week.

Required

1. Using the least-squares regression method, estimate the variable and fixed elements of etching cost.
2. Express the cost data in (1) above in the form $Y = a + bX$.
3. If the company processes five units next week, what would be the expected total etching cost?

E5–9   Harris Company manufactures and sells a single product. A partially completed schedule of the company's total and per unit costs over the relevant range of 30,000 to 50,000 units produced and sold annually is given below:

	Units Produced and Sold		
	30,000	**40,000**	**50,000**
Total costs:			
Variable costs	$180,000	240,000	300,500
Fixed costs	300,000	?	?
Total costs	$480,000	640,000	800,000
Cost per unit:			
Variable cost	6	8.5	10
Fixed cost	10	10	10
Total cost per unit	16	10? 6	20

Required

1. Complete the schedule of the company's total and unit costs above.
2. Assume that the company produces and sells 45,000 units during a year at a selling price of $16 per unit. Prepare an income statement in the contribution format for the year.

E5–10   The Alpine House, Inc., is a large retailer of winter sports equipment. An income statement for the company's Ski Department for a recent quarter is presented below:

THE ALPINE HOUSE, INC.
Income Statement—Ski Department
For the Quarter Ended March 31

Sales		$150,000
Less cost of goods sold		90,000
Gross margin		60,000
Less operating expenses:		
Selling expenses	$30,000 26,000	
Administrative expenses	10,000 6,000 40,000	
Net income		$ 20,000

Skis sell, on the average, for $750 per pair. Variable selling expenses are $50 per pair of skis sold. The remaining selling expenses are fixed. The administrative expenses are 20% variable and 80% fixed. The company does not manufacture its own skis; it purchases them from a supplier for $450 per pair.

Required
1. Prepare an income statement for the quarter using the contribution approach.
2. For every pair of skis sold during the quarter, what was the contribution toward covering fixed expenses and toward earning profits?

Problems

P5–11   High-Low Method; Contribution Income Statement   Morrisey & Brown, Ltd., of Sydney is a merchandising firm that is the sole distributor of a product that is increasing in popularity among Australian consumers. The company's income statements for the three most recent months follow:

MORRISEY & BROWN, LTD.
Income Statements
For the Three Months Ending September 30

	July	August	September
Sales in units	4,000	4,500	5,000
Sales revenue	A$400,000	A$450,000	A$500,000
Less cost of goods sold	240,000	270,000	300,000
Gross margin	160,000	180,000	200,000
Less operating expenses:			
Advertising expense	21,000	21,000	21,000
Shipping expense	34,000	36,000	38,000
Salaries and commissions	78,000	84,000	90,000
Insurance expense	6,000	6,000	6,000
Depreciation expense	15,000	15,000	15,000
Total operating expenses	154,000	162,000	170,000
Net income	A$ 6,000	A$ 18,000	A$ 30,000

(Note: Morrisey & Brown, Ltd.'s Australian-formatted income statement has been recast in the format common in Canada. The Australian dollar is denoted by A$.)

Required
1. Identify each of the company's expenses (including cost of goods sold) as being either variable, fixed, or mixed.
2. By use of the high-low method, separate each mixed expense into variable and fixed elements. State the cost formula for each mixed expense.
3. Redo the company's income statement at the 5,000-unit level of activity using the contribution format.

P5–12   Least-Squares Regression Method of Cost Analysis; Graphing (Appendix 5A) Professor John Morton has just been appointed chairperson of the Finance Department at Mary's University. In reviewing the department's cost records, Professor Morton has found the following total cost associated with Finance 101 over the last several terms:

Term	Number of Sections Offered	Total Cost
Fall, last year	4	$10,000
Winter, last year	6	14,000
Summer, last year	2	7,000
Fall, this year	5	13,000
Winter, this year	3	9,500

Professor Morton knows that there are some variable costs, such as amounts paid to graduate assistants, associated with the course. He would like to have the variable and fixed costs separated for planning purposes.

Required

1. Using the least-squares regression method, estimate the variable cost per section and the total fixed cost per term for Finance 101.
2. Express the cost data derived in (1) above in the linear equation form $Y = a + bX$.
3. Assume that because of the small number of sections offered during the Winter Term this year, Professor Morton will have to offer eight sections of Finance 101 during the fall term. Compute the expected total cost for Finance 101. Can you see any problem with using the cost formula from (2) above to derive this total cost figure? Explain.
4. Prepare a scattergraph and fit a regression line to the plotted points using the cost formula expressed in (2) above.

P5–13   Contribution versus Traditional Income Statement   Marwick's Pianos, Inc., purchases pianos from a large manufacturer and sells them at the retail level. The pianos cost, on the average, $2,450 each from the manufacturer. Marwick's Pianos, Inc., sells the pianos to its customers at an average price of $3,125 each. The selling and administrative costs that the company incurs in a typical month are presented below:

Costs	Cost Formula
Selling:	
Advertising	$700 per month
Sales salaries and commissions	$950 per month, plus 8% of sales
Delivery of pianos to customers	$30 per piano sold
Utilities	$350 per month
Depreciation of sales facilities	$800 per month
Administrative:	
Executive salaries	$2,500 per month
Insurance	$400 per month
Clerical	$1,000 per month, plus $20 per piano sold
Depreciation of office equipment	$300 per month

During August, Marwick's Pianos, Inc., sold and delivered 40 pianos.

Required

1. Prepare an income statement for Marwick's Pianos, Inc., for August. Use the traditional format, with costs organized by function.
2. Redo (1) above, this time using the contribution format, with costs organized by behaviour. Show costs and revenues on both total and a per unit basis down through contribution margin.
3. Refer to the income statement you prepared in (2) above. Why might it be misleading to show the fixed costs on a per unit basis?

P5–14   Identifying Cost Behaviour Patterns   On the next page are a number of cost behaviour patterns that might be found in a company's cost structure. The vertical axis on each graph represents total cost, and the horizontal axis on each graph represents level of activity (volume).

Required

1. For each of the following situations, identify the graph from the next page that illustrates the cost pattern involved. Any graph may be used more than once.
   a. Cost of raw materials used.
   b. Electricity bill—a flat fixed charge, plus a variable cost after a certain number of kilowatt-hours are used.
   c. City water bill, which is computed as follows:

First 1,000,000 litres or less	$1,000 flat fee
Next 10,000 litres	0.003 per litre used
Next 10,000 litres	0.006 per litre used
Next 10,000 litres	0.009 per litre used
Etc.	Etc.

d. Depreciation of equipment, where the amount is computed by the straight-line method. When the depreciation rate was established, it was anticipated that the obsolescence factor would be greater than the wear and tear factor.

e. Rent on a factory building donated by the city, where the agreement calls for a fixed fee payment unless 200,000 labour-hours or more are worked, in which case no rent need be paid.

f. Salaries of maintenance workers, where one maintenance worker is needed for every 1,000 hours of machine-hours or less (that is, 0 to 1,000 hours requires one maintenance worker, 1,001 to 2,000 hours requires two maintenance workers, etc.)

g. Cost of raw materials, where the cost decreases by 5 cents per unit for each of the first 100 units purchased, after which it remains constant at $2.50 per unit.

h. Rent on a factory building donated by the county, where the agreement calls for rent of $100,000 less $1 for each direct labour-hour worked in excess of 200,000 hours, but a minimum rental payment of $20,000 must be paid.

i. Use of a machine under a lease, where a minimum charge of $1,000 is paid for up to 400 hours of machine time. After 400 hours of machine time, an additional charge of $2 per hour is paid up to a maximum charge of $2,000 per period.

2. How would a knowledge of cost behaviour patterns such as those above be of help to a manager in analyzing the cost structure of his or her firm?

(CPA, adapted)

P5–15 High-Low Method of Cost Analysis Nova Company's total overhead costs at various levels of activity are presented below:

Month	Machine-Hours	Total Overhead Costs
April	70,000	$198,000
May	60,000	174,000
June	80,000	222,000
July	90,000	246,000

27.6   12.1

Assume that the total overhead costs above consist of utilities, supervisory salaries, and maintenance. The breakdown of these costs at the 60,000 machine-hour level of activity is:

Utilities (V)	$ 48,000
Supervisory salaries (F)	21,000
Maintenance (M)	105,000
Total overhead costs	$174,000

60.3

V = variable; F = fixed; M = mixed.

Nova Company's management wants to break down the maintenance cost into its basic variable and fixed cost elements.

Required

1. As shown above, overhead costs in July amounted to $246,000. Determine how much of this consisted of maintenance cost. (Hint: To do this, it may be helpful to first determine how much of the $246,000 consisted of utilities and supervisory salaries. Think about the behaviour of variable and fixed costs!)
2. By means of the high-low method, estimate a cost formula for maintenance.
3. Express the company's *total* overhead costs in the linear equation form $Y = a + bX$.
4. What *total* overhead costs would you expect to be incurred at an operating activity level of 75,000 machine-hours?

P5–16 High-Low Method of Cost Analysis   Sawaya Co., Ltd., of Japan is a manufacturing company whose total factory overhead costs fluctuate considerably from year to year according to increases and decreases in the number of direct labour-hours worked in the factory. Total factory overhead costs (in Japanese yen, denoted ¥) at high and low levels of activity for recent years are given below:

	Level of Activity	
	Low	**High**
Direct labour-hours	50,000	75,000
Total factory overhead costs	¥14,250,000	¥17,625,000

The factory overhead costs above consist of indirect materials, rent, and maintenance. The company has analyzed these costs at the 50,000-hour level of activity as follows:

Indirect materials (V)	¥5,000,000
Rent (F)	6,000,000
Maintenance (M)	3,250,000
Total factory overhead costs	¥14,250,000

V = variable; F = fixed; M = mixed.

To have data available for planning, the company wants to break down the maintenance cost into its variable and fixed cost elements.

Required

1. Estimate how much of the ¥17,625,000 factory overhead cost at the high level of activity consists of maintenance cost. (Hint: To do this, it may be helpful to first determine how much of the ¥17,625,000 consists of indirect materials and rent. Think about the behaviour of variable and fixed costs!)
2. By means of the high-low method of cost analysis, estimate a cost formula for maintenance.
3. What total factory overhead costs would you expect the company to incur at an operating level of 70,000 direct labour-hours?

P5–17 Manufacturing Statements; High-Low Method of Cost Analysis
Amfac Company manufactures a single product. The company keeps careful records of manufacturing activities from which the following information has been extracted:

	Level of Activity	
	March–Low	June–High
Number of units produced	6,000	9,000
Cost of goods manufactured	$168,000	$257,000
Work in process inventory, beginning	$ 9,000	$ 32,000
Work in process inventory, ending	$ 15,000	$ 21,000
Direct materials cost per unit	$ 6	$ 6
Direct labour cost per unit	$ 10	$ 10
Manufacturing overhead cost, total	?	?

The company's manufacturing overhead cost consists of both variable and fixed cost elements. To have data available for planning, management wants to determine how much of the overhead cost is variable with units produced and how much of it is fixed per month.

Required
1. For both March and June, determine the amount of manufacturing overhead cost added to production. The company had no under- or overapplied overhead in either month. (Hint: A useful way to proceed might be to construct a schedule of cost of goods manufactured.)
2. By means of the high-low method of cost analysis, estimate a cost formula for manufacturing overhead. Express the variable portion of the formula in terms of a variable rate per unit of product.
3. If 7,000 units are produced during a month, what would be the cost of goods manufactured? (Assume that work in process inventories do not change and that there is no under- or overapplied overhead cost for the month.)

P5–18   Scattergraph Method of Cost Analysis   Molina Company is a value-added computer resaler that specializes in providing services to small companies. The company owns and maintains several autos for use by the sales staff. All expenses of operating these autos have been entered into an Automobile Expense account on the company's books. Along with this record of expenses, the company has also kept a careful record of the number of miles the autos have been driven each month.

The company's records of miles driven and total auto expenses over the past 10 months are given below:

Month	Total Mileage (000)	Total Cost
January	4	$3,000
February	8	3,700
March	7	3,300
April	12	4,000
May	6	3,300
June	11	3,900
July	14	4,200
August	10	3,600
September	13	4,100
October	15	4,400

Molina Company's president wants to know the cost of operating the fleet of cars in terms of the fixed monthly cost and the variable cost per mile driven.

Required
1. Prepare a scattergraph using the data given above. Place cost on the vertical axis and activity (miles driven) on the horizontal axis. Fit a regression line to the plotted points by simple visual inspection.
2. By analyzing your scattergraph, estimate fixed cost per month and the variable cost per mile driven.
3. How would the formula change if it were changed to Canadian metric units?

P5–19   Least-Squares Regression Method of Cost Analysis   (Appendix 5A) Refer to the data for Molina Company in P5–18.

Required
1. Using the least-squares regression method, estimate the variable and fixed cost elements associated with the company's fleet of autos. (Since the Total Mileage is in thousands of miles, the variable rate you compute will also be in thousands of miles. The rate can be left in this form, or you can convert it to a per mile basis by dividing the rate you get by 1,000.)
2. From the data in (1) above, express the cost formula for auto use in the linear equation form $Y = a + bX$.

P5–20 Mixed Cost Analysis; High-Low and Scattergraph Methods

Pleasant View Hospital of British Columbia has just hired a new chief administrator who is anxious to employ sound management and planning techniques in the business affairs of the hospital. Accordingly, she has directed her assistant to summarize the cost structure existing in the various departments so that data will be available for planning purposes.

The assistant is unsure how to classify the utilities costs in the Radiology Department since these costs do not exhibit either strictly variable or fixed cost behaviour. Utilities costs are very high in the department due to a CAT scanner that draws a large amount of power and is kept running at all times. The scanner cannot be turned off due to the long warm-up period required for its use. When the scanner is used to scan a patient, it consumes an additional burst of power. The assistant has accumulated the following data on utilities costs and use of the scanner since the first of the year.

Month	Number of Scans	Utilities Cost
January	60	$2,200
February	70	2,600
March	90	2,900
April	120	3,300
May	100	3,000
June	130	3,600
July	150	4,000
August	140	3,600
September	110	3,100
October	80	2,500

The chief administrator has informed her assistant that the utilities cost is probably a mixed cost that will have to be broken down into its variable and fixed cost elements by use of a scattergraph. The assistant feels, however, that if an analysis of this type is necessary, then the high-low method should be used, since it is easier and quicker. The controller has suggested that there may be a better approach.

Required
1. Using the high-low method, estimate a cost formula for utilities. Express the formula in the form $Y = a + bX$. (The variable rate should be stated in terms of cost per scan.)
2. Prepare a scattergraph by plotting the above data on a graph. (The number of scans should be placed on the horizontal axis, and utilities cost should be placed on the vertical axis.) Fit a regression line to the plotted points by visual inspection and estimate a cost formula for utilities.

P5–21 Least-Squares Regression Method of Cost Analysis (Appendix 5A) Refer to the data for Pleasant View Hospital in P5–20.

Required
1. Using the least-squares regression method, estimate a cost formula for utilities. (Round the variable rate to two decimal places.)
2. Refer to the graph prepared in (2) of P5–20. Explain why in this case the high-low method would be the least accurate of the three methods in deriving a cost formula.

P5–22 Least-Squares Regression Analysis; Contribution Income Statement (Appendix 5A) Milden Company has an exclusive franchise to purchase a product from the manufacturer and distribute it on the retail level. As an aid in planning, the company has decided to start using the contribution approach to the income statement internally. To have data to prepare such a statement, the company has analyzed its expenses and developed the following cost formulas:

Cost	Cost Formula
Cost of good sold	$35 per unit sold
Advertising expense	$210,000 per quarter
Sales commissions	6% of sales
Shipping expense	?
Administrative salaries	$145,000 per quarter
Insurance expense	$9,000 per quarter
Depreciation expense	$76,000 per quarter

Management has concluded that shipping expense is a mixed cost, containing both variable and fixed cost elements. Units sold and the related shipping expense over the last eight quarters follow:

Quarter	Units Sold (000)	Shipping Expense
Year 1:		
First	10	$119,000
Second	16	175,000
Third	18	190,000
Fourth	15	164,000
Year 2:		
First	11	130,000
Second	17	185,000
Third	20	210,000
Fourth	13	147,000

Milden Company's president would like a cost formula derived for shipping expense so that a budgeted income statement using the contribution approach can be prepared for the next quarter.

Required

1. Using the least-square regression method, estimate a cost formula for shipping expense. (Since the Units Sold above are in thousands of units, the variable rate you compute will also be in thousands of units. It can be left in this form, or you can convert your variable rate to a per unit basis by dividing it by 1,000.)
2. In the first quarter of Year 3, the company plans to sell 12,000 units at a selling price of $100 per unit. Prepare an income statement for the quarter using the contribution format.

Cases

C5–23 Analysis of Mixed Costs, Job-Cost System, and Activity-Based Costing   Hokuriku-Seika Co., Ltd., of Yokohama, Japan, is a subcontractor to local manufacturing firms. The company specializes in precision metal cutting using focused high-pressure water jets and high-energy lasers. The company has a traditional job-cost system in which direct labour and direct materials costs are assigned directly to jobs, but factory overhead is applied using direct labour-hours as a base. Management uses this job cost data for valuing cost of goods sold and inventories for external reports. For internal decision making, management has largely ignored this cost data since direct labour costs are basically fixed and management believes overhead costs actually have little to do with direct labour-hours. Recently, management has become interested in activity-based costing (ABC) as a way of estimating job costs and other costs for decision-making purposes.

Management assembled a cross-functional team to design a prototype ABC system. Electrical costs was one of the factory overhead costs first investigated by the team. Electricity is used to provide light, to power equipment, and to heat the building in the winter and cool it in the summer. The ABC team proposed allocating electrical costs to jobs based on machine-hours since running the machines consumes significant amounts of electricity. Data assembled by the team concerning actual direct labour-hours, machine-hours, and electrical costs over a recent eight-week period appear below. (The Japanese currency is the yen, which is denoted by ¥.)

	Direct Labour-Hours	Machine-Hours	Electrical Costs
Week 1	8,920	7,200	¥ 77,100
Week 2	8,900	8,200	84,400
Week 3	8,950	8,700	80,400
Week 4	8,990	7,200	75,500
Week 5	8,840	7,400	81,100
Week 6	8,890	8,800	83,300
Week 7	8,950	6,400	79,200
Week 8	8,990	7,700	85,500
Total	71,340	61,600	¥646,500

To help assess the effect of the proposed change to machine-hours as allocation base, the eight-week totals were converted to annual figures by multiplying them by six.

	Direct Labour-Hours	Machine-Hours	Electrical Costs
Estimated annual total (eight-week total above × 6)	428,040	369,600	¥3,879,000

Required

1. Assume that the estimated annual totals from the above table are used to compute the company's predetermined overhead rate. What would be the predetermined overhead rate for electrical costs if the allocation base is direct labour-hours? Machine-hours?
2. Hokuriku-Seika Co. intends to bid on a job for a shipyard that would require 350 direct labour-hours and 270 machine-hours. How much electrical cost would be charged to this job using the predetermined overhead rate computed in (1) above if the allocation base is direct labour-hours? Machine-hours?
3. Prepare a scattergraph in which you plot direct labour-hours on the horizontal axis and electrical costs on the vertical axis. Prepare another scattergraph in which you plot machine-hours on the horizontal axis and electrical costs on the vertical axis. Do you agree with the ABC team that machine-hours is a better allocation base for electrical costs than direct labour-hours? Why?
4. Using machine-hours as the measure of activity, estimate the fixed and variable components of electrical costs using either the scattergraph (i.e., visual fit) method or least-squares regression.
5. How much electrical cost do you think would actually be caused by the shipyard job in (2) above? Explain.
6. What factors, apart from direct labour-hours and machine-hours, are likely to affect consumption of electrical power in the company?

C5–24 Mixed Cost Analysis by Three Methods (Appendix 5A) The Ramon Company manufactures a wide range of products at several plant locations. The Franklin plant, which manufactures electrical components, has been experiencing difficulties with fluctuating monthly overhead costs. The fluctuations have made it difficult to estimate the level of overhead that will be incurred for any one month.

Management wants to be able to estimate overhead costs accurately in order to better plan its operational and financial needs. A trade association publication to which Ramon Company subscribes indicates that for companies manufacturing electrical components, overhead tends to vary with direct labour-hours.

One member of the accounting staff has proposed the cost behaviour pattern of the overhead costs be determined. Then overhead costs could be predicted from the budgeted direct labour-hours.

Another member of the accounting staff has suggested that a good starting place for determining the cost behaviour pattern of overhead costs would be an analysis of historical data. The historical cost behaviour pattern would provide a basis for estimating future overhead costs. The methods that have been proposed for determining the cost behaviour pattern include high-low, scattergraph, least-squares regression, multiple regression, and exponential smoothing. Of these methods, Ramon Company has decided to employ the high-low method, the scattergraph method, and the least-squares regression method. Data on direct labour-hours and the respective overhead costs incurred have been collected for the past two years. The raw data are as follows:

| | 2000 | | 2001 | |
Month	Direct Labour-Hours	Overhead Costs	Direct Labour-Hours	Overhead Costs
January	20,000	$84,000	21,000	$86,000
February	25,000	99,000	24,000	93,000
March	22,000	89,500	23,000	93,000
April	23,000	90,000	22,000	87,000
May	20,000	81,500	20,000	80,000
June	19,000	75,500	18,000	76,500
July	14,000	70,500	12,000	67,500
August	10,000	64,500	13,000	71,000
September	12,000	69,000	15,000	73,500
October	17,000	75,000	17,000	72,500
November	16,000	71,500	15,000	71,000
December	19,000	78,000	18,000	75,000

All equipment in the Franklin plant is leased under an arrangement calling for a flat fee up to 19,500 direct labour-hours of activity in the plant, after which lease charges are assessed on an hourly basis. Lease expense is a major item of overhead cost.

Required

1. Using the high-low method, estimate the cost formula for overhead in the Franklin plant.
2. Repeat (1) above, this time using the least-squares regression method. Your assistant has computed the following amounts, which may be helpful in your analysis.

$$\Sigma X = 435,000$$
$$\Sigma Y = \$1,894,000$$
$$\Sigma XY = \$35,170,500,000$$
$$\Sigma X^2 = 8,275,000,000$$

(Round off your answers to three significant digits.)

3. Prepare a scattergraph, including on it all data for the two-year period. Fit a regression line or lines to the plotted points by visual inspection. In this part it is not necessary to compute the fixed and variable cost elements.
4. Assume that the Franklin plant works 22,500 direct labour-hours during a month. Compute the expected overhead cost for the month using the cost formulas developed above with:
   a. The high-low method.
   b. The least-squares regression method.
   c. The scattergraph method [read the expected costs directly off the graph prepared in (3) above].
5. Of the three proposed methods, which one should the Ramon Company use to estimate monthly overhead costs in the Franklin plant? Explain fully, indicating the reasons why the other methods are less desirable.
6. Would a relevant range concept probably be more or less important in the Franklin plant than in most companies?

(CMA, adapted)

C5–25   Analysis of Mixed Costs in a Pricing Decision   Maria Chavez owns a catering company that serves food and beverages at parties and business functions. Chavez's business is seasonal, with a heavy schedule during the summer months and holidays and a lighter schedule at other times.

One of the major events Chavez's customers request is a cocktail party. She offers a standard cocktail party and has estimated the cost per guest as follows:

Food and beverages	$15.00
Labour (0.5 hrs. @ $10.00/hr.)	5.00
Overhead (0.5 hrs. @ $13.98/hr.)	6.99
Total cost per guest	$26.99

The standard cocktail party lasts three hours and Chavez hires one worker for every six guests, so that works out to one-half hour of labour per guest. These workers are hired only as needed and are paid only for the hours they actually work.

When bidding on cocktail parties, Chavez adds a 15% markup to yield a price of about $31 per guest. She is confident about her estimates of the costs of food and beverages and labour but is not as comfortable with the estimate of overhead cost. The $13.98 overhead cost per labour hour was determined by dividing total overhead expenses for the last 12 months by total labour hours for the same period. Monthly data concerning overhead costs and labour-hours appear below:

Month	Labour-Hours	Overhead Expenses
January......................	2,500	$ 55,000
February.....................	2,800	59,000
March	3,000	60,000
April	4,200	64,000
May.........................	4,500	67,000
June	5,500	71,000
July.........................	6,500	74,000
August.......................	7,500	77,000
September	7,000	75,000
October......................	4,500	68,000
November	3,100	62,000
December	6,500	73,000
Total	57,600	$805,000

Chavez has received a request to bid on a 180-guest fund-raising cocktail party to be given next month by an important local charity. (The party would last the usual three hours.) She would really like to win this contract; the guest list for this charity event includes many prominent individuals she would like to land as future clients. Maria is confident that these potential customers would be favourably impressed by her company's services at the charity event.

Required
1. Estimate the contribution to profit of a standard 180-guest cocktail party if Chavez charges her usual price of $31 per guest. (In other words, by how much would her overall profit increase?)
2. How low could Chavez bid for the charity event in terms of a price per guest and still not lose money on the event itself?
3. The individual who is organizing the charity's fund-raising event has indicated that he has already received a bid under $30 from another catering company. Do you think Chavez should bid below her normal $31 per guest price for the charity event? Why or why not?

(CMA, adapted)

Group Exercises

GE5–26 Economies or Diseconomies of Scale? Increased efficiency and lower costs result from economies of scale. An increase in scale or size (i.e., capacity) seldom requires a proportional increase in investment, research and development, sales and marketing, or administration. Therefore, high-volume, large-scale facilities create the potential for lower unit cost. It has been estimated that scale-related costs decrease as volume increases, usually falling by 15% to 25% per unit each time volume doubles.

Many industries including steel, autos, electric power, and universities have used scale-based economies to lower the cost of their product or service. Throughout the 1980s, North American steel companies invested enormous sums to modernize their plants, lower their costs, and rise from the huge losses inflicted by foreign competition. But now, "minimills," smaller, more specialized plants, are a new threat that could cause the large North American steel companies' profits to come crashing down if they are unable to fully realize the benefits of their size.

Required

1. Explain what impact steel company investments in modernizing their plants had on total fixed costs, fixed cost per unit, total variable costs, variable cost per unit, total costs, and average unit cost. Place this information on two graphs. On both graphs, label the *X* axis Production Volume. The *Y* axis on one graph should be labelled Total Costs, and on the other graph label the *Y* axis Unit Cost.

2. Which fixed costs are increasing rapidly, committed fixed costs (the costs related to the facilities and equipment) or discretionary fixed costs (the costs related to people who support production and sales)? Develop a specific scenario explaining how a particular fixed cost could increase over time.

3. What could cause fixed costs to increase so rapidly in your scenario?

4. Explain how gains and losses of market share can have such a huge impact on operating profits and losses of North American steel companies.

IE5–27 Estimating Variable and Fixed Costs Carnival Corporation owns and operates a fleet of cruise ships. The company measures its activity in terms of passenger cruise-days. For example, a family of four on a five-day cruise is counted as 20 passenger cruise-days. Many of the expenses of cruise ships—for example, the costs of food served to passengers—vary with the number of passenger cruise-days. By accessing Carnival Corporation's annual report in the Investor Relations section of their web site www.carnivalcorp.com, you can find information about their expenses and passenger cruise-days for the last three years. Operating Expenses, Selling and Administrative Expenses, and Depreciation and Amortization Expenses are listed in the company's income statement. The passenger cruise-days are listed in the section of the annual report called Management's Discussion and Analysis of Financial Condition and Results of Operations.

Required

1. For each of the three categories of expenses listed above, do the following:
   a. Plot the expense against passenger cruise-days.
   b. Using the scattergraph method, estimate the fixed and variable components of the expense. Do you have much confidence in your estimates? Why or why not?
   c. Using the high-low method, estimate the fixed and variable components of the expense. Do you have much confidence in this estimate? Why or why not?

2. Use what you believe to be the best estimates of fixed and variable costs from your analyses above to estimate how the total cost of the company varies with the number of passenger cruise-days. Express the relation in terms of the cost formula $Y = a + bX$, where Y is total cost and X is passenger cruise-days. (Ignore interest expense and income tax expense. Only include Operating Expenses, Selling and Administrative, and Depreciation and Amortization in the total cost.)

Chapter Six
Cost-Volume-Profit Relationships

Business Focus

Mike volunteered to be the director of the organization sponsoring this year's Provincial Square Holiday Feed, an annual charitable event that provides a special holiday meal to the homeless and low-income residents of the downtown area. The event is supported by donations of cash, foodstuffs, and labour. There is a small charge for the meal, but the charge is voluntary.

Mike's organization will have to buy some groceries, including disposable tableware, and will have to hire a professional chef to make sure that health department guidelines are scrupulously followed. Mike would like to know how many meals his organization can afford to serve. This information will affect all of his planning.

Learning Objectives

After studying Chapter 6, you should be able to:

1 Explain how changes in activity affect contribution margin and net income.

2 Compute the contribution margin ratio (CM ratio) and use it to compute changes in contribution margin and net income.

3 Show the effects on contribution margin of changes in variable costs, fixed costs, selling price, and volume.

4 Compute the break-even point by both the equation method and the contribution margin method.

5 Prepare a cost-volume-profit (CVP) graph and explain the significance of each of its components.

6 Use the CVP formulas to determine the activity level needed to achieve a desired target profit.

Cost-volume-profit (CVP) analysis is one of the most powerful tools that managers have at their command. It helps them understand the interrelationship between cost, volume, and profit in an organization by focusing on interactions between the following five elements:

1. Prices of products.
2. Volume or level of activity.
3. Per unit variable costs.
4. Total fixed costs.
5. Mix of products sold.

Because CVP analysis helps managers understand the interrelationship between cost, volume, and profit, it is a vital tool in many business decisions. These decisions include, for example, what products to manufacture or sell, what pricing policy to follow, what marketing strategy to employ, and what type of productive facilities to acquire.

Managerial Accounting in Action

THE ISSUE

acoustic concepts, inc.

Acoustic Concepts, Inc., was founded by Prem Narayan, a graduate student in engineering, to market a radical new speaker he had designed for automobile sound systems. The speaker, called the Sonic Blaster, uses an advanced microprocessor chip to boost amplification to awesome levels. Prem contracted with a Taiwanese electronics manufacturer to produce the speaker. With seed money provided by his family, Prem placed an order with the manufacturer for completed units and ran advertisements in auto magazines.

The Sonic Blaster was an almost immediate success, and sales grew to the point that Prem moved the company's headquarters out of his apartment and into rented quarters in a neighbouring industrial park. He also hired a receptionist, an accountant, a sales manager, and a small sales staff to sell the speakers to retail stores. The accountant, Bob Luchinni, had worked for several small companies where he had acted as a business advisor as well as accountant and bookkeeper. The following discussion occurred soon after Bob was hired:

Prem: Bob, I've got a lot of questions about the company's finances that I hope you can help answer.
Bob: We're in great shape. The loan from your family will be paid off within a few months.

Prem: I know, but I am worried about the risks I've taken on by expanding operations. What would happen if a competitor entered the market and our sales slipped? How far could sales drop without putting us into the red? Another question I've been trying to resolve is how much our sales would have to increase in order to justify the big marketing campaign the sales staff is pushing for.

Bob: Marketing always wants more money for advertising.

Prem: And they are always pushing me to drop the selling price on the speaker. I agree with them that a lower price will boost our volume, but I'm not sure the increased volume will offset the loss in revenue from the lower price.

Bob: It sounds like these questions all are related in some way to the relationships between our selling prices, our costs, and our volume. We shouldn't have a problem coming up with some answers. I'll need a day or two, though, to gather some data.

Prem: Why don't we set up a meeting for three days from now? That would be Thursday.

Bob: That'll be fine. I'll have some preliminary answers for you as well as a model you can use for answering similar questions in the future.

Prem: Good. I'll be looking forward to seeing what you come up with. ∎

The Basics of Cost-Volume-Profit (CVP) Analysis

Bob Luchinni's preparation for the Thursday meeting begins where our study of cost behaviour in the preceding chapter left off—with the contribution income statement. The contribution income statement emphasizes the behaviour of costs and therefore is extremely helpful to a manager in judging the impact on profits of changes in selling price, cost, or volume. Bob will base his analysis on the following contribution income statement he prepared last month:

ACOUSTIC CONCEPTS, INC.
Contribution Income Statement
For the Month of June

	Total	Per Unit
Sales (400 speakers)	$100,000	$250
Less variable expenses	60,000	150
Contribution margin	40,000	$100
Less fixed expenses	35,000	
Net income	$ 5,000	

Notice that sales, variable expenses, and contribution margin are expressed on a per unit basis as well as in total. This is commonly done on income statements prepared for management's own use, since, as we shall see, it facilitates profitability analysis.

Objective 1

Explain how changes in activity affect contribution margin and net income.

Contribution Margin

As explained in Chapter 5, contribution margin is the amount remaining from sales revenue after variable expenses have been deducted. Thus, it is the amount available to cover fixed expenses and then to provide profits for the period. Notice the sequence here—contribution margin is used *first* to cover the fixed expenses, and then whatever remains goes toward profits. If the contribution margin is not sufficient to cover the fixed expenses, then a loss occurs for the period. To illustrate with an extreme example, assume that by the middle of a particular month Acoustic Concepts has been able to sell only one speaker. At that point, the company's income statement will appear as follows:

	Total	Per Unit
Sales (1 speaker)	$ 250	$250
Less variable expenses	150	150
Contribution margin	100	$100
Less fixed expenses	35,000	
Net loss	$(34,900)	

For each additional speaker that the company is able to sell during the month, $100 more in contribution margin will become available to help cover the fixed expenses. If a second speaker is sold, for example, then the total contribution margin will increase by $100 (to a total of $200) and the company's loss will decrease by $100, to $34,800:

	Total	Per Unit
Sales (2 speakers)	$ 500	$250
Less variable expenses	300	150
Contribution margin	200	$100
Less fixed expenses	35,000	
Net loss	$(34,800)	

If enough speakers can be sold to generate $35,000 in contribution margin, then all of the fixed costs will be covered and the company will have managed to at least *break even* for the month—that is, to show neither profit nor loss but just cover all of its costs. To reach the break-even point, the company will have to sell 350 speakers in a month, since each speaker sold yields $100 in contribution margin:

	Total	Per Unit
Sales (350 speakers)	$87,500	$250
Less variable expenses	52,500	150
Contribution margin	35,000	$100
Less fixed expenses	35,000	
Net income	$ –0–	

Break-even point   The level of sales at which profit is zero. The break-even point can also be defined as the point where total sales equals total expenses or as the point where total contribution margin equals total fixed expenses.

Computation of the break-even point is discussed in detail later in the chapter; for the moment, note that the **break-even point** can be defined as the level of sales at which profit is zero.

Once the break-even point has been reached, net income will increase by the unit contribution margin for each additional unit sold. If 351 speakers are sold in a month, for example, then we can expect that the net income for the month will be $100, since the company will have sold 1 speaker more than the number needed to break even:

	Total	Per Unit
Sales (351 speakers)	$87,750	$250
Less variable expenses	52,650	150
Contribution margin	35,100	$100
Less fixed expenses	35,000	
Net income	$ 100	

If 352 speakers are sold (2 speakers above the break-even point), then we can expect that the net income for the month will be $200, and so forth. To know what the profits will be at various levels of activity, therefore, it is not necessary for a manager to prepare a whole series of income statements. The manager can simply take the number of units to be sold over the break-even point and multiply that number by the unit contribution margin. The result represents the anticipated profits for the period. Or, to estimate the effect of a planned increase in sales on profits, the manager can simply multiply the increase in units sold by the unit contribution margin. The result will be the expected increase in profits. To illustrate, if Acoustic Concepts is currently selling 400 speakers per month and plans to increase sales to 425 speakers per month, the anticipated impact on profits can be computed as follows:

Increased number of speakers to be sold	25
Contribution margin per speaker	×$100
Increase in net income	$2,500

These calculations can be verified as follows:

	Sales Volume			
	400 Speakers	**425 Speakers**	**Difference 25 Speakers**	**Per Unit**
Sales	$100,000	$106,250	$6,250	$250
Less variable expenses	60,000	63,750	3,750	150
Contribution margin	40,000	42,500	2,500	$100
Less fixed expenses	35,000	35,000	-0-	
Net income	$ 5,000	$ 7,500	$2,500	

To summarize the series of examples given above, if there were no sales, the company's loss would equal its fixed expenses. Each unit that is sold reduces the loss by the amount of the unit contribution margin. Once the break-even point has been reached, each additional unit sold increases the company's profit by the amount of the unit contribution margin.

Focus on Current Practice

Elgin Sweeper Company, the leading manufacturer of street sweepers in North America, manufactures five distinct sweeper models in a single facility. Historically, the company has used the traditional format for the income statement, which shows cost of goods sold, gross margin, and so forth. However, the company abandoned this format for internal use and has adopted the contribution approach. By using the contribution approach, management has discovered that key differences exist between the five sweeper models. CM ratios differ by model due to differences in variable inputs. Also, due to differences in volume, the five models differ substantially in terms of the total amount of contribution margin generated each year. Income statements in the contribution format—with breakdowns of sales, contribution margin, and CM ratios by sweeper model—now serve as the basis for internal decision making by management.[1] ∎

---

1. John P. Callan, Wesley N. Tredup, and Randy S. Wissinger, "Elgin Sweeper Company's Journey toward Cost Management," *Management Accounting* 73, no. 1 (July 1991), p. 27; and telephone interviews with management.

Contribution Margin Ratio (CM Ratio)

In addition to being expressed on a per unit basis, sales revenues, variable expenses, and contribution margin for Acoustic Concepts can also be expressed as a percentage of sales:

	Total	Per Unit	Percent of Sales
Sales (400 speakers)	$100,000	$250	100%
Less variable expenses	60,000	150	60%
Contribution margin	40,000	$100	40%
Less fixed expenses	35,000		
Net income	$ 5,000		

The contribution margin as a percentage of total sales is referred to as the **contribution margin ratio (CM ratio).** This ratio is computed as follows:

$$\text{CM ratio} = \frac{\text{Contribution margin}}{\text{Sales}}$$

For Acoustic Concepts, the computations are as follows:

$$\frac{\text{Total contribution margin, \$40,000}}{\text{Total sales, \$100,000}} = 40\% \quad \text{or} \quad \frac{\text{Per unit contribution margin, \$100}}{\text{Per unit sales, \$250}} = 40\%$$

The CM ratio is extremely useful since it shows how the contribution margin will be affected by a change in total sales. To illustrate, notice that Acoustic Concepts has a CM ratio of 40%. This means that for each dollar increase in sales, total contribution margin will increase by 40 cents ($1 sales × CM ratio of 40%). Net income will also increase by 40 cents, assuming that there are no changes in fixed costs.

As this illustration suggests, *the impact on net income of any given dollar change in total sales can be computed in seconds by simply applying the CM ratio to the dollar change.* If Acoustic Concepts plans a $30,000 increase in sales during the coming month, for example, management can expect contribution margin to increase by $12,000 ($30,000 increased sales × CM ratio of 40%). As we noted above, net income will also increase by $12,000 if fixed costs do not change.

This is verified by the following table:

	Sales Volume			
	Present	Expected	Increase	Percent of Sales
Sales	$100,000	$130,000	$30,000	100%
Less variable expenses	60,000	78,000*	18,000	60%
Contribution margin	40,000	52,000	12,000	40%
Less fixed expenses	35,000	35,000	-0-	
Net income	$ 5,000	$ 17,000	$12,000	

*$130,000 expected sales ÷ $250 per unit = 520 units. 520 units × $150 per unit = $78,000.

Some managers prefer to work with the CM ratio rather than the unit contribution margin figure. The CM ratio is particularly valuable in those situations where the manager must make trade-offs between more dollar sales of one product versus more dollar sales of another. Generally speaking, when trying to increase sales, products that yield the greatest amount of contribution margin per dollar of sales should be emphasized.

Focus on Current Practice

Ultramar initiated its Value Plus ad campaign in mid-1996, which promised the lowest gasoline prices in the market. The result of the campaign was a price war that lasted about six weeks. During this time, prices fell as low as 19.9 cents just outside Montreal. Petro-Canada broke the costly war, elevating their prices to 58 cents per litre—still below the break-even point of 62 cents.

Some Applications of CVP Concepts

Objective 3

Show the effects on contribution margin of changes in variable costs, fixed costs, selling price, and volume.

Bob Luchinni, the accountant at Acoustic Concepts, wanted to demonstrate to the company's president Prem Narayan how the concepts developed on the preceding pages of this text can be used in planning and decision making. Bob gathered the following basic data:

	Per Unit	Percent of Sales
Sales price	$250	100%
Less variable expenses	150	60%
Contribution margin	$100	40%

Recall that fixed expenses are $35,000 per month. Bob Luchinni will use these data to show the effects of changes in variable costs, fixed costs, sales price, and sales volume on the company's profitability.

CHANGE IN FIXED COST AND SALES VOLUME Acoustic Concepts is currently selling 400 speakers per month (monthly sales of $100,000). The sales manager feels that a $10,000 increase in the monthly advertising budget would increase monthly sales by $30,000. Should the advertising budget be increased?

The following table shows the effect of the proposed change in monthly advertising budget:

	Current Sales	Sales with Additional Advertising Budget	Difference	Percent of Sales
Sales	$100,000	$130,000	$30,000	100%
Less variable expenses	60,000	78,000	18,000	60%
Contribution margin	40,000	52,000	12,000	40%
Less fixed expenses	35,000	45,000*	10,000	
Net income	$ 5,000	$ 7,000	$ 2,000	

*$35,000 plus additional $10,000 monthly advertising budget = $45,000.

Assuming there are no other factors to be considered, the increase in the advertising budget should be approved since it would lead to an increase in net income of $2,000. There are two shorter ways to present this solution. The first alternative solution follows:

Alternative Solution 1

Expected total contribution margin:	
$130,000 × 40% CM ratio	$52,000
Present total contribution margin:	
$100,000 × 40% CM ratio	40,000
Incremental contribution margin	12,000
Change in fixed costs:	
Less incremental advertising expense	10,000
Increased net income	$ 2,000

Since in this case only the fixed costs and the sales volume change, the solution can be presented in an even shorter format, as follows:

Alternative Solution 2

Incremental contribution margin:	
$30,000 × 40% CM ratio	$12,000
Less incremental advertising expense	10,000
Increased net income	$ 2,000

Incremental analysis
An analytical approach that focuses only on those items of revenue, cost, and volume that will change as a result of a decision.

Notice that this approach does not depend on a knowledge of previous sales. Also notice that it is unnecessary under either shorter approach to prepare an income statement. Both of the solutions above involve an **incremental analysis** in that they consider only those items of revenue, cost, and volume that will change if the new program is implemented. Although in each case a new income statement could have been prepared, most managers would prefer the incremental approach. The reason is that it is simpler and more direct, and it permits the decision maker to focus attention on the specific items involved in the decision.

CHANGE IN VARIABLE COSTS AND SALES VOLUME   Refer to the original data. Recall that Acoustic Concepts is currently selling 400 speakers per month. Management is contemplating the use of higher-quality components, which would increase variable costs (and thereby reduce the contribution margin) by $10 per speaker. However, the sales manager predicts that the higher overall quality would increase sales to 480 speakers per month. Should the higher-quality components be used?

The $10 increase in variable costs will cause the unit contribution margin to decrease from $100 to $90.

Solution

Expected total contribution margin with	
higher-quality components:	
480 speakers × $90	$43,200
Present total contribution margin:	
400 speakers × $100	40,000
Increase in total contribution margin	$ 3,200

Yes, based on the information above, the higher-quality components should be used. Since fixed costs will not change, net income should increase by the $3,200 increase in contribution margin shown above.

CHANGE IN FIXED COST, SALES PRICE, AND SALES VOLUME   Refer to the original data and recall again that the company is currently selling 400 speakers per month. To increase sales, the sales manager would like to cut the selling price by $20 per speaker and increase the advertising budget by $15,000 per month. The sales manager argues that if these two steps are taken, unit sales will increase by 50% to 600 speakers per month. Should the changes be made?

A decrease of $20 per speaker in the selling price will cause the unit contribution margin to decrease from $100 to $80.

Solution

Expected total contribution margin with lower selling price:	
600 speakers × $80	$48,000
Present total contribution margin:	
400 speakers × $100	40,000
Incremental contribution margin	8,000
Change in fixed costs:	
Less incremental advertising expense	15,000
Reduction in net income	$(7,000)

No, based on the information above, the changes should not be made. The same solution can be obtained by preparing comparative income statements:

	Present 400 Speakers per Month		Expected 600 Speakers per Month		
	Total	**Per Unit**	**Total**	**Per Unit**	**Difference**
Sales	$100,000	$250	$138,000	$230	$38,000
Less variable expenses	60,000	150	90,000	150	30,000
Contribution margin	40,000	$100	48,000	$ 80	8,000
Less fixed expenses	35,000		50,000*		15,000
Net income (loss)	$ 5,000		$ (2,000)		$ (7,000)

*35,000 + Additional monthly advertising budget of $15,000 = $50,000.

Notice that the effect on net income is the same as that obtained by the incremental analysis above.

CHANGE IN VARIABLE COST, FIXED COST, AND SALES VOLUME Refer to the original data. As before, the company is currently selling 400 speakers per month. The sales manager would like to place the sales staff on a commission basis of $15 per speaker sold, rather than on flat salaries that now total $6,000 per month. The sales manager is confident that the change will increase monthly sales by 15% to 460 speakers per month. Should the change be made?

Solution

Changing the sales staff from a salaried basis to a commission basis will affect both fixed and variable costs. Fixed costs will decrease by $6,000, from $35,000 to $29,000. Variable costs will increase by $15, from $150 to $165, and the unit contribution margin will decrease from $100 to $85.

Expected total contribution margin with sales staff on commissions:	
460 speakers × $85	$39,100
Present total contribution margin:	
400 speakers × $100	40,000
Decrease in total contribution margin	(900)
Change in fixed costs:	
Add salaries avoided if a commission is paid	6,000
Increase in net income	$ 5,100

Yes, based on the information above, the changes should be made. Again, the same answer can be obtained by preparing comparative income statements:

	Present 400 Speakers per Month		Expected 460 Speakers per Month		Difference: Increase or (Decrease) in Net Income
	Total	Per Unit	Total	Per Unit	
Sales	$100,000	$250	$115,000	$250	$15,000
Less variable expenses	60,000	150	75,900	165	(15,900)
Contribution margin	40,000	$100	39,100	$ 85	(900)
Less fixed expenses	35,000		29,000		6,000
Net income	$ 5,000		$ 10,100		$ 5,100

CHANGE IN REGULAR SALES PRICE   Refer to the original data where Acoustic Concepts is currently selling 400 speakers per month. The company has an opportunity to make a bulk sale of 150 speakers to a wholesaler if an acceptable price can be worked out. This sale would not disturb the company's regular sales. What price per speaker should be quoted to the wholesaler if Acoustic Concepts wants to increase its monthly profits by $3,000?

Variable cost per speaker	$150
Desired profit per speaker:	
$3,000 ÷ 150 speakers	20
Quoted price per speaker	$170

Notice that no element of fixed cost is included in the computation. This is because fixed costs are not affected by the bulk sale, so all of the additional revenue that is in excess of variable costs goes to increasing the profits of the company.

If Acoustic Concepts had been operating at a loss rather than at a profit, many managers would look at the situation somewhat differently. Instead of a modest profit of $3,000, many managers would attempt to reverse all or part of the company's overall loss by quoting a higher price. To illustrate this point, assume that Acoustic Concepts presently has a loss of $6,000 this month and that the company would like to make enough money on the bulk sale of speakers to turn this loss into a profit of $3,000. Under these circumstances, the quoted price on the 150 new speakers would be computed as shown below.

Variable cost per speaker	$150
Present net loss:	
$6,000 ÷ 150 speakers	40
Desired profit:	
$3,000 ÷ 150 speakers	20
Quoted price per speaker	$210

The $210 price we have computed represents a substantial discount from the $250 regular selling price per speaker. Thus, both the wholesaler and the company would benefit from the bulk order at this price. This will not always happen, however. By attempting to cover all of the company's losses on one special order, a manager may quote such a high price that the order is lost. Any price greater than $150 will help to reduce the company's loss. A manager must always keep such market considerations in mind when deciding on prices.

Importance of the Contribution Margin

As stated in the introduction to the chapter, CVP analysis seeks the most profitable combination of variable costs, fixed costs, selling price, and sales volume. The above examples show that the effect on the contribution margin is a major consideration in deciding on the most profitable combination of these factors. We have seen that profits can sometimes be improved by reducing the contribution margin if fixed costs can be reduced by a greater amount. More commonly, however, we have seen that the way to improve profits is to increase the total contribution margin figure. Sometimes this can be done by reducing the selling price and thereby increasing volume; sometimes it can be done by increasing the fixed costs (such as advertising) and thereby increasing volume; and sometimes it can be done by trading off variable and fixed costs with appropriate changes in volume. Many other combinations of factors are possible.

The size of the unit contribution margin figure (and the size of the CM ratio) will have a heavy influence on what steps a company is willing to take to improve profits. For example, the greater the unit contribution margin for a product, the greater is the amount that a company will be willing to spend in order to increase unit sales of the product by a given percentage. This explains in part why companies with high unit contribution margins (such as auto manufacturers) advertise so heavily, while companies with low unit contribution margins (such as dishware manufacturers) tend to spend much less for advertising.

In short, the effect on the contribution margin holds the key to many decisions.

Focus on Current Practice

According to a July 30, 1999, release by Canada News Wire, vehicle productivity, which is measured by the number of days needed to assemble an automobile, stands at 3.26 worker-days in Canada compared with 3.37 in the United States, giving Canada a 3.3% competitive edge. It is expected that in 1999, Canadian auto production in Canada will increase to a record 2.8 million vehicles, up from 2.6 million in 1998.

Canadian auto plants have assembled 19% of North American vehicle production. That is almost 2.5 times Canada's share of sales. Canadian auto manufacturers also have an advantage because U.S. companies pay higher health care costs. These two advantages give Canadian auto manufacturers a 33% labour cost advantage over their American counterparts. Canadian companies can break even at lower sales levels than comparative size American plants because of these cost advantages. ■

Break-Even Analysis

Objective 4

Compute the break-even point by both the equation method and the contribution margin method.

CVP analysis is sometimes referred to simply as break-even analysis. This is unfortunate because break-even analysis is only one element of CVP analysis—although an important element. Break-even analysis is designed to answer questions such as those asked by Prem Narayan, the president of Acoustic Concepts, concerning how far sales could drop before the company begins to lose money.

Break-Even Computations

Equation method A method of computing the break-even point that relies on the equation Sales = Variable expenses + Fixed expenses + Profits.

Earlier in the chapter we defined the break-even point to be the level of sales at which the company's profit is zero. The break-even point can be computed using either the *equation method* or the *contribution margin method*—the two methods are equivalent.

THE EQUATION METHOD The **equation method** centres on the contribution approach to the income statement illustrated earlier in the chapter. The format of this income statement can be expressed in equation form as follows:

$$Profits = Sales - (Variable\ expenses + Fixed\ expenses)$$

Rearranging this equation slightly yields the following equation, which is widely used in CVP analysis:

$$Sales = Variable\ expenses + Fixed\ expenses + Profits$$

At the break-even point, profits are zero. Therefore, the break-even point can be computed by finding that point where sales just equal the total of the variable expenses plus the fixed expenses. For Acoustic Concepts, the break-even point in unit sales, Q, can be computed as follows:

$$Sales = Variable\ expenses + Fixed\ expenses + Profits$$

$$\$250Q = \$150Q + \$35,000 + \$0$$
$$\$100Q = \$35,000$$
$$Q = \$35,000 \div 100$$
$$Q = 350\ speakers$$

where:

Q = Number (quantity) of speakers sold
$\$250$ = Unit sales price
$\$150$ = Unit variable expenses
$\$35,000$ = Total fixed expenses

The break-even point in sales dollars can be computed by multiplying the break-even level of unit sales by the selling price per unit:

$$350\ speakers \times \$250 = \$87,500$$

The break-even in total sales dollars, X, can also be directly computed as follows:

$$Sales = Variable\ expenses + Fixed\ expenses + Profits$$

$$X = 0.60X + \$35,000 + \$0$$
$$0.40X = \$35,000$$
$$X = \$35,000 \div 0.40$$
$$X = \$87,500$$

where:

X = Total sales dollars
0.60 = Variable expenses as a percentage of sales
$\$35,000$ = Total fixed expenses

Firms often have data available only in percentage form, and the approach we have just illustrated must then be used to find the break-even point. Notice that use of percentages in the equation yields a break-even point in sales dollars rather than in units sold. The break-even point in units sold is the following:

$$\$87,500 \div \$250 = 350\ speakers$$

Contribution margin method A method of computing the break-even point in which the fixed expenses are divided by the contribution margin per unit.

THE CONTRIBUTION MARGIN METHOD   The **contribution margin method** is actually just a shortcut version of the equation method already described. The approach centres on the idea discussed earlier that each unit sold provides a certain amount of contribution margin that goes toward covering fixed costs. To find how many units must be sold to break even, divide the total fixed costs by the unit contribution margin:

$$\text{Break-even point in units sold} = \frac{\text{Fixed expenses}}{\text{Unit contribution margin}}$$

Each speaker generates a contribution margin of $100 ($250 selling price, less $150 variable expenses). Since the total fixed expenses are $35,000, the break-even point is as follows:

$$\frac{\text{Fixed expenses}}{\text{Unit contribution margin}} = \frac{\$35,000}{\$100} = 350 \text{ speakers}$$

A variation of this method uses the CM ratio instead of the unit contribution margin. The result is the break-even in total sales dollars rather than in total units sold.

$$\text{Break-even point in total sales dollars} = \frac{\text{Fixed expenses}}{\text{CM ratio}}$$

In the Acoustic Concepts example, the calculations are as follows:

$$\frac{\text{Fixed expenses}}{\text{CM ratio}} = \frac{\$35,000}{40\%} = \$87,500$$

This approach, based on the CM ratio, is particularly useful in those situations where a company has multiple product lines and wishes to compute a single break-even point for the company as a whole. More is said on this point in a later section titled The Concept of Sales Mix.

Focus on Current Practice

Maritime Trading Co. (MTC), a catalogue retailer based in Halifax, estimated it would break even at sales of $650,000 in its 1998–99 fiscal year. In 1997, after MTC shipped out 10,000 catalogues, Canada Post went on strike. When MTC president Kent Groves spoke out against the strike his offices were picketed by striking postal workers shouting "corporate greed." Consequently MTC suffered a large loss. The company has since shifted its strategic focus from revenue generation to cost efficiency. MTC reduced staff from 20 to 15 and has renegotiated expenses such as accounting and graphic design fees. By reducing both variable costs and fixed costs, MTC believes it has taken its break-even point down to an achievable level.

CVP Relationships in Graphic Form

Objective 5

Prepare a cost-volume-profit (CVP) graph and explain the significance of each of its components.

The relationships among revenue, cost, profit, and volume can be expressed graphically by preparing a **cost-volume-profit (CVP) graph.** A CVP graph highlights CVP relationships over wide ranges of activity and can give managers a perspective that can be obtained in no other way. To help explain his analysis to Prem Narayan, Bob Luchinni decided to prepare a CVP graph for Acoustic Concepts.

PREPARING THE CVP GRAPH   Preparing a CVP graph (sometimes called a *break-even chart*) involves three steps. These steps are keyed to the graph in Exhibit 6–1:

Exhibit 6–1   Preparing the CVP Graph

Volume in speakers

Cost-volume-profit (CVP) graph   The relations between revenues, costs, and level of activity in an organization presented in graphic form.

1. Draw a line parallel to the volume axis to represent total fixed expenses. For Acoustic Concepts, total fixed expenses are $35,000.
2. Choose some volume of sales and plot the point representing total expenses (fixed and variable) at the activity level you have selected. In Exhibit 6–1, Bob Luchinni chose a volume of 600 speakers. Total expenses at that activity level would be as follows:

Fixed expenses	$ 35,000
Variable expenses (600 speakers × $150)	90,000
Total expenses	$125,000

    After the point has been plotted, draw a line through it back to the point where the fixed expenses line intersects the dollars axis.
3. Again choose some volume of sales and plot the point representing total sales dollars at the activity level you have selected. In Exhibit 6–1, Bob Luchinni again chose a volume of 600 speakers. Sales at that activity level total $150,000 (600 speakers × $250). Draw a line through this point back to the origin.

    The interpretation of the completed CVP graph is given in Exhibit 6–2. The anticipated profit or loss at any given level of sales is measured by the vertical distance between the total revenue line (sales) and the total expenses line (variable expenses plus fixed expenses).

    The break-even point is where the total revenue and total expenses lines cross. The break-even point of 350 speakers in Exhibit 6–2 agrees with the break-even point obtained for Acoustic Concepts in earlier computations.

Target Profit Analysis

Objective 6

Use the CVP formulas to determine the activity level needed to achieve a desired target profit.

CVP formulas can be used to determine the sales volume needed to achieve a target profit. Suppose that Prem Narayan of Acoustic Concepts would like to earn a target profit of $40,000 per month. How many speakers would have to be sold?

THE CVP EQUATION   One approach is to use the equation method discussed on page 256. Instead of solving for the unit sales where profits are zero, you instead solve for the unit sales where profits are $40,000.

Exhibit 6–2 The Completed CVP Graph

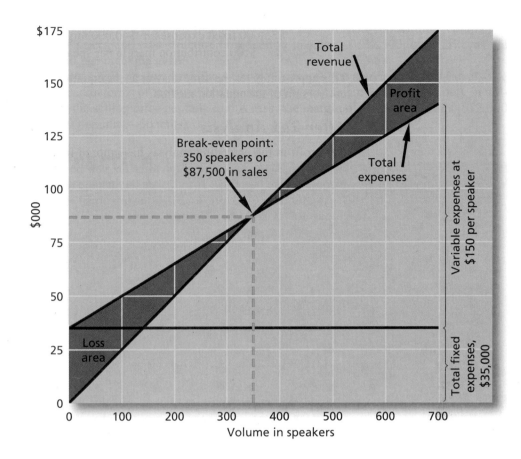

$$\text{Sales} = \text{Variable expenses} + \text{Fixed expenses} + \text{Profits}$$

$$\$250Q = \$150Q + \$35,000 + \$40,000$$
$$\$100Q = \$75,000$$
$$Q = \$75,000 \div \$100$$
$$Q = 750 \text{ speakers}$$

where:

Q =	Number of speakers sold
$\$250$ =	Unit sales price
$\$150$ =	Unit variable expenses
$\$35,000$ =	Total fixed expenses
$\$40,000$ =	Target profit

Thus, the target profit can be achieved by selling 750 speakers per month, which represents $187,500 in total sales ($250 × 750 speakers).

THE CONTRIBUTION MARGIN APPROACH A second approach involves expanding the contribution margin formula to include the target profit:

$$\text{Units sold to attain the target profit} = \frac{\text{Fixed expenses} + \text{Target profit}}{\text{Unit contribution margin}}$$

Management is anxious to improve the company's profit performance and has asked for several items of information.

Required

1. Compute the company's CM ratio and variable expense ratio.
2. Compute the company's break-even point in both units and sales dollars. Use the equation method.
3. Assume that sales increase by $400,000 next year. If cost behaviour patterns remain unchanged, by how much will the company's net income increase? Use the CM ratio to determine your answer.
4. Refer to original data. Assume that next year management wants the company to earn a minimum profit of $90,000. How many units will have to be sold to meet this target profit figure?
5. Refer to the original data. Compute the company's margin of safety in both dollar and percentage form.
6. a. Compute the company's degree of operating leverage at the present level of sales.
   b. Assume that through a more intense effort by the sales staff the company's sales increase by 8% next year. By what percentage would you expect net income to increase? Use the operating leverage concept to obtain your answer.
   c. Verify your answer to (b) by preparing a new income statement showing an 8% increase in sales.
7. In an effort to increase sales and profits, management is considering the use of a higher-quality speaker. The higher-quality speaker would increase variable costs by $3 per unit, but management could eliminate one quality inspector who is paid a salary of $30,000 per year. The sales manager estimates that the higher-quality speaker would increase annual sales by at least 20%.
   a. Assuming that changes are made as described above, prepare a projected income statement for next year. Show data on a total, per unit, and percentage basis.
   b. Compute the company's new break-even point in both units and dollars of sales. Use the contribution margin method.
   c. Would you recommend that the changes be made?

Solution to Review Problem

1. CM ratio: Variable expense ratio:

$$\frac{\text{Contribution margin, \$15}}{\text{Selling price, \$60}} = 25\% \qquad \frac{\text{Variable expense, \$45}}{\text{Selling price, \$60}} = 75\%$$

2.   Sales = Variable expenses + Fixed expenses + Profits

$$\begin{aligned}
\$60Q &= \$45Q + \$240{,}000 + \$0 \\
\$15Q &= \$240{,}000 \\
Q &= \$240{,}000 \div \$15 \\
Q &= 16{,}000 \text{ units; or at \$60 per unit, \$960,000}
\end{aligned}$$

Alternative solution:

$$\begin{aligned}
X &= 0.75X + \$240{,}000 + \$0 \\
0.25X &= \$240{,}000 \\
X &= \$240{,}000 \div 0.25 \\
X &= \$960{,}000; \text{ or at \$60 per unit, 16,000 units}
\end{aligned}$$

3.
Increase in sales...	$400,000
Multiply by the CM ratio.................................	× 25%
Expected increase in contribution margin............	$100,000

Since the fixed expenses are not expected to change, net income will increase by the entire $100,000 increase in contribution margin computed above.

4. Equation method:

Sales = Variable expenses + Fixed expenses + Profits

$$\begin{aligned}
\$60Q &= \$45Q + \$240{,}000 + \$90{,}000 \\
\$15Q &= \$330{,}000 \\
Q &= \$330{,}000 \div \$15 \\
Q &= 22{,}000 \text{ units}
\end{aligned}$$

Contribution margin method:

$$\frac{\text{Fixed expenses} + \text{Target profit}}{\text{Contribution margin per unit}} = \frac{\$240,000 + \$90,000}{\$15} = 22,000 \text{ units}$$

5.   Total sales − Break-even sales = Margin of safety in dollars
$1,200,000 − $960,000 = $240,000

$$\frac{\text{Margin of safety in dollars, } \$240,000}{\text{Total sales, } \$1,200,000} = 20\%$$

6. a. $$\frac{\text{Contribution margin, } \$300,000}{\text{Net income, } \$60,000} = 5 \text{ (degree of operating leverage)}$$

   b.
Expected increase in sales	8%
Degree of operating leverage	× 5
Expected increase in net income	40%

   c. If sales increase by 8%, then 21,600 units (20,000 × 1.08 = 21,600) will be sold next year. The new income statement will be as follows:

	Total	Per Unit	Percent of Sales
Sales (21,600 units)	$1,296,000	$60	100%
Less variable expenses	972,000	45	75%
Contribution margin	324,000	$15	25%
Less fixed expenses	240,000		
Net income	$ 84,000		

Thus, the $84,000 expected net income for next year represents a 40% increase over the $60,000 net income earned during the current year:

$$\frac{\$84,000 - \$60,000 = \$24,000}{\$60,000} = 40\% \text{ increase}$$

Note from the income statement above that the increase in sales from 20,000 to 21,600 units has resulted in increases in *both* total sales and total variable expenses. It is a common error to overlook the increase in variable expenses when preparing a projected income statement.

7. a. A 20% increase in sales would result in 24,000 units being sold next year: 20,000 units × 1.20 = 24,000 units.

	Total	Per Unit	Percent of Sales
Sales (24,000 units)	$1,440,000	$60	100%
Less variable expenses	1,152,000	48*	80%
Contribution margin	288,000	$12	20%
Less fixed expenses	210,000[†]		
Net income	$ 78,000		

   *$45 + $3 = $48; $48 ÷ $60 = 80%.
   [†]$240,000 − $30,000 = $210,000.

Note that the change in per unit variable expenses results in a change in both the per unit contribution margin and the CM ratio.

   b. $$\frac{\text{Fixed expenses, } \$210,000}{\text{Contribution margin per unit, } \$12} = 17,500 \text{ units}$$

$$\frac{\text{Fixed expenses, } \$210,000}{\text{CM ratio, } 20\%} = \$1,050,000 \text{ break-even sales}$$

c. Yes, based on these data the changes should be made. The changes will increase the company's net income from the present $60,000 to $78,000 per year. Although the changes will also result in a higher break-even point (17,500 units as compared to the present 16,000 units), the company's margin of safety will actually be wider than before:

Total sales − Break-even sales = Margin of safety in dollars
$1,400,000 − $1,050,000 = $390,000

As shown in (5) above, the company's present margin of safety is only $240,000. Thus, several benefits will result from the proposed changes.

Appendix 6A: Cost-Volume-Profit with Uncertainty

Objective 10

Understand cost-volume-profit with uncertainty.

CVP analysis is often employed to assess what future prospects might be under various arrangements. Given the compactness of the analysis, the CVP formula is a convenient approach to conducting such assessments. Consider the following example: Novelties Ltd. produces and sells highly faddish products directed toward the teenage market. A new product has come onto the market that the company is anxious to produce and sell. Enough capacity exists in the company's plant to produce 15,000 units each month. Variable costs to manufacture and sell one unit would be $1.60, and fixed costs would total $16,000 per month.

Management of Novelties wants to assess the implications of various alternatives. As part of the investigation, management wants an analysis of the profits before income taxes if various alternative sales volumes, selling prices, and variable expenses occur. Sales volumes would be 13,500 units or 15,000 units. Selling prices would be $3.50 or $4.00. Variable expenses were estimated as being $1.28 or $1.60 depending on a series of outcomes. First consider the eight (2 × 2 × 2) possible outcomes:

Alternatives	Variable Expenses	Selling Prices	Sales Volumes	Fixed Expenses	Profits before Taxes
1	$1.28	$3.50	13,500	$16,000	$13,970
2	1.28	3.50	15,000	16,000	17,300
3	1.28	4.00	13,500	16,000	20,720
4	1.28	4.00	15,000	16,000	24,800
5	1.60	3.50	13,500	16,000	9,650
6	1.60	3.50	15,000	16,000	12,500
7	1.60	4.00	13,500	16,000	16,400
8	1.60	4.00	15,000	16,000	20,000

By noticing the repetitions of variable expenses and selling prices, the preceding table can be represented in the form of a tree, commonly termed a *decision tree*, as shown in Exhibit 6A–1.

As a manager, one would like alternative 4 with a profit of $24,800. If a manager can force the future components of a profit to be the following—variable expenses, $1.28; selling price, $4.00; and sales volume, 15,000 units—a profit of $24,800 before taxes can be achieved. Unfortunately, managers do not have such a luxury.

Assume the best the manager can do is assess the chances of each alternative occurring. These chances are commonly termed *subjective probabilities* and can represent what the manager believes will occur. Each of the possible chances can also be placed on the tree as shown in Exhibit 6A–2.

Close observation reveals several important and general results to the manager of Novelties. First, the chances for each uncertain factor are expressed in decimal form

Exhibit 6A-1   A Decision Tree

Variable Expense	Selling Prices	Sales Volumes	Fixed Expenses	Profits before Taxes	Alternative Number
		13,500	$16,000	$13,970	1
	$3.50	15,000	$16,000	$17,300	2
	$4.00	13,500	$16,000	$20,720	3
$1.28		15,000	$16,000	$24,800	4
$1.60		13,500	$16,000	$ 9,650	5
	$3.50	15,000	$16,000	$12,500	6
	$4.00	13,500	$16,000	$16,400	7
		15,000	$16,000	$20,000	8

Exhibit 6A-2   A Decision Tree

Variable Expense Chances	Selling Price Chances	Sales Volume Chances	Product Results	Alternative Number
		.90	.60 × .70 × .90 = .38	1
	.70	.10	.60 × .70 × .10 = .04	2
	.30	.90	.60 × .30 × .90 = .16	3
.60		.10	.60 × .30 × .10 = .02	4
.40		.90	.40 × .70 × .90 = .25	5
	.70	.10	.40 × .70 × .10 = .03	6
	.30	.90	.40 × .30 × .90 = .11	7
		.10	.40 × .30 × .10 = .01	8
			Total 1.00	

and sum to one. Second, the chances are multiplied on the tree in the same sequence as the CVP elements. Third, no chance was assigned to fixed expenses because they are known in every case.

The manager notes that if the subjective probabilities are correct, there is only a 2% chance, or 2 chances in 100, of having a profit of $24,800.

To ascertain what Novelties might expect future profits to be, the expected value (often termed a mean) is computed as follows:

Alternatives	Profits	Chances	Products	
1	$13,970	.38	$5,308.60	($13,970 × .38)
2	17,300	.04	692.00	($17,300 × .04)
3	20,720	.16	3,315.20	
4	24,800	.02	496.00	
5	9,650	.25	2,412.50	
6	12,500	.03	375.00	
7	16,400	.11	1,804.00	
8	20,000	.01	200.00	
		1.00		
Total expected value			$14,603.30	

The expected value, $14,603.30, is a reasonable estimate of what the profit of Novelties might be for next period given the data and the chances supplied to the analysis.

The decision tree analysis is very powerful. A computer can facilitate the tedious calculations. However, it is important to note that the number of calculations increases dramatically with both the number of alternatives (e.g., 1.28 or 1.60 for variable expenses) considered (e.g., $3 \times 3 \times 3 = 27$, $4 \times 4 \times 4 = 64$) and the number of factors (e.g., selling prices, sales volumes, etc.) considered in the CVP formulation (e.g., $2 \times 2 \times 2 \times 2 = 16$, $2 \times 2 \times 2 \times 2 = 32$). Even a computer can be taxed very quickly.

Questions

6–1 What is meant by a product's CM ratio? How is this ratio useful in planning business operations?

6–2 Often the most direct route to a business decision is to make an incremental analysis based on the information available. What is meant by an *incremental analysis?*

6–3 Company A's cost structure includes costs that are mostly variable, whereas Company B's cost structure includes costs that are mostly fixed. In a time of increasing sales, which company will tend to realize the most rapid increase in profits? Explain.

6–4 What is meant by the term *operating leverage?*

6–5 A 10% decrease in the selling price of a product will have the same impact on net income as a 10% increase in the variable expenses. Do you agree? Why or why not?

6–6 What is meant by the term *break-even point?*

6–7 Name three approaches to break-even analysis. Briefly explain how each approach works.

6–8 In response to a request from your immediate supervisor, you have prepared a CVP graph portraying the cost and revenue characteristics of your company's product and operations. Explain how the lines on the graph and the break-even point would change if (a) the selling price per unit decreased, (b) fixed costs increased throughout the entire range of activity portrayed on the graph, and (c) variable costs per unit increased.

6–9 Al's Auto Wash charges $4 to wash a car. The variable costs of washing a car are 15% of sales. Fixed expenses total $1,700 monthly. How many cars must be washed each month for Al to break even?

6–10   What is meant by the margin of safety?

6–11   Companies X and Y are in the same industry. Company X is highly automated, whereas Company Y relies primarily on labour to make its products. If sales and total expenses in the two companies are about the same, which would you expect to have the lower margin of safety? Why?

6–12   What is meant by the term *sales mix*? What assumption is usually made concerning sales mix in CVP analysis?

6–13   Explain how a shift in the sales mix could result in both a higher break-even point and a lower net income.

6–14   Why do accountants commonly use linear CVP analysis rather than the curvilinear form?

6–15   What effect would a 30% income tax rate have on the CVP formula?

6–16   Why must inventories be assumed to be constant in the CVP formula?

6–17   What would happen to CVP analysis if worker productivity increased as the top of the relevant range was reached?

6–18   Describe how uncertainty can be explicitly considered in CVP analysis.

6–19   Does the concept of relevant range imply more than one break-even point? Explain.

Exercises

E6–1   Menlo Company manufactures and sells a single product. The company's sales and expenses for last quarter follow:

	Total	Per Unit
Sales	$450,000	$30
Less variable expenses	180,000	12
Contribution margin	270,000	$18
Less fixed expenses	216,000	
Net income	$ 54,000	

Required
1. What is the quarterly break-even point in units sold and in sales dollars?
2. Without resorting to computations, what is the total contribution margin at the break-even point?
3. How many units would have to be sold each quarter to earn a target profit of $90,000? Use the unit contribution method. Verify your answer by preparing a contribution income statement at the target level of sales.
4. Refer to the original data. Compute the company's margin of safety in both dollar and percentage terms.
5. What is the company's CM ratio? If sales increase by $50,000 per quarter and there is no change in fixed expenses, by how much would you expect quarterly net income to increase? (Do not prepare an income statement; use the CM ratio to compute your answer.)

E6–2   Lindon Company is the exclusive distributor for an automotive product. The product sells for $40 per unit and has a CM ratio of 30%. The company's fixed expenses are $180,000 per year.

Required

1. What are the variable expenses per unit?
2. Using the equation method:
   a. What is the break-even point in units and sales dollars?
   b. What sales level in units and in sales dollars is required to earn an annual profit of $60,000?
   c. Assume that by using a more efficient shipper, the company is able to reduce its variable expenses by $4 per unit. What is the company's new break-even point in units and sales dollars?
3. Repeat (2) above using the unit contribution method.

E6–3　The Halifax Symphony Guild is planning its annual dinner-dance. The dinner-dance committee has assembled the following expected costs for the event:

Dinner (per person)	$　18
Favours and program (per person)	2
Band	2,800
Rental of ballroom	900
Professional entertainment during intermission	1,000
Tickets and advertising	1,300

The committee members would like to charge $35 per person for the evening's activities.

Required

1. Compute the break-even point for the dinner-dance (in terms of the number of persons that must attend).
2. Assume that last year only 300 persons attended the dinner-dance. If the same number attend this year, what price per ticket must be charged in order to break even?
3. Refer to the original data ($35 ticket price per person). Prepare a CVP graph for the dinner-dance from a zero level of activity up to 900 tickets sold. Number of persons should be placed on the horizontal *(X)* axis, and dollars should be placed on the vertical *(Y)* axis.

E6–4　Magic Realm, Inc., has developed a new fantasy board game. The company sold 15,000 games last year at a selling price of $20 per game. Fixed costs associated with the game total $182,000 per year, and variable costs are $6 per game. Production of the game is entrusted to a printing contractor. Variable costs consist mostly of payments to this contractor.

Required

1. Prepare an income statement for the game last year and compute the degree of operating leverage.
2. Management is confident that the company can sell 18,000 games next year (an increase of 3,000 games, or 20%, over last year). Compute:
   a. The expected percentage increase in net income for next year.
   b. The expected total dollar net income for next year. (Do not prepare an income statement; use the degree of operating leverage to compute your answer.)

E6–5　Miller Company's most recent income statement is shown below:

	Total	Per Unit
Sales (20,000 units)	$300,000	$15.00
Less variable expenses	180,000	9.00
Contribution margin	120,000	$ 6.00
Less fixed expenses	70,000	
Net income	$ 50,000	

Required

Prepare a new income statement under each of the following conditions (consider each case independently):

1. The sales volume increases by 15%.
2. The selling price decreases by $1.50 per unit, and the sales volume increases by 25%.
3. The selling price increases by $1.50 per unit, fixed expenses increase by $20,000, and the sales volume decreases by 5%.

4. The selling price increases by 12%, variable expenses increase by 60 cents per unit, and the sales volume decreases by 10%.

E6–6 Fill in the missing amounts in each of the eight case situations below. Each case is independent of the others. (Hint: One way to find the missing amounts would be to prepare a contribution income statement for each case, enter the known data, and then compute the missing items.)

a. Assume that only one product is being sold in each of the four following case situations:

Case	Units Sold	Sales	Variable Expenses	Contribution Margin per Unit	Fixed Expenses	Net Income (Loss)
1	15,000	$180,000	$120,000	$?	$ 50,000	$?
2	?	100,000	?	10	32,000	8,000
3	10,000	?	70,000	13	?	12,000
4	6,000	300,000	?	?	100,000	(10,000)

b. Assume that more than one product is being sold in each of the four following case situations:

Case	Sales	Variable Expenses	Average Contribution Margin (percent)	Fixed Expenses	Net Income (Loss)
1	$500,000	$?	20	$?	$ 7,000
2	400,000	260,000	?	100,000	?
3	?	?	60	130,000	20,000
4	600,000	420,000	?	?	(5,000)

E6–7 Olongapo Sports Corporation is the distributor in the Philippines of two premium golf balls—the Flight Dynamic and the Sure Shot. Monthly sales and the contribution margin ratios for the two products follow:

	Product		
	Flight Dynamic	Sure Shot	Total
Sales	P150,000	P250,000	P400,000
CM ratio	80%	36%	?

Fixed expenses total P183,750 per month. (The currency in the Philippines is the peso, which is denoted by P.)

Required
1. Prepare an income statement for the company as a whole. Use the format shown in Exhibit 6–4 and carry computations to one decimal place.
2. Compute the break-even point for the company based on the current sales mix.
3. If sales increase by P100,000 a month, by how much would you expect net income to increase? What are your assumptions?

E6–8 Outback Outfitters manufactures and sells recreational equipment. One of the company's products, a small camp stove, sells for $50 per unit. Variable expenses are $32 per stove, and fixed expenses associated with the stove total $108,000 per month.

Required
1. Compute the break-even point in number of stoves and in total sales dollars.
2. If the variable expenses per stove increase as a percentage of the selling price, will it result in a higher or a lower break-even point? Why? (Assume that the fixed expenses remain unchanged.)
3. At present, the company is selling 8,000 stoves per month. The sales manager is convinced that a 10% reduction in the selling price would result in a 25% increase in monthly sales of stoves. Prepare two contribution income statements, one under present

operating conditions, and one as operations would appear after the proposed changes. Show both total and per unit data on your statements.

4. Refer to the data in (3) above. How many stoves would have to be sold at the new selling price to yield a minimum net income of $35,000 per month?

Problems

P6–9 Basic CVP Analysis; Graphing   The Fashion Shoe Company operates a chain of women's shoe shops around the country. The shops carry many styles of shoes that are all sold at the same price. Sales personnel in the shops are paid a substantial commission on each pair of shoes sold (in addition to a small basic salary) in order to encourage them to be aggressive in their sales efforts.

The following cost and revenue data relate to Shop 48 and are typical of one of the company's many outlets:

	Per Pair of Shoes
Sales price	$ 30.00
Variable expenses:	
Invoice cost	$ 13.50
Sales commission	4.50
Total variable expenses	$ 18.00

	Annual
Fixed expenses:	
Advertising	$ 30,000
Rent	20,000
Salaries	100,000
Total fixed expenses	$150,000

Required

1. Calculate the annual break-even point in dollar sales and in unit sales for Shop 48.
2. Prepare a CVP graph showing cost and revenue data for Shop 48 from a zero level of activity up to 20,000 pairs of shoes sold each year. Clearly indicate the break-even point on the graph.
3. If 12,000 pairs of shoes are sold in a year, what would be Shop 48's net income or loss?
4. The company is considering paying the store manager of Shop 48 an incentive commission of 75 cents per pair of shoes (in addition to the salesperson's commission). If this change is made, what will be the new break-even point in dollar sales and in unit sales?
5. Refer to the original data. As an alternative to (4) above, the company is considering paying the store manager 50 cents commission on each pair of shoes sold in excess of the break-even point. If this change is made, what will be the shop's net income or loss if 15,000 pairs of shoes are sold?
6. Refer to the original data. The company is considering eliminating sales commissions entirely in its shops and increasing fixed salaries by $31,500 annually. If this change is made, what will be the new break-even point in dollar sales and in unit sales for Shop 48? Would you recommend that the change be made? Explain.

P6–10 Basics of CVP Analysis; Cost Structure   Due to erratic sales of its sole product—a high-capacity battery for laptop computers—PEM, Inc., has been experiencing difficulty for some time. The company's income statement for the most recent month is given below:

Sales (19,500 units × $30)		$585,000
Less variable expenses		409,500
Contribution margin		175,500
Less fixed expenses		180,000
Net loss		$ (4,500)

Required

1. Compute the company's CM ratio and its break-even point in both units and dollars.
2. The president believes that a $16,000 increase in the monthly advertising budget, combined with an intensified effort by the sales staff, will result in an $80,000 increase in monthly sales. If the president is right, what will be the effect on the company's monthly net income or loss? (Use the incremental approach in preparing your answer.)
3. Refer to the original data. The sales manager is convinced that a 10% reduction in the selling price, combined with an increase of $60,000 in the monthly advertising budget, will cause unit sales to double. What will the new income statement look like if these changes are adopted?
4. Refer to the original data. The Marketing Department thinks that a fancy new package for the laptop computer battery would help sales. The new package would increase packaging costs by 75 cents per unit. Assuming no other changes, how many units would have to be sold each month to earn a profit of $9,750?
5. Refer to the original data. By automating certain operations, the company could reduce variable costs by $3 per unit. However, fixed costs would increase by $72,000 each month.
   a. Compute the new CM ratio and the new break-even point in both units and dollars.
   b. Assume that the company expects to sell 26,000 units next month. Prepare two income statements, one assuming that operations are not automated and one assuming that they are. (Show data on a per unit and percentage basis, as well as in total, for each alternative.)
   c. Would you recommend that the company automate its operations? Explain.

P6–11 Sales Mix Assumptions; Break-Even Analysis Gold Star Rice, Ltd., of Thailand exports Thai rice throughout Asia. The company grows three varieties of rice—Fragrant, White, and Loonzain. (The currency in Thailand is the baht, which is denoted by B.) Budgeted sales by product and in total for the coming month are shown below:

	Product White		Fragrant		Loonzain		Total	
Percentage of total sales	20%		52%		28%		100%	
Sales	B150,000	100%	B390,000	100%	B210,000	100%	B750,000	100%
Less variable expenses	108,000	72%	78,000	20%	84,000	40%	270,000	36%
Contribution margin	B 42,000	28%	B312,000	80%	B126,000	60%	480,000	64%
Less fixed expenses							449,280	
Net income							B 30,720	

$$\text{Break-even sales: } \frac{\text{Fixed expenses, B449,280}}{\text{CM ratio, 0.64}} = \text{B702,000}$$

As shown by these data, net income is budgeted at B30,720 for the month and break-even sales at B702,000.

Assume that actual sales for the month total B750,000 as planned. Actual sales by product are: White, B300,000; Fragrant, B180,000; and Loonzain, B270,000.

Required

1. Prepare a contribution income statement for the month based on actual sales data. Present the income statement in the format shown above.
2. Compute the break-even sales for the month based on your actual data.

3. Considering the fact that the company met its B750,000 sales budget for the month, the president is shocked at the results shown on your income statement in (1) above. Prepare a brief memo for the president explaining why both the operating results and break-even sales are different from what was budgeted.

P6–12   Basics of CVP Analysis   Feather Friends, Inc., makes a high-quality wooden birdhouse that sells for $20 per unit. Variable costs are $8 per unit, and fixed costs total $180,000 per year.

Required   Answer the following independent questions:

1. What is the product's CM ratio?
2. Use the CM ratio to determine the break-even point in sales dollars.
3. Due to an increase in demand, the company estimates that sales will increase by $75,000 during the next year. By how much should net income increase (or net loss decrease) assuming that fixed costs do not change?
4. Assume that the operating results for last year were:

Sales	$400,000
Less variable expenses	160,000
Contribution margin	240,000
Less fixed expenses	180,000
Net income	$ 60,000

    a. Compute the degree of operating leverage at the current level of sales.
    b. The president expects sales to increase by 20% next year. By what percentage should net income increase?

5. Refer to the original data. Assume that the company sold 18,000 units last year. The sales manager is convinced that a 10% reduction in the selling price, combined with a $30,000 increase in advertising, would cause annual sales in units to increase by one-third. Prepare two contribution income statements, one showing the results of last year's operations and one showing the results of operations if these changes are made. Would you recommend that the company do as the sales manager suggests?

6. Refer to the original data. Assume again that the company sold 18,000 units last year. The president does not want to change the selling price. Instead, he wants to increase the sales commission by $1 per unit. He thinks that this move, combined with some increase in advertising, would increase annual sales by 25%. By how much could advertising be increased with profits remaining unchanged? Do not prepare an income statement; use the incremental analysis approach.

P6–13   The Case of the Elusive Contribution Margin

The Shirt Works sells a large variety of tee shirts and sweat shirts. Steve Hooper, the owner, is thinking of expanding his sales by hiring local high school students, on a commission basis, to sell sweat shirts bearing the name and mascot of the local high school.

These sweat shirts would have to be ordered from the manufacturer six weeks in advance, and they could not be returned because of the unique printing required. The sweat shirts would cost Mr. Hooper $8 each with a minimum order of 75 sweat shirts. Any additional sweat shirts would have to be ordered in increments of 75.

Since Mr. Hooper's plan would not require any additional facilities, the only costs associated with the project would be the costs of the sweat shirts and the costs of the sales commissions. The selling price of the sweat shirts would be $13.50 each. Mr. Hooper would pay the students a commission of $1.50 for each shirt sold.

Required   1. To make the project worthwhile, Mr. Hooper would require a $1,200 profit for the first three months of the venture. What level of sales in units and in dollars would be required to reach this target net income? Show all computations.
2. Assume that the venture is undertaken and an order is placed for 75 sweat shirts. What would be Mr. Hooper's break-even point in units and in sales dollars? Show computations and explain the reasoning behind your answer.

P6–14 Interpretive Questions on the CVP Graph   A CVP graph such as the one shown below is a useful technique for showing relationships between costs, volume, and profits in an organization.

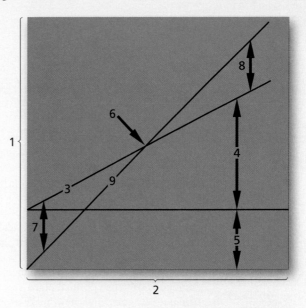

Required   1. Identify the numbered components in the CVP graph.
2. State the effect of each of the following actions on line 3, line 9, and the break-even point. For line 3 and line 9, state whether the action will cause the line to:

> Remain unchanged.
> Shift upward.
> Shift downward.
> Have a steeper slope (i.e., rotate upward).
> Have a flatter slope (i.e., rotate downward).
> Shift upward *and* have a steeper slope.
> Shift upward *and* have a flatter slope.
> Shift downward *and* have a steeper slope.
> Shift downward *and* have a flatter slope.

In the case of the break-even point, state whether the action will cause the break-even point to:

> Remain unchanged.
> Increase.
> Decrease.
> Probably change, but the direction is uncertain.

Treat each case independently.

> x. *Example.*   Fixed costs are reduced by $5,000 per period.
> *Answer* (see choices above):   Line 3:   Shift downward.
> Line 9:   Remain unchanged.
> Break-even point: Decrease.

a. The unit selling price is increased from $18 to $20.
b. Unit variable costs are decreased from $12 to $10.
c. Fixed costs are increased by $3,000 per period.
d. Two thousand more units are sold during the period than were budgeted.
e. Due to paying salespersons a commission rather than a flat salary, fixed costs are reduced by $8,000 per period and unit variable costs are increased by $3.
f. Due to an increase in the cost of materials, both unit variable costs and the selling price are increased by $2.
g. Advertising costs are increased by $10,000 per period, resulting in a 10% increase in the number of units sold.
h. Due to automating an operation previously done by workers, fixed costs are increased by $12,000 per period and unit variable costs are reduced by $4.

P6–15   Sales Mix; Break-Even Analysis; Margin of Safety   Island Novelties, Inc., of Cape Breton makes two products, Caper Fantasy and Island Joy. Present revenue, cost, and sales data on the two products follow:

	Caper Fantasy	Island Joy
Selling price per unit	$15	$100
Variable expenses per unit	9	20
Number of units sold annually	20,000	5,000

Fixed expenses total $475,800 per year.

Required
1. Assuming the sales mix given above, do the following:
   a. Prepare a contribution income statement showing both dollar and percent columns for each product and for the company as a whole.
   b. Compute the break-even point in dollars for the company as a whole and the margin of safety in both dollars and percent.
2. Another product, Highland Delight, has just come onto the market. Assume that the company could sell 10,000 units at $45 each. The variable expenses would be $36 each. The company's fixed expenses would not change.
   a. Prepare another contribution income statement, including sales of the Highland Delight (sales of the other two products would not change). Carry percentage computations to one decimal place.
   b. Compute the company's new break-even point in dollars and the new margin of safety in both dollars and percent.
3. The president of the company examines your figures and says, "There's something strange here. Our fixed costs haven't changed and you show greater total contribution margin if we add the new product, but you also show our break-even point going up. With greater contribution margin, the break-even point should go down, not up. You've made a mistake somewhere." Explain to the president what has happened.

P6–16   Sensitivity Analysis of Net Income; Changes in Volume   Minden Company introduced a new product last year for which it is trying to find an optimal selling price. Marketing studies suggest that the company can increase sales by 5,000 units for each $2 reduction in the selling price. The company's present selling price is $70 per unit, and variable expenses are $40 per unit. Fixed expenses are $540,000 per year. The present annual sales volume (at the $70 selling price) is 15,000 units.

Required
1. What is the present yearly net income or loss?
2. What is the present break-even point in units and in dollar sales?
3. Assuming that the marketing studies are correct, what is the *maximum* profit that the company can earn yearly? At how many units and at what selling price per unit would the company generate this profit?
4. What would be the break-even point in units and in dollar sales using the selling price you determined in (3) above (e.g., the selling price at the level of maximum profits)? Why is this break-even point different from the break-even point you computed in (2) above?

P6–17   Graphing; Incremental Analysis; Operating Leverage   Angie Silva has recently opened The Sandal Shop in Brisbane, Australia, a store that specializes in fashionable sandals. Angie has just received a degree in business and she is anxious to apply the principles she has learned to her business. In time, she hopes to open a chain of sandal shops. As a first step, she has prepared the following analysis for her new store:

Sales price per pair of sandals	$40
Variable expenses per pair of sandals	16
Contribution margin per pair of sandals	$24

Fixed expenses per year:

Building rental	$15,000
Equipment depreciation	7,000
Selling	20,000
Administrative	18,000
Total fixed expenses	$60,000

Required
1. How many pairs of sandals must be sold each year to break even? What does this represent in total dollar sales?
2. Prepare a CVP graph for the store from a zero level of activity up to 5,000 pairs of sandals sold each year. Indicate the break-even point on your graph.
3. Angie has decided that she must earn at least $18,000 the first year to justify her time and effort. How many pairs of sandals must be sold to reach this target profit?
4. Angie now has two salespersons working in the store—one full time and one part time. It will cost her an additional $8,000 per year to convert the part-time position to a full-time position. Angie believes that the change would bring in an additional $25,000 in sales each year. Should she convert the position? Use the incremental approach (do not prepare an income statement).
5. Refer to the original data. During the first year, the store sold only 3,000 pairs of sandals and reported the following operating results:

Sales (3,000 pair)	$120,000
Less variable expenses	48,000
Contribution margin	72,000
Less fixed expenses	60,000
Net income	$ 12,000

a. What is the store's degree of operating leverage?
b. Angie is confident that with a more intense sales effort and with a more creative advertising program she can increase sales by 50% next year. What would be the expected percentage increase in net income? Use the degree of operating leverage to compute your answer.

P6–18   Sales Mix; Commission Structure; Break-Even Point   Carbex, Inc., produces cutlery sets out of high-quality wood and steel. The company makes a standard cutlery set and a deluxe set and sells them to retail department stores throughout the country. The standard set sells for $60, and the deluxe set sells for $75. The variable expenses associated with each set are given below (in cost per set):

	Standard	Deluxe
Production costs	$15.00	$30.00
Sales commissions (15% of sales price)	9.00	11.25

The company's fixed expenses each month are:

Advertising	$105,000
Depreciation	21,700
Administrative	63,000

Salespersons are paid on a commission basis to encourage them to be aggressive in their sales efforts. Mary Parsons, the financial vice president, watches sales commissions carefully and has noted that they have risen steadily over the last year. For this reason, she was shocked to find that even though sales have increased, profits for the current month—May—are down substantially from April. Sales, in sets, for the last two months are given below:

	Standard	Deluxe	Total
April	4,000	2,000	6,000
May	1,000	5,000	6,000

Required   1. Prepare an income statement for April and an income statement for May. Use the contribution format, with the following headings:

	Standard		Deluxe		Total	
	Amount	Percent	Amount	Percent	Amount	Percent
Sales						
Etc						

   Place the fixed expenses only in the Total column. Carry percentage computations to one decimal place. Do not show percentages for the fixed expenses.
   2. Explain why there is a difference in net income between the two months, even though the same *total* number of sets was sold in each month.
   3. What can be done to the sales commissions to optimize the sales mix?
   4. a. Using April's figures, what was the break-even point for the month in sales dollars?
      b. Has May's break-even point gone up or down from that of April? Explain your answer without calculating the break-even point for May.

P6–19 Various CVP Questions: Break-Even Point; Cost Structure; Target Sales   Northwood Company manufactures basketballs. The company has a standard ball that sells for $25. At present, the standard ball is manufactured in a small plant that relies heavily on direct labour workers. Thus, variable costs are high, totalling $15 per ball.

Last year, the company sold 30,000 standard balls, with the following results:

Sales (30,000 standard balls)	$750,000
Less variable expenses	450,000
Contribution margin	300,000
Less fixed expenses	210,000
Net income	$ 90,000

Required   1. Compute (a) the CM ratio and the break-even point in balls, and (b) the degree of operating leverage at last year's level of sales.
   2. Due to an increase in labour rates, the company estimates that variable costs will increase by $3 per ball next year. If this change takes place and the selling price per ball remains constant at $25, what will be the new CM ratio and break-even point in balls?
   3. Refer to the data in (2) above. If the expected change in variable costs takes place, how many balls will have to be sold next year to earn the same net income ($90,000) as last year?
   4. Refer again to the data in (2) above. The president feels that the company must raise the selling price on the standard balls. If Northwood Company wants to maintain *the same CM ratio as last year,* what selling price per ball must it charge next year to cover the increased labour costs?
   5. Refer to the original data. The company is discussing the construction of a new, automated plant to manufacture the standard balls. The new plant would slash variable costs per ball by 40%, but it would cause fixed costs to double in amount per year. If the new plant is built, what would be the company's new CM ratio and new break-even point in balls?
   6. Refer to the data in (5) above.
      a. If the new plant is built, how many balls will have to be sold next year to earn the same net income ($90,000) as last year?
      b. Assume the new plant is built and that next year the company manufactures and sells 30,000 balls (the same number as sold last year). Prepare a contribution income statement and compute the degree of operating leverage.
      c. If you were a member of top management, would you have voted in favour of constructing the new plant? Explain.

P6–20 Changing Levels of Fixed and Variable Costs   Neptune Company produces toys and other items for use in beach and resort areas. A small, inflatable toy has come onto the market that the company is anxious to produce and sell. Enough capacity exists in the company's plant to produce 16,000 units of the toy each month. Variable costs to manufacture and sell one unit would be $1.25, and fixed costs associated with the toy would total $35,000 per month.

The company's Marketing Department predicts that demand for the new toy will exceed the 16,000 units that the company is able to produce. Additional manufacturing space can be rented from another company at a fixed cost of $1,000 per month. Variable costs in the rented facility would total $1.40 per unit, due to somewhat less efficient operations than in the main plant. The new toy will sell for $3 per unit.

Required
1. Compute the monthly break-even point for the new toy in units and in total dollar sales. Show all computations in good form.
2. How many units must be sold each month to make a monthly profit of $12,000?
3. If the sales manager receives a bonus of 10 cents for each unit sold in excess of the break-even point, how many units must be sold each month to earn a return of 25% on the monthly investment in fixed costs?

P6–21   Changes in Cost Structure   Morton Company's income statement for last month is given below:

Sales (15,000 units × $30)	$450,000
Less variable expenses	315,000
Contribution margin	135,000
Less fixed expenses	90,000
Net income	$ 45,000

The industry in which Morton Company operates is quite sensitive to cyclical movements in the economy. Thus, profits vary considerably from year to year according to general economic conditions. The company has a large amount of unused capacity and is studying ways of improving profits.

Required
1. New equipment has come onto the market that would allow Morton Company to automate a portion of its operations. Variable costs would be reduced by $9 per unit. However, fixed costs would increase to a total of $225,000 each month. Prepare two contribution-type income statements, one showing present operations and one showing how operations would appear if the new equipment is purchased. Show an Amount column, a Per Unit column, and a Percent column on each statement. Do not show percentages for the fixed costs.
2. Refer to the income statements in (1) above. For both present operations and the proposed new operations, compute (a) the degree of operating leverage, (b) the break-even point in dollars, and (c) the margin of safety in both dollar and percentage terms.
3. Refer again to the data in (1) above. As a manager, what factor would be paramount in your mind in deciding whether to purchase the new equipment? (You may assume that ample funds are available to make the purchase.)
4. Refer to the original data. Rather than purchase new equipment, the president is thinking about changing the company's marketing method. Under the new method, sales would increase by 20% each month and net income would increase by one-third. Fixed costs could be slashed to only $48,000 per month. Compute the break-even point for the company after the change in marketing method.

P6–22   Missing Data; Integration of CVP Factors   You were employed just this morning by Pyrrhic Company, a prominent and rapidly growing organization. As your initial assignment, you were asked to complete an analysis of one of the company's products for the board of directors meeting later in the day. After completing the analysis, you left your office for a few moments only to discover on returning that a broken sprinkler in the ceiling has destroyed most of your work. Only the following bits remained:

PYRRHIC COMPANY
Actual Income Statement
For the Month Ended June 30

	Total	Per Unit	Percent
Sales (? units)	$?	$?	100%
Less variable expenses	?	?	?%
Contribution margin	?	$?	?%
Less fixed expenses	?		
Net income	$?		

Break-even point:
| In units .... | | ? units | |
| In dollars .... | | $180,000 | |

Margin of safety:
In dollars		$?	
In percentage		20%	
Degree of operating leverage		?	

The computations above are all based on actual results for June. The company's *projected* income statement for this product for July follows:

PYRRHIC COMPANY
Projected Income Statement
For the Month Ended July 31

	Total	Per Unit	Percent
Sales (33,000 units)	$?	$?	?%
Less variable expenses	?	?	?%
Contribution margin	?	$?	?%
Less fixed expenses	?		
Net income	$40,500		

To add to your woes, the company's mainframe computer is down so no data are available from that source. You do remember that sales for July are projected to increase by 10% over sales for June. You also remember that June's net income was $27,000—the same amount as your annual salary from the company. Finally, you remember that the degree of operating leverage is highly useful to the manager as a predictive tool.

Total fixed expenses, the unit selling price, and the unit variable expenses are planned to be the same in July as they were in June.

The board of directors meets in just one hour.

Required
1. For the June data, do the following:
   a. Complete the June income statement (all three columns).
   b. Compute the break-even point in units and verify the break-even point in dollars. Use the unit contribution method.
   c. Compute the margin of safety in dollars and verify the margin of safety percentage.
   d. Compute the degree of operating leverage as of June 30.
2. For the July data, do the following:
   a. Complete the July projected income statement (all three columns).
   b. Compute the margin of safety in dollars and percent and compute the degree of operating leverage. Why has the margin of safety gone up and the degree of operating leverage gone down?
3. Brimming with confidence after having completed (1) and (2) above in less than one hour, you decide to give the board of directors some added data. You know that direct labour accounts for $1.80 of the company's per unit variable expenses. You have learned that direct labour costs may increase by one-third next year. Assuming that this cost increase

takes place and that selling price and other cost factors remain unchanged, how many units will the company have to sell in a month to earn a net income equal to 20% of sales?

P6–23 Break-Even Analysis and Sensitivity Tou Company produces a single product. It sold 32,000 units last year with the following results.

Sales		$800,000
Variable costs	$480,000	
Fixed costs	150,000	630,000
Net income before taxes		170,000
Income taxes (45%)		76,500
Net income		$ 93,500

In an attempt to improve its product in the coming year, Tou is considering replacing a component part in its product that has a cost of $3.50, with a new and better part costing $5.50 per unit. A new machine will also be needed to increase plant capacity. The machine would cost $18,000 with a useful life of six years and no salvage value. The company uses straight-line depreciation on all capital assets for both financial statements and tax purposes.

Required

1. What was Tou Company's break-even point in number of units last year?
2. How many units of product would Tou Company have had to sell in the last year to earn $99,000 in net income after taxes?
3. If Tou Company holds the sales price constant and makes the suggested changes, how many units of product must be sold in the coming year to break even?
4. If Tou Company holds the sales price constant and makes the suggested changes, how many units of product will the company have to sell to make the same net income after taxes as last year?
5. If Tou Company wishes to maintain the same contribution margin ratio after implementing the changes, what selling price per unit of product must it charge next year to cover the increased material costs?

(CGA, adapted)

P6-24 CVP under Uncertainty (Appendix 6A) The manager of Stereo-Fun wants to decide whether to move his store to the new Market Mall, or to keep it in its present location. Because of changing economic conditions, the market for stereo equipment may decline, remain the same, or increase, during the next year. The manager estimates the move to Market Mall will cost $10,000. Also he assesses market conditions and his associated net profits for the next year under both alternatives (not including cost of move) to be as follows:

		Net Profits ($000)	
State of Market	**Probability**	**Move to Market Mall**	**Do not Move**
Decline	0.2	−25	−10
Same	0.5	50	40
Increase	0.3	100	80

Required

1. Construct the decision tree for this problem.
2. Calculate the expected net profits for each alternative. What decision should the manager make?

(CGA, adapted)

P6–25 CVP, Uncertainty, and Bidding (Appendix 6A) Glace Bay has just announced plans to build a library and arts centre complex. To encourage development of creative design concepts, the city has indicated its intention to hold a design competition. The best entry will win the architectural contract, which will generate a revenue of $250,000 before the design costs.

A local firm of architects is considering submitting a proposal. They know that a well-thought-out design would greatly enhance their chance of winning. However, such a design is costly. On the other hand, a less costly design proposal has a limited chance of winning.

The architectural firm has two proposals under consideration. Each proposal has the following cost and probabilities associated with it:

	Cost of Design Proposal	Probability of Winning Contract
Proposal A	80,000	60
Proposal B	30,000	30

Design costs are assumed to be incurred at the beginning of the current year. Income taxes are 40%.

Required   Which proposal would you recommend the architectural firm submit to the design competition? Show all calculations.

(SMAC, adapted)

P6–26   CVP under Uncertainty   (Appendix 6A) New Fashion, Inc., is a manufacturer of several clothing lines based on oriental motifs. Aggressive advertising and sales campaigns have resulted in rapid growth up to existing capacity and the owner, Ying Yao, is now considering the purchase of additional production equipment to start up a new dress line.

Yao's purchasing manager has selected a machine with the following characteristics:

Initial cost per machine	$200,000
Estimated salvage in 5 years	$10,000
Capacity per year	600 units
Capital cost allowance, class 8	20%

In an effort to improve its own sagging fortunes, the company selling the machine has offered to sell Yao a second or any subsequent machine required at a 20% discount from the normal single unit cost.

Market research has indicated that annual demand for the new dress line can be established and stabilized at a static figure for a period of five years.

The production manager has estimated that the manufacturing cost for the new dress will be as follows:

Direct materials:	$40 per unit
Direct labour:	6 hours at $10 per hour
Variable overhead:	20% of direct labour cost

Required   1. The sales manager had estimated the probability distribution for annual demand based on a price of $220 as follows:

Demand Level	Probability
800	.20
1,000	.40
1,200	.30
1,400	.10

Determine the expected contribution before taxes.

2. Not satisfied with the uncertainty of this distribution, the sales manager hired an industrial specialist who had prior information regarding the fashion market. Using his prior information, the specialist predicted the following table of conditional probabilities:

Demand Level	Conditional Probabilities
800	.1250
1,000	.1875
1,200	.2500
1,400	.4375

Determine the expected contribution after receipt of this new information.

(SMAC, adapted)

P6–27 CVP under Uncertainty (Appendix 6A) Acme Sales Ltd., wishing to increase sales, has decided to change its strategy by adopting one of two alternatives. The first alternative is to expand the number of product lines, and the second is to improve the service provided on existing lines by streamlining existing lines and by retraining salespersons to provide better service. Besides selling effort, the company's success is also dependent on the economy. There is a 70% chance that the economy will continue to grow over the next year, and a 30% chance there will be no economic growth. The company has determined that the expansion of the product lines would cost $200,000 to implement, and the improvement in service alternative would cost $50,000 to implement. The table below gives the company's estimates of the profits and probabilities anticipated for each alternative. These estimates (in thousands of dollars) do not include the costs of implementing each alternative.

Alternatives	Economy Grows (P = .7)		No Change in Economy (P = 3)	
	Higher Sales (P = .8)	No Impact on Sales (P = .2)	Higher Sales (P = .4)	No Impact on Sales (P = .6)
Expansion of product lines	1,000	800	750	600
Improvement of service	900	700	550	400

Required
1. Draw and label the decision tree for this problem.
2. Which alternative should Acme choose to maximize expected net profit?

(CGA, adapted)

Cases

C6–28 Cost Structure; Break-Even; Target Profits Pittman Company is a small but growing manufacturer of telecommunications equipment. The company has no sales force of its own; rather, it relies completely on independent sales agents to market its products. These agents are paid a commission of 15% of selling price for all items sold.

Barbara Cheney, Pittman's controller, has just prepared the company's budgeted income statement for next year. The statement follows:

PITTMAN COMPANY
Budgeted Income Statement
For the Year Ended December 31

Sales		$16,000,000
Manufacturing costs:		
Variable	$7,200,000	
Fixed overhead	2,340,000	9,540,000
Gross margin		6,460,000

4. Refer to the original data. Whitney Company's board of directors believes that the company's problem lies in inadequate promotion. By how much can advertising be increased and still allow the company to earn a target return of 4.5% on sales of 60,000 units?

5. Refer to the original data. The company has been approached by an overseas distributor who wants to purchase 9,500 units on a special price basis. There would be no sales commission on these units. However, shipping costs would be increased by 50% and variable administrative costs would be reduced by 25%. In addition, a $5,700 special insurance fee would have to be paid by Whitney Company to protect the goods in transit. What unit price would have to be quoted on the 9,500 units by Whitney Company to allow the company to earn a profit of $14,250 on total operations? Regular business would not be disturbed by this special order.

C6–30   Break-Even Analysis with Step Fixed Costs   Wymont Nursing Home operates a general hospital with separate departments such as general care, ambulatory care, and surgical recovery. Wymont Nursing Home charges each separate department for services to its patients such as meals and laundry and for administrative services such as billing and collections. Space and bed charges are fixed for the year.

Last year, the General Care Department at Wymont Nursing Home charged its patients an average of $65 per day, had a capacity of 80 beds, operated 24 hours per day for 365 days, and had total revenue of $1,138,800.

Expenses charged by the nursing home to the General Care Department for the year were as follows:

	Basis for Allocation	
	Patient-Days (variable)	**Bed Capacity (fixed)**
Dietary	$ 42,952	
Janitorial		$ 12,800
Laundry	28,000	
Labouratory	47,800	
Pharmacy	33,800	
Repairs and maintenance	5,200	7,140
General administrative services		131,760
Rent		275,320
Billings and collections	87,000	
Other	18,048	25,980
	$262,800	$453,000

The only personnel directly employed by the General Care Department are supervising nurses, nurses, and aides. The nursing home has minimum personnel requirements for General Care based on total annual patient-days in General Care. Nursing home requirements, beginning at the minimum expected level of operation, follow:

Annual Patient-Days	Aides	Nurses	Supervising Nurses
10,000–14,000	21	11	4
14,001–17,000	22	12	4
17,001–23,725	22	13	4
23,726–25,550	25	14	5
25,551–27,375	26	14	5
27,376–29,200	29	16	6

These staffing levels represent full-time equivalents, and it should be assumed that the General Care Department always employs only the minimum number of required full-time equivalent personnel.

Annual salaries for each class of employee are: supervising nurses, $18,000; nurses, $13,000; and aides, $5,000. Salary expense for last year was $72,000, $169,000, and $110,000 for supervising nurses, nurses, and aides, respectively.

Required

1. Compute the following:
   a. The number of patient-days in the Pediatrics Department for last year. (Each day a patient is in the nursing home is known as a *patient-day*.)
   b. The variable cost per patient-day for last year.
   c. The total fixed costs, including both allocated fixed costs and personnel costs, in the General Care Department for each level of operation shown above (i.e., total fixed costs at the 10,000–14,000 patient-day level of operation, total fixed costs at the 14,001–17,000 patient-day level of operation, etc.).
2. Using the data computed in (1) above and any other data as needed, compute the *minimum* number of patient-days required for the General Care Department to break even. You may assume that variable and fixed cost behaviour and that revenue per patient-day will remain unchanged in the future.
3. Determine the minimum number of patient-days required for the General Care Department to earn an annual "profit" of $200,000.

(CPA, adapted)

C6–31 Individual Product Break-evens in a Multiproduct Company

Cheryl Montoya picked up the phone and called her boss, Wes Chan, the vice president of marketing at Piedmont Fasteners Corporation: "Wes, I'm not sure how to go about answering the questions that came up at the meeting with the president yesterday."

"What's the problem?"

"The president wanted to know each product's break-even, but I am having trouble figuring them out."

"I'm sure you can handle it, Cheryl. And, by the way, I need your analysis on my desk tomorrow morning at 8:00 sharp in time for the follow-up meeting at 9:00."

Piedmont Fasteners Corporation makes three different clothing fasteners in its manufacturing facility in Ontario. Data concerning these products appear below:

	Velcro	Metal	Nylon
Normal annual sales volume	100,000	200,000	400,000
Unit selling price	$1.65	$1.50	$0.85
Variable cost per unit	$1.25	$0.70	$0.25

Total fixed expenses are $400,000 per year.

All three products are sold in highly competitive markets, so the company is unable to raise its prices without losing unacceptable numbers of customers.

The company has an extremely effective just-in-time manufacturing system, so there are no beginning or ending work in process or finished goods inventories.

Required

1. What is the company's overall break-even in total sales dollars?
2. Of the total fixed costs of $400,000, $20,000 could be avoided if the Velcro product were dropped, $80,000 if the Metal product were dropped, and $60,000 if the Nylon product were dropped. The remaining fixed costs of $240,000 consist of common fixed costs such as administrative salaries and rent on the factory building that could be avoided only by going out of business entirely.
   a. What is the break-even quantity of each product?
   b. If the company sells exactly the break-even quantity of each product, what will be the overall profit of the company?

Group Exercises

GE6–32 CVP and Collegiate Sports

Revenue from major intercollegiate sports is an important source of funds for many colleges. Most of the costs of putting on a hockey or basketball game may be fixed and may increase very little as the size of the crowd increases. Thus, the revenue from every extra ticket sold may be almost pure profit.

Choose a sport played at your college or university, such as hockey or basketball, that generates significant revenue. Talk with the business manager of your college's sports programs before answering the following questions:

Exhibit 7–1   Cost
Classifications—
Absorption versus
Variable Costing

Absorption Costing		Variable Costing
Product costs	Direct materials Direct labour Variable manufacturing overhead	Product costs
	Fixed manufacturing overhead	Period costs
Period costs	{Selling and administrative expenses	

The concepts discussed so far in this section are illustrated in Exhibit 7–1, which shows the classification of costs under both absorption and variable costing.

Unit Cost Computations

To illustrate the computation of unit costs under both absorption and variable costing, consider Boley Company, a small company that produces a single product and has the following cost structure:

Number of units produced each year		6,000
Variable costs per unit:		
Direct materials	$	2
Direct labour		4
Variable manufacturing overhead		1
Variable selling and administrative expenses		3
Fixed costs per year:		
Fixed manufacturing overhead		30,000
Fixed selling and administrative expenses		10,000

Required

1. Compute the unit product cost under absorption costing.
2. Compute the unit product cost under variable costing.

Solution

Absorption Costing

Direct materials	$ 2
Direct labour	4
Variable manufacturing overhead	1
Total variable production cost	7
Fixed manufacturing overhead ($30,000 ÷ 6,000 units of product)	5
Unit product cost	$12

Variable Costing

Direct materials	$ 2
Direct labour	4
Variable manufacturing overhead	1
Unit product cost	$ 7

(The $30,000 fixed manufacturing overhead will be charged off in total against income as a period expense along with the selling and administrative expenses.)

Under the absorption costing method, notice that *all* production costs, variable and fixed, are included when determining the unit product cost. Thus, if the company sells a unit of product and absorption costing is being used, then $12 (consisting of $7 variable cost and $5 fixed cost) will be deducted on the income statement as cost of goods sold. Similarly, any unsold units will be carried as inventory on the balance sheet at $12 each.

Under the variable costing method, notice that only the variable production costs are included in product costs. Thus, if the company sells a unit of product, only $7 will be deducted as cost of goods sold, and unsold units will be carried in the balance sheet inventory account at only $7 each.

Income Comparison of Absorption and Variable Costing

Objective 2

Describe how fixed manufacturing overhead costs are deferred in inventory and released from inventory under absorption costing.

Income statements prepared under the absorption and variable costing approaches are shown in Exhibit 7–2. In preparing these statements, we use the date for Boley Company presented earlier, along with other information about the company as given below:

Units in beginning inventory	–0–
Units produced	6,000
Units sold	5,000
Units in ending inventory	1,000
Selling price per unit	$ 20
Selling and administrative expenses:	
Variable per unit	3
Fixed per year	10,000

	Absorption Costing	Variable Costing
Unit product cost:		
Direct materials	$ 2	$ 2
Direct labour	4	4
Variable manufacturing overhead	1	1
Fixed manufacturing overhead ($30,000 4 6,000 units)	5	
Unit product cost	$12	$ 7

Several points can be made from the financial statements in Exhibit 7–2:

Fixed manufacturing overhead cost deferred in inventory The portion of the fixed manufacturing overhead cost of a period that goes into inventory under the absorption costing method as a result of production exceeding sales.

1. Under the absorption costing method, if there is an increase in inventories then some of the fixed manufacturing costs of the current period will not appear on the income statement as part of cost of goods sold. Instead, these costs are deferred to a future period and are carried on the balance sheet as part of the inventory count. Such a deferral of costs is known as **fixed manufacturing overhead cost deferred in inventory.** The process involved can be explained by referring to the data for Boley Company. During the current period, Boley Company produced 6,000 units but sold only 5,000 units, thus leaving 1,000 unsold units in the ending inventory. Under the absorption costing method, each unit produced was assigned $5 in fixed overhead cost (see the unit cost computations above). Therefore, each of the 1,000 units going into inventory at the end of the period has $5 in fixed manufacturing overhead cost attached to it, or a total of $5,000 for the 1,000 units. *This fixed manufacturing overhead cost of the current period is deferred in inventory to the next period, when, hopefully, these units will be taken out of inventory and sold.* The deferral of $5,000 of fixed manufacturing overhead costs can be seen clearly by analyzing the ending inventory under the absorption costing method:

Exhibit 7–2

Comparison of Absorption and Variable Costing— Boley Company

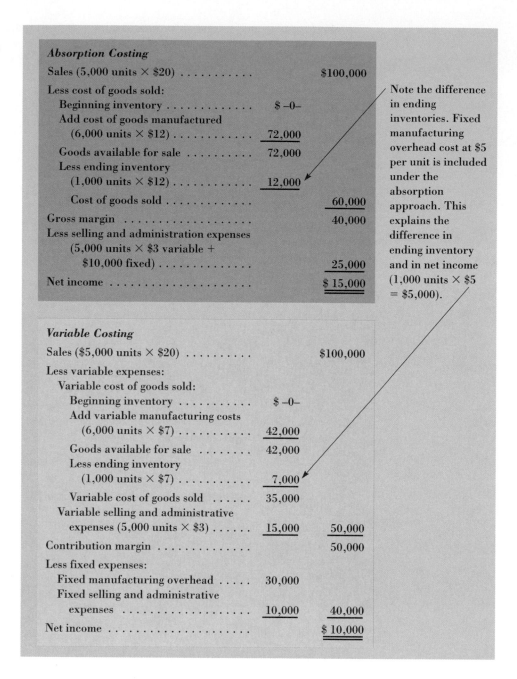

Absorption Costing

Sales (5,000 units × $20)		$100,000
Less cost of goods sold:		
Beginning inventory	$ –0–	
Add cost of goods manufactured (6,000 units × $12)	72,000	
Goods available for sale	72,000	
Less ending inventory (1,000 units × $12)	12,000	
Cost of goods sold		60,000
Gross margin		40,000
Less selling and administration expenses (5,000 units × $3 variable + $10,000 fixed)		25,000
Net income		$ 15,000

Note the difference in ending inventories. Fixed manufacturing overhead cost at $5 per unit is included under the absorption approach. This explains the difference in ending inventory and in net income (1,000 units × $5 = $5,000).

Variable Costing

Sales ($5,000 units × $20)		$100,000
Less variable expenses:		
Variable cost of goods sold:		
Beginning inventory	$ –0–	
Add variable manufacturing costs (6,000 units × $7)	42,000	
Goods available for sale	42,000	
Less ending inventory (1,000 units × $7)	7,000	
Variable cost of goods sold	35,000	
Variable selling and administrative expenses (5,000 units × $3)	15,000	50,000
Contribution margin		50,000
Less fixed expenses:		
Fixed manufacturing overhead	30,000	
Fixed selling and administrative expenses	10,000	40,000
Net income		$ 10,000

Variable manufacturing costs: 1,000 units × $7	$ 7,000
Fixed manufacturing overhead costs: 1,000 units × $5	5,000
Total inventory value	$12,000

In summary, under absorption costing, of the $30,000 in fixed manufacturing overhead costs incurred during the period, only $25,000 (5,000 units sold × $5) has been included in cost of goods sold. The remaining $5,000 (1,000 units *not* sold × $5) has been deferred in inventory to the next period.

2. Under the variable costing method, the entire $30,000 in fixed manufacturing overhead costs has been treated as an expense of the current period (see the bottom portion of the variable costing income statement).

3. The ending inventory figure under the variable costing method is $5,000 lower than it is under the absorption costing method. The reason is that under variable costing, only the variable manufacturing costs are assigned to units of product and therefore included in inventory:

Variable manufacturing costs: 1,000 units × $7 . . . . $7,000

The $5,000 difference in ending inventories explains the difference in net income reported between the two costing methods. Net income is $5,000 *higher* under absorption costing since, as explained above, $5,000 of fixed manufacturing overhead cost has been deferred in inventory to the next period under that costing method.

4. The absorption costing income statement makes no distinction between fixed and variable costs; therefore, it is not well suited for CVP computations, which are important for good planning and control. To generate data for CVP analysis, it would be necessary to spend considerable time reworking and reclassifying costs on the absorption statement.

5. The variable costing approach to costing units of product blends very well with the contribution approach to the income statement, since both concepts are based on the idea of classifying costs by behaviour. The variable costing data in Exhibit 7–2 could be used immediately in CVP computations.

Essentially, the difference between the absorption costing method and the variable costing method centres on timing. Advocates of variable costing say that fixed manufacturing costs should be expensed immediately in total, whereas advocates of absorption costing say that fixed manufacturing costs should be charged against revenues bit by bit as units of product are sold. Any units of product not sold under absorption costing result in fixed costs being inventoried and carried forward *as assets* to the next period. We will defer discussing the arguments presented by each side in this dispute until after we have a better understanding of the two methods. Nevertheless, as we shall see in the following situation, the use of absorption costing can sometimes produce strange effects on income statements.

Focus on Current Practice

The Shanghai Bund Steel Works (SBSW) of the Peoples' Republic of China is a large state-owned enterprise. In recent years, state-owned companies such as SBSW have been given a great deal of autonomy, providing that they meet their financial and nonfinancial targets. However, in state-owned enterprises, management has very little freedom to adjust the workforce—eliminating jobs would create political problems. Therefore, for internal management purposes, SBSW treats labour cost as a fixed cost that is part of fixed manufacturing overhead.[1] ■

---

1. Yau Shiu Wing Joseph, *Management Accounting* (UK), (October 1996), pp. 52–54.

Exhibit 7-3 (concluded)

Absorption Costing

	Year 1	Year 2	Year 3	Three Years Together
Sales	£500,000	£400,000	£600,000	£1,500,000
Less cost of goods sold:				
Beginning inventory	£ -0-	£ -0-	£ 65,000	£ -0-
Add cost of goods manufactured (25,000 units × £13)	325,000	325,000	325,000	975,000
Goods available for sale	325,000	325,000	390,000	975,000
Less ending inventory (5,000 units × £13)	-0-	65,000	-0-	-0-
Cost of goods sold	325,000	260,000	390,000	975,000
Gross margin	175,000	140,000	210,000	525,000
Less selling and administrative expenses	115,000*	110,000*	120,000*	345,000
Net income	£ 60,000	£ 30,000	£ 90,000	£ 180,000

*The selling and administrative expenses are computed as follows:
Year 1: 25,000 units × £1 variable plus £90,000 fixed = £115,000.
Year 2: 20,000 units × £1 variable plus £90,000 fixed = £110,000.
Year 3: 30,000 units × £1 variable plus £90,000 fixed = £120,000.

Variable Costing

	Year 1	Year 2	Year 3	Three Years Together
Sales	£500,000	£400,000	£600,000	£1,500,000
Less variable expenses:				
Variable cost of goods sold:				
Beginning inventory	-0-	-0-	35,000	-0-
Add variable manufacturing costs (25,000 units × £7)	175,000	175,000	175,000	525,000
Goods available for sale	175,000	175,000	210,000	525,000
Less ending inventory (5,000 units × £7)	-0-	35,000	-0-	-0-
Variable costs of goods sold	175,000*	140,000*	210,000*	525,000
Variable selling and administrative expenses (£1 per unit sold)	25,000	20,000	30,000	75,000
Contribution margin	300,000	240,000	360,000	900,000
Less fixed expenses:				
Fixed manufacturing overhead	150,000	150,000	150,000	450,000
Fixed selling and administrative expenses	90,000	90,000	90,000	270,000
	240,000	240,000	240,000	720,000
Net income	£ 60,000	£ -0-	£120,000	£ 180,000

*The variable cost of goods sold could have been computed more simply as follows:
Year 1: 25,000 units sold × £7 = £175,000.
Year 2: 20,000 units sold × £7 = £140,000.

Exhibit 7–4

Comparative Income Effects—Absorption and Variable Costing

Relation between Production and Sales for the Period	Effect on Inventories	Relation between Absorption and Variable Costing Net Incomes
Production = Sales	No change in inventories	Absorption costing net income = Variable costing net income
Production > Sales	Inventories increase	Absorption costing net income > Variable costing net income*
Production < Sales	Inventories decrease	Absorption costing net income < Variable costing net income†

*Net income is higher under absorption costing, since fixed manufacturing overhead cost is *deferred* in inventory under absorption costing as inventories increase.

†Net income is lower under absorption costing, since fixed manufacturing overhead cost is *released* from inventory under absorption costing as inventories decrease.

turing overhead incurred during the year flows through to the income statement as expense. And therefore, the net income under the two methods is the same.

2. When production exceeds sales, the net income reported under absorption costing will generally be greater than the net income reported under variable costing (see Year 2 in Exhibit 7–3). This occurs because under absorption costing, part of the fixed manufacturing overhead costs of the current period is deferred in inventory. In Year 2, for example, £30,000 of fixed manufacturing overhead costs (5,000 units × £6 per unit) has been applied to units in ending inventory. These costs are excluded from cost of goods sold.

   Under variable costing, however, *all* of the fixed manufacturing overhead costs of Year 2 have been charged immediately against income as a period cost. As a result, the net income for Year 2 under variable costing is £30,000 *lower* than it is under absorption costing. Exhibit 7–5 contains a reconciliation of the variable costing and absorption costing net income figures.

Fixed manufacturing overhead cost released from inventory The portion of the fixed manufacturing overhead cost of a *prior* period that becomes an expense of the current period under the absorption costing method as a result of sales exceeding production.

3. When production is less than sales, the net income reported under the absorption costing approach will generally be less than the net income reported under the variable costing approach (see Year 3 in Exhibit 7–3). This happens because inventories are drawn down and fixed manufacturing overhead costs that were previously deferred in inventory under absorption costing are released and charged against income (known as **fixed manufacturing overhead cost released from inventory**). In Year 3, for example, the £30,000 in fixed manufacturing overhead costs

Exhibit 7–5

Reconciliation of Variable Costing and Absorption Costing—Net Income Data from Exhibit 7–3

	Year 1	Year 2	Year 3
Variable costing net income	£60,000	£ –0–	£120,000
Add fixed manufacturing overhead costs deferred in inventory under absorption costing (5,000 units × £6 per unit)	–0–	30,000	–0–
Deduct fixed manufacturing overhead costs released from inventory under absorption costing (5,000 units × £6 per unit)	–0–	–0–	(30,000)
Absorption costing net income	£60,000	£30,000	£ 90,000

Variable Costing

Net income is *not* affected by changes in production under variable costing. Notice from Exhibit 7–6 that net income is the same for all three years under the variable costing approach, although production exceeds sales in one year and is less than sales in another year. In short, a change in production has no impact on net income when variable costing is in use.

Absorption Costing

Net income *is* affected by changes in production when absorption costing is in use, however. As shown in Exhibit 7–6, net income under the absorption approach goes up in Year 2, in response to the increase in production for that year, and then goes down in Year 3, in response to the drop in production for that year. Note particularly that net income goes up and down between these two years *even though the same number of units is sold in each year.* The reason for this effect can be traced to the shifting of fixed manufacturing overhead costs between periods under the absorption costing method as a result of changes in inventory.

As shown in Exhibit 7–6, production exceeds sales in Year 2, resulting in an increase of 10,000 units in inventory. Each unit produced during Year 2 has £6 in fixed manufacturing overhead costs attached to it (see the unit cost computations at the top of Exhibit 7–6). Therefore, £60,000 (10,000 units × £6) of the fixed manufacturing overhead costs of Year 2 are not charged against that year but rather are added to the inventory account (along with the variable manufacturing costs). The net income of Year 2 rises sharply, because of the deferral of these costs in inventories, even though the same number of units is sold in Year 2 as in the other years.

The reverse effect occurs in Year 3. Since sales exceed production in Year 3, that year is forced to cover all of its own fixed manufacturing overhead costs as well as the fixed manufacturing overhead costs carried forward in inventory from Year 2. A substantial drop in net income during Year 3 results from the release of fixed manufacturing overhead costs from inventories despite the fact that the same number of units is sold in that year as in the other years.

The variable costing and absorption costing net incomes are reconciled in Exhibit 7–7. This exhibit shows that the differences in net income can be traced to the effects of changes in inventories on absorption costing net income. Under absorption costing, fixed manufacturing overhead costs are deferred in inventory when inventories increase and are released from inventory when inventories decrease.

Exhibit 7–7
Reconciliation of Variable Costing and Absorption Costing—Net Income Data from Exhibit 7–6

	Year 1	Year 2	Year 3
Variable costing net income	£60,000	£ 60,000	£ 60,000
Add fixed manufacturing overhead costs deferred in inventory under absorption costing (10,000 units × £6 per unit)	–0–	60,000	–0–
Deduct fixed manufacturing overhead costs released from inventory under absorption costing (10,000 units × £6 per unit)	–0–	–0–	(60,000)
Absorption costing net income	£60,000	£120,000	£ –0–

Managerial Accounting in Action

THE WRAP-UP

After checking all of his work, Sean took the exhibits he had prepared to Mary's office where the following conversation took place:

Sean: I have some calculations I would like to show you.

Mary: Will this take long? I only have a few minutes before I have to meet with the buyer from Neiman Marcus.

Sean: Well, we can at least get started. These exhibits should help explain why our net income didn't increase this year as much as you thought it should have.

Mary: This first exhibit (i.e., Exhibit 7–3) looks like it just summarizes our income statements for the last three years.

Sean: Not exactly. There are actually two sets of income statements on this exhibit. The absorption costing income statements are the ones I originally prepared and we submitted to the bank. Below the absorption costing income statements are another set of income statements.

Mary: Those are the ones labelled variable costing.

Sean: That's right. You can see that the net incomes are the same for the two sets of income statements in our first year of operations, but they differ for the other two years.

Mary: I'll say! The variable costing statements indicate that we just broke even in the second year instead of earning a £30,000 profit. And the increase in net income between the second and third years is £120,000 instead of just £60,000. I don't know how you come up with two different net income figures, but the variable costing net income seems to be much closer to the truth. The second year was almost a disaster. We barely sold enough sweaters to cover all of our fixed costs.

Sean: You and I both know that, but the accounting rules view the situation a little differently. If we produce more than we sell, the accounting rules require that we take some of the fixed cost and assign it to the units that end up in inventories at year-end.

Mary: You mean that instead of appearing on the income statement as an expense, some of the fixed costs wind up on the balance sheet as inventories?

Sean: Precisely.

Mary: I thought accountants were conservative. Since when was it conservative to call an expense an asset?

Sean: We accountants have been debating whether fixed production costs are an asset or an expense for over 50 years.

Mary: It must have been a *fascinating* debate.

Sean: I have to admit that it ranks right up there with watching grass grow in terms of excitement level.

Mary: I don't know what the arguments are, but I can tell you for sure that we don't make any money by just producing sweaters. If I understand what you have shown me, I can increase my net income under absorption costing by simply making more sweaters—we don't have to sell them.

Sean: Correct.

Mary: So all I have to do to enjoy the lifestyle of the rich and famous is to hire every unemployed knitter in Ireland to make sweaters I can't sell.

Sean: We would have a major cash flow problem, but our net income would certainly go up.

Mary: Well, if the banks want us to use absorption costing so be it. I don't know why they would want us to report that way, but if that's what they want, that's what they'll get. Is there any reason why we can't use this variable costing method ourselves? The statements are easier to understand, and the net income figures make more sense to me. Can't we do both?

Sean: I don't see why not. Making the adjustment from one method to the other is very simple.

Mary: Good. Let's talk about this some more after I get back from the meeting with Neiman Marcus. ∎

The Impact on the Manager

Like Mary O'Meara, opponents of absorption costing argue that shifting fixed manufacturing overhead cost between periods can be confusing and can lead to misinterpretations and even to faulty decisions. Look again at the data in Exhibit 7–6; a manager might wonder why net income went up substantially in Year 2 under absorption costing when sales remained the same as in the prior year. Was it a result of lower selling costs, more efficient operations, or was some other factor involved? The manager is unable to tell, looking simply at the absorption costing income statement. Then in Year 3, net income drops sharply, even though again the same number of units is sold as in the other two years. Why would income rise in one year and then drop in the next? The figures seem erratic and contradictory and can lead to confusion and a loss of confidence in the integrity of the statement data.

By contrast, the variable costing income statements in Exhibit 7–6 are clear and easy to understand. Sales remain constant over the three-year period covered in the exhibit, so both contribution margin and net income also remain constant. The statements are consistent with what the manager would expect to happen under the circumstances, so they tend to generate confidence rather than confusion.

To avoid mistakes when absorption costing is used, readers of financial statements should be alert to changes in inventory levels. Under absorption costing, if there is an increase in inventories, fixed manufacturing overhead costs are deferred in inventories and net income is elevated. If there is a decrease in inventories, fixed manufacturing overhead costs are released from inventories and net income is depressed. Thus, fluctuations in net income can be due to changes in inventories rather than to changes in sales.

Focus on Current Practice

While managers can artificially increase net income under absorption costing by producing more than is really necessary and building up inventories, a few unscrupulous managers have stepped over the line into the area of outright fraud. By claiming inventories that don't exist, an unethical manager can produce instant profits and dress up the balance sheet. Since the value of ending inventories is subtracted from the cost of goods available for sale in order to arrive at the cost of goods sold, phantom inventories directly reduce cost of goods sold. Phantom inventories also beef up the balance sheet by increasing assets.

Auditors attempt to uncover such fraud by physically verifying the existence of inventory reported on the balance sheet. This is done by counting random samples of perhaps 5% to 10% of reported inventory items. However, this audit approach is not always effective. For example, managers at failing Laribee Wire Manufacturing Co. attempted to keep the company afloat by creating fictitious inventories. Investigations following the company's bankruptcy revealed that managers had fraudulently overstated income by claiming inventories of over 4 million pounds of copper rod that did not exist. Such inventory fraud at Laribee turned a loss of $6.5 million into an operating profit of $5.5 million in one year alone.[2]

Even worse is the 1997 Bre-X scandal. Bre-X was a Calgary-based gold mining company whose share prices went from $5 to over $200 before crashing into bankruptcy after an independent audit. In the biggest fraud of the century Bre-X claimed to have gold reserves worth over $70 billion U.S. in its operations in Busang, Indonesia. ∎

Choosing a Costing Method

Objective 5

Explain the advantages and limitations of both the variable and absorption costing methods.

In choosing between variable and absorption costing, several factors should be considered by the manager. These factors are discussed in this section.

CVP Analysis and Absorption Costing

Absorption costing is widely used for both internal and external reports. Many firms use the absorption approach exclusively because of its focus on *full* costing of units of product. A weakness of the method, however, is its inability to dovetail well with CVP analysis.

To illustrate, refer again to Exhibit 7–3. Let us compute the break-even point for Emerald Isle Knitters. To obtain the break-even point, we divide total fixed costs by the contribution margin per unit:

Selling price per unit	£ 20
Variable costs per unit	8
Contribution margin per unit	£ 12
Fixed manufacturing overhead costs	£150,000
Fixed selling and administrative costs	90,000
Total fixed costs	£240,000

$$\frac{\text{Total fixed costs}}{\text{Contribution margin per unit}} = \frac{£240,000}{£12} = 20,000 \text{ units}$$

The break-even point is 20,000 units. Notice from Exhibit 7–3 that in Year 2 the firm sold exactly 20,000 units, the break-even volume. Under the contribution approach, using variable costing, the firm does break even in Year 2, showing zero net income. *Under absorption costing, however, the firm shows a positive net income of £30,000 for Year 2.* How can this be? How can absorption costing produce a positive net income when the firm sold exactly the break-even volume of units?

The answer lies in the fact that £30,000 in fixed manufacturing overhead costs were deferred in inventory during Year 2 under absorption costing and therefore did not appear as charges against income. By deferring these fixed manufacturing overhead costs in inventory, the income statement shows a profit even though the company sold exactly the break-even volume of units. Absorption costing runs into similar kinds of difficulty in other areas of CVP analysis, which assumes that variable costing is being used.

---

2. Lee Burton, "Convenient Fiction: Inventory Chicanery Tempts More Firms, Fools More Auditors," *The Wall Street Journal,* December 14, 1992, pp. A1, A5.

since there is a direct relationship between ending inventory and net income. Those responsible for performance evaluation should look beyond the bottom line so as to identify such abuses.

At any rate, absorption costing is the generally accepted method for preparing mandatory external financial reports and income tax returns. Probably because of the cost and possible confusion of maintaining two separate costing systems—one for external reporting and one for internal reporting—most companies use absorption costing for both external and internal reports.

Variable Costing and the Theory of Constraints

A form of variable costing is used in the theory of constraints (TOC), one of the management approaches that was discussed in Chapter 1. In the TOC approach, direct labour is generally considered to be a fixed cost. As discussed in earlier chapters, in many companies direct labour is not really a variable cost. Even though direct labour workers may be paid on an hourly basis, many companies have a commitment—sometimes enforced in labour contracts or by law—to guarantee workers a minimum number of paid hours. In TOC companies, there are two additional reasons to consider direct labour to be a fixed cost.

First, direct labour is not usually the constraint. In the simplest cases, the constraint is a machine. In more complex cases, the constraint is a policy (such as a poorly designed compensation scheme for salespersons) that prevents the company from using its resources more effectively. If direct labour is not the constraint, there is no reason to increase it. Hiring more direct labour would increase costs without increasing the output of salable products and services.

Second, TOC emphasizes continuous improvement to maintain competitiveness. Without committed and enthusiastic employees, sustained continuous improvement is virtually impossible. Since layoffs often have devastating effects on employee morale, managers involved in TOC are extremely reluctant to lay off employees.

For these reasons, most managers in TOC companies believe that direct labour in their companies behaves much more like a committed fixed cost than a variable cost. Hence, in the modified form of variable costing used in TOC companies, direct labour is not included as a part of product costs.

Impact of JIT Inventory Methods

Objective 6

Explain how the use of JIT reduces the difference in net income reported under the variable and absorption costing methods.

As discussed in this chapter, variable and absorption costing will produce different net income figures whenever the number of units produced is different from the number of units sold—in other words, whenever there is a change in the number of units in inventory. We have also learned that the absorption costing net income figure can be erratic, sometimes moving in a direction that is opposite from the movement in sales.

When companies use just-in-time (JIT) methods, these problems are reduced. The erratic movement of net income under absorption costing and the difference in net income between absorption and variable costing occur because of changes in the number of units in inventory. Under JIT, goods are produced to customers' orders and the goal is to eliminate finished goods inventories entirely and reduce work in process inventory to almost nothing. If there is very little inventory, then changes in inventories will be very small and both variable and absorption costing will show basically the same net income figure. In that case, absorption costing net income will move in the same direction as movements in sales.

Of course, the cost of a unit of product will still be different between variable and absorption costing, as explained earlier in the chapter. But when JIT is used, the differences in net income will largely disappear.

Summary

Variable and absorption costing are alternative methods of determining unit product costs. Under variable costing, only those production costs that vary with output are treated as product costs. This includes direct materials, variable overhead, and ordinarily direct labour. Fixed manufacturing overhead is treated as a period cost and charged off against revenue as it is incurred, the same as selling and administrative expenses. By contrast, absorption costing treats fixed manufacturing overhead as a product cost, along with direct materials, direct labour, and variable overhead.

Since absorption costing treats fixed manufacturing overhead as a product cost, a portion of fixed manufacturing overhead is assigned to each unit as it is produced. If units of product are unsold at the end of a period, then the fixed manufacturing overhead costs attached to the units are carried with them into the inventory account and deferred to the next period. When these units are later sold, the fixed manufacturing overhead costs attached to them are released from the inventory account and charged against revenues as a part of cost of goods sold. Thus, under absorption costing, it is possible to defer a portion of the fixed manufacturing overhead costs of one period to the next period through the inventory account.

Unfortunately, this shifting of fixed manufacturing overhead costs between periods can cause net income to move in an erratic manner and can result in confusion and unwise decisions on the part of management. To guard against mistakes when they interpret income statement data, managers should be alert to any changes that may have taken place in inventory levels or in unit product costs during the period.

Practically speaking, variable costing cannot be used externally for either financial reporting or income tax purposes. However, it may be used internally for planning purposes. The variable costing approach dovetails well with CVP concepts that are often indispensable in profit planning and decision making.

Review Problem: Absorption and Direct Costing

Dexter Company produces and sells a single product. Selected cost and operating data relating to the product for a recent year are given below:

Opening inventory in units	1,000
Units produced during the year	10,000
Units sold during the year	8,000
Ending inventory in units	3,000
Selling price per unit	$ 50
Selling and administrative costs:	
Variable per unit	5
Fixed per year	70,000
Manufacturing costs—previous period:	
Variable per unit	$19
Fixed per unit	9
Total cost per unit	28
Manufacturing costs—current period:	
Variable per unit:	
Direct materials	11
Direct labour	6
Variable overhead	3
Fixed per year	100,000

Required   1. Assume that the company uses absorption costing.
  a. Compute the manufactured cost of one unit of product.
  b. Prepare an income statement for the year.
2. Assume that the company uses direct costing.
  a. Compute the manufactured cost of one unit of product.
  b. Prepare an income statement for the year.
3. Reconcile the direct costing and absorption costing net income figures.

Solution   1. a. Under absorption costing, all manufacturing costs, variable and fixed, are added to the cost of a unit of product:

Direct materials	$11
Direct labour	6
Variable overhead	3
Fixed overhead ($100,000 ÷ 10,000 units)	10
Total cost per unit	$30

b. The absorption costing income statement follows:

Sales (8,000 units × $50)		$400,000
Cost of goods sold:		
Opening inventory	$ 28,000	
Add cost of goods manufactured		
(10,000 units × $30)	300,000	
Goods available for sale	328,000	
Less ending inventory (3,000 units × $30) ...	90,000	238,000
Gross margin		162,000
Selling and administrative expense		110,000
Net income		$52,000

*Variable (8,000 units × $5)	$40,000	
Fixed per year	70,000	
Total	$110,000	

2. a. Under direct costing, only the variable manufacturing costs are added to the cost of a unit of product:

Direct materials	$11
Direct labour	6
Variable overhead	3
Total cost per unit	$20

b. The direct costing income statement follows:

Sales (8,000 units × $50)		$400,000
Less variable expenses:		
Opening inventory (1,000 units × $19)	$19,000	
Add variable cost of goods manufactured		
(10,000 units × $20)	$200,000	
Goods available for sale	219,000	
Less ending inventory (3,000		
units × $20)	60,000	
Variable cost of goods sold	159,000	
Variable selling and administrative		
expense (8,000 units × $5)	40,000	199,000
Contribution margin		201,000
Less fixed expenses:		
Fixed overhead cost for the year	100,000	
Fixed selling and administrative		
expense	70,000	170,000
Net income		$31,000

3. The reconciliation of the direct and absorption costing net income figures follows:

Direct costing net income	31,000
Add fixed overhead costs deferred in inventory under absorption costing (3,000 units × $10)	30,000
	61,000
Less fixed overhead costs charged in opening inventory under absorption costing (1,000 units × $9)	9,000
Absorption costing net income	$52,000

Questions

7–1 What is the basic difference between absorption costing and variable costing?

7–2 Are selling and administrative expenses treated as product costs or as period costs under variable costing?

7–3 Explain how fixed manufacturing overhead costs are shifted from one period to another under absorption costing.

7–4 What arguments can be advanced in favour of treating fixed manufacturing overhead costs as product costs?

7–5 What arguments can be advanced in favour of treating fixed manufacturing overhead costs as period costs?

7–6 If production and sales are equal, which method would you expect to show the higher net income, variable costing or absorption costing? Why?

7–7 If production exceeds sales, which method would you expect to show the higher net income, variable costing or absorption costing? Why?

7–8 If fixed manufacturing overhead costs are released from inventory under absorption costing, what does this tell you about the level of production in relation to the level of sales?

7–9 Parker Company had $5,000,000 in sales and reported a $300,000 loss in its annual report to shareholders. According to a CVP analysis prepared for management's use, $5,000,000 in sales is the break-even point for the company. Did the company's inventory level increase, decrease, or remain unchanged? Explain.

7–10 Under absorption costing, how is it possible to increase net income without increasing sales?

7–11 How is the use of variable costing limited?

7–12 Develop a reason from financial accounting theory that would support a recommendation of absorption costing for financial reporting purposes.

7–13 How does the use of JIT inventory methods reduce or eliminate the difference in reported net income between absorption and variable costing?

Exercises

E7–1   Alberta Grills, Inc., makes a single product—a handmade specialty barbecue grill that it sells for $210. Data for last year's operations follow:

Units in beginning inventory	–0–
Units produced	20,000
Units sold	19,000
Units in ending inventory	1,000

Variable costs per unit:		
Direct materials	$	50
Direct labour		80
Variable manufacturing overhead		20
Variable selling and administrative		10
Total variable cost per unit	$	160

Fixed costs:	
Fixed manufacturing overhead	$700,000
Fixed selling and administrative	285,000
Total fixed costs	$985,000

Required
1. Assume that the company uses variable costing. Compute the unit product cost for one barbecue grill.
2. Assume that the company uses variable costing. Prepare an income statement for the year in good form using the contribution format.
3. What is the company's break-even point in terms of the number of barbecue grills sold?

E7–2   Refer to the date in E7–1 for Alberta Grills. Assume in this exercise that the company uses absorption costing.

Required
1. Compute the unit product cost for one barbecue grill.
2. Prepare an income statement for the year in good form.

E7–3   Ida Sidha Karya Company is a family-owned company located in the village of Gianyar on the island of Bali in Indonesia. The company produces a handcrafted Balinese musical instrument called a gamelan that is similar to a xylophone. The sounding bars are cast from brass and hand-filed to attain just the right sound. The bars are then mounted on an intricately hand-carved wooden base. The gamelans are sold for 850 (thousand) rupiahs. (The currency in Indonesia is the rupiah, which is denoted by Rp.) Selected data for the company's operations last year follow (all currency values are in thousands of rupiahs):

Units in beginning inventory	–0–
Units produced	250
Units sold	225
Units in ending inventory	25

Variable costs per unit:	
Direct materials	Rp100
Direct labour	320
Variable manufacturing overhead	40
Variable selling and administrative	20

Fixed costs:	
Fixed manufacturing overhead	Rp60,000
Fixed selling and administrative	20,000

Required
1. Assume that the company uses absorption costing. Compute the unit product cost for one gamelan.
2. Assume that the company uses variable costing. Compute the unit product cost for one gamelan.

E7–4 Refer to the data in E7–3 for Ida Sidha Karya Company. An income statement prepared under the absorption costing method by the company's accountant appears below (all currency values are in thousands of rupiahs):

Sales (225 units × Rp850)		Rp191,250
Less cost of goods sold:		
Beginning inventory	Rp –0–	
Add cost of goods manufactured (250 units × Rp __?__)	175,000	
Goods available for sale	175,000	
Less ending inventory (25 units × Rp __?__)	17,500	157,500
Gross margin		33,750
Less selling and administrative expenses:		
Variable selling and administrative	4,500	
Fixed selling and administrative	20,000	24,500
Net income		Rp 9,250

Required
1. Determine how much of the ending inventory of Rp17,500 above consists of fixed manufacturing overhead cost deferred in inventory to the next period.
2. Prepare an income statement for the year using the variable costing method. Explain the difference in net income between the two costing methods.

E7–5 Sierra Company produces and sells a single product. The following costs relate to its production and sale:

Variable costs per unit:		
Direct materials	$	9
Direct labour		10
Manufacturing overhead		5
Selling and administrative expenses		3
Fixed costs per year:		
Fixed manufacturing overhead		150,000
Fixed selling and administrative expenses		400,000

During the last year, 25,000 units were produced and 22,000 units were sold. The Finished Goods inventory account at the end of the year shows a balance of $72,000 for the 3,000 unsold units.

Required
1. Is the company using absorption costing or variable costing to cost units in the Finished Goods inventory account? Show computations to support your answer.
2. Assume that the company wishes to prepare financial statements for the year to issue to its shareholders.
   a. Is the $72,000 figure for Finished Goods inventory the correct amount to use on these statements for external reporting purposes? Explain.
   b. At what dollar amount *should* the 3,000 units be carried in the inventory for external reporting purposes?

E7–6 Lynch Company manufactures and sells a single product. The following costs were incurred during the company's first year of operations:

Variable costs per unit:		
Production:		
Direct materials	$	6
Direct labour		9
Variable manufacturing overhead		3
Variable selling and administrative		4
Fixed costs per year:		
Fixed manufacturing overhead		300,000
Fixed selling and administrative		190,000

During the year, the company produced 25,000 units and sold 20,000 units. The selling price of the company's product is $50 per unit.

Required   1. Assume that the company uses the absorption costing method:
     a. Compute the unit product cost.
     b. Prepare an income statement for the year.
    2. Assume that the company uses the variable costing method:
     a. Compute the unit product cost.
     b. Prepare an income statement for the year.

E7–7   Whitman Company has just completed its first year of operations. The company's accountant has prepared an income statement for the year, as follows (absorption costing basis):

WHITMAN COMPANY
Income Statement

Sales (35,000 units at $25)		$875,000
Less cost of goods sold:		
Beginning inventory	$ –0–	
Add cost of goods manufactured (40,000 units at $16)	640,000	
Goods available for sale	640,000	
Less ending inventory (5,000 units at $16)	80,000	560,000
Gross margin		315,000
Less selling and administrative expenses		280,000
Net income		$ 35,000

The company's selling and administrative expenses consist of $210,000 per year in fixed expenses and $2 per unit sold in variable expenses. The $16 unit product cost given above is computed as follows:

Direct materials	$ 5
Direct labour	6
Variable manufacturing overhead	1
Fixed manufacturing overhead ($160,000 ÷ 40,000 units)	4
Unit product cost	$16

Required   1. Redo the company's income statement in the contribution format using variable costing.
    2. Reconcile any difference between the net income figure on your variable costing income statement and the net income figure on the absorption costing income statement above.

Problems

P7–8   Straightforward Comparison of Costing Methods   High Country, Inc., produces and sells many recreational products. The company has just opened a new plant to produce a folding camp cot that will be marketed throughout Canada. The following cost and revenue data relate to May, the first month of the plant's operation:

Beginning inventory		–0–
Units produced		10,000
Units sold		8,000
Selling price per unit	$	75
Selling and administrative expenses:		
Variable per unit		6
Fixed (total)		200,000
Manufacturing costs:		
Direct materials cost per unit		20
Direct labour cost per unit		8
Variable manufacturing overhead cost per unit		2
Fixed manufacturing overhead cost (total)		100,000

Management is anxious to see how profitable the new camp cot will be and has asked that an income statement be prepared for May.

Required
1. Assume that the company uses absorption costing.
   a. Determine the unit product cost.
   b. Prepare an income statement for May.
2. Assume that the company uses the contribution approach with variable costing.
   a. Determine the unit product cost.
   b. Prepare an income statement for May.
3. Explain the reason for any difference in the ending inventory under the two costing methods and the impact of this difference on reported net income.

P7–9   Straightforward Variable Costing Statements   During Heaton Company's first two years of operations, the company reported net income as follows (absorption costing basis):

	Year 1	Year 2
Sales (@ $25)	$1,000,000	$1,250,000
Less cost of goods sold:		
Beginning inventory	–0–	90,000
Add cost of goods manufactured (@ $18)	810,000	810,000
Goods available for sale	810,000	900,000
Less ending inventory (@ $18)	90,000	–0–
Cost of goods sold	720,000	900,000
Gross margin	280,000	350,000
Less selling and administrative expenses*	210,000	230,000
Net income	$ 70,000	$ 120,000

* $2 per unit variable; $130,000 fixed each year.

The company's $18 unit product cost is computed as follows:

Direct materials	$ 4
Direct labour	7
Variable manufacturing overhead	1
Fixed manufacturing overhead ($270,000 ÷ 45,000 units)	6
Unit product cost	$18

Production and cost data for the two years are:

	Year 1	Year 2
Units produced	45,000	45,000
Units sold	40,000	50,000

Required
1. Prepare an income statement for each year in the contribution format using variable costing.
2. Reconcile the absorption costing and the variable costing net income figures for each year.

P7–10   Prepare and Reconcile Variable Costing Statements   Denton Company manufactures and sells a single product. Cost data for the product are given below:

Variable costs per unit:		
Direct materials	$	7
Direct labour		10
Variable manufacturing overhead		5
Variable selling and administrative		3
Total variable cost per unit	$	25

Fixed costs per month:	
Fixed manufacturing overhead	$315,000
Fixed selling and administrative	245,000
Total fixed cost per month	$560,000

5. a. Explain how operations would have differed in Year 2 if the company had been using JIT inventory methods.
   b. If JIT has been in use during Year 2, what would the company's net income have been under absorption costing? Explain the reason for any difference between this income figure and the figure reported by the company in the statements above.

P7–15   Ethics and the Manager; Production Schedule   Carlos Cavalas, the manager of Echo Products' Brazilian Division, is trying to decide what production schedule to set for the last quarter of the year. The Brazilian Division had planned to sell 3,600 units during the year, but by September 30 only the following activity had been reported:

	Units
Inventory, January 1	–0–
Production	2,400
Sales	2,000
Inventory, September 30	400

The division can rent warehouse space to store up to 1,000 units. The minimum inventory level that the division should carry is 50 units. Mr. Cavalas is aware that production must be at least 200 units per quarter in order to retain a nucleus of key employees. Maximum production is 1,500 units per quarter.

Demand has been soft, and the sales forecast for the last quarter is only 600 units. Due to the nature of the division's operations, fixed manufacturing overhead is a major element of product cost.

Required

1. Assume that the division is using variable costing. How many units should be scheduled for production during the last quarter of the year? (The basic formula for computing the required production for a period in a company is: Expected sales + Desired ending inventory − Beginning inventory = Required production.) Show computations and explain your answer. Will the number of units scheduled for production affect the division's reported income or loss for the year? Explain.
2. Assume that the division is using absorption costing and that the divisional manager is given an annual bonus based on divisional operating income. If Mr. Cavalas wants to maximize his division's operating income for the year, how many units should be scheduled for production during the last quarter? [See the formula in (1) above.] Show computations and explain your answer.
3. Identify the ethical issues involved in the decision Mr. Cavalas must make.

P7–16   A Comparison of Costing Methods   For the year ended March 31, 2002 the following are the sales, production, and cost data for Saskatoon Company:

Sales (10,000 units)	$600,000
Manufacturing costs for the units produced:	
Prime cost	330,000
Variable overhead	110,000
Fixed overhead	85,600
Operating expenses:	
Variable selling	10,000
Fixed selling	35,000
Fixed administrative	55,000

Saskatoon Company produced 11,000 units during the year, which is 300 units more than normal capacity. In beginning finished goods inventory there were 1,000 units with a variable manufacturing cost of $38 per unit. Fixed overhead in beginning inventory was $7 per unit. Saskatoon uses the FIFO cost flow assumption.

Note:
Any over- or underapplied overhead is treated as a period expense.

Required Calculate:

1. The number of units in ending inventory.
2. The cost of ending inventory using direct costing.
3. The cost of ending inventory using absorption costing.
4. Saskatoon Company's gross margin percentage.
5. Saskatoon Company's total *manufacturing* contribution margin.
6. Saskatoon Company's contribution margin as a percentage of sales.
7. The difference in net income between the direct costing method and the absorption costing method.

(CGA, adapted)

P7–17   A Comparison of Costing Methods   You are provided with the following information for Singh Enterprises during the first quarter of 2000.

	January	February	March
Unit sales	12,000	14,000	18,000
Sales price per unit	$12	$12	$12
Variable manufacturing cost per unit	5	5	5
Variable selling expense per unit	2	2	2
Unit production	15,000	18,000	13,000

Additional information:

a. On January 1, there were 2,000 units on hand.

b. Fixed overhead cost is $3.00 per unit and is applied to units of product on the basis of a production volume of 14,000 units per month. The cost of goods sold is adjusted for any over- or underapplied fixed manufacturing overhead.

c. Singh Enterprises uses a FIFO inventory flow. Work in process inventories are immaterial and are to be ignored.

d. Fixed selling and administrative expenses total $20,000 per month.

Required

1. For each of the above three months, prepare income statements using:
   a. Absorption costing;
   b. Contribution approach with direct costing.

2. Explain in detail why, under absorption costing, over the three-month period profits have moved erratically and have not moved in correlation with the changes in sales volume. In your answer you should include a reconciliation of net income under absorption costing with net income under direct costing.

3. Identify the advantages and disadvantages of using the direct costing method for internal reporting purposes.

(CGA, adapted)

P7–18   Chun Lee Co. Ltd. is trying to determine the appropriate selling price of one of its products, Xamon. Each unit of Xamon has the following cost characteristics:

	Cost per Unit of Xamon
Direct materials	$ 6
Direct labour	12
Variable overhead	5
Fixed overhead	7
Variable selling expense	2
Fixed selling expense	4

Chun Lee expects to produce and sell 5,000 units of Xamon in the coming year. An investment of $100,000 is required for the production of Xamon.

RAYCO, INC.
Income Statements
For the First Two Quarters

	First Quarter		Second Quarter	
Sales		$480,000		$600,000
Less cost of goods sold:				
Beginning inventory	$ 80,000		$140,000	
Add cost of goods manufactured	300,000		180,000	
Goods available for sale	380,000		320,000	
Less ending inventory	140,000		20,000	
Cost of goods sold	240,000		300,000	
Add underapplied overhead	—	240,000	72,000	372,000
Gross margin		240,000		228,000
Less selling and administrative				
expenses		200,000		215,000
Net income		$ 40,000		$ 13,000

After studying the statements briefly, Mr. Yoder called in the controller to see if the mistake in the second quarter could be located before the figures were released to the press. The controller stated, "I'm sorry to say that those figures are correct, Ben. I agree that sales went up during the second quarter, but the problem is in production. You see, we budgeted to produce 15,000 units each quarter, but a strike on the west coast among some of our suppliers forced us to cut production in the second quarter back to only 9,000 units. That's what caused the drop in net income."

Mr. Yoder was confused by the controller's explanation. He replied, "This doesn't make sense. I ask you to explain why net income dropped when sales went up and you talk about production! So what if we had to cut back production? We still were able to increase sales by 25%. If sales go up, then net income should go up. If your statements can't show a simple thing like that, then it's time for some changes in your area!"

Budgeted production and sales for the year, along with actual production and sales for the first two quarters, are given below:

	Quarter			
	First	Second	Third	Fourth
Budgeted sales (units)	12,000	15,000	15,000	18,000
Actual sales (units)	12,000	15,000	—	—
Budgeted production (units)	15,000	15,000	15,000	15,000
Actual production (units)	15,000	9,000	—	—

The company's plant is heavily automated, and fixed manufacturing overhead amounts to $180,000 each quarter. Variable manufacturing costs are $8 per unit. The fixed manufacturing overhead is applied to units of product at a rate of $12 per unit (based on the budgeted production shown above). Any under- or overapplied overhead is taken directly to cost of goods sold for the quarter. The company had 4,000 units in inventory to start the first quarter and uses the FIFO inventory flow assumption. Variable selling and administrative expenses are $5 per unit.

Required

1. What characteristic of absorption costing caused the drop in net income for the second quarter and what could the controller have said to explain the problem more fully?
2. Prepare income statements for each quarter using the contribution approach, with variable costing.
3. Reconcile the absorption costing and the variable costing net income figures for each quarter.
4. Identify and discuss the advantages and disadvantages of using the variable costing method for internal reporting purposes.

5. Assume that the company had introduced JIT inventory methods at the beginning of the second quarter. (Sales and production during the first quarter remain the same.)
   a. How many units would have been produced during the second quarter under JIT?
   b. Starting with the third quarter, would you expect any difference between the net income reported under absorption costing and under variable costing? Explain why there would or would not be any difference.

C7–21 Absorption and Variable Costing; Uneven Production; Break-Even Analysis; Just-in-Time (JIT) Impact   "Now this doesn't make any sense at all," said Flora Fisher, financial vice president for Warner Company. "Our sales have been steadily rising over the last several months, but profits have been going in the opposite direction. In September we finally hit $2,000,000 in sales, but the bottom line for that month drops off to a $100,000 loss. Why aren't profits more closely correlated with sales?"

The statements to which Ms. Fisher was referring are shown below:

WARNER COMPANY
Monthly Income Statements

	July	August	September
Sales (@ $25)	$1,750,000	$1,875,000	$2,000,000
Less cost of goods sold:			
Beginning inventory	80,000	320,000	400,000
Cost applied to production:			
Variable manufacturing costs (@ $9)	765,000	720,000	540,000
Fixed manufacturing overhead	595,000	560,000	420,000
Cost of goods manufactured	1,360,000	1,280,000	960,000
Goods available for sale	1,440,000	1,600,000	1,360,000
Less ending inventory	320,000	400,000	80,000
Cost of goods sold	1,120,000	1,200,000	1,280,000
Underapplied or (overapplied) fixed overhead cost	(35,000)	—	140,000
Adjusted cost of goods sold	1,085,000	1,200,000	1,420,000
Gross margin	665,000	675,000	580,000
Less selling and administrative expenses	620,000	650,000	680,000
Net income (loss)	$ 45,000	$ 25,000	$ (100,000)

Hal Taylor, a recent university graduate who has just been hired by Warner Company, has stated to Ms. Fisher that the contribution approach, with variable costing, is a much better way to report profit data to management. Sales and production data for the last quarter follow:

	July	August	September
Production in units	85,000	80,000	60,000
Sales in units	70,000	75,000	80,000

Additional information about the company's operations is given below:

a. Five thousand units were in inventory on July 1.
b. Fixed manufacturing overhead costs total $1,680,000 per quarter and are incurred evenly throughout the quarter. This fixed manufacturing overhead cost is applied to units of product on the basis of a budgeted production volume of 80,000 units per month.
c. Variable selling and administrative expenses are $6 per unit sold. The remainder of the selling and administrative expenses on the statements above are fixed.
d. The company uses a FIFO inventory flow assumption. Work in process inventories are insignificant and can be ignored.

"I know production is somewhat out of step with sales," said Carla Vorhees, the company's controller. "But we had to build inventory early in the quarter in anticipation of a strike in September. Since the union settled without a strike, we then had to cut back production in September in order to work off the excess inventories. The income statements you have are completely accurate."

Required

1. Prepare an income statement for each month using the contribution approach with variable costing.
2. Compute the monthly break-even point under variable costing.
3. Explain to Ms. Fisher why profits have moved erratically over the three-month period shown in the absorption costing statements above and why profits have not been more closely related to changes in sales volume.
4. Reconcile the variable costing and absorption costing net income (loss) figures for each month. Show all computations, and show how you derive each figure used in your reconciliation.
5. Assume that the company had decided to introduce JIT inventory methods at the beginning of September. (Sales and production during July and August were as shown above.)
   a. How many units would have been produced during September under JIT?
   b. Starting with the next quarter (October, November, and December), would you expect any difference between the income reported under absorption costing and under variable costing? Explain why there would or would not be any difference.
   c. Refer to your computations in (2) above. How would JIT help break-even analysis "make sense" under absorption costing?

Group Exercises

GE7–22 One Size Fits All?   Nearly 70 years ago, economist J. Maurice Clarke stated that "accountants use different costs because of their differing objectives." The business world has certainly become a lot more complicated since Professor Clarke's time. Yet people often cling to the myth of a single, unique unit cost.

Required

1. How is accounting information used? That is, for what purposes, functions, or roles is cost information used?
2. Once you've identified the uses for cost information, how would you determine the makeup of the unit cost for each use. For example, one of the uses you should have identified is the need for a unit cost to value inventory and determine incomes for external financial reporting purposes. What do generally accepted accounting principles (GAAP) have to say about what is an inventoriable product cost for financial reporting purposes?

GE7–23 Who Needs Customers? I Can Make Money without Them
Tough times always seem to bring out the worst in people. When companies are desperate to stay in business or to report more favourable earnings to Bay Street, some managers just can't seem to resist the temptation to manipulate reported profits. Unfortunately, inventory is sometimes a tempting source of such manipulations. It is important to know how such earnings distortions can occur, whether they result from intentional actions or innocent miscalculations.

Required

1. What product cost concept is the basis for inventory valuation and cost of goods sold determination for external financial reporting purposes?
2. Explain the concept of "phantom" or "illusory" profits. Excluding inflation and changes in the selling prices of products, how could a firm with the same sales as last year report significantly higher profits without cutting any costs? Could a firm with sales below the break-even point report profits? Explain.
3. Are all such "fictitious" profits an attempt to distort profits and mislead investors and creditors? If not, under what economic conditions would this most likely occur?
4. Could the reverse situation occur? That is, could lower accounting profits be reported even though the firm is not economically worse off? Under what economic conditions would this most likely occur?

5. A far more serious manipulation is inventory fraud by reporting fictitious inventories. Explain how this could result in a serious overstatement of earnings and assets.

GE7–24   Changing Cost Structures and Product Costing   As firms automate their operations with advanced manufacturing technology and information technology, cost structures are becoming more fixed with higher proportions of overhead.

Required

1. What implications does this trend hold for arguments favouring absorption costing? What implications does this trend hold for arguments favouring variable costing?
2. If absorption costing continues to be used for external financial reporting, what impact will inventory buildups or inventory liquidations have on future reported earnings compared with the effects they have had on past reported earnings?
3. Most firms evaluate and compensate top management, in part, on the basis of reported income. Would top management have a preference for variable costing or full absorption costing? Explain.

IE7–25   Estimating Variable Costing Net Income from an Absorption Costing Income Statement   Magna International Corporation is the world's top automotive supplier. The company's manufacturing processes are highly automated, so most manufacturing costs are fixed. You can access the company's most recent annual report in the Sedar section of its web site www.sedar.com. Its most recent operating income figure is on its income statement, and the values of beginning and ending inventories are on its balance sheet.

Required   Assume that Magna uses absorption costing in its annual report and that 60% of the cost of its beginning and ending inventories consists of fixed manufacturing overhead costs. Estimate the company's operating income if it had used variable costing.

enormously to the complexity of activity-based costing. Even so, you are likely to find this chapter especially challenging.

In the traditional cost accounting systems described in Chapters 2, 3, and 4, the objective is to properly value inventories and cost of goods sold for external financial reports. In activity-based costing, the objective is to understand overhead and the profitability of products and customers. As a consequence of these differences in objectives, "best practice" activity-based costing differs in a number of ways from traditional cost accounting.

In activity-based costing:

1. Nonmanufacturing as well as manufacturing costs may be assigned to products.
2. Some manufacturing costs may be excluded from product costs.
3. There are a number of overhead cost pools, each of which is allocated to products and other costing objects using its own unique measure of activity.
4. The allocation bases often differ from those used in traditional costing systems.
5. The overhead rates, or *activity rates*, may be based on the level of activity at capacity rather than on the budgeted level of activity.

As we will see later in the chapter, these differences from traditional cost accounting systems can have dramatic impacts on the apparent costs of products and the profitability of products and customers. But first, we will briefly discuss the reasons for these departures from traditional cost accounting practices.

How Costs Are Treated Under Activity-Based Costing

Nonmanufacturing Costs and Activity-Based Costing

In traditional cost accounting, only manufacturing costs are assigned to products. Selling, general, and administrative expenses are treated as period expenses and are not assigned to products. However, many of these nonmanufacturing costs are also part of the costs of producing, selling, distributing, and servicing products. For example, commissions paid to salespersons, shipping costs, and warranty repair costs can be easily traced to individual products. To determine the profitability of products and services, such nonmanufacturing costs are assigned to products in activity-based costing.

Manufacturing Costs and Activity-Based Costing

In traditional cost accounting, *all* manufacturing costs are assigned to products— even manufacturing costs that are not caused by the products. For example, a portion of the factory security guard's wages would be allocated to each product even though the guard's wages are totally unaffected by which products are made or not made during a period. In activity-based costing, a cost is assigned to a product only if there is good reason to believe that the cost would be affected by decisions concerning the product.

PLANTWIDE OVERHEAD RATE   Our discussion in Chapter 3 assumed that a single overhead rate, called a *plantwide overhead rate,* was being used throughout an entire factory and that the allocation base was direct labour-hours or machine-hours. This simple approach to overhead assignment can result in distorted unit product costs when it is used for decision-making purposes.

When cost systems were developed in the 1800s, direct labour was a larger component of product costs than it is today. Data relating to direct labour were readily available and convenient to use, and managers believed there was a high positive correlation between direct labour and overhead costs. (A positive correlation between two things means that they tend to move in tandem.) Consequently, direct labour was a useful allocation base for overhead.

However, a plantwide overhead rate based on direct labour may no longer be satisfactory. First, in many companies, direct labour may no longer be highly correlated with (i.e., move in tandem with) overhead costs. Second, because of the large variety of activities encompassed in overhead, no single allocation base may be able to adequately reflect the demands that products place on overhead resources.

On an economywide basis, direct labour and overhead costs have been moving in opposite directions for a long time. As a percentage of total cost, direct labour has been declining, whereas overhead has been increasing.[1] Many tasks that used to be done by hand are now done with largely automated equipment—a component of overhead. Furthermore, product diversity has increased. Companies are creating new products and services at an ever-accelerating rate that differ in volume, batch size, and complexity. Managing and sustaining this product diversity requires many more overhead resources such as production schedulers and product design engineers, and many of these overhead resources have no obvious connection with direct labour.

Nevertheless, direct labour remains a viable base for applying overhead to products in many companies—particularly for external reports. In some companies there is still a high positive correlation between overhead costs and direct labour. And most companies throughout the world continue to base overhead allocations on direct labour or machine-hours. However, in those instances in which factorywide overhead costs do not move in tandem with factorywide direct labour, some other means of assigning costs must be found or product costs will be distorted.

DEPARTMENTAL OVERHEAD RATES   Rather than use a plantwide overhead rate, many companies use departmental overhead rates. The allocation bases used in these departmental overhead rates depend on the nature of the work performed in each department. For example, overhead costs in a machining department may be allocated on the basis of the machine-hours in that department. In contrast, the overhead costs in an assembly department may be allocated on the basis of direct labour-hours in that department.

Unfortunately, even departmental overhead rates will not correctly assign overhead costs in situations where a company has a range of products that differ in volume, batch size, or complexity of production.[2] The reason is that the departmental approach usually relies on volume as the factor in allocating overhead cost to products. For example, if the machining department's overhead is applied to products on the basis of machine-hours, it is assumed that the department's overhead costs are caused by, and are directly proportional to, machine-hours. However, the department's overhead costs are probably more complex than this and are caused by a variety of factors, including the range of products processed in the department, the number of batch setups that are required, the complexity of the products, and so on. Activity-based costing is a technique that is designed to reflect these diverse factors more accurately when costing products. It attempts to accomplish this goal by identifying the major *activities* such as batch setups, purchase order processing, and so on, that consume overhead resources. An **activity** is any event that causes the consumption of overhead resources. The costs of carrying out these activities are assigned to the products that cause the activities.

Activity   An event that causes the consumption of overhead resources in an organization.

---

1. Germain Böer provides some data concerning these trends in "Five Modern Management Accounting Myths," *Management Accounting* (January 1994), pp. 22–27. Data maintained by the U.S. Department of Commerce shows that since 1849, on average, material cost as a percentage of manufacturing cost has been fairly constant at 55% of sales. Labour cost has always been relatively less important and has declined steadily from 23% in 1849 to about 10% in 1987. Overhead has grown from about 18% of sales in 1947 to about 33% of sales 50 years later.
2. See Robin Cooper and Robert S. Kaplan, "How Cost Accounting Distorts Product Costs," *Management Accounting* (April 1988), pp. 20–27.

offices, providing a computer network, arranging for loans, preparing annual reports to shareholders, and so on. These activities are not consumed by the products or services.

When combining activities in an ABC system, activities should be grouped together at the appropriate level. Batch-level activities should not be combined with unit-level activities or product-level activities with batch-level activities and so on. In general, it is best to combine only those activities that are highly correlated with each other within a level. Activities are correlated with each other if they tend to move in tandem. For example, the number of customer orders received is likely to be highly correlated with the number of completed customer orders shipped, so these two batch-level activities (receiving and shipping orders) can usually be combined with little loss of accuracy.

At Classic Brass, the ABC team, in consultation with top managers, selected the following *activity cost pools* and *activity measures:*

Activity Cost Pools at Classic Brass

Activity Cost Pool	Activity Measure
Customer orders	Number of customer orders
Product design	Number of product designs
Order size	Machine-hours
Customer relations	Number of active customers
Other	Not applicable

Activity cost pool A "bucket" in which costs are accumulated that relate to a single activity in the activity-based costing system.

Activity measure An allocation base in an activity-based costing system; ideally, a measure of the amount of activity that drives the costs in an activity cost pool.

An **activity cost pool** is a "bucket" in which costs are accumulated that relate to a single activity in the ABC system. For example, the Customer Orders cost pool will be assigned all costs of resources that are consumed by taking and processing customer orders, including costs of processing paperwork and any costs involved in setting up machines. The measure of activity for this cost pool is simply the number of customer orders received. This is a batch-level activity, since each order generates work that occurs regardless of whether the order is for one unit or 1,000 units. The number of customer orders received is an example of an *activity measure*. An **activity measure** is an allocation base in an activity-based costing system.

The Product Design cost pool will be assigned all costs of resources consumed by designing products. The activity measure for this cost pool is the number of products designed. This is a product-level activity, since the amount of design work on a new product does not depend on the number of units ultimately ordered or batches ultimately run.

The Order Size cost pool will be assigned all costs of resources consumed as a consequence of the number of units produced, including the costs of miscellaneous factory supplies, power to run machines, and some equipment depreciation. This is a unit-level activity since each unit requires some of these resources. The activity measure for this cost pool is machine-hours.

The Customer Relations cost pool will be assigned all costs associated with maintaining relations with customers, including the costs of sales calls and the costs of entertaining customers. The activity measure for this cost pool is the number of customers the company has on its active customer list.

The Other cost pool will be assigned all overhead costs that are not associated with customer orders, product design, the size of the orders, or customer relations. These costs mainly consist of organization-sustaining costs and the costs of unused, idle capacity. These costs *will not* be assigned to products since they represent resources that are *not* consumed by products.

It is unlikely that any other company would use exactly the same activity cost pools and activities that were selected by Classic Brass. Because of the amount of judgment involved, there is considerable variation in the number and definitions of the activity cost pools and activity measures used by companies.

The Mechanics of Activity-Based Costing

After the ABC system had been designed, the team was ready to begin the process of actually computing the costs of products, customers, and other objects of interest.

Tracing Overhead Costs to Activities and Cost Objects

The second step in implementing an ABC system is to directly trace as many overhead costs as possible to the ultimate cost objects. At Classic Brass, the ultimate cost objects are products, customer orders, and customers. The company's manufacturing overhead and selling, general, and administrative costs are listed in Exhibit 8–2. In the ABC system at Classic Brass all of these costs are considered to be "overhead" and will be assigned to cost objects as appropriate.

One of these overhead costs—shipping—can be traced directly to customer orders. Classic Brass is directly billed for each customer order it ships, so it is a simple matter to trace these costs to the customer orders. Customers do not pay these actual shipping costs; instead they pay a standard shipping charge that can differ substantially from the actual bill that Classic Brass receives from the freight company.

No other overhead costs could be directly traced to products, customer orders, or customers. Consequently, the remainder of the overhead costs would be assigned to cost objects using the ABC system.

Assigning Costs to Activity Cost Pools

Objective 3

Assign costs to cost pools using a first-stage allocation.

First-stage allocation
The process by which overhead costs are assigned to activity cost pools in an activity-based costing system.

Most overhead costs are originally classified in the company's basic accounting system according to the departments in which they are incurred. For example, salaries, supplies, rent, and so forth, incurred by the marketing department are charged to that department. In some cases, some or all of these costs can be directly traced to one of the activity cost pools in the ABC system, which is the third step in implementing activity-based costing. For example, if the ABC system has an activity called *purchase order processing,* then all of the costs of the purchasing department could probably be traced to that activity. To the extent possible, costs should be traced directly to the activity cost pools. However, it is quite common for an overhead department to be involved in several of the activities that are tracked in the ABC system. In such situations, the costs of the department are divided among the activity cost pools via an allocation process called *first-stage allocation.* The **first-stage allocation** in an ABC system is the process by which overhead costs are assigned to activity cost pools.

Exhibit 8–2   Overhead Costs (both Manufacturing and Nonmanufacturing) at Classic Brass

Production Department:		
Indirect factory wages	$500,000	
Factory equipment depreciation	300,000	
Factory utilities	120,000	
Factory building lease	80,000	$1,000,000
Shipping costs *		40,000
General Administrative Department:		
Administrative wages and salaries	400,000	
Office equipment depreciation	50,000	
Administrative building lease	60,000	510,000
Marketing Department:		
Marketing wages and salaries	250,000	
Selling expenses	50,000	300,000
Total overhead costs		$1,850,000

*Shipping costs can be traced directly to customer orders.

Exhibit 8–5

Computation of Activity Rates

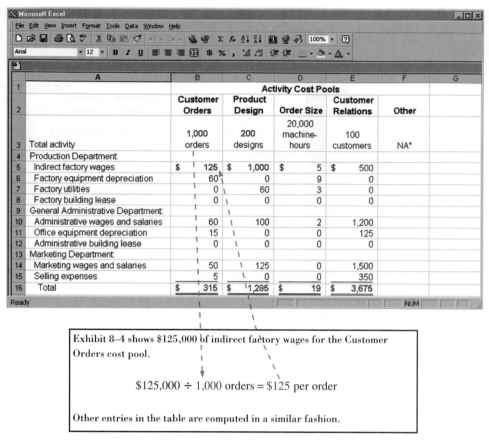

	Customer Orders	Product Design	Order Size	Customer Relations	Other	
			Activity Cost Pools			
Total activity	1,000 orders	200 designs	20,000 machine-hours	100 customers	NA*	
Production Department:						
Indirect factory wages	$ 125	$ 1,000	$ 5	$ 500		
Factory equipment depreciation	60	0	9	0		
Factory utilities	0	60	3	0		
Factory building lease	0	0	0	0		
General Administrative Department:						
Administrative wages and salaries	60	100	2	1,200		
Office equipment depreciation	15	0	0	125		
Administrative building lease	0	0	0	0		
Marketing Department:						
Marketing wages and salaries	50	125	0	1,500		
Selling expenses	5	0	0	350		
Total	$ 315	$ 1,285	$ 19	$ 3,675		

Exhibit 8–4 shows $125,000 of indirect factory wages for the Customer Orders cost pool.

$$\$125,000 \div 1,000 \text{ orders} = \$125 \text{ per order}$$

Other entries in the table are computed in a similar fashion.

*Activity rates are not computed for the Other cost pool since these costs will not be allocated further.

NA = Not applicable.

produce the company's present product mix and to serve its present customers. The activity at the top of each column was divided into each of the costs in the corresponding column in Exhibit 8–4 to arrive at the activity rates in Exhibit 8–5. For example, the $125,000 entry in Exhibit 8–4 for indirect factory wages under the Customer Orders column is divided by the total of 1,000 customer orders listed at the top of Exhibit 8–5 to arrive at the activity rate of $125 for indirect factory wages under the Customer Orders column in Exhibit 8–5. Similarly, the $200,000 entry in Exhibit 8–4 for indirect factory wages under the Product Design column is divided by the total number of designs (i.e., 200 product designs) to arrive at the activity rate of $1,000 per design for indirect factory wages. Note that activity rates are not computed for the Other category of costs. This is because these organization-sustaining costs and costs of idle capacity are not allocated to products and customers.

We urge you to study Exhibit 8–5 with care so that you are sure you know how each entry in the table was computed. Take each column in turn and divide each of the cost entries in Exhibit 8–4 under that column by the total activity at the top of the column in Exhibit 8–5. Once you see how the numbers were computed, it is really easy, although there are a lot of computations.

The entries at the bottom of Exhibit 8–5 indicate that on average a customer order consumes resources that cost $315; a product design consumes resources that cost $1,285; a unit of product consumes resources that cost $19 per machine-hour; and maintaining relations with a customer consumes resources that cost $3,675. Note that these are *average* figures. Some members of the ABC design team at Classic Brass argued that it would be unfair to charge all new products the same $1,285 product design cost regardless of how much design time they actually require. After discussing the pros and

Exhibit 8–6   The Activity-Based Costing Model at Classic Brass

cons, the team concluded that it would not be worth the effort at the present time to keep track of actual design time spent on each new product. Similarly, some team members were uncomfortable assigning the same $3,675 cost to each customer. Some customers are undemanding—ordering standard products well in advance of their needs. Others are very demanding and consume large amounts of marketing and administrative staff time. These are generally customers who order customized products, who tend to order at the last minute, and who change their minds. While everyone agreed with this observation, the data that would be required to measure individual customers' demands on resources was not currently available. Rather than delay implementation of the ABC system, the team decided to defer such refinements to a later date.

Before proceeding further, it would be helpful to get a better idea of the overall process of assigning costs to products and other cost objects in an ABC system. Exhibit 8–6 provides a visual perspective of the ABC system at Classic Brass. We recommend that you carefully go over this exhibit. In particular, note that the Other category, which contains organization-sustaining costs and costs of idle capacity, is not allocated to products or customers.

Targeting Process Improvements

Activity-based management (ABM)   A management approach that focuses on managing activities as a way of eliminating waste and reducing delays and defects.

Activity-based costing can be used to identify areas that would benefit from process improvements. Indeed, managers often cite this as the major benefit of activity-based costing.[4] When used in this way, activity-based costing is often called *activity-based management*. Basically, **activity-based management (ABM)** focuses on managing activities as a way of eliminating waste and reducing delays and defects. Activity-based management is used in organizations as diverse as manufacturing companies, hospitals, and the Royal Canadian Mint.[5] When "forty percent of the cost of running a

---

4. Dan Swenson, "The Benefits of Activity-Based Cost Management to the Manufacturing Industry," *Journal of Management Accounting Research* 7 (Fall 1995), pp. 168–80.
5. Michael Senyshen, "ABC/M in the Federal Government," *CGA Magazine* (December 1997), p. 19.

hospital involves storing, collecting and moving information," there is obviously a great deal of room for eliminating waste and for improvement.[6]

The first step in any improvement program is to decide what to improve. The theory of constraints approach discussed in Chapter 1 is a powerful tool for targeting the area in an organization whose improvement will yield the greatest benefit. Activity-based management provides another approach. The activity rates computed in activity-based costing can provide valuable clues concerning where there is waste and scope for improvement in an organization. For example, managers at Classic Brass were surprised at the high cost of customer orders. Some customer orders are for less than $100 worth of products, and yet it costs, on average, $315 to process an order according to the activity rates calculated in Exhibit 8–5. This seemed like an awful lot of money for an activity that adds no value to the product. As a consequence, the customer order processing activity was targeted for improvement using TQM and process reengineering as discussed in Chapter 1.

Benchmarking provides a systematic approach to identifying the activities with the greatest room for improvement. For example, the Marketing Resources Group of a telephone company, performed an ABC analysis of the activities carried out in the Accounting Department.[7] Managers computed the activity rates for the activities of the Accounting Department and then compared these rates to the costs of carrying out the same activities in other companies. Two benchmarks were used: (1) a sample of FORTUNE 100 companies, which are the largest 100 companies in the United States; and (2) a sample of "world-class" companies that had been identified by a consultant as having the best accounting practices in the world. These comparisons appear below:

Activity	Activity Measure	Telephone Co. Cost	FORTUNE 100 Benchmark	World-Class Benchmark
Processing accounts receivable	Number of invoices processed	$3.80 per invoice	$15.00 per invoice	$4.60 per invoice
Processing accounts payable	Number of invoices processed	$8.90 per invoice	$7.00 per invoice	$1.80 per invoice
Processing payroll cheques	Number of cheques processed	$7.30 per cheque	$5.00 per cheque	$1.72 per cheque
Managing customer credit	Number of customer accounts	$12.00 per account	$16.00 per account	$5.60 per account

It is clear from this analysis that the company did a good job of processing accounts receivables. Its average cost per invoice is $3.80, whereas the cost in other companies that were considered world class was even higher—$4.60 per invoice. On the other hand, the cost of processing payroll cheques was significantly higher at the telephone company than at benchmark companies. The cost per payroll cheque cost was $7.30 versus $5.00 at FORTUNE 100 companies and $1.72 at world-class companies. This suggests that it may be possible to wring some waste out of this activity using TQM, process reengineering, or some other method.

---

6. Kambiz Foroohar, "Rx: Software," *Forbes*, April 7, 1997, p. 114.
7. Steve Coburn, Hugh Grove, and Cynthia Fukami, "Benchmarking with ABCM," *Management Accounting* (January 1995), pp. 56–60.

Focus on Current Practice

Reports suggest Nortel was dissatisfied with the departmental collection and allocation of its research costs using departmental rates. To overcome this problem, they implemented an ABC approach to enable the research costs to be more understandable by managers and to enable managers to determine detailed activity driven costs.

The approach also permitted Nortel to satisfy the legal regulations associated with their worldwide activities. The project focus combined with ABC helped to achieve cost reductions as well as a better understanding of costs by R&D project managers.[8]

Assigning Costs to Cost Objects

Objective 5

Assign costs to a cost object using a second-stage allocation.

Second-stage allocation
The process by which activity rates are used to apply costs to products and customers in activity-based costing.

The fifth step in the implementation of activity-based costing is called *second-stage allocation*. In the **second-stage allocation**, activity rates are used to apply costs to products and customers. At Classic Brass, the ABC system might be used to apply activity costs to all of the company's products, customer orders, and customers. For purposes of illustration, we will consider only one customer—Windward Yachts. This customer ordered two different products—stanchions and a compass housing. The stanchions are a standard product that does not require any design work. In contrast, the compass housing is a custom product that required extensive designing. Data concerning these two products appear in Exhibit 8–7.

Overhead Costs Computed Using the ABC System

Direct materials and direct labour costs are the same under the old traditional cost accounting system and the new ABC system. However, the two systems handle overhead very differently.

The overhead calculations for the stanchions and compass housings are carried out in Exhibits 8–8A and 8–8B, respectively. Let's examine the ABC overhead

Exhibit 8–7 Data Concerning the Products Ordered by Windward Yachts

Standard Stanchions
1. This is a standard design that does not require any new design resources.
2. Four hundred units were ordered during the year, comprising two separate orders.
3. Each stanchion required 0.5 machine-hour, for a total of 200 machine-hours.
4. The selling price per unit was $34, for a total of $13,600.
5. Direct materials for 400 units totalled $2,110.
6. Direct labour for 400 units totalled $1,850.
7. Shipping costs for the two orders totalled $180.

Custom Compass Housing
1. This is a custom product that requires new design resources.
2. There was only one order for a single unit during the year.
3. The compass housing required 4 machine-hours.
4. The selling price was $650.
5. Direct materials was $13.
6. Direct labour was $50.
7. Shipping costs were $25.

---

8. Chris Dorey, "The ABC's of R&D at Nortel," *CMA Magazine* (March 1998), pp. 19–22, 26.

Exhibit 8–8A

Computation of the Overhead Cost of Two Orders for Standard Stanchions Totalling Four Hundred Units

	Customer Orders	Product Design	Order Size	Customer Relations	Total (action analysis)
Activity Cost Pools					
Total activity for stanchions:	2 orders	No new designing	200 machine-hours	NA	
Production Department:					
Indirect factory wages	$ 250	$ 0	$ 1,000	$ 0	$ 1,250
Factory equipment depreciation	120	0	1,800	0	1,920
Factory utilities	0	0	600	0	600
Factory building lease	0	0	0	0	0
General Administrative Department:					
Administrative wages and salaries	120	0	400	0	520
Office equipment depreciation	30	0	0	0	30
Administrative building lease	0	0	0	0	0
Marketing Department:					
Marketing wages and salaries	100	0	0	0	100
Selling expenses	10	0	0	0	10
Totals (activity view)	$ 630	$ 0	$ 3,800	$ 0	$ 4,430

> Exhibit 8–5 shows an activity rate of $125 for indirect factory wages for the Customer Orders cost pool.
>
> $125 per order × 2 orders = $250
>
> Other entries in the table are computed in a similar fashion.

NA = Not applicable.

Exhibit 8–8B

Computation of the Overhead Cost of One Order for One Unit of the Custom Compass Housing

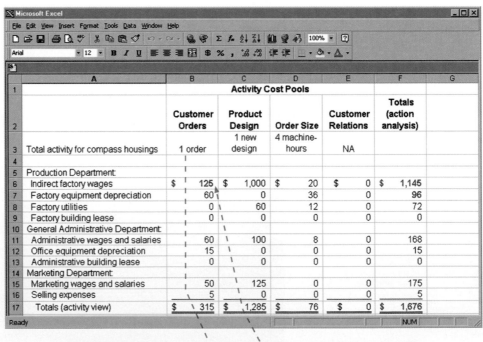

	Customer Orders	Product Design	Order Size	Customer Relations	Totals (action analysis)
Activity Cost Pools					
Total activity for compass housings	1 order	1 new design	4 machine-hours	NA	
Production Department:					
Indirect factory wages	$ 125	$ 1,000	$ 20	$ 0	$ 1,145
Factory equipment depreciation	60	0	36	0	96
Factory utilities	0	60	12	0	72
Factory building lease	0	0	0	0	0
General Administrative Department:					
Administrative wages and salaries	60	100	8	0	168
Office equipment depreciation	15	0	0	0	15
Administrative building lease	0	0	0	0	0
Marketing Department:					
Marketing wages and salaries	50	125	0	0	175
Selling expenses	5	0	0	0	5
Totals (activity view)	$ 315	$ 1,285	$ 76	$ 0	$ 1,676

> Exhibit 8–5 shows an activity rate of $125 for indirect factory wages for the Customer Orders cost pool.
>
> $125 per order × 1 order = $125
>
> Other entries in the table are computed in a similar fashion.

NA = Not applicable.

Exhibit 8–9 Product Margins—Activity-Based Costing System (Activity View)

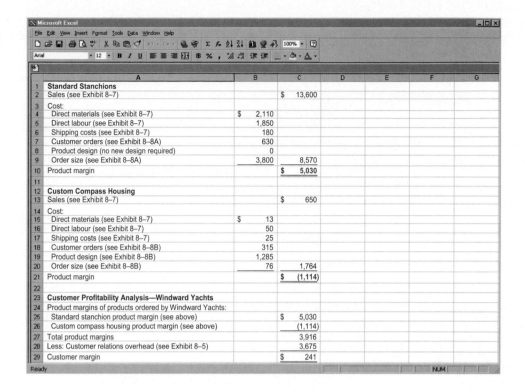

	A	B	C	D	E	F	G
1	**Standard Stanchions**						
2	Sales (see Exhibit 8–7)		$ 13,600				
3	Cost:						
4	Direct materials (see Exhibit 8–7)	$ 2,110					
5	Direct labour (see Exhibit 8–7)	1,850					
6	Shipping costs (see Exhibit 8–7)	180					
7	Customer orders (see Exhibit 8–8A)	630					
8	Product design (no new design required)	0					
9	Order size (see Exhibit 8–8A)	3,800	8,570				
10	Product margin		$ 5,030				
11							
12	**Custom Compass Housing**						
13	Sales (see Exhibit 8–7)		$ 650				
14	Cost:						
15	Direct materials (see Exhibit 8–7)	$ 13					
16	Direct labour (see Exhibit 8–7)	50					
17	Shipping costs (see Exhibit 8–7)	25					
18	Customer orders (see Exhibit 8–8B)	315					
19	Product design (see Exhibit 8–8B)	1,285					
20	Order size (see Exhibit 8–8B)	76	1,764				
21	Product margin		$ (1,114)				
22							
23	**Customer Profitability Analysis—Windward Yachts**						
24	Product margins of products ordered by Windward Yachts:						
25	Standard stanchion product margin (see above)		$ 5,030				
26	Custom compass housing product margin (see above)		(1,114)				
27	Total product margins		3,916				
28	Less: Customer relations overhead (see Exhibit 8–5)		3,675				
29	Customer margin		$ 241				

calculations for the stanchions in Exhibit 8–8A. First note that none of the Customer Relations costs have been allocated to the stanchions. A customer-level cost is assigned to customers directly; it is not assigned to products. The activities required to fill the two orders for stanchions totalling 400 units are listed across the top of the exhibit. Since this is a standard product, no new designing is required and hence no design costs are allocated to the order. However, there are two orders, so each of the activity rates under the Customer Orders column in Exhibit 8–5 is multiplied by 2 to determine the Customer Orders costs for this product. For example, the activity rate for indirect factory wages for Customer Orders in Exhibit 8–5 is $125 per order. Since there are two orders, 2 × $125 = $250 is allocated to this product and appears as the first entry under the Customer Orders column in Exhibit 8–8A. Similarly, the activity rate for factory equipment depreciation for Customer Orders in Exhibit 8–5 is $60 per order. Since there are two orders, the product is charged $120. This appears as the second entry under Customer Orders in Exhibit 8–8A.

As with Exhibit 8–5, we urge you to study Exhibits 8–8A and 8–8B carefully to make sure you know how each entry in the table was computed. Take each column in turn and multiply each of the activity rates in Exhibit 8–5 under that column by the total activity at the top of the column in Exhibit 8–8A (and 8–8B). As before, once you see how the numbers are computed, it is not difficult, although there are a lot of computations.

Product Margins Computed Using the ABC System

Objective 6

Prepare a report showing activity-based costing product margins from an activity view.

In Exhibit 8–9, the overhead costs computed from Exhibits 8–8A and 8–8B are combined with direct materials, direct labour, and shipping cost data. For each of the products, these combined costs are deducted from sales to arrive at product margins. Under the ABC system, the stanchions show a profit of $5,030, whereas the compass housing shows a loss of $1,114.

Note from Exhibit 8–9 that the new ABC system also includes a profitability analysis of Windward Yachts, the customer that ordered the stanchions and the custom compass housing. Such customer analyses can be easily accomplished by adding together the product margins for each of the products a customer has ordered and then subtracting the average charge of $3,675 for Customer Relations.

Comparison of Traditional and ABC Product Costs

Now that the product margins have been computed using activity-based costing, it would be interesting to compare them to the product margins computed using the company's traditional cost system.

Product Margins Computed Using the Traditional Cost System

The costs of the two products ordered by Windward Yachts are computed under the company's traditional cost accounting system in Exhibit 8–10. The company's traditional system uses a plantwide predetermined overhead rate based on machine-hours. Since the total manufacturing overhead cost is $1,000,000 (see Exhibit 8–2) and the total machine time is 20,000 machine-hours (see Exhibit 8–5), the predetermined manufacturing overhead rate for the company is $50 per machine-hour ($1,000,000 ÷ 20,000 machine-hours = $50 per machine-hour). From Exhibit 8–10, we see that when this predetermined manufacturing overhead rate is used to determine product costs, the stanchions show a loss of $360, whereas the compass housing shows a profit of $387.

The Differences between ABC and Traditional Product Costs

The costs of the products under the new ABC system are dramatically different from the costs computed using the old traditional costing system. The stanchions, which looked unprofitable under the traditional cost system, appear to be very profitable under the ABC system in Exhibit 8–9. And the compass housing, which looked profitable under the old cost system, appears to be unprofitable under the new costing system.

Exhibit 8–10 Product Margins—Traditional Cost Accounting System

Standard Stanchions		
Margin computed using the company's old cost accounting system:		
Sales (400 units × $34)		$13,600
Cost:		
Direct materials	$ 2,110	
Direct labour	1,850	
Manufacturing overhead (400 units × 0.5 machine-hours per unit		
× $50 per machine-hour*)	10,000	13,960
Product margin		$ (360)
Custom Compass Housing		
Margin computed using the company's old cost accounting system:		
Sales (1 unit × $650)		$ 650
Cost:		
Direct materials	13	
Direct labour	50	
Manufacturing overhead (1 unit × 4.0 machine-hours per unit		
× $50 per machine-hour*)	200	263
Product margin		$ 387

* Predetermined manufacturing overhead rate:

$$\frac{\text{Total manufacturing overhead, } \$1,000,000}{\text{Total machine-hours, } 20,000} = \$50 \text{ per machine-hour}$$

There are two major reasons for these changes in apparent profitability. First, under the old cost system the costs of designing products were spread across all products without regard to whether they actually required design work. Under the new ABC system, these costs are assigned only to products that actually require design work. Consequently, under the ABC system, design costs have been shifted from standard products like stanchions, which do not require any design work, to custom products like the compass housing.

Second, the Customer Orders costs, which are batch-level costs, were applied on the basis of machine-hours, a unit-level base, under the old cost system. Therefore, under the old cost system, high-volume products absorbed the bulk of these batch-level costs even though they caused no more of these costs than low-volume products that are ordered as frequently. Under the new cost system, these batch-level costs are assigned as a lump-sum to each customer order. Consequently, the new cost system shifts these costs from high-volume orders like the stanchions to low-volume orders like the compass housing.

When there are batch-level or product-level costs, activity-based costing will ordinarily shift costs from high-volume products produced in large batches to low-volume products produced in small batches. This cost shifting will usually have a greater impact on the *per unit* costs of low-volume products than on the per unit costs of high-volume products. For example, suppose that a total of $100 in batch-level cost is shifted from a high-volume, 100-unit product to a low-volume, 1-unit product. This shifting of cost will decrease the cost of the high-volume product by $1 per unit, on average, but will increase the cost of the low-volume product by $100 for the single unit. In summary, implementing activity-based costing will typically shift costs from high-volume to low-volume products, but the effects will be much more dramatic on the per unit costs of the low-volume products. The per unit costs of the low-volume products will increase far more than the per unit costs of the high-volume products will decrease.

It is important to remember another major difference between the costs of products as computed under the new ABC system at Classic Brass and product costs as computed under the old traditional cost system. Under a traditional system, only manufacturing costs are assigned to products. Under the new ABC system at Classic Brass, nonmanufacturing costs are assigned to products as well as the manufacturing costs. In addition, the organization-sustaining manufacturing costs and the costs of idle capacity are *not* assigned to products under the ABC system, whereas they *are* assigned to products under the old traditional costing system. For these reasons, the term *product cost* in this chapter has a different meaning than it had in Chapters 2, 3, and 4. In the context of an ABC system like the one implemented at Classic Brass, product costs include the costs of *all* resources consumed by the product, whether they are manufacturing costs or not.

Focus on Current Practice

The application of ABC concepts to different industries requires careful consideration that the design specifics should vary for different industries. Insurance, banking, telephone, railroads, and distribution industries all present peculiarities for the system's designer from those present in traditional manufacturing. Activities for distribution companies include market research, product acquisition, marketing and inventorying. Insurance companies have activities such as selling, claim processing, policy processing and sustaining. Telephone companies have service activities such as selling, service, billing and maintenance. Banking involves data centres, networks, and different products similar to insurance and telephone. The system for each of these industries should contain a careful identification of cost objects, activities and overall structure, not a pre-configured design applied from another industry.[9]

---

9. Paul Sharman, "ABC Systems Architecture," *CMA Magazine* (May 1998), pp. 15–18.

Managerial Accounting in Action

The ABC design team presented the results of its work in a meeting attended by all of the top managers of Classic Brass, including the president John Towers, the production manager Susan Richter, the marketing manager Tom Olafson, and the accounting manager Mary Goodman. The ABC team brought with them to the meeting copies of the chart showing the ABC design (Exhibit 8–6), the tables showing the product margins for the stanchions and compass housing under the company's old cost accounting system (Exhibit 8–7), the tables showing the ABC analysis of the same products (Exhibit 8–9), and the action analysis (Exhibit 8–12). After the formal presentation by the ABC team, the following discussion took place:

John: I would like to personally thank the ABC team for all of the work they have done and for an extremely interesting presentation. I am now beginning to wonder about a lot of the decisions we have made in the past using our old cost accounting system.

Mary: I hope I don't have to remind anyone that I have been warning everyone for quite some time about this problem.

John: No, you don't have to remind us Mary. I guess we just didn't understand the problem before.

John: Tom, why did we accept this order for standard stanchions in the first place if our old cost accounting system was telling us it was a big money loser?

Tom: Windward Yachts, the company that ordered the stanchions, has asked us to do a lot of custom work like the compass housing in the past. To get that work, we felt we had to accept their orders for money-losing standard products.

John: According to this ABC analysis, we had it all backwards. We are losing money on the custom products and making a fistful on the standard products.

Susan: I never did believe we were making a lot of money on the custom jobs. You ought to see all of the problems they create for us in production.

Tom: I hate to admit it, but the custom jobs always seem to give us headaches in marketing too.

John: Why don't we just stop soliciting custom work? This seems like a no-brainer to me. If we are losing money on custom jobs like the compass housing, why not suggest to our customers that they go elsewhere for that kind of work?

Tom: Wait a minute, we would lose a lot of sales.

Susan: So what, we would save a lot more costs.

Mary: Maybe yes, maybe no. Some of the costs would not disappear if we were to drop all of those products.

Tom: Like what?

Mary: Well Tom, part of your salary is included in the costs of the ABC model.

Tom: Where? I don't see anything listed that looks like my salary.

Mary: Tom, when the ABC team interviewed you they asked you what percentage of your time was spent in handling customer orders and how much was spent dealing with new product design issues. Am I correct?

Tom: Sure, but what's the point?

Mary: I believe you said that about 10% of your time is spent dealing with new products. As a consequence, 10% of your salary was allocated to the Product Design cost pool. If we were to drop all of the products requiring design work, would you be willing to take a 10% pay cut?

Tom: I trust you're joking.

Mary: Do you see the problem? Just because 10% of your time is spent on custom products doesn't mean that the company would save 10% of your salary if the custom products were dropped. Before we take a drastic action like dropping the custom products, we should identify which costs are really relevant.

John: I think I see what you are driving at. We wouldn't want to drop a lot of products just to find that our costs really haven't changed much. It is true that dropping the products would free up resources like Tom's time, but we had better be sure we have some good use for those resources *before* we take such an action.

Mary: That's why we put together the action analysis.

John: What's this red margin at the bottom of the action analysis? Isn't that a product margin?

Mary: Yes, it is. However, we call it a red margin because we should *stop* and think very, very carefully before taking any actions based on that margin.

John: Why is that?

Mary: We subtracted the costs of factory equipment depreciation to arrive at that red margin. We doubt that we could avoid any of that cost if we were to drop custom orders. We use the same machines on custom orders that we use on standard products. The factory equipment has no resale value, and it does not wear out through use.

John: What about this yellow margin?

Mary: Yellow means proceed with a great deal of caution. To get to the yellow margin we deducted from sales a lot of costs that could be adjusted only if the managers involved are willing to eliminate resources or shift them elsewhere in the organization.

John: If I understand the yellow margin correctly, the apparent loss of $1,018 on the custom stanchions is the result of the indirect factory wages of $1,145.

Susan: Right, that's basically the wages of our design engineers.

John: I wouldn't want to lay off any of our designers. Could we turn them into salespersons?

Tom: I'd love to have Shueli Park join our marketing team.

Susan: No way, she's our best designer.

John: Okay, I get the picture. We are not going to be cutting anyone's wages, we aren't going to be laying off anyone, and it looks like we may have problems getting agreement about moving people around. Where does that leave us?

Mary: What about raising prices on our custom products?

Tom: We should be able to do that. We have been undercutting the competition to make sure we got custom work. We were doing that because we thought custom work was very profitable.

John: Why don't we just charge directly for design work?

Tom: Some of our competitors already charge for design work. However, I don't think we would be able to charge enough to cover our design costs.

John: What about design work, can we do anything to make it more efficient so it costs us less? I'm not going to lay anyone off, but if we make the design process more efficient, we could lower the charge for design work and spread those costs across more customers.

Susan: That may be possible. I'll form a TQM team to look at it.

John: Let's get some benchmark data on design costs. If we set our minds to it, I'm sure we can be world class in no time.

Susan: Okay. Mary, will you help with the benchmark data?

Mary: Sure.

> **Tom:** There is another approach we can take too. Windward Yachts probably doesn't really need a custom compass housing. One of our standard compass housings would work just fine. If we start charging for the design work, I think they will see that it would be in their own interests to use the lower-cost standard product.
>
> **John:** Let's meet again in about a week to discuss our progress. Is there anything else on the agenda for today? ■

The points raised in the preceding discussion are extremely important. By measuring the resources consumed by products (and other cost objects), a "best practice" ABC system provides a much better basis for decision making than a traditional cost accounting system that spreads overhead costs around without much regard for what might be causing the overhead. A well-designed ABC system provides managers with estimates of potentially relevant costs that can be a very useful starting point for management analysis.

Activity-Based Costing and External Reports

Since activity-based costing generally provides more accurate product costs than traditional costing methods, why isn't it used for external reports? Some companies *do* use activity-based costing in their external reports, but most do not. There are a number of reasons for this. First, external reports are less detailed than internal reports prepared for decision making. On the external reports, individual product costs are not reported. Cost of goods sold and inventory valuations are disclosed, but there is no breakdown of these accounts by product. If some products are undercosted and some are overcosted, the errors tend to cancel each other when the product costs are added together.

Second, it is often very difficult to make changes in a company's accounting system. The official cost accounting systems in most large companies are usually embedded in complex computer programs that have been modified in-house over the course of many years. It is extremely difficult to make changes in such computer programs without causing numerous bugs.

Third, an ABC system such as the one described in this chapter may not conform to generally accepted accounting principles (GAAP). As discussed in Chapter 2, product costs computed for external reports must include all of the manufacturing costs and only manufacturing costs; but in an ABC system as described in this chapter, product costs exclude some manufacturing costs and include some nonmanufacturing costs. It is possible to adjust the ABC data at the end of the period to conform to GAAP, but that requires more work.

Fourth, auditors are likely to be uncomfortable with allocations that are based on interviews with the company's personnel. Such subjective data can be easily manipulated by management to make earnings and other key variables look more favourable.

For all of these reasons, most companies confine their ABC efforts to special studies for management, and they do not attempt to integrate activity-based costing into their formal cost accounting systems.

A Simplified Approach to Activity-Based Costing

If an action analysis like Exhibit 8–12 is not prepared, the process of computing product margins under activity-based costing can be considerably simplified. The first-stage allocation shown in Exhibit 8–4 is still necessary, but the remainder of the computations can be streamlined.

Objective 8

Use the simplified approach to compute activity-based costs and margins.

To use the simplified approach after the first-stage allocation is completed, compute activity rates for each activity cost pool as follows:

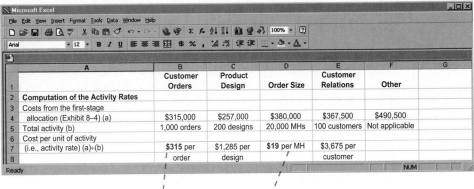

A	Customer Orders	Product Design	Order Size	Customer Relations	Other	G
Computation of the Activity Rates						
Costs from the first-stage						
allocation (Exhibit 8–4) (a)	$315,000	$257,000	$380,000	$367,500	$490,500	
Total activity (b)	1,000 orders	200 designs	20,000 MHs	100 customers	Not applicable	
Cost per unit of activity						
(i.e., activity rate) (a)÷(b)	$315 per order	$1,285 per design	$19 per MH	$3,675 per customer		

Note that these activity rates are exactly the same as the activity rates at the bottom of Exhibit 8–5. If there is to be no activity analysis, the other numbers in Exhibit 8–5 are not needed and do not have to be computed.

Using these activity rates, the product and customer margins can be directly computed as follows:

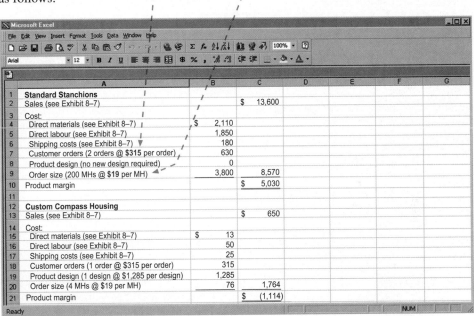

A	B	C	D	E	F	G
Standard Stanchions						
Sales (see Exhibit 8–7)		$ 13,600				
Cost:						
Direct materials (see Exhibit 8–7)	$ 2,110					
Direct labour (see Exhibit 8–7)	1,850					
Shipping costs (see Exhibit 8–7)	180					
Customer orders (2 orders @ $315 per order)	630					
Product design (no new design required)	0					
Order size (200 MHs @ $19 per MH)	3,800	8,570				
Product margin		$ 5,030				
Custom Compass Housing						
Sales (see Exhibit 8–7)		$ 650				
Cost:						
Direct materials (see Exhibit 8–7)	$ 13					
Direct labour (see Exhibit 8–7)	50					
Shipping costs (see Exhibit 8–7)	25					
Customer orders (1 order @ $315 per order)	315					
Product design (1 design @ $1,285 per design)	1,285					
Order size (4 MHs @ $19 per MH)	76	1,764				
Product margin		$ (1,114)				

A	B	C	D	E	F	G
Customer Profitability Analysis—Windward Yachts						
Product margins of products ordered by Windward Yachts:						
Standard stanchion product margin (see above)	$ 5,030					
Custom compass housing product margin (see above)	(1,114)					
Total product margins	3,916					
Less: Customer relations overhead (see above)	3,675					
Customer margin	$ 241					

Note that the numbers in this report match the numbers that appear in Exhibit 8–9. This simplified approach allows one to compute product and customer margins without having to do the detailed computations in all of the cells of Exhibit 8–5 and Exhibits 8–8A and 8–8B. However, this simplified approach does not provide the data that are needed to construct an action analysis.

Activity-Based Costing and Service Industries

Although initially conceived as a tool for manufacturing companies, activity-based costing is also being used in service industries. Successful implementation of an activity-based costing system depends on identifying the key activities that generate costs and being able to keep track of how many of those activities are performed for each service that is provided.

Two common problems exist in service firms that sometimes make implementation of activity-based costing relatively difficult. One problem is that a larger proportion of costs in service industries tend to be facility-level costs that cannot be traced to any particular billable service provided by the firm. Another problem is that it is more difficult to capture activity data in service companies, because so many of the activities tend to involve nonrepetitive human tasks that cannot be easily recorded.[11] Nevertheless, activity-based costing systems have been implemented in a number of service firms, including railroads, hospitals, banks, and data services companies.

Our discussion in this chapter has focused on the use of activity-based costing in manufacturing companies. We will defer further discussion of its use in service-type operations to Chapter 16, where we discuss its specific application in greater depth.

Focus on Current Practice

A 1992 survey of 352 large Canadian companies states that 67% had not considered activity-based costing (ABC) while 14% had implemented or were implementing ABC and 15% were currently assessing the methodology; 4% had considered ABC and decided not to implement it. The development of ABC in Canada appears to be behind that in the United States. Given that 9% of U.K. companies had considered ABC and rejected it, acceptance in Canada appears to be higher than in the U.K. The manufacturing sector shows the highest rate of development, while resource, retail, and communications sectors are further behind.[12] ∎

International Use of Activity-Based Costing

Activity-based costing was pioneered in the United States, although several of the early field studies were performed by American researchers on German companies. The concept is relatively new, with the term *activity-based costing* having been coined by the management of John Deere Company within the last 15 years.

To date, activity-based costing has not spread as rapidly throughout the world as has JIT and TQM. Perhaps the reason is traceable to the costs of implementation and to the fact that it is sometimes difficult to collect the data needed to operate the system. In Japan, activity-based costing is rarely used. Instead, Japanese managers seem to prefer volume measures such as direct labour-hours to assign overhead cost to products. This preference, according to Japanese researchers, can be explained by the fact that Japanese managers are "convinced that reducing direct labour is essential for ongoing cost improvement."[13] It is argued that by using direct labour as an overhead allocation

11. William Rotch, "Activity-Based Costing in Service Industries," *Journal of Cost Management* (Summer 1990), p. 8.
12. "Activity-Based Costing," *Management Accounting Issues Paper 3* (Hamilton, ON: Society of Management Accountants of Canada, 1993) pp. 9–13.
13. Toshiro Hiromoto, "Another Hidden Edge—Japanese Management Accounting," *Harvard Business Review* (July–August 1988), p. 23.

base, managers are forced to watch direct labour more closely and to seek ways to reduce it. In short, Japanese managers tend to be more concerned about cost reduction and working toward specific long-term company goals than they are about obtaining more accurate product costs.

The most extensive application of activity-based costing has been in the United States, with some applications having been made in Europe, particularly in Germany and Northern Europe.

Summary

Traditional cost accounting methods suffer from several defects that can result in distorted costs for decision-making purposes. All manufacturing costs—even those that are not caused by any specific product—are allocated to products. And nonmanufacturing costs that are caused by products are not assigned to products. Traditional methods also allocate the costs of idle capacity to products. In effect, products are charged for resources that they do not use. And finally, traditional methods tend to place too much reliance on unit-level allocation bases such as direct labour and machine-hours. This results in overcosting high-volume products and undercosting low-volume products and can lead to mistakes when making decisions.

Activity-based costing estimates the costs of the resources consumed by cost objects such as products and customers. The approach taken in activity-based costing assumes that cost objects generate activities that in turn consume costly resources. Activities form the link between costs and cost objects. Activity-based costing is concerned with overhead—both manufacturing overhead and selling, general, and administrative overhead. The accounting for direct labour and direct material is usually unaffected.

The steps that are involved in computing ABC product costs are summarized in Exhibit 8–13. Use this exhibit to trace through the key exhibits in the chapter.

To build an ABC system, companies typically choose a small set of activities that summarize much of the work performed in overhead departments. Associated with each activity is an activity cost pool. To the extent possible, overhead costs are directly traced to these activity cost pools. The remaining overhead costs are assigned to the activity cost pools in the first-stage allocation. Interviews with managers often form the basis for these allocations.

An activity rate is computed for each cost pool by dividing the costs assigned to the cost pool by the measure of activity for the cost pool. Activity rates provide useful information to managers concerning the costs of carrying out overhead activities. A particularly high cost for an activity may trigger efforts to improve the way the activity is carried out in the organization.

In the second-stage allocation, the activity rates are used to apply costs to cost objects such as products and customers. The costs computed under activity-based costing are often quite different from the costs generated by a company's traditional cost accounting system. While the ABC system is almost certainly more accurate, managers should nevertheless exercise caution before making decisions based on the ABC data. A vital part of any activity-based analysis of product or customer profitability is an action analysis that identifies who is ultimately responsible for each cost and the ease with which the cost can be adjusted.

Exhibit 8–13 How the ABC Steps Fit Together

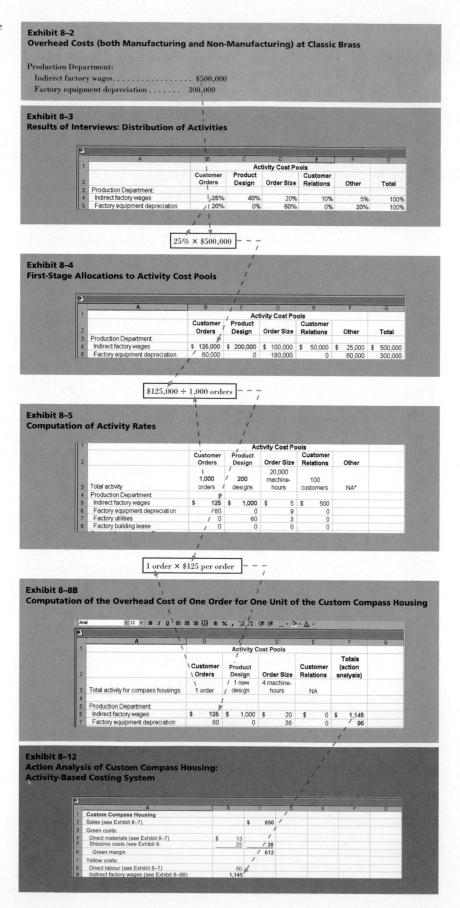

Exhibit 8–2
Overhead Costs (both Manufacturing and Non-Manufacturing) at Classic Brass

Production Department:
Indirect factory wages. $500,000
Factory equipment depreciation 300,000

Exhibit 8–3
Results of Interviews: Distribution of Activities

	Activity Cost Pools					
	Customer Orders	Product Design	Order Size	Customer Relations	Other	Total
Production Department:						
Indirect factory wages	25%	40%	20%	10%	5%	100%
Factory equipment depreciation	20%	0%	60%	0%	20%	100%

25% × $500,000

Exhibit 8–4
First-Stage Allocations to Activity Cost Pools

	Activity Cost Pools					
	Customer Orders	Product Design	Order Size	Customer Relations	Other	Total
Production Department:						
Indirect factory wages	$ 125,000	$ 200,000	$ 100,000	$ 50,000	$ 25,000	$ 500,000
Factory equipment depreciation	60,000	0	180,000	0	60,000	300,000

$125,000 ÷ 1,000 orders

Exhibit 8–5
Computation of Activity Rates

	Activity Cost Pools				
	Customer Orders	Product Design	Order Size	Customer Relations	Other
Total activity	1,000 orders	200 designs	20,000 machine-hours	100 customers	NA*
Production Department:					
Indirect factory wages	$ 125	$ 1,000	$ 5	$ 500	
Factory equipment depreciation	60	0	9	0	
Factory utilities	0	60	3	0	
Factory building lease	0	0	0	0	

1 order × $125 per order

Exhibit 8–8B
Computation of the Overhead Cost of One Order for One Unit of the Custom Compass Housing

	Activity Cost Pools				
	Customer Orders	Product Design	Order Size	Customer Relations	Totals (action analysis)
Total activity for compass housings	1 order	1 new design	4 machine-hours	NA	
Production Department:					
Indirect factory wages	$ 125	$ 1,000	$ 20	$ 0	$ 1,145
Factory equipment depreciation	60	0	36	0	96

Exhibit 8–12
Action Analysis of Custom Compass Housing:
Activity-Based Costing System

Custom Compass Housing		
Sales (see Exhibit 8–7)		$ 650
Green costs:		
Direct materials (see Exhibit 8–7)	$ 13	
Shipping costs (see Exhibit 8–	25	38
Green margin		612
Yellow costs:		
Direct labour (see Exhibit 8–7)	50	
Indirect factory wages (see Exhibit 8–8B)	1,145	

Review Problem: Activity-Based Costing

Ferris Corporation makes a single product—a fire-resistant commercial filing cabinet—that it sells to office furniture distributors. The company has a simple ABC system that it uses for internal decision making. The company has two overhead departments whose costs are listed below:

Manufacturing overhead	$500,000
Selling and administrative overhead	300,000
Total overhead costs	$800,000

The company's ABC system has the following activity cost pools and activity measures:

Activity Cost Pool	Activity Measure
Volume related	Number of units
Order related	Number of orders
Customer support	Number of customers
Other	Not applicable

Costs assigned to the "Other" activity cost pool have no activity measure; they consist of the costs of unused capacity and organization-sustaining costs—neither of which are assigned to products, orders, or customers.

Ferris Corporation distributes the costs of manufacturing overhead and of selling and administrative overhead to the activity cost pools based on employee interviews, the results of which are reported below:

Distribution of Resource Consumption Across Activities

	Volume Related	Order Related	Customer Support	Other	Total
Manufacturing overhead	50%	35%	5%	10%	100%
Selling and administrative overhead	10%	45%	25%	20%	100%
Total activity	1,000 units	250 orders	100 customers		

Required
1. Perform the first-stage allocations of overhead costs to the activity cost pools as in Exhibit 8–4.
2. Compute activity rates for the activity cost pools as in Exhibit 8–5.
3. OfficeMart is one of Ferris Corporation's customers. Last year, OfficeMart ordered filing cabinets four different times. OfficeMart ordered a total of 80 filing cabinets during the year. Construct a table as in Exhibit 8–8A showing the overhead costs of these 80 units and four orders.
4. The selling price of a filing cabinet is $595. The cost of direct materials is $180 per filing cabinet, and direct labour is $50 per filing cabinet. What is the product margin on the 80 filing cabinets ordered by OfficeMart? How profitable is OfficeMart as a customer? See Exhibit 8–9 for an example of how to complete this report.
5. Management of Ferris Corporation has assigned ease of adjustment codes to the various costs as follows:

Cost	Ease of Adjustment Code
Direct materials	Green
Direct labour	Yellow
Manufacturing overhead	Yellow
Selling and administrative overhead	Red

Prepare an activity analysis of the OfficeMart orders as in Exhibit 8–12.

Solution to Review Problem

1. The first-stage allocation of costs to the activity cost pools appears below:

	Activity Cost Pools				
	Volume Related	**Order Related**	**Customer Support**	**Other**	**Total**
Manufacturing overhead	$250,000	$175,000	$ 25,000	$ 50,000	$500,000
Selling and administrative overhead . .	30,000	135,000	75,000	60,000	300,000
Total cost	$280,000	$310,000	$100,000	$110,000	$800,000

2. The activity rates for the activity cost pools are:

	Volume Related	**Order Related**	**Customer Support**
Manufacturing overhead	$250	$ 700	$ 250
Selling and administrative overhead	30	540	750
Total cost	$280	$1,240	$1,000

3. The overhead cost for the four orders of a total of 80 filing cabinets would be computed as follows:

	Volume Related	**Order Related**	**Total**
Activity	80 units	4 orders	
Manufacturing overhead	$20,000	$2,800	$22,800
Selling and administrative overhead . .	2,400	2,160	4,560
Total cost	$22,400	$4,960	$27,360

4. The product and customer margins can be computed as follows:

Filing Cabinet Product Margin

Sales ($595 × 80)		$47,600
Cost:		
Direct materials ($180 × 80)	$14,400	
Direct labour ($50 × 80)	4,000	
Volume-related overhead (above)	22,400	
Order-related overhead (above)	4,960	45,760
Product margin		$ 1,840

Customer Profitability Analysis—OfficeMart

Product margin (above)	$ 1,840
Less: Customer support overhead (above)	1,000
Customer margin	$ 840

5. The activity analysis of the four orders for 80 filing cabinets in total is:

Action Analysis Report for Four Orders Totalling 80 Units

Sales		$47,600
Green costs:		
Direct materials	$14,400	14,400
Green margin		33,200
Yellow costs:		
Direct labour	4,000	
Manufacturing overhead	22,800	26,800
Yellow margin		6,400
Red costs:		
Selling and administrative overhead	4,560	4,560
Red margin		$ 1,840

Note: An action analysis report can also be completed for OfficeMart as a customer. The first step would be to calculate the overhead costs for OfficeMart as follows:

	Volume Related	Order Related	Customer Support	Total
Activity	80 units	4 orders	1 customer	
Manufacturing overhead	$20,000	$2,800	$ 250	$23,050
Selling and administrative overhead	2,400	2,160	750	5,310
Total cost	$22,400	$4,960	$1,000	$28,360

The action analysis report can then be easily prepared as follows:

Action Analysis Report for OfficeMart as a Customer

Sales		$47,600
Green costs:		
Direct materials	$14,400	14,400
Green margin		33,200
Yellow costs:		
Direct labour	4,000	
Manufacturing overhead	23,050	27,050
Yellow margin		6,150
Red costs:		
Selling and administrative overhead	5,310	5,310
Red margin		$ 840

Appendix 8A: Cost Flows in an Activity-Based Costing System

Objective 9

Record the flow of costs in an activity-based costing system.

As stated in the main body of the chapter, the flow of costs through Raw Materials, Work in Process, and other accounts is the same under activity-based costing as was illustrated in Chapter 3. Although the flow of costs is the same, a company must compute several predetermined overhead rates when activity-based costing is being used and that complicates the journal entries and T-accounts somewhat. Our purpose in this appendix is to provide a detailed example of cost flows in an activity-based costing system.

An Example of Cost Flows

Note that the company in the following example has five activity centres and therefore must compute five predetermined overhead rates. Also note from the example how underapplied and overapplied overhead costs are computed when activity-based costing is being used.

BASIC DATA.   Sarvik Company installed an activity-based costing system several years ago. The company has five activity centres for costing purposes. These activity centres are listed below, along with the estimated overhead cost and the expected level of activity in each centre for the coming year.

Activity Centre	Cost Driver	Estimated Overhead Cost	Expected Activity
Machine related	CPU hours	$175,000	5,000 CPU hours
Purchase orders	Number of orders	63,000	700 orders
Machine setups	Number of setups	92,000	460 setups
Product testing	Number of tests	160,000	200 tests
General factory	Machine-hours	300,000	25,000 machine-hours

At the beginning of the year, the company had inventory balances as follows:

Raw materials	$3,000
Work in process	4,000
Finished goods	–0–

Selected transactions recorded by the company during the year are given below:

a. Raw materials were purchased on account, $915,000.
b. Raw materials were requisitioned for use in production, $900,000 ($810,000 direct and $90,000 indirect). The indirect materials were traceable to the activity centres as follows:

Machine related	$16,000
Purchase orders	3,000
Machine setups	8,000
Product testing	21,000
General factory	42,000
Total	$90,000

c. Labour costs were incurred in the factory, $370,000 ($95,000 direct labour and $275,000 indirect labour). The indirect labour costs were traceable to the activity centres as follows:

Machine related	$ 30,000
Purchase orders	40,000
Machine setups	25,000
Product testing	60,000
General factory	120,000
Total	$275,000

d. Depreciation was recorded on factory assets, $180,000. This depreciation was traceable to the activity centres as follows:

Machine related	$ 72,000
Purchase orders	9,000
Machine setups	16,000
Product testing	48,000
General factory	35,000
Total	$180,000

e. Miscellaneous manufacturing overhead costs were incurred, $230,000. These overhead costs were traceable to the activity centres as follows:

Machine related	$ 50,000
Purchase orders	18,000
Machine setups	45,000
Product testing	27,000
General factory	90,000
Total	$230,000

f. Manufacturing overhead cost was applied to production. *Actual* activity in the various activity centres during the year was as follows:

Machine related	4,600 CPU hours
Purchase orders	800 orders issued
Machine setups	500 setups completed
Product testing	190 tests completed
General factory	23,000 machine-hours worked

g. Goods costing $1,650,000 to manufacture were completed during the year.

Required

1. Compute the predetermined overhead rate for each activity centre.
2. Prepare journal entries to record transactions (a) through (g) above. When applying overhead cost to production in entry (f), note that you have five predetermined overhead rates, rather than just one.
3. Post the entries in (2) above to T-accounts. As part of this posting, *create a T-account for each activity centre and treat these accounts as subsidiary accounts to Manufacturing Overhead.*
4. Compute the underapplied or overapplied overhead cost in the Manufacturing Overhead account and in each activity centre.

Solution

1. Predetermined overhead rates for the activity centres:

Activity Centre	(1) Estimated Overhead Cost	(2) Expected Activity	(1) ÷ (2) Predetermined Overhead Rate
Machine related	$175,000	5,000 CPU hours	$35/CPU hour
Purchase orders	63,000	700 orders	$90/order
Machine setups	92,000	460 setups	$200/setup
Product testing	160,000	200 tests	$800/test
General factory	300,000	25,000 machine-hours	$12/machine-hour

2. a. Raw Materials 915,000

       Accounts Payable 915,000

   b. Work in Process 810,000

     Manufacturing Overhead 90,000

       Raw Materials 900,000

   c. Work in Process 95,000

     Manufacturing Overhead 275,000

       Salaries and Wages Payable 370,000

   d. Manufacturing Overhead 180,000

       Accumulated Depreciation 180,000

   e. Manufacturing Overhead 230,000

       Accounts Payable 230,000

f. Recall from Chapter 3 that the formula for computing applied overhead cost is as follows:

Predetermined overhead rate × Actual activity = Applied overhead cost

Since we have *five* activity centres and *five* predetermined overhead rates, we must determine the amount of applied overhead cost for *each* activity centre. The computations are as follows:

Activity Centre	(1) Predetermined Overhead Rate	(2) Actual Activity	(1) × (2) Applied Overhead Cost
Machine related	$35/CPU hour	4,600 CPU hours	$161,000
Purchase orders	$90/order	800 orders issued	72,000
Machine setups	$200/setup	500 setups completed	100,000
Product testing	$800/test	190 tests completed	152,000
General factory	$12/machine-hour	23,000 machine-hours	276.000
Total			$761,000

By totalling these five applied overhead cost figures, we find that the company applied $761,000 in overhead cost to products during the year. The following entry records this application of overhead cost:

Work in Process	761,000	
Manufacturing Overhead		761,000
g. Finished Goods	1,650,000	
Work in Process		1,650,000

3. See the T-accounts in Exhibit 8A–1 on the following page. Note from these T-accounts that when amounts are posted to Manufacturing Overhead, the amounts must also be posted to the activity centre accounts to which they relate.

4. The underapplied or overapplied overhead cost is computed in the T-accounts in Exhibit 8A–1 for Manufacturing Overhead and for each of the activity centre accounts. These computations can be summarized as follows:

	Total	Machine Related	Purchase Orders	Machine Setups	Product Testing	General Factory
Actual overhead cost	$775,000	$168,000	$70,000	$ 94,000	$156,000	$287,000
Applied overhead cost	761,000	161,000	72,000	100,000	152,000	276,000
Underapplied or (overapplied) overhead cost	$ 14,000	$ 7,000	$ (2,000)	$ (6,000)	$4,000	$11,000

Note from the computations above that the $14,000 total underapplied overhead cost is equal to the sum of the underapplied and overapplied amounts from the five activity centres.

Exhibit 8A–1 T-Accounts Showing Activity Centres

Raw Materials			
Bal.	3,000	(b)	900,000
(a)	915,000		
Bal.	18,000		

Finished Goods		
Bal.	–0–	
(g)	1,650,000	

Accounts Payable		
	(a)	915,000
	(e)	230,000

Work in Process			
Bal.	4,000	(g)	1,650,000
(b)	810,000		
(c)	95,000		
(f)	761,000		
Bal.	20,000		

Accumulated Depreciation	
(d)	180,000

Salaries and Wages Payable	
(c)	370,000

Manufacturing Overhead			
(b)	90,000	(f)	761,000
(c)	275,000		
(d)	180,000		
(e)	230,000		
	775,000		761,000
Bal.	14,000		

Manufactuing overhead cost flows are detailed in the individual activity centre accounts, which form a subsidiary overhead ledger. For example, the $90,000 posted to Manufacturing Overhead in entry (b) above is detailed in the individual activity centre accounts under entry (b).

Machine-Related Activity Centre			
(b)	16,000	(f)	161,000
(c)	30,000		
(d)	72,000		
(e)	50,000		
	168,000		161,000
Bal.	7,000		

Purchase Orders Activity Centre			
(b)	3,000	(f)	72,000
(c)	40,000		
(d)	9,000		
(e)	18,000		
	70,000		721,000
		Bal.	2,000

Machine-Setups Activity Centre			
(b)	8,000	(f)	100,000
(c)	25,000		
(d)	16,000		
(e)	45,000		
	94,000		100,000
		Bal.	6,000

Product Testing Activity Centre			
(b)	21,000	(f)	152,000
(c)	60,000		
(d)	48,000		
(e)	27,000		
	156,000		152,000
Bal.	4,000		

General Factory Activity Centre			
(b)	42,000	(f)	276,000
(c)	120,000		
(d)	35,000		
(e)	90,000		
	287,000		276,000
Bal.	11,000		

Questions

8–1   In what fundamental ways does activity-based costing differ from traditional costing methods such as those described in Chapters 2 and 3?

8–2   Why is direct labour a poor base for allocating overhead in many companies?

8–3   Why are overhead rates in activity-based costing based on the level of activity at capacity rather than on the budgeted level of activity?

8–4   Why is top management support crucial when attempting to implement an activity-based costing system?

8–5   What are unit-level, batch-level, product-level, customer-level, and organization-sustaining activities?

8–6   What types of costs should not be assigned to products in an activity-based costing system?

8–7   Why are there two stages of allocation in activity-based costing?

8–8   Why is the first stage of the allocation process in activity-based costing often based on interviews?

8–9   How can the activity rates (i.e., cost per activity) for the various activities be used to target process improvements?

8–10   When activity-based costing is used, why are manufacturing overhead costs often shifted from high-volume products to low-volume products?

8–11   Why should an activity view of product margins such as in Exhibit 8–9 be supplemented with an action analysis such as in Exhibit 8–12 when making decisions about products or customers?

8–12   Why is the activity-based costing described in this chapter probably unacceptable for external financial reports?

8–13   In what three ways does activity-based costing improve the costing system of an organization?

8–14   What are the two chief limitations of activity-based costing?

8–15   Can activity-based costing be used in service organizations?

Exercises

E8–1   CD Express, Inc., provides CD duplicating services to software companies. The customer provides a master CD from which CD Express makes copies. An order from a customer can be for a single copy or for thousands of copies. Most jobs are broken down into batches to allow smaller jobs, with higher priorities, to have access to the machines.

Below are listed a number of activities carried out at CD Express.

a. Sales representatives' periodic visits to customers to keep them informed about the services provided by CD Express.
b. Ordering labels from the printer for a particular CD.
c. Setting up the CD duplicating machine to make copies from a particular master CD.
d. Loading the automatic labelling machine with labels for a particular CD.
e. Visually inspecting CDs and placing them by hand into protective plastic cases prior to shipping.
f. Preparation of the shipping documents for the order.

g. Periodic maintenance of equipment.
h. Lighting and heating the company's production facility.
i. Preparation of quarterly financial reports.

Required   Classify each of the activities above as either a unit-level, batch-level, product-level, customer-level, or organization-sustaining activity. (An order to duplicate a particular CD is a product-level activity.) Assume the order is large enough that it must be broken down into batches.

E8–2   Listed below are a number of activities that you have observed at Ming Company, a manufacturing company. Each activity has been classified as a unit-level, batch-level, product-level, or customer-level activity.

Activity	Level of Activity	Examples of Activity Measures
a. Direct labour workers assemble a product	Unit	
b. Products are designed by engineers	Product	
c. Equipment is set up	Batch	
d. Machines are used to shape and cut materials	Unit	
e. Monthly bills are sent out to regular customers	Customer	
f. Materials are moved from the receiving dock to production lines	Batch	
g. All completed units are inspected for defects	Unit	

Required   Complete the table by providing examples of activity measures for each activity that could be used to allocate its costs to products or customers.

E8–3   Listed below are a number of activities that you have observed at Vapo Ingman Oy, a Finnish manufacturing company. The company makes a variety of products at its plant outside Helsinki.

a. Machine settings are changed between batches of different products.
b. Parts inventories are maintained in the storeroom. (Each product requires its own unique parts.)
c. Products are milled on a milling machine.
d. New employees are hired by the personnel office.
e. New products are designed.
f. Periodic maintenance is performed on general-purpose production equipment.
g. A bill is sent to a customer who is late in making payments.
h. Yearly taxes are paid on the company's facilities.
i. Purchase orders are issued for materials to be used in production.

Required   1. Classify each of the activities above as either a unit-level, batch-level, product-level, customer-level, or organization-sustaining activity.
2. Where possible, for each activity name one or more activity measures that might be used to assign costs generated by the activity to products or customers.

E8–4   The operations vice president of Home Bank has been interested in investigating the efficiency of the bank's operations. She has been particularly concerned about the costs of handling routine transactions at the bank and would like to compare these costs at the bank's various branches. If the branches with the most efficient operations can be identified, their methods can be studied and then replicated elsewhere. While the bank maintains meticulous records of wages and other costs, there has been no attempt thus far to show how those costs are related to the various services provided by the bank. The operations vice president has asked for your help in conducting an activity-based costing study of bank operations. In particular, she would like to know the cost of opening an account, the cost of processing deposits and withdrawals, and the cost of processing other customer transactions.

The Westfield branch of Home Bank has submitted the following cost data for last year:

Teller wages	$160,000
Assistant branch manager salary	75,000
Branch manager salary	80,000
Total	$315,000

Virtually all of the other costs of the branch—rent, depreciation, utilities, and so on—are organization-sustaining costs that cannot be meaningfully assigned to individual customer transactions such as depositing cheques.

In addition to the cost data above, the employees of the Westfield branch have been interviewed concerning how their time was distributed last year across the activities included in the activity-based costing study. The results of those interviews appear below:

Distribution of Resource Consumption across Activities

	Opening Accounts	Processing Deposits and Withdrawals	Processing Other Customer Transactions	Other Activities	Total
Teller wages	5%	65%	20%	10%	100%
Assistant branch manager salary .	15%	5%	30%	50%	100%
Branch manager salary	5%	0%	10%	85%	100%

Required Prepare the first-stage allocation for the activity-based costing study. (See Exhibit 8–4 for an example of a first-stage allocation.)

E8–5 (This exercise is a continuation of E8–4; it should be assigned *only* if E8–4 is also assigned.) The manager of the Westfield branch of Home Bank has provided the following data concerning the transactions of the branch during the past year:

Activity	Total Activity at the Westfield Branch	
Opening accounts	500	new accounts opened
Processing deposits and withdrawals	100,000	deposits and withdrawals processed
Processing other customer transactions . . .	5,000	other customer transactions processed

The lowest costs reported by other branches for these activities are displayed below:

Activity	Lowest Cost among All Home Bank Branches	
Opening accounts	$26.75	per new account
Processing deposits and withdrawals	$ 1.24	per deposit or withdrawal
Processing other customer transactions . .	$11.86	per other customer transaction

Required
1. Using the first-stage allocation from E8–4 and the above data, compute the activity rates for the activity-based costing system. (Use Exhibit 8–5 as a guide.) Round all computations to the nearest whole cent.
2. What do these results suggest to you concerning operations at the Westfield branch?

E8–6 Durban Metal Products, Ltd., of the Republic of South Africa makes specialty metal parts used in applications ranging from the cutting edges of bulldozer blades to replacement parts for Land Rovers. The company uses an activity-based costing system for internal decision-making purposes. The company has four activity cost pools as listed below:

Activity Cost Pool	Activity Measure
Order size	Number of direct labour-hours
Customer orders	Number of customer orders
Product testing	Number of testing hours
Selling	Number of sales calls

The results of the first-stage allocation of the activity-based costing system, in which the activity rates were computed, appear below:

	Order Size	Customer Orders	Product Testing	Selling
Manufacturing:				
Indirect labour	R 8.25	R180.00	R30.00	R 0.00
Factory depreciation	8.00	0.00	40.00	0.00
Factory utilities	0.10	0.00	1.00	0.00
Factory administration	0.00	48.00	18.00	30.00
General selling and administrative:				
Wages and salaries	0.50	80.00	0.00	800.00
Depreciation	0.00	12.00	0.00	40.00
Taxes and insurance	0.00	0.00	0.00	20.00
Selling expenses	0.00	0.00	0.00	200.00
Total overhead cost	R16.85	R320.00	R89.00	R1,090.00

Note: The currency in South Africa is the Rand, denoted here by R.

The managing director of the company would like information concerning the cost of a recently completed order for heavy-duty trailer axles. The order required 200 direct labour-hours, 4 hours of product testing, and 2 sales calls.

Required

1. Prepare a report showing the overhead cost of the order for heavy-duty trailer axles according to the activity-based costing system. (Use Exhibit 8–8A as a guide.) What is the total overhead cost of the order according to the activity-based costing system?
2. Explain the two different perspectives this report gives to managers concerning the nature of the overhead costs involved in the order. (Hint: Look at the row and column totals of the report you have prepared.)

E8–7 Foam Products, Inc., makes foam seat cushions for the automotive and aerospace industries. The company's activity-based costing system has four activity cost pools, which are listed below:

Activity Cost Pool	Activity Measure
Volume	Number of direct labour-hours
Batch processing	Number of batches
Order processing	Number of orders
Customer service	Number of customers

The activity rates for the cost pools have been computed as follows:

		Activity Rates		
	Volume	Batch Processing	Order Processing	Customer Service
Production overhead:				
Indirect labour	$0.60	$ 60.00	$ 20.00	$ 0.00
Factory equipment depreciation	4.00	17.00	0.00	0.00
Factory administration	0.10	7.00	25.00	150.00
General selling and administrative overhead:				
Wages and salaries	0.40	20.00	160.00	1,600.00
Depreciation	0.00	3.00	10.00	38.00
Marketing expenses	0.45	0.00	60.00	675.00
Total	$5.55	$107.00	$275.00	$2,463.00

The company just completed a single order from Lyon Gate Trucking for 1,000 custom seat cushions. The order was produced in two batches. Each seat cushion required 0.25 direct labour-hours. The selling price was $20 per unit, the direct materials cost was $8.50 per unit, and the direct labour cost was $6.00 per unit. This was Lyon Gate Trucking's only order during the year.

Required
1. Prepare a report showing the product margin for this order from an activity viewpoint. (Use the product report in Exhibit 8–9 as a guide.) At this point, ignore the customer service costs.
2. Prepare a report showing the customer margin on sales to Lyon Gate Trucking from an activity viewpoint. (Use the customer profitability analysis in Exhibit 8–9 as a guide.)

E8–8   Refer to the data for Foam Products, Inc., in E8–7. In addition, management has provided their ease of adjustment codes for purposes of preparing action analyses.

	Ease of Adjustment Codes
Direct materials	Green
Direct labour	Yellow
Production overhead:	
Indirect labour	Yellow
Factory equipment depreciation .	Red
Factory administration	Red
General selling and administrative:	
Wages and salaries	Red
Depreciation	Red
Marketing expenses	Yellow

Required   Prepare an action analysis report on the order from Lyon Gate Trucking. (Use the report in Exhibit 8–12 as a guide.) Ignore the customer service costs.

E8–9   Refer to the data for Foam Products, Inc., in E8–7 and E8–8. Management would like an action analysis report for the customer similar to those prepared for products, but it is unsure of how this can be done. The customer service cost of $2,463 could be deducted directly from the product margin for the order, but this would obscure how much of the customer service cost consists of Green, Yellow, and Red costs.

Required   Prepare an action analysis report that shows the profitability of sales to Lyon Gate Trucking during the year. The best way to proceed is to prepare an analysis of overhead costs as in Exhibit 8–8A but include the customer service costs in the analysis.

E8–10   Advanced Products Corporation has supplied the following data from its activity-based costing system:

Overhead Costs

Wages and salaries	$300,000
Other overhead costs	100,000
Total overhead costs	$400,000

Activity Cost Pool	Activity Measure	Total Activity for the Year
Volume related	Number of direct labour-hours	20,000 DLHs
Order related	Number of customer orders	400 orders
Customer support . .	Number of customers	200 customers
Other	These costs are not allocated to products or customers	Not applicable

Distribution of Resource Consumption across Activities

	Volume Related	Order Related	Customer Support	Other Activities	Total
Wages and salaries	40%	30%	20%	10%	100%
Other overhead costs	30%	10%	20%	40%	100%

During the year, Advanced Products completed one order for a new customer, Shenzhen Enterprises. This customer did not order any other products during the year. Data concerning that order follow:

Data concerning the Shenzhen Enterprises Order

Units ordered	10 units
Direct labour-hours per unit	2 DLHs
Selling price	$300 per unit
Direct materials	$180 per unit
Direct labour	$ 50 per unit

Required

1. Prepare a report showing the first-stage allocations of overhead costs to the activity cost pools. (Use Exhibit 8–4 as a guide.)
2. Compute the activity rates for the activity cost pools. (Use Exhibit 8–5 as a guide.)
3. Prepare a report showing the overhead costs for the order from Shenzhen Enterprises. (Use Exhibit 8–8A as a guide. Do not include the customer support costs at this point in the analysis.)
4. Prepare a report from the activity viewpoint showing the product margin for the order and the customer margin for Shenzhen Enterprises. (Use Exhibit 8–9 as a guide.)
5. Prepare an action analysis of the order from Shenzhen Enterprises. (Use Exhibit 8–12 as a guide.) For purposes of this report, direct materials should be coded as a Green cost, direct labour and wages and salaries as Yellow costs, and other overhead costs as a Red cost.

E8–11 Hiram's Lakeside is a popular restaurant located on Lake George in Manitoba. The owner of the restaurant has been trying to better understand costs at the restaurant and has hired a student intern to conduct an activity-based costing study. The intern, in consultation with the owner, identified the following major activities:

Activity Cost Pool	Activity Measure
Serving a party of diners	Number of parties served
Serving a diner	Number of diners served
Serving drinks	Number of drinks ordered

A group of diners who ask to sit at the same table are counted as a party. Some costs, such as the costs of cleaning linen, are the same whether one person is at a table or the table is full. Other costs, such as washing dishes, depend on the number of diners served.

Data concerning last month's operations are displayed below. The intern has already completed the first-stage allocations of costs to the activity cost pools.

	Serving a Party	Serving a Diner	Serving Drinks	Total
Total cost	$33,000	$138,000	$24,000	$195,000
Total activity	6,000 parties	15,000 diners	10,000 drinks	

The above costs include all of the costs of the restaurant except for organization-sustaining costs such as rent, property taxes, and top-management salaries.

Prior to the activity-based costing study, the owner knew very little about the costs of the restaurant. She knew that the total cost for the month (including organization-sustaining costs) was $240,000 and that 15,000 diners had been served. Therefore, the average cost per diner was $16.

Required

1. According to the activity-based costing system, what is the total cost of serving each of the following parties of diners? (You can use the simplified approach described at the end of the chapter.)
   a. A party of four diners who order three drinks in total.
   b. A party of two diners who do not order any drinks.
   c. A lone diner who orders two drinks.
2. Convert the total costs you computed in (1) above to costs per diner. In other words, what is the average cost per diner for serving each of the following parties of diners?
   a. A party of four diners who order three drinks in total.
   b. A party of two diners who do not order any drinks.
   c. A lone diner who orders two drinks.
3. Why do the costs per diner for the three different parties differ from each other and from the overall average cost of $16 per diner?

Problems

P8–12 Activity Rates and Pricing Jobs   Mercer Asbestos Removal Company is in the business of removing potentially toxic asbestos insulation and related products from buildings. There has been a long-simmering dispute between the company's estimator and the work supervisors. The on-site supervisors claim that the estimators do not take enough care in distinguishing between routine work such as removal of asbestos insulation around heating pipes in older homes and nonroutine work such as removing asbestos-contaminated ceiling plaster in industrial buildings. The on-site supervisors believe that nonroutine work is far more expensive than routine work and should bear higher customer charges. The estimator sums up his position in this way: "My job is to measure the area to be cleared of asbestos. As directed by top management, I simply multiply the square metres by $20 to determine the bid price. Since our average cost is only $17.40 per square metre, that leaves enough cushion to take care of the additional costs of nonroutine work that shows up. Besides, it is difficult to know what is routine or not routine until you actually start tearing things apart."

Partly to shed light on this controversy, the company initiated an activity-based costing study of all of its costs. Data from the activity-based costing system follow:

Activity Cost Pool	Activity Measure
Job size	Thousands of square metres
Estimating and job setup	Number of jobs
Dealing with nonroutine jobs	Number of nonroutine jobs
Other (costs of idle capacity and organization-sustaining costs)	Not applicable; these costs are not allocated to jobs

Costs for the Year

Wages and salaries	$ 300,000
Disposal fees	700,000
Equipment depreciation	90,000
On-site supplies	50,000
Office expenses	200,000
Licensing and insurance	400,000
Total cost	$1,740,000

Distribution of Resource Consumption across Activities

	Job Size	Estimating and Job Setup	Dealing with Nonroutine Jobs	Other	Total
Wages and salaries	50%	10%	30%	10%	100%
Disposal fees	60%	0%	40%	0%	100%
Equipment depreciation . .	40%	5%	20%	35%	100%
On-site supplies	60%	30%	10%	0%	100%
Office expenses	10%	35%	25%	30%	100%
Licensing and insurance . .	30%	0%	50%	20%	100%

Activity Cost Pool	Activity for the Year
Job size	100 thousand square metres
Estimating and job setup	500 jobs
Dealing with nonroutine jobs	100 nonroutine jobs

Note: The 100 nonroutine jobs are included in the total of 500 jobs.
Both nonroutine jobs and routine jobs require estimating and setup.

Required

1. Perform the first-stage allocation of costs to the activity cost pools. (Use Exhibit 8–4 as a guide.)
2. Compute the activity rates for the activity cost pools. (Use Exhibit 8–5 as a guide or the simpler approach described at the end of the chapter.)
3. Using the activity rates you have computed, determine the total cost and the average cost per thousand square metres of each of the following jobs according to the activity-based costing system. (You will not be able to do an activity analysis because the ease of adjustment codes have not been provided.)
   a. A routine 125-square-metre asbestos removal job.
   b. A routine 250-square-metre asbestos removal job.
   c. A nonroutine 250-square-metre asbestos removal job.
4. Given the results you obtained in (3) above, do you agree with the estimator that the company's present policy for bidding on jobs is adequate?

P8–13 Action Analysis of a Market   Pixel Studio, Inc., is a small company that creates computer-generated animations for films and television. Much of the company's work consists of short commercials for television, but the company also does realistic computer animations for special effects in movies.

The young founders of the company have become increasingly concerned with the economics of the business—particularly since many competitors have sprung up recently in the local area. To help understand the company's cost structure, an activity-based costing system has been designed. Three major activities are carried out in the company: animation concept, animation production, and contract administration. The animation concept activity is carried out at the contract proposal stage when the company bids on projects. This is an intensive activity that involves individuals from all parts of the company in creating story boards and prototype stills to be shown to the prospective client. Once a project is accepted by the client, the animation goes into production and contract administration begins. Almost all of the work involved in animation production is done by the technical staff, whereas the administrative staff is largely responsible for contract administration. The activity cost pools and their activity measures are listed below:

Activity Cost Pool	Activity Measure
Animation concept	Number of proposals
Animation production	Minutes of completed animation
Contract administration	Number of contracts

The first-stage allocation has already been completed and the activity rates have been computed. These activity rates appear below:

	Activity Rates		
	Animation Concept	Animation Production	Contract Administration
Technical staff salaries	$4,000	$ 6,000	$1,600
Animation equipment depreciation	360	1,125	–0–
Administrative wages and salaries .	1,440	150	4,800
Supplies costs	120	300	160
Facility costs	120	150	240
Total cost	$6,040	$7,725	$6,800

These activity rates include all of the costs of the company, except for the costs of idle capacity and organization-sustaining costs.

Preliminary analysis using these activity rates has indicated that the local commercial segment of the market may be unprofitable. This segment is highly competitive. Producers of local commercials may ask three or four companies like Pixel Studio to bid, which results in an unusually low ratio of accepted contracts to bids. Furthermore, the animation sequences tend to be much shorter for local commercials than for other work. Since animation work is billed at fairly standard rates according to the running time of the completed animation, this means that the revenues from these short projects tend to be below average. Data concerning activity appear below:

Activity Measure	Total Activity	Local Commercials
Number of proposals	50	25
Minutes of completed animation	80	5
Number of contracts	25	10

The total sales from the 10 contracts for local commercials was $180,000.

Required

1. Determine the cost of the local commercial market according to the activity-based costing system using Exhibit 8–8A as a guide. (Think of the local commercial market as a product.)
2. Prepare a report showing the margin from the local commercial market using the product margin report in Exhibit 8–9 as a guide. (This company has no direct materials or direct labour costs. All of the company's costs have been included in the activity-based costing system.)
3. Prepare an action analysis report concerning the local commercial market using Exhibit 8–12 as a guide. For this purpose, management has coded the various costs as follows:

	Ease of Adjustment Code
Technical staff salaries	Red
Animation equipment depreciation . .	Red
Administrative wages and salaries . .	Yellow
Supplies costs	Green
Facility costs	Red

There was some controversy in the company concerning these codes. In particular, some administrators objected to coding their own salaries Yellow, while the technical staff salaries were coded Red. However, the founders of the firm squashed these objections by pointing out that "our technical staff are our most valuable assets. Good animators are extremely difficult to find, and they would be the last to go if we had to cut back."

4. What would you recommend to management concerning the local commercial market?

P8–14   Activity-Based Costing as an Alternative to Traditional Product Costing: Simplified Method   This chapter emphasizes the use of activity-based costing in internal decisions. However, a modified form of activity-based costing can also be used to develop product costs for external financial reports. For this purpose, product costs include all manufacturing overhead costs and exclude all nonmanufacturing costs. This problem illustrates such a costing system.

Ellix Company manufactures two models of ultra-high fidelity speakers, the X200 model and the X99 model. Data regarding the two products follow:

Product	Direct Labour-Hours per Unit	Annual Production	Total Direct Labour-Hours
X200	1.8	5,000 units	9,000
X99	0.9	30,000 units	27,000
			36,000

Additional information about the company follows:

a. Model X200 requires $72 in direct materials per unit, and model X99 requires $50.
b. The direct labour rate is $10 per hour.
c. The company has always used direct labour-hours as the base for applying manufacturing overhead cost to products.
d. Model X200 is more complex to manufacture than model X99 and requires the use of special equipment.
e. Because of the special work required in (d) above, the company is considering the use of activity-based costing to apply manufacturing overhead cost to products for external financial reports. Three activity cost pools have been identified as follows:

Activity Cost Pool	Activity Measure	Estimated Overhead Cost
Machine setups	Number of setups	$ 360,000
Special processing . . .	Machine-hours	180,000
General factory	Direct labour-hours	1,260,000
		$1,800,000

	Expected Activity		
Activity Measure	Model X200	Model X99	Total
Number of setups	50	100	150
Machine-hours	12,000	–0–	12,000
Direct labour-hours	9,000	27,000	36,000

Required

1. Assume that the company continues to use direct labour-hours as the base for applying overhead cost to products.
    a. Compute the predetermined overhead rate.
    b. Compute the unit product cost of each model.
2. Assume that the company decides to use activity-based costing to apply manufacturing overhead cost to products. (You can use the simplified approach described at the end of the chapter.)
    a. Compute the predetermined overhead rate for each activity cost pool and determine the amount of overhead cost that would be applied to each model using the activity-based costing system.
    b. Compute the unit product cost of each model.

3. Explain why manufacturing overhead cost shifted from the high-volume model to the low-volume model under activity-based costing.

P8–15 Activity Rates and Activity-Based Management   Aerotraiteur SA is a French company that provides passenger and crew meals to airlines operating out of the two international airports of Paris—Orly and Charles de Gaulle (CDG). The operations at Orly and CDG are managed separately, and top management believes that there may be benefits to greater sharing of information between the two operations.

To better compare the two operations, an activity-based costing system has been designed with the active participation of the managers at both Orly and CDG. The activity-based costing system is based on the following activity cost pools and activity measures:

Activity Cost Pool	Activity Measure
Meal preparation	Number of meals
Flight-related activities	Number of flights
Customer service	Number of customers
Other (costs of idle capacity and organization-sustaining costs) . . .	Not applicable

The operation at CDG airport serves 1.5 million meals annually on 7,500 flights for 10 different airlines. (Each airline is considered one customer.) The annual cost of running the CDG airport operation, excluding only the costs of raw materials for meals, totals 29,400,000 FF.

Note: The currency in France at the time of the activity-based costing study was the franc, denoted here by FF.

Annual Cost of the CDG Operation

Cooks and delivery personnel wages . .	24,000,000 FF
Kitchen supplies	300,000
Chef salaries	1,800,000
Equipment depreciation	600,000
Administrative wages and salaries	1,500,000
Building costs	1,200,000
Total cost	29,400,000 FF

The results of employee interviews at CDG are displayed below:

Distribution of Resource Consumption across Activities at the CDG Operation

	Meal Preparation	Flight Related	Customer Service	Other	Total
Cooks and delivery personnel wages . .	75%	20%	0%	5%	100%
Kitchen supplies	100%	0%	0%	0%	100%
Chef salaries	30%	20%	40%	10%	100%
Equipment depreciation	60%	0%	0%	40%	100%
Administrative wages and salaries . . .	0%	20%	60%	20%	100%
Building costs	0%	0%	0%	100%	100%

Required

1. Perform the first-stage allocation of costs to the activity cost pools. (Use Exhibit 8–4 as a guide.)
2. Compute the activity rates for the activity cost pools. (Use Exhibit 8–5 as a guide.)
3. The Orly operation has already concluded its activity-based costing study and has reported the following costs of carrying out activities at Orly:

	Meal Preparation	Flight Related	Customer Service
Cooks and delivery personnel wages	12.20 FF	780 FF	
Kitchen supplies	0.25		
Chef salaries	0.18	32	54,000 FF
Equipment depreciation	0.23		
Administrative wages and salaries .		45	68,000
Building costs	0.00	0	0
Total cost	12.86 FF	857 FF	122,000 FF

Comparing the activity rates for the CDG operation you computed in (2) above to the activity rates for Orly, do you have any suggestions for the top management of Aerotraiteur SA?

P8–16 Activity-Based Costing as an Alternative to Traditional Product Costing: Simplified Method This chapter emphasizes the use of activity-based costing in internal decisions. However, a modified form of activity-based costing can also be used to develop product costs for external financial reports. For this purpose, product costs include all manufacturing overhead costs and exclude all nonmanufacturing costs. This problem illustrates such a costing system.

Siegel Company manufactures a product that is available in both a deluxe model and a regular model. The company has manufactured the regular model for years. The deluxe model was introduced several years ago to tap a new segment of the market. Since introduction of the deluxe model, the company's profits have steadily declined and management has become increasingly concerned about the accuracy of its costing system. Sales of the deluxe model have been increasing rapidly.

Manufacturing overhead is assigned to products on the basis of direct labour-hours. For the current year, the company has estimated that it will incur $900,000 in manufacturing overhead cost and produce 5,000 units of the deluxe model and 40,000 units of the regular model. The deluxe model requires two hours of direct labour time per unit, and the regular model requires one hour. Material and labour costs per unit are as follows:

	Model	
	Deluxe	Regular
Direct materials	$40	$25
Direct labour	14	7

Required
1. Using direct labour-hours as the base for assigning overhead cost to products, compute the predetermined overhead rate. Using this rate and other data from the problem, determine the unit product cost of each model.
2. Management is considering using activity-based costing to apply manufacturing overhead cost to products for external financial reports. The activity-based costing system would have the following four activity cost centres:

Activity Cost Pool	Activity Measure	Estimated Overhead Cost
Purchasing	Purchase orders issued	$204,000
Processing	Machine-hours	182,000
Scrap/rework	Scrap/rework orders issued	379,000
Shipping	Number of shipments	135,000
		$900,000

| | Expected Activity | | |
Activity Measure	Deluxe	Regular	Total
Purchase orders issued	200	400	600
Machine-hours	20,000	15,000	35,000
Scrap/rework orders issued	1,000	1,000	2,000
Number of shipments	250	650	900

Using the simplified approach described at the end of the chapter, determine the predetermined overhead rate for each of the four activity cost pools.

3. Using the predetermined overhead rates you computed in (2) above, do the following:
   a. Compute the total amount of manufacturing overhead cost that would be applied to each model using the activity-based costing system. After these totals have been computed, determine the amount of manufacturing overhead cost per unit of each model.
   b. Compute the unit product cost of each model.

4. From the data you have developed in (1) through (3) above, identify factors that may account for the company's declining profits.

P8–17 Evaluating the Profitability of Jobs Gallatin Carpet Cleaning is a small, family-owned business operating out of Halifax, Nova Scotia. For its services, the company has always charged a flat fee per hundred square feet of carpet cleaned. The current fee is $28 per hundred square feet. However, there is some question about whether the company is actually making any money on jobs for some customers—particularly those located on remote farms that require considerable travel time. The owner's daughter, home for the summer from college, has suggested investigating this question using activity-based costing. After some discussion, a simple system consisting of four activity cost pools seemed to be adequate. The activity cost pools and their activity measures appear below:

Activity Cost Pool	Activity Measure	Activity for the Year
Cleaning carpets	Square feet cleaned (00s)	20,000 hundred square feet
Travel to jobs	Kilometres driven	60,000 kilometres
Job support	Number of jobs	2,000 jobs
Other (costs of idle capacity and organization-sustaining costs) . . .	None	Not applicable

The total cost of operating the company for the year is $430,000, which includes the following costs:

Wages	$150,000
Cleaning supplies	40,000
Cleaning equipment depreciation	20,000
Vehicle expenses	80,000
Office expenses	60,000
President's compensation	80,000
Total cost	$430,000

Resource consumption is distributed across the activities as follows:

Distribution of Resource Consumption across Activities

	Cleaning Carpets	Travel to Jobs	Job Support	Other	Total
Wages	70%	20%	0%	10%	100%
Cleaning supplies	100%	0%	0%	0%	100%
Cleaning equipment depreciation ..	80%	0%	0%	20%	100%
Vehicle expenses	0%	60%	0%	40%	100%
Office expenses	0%	0%	45%	55%	100%
President's compensation	0%	0%	40%	60%	100%

Job support consists of receiving calls from potential customers at the home office, scheduling jobs, billing, resolving issues, and so on.

Required

1. Prepare the first-stage allocation of costs to the activity cost pools. (Use Exhibit 8–4 as a guide.)
2. Compute the activity rates for the activity cost pools. (Use Exhibit 8–5 as a guide.)
3. The company recently completed a 500 square foot carpet cleaning job at the Miller Dairy Farm—a 75-kilometre round-trip journey from the company's offices in Halifax. Compute the cost of this job using the activity-based costing system. (Use Exhibit 8–8A as a guide.)
4. The revenue from the Miller Dairy Farm was $140 (5 hundred square feet @ $28 per hundred square feet). Prepare a report showing the margin from this job from an activity view. (Use Exhibit 8–9 as a guide. Think of the job as a product.)
5. Prepare an action analysis report of the Miller Dairy Farm job. (Use Exhibit 8–12 as a guide.) The president of Gallatin Carpet Cleaning considers all of the company's costs to be Green costs except for office expenses, which is coded Yellow, and his own compensation, which is coded Red. The people who do the actual carpet cleaning are all trained part-time workers who are paid only for work actually done.
6. What do you conclude concerning the profitability of the Miller Dairy Farm job? Explain.
7. What advice would you give the president concerning pricing jobs in the future?

P8–18   Activity-Based Costing as an Alternative to Traditional Product Costing: Simplified Method   This chapter emphasizes the use of activity-based costing in internal decisions. However, a modified form of activity-based costing can also be used to develop product costs for external financial reports. For this purpose, product costs include all manufacturing overhead costs and exclude all nonmanufacturing costs. This problem illustrates such a costing system.

For many years, Zapro Company manufactured a single product called a mono-relay. Then three years ago, the company automated a portion of its plant and at the same time introduced a second product called a bi-relay which has become increasingly popular. The bi-relay is a more complex product, requiring one hour of direct labour time per unit to manufacture and extensive machining in the automated portion of the plant. The mono-relay requires only 0.75 hour of direct labour time per unit and only a small amount of machining. Manufacturing overhead costs are currently assigned to products on the basis of direct labour-hours.

Despite the growing popularity of the company's new bi-relay, profits have been declining steadily. Management is beginning to believe that there may be a problem with the company's costing system. Material and labour costs per unit are as follows:

	Mono-Relay	Bi-Relay
Direct materials	$35	$48
Direct labour (0.75 hour and 1.0 hour @ $12 per hour)	9	12

Management estimates that the company will incur $1,000,000 in manufacturing overhead costs during the current year and 40,000 units of the mono-relay and 10,000 units of the bi-relay will be produced and sold.

Required

1. Compute the predetermined manufacturing overhead rate assuming that the company continues to apply manufacturing overhead cost on the basis of direct labour-hours. Using this rate and other data from the problem, determine the unit product cost of each product.

2. Management is considering using activity-based costing to apply manufacturing overhead cost to products for external financial reports. The activity-based costing system would have the following four activity cost pools:

Activity Cost Pool	Activity Measure	Estimated Overhead Cost
Maintaining parts inventory	Number of part types	$ 180,000
Processing purchase orders	Number of purchase orders	90,000
Quality control	Number of tests run	230,000
Machine related	Machine-hours	500,000
		$1,000,000

Activity Measure	Expected Activity		
	Mono-Relay	Bi-Relay	Total
Number of part types	75	150	225
Number of purchase orders	800	200	1,000
Number of tests run	2,500	3,250	5,750
Machine-hours	4,000	6,000	10,000

Using the simplified approach described at the end of the chapter, determine the predetermined overhead rate for each of the four activity cost pools.

3. Using the predetermined manufacturing overhead rates you computed in (2) above, do the following:
    a. Compute the total amount of manufacturing overhead cost that would be applied to each product using the activity-based costing system. After these totals have been computed, determine the amount of manufacturing overhead cost per unit of each product.
    b. Compute the unit product cost of each product.

4. Look at the data you have computed in (1) through (3) above. In terms of manufacturing overhead costs, what factors make the bi-relay more costly to produce than the mono-relay? Is the bi-relay as profitable as management believes? Explain.

Cases

C8–19 Evaluating the Profitability of Customers   Classic Windows is a small company that builds specialty wooden windows for local builders. For years the company has relied on a simple costing system based on direct labour-hours (DLHs) for determining the costs of its products. However, the company's president became interested in activity-based costing after reading an article about ABC in a trade journal. An activity-based costing design team was put together, and within a few months a simple system consisting of four activity cost pools had been designed. The activity cost pools and their activity measures appear below:

Activity Cost Pool	Activity Measure	Activity for the Year
Making windows	Direct labour-hours	100,000 DLHs
Processing orders	Number of orders	2,000 orders
Customer relations	Number of customers	100 customers
Other (costs of idle capacity and organization-sustaining costs)	None	Not applicable

The Processing Orders activity cost pool includes order taking, job setup, job scheduling, and so on. Direct materials and direct labour are directly assigned to jobs in both the traditional and activity-based costing systems. The total overhead cost (both nonmanufacturing and manufacturing) for the year is $1,370,000 and includes the following costs:

Manufacturing overhead costs:		
Indirect factory wages	$400,000	
Production equipment depreciation	300,000	
Other factory costs	80,000	$ 780,000
Selling and administrative expenses:		
Administrative wages and salaries	300,000	
Office expenses	40,000	
Marketing expenses	250,000	590,000
Total overhead cost		$1,370,000

Based largely on interviews with employees, the distribution of resource consumption across the activities has been estimated as follows:

Distribution of Resource Consumption across Activities

	Making Windows	Processing Orders	Customer Relations	Other	Total
Indirect factory wages	30%	40%	10%	20%	100%
Production equipment depreciation	90%	0%	0%	10%	100%
Other factory costs	30%	0%	0%	70%	100%
Administrative wages and salaries	0%	20%	30%	50%	100%
Office expenses	0%	30%	10%	60%	100%
Marketing expenses	0%	0%	60%	40%	100%

Management of the company is particularly interested in measuring the profitability of two customers. One of the customers, Kuszik Builders, is a low-volume purchaser. The other, Western Homes, is a relatively high-volume purchaser. Details of these two customers' orders for the year appear below:

	Kuszik Builders	Western Homes
Number of orders during the year	2 orders	3 orders
Total direct labour hours	300 DLHs	2,000 DLHs
Total sales	$12,500	$68,000
Total direct materials	$ 4,200	$18,500
Total direct labour cost	$ 5,400	$36,000

Required
1. The company's traditional costing system applies manufacturing overhead to jobs strictly on the basis of direct labour-hours. Using this traditional approach, carry out the following steps:
   a. Compute the predetermined manufacturing overhead rate.
   b. Compute the total margin for all of the windows ordered by Kuszik Builders according to the traditional costing system. Do the same for Western Homes.
2. Using activity-based costing, carry out the following steps:
   a. Perform the first-stage allocation of costs to the activity cost pools. (Use Exhibit 8–4 as a guide.)
   b. Compute the activity rates for the activity cost pools. (Use Exhibit 8–5 as a guide.)
   c. Compute the overhead costs of serving each of the two customers. (You will need to construct a table like Exhibit 8–8A for each of the customers. However, unlike Exhibit 8–8A, you should fill in the column for Customer Relations as well as the other columns. Exhibit 8–8A was constructed for a product; in this case we are interested in a customer.)
   d. Prepare an action analysis report showing the margin on business with Kuszik Builders. (The ease of adjustment codes appear below.) Repeat for Western Homes.

	Ease of Adjustment Code
Direct materials	Green
Direct labour	Yellow
Indirect factory wages	Yellow
Production equipment depreciation . .	Yellow
Other factory costs	Yellow
Administrative wages and salaries . . .	Red
Office expenses	Yellow
Marketing expenses	Yellow

3. Does Classic Windows appear to be losing money on either customer? Do the traditional and activity-based costing systems agree concerning the profitability of the customers? If they do not agree, which costing system do you believe? Why?

C8–20   Activity-Based Costing as an Alternative to Traditional Product Costing: Simplified Method[14]   "A dollar of gross margin per briefcase? That's ridiculous!" roared Art Dejans, president of CarryAll, Inc. "Why do we go on producing those standard briefcases when we're able to make over $15 per unit on our specialty items? Maybe it's time to get out of the standard line and focus the whole plant on specialty work."

Mr. Dejans is referring to a summary of unit costs and revenues that he had just received from the company's Accounting Department:

	Standard Briefcases	Specialty Briefcases
Selling price per unit	$36	$40
Unit product cost	35	25
Gross margin per unit	$ 1	$15

CarryAll produces briefcases from leather, fabric, and synthetic materials in a single plant. The basic product is a standard briefcase that is made from leather lined with fabric. The standard briefcase is a high-quality item and has sold well for many years.

Last year, the company decided to expand its product line and produce specialty briefcases for special orders. These briefcases differ from the standard in that they vary in size, they contain the finest synthetic materials, and they are imprinted with the buyer's name. To reduce labour costs on the specialty briefcases, most of the cutting and stitching is done by automated machines. These machines are used to a much lesser degree in the production of standard briefcases.

"I agree that the specialty business is looking better and better," replied Sally Henrie, the company's marketing manager. "And there seems to be plenty of specialty work out there, particularly since the competition hasn't been able to touch our price. Did you know that Armor Company, our biggest competitor, charges over $50 a unit for its specialty items? Now that's what I call gouging the customer!"

A breakdown of the manufacturing cost for each of CarryAll's product lines is given below:

14. Adapted from a case written by Harold P. Roth and Imogene Posey, "Management Accounting Case Study: CarryAll Company," *Management Accounting Campus Report,* Institute of Management Accountants (Fall 1991), p. 9. Used by permission.

	Standard Briefcases		Specialty Briefcases	
Units produced each month		10,000		2,500
Direct materials:				
Leather .... 1.0 sq. yd.		$15.00	0.5 sq. yd.	$ 7.50
Fabric .... 1.0 sq. yd.		5.00	1.0 sq. yd.	5.00
Synthetic		—		5.00
Total materials		20.00		17.50
Direct labour .... 0.5 hr. @ $12		6.00	0.25 hr. @ $12	3.00
Manufacturing overhead .... 0.5 hr. @ $18		9.00	0.25 hr. @ $18	4.50
Unit product cost		$35.00		$25.00

Manufacturing overhead is applied to products on the basis of direct labour-hours. The rate of $18 per direct labour-hour is determined by dividing the total manufacturing overhead cost for a month by the direct labour-hours:

$$\frac{\text{Manufacturing overhead cost, \$101,250}}{\text{Direct labour-hours, 5,625}} = \$18 \text{ per DLH}$$

The following additional information is available about the company and its products:

a. Standard briefcases are produced in batches of 200 units, and specialty briefcases are produced in batches of 25 units. Thus, the company does 50 setups for the standard items each month and 100 setups for the specialty items. A setup for the standard items requires one hour of time, whereas a setup for the specialty items requires two hours of time.

b. All briefcases are inspected to ensure that quality standards are met. A total of 300 hours of inspection time is spent on the standard briefcases and 500 hours of inspection time is spent on the specialty briefcases each month.

c. A standard briefcase requires 0.5 hour of machine time, and a specialty briefcase requires 2 hours of machine time.

d. The company is considering the use of activity-based costing as an alternative to its traditional costing system for computing unit product costs. Since these unit product costs will be used for external financial reporting, all manufacturing overhead costs are to be allocated to products and nonmanufacturing costs are to be excluded from product costs. The activity-based costing system has already been designed and costs allocated to the activity cost pools. The activity cost pools and activity measures are detailed below:

Activity Cost Pool	Activity Measure	Estimated Overhead Cost
Purchasing	Number of orders	$ 12,000
Material handling	Number of receipts	15,000
Production orders and setup	Setup hours	20,250
Inspection	Inspection-hours	16,000
Frame assembly	Assembly-hours	8,000
Machine related	Machine-hours	30,000
		$101,250

Activity Measure	Expected Activity		
	Standard Briefcase	Specialty Briefcase	Total
Number of orders:			
Leather	34	6	40
Fabric	48	12	60
Synthetic material	—	100	100
Number of receipts:			
Leather	52	8	60
Fabric	64	16	80
Synthetic material	—	160	160
Setup hours	?	?	?
Inspection-hours	?	?	?
Assembly-hours	800	800	1,600
Machine-hours	?	?	?

Required

1. Using activity-based costing and the simplified approach described at the end of the chapter, determine the amount of manufacturing overhead cost that would be applied to each standard briefcase and each specialty briefcase.

2. Using the data computed in (1) above and other data from the case as needed, determine the unit product cost of each product line from the perspective of the activity-based costing system.

3. Ideally, what changes should be made in CarryAll's activity-based costing system if it is to be used for making decisions about products?

4. Within the limitations of the data that have been provided, evaluate the president's concern about the profitability of the two product lines. Would you recommend that the company shift its resources entirely to production of specialty briefcases? Explain.

5. Sally Henrie stated that "the competition hasn't been able to touch our price" on specialty business. Why do you suppose the competition has not been able to touch CarryAll's price?

C8–21 Activity Analysis[15] Following is information on the Metalworks Company.
Background Mark Smith was hired as the controller of Metalworks Company two years ago. The family-owned company, located in Southwestern Ontario, has been in operation for about 20 years and until this year has always been a profitable operation. This year, however, Metalworks is operating at a deficit. The primary reason is that a strike in the automotive industry, which idled production, caused a decrease in Metalworks' orders. However, Mark Smith is not certain that the sales decrease was the only reason for Metalworks' losses. Exhibit 1 presents Metalworks' Income Statement for the fiscal year ending December 31, 1999.

Metalworks is in the business of producing metal components which are made out of powdered metals. Its product line includes about 150 parts made from various combinations of iron, copper, brass and stainless steel. Each part is specifically designed and produced for a customer—automotive customers represent about 65% of Metalworks' business, with the rest represented by power tool and home appliance manufacturers.

Processes Metalworks fabricates all its products out of powdered metal. Powdered metals are mixed in large vats—the company has about 80 different blends that are mixed according to a "recipe" by a powder blender technician. After the powder is blended and tested to see if the mix is correct, the press operator either pours or ladles the mixture into presses. Each Metalworks' contract requires a unique set of tools for the pressing operation. The life of the tools vary according to the part being made; some sets of tools are good for millions of parts (e.g., blender stems) while others must be replaced more frequently (certain automotive parts). After pressing,

---

15. Written by Priscilla S. Wisner and Harold P. Roth. Priscilla S. Wisner is an Assistant Professor at the American Graduate School of International Management and Harold P. Roth is a Professor at the University of Tennessee. This case is based on an actual company. The names and numbers have been changed to preserve anonymity. The authors wish to acknowledge the assistance of Jim Ross of the University of Tennessee Center for Industrial Studies. *Issues in Accounting Education*, Vol. 13, No. 4 (November 1998).

the parts are inspected to determine if they are properly formed. If they are not, the parts can be pressed again.

After the pressing operation, all parts go through a sintering process, where the powder blend is heated until the powders meld. "Meld" is a commonly used process term, formed by combining the words "melt" and "weld." It means to melt together. This process entails putting the pressed pieces onto a conveyor belt that moves through a long furnace. Depending on the part, the pieces are placed on skids, plates, or trays for the sintering operation. Both the furnace belt speed and temperature depend upon the chemical composition and size of the part. Certain powder blends meld at lower temperatures, while other blends require higher temperatures. The furnace operators manually adjust the belt speed depending on the part to be sintered. The furnace temperature is adjusted by varying the type and amount of gas used for heating. Nitrogen, ammonia, natural gas and other endothermic gases are used to heat the furnaces—the cost per cubic metre of these gases varies considerably. Ammonia, the most expensive gas, is used for all parts but in greater quantities for parts made of stainless steel (which require a very high temperature to meld). All gases are accounted for as utility costs.

As parts emerge from the furnace, they are inspected. Parts that fail inspection are either reground for use in other products or scrapped, depending on the metals used in the part.

After the sintering (furnace) process, all pieces go to a deburring station, where the pieces are washed in tumbling tubs, sometimes accompanied by smooth stones. The deburring process rids the parts of extraneous particles. Parts are then inspected to determine that they meet specifications. If not, they must be reground or scrapped.

Following deburring, 40% of the products are ready for finishing and shipping. The finishing process entails coating the product with a thin film of oil. These parts are then boxed and shipped. Shipping costs are typically paid by the customer, except when an order requires expediting due to Metalworks' processing delays. Of Metalworks' freight costs, approximately 80% are incurred due to expediting shipments.

The remaining products (60%) require secondary processing. The most common secondary process is machining. Machining involves changing the piece in some way, such as cutting a groove, boring a hole, or cutting threads into a hole. Another secondary processing operation entails combining Metalworks' parts with parts bought from another company. Parts are again inspected to determine if the machining and/or combining operation was successful. If not, the parts must be scrapped. After secondary processing, 75% of the pieces are returned to the deburring process, and are then finished and shipped.

The remainder of the pieces require a second heat-treating process, which is similar to the sintering process and uses the same furnaces. After this step they are ready for a second deburring operation, finishing and shipping.

Quality is a high priority at Metalworks. Some parts require 100% inspection, while others are inspected on a random basis. Scrap rates are as high as 10–15% on some parts, with the average scrap rate at about 6–7%. Scrap can be caused by a number of factors throughout the process. The inspection process is strongest after the pressing operation, prior to sintering. If a bad part passes through the sintering operation, additional processing is required to regrind the materials. Some materials cannot be reground after sintering and must be scrapped.

Accounting System   At the beginning of each job, a lot number is assigned to the batch of parts to be manufactured. On a daily basis, each production employee records how much time was worked by lot number and process, and also the quantity of parts processed. This daily record is entered into the computer system and forms the basis for hours worked by lot and process. Product costs are calculated by lot number, with each lot directly charged for labour, materials, any outside services, and sales commissions. Labour is charged at actual hours worded times a standard labour rate of either $7.50/hour or $8.50/hour (actual wage rates vary from $5 to $11/hour). Direct materials are charged according to the formula for the part. Outside services are charged at actual costs, and commissions equal 2.5% of the selling price for most products. Three categories of overhead are recognized: machining overhead, shipping and inspection overhead, and general and administrative overhead. These costs are allocated to each product as a percentage of various labour categories, according to the following formulas:

- machining overhead: 200% of machining labour
- shipping and inspection overhead: 50% of shipping and inspection labour
- general and administrative overhead: 350% of direct labour

Exhibit 2 explains the relationships between the income statement and the product costing system. Exhibit 3 contains an example of a product cost report at Metalworks.

Required

1. How can ABC concepts be used to better understand product costs at Metalworks? Discuss the potential ABC applications.
2. Develop a process map to illustrate the activities at Metalworks.

EXHIBIT 1
Income Statement
December 31, 1999

			%
Sales		$5,900,000	100.0
Labour			
Direct Labour	$255,000		4.3
Machining Labour	220,000		3.7
Pasting Labour	52,000		0.9
Heat Treat Labour	95,000		1.6
Eng'r. Tooling	96,000		1.6
Shipping	59,000		1.0
Quality Control	50,000		0.9
Total Labour		827,000	14.0
Direct Other			
Powdered Metals		1,960,000	33.2
Outside Processes		675,900	11.5
Overhead			
Supervisory Labour	167,200		2.8
Waste Management	136,500		2.3
Commissions	225,000		3.8
Utilities	360,000		6.1
Tooling Replacement	155,000		2.6
Supplies	114,000		1.9
Scheduling	22,000		0.4
Maintenance	168,000		2.8
Eng'r, Tooling, Selling	67,500		1.1
Insurance	140,500		2.4
Rent	103,500		1.8
Freight	100,000		1.7
Other	62,000		1.1
Total Overhead		1,821,200	30.8
General & Administrative			
G&A	550,000		9.3
Interest	65,000		1.1
Depreciation	185,000		3.2
Total G&A		800.000	13.6
Total Costs		6,084,100	103.1
Net Income		($ 184,100)	(3.1)

EXHIBIT 2
Relationship of Income Statement Expenses and Product Costs

Labour	Actual hours from timecards charged to lots at $8.50/hour for machining and inspection, $7.50 for all other processes.
Powdered Metals	Charged according to the blend formula for each lot
Outside Processes	Service bought from other companies—charged direct
Supervisory Labour	Overhead
Waste Management	Overhead
Commissions	2.5% of sales price
Utilities	Overhead
Tooling Replacement	3% of sales price charged direct to product
Supplies	Overhead
Scheduling	Overhead
Maintenance	Overhead
Eng'r, Tooling, Selling	Overhead
Insurance	Overhead
Rent	Overhead
Freight	Overhead (80% are expediting costs)
Other	Overhead
General & Administrative	Overhead

EXHIBIT 3
Product Costs—Product 400

		March 98 Lot 55	Sept. 98 Lot 61	April 99 Lot 65	April 99 Lot 68
	# pressed	49,000	41,064	17,000	35,550
Labour[a]					
Blend Powder (D)	hours × $7.50	.0020	.0021	.0014	.0026
Setup (D)	hours × $7.50	.0022	.0025	.0042	.0019
Press Adjustment (D)	hours × $7.50	.0025	.0022	.0043	.0025
Compact (D)	hours × $7.50	.0125	.0099	.0156	.0100
Sintering (D)	hours × $7.50	.0072	.0031	.0093	.0058
Duburr/Finish (S&I)	hours × $7.50	.0046	.0042	.0043	.0049
In-Process Inspection (S&I)	hours × $8.50	.0122	.0070	.0103	.0064
Final Inspection (S&I)	hours × $8.50	.0015	.0003	.0005	.0028
100% Inspection (S&I)	hours × $7.50	.0138	.0230	.0360	.0209
Repair & Maint. (M)	hours × $7.50	.0047	.0067	.0057	.0122
Boxing Parts (S&I)	hours × $7.50	.0029	.0051	.0030	.0029
1st Drilling (M)	hours × $7.50	.0298	.0357	.0342	.0328
Secondary Adj. (M)	hours × $7.50	.0076	.0073	.0108	.0102
First Piece Inspection (S&I)	hours × $7.50	.0000	.0000	.0000	.0000
Machining (M)	hours × $8.50	.0515	.0412	.0329	.0403
2nd Deburr (S&I)	hours × $7.50	.0033	.0006	.0023	.0020
Secondary Setup (M)	hours × $7.50	.0020	.0032	.0016	.0015
Counterbore (M)	hours × $7.50	.0142	.0126	.0140	.0141
Total Costs					
Total Direct Labour		.0264	.0198	.0348	.0228
Total Machining Labour		.1098	.1067	.0992	.1111
Total Ship & Inspect Labour		.0383	.0402	.0564	.0399
Materials	formula price	.1263	.1263	.1263	.1263
Other	outside processes	.0400	.0400	.0400	.0400
Tool Replacement	3% of price	.0201	.0205	.0205	.0205
G&A O/H	350% of DL	.0924	.0693	.1218	.0798
Machining O/H	Mach. Labour × 2.0	.2196	.2134	.1984	.2222
Ship & Inspect O/H	S&I labour × .5	.0192	.0201	.0282	.0200
Commissions	2.5% of price	.0168	.0171	.0171	.0171
Total Cost		.7089	.6734	.7427	.6997
Price per unit		.6714	.6822	.6822	.6822
Profit/Loss per unit		−.0375	.0088	−.0605	−.0175
% Profit/Loss		(5.59%)	1.30%	(8.85)%	(2.55)%

[a]D = direct labour
S&I = ship & inspect labour
M = machining labour

C8–22 Cost Flows under Activity-Based Costing; Partial T-Accounts

(Appendix 8A) Munoz Company installed an activity-based costing system several years ago. The company manufactures four products in a single facility and has identified five major activity centres, as listed below. Direct materials and direct labour costs for 2000, the current year, have been added to Work in Process and to the products. These costs are shown by entries (a) and (b) in the Work in Process account. However, no entries have been made for either actual or applied manufacturing overhead cost.

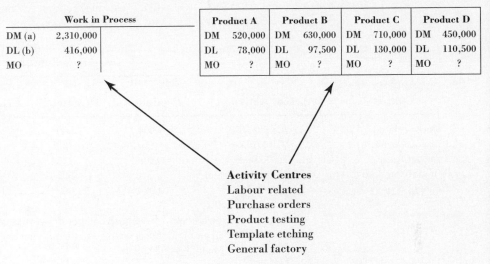

Work in Process			Product A		Product B		Product C		Product D	
DM (a)	2,310,000		DM	520,000	DM	630,000	DM	710,000	DM	450,000
DL (b)	416,000		DL	78,000	DL	97,500	DL	130,000	DL	110,500
MO	?		MO	?	MO	?	MO	?	MO	?

Activity Centres
Labour related
Purchase orders
Product testing
Template etching
General factory

At the beginning of the year, the company made the following estimates of cost and activity in the five activity centres for the purpose of computing predetermined overhead rates:

Activity Centre	Cost Driver	Estimated Overhead Cost—2000	Expected Activity
Labour related	Direct labour-hours	$210,000	35,000 direct labour-hours
Purchase orders	Number of orders	72,000	900 orders
Product testing	Number of tests	168,000	1,400 tests
Template etching	Number of templates	315,000	10,500 templates
General factory	Machine-hours	840,000	70,000 machine-hours

Required

1. Compute the predetermined overhead rate for each activity centre for 2000.
2. During 2000, actual manufacturing overhead cost and actual activity were recorded in the various activity centres as follows:

Activity Centre	Actual Overhead Cost—2000	Actual Activity
Labour related	$ 205,000	32,000 direct labour-hours
Purchase orders	74,000	950 orders
Product testing	160,000	1,300 tests
Template etching	338,000	11,500 templates
General factory	825,000	68,000 machine-hours
Total overhead cost	$1,602,000	

Prepare a journal entry to record the incurrence of actual manufacturing overhead cost for the year (credit Accounts Payable). Label this as entry (c). Prepare T-accounts for Manufacturing Overhead and for each of the activity centres, and post entry (c) to these accounts.

3. Refer to the "actual activity" data in (2) above.
   a. Determine the amount of overhead cost applied to production for the year. In determining this amount, remember that you have five predetermined overhead rates, rather than just one.
   b. Prepare a journal entry to record the amount of applied overhead cost for the year. Label this as entry (d), and post the entry to the appropriate T-accounts.
   c. Determine the amount of underapplied or overapplied manufacturing overhead cost for 2000 for each activity centre and for Manufacturing Overhead.
4. Refer again to the "actual activity" data in (2) above. Assume that these activities were traceable to the company's four products as follows:

Activity Centre	Actual Activity	Events or Transactions Relating to Products			
		Product A	Product B	Product C	Product D
Labour related	32,000 DLH	6,000	7,500	10,000	8,500
Purchase orders	950 orders	150	300	100	400
Product testing	1,300 tests	400	175	225	500
Template etching	11,500 templates	—	4,500	—	7,000
General factory	68,000 MH	10,000	20,000	17,000	21,000

a. Determine the amount of overhead cost for the year chargeable to each product.
b. Does the total amount of cost charged to the products in (a) above "tie in" to the T-accounts in any way? Explain.

Group Exercises

GE8–22 Traditional Product Cost Systems Are Out-of-Date   Many firms realize that there are fundamental problems with the methods they use to cost their products or services. But should they change from traditional product costing methods to activity-based costing (ABC) methods? It is important first of all to understand the limitations of existing product costing systems in today's competitive environment typified by a diverse product line populated by many low-volume complex products.

Required
1. What is wrong with traditional product costing systems that they no longer meet the needs of today's managers?
2. How does the cost structure of most manufacturing firms today differ from their cost structure of 20 years ago?
3. What caused this change in cost structure?
4. Why can't traditional product costing systems account for costs of product diversity? Volume diversity? Product complexity?

GE8–23 We're Doing Well but We Don't Know Why   "Many U.S. companies don't know where they are making money and where they are losing (money)," says Robert S. Kaplan, a Harvard University accounting professor. Kaplan was aiming his criticism directly at traditional cost accounting systems and, in particular, at the methods used to allocate overhead costs among the many different products produced by job shops, batch manufacturers, and assemblers. Source: Ford S. Worthy, "Accounting Bores You? Wake Up," *Fortune*, October 12, 1987, pp. 43, 44, 48–50.

Part I: Standard Products   Firms that sell a complete line of products usually have their bread-and-butter products. These high-volume standard or commodity products, while few in number (e.g., 20%–25% of the product line), may account for as much as 70%–80% of the business or sales volume of their firms.

Required

1. Looking at firms that manufacture a wide range of products, high-volume standard products tend to get systematically overcosted under conventional product costing systems. Describe these products along the following dimensions: competitive environment, how prices are set, stage of life cycle, market acceptance, profit margins (price less cost), general age of technology used to produce these products, degree of labour intensity in the manufacturing process, complexity of product, and batch size when manufactured.
2. Assuming the allocation of manufacturing overhead is based on direct labour cost, explain how these products get overcosted.
3. Since high-volume standard products face fierce price competition, what implications does overcosting have for reported product profitability, product emphasis, market share, future allocations of resources to support the product, and potential product discontinuance?

Part II: Specialty Products   Firms that sell a complete line of products will likely have a product line dominated by a large number of low-volume specialty or custom products. While the firm may produce a large number of specialty products (e.g., 70%–80% of the product line), the cumulative sales of low-volume custom products may amount to no more than 25%–30% of sales revenues.

Required

1. Low-volume specialty or custom products tend to get systematically undercosted under conventional product costing systems. These products meet the unique needs of a particular customer and, therefore, the level of sales of any one custom product is usually relatively low when compared to the sales volume of standard products. Describe these products along the following dimensions: competitive environment, how prices are set, stage of life cycle, market acceptance, profit margins (price less cost), general age of technology used to produce these products, degree of labour intensity in the manufacturing process, complexity of product, and batch size when manufactured.
2. Assuming the allocation of manufacturing overhead is based on direct labour cost, explain how these products get undercosted.
3. As a rule, low-volume specialty products do not face the kind of direct head-to-head price competition that high-volume products confront. Instead, they compete on their unique features or performance more so than price. What implications does undercosting have for reported product profitability, product emphasis, market share, future allocations of resources to support the product, and management's perception of the future role to be played by specialty products?

GE8–24   Impact of Changing Cost Systems on Product Costs   A manufacturing company is thinking of changing its method of computing product costs for the purposes of making decisions. Under the company's conventional direct labour-based costing system, manufacturing overhead costs are applied to products on the basis of direct labour-hours. Under the proposed activity-based costing (ABC) system, both manufacturing and nonmanufacturing overhead costs are applied to products using a variety of allocation bases at the unit, batch, and product levels.

Required

For each of the following products, indicate the impact on the product's apparent cost from switching from a conventional direct labour-based costing system to an activity-based costing system.

1. A low-volume product that is produced in small batches.
2. A high-volume product that is produced in large batches with automated equipment and that requires very few direct labour hours per unit.
3. A high-volume product that requires little machine work but a lot of direct labour.

GE8–25   Dividing Up the Bill   You and your friends go to a restaurant as a group. At the end of the meal, the issue arises of how the bill for the group should be shared. One alternative is to figure out the cost of what each individual consumed and divide up the bill accordingly. Another alternative is to split the bill equally among the individuals.

Required

Which system for dividing the bill is more equitable? Which system is easier to use? How does this issue relate to the material covered in this chapter?

IE8–26   Case Studies   ABC Technologies, a consulting and software company specializing in activity-based costing and activity-based management, maintains a library of case studies written by its clients on its web site www.abctech.com. You will be asked to register to access the library, but ABC Technologies promises not to sell or give the registration information to any other person or organization. After entering the library, access the by-industry index.

Required
1. In the Health Care industry category, Issue 30 is titled "Blue Cross and Blue Shield." Access and read this case study. What specific change in processing ASO disability claims resulted from implementation of activity-based costing? Why did the activity-based costing (ABC) study trigger this change?
2. In the Construction industry category, Issue 14 is titled "ABC in the Construction Industry." Access and read this case study. Explain how a conventional costing system in the construction industry can lead to a "death spiral" and how a properly implemented ABC system eliminates this problem.
3. In the Food & Grocery industry category, Issue 5 is titled "Oregon Freeze Dry." Explain how the company's old cost system misled managers into taking inappropriate actions.

Chapter Nine
Profit Planning

Business Focus

Budgets are perhaps even more important in small service organizations than they are in large manufacturing companies. The accounting firm of Carter, Young, Wolf and Dalhauser is typical of many small firms that must keep a constant eye on their cash flows. Because of high fixed costs, small changes in revenues or a client that is delinquent in paying bills can have potentially disastrous effects on the firm's cash flows.

Lucy Carter, the managing partner of the firm, uses a for-mal budget for keeping cash flow on an even keel. She says, "I don't know how small firms can survive without a budget in this business climate." The formal budget is based on estimated client billings (i.e., revenues) for the coming year. The annual budget is broken down into months, and each month the budget is compared to the actual financial results of the month. If the actuals fall short of the budget, adjustments may be necessary. For example, because of shortfalls in billings in one year, the firm

reduced its staff by three staff accountants and added a part-time staff accountant. Because of the critical nature of client billings, Carter's staff prepares daily reports on billings that indicate how well actual billings compare to the budgeted billings on a month-to-date basis.

Source: Gene R. Barrett, "How Small CPA Firms Manage Their Cash," Journal of Accountancy, *August 1993, pp. 56–59.*

Learning Objectives

After studying Chapter 9, you should be able to:

1 Understand why organizations budget and the processes they use to create budgets.

2 Prepare a sales budget, including a schedule of expected cash receipts.

3 Prepare a production budget.

4 Prepare a direct materials budget, including a schedule of expected cash disbursements for purchases of materials.

5 Prepare a direct labour budget.

6 Prepare a manufacturing overhead budget.

7 Prepare an ending finished goods inventory budget.

8 Prepare a selling and administrative expense budget.

9 Prepare a cash budget.

10 Prepare a budgeted income statement and a budgeted balance sheet.

11 (Appendix 9A) Compute the optimum inventory level and order size.

Strategic planning, defined in Chapter 2, is the term applied to the selection of policies, practices and procedures by management in an attempt to achieve the goals set for the organization. New businesses typically formalize their strategic planning in the form of a business plan. A business plan consists of information about the company's basic product or service and about the steps to be taken to reach its potential market. The plan includes information about production methods, the competition, the management team, and the details on how the business will be financed.

The Business Plan

The business plan is a key document for the internal management of the organization. It provides the basis for evaluation and control of the enterprise. It is also valuable for external use in attracting resources from potential creditors and investors. The answers to many of the questions raised by providers of funds can be found in the business plan.

Exhibit 9–1[1] shows a flowchart of the steps taken in a typical business plan. The 16-week time span is for illustrative purposes only. The actual length of the business plan varies with the nature and complexity of the venture and could span anywhere from a few weeks to several months. Note from the flowchart that it is essential that certain steps be completed before others are begun. It makes no sense, for example, to talk about forecasting sales (step 5) until a product or service has been picked (step 3) and the market has been researched (step 4). Continuing businesses formalize part of the financial aspects of their strategy in their annual budget.

Profit planning The steps taken by business organizations to achieve certain desired levels of profits.

In the remainder of this chapter we turn our attention to the financial aspects of the business plan and to the steps taken by business organizations to achieve certain desired levels of profits—a process that is generally called **profit planning**, step 13 in the sequence presented in Exhibit 9–1. Keep in mind as you work your way through the chapter that the process you see occurs after numerous steps involving strategy selection, market research, site and production design and personnel planning along with various legal and systems decisions. Only then can details of the profit plan be constructed.

In our study, we shall see that profit planning is accomplished through the preparation of a number of budgets, which, when brought together, form an integrated part of a business plan known as the *master budget*. We shall find that the data going into the preparation of the master budget focus heavily on the future, rather than on the past.

1. Adapted from Nicholas C. Siropolis, *Small Business Management: A Guide to Entrepreneurship*, 2nd ed. (Boston: Houghton Mifflin, 1982), pp. 138–41.

Exhibit 9-1 Flowchart of the Steps in Developing a Business Plan

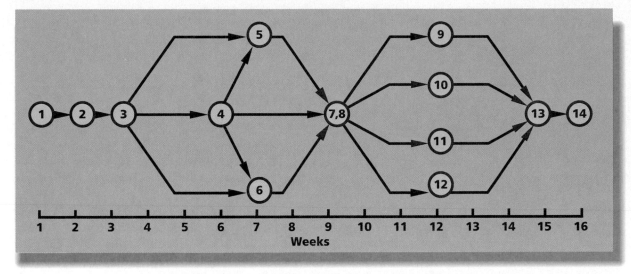

Key:

1. Decide to go into business.
2. Analyze yourself.
3. Pick product or service.
4. Research market.
5. Forecast sales revenues.
6. Pick site.
7. Develop production plan.

8. Develop marketing plan.
9. Develop personnel plan.
10. Decide whether to incorporate.
11. Explain need for records.
12. Develop insurance plan.
13. Develop financial plan.
14. Write summary overview.

The Basic Framework of Budgeting

Objective 1

Understand why organizations budget and the processes they use to create budgets.

Budget A detailed plan for the acquisition and use of financial and other resources over a specified time period.

Master budget A summary of a company's plans in which specific targets are set for sales, production, distribution, and financing activities and that generally culminates in a cash budget, budgeted income statement, and budgeted balance sheet.

Definition of Budgeting

A **budget** is a detailed plan for the acquisition and use of financial and other resources over a specified time period. It represents a plan for the future expressed in formal quantitative terms. The act of preparing a budget is called *budgeting*. The use of budgets to control a firm's activities is known as *budgetary control*.

The **master budget** is a summary of a company's plans that sets specific targets for sales, production, distribution, and financing activities. It generally culminates in a cash budget, a budgeted income statement, and a budgeted balance sheet. In short, it represents a comprehensive expression of management's plans for the future and how these plans are to be accomplished.

Personal Budgets

Nearly everyone budgets to some extent, even though many of the people who use budgets do not recognize what they are doing as budgeting. For example, most people make estimates of their income and plan expenditures for food, clothing, housing, and so on. As a result of this planning, people restrict their spending to some predetermined, allowable amount. While they may not be conscious of the fact, these people clearly go through a budgeting process. Income is estimated, expenditures are planned, and spending is restricted in accordance with the plan. Individuals also use budgets to forecast their future financial condition for purposes such as purchasing a home, financing college education, or setting aside funds for retirement. These budgets may exist only in the mind of the individual, but they are budgets nevertheless.

The budgets of a business firm serve much the same functions as the budgets prepared informally by individuals. Business budgets tend to be more detailed and to involve more work, but they are similar to the budgets prepared by individuals in most other respects. Like personal budgets, they assist in planning and controlling expenditures; they also assist in predicting operating results and financial condition in future periods.

Difference between Planning and Control

Planning Developing objectives and preparing budgets to achieve these objectives.

Control Those steps taken by management that attempt to increase the likelihood that the objectives set down at the planning stage are attained to ensure that all parts of the organization function in a manner consistent with organizational policies.

The terms *planning* and *control* are often confused, and occasionally these terms are used in such a way as to suggest that they mean the same thing. Actually, planning and control are two quite distinct concepts. **Planning** involves developing objectives and preparing various budgets to achieve these objectives. **Control** involves the steps taken by management to increase the likelihood that the objectives set down at the planning stage are attained, and to ensure that all parts of the organization function in a manner consistent with organizational policies. To be completely effective, a good budgeting system must provide for *both* planning and control. Good planning without effective control is time wasted. On the other hand, unless plans are laid down in advance, there are no objectives toward which control can be directed.

Advantages of Budgeting

There is an old saying to the effect that "a man is usually down on what he isn't up on." Managers who have never tried budgeting are usually quick to state that budgeting is a waste of time. These managers may argue that even though budgeting may work well in *some* situations, it would never work well in their companies because operations are too complex or because there are too many uncertainties. In reality, however, managers who argue this way usually will be deeply involved in planning (albeit on an informal basis). These managers will have clearly defined thoughts about what they want to accomplish and when they want it accomplished. The difficulty is that unless they have some way of communicating their thoughts and plans to others, the only way their companies will ever attain the desired objectives will be through accident. In short, even though companies may attain a certain degree of success without budgets, they never attain the heights that could have been reached with a coordinated system of budgets.

Companies realize many benefits from a budgeting program. Among these benefits are the following:

1. Budgets provide a means of *communicating* management's plans throughout the organization.
2. Budgets force managers to *think about* and plan for the future. In the absence of the necessity to prepare a budget, too many managers would spend all of their time dealing with daily emergencies.
3. The budgeting process provides a means of *allocating resources* to those parts of the organization where they can be used most effectively.
4. The budgeting process can uncover potential *bottlenecks* before they occur.
5. Budgets *coordinate* the activities of the entire organization by *integrating* the plans of the various parts. Budgeting helps to ensure that everyone in the organization is pulling in the same direction.
6. Budgets define goals and objectives that can serve as *benchmarks* for evaluating subsequent performance.

In the past, some managers have avoided budgeting because of the time and effort involved in the budgeting process. It can be argued that budgeting is actually "free" in that the manager's time and effort are more than offset by greater profits. Moreover, with the advent of computer spreadsheet programs, *any* company—large or small—can implement and maintain a budgeting program at minimal cost. Budgeting lends itself well to readily available spreadsheet application programs.

Focus on Current Practice

Consider the following situation encountered by one of the authors at a mortgage banking firm: For years, the company operated with virtually no system of budgets whatever. Management contended that budgeting wasn't well suited to the firm's type of operation. Moreover, management pointed out that the firm was already profitable. Indeed, outwardly the company gave every appearance of being a well-managed, smoothly operating organization. A careful look within, however, disclosed that day-to-day operations were far from smooth, and often approached chaos. The average day was nothing more than an exercise in putting out one brush fire after another. The Cash account was always at crisis levels. At the end of a day, no one ever knew whether enough cash would be available the next day to cover required loan closings. Departments were uncoordinated, and it was not uncommon to find that one department was pursuing a course that conflicted with the course pursued by another department. Employee mo-

rale was low, and turnover was high. Employees complained bitterly that when a job was well done, nobody ever knew about it.

The company was bought out by a new group of shareholders who required that an integrated budgeting system be established to control operations. Within one year's time, significant changes were evident. Brush fires were rare. Careful planning virtually eliminated the problems that had been experienced with cash, and departmental efforts were coordinated and directed toward predetermined overall company goals. Although the employees were wary of the new budgeting program initially, they became "converted" when they saw the positive effects that it brought about. The more efficient operations caused profits to jump dramatically. Communication increased throughout the organization. When a job was well done, everybody knew about it. As one employee stated, "For the first time, we know what the company expects of us." ■

Responsibility Accounting

> **Responsibility accounting** A system of accountability in which managers are held responsible for those items of revenue and cost—and only those items—over which the manager can exert significant control. The managers are held responsible for differences between budgeted and actual results.

An organization of accounts along with a management conception employing this organization or classification scheme is introduced in the upcoming discussions in this chapter and those that follow under the term *responsibility accounting*. Instead of organizing accounts by what is incurred or what activity was performed, accounts are grouped by the responsibility exercised by the manager.

The basic idea behind **responsibility accounting** is that a manager should be held responsible for those items—and *only* those items—that the manager can actually control to a significant extent. Each line item (i.e., revenue or cost) in the budget is made the responsibility of a manager, and that manager is held responsible for subsequent deviations between budgeted goals and actual results. In effect, responsibility accounting *personalizes* accounting information by looking at costs from a *personal control* standpoint. This concept is central to any effective profit planning and control system. Someone must be held responsible for each cost or else no one will be responsible, and the cost will inevitably grow out of control.

Being held responsible for costs does not mean that the manager is penalized if the actual results do not measure up to the budgeted goals. However, the manager should take the initiative to correct any unfavourable discrepancies, should understand the source of significant favourable or unfavourable discrepancies, and should be prepared to explain the reasons for discrepancies to higher management. The point of an effective responsibility system is to make sure that nothing "falls through the cracks," that the organization reacts quickly and appropriately to deviations from its plans, and that the organization learns from the feedback it gets by comparing budgeted goals to actual results. The point is *not* to penalize individuals for missing targets.

We will look at responsibility accounting in more detail in the upcoming chapters. For the moment, we can summarize the overall idea by noting that it rests on three basic premises. The first premise is that costs can be organized in terms of levels of management responsibility. The second premise is that the costs charged to a particular level are controllable at that level by its managers. And the third premise is that effective budget data can be generated as a basis for evaluating actual performance. This chapter on profit planning is concerned with the third of these premises in that the purpose of the chapter is to show the steps involved in budget preparation.

Choosing a Budget Period

Operating budgets are ordinarily set to cover a one-year period. The one-year period should correspond to the company's fiscal year so that the budget figures can be compared with the actual results. Many companies divide their budget year into four quarters. The first quarter is then subdivided into months, and monthly budget figures are established. These near-term figures can often be established with considerable accuracy. The last three quarters are carried in the budget at quarterly totals only. As the year progresses, the figures for the second quarter are broken down into monthly amounts, then the third-quarter figures are broken down, and so forth. This approach has the advantage of requiring periodic review and reappraisal of budget data throughout the year.

Continuous or **perpetual budget**   A 12-month budget that rolls forward one month as the current month is completed.

Continuous or *perpetual budgets* are used by a significant number of organizations. A **continuous** or **perpetual budget** is a 12-month budget that rolls forward one month (or quarter) as the current month (or quarter) is completed. In other words, one month (or quarter) is added to the end of the budget as each month (or quarter) comes to a close. This approach keeps managers focused on the future at least one year ahead. Advocates of continuous budgets argue that with this approach there is less danger that managers will become too focused on short-term results as the year progresses.

In this chapter, we will focus on one-year operating budgets. However, using basically the same techniques, operating budgets can be prepared for periods that extend over many years. It may be difficult to accurately forecast sales and required data much beyond a year, but even rough estimates can be invaluable in uncovering potential problems and opportunities that would otherwise be overlooked.

The Self-Imposed Budget

The success of a budget program will be determined in large part by the way in which the budget is developed. The most successful budget programs involve managers with cost control responsibilities in preparing their own budget estimates—rather than having a budget imposed from above. This approach to preparing budget data is particularly important if the budget is to be used to control and evaluate a manager's activities. If a budget is imposed on a manager from above, it will probably generate resentment and ill will rather than cooperation and increased productivity.

Self-imposed budget   A method of preparing budgets in which managers prepare their own budgets. These budgets are then reviewed by the manager's supervisor, and any issues are resolved by mutual agreement.

Participative budget   Same as *self-imposed budget*.

This budgeting approach in which managers prepare their own budget estimates—called a *self-imposed budget*—is generally considered to be the most effective method of budget preparation. A **self-imposed budget** or **participative budget** is a budget that is prepared with the full cooperation and participation of managers at all levels. Exhibit 9–2 illustrates this approach to budget preparation.

A number of advantages are commonly cited for such self-imposed budgets:

1. Individuals at all levels of the organization are recognized as members of the team whose views and judgments are valued by top management.
2. The person in direct contact with an activity is in the best position to make budget estimates. Therefore, budget estimates prepared by such persons tend to be more accurate and reliable.
3. People are more likely to work at fulfilling a budget that they have participated in setting than they are to work at fulfilling a budget that is imposed from above.

Exhibit 9–2   The
Initial Flow of Budget Data
in a Participative
Budgeting System

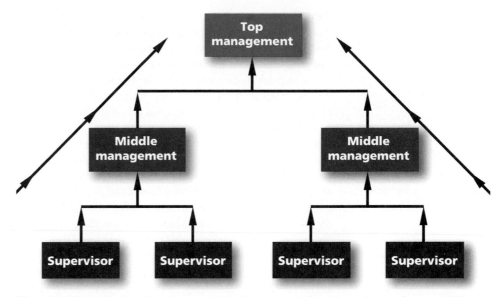

The initial flow of budget data in a participative system is from lower levels of responsibility to higher levels of responsibility. Each person with responsibility for cost control will prepare his or her own budget estimates and submit them to the next higher level of management. These estimates are reviewed and consolidated as they move upward in the organization.

4. A self-imposed budget contains its own unique system of control in that if people are not able to meet budget specifications, they have only themselves to blame. On the other hand, if a budget is imposed from above, they can always say that the budget was unreasonable or unrealistic to start with, and therefore was impossible to meet.

Once self-imposed budgets are prepared, are they subject to any kind of review? The answer is yes. Budget estimates prepared by lower-level managers cannot necessarily be accepted without question by higher levels of management. If no system of checks and balances is present, self-imposed budgets may be too loose and allow too much "budgetary slack." The result will be inefficiency and waste. Therefore, before budgets are accepted, they must be carefully reviewed by immediate superiors. If changes from the original budget seem desirable, the items in question are discussed and modified as necessary by mutual consent.

In essence, all levels of an organization should work together to produce the budget. Since top management is generally unfamiliar with detailed, day-to-day operations, it should rely on subordinates to provide detailed budget information. On the other hand, top management has a perspective on the company as a whole that is vital in making broad policy decisions in budget preparation. Each level of responsibility in an organization should contribute in the way that it best can in a *cooperative* effort to develop an integrated budget document.

To be successful, a self-imposed approach to setting budgets requires that all managers understand and agree with the organization's strategy. Otherwise, the budgets proposed by the lower-level managers will lack coherent direction. Differences in information can mean that different levels of managers do not operate consistently because they are working with different information. Certainly the individual managers can be expected to operate in a manner that optimizes their own interests, financial or otherwise.

An interesting, but unresolved, problem is how to design incentives to encourage subordinates to communicate accurate budget detail to top management. Subordinates can often control their own performance results by the nature of the budget information they feed through the system. This can be a problem for profit enterprises, not-for-profit enterprises, and government entities alike. Budgets can be used to set targets or quotas that in turn influence how top management allocates bonuses to managers and additional resources to the various units within the enterprise. Fundamentally, to provide incentives for a reward scheme, a designer needs to know what the alternative rewards will be from truthful forecasting rather than biased forecasting.[2] Unfortunately these alternatives cannot be known beforehand, which is when the incentive scheme has to be set. Thus, to be effective, organizations must rely on a cooperative atmosphere among subordinates, not a competitive or self-serving one, and on the ability of top management to assess the reasonableness of forecasts obtained from subordinates.

We have described an ideal budgetary process that involves self-imposed budgets prepared by the managers who are directly responsible for revenues and costs. Most companies deviate from this ideal. Typically, top managers initiate the budget process by issuing broad guidelines in terms of overall target profits or sales. Lower-level managers are directed to prepare budgets that meet those targets. The difficulty is that the targets set by top managers may be unrealistically high or may allow too much slack. If the targets are too high and employees know they are unrealistic, motivation will suffer. If the targets allow too much slack, waste will occur. And unfortunately top managers are often not in a position to know whether the targets they have set are appropriate. Admittedly, however, in a pure self-imposed budgeting system, lower-level managers may be tempted to build into their budgets a great deal of budgetary slack and there may be a lack of direction. Nevertheless, because of the motivational advantages of self-imposed budgets, top managers should be cautious about setting inflexible targets or otherwise imposing limits on the budgeting process.

The Matter of Human Relations

Whether or not a budget program is accepted by lower management personnel will be reflective of (1) the degree to which top management accepts the budget program as a vital part of the company's activities, and (2) the way in which top management uses budgeted data.

If a budget program is to be successful, it must have the complete acceptance and support of the persons who occupy key management positions. If lower or middle management personnel sense that top management is lukewarm about budgeting, or if they sense that top management simply tolerates budgeting as a necessary evil, then their own attitudes will reflect a similar lack of enthusiasm. Budgeting is hard work, and if top management is not enthusiastic about and committed to the budget program, then it is unlikely that anyone else in the organization will be either.

In administering the budget program, it is particularly important that top management not use the budget as a club to pressure employees or as a way to find someone to blame for a particular problem. This type of negative emphasis will simply breed hostility, tension, and mistrust rather than greater cooperation and productivity. Unfortunately, research suggests that the budget is often used as a pressure device and that great emphasis is placed on "meeting the budget" under all circumstances.[3]

Rather than being used as a pressure device, the budget should be used as a positive instrument to assist in establishing goals, in measuring operating results, and in isolating areas that are in need of extra effort or attention. Any misgivings that employees have about a budget program can be overcome by meaningful involvement at all

---

2. Anthony A. Atkinson, "Truth-Inducing Schemes in Budgeting and Resource Allocation," *Cost and Management* (May–June, 1985), pp. 38–42. For a broader study of this issue see Alan S. Dunk and Hossein Nouri, "Antecedents of Budgetary Slack: A Literature Review and Synthesis," *Journal of Accounting Literature* (1998), pp. 72–96.
3. Paul J. Carruth, Thurrell O. McClendon, and Milton R. Ballard, "What Supervisors Don't Like about Budget Evaluations," *Management Accounting* 64, no. 8 (February 1983), p. 42.

levels and by proper use of the program over a period of time. Administration of a budget program requires a great deal of insight and sensitivity on the part of management. The ultimate object must be to develop the realization that the budget is designed to be a positive aid in achieving both individual and company goals.

Management must keep clearly in mind that the human dimension in budgeting is of key importance. It is easy for the manager to become preoccupied with the technical aspects of the budget program to the exclusion of the human aspects. Indeed, the use of budget data in a rigid and inflexible manner is the greatest single complaint of persons whose performance is being evaluated through the budget process.[4] Management should remember that the purposes of the budget are to motivate employees and to coordinate efforts. Preoccupation with the dollars and cents in the budget, or being rigid and inflexible in budget administration, can only lead to frustration of these purposes.

Focus on Current Practice

In establishing a budget, how challenging should budget targets be? In practice, companies typically set their budgets either at a "stretch" level or a "highly achievable" level. A stretch-level budget is one that has only a small chance of being met and in fact may be met less than half the time by even the most capable managers. A highly achievable budget is one that is challenging, but which can be met through hard work.

Research shows that managers prefer highly achievable budgets.[5] Such budgets are generally coupled with bonuses that are given when budget targets are met, along with added bonuses when these targets are exceeded. Highly achievable budgets are believed to build a manager's confidence and to generate greater commitment to the budget program. ∎

A response to the competitive pressures of modern organizations is to organize and manage according to a strategy of innovation, service, quality, speed, and knowledge sharing. Using this strategy business managers need to be flexible and responsive to the demands of the marketplace. Some companies are suggesting that budgets combined with too rigid an application of responsibility accounting can create a rigidity and a culture that is inappropriate for the new environment. Observers of the business community suggest some successful banks, retailers, contractors, and manufacturers have altered their budget practices to enable a more responsive managerial culture while retaining an overall strategic direction and financial responsibility.[6]

The Budget Committee

Budget committee A group of key management persons who are responsible for overall policy matters relating to the budget program and for coordinating the preparation of the budget.

A standing **budget committee** will usually be responsible for overall policy matters relating to the budget program and for coordinating the preparation of the budget itself. This committee generally consists of the president; vice presidents in charge of various functions such as sales, production, and purchasing; and the controller. Difficulties and disputes between segments of the organization in matters relating to the budget are resolved by the budget committee. In addition, the budget committee approves the final budget and receives periodic reports on the progress of the company in attaining budgeted goals.

---

4. Carruth et al., "What Supervisors Don't Like . . . ," p. 91.
5. See Kenneth A. Merchant, *Rewarding Results: Motivating Profit Center Managers* (Boston, MA: Harvard Business School Press, 1989). For further discussion of budget targets, see Kenneth A. Merchant, "How Challenging Should Profit Budget Targets Be?" *Management Accounting* 72, no. 5 (November 1990), pp. 46–48.
6. Jeremy Hope and Robin Fraser, "Beyond Budgeting . . . Breaking through the Barrier to 'the Third Wave'," *Management Accounting UK* (December 1997 reprinted 1998) by the International Federation of Accountants at http://www.IFAC.org/standards and guidence/fmac/articlesofmerit98/

Disputes can (and do) erupt over budget matters. Because budgets allocate resources, the budgeting process to a large extent determines which departments get more resources and which get relatively less. Also, the budget sets the benchmarks by which managers and their departments will be at least partially evaluated. Therefore, it should not be surprising that managers take the budgeting process very seriously and invest considerable energy and even emotion in ensuring that their interests, and those of their departments, are protected. Because of this, the budgeting process can easily degenerate into a dispute in which the ultimate goal of working together toward common goals is forgotten.

Running a successful budgeting program that avoids such disputes requires considerable interpersonal skills in addition to purely technical skills. But even the best interpersonal skills will fail if, as discussed earlier, top management uses the budget process inappropriately as a club or as a way to find blame.

Focus on Current Practice

Budgeting is often an intensely political process in which managers jockey for resources and relaxed goals for the upcoming year. One group of consultants describes the process in this way: Annual budgets "have a particular urgency in that they provide the standard and most public framework against which managers are assessed and judged. It is, therefore, not surprising that budget-setting is taken seriously . . . Often budgets are a means for managers getting what they want. A relaxed budget will secure a relatively easy twelve months, a tight one means that their names will constantly be coming up in the monthly management review meeting. Far better to shift the burden of cost control and financial discipline to someone else. Budgeting is an intensely political exercise conducted with all the sharper managerial skills not taught at business school, such as lobbying and flattering superiors, forced haste, regretted delay, hidden truth, half-truths, and lies."[7] ■

The Master Budget Interrelationships

The master budget consists of a number of separate but interdependent budgets. Exhibit 9–3 provides an overview of the various parts of the master budget and how they are related.

Sales budget A detailed schedule showing the expected sales for coming periods; these sales are typically expressed in both dollars and units.

THE SALES BUDGET   A **sales budget** is a detailed schedule showing the expected sales for the budget period; typically, it is expressed in both dollars and units of product. An accurate sales budget is the key to the entire budgeting process. All of the other parts of the master budget are dependent on the sales budget in some way, as illustrated in Exhibit 9–3. Thus, if the sales budget is sloppily done, then the rest of the budgeting process is largely a waste of time.

The sales budget will help determine how many units will have to be produced. Thus, the production budget is prepared after the sales budget. The production budget in turn is used to determine the budgets for manufacturing costs including the direct materials budget, the direct labour budget, and the manufacturing overhead budget. These budgets are then combined with data from the sales budget and the selling and administrative expense budget to determine the cash budget. In essence, the sales budget triggers a chain reaction that leads to the development of the other budgets.

As shown in Exhibit 9–3, the selling and administrative expense budget is both dependent on and a determinant of the sales budget. This reciprocal relationship arises because sales will in part be determined by the funds committed for advertising and sales promotion.

---

7. Michael Morrow, ed., *Activity-Based Management* (New York: Woodhead-Faulkner, 1992), p. 91.

Exhibit 9–3
The Master Budget
Interrelationships

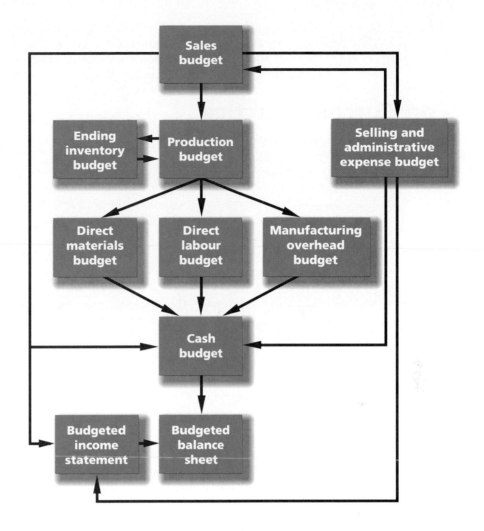

THE CASH BUDGET Once the operating budgets (sales, production, and so on) have been established, the cash budget and other financial budgets can be prepared. A **cash budget** is a detailed plan showing how cash resources will be acquired and used over some specified time period. Observe from Exhibit 9–3 that all of the operating budgets have an impact on the cash budget. In the case of the sales budget, the impact comes from the planned cash receipts to be received from sales. In the case of the other budgets, the impact comes from the planned cash expenditures within the budgets themselves.

Cash budget A detailed plan showing how cash resources will be acquired and used over some specific time period.

Sales Forecasting—A Critical Step

The sales budget is usually based on the company's *sales forecast*. Sales from prior years are commonly used as a starting point in preparing the sales forecast. In addition, the manager may examine the company's unfilled back orders, the company's pricing policy and marketing plans, trends in the industry, and general economic conditions. Sophisticated statistical tools may be used to analyze the data and to build models that are helpful in predicting key factors influencing the company's sales. The accompanying Focus on Current Practice box suggests how some companies are using computer simulations to enhance their marketing strategies and sales forecasts. We will not, however, go into the details of how sales forecasts are made.

Business intelligence is becoming an important means of gathering information for sales forecasting and cost estimation. For example, the Society of Competitive

Intelligence Professionals (SCIP) is a U.S.-based group of 6,500 members, 90 of whom are from Quebec. Canadian companies such as Bell, the Royal Bank, Pratt and Whitney and Bombardier use their services to gather information about competitors, opportunities, business practices and personnel to better budget costs and sales.[8]

Focus on Current Practice

Some companies are turning to elabourate computer simulations for help in forecasting sales. In one emerging approach, software designers create a "virtual economy" containing "virtual people." "These 'people,' constructed of bits of computer code, are endowed with ages, incomes, domiciles, genders and buying habits. [For example, some] buy a new music CD as soon as it hits the stores; others, only after a certain number of their neighbours own it or a certain number of radio stations have played it. All these assumptions are based on real data . . ." The computer model may contain millions of these virtual people who then react—sometimes in unpredictable ways—to advertising, sales promotions, new product offerings, and so on. Managers can use such a model to plan their marketing strategy and to forecast sales.[9] ■

Preparing the Master Budget

Managerial Accounting in Action

THE ISSUE

Tom Wills is the majority shareholder and chief executive officer of Hampton Freeze, Inc., a company he started in 1998. The company makes premium popsicles using only natural ingredients and featuring exotic flavours such as tangy tangerine and minty mango. The company's business is highly seasonal, with most of the sales occurring in spring and summer.

In 1999, the company's second year of operations, there was a major cash crunch in the first and second quarters that almost forced the company into bankruptcy. In spite of this cash crunch, 1999 turned out to be overall a very successful year in terms of both cash flow and net income. Partly as a result of that harrowing experience, Tom decided toward the end of 1999 to hire a professional financial manager. Tom interviewed several promising candidates for the job and settled on Larry Giano, who had considerable experience in the packaged foods industry. In the job interview, Tom questioned Larry about the steps he would take to prevent a recurrence of the 1999 cash crunch:

Tom: As I mentioned earlier, we are going to wind up 1999 with a very nice profit. What you may not know is that we had some very big financial problems this year.
Larry: Let me guess. You ran out of cash sometime in the first or second quarter.
Tom: How did you know?
Larry: Most of your sales are in the second and third quarter, right?

8. Rene Lewandowski, "Corporate Confidential," *The Financial Post Magazine* (March 1999), pp. 18–26. Also a detailed discussion of this area of business intelligence gathering is provided in *Developing Comprehensive Competitive Intelligence*, Management Accounting Guideline No. 39, The Society of Management Accountants of Canada, 1996.
9. Rita Koselka, "Playing the Game of Life," *Forbes*, April 7, 1997, pp. 100–108.

Tom: Sure, everyone wants to buy popsicles in the spring and summer, but nobody wants them when the weather turns cold.

Larry: So you don't have many sales in the first quarter?

Tom: Right.

Larry: And in the second quarter, which is the spring, you are producing like crazy to fill orders?

Tom: Sure.

Larry: Do your customers, the grocery stores, pay you the day you make your deliveries?

Tom: Are you kidding? Of course not.

Larry: So in the first quarter, you don't have many sales. In the second quarter, you are producing like crazy, which eats up cash, but you aren't paid by your customers until long after you have paid your employees and suppliers. No wonder you had a cash problem. I see this pattern all the time in food processing because of the seasonality of the business.

Tom: So what can we do about it?

Larry: The first step is to predict the magnitude of the problem before it occurs. If we can predict early in the year what the cash shortfall is going to be, we can go to the bank and arrange for credit before we really need it. Bankers tend to be leery of panicky people who show up begging for emergency loans. They are much more likely to make the loan if you look like you know what you are doing, you have done your homework, and you are in control of the situation.

Tom: How can we predict the cash shortfall?

Larry: You can put together a cash budget. While you're at it, you might as well do a master budget. You'll find it is well worth the effort.

Tom: I don't like budgets. They are too confining. My wife budgets everything at home, and I can't spend what I want.

Larry: Can I ask a personal question?

Tom: What?

Larry: Where did you get the money to start this business?

Tom: Mainly from our family's savings. I get your point. We wouldn't have had the money to start the business if my wife hadn't been forcing us to save every month.

Larry: Exactly. I suggest you use the same discipline in your business. It is even more important here because you can't expect your employees to spend your money as carefully as you would.

Tom: I'm sold. Welcome aboard. ■

With the full backing of Tom Wills, Larry Giano set out to create a master budget for the company for the year 2000. In his planning for the budgeting process, Larry drew up the following list of documents that would be a part of the master budget:

1. A sales budget, including a schedule of expected cash collections.
2. A production budget (or merchandise purchases budget for a merchandising company).
3. A direct materials budget, including a schedule of expected cash disbursements for raw materials.
4. A direct labour budget.
5. A manufacturing overhead budget.
6. An ending finished goods inventory budget.
7. A selling and administrative expense budget.

8. A cash budget.
9. A budgeted income statement.
10. A budgeted balance sheet.

Larry felt it was important to get everyone's cooperation in the budgeting process, so he asked Tom to call a companywide meeting in which the budgeting process would be explained. At the meeting there was initially some grumbling, but Tom was able to convince nearly everyone of the necessity for planning and getting better control over spending. It helped that the cash crisis earlier in the year was still fresh in everyone's minds. As much as some people disliked the idea of budgets, they liked their jobs even more.

In the months that followed, Larry worked closely with all of the managers involved in the master budget, gathering data from them and making sure that they understood and fully supported the parts of the master budget that would affect them. In subsequent years, Larry hoped to turn the whole budgeting process over to the managers and to take a more advisory role.

The interdependent documents that Larry Giano prepared for Hampton Freeze are Schedules 1 through 10 of his company's master budget. In this section, we will study these schedules.

Objective 2

Prepare a sales budget, including a schedule of expected cash receipts.

The Sales Budget

The sales budget is the starting point in preparing the master budget. As shown earlier in Exhibit 9–3, all other items in the master budget, including production, purchases, inventories, and expenses, depend on it in some way.

The sales budget is constructed by multiplying the budgeted sales in units by the selling price. Schedule 1 contains the sales budget for Hampton Freeze for the year

Schedule 1

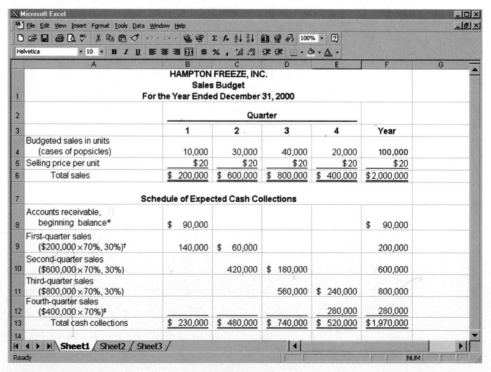

HAMPTON FREEZE, INC.
Sales Budget
For the Year Ended December 31, 2000

	Quarter				
	1	2	3	4	Year
Budgeted sales in units (cases of popsicles)	10,000	30,000	40,000	20,000	100,000
Selling price per unit	$20	$20	$20	$20	$20
Total sales	$ 200,000	$ 600,000	$ 800,000	$ 400,000	$2,000,000

Schedule of Expected Cash Collections

	1	2	3	4	Year
Accounts receivable, beginning balance*	$ 90,000				$ 90,000
First-quarter sales ($200,000 × 70%, 30%)†	140,000	$ 60,000			200,000
Second-quarter sales ($600,000 × 70%, 30%)		420,000	$ 180,000		600,000
Third-quarter sales ($800,000 × 70%, 30%)			560,000	$ 240,000	800,000
Fourth-quarter sales ($400,000 × 70%)‡				280,000	280,000
Total cash collections	$ 230,000	$ 480,000	$ 740,000	$ 520,000	$1,970,000

*Cash collections from last year's fourth-quarter sales. See the beginning-of-year balance sheet on page 422.

†Cash collections from sales are as follows: 70% collected in the quarter of sale, and the remaining 30% collected in the following quarter.

‡Uncollected fourth-quarter sales appear as accounts receivable on the company's end-of-year balance sheet (see Schedule 10 on page 421).

2000, by quarters. Notice from the schedule that the company plans to sell 100,000 cases of popsicles during the year, with sales peaking in the third quarter.

A schedule of expected cash collections, such as the one that appears in Schedule 1 for Hampton Freeze, is prepared after the sales budget. This schedule will be needed later to prepare the cash budget. Cash collections consist of collections on sales made to customers in prior periods plus collections on sales made in the current budget period. At Hampton Freeze, experience has shown that 70% of sales are collected in the quarter in which the sale is made and the remaining 30% are collected in the following quarter. So, for example, 70% of the first quarter sales of $200,000 (or $140,000) is collected during the first quarter and 30% (or $60,000) is collected during the second quarter.

The Production Budget

Objective 3

Prepare a production budget.

The production budget is prepared after the sales budget. The **production budget** lists the number of units that must be produced during each budget period to meet sales needs and to provide for the desired ending inventory. Production needs can be determined as follows:

Production budget A detailed plan showing the number of units that must be produced during a period in order to meet both sales and inventory needs.

Budgeted sales in units	XXXX
Add desired ending inventory	XXXX
Total needs	XXXX
Less beginning inventory	XXXX
Required production	XXXX

Schedule 2, which appears below, contains the production budget for Hampton Freeze.

Note that production requirements for a quarter are influenced by the desired level of the ending inventory. Inventories should be carefully planned. Excessive inventories tie up funds and create storage problems. Insufficient inventories can lead to lost sales or crash production efforts in the following period. At Hampton Freeze, management believes that an ending inventory equal to 20% of the next quarter's sales strikes the appropriate balance.

Inventory Purchases—Merchandising Firm

Hampton Freeze prepares a production budget, since it is a *manufacturing* firm. If it were a *merchandising* firm, then instead of a production budget it would prepare a

Schedule 2

HAMPTON FREEZE, INC.
Production Budget
For the Year Ended December 31, 2000
(in cases)

	Quarter				
	1	2	3	4	Year
Budgeted sales (Schedule 1)	10,000	30,000	40,000	20,000	100,000
Add desired ending inventory of finished goods*	6,000	8,000	4,000	3,000†	3,000
Total needs	16,000	38,000	44,000	23,000	103,000
Less beginning inventory of finished goods‡	2,000	6,000	8,000	4,000	2,000
Required production	14,000	32,000	36,000	19,000	101,000

*Twenty percent of the next quarter's sales.

†Estimated.

‡The same as the prior quarter's *ending* inventory.

Merchandise purchases budget A budget used by a merchandising company that shows the amount of goods that must be purchased from suppliers during the period.

merchandise purchases budget showing the amount of goods to be purchased from its suppliers during the period. The merchandise purchases budget is in the same basic format as the production budget, except that it shows goods to be purchased rather than goods to be produced, as shown below:

Budgeted cost of goods sold (in units or in dollars)	XXXXX
Add desired ending merchandise inventory	XXXXX
Total needs	XXXXX
Less beginning merchandise inventory	XXXXX
Required purchases (in units or in dollars)	XXXXX

The merchandising firm would prepare an inventory purchases budget such as the one above for each item carried in inventory. Some large retail organizations make such computations on a frequent basis (particularly at peak seasons) to ensure that adequate quantities are on hand to meet customer needs.

The Direct Materials Budget

Returning to Hampton Freeze's budget data, after the production requirements have been computed, a *direct materials budget* can be prepared. The **direct materials budget** details the raw materials that must be purchased to fulfill the production budget and to provide for adequate inventories. The required purchases of raw materials are computed as follows:

Raw materials needed to meet the production schedule	XXXXX
Add desired ending inventory of raw materials	XXXXX
Total raw materials needs	XXXXX
Less beginning inventory of raw materials	XXXXX
Raw materials to be purchased	XXXXX

Direct materials budget A detailed plan showing the amount of raw materials that must be purchased during a period to meet both production and inventory needs.

Material requirements planning (**MRP**) An operations management tool that uses a computer to help manage materials and inventories.

Preparing a budget of this kind is one step in a company's overall **material requirements planning (MRP).** MRP is an operations management tool that uses a computer to help manage materials and inventories. The objective of MRP is to ensure that the right materials are on hand, in the right quantities, and at the right time to support the production budget. The detailed operation of MRP is covered in most operations management books.

Schedule 3 contains the direct materials budget for Hampton Freeze. The only raw material included in that budget is high fructose sugar, which is the major ingredient in popsicles other than water. The remaining raw materials are relatively insignificant and are included in variable manufacturing overhead. Notice that materials requirements are first determined in units (kilograms, litres, and so on) and then translated into dollars by multiplying by the appropriate unit cost. Also note that the management of Hampton Freeze desires to maintain ending inventories of sugar equal to 10% of the following quarter's production needs.

The direct materials budget is usually accompanied by a schedule of expected cash disbursements for raw materials. This schedule is needed to prepare the overall cash budget. Disbursements for raw materials consist of payments for purchases on account in prior periods plus any payments for purchases in the current budget period. Schedule 3 contains such a schedule of cash disbursements.

The Direct Labour Budget

Direct labour budget A detailed plan showing labour requirements over some specific time period.

The **direct labour budget** is also developed from the production budget. Direct labour requirements must be computed so that the company will know whether sufficient labour

Schedule 3

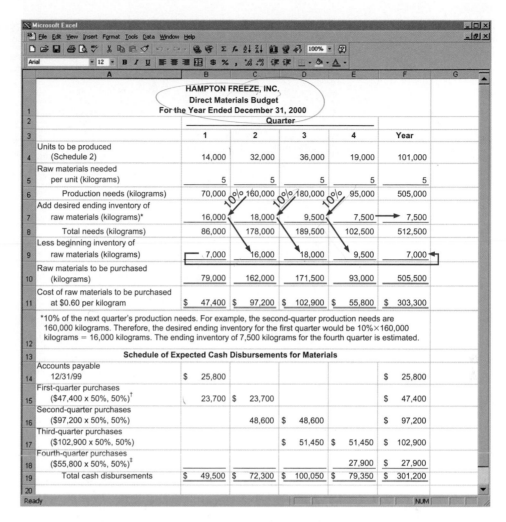

	HAMPTON FREEZE, INC. Direct Materials Budget For the Year Ended December 31, 2000				
	Quarter				
	1	**2**	**3**	**4**	**Year**
Units to be produced (Schedule 2)	14,000	32,000	36,000	19,000	101,000
Raw materials needed per unit (kilograms)	5	5	5	5	5
Production needs (kilograms)	70,000	160,000	180,000	95,000	505,000
Add desired ending inventory of raw materials (kilograms)*	16,000	18,000	9,500	7,500	7,500
Total needs (kilograms)	86,000	178,000	189,500	102,500	512,500
Less beginning inventory of raw materials (kilograms)	7,000	16,000	18,000	9,500	7,000
Raw materials to be purchased (kilograms)	79,000	162,000	171,500	93,000	505,500
Cost of raw materials to be purchased at $0.60 per kilogram	$ 47,400	$ 97,200	$ 102,900	$ 55,800	$ 303,300

*10% of the next quarter's production needs. For example, the second-quarter production needs are 160,000 kilograms. Therefore, the desired ending inventory for the first quarter would be 10%×160,000 kilograms = 16,000 kilograms. The ending inventory of 7,500 kilograms for the fourth quarter is estimated.

Schedule of Expected Cash Disbursements for Materials					
Accounts payable 12/31/99	$ 25,800				$ 25,800
First-quarter purchases ($47,400 x 50%, 50%)†	23,700	$ 23,700			$ 47,400
Second-quarter purchases ($97,200 x 50%, 50%)		48,600	$ 48,600		$ 97,200
Third-quarter purchases ($102,900 x 50%, 50%)			$ 51,450	$ 51,450	$ 102,900
Fourth-quarter purchases ($55,800 x 50%, 50%)‡				27,900	$ 27,900
Total cash disbursements	$ 49,500	$ 72,300	$ 100,050	$ 79,350	$ 301,200

*Cash payments for last year's fourth-quarter material purchases. See the beginning-of-year balance sheet on page 422.

†Cash payments for purchases are as follows: 50% paid for in the quarter of purchase, and the remaining 50% paid for in the quarter following.

‡Unpaid fourth-quarter purchases appear as accounts payable on the company's end-of-year balance sheet (see Schedule 10 on page 421).

time is available to meet production needs. By knowing in advance just what will be needed in the way of labour time throughout the budget year, the company can develop plans to adjust the labour force as the situation may require. Firms that neglect to budget run the risk of facing labour shortages or having to hire and lay off at awkward times. Erratic labour policies lead to insecurity and inefficiency on the part of employees.

To compute direct labour requirements, the number of units of finished product to be produced each period (month, quarter, and so on) is multiplied by the number of direct labour-hours required to produce a single unit. Many different types of labour may be involved. If so, then computations should be by type of labour needed. The direct labour requirements can then be translated into expected direct labour costs. How this is done will depend on the labour policy of the firm. In Schedule 4, the management of Hampton Freeze has assumed that the direct labour force will be adjusted as the work requirements change from quarter to quarter. In that case, the total direct labour cost is computed by simply multiplying the direct labour-hour requirements by the direct labour rate per hour as was done in Schedule 4.

However, many companies have employment policies or contracts that prevent them from laying off and rehiring workers as needed. Suppose, for example, that

Schedule 4

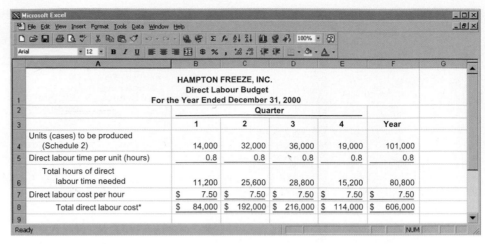

HAMPTON FREEZE, INC.
Direct Labour Budget
For the Year Ended December 31, 2000

	Quarter				
	1	2	3	4	Year
Units (cases) to be produced (Schedule 2)	14,000	32,000	36,000	19,000	101,000
Direct labour time per unit (hours)	0.8	0.8	0.8	0.8	0.8
Total hours of direct labour time needed	11,200	25,600	28,800	15,200	80,800
Direct labour cost per hour	$ 7.50	$ 7.50	$ 7.50	$ 7.50	$ 7.50
Total direct labour cost*	$ 84,000	$ 192,000	$ 216,000	$ 114,000	$ 606,000

*This schedule assumes that the direct labour workforce will be fully adjusted to the workload (i.e., "total hours of direct labour time needed") each quarter.

Schedule 5

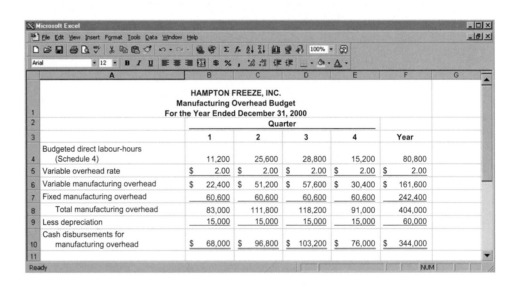

HAMPTON FREEZE, INC.
Manufacturing Overhead Budget
For the Year Ended December 31, 2000

	Quarter				
	1	2	3	4	Year
Budgeted direct labour-hours (Schedule 4)	11,200	25,600	28,800	15,200	80,800
Variable overhead rate	$ 2.00	$ 2.00	$ 2.00	$ 2.00	$ 2.00
Variable manufacturing overhead	$ 22,400	$ 51,200	$ 57,600	$ 30,400	$ 161,600
Fixed manufacturing overhead	60,600	60,600	60,600	60,600	242,400
Total manufacturing overhead	83,000	111,800	118,200	91,000	404,000
Less depreciation	15,000	15,000	15,000	15,000	60,000
Cash disbursements for manufacturing overhead	$ 68,000	$ 96,800	$ 103,200	$ 76,000	$ 344,000

Hampton Freeze has 50 workers who are classified as direct labour and each of them is guaranteed at least 480 hours of pay each quarter at a rate of $7.50 per hour. In that case, the minimum direct labour cost for a quarter would be as follows:

$$50 \text{ workers} \times 480 \text{ hours} \times \$7.50 = \$180,000$$

Note that in Schedule 4 the direct labour costs for the first and fourth quarters would have to be increased to a $180,000 level if Hampton Freeze's labour policy did not allow it to adjust the workforce at will.

The Manufacturing Overhead Budget

The **manufacturing overhead budget** provides a schedule of all costs of production other than direct materials and direct labour. Schedule 5 shows the manufacturing overhead budget for Hampton Freeze. Note how the production costs are separated into variable and fixed components. The variable component is $2 per direct labour-hour. The fixed component is $60,600 per quarter.

The last line of Schedule 5 for Hampton Freeze shows its budgeted cash disbursements for manufacturing overhead. Since some of the overhead costs are not cash

---

Objective 6

Prepare a manufacturing overhead budget.

Manufacturing overhead budget A detailed plan showing the production costs, other than direct materials and direct labour, that will be incurred over a specified time period.

Schedule 6

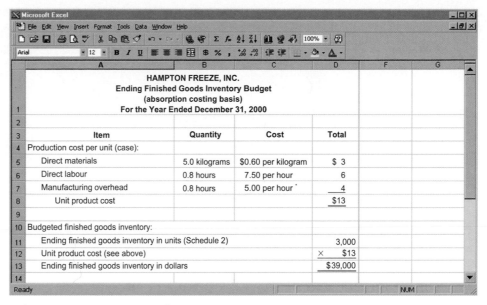

*$404,000 ÷ 80,800 hours = $5.

outflows, the total budgeted manufacturing overhead costs must be adjusted to determine the cash disbursements for manufacturing overhead. At Hampton Freeze, the only significant noncash manufacturing overhead cost is depreciation, which is $15,000 per quarter. These noncash depreciation charges are deducted from the total budgeted manufacturing overhead to determine the expected cash disbursements. Hampton Freeze pays all overhead costs involving cash disbursements in the quarter incurred.

Objective 7

Prepare an ending finished goods inventory budget.

Ending finished goods inventory budget   A budget showing the dollar amount of cost expected to appear on the balance sheet for unsold units at the end of a period.

Objective 8

Prepare a selling and administrative expense budget.

Selling and administrative expense budget   A detailed schedule of planned expenses that will be incurred in areas other than manufacturing during a budget period.

The Ending Finished Goods Inventory Budget

After completing Schedules 1–5, Larry Giano had all of the data he needed to compute unit product costs. This computation was needed for two reasons: first, to determine cost of goods sold on the budgeted income statement; and second, to know what amount to put on the balance sheet inventory account for unsold units. The carrying cost of the unsold units is computed on the **ending finished goods inventory budget.**

Larry Giano considered using variable costing in preparing Hampton Freeze's budget statements, but he decided to use absorption costing instead since the bank would very likely require that absorption costing be used. He also knew that it would be easy to convert the absorption costing financial statements to a variable costing basis later. At this point, the primary concern was to determine what financing, if any, would be required in the year 2000 and then to arrange for that financing from the bank.

The unit product cost computations are shown in Schedule 6. For Hampton Freeze, the absorption costing unit product cost is $13 per case of popsicles—consisting of $3 of direct materials, $6 of direct labour, and $4 of manufacturing overhead. For convenience, the manufacturing overhead is applied to units of product on the basis of direct labour-hours. The budgeted carrying cost of the expected ending inventory is $39,000.

The Selling and Administrative Expense Budget

The **selling and administrative expense budget** lists the budgeted expenses for areas other than manufacturing. In large organizations, this budget would be a compilation of many smaller, individual budgets submitted by department heads and other persons

Schedule 7

	HAMPTON FREEZE, INC. Selling and Administrative Expense Budget For the Year Ended December 31, 2000				
		Quarter			
	1	2	3	4	Year
Budgeted sales in units (cases)	10,000	30,000	40,000	20,000	100,000
Variable selling and administrative expense per unit*	× $1.80	× $1.80	× $1.80	× $1.80	× $1.80
Variable expense	$ 18,000	$ 54,000	$ 72,000	$ 36,000	$ 180,000
Fixed selling and administrative expenses:					
Advertising	40,000	40,000	40,000	40,000	160,000
Executive salaries	35,000	35,000	35,000	35,000	140,000
Insurance	9,912	9,913	9,912	9,913	39,650
Property taxes	4,538	4,537	4,538	4,537	18,150
Depreciation	2,000	2,000	2,000	2,000	8,000
Total budgeted selling and administrative expenses	$ 109,450	$ 145,450	$ 163,450	$ 127,450	$ 545,800

*Commissions, clerical, and shipping.

responsible for selling and administrative expenses. For example, the marketing manager in a large organization would submit a budget detailing the advertising expenses for each budget period.

Schedule 7 contains the selling and administrative expense budget for Hampton Freeze Company for 2000. The total insurance costs for the year are $39,650, of which $1,900 is paid in quarter 2 and $37,750 is paid in quarter 3. The total cost is divided equally among the quarters. Property tax is estimated at $18,150 to be paid in the fourth quarter. This cost is also prorated to each quarter according to normal accrual accounting practice.

The Cash Budget

Objective 9

Prepare a cash budget.

As illustrated in Exhibit 9–3, the cash budget pulls together much of the data developed in the preceding steps. It is a good idea to restudy Exhibit 9–3 to get the big picture firmly in mind before moving on.

The cash budget is composed of four major sections:

1. The receipts section.
2. The disbursements section
3. The cash excess or deficiency section.
4. The financing section.

The receipts section consists of a listing of all of the cash inflows, except for financing, expected during the budget period. Generally, the major source of receipts will be from sales.

The disbursements section consists of all cash payments that are planned for the budget period. These payments will include raw materials purchases, direct labour payments, manufacturing overhead costs, and so on, as contained in their respective budgets. In addition, other cash disbursements such as equipment purchases, dividends, and other cash withdrawals by owners are listed. For instance, we see in Schedule 8

Schedule 8

	Schedule	1	2	3	4	Year

HAMPTON FREEZE, INC.
Cash Budget
For the Year Ended December 31, 2000

	Schedule	Quarter 1	Quarter 2	Quarter 3	Quarter 4	Year
Cash balance, beginning		$42,500	$40,000	$40,000	$40,500	$42,500
Add receipts:						
Collections from customers	1	230,000	480,000	740,000	520,000	1,970,000
Total cash available before current financing		272,500	520,000	780,000	560,500	2,012,500
Less disbursements:						
Direct materials	3	49,500	72,300	100,050	79,350	301,200
Direct labour	4	84,000	192,000	216,000	114,000	606,000
Manufacturing overhead	5	68,000	96,800	103,200	76,000	344,000
Selling and administrative**	7	93,000	130,900	184,750	129,150	537,800
Income taxes*	9	10,500	10,500	10,500	10,500	42,000
Equipment purchases*		30,000	20,000	—	—	50,000
Dividends*		17,500	17,500	17,500	17,500	70,000
Total disbursements		352,500	540,000	632,000	426,500	1,951,000
Excess (deficiency) of cash available over disbursements		(80,000)	(20,000)	148,000	134,000	61,500
Financing:						
Borrowings (at beginning)		120,000*	60,000	—	—	180,000
Repayments (at ending)		—	—	(100,000)	(80,000)	(180,000)
Interest (at 10% per annum)		—	—	(7,500)†	(6,500)†	(14,000)
Total financing		120,000	60,000	(107,500)	(86,500)	(14,000)
Cash balance, ending		$40,000	$40,000	$40,500	$47,500	$47,500

*The company requires a minimum cash balance of $40,000. Therefore, borrowing must be sufficient to cover the cash deficiency of $80,000 and to provide for the minimum cash balance of $40,000. All borrowings and all repayments of principal are in round $1,000 amounts.

†The interest payments relate only to the principal being repaid at the time it is repaid. For example, the interest in quarter 3 relates only to the interest due on the $100,000 principal being repaid from quarter 1 borrowing, as follows: $100,000 \times 10\% \times 3/4 = $7,500$. The interest paid in quarter 4 is computed as follows:

$$\$20,000 \times 10\% \times 1 \text{ year} \dots \dots \$2,000$$
$$\$60,000 \times 10\% \times 3/4 \dots \dots \underline{4,500}$$
$$\text{Total interest paid} \dots \dots \underline{\$6,500}$$

**$107,450 − $9,912 − $4,538 = $93,000; $143,450 − $9,913 − $4,537 + $1,900 = $130,900; $161,450 − $9,912 − $4,538 + $37,750 = $184,750; $125,450 − $9,913 − $4,537 + $18,150 = $129,150

that management plans to spend $50,000 during the budget period on equipment purchases and $70,000 on dividends to the owners. This is additional information that does not appear on any of the earlier schedules.

The cash excess or deficiency section is computed as follows:

Cash balance, beginning	XXXX
Add receipts	XXXX
Total cash available before financing	XXXX
Less disbursements	XXXX
Excess (deficiency) of cash available over disbursements	XXXX

Schedule 9

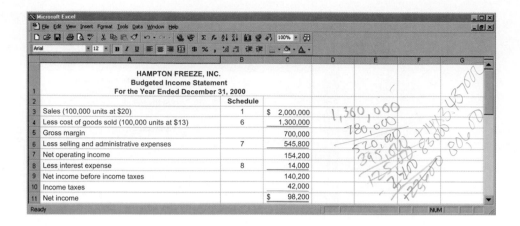

If there is a cash deficiency during any budget period, the company will need to borrow funds. If there is a cash excess during any budget period, funds borrowed in previous periods can be repaid or the idle funds can be placed in short-term or other investments.

The financing section provides a detailed account of the borrowings and repayments projected to take place during the budget period. It also includes a detail of interest payments that will be due on money borrowed. Banks are becoming increasingly insistent that firms in need of borrowed money give long advance notice of the amounts and times that funds will be needed. This permits the banks to plan and helps to assure that funds will be ready when needed. Moreover, careful planning of cash needs via the budgeting process avoids unpleasant surprises for companies as well. Few things are more disquieting to an organization than to run into unexpected difficulties in the Cash account. A well-coordinated budgeting program eliminates uncertainty as to what the cash situation will be in two months, six months, or a year from now.

Generally speaking, the cash budget should be broken down into time periods that are as short as feasible. There can be considerable fluctuations in cash balances that would be hidden by looking at a longer time period. While a monthly cash budget is most common, many firms budget cash on a weekly or even daily basis. Larry Giano has prepared a quarterly cash budget for Hampton Freeze that can be further refined as necessary. This budget appears in Schedule 8. Larry has assumed in the budget that an open line of credit can be arranged with the bank that can be used as needed to bolster the company's cash position. He has also assumed that the interest on any loans taken out with this line of credit would carry an interest rate of 10% per year. For simplicity, Larry has assumed that all borrowings and repayments are in round $1,000 amounts and that all borrowing occurs at the beginning of a quarter and all repayments are made at the end of a quarter.

In the case of Hampton Freeze, all loans have been repaid by year-end. If all loans are not repaid and a budgeted income statement or balance sheet is being prepared, then interest must be accrued on the unpaid loans. This interest will *not* appear on the cash budget (since it has not yet been paid), but it will appear as part of interest expense on the budgeted income statement and as a liability on the budgeted balance sheet.

The Budgeted Income Statement

Objective 10

Prepare a budgeted income statement and a budgeted balance sheet.

A budgeted income statement can be prepared from the data developed in Schedules 1–8. *The budgeted income statement is one of the key schedules in the budget process.* It shows the company's planned profit for the upcoming budget period, and it stands as a benchmark against which subsequent company performance can be measured.

Schedule 9 contains the budgeted income statement for Hampton Freeze.

Schedule 10

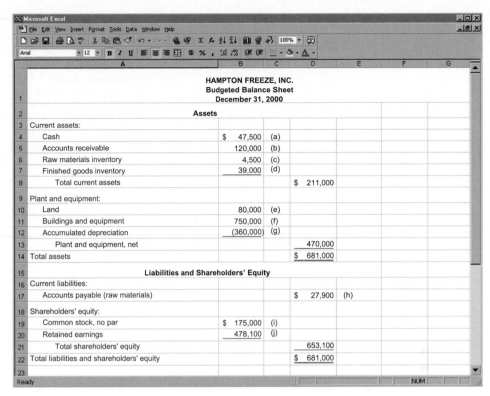

Explanation of December 31, 2000, balance sheet figures:

a. The ending cash balance, as projected by the cash budget in Schedule 8.

b. Thirty percent of fourth-quarter sales, from Schedule 1 ($400,000 × 30% = $120,000).

c. From Schedule 3, the ending raw materials inventory will be 7,500 kilograms. This material costs $0.60 per kilogram. Therefore, the ending inventory in dollars will be 7,500 kilograms × $0.60 = $4,500.

d. From Schedule 6.

e. From the December 31, 1999, balance sheet (no change).

f. The December 31, 1999, balance sheet indicated a balance of $700,000. During 2000, $50,000 additional equipment will be purchased (see Schedule 8), bringing the December 31, 2000, balance to $750,000.

g. The December 31, 1999, balance sheet indicated a balance of $292,000. During 2000, $68,000 of depreciation will be taken ($60,000 on Schedule 5 and $8,000 on Schedule 7), bringing the December 31, 2000, balance to $360,000.

h. One-half of the fourth-quarter raw materials purchases, from Schedule 3.

i. From the December 31, 1999, balance sheet (no change).

j.
December 31, 1999 balance	$449,900
Add net income, from Schedule 9	98,200
	548,100
Deduct dividends paid, from Schedule 8	70,000
December 31, 2000, balance	$478,100

The Budgeted Balance Sheet

The budgeted balance sheet is developed by beginning with the current balance sheet and adjusting it for the data contained in the other budgets. Hampton Freeze's budgeted balance sheet is presented in Schedule 10. Some of the data on the budgeted balance sheet have been taken from the company's end-of-year balance sheet for 1999 which appears below:

HAMPTON FREEZE, INC.
Balance Sheet
December 31, 1999

Assets

Current assets:

Cash	$ 42,500	
Accounts receivable	90,000	
Raw materials inventory (7,000 kilograms)	4,200	
Finished goods inventory (2,000 cases)	26,000	
Total current assets		$162,700

Plant and equipment:

Land	80,000	
Buildings and equipment	700,000	
Accumulated depreciation	(292,000)	
Plant and equipment, net		488,000
Total assets		$650,700

Liabilities and Shareholders' Equity

Current liabilities:

Accounts payable (raw materials)		$ 25,800

Shareholders' equity:

Common stock, no par	$175,000	
Retained earnings	449,900	
Total shareholders' equity		624,900
Total liabilities and shareholders' equity		$650,700

Managerial Accounting in Action

THE ISSUE

After completing the master budget, Larry Giano took the documents to Tom Wills, chief executive officer of Hampton Freeze, for his review. The following conversation took place:

Larry: Here's the budget. Overall, the net income is excellent, and the net cash flow for the entire year is positive.

Tom: Yes, but I see on this cash budget that we have the same problem with negative cash flows in the first and second quarters that we had last year.

Larry: That's true. I don't see any way around that problem. However, there is no doubt in my mind that if you take this budget to the bank today, they'll approve an open line of credit that will allow you to borrow enough to make it through the first two quarters without any problem.

Tom: Are you sure? They didn't seem very happy to see me last year when I came in for an emergency loan.

Larry: Did you repay the loan on time?

Tom: Sure.

Larry: I don't see any problem. You won't be asking for an emergency loan this time. The bank will have plenty of warning. And with this budget, you have a solid plan that shows when and how you are going to pay off the loan. Trust me, they'll go for it.

Tom: Fantastic! It would sure make life a lot easier this year. ∎

Careful observation of the income statement (Schedule 9), the balance sheet (Schedule 10) and the cash budget (Schedule 8) would note that a significant item represented by income taxes has been simplified. Income taxes, while pertinent to budgets, have been simplified to avoid overdoing the complexity of the presentation. Given income taxes can represent a significant percent of net income, this area is serious.

In organizations, income taxes may not be administered at the level of the responsibility centre being budgeted. The specialized nature of the area means that they may require management by specialists at the headquarters level. In addition, income taxation is a company wide charge that may be difficult to break down by responsibility centre.

Some of the detail about income taxes is partially described in Chapter 15 when capital budgeting (long-term) is presented. Here the complexity of capital cost allowance, capital gains and losses, recaptures and terminal losses are an integral part of the required budgets. To introduce the full operational aspects of income taxes to the master budget requires the consideration of Future Tax Liabilities and Assets, installments and loss carry overs. Advanced discussions of budgeting can present these issues within the analysis after the necessary background study is made of the tax rules.

Expanding the Budgeted Income Statement

The master budget income statement in Schedule 9 focuses on a single level of activity and has been prepared using absorption costing. Some managers prefer an alternate format that focuses on a *range* of activity and that is prepared using the contribution approach. An example of a master budget income statement using this alternative is format presented in Exhibit 9–4 below.

A statement such as that in Exhibit 9–4 is *flexible,* since it is geared to more than one level of activity. If, for example, the company planned to sell 2,000 units during a period but actually sold only 1,900 units, then the budget figures at the 1,900-unit level would be used to compare against actual costs and revenues. Other columns could be added to the budget as needed by simply applying the budget formulas provided.

In short, a master budget income statement in this expanded format can be very useful in planning and controlling operations. The concepts underlying a flexible approach to budgeting are discussed in later chapters.

Exhibit 9–4 Flexible Budget Income Statement

EXAMPLE COMPANY
Master Budget Income Statement

	Budget Formula (per unit)	Sales in Units		
		1,900	2,000	2,100
Sales	$ 75.00	$ 142,500	$ 150,000	$ 157,500
Less variable expenses:				
Direct materials	12.00	22,800	24,000	25,200
Direct labour	31.00	58,900	62,000	65,100
Variable manufacturing overhead	7.50	14,250	15,000	15,750
Variable selling and administrative	4.00	7,600	8,000	8,400
Total variable expenses	54.50	103,550	109,000	114,450
Contribution margin	$ 20.50	38,950	41,000	43,050
Less fixed expenses:				
Fixed manufacturing overhead		18,000	18,000	18,000
Fixed selling administrative		9,000	9,000	9,000
Total fixed expenses		27,000	27,000	27,000
Net income		$ 11,950	$ 14,000	$ 16,050

Budgeting for Not-for-Profit Entities

Up to this point we have discussed budgeting in the context of profit-seeking enterprises. The sales estimate is the critical ingredient around which the rest of the master budget depends. Inaccurate sales estimates create additional inaccuracies in all other budgets. With profit-oriented bodies there is an intricate relationship between expenses and revenues. With not-for-profit (NFP) entities there is often no relationship between revenue sources expected to be received and expenditures expected to be incurred. Examples of NFP entities include municipal, provincial, and federal governmental units as well as hospitals, universities, voluntary associations, professional associations, and many others. The profit motive is replaced with a service orientation in NFP organizations. Budget information is gathered to assist in decisions regarding what programs and expenditures the entity will undertake. Subsequently the NFP entity estimates what revenues are needed to support these programs and anticipated expenditures. Revenue sources may be in the form of grants, donations, or special tax or membership levies. The very survival of NFP organizations such as art galleries depends on their ability to attract donors.

Accountability is of critical importance to most NFP entities. To ensure continued support from contributors it is advantageous to have a budgeting process in place to assist in planning how resources are effectively and efficiently used. Budgets of NFP entities should be formally approved by the entity's governing body. A formally approved budget sends a signal to employees and volunteers alike that the governing body is committed to meeting revenue and expenditure goals.

A budget can be prepared either on an expenditure basis or on a program basis. An expenditure-based budget simply lists the total expected costs of such items as rent, insurance, salaries, and depreciation but does not detail how much of these various expenses relate to particular programs. For many NFP organizations there is a need to report information on the basis of programs rather than line-item expenses. Preparation of the budget on the basis of programs facilitates performance evaluation and allows for the comparison of budgeted with actual revenues and expenses of each program. This should aid decision making about resource allocation among various programs. Budgeting by program also facilitates a stewardship objective by providing information in a format permitting determination of whether designated funds are being spent as intended.

Zero-Based Budgeting

In the traditional approach to budgeting, the manager starts with last year's budget and adds to it (or subtracts from it) according to anticipated needs. This is an incremental approach to budgeting in which the previous year's budget is taken for granted as a baseline.

Zero-base budgeting is an alternative approach that is sometimes used—particularly in the governmental and not-for-profit sectors of the economy. Under a **zero-base budget,** managers are required to justify *all* budgeted expenditures, not just changes in the budget from the previous year. The baseline is zero rather than last year's budget.

Zero-based budget   A method of budgeting in which managers are required to justify all costs as if the programs involved were being proposed for the first time.

A zero-base budget requires considerable documentation. In addition to all of the schedules in the usual master budget, the manager must prepare a series of "decision packages" in which all of the activities of the department are ranked according to their relative importance and the cost of each activity is identified. Higher-level managers can then review the decision packages and cut back in those areas that appear to be less critical or whose costs do not appear to be justified.

Nearly everyone would agree that zero-base budgeting is a good idea. The only issue is the frequency with which a zero-base review is carried out. Under zero-base budgeting, the review is performed every year. Critics of zero-base budgeting charge that properly executed zero-base budgeting is too time-consuming and too costly to justify on an annual basis. In addition, it is argued that annual reviews soon become mechanical and that the whole purpose of zero-base budgeting is then lost.

Whether or not a company should use an annual review is a matter of judgment. In some situations, annual zero-base reviews may be justified; in other situations, they may not because of the time and cost involved. However, most managers would at least agree that on occasion zero-base reviews can be very helpful.

Activity-Based Budgeting

Activity-based budgeting A type of budgeting in which emphasis is placed on budgeting the costs of the activities needed to produce and market the firm's goods and services

In Chapter 8 we saw that activity-based costing has been developed to help provide the manager with more accurate product or service costs. More accurate costs should translate into better decision making and tighter control over costs. Activity-based costing principles can also be applied to budgeting. With **activity-based budgeting** the emphasis is on budgeting the costs of the activities needed to produce and market the firm's goods and services.

Activity-based budgeting involves several stages. First, the budgeted cost of accomplishing each unit of activity is determined. Recall that an activity is a cost driver such as machine setup, a purchase order, a quality inspection, or a maintenance request. Next, sales and production targets are used to estimate the demand for these activities. The unit cost of each activity is then multiplied by the expected demand to determine the total cost of each activity. The result is a budget based on activities that drive costs rather than the traditional budget based on business functions and expense classifications.

For activity budgeting, costs within the responsibility centre are classified by activity and activity drivers other than simple quantities produced or sold are identified. Activities such as quality inspections, material handling, assembly, shipping, purchasing, and so on are identified, measured and costed. These costs are then compiled to present the overall costs of the product or services if overall results are desired. The activity costing presented in Chapter 8 illustrates how activity budgets are presented.

International Aspects of Budgeting

A multinational company (MNC) faces special problems when preparing a budget. These problems arise because of fluctuations in foreign currency exchange rates, the high inflation rates found in some countries, and local economic conditions and governmental policies that affect everything from labour costs to marketing practices.

Fluctuations in foreign currency exchange rates create unique budgeting problems. Exporters may be able to predict with some accuracy their sales in the local foreign currency such as South African rands or Swiss francs. However, the amounts they eventually receive in their own currency will depend on the currency exchange rates that prevail at the time. If, for example, the currency exchange rates are less favourable than expected, the company will ultimately receive in its own currency less than it had anticipated.

Companies that are heavily involved in export operations often hedge their exposure to exchange rate fluctuations by buying and selling sophisticated financial contracts. These hedges ensure that if the company loses money in its exporting operations because of exchange rate fluctuations, it will make up that loss with gains on its financial contracts. The details of such hedging operations are covered in finance textbooks. When an MNC uses hedging operations, the costs of those activities should be budgeted along with other expenses.

Some MNCs have operations in countries with very high inflation rates—sometimes exceeding 100% a year. Such high inflation rates—called *hyperinflation*—can render a budget obsolete very quickly. A common budgeting tactic in such countries is to reduce the lead time for preparing the budget and to revise the budget frequently throughout the year in the light of the actual inflation experienced to date.

In addition to problems with exchange rates and inflation, MNCs must be sensitive to government policies in the countries in which they operate that might affect labour costs, equipment purchases, cash management, or other budget items.

Focus on Current Practice

"[In] 1985 the Toronto Blue Jays budgeted a loss for the season despite the fact that the team had the best win-loss record in the major leagues. The majority of team expenses were paid in U.S. dollars in contrast to their revenue, which was earned in Canadian dollars. To protect themselves against adverse changes in the exchange rate, the Blue Jays made forward purchases of U.S. dollars in late 1984 at 75 cents per Canadian dollar to cover a large portion of their budgeted 1985 U.S. dollar denominated expenses. In 1985, the Blue Jays profited on their hedged position when the Canadian dollar depreciated, which helped to offset losses on unhedged U.S. dollar denominated expenses during the same period."[10] ■

Summary

Our purpose has been to present an overview of the budgeting process and to show how the various operating budgets relate to each other. We have seen how the sales budget forms the foundation for profit planning. Once the sales budget has been set, the production budget and the selling and administrative budget can be prepared since they depend on how many units are to be sold. The production budget determines how many units are to be produced, so after it is prepared, the various manufacturing cost budgets can be prepared. All of these various budgets feed into the cash budget and the budgeted income statement and balance sheet. There are many connections between these various parts of the master budget. For example, the schedule of expected cash collections, which is completed in connection with the sales budget, provides data for both the cash budget and the budgeted balance sheet.

The material in this chapter is just an introduction to budgeting and profit planning. In later chapters, we will see how budgets are used to control day-to-day operations and how they are used in performance evaluation.

Review Problem: Budget Schedules

Mylar Company manufactures and sells a product that has seasonal variations in demand, with peak sales coming in the third quarter. The following information concerns operations for Year 2—the coming year—and for the first two quarters of Year 3:

a. The company's single product sells for $8 per unit. Budgeted sales in units for the next six quarters are as follows:

	Year 2 Quarter				Year 3 Quarter	
	1	2	3	4	1	2
Budgeted sales in units	40,000	60,000	100,000	50,000	70,000	80,000

b. Sales are collected in the following pattern: 75% in the quarter the sales are made, and the remaining 25% in the following quarter. On January 1, Year 2, the company's balance

---

10. Paul V. Mannino and Ken Milani, "Budgeting for an International Business," *Management Accounting* 73, no. 8 (February 1992), p. 37. Used by permission.

sheet showed $65,000 in accounts receivable, all of which will be collected in the first quarter of the year. Bad debts are negligible and can be ignored.

c. The company desires an ending inventory of finished units on hand at the end of each quarter equal to 30% of the budgeted sales for the next quarter. This requirement was met on December 31, Year 1, in that the company had 12,000 units on hand to start the new year.

d. Five kilograms of raw materials are required to complete one unit of product. The company requires an ending inventory of raw materials on hand at the end of each quarter equal to 10% of the production needs of the following quarter. This requirement was met on December 31, Year 1, in that the company had 23,000 kilograms of raw materials on hand to start the new year.

e. The raw material costs $0.80 per kilogram. Purchases of raw material are paid for in the following pattern: 60% paid in the quarter the purchases are made, and the remaining 40% paid in the following quarter. One January 1, Year 2, the company's balance sheet showed $81,500 in accounts payable for raw material purchases, all of which will be paid for in the first quarter of the year.

Required　Prepare the following budgets and schedules for the year, showing both quarterly and total figures:

1. A sales budget and a schedule of expected cash collections.
2. A production budget.
3. A direct materials purchases budget and a schedule of expected cash payments for material purchases.

Solution to Review Problem

1. The sales budget is prepared as follows:

| | | **Year 2 Quarter** | | | |
	1	2	3	4	Year
Budgeted sales in units ..	40,000	60,000	100,000	50,000	250,000
Selling price per unit .... ×	$8 ×	$8 ×	$8 ×	$8 ×	$8
Total sales	$320,000	$480,000	$800,000	$400,000	$2,000,000

Based on the budgeted sales above, the schedule of expected cash collections is prepared as follows:

| | | **Year 2 Quarter** | | | |
	1	2	3	4	Year
Accounts receivable, beginning balance	$ 65,000				$ 65,000
First-quarter sales ($320,000 × 75%, 25%)	240,000	$ 80,000			320,000
Second-quarter sales ($480,000 × 75%, 25%)		360,000	$120,000		480,000
Third-quarter sales ($800,000 × 75%, 25%)			600,000	$200,000	800,000
Fourth-quarter sales ($400,000 × 75%)				300,000	300,000
Total cash collections	$305,000	$440,000	$720,000	$500,000	$1,965,000

2. Based on the sales budget in units, the production budget is prepared as follows:

| | | **Year 2 Quarter** | | | | **Year 3 Quarter** | |
	1	2	3	4	Year	1	2
Budgeted sales (units)	40,000	60,000	100,000	50,000	250,000	70,000	80,000
Add desired ending inventory of finished goods*	18,000	30,000	15,000	21,000†	21,000	24,000	
Total needs	58,000	90,000	115,000	71,000	271,000	94,000	
Less beginning inventory of finished goods	12,000	18,000	30,000	15,000	12,000	21,000	
Required production	46,000	72,000	85,000	56,000	259,000	73,000	

*30% of the following quarter's budgeted sales in units.

†30% of the budgeted Year 3 first-quarter sales.

3. Based on the production budget figures, raw materials will need to be purchased as follows during the year:

	1	2	3	4	Year 2	Year 3 Quarter 1
Required production (units)	46,000	72,000	85,000	56,000	259,000	73,000
Raw materials needed per unit (kilograms)	× 5	× 5	× 5	× 5	× 5	× 5
Production needs (kilograms)	230,000	360,000	425,000	280,000	1,295,000	365,000
Add desired ending inventory of raw materials (kilograms)*	36,000	42,500	28,000	36,500†	36,500	
Total needs (kilograms)	266,000	402,500	453,000	316,500	1,331,500	
Less beginning inventory of raw materials (kilograms)	23,000	36,000	42,500	28,000	23,000	
Raw materials to be purchased (kilograms)	243,000	366,500	410,500	288,500	1,308,500	

*Ten percent of the following quarter's production needs in kilograms.

†Ten percent of the Year 3 first-quarter production needs in kilograms.

Based on the raw material purchases above, expected cash payments are computed as follows:

	Year 2 Quarter				
	1	2	3	4	Year 2
Cost of raw materials to be purchased at $0.80 per kilogram	$194,400	$293,200	$328,400	$230,800	$1,046,800
Accounts payable, beginning balance	$ 81,500				$ 81,500
First-quarter purchases ($194,400 × 60%, 40%)	116,640	$ 77,760			194,400
Second-quarter purchases ($293,200 × 60%, 40%) . . .		175,920	$117,280		293,200
Third-quarter purchases ($328,400 × 60%, 40%)			197,040	$131,360	328,400
Fourth-quarter purchases ($230,800 × 60%)				138,480	138,480
Total cash disbursements	$198,140	$253,680	$314,320	$269,840	$1,035,980

Appendix 9A: Inventory Decisions

Objective 11

Compute the optimum inventory level and order size.

Inventory planning and control decisions are an important aspect of the management of many organizations. Inventory levels are not left to chance but rather are carefully planned. Major questions left unanswered are: How does the manager know what inventory level is right for the firm? and Won't the level that is right vary from organization to organization? The purpose of this section is to examine the inventory control methods available to the manager to answer these questions and the relevant costs for these decisions.

Costs Associated with Inventory

Inventory ordering costs Those costs associated with the acquisition of inventory, such as clerical costs and transportation costs.

Three groups of costs are associated with inventory. The first group, known as **inventory ordering costs,** consists of costs associated with the acquisition of inventory. Examples include:

1. Clerical costs.
2. Transportation costs.

Inventory carrying costs Those costs associated with the acquisition of inventory, such as rental or storage space, handling costs, property taxes, insurance, and interest on funds.

The second group, known as **inventory carrying costs,** consists of costs that arise from having inventory on hand. Examples include:

1. Storage space costs.
2. Handling costs.
3. Property taxes.
4. Insurance.
5. Obsolescence losses.
6. Interest on capital invested in inventory.

Cost of not carrying sufficient inventory Those costs that result from not having enough inventory on hand to meet customers' needs; such costs would include customer ill will, quantity discounts forgone, erratic production, added transportation charges, and lost sales.

The third group, known as **costs of not carrying sufficient inventory,** consists of costs that result from not having enough inventory on hand to meet customers' needs. Costs in this group are more difficult to identify than costs in the other two groups, but nevertheless they can include items that are very significant to a firm. Examples of costs in this group are:

1. Customer ill will.
2. Quantity discounts forgone.
3. Erratic production (expediting of goods, extra setup, etc.).
4. Inefficiency of production runs.
5. Added transportation charges.
6. Lost sales.

In a broad conceptual sense, the right level of inventory to carry is the level that minimizes the total of these three groups of costs. Such a minimization is difficult to achieve, however, because certain of the costs involved are in direct conflict with one another. Notice, for example, that as inventory levels increase, the costs of carrying inventory also increase, but the costs of not carrying sufficient inventory decrease. In working toward total cost minimization, therefore, the manager must balance off the three groups of costs against one another. The problem really has two dimensions—how much to order (or how much to produce in a production run) and how often to do it.

Computing the Economic Order Quantity

The how-much-to-order question is commonly referred to as the **economic order quantity.** It is the order size that results in a minimization of the first two groups of cost just described. We consider two approaches to computing the economic order quantity—the tabular approach and the formula approach.

The Tabular Approach

Economic order quantity The order size for materials that results in a minimization of the costs of ordering inventory and carrying inventory.

Given a certain annual consumption of an item, a firm might place a few orders each year of a large quantity each, or it might place many orders of a small quantity each. Placing only a few orders will result in low inventory ordering costs but in high inventory carrying costs, as the average inventory level would be very large. On the other hand, placing many orders would result in high inventory ordering costs but in low inventory carrying costs; in this case the average inventory level would be quite small. As stated earlier, the economic order quantity seeks the order size that balances off these two groups of costs. To show how it is computed, assume that a manufacturer used 3,000 subassemblies (manufactured parts inserted in other manufactured items) in the manufacturing process each year. The subassemblies are purchased from a supplier at a cost of $20 each. Other cost data are given below:

Inventory carrying costs, per unit, per year . . . . $ 0.80
Cost of replacing a purchase order 10.00

Exhibit 9A–1 contains a tabulation of the total costs associated with various order sizes for the subassemblies. Notice the total annual cost is lowest (and is equal)

Exhibit 9A–1   Tabulation of Costs Associated with Various Order Sizes

Symbol*						Order Size in Units					
		25	50	100	200	250	300	400	1,000	3,000	
E/2	Average inventory in units	12.5	25	50	100	125	150	200	500	1,500	
Q/E	Number of purchase orders	120	60	30	15	12	10	7.5	3	1	
C(E/2)	Annual carrying cost at $0.80 per unit	$ 10	$ 20	$ 40	$ 80	$100	$120	$160	$400	$1,200	
p(Q/E)	Annual purchase order cost at $10 per order	1,200	600	300	150	120	100	75	30	10	
T	Total annual cost	$1,210	$620	$340	$230	$220	$220	$235	$430	$1,210	

*Symbols:

E = Order size in units (see headings above).

Q = Annual quantity used in units (3,000 in this example).

C = Annual cost of carrying one unit in stock.

P = Cost of placing one order.

T = Total annual cost = $P(Q/E) + C(E/2)$

Exhibit 9A–2

Graphic Solution to
Economic Order Size

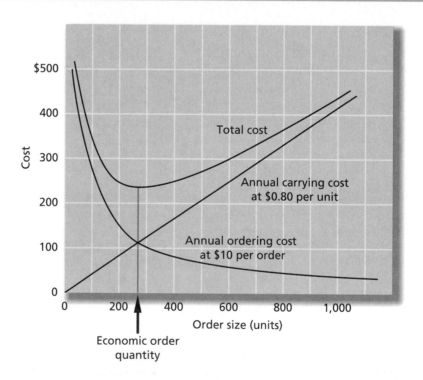

at the 250- and 300-unit order sizes. The economic order quantity lies somewhere between these two points. We could locate it precisely by adding more columns to the tabulation, and we would in time zero in on 274 units as being the exact economic order quantity.

The cost relationships from this tabulation are shown graphically in Exhibit 9A–2. Notice from the graph that total annual cost is minimized at that point when annual carrying costs and annual purchase order costs are equal. The same point identifies the economic order quantity, because the purpose of the computation is to find the point of exact trade-off between these two classes of costs.

Observe from the graph that total cost shows a tendency to flatten out between 200 and 400 units. Most firms look for this minimum cost range and choose an order size that falls within it, rather than choosing the exact economic order quantity. The primary reason is that suppliers will often ship goods only in round-lot sizes. The table in Exhibit 9A–1 is based on the formula:

$$T = P(Q/E) + C(E/2)$$

where P is a constant cost per order, and C is a unit cost of carrying a unit of inventory for the period of time under consideration. If quantity discounts can be obtained for orders of a certain size, another term representing the purchase costs of the particular lot size should be added to the formula or another line to the table. Other complications arise where annual or period demand is not known, lead times vary, or multiple deliveries are necessary for each order.

The Formula Approach

The economic order quantity can also be found by means of a formula. The formula is derived by solving the minimization of $T = P(Q/E) + C(E/2)$ for E using calculus. The result is

$$E = \sqrt{\frac{2\,QP}{C}}$$

where:

   E = order size in units
   Q = annual quantity used in units
   P = cost of placing one order
   C = annual cost of carrying one unit in stock

Substituting with the data used in our preceding example, we have:

   Q = $3,000 subassemblies used per year
   P = $10 cost to place one order
   C = $0.80 cost to carry one subassembly in stock for one year

$$E = \sqrt{\frac{2(3,000)(\$10)}{\$0.80}} = \sqrt{\frac{\$60,000}{\$0.80}} = \sqrt{75,000}$$

$$E = 274 \text{ (the economic order quantity)}$$

Although data can be obtained very quickly using the formula approach, it has the drawback of not providing as great a range of information as the method discussed previously, and it cannot be used where changes in purchase prices occur with changes in lot sizes.

JIT and the Economic Order Quantity

The EOQ will decrease under either of these circumstances:

1. The cost of placing an order decreases.
2. The cost of carrying inventory in stock increases.

Managers who advocate JIT purchasing argue that the cost of carrying inventory in stock is much greater than generally realized because of the waste and inefficiency that inventories create. These managers argue that this fact, combined with the fact that JIT purchasing dramatically reduces the cost of placing an order, is solid evidence that companies should purchase more frequently in smaller amounts. Assume, for example, that a company has used the following data to compute its EOQ:

$Q = 1,000$ units needed each year
$P = \$60$ cost to place one order
$C = \$3$ cost to carry one unit in stock for one year

Given these data, the EOQ would be:

$$E = \sqrt{\frac{2QP}{C}} = \sqrt{\frac{2(1,000)(\$60)}{\$3}} = \sqrt{40,000}$$

$$E = 200 \text{ units}$$

Now assume that as a result of JIT purchasing the company is able to decrease the cost of placing an order to only $10. Also assume that because of the waste and inefficiency caused by inventories, the true cost of carrying a unit in stock is $8 per year. The revised EOQ would be:

$$E = \sqrt{\frac{2QP}{C}} = \sqrt{\frac{2(1,000)(\$10)}{\$8}} = \sqrt{2,500}$$

$$E = 50 \text{ units}$$

Under JIT purchasing, the company would *not* necessarily order in 50-unit lots since purchases would be geared to current demand. This example shows quite dramatically, however, the economics behind the JIT concept as far as the purchasing of goods is concerned.

Production Lot Size

Economic production lot size The number of units produced in a production lot that results in a minimization of setup costs and the costs of carrying inventory.

The economic order quantity concept can also be applied to the problem of determining the **economic production lot size.** Deciding when to start and when to stop production runs is a problem that has plagued manufacturers for years. The problem can be solved quite easily by inserting the **setup cost** for a new production lot into the economic order quantity formula in place of the purchase order cost. The setup cost includes the labour and other costs involved in making facilities ready for a run of a different production item.

Setup costs Labour and other costs involved in getting facilities ready for a run of a different production item.

To illustrate, assume that Chittenden Company has determined that the following costs are associated with one of its product lines:

$Q = 15,000$ units produced each year
$P = \$150$ setup costs to change production from one product to another
$C = \$2$ to carry one unit in stock for one year

Managers involved in the theory of constraints would go even further in reducing lot sizes. When a particular work centre is not a constraint, the only significant cost involved in setups is typically direct labour wages. However, since direct labour wages are considered to be a fixed cost rather than a variable cost in the theory of constraints, the incremental cost of setups is considered to be zero. Therefore, at work centres that are not a constraint, the economic lot size in the theory of constraints is as small as a single unit. At the constraint itself, setup time is very costly, since each minute spent setting up is a minute taken away from producing output that could be sold. Therefore, setup reduction efforts should be focused on the constraint and lot sizes should be larger on the constraint than at other work centres.

Managers should be extremely cautious when applying the results of ABC analyses to computation of the economic lot size. Typically, one of the results of an ABC analysis is a dramatic increase in the apparent costs of setups. The reason for this is that under conventional costing systems, many of the costs that might be attributed to switching over from one product to another are lumped into the general manufacturing overhead cost pool and distributed to products based on direct labour-hours or some other measure of volume. When an ABC analysis is done, these costs are separately identified as setup costs. As a consequence, setup costs appear to increase, and this would seem to imply that the economic lot size should be increased. However, a close examination of the costs attributed to setups in the ABC analysis will usually reveal that most of the costs cannot actually be avoided by reducing the number of setups. For example, machinery depreciation may be included in setup costs. However, reducing the number of setups may have no impact at all on the amount of machinery depreciation actually incurred.

What is the optimal production lot size for this product line? It can be determined by using the same formula used to compute the economic order quantity:

$$O = \sqrt{\frac{2(15,000)(\$150)}{\$2}} = \sqrt{\frac{\$4,500,000}{\$2}} = \sqrt{2,250,000}$$

$O = 1,500$ (economic production lot size in units)

The Chittenden Company will minimize its overall costs by producing in lots of 1,500 units each. Tabular analysis can be used to provide a more flexible model for the planning of production lot sizes.

JIT systems are being touted as a total manufacturing system for repetitive manufacturing environments such as those used to produce food and beverages, electrical products, textiles, and automobiles. Small lot production and flexible manufacturing are key elements to the system.[11] Distances in Canada may pose a problem for some industries but not necessarily for all. The seasonal nature of some businesses may preclude the use of JIT because additional production capacity is simply too costly to permit production only when the need is evident in the form of customer orders. However, the potential improvements in productivity and quality together with the reduction in needed investment in inventory make JIT production an option to be seriously investigated for manufacturers and processors.

JIT production philosophy, when it was originated, examined carefully the assumptions in economic production lot size analysis. The typical analysis as presented earlier assumes setup time is a known fixed cost, for example, $150 per setup in the preceding example. JIT approached this production lot size problem by attempting to reduce setup costs to zero. If setup costs in the Chittenden Company example were $0.0, the economic production lot size in units would be one, a JIT production approach. The less the setup cost, the smaller the production lots. Production approaches have been redesigned in some operations so that many different products can be manufactured at little or no setup costs. For example, a world-class automobile manufacturer has been noted as being able to change from one model to another in 2.5 minutes, a complete retooling operation.[12]

Reorder Point and Safety Stock

We stated earlier that the inventory problem has two dimensions—how much to order and how often to do it. How often to do it involves what are commonly termed the *reorder point* and the *safety stock,* and seeks to find the optimal trade-off between the second two groups of inventory costs outlined earlier (the costs of carrying inventory and the costs of not carrying sufficient inventory). First, we will discuss the reorder

---

11. Alan T. G. Saipe, "Just-in-Time Holds Promise for Manufacturing Productivity," *Cost and Management* (May–June 1984), pp. 41–43.
12. Robert D'Amore. "Just-Time-Systems." *Cost Accounting, Robotics, and the New Manufacturing Environment,* ed. Robert Capettini and Donald K. Clancy (Sarasota, Fla.: American Accounting Association, 1987), p. 8.2.

point and the factors involved in its computation. Then, we discuss the circumstances under which a safety stock must be maintained.

The **reorder point** tells the manager when to place an order or when to initiate production to replenish depleted stocks. It is dependent on three factors—the economic order quantity (or economic production lot size), the *lead time,* and the rate of usage during the lead time. The **lead time** can be defined as the interval between the time that an order is placed and the time that the order is finally received from the supplier or from the production line.

CONSTANT USAGE DURING THE LEAD TIME   If the rate of usage during the lead time is known with certainty, the reorder point can be determined by the following formula:

$$\text{Reorder point} = \text{Lead time} \times \text{Average daily or weekly usage}$$

To illustrate the formula's use, assume that a company's economic order quantity is 500 units, that the lead time is 3 weeks, and that the average weekly usage is 50 units.

$$\text{Reorder point} = 3 \text{ weeks} \times 50 \text{ units per week} = 150 \text{ units}$$

The reorder point would be 150 units. That is, the company automatically places a new order for 500 units when inventory stock drops to a level of 150 units, or three weeks' supply, left on hand.

VARIABLE USAGE DURING THE LEAD TIME   The previous example assumed that the 50 units per week usage rate was constant and was known with certainty. Although some firms enjoy the luxury of certainty, the more common situation is to find considerable variation in the rate of usage of inventory items from period to period. If usage varies from period to period, the firm that reorders in the way computed earlier may soon find itself out of stock. A sudden spurt in demand, a delay in delivery, or a snag is processing an order may cause inventory levels to be depleted before a new shipment arrives.

Companies that experience problems in demand, delivery, or processing of orders have found that they need some type of buffer to guard against stock-outs. Such a buffer is usually called a **safety stock.** A safety stock serves as insurance against greater-than-usual demand and against problems in the ordering and delivery of goods. Its size is determined by deducting average usage from the maximum usage that can reasonably be expected during a period. For example, if the firm in the preceding example was faced with a situation of variable demand for its product, it would compute a safety stock as follows:

Maximum expected usage per week	73.3 units
Average usage per week	50
Excess	23.3 units
Lead time	× 3 weeks
Safety stock	70 units

The reorder point is then determined by *adding the safety stock to the average usage during the lead time.* In formula form, the reorder point will be:

$$\text{Reorder point} = (\text{Lead time} \times \text{Average daily or weekly usage}) + \text{Safety stock}$$

Computation of the reorder point by this approach is shown both numerically and graphically in Exhibit 9A–3. As shown in the exhibit, the company places a new order for 500 units when inventory stocks drop to a level of 220 units left on hand.

If management does not wish to assume the worst-case situation by using the maximum expected usage per week, then a slightly more complex calculation of the

Reorder point   The point in time when an order must be placed to replenish depleted stocks; it is determined by multiplying the lead time by the average daily or weekly usage.

Lead time   The interval between the time that an order is placed and the time that the order is finally received from the supplier.

Safety stock   The difference between average usage of materials and maximum usage of materials that can reasonably be expected during the lead time.

Exhibit 9A–3   Determining the Reorder Point—Variable Usage

Economic order quantity. . . . .500 units
Lead time. . . . . 3 weeks
Average weekly usage. . . . . . 50 units
Maximum weekly usage. . . . .77.3 units
Safety stock . . . . 70 units

Reorder point = (3 weeks × 50 units per week) + 70 units = 220 units

safety stock is necessary as shown in Exhibit 9A–4 and based on the data that follow. Assume management makes the following estimates for a yearly period:

Carrying cost per year, $1 per unit
Stock-out cost per unit, $0.60
Average usage per week, 50
Orders placed per year. 12

Demand	Probabilities
80	0.05
120	0.06
140	0.20
150	0.38
160	0.20
180	0.06
220	0.05
	1.00

These estimates reflect the uncertainty experienced by management when they face the various demand possibilities. The table of demand levels and corresponding probabilities presents how management has described the uncertainty they face. This description will, as we shall see, be incorporated in the safety stock calculation.

The calculation of the optimal safety stock begins by computing the various inventory quantities that the demand probabilities indicate could be satisfied by the safety stock. These, quantities are the demand quantities in excess of the expected demand during the lead time period. Calculation *a* in Exhibit 9A–4 illustrates the amounts. Each unit of safety stock inventory will be on hand for the year (the typical time period used), so the carrying costs per unit of inventory per year is used to determine the first cost element, the total carrying cost and the safety stock per year.

The second set of calculations computes the stock-out costs caused because demand exceeds the safety stock quantity. Column *b* in Exhibit 9A–4 reflects the excess demand possibilities above the safety stock and the average demand during the lead time, in other words, the stock-out quantity. The stock-out in units is multiplied by

Exhibit 9A–4   Safety Stock Level

(a) Safety Stock Level in Units	Total Carrying Cost per Year	(b) Stock-Out in Units	(c) Stock-Out Cost per Order Time	Number of Times Orders Placed	Probability of Stock-Out	(d) Expected Stock-Out Cost per Year	(e) Total Cost per Year
–0–	$–0–	10	$ 6.00	12	0.20	$14.40	
		30	18.00	12	0.06	12.96	
		70	42.00	12	0.05	25.20	$52.56
10	10	20	12.00	12	0.06	8.64	
		60	36.00	12	0.05	21.60	40.24
30	30	40	24.00	12	0.05	14.40	44.40
70	70	0	0.00	12	0.00	0.00	70.00

a. Safety stock level is possible demand minus expected demand (e.g., 180 − 150 = 30). Carrying cost of safety stock is units times cost per unit to carry (e.g., 30 × $1 = $30).

b. Stock-out in units is possible demand minus expected demand minus safety stocks (e.g., 220 − 150 − 10 = 60; 180 − 150 − 10 = 20).

c. Stock-out cost per order time is stock-out in unit times stock-out cost per unit (e.g., 30 × $0.60 = $18.00; 40 × 0.06 = $24.00).

d. Expected stock-out cost per year is stock-out cost per time the order is placed, times the number of orders placed per year, times the probability of a stock-out each time (e.g., $6 × 12 × 0.20 = $14.40; $12 × 12 × 0.06 = $8.64). The probability of a stock-out is obtained from the data for various demand levels in excess of the expected amount of 150 plus the safety stock.

e. Total cost per year is the carrying cost of the safety stock plus the expected stock-out cost per year for the appropriate demand levels (e.g., $0.0 + $14.40 + $12.96 + $25.20 = $52.56; $30 + $14.40 = $44.40).

the stock-out cost per unit of 60 cents to give the stock-out cost for each time an order is placed. Knowledge of the average inventory usage per year and the order size is used to determine the number of times orders are placed in a year. To determine the stock-out total costs, the stock-out cost per order is multiplied by the number of orders per year by the probability of each possible demand level to yield column *d*. The sum of the total carrying cost for the safety stock and the expected stock-out costs give the cost for each safety stock level. The lowest expected total costs provide the optimal level of safety stock. Notice that Exhibit 9A–4 suggests 10 is the optimal level, with a total cost of carrying the safety stock of $40.24. The conservative maximum safety stock level of 70 suggested earlier had an annual cost of $70 in this illustration.

Perishable Products

Inventory problems for perishable products or services such as hotel rooms pose an interesting and somewhat different inventory problem. Basically, if too much or many are ordered, the cost of the inventory is similar to a carrying cost, while ordering too few has the cost of contribution forgone from the lost sale. A firm cannot sell what it does not have, while it loses what it purchased but did not sell.

Assume the following:

Purchase cost $3 per unit.
Selling price $5 per unit.

Remember:

You cannot sell what you do not have.
What you buy but cannot sell is lost.

Carefully review the calculations in Exhibit 9A–5 to see how the information can be combined to select the optimum inventory level.

Exhibit 9A–5

Calculation of Optimal Inventory

		Profitability of Order/Demand Combinations and Probability/Demand					
		0.10	0.15	0.05	0.40	0.30	
Inventory		1	2	3	4	5	**Expected Profit**
1		$2	$2	$2	$2	$2	$2.00
2		−1	4	4	4	4	3.50
3		−4	1	6	6	6	4.25
4		−7	−2	3	8	8	4.75
5		−10	−5	0	5	10	3.25*

Note: Four units is the optimum level of inventory because it has the greatest profit, $4.75.

*Profit × probability; for example, $[0.10(-10) + 0.15(-5) + 0.05(0) + 0.40(5) + 0.30(10)] = \$3.25$

For perishable products, each unsold unit of inventory generally is lost; at best, it may receive a rebate from the inventory supplier. Comparison of the total revenue based on demand quantities time selling prices, with the purchase cost of the inventory adjusted for any rebates or returns, determines the cell profit or loss for each combination of demand and inventory shown in Exhibit 9A–5. Because the demand levels are uncertain, each possible net income before income taxes for the particular inventory level is multiplied by the probability of the demand level to yield the expected profits. The maximum expected profit is considered to be the indicator of the optimum inventory level.

Questions

9–1 What is a budget? What is budgetary control?

9–2 Discuss some of the major benefits to be gained from budgeting.

9–3 What is meant by the term *responsibility accounting?*

9–4 What is a master budget? Briefly describe its contents.

9–5 Why is the sales forecast the starting point in budgeting?

9–6 "As a practical matter, planning and control mean exactly the same thing." Do you agree? Explain.

9–7 Describe the flow of budget data in an organization. Who are the participants in the budgeting process, and how do they participate?

9–8 What is a self-imposed budget? What are the major advantages of self-imposed budgets? What caution must be exercised in their use.

9–9 How can budgeting assist a firm in its employment policies?

9–10 "The principal purpose of the cash budget is to see how much cash the company will have in the bank at the end of the year." Do you agree? Explain.

9–11 How does zero-base budgeting differ from traditional budgeting?

9–12   "Budgeting is designed primarily for organizations that have few complexities and uncertainties in their day-to-day operations." Do you agree? Why or why not?

9–13   Which is a better basis for judging actual results, budgeted performance or past performance? Why?

9–14   Is there any difference between a sales forecast and a sales budget? Explain.

9–15   "To a large extent, the success of a budget program hinges on education and good salesmanship." Do you agree? Explain.

9–16   "With profit, not-for-profit, and government entities there is generally a direct relationship between revenues and expenditures." Do you agree with this statement? Why or why not?

9–17   Some people argue budgets should be done away with by organizations facing stiff competition. Why would this be ? Can the budgeting process be modified to cope with the pressures of competition?

9–18   (Appendix 9A) What three classes of costs are balanced by a company's inventory policy?

9–19   (Appendix 9A) What trade-offs in costs are involved in computing the EOQ (economic order quantity)?

9–20   (Appendix 9A) Define *lead time* and *safety stock*.

9–21   (Appendix 9A) List at least three costs associated with a company's inventory policy that do not appear as an expense on the income statement.

9–22   (Appendix 9A) "Managers are more interested in a minimum cost *range* than they are in a minimum cost point." Explain.

9–23   (Appendix 9A) What implications exist when management can reduce setup costs?

9–24   (Appendix 9A) What modifications are necessary to the economic order quantity calculations when purchase discounts are possible?

9–25   (Appendix 9A) What are the inventory costs associated with perishable products?

Exercises

E9–1   Silver Company makes a product that is very popular as a Mother's Day gift. Thus, peak sales occur in May of each year. These peak sales are shown in the company's sales budget for the second quarter given below:

	April	May	June	Total
Budgeted sales	$300,000	$500,000	$200,000	$1,000,000

From past experience, the company has learned that 20% of a month's sales are collected in the month of sale, that another 70% is collected in the month following sale, and that the remaining 10% is collected in the second month following sale. Bad debts are negligible and can be ignored. February sales totalled $230,000, and March sales totalled $260,000.

Required   1. Prepare a schedule of expected cash collections from sales, by month and in total, for the second quarter.

2. Assume that the company will prepare a budgeted balance sheet as of June 30. Compute the accounts receivable as of that date.

E9–2 Down Under Products, Ltd., of Australia has budgeted sales of its popular boomerang for the next four months as follows:

	Sales in Units
April	50,000
May	75,000
June	90,000
July	80,000

The company is now in the process of preparing a production budget for the second quarter. Past experience has shown that end-of-month inventory levels must equal 10% of the following month's sales. The inventory at the end of March was 5,000 units.

Required Prepare a production budget for the second quarter; in your budget, show the number of units to be produced each month and for the quarter in total.

E9–3 Three grams of musk oil are required for each bottle of Mink Caress, a very popular perfume made by a small company in western Siberia. The cost of the musk oil is 150 roubles per gram. (Siberia is located in Russia, whose currency is the rouble.) Budgeted production of Mink Caress is given below by quarters for Year 2 and for the first quarter of Year 3.

	Year 2 Quarter				Year 3 Quarter
	First	Second	Third	Fourth	First
Budgeted production, in bottles	60,000	90,000	150,000	100,000	70,000

Musk oil has become so popular as a perfume base that it has become necessary to carry large inventories as a precaution against stock-outs. For this reason, the inventory of musk oil at the end of a quarter must be equal to 20% of the following quarter's production needs. Some 36,000 grams of musk oil will be on hand to start the first quarter of Year 2.

Required Prepare a materials purchases budget for musk oil, by quarter and in total, for Year 2. At the bottom of your budget, show the amount of purchases in roubles for each quarter and for the year in total.

E9–4 You have been asked to prepare a December cash budget for Ashton Company, a distributor of exercise equipment. The following information is available about the company's operations:

a. The cash balance on December 1 will be $40,000.
b. Actual sales for October and November and expected sales for December are as follows:

	October	November	December
Cash sales	$ 65,000	$ 70,000	$ 83,000
Sales on account	400,000	525,000	600,000

Sales on account are collected over a three-month period in the following ratio: 20% collected in the month of sale, 60% collected in the month following sale, and 18% collected in the second month following sale. The remaining 2% is uncollectible.

c. Purchases of inventory will total $280,000 for December. Thirty percent of a month's inventory purchases are paid during the month of purchase. The accounts payable remaining from November's inventory purchases total $161,000, all of which will be paid in December.

d. Selling and administrative expenses are budgeted at $430,000 for December. Of this amount, $50,000 is for depreciation.
e. A new web server for the Marketing Department costing $76,000 will be purchased for cash during December, and dividends totalling $9,000 will be paid during the month.
f. The company must maintain a minimum cash balance of $20,000. An open line of credit is available from the company's bank to bolster the cash position as needed.

Required
1. Prepare a schedule of expected cash collections for December.
2. Prepare a schedule of expected cash disbursements for materials during December to suppliers for inventory purchases.
3. Prepare a cash budget for December. Indicate in the financing section any borrowing that will be needed during the month.

E9–5 A cash budget, by quarters, is given below for a retail company. Fill in the missing amounts (000 omitted). The company requires a minimum cash balance of at least $5,000 to start each quarter.

	1	2	3	4	Year
Cash balance, beginning	$ 6	$?	$?	$?	$?
Add collections from customers	?	?	96	?	323
Total cash available before current financing	71	?	?	?	?
Less disbursements:					
Purchase of inventory	35	45	?	35	?
Operating expenses	?	30	30	?	113
Equipment purchases	8	8	10	?	36
Dividends	2	2	2	2	?
Total disbursements	?	85	?	?	?
Excess (deficiency) of cash available over disbursements	(2)	?	11	?	?
Financing:					
Borrowings	?	15	—	—	?
Repayments (including interest)*	—	—	(?)	(17)	(?)
Total financing	?	?	?	?	?
Cash balance, ending	$?	$?	$?	$?	$?

*Interest will total $1,000 for the year.

E9–6 (Appendix 9A) Bedford Motor Company uses 4,500 units of Part S-10 each year. The cost of placing one order for Part S-10 is estimated to be about $20. Other costs associated with carrying Part S-10 in inventory are:

	Annual Cost per Part
Insurance	$0.20
Property taxes	0.09
Interest on funds invested	0.15
Other	0.06
Total cost	$0.50

Required
1. Compute the economic order quantity (EOQ) for Part S-10.
2. Assume that the company has been able to reduce the cost of placing an order to only $1. Also assume that when the waste and inefficiency caused by inventories is considered, the cost to carry a part in inventory jumps to $1.60 per unit. Under these conditions, what would be the EOQ?

E9–7   (Appendix 9A) Kaufheim A.G. of Dresden, Germany, distributes medical supplies throughout Germany. Selected information relating to a quick-developing X-ray film carried by the company is given below:

Economic order quantity (EOQ)	700 units
Maximum weekly usage	60 units
Lead time	4 weeks
Average weekly usage	50 units

Management is trying to determine the proper safety stock to carry on this inventory item and to determine the proper reorder point.

Required   1.   Assume that no safety stock is to be carried. What is the reorder point?
2.   Assume that a full safety stock is to be carried.
   a.   What would be the size of the safety stock in units?
   b.   What would be the reorder point?

E9–8   (Appendix 9A) Flint Company uses 9,000 units of part AK-4 each year. To get better control over its inventories, the company is anxious to determine the economic order quantity (EOQ) for this part.

Required   1.   The company has determined that the cost to place an order for the part is $30, and it has determined that the cost to carry one part in inventory for one year is $1.50. Compute the EOQ for the part.
2.   Assume that the cost to place an order increases from $30 to $40 per order. What will be the effect on the EOQ? Show computations.
3.   Assume that the cost to carry a part in inventory increases from $1.50 to $2.00 per part. (Ordering costs remain unchanged at $30 per order.) What will be the effect on the EOQ? Show computations.
4.   In (2) and (3) above, why does an increase in cost cause the EOQ to go up in one case and to go down in the other?

E9–9   (Appendix 9A) Classify the following as either (a) costs of carrying inventory or (b) costs of not carrying sufficient inventory:

1.   Airfreight on a rush order of a critical part needed in production.
2.   Interest paid on investment funds.
3.   Municipal taxes on inventory.
4.   Spoilage of perishable goods.
5.   Excessive setup costs.
6.   Customers lost through inability of the company to make prompt delivery.
7.   Quantity discounts lost as a result of purchasing in small lots.
8.   Fire insurance on inventory.
9.   Loss sustained when a competitor comes out with a less expensive, more efficient product.
10. A general feeling of ill will among customers, due to broken delivery promises.

Problems

P9–10   Cash Budget   Herbal Care Corp., a distributor of herb-based sun screens, is ready to begin its third quarter, in which peak sales occur. The company has requested a $40,000, 90-day loan from its bank to help meet cash requirements during the quarter. Since Herbal Care has experienced difficulty in paying off its loans in the past, the loan officer at the bank has asked the company to prepare a cash budget for the quarter. In response to this request, the following data have been assembled:

a.   On July 1, the beginning of the third quarter, the company will have a cash balance of $44,500.
b.   Actual sales for the last two months and budgeted sales for the third quarter follow:

May (actual)	$250,000
June (actual)	300,000
July (budgeted)	400,000
August (budgeted)	600,000
September (budgeted)	320,000

(handwritten: 25% / 3%)

Past experience shows that 25% of a month's sales are collected in the month of sale, 70% in the month following sale, and 3% in the second month following sale. The remainder is uncollectible.

c. Budgeted merchandise purchases and budgeted expenses for the third quarter are given below:

	July	August	September
Merchandise purchases	$240,000	$350,000	$175,000
Salaries and wages	45,000	50,000	40,000
Advertising	130,000	145,000	80,000
Rent payments	9,000	9,000	9,000
Depreciation	10,000	10,000	10,000

Merchandise purchases are paid in full during the month following purchase. Accounts payable for merchandise purchases on June 30, which will be paid during July, total $180,000.

d. Equipment costing $10,000 will be purchased for cash during July.

e. In preparing the cash budget, assume that the $40,000 loan will be made in July and repaid in September. Interest on the loan will total $1,200.

Required
1. Prepare a schedule of expected cash collections for July, August, and September and for the quarter in total.
2. Prepare a cash budget, by month and in total, for the third quarter.
3. If the company needs a minimum cash balance of $20,000 to start each month, can the loan be repaid as planned? Explain.

P9–11   Production and Purchases Budgets   Pearl Products Limited of Shenzhen, China, manufactures and distributes toys throughout South East Asia. Three cubic centimetres (cc) of solvent H300 are required to manufacture each unit of Supermix, one of the company's products. The company is now planning raw materials needs for the third quarter, the quarter in which peak sales of Supermix occur. To keep production and sales moving smoothly, the company has the following inventory requirements:

a. The finished goods inventory on hand at the end of each month must be equal to 3,000 units of Supermix plus 20% of the next month's sales. The finished goods inventory on June 30 is budgeted to be 10,000 units.

b. The raw materials inventory on hand at the end of each month must be equal to one-half of the following month's production needs for raw materials. The raw materials inventory on June 30 is budgeted to be 54,000 cc of solvent H300.

c. The company maintains no work in process inventories.

A sales budget for Supermix for the last six months of the year follows.

	Budgeted Sales in Units
July	35,000
August	40,000
September	50,000
October	30,000
November	20,000
December	10,000

Required
1. Prepare a production budget for Supermix for the months July–October.

2. Examine the production budget that you prepared in (1) above. Why will the company produce more units than it sells in July and August, and fewer units than it sells in September and October?
3. Prepare a budget showing the quantity of solvent H300 to be purchased for July, August, and September, and for the quarter in total.

P9–12   Master Budget Preparation   Minden Company is a wholesale distributor of premium European chocolates. The company's balance sheet as of April 30 is given below:

MINDEN COMPANY
Balance Sheet
April 30

Assets

Cash	$ 9,000
Accounts receivable, customers	54,000
Inventory	30,000
Buildings and equipment, net of depreciation	207,000
Total assets	$300,000

Liabilities and Shareholders' Equity

Accounts payable, suppliers	$ 63,000
Note payable	14,500
Capital stock, no par	180,000
Retained earnings	42,500
Total liabilities and shareholders' equity	$300,000

The company is in the process of preparing budget data for May. A number of budget items have already been prepared, as stated below:

a. Sales are budgeted at $200,000 for May. Of these sales, $60,000 will be for cash; the remainder will be credit sales. One-half of a month's credit sales are collected in the month the sales are made, and the remainder is collected in the following month. All of the April 30 receivables will be collected in May.
b. Purchases of inventory are expected to total $120,000 during May. These purchases will all be on account. Forty percent of all purchases are paid for in the month of purchase; the remainder is paid in the following month. All of the April 30 accounts payable to suppliers will be paid during May.
c. The May 31 inventory balance is budgeted at $40,000.
d. Operating expenses for May are budgeted at $72,000, exclusive of depreciation. These expenses will be paid in cash. Depreciation is budgeted at $2,000 for the month.
e. The note payable on the April 30 balance sheet will be paid during May, with $100 in interest. (All of the interest relates to May.)
f. New refrigerating equipment costing $6,500 will be purchased for cash during May.
g. During May, the company will borrow $20,000 from its bank by giving a new note payable to the bank for that amount. The new note will be due in one year.

Required 1. Prepare a cash budget for May. Support your budget with schedules showing budgeted cash receipts from sales and budgeted cash payments for inventory purchases.
2. Prepare a budgeted income statement for May. Use the traditional income statement format.
3. Prepare a budgeted balance sheet as of May 31.

P9–13   Ethics and the Manager   Norton Company, a manufacturer of infant furniture and carriages, is in the initial stages of preparing the annual budget for next year. Scott Ford has recently joined Norton's accounting staff and is interested to learn as much as possible about the company's budgeting process. During a recent lunch with Marge Atkins, sales manager, and Pete Granger, production manager, Ford initiated the following conversation.

Ford: Since I'm new around here and am going to be involved with the preparation of the annual budget, I'd be interested to learn how the two of you estimate sales and production numbers.

Atkins: We start out very methodically by looking at recent history, discussing what we know about current accounts, potential customers, and the general state of consumer spending. Then, we add that usual dose of intuition to come up with the best forecast we can.

Granger: I usually take the sales projections as the basis for my projections. Of course, we have to make an estimate of what this year's ending inventories will be, which is sometimes difficult.

Ford: Why does that present a problem? There must have been an estimate of ending inventories in the budget for the current year.

Granger: Those number aren't always reliable since Marge makes some adjustments to the sales number before passing them on to me.

Ford: What kind of adjustments?

Atkins: Well, we don't want to fall short of the sales projections so we generally give ourselves a little breathing room by lowering the initial sales projection anywhere from 5% to 10%.

Granger: So, you can see why this year's budget is not a very reliable starting point. We always have to adjust the projected production rates as the year progresses and, of course, this changes the ending inventory estimates. By the way, we make similar adjustments to expenses by adding at least 10% to the estimates; I think everyone around here does the same thing.

Required

1. Marge Atkins and Pete Granger have described the use of what is sometimes called *budgetary slack*.
   a. Explain why Atkins and Granger behave in this manner and describe the benefits they expect to realize from the use of budgetary slack.
   b. Explain how the use of budgetary slack can adversely affect Atkins and Granger.
2. As a management accountant, Scott Ford believes that the behaviour described by Marge Atkins and Pete Granger may be unethical. By referring to the Standards of Ethical Conduct for Management Accountants in Chapter 1, explain why the use of budgetary slack may be unethical.

(CMA, adapted)

P9–14   Tabulation Approach to Economic Order Quantity (EOQ)
(Appendix 9A) Hermanos, S.A., of Mexico City uses 15,000 ingots of a special silver alloy each year to manufacture jewellery. The ingots are purchased from a supplier in another state according to the following price schedule:

Ingots	Per Ingot
500	$30.00
1,000	29.90
1,500	29.85
2,000	29.80
2,500	29.75

The currency in Mexico is the new peso, which can be denoted by a $ sign.

Hermanos, S.A., sends its own truck to the supplier's plant to pick up the ingots. The truck's capacity is 2,500 ingots per trip. The company has been getting a full load of ingots each trip, making six trips each year. The cost of making one round trip to the supplier's plant is $500. The cost of the paperwork associated with each trip is $30.

The supplier requires that all purchases be made in round 500-ingot lots. The cost of storing one ingot for one year is $10.

Required

1. Using the tabulation approach to EOQ, compute the volume in which the company should be purchasing its ingots. Treat the savings arising from quantity discounts as a reduction in total annual trucking and storing costs.
2. Compute the annual cost savings that will be realized if the company purchases in the volume which you have determined in (1) above, as compared to its present purchase policy.

P9–15 Integration of the Sales, Production, and Purchases Budgets
Milo Company manufactures beach umbrellas. The company is now preparing detailed budgets for the third quarter and has assembled the following information to assist in the budget preparation:

a. The Marketing Department has estimated sales as follows for the remainder of the year (in units):

July	30,000	October	20,000
August	70,000	November	10,000
September	50,000	December	10,000

The selling price of the beach umbrellas is $12 per unit.

b. All sales are on account. Based on past experience, sales are collected in the following pattern:

> 30% in the month of sale
> 65% in the month following sale
> 5% uncollectible

Sales for June totalled $300,000.

c. The company maintains finished goods inventories equal to 15% of the following month's sales. This requirement will be met at the end of June.

d. Each beach umbrella requires 1 metre of Gilden, a material that is sometimes hard to get. Therefore, the company requires that the inventory of Gilden on hand at the end of each month be equal to 50% of the following month's production needs. The inventory of Gilden on hand at the beginning and end of the quarter will be:

> June 30 .... 18,000 metres
> September 30 ...... ? metres

e. The Gilden costs $3.20 per metre. One-half of a month's purchases of Gilden is paid for in the month of purchase; the remainder is paid for in the following month. The accounts payable on July 1 for purchases of Gilden during June will be $76,000.

Required
1. Prepare a sales budget, by month and in total, for the third quarter. (Show your budget in both units and dollars.) Also prepare a schedule of expected cash collections, by month and in total, for the third quarter.
2. Prepare a production budget for each of the months July–October.
3. Prepare a materials purchases budget for Gilden, by month and in total, for the third quarter. Also prepare a schedule of expected cash payments for Gilden, by month and in total, for the third quarter.

P9–16 Cash Budget with Supporting Schedules Garden Sales, Inc., sells garden supplies. Management is planning its cash needs for the second quarter. The company usually has to borrow money during this quarter to support peak sales of lawn care equipment, which occur during May. The following information has been assembled to assist in preparing a cash budget for the quarter:

a. Budgeted monthly income statements for April–July are:

	April	May	June	July
Sales	$600,000	$900,000	$500,000	$400,000
Cost of goods sold	420,000	630,000	350,000	280,000
Gross margin	180,000	270,000	150,000	120,000
Less operating expenses:				
Selling expense	79,000	120,000	62,000	51,000
Administrative expense*	45,000	52,000	41,000	38,000
Total expenses	124,000	172,000	103,000	89,000
Net income	$ 56,000	$ 98,000	$ 47,000	$ 31,000

*Includes $20,000 depreciation each month.

b. Sales are 20% for cash and 80% on account.
c. Sales on account are collected over a three-month period in the following ratio: 10% collected in the month of sale; 70% collected in the first month following the month of sale; and the remaining 20% collected in the second month following the month of sale. February's sales totalled $200,000, and March's sales totalled $300,000.
d. Inventory purchases are paid for within 15 days. Therefore, 50% of a month's inventory purchases are paid for in the month of purchase. The remaining 50% is paid in the following month. Accounts payable at March 31 for inventory purchases during March total $126,000.
e. At the end of each month, inventory must be on hand equal to 20% of the cost of the merchandise to be sold in the following month. The merchandise inventory at March 31 is $84,000.
f. Dividends of $49,000 will be declared and paid in April.
g. Equipment costing $16,000 will be purchased for cash in May.
h. The cash balance at March 31 is $52,000; the company must maintain a cash balance of at least $40,000 at all times.
i. The company can borrow from its bank as needed to bolster the Cash account. Borrowings and repayments must be in multiples of $1,000. All borrowings take place at the beginning of a month, and all repayments are made at the end of a month. The annual interest rate is 12%. Compute interest on whole months ($\frac{1}{12}$, $\frac{2}{12}$, and so forth).

Required

1. Prepare a schedule of expected cash collections from sales for each of the months April, May, and June, and for the quarter in total.
2. Prepare the following for merchandise inventory:
    a. An inventory purchases budget for each of the months April, May, and June.
    b. A schedule of expected cash disbursements for inventory for each of the months April, May, and June, and for the quarter in total.
3. Prepare a cash budget for the second quarter, by month as well as in total for the quarter. Show borrowings from the company's bank and repayments to the bank as needed to maintain the minimum cash balance.

P9–17 Planning Bank Financing by Means of a Cash Budget Westex Products is a wholesale distributor of industrial cleaning products. When the treasurer of Westex Products approached the company's bank in late 1999 seeking short-term financing, he was told that money was very tight and that any borrowing over the next year would have to be supported by a detailed statement of cash receipts and disbursements. The treasurer also was told that it would be very helpful to the bank if borrowers would indicate the quarters in which they would be needing funds, as well as the amounts that would be needed, and the quarters in which repayments could be made.

Since the treasurer is unsure as to the particular quarters in which the bank financing will be needed, he has assembled the following information to assist in preparing a detailed cash budget:

a. Budgeted sales and merchandise purchases for the year 2000, as well as actual sales and purchases for the last quarter of 1999, are:

	Sales	Merchandise Purchases
1999:		
Fourth quarter actual	$200,000	$126,000
2000:		
First quarter estimated	300,000	186,000
Second quarter estimated	400,000	246,000
Third quarter estimated	500,000	305,000
Fourth quarter estimated	200,000	126,000

b. The company normally collects 65% of a quarter's sales before the quarter ends and another 33% in the following quarter. The remainder is uncollectible. This pattern of collections is now being experienced in the 1999 fourth-quarter actual data.

c. Eighty percent of a quarter's merchandise purchases are paid for within the quarter. The remainder is paid in the following quarter.

d. Operating expenses for the year 2000 are budgeted quarterly at $50,000 plus 15% of sales. Of the fixed amount, $20,000 each quarter is depreciation.

e. The company will pay $10,000 in dividends each quarter.

f. Equipment purchases of $75,000 will be made in the second quarter, and purchases of $48,000 will be made in the third quarter. These purchases will be for cash.

g. The Cash account contained $10,000 at the end of 1999. The treasurer feels that this represents a minimum balance that must be maintained.

h. Any borrowing will take place at the beginning of a quarter, and any repayments will be made at the end of a quarter at an annual interest rate of 10%. Interest is paid only when principal is repaid. All borrowings and all repayments of principal must be in round $1,000 amounts. Interest payments can be in any amount. (Compute interest on whole months, e.g., $\frac{1}{12}$, $\frac{2}{12}$.)

i. At present, the company has no loans outstanding.

Required

1. Prepare the following by quarter and in total for the year 2000:
   a. A schedule of expected cash collections.
   b. A schedule of budgeted cash disbursements for merchandise purchases.

2. Compute the expected cash payments for operating expenses, by quarter and in total, for the year 2000.

3. Prepare a cash budget, by quarter and in total, for the year 2000. Show clearly in your budget the quarter(s) in which borrowing will be necessary and the quarter(s) in which repayments can be made, as requested by the company's bank.

P9–18 Master Budget Preparation Hillyard Company, an office supplies specialty store, prepares its master budget on a quarterly basis. The following data have been assembled to assist in preparation of the master budget for the first quarter:

a. As of December 31 (the end of the prior quarter), the company's general ledger showed the following account balances:

	Debits	Credits
Cash	$ 48,000	
Accounts Receivable	224,000	
Inventory	60,000	
Buildings and Equipment (net)	370,000	
Accounts Payable		$ 93,000
Capital Stock		500,000
Retained Earnings		109,000
	$702,000	$702,000

b. Actual sales for December and budgeted sales for the next four months are as follows:

December (actual)	$280,000
January	400,000
February	600,000
March	300,000
April	200,000

c. Sales are 20% for cash and 80% on credit. All payments on credit sales are collected in the month following sale. The accounts receivable at December 31 are a result of December credit sales.

d. The company's gross profit rate is 40% of sales.

e. Monthly expenses are budgeted as follows: salaries and wages, $27,000 per month: advertising, $70,000 per month; shipping, 5% of sales; depreciation, $14,000 per month; other expense, 3% of sales.

f. At the end of each month, inventory is to be on hand equal to 25% of the following month's sales needs, stated at cost.

g. One-half of a month's inventory purchases is paid for in the month of purchase; the other half is paid for in the following month.

h. During February, the company will purchase a new copy machine for $1,700 cash. During March, other equipment will be purchased for cash at a cost of $84,500.

i. During January, the company will declare and pay $45,000 in cash dividends.

j. The company must maintain a minimum cash balance of $30,000. An open line of credit is available at a local bank for any borrowing that may be needed during the quarter. All borrowing is done at the beginning of a month, and all repayments are made at the end of a month. Borrowings and repayments of principal must be in multiples of $1,000. Interest is paid only at the time of payment of principal. The annual interest rate is 12%. (Figure interest on whole months, e.g., $\frac{1}{12}$, $\frac{2}{12}$.)

Required   Using the data above, complete the following statements and schedules for the first quarter:

1. Schedule of expected cash collections:

	January	February	March	Quarter
Cash sales	$ 80,000	120,000	60,000	260,000
Credit sales	224,000	320,000	480,000	1,024,000
Total cash collections	$304,000	440,000	540,000	1,289,000

2. a. Inventory purchases budget:

	January	February	March	Quarter
Budgeted cost of goods sold	$240,000*	$360,000	180,000	780,000
Add desired ending inventory	90,000†	45,000	30,000	185,000
Total needs	330,000	405,000	210,000	965,000
Less beginning inventory	60,000	90,000	45,000	195,000
Required purchases	$270,000	315,000	185,000	770,000

*For January sales: $400,000 sales × 60% cost ratio = $240,000.

†$360,000 × 25% = $90,000.

770

b. Schedule of cash disbursements for purchases:

	January	February	March	Quarter
December purchases	$ 93,000			$ 93,000
January purchases ($270,000)	135,000	135,000		270,000
February purchases		157,500	157,500	315,000
March purchases			92.5	92,500
Total cash disbursements for purchases	$228,000	292,500	250,000	770,500

3. Schedule of cash disbursements for expenses:

	January	February	March	Quarter
Salaries and wages	$ 27,000			81,000
Advertising	70,000			210,000
Shipping	20,000	30,000	15,000	65,000
Other expenses	12,000	18,000	9,000	39,000
Total cash disbursements for operating expenses	$129,000	145,000	121,000	375,000

595

4. Cash budget:

	January	February	March	Quarter
Cash balance, beginning	$ 48,000			
Add cash collections	304,000			
Total cash available	352,000			
Less disbursements:				
Purchases of inventory	228,000			
Operating expenses	129,000			
Purchases of equipment	—			
Cash dividends	45,000			
Total disbursements	402,000			
Excess (deficiency) of cash	(50,000)			
Financing:				
Etc.				

5. Prepare an income statement for the quarter ending March 31 as shown in Schedule 9 in the chapter.
6. Prepare a balance sheet as of March 31.

P9–19   Tabulation Approach; Economic Order Quantity (EOQ); Reorder Point   (Appendix 9A) You have been engaged to install an inventory control system for Kiwi Electronics, Ltd., of Christchurch, New Zealand. Among the inventory control features that Kiwi Electronics desires are indicators of "how much" to order "when." The following information is furnished for one item, called a duosonic, that is carried in inventory.

a. Duosonics are sold by the gross (12 dozen) at a list price of $NZ800 per gross. (The currency in New Zealand is the New Zealand dollar, denoted here by $NZ.) Kiwi Electronics receives a 40% trade discount off list price on purchases in gross lots.
b. Freight cost is $NZ20 per gross from the shipping point to Kiwi Electronics' plant.
c. Kiwi Electronics uses about 5,000 duosonics during a 259-day production year but must purchase a total of 36 gross per year to allow for normal breakage. Minimum and maximum usages are 12 and 28 duosonics per day, respectively.
d. Normal delivery time to receive an order is 20 working days from the date that a purchase request is initiated. A stock-out (complete exhaustion of the inventory) of duosonics would stop production, and Kiwi Electronics would purchase duosonics locally at list price rather than shut down.
e. The cost of placing an order is $NZ30.
f. Space storage cost is $NZ24 per year per average gross in storage.
g. Insurance and taxes are approximately 12% of the net delivered cost of average inventory, and Kiwi Electronics expects a return of at least 8% on its average investment. (Ignore ordering costs and carrying costs in making these computations.)

Required

1. Prepare a schedule computing the total annual cost of duosonics based on uniform order lot sizes of one, two, three, four, and five gross of duosonics. (The schedule should show the total annual cost according to each lot size.) Indicate the EOQ.
2. Prepare a schedule computing the minimum stock reorder point for duosonics. This is the point below which reordering is necessary to guard against a stock-out. Factors to be considered include average lead period usage and safety stock requirements.

(CPA, adapted)

P9–20   Economic Order Quantity (EOQ); Safety Stock   (Appendix 9A) Myron Metal Works, Inc., uses a small casting in one of its finished products. The castings are purchased from a foundry located in another province. In total, Myron Metal Works, Inc., purchases 54,000 castings per year at a cost of $8 per casting.

The castings are used evenly throughout the year in the production process on a 360-day-per-year basis. The company estimates that it costs $90 to place a single purchase order and about $3 to carry one casting in inventory for a year. The high carrying costs result from the need to keep the castings in carefully controlled temperature and humidity conditions, and from the high cost of insurance.

Delivery from the foundry generally takes 6 days, but it can take as much as 10 days. The days of delivery time and the percentage of their occurrence are shown in the following tabulation:

Delivery Time (days)	Percentage of Occurrence
6	75
7	10
8	5
9	5
10	5
	100

Required

1. Compute the economic order quantity (EOQ).
2. Assume that the company is willing to assume a 15% risk of being out of stock. What would be the safety stock? The reorder point?
3. Assume that the company is willing to assume only a 5% risk of being out of stock. What would be the safety stock? The reorder point?
4. Assume a 5% stock-out risk as stated in (3) above. What would be the total cost of ordering and carrying inventory for one year?
5. Refer to the original data. Assume that using process reengineering the company reduces its cost of placing a purchase order to only $6. Also, the company estimates that when the waste and inefficiency caused by inventories are considered, the true cost of carrying a unit in stock is $7.20 per year.
   a. Compute the new EOQ.
   b. How frequently would the company be placing an order, as compared to the old purchasing policy?

P9–21 Master Budget Completion   Following is selected information relating to the operations of Shilow Company, a wholesale distributor:

Current assets as of March 31:

Cash	$ 8,000
Accounts receivable	20,000
Inventory	36,000
Plant and equipment, net	120,000
Accounts payable	21,750
Capital stock	150,000
Retained earnings	12,250

a. Gross profit is 25% of sales.
b. Actual and budgeted sales data:

March (actual)	$50,000
April	60,000
May	72,000
June	90,000
July	48,000

c. Sales are 60% for cash and 40% on credit. Credit sales are collected in the month following sale. The accounts receivable at March 31 are a result of March credit sales.
d. At the end of each month, inventory is to be on hand equal to 80% of the following month's sales needs, stated at cost.
e. One-half of a month's inventory purchases is paid for in the month of purchase; the other half is paid for in the following month. The accounts payable at March 31 are a result of March purchases of inventory.

f. Monthly expenses are as follows: salaries and wages, 12% of sales; rent, $2,500 per month; other expenses (excluding depreciation), 6% of sales. Assume that these expenses are paid monthly. Depreciation is $900 per month (includes depreciation on new assets).
g. Equipment costing $1,500 will be purchased for cash in April.
h. The company must maintain a minimum cash balance of $4,000. An open line of credit is available at a local bank. All borrowing is done at the beginning of a month, and all repayments are made at the end of a month; borrowing must be in multiples of $1,000. The annual interest rate is 12%. Interest is paid only at the time of repayment of principal; figure interest on whole months ($\frac{1}{12}$, $\frac{2}{12}$, and so forth).

Required   Using the data above:

1. Complete the following schedule:

Schedule of Expected Cash Collections

	April	May	June	Quarter
Cash sales	$36,000			
Credit sales	20,000			
Total collections	$56,000			

2. Complete the following:

Inventory Purchases Budget

	April	May	June	Quarter
Budgeted cost of goods sold	$45,000*	$54,000		
Add desired ending inventory	43,200†			
Total needs	88,200			
Less beginning inventory	36,000			
Required purchases	$52,200			

*For April sales: $60,000 sales × 75% cost ratio = $45,000.

†$54,000 × 80% = $43,200

Schedule of Expected Cash Disbursements—Purchases

	April	May	June	Quarter
March purchases	$21,750			$21,750
April purchases	26,100	$26,100		52,200
May purchases				
June purchases				
Total disbursements	$47,850			

3. Complete the following:

Schedule of Expected Cash Disbursements—Operating Expenses

	April	May	June	Quarter
Salaries and wages	$ 7,200			
Rent	2,500			
Other expenses	3,600			
Total disbursements	$13,300			

4. Complete the following cash budget:

Cash Budget

	April	May	June	Quarter
Cash balance, beginning	$ 8,000			
Add cash collections	56,000	___	___	___
Total cash available	64,000	___	___	___
Less cash disbursements:				
For inventory	47,850			
For expenses	13,300			
For equipment	1,500	___	___	___
Total cash disbursements . . .	62,650	___	___	___
Excess (deficiency) of cash	1,350			
Financing:				
Etc.				

5. Prepare an income statement for the quarter ended June 30. (Use the functional format in preparing your income statement, as shown in Schedule 9 in the text.)
6. Prepare a balance sheet as of June 30.

P9–22   Integrated Operating Budgets   The West Division of Vader Corporation produces an intricate component part used in Vader's major product line. The divisional manager has recently been concerned about a lack of coordination between purchasing and production personnel and believes that a monthly budgeting system would be better than the present system.

The manager of West Division has decided to develop budget information for the third quarter of the current year as a trial before the budget system is implemented for an entire fiscal year. In response to the manager's request for data that could be used to develop budget information, the controller of West Division accumulated the following data:

Sales   Sales through June 30, the first six months of the current year, were 24,000 units. Actual sales in units for May and June and estimated unit sales for the next five months are detailed as follows:

May (actual)	4,000
June (actual)	4,000
July (estimated)	5,000
August (estimated)	6,000
September (estimated)	7,000
October (estimated)	7,500
November (estimated)	8,000

West Division expects to sell 65,000 units during the year ending December 31.

Direct Material   Data regarding the materials used in the component are shown in the following schedule. The desired monthly ending inventory for all direct materials is to have sufficient materials on hand to provide for 50% of the next month's production needs.

Direct Material	Units of Direct Materials per Finished Component	Cost per Unit	Inventory Level June 30
No. 101	6 grams	$2.40	35,000 grams
No. 211	4 kilograms	5.00	30,000 kilograms

Direct Labour   Each component must pass through three processes to be completed. Data regarding the direct labour are as follows:

Process	Direct Labour-Hours per Finished Component	Cost per Direct Labour-Hour
Forming	0.80	$8.00
Assembly	2.00	5.50
Finishing	0.25	6.00

Manufacturing Overhead   West Division produced 27,000 components during the six-month period through June 30. The actual variable overhead costs incurred during this six-month period are shown below. The controller of West Division believes that the variable overhead costs will be incurred at the same rate during the last six months of the year.

Supplies	$ 59,400
Electricity	27,000
Indirect labour	54,000
Other	8,100
Total variable overhead	$148,500

The fixed manufacturing overhead costs incurred during the first six months amounted to $93,500. Fixed manufacturing overhead costs are budgeted for the full year as follows:

Supervision	$ 60,000
Taxes	7,200
Depreciation	86,400
Other	32,400
Total fixed manufacturing overhead	$186,000

Finished Goods Inventory   The desired monthly ending inventory in units of completed components is 80% of the next month's estimated sales. There are 4,000 finished units in inventory on June 30.

Required

1. Prepare a production budget for the West Division for the third quarter ending September 30. Show computations by month and in total for the quarter.
2. Prepare a direct materials purchases budget in units and in dollars for each type of material for the third quarter ending September 30. Again show computations by month and in total for the quarter.
3. Prepare a direct labour budget in hours and in dollars for the third quarter ending September 30. This time it is *not* necessary to show monthly figures; show quarterly totals only. Assume that the workforce is adjusted as work requirements change.
4. Assume that the company plans to produce a total of 65,000 units for the year. Prepare a manufacturing overhead budget for the six-month period ending December 31. Again, it is *not* necessary to show monthly figures.

(CMA, adapted)

P9–23   Cash Budget for One Month[13]   Wallace Products, Ltd., is planning its cash needs for July. Since the company will be buying some new equipment during the month, the treasurer is sure that some borrowing will be needed, but he is uncertain how much. The following data have been assembled to assist the treasurer in preparing a cash budget for the month:

a. Equipment will be purchased during July for cash at a cost of $45,000.
b. Selling and administrative expenses will be:

---

13. Adapted from Sherry Penny, "What a University Has Learned from 4 Years of Financial Stress," *The Chronicle of Higher Education,* May 5, 1993, pp. B1–B3.

Advertising	$110,000
Sales salaries	50,000
Administrative salaries	35,000
Shipping	2,100

c. Sales are budgeted at $800,000 for July. Customers are allowed a 2½% cash discount on accounts paid within 10 days after the end of the month of sale. Only 50% of the payments made in the month following sale fall within the discount period. (All of the company's sales are on account.)

d. On June 30, the company will have the following accounts receivable outstanding:

Month	Sales	Accounts Receivable at June 30	Percentage of Sales Uncollected at June 30	Percentage to Be Collected in July
March	$430,000	$ 6,450	1½%	?
April	590,000	35,400	6%	?
May	640,000	128,000	20%	?
June	720,000	720,000	100%	?

Bad debts are negligible. All March receivables shown above will have been collected by the end of July, and the collection pattern implicit in the schedule above will be the same in July as in previous months.

e. Production costs are budgeted as follows for July:

Prime costs:		
Raw materials to be used in production		$342,000
Direct labour		95,000
Overhead costs:		
Indirect labour	$36,000	
Utilities	1,900	
Payroll benefits	14,800	
Depreciation	28,000	
Property taxes	1,100	
Fire insurance	1,700	
Amortization of patents	3,500	
Scrapping of obsolete goods	2,600	89,600
Total production costs		$526,600

f. The raw materials inventory is budgeted to increase by $18,000 during July; other inventories will not change.

g. Half of the raw materials purchased each month is paid for in the month of purchase; the other half is paid for in the following month. Accounts payable at June 30 for raw materials purchases will be $172,000.

h. All July payroll amounts will be paid for within the month of July.

i. Utilities costs are paid for within the month.

j. The $14,800 monthly charge above for "Payroll benefits" includes the following items:

Company pension plan, including ½ of a $9,600 special adjustment that was paid in April	$7,000
Group insurance (payable semiannually, with the last payment having been made in January)	900
Unemployment insurance (payable monthly)	1,300
Vacation pay, which represents ½ of the annual cost (July's vacations will require $14,100)	5,600

k. Property taxes are paid in June of each year.

l. Fire insurance premiums were paid in January, in advance.

m. The company has an open line of credit with the Royal Calgary Bank. All borrowing from the bank must be in round $1,000 amounts.

n. The cash balance on June 30 will be $78,000; the company must maintain a cash balance of at least $75,000 at all times.

Required

1. Prepare a schedule showing expected cash collections for July.
2. Compute (a) budgeted cash disbursements for raw materials purchases, and (b) budgeted cash disbursements for overhead for July.
3. Prepare a cash budget for July in good form.
4. A member of the board of directors of Wallace Products stated, "The monthly cash budget shows the company's cash surplus or deficiency and assures us that an unexpected cash shortage will not occur." Comment on this statement.

(SMAC, adapted)

P9–24 Economic Order Quantity, Safety Stock, and JIT Purchasing Impact   (Appendix 9A) Stoffer Manufacturing Company uses 7,200 units of material X each year. The material is used evenly throughout the year in the company's production process. A recent cost study indicates that it costs $3.20 to carry one unit in inventory for a year. The company estimates that the cost of placing an order for material X is $180.

On the average, it takes 7 days to receive an order from the supplier. Sometimes, orders do not arrive for 10 days, and at rare intervals (about 2% of the time) they do not arrive for 12 days. Each unit of material X costs the company $15. Stoffer works an average of 360 days per year.

Required

1. Compute the EOQ.
2. What size safety stock would you recommend for material X? Why?
3. What is the reorder point for material X in units?
4. Compute the total cost associated with ordering and carrying material X in inventory for a year. (Do *not* include the $15 purchase cost in this computation.)
5. Refer to the original data. Assume that as a result of adopting JIT purchasing policies, the company is able to reduce the cost of placing a purchase order to only $5. Also assume that after considering the waste and inefficiency caused by inventories, the actual cost of carrying one unit of material X in inventory for a year is $18.
   a. Compute the new EOQ.
   b. How frequently would the company be placing a purchase order, as compared to the old purchasing policy?

P9–25 Inventory of Perishable Products   (Appendix 9A) Bruno's Bakery stocks fresh baked doughnuts that sell for $6 per dozen and cost $4 per dozen to produce. Unsold day-old doughnuts are reduced in price to $3 per dozen and are always completely sold without affecting the current day's demand for fresh doughnuts. Bruno, the owner of the bakery, estimates daily demand characteristics for fresh doughnuts as follows:

Demand (Dozens)	Probability
20	0.1
22	0.2
24	0.3
26	0.3
28	0.1

Required How many dozens of doughnuts should Bruno's Bakery produce each morning to maximize net income? Support your decision by preparing an appropriate payoff table.

(SMAC, adapted)

Cases

C9–26 Master Budget with Supporting Schedules   You have just been hired as a new management trainee by Earrings Unlimited, a distributor of earrings to various retail outlets located in shopping malls across the country. In the past, the company has done very little in the way of budgeting and at certain times of the year has experienced a shortage of cash.

Since you are well trained in budgeting, you have decided to prepare comprehensive budgets for the upcoming second quarter in order to show management the benefits that can be gained from an integrated budgeting program. To this end, you have worked with accounting and other areas to gather the information assembled below.

The company sells many styles of earrings, but all are sold for the same price—$10 per pair. Actual sales of earrings for the last three months and budgeted sales for the next six months follow (in pairs of earrings):

January (actual)	20,000	June (budget)	50,000
February (actual)	26,000	July (budget)	30,000
March (actual)	40,000	August (budget)	28,000
April (budget)	65,000	September (budget)	25,000
May (budget)	100,000		

The concentration of sales before and during May is due to Mother's Day. Sufficient inventory should be on hand at the end of each month to supply 40% of the earrings sold in the following month.

Suppliers are paid $4 for a pair of earrings. One-half of a month's purchases is paid for in the month of purchase; the other half is paid for in the following month. All sales are on credit, with no discount, and payable within 15 days. The company has found, however, that only 20% of a month's sales are collected in the month of sale. An additional 70% is collected in the following month, and the remaining 10% is collected in the second month following sale. Bad debts have been negligible.

Monthly operating expenses for the company are given below:

Variable:	
Sales commissions	4% of sales
Fixed:	
Advertising	$200,000
Rent	18,000
Salaries	106,000
Utilities	7,000
Insurance expired	3,000
Depreciation	14,000

Insurance is paid on an annual basis, in November of each year.

The company plans to purchase $16,000 in new equipment during May and $40,000 in new equipment during June; both purchases will be for cash. The company declares dividends of $15,000 each quarter, payable in the first month of the following quarter.

A listing of the company's ledger accounts as of March 31 is given below:

Assets	
Cash	$ 74,000
Accounts receivable ($26,000 February sales; $320,000 March sales)	346,000
Inventory	104,000
Prepaid insurance	21,000
Property and equipment (net)	950,000
Total assets	$1,495,000

Liabilities and Shareholders' Equity

Accounts payable	$ 100,000
Dividends payable	15,000
Capital stock	800,000
Retained earnings	580,000
Total liabilities and shareholders' equity	$1,495,000

Part of the use of the budgeting program will be to establish an ongoing line of credit at a local bank. Therefore, determine the borrowing that will be needed to maintain a minimum cash balance of $50,000. All borrowing will be done at the beginning of a month; any repayments will be made at the end of a month.

The annual interest rate will be 12%. Interest will be computed and paid at the end of each quarter on all loans outstanding during the quarter. Compute interest on whole months ($\frac{1}{12}$, $\frac{2}{12}$, and so forth).

Required   Prepare a master budget for the three-month period ending June 30. Include the following detailed budgets:

1. a. A sales budget, by month and in total.
   b. A schedule of expected cash collections from sales, by month and in total.
   c. A merchandise purchases budget in units and in dollars. Show the budget by month and in total.
   d. A schedule of expected cash disbursements for merchandise purchases, by month and in total.
2. A cash budget. Show the budget by month and in total.
3. A budgeted income statement for the three-month period ending June 30. Use the contribution approach.
4. A budgeted balance sheet as of June 30.

C9–27 Integration of Purchases Budget, Reorder Point, and Safety Stock   (Appendix 9A) The Press Company manufactures and sells industrial components. The Whitmore Plant is responsible for producing two components. AD-5 and FX-3, Plastic, brass, and aluminum are used in the production of these two products.

Press Company has adopted a 13-period reporting cycle in all of its plants for budgeting purposes. Each period is four weeks long and has 20 working days. The projected inventory levels for AD-5 and FX-3 at the end of the current (seventh) period and the projected sales for these two products for the next three four-week periods are as follows:

		Projected Sales (in Units)		
Component	Projected Inventory Level (in Units) End of 7th Period	8 Period	9 Period	10 Period
AD-5	3,000	7,500	8,750	9,500
FX-3	2,800	7,000	4,500	4,000

Past experience has shown that adequate inventory levels for AD-5 and FX-3 can be maintained if 40% of the next period's projected sales are on hand at the end of a reporting period. Based on this experience and the projected sales, the Whitmore Plant has budgeted production of 8,000 units of AD-5 and 6,000 units of FX-3 in the eighth period. Production is assumed to be uniform for both products within each four-week period.

The raw material specifications for AD-5 and FX-3 are as follows:

	AD-5 (Kilograms)	FX-3 (Kilograms)
Plastic	2.0	1.0
Brass	0.5	—
Aluminum	—	1.5

Data relating to the purchase of raw materials are:

	Purchase Price per Kilogram	Standard Purchase Lot (Kilograms)	Reorder Point (Kilograms)	Projected Inventory Status at the End of the Seventh Period (Kilograms)		Lead Time in Working Days
				On Hand	On Order	
Plastic	$0.40	15,000	12,000	16,000	15,000	10
Brass	0.95	5,000	7,500	9,000	—	30
Aluminum . . .	0.55	10,000	10,000	14,000	10,000	20

The sales of AD-5 and FX-3 do not vary significantly from month to month. Consequently, the safety stock incorporated into the reorder point for each of the raw materials is adequate to compensate for variations in the sales of the finished products.

Raw material orders are placed the day the quantity on hand falls below the reorder point. Whitmore Plant's suppliers are very dependable so that the given lead times are reliable. The outstanding orders for plastic and aluminum are due to arrive on the 10th and 4th working days of the eighth period, respectively. Payments for all raw material orders are remitted in the month of delivery.

Required   Whitmore Plant is required to submit a report to corporate headquarters of Press Company summarizing the projected raw material activities before each period commences. The data for the eighth period report are being assembled. Determine the following items for plastic, brass, and aluminum for inclusion in the eighth period report:

1. Project quantities (in kilograms) of each raw material to be issued to production.
2. Projected quantities (in kilograms) of each raw material ordered and the date (in terms of working days) the order is to be placed.
3. The projected inventory balance (in kilograms) of each raw material at the end of the period.
4. The payments for purchases of each raw material.

(CMA, adapted)

C9–28   Evaluating a Company's Budget Procedures   Springfield Corporation operates on a calendar-year basis. It begins the annual budgeting process in late August, when the president establishes targets for the total dollar sales and net income before taxes for the next year.

The sales target is given to the Marketing Department, where the marketing manager formulates a sales budget by product line in both units and dollars. From this budget, sales quotas by product line in units and dollars are established for each of the corporation's sales districts.

The marketing manager also estimates the cost of the marketing activities required to support the target sales volume and prepares a tentative marketing expense budget.

The executive vice president uses the sales and profit targets, the sales budget by product line, and the tentative marketing expense budget to determine the dollar amounts that can be devoted to manufacturing and corporate office expense. The executive vice president prepares the budget for corporate expenses, and then forwards to the Production Department the product-line sales budget in units and the total dollar amount that can be devoted to manufacturing.

The production manager meets with the factory managers to develop a manufacturing plan that will produce the required units when needed within the cost constraints set by the executive vice president. The budgeting process usually comes to a halt at this point because the Production Department does not consider the financial resources allocated to be adequate.

When this standstill occurs, the vice president of finance, the executive vice president, the marketing manager, and the production manager meet to determine the final budgets for each of the areas. This normally results in a modest increase in the total amount available for manufacturing costs, while the marketing expense and corporate office expense budgets are cut. The total sales and net income figures proposed by the president are seldom changed. Although the participants are seldom pleased with the compromise, these budgets are final. Each executive then develops a new detailed budget for the operations in his or her area.

None of the areas has achieved its budget in recent years. Sales often run below the target. When budgeted sales are not achieved, each area is expected to cut costs so that the president's profit target can still be met. However, the profit target is seldom met because costs are not cut enough. In fact, costs often run above the original budget in all functional areas. The president is disturbed that Springfield has not been able to meet the sales and profit targets. He hired a consultant with considerable experience with companies in Springfield's industry. The consultant reviewed the budgets for the past four years. He concluded that the product-line sales budgets were reasonable and that the cost and expense budgets were adequate for the budgeted sales and production levels.

Required
1. Discuss how the budgeting process as employed by Springfield Corporation contributes to the failure to achieve the president's sales and profit targets.
2. Suggest how Springfield Corporation's budgeting process could be revised to correct the problem.
3. Should the functional areas be expected to cut their costs when sales volume falls below budget? Explain your answer.

(CMA, adapted)

C9–29 Evaluating a Company's Budget Procedures Tom Emory and Jim Morris strolled back to their plant from the administrative offices of Ferguson & Son Mfg. Company. Tom is manager of the machine shop in the company's factory; Jim is manager of the equipment maintenance department.

The men had just attended the monthly performance evaluation meeting for plant department heads. These meetings had been held on the third Tuesday of each month since Robert Ferguson, Jr., the president's son, had become plant manager a year earlier.

As they were walking, Tom Emory spoke: "Boy, I hate those meetings! I never know whether my department's accounting reports will show good or bad performance. I'm beginning to expect the worst. If the accountants say I saved the company a dollar, I'm called 'Sir,' but if I spend even a little too much—boy, do I get in trouble. I don't know if I can hold on until I retire."

Tom had just been given the worst evaluation he had ever received in his long career with Ferguson & Son. He was one of the most respected of the experienced machinists in the company. He had been with Ferguson & Son for many years and was promoted to supervisor of the machine shop when the company expanded and moved to its present location. The president (Robert Ferguson, Sr.) had often stated that the company's success was due to the high quality of the work of machinists like Tom. As supervisor, Tom stressed the importance of craftsmanship and told his workers that he wanted no sloppy work coming from his department.

When Robert Ferguson, Jr., became the plant manager, he directed that monthly performance comparisons be made between actual and budgeted costs for each department. The departmental budgets were intended to encourage the supervisors to reduce inefficiencies and to seek cost reduction opportunities. The company controller was instructed to have his staff "tighten" the budget slightly whenever a department attained its budget in a given month; this was done to reinforce the plant manager's desire to reduce costs. The young plant manager often stressed the importance of continued progress toward attaining the budget; he also made it know that he kept a file of these performance reports for future reference when he succeeded his father.

Tom Emory's conversation with Jim Morris continued as follows:

Emory: I really don't understand. We've worked so hard to get up to budget, and the minute we make it they tighten the budget on us. We can't work any faster and still maintain quality. I think my men are ready to quit trying. Besides, those reports don't tell the whole story. We always seem to be interrupting the big jobs for all those small rush orders. All that setup and machine adjustment time is killing us. And quite frankly, Jim, you were no help. When our hydraulic press broke down last month, your people were nowhere to be found. We had to take it apart ourselves and got stuck with all that idle time.

Morris: I'm sorry about that, Tom, but you know my department has had trouble making budget, too. We were running well behind at the time of that problem, and if we'd spent a day on that old machine, we would never have made it up. Instead we made the scheduled inspections of the forklift trucks because we knew we could do those in less than the budgeted time.

Emory: Well, Jim, at least you have some options. I'm locked into what the scheduling department assigns to me and you know they're being harassed by sales for those special orders. Incidentally, why didn't your report show all the supplies you guys wasted last month when you were working in Bill's department?

Morris: We're not out of the woods on that deal yet. We charged the maximum we could to other work and haven't even reported some of it yet.

Emory: Well, I'm glad you have a way of getting out of the pressure. The accountants seem to know everything that's happening in my department, sometimes even before I do. I thought all that budget and accounting stuff was supposed to help, but it just gets me into trouble. It's all a big pain. I'm trying to put out quality work; they're trying to save pennies.

Required

1. Identify the problems that appear to exist in Ferguson & Son Mfg. Company's budgetary control system and explain how the problems are likely to reduce the effectiveness of the system.

2. Explain how Ferguson & Son Mfg. Company's budgetary control system could be revised to improve its effectiveness.

(CMA, adapted)

C9–30   Cash Budget for a Growing Company   CrossMan Corporation, a rapidly expanding crossbow distributor to retail outlets, is in the process of formulating plans for next year. Joan Caldwell, director of marketing, has completed her sales budget and is confident that sales estimates will be met or exceeded. The following budgeted sales figures show the growth expected and will provide the planning basis for other corporate departments.

	Budgeted Sales		Budgeted Sales
January	$1,800,000	July	$3,000,000
February	2,000,000	August	3,000,000
March	1,800,000	September	3,200,000
April	2,200,000	October	3,200,000
May	2,500,000	November	3,000,000
June	2,800,000	December	3,400,000

George Brownell, assistant controller, has been given the responsibility for formulating the cash budget, a critical element during a period of rapid expansion. The following information provided by operating managers will be used in preparing the cash budget.

a. CrossMan has experienced an excellent record in accounts receivable collection and expects this trend to continue. Sixty percent of billings are collected in the month after the sale and 40% in the second month after the sale. Uncollectible accounts are negligible and will not be considered in this analysis.

b. The purchase of the crossbows is CrossMan's largest expenditure; the cost of these items equals 50% of sales. Sixty percent of the crossbows are received one month prior to sale and 40% are received during the month of sale.

c. Prior experience shows that 80% of accounts payable are paid by CrossMan one month after receipt of the purchased crossbows, and the remaining 20% are paid the second month after receipt.

d. Hourly wages, including fringe benefits, depend on sales volume and are equal to 20% of the current month's sales. These wages are paid in the month incurred.

e. General and administrative expenses are budgeted to be $2,640,000 for the year. The composition of these expenses is given below. All of these expenses are incurred evenly throughout the year except the property taxes. Property taxes are paid in four equal installments in the last month of each quarter.

Salaries	$ 480,000
Promotion	660,000
Property taxes	240,000
Insurance	360,000
Utilities	300,000
Depreciation	600,000
Total	$2,640,000

f. Income tax payments are made by CrossMan in the first month of each quarter based on the income for the prior quarter. CrossMan's income tax rate is 40%. CrossMan's net income for the first quarter is projected to be $612,000.

g. Equipment and warehouse facilities are being acquired to support the company's rapidly growing sales. Purchases of equipment and facilities are budgeted at $28,000 for April and $324,000 for May.

h. CrossMan has a corporate policy of maintaining an end-of-month cash balance of $100,000. Cash is borrowed or invested monthly, as needed, to maintain this balance. Interest expense on borrowed funds is budgeted at $8,000 for the second quarter, all of which will be paid during June.

i. CrossMan uses a calendar year reporting period.

Required

1. Prepare a cash budget for CrossMan Corporation by month and in total for the second quarter. Be sure that all receipts, disbursements, and borrowing/investing amounts are shown for each month. Ignore any interest income associated with amounts invested.

2. Discuss why cash budgeting is particularly important for a rapidly expanding company such as CrossMan Corporation.

(CMA, adapted)

C9–31 Spreadsheet Budget The Ray Company Ltd. is a small retail store located in Dartmouth. Its sales budget for the first three months of 2000 is shown below.

January	$40,000
February	50,000
March	60,000

Sales consist of 60% cash and 40% credit. According to the experience of 1999, half of the credit sales are collected in the month of sale, and the rest are collected in the month following the sale. Bad debts are minimal and can be ignored. Total sales in December 1999 were $70,000.

The following spreadsheet contains some information about the budgeted cash collections from sales for the first quarter of 2000.

RAY COMPANY
Budgeted Cash Collections from Sales
For the First Quarter, 2000

	January	February	March	Quarter
Total sales	$40,000	$50,000	$60,000	
Less credit sales	16,000			
Cash sales	$24,000			
Add collections on credit sales from previous month				
Add collections on credit sales from current month				
....				

Required

1. What formulas, values, or labels must the following cells contain to facilitate the completion of this budget? List the cell reference on the left with the formula, value, or label on the right.

Cell Reference	Answer	Cell Reference	Answer
A18		F10	
D13		F13	
D16		F16	
D18		F18	
E8		G7	
E10		G8	
E13		G10	
E16		G13	
E18		G16	
F8		G18	

2. Suppose that the total budgeted sales for January were $80,000. Recalculate the value of cell D18.

(CGA, adapted)

C9–32   Budgeted Income Statement and Balance Sheet   Chen Company is a retail book store that sells both to nonbusiness and other retail stores. Su Chen, the manager, is interested in preparing a budget balance sheet and income statement for the upcoming year.

Su prepared the following estimates for the upcoming year: Sales, $100,000, one-half made on credit; depreciation expense, $20,000; capital asset additions, $10,000; $1,500 in unpaid income taxes at the year-end, and no payments for the long-term note. Interest, however, will be paid. Dividends should be $12,000. Receivables and inventory were expected to be in the same proportion as the current year. Similarly, accounts payable, income taxes, and gross margin should continue as before.

The financial statements for Chen Company for 1999 were:

Income Statement

Sales	$ 95,000
Cost of goods sold	46,000
Gross Margin	49,000
Expenses (including depreciation $18,000 and $3,000 interest)	33,000
Pretax income	16,000
Income tax (22%)	3,520
Net income	$ 12,480

Balance Sheet
Assets

Cash	$ 20,000
Accounts receivable	30,000
Inventory	40,000
Capital asset (net)	100,000
Total assets	$190,000

Liabilities

Accounts payable	$ 50,000
Income taxes payable	1,000
Notes payable, long-term	25,000
	76,000

Shareholders' Equity

Capital stock (8,000 no par shares)	80,000
Retained earnings	34,000
	114,000
Total liabilities and shareholders' equity	$190,000

Required Prepare a budgeted income statement and balance sheet for 2000.

C9–33 Not-for-Profit Cash Collections Jane Conrad, city manager for the Halifax Regional Municipality, is engaged in some preliminary analysis of the city's revenues for the upcoming year. Revenue estimation is an important aspect of budgeting for the city because it helps to determine what revenues will be available for program expenditures set by city council.

City revenues are a function of property tax assessments, the tax rate, and new construction as well as various fines and fees. Fines and fees are in turn related to population growth. Government grants from the province are a particularly difficult matter because they are unknown until the province sets its budget, usually after the city has set a tax rate. Thus grant projections are typically estimated based on the rate of inflation and last year's amount. If errors do occur in the estimate they can be offset by program expenditure adjustments later in the year.

Jane uses the following formulae to estimate the revenue components:

$$Pt_t = rA_t \text{ where}$$

Pt_t is the property tax revenue for year t
  r is the tax rate per $1,000 of assessment
A_t is the assessment in $1,000 units for year t

$A_t = 1.05\, A_{t-1} + .5S$ where this regression formula relates last year's assessment A_{t-1} and new construction S and includes the fact that all new construction does not happen at the beginning of the year.

Fines and fees (Ff) relate to population by the following formula:

$$Ff_t = [(1 + G)\, P_{t-1}]*\$5$$

where

  G is the population growth percentage
P_{t-1} is the population for last year, t − 1.

Government grants (Gg) from the province are set as follows:

$$Gg_t = (1 + I)\, Gg_{t-1}$$

where

  I is the inflation rate for the current year.

Collection of tax revenue and fines and fees is scattered throughout the year. Monthly revenues are an important factor in minimizing financial borrowing. Government grants are paid to the city twice per year, September and January so these require little estimation of collection dates. However, the tax revenue is typically collected according to the following pattern:

April	. . . .	2%	October	25%
May	. . . .	30%	November	3%
June	. . . .	18%	December	3%
July	. . . .	2%	January	2%
August	. . . .	1%	February	1%
September	. . . .	10%	March	1%
				98%

2% of revenue is lost from bad debts.

Fines and fees are collected in a relatively even pattern throughout the year, April to March.

The following data were collected by Jane to assist with the calculations.

$$A_{t-1} = \$80,000,000 \text{ in } 1.000 \text{ units}$$
$$r = \$6.50 \text{ per } \$1,000 \text{ assessed value}$$
$$S = \$1,000,000 \text{ in } 1,000 \text{ units}$$
$$P_{t-1} = 375,000 \text{ people}$$
$$G = 12\%$$
$$I = 3\%$$
$$Gg_{t-1} = \$10,000,000$$

Required   Estimate the monthly collections for Halifax Regional Municipality.

C9–34 **Activity-Based Budgets**
Able Company employs activity based analysis to its budget preparation. The following data was gathered by a team of analysts using both historical data and forecasts of future expected costs.

The company has identified the five activity centres that are listed below, along with the estimated overhead cost and expected level of activity in each centre for the coming year.

Activity Centre	Cost Driver	Estimated Overhead Cost	Expected Activity
Machining	Computer-hours	$250,000	10,000 computer-hours
Purchase orders ...	Number of orders	120,000	2,000 orders
Parts management .	Number of part types	40,000	500 part types
Testing	Number of tests	125,000	5,000 tests
General factory	Machine-hours	350,000	50,000 machine-hours

At the beginning of the year, the company had inventory balances as follows:

Raw materials	$25,000
Work in process	70,000
Finished goods	45,000

The following transactions were expected during the year:

a. Raw materials expected to be purchased on account, $375,000.
b. Raw materials expected to be used in production, $390,000 ($340,000 direct and $50,000 indirect). The indirect materials traceable to activity centres were expected to be as follows:

Machining	$30,000
Purchase orders	8,000
Testing	12,000
Total	$50,000

c. The following costs were estimated for employee services: direct labour, $110,000; indirect labour, $280,000; sales commissions, $90,000; and administrative salaries, $240,000. The indirect labour costs for the activity centres were as follows:

Purchase orders	$80,000
Parts management	25,000
Testing	65,000
General factory	110,000
Total	$280,000

d. Sales travel costs were estimated to be $42,000.
e. Miscellaneous manufacturing overhead costs were expected to be $68,000. These overhead costs were traceable to activity centres as follows:

Machining	$19,000
Purchase orders	11,000
Parts management	2,000
Testing	7,000
General factory	29,000
Total	$68.000

f. Advertising costs were expected to be $165,000.
g. Depreciation estimated for the year, $320,000 ($270,000 related to factory operations and $50,000 related to selling and administrative activities). The depreciation related to factory operations was traceable to activity centres as follows:

Machining	$130,000
Parts management	4,000
Testing	28,000
General factory	108,000
Total	$270,000

h. Miscellaneous manufacturing overhead costs were expected to be $220,000. These overhead costs were traceable to activity centres as follows:

Machining	$ 70,000
Purchase orders	21,000
Parts management	12,000
Testing	15,000
General factory	102,000
Total	$220,000

i. Manufacturing overhead cost will be applied to production. Estimated activity for expected production levels in the various activity centres during the year is as follows:

Machining	10,200 computer hours
Purchase orders	2,050 orders issued
Parts management	475 part types held in stock
Testing	4,880 tests completed
General factory	51,000 machine-hours worked

j. Goods expected to cost $1,365,000 to manufacture were expected to be completed during the year.
k. Goods estimated to be sold on account to customers during the year were expected to amount to a total selling price of $1,975,000. The goods were expected to cost $1,360,000 to manufacture.

Required
1. Compute the overhead rates to be assigned to activities of the five centres listed above.
2. Prepare the expected income statement for next year.
3. Include in cost of goods sold the expected overhead under- or overapplied amount.

Group Exercises

GE9–35 Financial Pressures Hit Higher Education In the late eighties and early nineties, public universities found that they were no longer immune to the financial stress faced by the rest of the private sector. Budget cuts were in the air across the land. When the budget axe hit, the cuts often came without warning and their size was sometimes staggering. Government support for some institutions dropped. Most university administrators had only experienced budget increases, never budget cuts. Also, the budget setbacks usually occurred at the most inopportune time—during the school year when contractual commitments with faculty and staff had been signed, programs had been planned, and students were enrolled and taking classes.

Required

1. Should the administration be "fair" to all affected and institute a round of across-the-board cuts whenever the province announces another subsidy reduction?
2. If not across-the-board cutbacks in programs, then would you recommend more focused reductions, and if so, what priorities would you establish for bringing spending in line with revenues?
3. Since these usually are not one-time-only cutbacks, how would you manage continuous, long-term reductions in budgets extending over a period of years?
4. Should the decision-making process be top-down (centralized with top administrators) or bottom-up (participative)? Why?
5. How should issues such as protect-your-turf mentality, resistance to change, and consensus building be dealt with?
6. Since no university can afford a reputation of "going downhill," what innovative ideas or initiatives would you recommend that would return a university to a more stable, predictable environment?

GE9–36   Budgeting 101[14]   Who better to tell new students about the ins and outs of budgeting for university than those who have recently lived the experience—you. Suppose you are advising incoming first-year students, or those living off campus for the first time, on money matters and how to live within a budget.

Required

1. Provide a list of typical expenses for a new student living on campus. What is different about a student who is living off campus?
2. What advice should parents give to new students before sending them off to live on their own for the first time?
3. Which expenses should be split between parents and students? How will they be divided?
4. Which expenses can be reduced? How?
5. What role should work play?
6. What are the advantages and disadvantages of credit cards?
7. How would you suggest handling a situation where a student has spent more than his or her budget? Should parents bail the student out?
8. If the student were living off campus with several other roommates, what options do they have for handling expenses such as utilities, rent, and food? How would you advise them?
9. What should a student do if a roommate is not financially responsible and does not pay his or her share of expenses?
10. What do you do with a roommate who eats or drinks more than his or her share?

IE9–37   Talk with a Controller about Budgeting   Use an on-line yellow pages directory to find a business or nonprofit organization in your area with a web site. Find out as much as you can about the organization's operations from its web site.

Required

Make an appointment with the controller or chief financial officer of the organization you have identified. In the meeting, find out the answers to the following questions:

1. How are the overall budget goals set?
2. What is the process used to build the budget? Who does it? How much input do operating managers have in the process? How long does it take to build the budget?
3. What are the main benefits of budgeting? How are the budgets used?

---

14. Adapted from Deborah Lohse, "Students Can Learn a Lesson on Budgeting," *The Wall Street Journal*, August 23, 1995, p. C1; and Bill Lubinger, "College Tests Your Money Handling Skills," *The Plain Dealer*, September 2, 1995, p. 3–E.

IE9–38 **Business Intelligence**   Using the WWW, investigate the nature of the business conducted by a major Canadian company such as Bombardier, Alcan, Pratt and Whitney, or the Royal Bank. Once the nature of the business is established investigate a key aspect of the business environment that is critical to the next budget period of your selection such as major expansion plans for a subway, a new aircraft type, labour rate increases, changes in metal prices or interest rates, and housing starts.

Required   Prepare a five-page report of your findings that may help the budget committee evaluate sales forecasts and budgets.

IE9–39 **Budget Research**   A recent article concerning Nortel Network's parts shortage suggests that a software problem in its order processing and procurement of parts for its fibre-optic telephone equipment may result in a decline in earnings for the quarter and perhaps lost sales to its competitors, Hitachi and Fujitsu.[15]

Required   Using the WWW or business databases, ascertain if fibre-optic products and parts continue in short supply and why this shortage may continue. Are JIT inventory practices part of the problem?

---

15. Michael Lewis, "Nortel Squeezed by Parts Shortage," *The Financial Post,* July 9, 1999, p. c3.

Chapter Ten

Standard Costs and the Balanced Scorecard

Business Focus

Special effects, such as the computer-generated action shots of dinosaurs in Jurassic Park, are expensive to produce. A single visual effect, lasting three to seven seconds, can cost up to $50,000. And a high-profile film may contain hundreds of these shots.

Competition is fierce. Since visual effects are produced under fixed-price contracts, visual-effects companies must carefully estimate their costs. And once a bid has been accepted, costs must be zeal-ously monitored to make sure they do not spin out of control. Buena Vista Visual Effects, a part of Walt Disney Studios, uses a standard cost system to estimate and control costs. A "storyboard" is created for each special-effects shot; it sketches the visual effect, details the length of the shot (measured in frames—24 frames equals one second of film), and describes the work that will need to be done to create the effect. A detailed budget is then prepared using standard costs. For example, a shot may require a miniature model maker working full time for 12 weeks at a specified weekly wage. As the job progresses, this stan-dard cost is compared to actual costs and significant cost over-runs are investigated. Management attention is directed to significant vari-ances.

Source: Ray Scalice, "Lights! Cameras! . . . Accountants?" Management Accounting, *June 1996, pp. 42–46.*

Learning Objectives

After studying Chapter 10, you should be able to:

1 Explain how direct materials standards and direct labour stan-dards are set.

2 Compute the direct materials price and quantity variances and explain their significance.

3 Complete the mix and yield variances for materials and explain their significance.

4 Compute the direct labour rate and efficiency variances and explain their significance.

5 Compute the variable manu-facturing overhead spending and efficiency variances.

6 Understand the advantages of and the potential problems with using standard costs.

7 Understand how a balanced scorecard fits together and how it supports a company's strategy.

8 Compute the delivery cycle time, the throughput time, and the manufacturing cycle efficiency (MCE).

9 (Appendix 10A) Prepare journal entries to record standard costs and variances.

10 (Appendix 10B) Explain the concept of learning curves.

In this chapter we begin our study of management

control and performance measures. Quite often, these terms carry with them negative connotations—we may have a tendency to think of performance measurement as something to be feared. And indeed, performance measurements can be used in very negative ways—to cast blame and to punish. However, that is not the way they should be used. As explained in the following quotation, performance measurement serves a vital function in both personal life and in organizations:

> Imagine you want to improve your basketball shooting skill. You know that practice will help, so you [go] to the basketball court. There you start shooting toward the hoop, but as soon as the ball gets close to the rim your vision goes blurry for a second, so that you cannot observe where the ball ended up in relation to the target (left, right, in front, too far back, inside the hoop?). It would be pretty difficult to improve under those conditions. . . . (And by the way, how long would [shooting baskets] sustain your interest if you couldn't observe the outcome of your efforts?)
>
> Or imagine someone engaging in a weight loss program. A normal step in such programs is to purchase a scale to be able to track one's progress: Is this program working? Am I losing weight? A positive answer would be encouraging and would motivate me to keep up the effort, while a negative answer might lead me to reflect on the process: Am I working on the right diet and exercise program? Am I doing everything I am supposed to?, etc. Suppose you don't want to set up a sophisticated measurement system and decide to forgo the scale. You would still have some idea of how well you are doing from simple methods such as clothes feeling looser, a belt that fastens at a different hole, or simply via observation in a mirror! Now, imagine trying to sustain a weight loss program without *any* feedback on how well you are doing.
>
> In these . . . examples, availability of quantitative measures of performance can yield two types of benefits: First, performance feedback can help improve the "production process" through a better understanding of what works and what doesn't; e.g., shooting this way works better than shooting that way. Secondly, feedback on performance can sustain motivation and effort, because it is encouraging and/or because it suggests that more effort is required for the goal to be met.[1]

In the same way, performance measurement can be helpful in an organization. It can provide feedback concerning what works and what does not work, and it can help motivate people to sustain their efforts.

Our study of performance measurement begins in this chapter with the lowest levels in the organization. We work our way up the organizational ladder in subsequent chapters. In this chapter we see how various measures are used to control operations and to evaluate performance. Even though we are starting with the lowest levels in the organization, keep in mind that the performance measures used should be derived from the organization's overall strategy. For example, a company like Sony that bases its strategy on rapid introduction of innovative consumer products should use different

---

1. Soumitra Dutta and Jean-François Manzoni, *Process Reengineering, Organizational Change and Performance Improvement* (New York: McGraw-Hill, 1999), Chapter IV.

performance measures than a company like Purolator Courier Ltd. where on-time delivery, customer convenience, and low cost are key competitive advantages. Sony may want to keep close track of the percentage of revenues from products introduced within the last year; whereas Purolator may want to closely monitor the percentage of packages delivered on time. Later in this chapter when we discuss the *balanced score-card,* we will have more to say concerning the role of strategy in the selection of performance measures. But first we will see how *standard costs* are used by managers to help control costs.

Companies in highly competitive industries like Nortel, Purolator, Air Canada, Corel Computer, Imperial Oil, and Toyota must be able to provide high-quality goods and services at low cost. If they do not, they will perish. Stated in the starkest terms, managers must obtain inputs such as raw materials and electricity at the lowest possible prices and must use them as effectively as possible—while maintaining or increasing the quality of the output. If inputs are purchased at prices that are too high or more input is used than is really necessary, higher costs will result.

How do managers control the prices that are paid for inputs and the quantities that are used? They could examine every transaction in detail, but this obviously would be an inefficient use of management time. For many companies, the answer to this control problem lies at least partially in standard costs.

Standard Costs—Management by Exception

A *standard* is a benchmark or "norm" for measuring performance. Standards are found everywhere. Your doctor evaluates your weight using standards that have been set for individuals of your age, height, and gender. The food we eat in restaurants must be prepared under specified standards of cleanliness. The buildings we live in must conform to standards set in building codes. Standards are also widely used in managerial accounting where they relate to the *quantity* and *cost* of inputs used in manufacturing goods or providing services.

Managers—often assisted by engineers and accountants—set quantity and cost standards for each major input such as raw materials and labour time. *Quantity standards* indicate how much of an input should be used in manufacturing a unit of product or in providing a unit of service. *Cost (price) standards* indicate what the cost, or purchase price, of the input should be. Actual quantities and actual costs of inputs are compared to these standards. If either the quantity or the cost of inputs departs significantly from the standards, managers investigate the discrepancy. The purpose is to find the cause of the problem and then eliminate it so that it does not recur. This process is called **management by exception.**

Management by exception A system of management in which standards are set for various operating activities, with actual results then compared to these standards. Any differences that are deemed significant are brought to the attention of management as "exceptions."

In our daily lives, we operate in a management by exception mode most of the time. Consider what happens when you sit down in the driver's seat of your car. You put the key in the ignition, you turn the key, and your car starts. Your expectation (standard) that the car will start is met; you do not have to open the car hood and check the battery, the connecting cables, the fuel lines, and so on. If you turn the key and the car does not start, then you have a discrepancy (variance). Your expectations are not met, and you need to investigate why. Note that even if the car starts after a second try, it would be wise to investigate anyway. The fact that the expectation was not met should be viewed as an opportunity to uncover the cause of the problem rather than as simply an annoyance. If the underlying cause is not discovered and corrected, the problem may recur and become much worse.

Who Uses Standard Costs?

Manufacturing, service, food, and not-for-profit organizations all make use of standards to some extent. Auto service centres like Canadian Tire, for example, often set specific labour time standards for the completion of certain work tasks, such as installing a carburetor or doing a valve job, and then measure actual performance against these standards. Fast-food outlets such as Harvey's have exacting standards as to the quantity of meat going into a sandwich, as well as standards for the cost of the meat. Hospitals have standard costs (for food, laundry, and other items) for each occupied bed per day, as well as standard time allowances for certain routine activities, such as laboratory tests. In short, you are likely to run into standard costs in virtually any line of business that you enter.

Focus on Current Practice

A survey of manufacturing companies with annual sales in excess of $500 million found that 87% use standard costing. The survey also found that the use of standard cost systems is increasing and that standards are being applied to smaller and smaller units within the firms.[2]

Another study of 244 companies involved in traditional manufacturing, high-tech operations, and service activities found that 67% use standard cost systems. No statistically significant difference was found between companies in the use of standard costs based on either type of operation or size of company.[3] ■

Standard cost card A detailed listing of the standard amounts of materials, labour, and overhead that should go into a unit of product, multiplied by the standard price or rate that has been set for each cost element.

Manufacturing companies often have highly developed standard costing systems in which standards relating to materials, labour, and overhead are developed in detail for each separate product. These standards are listed on a **standard cost card** that provides the manager with a great deal of information concerning the inputs that are required to produce a unit and their costs. In the following section, we provide a detailed example of the setting of standard costs and the preparation of a standard cost card.

Setting Standard Costs

Setting price and quantity standards is more an art than a science. It requires the combined expertise of all persons who have responsibility over input prices and over the effective use of inputs. In a manufacturing setting, this might include accountants, purchasing managers, engineers, production supervisors, line managers, and production workers. Past records of purchase prices and of input usage can be helpful in setting standards. However, the standards should be designed to encourage efficient *future* operations, not a repetition of *past* inefficient operations.

Ideal versus Practical Standards

Should standards be attainable all of the time, should they be attainable only part of the time, or should they be so tight that they become, in effect, "the impossible dream"? Opinions among managers vary, but standards tend to fall into one of two categories—either ideal or practical.

Ideal standards
Standards that allow for no machine breakdowns or other work interruptions and that require peak efficiency at all times.

Ideal standards are those that can be attained only under the best circumstances. They allow for no machine breakdowns or other work interruptions, and they call for a level of effort that can be attained only by the most skilled and efficient employees working at peak effort 100% of the time. Some managers feel that such standards have a motivational value. These managers argue that even though employees know they will rarely meet the standard, it is a constant reminder of the need for ever-increasing efficiency and effort. Few firms use ideal standards. Most managers feel that ideal

2. Bruce R. Gaumnitz and Felix P. Kollaritsch, "Manufacturing Cost Variances: Current Practice and Trends," *Journal of Cost Management* 5, no. 1 (Spring 1991), pp. 58–64.
3. Jeffrey R. Cohen and Laurence Paquette, "Management Accounting Practices: Perceptions of Controllers," *Journal of Cost Management* 5, no. 3 (Fall 1991), pp. 73–83

standards tend to discourage even the most diligent workers. Moreover, when ideal standards are used, variances from the standards have little meaning. Because of the ideal standards, large variances are normal and it is difficult to "manage by exception."

Practical standards
Standards that allow for normal machine downtime and other work interruptions and that can be attained through reasonable, though highly efficient, efforts by the average worker.

Practical standards are defined as standards that are "tight but attainable." They allow for normal machine downtime and employee rest periods, and they can be attained through reasonable, though highly efficient, efforts by the average worker. Variances from such a standard are very useful to management in that they represent deviations that fall outside of normal operating conditions and signal a need for management attention. Furthermore, practical standards can serve multiple purposes. In addition to signalling abnormal conditions, they can also be used in forecasting cash flows and in planning inventory. By contrast, ideal standards cannot be used in forecasting and planning; they do not allow for normal inefficiencies, and therefore they result in unrealistic planning and forecasting figures.

Throughout the remainder of this chapter, we will assume the use of practical rather than ideal standards.

Managerial Accounting in Action

THE ISSUE

The Colonial Pewter Company was organized a year ago. The company's only product at present is a reproduction of an eighteenth century pewter bookend. The bookend is made largely by hand, using traditional metalworking tools. Consequently, the manufacturing process is labour intensive and requires a high level of skill.

Colonial Pewter has recently expanded its workforce to take advantage of unexpected demand for the bookends as gifts. The company started with a small cadre of experienced pewter workers but has had to hire less experienced workers as a result of the expansion. The president of the company, J. D. Wriston, has called a meeting to discuss production problems. Attending the meeting are Tom Kuchel, the production manager; Janet Warner, the purchasing manager; and Terry Sherman, the corporate controller.

J. D.: I've got a feeling that we aren't getting the production we should out of our new people.

Tom: Give us a chance. Some of the new people have been on board for less than a month.

Janet: Let me add that production seems to be wasting an awful lot of material—particularly pewter. That stuff is very expensive.

Tom: What about the shipment of defective pewter you bought a couple of months ago—the one with the iron contamination? That caused us major problems.

Janet: That's ancient history. How was I to know it was off-grade? Besides, it was a great deal.

J. D.: Calm down everybody. Let's get the facts before we start sinking our fangs into each other.

Tom: I agree. The more facts the better.

J. D.: Okay, Terry, it's your turn. Facts are the controller's department.

Terry: I'm afraid I can't provide the answers off the top of my head, but it won't take me too long to set up a system that can routinely answer questions relating to worker productivity, material waste, and input prices.

J. D.: How long is "not too long"?

Terry: I will need all of your cooperation, but how about a week from today?

J. D.: That's okay with me. What about everyone else?

Tom: Sure.

Janet: Fine with me.

J. D.: Let's mark it on our calendars. ■

Setting Direct Materials Standards

Terry Sherman's first task was to prepare price and quantity standards for the company's only significant raw material, pewter ingots. The **standard price per unit** for direct materials should reflect the final, delivered cost of the materials, net of any discounts taken. After consulting with purchasing manager Janet Warner, Terry prepared the following documentation for the standard price of a pound of pewter in ingot form:

Purchase price, top-grade pewter ingots, in 15 kilogram ingots	$ 3.60
Freight, by truck, from the supplier's warehouse	0.44
Receiving and handling	0.05
Less purchase discount	(0.09)
Standard price per pound	$ 4.00

Standard price per unit
The price that should be paid for a single unit of materials, including allowances for quality, quantity purchased, shipping, receiving, and other such costs, net of any discounts allowed.

Notice that the standard price reflects a particular grade of material (top grade), purchased in particular lot sizes (15 kilogram ingots), and delivered by a particular type of carrier (truck). Allowances have also been made for handling and discounts. If everything proceeds according to these expectations, the net standard price of a kilogram of pewter should therefore be $4.00.

Standard quantity per unit The amount of materials that should be required to complete a single unit of product, including allowances for normal waste, spoilage, rejects, and similar inefficiencies.

The **standard quantity per unit** for direct materials should reflect the amount of material going into each unit of finished product, as well as an allowance for unavoidable waste, spoilage, and other normal inefficiencies. After consulting with the production manager, Tom Kuchel, Terry Sherman prepared the following documentation for the standard quantity of pewter going into a pair of bookends:

Material requirements as specified in the bill of materials	
for a pair of bookends, in kilograms	2.7
Allowance for waste and spoilage, in kilograms	0.2
Allowance for rejects, in kilograms	0.1
Standard quantity per pair of bookends, in kilograms	3.0

Bill of materials A listing of the quantity of each type of material required to manufacture a unit of product.

A **bill of materials** is a list that shows the type and quantity of each item of material going into a unit of finished product. It is a handy source for determining the basic material input per unit, but it should be adjusted for waste and other factors, as shown above, when determining the standard quantity per unit of product. "Waste and spoilage" in the table above refers to materials that are wasted as a normal part of the production process or that spoil before they are used. "Rejects" refers to the direct material contained in units that are defective and must be scrapped.

Focus on Current Practice

After many years of operating a standard cost system, a major wood products company reviewed the materials standards for its products by breaking each standard down into its basic elements. In doing so, the company discovered that there was a 20% waste factor built into the standard cost for every product. Management was dismayed to learn that the dollar amount of "allowable" waste was so large. Since the quantity standards had not been scrutinized for many years, management was unaware of the existence of this significant cost improvement potential in the company.[4] ■

---

4. James M. Reeve, "The Impact of Variation on Operating System Performance," *Performance Excellence* (Sarasota, FL: American Accounting Association, 1990), p. 77.

Although it is common to recognize allowances for waste, spoilage, and rejects when setting standard costs, this practice is now coming into question. Those involved in TQM (total quality management) and similar management approaches argue that no amount of waste or defects should be tolerated. If allowances for waste, spoilage, and rejects are built into the standard cost, the levels of those allowances should be periodically reviewed and reduced over time to reflect improved processes, better training, and better equipment.

Once the price and quantity standards have been set, the standard cost of material per unit of finished product can be computed as follows:

$$\text{3.0 kilograms per unit} \times \text{\$4.00 per kilograms} = \text{\$12 per unit}$$

This $12 cost figure will appear as one item on the standard cost card of the product.

Setting Direct Labour Standards

Standard rate per hour
The labour rate that should be incurred per hour of labour time, including employment taxes, fringe benefits, and other such labour costs.

Direct labour price and quantity standards are usually expressed in terms of a labour rate and labour-hours. The **standard rate per hour** for direct labour would include not only wages earned but also fringe benefits and other labour costs. Using last month's wage records and in consultation with the production manager, Terry determined the standard rate per hour at the Colonial Pewter Company as follows:

Basic wage rate per hour	$10
Employment taxes at 10% of the basic rate . . .	1
Fringe benefits at 30% of the basic rate	3
Standard rate per direct labour-hour	$14

Many companies prepare a single standard rate for all employees in a department. This standard rate reflects the expected "mix" of workers, even though the actual wage rates may vary somewhat from individual to individual due to differing skills or seniority. A single standard rate simplifies the use of standard costs and also permits the manager to monitor the use of employees within departments. More is said on this point a little later. According to the standard computed above, the direct labour rate for Colonial Pewter should average $14 per hour.

Standard hours per unit
The amount of labour time that should be required to complete a single unit of product, including allowances for breaks, machine downtime, cleanup, rejects, and other normal inefficiencies.

The standard direct labour time required to complete a unit of product (generally called the **standard hours per unit**) is perhaps the single most difficult standard to determine. One approach is to divide each operation performed on the product into elemental body movements (such as reaching, pushing, and turning over). Published tables of standard times for such movements are available. These times can be applied to the movements and then added together to determine the total standard time allowed per operation. Another approach is for an industrial engineer to do a time and motion study, actually clocking the time required for certain tasks. As stated earlier, the standard time should include allowances for coffee breaks, personal needs of employees, cleanup, and machine downtime. After consulting with the production manager, Terry prepared the following documentation for the standard hours per unit:

Basic labour time per unit, in hours	1.9
Allowance for breaks and personal needs	0.1
Allowance for cleanup and machine downtime	0.3
Allowance for rejects	0.2
Standard labour-hours per unit of product . . .	2.5

Once the rate and time standards have been set, the standard labour cost per unit of product can be computed as follows:

$$\text{2.5 hours per unit} \times \text{\$14 per hour} = \text{\$35 per unit}$$

This $35 cost figure appears along with direct materials as one item on the standard cost card of the product.

Standard labour-hours have declined in relative importance for some organizations. This is particularly true in highly automated manufacturing firms. Service organizations and numerous other construction and processing organizations, however, still retain a major interest in labour and want to know how it performs. Standard labour-hours inform workers and managers what is expected and how labour should be used. Standard labour-hours assist in formulating, testing, and revising the plans of the organization. More specifically, standards and the resulting comparisons to actual labour-hours may serve to motivate workers and managers. Labour standards can influence individuals in setting their own goals. If standards are perceived as realistic and if the variances from these standards are used fairly and constructively, then employees will generally be motivated to work for the organizational objectives conveyed by the standards. Feelings of success or failure impact on performance, but pressure can invigorate or intimidate employees. Erosion of effort and performance levels can result when standards are set inappropriately and used incorrectly.

Focus on Current Practice

Industrie Natuzzi SpA, founded and run by Pasquale Natuzzi, produces handmade leather furniture for the world market in Santaeramo Del Colle in southern Italy. Natuzzi is export-oriented and has, for example, about 25% of the U.S. leather furniture market. The company's furniture is handmade by craftsmen, each of whom has a computer terminal that is linked to a sophisticated computer network. The computer terminal provides precise instructions on how to accomplish a particular task in making a piece of furniture. And the computer keeps track of how quickly the craftsman completes the task. If the craftsman beats the standard time to complete the task, the computer adds a bonus to the craftsman's pay.

The company's computers know exactly how much thread, screws, foam, leather, labour, and so on, is required for every model. "Should the price of Argentinean hides or German dyes rise one day, employees in Santaeramo enter the new prices into the computer, and the costs for all sofas with that leather and those colours are immediately recalculated. 'Everything has to be clear for me,' says Natuzzi. 'Why this penny? Where is it going?'"[5] ■

Setting Variable Manufacturing Overhead Standards

As with direct labour, the price and quantity standards for variable manufacturing overhead are generally expressed in terms of rate and hours. The rate represents *the variable portion of the predetermined overhead rate* discussed in Chapter 3; the hours represent whatever hours base is used to apply overhead to units of product (usually machine-hours or direct labour-hours, as we learned in Chapter 3). At Colonial Pewter, the variable portion of the predetermined overhead rate is $3 per direct labour-hour. Therefore, the standard variable manufacturing overhead cost per unit is computed as follows:

Standard cost per unit
The standard cost of a unit of product as shown on the standard cost card; it is computed by multiplying the standard quantity or hours by the standard price or rate for each cost element.

$$\text{2.5 hours per unit} \times \text{\$3 per hour} = \text{\$7.50 per unit}$$

This $7.50 cost figure appears along with direct materials and direct labour as one item on the standard cost card in Exhibit 10–1. Observe that the **standard cost per unit** is computed by multiplying the standard quantity or hours by the standard price or rate.

---

5. Richard C. Morais, "A Methodical Man," *Forbes*, August 11, 1997, pp. 70–72.

Exhibit 10–1
Standard Cost Card—
Variable Production Cost

Inputs	(1) Standard Quantity or Hours	(2) Standard Price or Rate	(3) Standard Cost (1) × (2)
Direct materials	3.0 kilograms	$ 4.00	$12.00
Direct labour	2.5 hours	14.00	35.00
Variable manufacturing overhead . .	2.5 hours	3.00	7.50
Total standard cost per unit			$54.50

Are Standards the Same as Budgets?

Standards and budgets are very similar. The major distinction between the two terms is that a standard is a *unit* amount, whereas a budget is a *total* amount. The standard cost for materials at Colonial Pewter is $12 per pair of bookends. If 1,000 pairs of bookends are to be manufactured during a budgeting period, then the budgeted cost of materials would be $12,000. In effect, *a standard can be viewed as the budgeted cost for one unit of product.*

A General Model for Variance Analysis

An important reason for separating standards into two categories—price and quantity—is that different managers are usually responsible for buying and for using inputs and these two activities occur at different points in time. In the case of raw materials, for example, the purchasing manager is responsible for the price, and this responsibility is exercised at the time of purchase. In contrast, the production manager is responsible for the amount of the raw material used, and this responsibility is exercised when the materials are used in production, which may be many weeks or months after the purchase date. It is important, therefore, that we cleanly separate discrepancies due to deviations from price standards from those due to deviations from quantity standards. Differences between *standard* prices and *actual* prices and *standard* quantities and *actual* quantities are called **variances**. The act of computing and interpreting variances is called *variance analysis*.

Variance The difference between standard prices and quantities and actual prices and quantities.

Price and Quantity Variances

A general model for computing standard cost variances for variable costs is presented in Exhibit 10–2. This model isolates price variances from quantity variances and shows how each of these variances is computed.[6] We will be using this model throughout the chapter to compute variances for direct materials, direct labour, and variable manufacturing overhead.

Three things should be noted from Exhibit 10–2. First, note that a price variance and a quantity variance can be computed for all three variable cost elements—direct materials, direct labour, and variable manufacturing overhead—even though the variance is not called by the same name in all cases. For example, a price variance is called a *materials price variance* in the case of direct materials but a *labour rate variance* in the case of direct labour and an *overhead spending variance* in the case of variable manufacturing overhead.

Second, note that even though a price variance may be called by different names, it is computed in exactly the same way regardless of whether one is dealing with direct

---

6. Variance analysis of fixed costs is reserved until Chapter 11.

Exhibit 10–2   A
General Model for Variance
Analysis—Variable
Production Costs

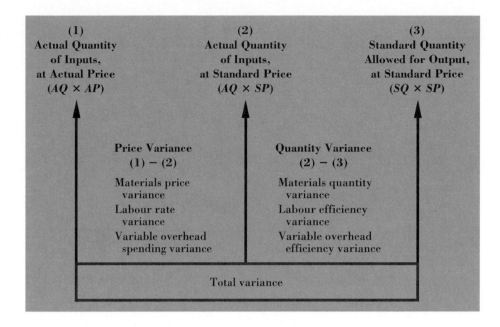

| (1) Actual Quantity of Inputs, at Actual Price ($AQ \times AP$) | (2) Actual Quantity of Inputs, at Standard Price ($AQ \times SP$) | (3) Standard Quantity Allowed for Output, at Standard Price ($SQ \times SP$) |

Price Variance
(1) − (2)

Materials price variance
Labour rate variance
Variable overhead spending variance

Quantity Variance
(2) − (3)

Materials quantity variance
Labour efficiency variance
Variable overhead efficiency variance

Total variance

Standard quantity allowed   The amount of materials that should have been used to complete the period's output as computed by multiplying the actual number of units produced by the standard quantity per unit.

Standard hours allowed   The time that should have been taken to complete the period's output as computed by multiplying the actual number of units produced by the standard hours per unit.

materials, direct labour, or variable manufacturing overhead. The same is true with the quantity variance.

Third, note that variance analysis is actually a type of input-output analysis. The inputs represent the actual quantity of direct materials, direct labour, and variable manufacturing overhead used; the output represents the good production of the period, expressed in terms of the *standard quantity (or the standard hours) allowed for the actual output* (see column 3 in Exhibit 10–2). By **standard quantity allowed** or **standard hours allowed,** we mean the amount of direct materials, direct labour, or variable manufacturing overhead *that should have been used* to produce the actual output of the period. This could be more or could be less materials, labour, or overhead than was *actually* used, depending on the efficiency or inefficiency of operations. The standard quantity allowed is computed by multiplying the actual output in units by the standard input allowed per unit.

With this general model as a foundation, we will now examine the price and quantity variances in more detail.

Using Standard Costs—Direct Materials Variances

Objective 2

Compute the direct materials price and quantity variances and explain their significance.

After determining Colonial Pewter Company's standard costs for direct materials, direct labour, and variable manufacturing overhead, Terry Sherman's next step was to compute the company's variances for June, the most recent month. As discussed in the preceding section, variances are computed by comparing standard costs to actual costs. To facilitate this comparison, Terry referred to the standard cost data contained in Exhibit 10–1. This exhibit shows that the standard cost of direct materials per unit of product is as follows:

3.0 kilograms per unit × $4.00 per kilogram = $12 per unit

Colonial Pewter's purchasing records for June showed that 6,500 kilograms of pewter were purchased at a cost of $3.80 per kilogram. This cost figure included freight and handling and was net of the quantity discount. All of the material purchased was used during June to manufacture 2,000 pairs of pewter bookends. Using these data and the standard costs from Exhibit 10–1, Terry computed the price and quantity variances shown in Exhibit 10–3.

Exhibit 10–3 Variance
Analysis—Direct Materials

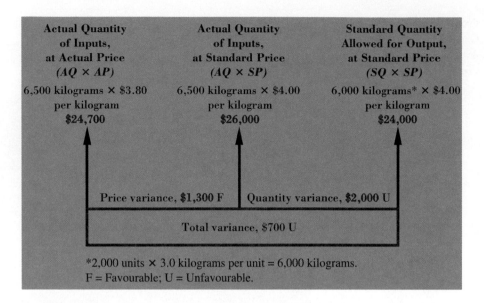

Actual Quantity of Inputs, at Actual Price (AQ × AP)	Actual Quantity of Inputs, at Standard Price (AQ × SP)	Standard Quantity Allowed for Output, at Standard Price (SQ × SP)
6,500 kilograms × $3.80 per kilogram $24,700	6,500 kilograms × $4.00 per kilogram $26,000	6,000 kilograms* × $4.00 per kilogram $24,000

Price variance, $1,300 F   Quantity variance, $2,000 U

Total variance, $700 U

*2,000 units × 3.0 kilograms per unit = 6,000 kilograms.
F = Favourable; U = Unfavourable.

The three arrows in Exhibit 10–3 point to three different total cost figures. The first, $24,700, refers to the actual total cost of the pewter that was purchased during June. The second, $26,000, refers to what the pewter would have cost if it had been purchased at the standard price of $4.00 a kilogram rather than the actual price of $3.80 a kilogram. The difference between these two figures, $1,300 ($26,000 − $24,700), is the price variance. It exists because the actual purchase price was $0.20 per kilogram less than the standard purchase price. Since 6,500 kilograms were purchased, the total amount of the variance is $1,300 ($0.20 per kilogram × 6,500 kilograms). This variance is labelled favourable (denoted by F), since the actual purchase price was less than the standard purchase price. A price variance is labelled unfavourable (denoted by U) if the actual price exceeds the standard price.

The third arrow in Exhibit 10–3 points to $24,000—the cost that the pewter would have been had it been purchased at the standard price and only the amount allowed by the standard quantity had been used. The standards call for 3 kilograms of pewter per unit. Since 2,000 units were produced, 6,000 kilograms of pewter should have been used. This is referred to as the standard quantity allowed for the output. If this 6,000 kilograms of pewter had been purchased at the standard price of $4.00 per kilogram, the company would have spent $24,000. The difference between this figure, $24,000, and the figure at the end of the middle arrow in Exhibit 10–3, $26,000, is the quantity variance of $2,000.

To understand this quantity variance, note that the actual amount of pewter used in production was 6,500 kilograms. However, the standard amount of pewter allowed for the actual output is only 6,000 kilograms. Therefore, a total of 500 kilograms too much pewter was used to produce the actual output. To express this in dollar terms, the 500 kilograms is multiplied by the standard price of $4.00 per kilogram to yield the quantity variance of $2,000. Why is the standard price, rather than the actual price, of the pewter used in this calculation? The production manager is ordinarily responsible for the quantity variance. If the actual price were used in the calculation of the quantity variance, the production manager would be held responsible for the efficiency or inefficiency of the purchasing manager. Apart from being unfair, fruitless arguments between the production manager and purchasing manager would occur every time the actual price of an input is above its standard price. To avoid these arguments, the standard price is used when computing the quantity variance.

The quantity variance in Exhibit 10–3 is labelled unfavourable (denoted by U). This is because more pewter was used to produce the actual output than is called for by the standard. A quantity variance is labelled unfavourable if the actual quantity exceeds the standard quantity and is labelled favourable if the actual quantity is less than the standard quantity.

Exhibit 10–4 Variance Analysis—Direct Materials, When the Amount Purchased Differs from the Amount Used

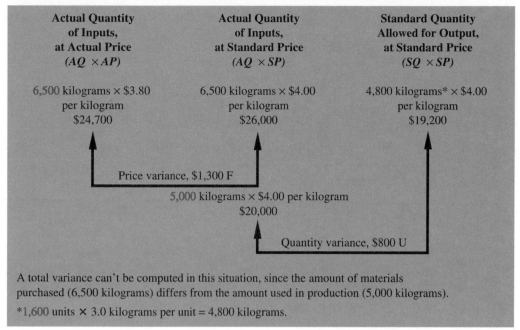

Actual Quantity of Inputs, at Actual Price $(AQ \times AP)$	Actual Quantity of Inputs, at Standard Price $(AQ \times SP)$	Standard Quantity Allowed for Output, at Standard Price $(SQ \times SP)$
6,500 kilograms × $3.80 per kilogram $24,700	6,500 kilograms × $4.00 per kilogram $26,000	4,800 kilograms* × $4.00 per kilogram $19,200

Price variance, $1,300 F

5,000 kilograms × $4.00 per kilogram
$20,000

Quantity variance, $800 U

A total variance can't be computed in this situation, since the amount of materials purchased (6,500 kilograms) differs from the amount used in production (5,000 kilograms).

*1,600 units × 3.0 kilograms per unit = 4,800 kilograms.

The computations in Exhibit 10–3 reflect the fact that all of the material purchased during June was also used during June. How are the variances computed if a different amount of material is purchased than is used? To illustrate, assume that during June the company purchased 6,500 kilograms of materials, as before, but that it used only 5,000 kilograms of material during the month and produced only 1,600 units. In this case, the price variance and quantity variance would be as shown in Exhibit 10–4.

Most firms compute the materials price variance, for example, when materials *are purchased* rather than when the materials are placed into production.[7] This permits earlier isolation of the variance, since materials may remain in storage for many months before being used in production. Isolating the price variance when materials are purchased also permits the company to carry its raw materials in the inventory accounts at standard cost. This greatly simplifies assigning raw materials costs to work in process when raw materials are later placed into production.[8]

Note from the exhibit that the price variance is computed on the entire amount of material purchased (6,500 kilograms), as before, whereas the quantity variance is computed only on the portion of this material used in production during the month (5,000 kilograms). A quantity variance on the 1,500 kilograms of material that was purchased during the month but *not* used in production (6,500 kilograms purchased − 5,000 kilograms used = 1,500 kilograms unused) will be computed in a future period when these materials are drawn out of inventory and used in production. The situation illustrated in Exhibit 10–4 is common for companies that purchase materials well in advance of use and store the materials in warehouses while awaiting the production process.

Materials price variance A measure of the difference between the actual unit price paid for an item and the standard price, multiplied by the quantity purchased.

Materials Price Variance—A Closer Look

A **materials price variance** measures the difference between what is paid for a given quantity of materials and what should have been paid according to the standard that has been set. From Exhibit 10–3, this difference can be expressed by the following formula:

---

7. Max Laudeman and F. W. Schaeberle, "The Cost Accounting Practices of Firms Using Standard Costs," *Cost and Management* 57, no. 4 (July–August 1983), p. 24.
8. See Appendix 10A at the end of the chapter for an illustration of journal entries in a standard cost system.

$$\text{Materials price variance} = (AQ \times AP) - (AQ \times SP)$$

Actual   Actual   Standard
Quantity   Price   Price

The formula can be factored into simpler form as follows:

$$\text{Materials price variance} = AQ(AP - SP)$$

Some managers prefer this simpler formula, since it permits variance computations to be made very quickly. Using the data from Exhibit 10–3 in this formula, we have the following:

$$6{,}500 \text{ kilograms } (\$3.80 \text{ per kilogram} - \$4.00 \text{ per kilogram}) = \$1{,}300 \text{ F}$$

Notice that the answer is the same as that yielded in Exhibit 10–3. If the company wanted to put these data into a performance report, the data might appear as follows:

COLONIAL PEWTER COMPANY
Performance Report—Purchasing Department

Item Purchased	(1) Quantity Purchased	(2) Actual Price	(3) Standard Price	(4) Difference in Price (2) − (3)	(5) Total Price Variance (1) × (4)	Explanation
Pewter	6,500 kilograms	$3.80	$4.00	$0.20	$1,300 F	Bargained for an especially favourable price.

F = Favourable; U = Unfavourable.

ISOLATION OF VARIANCES   At what point should variances be isolated and brought to the attention of management? The answer is, the earlier the better. The sooner deviations from standard are brought to the attention of management, the sooner problems can be evaluated and corrected. If long periods are allowed to elapse before variances are computed, costs that could otherwise have been controlled may accumulate to the point of doing significant damage to profits. Most firms compute the materials price variance, for example, when materials are *purchased* rather than when the materials are placed in production. This permits earlier isolation of the variance, since materials may remain in the warehouse before being used in production. Isolating the price variance in the inventory accounts when purchased also permits the company to carry its raw materials in the inventory at standard cost. This greatly simplifies the selection of the proper costs figure to use when raw materials are later placed into production.[9] Note however that the problem of determining the purchase price variance at a different time than the materials usage variance would not occur in a strict JIT environment.

Once a performance report has been prepared, what does management do with the price variance data? The most significant variances should be viewed as "red

---

9. See Appendix 10A at the end of this chapter for an illustration of journal entries in a standard cost system.

flags," calling attention to the fact that an exception has occurred that will require some explanation and perhaps follow-up effort. Normally, the performance report itself will contain some explanation of the reason for the variance, as shown above. In the case of Colonial Pewter Company, the purchasing manager, Janet Warner, said that the favourable price variance resulted from bargaining for an especially favourable price.

Focus on Current Practice

The Gaumnitz and Kollaritsch study of large manufacturing companies cited earlier found that about 60% prepare variance reports on a monthly basis, another 13% prepare reports on a weekly basis, and nearly 22% prepare reports on a daily basis. The number of companies preparing daily reports has more than doubled in recent years.[10] The Cohen and Paquette study cited earlier reported essentially the same results, with only slightly fewer companies preparing monthly reports and only slightly more preparing weekly or daily reports.[11] ■

RESPONSIBILITY FOR THE VARIANCE   Who is responsible for the materials price variance? Generally speaking, the purchasing manager has control over the price paid for goods and is therefore responsible for any price variances. Many factors influence the prices paid for goods, including how many units are ordered in a lot, how the order is delivered, whether the order is a rush order, and the quality of materials purchased. A deviation in any of these factors from what was assumed when the standards were set can result in a price variance. For example, purchase of second-grade materials rather than top-grade materials may result in a favourable price variance, since the lower-grade materials would generally be less costly (but perhaps less suitable for production).

There may be times, however, when someone other than the purchasing manager is responsible for a materials price variance. Production may be scheduled in such a way, for example, that the purchasing manager must request delivery by airfreight, rather than by truck. In these cases, the production manager would bear responsibility for the resulting price variances.

A word of caution is in order. Variance analysis should not be used as an excuse to conduct witch hunts or as a means of beating line managers and workers over the head. The emphasis must be on the control function in the sense of *supporting* the line managers and *assisting* them in meeting the goals that they have participated in setting for the company. In short, the emphasis should be positive rather than negative. Excessive dwelling on what has already happened, particularly in terms of trying to find someone to blame, can be destructive to the functioning of an organization.

Materials quantity variance   A measure of the difference between the actual quantity of materials used in production and the standard quantity allowed, multiplied by the standard price per unit of materials.

Materials Quantity Variance—A Closer Look

The **materials quantity variance** measures the difference between the quantity of materials used in production and the quantity that should have been used according to the standard that has been set. Although the variance is concerned with the physical usage of materials, it is generally stated in dollar terms, as shown in Exhibit 10–3. The formula for the materials quantity variance is as follows:

---

10. See Gaumnitz and Kollaritsch, "Manufacturing Cost Variances: Current Practice and Trends," p. 60.
11. See Cohen and Pacquette, "Management Accounting Practices: Perceptions of Controllers," p. 77.

$$\text{Materials quantity variance} = (AQ \times SP) - (SQ \times SP)$$

Actual Quantity   Standard Price   Standard Quantity Allowed for Output

Again, the formula can be factored into simpler terms:

$$\text{Materials quantity variance} = SP(AQ - SQ)$$

Using the data from Exhibit 10–3 in the formula, we have the following:

$$\$4.00 \text{ per kilogram}(6,500 \text{ kilograms} - 6,000 \text{ kilograms*}) = \$2,000 \text{ U}$$

*2,000 units × 3.0 kilograms per unit = 6,000 kilograms.

The answer, of course, is the same as that yielded in Exhibit 10–3. The data might appear as follows if a formal performance report were prepared:

COLONIAL PEWTER COMPANY
Performance Report—Production Department

Type of Materials	(1) Standard Price	(2) Actual Quantity	(3) Standard Quantity Allowed	(4) Difference in Quantity (2) − (3)	(5) Total Quantity Variance (1) × (4)	Explanation
Pewter	$4.00	6,500 kg	6,000 kg	500 kg	$2,000 U	Second-grade materials unsuitable for production

F = Favourable; U = Unfavourable.

The materials quantity variance is best isolated at the time that materials are placed into production. Materials are drawn for the number of units to be produced, according to the standard bill of materials for each unit. Any additional materials are usually drawn with an excess materials requisition slip, which is different in colour from the normal requisition slips. This procedure calls attention to the excessive usage of materials *while production is still in process* and provides an opportunity for early control of any developing problem.

Excessive usage of materials can result from many factors, including faulty machines, inferior quality of materials, untrained workers, and poor supervision. Generally speaking, it is the responsibility of the production department to see that material usage is kept in line with standards. There may be times, however, when the *purchasing* department may be responsible for an unfavourable materials quantity variance. If the purchasing department obtains inferior quality materials in an effort to economize on price, the materials may be unsuitable for use and may result in excessive waste. Thus, purchasing rather than production would be responsible for the quantity variance. At Colonial Pewter, the production manager, Tom Kuchel, said that second-grade materials were the cause of the unfavourable materials quantity variance for June.

Exhibit 10–5   Extended Model for Variance Analysis—Materials

Note: the following represents the diagram content in Exhibit 10–5.

Actual Quantity of Inputs, at Actual Price $(AQ \times AP)$	Actual Quantity of Inputs, at Standard Price $(AQ \times SP)$	Actual Quantity of Inputs, at Standard Mix and Standard Price $(M \times SP)$	Standard Quantity of Inputs, at Standard Mix and Standard Price $(SQ \times SP)$

Prime variance*   Mix variance $(AQ - M)SP$ Yield variance $(M - SQ)SP$

Usual quantity variance $(AQ - SQ)SP$

Usual total variance

*Same as previous analysis, e.g., Exhibit 10–2.

Further Analysis of Material Variances

Objective 3

Compute mix and yield variances for materials and explain their significance.

A survey of the cost accounting practices of the 1,000 largest U.S. industrial companies[12] found that two other types of standard cost variances are frequently computed.[13] These are subcomponents of the material usage variance: a *material mix* and *material yield variance*. A representation of these variances is presented in Exhibit 10–5.

The production of most goods generally requires input from more than one material. Chemical firms, for example, may use varying proportions of interchangeable materials. The same is true with food processing companies. For example, a company that produces flour with a mixture of red and white wheat may, on occasion, substitute one kind of wheat for the other. When legally permitted, a manufacturer of canned fruit may substitute peaches for pears and a manufacturer of sausages may substitute pork for beef. The calculation of mix and yield variances is appropriate only if different types of material can be substituted for one another. A **mix variance** results if the actual mix of materials differs from the budgeted mix of materials. The budgeted mix reflects a proportional mix of materials that is expected to be used to produce a given product. A mix variance is calculated to determine the effects of a change in the material mix on the total material cost. Where a manager has control over the composition of the mix, the mix variance can be a useful measure of the manager's performance.

Mix variance   The dollar effect of a difference between the actual mix of materials and the budgeted mix of materials on total material cost.

The amount of quantity variance remaining after deducting the mix variance from the total quantity variance is the **yield variance.** A yield variance occurs when the actual combination of inputs generates a different rate of output from what would have been produced by the input mix used in setting the standards. In other words, the actual yield differs from the standard yield expected from a given mix of inputs.

Yield variance   The portion of the efficiency variance which is not the mix variance. It occurs when the actual yield differs from the standard yield expected from a given mix of inputs.

To illustrate the calculation of the mix and yield variances assume that Cape Breton Chemical Company combines secret ingredients A and B to make a product known as super cleaner Bjax. The standard composition calls for a mix of 2 kilograms of A and 3 kilograms of B to produce one unit of Bjax. The standard mix for A and B is therefore ⅖ and ⅗ respectively. Assume that 150 units were produced using 350 kilograms of A and 450 kilograms of B. Material A has a standard unit price of $1.50 and material B has a standard price of $2.50 per unit.

12. Max Laudeman and F. W. Schaeberle, "The Cost Accounting Practices of Firms Using Standard Costs," *Cost and Management* (July–August 1985), pp. 21–25.
13. Ibid.

For a given input, the mix variance can be calculated in two steps. First, multiply the budgeted mix percentage by the actual *total* input and subtract the actual quantity. This is the mix variance expressed in physical terms. Second, multiply your answer from step one by the standard cost of the input.

$$\text{Mix variance} = \left[\text{Actual quantity} - \left(\text{Budgeted \%} \times \text{Total input} \right) \right] \times \text{Standard price}$$

For material A this would be:

$$[350 - \tfrac{2}{5}(350 + 450)] \times \$1.50 = \$45U$$

Similarly, for material B the mix variance is

$$[450 - \tfrac{3}{5}(350 + 450)] \times \$2.50 = \$75F$$

The budgeted percent times the total input of material A is 320 [$\tfrac{2}{5}(350 + 450)$] kilograms. This is the amount of material A that would have been used if the budget had been adhered to. Since the amount of material used, 350 kilograms, exceeds the budgeted amount, the mix variance is unfavourable. If the budget had been adhered to in the case of material B, 480 [$\tfrac{3}{5}(350 + 450)$] kilograms would have been used. Since the actual usage of material B was only 450 kilograms, the material mix variance of material B is favourable.

The variances can also be calculated using the following notation. For material A:

$$\text{Mix variance} = (AQ_A - M_A)SP_A$$
$$= [350 - \tfrac{2}{5}(350 + 450)]\$1.50 = \$45U$$
$$\text{Yield variance} = (M_A - SQ_A)SP_A$$
$$= [\tfrac{2}{5}(350 + 450) - 150(2)]\$1.50 = \$30U$$
$$\text{Total material quantity variance} = (AQ_A - SQ_A)SP_A$$
$$= (350 - 150(2))\$1.50 = \$75U$$

or mix variance + yield variance
$$\$45U + \$30U = \$75U$$

where

AQ_A is the actual quantity used of material A.
M_A is the standard mix of material A actually used.
SQ_A is the standard quantity of material A.

For material B:

$$\text{Mix variance} = [450 - \tfrac{3}{5}(350 + 450)]\$2.50 = -\$75F$$
$$\text{Yield variance} = [\tfrac{3}{5}(350 + 450) - 3(150)]\$2.50 = \$75U$$
$$\text{Total material quantity variance} = [450 - 3(150)]\$2.50 = \$0.0$$

or

$$\$75F - \$75U = \$0.0$$

Labour efficiency variances, described in the section to follow, can be analyzed in a similar manner if the composition of a work group is provided in the standard. For example, if all junior staff are assigned to other jobs a public accounting firm might assign senior staff to a job that would normally be done by more junior personnel. The standard mix of employees can be applied to the total hours worked in the group to determine the standard mix for each employee group.

The calculation of mix and yield variances provides a means of separating the quantity variance into a set of constituents. This breakdown can be meaningful where managers are able to change the mix in production, thereby affecting the quantities of each type of material used. If the standard mix is the ideal, then departures from this mix should be made evident to statement users.

Managers, however, should carefully examine the effect of mix and yield variances to see how other costs such as labour and overhead are affected by the change in mix and its effect on yield. Often there are interrelationships among the mix, yield, and material price variances. For example, a production manager may respond to changes in relative prices of inputs by changing the mix. The new mix may, in turn, affect the yield. If examined in isolation, the appropriateness of the decision to change the mix could not be properly assessed. This raises performance evaluation issues. The budgeted mix is no longer optimal and, therefore, cannot be used as a valid benchmark for evaluating the manager's performance.

One problem of mix and yield variances stems from its use of standard prices. When prices differ from standard, it is the change in actual relative prices within the materials composition which may make changes in the mix and yield worthwhile. The fact that these price changes are held constant when calculating the mix and usage variances makes it difficult to interpret the effectiveness of managerial decisions to make changes in the mix of inputs. Conceptually, these variances can be left in physical units. Multiplying by standard prices is to facilitate aggregation by providing a common denominator.

Using Standard Costs—Direct Labour Variances

Objective 4

Compute the direct labour rate and efficiency variances and explain their significance.

Terry's next step in determining Colonial Pewter's variances for June was to compute the direct labour variances for the month. Recall from Exhibit 10–1 that the standard direct labour cost per unit of product is $35, computed as follows:

$$2.5 \text{ hours per unit} \times \$14.00 \text{ per hour} = \$35 \text{ per unit}$$

During June, the company paid its direct labour workers $74,250, including employment taxes and fringe benefits, for 5,400 hours of work. This was an average of $13.75 per hour. Using these data and the standard costs from Exhibit 10–1, Terry computed the direct labour rate and efficiency variances that appear in Exhibit 10–6.

Notice that the column headings in Exhibit 10–6 are the same as those used in the prior two exhibits, except that in Exhibit 10–6 the terms *hours* and *rate* are used in place of the terms *quantity* and *price*.

Labour Rate Variance—A Closer Look

Labour rate variance
A measure of the difference between the actual hourly labour rate and the standard rate, multiplied by the number of hours worked during the period.

As explained earlier, the price variance for direct labour is commonly termed a **labour rate variance.** This variance measures any deviation from standard in the average hourly rate paid to direct labour workers. The formula for the labour rate variance is expressed as follows:

$$\text{Labour rate variance} = (AH \times AR) - (AH \times SR)$$

Actual	Actual	Standard
Hours	Rate	Rate

Exhibit 10–6   Variance Analysis—Direct Labour

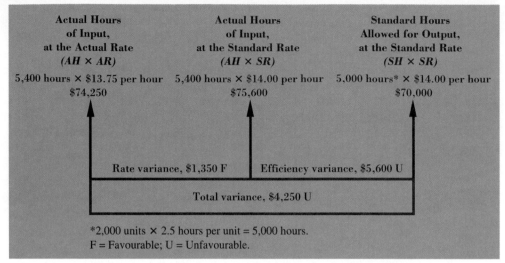

Actual Hours of Input, at the Actual Rate (AH × AR)	Actual Hours of Input, at the Standard Rate (AH × SR)	Standard Hours Allowed for Output, at the Standard Rate (SH × SR)
5,400 hours × $13.75 per hour $74,250	5,400 hours × $14.00 per hour $75,600	5,000 hours* × $14.00 per hour $70,000

Rate variance, $1,350 F   Efficiency variance, $5,600 U

Total variance, $4,250 U

*2,000 units × 2.5 hours per unit = 5,000 hours.
F = Favourable; U = Unfavourable.

The formula can be factored into simpler form as follows:

$$\text{Labour rate variance} = AH(AR - SR)$$

Using the data from Exhibit 10–6 in the formula, we have the following:

$$5{,}400 \text{ hours } (\$13.75 \text{ per hour} - \$14.00 \text{ per hour}) = \$1{,}350 \text{ F}$$

In most firms, the rates paid to workers are quite predictable. Nevertheless, rate variances can arise through the way labour is used. Skilled workers with high hourly rates of pay may be given duties that require little skill and call for low hourly rates of pay. This will result in unfavourable labour rate variances, since the actual hourly rate of pay will exceed the standard rate specified for the particular task being performed. A reverse situation exists when unskilled or untrained workers are assigned to jobs that require some skill or training. The lower pay scale for these workers will result in favourable rate variances, although the workers may be inefficient. Finally, unfavourable rate variances can arise from overtime work at premium rates if any portion of the overtime premium is added to the direct labour account.

Who is responsible for controlling the labour rate variance? Since rate variances generally arise as a result of how labour is used, supervisors bear responsibility for seeing that labour rate variances are kept under control.

Labour Efficiency Variance—A Closer Look

Labour efficiency variance   A measure of the difference between the actual hours taken to complete a task and the standard hours allowed, multiplied by the standard hourly labour rate.

The quantity variance for direct labour, more commonly called the **labour efficiency variance,** measures the productivity of labour time. No variance is more closely watched by management, since it is widely believed that increasing the productivity of direct labour time is vital to reducing costs. The formula for the labour efficiency variance is expressed as follows:

$$\text{Labour efficiency variance} = (AH \times SR) - (SH \times SR)$$

Actual Hours   Standard Rate   Standard Hours Allowed for Output

Factored into simpler terms, the formula is as follows:

$$\text{Labour efficiency variance} = SR(AH - SH)$$

Using the data from Exhibit 10–6 in the formula, we have the following:

$$\$14.00 \text{ per hour}(5,400 \text{ hours} - 5,000 \text{ hours*}) = \$5,600 \text{ U}$$

*2,000 units $\times$ 2.5 hours per unit = 5,000 hours.

Possible causes of an unfavourable labour efficiency variance include poorly trained or motivated workers; poor quality materials, requiring more labour time in processing; faulty equipment, causing breakdowns and work interruptions; poor supervision of workers; and inaccurate standards. The managers in charge of production would generally be responsible for control of the labour efficiency variance. However, the variance might be chargeable to purchasing if the acquisition of poor materials resulted in excessive labour processing time.

When the labour force is essentially fixed in the short term, another important cause of an unfavourable labour efficiency variance is insufficient demand for the output of the factory. In some firms, the actual labour-hours worked is basically fixed—particularly in the short term. Managers in these firms argue that it is difficult, and perhaps even unwise, to constantly adjust the workforce in response to changes in the workload. Therefore, the only way a work centre manager can avoid an unfavourable labour efficiency variance in such firms is by keeping everyone busy all of the time. The option of reducing the number of workers on hand is not available.

Thus, if there are insufficient orders from customers to keep the workers busy, the work centre manager has two options—either accept an unfavourable labour efficiency variance or build inventory.[14] A central lesson of just-in-time (JIT) is that building inventory with no immediate prospect of sale is a bad idea. Inventory—particularly work in process inventory—leads to high defect rates, obsolete goods, and generally inefficient operations. As a consequence, when the workforce is basically fixed in the short term, managers must be cautious about how labour efficiency variances are used. Some managers advocate dispensing with labour efficiency variances entirely in such situations—at least for the purposes of motivating and controlling workers on the shop floor.

Using Standard Costs—Variable Manufacturing Overhead Variances

Objective 5

Compute the variable manufacturing overhead spending and efficiency variances.

The final step in Terry's analysis of Colonial Pewter's variances for June was to compute the variable manufacturing overhead variances. The variable portion of manufacturing overhead can be analyzed using the same basic formulas that are used to analyze direct materials and direct labour. Recall from Exhibit 10–1 that the standard variable manufacturing overhead is $7.50 per unit of product, computed as follows:

$$2.5 \text{ hours per unit} \times \$3.00 \text{ per hour} = \$7.50 \text{ per unit}$$

Colonial Pewter's cost records showed that the total actual variable manufacturing overhead cost for June was $15,390. Recall from the earlier discussion of the direct labour variances that 5,400 hours of direct labour time were recorded during the month and that the company produced 2,000 pairs of bookends. Terry's analysis of this overhead data appears in Exhibit 10–7.

---

14. For further discussion, see Eliyahu M. Goldratt and Jeff Cox, *The Goal*, 2nd rev. ed. (Croton-on-Hudson, NY: North River Press, 1992).

Exhibit 10–7 Variance Analysis—Variable Manufacturing Overhead

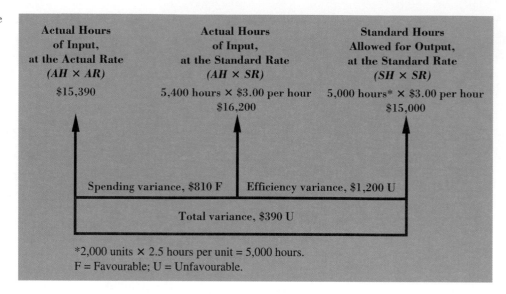

Notice the similarities between Exhibits 10–6 and 10–7. These similarities arise from the fact that direct labour-hours are being used as a base for allocating overhead cost to units of product; thus, the same hourly figures appear in Exhibit 10–7 for variable manufacturing overhead as in Exhibit 10–6 for direct labour. The main difference between the two exhibits is in the standard hourly rate being used, which in this company is much lower for variable manufacturing overhead.

Manufacturing Overhead Variances—A Closer Look

Variable overhead spending variance The difference between the actual variable overhead cost incurred during a period and the standard cost that should have been incurred based on the actual activity of the period.

The formula for **variable overhead spending variance** is expressed as follows:

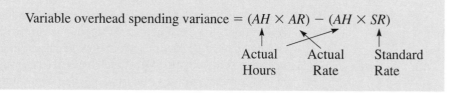

Or, factored into simpler terms:

$$\text{Variable overhead spending variance} = AH(AR - SR)$$

Using the data from Exhibit 10–7 in the formula, we have the following:

$$5{,}400 \text{ hours}(\$2.85 \text{ per hour}^* - \$3.00 \text{ per hour}) = \$810 \text{ F}$$

*$15,390 ÷ 5,400 hours = $2.85 per hour.

Variable overhead efficiency variance The difference between the actual activity (direct labour-hours, machine-hours, or some other base) of a period and the standard activity allowed, multiplied by the variable part of the predetermined overhead rate.

The formula for the **variable overhead efficiency variance** is expressed as follows:

$$\text{Variable overhead efficiency variance} = (AH \times SR) - (SH \times SR)$$

Actual Hours   Standard Rate   Standard Hours Allowed for Output

Or, factored into simpler terms:

$$\text{Variable overhead efficiency variance} = SR(AH - SH)$$

Again using the data from Exhibit 10–7, the computation of the variance would be as follows:

$$\$3.00 \text{ per hour}(5,400 \text{ hours} - 5,000 \text{ hours*}) = \$1,200 \text{ U}$$

*2,000 units × 2.5 hours per unit = 5,000 hours.

We will reserve further discussion of the variable overhead spending and efficiency variances until Chapter 11, where overhead analysis is discussed in depth.

Before proceeding further, we suggest that you pause at this point and go back and review the data contained in Exhibits 10–1 through 10–7. These exhibits and the accompanying text discussion provide a comprehensive, integrated illustration of standard setting and variance analysis.

Managerial Accounting in Action

THE ISSUE

COLONIAL PEWTER COMPANY

In preparation for the scheduled meeting to discuss Terry's analysis of Colonial Pewter's standard costs and variances, Terry distributed Exhibits 10–1 through 10–7, with supporting explanations, to the management group of Colonial Pewter. This included J. D. Wriston, the president of the company; Tom Kuchel, the production manager; and Janet Warner, the purchasing manager. J. D. Wriston opened the meeting with the following question:

J. D.: Terry, I think I understand the report you distributed, but just to make sure, would you mind summarizing the highlights of what you found?

Terry: As you can see, the biggest problems are the unfavourable materials quantity variance of $2,000 and the unfavourable labour efficiency variance of $5,600.

J. D.: Tom, you're the production boss. What do you think is responsible for the unfavourable labour efficiency variance?

Tom: It pretty much has to be the new production workers. Our experienced workers shouldn't have much problem meeting the standard of 2.5 hours per unit. We all knew that there would be some inefficiency for a while as we brought new people on board.

J. D.: No one is disputing that, Tom. However, $5,600 is a lot of money. Is this problem likely to go away very soon?

Tom: I hope so. If we were to contrast the last two weeks of June with the first two weeks, I'm sure we would see some improvement.

J. D.: I don't want to beat up on you, Tom, but this is a significant problem. Can you do something to accelerate the training process?

Tom: Sure. I could pair up each of the new guys with one of our old-timers and have them work together for a while. It would slow down our older guys a bit, but I'll bet the new workers would learn a lot.

J. D.: Let's try it. Now, what about that $2,000 unfavourable materials quantity variance?

Tom: Are you asking me?

J. D.: Well, I would like someone to explain it.

Tom: Don't look at me. It's that iron-contaminated pewter that Janet bought on her "special deal."

Janet: We got rid of that stuff months ago.

J. D.: Hold your horses. We're not trying to figure out who to blame here. I just want to understand what happened. If we can understand what happened, maybe we can fix it.

Terry: Tom, are the new workers generating a lot of scrap?

Tom: Yeah, I guess so.

J. D.: I think that could be part of the problem. Can you do anything about it?

Tom: I can watch the scrap real closely for a few days to see where it's being generated. If it is the new workers, I can have the old-timers work with them on the problem when I team them up.

J. D.: Good. Let's reconvene in a few weeks and see what has happened. Hopefully, we can get those unfavourable variances under control. ■

Structure of Performance Reports

On preceding pages we have learned that performance reports are used in a standard cost system to communicate variance data to management. Exhibit 10–8 provides an example of how these reports can be integrated in a responsibility reporting system.

Note from the exhibit that the performance reports *start at the bottom and build upward,* with managers at each level receiving information on their own performance as well as information on the performance of each manager under them in the chain of responsibility. This variance information flows upward from level to level in a pyramid fashion, with the president finally receiving a summary of all activities in the organization. If the manager at a particular level (such as the production superintendent) wants to know the reasons behind a variance, he or she can ask for the detailed performance reports prepared by the various operations or departments.

In the following section, we turn our attention to the question of how a manager can determine which variances on these reports are significant enough to warrant further attention.

Variance Analysis and Management by Exception

Variance analysis and performance reports are important elements of *management by exception.* Simply put, management by exception means that the manager's attention should be directed toward those parts of the organization where plans are not working out for one reason or another. Time and effort should not be wasted attending to those parts of the organization where things are going smoothly.

The budgets and standards discussed in this chapter and in the preceding chapter reflect management's plans. If all goes according to plan, there will be little difference between actual results and the results that would be expected according to the budgets and standards. If this happens, managers can concentrate on other issues. However, if actual results do not conform to the budget and to standards, the performance reporting system sends a signal to the manager that an "exception" has occurred. This signal is in the form of a variance from the budget or standards.

However, are all variances worth investigating? The answer is no. Differences between actual results and what was expected will almost always occur. If every variance were investigated, management would waste a great deal of time tracking down nickel-and-dime differences. Variances may occur for any of a variety of reasons— only some of which are significant and warrant management attention. For example,

Exhibit 10–8 Upward Flow of Performance Reports

President's Report
The president's performance report summarizes all company data. The president can trace the variances downward through the company as needed to determine where top-management time should be spent.

Responsibility centre:	Budget	Actual	Variance
Sales manager	X	X	X
Production superintendent	$26,000	$29,000	$3,000 U
Engineering head	X	X	X
Personnel supervisor	X	X	X
Controller	X	X	X
	$54,000	$61,000	$7,000 U

Production Superintendent
The performance of each department head is summarized for the production superintendent. The totals on the superintendent's performance report are then passed upward to the next level of responsibility.

Responsibility centre:	Budget	Actual	Variance
Cutting department	X	X	X
Machining department	X	X	X
Finishing department	$11,000	$12,500	$1,500 U
Packaging department	X	X	X
	$26,000	$29,000	$3,000 U

Finishing Department Head
The performance report of each supervisor is summarized on the performance report of the department head. The department totals are then passed upward to the production superintendent.

Responsibility centre:	Budget	Actual	Variance
Sanding operation	X	X	X
Wiring operation	$ 5,000	$ 5,800	$ 800 U
Assembly operation	X	X	X
	$11,000	$12,500	$1,500 U

Wiring Operation Supervisor
The supervisor of each operation receives a performance report. The totals on these reports are then communicated upward to the next higher level of responsibility.

Variable costs:	Budget	Actual	Variance
Direct materials	X	X	X
Direct labour	X	X	X
Manufacturing overhead	X	X	X
	$ 5,000	$ 5,800	$ 800 U

hotter-than-normal weather in the summer may result in higher-than-expected electrical bills for air conditioning. Or, workers may work slightly faster or slower on a particular day. Because of unpredictable random factors, one can expect that virtually every cost category will produce a variance of some kind.

How should managers decide which variances are worth investigating? One clue is the size of the variance. A variance of $5 is probably not big enough to warrant attention, whereas a variance of $5,000 might well be worth tracking down. Another clue is the size of the variance relative to the amount of spending involved. A variance that is only 0.1% of spending on an item is likely to be well within the bounds one would normally expect due to random factors. On the other hand, a variance of 10% of spending is much more likely to be a signal that something is basically wrong.

A more dependable approach is to plot variance data on a statistical control chart, such as illustrated in Exhibit 10–9. The basic idea underlying a statistical control chart is that some random fluctuations in variances from period to period are normal and to be expected even when costs are well under control. A variance should only be investigated when it is unusual relative to that normal level of random fluctuation. Typically the standard deviation of the variances is used as the measure of the normal level of fluctuations. A rule of thumb is adopted such as "investigate all variances that are more than X standard deviations from zero." In the control chart in Exhibit 10–9, X is 1.0.

Exhibit 10–9 A
Statistical Control Chart

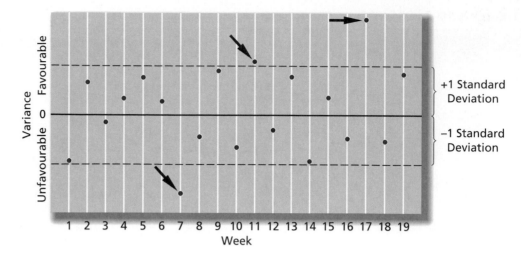

That is, the rule of thumb in this company is to investigate all variances that are more than one standard deviation in either direction (favourable or unfavourable) from zero. This means that the variances in weeks 7, 11, and 17 would have been investigated, but none of the others.

What value of X should be chosen? The bigger the value of X, the wider the band of acceptable variances that would not be investigated. Thus, the bigger the value of X, the less time will be spent tracking down variances, but the more likely it is that a real out-of-control situation would be overlooked. Ordinarily, if X is selected to be 1.0, roughly 30% of all variances will trigger an investigation even when there is no real problem. If X is set at 1.5, the figure drops to about 13%. If X is set at 2.0, the figure drops all the way to about 5%. Don't forget, however, that selecting a big value of X will result not only in fewer investigations but also a higher probability that a real problem will be overlooked.

In addition to watching for unusually large variances, the pattern of the variances should be monitored. For example, a run of steadily mounting variances should trigger an investigation even though none of the variances is large enough by itself to warrant investigation.

International Uses of Standard Costs

Standard costs are used by companies worldwide. A comparative study of cost accounting practices found that three-fourths of the companies surveyed in the United Kingdom, two-thirds of the companies surveyed in Canada, and 40% of the companies surveyed in Japan used standard cost systems.[15]

Standard costs were first introduced in Japan after World War II, with Nippon Electronics Company (NEC) being one of the first Japanese companies to adopt standard costs for all of its products. Many other Japanese companies followed NEC's lead after the war and developed standard cost systems. The ways in which these standard costs are used in Japan—and also in the other countries cited above—are shown in Exhibit 10–10.

Over time, the pattern of use shown in Exhibit 10–10 may change, but at present managers can expect to encounter standard costs in most industrialized nations.

---

15. Shin'ichi Inoue, "Comparative Studies of Recent Development of Cost Management Problems in U.S.A., U.K., Canada, and Japan," Research Paper No. 29, Kagawa University (March 1988), p. 17. The study included 95 United States companies, 52 United Kingdom companies, 82 Canadian companies, and 646 Japanese companies.

Exhibit 10–10 Uses of Standard Costs in Four Countries

	Canada	United States	United Kingdom	Japan
Cost management	2	1*	2	1
Budgetary planning and control†	1	2	3	3
Pricing decisions	3	3	1	2
Financial statement preparation	4	4	4	4

*The numbers 1 through 4 denote importance of use, from greatest to least.

†Includes management planning.

Source: Compiled from data in a study by Shin'ichi Inoue, "Comparative Studies of Recent Development of Cost Management Problems in U.S.A., U.K., Canada, and Japan," Research Paper No. 29, Kagawa University (March 1988), p. 20.

Moreover, the most important uses are for cost management and budgetary planning purposes.

Evaluation of Controls Based on Standard Costs

Advantages of Standard Costs

Objective 6

Understand how a balanced scorecard fits together and how it supports a company's strategy.

Standard cost systems have a number of advantages.

1. As stated earlier, the use of standard costs is a key element in a management by exception approach. So long as costs remain within the standards, managers can focus on other issues. When costs fall significantly outside the standards, managers are alerted that there may be problems requiring attention. This approach helps managers focus on important issues.
2. So long as standards are viewed as reasonable by employees, they can promote economy and efficiency. They provide benchmarks that individuals can use to judge their own performance.
3. Standard costs can greatly simplify bookkeeping. Instead of recording actual costs for each job, the standard costs for materials, labour, and overhead can be charged to jobs.
4. Standard costs fit naturally in an integrated system of "responsibility accounting." The standards establish what costs should be, who should be responsible for them, and whether actual costs are under control.

Potential Problems with the Use of Standard Costs

The use of standard costs can present a number of potential problems. Most of these problems result from improper use of standard costs and the management by exception principle or from using standard costs in situations in which they are not appropriate.

1. Standard cost variance reports are usually prepared on a monthly basis and often are released days or even weeks after the end of the month. As a consequence, the information in the reports may be so stale that it is almost useless. Timely, frequent reports that are approximately correct are better than infrequent reports that are very precise but out of date by the time they are released. As mentioned earlier, some companies are now reporting variances and other key operating data daily or even more frequently.
2. If managers are insensitive and use variance reports as a club, morale may suffer. Employees should receive positive reinforcement for work well done. Management by exception, by its nature, tends to focus on the negative. If

variances are used as a club, subordinates may be tempted to cover up unfavourable variances or take actions that are not in the best interests of the company to make sure the variances are favourable. For example, workers may put on a crash effort to increase output at the end of the month to avoid an unfavourable labour efficiency variance. In the rush to produce output, quality may suffer.

3. Labour quantity standards and efficiency variances make two important assumptions. First, they assume that the production process is labour-paced; if labour works faster, output will go up. However, output in many companies is no longer determined by how fast labour works; rather, it is determined by the processing speed of machines. Second, the computations assume that labour is a variable cost. However, as discussed in earlier chapters, in many companies, direct labour may be essentially fixed. If labour is fixed, then an undue emphasis on labour efficiency variances creates pressure to build excess work in process and finished goods inventories.

Focus on Current Practice

In an article about the big three auto makers in North America, *The Wall Street Journal* reported the following:

General Motors is wrestling with how to change a way of life in a sprawling, hidebound bureaucracy . . . That's why GM has spent more than a year overhauling how it measures success.

"Traditionally, we measured labour efficiency in the plants," Mr. Hoglund [a GM executive vice president] says, to elicit greater output per unit of labour. "Then we found out it drove all the wrong behaviours—people got rewarded for higher and higher volumes, but there was no incentive for quality." Moreover, all the comparisons were internal. Now, he says, the key measures are customer satisfaction and how various processes stack up against the best of the competition.[16] ∎

4. In some cases, a "favourable" variance can be as bad or worse than an "unfavourable" variance. For example, McDonald's has a standard for the amount of hamburger meat that should be in a Big Mac. If there is a "favourable" variance, it means that less meat was used than the standard specifies. The result is a substandard Big Mac and possibly a dissatisfied customer.

5. There may be a tendency with standard cost reporting systems to emphasize meeting the standards to the exclusion of other important objectives such as maintaining and improving quality, on-time delivery, and customer satisfaction. This tendency can be reduced by using supplemental performance measures that focus on these other objectives.

6. Just meeting standards may not be sufficient; continual improvement may be necessary to survive in the current competitive environment. For this reason, some companies focus on the trends in the standard cost variances—aiming for continual improvement rather than just meeting the standards. In other companies, engineered standards are being replaced either by a rolling average of actual costs, which is expected to decline, or by very challenging target costs.

In summary, managers should exercise considerable care in their use of a standard cost system. It is particularly important that managers go out of their way to focus on the positive, rather than just on the negative, and to be aware of possible unintended consequences.

Nevertheless, standard costs are still found in the vast majority of manufacturing companies and in many service companies, although their use is changing. For evaluating performance, standard cost variances may be supplanted in the future by a par-

---

16. "Tooling Along: With Auto Profits Up, Big Three Again Get a Major Opportunity," *The Wall Street Journal,* May 4, 1994, pp. A1, A11.

ticularly interesting development known as the *balanced scorecard,* which is discussed in the next section. While the balanced scorecard concept is new in most of the world, it has been eagerly embraced by a wide variety of organizations including Analog Devices, KPMG Peat Marwick, Tenneco, Allstate, AT&T, Elf Atochem, Conair-Franklin, Chemical Bank, 3COM, Rockwater, Apple Computer, Advanced Micro Devices (AMD), FMC, the Bank of Montreal, and Domeco Limited.

Balanced Scorecard

Objective 7

Understand how a balanced scorecard fits together and how it supports a company's strategy.

Balanced scorecard An integrated set of performance measures that is derived from and supports the organization's strategy.

A **balanced scorecard** consists of an integrated set of performance measures that are derived from the company's strategy and that support the company's strategy throughout the organization.[17,18] A strategy is essentially a theory about how to achieve the organization's goals. For example, Air Canada could adopt a strategy to offer passengers low prices and fun on short-haul jet service. The low prices result from the absence of costly frills such as meals, assigned seating, and interline baggage checking. The fun is provided by flight attendants who go out of their way to entertain passengers with their antics. This is an interesting strategy. The airline could consciously hire people who have a sense of humor and who enjoy their work. Hiring and retaining such employees probably costs no more—and may cost less—than retaining grumpy flight attendants who view their jobs as a chore. The purpose of this strategy is to build loyal customers through a combination of "fun"—which does not cost anything to provide—and low prices that are possible because of the lack of costly frills offered by competing airlines. The theory is that low prices and fun will lead to loyal customers, which, in combination with low costs, will lead to high profits.

Under the balanced scorecard approach, top management translates its strategy into performance measures that employees can understand and can do something about. For example, the amount of time passengers have to wait in line to have their baggage checked might be a performance measure for the supervisor in charge of the Air Canada check-in counter at the Vancouver airport. This performance measure is easily understood by the supervisor, and can be improved by the supervisor's actions.

Common Characteristics of Balanced Scorecards

Performance measures used in the balanced scorecard approach tend to fall into the four groups illustrated in Exhibit 10–11: financial, customer, internal business processes, and learning and growth. Internal business processes are what the company does in an attempt to satisfy customers. For example, in a manufacturing company, assembling a product is an internal business process. In an airline, handling baggage is an internal business process. The basic idea is that learning is necessary to improve internal business processes; improving business processes is necessary to improve

---

17. The balanced scorecard concept was developed by Robert Kaplan and David Norton. For further details, see their articles "The Balanced Scorecard—Measures That Drive Performance," *Harvard Business Review* (January/February 1992), pp. 71–79; "Using the Balanced Scorecard as a Strategic Management System," *Harvard Business Review* (January/February 1996), pp. 75–85; "Why Does a Business Need a Balanced Scorecard?" *Journal of Cost Management* (May/June 1997), pp. 5–10; and their book *Translating Strategy into Action: The Balanced Scorecard* (Boston, MA: Harvard Business School Press, 1996).

18. In the 1960s, the French developed a concept similar to the balanced scorecard called Tableau de Bord or "dashboard." For details, see Michel Lebas, "Managerial Accounting in France: Overview of Past Tradition and Current Practice," *The European Accounting Review* 3, no. 3 (1994), pp. 471–87; and Marc Epstein and Jean-François Manzoni, "The Balanced Scorecard and the Tableau de Bord: Translating Strategy into Action," *Management Accounting* (August 1997), pp. 28–36.

Exhibit 10–11 From Strategy to Performance Measures: The Balanced Scorecard

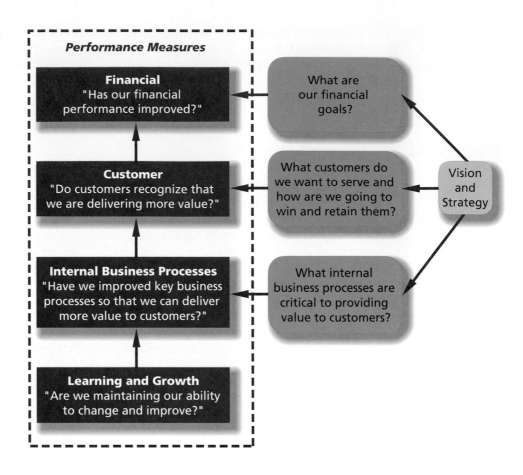

customer satisfaction; and improving customer satisfaction is necessary to improve financial results.

Note that the emphasis in Exhibit 10–11 is on *improvement*—not on just attaining some specific objective such as profits of $10 million. In the balanced scorecard approach, continual improvement is encouraged. In many industries, this is a matter of survival. If an organization does not continually improve, it will eventually lose out to competitors that do.

Financial performance measures appear at the top of Exhibit 10–11. Ultimately, most companies exist to provide financial rewards to owners. There are exceptions. Some companies—for example, The Body Shop—may have loftier goals such as providing environmentally friendly products to consumers. However, even nonprofit organizations must generate enough financial resources to stay in operation.

Ordinarily, top managers are responsible for the financial performance measures—not lower-level managers. The supervisor in charge of checking in passengers can be held responsible for how long passengers have to wait in line. However, this supervisor cannot reasonably be held responsible for the entire company's profit. That is the responsibility of the airline's top managers. We will have more to say about financial performance measures in Chapter 12.

Exhibit 10–12 lists some examples of performance measures that can be found on the balanced scorecards of companies. However, few companies, if any, would use all of these performance measures, and almost all companies would add other performance measures. Managers should carefully select the performance measures for their company's balanced scorecard, keeping the following points in mind. First and foremost, the performance measures should be consistent with, and follow from, the

Exhibit 10–12

Examples of Performance
Measures for Balanced
Scorecards

Customer Perspective	
Performance Measure	**Desired Change**
Customer satisfaction as measured by survey results	+
Number of customer complaints	−
Market share	+
Product returns as a percentage of sales	−
Percentage of customers retained from last period	+
Number of new customers	+

Internal Business Processes Perspective	
Performance Measure	**Desired Change**
Percentage of sales from new products	+
Time to introduce new products to market	−
Percentage of customer calls answered within 20 seconds	+
On-time deliveries as a percentage of all deliveries	+
Work in process inventory as a percentage of sales	−
Unfavourable standard cost variances	−
Defect-free units as a percentage of completed units	+
Delivery cycle time*	−
Throughput time*	−
Manufacturing cycle efficiency*	+
Quality costs†	−
Setup time	−
Time from call by customer to repair of product	−
Percent of customer complaints settled on first contact	+
Time to settle a customer claim	−

Learning and Growth Perspective	
Performance Measure	**Desired Change**
Suggestions per employee	+
Value-added employee‡	+
Employee turnover	−
Hours of in-house training per employee	+

*Explained later in this chapter.

†See Appendix B, Cost of Quality, at the back of the text.

‡Value-added is revenue less externally purchased materials, supplies, and services.

company's strategy. If the performance measures are not consistent with the company's strategy, people will find themselves working at cross-purposes. Second, the scorecard should not have too many performance measures. This can lead to a lack of focus and confusion.

While the entire organization will have an overall balanced scorecard, each responsible individual will have his or her own personal scorecard as well. This scorecard should consist of items the individual can personally influence that relate directly to the performance measures on the overall balanced scorecard. The performance measures on this personal scorecard should not be overly influenced by actions taken by others in the company or by events that are outside of the individual's control.

With those broad principles in mind, we will now take a look at how a company's strategy affects its balanced scorecard.

Focus on Current Practice

Customer satisfaction can be measured in a variety of ways. Every month Hershey Foods Corporation mails a one-page survey to a sample of its customers (i.e., food distributors, wholesalers, and grocery chains). The survey asks customers to rate Hershey on a number of characteristics including the following:

- Courtesy, speed, and accuracy of customer service personnel.
- Quality of Hershey's carriers.
- Delivery dependability.
- Completeness of shipments.
- Condition of products when delivered.

- Speed and accuracy of Hershey's invoicing.

Customers are asked to rate Hershey in comparison with their very best suppliers, not just Hershey's direct competitors. "Whenever we see a 'poorer than' rating, the customer gets a follow-up phone call from the manager of the customer service centre. This call probes for more information about the problem. Once the manager has additional information, he or she involves others in the company who can help rectify the situation. We then thank the customer for the information, explain how we will correct it, and ask them to let us know if things change."[19] ∎

A Company's Strategy and the Balanced Scorecard

Returning to the performance measures in Exhibit 10–11, each company must decide which customers to target and what internal business processes are crucial to attracting and retaining those customers. Different companies, having different strategies, will target different customers with different kinds of products and services. Take the automobile industry as an example. BMW stresses engineering and handling; Volvo, safety; Jaguar, luxury detailing; Corvette, racy styling; and Toyota, reliability. Because of these differences in emphases, a one-size-fits-all approach to performance measurement will not work even within this one industry. Performance measures must be tailored to the specific strategy of each company.

Suppose, for example, that Jaguar's strategy is to offer distinctive, richly finished luxury automobiles to wealthy individuals who prize handcrafted, individualized products. Part of Jaguar's strategy might be to create such a large number of options for details, such as leather seats, interior and exterior colour combinations, and wooden dashboards, that each car becomes virtually one of a kind. For example, instead of just offering tan or blue leather seats in standard cowhide, the company may offer customers the choice of an almost infinite palate of colours in any of a number of different exotic leathers. For such a system to work effectively, Jaguar would have to be able to deliver a completely customized car within a reasonable amount of time—and without incurring more cost for this customization than the customer is willing to pay. Exhibit 10–13 suggests how Jaguar might reflect this strategy in its balanced scorecard.

If the balanced scorecard is correctly constructed, the performance measures should be linked together on a cause-and-effect basis. Each link can then be read as a hypothesis in the form "If we improve this performance measure, then this other performance measure should also improve." Starting from the bottom of Exhibit 10–13, we can read the links between performance measures as follows. If employees acquire the skills to install new options more effectively, then the company can offer more options and the options can be installed in less time. If more options are available and they are installed in less time, then customer surveys should show greater satisfaction with the range of options available. If customer satisfaction improves, then the num-

---

19. Randy O. Main, "Creating Customer Satisfaction," *Sustaining Total Quality*, The Conference Board Report Number 1025 (New York, 1993), pp. 34–35.

Exhibit 10–13 A Possible Strategy at Jaguar and the Balanced Scorecard

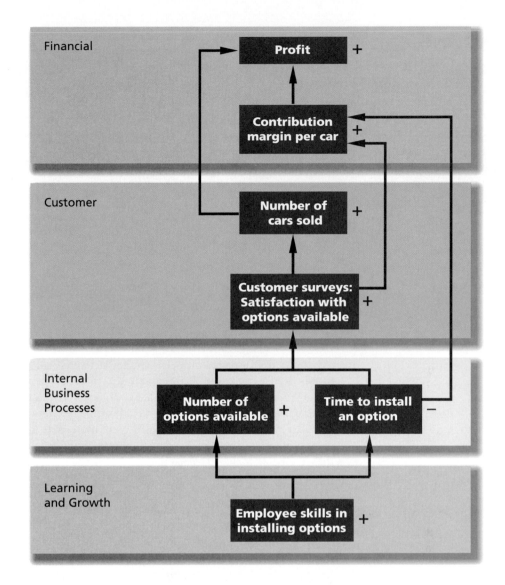

ber of cars sold should increase. In addition, if customer satisfaction improves, the company should be able to maintain or increase its selling prices, and if the time to install options decreases, the costs of installing the options should decrease. Together, this should result in an increase in the contribution margin per car. If the contribution margin per car increases and more cars are sold, the result should be an increase in profits.

In essence, the balanced scorecard articulates a theory of how the company can attain its desired outcomes (financial, in this case) by taking concrete actions. While the strategy laid out in Exhibit 10–13 seems plausible, it should be regarded as only a theory that should be discarded if it proves to be invalid. For example, if the company succeeds in increasing the number of options available and in decreasing the time required to install options and yet there is no increase in customer satisfaction, the number of cars sold, the contribution margin per car, or profits, the strategy would have to be reconsidered. One of the advantages of the balanced scorecard is that it continually tests the theories underlying management's strategy. If a strategy is not working, it should become evident when some of the predicted effects (i.e., more car sales) do not occur. Without this feedback, management may drift on indefinitely with an ineffective strategy based on faulty assumptions.

Focus on Current Practice

MBNA Corporation services special customized Visa and MasterCard credit cards for over 4,000 different affinity groups such as the National Education Association, Georgetown University, and the Ringling Brothers circus. This is a desirable market niche because members of such affinity groups have significantly higher incomes and carry significantly higher credit card balances than the public at large.

To retain these profitable customers, MBNA emphasizes service—particularly speedy service. The company has set 15 different standards for service. For example, customer address changes must be processed in one day, the telephone at customer service desks must be picked up within two rings, and calls that come into the switchboard must be routed to the correct person within 21 seconds. The current goal is to meet or exceed these standards 98.5% of the time. High technology hardware and software automatically tracks each of these performance measures on a continuous basis, and the results are posted daily for all employees to see. At the end of the year, employees can earn a bonus of up to $1,000, depending on how many days the 98.5% standard has been met.[20] ■

Advantages of Timely and Graphic Feedback

Whatever performance measures are used, they should be reported on a frequent and timely basis. For example, data about defects should be reported to the responsible managers at least once a day so that action can be quickly taken if an unusual number of defects occurs. In the most advanced companies, any defect is reported *immediately*, and its cause is tracked down before any more defects can occur. Another common characteristic of the performance measures under the balanced scorecard approach is that managers focus on *trends* in the performance measures over time. The emphasis is on progress and *improvement* rather than on meeting any specific standard.

For tracking trends and improvement over time, graphic displays are often far more informative than rows or columns of numbers. Consider, for example, the problem of passengers who reserve seats but do not show up to buy their tickets. Because of these "no-show" passengers, airlines routinely overbook popular flights. The airlines gamble that there will be enough no-shows that no passenger will be bumped from the flight. Sometimes airlines lose this gamble. This results in the airline incurring substantial additional costs to either pay passengers with reservations to give them up or to house and feed excess passengers until suitable replacement flights can be found. Because of these costs (and the ill will created among passengers), airlines carefully monitor the percentage of overbooked seats that actually turn out to be a problem and result in a passenger being bumped from a flight. Suppose, for example, that an airline has recorded the following data over the last 20 weeks:

	Bumped passengers per hundred overbooked seats			Bumped passengers per hundred overbooked seats
Week 1	7.1		Week 11	6.4
Week 2	6.5		Week 12	6.3
Week 3	6.7		Week 13	6.7
Week 4	7.2		Week 14	5.8
Week 5	7.0		Week 15	6.6
Week 6	7.3		Week 16	6.6
Week 7	6.7		Week 17	6.9
Week 8	6.5		Week 18	7.1
Week 9	6.2		Week 19	7.4
Week 10	5.8		Week 20	7.8

20. Justin Martin, "Are You as Good as You Think You Are?" *Fortune*, September 30, 1996, pp. 94–99.

Exhibit 10-14 The Number of Passengers Bumped per Hundred Overbooked Seats

These data are plotted in Exhibit 10–14. Note how much easier it is to spot trends and unusual points when the data are plotted than when they are displayed in the form of a table. In particular, the worrisome increase in bumped passengers over the final seven weeks is very evident in the plotted data.

Some Measures of Internal Business Process Performance

Most of the performance measures listed in Exhibit 10–12 are self-explanatory. However, three are not—*delivery cycle time, throughput time,* and *manufacturing cycle efficiency (MCE).* These three important performance measures are discussed next.

Delivery cycle time
The amount of time required from receipt of an order from a customer to shipment of the completed goods.

DELIVERY CYCLE TIME The amount of time from when an order is received from a customer to when the completed order is shipped is called **delivery cycle time.** This time is clearly a key concern to many customers, who would like the delivery cycle time to be as short as possible. Cutting the delivery cycle time may give a company a key competitive advantage—and may be necessary for survival—and therefore many companies would include this performance measure on their balanced scorecard.

Objective 8

Compute the delivery cycle time, the throughput time, and the manufacturing cycle efficiency (MCE).

Throughput time The amount of time required to turn raw materials into completed products.

THROUGHPUT (MANUFACTURING CYCLE) TIME The amount of time required to turn raw materials into completed products is called **throughput time,** or *manufacturing cycle time.* The relationship between the delivery cycle time and the throughput (manufacturing cycle) time is illustrated in Exhibit 10–15.

Note that, as shown in Exhibit 10–15, the throughput time, or manufacturing cycle time, is made up of process time, inspection time, move time, and queue time. *Process time* is the amount of time in which work is actually done on the product. *Inspection time* is the amount of time spent ensuring that the product is not defective. *Move time* is the time required to move materials or partially completed products from workstation to workstation. *Queue time* is the amount of time a product spends waiting to be worked on, to be moved, to be inspected, or in storage waiting to be shipped.

As shown at the bottom of Exhibit 10–15, the only one of these four activities that adds value to the product is process time. The other three activities—

Exhibit 10–15   Delivery Cycle Time and Throughput (Manufacturing Cycle) Time

Value-Added Time	**Non-Value-Added Time**
Process Time	Wait Time
	Inspection Time
	Move Time
	Queue Time

inspecting, moving, and queueing—add no value and should be eliminated as much as possible.

MANUFACTURING CYCLE EFFICIENCY (MCE)   Through concerted efforts to eliminate the *non-value-added* activities of inspecting, moving, and queueing, some companies have reduced their throughput time to only a fraction of previous levels. In turn, this has helped to reduce the delivery cycle time from months to only weeks or hours. The throughput time, which is considered to be a key measure in delivery performance, can be put into better perspective by computing the **manufacturing cycle efficiency (MCE)**. The MCE is computed by relating the value-added time to the throughout time. The formula is as follows:

> **Manufacturing cycle efficiency (MCE)** Process (value-added) time as a percentage of throughput time.

$$MCE = \frac{\text{Value-added time}}{\text{Throughput (manufacturing cycle) time}}$$

If the MCE is less than 1, then non-value-added time is present in the production process. An MCE of 0.5, for example, would mean that half of the total production time consisted of inspection, moving, and similar non-value-added activities. In many manufacturing companies, the MCE is less than 0.1 (10%), which means that 90% of the time a unit is in process is spent on activities that do not add value to the product.[21] By monitoring the MCE, companies are able to reduce non-value-added activities and thus get products into the hands of customers more quickly and at a lower cost.

To provide a numeric example of these measures, assume the following data for Novex Company:

Novex Company keeps careful track of the time relating to orders and their production. During the most recent quarter, the following average times were recorded for each unit or order:

---

21. Callie Berlinger and James A. Brimson, eds., *Cost Management for Today's Advanced Manufacturing* (Boston, MA: Harvard Business School Press, 1988), p. 4.

	Days
Wait time	17.0
Inspection time	0.4
Process time	2.0
Move time	0.6
Queue time	5.0

Goods are shipped as soon as production is completed.

Required
1. Compute the throughput time, or velocity of production.
2. Compute the manufacturing cycle efficiency (MCE).
3. What percentage of the production time is spent in non-value-added activities?
4. Compute the delivery cycle time.

Solution
1. Throughput time = Process time + Inspection time + Move time + Queue time
   = 2.0 days + 0.4 days + 0.6 days + 5.0 days
   = 8.0 days
2. Only process time represents value-added time; therefore, the computation of the MCE would be as follows:

$$\text{MCE} = \frac{\text{Value-added time, 2.0 days}}{\text{Throughput time, 8.0 days}}$$
$$= 0.25$$

Thus, once put into production, a typical unit is actually being worked on only 25% of the time.
3. Since the MCE is 25%, the complement of this figure, or 75% of the total production time, is spent in non-value-added activities.
4. Delivery cycle time = Wait time + Throughput time
   = 17.0 days + 8.0 days
   = 25.0 days

Focus on Current Practice

Banks ordinarily require three to four weeks to approve an application for a mortgage loan on a house. The application form includes the individual's employment history, income, and financial assets and liabilities. Personnel at the bank check credit references and review the entire application before granting the loan. A manager at one bank wondered why this process takes so long and asked employees to keep track of how much time they actually worked on processing an application. He discovered that processing an application took on average 26 days, but only about 15 minutes of this time was actual work. All of the rest of the time the application was waiting in someone's in-basket. The manufacturing cycle efficiency (MCE) was therefore only 0.0004 (15 minutes/[26 days × 24 hours per day × 60 minutes per hour]). By redesigning and automating the process, the cycle time was cut down to 15 minutes and the MCE rose to 1.0. Loan applicants can now have a cup of coffee while waiting for approval.[22] ∎

SOME FINAL OBSERVATIONS CONCERNING THE BALANCED SCORE-CARD We would like to emphasize a few points concerning the balanced scorecard. First, the balanced scorecard should be tailored to the company's strategy; each company's balanced scorecard should be unique. The examples given in this chapter

---

22. Kaplan and Norton, *Translating Strategy into Action: The Balanced Scoreboard*, pp. 118–19.

are just that—examples. They should not be interpreted as general templates to be fitted to each company. Second, the balanced scorecard reflects a particular strategy, or theory, about how a company can further its objectives by taking specific actions. The theory should be viewed as tentative and subject to change if the actions do not in fact lead to attaining the company's financial and other goals. If the theory (i.e., strategy) changes, then the performance measures on the balanced scorecard should also change. The balanced scorecard should be viewed as a dynamic system that evolves as the company's strategy evolves.

Summary

A standard is a benchmark or "norm" for measuring performance. In business organizations, standards are set for both the cost and the quantity of inputs needed to manufacture goods or to provide services. Quantity standards indicate how much of a cost element, such as labour time or raw materials, should be used in manufacturing a unit of product or in providing a unit of service. Cost standards indicate what the cost of the time or the materials should be.

Standards are normally practical in nature, meaning that they can be attained by reasonable, though highly efficient, efforts. Such standards are generally felt to have a favourable motivational impact on employees.

When standards are compared to actual performance, the difference is referred to as a *variance*. Variances are computed and reported to management on a regular basis for both the price and the quantity elements of materials, labour, and overhead. Price and rate variances for inputs are computed by taking the difference between the actual and standard prices of the inputs and multiplying the result by the amount of input purchased. Quantity and efficiency variances are computed by taking the difference between the actual amount of the input used and the amount of input that is allowed for the actual output, and then multiplying the result by the standard price of the input.

Not all variances require management time or attention. Only unusual or particularly significant variances should be investigated—otherwise a great deal of time would be spent investigating unimportant matters. Additionally, it should be emphasized that the point of the investigation should not be to find someone to blame. The point of the investigation is to pinpoint the problem so that it can be fixed and operations improved.

Traditional standard cost variance reports should often be supplemented with other performance measures. Overemphasis on standard cost variances may lead to problems in other critical areas such as product quality, inventory levels, and on-time delivery.

The balanced scorecard is a promising approach to managing organizations. A balanced scorecard consists of an integrated system of performance measures that are derived from and support the company's strategy. Different companies will have different balanced scorecards because they have different strategies. A well-constructed balanced scorecard provides a means for guiding the company and also provides feedback concerning the effectiveness of the company's strategy.

Review Problem: Standard Costs

Xavier Company produces a single product. Variable manufacturing overhead is applied to products on the basis of direct labour-hours. The standard costs for one unit of product are as follows:

Direct material: 6 grams at $0.50 per gram	$ 3
Direct labour: 1.8 hours at $10 per hour	18
Variable manufacturing overhead: 1.8 hours at $5 per hour . . .	9
Total standard variable cost per unit	$30

During June, 2,000 units were produced. The costs associated with June's operations were as follows:

Material purchased: 18,000 grams at $0.60 per gram $10,800
Material used in production: 14,000 grams . . . .   —
Direct labour: 4,000 hours at $9.75 per hour   39,000
Variable manufacturing overhead costs incurred   20,800

Required   Compute the materials, labour, and variable manufacturing overhead variances.

Materials Variances

A total variance cannot be computed in this situation, since the amount of materials purchased (18,000 grams) differs from the amount of materials used in production (14,000 grams).

*2,000 units × 6 grams per unit = 12,000 grams.

Using the formulas in the chapter, the same variances would be computed as:

Materials price variance = AQ(AP − SP)
18,000 grams($0.60 per gram − $0.50 per gram) = $1,800 U
Materials quantity variance = SP(AQ − SQ)
$0.50 per gram(14,000 grams − 12,000 grams) = $1,000 U

Labour Variances

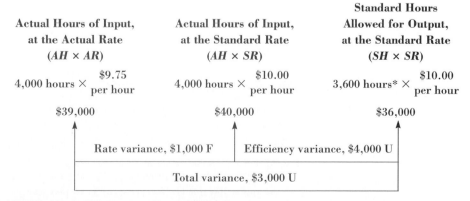

*2,000 units × 1.8 hours per unit = 3,600 hours.

Using the formulas in the chapter, the same variances would be computed as:

$$\text{Labour rate variance} = AH(AR - SR)$$
$$4{,}000 \text{ hours}(\$9.75 \text{ per hour} - \$10.00 \text{ per hour}) = \$1{,}000 \text{ F}$$
$$\text{Labour efficiency variance} = SR(AH - SH)$$
$$\$10.00 \text{ per hour}(4{,}000 \text{ hours} - 3{,}600 \text{ hours}) = \$4{,}000 \text{ U}$$

Variable Manufacturing Overhead Variances

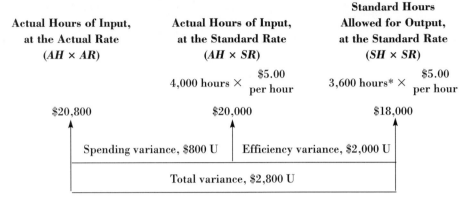

*2,000 units × 1.8 hours per unit = 3,600 hours.

Using the formulas in the chapter, the same variances would be computed as:

$$\text{Variable overhead spending variance} = AH(AR - SR)$$
$$4{,}000 \text{ hours}(\$5.20 \text{ per hour*} - \$5.00 \text{ per hour}) = \$800 \text{ U}$$

*$20,800 ÷ 4,000 hours = $5.20 per hour.

$$\text{Variable overhead efficiency variance} = SR(AH - SH)$$
$$\$5.00 \text{ per hour}(4{,}000 \text{ hours} - 3{,}600 \text{ hours}) = \$2{,}000 \text{ U}$$

Appendix 10A: General Ledger Entries to Record Variances

Objective 9

Prepare journal entries to record standard costs and variances.

Although standard costs and variances can be computed and used by management without being formally entered into the accounting records, most organizations prefer to make formal entries. Formal entry tends to give variances a greater emphasis than informal, off-the-record computations. This emphasis gives a clear signal of management's desire to keep costs within the limits that have been set. In addition, formal use of standard costs simplifies the bookkeeping process enormously. Inventories and cost of goods sold can be valued at their standard costs—eliminating the need to keep track of the actual cost of each unit.

Direct Materials Variances

To illustrate the general ledger entries needed to record standard cost variances, we will return to the data contained in the review problem at the end of the chapter. The entry to record the purchase of direct materials would be as follows:

Raw Materials (18,000 grams at $0.50 per gram)	9,000	
Materials Price Variance (18,000 grams at $0.10 per gram U)	1,800	
Accounts Payable (18,000 grams at $0.60 per gram)		10,800

Notice that the price variance is recognized when purchases are made, rather than when materials are actually used in production. This permits the price variance to be isolated early, and it also permits the materials to be carried in the inventory account at standard cost. As direct materials are later drawn from inventory and used in production, the quantity variance is isolated as follows:

Work in Process (12,000 grams at $0.50 per gram)	6,000	
Materials Quantity Variance (2,000 grams U at $0.50 per gram)	1,000	
Raw Materials (14,000 grams at $0.50 per gram)		7,000

Thus, direct materials enter into the Work in Process account at standard cost, in terms of both price and quantity.

Notice that both the price variance and the quantity variance above are unfavourable and are debit entries. If these variances had been favourable, they would have appeared as credit entries, as in the case of the direct labour rate variance below.

Direct Labour Variances

Referring again to the cost data in the review problem at the end of the chapter, the general ledger entry to record the incurrence of direct labour cost would be:

Work in Process (3,600 hours at $10.00 per hour)	36,000	
Labour Efficiency Variance (400 hours U at $10.00 per hour)	4,000	
Labour Rate Variance (4,000 hours at $0.25 per hour F)		1,000
Wages Payable (4,000 hours at $9.75 per hour)		39,000

Thus, as with direct materials, direct labour costs enter into the Work in Process account at standard, both in terms of the rate and in terms of the hours allowed for the actual production of the period.

Variable Manufacturing Overhead Variances

Variable manufacturing overhead variances generally are not recorded in the accounts separately but rather are determined as part of the general analysis of overhead, which is discussed in Chapter 11.

Cost Flows in a Standard Cost System

The flows of costs through the company's accounts are illustrated in Exhibit 10A–1. Note that entries into the various inventory accounts are made at standard cost—not actual cost. The differences between actual and standard costs are entered into special accounts that accumulate the various standard cost variances. Ordinarily, these standard cost variance accounts are closed out to Cost of Goods Sold at the end of the period. Unfavourable variances increase Cost of Goods Sold, and favourable variances decrease Cost of Goods Sold.

Appendix 10B: Learning Curves

Objective 10

Explain the concept of learning curves.

Most workers become more proficient at their tasks the more they do them. Learning takes place especially through the early stages of a job. For example, contractors constructing a high-rise apartment building find the 20th story goes on faster than the 8th story. This effect means break-even analysis would multiple break-even points when learning occurs because the assumption of constant worker and machine productivity stated in Chapter 6 would be violated.[23] Studies of the learning of workers suggests the pattern illustrated in Exhibit 10–B1.

---

23. Woody M. Liao, "The Effects of Learning on Cost-Volume-Profit Analysis," *Cost and Management* (November/December 1983), pp. 38–40, illustrates this issue.

Exhibit 10A–1   Cost Flows in a Standard Cost System*

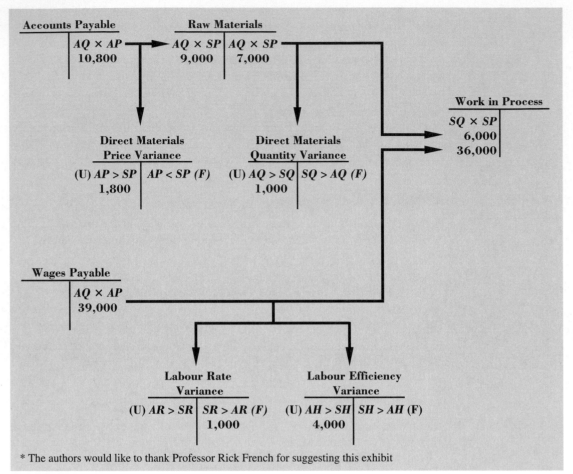

* The authors would like to thank Professor Rick French for suggesting this exhibit

The learning curve represents the fact that the time spent per unit declines by a constant percentage as the number of units produced doubles. This phenomenon has been observed where new long-term production activities are undertaken or where a long production cycle is conducted, such as building construction projects, airplane manufacture, and shipbuilding. Selling prices and workforce needs, as well as standards for time, can be assessed from such an analysis. Care is needed, however, because management practices, design, production technology, and quality requirements can interfere with the actual time spent by employees. Behaviour considerations can also affect learning. Factors such as peer pressure, union imposed constraints, and the state of management-worker relationships can affect productivity and limit learning.

The functional form of the pattern in Exhibit 10–B1 can be expressed as follows:

$$y = aQ^b$$

where

> Q is the cumulative production in units.
> b is a number representing the learning rate and expressed as follows:
>   log (learning rate)/log 2
> a is the hours required to produce the first unit.
> y is the average time required to produce one unit.

If the learning rate is, say, 80%, then b = log.80/log 2 = −.09691/.30103 = −.32193. The pattern of an 80% learning curve is as shown in the table below. Note

Exhibit 10–B1
Learning Curve

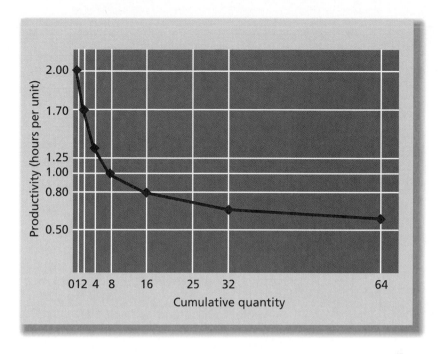

that every time experience doubles, the average hours to complete each unit drops to 80% of the preceding level. In other words, an 80% learning curve means that as cumulative production quantities double, the average time per unit falls by 20%.

Cumulative Quantity	Average Hours per Unit	Total Hours to Produce Cumulative Quantity
1	2	2
2	1.6(2 hours × .80)	3.2(2 × 1.6 hours)
4	1.3(1.6 hours × .80)	5.2(4 × 1.3 hours)
8	1.0(1.3 hours × .80)	8.0(8 × 1.0 hour)
16	0.8(1.0 hours × .80)	12.8(16 × 0.8 hour)
32	0.6(0.8 hour × .80)	19.2(32 × 0.6 hour)

With a computer, functional forms are often more convenient than tables. The total number of hours needed to produce Q units would be:

$$T = Q_y = Q_a Q^b = aQ^{b+1}$$

For a situation where T hours are available, the possible quantity of units that can be produced (Q) would be:

$$Q = (T/a)^x$$

where

$$x = 1/(b + 1)$$

Care is needed when using this formula. Assume, for example, a firm has produced 16 units already and wants to know the time required for another 16 units. By examining the earlier example, you can see the type of calculation required. Total time to produce 32 units is 19.2 hours. Total time to produce 16 units is 12.8 hours. Therefore, the last 16 units would take (19.2 − 12.8) or 6.4 hours; that is, 0.4 hours per unit. Mathematically, the exact answer can be determined by the following difference:

$$IT = a(Q_2)^{b+1} - a(Q_1)^{b+1}$$

where *IT* is the incremental time required, the 6.4 hours.

Interestingly, regression analysis, as described in Chapter 5, can be used to derive the parameters of a learning curve of the past history of an operation.

$$T = aQ^{b+1}$$

is the same as:

$$\log(T) = \log(a) + (b + 1)\log(Q)$$

If each *T* value and each *Q* amount is logged, a regression result can be calculated for the slope $(b + 1)$ and the intercept, log *a*. The regression value for log *a* can be converted to *a* by the following calculation, $10^{(\log a)}$, the y^x calculation on most standard hand calculators. The purpose of the log function is to convert the curved line displayed in Exhibit 10–B1 into a straight line so that the linear regression gives an accurate result.

Learning curves can serve as a method of setting and revising standard labour hours in a repetitive task environment. The use of the approach would be most appropriate where many workers are learning a task over a reasonably extended period of time. Short-run learning effects can be dealt with within a single accounting period using an average performance rate. Single employees can have labour efficiency variances occurring during their learning periods without serious inaccuracies being introduced to the standard cost variances. However, large groups functioning at the same stage, particularly early in a production sequence when the effects of learning are pronounced, need evaluation relative to their projected learning curve. Incorporating the learning curve times into the standard times should help avoid misleading standard cost variances.

It should be borne in mind that learning curve phenomena are applicable for labour-intensive manufacturing. Learning curve effects were originally studied in connection with aircraft manufacture in World War II. The learning curve has typically been employed in industries such as construction, shipbuilding, and electronics. In the new manufacturing environment, learning curves have less relevance. Automated manufacturing is unlikely to have much variation or to display a regular learning curve. In less-automated processes, however, where learning curves do occur, it is important to take the resulting decline in labour hours and costs into account in setting standards, determining prices, planning production, or setting up work schedules.

Questions

10–1 What is a quantity standard? What is a price standard?

10–2 Distinguish between ideal and practical standards.

10–3 If employees are chronically unable to meet a standard, what effect would you expect this to have on their productivity?

10–4 What is the difference between a standard and a budget?

10–5 What is meant by the term *variance*?

10–6 What is meant by the term *management by exception*?

10–7 Why are variances generally segregated in terms of a price variance and a quantity variance?

10–8 Who is generally responsible for the materials price variance? The materials quantity variance? The labour efficiency variance?

10–9 The materials price variance can be computed at what two different points in time? Which point is better? Why?

10–10 An examination of the cost records of the Chittenden Furniture Company reveals that the materials price variance is favourable but that the materials quantity variance is unfavourable by a substantial amount. What might this indicate?

10–11 What dangers lie in using standards as punitive tools?

10–12 "Our workers are all under labour contracts; therefore, our labour rate variance is bound to be zero." Discuss.

10–13 What effect, if any, would you expect poor quality materials to have on direct labour variances?

10–14 If variable manufacturing overhead is applied to production on the basis of direct labour-hours and the direct labour efficiency variance is unfavourable, will the variable overhead efficiency variance be favourable or unfavourable, or could it be either? Explain.

10–15 What is a statistical control chart, and how is it used?

10–16 Why can undue emphasis on labour efficiency variances lead to excess work in process inventories?

10–17 Why does the balanced scorecard differ from company to company?

10–18 Why does the balanced scorecard include financial performance measures as well as measures of how well internal business processes are doing?

10–19 What is the difference between the delivery cycle time and the throughput time? What four elements make up the throughput time? Into what two classes can these four elements be placed?

10–20 If a company has a manufacturing cycle efficiency (MCE) of less than 1, what does it mean? How would you interpret an MCE of 0.40?

10–21 (Appendix 10A) What are the advantages of making formal journal entries in the accounting records for variances?

10–22 What is a mix variance?

10–23 Can standard costs be used for financial reporting purposes? Explain.

10–24 (Appendix 10B) What is a learning curve?

10–25 (Appendix 10B) If production workers perform according to an 80% learning curve, what pattern of labour times does this suggest?

10–26 (Appendix 10B) The cost function for Lapp Co. reflects a 75% learning curve. The average time to complete a task with 50 units is 6 minutes. What is the projected time required for completion of the next 100 units?

Exercises

E10–1 Martin Company manufactures a powerful cleaning solvent. The main ingredient in the solvent is a raw material called Echol. Information on the purchase and use of Echol follows:

Purchase of Echol   Echol is purchased in 60 litre containers at a cost of $115 per container. A discount of 2% is offered by the supplier for payment within 10 days, and Martin Company takes all discounts. Shipping costs, which Martin Company must pay, amount to $130 for an average shipment of 100 sixty-litre containers of Echol.

Use of Echol   The bill of materials calls for 7.6 litres of Echol per bottle of cleaning solvent. About 5% of all Echol used is lost through spillage or evaporation (the 7.6 litres above is the *actual* content per bottle). In addition, statistical analysis has shown that every 41st bottle is rejected at final inspection because of contamination.

Required
1. Compute the standard purchase price for one litre of Echol.
2. Compute the standard quantity of Echol (in litres) per salable bottle of cleaning solvent.
3. Using the data from (1) and (2) above, prepare a standard cost card showing the standard cost of Echol per bottle of cleaning solvent.

E10–2   Bandar Industries Berhad of Malaysia manufactures sporting equipment. One of the company's products, a football helmet for the North American market, requires a special plastic. During the quarter ending June 30, the company manufactured 35,000 helmets, using 22,500 kilograms of plastic in the process. The plastic cost the company RM 171,000. (The currency in Malaysia is the ringgit, which is denoted here by RM.)

According to the standard cost card, each helmet should require 0.6 kilograms of plastic, at a cost of RM 8 per kilogram.

Required
1. What cost for plastic should have been incurred in the manufacture of the 35,000 helmets? How much greater or less is this than the cost that was incurred?
2. Break down the difference computed in (1) above in terms of a materials price variance and a materials quantity variance.

E10–3   Huron Company produces a commercial cleaning compound known as Zoom. The direct materials and direct labour standards for one unit of Zoom are given below:

	Standard Quantity or Hours	Standard Price or Rate	Standard Cost
Direct materials	4.6 kilograms	$ 2.50 per kilogram	$11.50
Direct labour	0.2 hours	12.00 per hour	2.40

During the most recent month, the following activity was recorded:

a. Twenty thousand kilograms of material were purchased at a cost of $2.35 per kilogram.
b. All of the material purchased was used to produce 4,000 units of Zoom.
c. A total of 750 hours of direct labour time was recorded at a total labour cost of $10,425.

Required
1. Compute the direct materials price and quantity variances for the month.
2. Compute the direct labour rate and efficiency variances for the month.

E10–4   Refer to the data in E10–3. Assume that instead of producing 4,000 units during the month, the company produced only 3,000 units, using 14,750 kilograms of material in the production process. (The rest of the material purchased remained in inventory.)

Required   Compute the direct materials price and quantity variances for the month.

E10–5   Erie Company manufactures a small cassette player called the Jogging Mate. The company uses standards to control its costs. The labour standards that have been set for one Jogging Mate cassette player are as follows:

Standard Hours	Standard Rate per Hour	Standard Cost
18 minutes	$12.00	$3.60

During August, 5,750 hours of direct labour time were recorded in the manufacture of 20,000 units of the Jogging Mate. The direct labour cost totalled $73,600 for the month.

Required
1. What direct labour cost should have been incurred in the manufacture of the 20,000 units of the Jogging Mate? By how much does this differ from the cost that was incurred?
2. Break down the difference in cost from (1) above into a labour rate variance and a labour efficiency variance.
3. The budgeted variable manufacturing overhead rate is $4 per direct labour-hour. During August, the company incurred $21,850 in variable manufacturing overhead cost. Compute the variable overhead spending and efficiency variances for the month.

E10–6 Dawson Toys, Ltd., produces a toy called the Maze. The company has recently established a standard cost system to help control costs and has established the following standards for the Maze toy:

> Direct materials: 6 microns per toy at $0.50 per micron
> Direct labour: 1.3 hours per toy at $8 per hour

During July, the company produced 3,000 Maze toys. Production data for the month on the toy follow:

Direct materials: 25,000 microns were purchased for use in production at a cost of $0.48 per micron. Some 5,000 of these microns were still in inventory at the end of the month.
Direct labour: 4,000 direct labour-hours were worked at a cost of $36,000.

Required
1. Compute the following variances for July:
   a. Direct materials price and quantity variances.
   b. Direct labour rate and efficiency variances.
2. Prepare a brief explanation of the significance and possible causes of each variance.

E10–7 The auto repair shop of Quality Motor Company uses standards to control the labour time and labour cost in the shop. The standard labour cost for a motor tune-up is given below:

Job	Standard Hours	Standard Rate	Standard Cost
Motor tune-up	2.5	$9	$22.50

The record showing the time spent in the shop last week on motor tune-ups has been misplaced. However, the shop supervisor recalls that 50 tune-ups were completed during the week, and the controller recalls the following variance data relating to tune-ups:

> Labour rate variance .... $87 F
> Total labour variance .... 93 U

Required
1. Determine the number of actual labour-hours spent on tune-ups during the week.
2. Determine the actual hourly rate of pay for tune-ups last week.

(Hint: A useful way to proceed would be to work from known to unknown data either by using the variance formulas or by using the columnar format shown in Exhibit 10–5.)

E10–8 Management of Mittel Rhein AG of Köln, Germany, would like to reduce the amount of time between when a customer places an order and when the order is shipped. For the first quarter of operations during the current year the following data were reported:

	Days
Inspection time	0.3
Wait time (from order to start of production)	14.0
Process time	2.7
Move time	1.0
Queue time	5.0

Required
1. Compute the throughput time, or velocity of production.
2. Compute the manufacturing cycle efficiency (MCE) for the quarter.

3. What percentage of the throughput time was spent in non-value-added activities?
4. Compute the delivery cycle time.
5. If by use of just-in-time (JIT) all queue time during production is eliminated, what will be the new MCE?

E10–9   (Appendix 10A) Genola Fashions began production of a new product on June 1. The company uses a standard cost system and has established the following standards for one unit of the new product:

	Standard Quantity or Hours	Standard Price or Rate	Standard Cost
Direct materials	2.5 metres	$14 per metres	$35.00
Direct labour	1.6 hours	8 per hour	12.80

During June, the following activity was recorded relative to the new product:

a. Purchasing acquired 10,000 metres of material at a cost of $13.80 per metres.
b. Production used 8,000 metres of the material to manufacture 3,000 units of the new product.
c. Production reported 5,000 hours of labour time worked directly on the new product; the cost of this labour time was $43,000.

Required

1. For materials:
   a. Compute the direct materials price and quantity variances.
   b. Prepare journal entries to record the purchase of materials and the use of materials in production.
2. For direct labour:
   a. Compute the direct labour rate and efficiency variances.
   b. Prepare a journal entry to record the incurrence of direct labour cost for the month.
3. Post the entries you have prepared to the following T-accounts:

Raw Materials		Accounts Payable	
?	?		138,000
Bal. ?			

Materials Price Variance		Wages Payable	
			43,000

Materials Quantity Variance		Labour Rate Variance	

Work in Process—Product A		Labour Efficiency Variance	
Materials used ?			
Labour cost ?			

Problems

P10–10   Health Clinic: Basic Variance Analysis   John Fleming, chief administrator for Valley View Clinic, is concerned about costs for tests in the clinic's lab. Charges for lab tests are consistently higher at Valley View than at other hospitals and have resulted in many complaints. Also, because of strict regulations on amounts reimbursed for lab tests, payments received from insurance companies and governmental units have not been high enough to provide an acceptable level of profit for the lab.

Mr. Fleming has asked you to evaluate costs in the clinic's lab for the past month. The following information is available:

a.   Basically, two types of tests are performed in the lab—blood tests and smears. During the past month, 1,800 blood tests and 2,400 smears were performed in the lab.

b.   Small glass plates are used in both types of tests. During the past month, the hospital purchased 12,000 plates at a cost of $28,200. This cost is net of a 6% quantity discount. Some 1,500 of these plates were still on hand unused at the end of the month; there were no plates on hand at the beginning of the month.

c.   During the past month, 1,150 hours of labour time were recorded in the lab. The cost of this labour time was $13,800.

d.   Variable overhead cost last month in the lab for utilities and supplies totalled $7,820.

Valley View Clinic has never used standard costs. By searching industry literature, however, you have determined the following nationwide averages for clinical labs:

Plates: Two plates are required per lab test. These plates cost $2.50 each and are disposed of after the test is completed.

Labour: Each blood test should require 0.3 hours to complete, and each smear should require 0.15 hours to complete. The average cost of this lab time is $14 per hour.

Overhead: Overhead cost is based on direct labour-hours. The average rate for variable overhead is $6 per hour.

Mr. Fleming would like a complete analysis of the cost of plates, labour, and overhead in the lab for the last month so that he can get to the root of the lab's cost problem.

Required

1.   Compute a materials price variance for the plates purchased last month and a materials quantity variance for the plates used last month.

2.   For labour cost in the lab:
   a.   Compute a labour rate variance and a labour efficiency variance.
   b.   In most clinics, one-half of the workers in the lab are senior technicians and one-half are assistants. In an effort to reduce costs, Valley View Clinic employs only one-fourth senior technicians and three-fourths assistants. Would you recommend that this policy be continued? Explain.

3.   Compute the variable overhead spending and efficiency variances. Is there any relationship between the variable overhead efficiency variance and the labour efficiency variance? Explain.

P10–11   Straightforward Variance Analysis   Becton Labs, Inc., produces various chemical compounds for industrial use. One compound, called Fludex, is prepared by means of an elaborate distilling process. The company has developed standard costs for one unit of Fludex, as follows:

	Standard Quantity	Standard Price or Rate	Standard Cost
Direct materials	2.5 kilograms	$20.00 per kilogram	$50.00
Direct labour	1.4 hours	12.50 per hour	17.50
Variable manufacturing overhead	1.4 hours	3.50 per hour	4.90
			$72.40

During November, the following activity was recorded by the company relative to production of Fludex:

a. Materials purchased, 12,000 kilograms at a cost of $225,000.
b. There was no beginning inventory of materials on hand to start the month; at the end of the month, 2,500 kilograms of material remained in the warehouse unused.
c. The company employs 35 lab technicians to work on the production of Fludex. During November, each worked an average of 160 hours at an average rate of $12 per hour.
d. Variable manufacturing overhead is assigned to Fludex on the basis of direct labour-hours. Variable manufacturing overhead costs during November totalled $18,200.
e. During November, 3,750 good units of Fludex were produced.

The company's management is anxious to determine the efficiency of the activities surrounding the production of Fludex.

Required

1. For materials used in the production of Fludex:
   a. Compute the price and quantity variances.
   b. The materials were purchased from a new supplier who is anxious to enter into a long-term purchase contract. Would you recommend that the company sign the contract? Explain.
2. For direct labour employed in the production of Fludex:
   a. Compute the rate and efficiency variances.
   b. In the past, the 35 technicians employed in the production of Fludex consisted of 20 senior technicians and 15 assistants. During November, the company experimented with only 15 senior technicians and 20 assistants in order to save costs. Would you recommend that the new labour mix be continued? Explain.
3. Compute the variable overhead spending and efficiency variances. What relationship can you see between this efficiency variance and the labour efficiency variance?

P10–12 Basic Variance Analysis Miller Toy Company manufactures a plastic swimming pool at its Westwood Plant. The plant has been experiencing problems for some time as shown by its June income statement below:

	Budgeted	Actual
Sales (15,000 pools)	$450,000	$450,000
Less variable expenses:		
Variable cost of goods sold*	180,000	196,290
Variable selling expenses	20,000	20,000
Total variable expenses	200,000	216,290
Contribution margin	250,000	233,710
Less fixed expenses:		
Manufacturing overhead	130,000	130,000
Selling and administrative	84,000	84,000
Total fixed expenses	214,000	214,000
Net income	$ 36,000	$ 19,710

*Contains direct materials, direct labour, and variable manufacturing overhead.

Janet Dunn, who has just been appointed general manager of the Westwood Plant, has been given instructions to "get things under control." Upon reviewing the plant's income statement, Ms. Dunn has concluded that the major problem lies in the variable cost of goods sold. She has been provided with the following standard cost per swimming pool:

	Standard Quantity or Hours	Standard Price or Rate	Standard Cost
Direct materials	3.0 kilograms	$2.00 per kilogram	$ 6.00
Direct labour	0.8 hours	6.00 per hour	4.80
Variable manufacturing overhead . . .	0.4 hours*	3.00 per hour	1.20
Total standard cost			$12.00

*Based on machine-hours.

Ms. Dunn has determined that during June the plant produced 15,000 pools and incurred the following costs:

a. Purchased 60,000 kilograms of materials at a cost of $1.95 per kilogram.
b. Used 49,200 kilograms of materials in production. (Finished goods and work in process inventories are insignificant and can be ignored.)
c. Worked 11,800 direct labour-hours at a cost of $7.00 per hour.
d. Incurred variable manufacturing overhead cost totalling $18,290 for the month. A total of 5,900 machine-hours was recorded.

It is the company's policy to close all variances to cost of goods sold on a monthly basis.

Required   1. Compute the following variances for June:
   a. Direct materials price and quantity variances.
   b. Direct labour rate and efficiency variances.
   c. Variable overhead spending and efficiency variances.
2. Summarize the variances that you computed in (1) above by showing the net overall favourable or unfavourable variance for the month. What impact did this figure have on the company's income statement? Show computations.
3. Pick out the two most significant variances that you computed in (1) above. Explain to Ms. Dunn possible causes of these variances.

P10–13   Variances; Unit Costs; Journal Entries   (Appendix 10A) Trueform Products, Inc., produces a broad line of sports equipment and uses a standard cost system for control purposes. Last year the company produced 8,000 of its varsity footballs. The standard costs associated with this football, along with the actual costs incurred last year, are given below (per football):

	Standard Cost	Actual Cost
Direct materials:		
Standard: 1.4 metres at $16.00 per metre	$18.24	
Actual: 1.25m at $15.36 per metre		$19.20
Direct labour:		
Standard: 0.9 hours at $7.50 per hour	6.75	
Actual: 0.8 hours at $8.00 per hour		6.40
Variable manufacturing overhead:		
Standard: 0.9 hours at $2.50 per hour	2.25	
Actual: 0.8 hours at $2.75 per hour		2.20
Total cost per football	$27.24	$27.80

The president was elated when he saw that actual costs exceeded standard costs by only $0.56 per football. He stated, "I was afraid that our unit cost might get out of hand when we gave out those raises last year in order to stimulate output. But it's obvious our costs are well under control."

There was no inventory of materials on hand to start the year. During the year, 10,000 metres of materials were purchased and used in production.

Required
1. For direct materials:
   a. Compute the price and quantity variances for the year.
   b. Prepare journal entries to record all activity relating to direct materials for the year.
2. For direct labour:
   a. Compute the rate and efficiency variances.
   b. Prepare a journal entry to record the incurrence of direct labour cost for the year.
3. Compute the variable overhead spending and efficiency variances.
4. Was the president correct in his statement that "our costs are well under control"? Explain.
5. State possible causes of each variance that you have computed.

P10–14   Internal Business Process Performance Measures   DataSpan, Inc., automated its plant at the start of the current year and installed a flexible manufacturing system. The company is also evaluating its suppliers and moving toward a just-in-time (JIT) inventory system. Many adjustment problems have been encountered, among which are problems relating to performance measurement. After much study, the company has decided to use the performance measures below as part of its balanced scorecard, and it has gathered data relating to these measures for the first four months of operations.

	Month			
	1	2	3	4
Throughput time (days)	?	?	?	?
Delivery cycle time (days)	?	?	?	?
Manufacturing cycle efficiency (MCE) . .	?	?	?	?
Percentage of on-time deliveries	91%	86%	83%	79%
Total throughput (units)	3,210	3,072	2,915	2,806

Management has asked for your help in computing throughput time, delivery cycle time, and MCE. The following average times have been logged over the last four months:

	Average per Month (in days)			
	1	2	3	4
Move time per unit	0.4	0.3	0.4	0.4
Process time per unit	2.1	2.0	1.9	1.8
Wait time per order before start				
of production	16.0	17.5	19.0	20.5
Queue time per unit	4.3	5.0	5.8	6.7
Inspection time per unit	0.6	0.7	0.7	0.6

Required
1. For each month, compute the following operating performance measures:
   a. The throughput time, or velocity of production.
   b. The MCE.
   c. The delivery cycle time.
2. Evaluate the company's performance over the last four months
3. Refer to the move time, process time, and so forth, given above for month 4.
   a. Assume that in month 5 the move time, process time, and so forth, are the same as in month 4, except that through the use of JIT inventory methods the company is able to completely eliminate the queue time during production. Compute the new throughput time and MCE.
   b. Assume in month 6 that the move time, process time, and so forth, are again the same as in month 4, except that the company is able to completely eliminate both the queue time during production and the inspection time. Compute the new throughput time and MCE.

P10–15   Developing Standard Costs   Danson Company is a chemical manufacturer that supplies various products to industrial users. The company plans to introduce a new chemical solution, called Nysap, for which it needs to develop a standard product cost. The following information is available on the production of Nysap:

a. Nysap is made by combining a chemical compound (nyclyn) and a solution (salex), and boiling the mixture. A 20% loss in volume occurs for both the salex and the nyclyn during boiling. After boiling, the mixture consists of 9.6 litres of salex and 12 kilograms of nyclyn per 10-litre batch of Nysap.

b. After the boiling process is complete, the solution is cooled slightly before 5 kilograms of protet are added per 10-litre batch of Nysap. The addition of the protet does not affect the total liquid volume. The resulting solution is then bottled in 10-litre containers.

c. The finished product is highly unstable, and one 10-litre batch out of six is rejected at final inspection. Rejected batches have no commercial value and are thrown out.

d. It takes a worker 35 minutes to process one 10-litre batch of Nysap. Employees work an eight-hour day, including one hour per day for rest breaks and cleanup.

Required
1. Determine the standard quantity for each of the raw materials needed to produce an acceptable 10-litre batch of Nysap.
2. Determine the standard labour time to produce an acceptable 10-litre batch of Nysap.
3. Assuming the following purchase prices and costs, prepare a standard cost card for materials and labour for one acceptable 10-litre batch of Nysap:

Salex	$1.50 per litre
Nyclyn	2.80 per kilogram
Protet	3.00 per kilogram
Direct labour cost	9.00 per hour

(CMA, adapted)

P10–16 Standards and Variances from Incomplete Data Highland Company produces a lightweight backpack that is popular with college students. Standard variable costs relating to a single backpack are given below:

	Standard Quantity or Hours	Standard Price or Rate	Standard Cost
Direct materials	?	$6 per metre	$?
Direct labour	?	?	?
Variable manufacturing overhead .	?	$3 per hour	?
Total standard cost			$?

During March, 1,000 backpacks were manufactured and sold. Selected information relating to the month's production is given below:

	Materials Used	Direct Labour	Variable Manufacturing Overhead
Total standard cost allowed*	$16,800	$10,500	$4,200
Actual costs incurred	15,000	?	3,600
Materials price variance	?		
Materials quantity variance	1,200 U		
Labour rate variance		?	
Labour efficiency variance		?	
Variable overhead spending variance . . .			?
Variable overhead efficiency variance . .			?

*For the month's production.

The following additional information is available for March's production:

Actual direct labour-hours	1,500
Standard overhead rate per hour	$3.00
Standard price of one metre of materials . . .	6.00
Difference between standard and actual cost per backpack produced during March . . .	0.15 F

Overhead is applied to production on the basis of direct labour-hours.

Required
1. What is the standard cost of a single backpack?
2. What was the actual cost per backpack produced during March?
3. How many metres of material are required at standard per backpack?
4. What was the materials price variance for March?
5. What is the standard direct labour rate per hour?
6. What was the labour rate variance for March? The labour efficiency variance?
7. What was the variable overhead spending variance for March? The variable overhead efficiency variance?
8. Prepare a standard cost card for one backpack.

P10–17 Computations from Incomplete Data

Sharp Company manufactures a product for which the following standards have been set:

	Standard Quantity or Hours	Standard Price or Rate	Standard Cost
Direct materials	3 metres	$5 per metre	$15
Direct labour	? hours	? per hour	?

During March, the company purchased direct materials at a cost of $55,650, all of which were used in the production of 3,200 units of product. In addition, 4,900 hours of direct labour time were worked on the product during the month. The cost of this labour time was $36,750. The following variances have been computed for the month:

Materials quantity variance	$4,500 U
Total labour variance	1,650 F
Labour efficiency variance	800 U

Required
1. For direct materials:
   a. Compute the actual cost per metre for materials for March.
   b. Compute the materials price variance and a total variance for materials.
2. For direct labour:
   a. Compute the standard direct labour rate per hour.
   b. Compute the standard hours allowed for the month's production.
   c. Compute the standard hours allowed per unit of product.

(Hint: In completing the problem, it may be helpful to move from known to unknown data either by using the columnar format shown in Exhibits 10–3 and 10–5 or by using the variance formulas.)

P10–18 Variance Analysis with Multiple Lots

Hillcrest Leisure Wear, Inc., manufactures men's clothing. The company has a single line of slacks that is produced in lots, with each lot representing an order from a customer. As a lot is completed, the customer's store label is attached to the slacks before shipment.

Hillcrest has a standard cost system and has established the following standards for a dozen slacks:

	Standard Quantity or Hours	Standard Price or Rate	Standard Cost
Direct materials	32 metres	$2.40 per metre	$76.80
Direct labour	6 hours	7.50 per hour	45.00

During October, Hillcrest worked on three orders for slacks. The company's job cost records for the month reveal the following:

Lot	Units in Lot (dozens)	Materials Used (metres)	Hours Worked
48	1,500	48,300	8,900
49	950	30,140	6,130
50	2,100	67,250	10,270

The following additional information is available:

a. Hillcrest purchased 180,000 metres of material during October at a cost of $424,800.
b. Direct labour cost incurred during the month for production of slacks amounted to $192,280.
c. There was no work in process inventory on October 1. During October, lots 48 and 49 were completed, and lot 50 was 100% complete as to materials and 80% complete as to labour.

Required
1. Compute the materials price variance for the materials purchased during October.
2. Determine the materials quantity variance for October in both metres and dollars:
   a. For each lot worked on during the month.
   b. For the company as a whole.
3. Compute the labour rate variance for October.
4. Determine the labour efficiency variance for the month in both hours and dollars:
   a. For each lot worked on during the month.
   b. For the company as a whole.
5. In what situations might it be better to express variances in units (hours, metres, and so on) rather than in dollars? In dollars rather than in units?

(CPA, adapted)

P10–19   Variance Analysis; Incomplete Data; Journal Entries   (Appendix 10A) Maple Products, Ltd., manufactures a hockey stick that is used worldwide. The standard cost of one hockey stick is:

	Standard Quantity or Hours	Standard Price or Rate	Standard Cost
Direct materials	? metres	$9.00 per metre	$?
Direct labour	2 hours	? per hour	?
Variable manufacturing overhead	? hours	1.30 per hour	?
Total standard cost			$27.00

Last year, 8,000 hockey sticks were produced and sold. Selected cost data relating to last year's operations follow:

	Dr.	Cr.
Direct materials purchased (20,000 metres)	$174,000	
Wages payable (? hours)		$79,200*
Work in process—direct materials	115,200	
Direct labour rate variance		3,300
Variable overhead efficiency variance	650	

*Relates to the actual direct labour cost for the year.

The following additional information is available for last year's operations:

a. No materials were on hand at the start of last year. Some of the materials purchased during the year were still on hand in the warehouse at the end of the year.
b. The variable manufacturing overhead rate is based on direct labour-hours. Total actual variable manufacturing overhead cost for last year was $19,800.
c. Actual direct materials usage for last year exceeded the standard by 0.06 metres per stick.

Required
1. For direct materials:
   a. Compute the price and quantity variances for last year.
   b. Prepare journal entries to record all activities relating to direct materials for last year.
2. For direct labour:
   a. Verify the rate variance given above and compute the efficiency variance for last year.
   b. Prepare a journal entry to record activity relating to direct labour for last year.

3. Compute the variable overhead spending variance for last year and verify the variable overhead efficiency variance given above.
4. State possible causes of each variance that you have computed.
5. Prepare a completed standard cost card for one hockey stick.

P10–20   Perverse Effects of Some Performance Measures   There is often more than one way to improve a performance measure. Unfortunately, some of the actions taken by managers to make their performance look better may actually harm the organization. For example, suppose the marketing department is held responsible only for increasing the performance measure "total revenues." Increases in total revenues may be achieved by working harder and smarter, but they can also usually be achieved by simply cutting prices. The increase in volume from cutting prices almost always results in greater total revenues; however, it does not always lead to greater total profits. Those who design performance measurement systems need to keep in mind that managers who are under pressure to perform may take actions to improve performance measures that have negative consequences elsewhere.

Required   For each of the following situations, describe actions that managers might take to show improvement in the performance measure but which do not actually lead to improvement in the organization's overall performance.

1. Concerned with the slow rate at which new products are brought to market, top management of a consumer electronics company introduces a new performance measure—speed-to-market. The research and development department is given responsibility for this performance measure, which measures the average amount of time a product is in development before it is released to the market for sale.
2. The CEO of a telephone company has been under public pressure from city officials to fix the large number of public pay phones that do not work. The company's repair people complain that the problem is vandalism and damage caused by theft of coins from coin boxes—particularly in high-crime areas in the city. The CEO says she wants the problem solved and has pledged to city officials that there will be substantial improvement by the end of the year. To ensure that this is done, she makes the managers in charge of installing and maintaining pay phones responsible for increasing the percentage of public pay phones that are fully functional.
3. A manufacturing company has been plagued by the chronic failure to ship orders to customers by the promised date. To solve this problem, the production manager has been given the responsibility of increasing the percentage of orders shipped on time. When a customer calls in an order, the production manager and the customer agree to a delivery date. If the order is not completed by that date, it is counted as a late shipment.
4. Concerned with the productivity of employees, the board of directors of a large multinational corporation has dictated that the manager of each subsidiary will be held responsible for increasing the revenue per employee of his or her subsidiary.

P10–21   Internal Business Process Performance Measures   Tombro Industries is in the process of automating one of its plants and developing a flexible manufacturing system. The company is finding it necessary to make many changes in operating procedures. Progress has been slow, particularly in trying to develop new performance measures for the factory.

In an effort to evaluate performance and determine where improvements can be made, management has gathered the following data relating to activities over the last four months:

	Month			
	1	**2**	**3**	**4**
Quality control measures:				
Number of defects	185	163	124	91
Number of warranty claims	46	39	30	27
Number of customer complaints	102	96	79	58
Material control measures:				
Purchase order lead time	8 days	7 days	5 days	4 days
Scrap as a percent of total cost	1%	1%	2%	3%
Machine performance measures:				
Percentage of machine downtime	3%	4%	4%	6%
Use as a percentage of availability	95%	92%	89%	85%
Setup time (hours)	8	10	11	12
Delivery performance measures:				
Throughput time, or velocity	?	?	?	?
Manufacturing cycle efficiency (MCE)	?	?	?	?
Delivery cycle time	?	?	?	?
Percentage of on-time deliveries	96%	95%	92%	89%

The president has read in industry journals that the throughput time, the MCE, and the delivery cycle time are important measures of performance, but no one is sure how they are computed. You have been asked to assist the company, and you have gathered the following data relating to these measures:

	Average per Month (in days)			
	1	**2**	**3**	**4**
Wait time per order before start				
of production	9.0	11.5	12.0	14.0
Inspection time per unit	0.8	0.7	0.7	0.7
Process time per unit	2.1	2.0	1.9	1.8
Queue time per unit	2.8	4.4	6.0	7.0
Move time per unit	0.3	0.4	0.4	0.5

As part of its modernization process, the company is also moving toward a just-in-time (JIT) inventory system. Over the next year, the company hopes to have the bulk of its raw materials and parts on a JIT basis.

Required
1. For each month, compute the following performance measures:
    a. The throughput time, or velocity of production.
    b. The MCE.
    c. The delivery cycle time.
2. Using the performance measures given in the main body of the problem and the performance measures computed in (1) above, do the following:
    a. Identify the areas where the company seems to be improving.
    b. Identify the areas where the company seems to be deteriorating.
3. Refer to the inspection time, process time, and so forth, given above for month 4.
    a. Assume that in month 5 the inspection time, process time, and so forth, are the same as for month 4, except that the company is able to completely eliminate the queue time during production. Compute the new throughput time and MCE.
    b. Assume that in month 6 the inspection time, process time, and so forth, are the same as in month 4, except that the company is able to eliminate both the queue time during production and the inspection time. Compute the new throughput time and MCE.

P10–22 Internal Business Process Performance Measures and Standard Costs "I've never seen such awful results," roared Ben Carrick, manufacturing vice president of Vorelli Industries. "I thought JIT and automation were supposed to make us more efficient, but just look at last month's efficiency report on Zets, our major product in this plant. The labour efficiency variance was $120,000 *unfavourable*. That's four times higher than it's ever been before. If you add on the $102,000 unfavourable material price variance on Zets, that's over $220,000 down the drain in a single month on just one product. Have you people in purchasing and production lost control over everything?"

"Now take it easy, Ben," replied Sandi Shipp, the company's purchasing agent. "We knew when we adopted JIT that our material costs would go up somewhat. But we're locking onto the very best suppliers, and they're making deliveries three times a day for our Zets product. In a few months, we'll be able to offset most of our higher purchasing costs by completely vacating three rented warehouses."

"And I know our labour efficiency variance looks bad," responded Raul Duvall, the company's production superintendent, "but it doesn't tell the whole story. With JIT flow lines and our new equipment, we've never been more efficient in the plant."

"How can you say you're efficient when you took 90,000 direct labour-hours to produce just 30,000 Zets last month?" asked Ben Carrick. "That works out to be 3 hours per unit, but according to the standard cost card you should be able to produce a Zet in just 2.5 hours. Do you call that efficient?"

"The problem is that the president wants us to use JIT on the finished goods side of the plant as well as on the raw materials side," explained Raul. "So we're trying to gear production to demand, but at the moment we have to cut production back somewhat in order to work off our finished goods inventory of Zets. This will go on for several more months before we'll be able to get production completely in balance with current demand. And don't forget that our line people aren't just standing around when their machines are idle. Under the new system, they're doing their own inspections and they do maintenance on their own equipment."

"It had better *not* go on for several more months," roared Ben Carrick, "at least not if you people down in production want any bonuses this year. I've been looking at these reports for 30 years, and I know inefficiency when I see it. Let's get things back under control."

After leaving Ben Carrick's office, Raul Duvall has approached you for help in developing some performance measures that will show the actual efficiency of the company's production process. Working with Raul, you have gathered the following information:

a. The company manufactures several products in this plant. A standard cost card for Zets is given below:

	Standard Quantity or Hours	Standard Price or Rate	Standard Cost
Direct materials	18 metres	$3.00 per metre	$54.00
Direct labour	2.5 hours	8.00 per hour	20.00
Variable manufacturing overhead	2.5 hours	2.80 per hour	7.00
Total standard cost			$81.00

b. During June, the most recent month, the company purchased 510,000 metres of material for production of Zets at a cost of $3.20 per metre. All of this material was used in the production of 30,000 units during the month. A large part of the production process is now automated, and the company is experiencing less waste each month.

c. The company maintains a stable workforce to produce Zets. Persons who previously were inspectors and on the maintenance crew have been reassigned as direct labour workers. During June, 90,000 hours were logged by direct labour workers on the Zets flow lines. The average pay rate was $7.85 per hour.

d. Variable manufacturing overhead cost is assigned to products on the basis of direct labour-hours. During June, the company incurred $207,000 in variable manufacturing overhead costs associated with the manufacture of Zets.

e. Demand for Zets is increasing over time, and top management is discussing the possibility of constructing additional production facilities.

f. The following information has been gathered from computers located on the production line. This information is expressed in hours per unit of the Zets product.

Processing: As workers have become more familiar with the new equipment and procedures, average processing time per unit has declined over the last three months, from 2.6 hours in April, to 2.5 hours in May, to 2.4 hours in June.

Inspection: Workers are now directly responsible for quality control, which accounts for the following changes in inspection time per unit over the last three months: April, 1.3 hours; May, 0.9 hours; and June, 0.1 hours.

Movement of goods: With the change to JIT flow lines, goods now move shorter distances between machines. Move time per unit over the past three months has been: April, 1.9 hours; May, 1.4 hours; and June, 0.6 hours.

Queue time in cells: Better coordination of production with demand has resulted in less queue time as goods move along the production line. The data for the last three months are: April, 8.2 hours; May, 5.2 hours; and June, 1.9 hours.

Required

1. Compute the materials price and quantity variances using traditional variance analysis. Is the decrease in waste apparent in this computation? Explain. If the company wants to compute the materials price variance, what should be done to make this computation more appropriate?
2. Compute the direct labour rate and efficiency variances using traditional variance analysis. Do you agree with Ben Carrick that the efficiency variance is still appropriate as a measure of performance for the company? Explain why you do or do not agree.
3. Compute the variable manufacturing overhead spending and efficiency variances using traditional variance analysis. Would you expect that a correlation still exists between direct labour and the incurrence of variable manufacturing overhead cost in the company? Explain, using data from your variance computations to support your position.
4. Compute the following for April, May, and June for Zets:
    a. The throughput time per unit.
    b. The manufacturing cycle efficiency (MCE).
5. Which performance measures do you think are more appropriate in this situation—the labour efficiency variance or throughput time per unit and manufacturing cycle efficiency?

P10–23 Developing Standard Costs   ColdKing Company is a small producer of fruit-flavoured frozen desserts. For many years, ColdKing's products have had strong regional sales on the basis of brand recognition; however, other companies have begun marketing similar products in the area, and price competition has become increasingly important. John Wakefield, the company's controller, is planning to implement a standard cost system for ColdKing and has gathered considerable information from his co-workers on production and material requirements for ColdKing's products. Wakefield believes that the use of standard costing will allow ColdKing to improve cost control and make better pricing decisions.

ColdKing's most popular product is raspberry sherbet. The sherbet is produced in 10-bottle batches. Each bottle contains 4 litres and each batch requires 6 litres of good raspberries. The fresh raspberries are sorted by hand before they enter the production process. Because of imperfections in the raspberries and normal spoilage, 1 litre of berries is discarded for every 4 litres of acceptable berries. Three minutes is the standard direct labour time for the sorting that is required to obtain 1 litre of acceptable raspberries. The acceptable raspberries are then blended with the other ingredients; blending requires 12 minutes of direct labour time per batch. After blending, the sherbet is packaged in litre containers. Wakefield has gathered the following pricing information:

a. ColdKing purchases raspberries at a cost of $0.80 per litre. All other ingredients cost a total of $0.45 per bottle.
b. Direct labour is paid at the rate of $9.00 per hour.
c. The total cost of material and labour required to package the sherbet is $0.38 per litre.

Required

1. Develop the standard cost for the direct cost components (materials, labour, and packaging) of a 10-bottle batch of raspberry sherbet. The standard cost should identify the standard quantity, standard rate, and standard cost per batch for each direct cost component of a batch of raspberry sherbet.

2. As part of the implementation of a standard cost system at ColdKing, John Wakefied plans to train those responsible for maintaining the standards on how to use variance analysis. Wakefield is particularly concerned with the causes of unfavourable variances.
   a. Discuss possible causes of unfavourable materials price variances and identify the individual(s) who should be held responsible for these variances.
   b. Discuss possible causes of unfavourable labour efficiency variances and identify the individual(s) who should be held responsible for these variances.

(CMA, adapted)

P10–24 Standard Costs and Variance Analysis   Marvel Parts, Inc., manufactures auto accessories. One of the company's products is a set of seat covers that can be adjusted to fit nearly any small car. The company has a standard cost system in use for all of its products. According to the standards that have been set for the seat covers, the factory should work 2,850 hours each month to produce 1,900 sets of covers. The standard costs associated with this level of production activity are:

	Total	Per Set of Covers
Direct materials	$42,560	$22.40
Direct labour	17,100	9.00
Variable manufacturing overhead		
(based on direct labour-hours)	6,840	3.60
		$35.00

During August, the factory worked only 2,800 direct labour-hours and produced 2,000 sets of covers. The following actual costs were recorded during the month:

	Total	Per Set of Covers
Direct materials (12,000 metres)	$45,600	$22.80
Direct labour	18,200	9.10
Variable manufacturing overhead	7,000	3.50
		$35.40

At standard, each set of covers should require 5.6 metres of material. All of the materials purchased during the month were used in production.

Required   Compute the following variances for August:

1. The materials price and quantity variances.
2. The labour rate and efficiency variances.
3. The variable overhead spending and efficiency variances.

P10–25 Mix and Yield Variances   Acadia Company uses standard costs to account for its production product ZIP. The standard cost of one unit is given below:

Material A:	20.00 kilograms @ $ .90 =	$18.00
Material B:	5.00 kilograms @ 2.50 =	12.50
Direct labour: 4.75 hours @	15.00 =	71.25

Each material is added at the beginning of the process. Production data for 2001 are as follows:

a. Beginning work in process, 15,000 units, 20% complete.
b. Started during the month, 37,000.
c. Ending work in process, 14,000 units, 75% complete.
d. Material A issued to production, 750,000 kilograms.
e. Material B issued to production, 180,000 kilograms.
f. Direct labour cost was $3,248,250 for 213,000 hours.
g. Assume that materials A and B are perfect substitutes.

Required Calculate the following variances for Acadia Company:

a. Material mix variance.
b. Material yield variance.
c. Labour rate variance.
d. Labour efficiency variance.

P10–26 Mix and Yield Variances The product Zano is made from three secret ingredients code-named Ray, Matt, and Nat. The materials are mixed in the following standard proportions to produce 100 litres of Zano:

Material	Quantity	Cost per litre
Ray	45 litres	$ 4.00
Matt	20 litres	8.00
Nat	15 litres	20.00

It takes 100 hours of direct labour at $15 per hour to produce 100 litres of Zano. Average monthly production and sales has been 150,000 litres of Zano. Last month the company produced 170,000 litres of Zano using the following resources:

Material	Quantity	Total Cost
Ray	79,000	$ 320,500
Matt	36,000	280,000
Nat	22,000	444,000
	137,000	$1,040,500
Direct labour	92,000 hrs.	$1,426,000

Required Determine the following variances:

a. Material price variance.
b. Material quantity variance.
c. Material mix variance.
d. Material yield variance.

P10–27 Variance Analysis; Journal Entries Azim's Shirts Inc. manufactures blankets for large stores. The standard costs for a dozen blankets include:

Direct materials—24 metres at $1.10/metre = $26.40
Direct labour—3 hours at $7.35/DLH = $22.05

During February, Azim worked on three separate orders of blankets. Job cost records for the month disclose the following:

Lot	Units in Lot	Materials Used	Hours Worked
4503	1,000 dozen	24,100 metres	2,980
4504	1,700 dozen	40,440 metres	5,130
4505	1,200 dozen	28,825 metres	2,890

You have been able to gather the following information:

a. Azim purchased 95,000 metres of material during February at a cost of $106,400. The material price variance is recorded when goods are purchased, and all inventories are carried at standard cost.
b. The payroll department reported that production employees were paid $7.50 per hour.
c. There was no beginning work in process. During February, lots 4503 and 4504 were completed, and all materials were issued for lot 4505, which was 80% complete as to labour.

Required 1. Compute the material price variance *and* make the appropriate journal entry.
2. Compute the remaining relevant variances for total production.
3. Prepare journal entries to charge materials and labour to production.

(CGA, adapted)

P10–28 Mix and Yield Variances   The Fido Company manufactures a popular brand of dog food. The dog food is mixed in 450-kilogram batches. The standard input for material per batch is as follows:

	Kilograms	Standard Price per Kilogram
Cereal	200	$.15
Horse meat	150	.40
Fish parts	100	.36
Input.	450	
Output	400	

The dog food is packed in cans weighing five kilograms. During the month of September, 11,200 cans were produced. The following materials were used during September:

	Kilograms
Cereal	29,200
Horse meat	19,800
Fish parts	14,300
Total input	63,300

Purchases for September were as follows:

	Kilograms	Total Cost
Cereal	30,200	$4,500
Horse meat	19,500	7,950
Fish parts	14,600	5,190
	64,300	$17,640

Fido Company uses a standard cost system and calculates material price variances at time of purchase.

Required   1. Compute the material mix variance for the month.
2. Compute the material yield variance for the month.

(SMAC, adapted)

P10–29 Learning Curves   (Appendix 10B) Halifax Instruments has just completed the assembly of some 400 sonic buoys for the Canadian Forces; these buoys are especially equipped to detect undersea vessels. The company is now being asked to submit an estimate of the cost of an additional 800 units. Its management has noted that the direct labour-hours (DLH) on each unit seem to be declining. For the first 200 units produced, the average hours per unit were 2.1. For the assembly of the 400 units, however, the average hours per unit dropped to 1.68.

Required   1. Using these values, calculate the total labour hours required to assemble 1,600 units.
2. Suppose incremental costs (labour plus variable overhead costs) are $15 per direct labour-hour. What would be the incremental assembly costs for a new order of 800 units?
3. Using the following data, determine the formula for total hours for various cumulative units produced using the high-low approach.

Cumulative Units Produced	Labour-Hours Average per Unit	Total
200	2.100	420.0
400	1.680	672.0
800	1.344	1,075.2

4. Halifax fills the order for the additional 800 units, and produces another 100 units for a second customer. Its cumulative experience with producing these 100 buoys shows 90 total direct labour-hours or an average of 0.90 DLH per buoy. Is this consistent with the learning curve you estimated? If not, suggest an explanation for the deviation.

Cases

C10–30 Ethics and the Manager Stacy Cummins, the newly hired controller at Merced Home Products, Inc., was disturbed by what she had discovered about the standard costs at the Home Security Division. In looking over the past several years of quarterly earnings reports at the Home Security Division, she noticed that the first-quarter earnings were always poor, the second-quarter earnings were slightly better, the third-quarter earnings were again slightly better, and then the fourth quarter and the year always ended with a spectacular performance in which the Home Security Division always managed to meet or exceed its target profit for the year. She also was concerned to find letters from the company's external auditors to top management warning about an unusual use of standard costs at the Home Security Division.

When Ms. Cummins ran across these letters, she asked the assistant controller, Gary Farber, if he knew what was going on at the Home Security Division. Gary said that it was common knowledge in the company that the vice president in charge of the Home Security Division, Preston Lansing, had rigged the standards at the Home Security Division in order to produce the same quarterly earnings pattern every year. According to company policy, variances are taken directly to the income statement as an adjustment to cost of goods sold.

Favourable variances have the effect of increasing net income, and unfavourable variances have the effect of decreasing net income. Lansing had rigged the standards so that there were always large favourable variances. Company policy was a little vague about when these variances have to be reported on the divisional income statements. While the intent was clearly to recognize variances on the income statement in the period in which they arise, nothing in the company's accounting manuals actually explicitly required this. So for many years Lansing had followed a practice of saving up the favourable variances and using them to create a nice smooth pattern of earnings growth in the first three quarters, followed by a big "Christmas present" of an extremely good fourth quarter. (Financial reporting regulations forbid carrying variances forward from one year to the next on the annual audited financial statements, so all of the variances must appear on the divisional income statement by the end of the year.)

Ms. Cummins was concerned about these revelations and attempted to bring up the subject with the president of Merced Home Products but was told that "we all know what Lansing's doing, but as long as he continues to turn in such good reports, don't bother him." When Ms. Cummins asked if the board of directors was aware of the situation, the president somewhat testily replied, "Of course they are aware."

Required

1. How did Preston Lansing probably "rig" the standard costs—are the standards set too high or too low? Explain.
2. Should Preston Lansing be permitted to continue his practice of managing reported earnings?
3. What should Stacy Cummins do in this situation?

C10–31 Behavioural Impact of Standard Costs and Variances Terry Travers is the manufacturing supervisor of Aurora Manufacturing Company, which produces a variety of plastic products. Some of these products are standard items that are listed in the company's catalogue, while others are made to customer specifications. Each month, Travers receives a performance report showing the budget for the month, the actual activity, and the variance between budget and actual. Part of Travers' annual performance evaluation is based on his department's performance against budget. Aurora's purchasing manager, Sally Christensen, also receives monthly performance reports and she, too, is evaluated in part on the basis of these reports.

The monthly reports for June had just been distributed when Travers met Christensen in the hallway outside their offices. Scowling, Travers began the conversation, "I see we have another set of monthly performance reports hand-delivered by that not very nice junior employee in the budget office. He seemed pleased to tell me that I'm in trouble with my performance again."

> **Christensen:** I got the same treatment. All I ever hear about are the things I haven't done right. Now I'll have to spend a lot of time reviewing the report and preparing explanations. The worst part is that it's now the 21st of July so the information is almost a month old, and we have to spend all this time on history.
>
> **Travers:** My biggest gripe is that our production activity varies a lot from month to month, but we're given an annual budget that's written in stone. Last month we were shut down for three days when a strike delayed delivery of the basic ingredient used in our plastic formulation, and we had already exhausted our inventory. You know about that problem, though, because we asked you to call all over the country to find an alternate source of supply. When we got what we needed on a rush basis, we had to pay more than we normally do.
>
> **Christensen:** I expect problems like that to pop up from time to time—that's part of my job—but now we'll both have to take a careful look at our reports to see where the charges are reflected for that rush order. Every month I spend more time making sure I should be charged for each item reported than I do making plans for my department's daily work. It's really frustrating to see charges for things I have no control over.
>
> **Travers:** The way we get information doesn't help, either. I don't get copies of the reports you get, yet a lot of what I do is affected by your department, and by most of the other departments we have. Why do the budget and accounting people assume that I should only be told about my operations even though the president regularly gives us pep talks about how we all need to work together as a team?
>
> **Christensen:** I seem to get more reports than I need, and I am never asked to comment on them until top management calls me on the carpet about my department's shortcomings. Do you ever hear comments when your department shines?
>
> **Travers:** I guess they don't have time to review the good news. One of my problems is that all the reports are in dollars and cents. I work with people, machines, and materials. I need information to help me *this* month to solve *this* month's problems—not another report of the dollars expended *last* month or the month before.

Required
1. Based on the conversation between Terry Travers and Sally Christensen, describe the likely motivation and behaviour of these two employees resulting from Aurora Manufacturing Company's standard cost and variance reporting system.
2. When properly implemented, both employees and companies should benefit from a system involving standard costs and variances.
   a. Describe the benefits that can be realized from a standard cost system.
   b. Based on the situation presented above, recommend ways for Aurora Manufacturing Company to improve its standard cost and variance reporting system so as to increase employee motivation.

(CMA, adapted)

C10–32 Unit Costs, Variances, and Journal Entries from Incomplete Data (Appendix 10A) You are employed by Olster Company, which manufactures products for the senior citizen market. As a rising young executive in the company, you are scheduled to make a presentation in a few hours to your superior. This presentation relates to last week's production of Maxitol, a popular health tonic that is manufactured by Olster Company. Unfortunately, while studying ledger sheets and variance summaries by poolside in the company's fitness area, you were bumped and dropped the papers into the pool. In desperation, you fished the papers from the water, but you have discovered that only the following fragments are readable:

Maxitol—Standard Cost Card

	Standard Quantity or Hours	Standard Price or Rate	Standard Cost
Material A	6 litres	$8 per lit	$
Material B		per kil	
Direct labour		per ho	0
Standard cost per batc			$99.50

Maxitol—General Ledger Accounts

Raw Materials—A

Bal. 3/1	0		
Bal. 3/7	2,000		

Work in Process

Bal. 3/1	0		
Material A	5,760		
Bal. 3/7	0		

Material A—Price Variance

	300

Wages Payable

	4,100

Raw Materials—B

Bal. 3/1	700	2,500	
Bal. 3/7	1,400		

Labour Rate Variance

500	

Material B—Quantity Variance

100	

Accounts Payable

	11,460

You remember that the accounts payable are for purchases of both material A and material B. You also remember that only 10 direct labour workers are involved in the production of Maxitol and that each worked 40 hours last week. The wages payable above are for wages earned by these workers.

You realize that to be ready for your presentation, you must reconstruct all data relating to Maxitol very quickly. As a start, you have called purchasing and found that 1,000 litres of material A and 800 kilograms of material B were purchased last week.

Required
1. How many batches of Maxitol were produced last week? (This is a key figure; be sure it's right before going on.)
2. For material A:
   a. What was the cost of material A purchased last week?
   b. How many litres were used in production last week?
   c. What was the quantity variance?
   d. Prepare journal entries to record all activity relating to material A for last week.
3. For material B:
   a. What is the standard cost per kilogram for material B?
   b. How many kilograms of material B were used in production last week? How many kilograms should have been used at standard?
   c. What is the standard quantity of material B per batch?
   d. What was the price variance for material B last week?
   e. Prepare journal entries to record all activity relating to material B for last week.
4. For direct labour:
   a. What is the standard rate per direct labour-hour?
   b. What are the standard hours per batch?
   c. What were the standard hours allowed for last week's production?
   d. What was the labour efficiency variance for last week?
   e. Prepare a journal entry to record all activity relating to direct labour for last week.
5. Complete the standard cost card shown above for one batch of Maxitol.

C10–33 Balanced Scorecard Weierman Department Store is located in the downtown area of a medium-sized city in Western Canada. While the store had been profitable for many years, it is facing increasing competition from large national chains that have set up stores in the city's suburbs. Recently the downtown area has been undergoing revitalization, and the owners of Weierman Department Store are somewhat optimistic that profitability can be restored.

In an attempt to accelerate the return to profitability, the management of Weierman Department Store is in the process of designing a balanced scorecard for the company. Management believes the company should focus on two key problems. First, customers are taking longer and longer to pay the bills they incur on the department store's charge card and they have far more bad debts than are normal for the industry. If this problem were solved, the company would have far more cash to make much needed renovations. Investigation has revealed that much of the problem with late payments and unpaid bills is apparently due to disputed bills that are the result of incorrect charges on the customer bills. These incorrect charges usually occur because salesclerks enter data incorrectly on the charge account slip. Second, the company has been incurring large losses on unsold seasonal apparel. Such items are ordinarily resold at a loss to discount stores that specialize in such distress items.

The meeting in which the balanced scorecard approach was discussed was disorganized and ineffectively led—possibly because no one other than one of the vice presidents had read anything about how to put a balanced scorecard together. Nevertheless, a number of potential performance measures were suggested by various managers. These potential performance measures are listed below:

Performance measures suggested by various managers:

- Total sales revenue.
- Percentage of salesclerks trained to correctly enter data on charge account slips.
- Customer satisfaction with accuracy of charge account bills from monthly customer survey.
- Sales per employee.
- Travel expenses for buyers for trips to fashion shows.
- Average age of accounts receivables.
- Courtesy shown by junior staff members to senior staff members based on surveys of senior staff.
- Unsold inventory at the end of the season as a percentage of total cost of sales.
- Sales per square metre of floor space.
- Percentage of suppliers making just-in-time deliveries.
- Quality of food in the staff cafeteria based on staff surveys.
- Written-off accounts receivables (bad debts) as a percentage of sales.
- Percentage of charge account bills containing errors.
- Percentage of employees who have attended the city's cultural diversity workshop.
- Total profit.
- Profit per employee.

Required
1. As someone with more knowledge of the balanced scorecard than almost anyone else in the company, you have been asked to build an integrated balanced scorecard. In your scorecard, use only performance measures suggested by the managers above. You do not have to use all of the performance measures suggested by the managers, but you should build a balanced scorecard that reveals a strategy for dealing with the problems with accounts receivable and with unsold merchandise. Construct the balanced scorecard following the format used in Exhibit 10–13. Do not be particularly concerned with whether a specific performance measure falls within the learning and growth, internal business process, customer, or financial perspective. However, clearly show the causal links between the performance measures with arrows and whether the performance measures should show increases or decreases.
2. Assume that the company adopts your balanced scorecard. After operating for a year, there are improvements in some performance measures but not in others. What should management do next?
3. a. Suppose that customers express greater satisfaction with the accuracy of their charge account bills but the performance measures for the average age of receivables and for bad debts do not improve. Explain why this might happen.

b. Suppose that the performance measures for the average age of accounts receivable, bad debts, and unsold inventory improve, but total profits do not. Explain why this might happen. Assume in your answer that the explanation lies within the company.

Group Exercises

GE10–34 Conventional Production Practices Traditional manufacturing systems were based on the economies of mass production and, therefore, focused primarily on productivity (average output per employee) and unit cost. Work processes were standardized, and production volume was maximized by increasing investments in economies of scale. Historically, direct labour costs amounted to approximately 30% to 40% of total manufacturing costs. To control high labour costs, North American plant managers were constantly exhorted to increase output, produce at or below standard unit costs, and minimize unfavourable cost variances.

Required

1. Can you cite service industries that have used the same mass production and economies of scale philosophy to prosper?
2. Describe the traditional manufacturing environment and how North American companies manage costs by maximizing production volume.
3. Traditionally, what performance measures were used to measure and evaluate the performance of direct labour and shop floor personnel?
4. Given that everyone from the plant manager on down wants to perform well, what incentives did these performance measures provide factory workers and shop floor supervisors?
5. What potential results did these performance incentives have?
6. Cycle time or throughput time, the time it takes to complete a job once it is started, is very important to customers. What impact did the combination of production factors—the factory layout, increasing volume, and decreasing unit cost—have on cycle times?
7. Today, production management is not only under pressure to contain (if not reduce) costs but customers are also demanding (and getting) increasing quality and a wider choice of products and services. How would production managers likely respond to demands for higher quality parts and a wider variety of finished products while still functioning under traditional mass-production systems?

GE10–35 Lean (i.e., JIT) Production Systems Lean production systems are one of the most important business innovations of this century. Toyota Motor Company deserves much credit for developing many of the key features of modern-day lean production systems. Lean production is delivering materials to the shop floor just in time for use and producing just in time to meet present demand. Successful implementations of lean production techniques eliminate a lot of the waste, excess, delay, and uncertainty associated with traditional manufacturing systems.

Required

1. What is lean (i.e., JIT) production?
2. Describe the JIT manufacturing environment and how Canadian companies manage costs by producing just in time.
3. If properly implemented, how does lean production benefit the firm? How does JIT manufacturing affect traditional performance measures such as direct labour efficiency, direct labour utilization, and machine utilization? What sort of performance measures must be implemented to achieve rather than defeat the objectives of JIT manufacturing?
4. How does the performance measurement system differ under JIT production from that under traditional production systems? Give specific examples of JIT performance measures.
5. How is the cost accounting system affected by a change to lean production?
6. Today, production managers are not only under pressure to reduce costs but to increase quality and shorten lead times. How do lean production systems manage to improve these three seemingly conflicting demands?

GE10–36   Standards in an Auto Repair Shop   Make an appointment to meet with the manager of an auto repair shop that uses standards. In most cases, this would be an auto repair shop that is affiliated with a national chain such as Goodrich or Canadian Tire or the service department of a new-car dealer.

Required   At the scheduled meeting, find out the answers to the following questions:

1. How are standards set?
2. Are standards practical or ideal?
3. How are the standards used?
4. Is the actual time taken to complete a task compared to the standard time?
5. What are the consequences of unfavourable variances? Of favourable variances?
6. Do the standards and variances create any potential problems?

GE10–37   Standards in Practice   Identify a company in your local area that is likely to use standards such as a commercial bakery, commercial printer, chain restaurant, or manufacturer. After verifying that the company uses standards, make an appointment to meet with the manager, controller, or chief financial officer of the organization.

Required   At the scheduled meeting, find out the answers to the following questions:

1. How are standards set?
2. Are standards practical or ideal?
3. How are the standards used?
4. What are the consequences of unfavourable variances? Of favourable variances?
5. Do the standards and variances create any potential problems?

IE10–38   Interpreting the Scores on the Balanced Scorecard   A balanced scorecard involves many different measures of performance ranging from the company's net income to the amount of time a customer must wait in line. How does a manager looking at a balanced scorecard know whether a particular score is good or bad? If a customer waits on average 30 seconds, is that good or bad? Is a net income of $10 million good or bad? CorVu Corporation is one of a number of companies that have developed balanced scorecard software. The company discusses the problem of interpreting performance measures on its web site www.corvu.com/papers/bsc.htm. Another software developer, Ergometrics, shows how balanced scorecard data can be visually displayed in the form of gauges on its web site www.ergometrics.com.

Required   1. Explain how CorVu Corporation computes its normalized scores.
2. Indicate how each of the Key Performance Indicators (KPIs) in CorVu Corporation's example could be displayed as gauges.
3. Suggest alternative methods for normalizing scores that might be useful to managers. Your alternatives should allow managers to tell at a glance whether performance is good or bad and improving or deteriorating.

Chapter Eleven

Flexible Budgets and Overhead Analysis

Business Focus

Dr. Salinas had just been unexpectedly appointed director of Provincial Medical Centre. The previous director, who had instituted tight budgetary controls, was extremely unpopular with the hospital's staff. This had led to his sacking by the hospital's board of directors. Dr. Salinas suspected that he had been chosen for the job because of his popularity rather than any innate management ability. He thought of himself as a physician rather than as a manager.

Shortly after taking over as director, the hospital's lab supervisor came storming into Dr. Salinas's office, threw a computer-generated report on Dr. Salinas's desk, and angrily stated: "Here, look at this report. It says we spent too much money in the Lab Department. We spent 5% more than had been authorized in the annual budget. Well, of course we did! Practically every department in the hospital asked for more tests that they had predicted at budget time! What are we supposed to do, refuse to run tests once we ran over budget?" Dr . Salinas responded: "Of course not. You have to run the tests. However, we also have to keep some control over our spending. On the other hand, I agree it isn't fair to hold you to the original budget. I don't see the solution right now, but I will work on it."

Learning Objectives

After studying Chapter 11, you should be able to:

1 Prepare a flexible budget and explain the advantages of the flexible budget approach over the static budget approach.

2 Prepare a performance report for both variable and fixed overhead costs using the flexible budget approach.

3 Use the flexible budget to prepare a variable overhead performance report containing only a spending variance.

4 Use the flexible budget to prepare a variable overhead performance report containing both a spending and an efficiency variance.

5 Explain the significance of the denominator activity figure in determining the standard cost of a unit of product.

6 Apply overhead cost to units of product in a standard cost system.

7 Compute and interpret the fixed overhead budget and volume variances.

$\mathbf{C}$ontrolling overhead costs is a major preoccupation of managers in business, in government, and in not-for-profit organizations. Overhead is a major cost, if not *the* major cost, in most large organizations. It costs Microsoft very little to download copies of its software onto hard disks and to provide purchasers with software manuals; almost all of Microsoft's costs are in research and development and marketing—elements of overhead. Or consider the Canadian National Exhibition. The only direct cost of serving a particular guest is the cost of the food the guest consumes at the park; virtually all of the other costs of running the exhibition are overhead. At Bombardier, there are far more direct costs, but there are still huge amounts of overhead in the form of engineering salaries, buildings, insurance, administrative salaries, and marketing costs.

Control of overhead costs poses special problems. Costs like direct materials and direct labour are often easier to understand, and therefore to control, than overhead, which can include everything from the disposable coffee cup in the visitor's waiting area to the president's salary. Overhead is usually made up of many separate costs—many of which may be small. This makes it impractical to control them in the same way that costs such as direct materials and direct labour are controlled. And some overhead costs are variable, some are fixed, and some are a mixture of fixed and variable. These particular problems can be largely overcome by the use of flexible budgets—a topic that was briefly discussed in Chapter 9. In this chapter, we study flexible budgets in greater detail and learn how they can be used to control costs. We also expand the study of overhead variances that we started in Chapter 10.

Objective 1

Prepare a flexible budget and explain the advantages of the flexible budget approach over the static budget approach.

Flexible Budgets

Characteristics of a Flexible Budget

Static budget A budget designed for only one level of activity.

The budgets that we studied in Chapter 9 were *static budgets*. A **static budget** is prepared for only the planned level of activity. This approach is suitable for planning purposes, but it is inadequate for evaluating how well costs are controlled. If the actual activity during a period differs from what was planned, it would be misleading to simply compare actual costs to the static budget. If activity is higher than expected, the variable costs should be higher than expected; and if activity is lower than expected, the variable costs should be lower than expected.

Flexible budgets take into account changes in costs that should occur as a consequence of changes in activity. A **flexible budget** provides estimates of what cost should be for any level of activity within a specified range. When a flexible budget is used in performance evaluation, actual costs are compared to what the *costs should have been for the actual level of activity during the period* rather than to the budgeted costs from the original budget. This is a very important distinction—particularly for variable costs. If adjustments for the level of activity are not made, it is very difficult to interpret discrepancies between budgeted and actual costs.

Flexible budget A budget that is designed to cover a range of activity and that can be used to develop budgeted costs at any point within that range to compare to actual costs incurred.

Deficiencies of the Static Budget

To illustrate the differences between a static budget and a flexible budget we will consider the case of Rick's Hairstyling salon located in Toronto that is owned and managed by Rick Manzi. The salon has very loyal customers—many of whom are associated with the Toronto Blue Jays. Despite the glamour associated with the salon, Rick is a very shrewd businessperson. Recently he has been attempting to get better control over his overhead, and with the urging of his accounting and business advisor, Victoria Kho, he has begun to prepare monthly budgets. Victoria Kho is a public accountant and a certified management accountant in independent practice that specializes in small service-oriented businesses like Rick's Hairstyling.

At the end of March, Rick carefully prepared a performance report for March as shown in Exhibit 11–1. Rick believes that the number of customers served in a month is the best way to measure the overall level of activity in his salon. Rick refers to these visits as client-visits. A customer who comes into the salon and has his or her hair styled is counted as one client-visit. Rick's Hairstyling budgeted for 5,000 client visits. However, this goal was exceeded since the business had 5,200 client visits. Using a *static budget approach* the company's overall performance is illustrated in Exhibit 11–1.

Exhibit 11–1

RICK'S HAIRSTYLING
Income Statement
For the Month Ended March 31

	Actual	Budget	Variance
Number of client visits	5,200	5,000	200 F
Sales	$156,000	$150,000	$6,000 F
Less variable expenses:			
Direct materials	5,600	5,000	600 U
Direct labour	21,000	20,000	1,000 U
Variable overhead	29,720	27,000	2,720 U
Selling and administrative	500	500	0
Total variable expenses	56,820	52,500	4,320 U
Contribution margin	99,180	97,500	1,680 U
Less fixed expenses:			
Overhead	29,720	21,500	8,220 U
Selling and administrative	10,000	10,000	0
Total fixed expenses	39,720	31,500	8,220 U
Net income	$59,460	$66,000	6,540 U

What is wrong with the income statement information presented in Exhibit 11–1 for performance evaluation? The static budget approach used to prepare the statement has a major deficiency in that it fails to distinguish between *activity* control and the *cost control* dimensions of a manager's responsibility. Activity control is involved with seeing that sales and production or service goals are met. Cost control is concerned with ensuring that sales, service and production is accomplished with the least possible costs consistent with quality standards. These are different responsibilities, and they must be kept separate in attempting to assess how well a manager is doing his or her job.

Of these two responsibilities, the static budget does a good job of determining whether or not activity control is being maintained. Look again at Exhibit 11–1. The data on the top line relate to service activity for the year. These data properly reflect the fact that activity control was exceeded since the business surpassed its goal of 5,000 client visits.

The remainder of the data in the statement deal with cost control. The problem with the report in Exhibit 11–1, as Rick immediately realized, is that it compares costs at one level of activity (5,200 client visits) to costs at a different level of activity (5,000 client visits). Since Rick had 200 more client-visits than expected his variable costs should be higher than budgeted. The static budget performance report confuses control over activity and control over costs. From Rick's standpoint, the increase in client visits was good and should be counted as a favourable variance, but the increase in activity has a negative impact on the costs in the report. Rick knew that something would have to be done to make the report more meaningful, but he was unsure of what to do. So he made an appointment to meet Victoria Kho to discuss the next step. After some discussion with Victoria Kho, Rick identified three major categories of variable overhead costs—hairstyling supplies, client gratuities, and electricity—and four major categories of fixed costs—support staff wages and salaries, rent, insurance, and utilities other than electricity. Client gratuities consist of flowers, candies, and glasses of champagne that Rick gives to his customers while they are in the salon. Rick considers electricity to be a variable cost, since almost all of the electricity in the salon is consumed in running blow dryers, curling irons, and other hairstyling equipment.

Managerial Accounting in Action

Victoria: How is the budgeting going?

Rick: Pretty well. I didn't have any trouble putting together the budget for March. At the end of the month I compared the actual costs for March with the budgeted costs, but the report isn't giving me what I really want to know.

Victoria: Because your actual level of activity didn't match your budgeted activity?

Rick: Right. I know that shouldn't affect my fixed costs, but we had a lot more clients-visits than I had expected and that had to affect my variable costs.

Victoria: So you want to know whether the actual level of activity justifies the actual costs you had in March?

Rick: Precisely.

Victoria: If you leave your reports and data with me, I can work on it later today, and by tomorrow I'll have a report to show to you. Actually, I have a styling appointment for later this week. Why don't I move my appointment up to tomorrow, and I will bring along the analysis so we can discuss it.

Rick: That's great.

Exhibit 11–2

	Budget Formula				
		RICK'S HAIRSTYLING			
		Flexible Budget			
		For the Month Ended March 31			
		Activity in Client Units			
		4,900	5,000	5,100	5,200
Sales		$147,000	$150,000	$153,000	$156,000
Less variable expenses:					
Direct material	1	4,900	5,000	5,100	5,200
Direct labour	4	19,600	20,000	20,400	20,800
Variable overhead	5.4	26,460	27,000	27,540	28,080
Selling and administrative	0.1	490	500	510	520
Total variable expenses	6.0	51,450	52,500	53,550	54,600
Contribution margin		95,550	97,500	99,450	101,400
Fixed overhead					
Manufacturing overhead		21,500	21,500	21,500	21,500
Selling and administrative		10,000	10,000	10,000	10,000
Total fixed expenses		31,500	31,500	31,500	31,500
Net income		$ 64,050	$ 66,000	$ 67,950	$ 69,900

How a Flexible Budget Works

Objective 2

Prepare a performance report for both variable and fixed overhead costs using the flexible budget approach.

The basic idea of the flexible budget is that a budget does not have to be static. Depending on the actual level of activity, a budget can be adjusted to show what costs *should be* for that specific level of activity. To illustrate how flexible budgets work, Victoria wrote a report for Rick that is simple to prepare (Exhibit 11–2). It shows how service revenue and costs can be expected to change, depending on the monthly level of activity. Within the activity range of 4,900 to 5,200 client-visits the fixed costs are expected to remain the same. For the variable costs Victoria multiplied Rick's per client costs (for example $1.00 for direct materials and $5.40 for variable overhead) by the appropriate number of client-visits in each column. For example, the $5.40 variable overhead cost was multiplied by 4,900 client-visits to give the total costs of $26,460.

At the end of a period Rick can readily compare actual results against appropriate budget figures at any service level within the relevant range. This is why the budget is called *flexible*. Rick's Hairstyling actually had 5,200 client visits during the month of March. Using the flexible budget approach the company performance is illustrated in Exhibit 11–3.

Note that in Exhibit 11–3 Victoria constructed the budget based on the *actual* number of client-visits for the month. The budget for the variable components is prepared by multiplying the actual level of activity by the variable dollar amount. For example, using the $5.40 per client-visit for variable overhead, the total cost for this item *should* be $28,080 for 5,200 client visits ($5.40 × 5,200). Since the actual cost for variable overhead was $29,720, the unfavourable variance was $1,640 rather than $2,720 reported in a static budget.

What if actual client-visits had been some odd figure such as 4,926 client visits rather than 5,200. The manager would have used the flexible budgeting formulas to develop budget figures for the 4,926 client-visit level of activity to compare against actual results. Herein lies the strength and dynamism of the flexible budget approach. A budget can be developed for any level of client-visits within the relevant range.

Exhibit 11–3

	RICK'S HAIRSTYLING Income Statement For the Month Ended March 31		
Budgeted number of client visits	5,000		
Actual number of client visits	5,200		
Client visits	**Actual 5,200**	**Budget based on 5,200**	**Variance**
Sales	$156,000	156,000	$ —
Less variable expenses:			
Direct material	5,600	5,200	400 U
Direct labour	21,000	20,800	200 U
Variable overhead	29,720	28,080	1,640 U
Selling and administrative	500	520	—
Total variable expenses	56,820	54,600	2,220 U
Contribution margin	99,180	101,400	2,220 U
Fixed overhead			
Manufacturing overhead	22,000	21,500	500 U
Selling and administrative	10,000	10,000	20 F
Total fixed expenses	32,000	31,500	500 U
Net income	$67,180	$69,900	$2,720 U

Reconciliation of Income Figures

To summarize the analysis Victoria prepared the net income figures shown in exhibit.

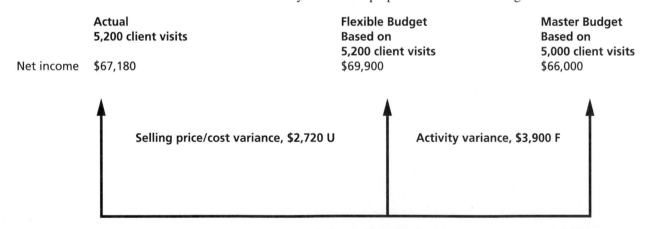

	Actual 5,200 client visits	Flexible Budget Based on 5,200 client visits	Master Budget Based on 5,000 client visits
Net income	$67,180	$69,900	$66,000

Selling price/cost variance, $2,720 U   Activity variance, $3,900 F

Activity variance The net income lost through failure to achieve the budgeted sales in units for the period.

The **activity variance** represents the net income gained (lost) through success (failure) to achieve the budgeted sales in units for the period. This variance is also known as the *sales volume variance*. It is computed by multiplying the difference between budgeted sales and actual sales (in units) by the budgeted contribution margin per unit. For Rick's Hairstyling, the computation would be:

$$(5,000 \text{ client-visits} - 5,200 \text{ client visits}) \times \$19.50^* = \$3,900$$

*$30 − $10.50 = $19.50

In short, the business gained $3,900 in contribution margin (and net income) by exceeding budgeted sales by 200 client-visits.

Selling price/cost variance Net income lost through failure to maintain control over selling price and over various costs incurred by the business.

The **selling price/cost variance** measures the net income lost through failure to maintain control over selling price and over various costs incurred by the business. The selling price element is computed by multiplying any difference between budgeted selling price and actual selling price per client-visit by the number of client-visits achieved. Because Rick's Hairstyling maintained its selling price at $30 per client-visit during March, there is no selling price variance in Exhibit 11–3. The cost element consists of the total amount of all cost variances on a company's income statement: for March, this amounted to $2,720 for Rick's Hairstyling (see Exhibit 11–3).

Using Flexible Budgeting for Overhead Control

Flexible budgeting can also be applied to focus attention on specific cost or revenue items. If Rick is concerned with overhead, for example, then the $5.40 variable cost shown earlier may be broken down into its individual components. For variable overhead costs, the per-client costs consists of $1.20 for hairstyling supplies, $4.00 for client gratuities, and $0.20 for electricity. Rick has asked Victoria to prepare an additional flexible budget performance report focusing on overhead costs.

Managerial Accounting in Action

THE ISSUE

The following discussion took place the next day at Rick's salon.

Victoria: Let's see what I've got. I multiplied the costs per client-visit for each overhead item by the actual number of client visits you had in March.
Rick: That is what you labelled the "budget based on 5,200 Client-Visits"?
Victoria: That's right. The original budget based on 5,000 client-visits understates what the variable costs should be when you actually serve 5,200 clients. We should expect the variable overhead costs to be higher at a higher level of customer service.
Rick: Why are some of my actual fixed costs different from what I budgeted? Doesn't fixed mean that they don't change?
Victoria: We call these costs fixed because they should not be affected by changes in the level of activity. However, they can change for other reasons. For example, your utilities bill, which included natural gas for heating, varies with the weather.
Rick: I see. A warmer than normal March gave me lower utilities bills than expected.
Victoria: The use of the term fixed also suggests that the costs can't be controlled, but that isn't true. It may be easier to control fixed costs than variable costs. For example, you can easily change your insurance bill by adjusting the amount of insurance you carry. It would be more difficult to have much effect on the variable electric bill, which is a necessary part of serving customers.
Rick: I think I understand but it is confusing.
Victoria: Just remember that a variable costs changes in proportion to activity but fixed costs do not depend on the level of activity. Fixed costs can change for reasons unrelated to activity. Also, controllability has little to do about whether a cost is variable or fixed. Fixed costs are often more controllable than variable costs.

Budgeted number of client-visits	5,000			
Actual number of client-visits	5,200			

Overhead Costs	Cost Formula (per client-visit)	Actual Costs Incurred for 5,200 Client-Visits	Budget Based on 5,200 Client-Visits	Variance
Variable overhead costs:				
Hairstyling supplies	$1.20	$ 6,400	$ 6,240	$ 160 U
Client gratuities	4.00	22,300	20,800	1,500 U
Electricity (variable)	0.20	1,020	1,040	20 F
Total variable overhead cost	$5.40	29,720	28,080	1,640 U

Fixed overhead costs:			
Support staff wages and salaries	8,100	8,000	100 U
Rent	12,000	12,000	–0–
Insurance	1,000	1,000	–0–
Utilities other than electricity	470	500	30 F
Total fixed overhead cost	21,570	21,500	70 U
Total overhead cost	$51,290	$49,580	$1,710 U

Using the flexible budget approach, Rick Manzi now has a much better way of assessing whether overhead costs are under control. The analysis is not so simple, however, in companies that provide a variety of products and services. The number of units produced or customers served may not be an adequate measure of overall activity. For example, does it make sense to count a Sony floppy diskette, worth a few dollars, as equivalent to a large-screen Sony TV? If the number of units produced is used as a measure of overall activity, then the floppy diskette and the large-screen TV will be counted as equivalent. Clearly, the number of units produced (or customers served) may not be appropriate as an overall measure of activity when the organization produces a variety of products or services; a common denominator may be needed.

The Measure of Activity—A Critical Choice

What should be used as the measure of activity when the company produces a variety of products and services? At least three factors are important in selecting an activity base for an overhead flexible budget:

1. There should be a causal relationship between the activity base and variable overhead costs. Changes in the activity base should cause, or at least be highly correlated with, changes in the variable overhead costs in the flexible budget. Ideally, the variable overhead costs in the flexible budget should vary in direct proportion to changes in the activity base. For example, in a carpentry shop specializing in handmade wood furniture, the costs of miscellaneous supplies such as glue, wooden dowels, and sandpaper can be expected to vary with the number of direct labour-hours. Direct labour-hours would therefore be a good measure of activity to use in a flexible budget for the costs of such supplies.
2. The activity base should not be expressed in dollars or other currency. For example, direct labour cost is usually a poor choice for an activity base in flexible budgets. Changes in wage rates affect the activity base but do not usually result in a proportionate change in overhead. For example, we would not ordinarily expect to see a 5% increase in the consumption of glue in a carpentry shop if the workers receive a 5% increase in pay. Therefore, it is normally best to use physical rather than financial measures of activity in flexible budgets.
3. The activity base should be simple and easily understood. A base that is not easily understood will probably result in confusion and misunderstanding. It is difficult to control costs if people don't understand the reports or do not accept them as valid.

Variable Overhead Variances—A Closer Look

A special problem arises when the flexible budget is based on *hours* of activity (such as direct labour-hours) rather than on units of product or number of customers served. The problem relates to whether actual hours or standard hours should be used to develop the flexible budget on the performance report.

The Problem of Actual versus Standard Hours

The nature of the problem can best be seen through a specific example. MicroDrive Corporation is an automated manufacturer of precision personal computer disk-drive motors. Data concerning the company's variable manufacturing overhead costs are shown in Exhibit 11–4.

MicroDrive Corporation uses machine-hours as the activity base in its flexible budget. Based on the budgeted production of 25,000 motors and the standard of 2 machine-hours per motor, the budgeted level of activity was 50,000 machine-hours. However, actual production for the year was only 20,000 motors, and 42,000 hours of machine time were used to produce these motors. According to the standard, only 40,000 hours of machine time should have been used (40,000 hours = 2 hours per motor × 20,000 motors).

In preparing an overhead performance report for the year, MicroDrive could use the 42,000 machine-hours actually worked during the year *or* the 40,000 machine-hours that should have been worked according to the standard. If the actual hours are used, only a spending variance will be computed. If the standard hours are used, both a spending *and* an efficiency variance will be computed. Both of these approaches are illustrated in the following sections.

Spending Variance Alone

If MicroDrive Corporation bases its overhead performance report on the 42,000 machine-hours actually worked during the year, then the performance report will show only a spending variance for variable overhead. A performance report prepared in this way is shown in Exhibit 11–5.

The formula for the spending variance was introduced in the preceding chapter. That formula is:

Objective 3

Use the flexible budget to prepare a variable overhead performance report containing only a spending variance.

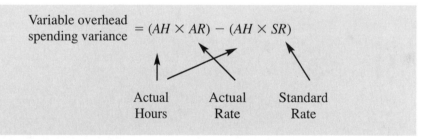

$$\text{Variable overhead spending variance} = (AH \times AR) - (AH \times SR)$$

Actual Hours　　　Actual Rate　　　Standard Rate

Exhibit 11–4

MicroDrive Corporation Data

Budgeted production	25,000	motors
Actual production	20,000	motors
Standard machine-hours per motor	2	machine-hours per motor
Budgeted machine-hours (2 × 25,000)	50,000	machine-hours
Standard machine-hours allowed for the actual production (2 × 20,000)	40,000	machine-hours
Actual machine-hours	42,000	machine-hours
Variable overhead costs per machine-hour:		
Indirect labour	$0.80	per machine-hour
Lubricants	0.30	per machine-hour
Power	0.40	per machine-hour
Actual total variable overhead costs:		
Indirect labour	$36,000	
Lubricants	11,000	
Power	24,000	
Total actual variable overhead cost	$71,000	

Exhibit 11–5

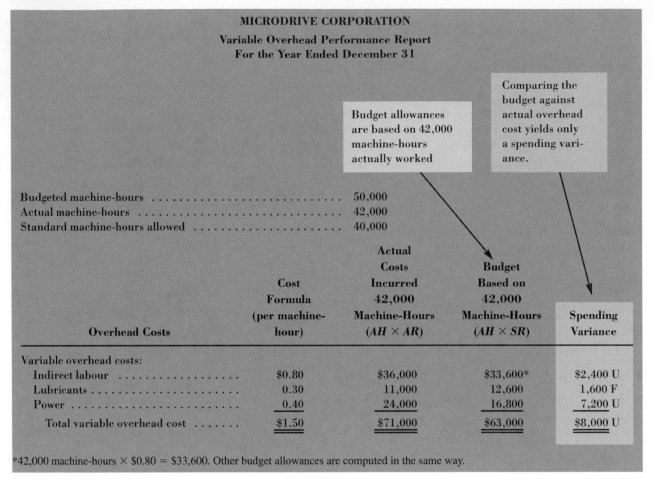

MICRODRIVE CORPORATION
Variable Overhead Performance Report
For the Year Ended December 31

> Budget allowances are based on 42,000 machine-hours actually worked

> Comparing the budget against actual overhead cost yields only a spending variance.

Budgeted machine-hours 50,000
Actual machine-hours 42,000
Standard machine-hours allowed 40,000

Overhead Costs	Cost Formula (per machine-hour)	Actual Costs Incurred 42,000 Machine-Hours (AH × AR)	Budget Based on 42,000 Machine-Hours (AH × SR)	Spending Variance
Variable overhead costs:				
Indirect labour	$0.80	$36,000	$33,600*	$2,400 U
Lubricants	0.30	11,000	12,600	1,600 F
Power	0.40	24,000	16,800	7,200 U
Total variable overhead cost	$1.50	$71,000	$63,000	$8,000 U

*42,000 machine-hours × $0.80 = $33,600. Other budget allowances are computed in the same way.

Or, in factored form:

$$\text{Variable overhead spending variance} = AH\,(AR - SR)$$

The report in Exhibit 11–5 is structured around the first, or unfactored, format.

INTERPRETING THE SPENDING VARIANCE   The variable overhead spending variance is useful only if the cost driver for variable overhead really is the actual hours worked. Then the flexible budget based on the actual hours worked is a valid benchmark that tells us how much *should* have been spent in total on variable overhead items during the period. The actual overhead costs would be larger than this benchmark, resulting in an unfavourable variance, if either (1) the variable overhead items cost more to purchase than the standards allow or (2) more variable overhead items were used than the standards allow. So the spending variance includes both price and quantity variances. In principle, these variances could be separately reported, but this is seldom done. Ordinarily, the price element in this variance will be small, so the variance will mainly be influenced by how efficiently variable overhead resources such as production supplies are used.

Exhibit 11-6

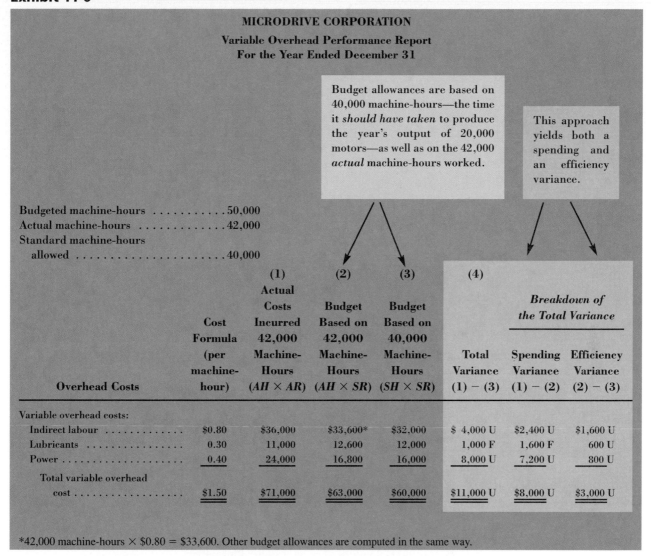

MICRODRIVE CORPORATION
Variable Overhead Performance Report
For the Year Ended December 31

Budget allowances are based on 40,000 machine-hours—the time it *should have taken* to produce the year's output of 20,000 motors—as well as on the 42,000 *actual* machine-hours worked.

This approach yields both a spending and an efficiency variance.

Budgeted machine-hours 50,000
Actual machine-hours 42,000
Standard machine-hours
  allowed 40,000

Overhead Costs	Cost Formula (per machine-hour)	(1) Actual Costs Incurred 42,000 Machine-Hours (AH × AR)	(2) Budget Based on 42,000 Machine-Hours (AH × SR)	(3) Budget Based on 40,000 Machine-Hours (SH × SR)	(4) Total Variance (1) − (3)	Breakdown of the Total Variance — Spending Variance (1) − (2)	Breakdown of the Total Variance — Efficiency Variance (2) − (3)
Variable overhead costs:							
Indirect labour	$0.80	$36,000	$33,600*	$32,000	$ 4,000 U	$2,400 U	$1,600 U
Lubricants	0.30	11,000	12,600	12,000	1,000 F	1,600 F	600 U
Power	0.40	24,000	16,800	16,000	8,000 U	7,200 U	800 U
Total variable overhead cost	$1.50	$71,000	$63,000	$60,000	$11,000 U	$8,000 U	$3,000 U

*42,000 machine-hours × $0.80 = $33,600. Other budget allowances are computed in the same way.

Both Spending and Efficiency Variances

Objective 4

Use the flexible budget to prepare a variable overhead performance report containing both a spending and an efficiency variance.

If management of MicroDrive Corporation wants both a spending and an efficiency variance for variable overhead, then it should compute budget allowances for *both* the 40,000 machine-hour and the 42,000 machine-hour levels of activity. A performance report prepared in this way is shown in Exhibit 11–6.

Note from Exhibit 11–6 that the spending variance is the same as the spending variance shown in Exhibit 11–5. The performance report in Exhibit 11–6 has simply been expanded to include an efficiency variance as well. Together, the spending and efficiency variances make up the total variance.

INTERPRETING THE EFFICIENCY VARIANCE Like the variable overhead spending, the variable overhead efficiency variance is useful only if the cost driver for variable overhead really is the actual hours worked. Then any increase in hours actually worked should result in additional variable overhead costs. Consequently, if too many hours were used to create the actual output, this is likely to result in an increase in variable overhead. The variable overhead efficiency variance is an estimate of the effect on variable overhead costs of inefficiency in the use of the base (i.e., hours). In a sense, the term *variable overhead efficiency variance* is a misnomer. It seems to suggest that it measures the efficiency with which variable overhead resources were used. It does not. It is an estimate of the indirect effect on variable overhead costs of inefficiency in the use of the activity base.

Recall from the preceding chapter that the variable overhead efficiency variance is a function of the difference between the actual hours incurred and the hours that should have been used to produce the period's output:

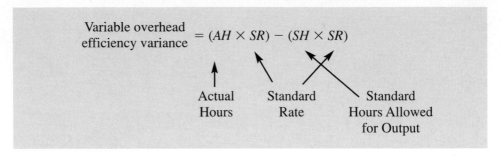

$$\text{Variable overhead efficiency variance} = (AH \times SR) - (SH \times SR)$$

Actual Hours   Standard Rate   Standard Hours Allowed for Output

Or, in factored form:

$$\text{Variable overhead efficiency variance} = SR(AH - SH)$$

If more hours are worked than are allowed at standard, then the overhead efficiency variance will be unfavourable. However, as discussed above, the inefficiency is not in the use of overhead *but rather in the use of the base itself.*

This point can be illustrated by looking again at Exhibit 11–6. Two thousand more machine-hours were used during the period than should have been used to produce the period's output. Each of these hours presumably required the incurrence of $1.50 of variable overhead cost, resulting in an unfavourable variance of $3,000 (2,000 hours $\times$ $1.50 = $3,000). Although this $3,000 variance is called an overhead efficiency variance, it could better be called a machine-hours efficiency variance, since it results from using too many machine-hours rather than from inefficient use of overhead resources. However, the term *overhead efficiency variance* is so firmly ingrained in day-to-day use that a change is unlikely. Even so, be careful to interpret the variance with a clear understanding of what it really measures.

CONTROL OF THE EFFICIENCY VARIANCE   Who is responsible for control of the overhead efficiency variance? Since the variance really reflects efficiency in the utilization of the base underlying the flexible budget, whoever is responsible for control of this base is responsible for control of the variance. If the base is direct labour-hours, then the supervisor responsible for the use of labour time will be responsible for any overhead efficiency variance.

Activity-Based Costing and the Flexible Budget

It is unlikely that all of the variable overhead in a complex organization is driven by a single factor such as the number of units produced or the number of labour-hours or machine-hours. Activity-based costing provides a way of recognizing a variety of overhead cost drivers and thereby increasing the accuracy of the costing system. In activity-based costing, each overhead cost pool has its own measure of activity. The actual spending in each overhead cost pool can be independently evaluated using the techniques discussed in this chapter. The only difference is that the cost formulas for variable overhead costs will be stated in terms of different kinds of activities instead of all being stated in terms of units or a common measure of activity such as direct labour-hours or machine-hours. If done properly, activity-based costing can greatly enhance the usefulness of overhead performance reports by recognizing multiple causes of overhead costs. But the usefulness of overhead performance reports depends on how carefully the reports are done. In particular, managers must take care to separate the variable from the fixed costs in the flexible budgets.[1]

Focus on Current Practice

Caterpillar, Inc., a manufacturer of heavy equipment and a pioneering company in the development and use of activity-based costing, divides its overhead costs into three large pools—the logistics cost pool, the manufacturing cost pool, and the general cost pool. In turn, these three cost pools are subdivided into scores of activity centres, with each centre having its own flexible budget from which variable and fixed overhead rates are developed. In an article describing the company's cost system, the systems manager stated that "the many manufacturing cost centre rates are the unique elements that set Caterpillar's system apart from simple cost systems."[2] ■

Overhead Rates and Fixed Overhead Analysis

The detailed analysis of fixed overhead differs considerably from the analysis of variable overhead, simply because of the difference in the nature of the costs involved. To provide a background for our discussion, we will first review briefly the need for, and computation of, predetermined overhead rates. This review will be helpful, since the predetermined overhead rate plays a major role in fixed overhead analysis. We will then show how fixed overhead variances are computed and make some observations as to their usefulness to managers.

Flexible Budgets and Overhead Rates

Objective 5

Explain the significance of the denominator activity figure in determining the standard cost of a unit of product.

Fixed costs come in large, indivisible pieces that by definition do not change with changes in the level of activity within the relevant range. As we learned in Chapter 3, this creates a problem in product costing, since a given level of fixed overhead cost spread over a small number of units will result in a higher cost per unit than if the same amount of cost is spread over a large number of units. Consider the data in the following table:

Month	(1) Fixed Overhead Cost	(2) Number of Units Produced	(3) Unit Cost (1)÷(2)
January	$6,000	1,000	$6.00
February	6,000	1,500	4.00
March	6,000	800	7.50

Notice that the large number of units produced in February results in a low unit cost ($4.00), whereas the small number of units produced in March results in a high unit cost ($7.50). This problem arises only in connection with the fixed portion of overhead, since by definition the variable portion of overhead remains constant on a per unit basis, rising and falling in total proportionately with changes in the activity

1. See Mak and Roush, "Managing Activity Costs with Flexible Budgeting and Variance Analysis," *Accounting Horizons* (September 1996), pp. 141–46, for an insightful discussion of activity-based costing and overhead variance analysis.
2. Lou F. Jones, "Product Costing at Caterpillar," *Management Accounting* 72, no. 8 (February 1991), p. 39.

level. Most managers feel that the fixed portion of unit cost should be stabilized so that a single unit cost figure can be used throughout the year. As we learned in Chapter 3, this stability can be accomplished through use of the predetermined overhead rate.

Throughout the remainder of this chapter, we will be analyzing the fixed overhead costs of MicroDrive Corporation. To assist us in that task, the flexible budget of the company—including fixed costs—is displayed in Exhibit 11–7. Note that the total fixed overhead costs amount to $300,000 within the range of activity in the flexible budget.

DENOMINATOR ACTIVITY　The formula that we used in Chapter 3 to compute the predetermined overhead rate is given below

$$\text{Predetermined overhead rate} = \frac{\text{Estimated total manufacturing overhead cost}}{\text{Estimated total units in the base (MH, DLH, etc.)}}$$

Denominator activity
The activity figure used to compute the predetermined overhead rate.

The estimated total units in the base in the formula for the predetermined overhead rate is called the **denominator activity.** Recall from our discussion in Chapter 3 that once an estimated activity level (denominator activity) has been chosen, it remains unchanged throughout the year, even if the actual activity turns out to be different from what was estimated. The reason for not changing the denominator is to maintain stability in the amount of overhead applied to each unit of product regardless of when it is produced during the year.

COMPUTING THE OVERHEAD RATE　When we discussed predetermined overhead rates in Chapter 3, we didn't explain how the estimated total manufacturing cost was determined. This figure can be derived from the flexible budget. Once the denominator level of activity has been chosen, the flexible budget can be used to determine the total amount of overhead cost that should be incurred at that level of activity. The predetermined overhead rate can then be computed using the following variation on the basic formula for the predetermined overhead rate:

Exhibit 11–7

MICRODRIVE CORPORATION
Flexible Budgets at Various Levels of Activity

Overhead Costs	Cost Formula (per machine-hour)	Activity (in machine-hours)			
		40,000	45,000	50,000	55,000
Variable overhead costs:					
Indirect labour	$0.80	$ 32,000	$ 36,000	$ 40,000	$ 44,000
Lubricants	0.30	12,000	13,500	15,000	16,500
Power	0.40	16,000	18,000	20,000	22,000
Total variable overhead cost	$1.50	60,000	67,500	75,000	82,500
Fixed overhead costs:					
Depreciation		100,000	100,000	100,000	100,000
Supervisory salaries		160,000	160,000	160,000	160,000
Insurance		40,000	40,000	40,000	40,000
Total fixed overhead cost		300,000	300,000	300,000	300,000
Total overhead cost		$360,000	$367,500	$375,000	$382,500

$$\text{Predetermined overhead rate} = \frac{\text{Overhead from the flexible budget at the denominator level of activity}}{\text{Denominator level of activity}}$$

To illustrate, refer to MicroDrive Corporation's flexible budget for manufacturing overhead in Exhibit 11–7. Suppose that the budgeted activity level for the year is 50,000 machine-hours and that this will be used as the denominator activity in the formula for the predetermined overhead rate. The numerator in the formula is the estimated total overhead cost of $375,000 when the activity is 50,000 machine-hours. This figure is taken from the flexible budget in Exhibit 11–7. In sum, the predetermined overhead rate for MicroDrive Corporation will be computed as follows:

$$\frac{\$375,000}{50,000 \text{ MH}} = \$7.50 \text{ per machine-hour}$$

Or the company can break its predetermined overhead rate down into variable and fixed elements rather than using a single combined figure:

$$\text{Variable element: } \frac{\$75,000}{50,000 \text{ MH}} = \$1.50 \text{ per machine-hour (MH)}$$

$$\text{Fixed element: } \frac{\$300,000}{50,000 \text{ MH}} = \$6 \text{ per machine-hour (MH)}$$

For every standard machine-hour of operation, work in process will be charged with $7.50 of overhead, of which $1.50 will be variable overhead and $6.00 will be fixed overhead. If a disk-drive motor should take two machine-hours to complete, then its cost will include $3 variable overhead and $12 fixed overhead, as shown on the following standard cost card:

Standard Cost Card—Per Motor

Direct materials (assumed)	$14
Direct labour (assumed)	6
Variable overhead (2 machine-hours at $1.50)	3
Fixed overhead (2 machine-hours at $6)	12
Total standard cost per motor	$35

In summary, the flexible budget provides the estimated overhead cost needed to compute the predetermined overhead rate. Thus, the flexible budget plays a key role in determining the amount of fixed and variable overhead cost that will be charged to units of product.

Overhead Application in a Standard Cost System

Objective 6

Apply overhead cost to units of product in a standard cost system.

To understand the fixed overhead variances, it is necessary first to understand how overhead is applied to work in process in a standard cost system. In Chapter 3, recall that we applied overhead to work in process on the basis of actual hours of activity (multiplied by the predetermined overhead rate). This procedure was correct, since at the time we were dealing with a normal cost system.[3] However, we are now dealing with a standard cost system. In such a system, overhead is applied to work in process on the basis of the *standard hours allowed for the output of the period* rather than on the basis of the actual number of hours worked. This point is illustrated in Exhibit 11–8. In a standard cost system, every unit of product moving along the production

---

3. Normal cost systems are discussed in Chapter 3.

Exhibit 11–8 Applied Overhead Costs: Normal Cost System versus Standard Cost System

Normal Cost System		Standard Cost System	
Manufacturing Overhead		**Manufacturing Overhead**	
Actual overhead costs incurred.	Applied overhead costs: Actual hours × Pre-determined overhead rate.	Actual overhead costs incurred.	Applied overhead costs: Standard hours allowed for output × Predetermined overhead rate.
	Under- or overapplied overhead		Under- or overapplied overhead

line bears the same amount of overhead cost, regardless of any variations in efficiency that may have been involved in its production.

The Fixed Overhead Variances

Objective 7

Compute and interpret the fixed overhead budget and volume variances.

To illustrate the computation of fixed overhead variances, we will refer again to the data for MicroDrive Corporation.

Denominator activity in machine-hours	50,000
Budgeted fixed overhead costs	$300,000
Fixed portion of the predetermined overhead rate (computed earlier)	$6

Let us assume that the following actual operating results were recorded for the year:

Actual machine-hours	42,000
Standard machine-hours allowed*	40,000
Actual fixed overhead costs:	
Depreciation	$100,000
Supervisory salaries	172,000
Insurance	36,000
Total actual cost	$308,000

*For the actual production of the year.

From these data, two variances can be computed for fixed overhead—a *budget variance* and a *volume variance*. The variances are shown in Exhibit 11–9.

Notice from the exhibit that overhead has been applied to work in process on the basis of 40,000 standard hours allowed for the output of the year rather than on the basis of 42,000 actual hours worked. As stated earlier, this keeps unit costs from being affected by any variations in efficiency.

The Budget Variance—A Closer Look

Budget variance A measure of the difference between the actual fixed overhead costs incurred during the period and budgeted fixed overhead costs as contained in the flexible budget.

The **budget variance** is the difference between the actual fixed overhead costs incurred during the period and the budgeted fixed overhead costs as contained in the flexible budget. It can be computed as shown in Exhibit 11–9 or by using the following formula:

$$\text{Budget variance} = \text{Actual fixed overhead cost} - \text{Flexible budget fixed overhead cost}$$

Exhibit 11–9
Computation of the Fixed
Overhead Variances

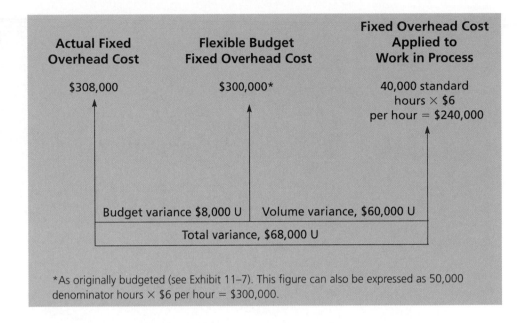

*As originally budgeted (see Exhibit 11–7). This figure can also be expressed as 50,000 denominator hours × $6 per hour = $300,000.

Applying this formula to MicroDrive Corporation, the budget variance would be as follows:

$$\$308,000 - \$300,000 = \$8,000 \text{ U}$$

The variances computed for the fixed costs at Rick's Hairstyling in Exhibit 11–2 are all budget variances, since they represent the difference between the actual fixed overhead cost and the budgeted fixed overhead cost from the flexible budget.

An expanded overhead performance report for MicroDrive Corporation appears in Exhibit 11–10. This report now includes the budget variances for fixed overhead as well as the spending variances for variable overhead that were in Exhibit 11–5.

The budget variances for fixed overhead can be very useful, since they represent the difference between how much *should* have been spent (according to the flexible budget) and how much was actually spent. For example, supervisory salaries has a $12,000 unfavourable variance. There should be some explanation for this large variance. Was it due to an increase in salaries? Was it due to overtime? Was another supervisor hired? If so, why was another supervisor hired—this was not included in the budget when activity for the year was planned.

The Volume Variance—A Closer Look

Volume variance The variance that arises whenever the standard hours allowed for the output of a period are different from the denominator activity level that was used to compute the predetermined overhead rate.

The **volume variance** is a measure of utilization of plant facilities. The variance arises whenever the standard hours allowed for the output of a period are different from the denominator activity level that was planned when the period began. It can be computed as shown in Exhibit 11–9 or by means of the following formula:

$$\begin{array}{c} \text{Volume} \\ \text{variance} \end{array} = \begin{array}{c} \text{Fixed portion of} \\ \text{the predetermined} \\ \text{overhead rate} \end{array} \times \left(\begin{array}{c} \text{Denominator} \\ \text{hours} \end{array} - \begin{array}{c} \text{Standard hours} \\ \text{allowed} \end{array} \right)$$

Applying this formula to MicroDrive Corporation, the volume variance would be computed as follows:

$$\$6 \text{ per MH } (50,000 \text{ MH} - 40,000 \text{ MH}) = \$60,000 \text{ U}$$

Exhibit 11–10 Fixed Overhead Costs on the Overhead Performance Report

MICRODRIVE CORPORATION
Overhead Performance Report
For the Year Ended December 31

Budgeted machine-hours 50,000
Actual machine-hours 42,000
Standard machine-hours allowed 40,000

Overhead Costs	Cost Formula (per machine-hour)	Actual Costs 42,000 Machine-Hours	Budget Based on 42,000 Machine-Hours	Spending or Budget Variance
Variable overhead costs:				
Indirect labour	$0.80	$ 36,000	$ 33,600	$ 2,400 U
Lubricants	0.30	11,000	12,600	1,600 F
Power	0.40	24,000	16,800	7,200 U
Total variable overhead cost	$1.50	71,000	63,000	8,000 U
Fixed overhead costs:				
Depreciation		100,000	100,000	—
Supervisory salaries		172,000	160,000	12,000 U
Insurance		36,000	40,000	4,000 F
Total fixed overhead cost		308,000	300,000	8,000 U
Total overhead cost		$379,000	$363,000	$16,000 U

Note that this computation agrees with the volume variance as shown in Exhibit 11–9. As stated earlier, the volume variance is a measure of utilization of available plant facilities. An unfavourable variance, as above, means that the company operated at an activity level *below* that planned for the period. A favourable variance would mean that the company operated at an activity level *greater* than that planned for the period.

It is important to note that the volume variance does not measure over- or under-spending. A company normally would incur the same dollar amount of fixed overhead cost regardless of whether the period's activity was above or below the planned (denominator) level. In short, the volume variance is an activity-related variance. It is explainable only by activity and is controllable only through activity.

To summarize:

1. If the denominator activity and the standard hours allowed for the output of the period are the same, then there is no volume variance.
2. If the denominator activity is greater than the standard hours allowed for the output of the period, then the volume variance is unfavourable, signifying an underutilization of available facilities.
3. If the denominator activity is less than the standard hours allowed for the output of the period, then the volume variance is favourable, signifying a higher utilization of available facilities than was planned.

Graphic Analysis of Fixed Overhead Variances

Some insights into the budget and volume variances can be gained through graphic analysis. A graph containing these variances is presented in Exhibit 11–11.

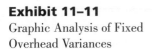

Exhibit 11–11

Graphic Analysis of Fixed
Overhead Variances

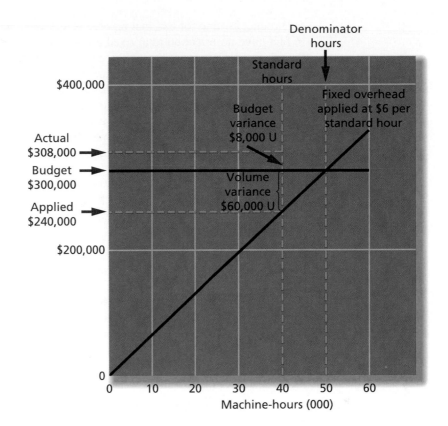

As shown in the graph, fixed overhead cost is applied to work in process at the predetermined rate of $6 for each standard hour of activity. (The applied-cost line is the upward-sloping line on the graph.) Since a denominator level of 50,000 machine-hours was used in computing the $6 rate, the applied-cost line crosses the budget-cost line at exactly the 50,000 machine-hour point. Thus, if the denominator hours and the standard hours allowed for the output are the same, there can be no volume variance, since the applied-cost line and the budget-cost line will exactly meet on the graph. It is only when the standard hours differ from the denominator hours that a volume variance can arise.

In the case at hand, the standard hours allowed for the actual output (40,000 hours) are less than the denominator hours (50,000 hours); the result is an unfavourable volume variance, since less cost was applied to production than was originally budgeted. If the situation had been reversed and the standard hours allowed for the actual output had exceeded the denominator hours, then the volume variance on the graph would have been favourable.

Cautions in Fixed Overhead Analysis

The reason we get a volume variance for fixed overhead is that the total fixed cost does not depend on activity; yet when applying the costs to work in process, we act *as if* the fixed costs were variable and depended on activity. This point can be seen from the graph in Exhibit 11–11. Notice from the graph that the fixed overhead costs are applied to work in process at a rate of $6 per hour *as if* they were variable. Treating these costs as if they were variable is necessary for product costing purposes, but there are some real dangers here. The manager can easily become misled and start thinking of the fixed costs as if they were *in fact* variable.

The manager must keep clearly in mind that fixed overhead costs come in large, indivisible pieces. Expressing fixed costs on a unit or per hour basis, though necessary for product costing for external reports, is artificial. Increases or decreases in activity in fact have no effect on total fixed costs within the relevant range of activity. Even though fixed costs are expressed on a unit or per hour basis, they are *not* proportional to activity. In a sense, the volume variance is the error that occurs as a result of treating fixed costs as variable costs in the costing system.

Because of the confusion that can arise concerning the interpretation of the volume variance, some companies present the volume variance in physical units (hours) rather than in dollars. These companies feel that stating the variance in physical units gives management a clearer signal concerning the cause of the variance.

Overhead Variances and Under- or Overapplied Overhead Cost

Four variances relating to overhead cost have been computed for MicroDrive Corporation in this chapter. These four variances are as follows:

Variable overhead spending variance (p. 544) ..	$ 8,000 U
Variable overhead efficiency variance (p. 545)..	3,000 U
Fixed overhead budget variance (p. 551)	8,000 U
Fixed overhead volume variance (p. 551)	60,000 U
Total overhead variance	$79,000 U

Recall from Chapter 3 that under- or overapplied overhead is the difference between the amount of overhead applied to products and the actual overhead costs incurred during a period. Basically, the overhead variances we have computed in this chapter break the under- or overapplied overhead down into variances that can be used by managers for control purposes. Consequently, *the sum of the overhead variances equals the under- or overapplied overhead cost for a period.*

Furthermore, in a standard cost system, unfavourable variances are equivalent to underapplied overhead and favourable variances are equivalent to overapplied overhead. Unfavourable variances occur because more was spent on overhead than the standards allow. Underapplied overhead occurs when more was spent on overhead than was applied to products during the period. But in a standard costing system, the standard amount of overhead allowed is exactly the same amount of overhead applied to products. Therefore, in a standard costing system, unfavourable variances and underapplied overhead are the same thing, as are favourable variances and overapplied overhead.

For MicroDrive Corporation, the total overhead variance was $79,000 unfavourable. Therefore, its overhead cost was underapplied by $79,000 for the year. To solidify this point in your mind, *carefully study the review problem at the end of the chapter!* This review problem provides a comprehensive summary of overhead analysis, including the computation of under- or overapplied overhead cost in a standard cost system.

Review Problem: Overhead Analysis

(This problem provides a comprehensive review of Chapter 11, including the computation of under- or overapplied overhead and its breakdown into the four overhead variances.)

Data for the manufacturing overhead of Aspen Company are given below:

Overhead Costs	Cost Formula (per machine-hour)	Machine-Hours 5,000	6,000	7,000
Variable overhead costs:				
Supplies	$0.20	$ 1,000	$ 1,200	$ 1,400
Indirect labour	0.30	1,500	1,800	2,100
Total variable overhead cost	$0.50	2,500	3,000	3,500
Fixed overhead costs:				
Depreciation		4,000	4,000	4,000
Supervision		5,000	5,000	5,000
Total fixed overhead cost		9,000	9,000	9,000
Total overhead cost		$11,500	$12,000	$12,500

Five hours of machine time are required per unit of product. The company has set denominator activity for the coming period at 6,000 machine-hours (or 1,200 units). The computation of the predetermined overhead rate would be as follows:

$$\text{Total:} \frac{\$12,000}{6,000 \text{ MH}} = \$2.00 \text{ per machine-hour}$$

$$\text{Variable element:} \frac{\$3,000}{6,000 \text{ MH}} = \$0.50 \text{ per machine-hour}$$

$$\text{Fixed element:} \frac{\$9,000}{6,000 \text{ MH}} = \$1.50 \text{ per machine-hour}$$

Assume the following *actual* results for the period:

Number of units produced	1,300 units
Actual machine-hours	6,800 machine-hours
Standard machine-hours allowed*	6,500 machine-hours
Actual variable overhead cost	$4,200
Actual fixed overhead cost	9,400

*1,300 units × 5 machine-hours per unit.

Therefore, the company's Manufacturing Overhead account would appear as follows at the end of the period:

Manufacturing Overhead

Actual overhead costs	13,600*	13,000†	Applied overhead costs
Underapplied overhead	600		

* $4,200 variable + $9,400 fixed = $13,600

† 6,500 standard hours × $2 per machine hour = $13,000. In a standard cost system, overhead is applied on the basis of standard hours, not actual hours.

Analyze the $600 underapplied overhead in terms of:

1. A variable overhead spending variance.
2. A variable overhead efficiency variance.
3. A fixed overhead budget variance.
4. A fixed overhead volume variance.

Variable Overhead Variances

These same variances in the alternative format would be as follows:

Variable overhead spending variance:

$$\text{Spending variance} = (AH \times AR) - (AH \times SR)$$
$$(\$4,200^*) - (6,800 \text{ hours} \times \$0.50 \text{ per hour}) = \$800 \text{ U}$$

*$AH \times AR$ equals the total actual cost for the period.

Variable overhead efficiency variance:

$$\text{Efficiency variance} = SR(AH - SH)$$
$$\$0.50 \text{ per hour } (6,800 \text{ hours} - 6,500 \text{ hours}) = \$150 \text{ U}$$

Fixed Overhead Variances

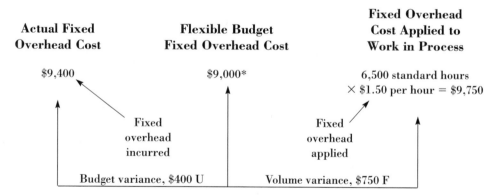

*Can be expressed as: 6,000 denominator hours $\times$ \$1.50 per hour = \$9,000.

These same variances in the alternative format would be as follows:

Fixed overhead budget variance:

$$\frac{\text{Budget}}{\text{variance}} = \frac{\text{Actual fixed}}{\text{overhead cost}} - \frac{\text{Flexible budget}}{\text{fixed overhead cost}}$$

$$\$9,400 - \$9,000 = \$400 \text{ U}$$

Fixed overhead volume variance:

$$\text{Volume variance} = \frac{\text{Fixed portion}}{\text{of the predetermined}} \times \frac{(\text{Denominator hours} -}{\text{Standard hours})}$$
$$\text{overhead rate}$$

$$\$1.50 \text{ per hour } (6,000 \text{ hours} - 6,500 \text{ hours}) = \$750 \text{ F}$$

Summary of Variances

A summary of the four overhead variances is given below:

Variable overhead:
    Spending variance .... $800 U
    Efficiency variance .... 150 U

Fixed overhead:
    Budget variance .... 400 U
    Volume variance .... __750 F__
    Underapplied overhead $600

Notice that the $600 summary variance figure agrees with the underapplied balance in the company's Manufacturing Overhead account. This agreement verifies the accuracy of our variance analysis.

Questions

11–1   What is a static budget?

11–2   What is a flexible budget and how does it differ from a static budget?

11–3   What does the activity variance measure and how is it computed?

11–4   Name three criteria that should be considered in choosing an activity base on which to construct a flexible budget.

11–5   In comparing budgeted data with actual data in a performance report for variable overhead, what variance(s) will be produced if the budgeted data are based on actual hours worked? On both actual hours worked and standard hours allowed?

11–6   What is meant by the term *standard hours allowed?*

11–7   How does the variable manufacturing overhead spending variance differ from the materials price variance?

11–8   Why is the term *overhead efficiency variance* a misnomer?

11–9   In what way is the flexible budget involved in product costing?

11–10   What is meant by the term *denominator level of activity?*

11–11   Why do we apply overhead to work in process on the basis of standard hours allowed in Chapter 11 when we applied it on the basis of actual hours in Chapter 3? What is the difference in costing systems between the two chapters?

11–12   In a standard cost system, what two variances are computed for fixed manufacturing overhead?

11–13   What does the fixed overhead budget variance measure?

11–14   Under what circumstances would you expect the volume variance to be favourable? Unfavourable? Does the variance measure deviations in spending for fixed overhead items? Explain.

11–15   How might the volume variance be measured, other than in dollars?

11–16   What dangers are there in expressing fixed costs on a per unit basis?

11–17   In Chapter 3, you became acquainted with the concept of under- or overapplied overhead. The under- or overapplied overhead can be broken down into what four variances?

11–18   If factory overhead is overapplied for August, would you expect the total of the overhead variances to be favourable or unfavourable?

Exercises

E11–1   An incomplete flexible budget is given below for Lavage Rapide, a Swiss company that owns and operates a large automatic carwash facility near Geneva. The Swiss currency is the Swiss franc, which is denoted by SFr.

LAVAGE RAPIDE
Flexible Budget
For the Month Ended August 31

Overhead Costs	Cost Formula (per car)	Activity(cars)		
		8,000	9,000	10,000
Variable overhead costs:				
Cleaning supplies	?	?	7,200 SFr	?
Electricity	?	?	2,700	?
Maintenance	?	?	1,800	?
Total variable overhead cost	?	?	?	?
Fixed overhead costs:				
Operator wages		?	9,000	?
Depreciation		?	6,000	?
Rent		?	8,000	?
Total fixed overhead cost		?	?	?
Total overhead cost		?	?	?

Required   Fill in the missing data.

E11–2   Refer to the data in Exercise 11–1. Lavage Rapide's owner-manager would like to prepare a budget for August assuming an activity level of 8,800 cars.

Required   Prepare a static budget for August. Use Exhibit 11–1 in the chapter as your guide.

E11–3   Refer to the data in Exercise 11–1. Lavage Rapide's actual level of activity during August was 8,900 cars, although the owner had constructed his static budget for the month assuming the level of activity would be 8,800 cars. The actual overhead costs incurred during August are given below:

	Actual Costs Incurred for 8,900 Cars
Variable overhead costs:	
Cleaning supplies	7,080 SFr
Electricity	2,460
Maintenance	1,550
Fixed overhead costs:	
Operator wages	9,100
Depreciation	7,000
Rent	8,000

Required Prepare a flexible budget performance report for both the variable and fixed overhead costs for August. Use Exhibit 11–2 in the chapter as your guide.

E11–4 The cost formulas for Emory Company's manufacturing overhead costs are given below. These cost formulas cover a relevant range of 15,000 to 25,000 machine-hours each year.

Overhead Costs	Cost Formula
Utilities	$0.30 per machine-hour
Indirect labour	$52,000 plus $1.40 per machine-hour
Supplies	$0.20 per machine-hour
Maintenance	$18,000 plus $0.10 per machine-hour
Depreciation	$90,000

Required Prepare a flexible budget in increments of 5,000 machine-hours. Include all costs in your budget.

E11–5 The variable portion of Murray Company's flexible budget for manufacturing overhead is given below:

Variable Overhead Costs	Cost Formula (per machine-hour)	Machine-Hours		
		10,000	12,000	14,000
Supplies	$0.20	$ 2,000	$ 2,400	$ 2,800
Maintenance	0.80	8,000	9,600	11,200
Utilities	0.10	1,000	1,200	1,400
Rework time	0.40	4,000	4,800	5,600
Total variable overhead cost	$1.50	$15,000	$18,000	$21,000

During a recent period, the company recorded 11,500 machine-hours of activity. The variable overhead costs incurred were:

Supplies	$2,400
Maintenance	8,000
Utilities	1,100
Rework time	5,300

The budgeted activity for the period had been 12,000 machine-hours.

Required
1. Prepare a variable overhead performance report for the period. Indicate whether variances are favourable (F) or unfavourable (U). Show only a spending variance on your report.
2. Discuss the significance of the variances. Might some variances be the result of others? Explain.

E11–6 The cheque-clearing office of Columbia National Bank is responsible for processing all cheques that come to the bank for payment. Managers at the bank believe that variable overhead costs are essentially proportional to the number of labour-hours worked in the office, so labour-hours is used as the activity base for budgeting and for performance reports for variable overhead costs in the department. Data for September, the most recent month, appear below:

Budgeted labour-hours	3,080
Actual labour-hours	3,100
Standard labour-hours allowed for the actual number of cheques processed	3,200

	Cost Formula (per labour-hour)	Actual Costs Incurred in September
Variable overhead costs:		
Office supplies	$0.10	$ 365
Staff coffee lounge	0.20	520
Indirect labour	0.90	2,710
Total variable overhead cost	$1.20	$3,595

Required   Prepare a variable overhead performance report for September for the cheque-clearing office that includes both spending and efficiency variances. Use Exhibit 11–6 as a guide.

E11–7   Operating at a normal level of 30,000 direct labour-hours, Lasser Company produces 10,000 units of product each period. The direct labour wage rate is $6 per hour. Two and one-half metres of direct materials go into each unit of product; the material costs $8.60 per metre. The flexible budget used to plan and control manufacturing overhead costs is given below (in condensed form):

	Cost Formula (per direct labour-hour	Direct Labour-Hours		
Overhead Costs		20,000	30,000	40,000
Variable costs	$1.90	$ 38,000	$ 57,000	$ 76,000
Fixed costs		168,000	168,000	168,000
Total overhead cost		$206,000	$225,000	$244,000

Required
1. Using 30,000 direct labour-hours as the denominator activity, compute the predetermined overhead rate and break it down into variable and fixed elements.
2. Complete the standard cost card below for one unit of product:

> Direct materials, 2.5 metres at $8.60 .... $21.50
> Direct labour,   ? ....   ?
> Variable overhead,   ? ....   ?
> Fixed overhead,   ? ....   ?
> Total standard cost per unit .... $?

E11–8   Norwall Company's flexible budget for manufacturing overhead (in condensed form) is given below:

	Cost Formula (per machine-hour)	Machine-Hours		
Overhead Costs		50,000	60,000	70,000
Variable costs	$3	$150,000	$180,000	$210,000
Fixed costs		300,000	300,000	300,000
Total overhead cost		$450,000	$480,000	$510,000

The following information is available for a recent period:
a. A denominator activity of 60,000 machine-hours is used to compute the predetermined overhead rate.

  b. At the 60,000 standard machine-hours level of activity, the company should produce 40,000 units of product.
  c. The company's actual operating results were:

Number of units produced	42,000
Actual machine-hours	64,000
Actual variable overhead costs	$185,000
Actual fixed overhead costs	302,400

Required

1. Compute the predetermined overhead rate and break it down into variable and fixed cost elements.
2. Compute the standard hours allowed for the actual production.
3. Compute the variable overhead spending and efficiency variances and the fixed overhead budget and volume variances.

E11–9   Selected operating information on three different companies for a recent year is given below:

	Company		
	A	**B**	**C**
Full-capacity machine-hours	10,000	18,000	20,000
Budgeted machine-hours*	9,000	17,000	20,000
Actual machine-hours	9,000	17,800	19,000
Standard machine-hours allowed for actual production	9,500	16,000	20,000

*Denominator activity for computing the predetermined overhead rate.

Required

For each company, state whether the company would have a favourable or unfavourable volume variance and why.

E11–10   The standard cost card for the single product manufactured by Cutter, Inc., is given below:

Standard Cost Care—per Unit

Direct materials, 3 metres at $6	$18
Direct labour, 4 hours at $7.75	31
Variable overhead, 4 hours at $1.50	6
Fixed overhead, 4 hours at $5	20
Total standard cost per unit	$75

Manufacturing overhead is applied to production on the basis of direct labour-hours. During the year, the company worked 37,000 hours and manufactured 9,500 units of product. Selected data relating to the company's fixed manufacturing overhead cost for the year are shown below:

Actual Fixed Overhead Cost	Flexible Budget Fixed Overhead Cost	Fixed Overhead Cost Applied to Work in Process
$198,700	?	? hrs. × $? = $?

Budget variance, $?   Volume variance, $10,000 U

Required

1. What were the standard hours allowed for the year's production?

2. What was the amount of fixed overhead cost contained in the flexible budget for the year?
3. What was the fixed overhead budget variance for the year?
4. What denominator activity level did the company use in setting the predetermined overhead rate for the year?

E11–11   Selected information relating to Yost Company's operations for the most recent year is given below:

Activity:
Denominator activity (machine-hours) .   45,000
Standard hours allowed per unit   3
Number of units produced   14,000

Costs:
Actual fixed overhead costs incurred . . $267,000
Fixed overhead budget variance . . . . . .   3,000 F

The company applies overhead cost to products on the basis of machine-hours.

Required
1. What were the standard hours allowed for the actual production?
2. What was the fixed portion of the predetermined overhead rate?
3. What was the volume variance?

Problems

P11–12   Preparing a Revised Performance Report   Several years ago, Westmont Company developed a comprehensive budgeting system for profit planning and control purposes. The line supervisors have been very happy with the system and with the reports being prepared on their performance, but both middle and upper management have expressed considerable dissatisfaction with the information being generated by the system. A typical manufacturing overhead performance report for a recent period is as follows:

WESTMONT COMPANY
Overhead Performance Report—Assembly Department
For the Quarter Ended March 31

	Actual	Budget	Variance
Machine-hours	35,000	40,000	
Variable overhead costs:			
Indirect materials	$ 29,700	$ 32,000	$2,300 F
Rework time	7,900	8,000	100 F
Utilities	51,800	56,000	4,200 F
Machine setup	11,600	12,000	400 F
Total variable overhead cost . . .	101,000	108,000	7,000 F
Fixed overhead costs:			
Maintenance	79,200	80,000	800 F
Inspection	60,000	60,000	—
Total fixed overhead cost	139,200	140,000	800 F
Total overhead cost	$240,200	$248,000	$7,800 F

After receiving a copy of this overhead performance report, the supervisor of the Assembly Department stated, "These reports are super. It makes me feel really good to see how well things are going in my department. I can't understand why those people upstairs complain so much."

The budget data above are for the original planned level of activity for the quarter.

Required
1. The company's vice president is uneasy about the performance reports being prepared and would like you to evaluate their usefulness to the company.

2. What changes, if any, would you recommend be made in the overhead performance report above in order to give better insight into how well the supervisor is controlling costs?
3. Prepare a new overhead performance report for the quarter, incorporating any changes you suggested in (2) above. (Include both the variable and the fixed costs in your report.)

P11–13 Applying the Flexible Budget Approach   The St. Lucia Blood Bank, a private charity partly supported by government grants, is located on the Caribbean island of St. Lucia. The Blood Bank has just finished its operations for September, which was a particularly busy month due to a powerful hurricane that hit neighbouring islands causing many injuries. The hurricane largely bypassed St. Lucia, but residents of St. Lucia willingly donated their blood to help people on other islands. As a consequence, the blood bank collected and processed over 20% more blood than had been originally planned for the month.

A report prepared by a government official comparing actual costs to budgeted costs for the Blood Bank appears below. (The currency on St. Lucia is the East Caribbean dollar.) Continued support from the government depends on the Blood Bank's ability to demonstrate control over their costs.

ST. LUCIA BLOOD BANK
Cost Control Report
For the Month Ended September 30

	Actual	Budget	Variance
Litres of blood collected	620	500	120 F
Variable costs:			
Medical supplies	$ 9,350	$ 7,500	$1,850 U
Lab tests	6,180	6,000	180 U
Refreshments for donors	1,340	1,000	340 U
Administrative supplies	400	250	150 U
Total variable cost	17,270	14,750	2,520 U
Fixed costs:			
Staff salaries	10,000	10,000	—
Equipment depreciation	2,800	2,500	300 U
Rent	1,000	1,000	—
Utilities	570	500	70 U
Total fixed cost	14,370	14,000	370 U
Total cost	$31,640	$28,750	$2,890 U

The managing director of the Blood Bank was very unhappy with this report, claiming that his costs were higher than expected due to the emergency on the neighbouring islands. He also pointed out that the additional costs had been fully covered by payments from grateful recipients on the other islands. The government official who prepared the report countered that all of the figures had been submitted by the Blood Bank to the government; he was just pointing out that actual costs were a lot higher than promised in the budget.

Required
1. Prepare a new performance report for September using the flexible budget approach. (Note: Even though some of these costs might be classified as direct costs rather than as overhead, the flexible budget approach can still be used to prepare a flexible budget performance report.)
2. Do you think any of the variances in the report you prepared should be investigated? Why?

P11–14 Standard Cost Card: Materials, Labour, and All Overhead Variances   Flandro Company uses a standard cost system and sets predetermined overhead rates on the basis of direct labour-hours. The following data are taken from the company's budget for the current year:

Denominator activity (direct labour-hours)	10,000
Variable manufacturing overhead cost	$25,000
Fixed manufacturing overhead cost	59,000

The standard cost card for the company's only product is given below:

Direct materials, 3 metres at $4.40 . . . . $13.20
Direct labour, 2 hours at $6 . . . . 12.00
Manufacturing overhead, 140% of direct labour cost 16.80
Standard cost per unit $42.00

During the year, the company produced 6,000 units of product and incurred the following costs:

Materials purchased, 24,000 metres at $4.80 . . . . $115,200
Materials used in production (in metres)   18,500
Direct labour cost incurred, 11,600 hours at $6.50 . . . . . $ 75,400
Variable manufacturing overhead cost incurred   29,580
Fixed manufacturing overhead cost incurred   60,400

Required

1. Redo the standard cost card in a clearer, more usable format by detailing the variable and fixed overhead cost elements.
2. Prepare an analysis of the variances for materials and labour for the year.
3. Prepare an analysis of the variances for variable and fixed overhead for the year.
4. What effect, if any, does the choice of a denominator activity level have on unit standard costs? Is the volume variance a controllable variance from a spending point of view? Explain.

P11–15 Basic Overhead Analysis   Chilczuk, S.A., of Gdansk, Poland, is a major producer of classic Polish sausage. The company uses a standard cost system to help in the control of costs. Overhead is applied to production on the basis of labour-hours. According to the company's flexible budget, the following manufacturing overhead costs should be incurred at an activity level of 35,000 labour-hours (the denominator activity level):

Variable overhead costs . . . . . PZ 87,500
Fixed overhead costs   210,000
Total overhead cost PZ297,500

The currency in Poland is the zloty, which is denoted here by PZ.
During the most recent year, the following operating results were recorded:

Activity:
Actual labour-hours worked   30,000
Standard labour-hours allowed for output   32,000

Cost:
Actual variable overhead cost incurred . . . . PZ 78,000
Actual fixed overhead cost incurred   209,400

At the end of the year, the company's Manufacturing Overhead account contained the following data:

Manufacturing Overhead

Actual	287,400	Applied	272,000
	15,400		

Management would like to determine the cause of the PZ15,400 underapplied overhead.

Required

1. Compute the predetermined overhead rate. Break the rate down into variable and fixed cost elements.
2. Show how the PZ272,000 Applied figure in the Manufacturing Overhead account was computed.
3. Analyze the PZ15,400 underapplied overhead figure in terms of the variable overhead spending and efficiency variances and the fixed overhead budget and volume variances.
4. Explain the meaning of each variance that you computed in (3) above.

P11–16   Integration of Materials, Labour, and Overhead Variances

"Wonderful! Not only did our salespeople do a good job in meeting the sales budget this year, but our production people did a good job in controlling costs as well," said Kim Clark, president of Martell Company. "Our $18,000 overall manufacturing cost variance is only 1.5% of the $1,200,000 standard cost of products sold during the year. That's well within the 3% parameter set by management for acceptable variances. It looks like everyone will be in line for a bonus this year."

The company produces and sells a single product. A standard cost card for the product follows:

Standard Cost Card—per Unit of Product

Direct materials, 2 metres at $8.45	$16.90
Direct labour, 1.4 hours at $8	11.20
Variable overhead, 1.4 hours at $2.50	3.50
Fixed overhead, 1.4 hours at $6	8.40
Standard cost per unit	$40.00

The following additional information is available for the year just completed:

a.   The company manufactured 30,000 units of product during the year.
b.   A total of 64,000 metres of material was purchased during the year at a cost of $8.55 per metre. All of this material was used to manufacture the 30,000 units. There were no beginning or ending inventories for the year.
c.   The company worked 45,000 direct labour-hours during the year at a cost of $7.80 per hour.
d.   Overhead is applied to products on the basis of direct labour-hours. Data relating to manufacturing overhead costs follow:

Denominator activity level (direct labour-hours)	35,000
Budgeted fixed overhead costs (from the overhead flexible budget)	$210,000
Actual variable overhead costs incurred	108,000
Actual fixed overhead costs incurred	211,800

Required
1.   Compute the direct materials price and quantity variances for the year.
2.   Compute the direct labour rate and efficiency variances for the year.
3.   For manufacturing overhead compute:
     a.   The variable overhead spending and efficiency variances for the year.
     b.   The fixed overhead budget and volume variances for the year.
4.   Total the variances you have computed, and compare the net amount with the $18,000 mentioned by the president. Do you agree that bonuses should be given to everyone for good cost control during the year? Explain.

P11–17   Flexible Budget and Overhead Performance Report

You have just been hired by FAB Company, the manufacturer of a revolutionary new garage door opening device. John Foster, the president, has asked that you review the company's costing system and "do what you can to help us get better control of our manufacturing overhead costs." You find that the company has never used a flexible budget, and you suggest that preparing such a budget would be an excellent first step in overhead planning and control.

After much effort and analysis, you are able to determine the following cost formulas for the company's normal operating range of 20,000 to 30,000 machine-hours each month:

Overhead Costs	Cost Formula
Utilities	$0.90 per machine-hour
Maintenance	$1.60 per machine-hour plus $40,000 per month
Machine setup	$0.30 per machine-hour
Indirect labour	$0.70 per machine-hour plus $130,000 per month
Depreciation	$70,000 per month

To show the president how the flexible budget concept works, you have gathered the following actual cost data for the most recent month, March, in which the company worked 26,000 machine-hours and produced 15,000 units:

Utilities	$ 24,200
Maintenance	78,100
Machine setup	8,400
Indirect labour	149,600
Depreciation	71,500
Total cost	$331,800

The only variance in the fixed costs for the month was with depreciation, which was increased as a result of a purchase of new equipment.

The company had originally planned to work 30,000 machine-hours during March.

Required

1. Prepare a flexible budget for the company in increments of 5,000 hours.
2. Prepare an overhead performance report for the company for March. (Use the format illustrated in Exhibit 11–10.)
3. What additional information would you need to compute an overhead efficiency variance for the company?

P11–18 Spending and Efficiency Variances; Evaluating an Overhead Performance Report Frank Western, supervisor of the Machining Department for Freemont Company, was visibly upset after being reprimanded for his department's poor performance over the prior month. The department's performance report is given below:

FREEMONT COMPANY

Performance Report—Machining Department

	Cost Formula (per machine-hour)	Actual	Budget	Variance
Machine-hours		38,000	35,000	
Variable overhead costs:				
Utilities	$0.40	$ 15,700	$ 14,000	$ 1,700 U
Indirect labour	2.30	86,500	80,500	6,000 U
Supplies	0.60	26,000	21,000	5,000 U
Maintenance	1.20	44,900	42,000	2,900 U
Total variable overhead cost	$4.50	173,100	157,500	15,600 U
Fixed overhead costs:				
Supervision		38,000	38,000	—
Maintenance		92,400	92,000	400 U
Depreciation		80,000	80,000	—
Total fixed overhead cost		210,400	210,000	400 U
Total overhead cost		$383,500	$367,500	$16,000 U

"I just can't understand all the red ink," said Western to Sarah Mason, supervisor of another department. "When the boss called me in, I thought he was going to give me a pat on the back because I know for a fact that my department worked more efficiently last month than it has ever worked before. Instead, he tore me apart. I thought for a minute that it might be over the supplies that were stolen out of our warehouse last month. But they only amounted to a couple of thousand dollars, and just look at this report. *Everything* is unfavourable, and I don't even know why."

The budget for the Machining Department had called for production of 14,000 units last month, which is equal to a budgeted activity level of 35,000 machine-hours (at a standard time of 2.5 hours per unit). Actual production in the Machining Department for the month was 16,000 units.

Required
1. Evaluate the overhead performance report given above and explain why the variances are all unfavourable.
2. Prepare a new overhead performance report that will help Mr. Western's superiors assess efficiency and cost control in the Machining Department. (Hint: Exhibit 11–6 may be helpful in structuring your report; however, the report you prepare should include both variable and fixed costs.)
3. Would the supplies stolen out of the warehouse be included as part of the variable overhead spending variance or as part of the variable overhead efficiency variance for the month? Explain.

P11–19 Detailed Performance Report The cost formulas for variable overhead costs in a machining operation are given below:

Variable Overhead Costs	Cost Formula (per machine-hour)
Power	$0.30
Setup time	0.20
Polishing wheels	0.16
Maintenance	0.18
Total variable overhead cost	$0.84

During August, the machining operation was scheduled to work 11,250 machine-hours and to produce 4,500 units of product. The standard machine time per unit of product is 2.5 hours. A strike near the end of the month forced a cutback in production. Actual results for the month were:

Actual machine-hours worked ... 9,250
Actual number of units produced . 3,600

Actual costs for the month were:

Variable Overhead Costs	Total Actual Costs	Per Machine-Hour
Power	$2,405	$0.26
Setup time	2,035	0.22
Polishing wheels	1,110	0.12
Maintenance	925	0.10
Total variable overhead cost	$6,475	$0.70

Required Prepare an overhead performance report for the machining operation for August. Use column headings in your report as shown below:

Overhead Costs	Cost Formula (per machine-hour)	Actual Costs Incurred 9,250 Machine-Hours	Budget Based on ? Machine-Hours	Budget Based on ? Machine-Hours	Total Variance	Breakdown of the Total Variance	
						Spending Variance	Efficiency Variance

P11–20 Standard Cost Card and Overhead Analysis Lane Company manufactures a single product that requires a great deal of hand labour. Overhead cost is applied on the basis of direct labour-hours. The company's condensed flexible budget for manufacturing overhead is given below:

Overhead Costs	Cost Formula (per direct labour-hour)	Direct Labour-Hours		
		45,000	60,000	75,000
Variable costs	$2	$ 90,000	$120,000	$150,000
Fixed costs		480,000	480,000	480,000
Total overhead cost ...		$570,000	$600,000	$630,000

The company's product requires 3 kilograms of material that has a standard cost of $7 per kilogram and 1.5 hours of direct labour time that has a standard rate of $6 per hour.

The company planned to operate at a denominator activity level of 60,000 direct labour-hours and to produce 40,000 units of product during the most recent year. Actual activity and costs for the year were as follows:

Number of units produced	42,000
Actual direct labour-hours worked	65,000
Actual variable overhead cost incurred	$123,500
Actual fixed overhead cost incurred	483,000

Required

1. Compute the predetermined overhead rate for the year. Break the rate down into variable and fixed elements.
2. Prepare a standard cost card for the company's product; show the details for all manufacturing costs on your standard cost card.
3. Do the following:
   a. Compute the standard hours allowed for the year's production.
   b. Complete the following Manufacturing Overhead T-account for the year:

Manufacturing Overhead

?	?
?	?

4. Determine the reason for any under- or overapplied overhead for the year by computing the variable overhead spending and efficiency variances and the fixed overhead budget and volume variances.
5. Suppose the company had chosen 65,000 direct labour-hours as the denominator activity rather than 60,000 hours. State which, if any, of the variances computed in (4) above would have changed, and explain how the variance(s) would have changed. No computations are necessary.

P11–21 Standard Cost Card; Fixed Overhead Analysis; Graphing When planning operations for the year, Southbrook Company chose a denominator activity of 40,000 direct labour-hours. According to the company's flexible budget, the following manufacturing overhead costs should be incurred at this activity level:

Variable overhead costs	$ 72,000
Fixed overhead costs	360,000

The company produces a single product that requires 2.5 hours to complete. The direct labour rate is $6 per hour. Eight metres of material are needed to complete one unit of product; the material has a standard cost of $4.50 per metre. Overhead is applied to production on the basis of direct labour-hours.

Required

1. Compute the predetermined overhead rate. Break the rate down into variable and fixed cost elements.
2. Prepare a standard cost card for one unit of product using the following format:

Direct materials, 8 metres at $4.50	$36	
Direct labour, ?	?	
Variable overhead, ?	?	
Fixed overhead, ?	?	
Standard cost per unit	$?	

3. Prepare a graph with cost on the vertical (Y) axis and direct labour-hours on the horizontal (X) axis. Plot a line on your graph from a zero level of activity to 60,000 direct labour-hours for each of the following costs:
   a. Budgeted fixed overhead (in total).
   b. Applied fixed overhead [applied at the hourly rate computed in (1) above].
4. Assume that during the year actual activity is as follows:

Number of units produced	14,000
Actual direct labour-hours worked	33,000
Actual fixed overhead cost incurred	$361,800

   a. Compute the fixed overhead budget and volume variances for the year.
   b. Show the volume variance on the graph you prepared in (3) above.
5. Disregard the data in (4) above. Assume instead that actual activity during the year is as follows:

Number of units produced	20,000
Actual direct labour-hours worked	52,000
Actual fixed overhead costs incurred	$361,800

   a. Compute the fixed overhead budget and volume variances for the year.
   b. Show the volume variance on the graph you prepared in (3) above.

P11–22 Flexible Budget and Overhead Analysis Harper Company assembles all of its products in the Assembly Department. Budgeted costs for the operation of this department for year have been set as follows:

Variable overhead costs:	
Direct materials	$ 900,000
Direct labour	675,000
Utilities	45,000
Indirect labour	67,500
Supplies	22,500
Total variable overhead cost . . .	1,710,000
Fixed overhead costs:	
Insurance	8,000
Supervisory salaries	90,000
Depreciation	160,000
Equipment rental	42,000
Total fixed overhead cost	300,000
Total budgeted overhead cost	$2,010,000
Budgeted direct labour-hours	75,000

Since the assembly work is done mostly by hand, operating activity in this department is best measured by direct labour-hours. The cost formulas used to develop the budgeted costs above are valid over a relevant range of 60,000 to 90,000 direct labour-hours per year.

Required
1. Prepare a manufacturing overhead flexible budget in good form for the Assembly Department. Make your budget in increments of 15,000 direct labour-hours. (The company does not include direct materials and direct labour costs in the flexible budget.)
2. Assume that the company computes predetermined overhead rates by department. Compute the rates that will be used by the Assembly Department to apply overhead costs to production. Break this rate down into variable and fixed cost elements.

3. Suppose that during the year the following actual activity and costs are recorded by the Assembly Department:

Actual direct labour-hours worked	73,000
Standard direct labour-hours allowed	
for the output of the year	70,000
Actual variable overhead cost incurred . . .	$124,100
Actual fixed overhead cost incurred	301,600

Complete the following:

a. A T-account for manufacturing overhead costs in the Assembly Department for the year is given below. Determine the amount of applied overhead cost for the year, and compute the under- or overapplied overhead.

Manufacturing Overhead

Actual cost   425,700

b. Analyze the under- or overapplied overhead figure in terms of the variable overhead spending and efficiency variances and the fixed overhead budget and volume variances.

P11–23   Flexible Budget; Overhead Performance Report   Gant Products, Inc., has recently introduced budgeting as an integral part of its corporate planning process. The company's first effort at constructing a flexible budget for manufacturing overhead is shown below:

Percentage of capacity	80%	100%
Machine-hours	4,800	6,000
Maintenance	$1,480	$ 1,600
Supplies	1,920	2,400
Utilities	1,940	2,300
Supervision	3,000	3,000
Machine setup	960	1,200
Total overhead cost	$9,300	$10,500

The budgets above are for costs over a relevant range of 80% to 100% of capacity on a monthly basis. The managers who will be working under these budgets have control over both fixed and variable costs.

Required

1. Redo the company's flexible budget, presenting it in better format. Show the budget at 80%, 90%, and 100% levels of capacity. (Use the high-low method to separate fixed and variable costs.)
2. Express the budget prepared in (1) above in cost formula form using a single cost formula to express all overhead costs.
3. The company operated at 95% of capacity during April in terms of actual hours of machine time recorded in the factory. Five thousand six hundred standard machine-hours were allowed for the output of the month. Actual overhead costs incurred were:

Maintenance	$ 2,083
Supplies	3,420
Utilities	2,666
Supervision	3,000
Machine setup	855
Total overhead cost	$12,024

The fixed costs had no variances. Prepare an overhead performance report for April. Structure your report so that it shows only a spending variance for overhead. You may assume that the master budget for April called for an activity level during the month of 6,000 machine-hours.

4. Upon receiving the performance report you have prepared, the production manager commented, "I have two observations to make. First, I think there's an error on your report. You show an unfavourable spending variance for supplies, yet I know that we paid exactly the budgeted price for all the supplies we used last month. Pat Stevens, the purchasing agent, made a comment to me that our supplies prices haven't changed in over a year. Second, I wish you would modify your report to include an efficiency variance for overhead. The reason is that waste has been a problem in the factory for years and the efficiency variance would help us get overhead waste under control."
   a. Explain the probable cause of the unfavourable spending variance for supplies.
   b. Compute an efficiency variance for *total* variable overhead and explain to the production manager why it would or would not contain elements of overhead waste.

P11–24 Activity-Based Costing and the Flexible Budget Approach The Little Theatre is a nonprofit organization devoted to staging theatre productions of plays for children in Manchester, England. The theatre has a very small full-time professional administrative staff. Through a special arrangement with the actors' union, actors and directors rehearse without pay and are paid only for actual performances.

The costs of 2000's operations appear below. (The currency in England was the pound, denoted £.) During 2000, The Little Theatre had six different productions—each of which was performed 18 times. For example, one of the productions was Peter the Rabbit, which had the usual six-week run with three performances on each weekend.

THE LITTLE THEATRE
Cost Report
For the Year Ended 31 December 2000

Number of productions	6
Number of performance of each production	18
Total number of performances	108
Actual costs incurred:	
Actors' and directors' wages	£216,000
Stagehands' wages	32,400
Ticket booth personnel and ushers' wages	16,200
Scenery, costumes, and props	108,000
Theatre hall rent	54,000
Printed programs	27,000
Publicity	12,000
Administrative expenses	43,200
Total cost	£508,800

Some of the costs vary with the number of productions, some with the number of performances, and some are relatively fixed and depend on neither the number of productions nor the number of performances. The costs of scenery, costumes, and props and of publicity vary with the number of productions. It does not make any difference how many times Peter the Rabbit is performed, the cost of the scenery is the same. Likewise, the cost of publicizing a play with posters and radio commercials is the same whether there are 10, 20, or 30 performances of the play. On the other hand, the wages of the actors, directors, stagehands, ticket booth personnel, and ushers vary with the number of performances. The greater the number of performances, the higher the wage costs will be. Similarly, the costs of renting the hall and printing the programs will vary with the number of performances. Administrative expenses are more difficult to pin down, but the best estimate is that approximately 75% of these costs are fixed, 15% depend on the number of productions staged, and the remaining 10% depend on the number of performances.

At the end of 2000, the board of directors of the theatre authorized expanding the theatre's program in 2001 to seven productions, with 24 performances each. Not surprisingly, actual costs for 2001 were considerably higher than the costs for 2000. (Grants from donors and ticket sales were also correspondingly higher.) Data concerning 2001's operations appears on next page:

THE LITTLE THEATRE
Cost Report
For the Year Ended 31 December 2001

Number of productions	7
Number of performances of each production	24
Total number of performances	168

Actual costs incurred:

Actors' and directors' wages	£341,800
Stagehands' wages	49,700
Ticket booth personnel and ushers' wages	25,900
Scenery, costumes, and props	130,600
Theatre hall rent	78,000
Printed programs	38,300
Publicity	15,100
Administrative expenses	47,500
Total cost	£726,900

Even though many of the costs above may be considered direct costs rather than overhead, the flexible budget approach covered in the chapter can still be used to evaluate how well these costs are controlled. The principles are the same whether a cost is a direct cost or is overhead.

Required
1. Use the actual results from 2000 to estimate the cost formulas for the flexible budget for The Little Theatre. Keep in mind that the theatre has two measures of activity—the number of productions and the number of performances.
2. Prepare a performance report for 2001 using the flexible budget approach and both measures of activity. Assume there was no inflation. (Note: To evaluate administrative expenses, first determine the flexible budget amounts for the three elements of administrative expenses. Then compare the total of the three elements to the actual administrative expense of £47,500.)
3. If you were on the board of directors of the theatre, would you be pleased with how well costs were controlled during 2001? Why or why not?
4. The cost formulas provide figures for the average cost per production and average cost per performance. How accurate do you think these figures would be for predicting the cost of a new production or of an additional performance of a particular production?

P11–25 Selection of a Denominator; Overhead Analysis Morton Company's condensed flexible budget for manufacturing overhead is given below:

Overhead Costs	Cost Formula (per direct labour-hour)	Direct Labour-Hours		
		20,000	30,000	45,000
Variable costs	$4.50	$ 90,000	$135,000	$180,000
Fixed costs		270,000	270,000	270,000
Total overhead cost ...		$360,000	$405,000	$450,000

The company manufactures a single product that requires two direct labour-hours to complete. The direct labour wage rate is $5 per hour. Four metres of raw material are required for each unit of product; the standard cost of the material is $8.75 per metre.

Although long-run normal activity is 30,000 direct labour-hours each year, the company expects to operate at a 40,000-hour level of activity this year.

Required
1. Assume that the company chooses 30,000 direct labour-hours as the denominator level of activity. Compute the predetermined overhead rate, breaking it down into variable and fixed cost elements.
2. Assume that the company chooses 40,000 direct labour-hours as the denominator level of activity. Repeat the computations in (1) above.

3. Complete two standard cost cards as outlined below. Each card should relate to a single unit of product.

Denominator Activity: 30,000 Direct Labour-Hours

Direct materials, 4 metres at $8.75 . . . . $35.00
Direct labour,   ? . . . .   ?
Variable overhead, ? . . . .   ?
Fixed overhead,   ? . . . .   ?

Standard cost per unit . . . . $?

Denominator Activity: 40,000 Direct Labour-Hours

Direct materials, $4 metres at $8.75 . . . . $35.00
Direct labour,   ? . . . .   ?
Variable overhead, ? . . . .   ?
Fixed overhead,   ? . . . .   ?

Standard cost per unit . . . . $?

4. Assume that the company produces 18,000 units and works 38,000 actual direct labour-hours during the year. Actual manufacturing overhead costs for the year are:

Variable costs $174,800
Fixed costs   271,600

Total overhead cost $446,400

Do the following:
a. Compute the standard hours allowed for this year's production.
b. Complete the Manufacturing Overhead account below. Assume that the company uses 30,000 direct labour-hours (long-run normal activity) as the denominator activity figure in computing predetermined overhead rates, as you have done in (1) above.

Manufacturing Overhead

Actual costs	446,400	?
?		?

c. Determine the cause of the under- or overapplied overhead for the year by computing the variable overhead spending and efficiency variances and the fixed overhead budget and volume variances.
5. Looking at the variances you have computed, what appears to be the major disadvantage of using long-run normal activity rather than expected actual activity as a denominator in computing the predetermined overhead rate? What advantages can you see to offset this disadvantage?

P11–26 Detailed Variance Analysis   XYZ Manufacturing Co. uses the weighted-average method and actual costs for financial reporting purposes. For better management control, XYZ uses a standard costing system. The standards that XYZ has developed for the single product that it produces are:

Materials per unit	10 kg	at	$15 per kg
Direct labour per unit . . .	10 DLH	at	$30 per DLH (Direct Labour-Hour)
Overhead per unit	10 DLH	at	$10 per DLH

All materials are added at the beginning of the process. Labour and overhead are applied evenly during the process.

For the most recent month, *budgeted* overhead was $145,000. In addition, you are provided with the following information for the most recent month:

	Number of Units
Beginning work in process (25% complete)	500
Started during month	1,240
Ending work in process (75% complete)	240

	Actual Costs $
Beginning work in process	
Materials	80,000
Direct labour	39,000
Overhead	13,000
Materials, 12,500 kg (all used during the month)	200,000
Direct labour, 17,000 hours	476,000
Overhead	150,000

Required   Part A

1. Calculate the equivalent units of performance for materials.
2. Calculate the equivalent units of performance for conversion costs.
3. Calculate materials costs used in the computation of cost per equivalent unit for materials.
4. Calculate direct labour costs used in the computation of cost per equivalent unit for labour.
5. Calculate overhead costs used in the computation of cost per equivalent unit or overhead.
6. Calculate actual cost of the ending work in process.

Part B
Using the information given in Part 1, compute the following:

7. Materials price variance.
8. Materials usage variance.
9. Direct labour rate variance.
10. Direct labour efficiency variance.
11. Overhead budget variance.
12. Overhead volume variance.
13. Total overhead variance.
14. Give brief explanation as to why the following variances might occur: (This is independent of the previous parts to this question.)
    a. An unfavourable materials quantity variance
    b. An unfavourable labour rate variance
    c. A favourable labour efficiency variance
    d. A favourable variable overhead spending variance

(CGA, adapted)

Cases

C11–27 Ethics and the Manager   Tom Kemper is the controller of the Quebec manufacturing facility of Prudhom Enterprises, Incorporated. Among the many reports that must be filed with corporate headquarters is the annual overhead performance report. The report covers an entire fiscal year, which ends on December 31, and is due at corporate headquarters shortly after the beginning of the New Year. Kemper does not like putting work off to the last minute, so just before Christmas he put together a preliminary draft of the overhead performance report. Some adjustments would be required for transactions that occur between Christmas and New Year's Day, but there are generally very few of these. A copy of the preliminary draft report, which Kemper completed on December 21, follows:

QUEBUE MANUFACTURING FACILITY
Overhead Performance Report
December 21 Preliminary Draft

Budgeted machine-hours 200,000
Actual machine-hours 180,000

Overhead Costs	Cost Formula (per machine-hour)	Actual Costs 180,000 Machine-Hours	Budget Based on 180,000 Machine-Hours	Spending or Budget Variance
Variable overhead costs:				
Power	$0.10	$ 19,750	$ 18,000	$ 1,750 U
Supplies	0.25	47,000	45,000	2,000 U
Abrasives	0.30	58,000	54,000	4,000 U
Total variable overhead cost	$0.65	124,750	117,000	7,750 U
Fixed overhead costs:				
Depreciation		345,000	332,000	13,000 U
Supervisory salaries		273,000	275,000	2,000 F
Insurance		37,000	37,000	—
Industrial engineering		189,000	210,000	21,000 F
Factory building lease		60,000	60,000	—
Total fixed overhead cost		904,000	914,000	10,000 F
Total overhead cost		$1,028,750	$1,031,000	$ 2,250 F

Melissa Comeau, the general manager at the Quebec facility, asked to see a copy of the preliminary draft report at 4:45 P.M. on December 23. Kemper carried a copy of the report to her office where the following discussion took place:

Comeau: Ouch! Almost all of the variances on the report are unfavourable. The only thing that looks good at all are the favourable variances for supervisory salaries and for industrial engineering. How did we have an unfavourable variance for depreciation?

Kemper: Do you remember that milling machine that broke down because the wrong lubricant was used by the machine operator?

Comeau: Only vaguely.

Kemper: It turned out we couldn't fix it. We had to scrap the machine and buy a new one.

Comeau: This report doesn't look good. I was raked over the coals last year when we had just a few unfavourable variances.

Kemper: I'm afraid the final report is going to look even worse.

Comeau: Oh?

Kemper: The line item for industrial engineering on the report is for work we hired Ferguson Engineering to do for us on a contract basis. The original contract was for $210,000, but we asked them to do some additional work that was not in the contract. Under the terms of the contract, we have to reimburse Ferguson Engineering for the costs of the additional work. The $189,000 in actual costs that appear on the preliminary draft report reflects only their billings up through December 21. The last bill they had sent us was on November 28, and they completed the project just last week. Yesterday I got a call from Laura Sunder over at Ferguson and she said they would be sending us a final bill for the project before the end of the year. The total bill, including the reimbursements for the additional work, is going to be . . .

Comeau: I am not sure I want to hear this.

Kemper: $225,000

Comeau: Ouch! Ouch! Ouch!

Kemper: The additional work we asked them to do added $15,000 to the cost of the project.

Comeau: No way can I turn in a performance report with an overall unfavourable variance. They'll kill me at corporate headquarters. Call up Laura in Montreal and ask her not to send the bill until after the first of the year. We have to have that $21,000 favourable variance for industrial engineering on the performance report.

Required   What should Tom Kemper do? Explain.

C11–28   Incomplete Data   Each of the cases below is independent. You may assume that each company uses a standard cost system and that each company's flexible budget for manufacturing overhead is based on standard machine-hours.

Item	Company A	Company B
1. Denominator activity in hours	?	40,000
2. Standard hours allowed for units produced . .	32,000	?
3. Actual hours worked	30,000	?
4. Flexible budget variable overhead per machine-hour	$?	$ 2.80
5. Flexible budget fixed overhead (total)	?	?
6. Actual variable overhead cost incurred	54,000	117,000
7. Actual fixed overhead cost incurred	209,400	302,100
8. Variable overhead cost applied to production*	?	117,600
9. Fixed overhead cost applied to production*	192,000	?
10. Variable overhead spending variance	?	?
11. Variable overhead efficiency variance	3,500 F	8,400 U
12. Fixed overhead budget variance	?	2,100 U
13. Fixed overhead volume variance	18,000 U	?
14. Variable portion of the predetermined overhead rate	?	?
15. Fixed portion of the predetermined overhead rate	?	?
16. Underapplied (or overapplied) overhead	?	?

*Based on standard hours allowed for units produced

Required   Compute the unknown amounts. (Hint: One way to proceed would be to use the format for variance analysis found in Exhibit 10–7 for variable overhead and in Exhibit 11–9 for fixed overhead.)

C11–29   Working Backwards from Variance Data   You have recently graduated from university and have accepted a position with Vitex, Inc., the manufacturer of a popular consumer product. During your first week on the job, the vice president has been favourably impressed with your work. She has been so impressed, in fact, that yesterday she called you into her office and asked you to attend the executive committee meeting this morning for the purpose of leading a discussion on the variances reported for last period. Anxious to favourably impress the executive committee, you took the variances and supporting data home last night to study.

On your way to work this morning, the papers were laying on the seat of your new, red convertible. As you were crossing a bridge on the highway, a sudden gust of wind caught the papers and blew them over the edge of the bridge and into the stream below. You managed to retrieve only one page, which contains the following information:

Standard Cost Card

Direct materials, 6 kilograms at $3 . . . . $18.00
Direct labour, 0.8 hours at $5 . . . .   4.00
Variable overhead, 0.8 hours at $3 . . . .   2.40
Fixed overhead, 0.8 hours at $7 . . . .   5.60
Standard cost per unit $30.00

	Total Standard Cost*	Price or Rate	Spending or Budget	Quantity or Efficiency	Volume
		Variances Reported			
Direct materials	$405,000	$6,900 F		$9,000 U	
Direct labour	90,000	4,850 U		7,000 U	
Variable overhead	54,000		$1,300 F	?† U	
Fixed overhead	126,000		500 F		$14,000 U

* Applied to Work in Process during the period.

† Figure obliterated.

You recall that manufacturing overhead cost is applied to production on the basis of direct labour-hours and that all of the materials purchased during the period were used in production. Since the company uses JIT to control work flows, work in process inventories are insignificant and can be ignored.

It is now 8:30 A.M. The executive committee meeting starts in just one hour; you realize that to avoid looking like a bungling fool you must somehow generate the necessary "backup" data for the variances before the meeting begins. Without backup data it will be impossible to lead the discussion or answer any questions.

Required

1. How many units were produced last period? (Think hard about this one!)
2. How many kilograms of direct material were purchased and used in production?
3. What was the actual cost per kilogram of material?
4. How many actual direct labour-hours were worked during the period?
5. What was the actual rate paid per direct labour-hour?
6. How much actual variable manufacturing overhead cost was incurred during the period?
7. What is the total fixed manufacturing overhead cost in the company's flexible budget?
8. What were the denominator hours for last period?

C11–30   Preparing a Performance Report Using Activity-Based Costing
A university offers an extensive continuing education program in many cities throughout the province. For the convenience of its faculty and administrative staff and to save costs, the university employs a supervisor to operate a motor pool. The motor pool operated with 20 vehicles until February, when an additional automobile was acquired. The motor pool furnishes gasoline, oil, and other supplies for its automobiles. A mechanic does routine maintenance and minor repairs. Major repairs are done at a nearby commercial garage.

Each year, the supervisor prepares an operating budget that informs the university administration of the funds needed for operating the motor pool. Depreciation (straight line) on the automobiles is recorded in the budget in order to determine the cost per kilometre of operating the vehicles.

The following schedule presents the operating budget for the current year, which has been approved by the university. The schedule also shows actual operating costs for March of the current year compared to one-twelfth of the annual operating budget.

UNIVERSITY MOTOR POOL
Budget Report for March

	Annual Operating Budget	Monthly Budget*	March Actual	(Over) Under Budget
Gasoline	$ 42,000	$ 1,500	$ 1,750	$(2,550)
Oil, minor repairs, parts	3,600	300	380	(80)
Outside repairs	2,700	225	50	175
Insurance	6,000	500	525	(25)
Salaries and benefits	30,000	2,500	2,500	—
Depreciation of vehicles	26,400	2,200	2,310	(110)
Total costs	$110,700	$20,725	$23,265	$(2,590)
Total kilometres	1,200,000	100,000	12,000	
Cost per kilometre	$ 0.2497	$0.2497	$0.2497	
Number of automobiles in use	20	20	21	

* Annual operating budget ÷ 12 months.

The annual operating budget was constructed on the following assumptions:

a.   Twenty automobiles in the motor pool.
b.   Fifty thousand kilometres driven per year per automobile.
c.   Fifteen kilometres per litre per automobile.
d. $0.60 per litre of gasoline.
e. $0.01 cost per kilometre for oil, minor repairs, and parts.
f. $135 cost per automobile per year for outside repairs.
g. $300 cost per automobile per year for insurance.

The supervisor of the motor pool is unhappy with the monthly report comparing budget and actual costs for March, claiming it presents an unfair picture of performance. A previous employer used flexible budgeting to compare actual costs to budgeted amounts.

Required

1.   Prepare a new performance report for March showing budgeted costs, actual costs, and variances. In preparing your report, use flexible budgeting techniques to compute the monthly budget figures.
2.   What are the deficiencies in the performance report presented above? How does the report that you prepared in (1) above overcome these deficiencies?

(CMA, adapted)

C11–31   Budgets and Standards   You are the recently hired manager of the Food Section of the Bedford Foundation. The Foundation was established as a not-for-profit organization to provide various services (food, clothing, shelter, and medical care) to the needy. The Food Section receives funding from the Foundation and from various departments of the government based on the number of meals it is able to provide each year. All funding is established at the beginning of each year (based on meals provided in the previous year) and all expenditures are controlled through a "line-item" budget. The objectives of your division are to provide daily meals to as many needy people as possible (the government makes the decision as to which people qualify as needy and informs you of this decision).

On your first day of work, you met with Mr. Health, the president of the Foundation, who welcomed you to your new position with the following statement:

I see you have a strong background in various industries as a management accountant. Unfortunately, I don't think you will have a chance to implement much of your knowledge here since we are a not-for-profit organization which operates considerably differently from the industries you are acquainted with. Budgeting in this organization consists of a line-item budget that we establish at the beginning of each year. Your evaluation will be based on your ability to keep expenditures within the limit for each item and serve the maximum number of meals. The Foundation does not prepare a master budget or any cash budgets since all cash levels are predetermined at the beginning of the year, and it is impossible to predict accurately what the demand will be. Any budget that might be prepared would not be accurate, so what purpose would it serve?

I understand that in industry, you made much use of flexible budgets, which seem to me to be a complete waste of time. Flexible budgets are prepared after the fact, so of course they are accurate. Anyone can do an accurate budget if they wait until after the event before predicting what will happen. Obviously, the flexible budget will be equal to the actual results, so what purpose does it serve?

If you have any intentions of instituting a standard cost system, you had better forget about that as well. That would work in an industrial setting only. I've heard some mention of program budgeting from various people in the government; I don't know what it is, but I'm sure it is something that might apply to various government departments, but would not have any applications in an organization such as ours.

Required   Write a report to the president of the Foundation responding to his comments. Make specific reference to the budget system currently in use and the applicability to the Foundation of the various management systems mentioned.

(SMAC, adapted)

C11–32   Overhead Variance Analysis and Responsibility   The Collins Company produces a single product in its manufacturing plant. Overhead is applied to production on the basis of standard direct labour-hours (DLH). The following schedule has been prepared as a flexible budget for overhead cost review purposes:

DLH in Month	Overhead Cost Should Be
3,000	$30,000
4,000	35,000
5,000	40,000
6,000	45,000

The standard costs for one unit of product have been determined as follows:

Direct labour, 4 hours at $25	$100.00
Direct materials, 10 kg at $6	60.00
Overhead	32.00
Total standard cost	$192.00

During the month of May, the company produced 1,200 units, actually worked 5,100 direct labour-hours and incurred overhead costs of $40,400 of which $15,100 were fixed.

Required
1. Prepare an analysis of overhead variances for the month of May to the extent possible with the information provided above.
2. As controller of the company, prepare a brief report (memorandum format) to the president discussing how well control over overhead costs was maintained during May. Indicate who should be held responsible for the variances you have calculated.

(SMAC, adapted)

C11–33   Variance Analysis   The Ripe Company uses a standard cost system in accounting for its production of chairs. Company policy is to isolate all variances as soon as possible. They began the year 2001 with the following standards based on an expected volume of 60,000 chairs for the year:

	Per Unit
Direct materials (3 metres at $10 per metre)	$ 30
Direct labour, type A (4 hours at $8 per hour)	32
Direct labour, type B (6 hours at $15 per hour)	90
Variable overhead (10 hours at $2 per hour)	20
Fixed overhead (10 hours at $4 per hour)	40
Total manufacturing costs	$212

Other expected revenues and expenses:

Selling price	$420 per unit
Variable selling and administration. . . .	$40 per unit
Fixed selling and administration	$20,000 per month
Expected total industry demand	25,000 units per month

Actual results for the month of February 2001 were as follows:

a. The company actually produced and sold 5,500 chairs at an average selling price of $400 per chair, and actual total industry sales totalled 30,000 units for the month.

b. Direct material purchases for the month totalled 15,000 metres at an average cost of $11 per metre. Production in the month used a total of 17,100 metres.

c. Due to the difference in labour rates for the two different classes of labour, the production foreperson decided to employ more of the type A workers and less of the type B workers. Actual results for the month were:

> Type A—40,000 hours at a total cost of $324,000.
> Type B—29,000 hours at a total cost of $435,000.

d. Actual overhead results for the month were:

Variable overhead	$130,000
Fixed overhead	$210,000

e. All other revenues and expenses behaved as expected.

Required
1. Calculate all the appropriate variances for the manufacturing costs.
2. Evaluate the decision of the production foreperson to change the composition of the direct labour force.
3. At the end of the month, the vice president of marketing made the following statement:

> I feel the sales force deserves a bonus for the month as they were able to exceed budgeted sales for the month by 10% (500 units). I don't know the total increase in company profits as I have no control over the production costs, but I'm sure it's enough to justify a $50,000 bonus.

> Calculate all appropriate variances and evaluate the vice president's statement.

(SMAC, adapted)

Group Exercises

GE11–34 Overhead Control For years, North American manufacturers followed a strategy of low-cost mass production to gain competitive advantage by pursuing economics of scale—maximizing production of a single product in a single facility. In order to leverage economies of scale into further reductions in unit cost, firms built bigger factories and filled those plants with bigger, faster, and more specialized machines. With total overhead costs increasing, plant managers ran larger lots and pushed costs lower by maximizing the volume of throughput in each department and at each workstation.

Of necessity, the variety of products made had to increase in order to gain the volume necessary to fully utilize the ever-larger and more costly facilities and machinery. As the variety of parts and products produced in any single plant increased, the need for support staff to manage and control production through the plant increased. In time, overhead costs had increased to 30%–40% of total manufacturing costs, while direct labour decreased to 10%–15% of total manufacturing costs and is still dropping.

Required
1. How did plant management control machine-related costs? Traditionally, what performance measures were used to measure and evaluate the performance of machinery?
2. What incentives did these machine-based performance measures provide plant management and shop floor supervisors? What potential results did these performance incentives have?
3. What is production support? Describe how and why production support increased over time.

4. How did plant management attempt to control this increasing category of production support overhead?
5. What is the overhead absorption variance? How was underapplied overhead interpreted?
6. Because of the increasing complexity of the plant, quality problems became an ever-present problem in the operations of a factory. How did plant management view quality in this environment, and what role did quality play in the day-to-day operations of the factory? What is the concept of an acceptable quality level (AQL)?
7. How did cost accounting account for scrap, spoilage, and rework?
8. Who was responsible for quality? How was their performance measured? What implications did this have for understanding and controlling the costs of poor quality?
9. Traditional cost accounting systems encourage some highly questionable behaviour. Can you identify any other questionable actions not already identified above?

GE11–35 Cost Control and Company Size Suppose two factories are located side by side. One plant is extremely large and complex with more than 4,000 employees, 40 production departments, 25 production support departments (e.g., production scheduling), three eight-hour shifts, and an annual budget in excess of $250 million. This plant, one of 20 National Motors assembly plants, makes NM's Great Iroquois sport-utility vehicle.

The other factory is much smaller and is managed by its owner. This plant employs 105 workers, has two 10-hour shifts, and has a budget of $4.5 million annually. Although machines of a similar type are grouped together in the plant, the facility is not large enough to be divided into different production departments. In addition to the owner, there is an engineer who designs the products on a computer-aided design system, an accountant, a secretary, and two shift forepersons. This job shop makes molds that are used to produce a variety of products. For example, one recent job was for a mold that would produce the front panel of the disk drive on an MBI Activa personal computer.

Required
1. What are the primary concerns or issues for each plant?
2. What should the objectives of each plant's cost system be?
3. Given these objectives, what kind of accounting reports and performance measures would be appropriate for managing each factory? Be sure to explain your reasoning for using the reports and performance measures that you recommend.
4. To report timely and relevant information, how often would you issue such reports and measures of performance?

GE11–36 Choice of Denominator Activity Level Canadian Widget, Inc., makes a number of high-volume standard products that are sold in highly competitive markets. As a result, its cost system stresses cost control. Canadian uses a standard cost system and updates standards on a regular and timely basis. Until recently, expected annual capacity was the basis for determining predetermined factory overhead rates. This rate was used for internal planning and reporting and performance evaluation purposes, as well as for inventory valuation.

Recently, John Phillips, controller, has proposed changing the basis for internal planning and reporting from expected annual capacity to practical capacity. Since practical capacity remains relatively constant unless there is a plant expansion or purchase of new manufacturing machinery, Phillips believes this change would facilitate planning and budgeting.

Phillips has held one meeting with department managers and presented them with their new annual budgets prepared on the basis of the new, proposed practical capacity standard. There was little discussion. Later, a member of the cost accounting staff pointed out that the new standard for determining predetermined overhead rates would be tighter than the old standard.

Required
1. If the new annual budgets for Canadian Widget reflect the implementation of tighter standards based on practical capacity:
   a. What negative behavioural implications for employees and department managers could occur as a result of this change?
   b. What could Canadian Widget management do to mitigate the negative behavioural effects?
2. Explain how tight cost standards within an organization could have positive behavioural effects.

3. Identify the individuals who should participate in setting standards and describe the benefits to an organization of their participation in the standard setting process.

(CMA, adapted)

GE11–37 Analyzing Your College's Budget Obtain a copy of your college or university's budget and actual results for the most recently completed year.

Required

1. Determine the major assumptions used in the last budget (e.g., number of students; tuition per student; number of employees; increases in wages, salaries, benefits; changes in occupancy costs; etc.).
2. Compare the budgeted revenue amounts with the actual results. Try to determine the reasons for any differences.
3. Compare budgeted expenses with the actual results. Try to determine the reasons for any differences.

IE11–38 Talk with a Controller about Overhead Analysis Use an online yellow pages directory such as www.canadayellowpages.com to find a business or nonprofit organization in your area with a web site. Find out as much as you can about the organization's operations from its web site.

Required

Make an appointment with the controller or chief financial officer of the organization you have identified. In the meeting, find out the answers to the following questions:

1. Are actual overhead costs compared to a static budget, to a flexible budget, or to something else?
2. Does the organization distinguish between variable and fixed overhead costs in its performance reports?
3. What are the consequences of an unfavourable variance? Of a favourable variance?

Chapter Twelve

Decentralization and Segment Reporting

Business Focus

E & A Company (the name has been changed to conceal the company's true identity) provides a wide range of engineering and architectural consulting services to both government and industry. For many years, the company pooled all operating costs and allocated them to its three branch offices on the basis of labour cost. When it abandoned this practice and started tracing costs such as rent directly to the offices, while at the same time assigning other costs on a more appropriate basis, the reported profits of one branch office doubled, the reported profits of another branch office changed from a loss to a profit, and the reported profits of the third branch office changed from a profit to a loss.

Source: Beth M. Chaffman and John Talbott, "Activity-Based Costing in a Service Organization," CMA 64, no. 10 (December/January 1991), p. 18.

Learning Objectives

After studying Chapter 12, you should be able to:

1 Differentiate between cost centres, profit centres, and investment centres, and explain how performance is measured in each.

2 Prepare a segmented income statement using the contribution format, and explain the difference between traceable fixed costs and common fixed costs.

3 Identify three business practices that hinder proper cost assignment.

4 Analyze variances from revenue targets.

5 Analyze marketing expenses using cost drivers.

6 Compute the return on investment (ROI).

7 Show how changes in sales, expenses, and assets affect an organization's ROI.

8 Compute residual income and understand the strengths and weaknesses of this method of measuring performance.

9 (Appendix 12A) Determine the range, if any, within which a negotiated transfer price should fall.

Managers of organizations determine the direction they wish the organization to take. Strategic planning as described in Chapter 2 is the term applied to this planning process. Budgeting is the financial expression of the plans. The short-term version of budgeting was presented in Chapter 9 while Chapter 15 describes long-term capital budgets. Planning, however, is only part of the management process. Managers through a combination of feedback of actual results, comparisons to budgets, comparisons to results of previous periods, and even comparisons to other organizations attempt to assure that the organization moves in the planned direction.

Managers control the organization using a variety of approaches. Accounting reports of financial results represent one important approach to controlling operations because such reports provide a means of obtaining comparisons to budgets, to previous results, and to the results of other organizations as well as a knowledge of actual results. Such financial comparisons also serve as a base for reward schemes used to motivate managers to work toward the achievement of planned goals and objectives.

These financial performance reports can be constructed in various ways so that they better serve the specific control functions that management desires. As this chapter illustrates, segment reporting, profitability analysis, and investment performance are three commonly used reporting structures that provide somewhat different types of information. For each it is important to understand what purpose is served by the report. Each presents information in a manner that permits a different view of the organization and a different aspect of organizational control. Understanding how the aspects change and why managers would want these changes will permit you to integrate the concepts of control with reports about standard cost variances, cost of production, and flexible budget analyses described in earlier chapters.

The modern manufacturing environment has promoted the need for flexibility in management to accompany flexibility in production. Flexibility in management requires timely and accurate decisions by members of the organization ranging from top management to the production worker. Timely and accurate decisions require timely and accurate control information appropriate to this wide range of organizational personnel. Extensions of control information to operating or production workers so they can control their operations has posed an interesting challenge for accountants. Traditional reports have been too aggregated for operating workers. Accounting formats often represent approaches that are not well understood by production workers. Monthly, reports, the common management accounting reporting period, are not timely enough to provide a review of operations that must change daily. Some accounting conventions such as expensing items that some view as assets can distort realities or misdirect attention so that incorrect control decisions can occur.

Study is ongoing to rectify some of the deficiencies. Focused indicators of performance such as scrap levels, rework efforts, market share, employee morale, pollutant discharges, and customer profitability are some of the approaches being used or refined. Some measures are financial; some are physical. Aggregations of physical results is the focus of intense study because of the difficulty of having a meaningful total when financial numbers are not used.[1]

This chapter provides an explanation of common financial performance indicators. Such reports represent the cornerstone of performance measurements to managers. Integrating material on performance from previous chapters with discussions in this and later chapters will provide you with a foundation for understanding developments in performance assessment.

---

1. "Developing Comprehensive Performance Indicators," *Management Accounting Guideline* 31 (Hamilton, ON: The Society of Management Accountants of Canada. 1994).

Decentralization in Organizations

Decentralized organization An organization in which decision making is not confined to a few top executives but rather is spread throughout the organization.

Once an organization grows beyond a few people, it becomes impossible for the top manager to make decisions about everything. For example, the CEO of the Delta Hotel chain cannot be expected to decide whether a particular hotel guest at the Delta Hotel on Vancouver Island should be allowed to check out later than the normal checkout time. To some degree, managers have to delegate decisions to those who are at lower levels in the organization. However, the degree to which decisions are delegated varies from organization to organization.

A **decentralized organization** is one in which decision making is not confined to a few top executives but rather is spread throughout the organization, with managers at various levels making key operating decisions relating to their sphere of responsibility. Decentralization is a matter of degree, since all organizations are decentralized to some extent out of necessity. At one extreme, a strongly decentralized organization is one in which there are few, if any, constraints on the freedom of even the lowest-level managers and employees to make decisions. At the other extreme, in a strongly centralized organization, lower-level managers have little freedom to make a decision. Although most organizations fall somewhere between these two extremes, there is a pronounced trend toward more and more decentralization.

Advantages and Disadvantages of Decentralization

Decentralization has many benefits, including:

1. Top management is relieved of much day-to-day problem solving and is left free to concentrate on strategy, on higher-level decision making, and on coordinating activities.
2. Decentralization provides lower-level managers with vital experience in making decisions. Without such experience, they would be ill-prepared to make decisions when they are promoted into higher-level positions.
3. Added responsibility and decision-making authority often result in increased job satisfaction. It makes the job more interesting and provides greater incentives for people to put out their best efforts.
4. Lower-level managers generally have more detailed and up-to-date information about conditions in their own area of responsibility than top managers. Therefore, the decisions of lower-level managers are often based on better information.
5. It is difficult to evaluate a manager's performance if the manager is not given much latitude in what he or she can do.

Decentralization has four major disadvantages:

1. Lower-level managers may make decisions without fully understanding the "big picture." While top-level managers typically have less detailed information about operations than the lower-level managers, they usually have more information about the company as a whole and may have a better understanding of the company's strategy. This situation can be avoided to some extent with the use of modern management information systems that can, in principle, give every manager at every level the same information that goes to the CEO and other top-level managers.
2. In a truly decentralized organization, there may be a lack of coordination among autonomous managers. This problem can be reduced by clearly defining the company's strategy and communicating it effectively throughout the organization.
3. Lower-level managers may have objectives that are different from the objectives of the entire organization. For example, some managers may be more interested in increasing the sizes of their departments than in increasing the profits of the

company.[2] To some degree, this problem can be overcome by designing performance evaluation systems that motivate managers to make decisions that are in the best interests of the company.

4. In a strongly decentralized organization, it may be more difficult to effectively spread innovative ideas. Someone in one part of the organization may have a terrific idea that would benefit other parts of the organization, but without strong central direction the idea may not be shared with and adopted by other parts of the organization.

Decentralization and Segment Reporting

Segment Any part or activity of an organization about which the manager seeks cost, revenue, or profit data.

Effective decentralization requires *segmental reporting*. In addition to the companywide income statement, reports are needed for individual segments of the organization. A **segment** is a part or activity of an organization about which managers would like cost, revenue, or profit data. Examples of segments include divisions of a company, sales territories, individual stores, service centres, manufacturing plants, marketing departments, individual customers, and product lines. As we shall see, a company's operations can be segmented in many ways. For example, a grocery store chain like Loblaws or Sobeys can segment their businesses by geographic region, by individual store, by the nature of the merchandise (i.e., green groceries, canned goods, paper goods), by brand name, and so on. In this chapter, we learn how to construct income statements for such business segments. These segmented income statements are useful in analyzing the profitability of segments and in measuring the performance of segment managers.

Cost, Profit, and Investment Centres

Decentralized companies typically categorize their business segments into cost centres, profit centres, and investment centres—depending on the responsibilities of the managers of the segments.[3]

Objective 1

Differentiate between cost centres, profit centres, and investment centres, and explain how performance is measured in each.

COST CENTRE   A **cost centre** is a business segment whose manager has control over costs but not over revenue or investment funds. Service departments such as accounting, finance, general administration, legal, personnel, and so on, are usually considered to be cost centres. In addition, manufacturing facilities are often considered to be cost centres. The managers of cost centres are expected to minimize cost while providing the level of services or the amount of products demanded by the other parts of the organization. For example, the manager of a production facility would be evaluated at least in part by comparing actual costs to how much the costs should have been for the actual number of units produced during the period.

Cost centre A business segment whose manager has control over cost but has no control over revenue or the use of investment funds.

PROFIT CENTRE   In contrast to a cost centre, a **profit centre** is any business segment whose manager has control over both cost and revenue. Like a cost centre, however, a profit centre generally does not have control over investment funds. For

Profit centre A business segment whose manager has control over cost and revenue but has no control over the use of investment funds.

---

2. There is a similar problem with top-level managers as well. The shareholders of the company have, in effect, decentralized by delegating their decision-making authority to the top managers. Unfortunately, top managers may abuse that trust by spending too much company money on palatial offices, rewarding themselves and their friends too generously, and so on. The issue of how to ensure that top managers act in the best interests of the owners of the company continues to puzzle experts. To a large extent, the owners rely on performance evaluation using return on investment and residual income measures as discussed later in the chapter and on bonuses and stock options. The stock market is also an important disciplining mechanism. If top managers squander the company's resources, the price of the company's stock will almost surely fall—resulting in a loss of prestige, bonuses, and possibly a job.

3. Some companies classify business segments that are responsible mainly for generating revenue, such as an insurance sales office, as *revenue centres*. Other companies would consider this to be just another type of profit centre, since costs of some kind (salaries, rent, utilities) are usually deducted from the revenues in the segment's income statement.

Investment centre A business segment whose manager has control over cost and over revenue and that also has control over the use of investment funds.

Responsibility centre Any business segment whose manager has control over cost, revenue, or the use of investment funds.

example, the manager in charge of one of six resorts would be responsible for both the revenues and costs, and hence the profits, of the resort but may not have control over major investments in the resort. Profit centre managers are often evaluated by comparing actual profit to targeted or budgeted profit.

INVESTMENT CENTRE An **investment centre** is any segment of an organization whose manager has control over cost, revenue, and investments in operating assets. For example, the president of General Motors Canada would have a great deal of discretion over investments in the division. The president of the Division would be responsible for initiating investment proposals, such as funding research into more fuel-efficient engines for sport-utility vehicles. Once the proposal has been approved by the top level of managers at General Motors Canada and the board of directors, the president of the Division would then be responsible for making sure that the investment pays off. Investment centre managers are usually evaluated using return on investment or residual income measures as discussed later in the chapter.

Responsibility Centres

Responsibility centre is broadly defined as any part of an organization whose manager has control over cost, revenue, or investment funds. Cost centres, profit centres, and investment centres are *all* known as responsibility centres.

A partial organization chart for Universal Foods Corporation, a company in the snack food and beverage industry, appears in Exhibit 12–1. This partial organization chart indicates how the various business segments of the company are classified in

Exhibit 12–1   Business Segments Classified as Cost, Profit, and Investment Centres

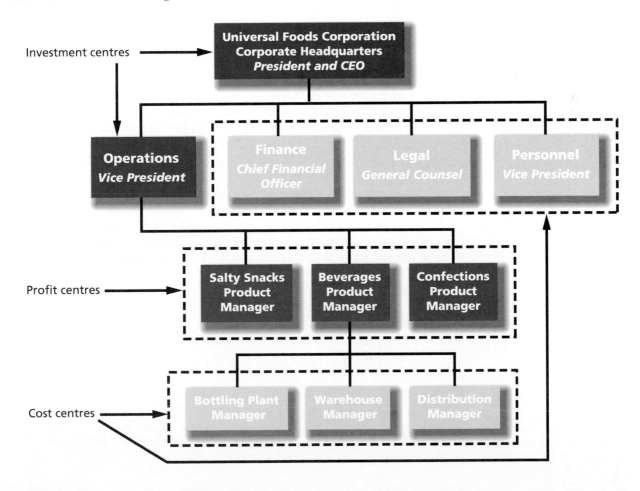

terms of responsibility. Note that the cost centres are the departments and work centres that do not generate significant revenues by themselves. These are staff departments such as finance, legal, and personnel, and operating units such as the bottling plant, warehouse, and beverage distribution centre. The profit centres are business segments that generate revenues and include the beverage, salty snacks, and confections product segments. The vice president of operations oversees allocation of investment funds across the product segments and is responsible for revenues and costs and so is treated as an investment centre. And finally, corporate headquarters is an investment centre, since it is responsible for all revenues, costs, and investments.

Segment Reporting and Profitability Analysis

As previously discussed, a different kind of income statement is required for evaluating the performance of business segments—an income statement that emphasizes segments rather than the performance of the company as a whole. This point is illustrated in the following discussion.

Managerial Accounting in Action

THE ISSUE

softsolutionsinc.

SoftSolutions, Inc., is a rapidly growing computer software company founded by Lori Saffer, who had previously worked in a large software company, and Marjorie Matsuo, who had previously worked in the hotel industry as a general manager. They formed the company to develop and market user-friendly accounting and operations software designed specifically for hotels. They quit their jobs, pooled their savings, hired several programmers, and got down to work.

The first sale was by far the most difficult. No hotel wanted to be the first to use an untested product from an unknown company. After overcoming this obstacle with persistence, good luck, dedication to customer service, and a very low introductory price, the company's sales burgeoned.

The company quickly developed similar business software for other specialized markets and then branched out into clip art and computer games. Within four years of its founding, the organization had grown to the point where Saffer and Matsuo were no longer able to personally direct all of the company's activities. Decentralization had become a necessity.

Accordingly, the company was split into two divisions—Business Products and Consumer Products. By mutual consent, Matsuo took the title president and Saffer took the title vice president of the Business Products Division. Chris Worden, a programmer who had spearheaded the drive into the clip art and computer games markets, was designated vice president of the Consumer Products Division.

Almost immediately, the issue arose of how best to evaluate the performance of the divisions. Matsuo called a meeting to consider this issue and asked Saffer, Worden, and the controller, Bill Carson, to attend. The following discussion took place at that meeting:

Marjorie Matsuo: We need to find a better way to measure the performance of the divisions.

Chris Worden: I agree. Consumer Products has been setting the pace in this company for the last two years, and we should be getting more recognition.

Lori Saffer: Chris, we are delighted with the success of the Consumer Products Division.

Chris Worden: I know. But it is hard to figure out just how successful we are with the present accounting reports. All we have are sales and cost of goods sold figures for the division.

Bill Carson: What's the matter with those figures? They are prepared using generally accepted accounting principles.

Chris Worden: The sales figures are fine. However, cost of goods sold includes some costs that really aren't the costs of our division, and it excludes some costs that are. Let's take a simple example. Everything we sell in the Consumer Products Division has to pass through the automatic bar-coding machine, which applies a unique bar code to the product.

Lori Saffer: We know. Every item we ship must have a unique identifying bar code. That's true for items from the Business Products Division as well as for items from the Consumer Products Division.

Chris Worden: That's precisely the point. Whether an item comes from the Business Products Division or the Consumer Products Division, it must pass through the automatic bar-coding machine after the software has been packaged. How much of the cost of the automatic bar coder would be saved if we didn't have any consumer products?

Marjorie Matsuo: Since we have only one automatic bar coder and we would need it anyway to code the business products, I guess none of the cost would be saved.

Chris Worden: That's right. And since none of the cost could be saved even if the entire Consumer Products Division were eliminated, how can we logically say that some of the cost of the automatic bar coder is a cost of the Consumer Products Division?

Lori Saffer: Just a minute, Chris, are you saying that my Business Products Division should be charged with the entire cost of the automatic bar coder?

Chris Worden: No, that's not what I am saying.

Marjorie Matsuo: But Chris, I don't see how we can have sensible performance reports without making someone responsible for costs like the cost of the automatic bar coder. Bill, as our accounting expert, what do you think?

Bill Carson: I have some ideas for handling issues like the automatic bar coder. The best approach would probably be for me to put together a draft performance report. We can discuss it at the next meeting when everyone has something concrete to look at.

Marjorie Matsuo: Okay, let's see what you come up with. ■

Bill Carson, the controller of SoftSolutions, realized that segmented income statements would be required to more appropriately evaluate the performance of the two divisions. To construct the segmented reports, he would have to carefully segregate costs that are attributable to the two divisions from costs that are not. Since most of the disputes over costs would be about fixed costs such as the automatic bar-coding machine, he knew he would also have to separate fixed from variable costs. Under the conventional absorption costing income statement prepared for the entire company, variable and fixed production costs were being commingled in the cost of goods sold.

Largely for these reasons, Bill Carson decided to use the contribution format income statement discussed in earlier chapters. Recall that when the contribution format is used: (1) the cost of goods sold consists only of the variable manufacturing costs; (2) the variable and fixed costs are listed in separate sections; and (3) a contribution margin is computed. When such a statement is segmented as in this chapter, fixed costs are broken down further into what are called traceable and common costs as discussed later. This breakdown allows a *segment margin* to be computed for each segment of the company. The segment margin is a valuable tool for assessing the long-run profitability of a segment and is also a much better tool for evaluating performance than the usual absorption costing reports.

Levels of Segmented Statements

A portion of the segmented report Bill Carson prepared is shown in Exhibit 12–2. The contribution format income statement for the entire company appears at the very top of the exhibit under the column labelled Total Company. Immediately to the right of this column are two columns—one for each of the two divisions. We can see that the divisional segment margin is $60,000 for the Business Products Division and $40,000 for the Consumer Products Division. This is the portion of the report that was specifically requested by the company's divisional managers. They wanted to know how much each of their divisions was contributing to the company's profits.

However, segmented income statements can be prepared for activities at many levels in a company. To provide more information to the company's divisional managers, Bill Carson has further segmented the divisions according to their major product lines. In the case of the Consumer Products Division, the product lines are clip art and computer games. Going even further, Bill Carson has segmented each of the product lines according to how they are sold—in retail computer stores or by catalogue sales. In Exhibit 12–2, this further segmentation is illustrated for the computer games product line. Notice that as we go from one segmented statement to another, we look at smaller and smaller pieces of the company. While not shown in Exhibit 12–2, Bill Carson also prepared segmented income statements for the major product lines in the Business Products Division.

Substantial benefits are received from a series of statements such as those contained in Exhibit 12–2. By carefully examining trends and results in each segment, a manager is able to gain considerable insight into the company's operations viewed from many different angles. And advanced computer-based information systems are making it easier and easier to construct such statements and to keep them continuously current.

Sales and Contribution Margin

To prepare an income statement for a particular segment, variable expenses are deducted from the sales to yield the contribution margin for the segment. It is important to keep in mind that the contribution margin tells us what happens to profits as volume changes—holding a segment's capacity and fixed costs constant. The contribution margin is especially useful in decisions involving temporary uses of capacity such as special orders. Decisions concerning the most effective uses of existing capacity often involve only variable costs and revenues, which of course are the very elements involved in contribution margin. Such decisions will be discussed in detail in Chapter 13.

Traceable and Common Fixed Costs

The most puzzling aspect of Exhibit 12–2 is probably the treatment of fixed costs. The report has two kinds of fixed costs—traceable and common. Only the *traceable fixed costs* are charged to the segments in the segmented income statements in the report. If a cost is not traceable to a segment, then it is not assigned to the segment.

A **traceable fixed cost** of a segment is a fixed cost that is incurred because of the existence of the segment—if the segment had never existed, the fixed cost would not have been incurred; and/or if the segment were eliminated, the fixed cost would disappear. Examples of traceable fixed costs include the following:

Traceable fixed cost A fixed cost that is incurred because of the existence of a particular business segment.

- The salary of the Fritos product manager at PepsiCo is a *traceable* fixed cost of the Fritos business segment of PepsiCo.

Exhibit 12–2
SoftSolutions, Inc.—
Segmented Income
Statements in the
Contribution Format

Segments Defined as Divisions

	Total Company	Divisions Business Products Division	Consumer Products Division
Sales	$500,000	$300,000	$200,000
Less variable expenses:			
Variable cost of goods sold	180,000	120,000	60,000
Other variable expenses	50,000	30,000	20,000
Total variable expenses	230,000	150,000	80,000
Contribution margin	270,000	150,000	120,000
Less traceable fixed expenses	170,000	90,000	80,000*
Divisional segment margin	100,000	$ 60,000	$ 40,000
Less common fixed expenses not traceable to the individual divisions	85,000		
Net income	$ 15,000		

Segments Defined as Product Lines of the Consumer Products Division

	Consumer Products Division	Product Line Clip Art	Computer Games
Sales	$200,000	$ 75,000	$125,000
Less variable expenses:			
Variable cost of goods sold	60,000	20,000	40,000
Other variable expenses	20,000	5,000	15,000
Total variable expenses	80,000	25,000	55,000
Contribution margin	120,000	50,000	70,000
Less traceable fixed expenses	70,000	30,000	40,000
Product-line segment margin	50,000	$ 20,000	$ 30,000
Less common fixed expenses not traceable to the individual product lines	10,000		
Divisional segment margin	$ 40,000		

Segments Defined as Sales Channels for One Product Line, Computer Games, of the Consumer Products Division

	Computer Games	Sales Channels Retail Stores	Catalogue Sales
Sales	$125,000	$100,000	$ 25,000
Less variable expenses:			
Variable cost of goods sold	40,000	32,000	8,000
Other variable expenses	15,000	5,000	10,000
Total variable expenses	55,000	37,000	18,000
Contribution margin	70,000	63,000	7,000
Less traceable fixed expenses	25,000	15,000	10,000
Sales-channel segment margin	45,000	$ 48,000	$ (3,000)
Less common fixed expenses not traceable to the individual sales channels	15,000		
Product-line segment margin	$ 30,000		

*Notice that this $80,000 in traceable fixed expense is divided into two parts—$70,000 traceable and $10,000 common—when the Consumer Products Division is broken down into product lines. The reasons for this are discussed later under Traceable Costs Can Become Common Costs.

- The maintenance cost for the building in which Boeing 747s are assembled is a *traceable* fixed cost of the 747 business segment of Boeing.
- The liability insurance at Delta Hotels is a *traceable* fixed cost of the Delta Hotel business segment of the C. P. Hotels.

Common fixed cost   A fixed cost that supports more than one business segment, but is not traceable in whole or in part to any one of the business segments.

A **common fixed cost** is a fixed cost that supports the operations of more than one segment but is not traceable in whole or in part to any one segment. Even if a segment were entirely eliminated, there would be no change in a true common fixed cost. Note the following:

- The salary of the CEO of General Motors Canada is a *common* fixed cost of the various divisions of General Motors Canada.
- The cost of the automatic bar-coding machine at SoftSolutions is a *common* fixed cost of the Consumer Products Division and of the Business Products Division.
- The cost of the receptionist's salary at an office shared by a number of doctors is a *common* fixed cost of the doctors. The cost is traceable to the office, but not to any one of the doctors individually.

IDENTIFYING TRACEABLE FIXED COSTS   The distinction between traceable and common fixed costs is crucial in segment reporting, since traceable fixed costs are charged to the segments, whereas common fixed costs are not. In an actual situation, it is sometimes hard to determine whether a cost should be classified as traceable or common.

The general guideline is to treat as traceable costs *only those costs that would disappear over time if the segment itself disappeared*. For example, if the Consumer Products Division were sold or discontinued, it would no longer be necessary to pay the division manager's salary. Therefore the division manager's salary should be classified as a traceable fixed cost of the division. On the other hand, the president of the company undoubtedly would continue to be paid even if the Consumer Products Division were dropped. In fact, he or she might even be paid more if dropping the division was a good idea. Therefore, the president's salary is common to both divisions. The same idea can be expressed in another way: *treat as traceable costs only those costs that are added as a result of the creation of a segment.*

ACTIVITY-BASED COSTING   Some costs are easy to identify as traceable costs. For example, the costs of advertising Crest toothpaste on television are clearly traceable to Crest. A more difficult situation arises when a building, machine, or other resource is shared by two or more segments. For example, assume that a multiproduct company leases warehouse space that is used for storing the full range of its products. Would the lease cost of the warehouse be a traceable or a common cost of the products? Managers familiar with activity-based costing might argue that the lease cost is traceable and should be assigned to the products according to how much space the products use in the warehouse. In like manner, these managers would argue that order processing costs, sales support costs, and other selling, general, and administrative (SG&A) expenses should also be charged to segments according to the segments' consumption of SG&A resources.

To illustrate, consider Holt Corporation, a company that manufactures concrete pipe for industrial uses. The company has three products—9-inch pipe, 12-inch pipe, and 18-inch pipe. Space is leased in a large warehouse on a yearly basis as needed. The lease cost of this space is $4 per square metre per year. The 9-inch pipe occupies 1,000 square metres of space, 12-inch pipe occupies 4,000 square metres, and 18-inch pipe occupies 5,000 square metres. The company also has an order processing department that incurred $150,000 in order processing costs last year. Management believes that order processing costs are driven by the number of orders placed by customers in a year. Last year 2,500 orders were placed, of which 1,200 were for 9-inch pipe, 800 were for 12-inch pipe, and 500 were for 18-inch pipe. Given these data, the following costs would be assigned to each product using the activity-based costing approach:

Warehouse space cost:
9-inch pipe: $4 × 1,000 square metres . . . . $ 4,000
12-inch pipe: $4 × 4,000 square metres   16,000
18-inch pipe: $4 × 5,000 square metres   20,000

Total cost assigned . . . . $ 40,000

Order processing costs:
$150,000 ÷ 2,500 orders = $60 per order
9-inch pipe: $60 × 1,200 orders . . . . $ 72,000
12-inch pipe: $60 × 800 orders   48,000
18-inch pipe: $60 × 500 orders   30,000

Total cost assigned $150,000

This method of assigning costs combines the strength of activity-based costing with the power of the contribution approach and greatly enhances the manager's ability to measure the profitability and performance of segments. However, managers must still ask themselves if the costs would in fact disappear over time if the segment itself disappeared. In the case of Holt Corporation, it is clear that the $20,000 in warehousing costs for the 18-inch pipe would be eliminated if 18-inch pipes were no longer being produced. The company would simply rent less warehouse space the following year. However, suppose the company owns the warehouse. Then it is not so clear that $20,000 of the cost of the warehouse would really disappear if the 18-inch pipes were discontinued as a product. The company might be able to sublease the space, or use it for other products, but then again the space might simply be empty while the costs of the warehouse continue to be incurred.

In assigning costs to segments, the key point is to resist the temptation to allocate costs (such as depreciation of corporate facilities) that are clearly common in nature and that would continue regardless of whether the segment exists or not. *Any allocation of common costs to segments will reduce the value of the segment margin as a guide to long-run segment profitability and segment performance.* This point will be discussed at length later in the chapter.

Traceable Costs Can Become Common Costs

Fixed costs that are traceable to one segment may be a common cost of another segment. For example, an airline might want a segmented income statement that shows the segment margin for a particular flight from Montreal to Paris, further broken down into first-class, business-class, and economy-class segment margins. The airline must pay a substantial landing fee at Charles DeGaulle airport in Paris. This fixed landing fee is a traceable cost of the flight, but it is a common cost of the first-class, business-class, and economy-class segments. Even if the first-class cabin is empty, the entire landing fee must be paid. So the landing fee is not a traceable cost of the first-class cabin. But on the other hand, paying the fee is necessary in order to have any first-class, business-class, or economy-class passengers. So the landing fee is a common cost of these three classes.

The dual nature of some of the fixed costs can be seen from the diagram in Exhibit 12–3. Notice from the diagram that when segments are defined as divisions, the Consumer Products Division has $80,000 in traceable fixed expenses. Only $70,000 of this amount remains traceable, however, when we narrow the definition of a segment from divisions to product lines. Notice that the other $10,000 then becomes a common cost of the two product lines of the Consumer Products Division.

Why would $10,000 of traceable fixed cost become a common cost when the division is divided into product lines? The $10,000 is the monthly salary of the manager of the Consumer Products Division. This salary is a traceable cost of the division as a whole, but it is a common cost of the division's product lines. The

Exhibit 12–3

Reclassification of Traceable Fixed Expenses from Exhibit 12–2.

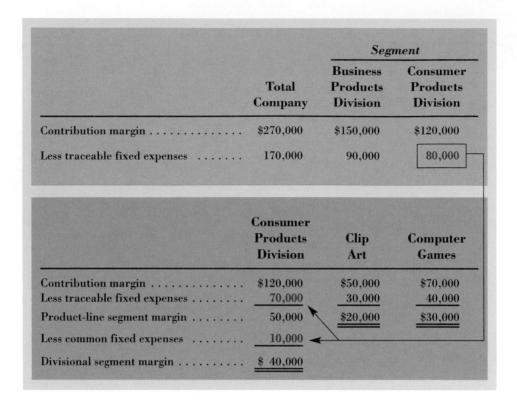

	Total Company	Segment	
		Business Products Division	**Consumer Products Division**
Contribution margin	$270,000	$150,000	$120,000
Less traceable fixed expenses	170,000	90,000	80,000

	Consumer Products Division	Clip Art	Computer Games
Contribution margin	$120,000	$50,000	$70,000
Less traceable fixed expenses	70,000	30,000	40,000
Product-line segment margin	50,000	$20,000	$30,000
Less common fixed expenses	10,000		
Divisional segment margin	$ 40,000		

manager's salary is a necessary cost of having the two product lines, but even if one of the product lines were discontinued entirely, the manager's salary would probably not be cut. Therefore, none of the manager's salary can be really traced to the individual products.

The $70,000 traceable fixed cost of the product lines consists of the costs of product-specific advertising. A total of $30,000 was spent on advertising clip art and $40,000 was spent on advertising computer games. These costs can clearly be traced to the individual product lines.

Segment Margin

Segment margin The amount computed by deducting the traceable fixed costs of a segment from the segment's contribution margin. It represents the margin available after a segment has covered all of its own costs.

Observe from Exhibit 12–2 that the **segment margin** is obtained by deducting the traceable fixed costs of a segment from the segment's contribution margin. It represents the margin available after a segment has covered all of its own costs. *The segment margin is the best gauge of the long-run profitability of a segment,* since it includes only those costs that are caused by the segment. If a segment cannot cover its own costs, then that segment probably should not be retained (unless it has important side effects on other segments). Notice from Exhibit 12–2, for example, that Catalogue Sales has a negative segment margin. This means that the segment is not covering its own costs; it is generating more costs than it collects in revenue.[4]

From a decision-making point of view, the segment margin is most useful in major decisions that affect capacity such as dropping a segment. By contrast, as we noted earlier, the contribution margin is most useful in decisions relating to short-run changes in volume, such as pricing special orders that involve utilization of existing capacity.

---

4. Retention or elimination of product lines and other segments is covered in more depth in Chapter 13.

Managerial Accounting in Action

THE WRAP-UP

softsolutionsinc.

Shortly after Bill Carson, the SoftSolutions, Inc., controller, completed the draft segmented income statement, he sent copies to the other managers and scheduled a meeting in which the report could be explained. The meeting was held on the Monday following the first meeting; and Marjorie Matsuo, Lori Saffer, and Chris Worden were all in attendance.

Lori Saffer: I think these segmented income statements are fairly self-explanatory. However, there is one thing I wonder about.
Bill Carson: What's that?
Lori Saffer: What is this common fixed expense of $85,000 listed under the total company? And who is going to be responsible for it if neither Chris nor I have responsibility?
Bill Carson: The $85,000 of common fixed expenses represents expenses like general administrative salaries and the costs of common production equipment such as the automatic bar-coding machine. Marjorie, do you want to respond to the question about responsibility for these expenses?
Marjorie Matsuo: Sure. Since I'm the president of the company, I'm responsible for those costs. Some things can be delegated, others cannot be. It wouldn't make any sense for either you or Chris to make decisions about the bar coder, since it affects both of you. That's an important part of my job—making decisions about resources that affect all parts of the organization. This report makes it much clearer who is responsible for what. I like it.
Chris Worden: So do I—my division's segment margin is higher than the net income for the entire company.
Marjorie Matsuo: Don't get carried away, Chris. Let's not misinterpret what this report means. The segment margins *have* to be big to cover the common costs of the company. We can't let the big segment margins lull us into a sense of complacency. If we use these reports, we all have to agree that our objective is to increase all of the segment margins over time.
Lori Saffer: I'm willing to give it a try.
Chris Worden: The reports make sense to me.
Marjorie Matsuo: So be it. Then the first item of business would appear to be a review of catalogue sales of computer games, where we appear to be losing money. Chris, could you brief us on this at our next meeting?
Chris Worden: I'd be happy to. I have been suspecting for some time that our catalogue sales strategy could be improved.
Marjorie Matsuo: We look forward to hearing your analysis. Meeting's adjourned. ■

There Is More Than One Way to Segment a Company

SoftSolutions segmented its sales by division, by product line within each division, and by sales channel. An organization can be segmented in many ways. For example, two different ways of segmenting the sales of the General Electric Company are displayed in Exhibit 12–4. In the first diagram, the company's sales are segmented by geographic region. In the second diagram, they are segmented by products. Note that each of the diagrams could be continued, providing progressively more detailed segment data. For example, the sales in France could be broken down by major product line, then by product. Similar breakdowns could be done of General Electric's costs and segment margins, although that would require substantial additional analytical work to identify the segments to which various costs should be assigned.

Segment breakdowns such as those shown in Exhibit 12–4 give a company's managers the ability to look at the company from many different directions. With the

Exhibit 12–4
General Electric Company's Revenues Segmented by Geographic Region and Products

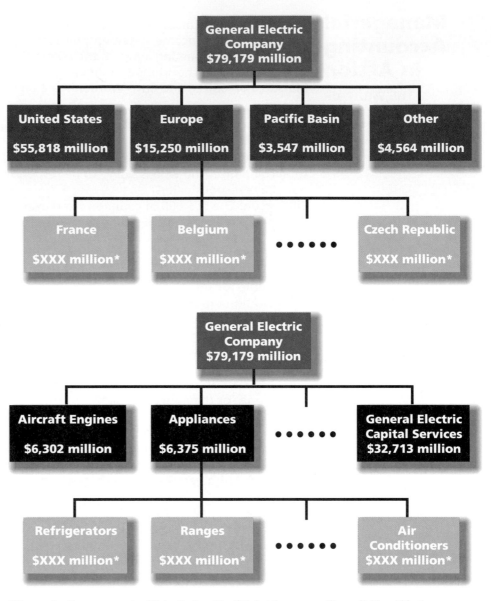

*These sales figures are not publicly disclosed by GE, but they are readily available within the company to managers.

increasing availability of companywide databases and sophisticated management information system software, detailed segmental reports of revenues, costs, and margins are becoming much easier to do.

Hindrances to Proper Cost Assignment

Objective 3

Identify three business practices that hinder proper cost assignment.

For segment reporting to accomplish its intended purposes, costs must be properly assigned to segments. If the purpose is to determine the profits being generated by a particular division, then all of the costs attributable to that division—and only those costs—should be assigned to it. Unfortunately, three business practices greatly hinder proper cost assignment: (1) omission of some costs in the assignment process, (2) the use of inappropriate methods for allocating costs among segments of a company, and (3) assignment to segments of costs that are really common costs.

Exhibit 12–5 Business Functions Making Up the Value Chain

Research and Development	Product Design	Manufacturing	Marketing	Distribution	Customer Service

Omission of Costs

Value chain The major business functions that add value to a company's products and services. These functions consist of research and development, product design, manufacturing, marketing, distribution, and customer service.

The costs assigned to a segment should include all costs attributable to that segment from the company's entire *value chain*. The **value chain,** which is illustrated in Exhibit 12–5, consists of the major business functions activities that add value to a company's products and services. All of these functions, from research and development, through product design, manufacturing, marketing, distribution, and customer service, are required to bring a product or service to the customer and generate revenues.

However, as discussed in Chapters 2, 3, and 7, only manufacturing costs are included in product costs for financial reporting purposes. Consequently, when trying to determine product profitability for internal decision-making purposes, some companies deduct only manufacturing costs from product revenues. As a result, such companies omit from their profitability analysis part or all of the "upstream" costs in the value chain, which consist of research and development and product design, and the "downstream" costs, which consist of marketing, distribution, and customer service. Yet these nonmanufacturing costs are just as essential in determining product profitability as are the manufacturing costs. These upstream and downstream costs, which are usually titled *Selling, General, and Administrative (SG&A)* on the income statement, can represent half or more of the total costs of an organization. If either the upstream or downstream costs are omitted in profitability analysis, then the product is undercosted and management may unwittingly develop and maintain products that in the long run result in losses rather than profits for the company.

Life cycle costing A costing approach that focuses on all costs along the value chain that will be generated throughout the entire life of a product.

Partly to avoid omitting costs that are an essential part of profitability analysis, some firms are turning to a concept known as *life cycle costing*. Essentially, **life cycle costing** focuses on all costs along the value chain that will be generated throughout the entire life of the product. This approach to costing helps ensure that no costs are omitted in profitability analysis.

Value chain analysis serves as a means of analyzing the internal operations or activities that contribute to the value on the product or service provided.[5] Separating the activities of an organization into those that contribute to the value perceived by the customer and those that do not provides an opportunity to focus management control on activities rather than responsibility departments in much the same way activity costing or activity management was presented in Chapters 8 and 9. Questions of spinning off non strategic non-value-added activities is an additional part of the value chain analysis that will be discussed in Chapters 13 and 15. Nevertheless, the focus on activity analysis as part of value chains can provide an instructive look at what is important to customers and hopefully avoid inappropriate costing or allocation.

---

5. Joseph G. Donelan and Edward A. Kaplan, "Value Chain Analysis: A Strategic Approach to Cost Management," *Journal of Cost Management* (March/April 1998). Also *Value Chain Analysis for Assessing Competitive Advantage,* Management Accounting Guideline #41, The Society of Management Accountants of Canada, 1996, provides an extensive discussion of the nature and role of value chains.

Inappropriate Methods for Allocating Costs among Segments

Cross-subsidization, or cost distortion, occurs when costs are improperly assigned among a company's segments. Cross-subsidization can occur in two ways; first, when companies fail to trace costs directly to segments in those situations where it is feasible to do so; and second, when companies use inappropriate bases to allocate costs.

FAILURE TO TRACE COSTS DIRECTLY   Costs that can be traced directly to a specific segment of a company should not be allocated to other segments. Rather, such costs should be charged directly to the responsible segment. For example, the rent for a branch office of an insurance company should be charged directly against the branch to which it relates rather than included in a companywide overhead pool and then spread throughout the company.

INAPPROPRIATE ALLOCATION BASE   Some companies allocate costs to segments using arbitrary bases such as sales dollars or cost of goods sold. For example, under the sales dollars approach, costs are allocated to the various segments according to the percentage of company sales generated by each segment. Thus, if a segment generates 20% of total company sales, it would be allocated 20% of the company's SG&A expenses as its "fair share." This same basic procedure is followed if costs of goods sold or some other measure is used as the allocation base.

For this approach to be valid, the allocation base must actually drive the overhead cost. (Or at least the allocation base should be highly correlated with the cost driver of the overhead cost.) For example, when sales dollars is used as the allocation base for SG&A expenses, it is implicitly assumed that SG&A expenses change in proportion to changes in total sales. If that is not true, the SG&A expenses allocated to segments will be misleading.

Arbitrarily Dividing Common Costs among Segments

The third business practice that leads to distorted segment costs is the practice of assigning nontraceable costs to segments. For example, some companies allocate the costs of the corporate headquarters building to products on segment reports. However, in a multiproduct company, no single product is likely to be responsible for any significant amount of this cost. Even if a product were eliminated entirely, there would usually be no significant effect on any of the costs of the corporate headquarters building. In short, there is no cause-and-effect relation between the cost of the corporate headquarters building and the existence of any one product. As a consequence, any allocation of the cost of the corporate headquarters building to the products must be arbitrary.

Common costs like the costs of the corporate headquarters building are necessary, of course, to have a functioning organization. The common practice of arbitrarily allocating these costs to segments is often justified on the grounds that "someone" has to "cover the common costs." While it is undeniably true that the common costs must be covered, arbitrarily allocating common costs to segments does not ensure that this will happen. In fact, adding a share of common costs to the real costs of a segment may make an otherwise profitable segment appear to be unprofitable. If a manager erroneously eliminates the segment, the revenues will be lost, the real costs of the segment will be saved, but the common costs will still be there. The net effect will be to reduce the profits of the company as a whole and make it even more difficult to "cover the common costs."

In summary, the way many companies handle segment reporting results in cost distortion. This distortion results from three practices—the failure to trace costs directly to a specific segment when it is feasible to do so, the use of inappropriate bases for allocating costs, and the allocation of common costs to segments. These practices are widespread. One study found that 60% of the companies surveyed made no attempt to assign SG&A costs to segments on a cause-and-effect basis.[6]

Customer Profitability Analysis

In prior sections, we have noted that companies analyze profitability in many ways, including by product, by market segment, and by channel of distribution. One frequently overlooked way to analyze profitability is by customer. Although managers generally assume that a dollar of sales to one customer is just as profitable as a dollar of sales to any other customer, this assumption may not be correct. The reason is that customers have varying demands for resource-consuming activities, just as products, markets, or other segments of a company have varying demands. For example, some customers order in smaller lots and more frequently than other customers, requiring more paperwork and materials handling. Some customers order nonstandard parts that require special engineering work, special machinery setups, and perhaps special packaging and handling. Other customers always seem to be in a hurry and want special expediting and delivery services. Customers who demand high levels of these resource-consuming activities should not be cross-subsidized by customers who demand little in the way of customized services, special packaging, and so forth. However, unless the activities that are provided for customer support are traced to the company's various customers, cross-subsidization almost certainly will occur.

After the various customer-support activities in a company have been identified, the costs of providing these activities should be charged to the customers who require them. Thus, a customer who requires special accounts receivable terms, many small orders and deliveries, the packing of goods in shop-ready containers, and specialized field service should be quoted a price that reflects these costly activities. This is why we stated in earlier chapters that suppliers who make deliveries to customers in a JIT environment frequently quote prices that are somewhat higher than prices charged by other suppliers. The higher prices are needed to compensate these suppliers for the special activities required on their part to support JIT customers.

Businesses that have analyzed customer profitability have been surprised to find that a fairly small number of customers are apparently responsible for most of their profits. It is also common to find that a small number of customers consume far more resources than are warranted by their revenues.

Revenue Variance Analysis

Objective 4

Analyze variances from revenue targets.

Segmented profitability analysis combined with the variance analysis discussed in Chaptera 10 and 11 can be used to generate a series of performance reports so that price and volumes (quantities) can be compared to targets set by the budgeting process. The interaction of price and quantity represents important information for businesses to analyze to determine why the strategic goals and specific budgeted targets were not achieved. Managers want to know the effects of market volume changes, market penetration or share changes, sales mix changes, and price changes. Each of these elements can be isolated but the true test of management is to reconstitute the combination needed for a new marketing strategy. Variances from previous results can provide a valuable start for this process.

The ability to have segment revenue data for analysis depends on the coding attached to the revenue information. Geographic, product line, customer, and sales personnel are common classifications. Managers, with the assistance of the accountant, must decide what they wish to know and what classifications can be realistically structured given the degree of substitutes and complements that exist, the number of products that exist, and the nature of meaningful groupings.

---

6. James R. Emore and Joseph A. Ness, "The Slow Pace of Meaningful Change in Cost Systems," *Journal of Cost Management* 4, no. 4 (Winter 1991), p. 39.

Exhibit 12–6   Actual and Budgeted Results

Actual Results		Flexible Budget		Master Budget	
Revenue:					
Deluxe (12,000 × $18)	$216,000	(12,000 × $20)	$240,000	(10,000 × $20)	$200,000
Standard (4,000 × $11)	44,000	(4,000 × $10)	40,000	(5,000 × $10)	50,000
	260,000		280,000		250,000
Variable expenses:					
Deluxe (12,000 × $8)	96,000	(12,000 × $8)	96,000	(10,000 × $8)	80,000
Standard (4,000 × $5)	20,000	(4,000 × $5)	20,000	(5,000 × $5)	25,000
	116,000		116,000		105,000
Contribution margin	$144,000		$164,000		$145,000
		Sales Price Variance		**Sales Volume Variance**	
Total variances		$20,000 U		$19,000 F	

To illustrate the nature of the variance reporting in the revenue area, consider the following example for Ace Video Company.

Budget sales in units:	
Deluxe video game	10,000
Standard video game	5,000
Budget price:	
Deluxe	$20
Standard	$10
Market volume expected:	
Deluxe	70,000
Standard	90,000
Budget variable expense:	
Deluxe	$8
Standard	$5

The sales price for the deluxe video game was reduced to $18 from the anticipated $20. This resulted in a $16,000 increase in revenue. The standard video game price was increased by $1 per unit resulting in a revenue decrease of $6,000. The reasoning behind the price and revenue changes is something marketing management should explain so that a new pricing strategy can be considered.

Actual results for the period were:

Unit sales:	
Deluxe	12,000
Standard	4,000
Sales prices:	
Deluxe	$18
Standard	$11
Market volume:	
Deluxe	75,000
Standard	85,000

Exhibit 12–6 presents a summary of the relations among budgeted and actual results.

Analysis of revenue variances can proceed as follows:

Sales price variance
Actual sales price minus budgeted sales price all times actual sales quantity.

$$\text{Sales price variance} = \left(\begin{array}{c} \text{Actual} \\ \text{sales price} \end{array} - \begin{array}{c} \text{Budgeted} \\ \text{sales price} \end{array} \right) \times \begin{array}{c} \text{Actual} \\ \text{sales volume} \end{array}$$

Deluxe	($18 − $20) × 12,000 units =	$24,000 U
Standard	($11 − $10) × 4,000 units =	4,000 F
	Total sales price variance =	$20,000 U

Market volume variance
Actual market volume minus budget market volume times anticipated market share all times budget contribution margin.

$$\begin{array}{c}\textbf{Market}\\\textbf{volume}\\\textbf{variance}\end{array} = \left[\left(\begin{array}{c}\text{Actual}\\\text{market}\\\text{volume}\end{array} - \begin{array}{c}\text{Budget}\\\text{market}\\\text{volume}\end{array}\right) \times \begin{array}{c}\text{Anticipated market}\\\text{share percentage}\end{array} \times \begin{array}{c}\text{Budgeted}\\\text{contribution}\\\text{margin per unit}\end{array}\right]$$

Deluxe	(75,000 − 70,000) × (10,000/70,000) × ($20 − $8) =	$8,571 F
Standard	(85,000 − 90,000) × (5,000/90,000) × ($10 − $5) =	$1,389 U
Total		$7,182 F

Market share variance
Actual sales volume minus the anticipated portion of the actual market volume all times budgeted contribution margin per unit.

$$\begin{array}{c}\textbf{Market}\\\textbf{share}\\\textbf{variance}\end{array} = \left[\begin{array}{c}\text{Actual}\\\text{sales}\\\text{quantity}\end{array} - \left(\begin{array}{c}\text{Actual}\\\text{market} \times\\\text{volume}\end{array} \begin{array}{c}\text{Anticipated}\\\text{market}\\\text{share}\end{array}\right)\right] \times \begin{array}{c}\text{Budgeted}\\\text{contribution}\\\text{margin per unit}\end{array}$$

Deluxe	(12,000 − [75,000 × (10,000/70,000)]) × ($20 − $8) =	$15,432 F
Standard	(4,000 − [85,000 × (5,000/90,000)]) × ($10 − $5) =	3,610 U
Total		$11,822 F

The market volume analysis and market share variances were calculated using the budget contribution margin. The use of the budget contribution numbers permits the isolation of volume effects from price effects at least for purposes of presentation. Ultimately managers may wish to consider the elasticity of the market in setting their future strategies.

The market volume variance used contribution margins. This is a common approach so that the profit effect of volume changes can be viewed. Alternative valuations could be used such as budgeted sales prices or budgeted gross margins if managers find these values more relevant.

The total market volume variance and market share variance help to analyze why sales quantities were 12,000 deluxe and 4,000 standard instead of the anticipated 10,000 deluxe and 5,000 standard. These quantity shifts resulted in a change in budgeted contribution as follows:

Deluxe	(12.000 − 10,000) × ($20 − $8) =	$24,000 F
Standard	(4,000 − 5,000) × ($10 − $5) =	5,000 U
Total		$19,000 F
Composition:	Market volume =	$7,182 F
	Market share =	11,822 F
		$19,004 F*

*$4 due to rounding

An alternative view of sales volume variances can be generated by examining sales mix and sales quantity variances in terms of their relationship to the budgeted contribution margin. To be meaningful, management must be in a position to control the mix of products it sells in the market. While alternative formulations are possible using gross margins, sales prices, or weighted average contribution margins, the straightforward use of contributions will be employed in the illustration that follows so the principle can be understood.

Sales mix variance
Actual sales quantity minus actual sales quantity based on budgeted mix all times budgeted sales price.

$$\begin{array}{c}\textbf{Sales}\\\textbf{mix}\\\textbf{variance}\end{array} = \left(\begin{array}{c}\text{Actual}\\\text{sales}\\\text{quantity}\end{array} - \begin{array}{c}\text{Actual sales}\\\text{quantity at}\\\text{anticipated}\\\text{sales mix}\end{array}\right) \times \begin{array}{c}\text{Budgeted}\\\text{contribution}\\\text{margin per unit}\end{array}$$

Deluxe $[12{,}000 - 16.000 \times (10/15)] \times (\$20 - \$8) =$ $\$15{,}996$ F

Standard $[4{,}000 - 16.000 \times (5/15)] \times (\$10 - \$5) =$ $6{,}665$ U

Total sales mix variance $=$ $\underline{\$\ 9{,}331\ F}$

where 16,000 units $= (12{,}000 + 4{,}000)$ and 10/15 is the anticipated proportion of deluxe sales while 5/15 is the anticipated standard mix proportion.

Sales quantity variance
Actual sales quantity based on budgeted mix minus budgeted sales quantity all times budgeted sales price.

$$\begin{array}{c} \text{Sales} \\ \text{quantity} \\ \text{variance} \end{array} = \left[\left(\begin{array}{c} \text{Actual sales} \\ \text{quantity at} \\ \text{anticipated} \\ \text{sales mix} \end{array} \right) - \begin{array}{c} \text{Anticipated} \\ \text{sales} \\ \text{quantity} \end{array} \right] \times \begin{array}{c} \text{Budgeted} \\ \text{contribution} \\ \text{margin per unit} \end{array}$$

Deluxe $\{[16{,}000 \times (10/15)] - 10{,}000\} \times (\$20 - \$8) =$ $\$8{,}004$ F

Standard $\{[16{,}000 \times (5/15)] - \ \ 5{,}000\} \times (\$10 - \$5) =$ $1{,}665$ F

Total sales quantity variance $\underline{\$9{,}669\ F}$

The total sales volume variance was $19,000, composed of the following:

Sales mix . . . . $\$\ 9{,}331$ F

Sales quantity . . . . $9{,}669$ F

Total . . . . $\underline{\$19{,}000\ F}$

Incentives

Sales personnel are often rewarded with incentives based on their sales performance. Two bases are used to calculate the commissions. One is to base commissions on sales revenue generated; the other uses contribution margin. Consider the following example from Hall Company.

Product	Sales Revenue	Contribution Margin
X	$40,000	$4,000
Y	20,000	3,000

If Joan Davidson receives 1% of total sales, her commission based on our example would be $1\% \times (\$40{,}000 + \$20{,}000)$ or $600. Joan, if she was expected to promote one or the other product, would not care which she sold because she receives the same for each. On the other hand, assume Joan receives 8.6% of the contribution margin. Joan's total commission would be $.086 \times (\$4{,}000 + \$3{,}000)$ or $602. However, if Joan were expected to trade off units of *X* for units of *Y* in her sales effort, she would be more inclined to sell *Y* than she would *X* because she receives $.086 \times \$3{,}000/\$20{,}000$ or 1.29% per sales dollar for *Y* compared to $.086 \times 4{,}000/40{,}000$ or .86% per sales dollar for product *X*. By determining incentives using contributions, Joan would be consistent in her objectives with the objectives of Hall company because Hall receives 15% per sales dollar for *Y* compared to 10% for product *X*.

Corel Corp. is attempting to gain market share from Microsoft with its Wordperfect Suite. Using both advertising and a very competitive cost of production Corel hopes to obtain better than 50% of the market. Costs to manufacture are quoted as $5 per unit of Office Suite. Retail prices are in the order of $350 U.S. Costs are kept low by using a CD-Roms instead of 30 to 40 diskettes. CD Roms cost less than $1 U.S. to manufacture, $2 to $3 for the manuals and $1 to $2 for packaging used in house production. Marketing and research, however, are added, 23% of sales for research and 50% for advertising, selling and administrative.[7]

Marketing Expense

Knowledge of the nature and behaviour of marketing expenses provides managers with information about the costs of their marketing endeavours. Such information represents a significant aspect of marketing efforts, one that is needed to complement the pricing strategy previously discussed. Transport, warehousing, selling, advertising, and credit are some of the key factors managers need to consider in their marketing strategy. Accurate cost behaviour and allocation by the accounting function can assist marketing decision makers.

Accountants typically decompose marketing expense into two general categories, order getting and order filling. Order getting costs are the pure marketing costs such as advertising, selling commissions, and travel. Order filling includes the costs of warehousing, transportation, packing, and credit. Order getting costs tend to be somewhat more discretionary than order filling because order filling occurs after the sale rather than to obtain the sale. Nevertheless, marketing managers need to understand the cost behaviour associated with both sets of costs so that analysis can be conducted to decide on what should be done and how. The simplified fixed variable analysis using sales dollars or sales units is too crude to provide suitable answers for many situations. Consider the following illustration:

Driver Analysis	Total for Period
Transport (kilometres to customer)	390 km
Jones Ltd.—30 km	
Smith Ltd.—60 km	
Selling (hours spent to call on per period)	500 hours
Jones Ltd.—200 hours	
Smith Ltd.—300 hours	
Advertising (relative cost of medium per period)	—
Jones Ltd.—3 weight	
Smith Ltd.—1 weight	
Warehousing (weight of product per unit)	13,000 kg
Product A—500 kg	
Product B—800 kg	
Credit/Collection (invoice ratio per shipment—Jones requires more time to pay and line item invoicing):	
Jones Ltd. 2 invoices per shipment, 10 units per invoice (4 of A, 6 of B)	5 shipments
Smith Ltd. 1 invoice per shipment, 10 units per invoice (6 of A, 4 of B)	5 shipments

	Costs for Period	
	Total	**Unit**
Transport	$ 1,950	$5 per km
Selling	7,500	$15 per hr
Advertising	4,000	—
Warehousing	6,500	$0.50 per kg
Credit/Collection	750	$50 per invoice
Total	$20,700	

7. Donald Rumball. "The Perfect Pitch," *The Financial Post Magazine* (December 1996), pp. 24–34.

	Costs to Customer		
	Jones Ltd.	**Smith Ltd.**	**Total**
Transport:			
$5/km × 5 × 30	$750		
$5/km × 4 × 60		$1,200	$1,950
Selling:			
$15/hr × 200 hours.............	3,000		
$15/hr × 300 hours.............		4,500	7,500
Advertising: 3/4 × $4,000..........	3,000		
1/4 × $4,000		1,000	4,000
Warehousing:			
$.50/kg × [(4 × 500) + (6 × 800)]..	3,400		
$.50/kg × [(6 × 500) + (4 × 800)]..		3,100	6,500
Credit/Collection:			
$50/invoice × 2 × 5	500		
$50/invoice × 1 × 5		250	750
	$10,650	$10,050	$20,700

When costs for a period are associated with their drivers and drivers can be associated with customers, marketing costs demonstrate the costs associated with particular customers.

	Costs to Products		
	Product A	**Product B**	**Total**
Transport—common	—	—	$1,950
Selling—common	—	—	7,500
Advertising—common	—	—	4,000
Warehousing:			
10 × 500 kg × $.50	$2,500		
10 × 800 kg × $.50		$4,000	$6,500
Credit/Collection—common	—	—	750
	$2,500	$4,000	$20,700

Because transport, selling, and advertising are independent of the type of product, they are treated as common costs for the product breakdown above. A similar situation exists for credit/collection since invoicing and collection costs are irrespective of the type of product. Only warehousing is a function of the product type and thus can be broken down by product type as well as customer.

Marketing expense analysis uses the concepts of drivers to provide alternative views of the relationship of marketing costs to sales. The complexity of the analysis depends on the ability to define appropriate cost drivers for the marketing costs in a manner similar to the approach used with overhead costs as explained in Chapter 8. To avoid unnecessarily arbitrary allocations, expenses that do not have suitable drivers should be treated as common costs that are not incremental for the particular categories of the breakdown attempted. Management may decide that further analysis of these common costs can result in refined driver definitions, which in turn will permit cause/effect allocations of common marketing costs.

Rate of Return for Measuring Managerial Performance

When a company is truly decentralized, segment managers are given a great deal of autonomy. So great is this autonomy that the various profit and investment centres are often viewed as being virtually independent businesses, with their managers having

Objective 6

Compute the return on investment (ROI).

about the same control over decisions as if they were in fact running their own independent firms. With this autonomy, fierce competition often develops among managers, with each striving to make his or her segment the "best" in the company.

Competition between investment centres is particularly keen for investment funds. How do top managers in corporate headquarters go about deciding who gets new investment funds as they become available, and how do these managers decide which investment centres are most profitably using the funds that have already been entrusted to their care? One of the most popular ways of making these judgments is to measure the rate of return that investment centre managers are able to generate on their assets. This rate of return is called the *return on investment (ROI)*.

The Return on Investment (ROI) Formula

Return on investment (ROI) Net operating income divided by average operating assets. It also equals margin multiplied by turnover.

The **return on investment (ROI)** is defined as net operating income divided by average operating assets:

$$ROI = \frac{\text{Net operating income}}{\text{Average operating assets}}$$

There are some issues about how to measure net operating income and average operating assets, but this formula seems clear enough. The higher the return on investment (ROI) of a business segment, the greater the profit generated per dollar invested in the segment's operating assets.

Net Operating Income and Operating Assets Defined

Net operating income Income before interest and income taxes have been deducted.

Note that *net operating income,* rather than net income, is used in the ROI formula. **Net operating income** is income before interest and taxes and is sometimes referred to as EBIT (earnings before interest and taxes). The reason for using net operating income in the formula is that the income figure used should be consistent with the base to which it is applied. Notice that the base (i.e., denominator) consists of *operating assets*. Thus, to be consistent we use net operating income in the numerator.

Operating assets Cash, accounts receivable, inventory, plant and equipment, and all other assets held for productive use in an organization.

Operating assets include cash, accounts receivable, inventory, plant and equipment, and all other assets held for productive use in the organization. Examples of assets that would not be included in the operating assets category, (i.e., examples of nonoperating assets) would include land held for future use, an investment in another company, or a factory building rented to someone else. The operating assets base used in the formula is typically computed as the average of the operating assets between the beginning and the end of the year.

Plant and Equipment: Net Book Value or Gross Cost?

A major issue in ROI computations is the dollar amount of plant and equipment that should be included in the operating assets base. To illustrate the problem involved, assume that a company reports the following amounts for plant and equipment on its balance sheet:

Plant and equipment	$3,000,000
Less accumulated depreciation	900,000
Net book value	$2,100,000

What dollar amount of plant and equipment should the company include with its operating assets in computing ROI? One widely used approach is to include only the plant and equipment's *net book value*—that is, the plant's original cost less accumulated depreciation ($2,100,000 in the example above). A second approach is to ignore depreciation and include the plant's entire *gross cost* in the operating assets base ($3,000,000 in the example above). Both of these approaches are used in actual practice, even though they will obviously yield very different operating asset and ROI figures.

The following arguments can be raised for using net book value to measure operating assets and for using gross cost to measure operating assets in ROI computation:

Arguments for Using Net Book Value to Measure Operating Assets in ROI Computations:

1. The net book value method is consistent with how plant and equipment are reported on the balance sheet (i.e., cost less accumulated depreciation to date).
2. The net book value method is consistent with the computation of operating income, which includes depreciation as an operating expense.

Arguments for Using Gross Cost to Measure Operating Assets in ROI Computations:

1. The gross cost method eliminates both the age of equipment and the method of depreciation as factors in ROI computations. (Under the net book value method, ROI will tend to increase over time as net book value declines due to depreciation.)
2. The gross cost method does not discourage replacement of old, worn-out equipment. (Under the net book value method, replacing fully depreciated equipment with new equipment can have a dramatic, adverse effect on ROI.)

Managers generally view consistency as the most important of the considerations above. As a result, a majority of companies use the net book value approach in ROI computations. In this text, we will also use the net book value approach unless a specific exercise or problem directs otherwise.

Controlling the Rate of Return

Objective 7

Show how changes in sales, expenses, and assets affect an organization's ROI.

When we first defined the return on investment, we used the following formula:

$$\text{ROI} = \frac{\text{Net operating income}}{\text{Average operating assets}}$$

We can modify this formula slightly by introducing sales as follows:

$$\text{ROI} = \frac{\text{Net operating income}}{\text{Sales}} \times \frac{\text{Sales}}{\text{Average operating assets}}$$

The first term on the right-hand side of the equation is the *margin*, which is defined as follows:

Margin Net operating income divided by sales.

$$\text{Margin} = \frac{\text{Net operating income}}{\text{Sales}}$$

The **margin** is a measure of management's ability to control operating expenses in relation to sales. The lower the operating expenses per dollar of sales, the higher the margin earned.

The second term on the right-hand side of the preceding equation is *turnover* which is defined as follows:

$$\text{Turnover} = \frac{\text{Sales}}{\text{Average operating assets}}$$

Turnover The amount of sales generated in an investment centre for each dollar invested in operating assets. It is computed by dividing sales by the average operating assets figure.

Turnover is a measure of the sales that are generated for each dollar invested in operating assets.

The following alternative form of the ROI formula, which we will use most frequently, combines margin and turnover:

$$\text{ROI} = \text{Margin} \times \text{Turnover}$$

Which formula for ROI should be used—the original one stated in terms of net operating income and average operating assets or this one stated in terms of margin and turnover? Either can be used—they will always give the same answer. However, the margin and turnover formulation provides some additional insights.

Some managers tend to focus too much on margin and ignore turnover. To some degree at least, the margin can be a valuable indicator of a manager's performance. Standing alone, however, it overlooks one very crucial area of a manager's responsibility—the investment in operating assets. Excessive funds tied up in operating assets, which depresses turnover, can be just as much of a drag on profitability as excessive operating expenses, which depresses margin. One of the advantages of ROI as a performance measure is that it forces the manager to control the investment in operating assets as well as to control expenses and the margin.

Du Pont pioneered the ROI concept and recognized the importance of looking at both margin and turnover in assessing the performance of a manager. The ROI formula is now widely used as the key measure of the performance of an investment centre. The ROI formula blends together many aspects of the manager's responsibilities into a single figure that can be compared to the returns of competing investment centres, the returns of other firms in the industry, and to the past returns of the investment centre itself.

Du Pont also developed the diagram that appears in Exhibit 12–7. This exhibit helps managers understand how they can control ROI. An investment centre manager can increase ROI in basically three ways:

1. Increase sales.
2. Reduce expenses.
3. Reduce assets.

To illustrate how the rate of return can be improved by each of these three actions, consider how the manager of the Monthaven Burger Grill is evaluated. Burger Grill is a small chain of upscale casual restaurants that has been rapidly adding outlets via franchising. The Monthaven franchise is owned by a group of local surgeons who have little time to devote to management and little expertise in business matters. Therefore, they delegate operating decisions—including decisions concerning investment in operating assets such as inventories—to a professional manager they have hired. The manager is evaluated largely based on the ROI the franchise generates.

The following data represent the results of operations for the most recent month:

Net operating income	$ 10,000
Sales	100,000
Average operating assets	50,000

The rate of return generated by the Monthaven Burger Grill investment centre is as follows:

Exhibit 12–7   Elements of Return on Investment (ROI)

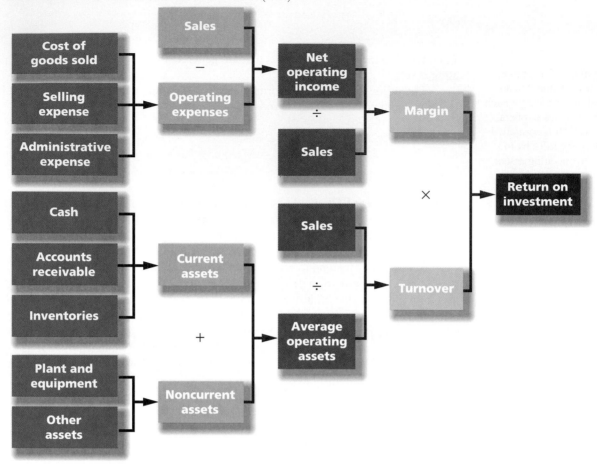

$$ROI = \quad \text{Margin} \quad \times \quad \text{Turnover}$$

$$\frac{\text{Net operating income}}{\text{Sales}} \times \frac{\text{Sales}}{\text{Average operating assets}}$$

$$\frac{\$10,000}{\$100,000} \times \frac{\$100,000}{\$50,000}$$

$$10\% \quad \times \quad 2 \quad = 20\%$$

As we stated above, to improve the ROI figure, the manager can (1) increase sales, (2) reduce expenses, or (3) reduce the operating assets.

APPROACH 1: INCREASE SALES   Assume that the manager of the Monthaven Burger Grill is able to increase sales from $100,000 to $110,000. Assume further that either because of good cost control or because some costs in the company are fixed, the net operating income increases even more rapidly, going from $10,000 to $12,000 per period. The operating assets remain constant.

$$ROI = \frac{\$12,000}{\$110,000} \times \frac{\$110,000}{\$50,000}$$

$$10.91\% \quad \times \quad 2.2 \quad = 24\% \text{ (as compared to 20\% above)}$$

APPROACH 2: REDUCE EXPENSES   Assume that the manager of the Monthaven Burger Grill is able to reduce expenses by $1,000 so that net operating income increases from $10,000 to $11,000. Both sales and operating assets remain constant.

$$ROI = \frac{\$11,000}{\$100,000} \times \frac{\$100,000}{\$50,000}$$

$$11\% \quad \times \quad 2 \quad = 22\% \text{ (as compared to 20\% above)}$$

APPROACH 3: REDUCE ASSETS   Assume that the manager of the Monthaven Burger Grill is able to reduce operating assets from $50,000 to $40,000. Sales and net operating income remain unchanged.

$$ROI = \frac{\$10,000}{\$100,000} \times \frac{\$100,000}{\$40,000}$$

$$10\% \quad \times \quad 2.5 \quad = 25\% \text{ (as compared to 20\% above)}$$

A clear understanding of these three approaches to improving the ROI figure is critical to the effective management of an investment centre. We will now look at each approach in more detail.

Increase Sales

In first looking at the ROI formula, one is inclined to think that the sales figure is neutral, since it appears as the denominator in the margin computation and as the numerator in the turnover computation. We *could* cancel out the sales figure, but we do not do so for two reasons. First, this would tend to draw attention away from the fact that the rate of return is a function of *two* variables, margin and turnover. And second, it would tend to conceal the fact that a change in sales can affect both the margin and the turnover in an organization. To explain, a change in sales can affect the *margin* if expenses increase or decrease at a different rate than sales. For example, a company may be able to keep a tight control on its costs as its sales go up, with the result that net operating income increases more rapidly than sales and increases the margin. Or a company may have fixed expenses that remain constant as sales go up, resulting in an increase in the net operating income and in the margin. Either (or both) of these factors could have been responsible for the increase in the margin percentage from 10% to 10.91% illustrated in approach 1 above.

Further, a change in sales can affect the *turnover* if sales either increase or decrease without a proportionate increase or decrease in the operating assets. In the first approach above, for example, sales increased from $100,000 to $110,000, but the operating assets remained unchanged. As a result, the turnover increased from 2 to 2.2 for the period.

Reduce Expenses

Often the easiest route to increased profitability and to a stronger ROI figure is to simply cut the "fat" out of an organization through a concerted effort to control expenses. When margins begin to be squeezed, this is generally the first line of attack by a manager. Discretionary fixed costs usually come under scrutiny first, and various programs are either curtailed or eliminated in an effort to cut costs. Managers must be careful, however, not to cut out muscle and bone along with the fat. Also, they must remember that frequent cost-cutting binges can destroy morale. Most managers now agree that it is best to stay "lean and mean" all of the time.

Reduce Operating Assets

Managers have always been sensitive to the need to control sales, operating expenses, and operating margins. However, they have not always been equally sensitive to the need to control investment in operating assets. Firms that have adopted the ROI approach to measuring managerial performance report that one of the first reactions of investment centre managers is to trim their investment in operating assets. The reason, of course, is that these managers soon realize that an excessive investment in operating assets reduces turnover and hurts the ROI. As these managers reduce their investment in operating assets, funds are released that can be used elsewhere in the organization.

How can an investment centre manager control the investment in operating assets? One approach is to eliminate unneeded inventory. JIT purchasing and JIT manufacturing have been extremely helpful in reducing inventories of all types, with the result that ROI figures have improved dramatically in some companies. Another approach is to devise various methods of speeding up the collection of receivables. For example, many firms now employ the lockbox technique by which customers in distant locations send their payments directly to post office boxes in their area. The funds are received and deposited by a local bank on behalf of the payee firm. This speeds up the collection process, since the payments are not delayed in the postal system. As a result of the speedup in collection, the accounts receivable balance is reduced and the asset turnover is increased.

ROI and the Balanced Scorecard

Simply exhorting managers to increase ROI is not sufficient. Managers who are told to increase ROI will naturally wonder how this is to be accomplished. The Du Pont scheme, which is illustrated in Exhibit 12–7, provides managers with *some* guidance. Generally speaking, ROI can be increased by increasing sales, decreasing costs, and/or decreasing investments in operating assets. However, it may not be obvious to managers *how* they are supposed to increase sales, decrease costs, and decrease investments in a way that is consistent with the company's strategy. For example, a manager who is given inadequate guidance may cut back on investments that are critical to implementing the company's strategy.

For that reason, as discussed in Chapter 10, when managers are evaluated based on ROI, a balanced scorecard approach is advised. And indeed, ROI, or residual income (discussed below), is typically included as one of the financial performance measures on a company's balanced scorecard. As we discussed in Chapter 10, the balanced scorecard provides a way of communicating a company's strategy to managers throughout the organization. The scorecard indicates *how* the company intends to improve its financial performance. A well-constructed balanced scorecard should answer questions like: "What internal business processes should be improved?" and "Which customer should be targeted and how will they be attracted and retained at a profit?" In short, a well-constructed balanced scorecard can provide managers with a road map that indicates how the company intends to increase its ROI. In the absence of such a road map of the company's strategy, managers may have difficulty understanding what they are supposed to do to increase ROI and they may work at cross-purposes rather than in harmony with the overall strategy of the company.

Criticisms of ROI

Although ROI is widely used in evaluating performance, it is not a perfect tool. The method is subject to the following criticisms:

1. Just telling managers to increase ROI may not be enough. Managers may not know how to increase ROI; they may increase ROI in a way that is inconsistent with the company's strategy; or they may take actions that increase ROI in the short run but harm the company in the long run (such as cutting back on research and development). This is why ROI is best used as part of a balanced scorecard as discussed above. A balanced scorecard can provide concrete guidance to managers, make it more likely that actions taken are consistent with the company's strategy, and reduce the likelihood that short-run performance will be enhanced at the expense of long-term performance.
2. A manager who takes over a business segment typically inherits many committed costs over which the manager has no control. These committed costs may be

relevant in assessing the performance of the business segment as an investment but make it difficult to fairly assess the performance of the manager relative to other managers.

3. As discussed in the next section, a manager who is evaluated based on ROI may reject profitable investment opportunities.

Residual Income—Another Measure of Performance

Objective 8

Compute residual income and understand the strengths and weaknesses of this method of measuring performance.

Residual income The net operating income that an investment centre earns above the required return on its operating assets.

Economic value added (EVA) A concept similar to residual income.

Another approach to measuring an investment centre's performance focuses on a concept known as *residual income*. **Residual income** is the net operating income that an investment centre earns above the minimum required return on its operating assets. **Economic value added (EVA)** is a similar concept that differs in some details from residual income.[8] For example, under the economic value added concept, funds used for research and development are treated as investments rather than as expenses.[9] However, for our purposes, we will not draw any distinction between residual income and economic value added.

When residual income or economic value added is used to measure performance, the purpose is to maximize the total amount of residual income or economic value added, not to maximize overall ROI. Organizations as diverse as Coca-Cola, Quaker Oats, the Maritime Tel & Tel, Domtar, and Nortel have embraced some version of residual income in recent years.

For purposes of illustration, consider the following data for an investment centre—the Ketchican Division of Alaskan Marine Services Corporation.

ALASKAN MARINE SERVICES CORPORATION
Ketchican Division
Basic Data for Performance Evaluation

Average operating assets	$100,000
Net operating income	$ 20,000
Minimum required rate of return	15%

Alaskan Marine Services Corporation has long had a policy of evaluating investment centre managers based on ROI, but it is considering a switch to residual income. The controller of the company, who is in favour of the change to residual income, has provided the following table that shows how the performance of the division would be evaluated under each of the two methods:

ALASKAN MARINE SERVICES CORPORATION
Ketchican Division

	Alternative Performance Measures	
	ROI	**Residual Income**
Average operating assets	$100,000 (a)	$100,000
Net operating income	$ 20,000 (b)	$ 20,000
ROI, (b) ÷ (a)	20%	
Minimum required return (15% × $100,000)		15,000
Residual income		$ 5,000

---

8. The basic idea underlying residual income and economic value added has been around for over 100 years. In recent years, economic value added has been popularized and trademarked by the consulting firm Stern, Stewart & Co.

9. Over 100 different adjustments could be made for deferred taxes, LIFO reserves, provisions for future liabilities, mergers and acquisitions, gains or losses due to changes in accounting rules, operating leases, and other accounts, but most companies make only a few. For further details, see S. David Young, *Economic Value Added*, INSEAD working paper 02/97–4667, INSEAD, 77305 Fontainebleau, France.

The reasoning underlying the residual income calculation is straightforward. The company is able to earn a rate of return of at least 15% on its investments. Since the company has invested $100,000 in the Ketchican Division in the form of operating assets, the company should be able to earn at least $15,000 (15% × $100,000) on this investment. Since the Ketchican Division's net operating income is $20,000, the residual income above and beyond the minimum required return is $5,000. If residual income is adopted as the performance measure to replace ROI, the manager of the Ketchican Division would be evaluated based on the growth from year to year in residual income.

Motivation and Residual Income

One of the primary reasons why the controller of Alaskan Marine Services Corporation would like to switch from ROI to residual income has to do with how managers view new investments under the two performance measurement schemes. The residual income approach encourages managers to make investments that are profitable for the entire company but that would be rejected by managers who are evaluated by the ROI formula.

To illustrate this problem, suppose that the manager of the Ketchican Division is considering purchasing a computerized diagnostic machine to aid in servicing marine diesel engines. The machine would cost $25,000 and is expected to generate additional operating income of $4,500 a year. From the standpoint of the company, this would be a good investment since it promises a rate of return of 18% ($4,500 ÷ $25,000), which is in excess of the company's minimum required rate of return of 15%.

If the manager of the Ketchican Division is evaluated based on residual income, she would be in favour of the investment in the diagnostic machine as shown below:

ALASKAN MARINE SERVICES CORPORATION
Ketchican Division
Performance Evaluated Using Residual Income

	Present	New Project	Overall
Average operating assets	$100,000	$25,000	$125,000
Net operating income	$ 20,000	$ 4,500	$ 24,500
Minimum required return	15,000	3,750*	18,750
Residual income	$ 5,000	$ 750	$ 5,750

*$25,000 × 15% = $3,750.

Since the project would increase the residual income of the Ketchican Division, the manager would want to invest in the new diagnostic machine.

Now suppose that the manager of the Ketchican Division is evaluated based on ROI. The effect of the diagnostic machine on the division's ROI is computed below:

ALASKAN MARINE SERVICES CORPORATION
Ketchican Division
Performance Evaluated Using ROI

	Present	New Project	Overall
Average operating assets (a)	$100,000	$25,000	$125,000
Net operating income (b)	$ 20,000	$ 4,500[†]	$ 24,500
ROI, (b) ÷ (a)	20%	18%	19.6%

[†]$25,000 × 18% = $4,500.

The new project reduces the division's ROI from 20% to 19.6%. This happens because the 18% rate of return on the new diagnostic machine, while above the company's 15% minimum rate of return, is below the division's present ROI of 20%. Therefore, the new diagnostic machine would drag the division's ROI down even though it would be a good investment from the standpoint of the company as a whole. If the manager of the division is evaluated based on ROI, she will be reluctant to even propose such an investment.

Basically, a manager who is evaluated based on ROI will reject any project whose rate of return is below the division's current ROI even if the rate of return on the project is above the minimum required rate of return for the entire company. In contrast, any project whose rate of return is above the minimum required rate of return for the company will result in an increase in residual income. Since it is in the best interests of the company as a whole to accept any project whose rate of return is above the minimum required rate of return, managers who are evaluated based on residual income will tend to make better decisions concerning investment projects than managers who are evaluated based on ROI.

Divisional Comparison and Residual Income

The residual income approach has one major disadvantage. It cannot be used to compare the performance of divisions of different sizes. You would expect larger divisions to have more residual income than smaller divisions, not necessarily because they are better managed but simply because of the bigger numbers involved.

As an example, consider the following residual income computations for Division X and Division Y:

	Division	
	X	**Y**
Average operating assets (a)	$1,000,000	$250,000
Net operating income	$ 120,000	$ 40,000
Minimum required return: 10% × (a)	100,000	25,000
Residual income	$ 20,000	$ 15,000

Observe that Division X has slightly more residual income than Division Y, but that Division X has $1,000,000 in operating assets as compared to only $250,000 in operating assets for Division Y. Thus, Division X's greater residual income is probably more a result of its size than the quality of its management. In fact, it appears that the smaller division is better managed, since it has been able to generate nearly as much residual income with only one-fourth as much in operating assets to work with. This problem can be reduced to some degree by focusing on the percentage change in residual income from year to year rather than on the absolute amount of the residual income.

RI/EVA Summary

Residual income and its derivative EVA include in the final result a composite picture of revenue, expenses, assets and the cost of investment capital (debt and equity). This measure is suggested to be more closely related to share price activity than any of the individual or other composites such as revenue growth, net income however defined, or ROI. Thus the advantage of the measure of performance is its focus on a key strategic objective, shareholder returns. Other suggested advantages include a more direct link to capital budgets similar to that shown in Chapter 14 when comparing ROI to net present value. The more direct relation of EVA to share prices provides a base for senior executive bonuses that helps to direct these executives in a manner that is consistent with shareholder interests.

EVA and residual income are not without their detractors. Both are historical based which means that particularly capital assets can suffer from being out of date in the same ways as mentioned with ROI. EVA/RI do not suggest whether the results achieved are the "best" that could have been achieved, thus a means of comparison is needed to evaluate results. EVA requires numerous adjustments that can increase the cost of preparing the information. EVA and residual income provide a single composite result that lacks the comprehensiveness of balance scorecards (see Chapter 10). However, regardless of the difficulties, EVA represents an example of the attempts to measure performance in a manner that focuses results on the strategic objectives of the firm.[10]

Summary

Segment reports can provide information for evaluating the profitability and performance of divisions, product lines, sales territories, and other segments of a company. Under the contribution approach to segment reporting, only those costs that are traceable are assigned to a segment. Fixed common costs and other nontraceable costs are not allocated to a segment. A cost is considered to be traceable to a segment only if the cost is caused by the segment and eliminating the segment would result in avoiding the cost.

Analysis provided by accountants can help managers view the important segment of marketing in a new light. Revenue and sales quantity analysis provide information about the effects of market changes or sales mix changes on profits. Association of marketing expenses with drivers that cause these expenses permits a review of how marketing activities cause expenses. Activity analysis is a powerful tool for assisting managers to understand marketing activities and their costs.

Costs that are traceable to a segment are further classified as either variable or fixed. The contribution margin is sales less variable costs. The segment margin is the contribution margin less the traceable fixed costs of the segment.

For purposes of evaluating the performance of managers, there are at least three kinds of business segments—cost centres, profit centres, and investment centres. Return on investment (ROI) is widely used to evaluate investment centre performance. However, there is a trend toward using residual income or economic value added instead of ROI. The residual income and economic value added approaches encourage profitable investments in many situations where the ROI approach would discourage investment.

Review Problem 1: Segmented Statements

The business staff of the legal firm Frampton, Davis & Smythe has constructed the following report which breaks down the firm's overall results for last month in terms of its two main business segments—family law and commercial law:

	Total	Family Law	Commercial Law
Revenues from clients	$1,000,000	$400,000	$600,000
Less variable expenses	220,000	100,000	120,000
Contribution margin	780,000	300,000	480,000
Less traceable fixed expenses	670,000	280,000	390,000
Segment margin	110,000	20,000	90,000
Less common fixed expenses	60,000	24,000	36,000
Net income	$ 50,000	$ (4,000)	$ 54,000

However, this report is not quite correct. The common fixed expenses such as the managing partner's salary, general administrative expenses, and general firm advertising have been allocated to the two segments based on revenues from clients.

---

10. For more technical discussions and alternative measures of EVA see Michael Senyshen, "Touch of EVA," *CGA Magazine* (February 1999), pp. 20–27; or see *Measuring and Managing Shareholder Value Creation,* Management Accounting Guideline #44, The Society of Management Accountants of Canada, 1997.

Required

1. Redo the segment report, eliminating the allocation of common fixed expenses. Show both Amount and Percent columns for the firm as a whole and for each of the segments. Would the firm be better off financially if the family law segment were dropped? (Note: Many of the firm's commercial law clients also use the firm for their family law requirements such as drawing up wills.)

2. The firm's advertising agency has proposed an ad campaign targeted at boosting the revenues of the family law segment. The ad campaign would cost $20,000, and the advertising agency claims that it would increase family law revenues by $100,000. The managing partner of Frampton, Davis & Smythe believes this increase in business could be accommodated without any increase in fixed expenses. What effect would this ad campaign have on the family law segment margin and on overall net income of the firm?

Solution to Review Problem 1

1. The corrected segmented income statement appears below:

	Total		Family Law		Commercial Law	
	Amount	Percent	Amount	Percent	Amount	Percent
Revenues from clients	$1,000,000	100%	$400,000	100%	$600,000	100%
Less variable expenses	220,000	22%	100,000	25%	120,000	20%
Contribution margin	780,000	78%	300,000	75%	480,000	80%
Less traceable fixed expenses	670,000	67%	280,000	70%	390,000	65%
Segment margin	110,000	11%	$ 20,000	5%	$ 90,000	15%
Less common fixed expenses	60,000	6%				
Net income	$ 50,000	5%				

No, the firm would not be financially better off if the family law practice were dropped. The family law segment is covering all of its own costs and is contributing $20,000 to covering the common fixed expenses of the firm. While the segment margin as a percent of sales is much lower for family law than for commercial law, it is still profitable; and it is likely that family law is a service that the firm must provide to its commercial clients in order to remain competitive.

2. The ad campaign would be expected to add $55,000 to the family law segment as follows:

Increased revenues from clients	$100,000
Family law contribution margin ratio	×75%
Incremental contribution margin	75,000
Less cost of the ad campaign	20,000
Increased segment margin	$ 55,000

Since there would be no increase in fixed expenses (including common fixed expenses), the increase in overall net income should also be $55,000.

Review Problem 2: Return on Investment (ROI) and Residual Income

The Magnetic Imaging Division of Medical Diagnostics, Inc., has reported the following results for last year's operations:

Sales	$25 million
Net operating income	3 million
Average operating assets	10 million

Required
1. Compute the margin, turnover, and ROI for the Magnetic Imaging Division.
2. Top management of Medical Diagnostics, Inc., has set a minimum required rate of return on average operating assets of 25%. What is the Magnetic Imaging Division's residual income for the year?

Solution to Review Problem 2

1. The required calculations appear below:

$$\text{Margin} = \frac{\text{Net operating income, \$3,000,000}}{\text{Sales, \$25,000,000}}$$

$$= 12\%$$

$$\text{Turnover} = \frac{\text{Sales, \$25,000,000}}{\text{Average operating assets, \$10,000,000}}$$

$$= 2.5$$

$$\text{ROI} = \text{Margin} \times \text{Turnover}$$
$$= 12\% \times 2.5$$
$$= 30\%$$

2. The residual income for the Magnetic Imaging Division is computed as follows:

Average operating assets	$10,000,000
Net operating income	$ 3,000,000
Minimum required return (25% × $10,000,000)	2,500,000
Residual income	$ 500,000

Appendix 12A: Transfer Pricing

Transfer price The price charged when one division or segment provides goods or services to another division or segment of an organization.

There are special problems in evaluating the performance of business segments when goods or services are transferred from one division to another. The problems revolve around the question of what *transfer price* to charge between the segments. A **transfer price** is the price charged when one segment of a company provides goods or services to another segment of the company. For example, most companies in the oil industry, such as Imperial, Shell, and Petro Canada, have petroleum refining and retail sales divisions that are evaluated on the basis of ROI or residual income. The petroleum refining division processes crude oil into gasoline, kerosene, lubricants, and other end products. The retail sales division takes gasoline and other products from the refining division and sells them through the company's chain of service stations. Each product has a price for transfers within the company. Suppose the transfer price for gasoline is $0.20 a litre. Then the refining division gets credit for $0.20 a litre of revenue on its segment report and the retailing division must deduct $0.20 a litre as an expense on its segment report. Clearly, the refining division would like the transfer price to be as high as possible, whereas the retailing division would like the transfer price to be as low as possible. However, the transaction has no direct effect on the entire company's reported profit. It is like taking money out of one pocket and putting it into the other.

Managers are intensely interested in how transfer prices are set, since they can have a dramatic effect on the apparent profitability of a division. Three common approaches are used to set transfer prices:

1. Allow the managers involved in the transfer to negotiate their own transfer price.
2. Set transfer prices at cost using:
   a. Variable cost.
   b. Full (absorption) cost.
3. Set transfer prices at the market price.

We will consider each of these transfer pricing methods in turn, beginning with negotiated transfer prices. Throughout the discussion we should keep in mind that *the fundamental objective in setting transfer prices is to motivate the managers to act in the best interests of the overall company.* In contrast, **suboptimization** occurs when managers do not act in the best interests of the overall company or even in the best interests of their own segment.

Negotiated Transfer Prices

Suboptimization An overall level of profitability that is less than a segment or a company is capable of earning.

Objective 9

Determine the range, if any, within which a negotiated transfer price should fall.

Negotiated transfer price A transfer price agreed on between buying and selling divisions.

A **negotiated transfer price** is a transfer price that is agreed on between the selling and purchasing divisions. Negotiated transfer prices have several important advantages. First, this approach preserves the autonomy of the divisions and is consistent with the spirit of decentralization. Second, the managers of the divisions are likely to have much better information about the potential costs and benefits of the transfer than others in the company.

When negotiated transfer prices are used, the managers who are involved in a proposed transfer within the company meet to discuss the terms and conditions of the transfer. They may decide not to go through with the transfer, but if they do, they must agree to a transfer price. Generally speaking, we cannot predict the exact transfer price they will agree to. However, we can confidently predict two things: (1) the selling division will agree to the transfer only if the profits of the selling division increase as a result of the transfer, and (2) the purchasing division will agree to the transfer only if the profits of the purchasing division also increase as a result of the transfer. This may seem obvious, but it is an important point.

Clearly, if the transfer price is below the selling division's cost, a loss will occur on the transaction and the selling division will refuse to agree to the transfer. Likewise, if the transfer price is set too high, it will be impossible for the purchasing division to make any profit on the transferred item. For any given proposed transfer, the transfer price has both a lower limit (determined by the situation of the selling division) and an upper limit (determined by the situation of the purchasing division). The actual transfer price agreed to by the two division managers can fall anywhere between those two limits. These limits determine the **range of acceptable transfer prices**—the range of transfer prices within which the profits of both divisions participating in a transfer would increase.

Range of acceptable transfer prices The range of transfer prices within which the profits of both the selling division and the purchasing division would increase as a result of a transfer.

An example will help us to understand negotiated transfer prices. Harris & Louder, Ltd. owns fast-food restaurants and snack food and beverage manufacturers in the United Kingdom. One of the restaurants, Pizza Maven, serves a variety of beverages along with pizzas. One of the beverages is ginger beer, which is served on tap. Harris & Louder has just purchased a new division, Imperial Beverages, that produces ginger beer. The managing director of Imperial Beverages has approached the managing director of Pizza Maven about purchasing Imperial Beverage ginger beer for sale at Pizza Maven restaurants rather than its usual brand of ginger beer. Managers at Pizza Maven agree that the quality of Imperial Beverages' ginger beer is comparable to the quality of their regular brand. It is just a question of price. The basic facts are listed below:

Imperial Beverage:
Ginger beer production capacity per month	10,000	barrels
Variable cost per barrel of ginger beer	£8	per barrel
Fixed costs per month	£70,000	
Selling price of Imperial Beverage ginger beer on the outside market	£20	per barrel

Pizza Maven:
Purchase price of regular brand of ginger beer	£18	per barrel
Monthly consumption of ginger beer	2,000	barrels

THE SELLING DIVISION'S LOWEST ACCEPTABLE TRANSFER PRICE

The selling division, Imperial Beverage will be interested in a proposed transfer only if its profit increases. Clearly, the transfer price must not fall below the variable cost per barrel of £8. In addition, if Imperial Beverage has insufficient capacity to fill the Pizza Maven order, then it would have to give up some of its regular sales. Imperial Beverages would expect to be compensated for the contribution margin on these lost sales. In summary, if the transfer has no effect on fixed costs, then from the selling division's standpoint, the transfer price must cover both the variable costs of producing the transferred units and any opportunity costs from lost sales.

Seller's perspective:

$$\text{Transfer price} \geq \frac{\text{Variable cost}}{\text{per unit}} + \frac{\text{Total contribution margin on lost sales}}{\text{Number of units transferred}}$$

THE PURCHASING DIVISION'S HIGHEST ACCEPTABLE TRANSFER PRICE   The purchasing division, Pizza Maven, will be interested in the proposal only if its profit increases. In cases like this where a purchasing division has an outside supplier, the purchasing division's decision is simple. Buy from the inside supplier if the price is less than the price offered by the outside supplier.

Purchaser's perspective:

$$\text{Transfer price} \leq \text{Cost of buying from outside supplier}$$

We will consider several different hypothetical situations and see what the range of acceptable transfer prices would be in each situation.

SELLING DIVISION WITH IDLE CAPACITY   Suppose that Imperial Beverages has sufficient idle capacity to satisfy the demand for ginger beer from Pizza Maven without cutting into sales of ginger beer to its regular customers. To be specific, let's suppose that Imperial Beverages is selling only 7,000 barrels of ginger beer a month on the outside market. That leaves unused capacity of 3,000 barrels a month—more than enough to satisfy Pizza Maven's requirement of 2,000 barrels a month. What range of transfer prices, if any, would make both divisions better off with the transfer of 2,000 barrels a month?

1. The selling division, Imperial Beverage, will be interested in the proposal only if:

$$\text{Transfer price} \geq \frac{\text{Variable cost}}{\text{per unit}} + \frac{\text{Total contribution margin on lost sales}}{\text{Number of units transferred}}$$

   Since Imperial Beverage has ample idle capacity, there are no lost outside sales. And since the variable cost per unit is £8, the lowest acceptable transfer price as far as the selling division is concerned is also £8.

$$\text{Transfer price} \geq £8 + \frac{£0}{2,000} = £8$$

2. The purchasing division, Pizza Maven, can buy similar ginger beer from an outside vendor for £18. Therefore, Pizza Maven would be unwilling to pay more than £18 per barrel for Imperial Beverage's ginger beer.

$$\text{Transfer price} \leq \text{Cost of buying from outside supplier} = £18$$

3. Combining the requirements of both the selling division and the purchasing division, the acceptable range of transfer prices in this situation is:

$$£8 \leq \text{Transfer price} \leq £18$$

Assuming that the managers understand their own businesses and that they are cooperative, they should be able to agree on a transfer price within this range.

Focus on Current Practice

Teva Pharmaceutical Industries Ltd. of Israel rejected the negotiated transfer price approach because senior executives believed that this approach would lead to endless, nonproductive arguments. Instead, the company uses activity-based costing to set its transfer prices. Marketing divisions are charged for unit-level costs based on the actual quantities of each product they acquire. In addition, they are charged batch-level costs based on the actual number of batches their orders require. Product-level and facility-level costs are charged to the marketing divisions annu-ally in lump sums—the details will be covered in Chapter 16. Essentially, Teva Pharmaceutical Industries sets its transfer prices at carefully com-puted variable costs. As long as Teva Pharmaceutical Industries has unused capacity, this system sends the marketing managers the cor-rect signals about how much it really costs the company to produce each product. With this information, the marketing managers are much better equipped to make pricing and other deci-sions regarding the products.[11] ■

SELLING DIVISION WITH NO IDLE CAPACITY Suppose that Imperial Beverages has *no* idle capacity; it is selling 10,000 barrels of ginger beer a month on the outside market at £20 per barrel. To fill the order from Pizza Maven, Imperial Beverages would have to divert 2,000 barrels from its regular customers. What range of transfer prices, if any, would make both divisions better off transferring the 2,000 barrels within the company?

1. The selling division, Imperial Beverage, will be interested in the proposal only if:

$$\text{Transfer price} \geq \frac{\text{Variable cost}}{\text{per unit}} + \frac{\text{Total contribution margin on lost sales}}{\text{Number of units transferred}}$$

Since Imperial Beverage has no idle capacity, there *are* lost outside sales. The contribution margin per barrel on these outside sales is £12 (£20 − £8).

$$\text{Transfer price} \geq £8 + \frac{(£20 - £8) \times 2,000}{2,000} = £8 + (£20 - £8) = £20$$

Thus, as far as the selling division is concerned, the transfer price must at least cover the revenue on the lost sales, which is £20 per barrel. This makes sense since the cost of producing the 2,000 barrels is the same whether they are sold on the inside market or on the outside. The only difference is that the selling division loses the revenue of £20 per barrel if it transfers the barrels to Pizza Maven.

2. As before, the purchasing division, Pizza Maven, would be unwilling to pay more than the £18 per barrel it is already paying for similar ginger beer from its regular supplier.

$$\text{Transfer price} \leq \text{Cost of buying from outside supplier} = £18$$

3. Therefore, the selling division would insist on a transfer price of at least £20. But the purchasing division would refuse any transfer price above £18. It is

---

11. Robert S. Kaplan, Dan Weiss, and Eyal Desheh, "Transfer Pricing with ABC," *Management Accounting* (May 1997), pp. 20–28.

impossible to satisfy both division managers simultaneously; there can be no agreement on a transfer price and no transfer will take place. Is this good? The answer is yes. From the standpoint of the entire company, the transfer does not make sense. Why give up sales of £20 to save £18?

Basically, the transfer price is a mechanism for dividing between the two divisions any profit the entire company earns as a result of the transfer. If the company loses money on the transfer, there will be no profit to divide up, and it will be impossible for the two divisions to come to an agreement. On the other hand, if the company makes money on the transfer, there will be a potential profit to share, and it will always be possible for the two divisions to find a mutually agreeable transfer price that increases the profits of both divisions. If the pie is bigger, it is always possible to divide it up in such a way that everyone has a bigger piece.

SELLING DIVISION HAS SOME IDLE CAPACITY   Suppose now that Imperial Beverages is selling 9,000 barrels of ginger beer a month on the outside market. Pizza Maven can only sell one kind of ginger beer on tap. They cannot buy 1,000 barrels from Imperial Beverages and 1,000 barrels from their regular supplier; they must buy all of their ginger beer from one source.

To fill the entire 2,000-barrel a month order from Pizza Maven, Imperial Beverages would have to divert 1,000 barrels from its regular customers who are paying £20 per barrel. The other 1,000 barrels can be made using idle capacity. What range of transfer prices, if any, would make both divisions better off transferring the 2,000 barrels within the company?

1. As before, the selling division, Imperial Beverage, will insist on a transfer price that at least covers their variable cost and opportunity cost:

$$\text{Transfer price} \geq \frac{\text{Variable cost}}{\text{per unit}} + \frac{\text{Total contribution margin on lost sales}}{\text{Number of units transferred}}$$

Since Imperial Beverage does not have enough idle capacity to fill the entire order for 2,000 barrels, there *are* lost outside sales. The contribution margin per barrel on the 1,000 barrels of lost outside sales is £12 (£20 − £8).

$$\text{Transfer price} \geq £8 + \frac{(£20 - £8) \times 1,000}{2,000} = £8 + £6 = £14$$

Thus, as far as the selling division is concerned, the transfer price must cover the variable cost of £8 plus the average opportunity cost of lost sales of £6.

2. As before, the purchasing division, Pizza Maven, would be unwilling to pay more than the £18 per barrel it pays its regular supplier.

$$\text{Transfer price} \leq \text{Cost of buying from outside suppliers} = £18$$

3. Combining the requirements for both the selling and purchasing divisions, the range of acceptable transfer prices is:

$$£14 \leq \text{Transfer price} \leq £18$$

Again, assuming that the managers understand their own businesses and that they are cooperative, they should be able to agree on a transfer price within this range.

NO OUTSIDE SUPPLIER   If Pizza Maven has no outside supplier for the ginger beer, the highest price the purchasing division would be willing to pay depends on how much the purchasing division expects to make on the transferred units—excluding the transfer price. If, for example, Pizza Maven expects to earn £30 per barrel of ginger beer after paying its own expenses, then it should be willing to pay up to £30 per barrel to Imperial Beverages. Remember, however, that this assumes Pizza Maven cannot buy ginger beer from other sources.

EVALUATION OF NEGOTIATED TRANSFER PRICES   As discussed earlier, if a transfer within the company would result in higher overall profits for the company, there is always a range of transfer prices within which both the selling and purchasing division would also have higher profits if they agree to the transfer. Therefore, if the managers understand their own businesses and are cooperative, then they should always be able to agree on a transfer price if it is in the best interests of the company that they do so.

The difficulty is that not all managers understand their own businesses and not all managers are cooperative. As a result, negotiations often break down even when it would be in the managers' own best interests to come to an agreement. Sometimes that is the fault of the way managers are evaluated. If managers are pitted against each other rather than against their own past performance or reasonable benchmarks, a non-cooperative atmosphere is almost guaranteed. Nevertheless, it must be admitted that even with the best performance evaluation system, some people by nature are not cooperative.

Possibly because of the fruitless and protracted bickering that often accompanies disputes over transfer prices, most companies rely on some other means of setting transfer prices. Unfortunately, as we will see below, all of the alternatives to negotiated transfer prices have their own serious drawbacks.

Transfers at the Cost to the Selling Division

Many companies set transfer prices at either the variable cost or full (absorption) cost incurred by the selling division. Although the cost approach to setting transfer prices is relatively simple to apply, it has some major defects.

First, the use of cost—particularly full cost—as a transfer price can lead to bad decisions and thus suboptimization. Return to the example involving the ginger beer. The full cost of ginger beer can never be less than £15 per barrel (£8 per barrel variable cost + £7 per barrel fixed cost at capacity). What if the cost of buying the ginger beer from an outside supplier is less than £15—for example, £14 per barrel? If the transfer price were bureaucratically set at full cost, then Pizza Maven would never want to buy ginger beer from Imperial Beverage, since it could buy its ginger beer from the outside supplier at less cost. However, from the standpoint of the company as a whole, ginger beer should be transferred from Imperial Beverage to Pizza Maven whenever Imperial Beverage has idle capacity. Why? Because when Imperial Beverage has idle capacity, it only costs the company £8 in variable cost to produce a barrel of ginger beer, but it costs £14 per barrel to buy from outside suppliers.

Second, if cost is used as the transfer price, the selling division will never show a profit on any internal transfer. The only division that shows a profit is the division that makes the final sale to an outside party.

A third problem with cost-based prices is that they do not provide incentives to control costs. If the costs of one division are simply passed on to the next, then there is little incentive for anyone to work to reduce costs. This problem can be overcome to some extent by using standard costs rather than actual costs for transfer prices.

Despite these shortcomings, cost-based transfer prices are commonly used in practice. Advocates argue that they are easily understood and convenient to use.

Transfers at Market Price

Market price   The price being charged for an item on the open (intermediate) market.

Some form of competitive **market price** (i.e., the price charged for an item on the open market) is often regarded as the best approach to the transfer pricing problem—particularly if transfer price negotiations routinely become bogged down.

Intermediate market A market in which a transferred product or service is sold in its present form to outside customers.

The market price approach is designed for situations in which there is an *intermediate market* for the transferred product or service. By **intermediate market,** we mean a market in which the product or service is sold in its present form to outside customers. If the selling division has no idle capacity, the market price in the intermediate market is the perfect choice for the transfer price. The reason for this is that if the selling division can sell a transferred item on the outside market instead, then the real cost of the transfer as far as the company is concerned is the opportunity cost of the lost revenue on the outside sale. Whether the item is transferred internally or sold on the outside intermediate market, the production costs are exactly the same. If the market price is used as the transfer price, the selling division manager will not lose anything by making the transfer, and the purchasing division manager will get the correct signal about how much it really costs the company for the transfer to take place.

While the market price works beautifully when there is no idle capacity, difficulties occur when the selling division has idle capacity. Recalling once again the ginger beer example, the outside market price for the ginger beer produced by Imperial Beverage is £20 per barrel. However, Pizza Maven can purchase all of the ginger beer it wants from outside suppliers for £18 per barrel. Why would Pizza Maven ever buy from Imperial Beverage if Pizza Maven is forced to pay Imperial Beverage's market price? In some market price-based transfer pricing schemes, the transfer price would be lowered to £18, the outside vendor's market price, and Pizza Maven would be directed to buy from Imperial Beverage as long as Imperial Beverage is willing to sell. This scheme can work reasonably well, but a drawback is that managers at Pizza Maven will regard the cost of ginger beer as £18 rather than the £8, which is the real cost to the company when the selling division has idle capacity. Consequently, the managers of Pizza Maven will make pricing and other decisions based on an incorrect cost.

Unfortunately, none of the possible solutions to the transfer pricing problem are perfect—not even market-based transfer prices.

Divisional Autonomy and Suboptimization

A question often arises as to how much autonomy should be granted to divisions in setting their own transfer prices and in making decisions concerning whether to sell internally or to sell outside. Should the divisional heads have complete authority to make these decisions, or should top corporate management step in if it appears that a decision is about to be made that would result in suboptimization? For example, if the selling division has idle capacity and divisional managers are unable to agree on a transfer price, should top corporate management step in and *force* a settlement?

Efforts should always be made, of course, to bring disputing managers together. But the almost unanimous feeling among top corporate executives is that divisional heads should not be forced into an agreement over a transfer price. That is, if a manager flatly refuses to change his or her position in a dispute, *then this decision should be respected* even if it results in suboptimization. This is simply the price that is paid for divisional autonomy. If top corporate management steps in and forces the decisions in difficult situations, then the purposes of decentralization are defeated and the company simply becomes a centralized operation with decentralization of only minor decisions and responsibilities. In short, if a division is to be viewed as an autonomous unit with independent profit responsibility, then it must have control over its own destiny—even to the extent of having the right to make bad decisions.

We should note, however, that if a division consistently makes bad decisions, the results will sooner or later reduce its profit and rate of return, and the divisional manager may find that he or she has to defend the division's performance. Even so, the manager's right to get into an embarrassing situation must be respected if decentralization is to operate successfully. Divisional autonomy and independent profit responsibility generally lead to much greater success and profitability than do closely controlled, centrally administered operations. Part of the price of this success is occasional suboptimization due to pettiness, bickering, or just plain stubbornness.

Furthermore, one of the major reasons for decentralizing is that top managers cannot know enough about every detail of operations to make every decision themselves. To impose the correct transfer price, top managers would have to know details about the intermediate market, variable costs, and capacity utilization. If top managers have all of this information, it is not clear why they decentralized in the first place.

International Aspects of Transfer Pricing

Transfer pricing is used worldwide to control the flow of goods and services between segments of an organization. However, the objectives of transfer pricing change when a multinational corporation (MNC) is involved and the goods and services being transferred must cross international borders. The objectives of international transfer pricing, as compared to domestic transfer pricing, are summarized in Exhibit 12A–1.

As shown in the exhibit, the objectives of international transfer pricing focus on minimizing taxes, duties, and foreign exchange risks, along with enhancing a company's competitive position and improving its relations with foreign governments. Although domestic objectives such as managerial motivation and divisional autonomy are always desirable in an organization, they usually become secondary when international transfers are involved. Companies will focus instead on charging a transfer price that will slash its total tax bill or that will strengthen a foreign subsidiary.

For example, charging a low transfer price for parts shipped to a foreign subsidiary may reduce customs duty payments as the parts cross international borders, or it may help the subsidiary to compete in foreign markets by keeping the subsidiary's costs low. On the other hand, charging a high transfer price may help an MNC draw profits out of a country that has stringent controls on foreign remittances, or it may allow an MNC to shift income from a country that has high income tax rates to a country that has low rates.

As previously mentioned, transfer prices can have a significant impact on a firm's income taxes. Firms prefer to shift products to countries which have lower tax rates by means of various transfer pricing schemes. On the other hand Revenue Canada seeks its fair share of the global tax pie, and its auditors demand hard documentary support of how transfer prices have been established. In general, Revenue Canada accepts fair-market value for determining the price of tangible products. For services such as management or marketing fees, transfer prices are generally based on costs with an appropriate markup added. Management, of course, has an incentive to set transfer prices to minimize its tax liability.[13]

The actual determination of transfer prices can become contentious. Alternative cost or revenue allocation methods can result in very different transfer prices. It is not surprising that disputes arise from time to time. For example, in a $200 million case, Revenue Canada claimed that Irving Oil owed taxes resulting from the sale of crude oil bought from its Bermuda subsidiary in 1971 to 1975. In February of 1991, the Federal

---

12. The exhibit is adapted from Wagdy M. Abdallah, "Guidelines for CEOs in Transfer Pricing Policies," *Management Accounting* 70, no. 3 (September 1988), p. 61.
13. Paul Glover. "Transfer Pricing: Are You Prepared?" *CMA Magazine* (October 1989), p. 24.

Court of Appeal ruled in favour of Irving. The court acknowledged that Irving was practicing tax avoidance, not tax evasion. Acting within the law, Irving had paid fair market value for its crude.

Recent legislative changes require clear documentation of the efforts made to set a transfer price if an arm's-length price (normal market price) is not used. Benchmarking and financial analysis may be needed to support the price. Arbitrary pricing is not permissible for these international transfer prices.[14]

Analysis of this requirement by Revenue Canada suggests that some companies who have gained advantages resulting from their integrated multinational operations can be subjected to double taxation from this new rule. The double taxation results from the fact that their operations have savings that may not be reflected in the arm's-length calculations required by Revenue Canada. Internal cost savings from the multinational operations can result in transfer prices below the arm's-length transfer price required.[15]

In summary, managers must be sensitive to the geographic, political, and economic circumstances in which they are operating, and set transfer prices in such a way as to optimize total company performance.

Review Problem 3: Transfer Pricing

Situation A

Collyer Products, Inc., has a Valve Division that manufactures and sells a standard valve as follows:

Capacity in units	100,000
Selling price to outside customers on the intermediate market	$30
Variable costs per unit	16
Fixed costs per unit (based on capacity)	9

The company has a Pump Division that could use this valve in the manufacture of one of its pumps. The Pump Division is currently purchasing 10,000 valves per year from an overseas supplier at a cost of $29 per valve.

Required

1. Assume that the Valve Division has ample idle capacity to handle all of the Pump Division's needs. What is the acceptable range, if any, for the transfer price between the two divisions?
2. Assume that the Valve Division is selling all that it can produce to outside customers on the intermediate market. What is the acceptable range, if any, for the transfer price between the two divisions?
3. Assume again that the Valve Division is selling all that it can produce to outside customers on the intermediate market. Also assume that $3 in variable expenses can be avoided on transfers within the company, due to reduced selling costs. What is the acceptable range, if any, for the transfer price between the two divisions?

Solution to Situation A

1. Since the Valve Division has idle capacity, it does not have to give up any outside sales to take on the Pump Division's business. Applying the formula for the lowest acceptable transfer price from the viewpoint of the selling division, we get:

$$\text{Transfer price} \geq \frac{\text{Variable cost}}{\text{per unit}} + \frac{\text{Total contribution margin on lost sales}}{\text{Number of units transferred}}$$

$$\text{Transfer price} \geq \$16 + \frac{\$0}{10,000} = \$16$$

14. Stephanie de Breyne, "Transfer Pricing: Get It in Writing," *CMA Magazine* (February 1998), p. 36.
15. David Hogan, "Transfer Pricing Inadequate," *Canadian Tax Highlights* (June 1998).

The Pump Division would be unwilling to pay more than $29, the price it is currently paying an outside supplier for its valves. Therefore, the transfer price must fall within the range:

$$\$16 \leq \text{Transfer price} \leq \$29$$

2. Since the Valve Division is selling all that it can produce on the intermediate market, it would have to give up some of these outside sales to take on the Pump Division's business. Thus, the Valve Division has an opportunity cost that is the total contribution margin on lost sales:

$$\text{Transfer price} \geq \frac{\text{Variable cost}}{\text{per unit}} + \frac{\text{Total contribution margin on lost sales}}{\text{Number of units transferred}}$$

$$\text{Transfer price} \geq \$16 + \frac{(\$30 - \$16) \times 10{,}000}{10{,}000} = \$16 + \$14 = \$30$$

Since the Pump Division can purchase valves from an outside supplier at only $29 per unit, no transfers will be made between the two divisions.

3. Applying the formula for the lowest acceptable price from the viewpoint of the selling division, we get:

$$\text{Transfer price} \geq \frac{\text{Variable cost}}{\text{per unit}} + \frac{\text{Total contribution margin on lost sales}}{\text{Number of units transferred}}$$

$$\text{Transfer price} \geq (\$16 - \$3) + \frac{(\$30 - \$16) \times 10{,}000}{10{,}000} = \$13 + \$14 = \$27$$

In this case, the transfer price must fall within the range:

$$\$27 \leq \text{Transfer price} \leq \$29$$

Situation B

Refer to the original data in situation A above. Assume that the Pump Division needs 20,000 special high-pressure valves per year. The Valve Division's variable costs to manufacture and ship the special valve would be $20 per unit. To produce these special valves, the Valve Division would have to reduce its production and sales of regular valves from 100,000 units per year to 70,000 units per year.

Required   As far as the Valve Division is concerned, what is the lowest acceptable transfer price?

Solution to Situation B   To produce the 20,000 special valves, the Valve Division will have to give up sales of 30,000 regular valves to outside customers. Applying the formula for the lowest acceptable price from the viewpoint of the selling division, we get:

$$\text{Transfer price} \geq \frac{\text{Variable cost}}{\text{per unit}} + \frac{\text{Total contribution margin on lost sales}}{\text{Number of units transferred}}$$

$$\text{Transfer price} \geq \$20 + \frac{(\$30 - \$16) \times 30{,}000}{20{,}000} = \$20 + \$21 = \$41$$

Questions

12–1   What is meant by the term *decentralization?*

12–2   What benefits result from decentralization?

12–3   Distinguish between a cost centre, a profit centre, and an investment centre.

12–4   Define a segment of an organization. Give several examples of segments.

12–5   How does the contribution approach assign costs to segments of an organization?

12–6   Distinguish between a traceable cost and a common cost. Give several examples of each.

12–7   Explain how the segment margin differs from the contribution margin.

12–8   Why aren't common costs allocated to segments under the contribution approach?

12–9   How is it possible for a cost that is traceable to a segment to become a common cost if the segment is divided into further segments?

12–10   What is meant by the terms *margin* and *turnover?*

12–11   What are the three basic approaches to improving return on investment (ROI)?

12–12   What is meant by residual income?

12–13   In what way can the use of ROI as a performance measure for investment centres lead to bad decisions? How does the residual income approach overcome this problem?

12–14   What is gained by examining costs from a life cycle perspective?

12–15   Why is value chain analysis an important viewpoint for revenue and cost analysis?

12–16   What is the advantage of examining a customer's profits over other segment analysis?

12–17   EVA provides a strategic focus for management. Analyze this statement.

12–18   (Appendix 12A) What is meant by the term *transfer price,* and why are transfer prices needed?

12–19   (Appendix 12A) From the standpoint of a selling division that has idle capacity, what is the minimum acceptable transfer price for an item?

12–20   (Appendix 12A) From the standpoint of a selling division that has *no* idle capacity, what is the minimum acceptable transfer price for an item?

12–21   (Appendix 12A) What are the advantages and disadvantages of cost-based transfer prices?

12–22   (Appendix 12A) If a market price for a product can be determined, why isn't it always the best transfer price?

Exercises

E12–1   Royal Lawncare Company produces and sells two packaged products, Weedban and Greengrow. Revenue and cost information relating to the products follow:

	Product	
	Weedban	**Greengrow**
Selling price per unit	$ 6.00	$ 7.50
Variable expenses per unit	2.40	5.25
Traceable fixed expenses per year	45,000	21,000

Common fixed expenses in the company total $33,000 annually. Last year the company produced and sold 15,000 units of Weedban and 28,000 units of Greengrow.

Required Prepare an income statement segmented by product lines. Show both Amount and Percent columns for the company as a whole and for each of the products.

E12–2 Raner, Harris, & Chan is a consulting firm that specializes in information systems for medical and dental clinics. The firm has two offices—one in Vancouver and one in Winnipeg. The firm classifies the direct costs of consulting jobs as variable costs. A segmented income statement for the company's most recent year is given below:

	Total Company		Segment Vancouver		Winnipeg	
Sales	$450,000	100%	$150,000	100%	$300,000	100%
Less variable expenses	225,000	50%	45,000	30%	180,000	60%
Contribution margin	225,000	50%	105,000	70%	120,000	40%
Less traceable fixed expenses	126,000	28%	78,000	52%	48,000	16%
Office segment margin	99,000	22%	$ 27,000	18%	$ 72,000	24%
Less common fixed expenses not traceable to segments	63,000	14%				
Net income	$ 36,000	8%				

Required

1. By how much would the company's net income increase if Winnipeg increased its sales by $75,000 per year? Assume no change in cost behaviour patterns.
2. Refer to the original data. Assume that sales in Vancouver increase by $50,000 next year and that sales in Winnipeg remain unchanged. Assume no change in fixed costs.
   a. Prepare a new segmented income statement for the company using the format above. Show both amounts and percentages.
   b. Observe from the income statement you have prepared that the contribution margin ratio for Vancouver has remained unchanged at 70% (the same as in the data above) but that the segment margin ratio has changed. How do you explain the change in the segment margin ratio?

E12–3 Refer to the data in E12–2. Assume that Winnipeg's sales by major market are:

	Segment Winnipeg		Medical		Dental	
Sales	$300,000	100%	$200,000	100%	$100,000	100%
Less variable expenses	180,000	60%	128,000	64%	52,000	52%
Contribution margin	120,000	40%	72,000	36%	48,000	48%
Less traceable fixed expenses	33,000	11%	12,000	6%	21,000	21%
Product-line segment margin	87,000	29%	$ 60,000	30%	$ 27,000	27%
Less common fixed expenses not traceable to markets	15,000	5%				
Divisional segment margin	$ 72,000	24%				

The company would like to initiate an intensive advertising campaign in one of the two market segments during the next month. The campaign would cost $5,000. Marketing studies indicate that such a campaign would increase sales in the Medical market by $40,000 or increase sales in the Dental market by $35,000.

Required

1. In which of the markets would you recommend that the company focus its advertising campaign? Show computations to support your answer.
2. In E12–2, Winnipeg shows $48,000 in traceable fixed expenses. What happened to the $48,000 in this exercise?

E12–4 Wingate Company, a wholesale distributor of videotapes, has been experiencing losses for some time, as shown by its most recent monthly income statement below:

Sales	$1,000,000
Less variable expenses	390,000
Contribution margin	610,000
Less fixed expenses	625,000
Net income (loss)	$ (15,000)

In an effort to isolate the problem, the president has asked for an income statement segmented by division. Accordingly, the Accounting Department has developed the following information:

	Division		
	East	Central	West
Sales	$250,000	$400,000	$350,000
Variable expenses as a percentage of sales	52%	30%	40%
Traceable fixed expenses	$160,000	$200,000	$175,000

Required
1. Prepare an income statement segmented by divisions, as desired by the president. Show both Amount and Percent columns for the company as a whole and for each division.
2. As a result of a marketing study, the president believes that sales in the West Division could be increased by 20% if advertising in that division were increased by $15,000 each month. Would you recommend the increased advertising? Show computations.

E12–5 You have a client who operates a large upscale grocery store that has a full range of departments. The management has encountered difficulty in using accounting data as a basis for decisions as to possible changes in departments operated, products, marketing methods, and so forth. List several overhead costs, or costs not applicable to a particular department, and explain how the existence of such costs (sometimes called *common costs*) complicates and limits the use of accounting data in making decisions in such a store.

(CPA, adapted)

E12–6 Selected operating data for two divisions of Outback Brewing, Ltd., of Australia are given below:

	Division	
	Queensland	New South Wales
Sales	$4,000,000	$7,000,000
Average operating assets	2,000,000	2,000,000
Net operating income	360,000	420,000
Property, plant, and equipment (net)	950,000	800,000

Required
1. Compute the rate of return for each division using the return on investment (ROI) formula stated in terms of margin and turnover.
2. So far as you can tell from the data, which divisional manager seems to be doing the better job? Why?

E12–7 Meiji Isetan Corp. of Japan has two regional divisions with headquarters in Osaka and Yokohama. Selected data on the two divisions follow (in millions of yen, denoted by ¥):

	Division	
	Osaka	Yokohama
Sales	¥3,000,000	¥9,000,000
Net operating income	210,000	720,000
Average operating assets	1,000,000	4,000,000

Required
1. For each division, compute the return on investment (ROI) in terms of margin and turnover. Where necessary, carry computations to two decimal places.
2. Assume that the company evaluates performance by use of residual income and that the minimum required return for any division is 15%. Compute the residual income for each division.
3. Is Yokohama's greater amount of residual income an indication that it is better managed? Explain.

E12–8 Selected sales and operating data for three divisions of a multinational structural engineering firm are given below:

	Division		
	Asia	**Europe**	**North America**
Sales	$12,000,000	$14,000,000	$25,000,000
Average operating assets	3,000,000	7,000,000	5,000,000
Net operating income	600,000	560,000	800,000
Minimum required rate of return	14%	10%	16%

Required
1. Compute the return on investment (ROI) for each division using the formula stated in terms of margin and turnover.
2. Compute the residual income for each division.
3. Assume that each division is presented with an investment opportunity that would yield a 15% rate of return.
   a. If performance is being measured by ROI, which division or divisions will probably accept the opportunity? Reject? Why?
   b. If performance is being measured by residual income, which division or divisions will probably accept the opportunity? Reject? Why?

E12–9 A family friend has asked your help in analyzing the operations of three anonymous companies. Supply the missing data in the tabulation below:

	Company		
	A	**B**	**C**
Sales	$9,000,000	$7,000,000	$4,500,000
Net operating income	?	280,000	?
Average operating assets	3,000,000	?	1,800,000
Return on investment (ROI)	18%	14%	?
Minimum required rate of return:			
Percentage	16%	?	15%
Dollar amount	?	320,000	?
Residual income	?	?	90,000

E12–10 Sarsfield Ltd. sells three products, X, Y, and Z. Actual revenue for the period was:

	Units	**Sales Price**
X	40,000	$3.00
Y	30,000	$4.25
Z	15,000	$8.50

Budget estimates for the same period were as follows:

	X	**Y**	**Z**
Sales	$300,000	$200,000	$100,000
Variable expenses	150,000	110,000	60,000
Fixed expenses	70,000	80,000	30,000
Income	$ 80,000	$ 10,000	$ 10,000
Units sales	55,000	35,000	10,000
Market sales in units	110,000	70,000	30,000
Actual market sales for the period were:	90,000	150,000	50,000

Required   Prepare a report to the marketing manager concerning the sales of X, Y, and Z. Support the report with a full revenue analysis.

E12–11   Zareski Products Limited is concerned about its marketing strategy. The marketing manager, Joan Anthony, wants a full analysis of its customers. The following facts were retrieved from the accounting data base:

	Customer Classes			Total Cost
	Small	Average	Large	
Sales in units	1,000	3,600	4,200	$15,900
Orders received	300	140	60	2,500
Coupons circulated	20,000	30,000	50,000	4,000
Portion of salaries	$ 5,000	$34,000	$33,000	72,000
				$94,400

Required   1. Determine the cost per customer class.
2. Calculate the cost per sales unit.

E12–12   (Appendix 12A) Sako Company's Audio Division produces a speaker that is widely used by manufacturers of various audio products. Sales and cost data on the speaker follow:

Selling price per unit on the intermediate market	$60
Variable costs per unit	42
Fixed costs per unit (based on capacity)	8
Capacity in units	25,000

Sako Company has just organized a Hi-Fi Division that could use this speaker in one of its products. The Hi-Fi Division will need 5,000 speakers per year. It has received a quote of $57 per speaker from another manufacturer. Sako Company evaluates divisional managers on the basis of divisional profits.

Required   1. Assume that the Audio Division is now selling only 20,000 speakers per year to outside customers on the intermediate market.
   a. From the standpoint of the Audio Division, what is the lowest acceptable transfer price for speakers sold to the Hi-Fi Division?
   b. From the standpoint of the Hi-Fi Division, what is the highest acceptable transfer price for speakers purchased from the Audio Division?
   c. If left free to negotiate without interference, would you expect the division managers to voluntarily agree to the transfer of 5,000 speakers from the Audio Division to the Hi-Fi Division? Why or why not?
   d. From the standpoint of the entire company, should the transfer take place? Why or why not?
2. Assume that the Audio Division is selling all of the speakers it can produce to outside customers on the intermediate market.
   a. From the standpoint of the Audio Division, what is the lowest acceptable transfer price for speakers sold to the Hi-Fi Division?
   b. From the standpoint of the Hi-Fi Division, what is the highest acceptable transfer price for speakers purchased from the Audio Division?
   c. If left free to negotiate without interference, would you expect the division managers to voluntarily agree to the transfer of 5,000 speakers from the Audio Division to the Hi-Fi Division? Why or why not?
   d. From the standpoint of the entire company, should the transfer take place? Why or why not?

E12–13   (Appendix 12A) In each of the cases below, assume that Division X has a product that can be sold either to outside customers on an intermediate market or to Division Y of the same company for use in its production process. The managers of the divisions are evaluated based on their divisional profits.

	Case	
	A	**B**
Division X:		
Capacity in units	200,000	200,000
Number of units being sold on the intermediate market	200,000	160,000
Selling price per unit on the intermediate market	$90	$75
Variable costs per unit	70	60
Fixed costs per unit (based on capacity)	13	8
Division Y:		
Number of units needed for production	40,000	40,000
Purchase price per unit now being paid to an outside supplier	$86	$74

Required
1. Refer to the data in case A above. Assume in this case that $3 per unit in variable costs can be avoided on intracompany sales. If the managers are free to negotiate and make decisions on their own, will a transfer take place? If so, within what range will the transfer price fall? Explain.
2. Refer to the data in case B above. In this case there will be no savings in variable costs on intracompany sales. If the managers are free to negotiate and make decisions on their own, will a transfer take place? If so, within what range will the transfer price fall? Explain.

E12–14   (Appendix 12A) Division A manufactures electronic circuit boards. The boards can be sold either to Division B of the same company or to outside customers. Last year, the following activity occurred in Division A:

Selling price per circuit board	$125
Production cost per circuit board	90
Number of circuit boards:	
Produced during the year	20,000
Sold to outside customers	16,000
Sold to Division B	4,000

Sales to Division B were at the same price as sales to outside customers. The circuit boards purchased by Division B were used in an electronic instrument manufactured by that division (one board per instrument). Division B incurred $100 in additional cost per instrument and then sold the instruments for $300 each.

Required
1. Prepare income statements for Division A, Division B, and the company as a whole.
2. Assume that Division A's manufacturing capacity is 20,000 circuit boards. Next year, Division B wants to purchase 5,000 circuit boards from Division A rather than 4,000. (Circuit boards of this type are not available from outside sources.) From the standpoint of the company as a whole, should Division A sell the 1,000 additional circuit boards to Division B or continue to sell them to outside customers? Explain.

Problems

P12–15   Segment Reporting   Vulcan Company's income statement for last month is given below:

VULCAN COMPANY
Income Statement
For the Month Ended June 30

Sales	$750,000
Less variable expenses	336,000
Contribution margin	414,000
Less fixed expenses	378,000
Net income	$ 36,000

Management is disappointed with the company's performance and is wondering what can be done to improve profits. By examining sales and cost records, you have determined the following:

a. The company is divided into two sales territories—Northern and Southern. The Northern territory recorded $300,000 in sales and $156,000 in variable expenses during June; the remaining sales and variable expenses were recorded in the Southern territory. Fixed expenses of $120,000 and $108,000 are traceable to the Northern and Southern territories, respectively. The rest of the fixed expenses are common to the two territories.

b. The company sells two products—Paks and Tibs. Sales of Paks and Tibs totalled $50,000 and $250,000, respectively, in the Northern territory during June. Variable expenses are 22% of the selling price for Paks and 58% for Tibs. Cost records show that $30,000 of the Northern territory's fixed expenses are traceable to Paks and $40,000 to Tibs, with the remainder common to the two products.

Required

1. Prepare segmented income statements first showing the total company broken down between sales territories and then showing the Northern territory broken down by product line. Show both Amount and Percent columns for the company in total and for each segment.

2. Look at the statement you have prepared showing the total company segmented by sales territory. What points revealed by this statement should be brought to the attention of management?

3. Look at the statement you have prepared showing the Northern territory segmented by product lines. What points revealed by this statement should be brought to the attention of management?

P12–16   Segment Reporting; Activity-Based Cost Assignment

Diversified Products, Inc., has recently acquired a small publishing company that Diversified Products intends to operate as one of its investment centres. The newly acquired company has three books that it offers for sale—a cookbook, a travel guide, and a handy speller. Each book sells for $10. The publishing company's most recent monthly income statement is given below:

	Total Company		Cookbook	Travel Guide	Handy Speller
			Product Line		
Sales	$300,000	100%	$90,000	$150,000	$60,000
Less expenses:					
Printing costs	102,000	34%	27,000	63,000	12,000
Advertising	36,000	12%	13,500	19,500	3,000
General sales	18,000	6%	5,400	9,000	3,600
Salaries	33,000	11%	18,000	9,000	6,000
Equipment depreciation	9,000	3%	3,000	3,000	3,000
Sales commissions	30,000	10%	9,000	15,000	6,000
General administration	42,000	14%	14,000	14,000	14,000
Warehouse rent	12,000	4%	3,600	6,000	2,400
Depreciation—office facilities	3,000	1%	1,000	1,000	1,000
Total expenses	285,000	95%	94,500	139,500	51,000
Net income (loss)	$ 15,000	5%	$(4,500)	$ 10,500	$ 9,000

The following additional information is available about the company:

a. Only printing costs and sales commissions are variable; all other costs are fixed. The printing costs (which include materials, labour, and variable overhead) are traceable to the three product lines as shown in the statement above. Sales commissions are 10% of sales for any product.

b. The same equipment is used to produce all three books, so the equipment depreciation cost has been allocated equally among the three product lines. An analysis of the company's activities indicates that the equipment is used 30% of the time to produce cookbooks, 50% of the time to produce travel guides, and 20% of the time to produce handy spellers.

c. The warehouse is used to store finished units of product, so the rental cost has been allocated to the product lines on the basis of sales dollars. The warehouse rental cost is $9 per square metre per year. The warehouse contains 16,000 square metres of space, of which 2,400 square metres is used by the cookbook line, 8,000 square metres by the travel guide line, and 5,600 square metres by the handy speller line.

d. The general sales cost above includes the salary of the sales manager and other sales costs not traceable to any specific product line. This cost has been allocated to the product lines on the basis of sales dollars.

e. The general administration cost and depreciation of office facilities both relate to overall administration of the company as a whole. These costs have been allocated equally to the three product lines.

f. All other costs are traceable to the three product lines in the amounts shown on the statement above.

The management of Diversified Products, Inc., is anxious to improve the new investment centre's 5% return on sales.

Required

1. Prepare a new segmented income statement for the month using the contribution approach. Show both an Amount column and a Percent column for the company as a whole and for each product line. Adjust allocations of equipment depreciation and of warehouse rent as indicated by the additional information provided.

2. After seeing the income statement in the main body of the problem, management has decided to eliminate the cookbook, since it is not returning a profit, and to focus all available resources on promoting the travel guide.
    a. Based on the statement you have prepared, do you agree with the decision to eliminate the cookbook? Explain.
    b. Based on the statement you have prepared, do you agree with the decision to focus all available resources on promoting the travel guide? Explain. (You may assume that an ample market is available for all three product lines.)

3. What additional points would you bring to the attention of management that might help to improve profits?

P12–17 Return on Investment (ROI) and Residual Income Financial data for Joel de Paris, Inc., for last year follow:

JOEL DE PARIS, INC.
Balance Sheet

	Ending Balance	Beginning Balance
Assets		
Cash	$ 120,000	$ 140,000
Accounts receivable	530,000	450,000
Inventory	380,000	320,000
Plant and equipment, net	620,000	680,000
Investment in Buisson, S.A.	280,000	250,000
Land (undeveloped)	170,000	180,000
Total assets	$2,100,000	$2,020,000
Liabilities and Shareholders' Equity		
Accounts payable	$ 310,000	$ 360,000
Long-term debt	1,500,000	1,500,000
Shareholders' equity	290,000	160,000
Total liabilities and shareholders' equity	$2,100,000	$2,020,000

JOEL DE PARIS, INC.
Income Statement

Sales		$4,050,000
Less operating expenses		3,645,000
Net operating income		405,000
Less interest and taxes:		
Interest expense	$ 150,000	
Tax expense	110,000	260,000
Net income		$ 145,000

The company paid dividends of $15,000 last year. The "Investment in Buisson, S.A.," on the balance sheet represents an investment in the shares of another company.

Required

1. Compute the company's margin, turnover, and ROI for last year.
2. The board of directors of Joel de Paris, Inc., has set a minimum required return of 15%. What was the company's residual income last year?

P12–18   Return on Investment (ROI) and Residual Income   "I know headquarters wants us to add on that new product line," said Dell Havasi, manager of Billings Company's Office Products Division. "But I want to see the numbers before I make any move. Our division has led the company for three years, and I don't want any letdown."

Billings Company is a decentralized organization with five autonomous divisions. The divisions are evaluated on the basis of the return that they are able to generate on invested assets, with year-end bonuses given to the divisional managers who have the highest ROI figures. Operating results for the company's Office Products Division for the most recent year are given below:

Sales	$10,000,000
Less variable expenses	6,000,000
Contribution margin	4,000,000
Less fixed expenses	3,200,000
Net operating income	$ 800,000
Divisional operating assets	$ 4,000,000

The company had an overall ROI of 15% last year (considering all divisions). The Office Products Division has an opportunity to add a new product line that would require an additional investment in operating assets of $1,000,000. The cost and revenue characteristics of the new product line per year would be:

Sales	$2,000,000
Variable expenses	60% of sales
Fixed expenses	$640,000

Required

1. Compute the Office Products Division's ROI for the most recent year; also compute the ROI as it will appear if the new product line is added.
2. If you were in Dell Havasi's position, would you be inclined to accept or reject the new product line? Explain.
3. Why do you suppose headquarters is anxious for the Office Products Division to add the new product line?
4. Suppose that the company views a return of 12% on invested assets as being the minimum that any division should earn and that performance is evaluated by the residual income approach.
   a. Compute the Office Products Division's residual income for the most recent year; also compute the residual income as it will appear if the new product line is added.
   b. Under these circumstances, if you were in Dell Havasi's position, would you accept or reject the new product line? Explain.

P12–19   Transfer Price; Well-Defined Intermediate Market
(Appendix 12A) Hrubec Products, Inc., operates a Pulp Division that manufactures wood pulp for use in the production of various paper goods. Revenue and costs associated with tonnes of pulp follow:

Selling price	$70
Less expenses:	
Variable $42	
Fixed (based on a capacity of	
50,000 tonnes per year) 18	60
Net income	$10

Hrubec Products has just acquired a small company that manufactures paper cartons. This company will be treated as a division of Hrubec with full profit responsibility. The newly formed Carton Division is currently purchasing 5,000 tonnes of pulp per year from a supplier at a cost of $70 per tonne, less a 10% quantity discount. Hrubec's president is anxious for the Carton Division to begin purchasing its pulp from the Pulp Division if an acceptable transfer price can be worked out.

Required

For (1) and (2) below, assume that the Pulp Division can sell all of its pulp to outside customers at the normal $70 price.

1. Are the managers of the Carton and Pulp Divisions likely to agree to a transfer price for 5,000 tonnes of pulp next year? Why or why not?
2. If the Pulp Division meets the price that the Carton Division is currently paying to its supplier and sells 5,000 tonnes of pulp to the Carton Division each year, what will be the effect on the profits of the Pulp Division, the Carton Division, and the company as a whole?

For (3)–(6) below, assume that the Pulp Division is currently selling only 30,000 tonnes of pulp each year to outside customers at the stated $70 price.

3. Are the managers of the Carton and Pulp Divisions likely to agree to a transfer price for 5,000 tonnes of pulp next year? Why or why not?
4. Suppose that the Carton Divisions outside supplier drops its price (net of the quantity discount) to only $59 per tonne. Should the Pulp Division meet this price? Explain. If the Pulp Division does *not* meet the $59 price, what will be the effect on the profits of the company as a whole?
5. Refer to (4) above. If the Pulp Division refuses to meet the $59 price, should the Carton Division be required to purchase from the Pulp Division at a higher price for the good of the company as a whole?
6. Refer to (4) above. Assume that due to inflexible management policies, the Carton Division is required to purchase 5,000 tonnes of pulp each year from the Pulp Division at $70 per tonne. What will be the effect on the profits of the company as a whole?

P12–20 Basic Transfer Pricing (Appendix 12A) Alpha and Beta are divisions within the same company. The managers of both divisions are evaluated based on their own division's return on investment (ROI). Assume the following information relative to the two divisions:

	Case			
	1	**2**	**3**	**4**
Alpha Division:				
Capacity in units	80,000	400,000	150,000	300,000
Number of units now being				
sold to outside customers				
on the intermediate market	80,000	400,000	100,000	300,000
Selling price per unit on the				
intermediate market	$30	$90	$75	$50
Variable costs per unit	18	65	40	26
Fixed costs per unit (based				
on capacity)	6	15	20	9
Beta Division:				
Number of units needed annually	5,000	30,000	20,000	120,000
Purchase price now being paid				
to an outside supplier	$27	$89	$75*	—

*Before any quantity discount.

Managers are free to decide if they will participate in any internal transfers. All transfer prices are negotiated.

Required

1. Refer to case 1 above. Alpha Division can avoid $2 per unit in commissions on any sales to Beta Division. Will the managers agree to a transfer and if so, within what range will the transfer price be? Explain.

2. Refer to case 2 above. A study indicates that Alpha Division can avoid $5 per unit in shipping costs on any sales to Beta Division.
   a. Would you expect any disagreement between the two divisional managers over what the transfer price should be? Explain.
   b. Assume that Alpha Division offers to sell 30,000 units to Beta Division for $88 per unit and that Beta Division refuses this price. What will be the loss in potential profits for the company as a whole?

3. Refer to case 3 above. Assume that Beta Division is now receiving an 8% quantity discount from the outside supplier.
   a. Will the managers agree to a transfer? If so, what is the range within which the transfer price would be?
   b. Assume that Beta Division offers to purchase 20,000 units from Alpha Division at $60 per unit. If Alpha Division accepts this price, would you expect its ROI to increase, decrease, or remain unchanged? Why?

4. Refer to case 4 above. Assume that Beta Division wants Alpha Division to provide it with 120,000 units of a *different* product from the one that Alpha Division is now producing. The new product would require $21 per unit in variable costs and would require that Alpha Division cut back production of its present product by 45,000 units annually. What is the lowest acceptable transfer price from Alpha Division's perspective?

P12–21 Activity-Based Segment Reporting "That commercial market has been dragging us down for years," complained Shanna Reynolds, president of Morley Products. "Just look at that anemic income figure for the commercial market. That market had three million dollars more in sales than the home market, but only a few thousand dollars more in profits. What a loser it is!"

The income statement to which Ms. Reynolds was referring follows:

	Total Company		Commercial Market	Home Market	School Market
Sales	$20,000,000	100.0%	$8,000,000	$5,000,000	$7,000,000
Less expenses:					
Cost of goods sold	9,500,000	47.5%	3,900,000	2,400,000	3,200,000
Sales support	3,600,000	18.0%	1,440,000	900,000	1,260,000
Order processing	1,720,000	8.6%	688,000	430,000	602,000
Warehousing	940,000	4.7%	376,000	235,000	329,000
Packing and shipping	520,000	2.6%	208,000	130,000	182,000
Advertising	1,690,000	8.5%	676,000	422,500	591,500
General management	1,310,000	6.6%	524,000	327,500	458,500
Total expenses	19,280,000	96.4%	7,812,000	4,845,000	6,623,000
Net income	$ 720,000	3.6%	$ 188,000	$ 155,000	$ 377,000

"I agree," said Walt Divot, the company's vice president. "We need to focus more of our attention on the school market, since it's our best segment. Maybe that will bolster profits and get the shareholders off our backs."

The following additional information is available about the company:

a. Morley Products is a wholesale distributor of various goods; the cost of goods sold figures above are traceable to the markets in the amounts shown.

b. Sales support, order processing, and packing and shipping are considered by management to be variable costs. Warehousing, general management, and advertising are fixed costs. These costs have all been allocated to the markets on the basis of sales dollars—a practice that the company has followed for years.

c. You have compiled the following data.

Cost Pool and Allocation Base	Total Cost	Amount of Activity			
		Total	Commercial Market	Home Market	School Market
Sales support (number of calls)	$3,600,000	24,000	8,000	5,000	11,000
Order processing (number of orders)	1,720,000	8,600	1,750	5,200	1,650
Warehousing (square metres of space)	940,000	39,000	11,000	22,000	6,000
Packing and shipping (kilograms shipped)	520,000	52,000	12,000	8,000	32,000

d. You have determined the following breakdown of the company's advertising expense and general management expense:

	Total	Market		
		Commercial	Home	School
Advertising:				
Traceable	$1,460,000	$700,000	$180,000	$580,000
Common	230,000			
General management:				
Traceable—salaries	410,000	150,000	120,000	140,000
Common	900,000			

The company is searching for ways to improve profit, and you have suggested that a segmented statement in which costs are assigned on the basis of activities might provide some useful insights for management.

Required

1. Refer to the data in (c) above. Determine a rate for each cost pool. Then, using this rate, compute the amount of cost assignable to each market.
2. Using the data from (1) above and other data from the problem, prepare a revised segmented statement for the company. Use the contribution format. Show an Amount column and a Percent column for the company as a whole and for each market segment. Carry percentage figures to one decimal place. (Remember to include warehousing among the fixed expenses.)
3. What, if anything, in your segmented statement should be brought to the attention of management? Explain.

P12–22 Variance Analysis The Leo Company produces and sells two product lines with the following budgeted revenues and expenses:

	Spars	Masts
Expected total industry sales	48,000 units	85,000 units
Expected Leo Company sales	4,200 units	17,000 units
Expected selling price	$200 per unit	$300 per unit
Expected cost of manufacturing (40% fixed)	110 per unit	180 per unit
Expected selling and administration costs (70% fixed) ...	60 per unit	70 per unit
Expected product profit margin	$30 per unit	$50 per unit
Actual results for 2000 included:		
Actual total industry sales	60,000 units	100,000 units
Actual Leo Company sales	6,000 units	18,000 units
Actual selling price	$180 per unit	$300 per unit

All costs behaved exactly as expected.

W. Gallant, vice president of marketing and sales, has requested that the employees of his department be paid a bonus for the year based on the fact that they have been able to increase sales by 2,800 units over the budget level for the year, an increase of over 13%.

Raddington evaluates its divisions on the basis of ROI. Management bonuses are also based on ROI. All investments in operating assets are expected to earn a minimum rate of return of 11%.

Reigis' ROI has ranged from 14% to 17% since it was acquired by Raddington. During the past year, Reigis had an investment opportunity that would yield an estimated rate of return of 13%. Reigis' management decided against the investment because it believed the investment would decrease the division's overall ROI.

Last year's income statement for Reigis Steel Division is given below. The division's operating assets employed were $12,960,000 at the end of the year, which represents an 8% increase over the previous year-end balance.

REIGIS STEEL DIVISION
Divisional Income Statement
For the Year Ended December 31

Sales		$31,200,000
Cost of goods sold		16,500,000
Gross margin		14,700,000
Less operating expenses:		
Selling expenses	$5,620,000	
Administrative expenses	7,208,000	12,828,000
Net operating income		$ 1,872,000

Required

1. Compute the following performance measures for the Reigis Steel Division:
   a. ROI. (Remember, ROI is based on the *average* operating assets, computed from the beginning-of-year and end-of-year balances.) State ROI in terms of margin and turnover.
   b. Residual income.
2. Would the management of Reigis Steel Division have been more likely to accept the investment opportunity it had last year if residual income were used as a performance measure instead of ROI? Explain.
3. The Reigis Steel Division is a separate investment centre within Raddington Industries. Identify the items Reigis must be free to control if it is to be evaluated fairly by either the ROI or residual income performance measures.

(CMA, adapted)

P12–26 Cost-Volume-Profit Analysis; Return on Investment (ROI); Transfer Pricing The Valve Division of Bendix, Inc., produces a small valve that is used by various companies as a component part in their products. Bendix, Inc., operates its divisions as autonomous units, giving its divisional managers great discretion in pricing and other decisions. Each division is expected to generate a rate of return of at least 14% on its operating assets. The Valve Division has average operating assets of $700,000. The valves are sold for $5 each. Variable costs are $3 per valve, and fixed costs total $462,000 per year. The division has a capacity of 300,000 valves each year.

Required

1. How many valves must the Valve Division sell each year to generate the desired rate of return on its assets?
   a. What is the margin earned at this level of sales?
   b. What is the turnover at this level of sales?
2. Assume that the Valve Division's current ROI is just equal to the minimum required 14%. In order to increase the division's ROI, the divisional manager wants to increase the selling price per valve by 4%. Market studies indicate that an increase in the selling price would cause sales to drop by 20,000 units each year. However, operating assets could be reduced by $50,000 due to decreased needs for accounts receivable and inventory. Compute the margin, turnover, and ROI if these changes are made.
3. Refer to the original data. Assume again that the Valve Division's current ROI is just equal to the minimum required 14%. Rather than increase the selling price, the sales manager wants to reduce the selling price per valve by 4%. Market studies indicate that this would fill the plant to capacity. In order to carry the greater level of sales, however, operating

assets would increase by $50,000. Compute the margin, turnover, and ROI if these changes are made.

4. Refer to the original data. Assume that the normal volume of sales is 280,000 valves each year at a price of $5 per valve. Another division of the company is currently purchasing 20,000 valves each year from an overseas supplier, at a price of $4.25 per valve. The manager of the Valve Division has adamantly refused to meet this price, pointing out that it would result in a loss for his division:

Selling price per valve		$ 4.25
Cost per valve:		
Variable	$3.00	
Fixed ($462,000 ÷ 300,000 valves)	1.54	4.54
Net loss per valve		$(0.29)

The manager of the Valve Division also points out that the normal $5 selling price barely allows his division the required 14% rate of return. "If we take on some business at only $4.25 per unit, then our ROI is obviously going to suffer," he reasons, "and maintaining that ROI figure is the key to my future. Besides, taking on these extra units would require us to increase our operating assets by at least $50,000 due to the larger inventories and receivables we would be carrying." Would you recommend that the Valve Division sell to the other division at $4.25? Show ROI computations to support your answer.

P12–27 **Market-Based Transfer Price** (Appendix 12A) Stavos Company's Cabinet Division manufactures a standard cabinet for television sets. The cost per cabinet is:

Variable cost per cabinet	$ 70
Fixed cost per cabinet	30*
Total cost per cabinet	$100

*Based on a capacity of 10,000 cabinets per year.

Part of the Cabinet Division's output is sold to outside manufacturers of television sets and part is sold to Stavos Company's Quark Division, which produces a TV set under its own name. The Cabinet Division charges $140 per cabinet for all sales.

The costs, revenue, and net income associated with the Quark Division's TV set is given below:

Selling price per TV set		$480
Less variable cost per TV set:		
Cost of the cabinet	$140	
Variable cost of electronic parts	210	
Total variable cost		350
Contribution margin		130
Less fixed costs per TV set		80*
Net income per TV set		$ 50

*Based on a capacity of 3,000 sets per year.

The Quark Division has an order from an overseas source for 1,000 TV sets. The overseas source wants to pay only $340 per set.

Required
1. Assume that the Quark Division has enough idle capacity to fill the 1,000-set order. Is the division likely to accept the $340 price or to reject it? Explain.
2. Assume that both the Cabinet Division and the Quark Division have idle capacity. Under these conditions, would it be an advantage or a disadvantage to the company as a whole for the Quark Division to reject the $340 price? Show computations to support your answer.
3. Assume that the Quark Division has idle capacity but that the Cabinet Division is operating at capacity and could sell all of its cabinets to outside manufacturers. Compute

the dollar advantage or disadvantage of the Quark Division accepting the 1,000-set order at the $340 unit price.

4. What conclusions do you draw concerning the use of market price as a transfer price in intracompany transactions?

P12–28   Negotiated Transfer Price   (Appendix 12A) Ditka Industries has several independent divisions. The company's Tube Division manufactures a picture tube used in television sets. The Tube Division's income statement for last year, in which 8,000 tubes were sold, is given below:

	Total	Unit
Sales	$1,360,000	$170.00
Less cost of goods sold	840,000	105.00
Gross margin	520,000	65.00
Less selling and administrative expenses	390,000	48.75
Divisional net income	$ 130,000	$ 16.25

As shown above, it costs the Tube Division $105 to produce a single tube. This figure consists of the following costs:

Direct materials	$ 38
Direct labour	27
Manufacturing overhead (75% fixed)	40
Total cost per tube	$105

The Tube Division has fixed selling and administrative expenses of $350,000 per year.

Ditka Industries has just formed a new division, called the TV Division, that will produce a television set that requires a high-resolution picture tube. The Tube Division has been asked to manufacture 2,500 of these tubes each year and sell them to the TV Division. As one step in determining the price that should be charged to the TV Division, the Tube Division has estimated the following cost for each of the new high-resolution tubes:

Direct materials	$ 60
Direct labour	49
Manufacturing overhead (⅔ fixed)	54
Total cost per tube	$163

To manufacture the new tubes, the Tube Division would have to reduce production of its regular tubes by 3,000 units per year. There would be no variable selling and administrative expenses on the intracompany business, and total fixed overhead costs would not change. Assume direct labour is a variable cost.

Required

1. Determine the lowest acceptable transfer price from the perspective of the Tube Division for each of the new high-resolution tubes.
2. Assume that the TV Division has found an outside supplier that will provide the new tubes for only $200 each. If the Tube Division meets this price, what will be the effect on the profits of the company as a whole?

P12–29   Segmented Statements; Product-Line Analysis   "At last, I can see some light at the end of the tunnel," said Steve Adams, president of Jelco Products. "Our losses have shrunk from over $75,000 a month at the beginning of the year to only $26,000 for August. If we can just isolate the remaining problems with products A and C, we'll be in the black by the first of next year."

The company's income statement for the latest month (August) is presented below (absorption costing basis):

JELCO PRODUCTS
Income Statement
For August

	Total Company	Product A	B	C
Sales	$1,500,000	$600,000	$400,000	$500,000
Less cost of goods sold	922,000	372,000	220,000	330,000
Gross margins	578,000	228,000	180,000	170,000
Less operating expenses:				
Selling	424,000	162,000	112,000	150,000
Administrative	180,000	72,000	48,000	60,000
Total operating expenses	604,000	234,000	160,000	210,000
Net income (loss)	$ (26,000)	$ (6,000)	$ 20,000	$(40,000)

"What recommendations did that business consultant make?" asked Mr. Adams. "We paid the guy $100 an hour; surely he found something wrong." "He says our problems are concealed by the way we make up our statements," replied Sally Warren, the executive vice president. "He left us some data on what he calls 'traceable' and 'common' costs that he says we should be isolating in our reports." The data to which Ms. Warren was referring are shown below:

	Total Company	Product A	B	C
Variable costs:*				
Production (materials, labour, and variable overhead)	—	18%	32%	20%
Selling	—	10%	8%	10%
Traceable fixed costs:				
Production	$376,000	$180,000	$36,000	$160,000
Selling	282,000	102,000	80,000	100,000
Common fixed costs:				
Production	210,000	—	—	—
Administrative	180,000	—	—	—

*As a percentage of sales.

"I don't see anything wrong with our statements," said Mr. Adams. "Bill, our chief accountant, says that he has been using this format for over 30 years. He's also very careful to allocate all of our costs to the products."

"I'll admit that Bill always seems to be on top of things," replied Ms. Warren. "By the way, purchasing says that the X7 chips we use in products A and B are on back order and won't be available for several weeks. From the looks of August's income statement, we had better concentrate our remaining inventory of X7 chips on product B." (Two X7 chips are used in both product A and product B.)

The following additional information is available on the company:

a. Work in process and finished goods inventories are negligible and can be ignored.
b. Products A and B each sell for $250 per unit, and product C sells for $125 per unit. Strong market demand exists for all three products.

Required
1. Prepare a new income statement for August, segmented by product and using the contribution approach. Show both Amount and Percent columns for the company in total and for each product.
2. Assume that Mr. Adams is considering the elimination of product C due to the losses it is incurring. Based on the statement you prepared in (1) above, what points would you make for or against elimination of product C?

3. Do you agree with the company's decision to concentrate the remaining inventory of X7 chips on product B? Why or why not?

4. Product C is sold in both a vending and a home market with sales and cost data as follows:

| | | Market | |
	Total	Vending	Home
Sales	$500,000	$50,000	$450,000
Variable costs:*			
Production	—	20%	20%
Selling	—	28%	8%
Traceable fixed costs:			
Selling	$ 75,000	$45,000	$ 30,000

*As a percentage of sales.

The remainder of product C's fixed selling costs and all of product C's fixed production costs are common to the markets in which product C is sold.

  a. Prepare an income statement showing product C segmented by market. Use the contribution approach and show both Amount and Percent columns for the product in total and for each market.

  b. What points revealed by this statement would you be particularly anxious to bring to the attention of management?

P12–30 Transfer Pricing with and without Idle Capacity (Appendix 12A)

The Electronics Division of Far North Telecom, Ltd., of Canada manufactures an electrical switching unit that can be sold either to outside customers or to the Fiber Optics Division of Far North Telecom. Selected operating data on the two divisions are given below:

Electronics Division:	
Unit selling price to outside customers	$ 80
Variable production cost per unit	52
Variable selling and administrative expense per unit	9
Fixed production cost in total	300,000*
Fiber Optics Division:	
Outside purchase price per unit (before any quantity discount)	80

*Capacity 25,000 units per year.

The Fiber Optics Division now purchases the switch from an outside supplier at the regular $80 intermediate price less a 5% quantity discount. Since the switch manufactured by the Electronics Division is of the same quality and type used by the Fiber Optics Division, consideration is being given to buying internally rather than from the outside supplier. As the company's president stated, "It's just plain smart to buy and sell within the corporate family."

A study has determined that the variable selling and administrative expenses of the Electronics Division would be cut by one-third for any sales to the Fiber Optics Division. Top management wants to treat each division as an autonomous unit with independent profit responsibility.

Required

1. Assume that the Electronics Division is currently selling only 20,000 units per year to outside customers and that the Fiber Optics Division needs 5,000 units per year.

  a. What is the lowest acceptable transfer price from the perspective of the Electronics Division? Explain.

  b. What is the highest acceptable transfer price from the perspective of the Fiber Optics Division? Explain.

  c. Assume that the Fiber Optics Division finds an outside supplier that will sell the electrical unit for only $65 per unit. Should the Electronics Division be required to meet this price? Explain.

d. Refer to the original data. Assume that the Electronics Division decides to raise its price to $85 per unit. If the Fiber Optics Division is forced to pay this price and to start purchasing from the Electronics Division, will this result in greater or less total corporate profits? How much per unit?

e. Under the circumstances posed in (d) above, should the Fiber Optics Division be forced to purchase from the Electronics Division? Explain.

2. Assume that the Electronics Division can sell all that it produces to outside customers. Repeat (a) through (e) above.

P12–31 **Service Organization; Segment Reporting** Music Teachers, Inc., is an educational association for music teachers that has 20,000 members. The association operates from a central headquarters but has local membership chapters throughout the United States. Monthly meetings are held by the local chapters to discuss recent developments on topics of interest to music teachers. The association's journal, *Teachers' Forum,* is issued monthly with features about recent developments in the field. The association publishes books and reports and also sponsors professional courses that qualify for continuing professional education credit. The association's statement of revenues and expenses for the current year is presented below.

MUSIC TEACHERS, INC.
Statement of Revenues and Expenses
For the Year Ended November 30

Revenues	$3,275,000
Less expenses:	
Salaries	920,000
Personnel costs	230,000
Occupancy costs	280,000
Reimbursement of member costs to local chapters	600,000
Other membership services	500,000
Printing and paper	320,000
Postage and shipping	176,000
Instructors' fees	80,000
General and administrative	38,000
Total expenses	3,144,000
Excess of revenues over expenses	$ 131,000

The board of directors of Music Teachers, Inc., has requested that a segmented statement of operations be prepared showing the contribution of each profit centre to the association. The association has four profit centres: Membership Division, Magazine Subscriptions Division, Books and Reports Division, and Continuing Education Division. Mike Doyle has been assigned responsibility for preparing the segmented statement, and he has gathered the following data prior to its preparation.

a. Membership dues are $100 per year, of which $20 is considered to cover a one-year subscription to the association's journal. Other benefits include membership in the association and chapter affiliation. The portion of the dues covering the magazine subscription ($20) should be assigned to the Magazine Subscription Division.

b. One-year subscriptions to *Teachers' Forum* were sold to nonmembers and libraries at $30 per subscription. A total of 2,500 of these subscriptions were sold last year. In addition to subscriptions, the magazine generated $100,000 in advertising revenues. The costs per magazine subscription were $7 for printing and paper and $4 for postage and shipping.

c. A total of 28,000 technical reports and professional texts were sold by the Books and Reports Division at an average unit selling price of $25. Average costs per publication were $4 for printing and paper and $2 for postage and shipping.

d. The association offers a variety of continuing education courses to both members and nonmembers. The one-day courses had a tuition cost of $75 each and were attended by 2,400 students. A total of 1,760 students took two-day courses at a tuition cost of $125 for each student. Outside instructors were paid to teach some courses.

e. Salary costs and space occupied by division follow:

	Salaries	Space Occupied (square feet)
Membership	$210,000	2,000
Magazine Subscriptions	150,000	2,000
Books and Reports	300,000	3,000
Continuing Education	180,000	2,000
Corporate staff	80,000	1,000
Total	$920,000	10,000

Personnel costs are 25% of salaries in the separate divisions as well as for the corporate staff. The $280,000 in occupancy costs includes $50,000 in rental cost for a warehouse used by the Books and Reports Division for storage purposes.

f. Printing and paper costs other than for magazine subscriptions and for books and reports relate to the Continuing Education Division.

g. General and administrative expenses include costs relating to overall administration of the association as a whole. The company's corporate staff does some mailing of materials for general administrative purposes.

The expenses that can be traced or assigned to the corporate staff, as well as any other expenses that are not traceable to the profit centres, will be treated as common costs. It is not necessary to distinguish between variable and fixed costs.

Required
1. Prepare a segmented statement of revenues and expenses for Music Teachers, Inc. This statement should show the segment margin for each division as well as results for the association as a whole.
2. Give arguments for and against allocating *all* costs of the association to the four divisions.

(CMA, adapted)

P12–32 Costing for Customers   Brink Manufacturing and Distributing Ltd. distributes its preformed concrete slabs throughout eastern Canada to two classes of customers, wholesalers and contractors. In an effort to analyze its marketing expenses by distribution channel, the following statistics were obtained:

	Wholesalers	Contractors
Units sold	2,000	2,500
Kilometres travelled	30,000	42,000
Orders	1,200	1,500
Customers	38	160
Costs:		
Warehousing per unit	$10.00	$13.00
Transport	$1.20 per kilometre	
Credit and collection	$0.60 per order plus $150 per customer	
Selling	$2.00 per order	
Advertising	$100.00 per customer	

Required
1. Analyze the marketing costs by customer class.
2. Brink is considering purchasing its own truck and hiring a driver for $36,000 per year. Determine how much it could afford to spend on a truck in year one to equal its current costs.

P12–33 Customer Profitability   William Watson, sales manager for WW Ltd., is concerned about the focus and direction of the sales activities at WW. To help analyze the situation, the following statistics have been gathered:

Range of sales per customer	$10,000 or more	$1,000 to $9,999	$0 to $999
Number of customers	50	350	3,500*
Sales calls	250	1,500	9,000†
Orders per year	700	1,800	5,000
Average sales per year (based on active customers)	$18,000	$3,500	$120
Total sales	$900,000	$1,225,000	$408,000
Gross margin percentage	20%	25%	30%
Contribution margin percentage	30%	40%	45%
Sales department costs:			
Supervision	$ 48,000		
Sales salaries and benefits	280,000		
Clerical	18,000		
Travel	45,000		
Entertainment	12,000		
Samples	7,000		
Rent	6,900		
Other	3,800		
	$420,700		

*1,900 no sales included.

†3,800 on no sales.

The following analysis of the time salespeople spend on a call was made:

Customer	50%
Travel time	30
Office time	20
	100%

The eight-person sales force averages the above time allocation of call time.

Office time cost per order averages $2.40. This cost represents the clerical costs of processing orders from the salespeople and direct phone orders from customers.

Required Provide an analysis of the situation for Mr. Watson and make some recommendations for him to consider.

P12–34 Customer Profitability Ricky Hayden Limited manufactures and sells electronic components to three classes of customers: computer assemblers and repair technicians, pulp and paper plants, and provincial governments. The sales to provincial governments represent purchases for junior colleges and some repair work for government equipment. The following information represents data for the past year.

	Assemblers	Governments	Pulp Plants
Sales	$3,000,000	$1,200,000	$800,000
Standard cost of goods sold	2,400,000	1,000,000	500,000
Gross margin	$ 600,000	$ 200,000	$300,000

The standard cost of goods sold is based on the absorption cost approach where variances have been allocated using normal allocation procedures. Variable standard production costs were determined to be the following percentages of standard cost of goods sold after variances were allocated:

Assemblers	75%
Governments	70%
Pulp plants	80%

Cost analyses determined the following incremental costs for fixed overhead:

Assemblers	$500,000
Governments	100,000
Pulp plants	200,000
	$800,000

Cost records associated with selling and administrative activities reflect the following information:

Computer services:
Total cost—$150,000
Base: Invoice lines
Number of lines:

Assemblers	6,000
Governments	4,000
Pulp plants	20,000

Warehousing of finished goods:
Salaries and wages—$68,000
Base: Standard absorption cost except that government contracts are based on immediate transfer upon completion of production.

Research and development:
Cost of salaries and wages plus equipment costs—$100,000
Base: These fixed costs are unrelated to the type of customer or the value of products sold.

Selling:
$250,000 in various costs
Base: $50,000 represents the costs of a full-time representative to the governments. The remainder is associated with the number of calls and the time each requires as made by sales representatives:
Assemblers—500 calls
Pulp plants—2,500 calls
Calls to assemblers are estimated to take three times as long as those to pulp plants because of the central purchasing departments used by pulp plants and their specific locations.

General administration:
Cost—$100,000
Base: No satisfactory base has been found to allocate these costs.

Advertising:
Cost—$100,000
Base: $30,000 general
70,000 specific to assemblers

Space:
Cost—$200,000
Base: Size of occupancy—17,000 square metres total

Executive offices	1,200 m^2
Sales offices	600 m^2
Computer services	600 m^2
Research and development	240 m^2
Factory	8,160 m^2
Warehouse	1,200 m^2

Factory costs are presently included in factory overhead standard costs. However, the $200,000 cannot be saved by renting space to other operations.

Required
1. Prepare a customer profitability report for the year based on the above information.
2. What further analysis might be possible that could improve cost allocations?
3. Would you recommend any change in customer focus for Ricky Hayden Limited?

Cases

C12–35 Transfer Pricing; Divisional Performance (Appendix 12A) Weller Industries is a decentralized organization with six divisions. The company's Electrical Division produces a variety of electrical items, including an X52 electrical fitting. The Electrical Division (which is operating at capacity) sells this fitting to its regular customers for $7.50 each; the fitting has a variable manufacturing cost of $4.25.

The company's Brake Division has asked the Electrical Division to supply it with a large quantity of X52 fittings for only $5 each. The Brake Division, which is operating at 50% of capacity, will put the fitting into a brake unit that it will produce and sell to a large commercial airline manufacturer. The cost of the brake unit being built by the Brake Division follows:

Purchased parts (from outside vendors)	$22.50
Electrical fitting X52	5.00
Other variable costs	14.00
Fixed overhead and administration	8.00
Total cost per brake unit	$49.50

Although the $5 price for the X52 fitting represents a substantial discount from the regular $7.50 price, the manager of the Brake Division believes that the price concession is necessary if his division is to get the contract for the airplane brake units. He has heard "through the grapevine" that the airplane manufacturer plans to reject his bid if it is more than $50 per brake unit. Thus, if the Brake Division is forced to pay the regular $7.50 price for the X52 fitting, it will either not get the contract or it will suffer a substantial loss at a time when it is already operating at only 50% of capacity. The manager of the Brake Division argues that the price concession is imperative to the well-being of both his division and the company as a whole.

Weller Industries uses return on investment (ROI) and dollar profits in measuring divisional performance.

Required

1. Assume that you are the manager of the Electrical Division. Would you recommend that your division supply the X52 fitting to the Brake Division for $5 each as requested? Why or why not? Show all computations.
2. Would it be to the economic advantage of the company as a whole for the Electrical Division to supply the fittings to the Brake Division if the airplane brakes can be sold for $50? Show all computations, and explain your answer.
3. In principle, should it be possible for the two managers to agree to a transfer price in this particular situation? If so, within what range would that transfer price lie?
4. Discuss the organizational and manager behaviour problems, if any, inherent in this situation. What would you advise the company's president to do in this situation?

(CMA, adapted)

C12–36 Organizational Structure, Performance Evaluation, and International Transfer Pricing Rupert Jones was recently hired as the corporate controller of Dreamland Manufacturing, a full-line manufacturer of fabric, beds, bed linens, and drapery. Dreamland is headquartered in a major Canadian city and has three nearby domestic operating divisions: fabrics, frames, and furnishings. A fourth division, Yamalian, is located in the country of Yamalia.

Currently, all divisions and divisional managers are evaluated based on maximizing divisional income. Except for the frames division, Dreamland's divisions have full freedom to source and sell any material or product in the outside market and to set their own transfer prices. An illustration of the product flows among divisions is shown in Exhibit 1.

The Yamalian division produces specialty fabrics; it transfers some to a fabrics and furnishings divisions in Canada and sells the rest in the Yamalian market. Transfers are subject to Canadian duty and excise taxes, as well as significant shipping costs.

The fabrics division produces fabric for the furnishings division and for large Canadian retail chains and wholesale distributors. The fabrics division also sews its fabric (or fabric

Exhibit 1

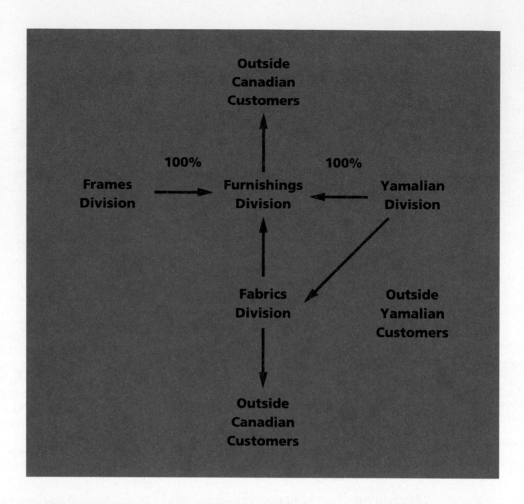

transferred from the Yamalian division) into components for other Dreamland products that are assembled and finished by the furnishings division.

The frames division manufactures steel and wooden bed frames and box spring liners. All of the products manufactured by the frames division are transferred to the furnishings division.

The furnishings division is the main manufacturing and assembling centre of Dreamland's operations. This division manufactures and assembles mattresses and beds, and also sews bed linens and draperies. All of the output of the furnishings division is sold in the Canadian market.

Recently, the furnishings division negotiated a contract to produce specialty hospital mattresses for several large city hospitals at a price of $900 per mattress. Costs to fill this contract are $600 per mattress ($400 variable and $200 fixed) plus the cost of producing the special mattress covers needed for these mattresses. There are three options for sourcing the special fabric required for the mattress covers and two options for sewing and completing the mattress covers.

Fabric Sewing Options

1. Source the special fabric from the fabrics division at a transfer price of $92 per unit (see Exhibit 2).
2. Source the special fabric from the Yamalian division at a cost of $81.00 per unit (see Exhibit 2).
3. Purchase the special fabric from a reputable outside supplier at a price of $75 per unit.

(*Note:* 1 unit = the amount of fabric required to make one mattress cover.)

Sewing and Completing Each Mattress Cover

1. The furnishings division can cut, sew, and complete each mattress cover for a cost which includes the fabric plus the following nonfabric items:

Exhibit 2

DREAMLAND MANUFACTURING
Calculation of Transfer Prices
For Special Mattress Covers
And Special Fabric

Fabrics Division

The proposed transfer price from the fabrics division for the special fabric
needed to produce one mattress cover was computed as follows:

Direct materials	$ 15.00
Weaving labour	30.00
Variable overhead	5.00
Fixed overhead	30.00
Total manufacturing cost	80.00
Normal profit allowance (15%)	12.00
Transfer price of fabric	$ 92.00

The proposed transfer price from the fabrics division for a completed
mattress cover was computed as follows:

Transfer price for fabric	$ 92.00
Cutting and sewing labour	15.00
Variable overhead	5.00
Fixed overhead	15.00
Total manufacturing cost	127.00
Normal profit allowance (15%)	19.05
Transfer price of fabric	$146.05

Yamalian Division

The proposed transfer price from the Yamalian division for the special
fabric needed to produce one mattress cover was computed as follows
(all costs represent translated Canadian currency):

Direct materials	$ 10.00
Weaving labour	8.00
Variable overhead	6.00
Fixed overhead	24.00
Total manufacturing cost	48.00
Normal profit allowance (25%)	12.00
Transfer price of fabric	60.00
Other cost incurred by Dreamland:	
Canadian duty and excise taxes	
(based on 25% of fair market value of $62)	15.50
Shipping costs	5.50
Total cost of fabric	$ 81.00

Cutting and sewing labour	$19.00
Variable overhead	5.00
Fixed overhead	18.00
Total conversion (nonfabric) costs	$42.00

2. The fabrics division has offered to cut, sew, and supply completed mattress covers to the
furnishings division at a total transfer price of $146.05 per cover (see Exhibit 2).

All divisions have enough capacity available to fulfill the requirements of the contract
without disrupting any of their other operations.

The furnishings division manager knows that the Fabrics and Yamalian divisions added standard markups to their costs in arriving at transfer prices (see Exhibit 2) and would prefer to deal with an internal division if he could convince one or the other to match the $75 price from the outside supplier. With this in mind, the furnishings division manager asked the president for his help in negotiating with the other internal divisions.

In response, the president asked Rupert Jones, the new corporate controller, to analyze the hospital mattress situation and recommend a production plan that would maximize overall company profitability. The president also asked Rupert to review the structure of Dreamland and to recommend an appropriate performance evaluation and transfer pricing system.

Required As Rupert Jones, the newly appointed corporate controller, analyze the situation and recommend the best production plan for the hospital mattress covers. Also, as requested by the president, review the structure of Dreamland and recommend an appropriate performance evaluation and transfer pricing system.

(SMAC, adapted)

C12–37 Value Chain Analysis Jack Gray, the general manager of the Windsor Bull Dogs junior A hockey team, asked you to assess the ticket prices for games at the Windsor arena. He would like you to compare this value chain with what he estimates to be the Dartmouth's operation. The average ticket price is $5.00 for Windsor based on an average attendance of 2,500 persons per game. Dartmouth averages 4,500 fans at an average price of $8.50 per ticket.

Costs per Attendee	Windsor	Dartmouth
Advertising & marketing	$0.50	$0.55
Ticket sales	0.30	0.25
Arena operations	0.70	0.80
Management compensation	0.25	0.20
Players' compensation	1.00	1.10
Security, etc.	0.25	0.70
Total costs	$3.00	$3.60

Required Assess the ticket prices.

Group Exercises

GE12–38 Performance Measurement at a Service Firm How do service-oriented firms' performance measurement and compensation systems compare with those of manufacturing firms? To study one well-run service business, ask the manager of your local McDonald's if he or she could spend some time discussing what performance measures McDonald's uses to evaluate store managers and how these performance measures tie in with the compensation of the store managers.

Required Organize your analysis into the following areas:

1. What are McDonald's goals, that is, the broad, long-range plans of the company (e.g., to increase market share)?
2. What are the critical success factors (CSF), that is, the key areas in which things must go right if the company is to be successful (e.g., low selling prices based on low production costs)?
3. What are the performance measures that help to motivate and monitor progress toward achieving each CSF (e.g., continuous reduction in cost of quality)?
4. Are performance measures consistent with the store manager's compensation plan?

GE12–39 Evaluating Innovative and Standard Products Some firms choose a strategy that involves competing in established markets by selling high-volume standard products that have wide acceptance. Other firms choose a strategy that emphasizes competing in niche markets by selling low-volume innovative products that have a more narrow application.

Required
1. What criteria do customers use when choosing to purchase each type of product?
2. What measures should plant managers use to control and evaluate the financial performance of each product?
3. From your reading of Chapters 9–12, how do you think plant managers would control and evaluate the financial performance of each product?

GE12–40   How Do Capital Markets Evaluate Performance?   Internally, companies usually use accounting measures to motivate and evaluate the performance of managers of corporate groups, divisions, product lines, and departments. How do investors use accounting information in determining whether to buy, sell, or hold onto a share?

Most companies pay their top managers a salary and a bonus. The bonus part of their compensation is usually based on how well the executive performs against some accounting-based performance target. For example, some percentage of the CEO's bonus may be earned when he or she achieves a certain increase in earnings per share or, in the case of a division manager, when he or she exceeds a certain percentage increase in operating profits. Yet, there are numerous examples of CEOs and other top officers who have met their performance targets, but the share price of the company lags or flounders for years on end. Top management prospers but shareholders may not.

Required
1. If a company consistently earns a profit year-in and year-out, do shareholders and prospective shareholders have a right to expect anything more than that from corporate management?
2. Is there any cost to holding large amounts of inventory? Is there any cost associated with the fixed assets—property, plant, and equipment—of capital-intensive businesses? Is there any cost of having idle assets or underutilized assets like buildings and equipment?
3. Is there any internal accounting charge for the money invested in working capital and fixed assets?
4. What is the cost of debt? Is there a similar cost associated with shareholders' equity? Explain.
5. Based on the discussion in (2) through (4) above, how does management create value (increase the share price)? Under what conditions would the share price languish or even decrease?
6. How would knowledge of this information influence how top management allocates the company's scarce cash resources within the firm?
7. Design a performance measurement system for senior-level officers and for divisional managers that is more consistent with enhancing a company's market value.
8. Do general economic conditions have any impact on a company's market value? How would you change the design of the performance measurement and compensation system to control for the fortune (or misfortune) of managing a company or division when general economic conditions were improving (or deteriorating)?

GE12–41   College Segment Reports   Obtain a copy of your college or university's most recent financial report prepared for internal use.

Required
1. Does the financial report break down the results into major segments such as schools, academic departments, intercollegiate sports, and so on? Can you determine the financial contribution (i.e., revenues less expenses) of each segment from the report?
2. If the report attempts to show the financial contribution of each major segment, does the report follow the principles for segment reporting in this chapter? If not, what principles are violated and what harm, if any, can occur as a result from violating those principles?

IE12–42   Return on Investment (ROI) Analysis   ROI is the product of a company's margin and turnover. In this exercise you will be computing margin, turnover, and ROI using data from the annual reports of several companies. Before starting on this exercise, you should know that in some cases it will not be completely clear which assets should be considered operating assets. Do not worry about this. Do the best you can and just be consistent from year to year within the same company.

Required   On the web site www.sedar.com you should be able to find directions to the company's annual report. Using data from the company's two most recent annual reports, compute the company's margin, turnover, and ROI for the two most recent years. Using these ratios, briefly discuss the company's performance.

1. Royal Bank of Canada
2. Loblaws
3. Nortel
4. Rogers Communications

GE12–43   Value Chain   Select a product that is familiar to you. Using its current market price as an indicator of its overall value, break down this price into individual value components in terms of what you would expect its value chain to look like. Using estimates of materials, labour and other costs construct the cost components for the value chain.

Required   Comment on which elements of the value chain contribute positively to customer value.

GE12–44   Economic Value Added   Obtain the latest annual report for INCO, Thompson Group, BCE Inc., Newbridge Networks, or Maritime Tel and Tel.

Required   Review the management discussion materials to determine how your selection determined economic value added. Was the EVA positive and if so, was the amount what you would have expected from the chapter discussion?

Chapter Thirteen

Relevant Costs for Decision Making

Business Focus

A failure to recognize the existence of sunk costs can lead to bad business decisions. As evidence, consider the following incident related by a business consultant after encountering a frustrated and angry fellow traveller ("Mr. Smith") whose flight home faced a lengthy delay:

Mr. Smith had recently flown into St. Louis on a commercial airline for a two-day business trip. While there, he learned that his company's private airplane had flown in the day before and would leave on the same day that he was scheduled to leave. Mr. Smith immediately cashed in his $200 commercial airline ticket and made arrangements to fly back on the company plane. He flew home feeling pretty good about saving his company the $200 fare and being able to depart on schedule.

About two weeks later, however, Mr. Smith's boss asked him why the department had been cross-charged $400 for his return trip when the commercial airfare was only $200. Mr. Smith explained that "the company plane was flying back regardless, and there were a number of empty seats."

How could Mr. Smith's attempt to save his company $200 end up "costing" his department $400? The problem is that Mr. Smith recognized something that his company's cost allocation system did not: namely, that the vast majority of the costs associated with flying the plane home were already sunk and, thus, unavoidable at the time he made the decision to fly home. By failing to distinguish between sunk (i.e., unavoidable) and avoidable costs, the cost allocation system was causing the firm and its managers to make uneconomic business decisions.

It is now clear why Mr. Smith was so frustrated the day I ran into him in St. Louis. His company's plane was sitting on the runway with a number of empty seats and ready to take off for the very same destination. Yet there was no way Mr. Smith was going to fly on that plane even though doing so was the "best business decision."

Source: Dennis L. Weisman, "How Cost Allocation Systems Can Lead Managers Astray," Journal of Cost Management 5, *no. 1 (Spring 1991), p. 4. Used by permission.*

Making decisions is one of the basic functions of a manager. Managers are constantly faced with problems of deciding what products to sell, what production methods to use, whether to make or buy component parts, what prices to charge, what channels of distribution to use, whether to accept special orders at special prices, and so forth. Decision making is often a difficult task that is complicated by the existence of numerous alternatives and massive amounts of data, only some of which may be relevant.

Every decision involves choosing from among at least two alternatives. In making a decision, the costs and benefits of one alternative must be compared to the costs and benefits of other alternatives. Costs that differ between alternatives are called **relevant costs.** Distinguishing between relevant and irrelevant cost and benefit data is critical for two reasons. First, irrelevant data can be ignored and need not be analyzed. This can save decision makers tremendous amounts of time and effort. Second, bad decisions can easily result from erroneously including irrelevant cost and benefit data when analyzing alternatives. To be successful in decision making, managers must be able to tell the difference between relevant and irrelevant data and must be able to correctly use the relevant data in analyzing alternatives. The purpose of this chapter is to develop these skills by illustrating their use in a wide range of decision-making situations. We hasten to add that these decision-making skills are as important in your personal life as they are to managers. After completing your study of the material in this chapter, you should be able to think more clearly about decisions in all facets of your life.

Relevant cost A cost that differs between alternatives in a particular decision. In managerial accounting, this term is synonymous with *avoidable cost* and *differential cost.*

Cost Concepts for Decision Making

Four cost terms discussed in Chapter 2 are particularly applicable to this chapter. These terms are *differential costs, incremental costs, opportunity costs,* and *sunk costs.* You may find it helpful to turn back to Chapter 2 and refresh your memory concerning these terms before reading on.

Identifying Relevant Costs and Benefits

Objective 1

Distinguish between relevant and irrelevant costs in decisions.

Only those costs and benefits that differ in total between alternatives are relevant in a decision. If a cost will be the same regardless of the alternative selected, then the decision has no effect on the cost and it can be ignored. For example, if you are trying to decide whether to go to a movie or to rent a videotape for the evening, the rent on your apartment is irrelevant. Whether you go to a movie or rent a videotape, the rent on your apartment will be exactly the same and is therefore irrelevant in the decision. On the other hand, the cost of the movie ticket and the cost of renting the videotape would be relevant in the decision since they are *avoidable costs.*

Avoidable cost Any cost that can be eliminated (in whole or in part) by choosing one alternative over another in a decision-making situation. In managerial accounting, this term is synonymous with *relevant cost* and *differential cost.*

An **avoidable cost** is a cost that can be eliminated in whole or in part by choosing one alternative over another. By choosing the alternative of going to the movie, the cost of renting the videotape can be avoided. By choosing the alternative of renting the videotape, the cost of the movie ticket can be avoided. Therefore, the cost of the movie ticket and the cost of renting the videotape are both avoidable costs. On the other hand, the rent on the apartment is not an avoidable cost of either alternative. You would continue to rent your apartment under either alternative. Avoidable costs are relevant costs. Unavoidable costs are irrelevant costs.

Two broad categories of costs are never relevant in decisions. These irrelevant costs are:

1. Sunk costs.
2. Future costs that do not differ between the alternatives.

Sunk cost Any cost that has already been incurred and that cannot be changed by any decision made now or in the future.

As we learned in Chapter 2, a **sunk cost** is a cost that has already been incurred and that cannot be avoided regardless of what a manager decides to do. Sunk costs are always the same, no matter what alternatives are being considered, and they are therefore always irrelevant and should be ignored. On the other hand, future costs that do differ between alternatives *are* relevant. For example, when deciding whether to go to a movie or rent a videotape, the cost of buying a movie ticket and the cost of renting a videotape have not yet been incurred. These are future costs that differ between alternatives when the decision is being made and therefore are relevant.

Differential cost Any cost that differs between alternatives in a decision-making situation. In managerial accounting, this term is synonymous with *avoidable cost* and *relevant cost.*

Along with sunk cost, the term **differential cost** was introduced in Chapter 2. In managerial accounting, the terms *avoidable cost, differential cost, incremental cost,* and *relevant cost* are often used interchangeably. To identify the costs that are avoidable (differential) in a particular decision situation and are therefore relevant, these steps can be followed:

1. Eliminate costs and benefits that do not differ between alternatives. These irrelevant costs consist of (a) sunk costs and (b) future costs that do not differ between alternatives.
2. Use the remaining costs and benefits that do differ between alternatives in making the decision. The costs that remain are the differential, or avoidable, costs.

Different Costs for Different Purposes

We need to recognize from the outset of our discussion that costs that are relevant in one decision situation are not necessarily relevant in another. Simply put, this means that *the manager needs different costs for different purposes.* For one purpose, a particular group of costs may be relevant; for another purpose, an entirely different group of costs may be relevant. Thus, in *each* decision situation the manager must examine the data at hand and isolate the relevant costs. Otherwise, the manager runs the risk of being misled by irrelevant data.

The concept of "different costs for different purposes" is basic to managerial accounting; we shall see its application frequently in the pages that follow.

Sunk Costs Are Not Relevant Costs

One of the most difficult conceptual lessons that managers have to learn is that sunk costs are never relevant in decisions. The temptation to include sunk costs in the analysis is especially strong in the case of book value of old equipment. We focus on book value of old equipment below, and then we consider other kinds of sunk costs in other parts of the chapter. We shall see that regardless of the kind of sunk cost involved, the conclusion is always the same—sunk costs are not avoidable, and therefore they should be ignored in decisions.

Managerial Accounting in Action

THE ISSUE

SoaringWings, Inc., is a small manufacturer of high-quality hang gliders. The most critical component of a hang glider is its metal frame, which must be very strong and yet very light. The frames are made by brazing together tubes of high-strength, but lightweight, metal alloys. Most of the brazing must be done by hand, but some can be done in an automated process by machine. Pete Kronski, the production manager of SoaringWings, Inc., has been trying to convince J. J. Marker, the company's president, to purchase a new brazing machine from Furimoro Industries. This machine would replace an old brazing machine from Bryston, Inc., that generates a large amount of scrap and waste.

On a recent blustery morning, Pete and J. J. happened to drive into the company's parking lot at the same time. The following conversation occurred as they walked together into the building.

Pete: Morning, J. J. Have you had a chance to look at the specifications on the new brazing machine from Furimoro Industries that I gave you last week?

J. J.: Are you still bugging me about the brazing machine?

Pete: You know it's almost impossible to keep that old Bryston brazing machine working within tolerances.

J. J.: I know, I know. But we're carrying the Bryston machine on the books for $140,000.

Pete: That's right. But I've done some investigating, and we could sell it for $90,000 to a plumbing company in town that doesn't require as tight tolerances as we do.

J. J.: Pete, that's just brilliant! You want me to sell a $140,000 machine for $90,000 and take a loss of $50,000. Do you have any other great ideas this morning?

Pete: J. J., I know it sounds far-fetched, but we would actually save money buying the new machine.

J. J.: I'm skeptical. However, if you can show me the hard facts, I'll listen.

Pete: Fair enough. I'll do it. ∎

Objective 2

Prepare an analysis showing whether to keep or replace old equipment.

Book Value of Old Equipment

Pete first gathered the following data concerning the old machine and the proposed new machine:

Old Machine		Proposed New Machine	
Original cost	$175,000	List price new	$200,000
Remaining book value	140,000	Expected life	4 years
Remaining life	4 years	Disposal value in four years	$ –0–
Disposal value now	$ 90,000	Annual variable expenses	
Disposal value in four years	–0–	to operate	300,000
Annual variable expenses		Annual revenue from sales	500,000
to operate	345,000		
Annual revenue from sales	500,000		

Should the old machine be disposed of and the new machine purchased? The first reaction of SoaringWings' president was to say no, since disposal of the old machine would result in a "loss" of $50,000:

Old Machine

Remaining book value	$140,000
Disposal value now	90,000
Loss if disposed of now	$ 50,000

Given this potential loss if the old machine is sold, a manager may reason, "We've already made an investment in the old machine, so now we have no choice but to use it until our investment has been fully recovered." A manager may tend to think this way even though the new machine is clearly more efficient than the old machine. An error made in the past cannot be corrected by simply *using* the machine. The investment that has been made in the old machine is a sunk cost. The portion of this investment that remains on the company's books (the book value of $140,000) should not be considered in a decision about whether to buy the new machine. Pete Kronski verified the irrelevance of the book value of the old machine by the following analysis:[1]

Total Cost and Revenues—Four Years

	Keep Old Machine	Purchase New Machine	Differential Costs and Benefits
Sales	$ 2,000,000	$ 2,000,000	$ –0–
Variable expenses	(1,380,000)	(1,200,000)	180,000
Cost (depreciation) of the new machine	—	(200,000)	(200,000)
Depreciation of the old machine or book value write-off	(140,000)	(140,000)*	–0–
Disposal value of the old machine	—	90,000*	90,000
Total net operating income over the four years	$ 480,000	$ 550,000	$ 70,000

*For external reporting purposes, the $140,000 remaining book value of the old machine and the $90,000 disposal value would be netted together and deducted as a single $50,000 "loss" figure.

Looking at all four years together, notice that the firm will be $70,000 better off by purchasing the new machine. Also notice that the $140,000 book value of the old machine had *no effect* on the outcome of the analysis. Since this book value is a sunk cost, it must be absorbed by the firm regardless of whether the old machine is kept and used or whether it is sold. If the old machine is kept and used, then the $140,000 book value is deducted in the form of depreciation. If the old machine is sold, then the $140,000 book value is deducted in the form of a lump-sum write-off. Either way, the company bears the same $140,000 cost and the differential cost is zero.

---

1. The computations involved in this example are taken one step further in Chapters 14 and 15 where we discuss the time value of money and the use of present value in decision making.

FOCUSING ON RELEVANT COSTS   What costs in the example above are relevant in the decision concerning the new machine? Looking at the original cost data, we should eliminate (1) the sunk costs and (2) the future costs and benefits that do not differ between the alternatives at hand.

1. The sunk costs:
   a. The remaining book value of the old machine ($140,000).
2. The future costs and benefits that do not differ:
   a. The sales revenue ($500,000 per year or $2,000,000 total).
   b. The variable expenses (to the extent of $300,000 per year or $1,200,000 total).

The costs and benefits that remain will form the basis for a decision. The analysis is as follows:

	Differential Costs and Benefits— Four Years
Reduction in variable expense promised by the new machine ($45,000* per year × 4 years)	$ 180,000
Cost of the new machine	(200,000)
Disposal value of the old machine	90,000
Net advantage of the new machine	$ 70,000

*$345,000 − $300,000 = $45,000.

Note that the items above are the same as those in the last column of the earlier analysis and represent those costs and benefits that differ between the two alternatives. Armed with this analysis, Pete felt confident that he would be able to explain the financial advantages of the new machine to the president of the company.

Managerial Accounting in Action

THE ISSUE

Pete Kronski took his analysis to the office of J. J. Marker, the president of SoaringWings, where the following conversation took place.

Pete: J. J., do you remember that discussion we had about the proposed new brazing machine?

J. J.:   Sure I remember. Did you find out that I'm right?

Pete: Not exactly. Here's the analysis where I compare the profit with the old machine over the next four years to the profit with the new machine.

J. J.:   I see you're claiming the profit is $70,000 higher with the new machine. Are you assuming higher sales with the new machine?

Pete: No, I have assumed total sales of $2,000,000 over the four years in either situation. The real advantage comes with the reduction in variable expenses of $180,000.

J. J.:   Where are those reductions going to come from?

Pete: The new brazing machine should cut our scrap and rework rate at least in half. That results in substantial savings in materials and labour costs.

J. J.:   What about the $50,000 loss on the old machine?

Pete: What really matters is the $200,000 cost of the new machine and the $90,000 salvage value of the old machine. The book value of the old machine is irrelevant. No matter what we do, that cost will eventually flow through the income statement as a charge in one form or another.

J. J.: I find that hard to accept, but it is difficult to argue with your analysis.

Pete: The analysis actually understates the advantages of the new machine. We don't catch all of the defects caused by the old machine, and defective products are sometimes sold to customers. With the new machine, I expect our warranty costs to decrease and our repeat sales to increase. And I would hate to be held responsible for any accidents caused by defective brazing by our old machine.

Pete: Okay, I'm convinced. Put together a formal proposal, and we'll present it at the next meeting of the board of directors. ■

Future Costs That Do Not Differ Are Not Relevant Costs

We stated above that people often have difficulty accepting the idea that sunk costs are never relevant in a decision. Some people also have difficulty accepting the principle that future costs that do not differ between alternatives are never relevant in a decision. An example will help illustrate how future costs *should* be handled in a decision.

An Example of Irrelevant Future Costs

A company is contemplating the purchase of a new labour-saving machine that will cost $30,000 and have a 10-year useful life. Data concerning the company's annual sales and costs with and without the new machine are shown below:

	Current Situation	Situation with the New Machine
Units produced and sold	5,000	5,000
Selling price per unit	$ 40	$ 40
Direct materials cost per unit	14	14
Direct labour cost per unit	8	5
Variable overhead cost per unit	2	2
Fixed costs, other	62,000	62,000
Fixed costs, new machine	—	3,000

The new machine promises a saving of $3 per unit in direct labour costs ($8 − $5 = $3), but it will increase fixed costs by $3,000 per year. All other costs, as well as the total number of units produced and sold, will remain the same. Following the steps outlined earlier, the analysis is as follows:

1. Eliminate the sunk costs. (No sunk costs are included in this example.)
2. Eliminate the future costs and benefits that do not differ between the alternatives.
   a. The selling price per unit and the number of units sold do not differ between the alternatives. (Therefore, total future sales revenues will not differ.)
   b. The direct materials cost per unit, the variable overhead cost per unit, and the number of units produced do not differ between the alternatives. (Therefore, total future direct materials costs and variable overhead costs will not differ.)
   c. The "Fixed costs, other" do not differ between the alternatives.

The remaining costs—direct labour costs and the fixed costs associated with the new machine—are the only relevant costs.

Exhibit 13–1
Differential Cost Analysis

	5,000 Units Produced and Sold		
	Present Method	**New Machine**	**Differential Costs and Benefits**
Sales	$200,000	$200,000	$ –0–
Variable expenses:			
Direct materials	70,000	70,000	–0–
Direct labour	40,000	25,000	15,000
Variable overhead	10,000	10,000	–0–
Total variable expenses	120,000	105,000	
Contribution margin	80,000	95,000	
Less fixed expenses:			
Other	62,000	62,000	–0–
New machine	–0–	3,000	(3,000)
Total fixed expenses	62,000	65,000	
Net operating income	$ 18,000	$ 30,000	$12,000

Savings in direct labour costs (5,000 units at a cost saving of $3 per unit)	$15,000
Less increase in fixed costs	3,000
Net annual cost savings promised by the new machine	$12,000

This solution can be verified by looking at *all* of the cost data (both those that are relevant and those that are not) under the two alternatives. This is done in Exhibit 13–1. Notice from the exhibit that the net advantage in favour of buying the machine is $12,000—the same answer we obtained by focusing on just the relevant costs. Thus, we can see that future costs that do not differ between alternatives are indeed irrelevant in the decision-making process and can be safely eliminated from the analysis.

Why Isolate Relevant Costs?

In the preceding example, we used two different approaches to analyze the alternatives. First, we considered only the relevant costs; and second, we considered all costs, both those that were relevant and those that were not. We obtained the same answer under both approaches. It would be natural to ask, "Why bother to isolate relevant costs when total costs will do the job just as well?" Isolating relevant costs is desirable for at least two reasons.

First, only rarely will enough information be available to prepare a detailed income statement for both alternatives such as we have done in the preceding examples. Assume, for example, that you are called on to make a decision relating to a *single operation* of a multidepartmental, multiproduct firm. Under these circumstances, it would be virtually impossible to prepare an income statement of any type. You would have to rely on your ability to recognize which costs are relevant and which are not in order to assemble that data necessary to make a decision.

Second, mingling irrelevant costs with relevant costs may cause confusion and distract attention from the matters that are really critical. Furthermore, the danger always exists that an irrelevant piece of data may be used improperly, resulting in an incorrect decision. The best approach is to ignore irrelevant data and base the decision entirely on the relevant data.

Exhibit 13–2
Discount Drug Company
Product Lines

	Total	**Drugs**	**Cosmetics**	**House-wares**
			Product Line	
Sales	$250,000	$125,000	$75,000	$50,000
Less variable expenses	105,000	50,000	25,000	30,000
Contribution margin	145,000	75,000	50,000	20,000
Less fixed expenses:				
Salaries	50,000	29,500	12,500	8,000
Advertising	15,000	1,000	7,500	6,500
Utilities	2,000	500	500	1,000
Depreciation—fixtures	5,000	1,000	2,000	2,000
Rent	20,000	10,000	6,000	4,000
Insurance	3,000	2,000	500	500
General administrative	30,000	15,000	9,000	6,000
Total fixed expenses	125,000	59,000	38,000	28,000
Net operating income (loss)	$ 20,000	$ 16,000	$12,000	$ (8,000)

Relevant cost analysis, combined with the contribution approach to the income statement, provides a powerful tool for making decisions. We will investigate various uses of this tool in the remaining sections of this chapter.

Adding and Dropping Product Lines and Other Segments

Objective 3

Prepare an analysis showing whether a product line or other organizational segment should be dropped or retained.

Decisions relating to whether old product lines or other segments of a company should be dropped and new ones added are among the most difficult that a manager has to make. In such decisions, many qualitative and quantitative factors must be considered. Ultimately, however, any final decision to drop an old segment or to add a new one is going to hinge primarily on the impact the decision will have on net operating income. To assess this impact, it is necessary to make a careful analysis of the costs involved.

An Illustration of Cost Analysis

Consider the three major product lines of the Discount Drug Company—drugs, cosmetics, and housewares. Sales and cost information for the preceding month for each separate product line and for the store in total are given in Exhibit 13–2.

What can be done to improve the company's overall performance? One product line—housewares—shows a net operating loss for the month. Perhaps dropping this line would cause profits in the company as a whole to improve. In deciding whether the line should be dropped, management should reason as follows:

If the housewares line is dropped, then the company will lose $20,000 per month in contribution margin. By dropping the line, however, it may be possible to avoid some fixed costs. It may be possible, for example, to discharge certain employees, or it may be possible to reduce advertising costs. If by dropping the housewares line the company is able to avoid more in fixed costs than it loses in contribution margin, then it will be better off if the line is eliminated, since overall net income should improve. On the other hand, if the company is not able to avoid as much in fixed costs as it loses in contribution margin, then the housewares line should be retained. In short, the manager should ask, "What costs can I avoid if I drop this product line?"

As we have seen from our earlier discussion, not all costs are avoidable. For example, some of the costs associated with a product line may be sunk costs. Other costs may be allocated common costs that will not differ in total regardless of whether the product line is dropped or retained. As discussed in Chapter 8, an activity-based costing analysis may be used to help identify the relevant costs.

To show how the manager should proceed in a product-line analysis, suppose that the management of the Discount Drug Company has analyzed the costs being charged to the three product lines and has determined the following:

1. The salaries expense represents salaries paid to employees working directly in each product-line area. All of the employees working in housewares would be discharged if the line is dropped.
2. The advertising expense represents direct advertising of each product line and is avoidable if the line is dropped.
3. The utilities expense represents utilities costs for the entire company. The amount charged to each product line is an allocation based on space occupied and is not avoidable if the product line is dropped.
4. The depreciation expense represents depreciation on fixtures used for display of the various product lines. Although the fixtures are nearly new, they are custom-built and will have little resale value if the housewares line is dropped.
5. The rent expense represents rent on the entire building housing the company; it is allocated to the product lines on the basis of sales dollars. The monthly rent of $20,000 is fixed under a long-term lease agreement.
6. The insurance expense represents insurance carried on inventories within each of the three product-line areas.
7. The general administrative expense represents the costs of accounting, purchasing, and general management, which are allocated to the product lines on the basis of sales dollars. Total administrative costs will not change if the housewares line is dropped.

With this information, management can identify costs that can and cannot be avoided if the product line is dropped:

	Total Cost	Not Avoidable*	Avoidable
Salaries	$ 8,000		$ 8,000
Advertising	6,500		6,500
Utilities	1,000	$ 1,000	
Depreciation—fixtures	2,000	2,000	
Rent	4,000	4,000	
Insurance	500		500
General administrative	6,000	6,000	
Total fixed expenses	$28,000	$13,000	$15,000

*These costs represent either (1) sunk costs or (2) future costs that will not change if the housewares line is retained or discontinued.

To determine how dropping the line will affect the overall profits of the company, we can compare the contribution margin that will be lost to the costs that can be avoided if the line is dropped:

Contribution margin lost if the housewares line is discontinued (see Exhibit 13–2) .... $(20,000)
Less fixed costs that can be avoided if the housewares line is discontinued (see above) 15,000
Decrease in overall company net operating income ..... $ (5,000)

In this case, the fixed costs that can be avoided by dropping the product line are less than the contribution margin that will be lost. Therefore, based on the data given, the housewares line should not be discontinued unless a more profitable use can be found for the floor and counter space that it is occupying.

Exhibit 13–3

A Comparative Format for Product-Line Analysis

	Keep Housewares	Drop Housewares	Difference: Net Income Increase or (Decrease)
Sales	$50,000	$ –0–	$(50,000)
Less variable expenses	30,000	–0–	30,000
Contribution margin	20,000	–0–	(20,000)
Less fixed expenses:			
Salaries	8,000	–0–	8,000
Advertising	6,500	–0–	6,500
Utilities	1,000	1,000	–0–
Depreciation—fixtures	2,000	2,000	–0–
Rent	4,000	4,000	–0–
Insurance	500	–0–	500
General administrative	6,000	6,000	–0–
Total fixed expenses	28,000	13,000	15,000
Net operating income (loss)	$ (8,000)	$(13,000)	$ (5,000)

A Comparative Format

Some managers prefer to approach decisions of this type by preparing comparative income statements showing the effects on the company as a whole of either keeping or dropping the product line in question. A comparative analysis of this type for the Discount Drug Company is shown in Exhibit 13–3.

As shown by column 3 in the exhibit, overall company net operating income will decrease by $5,000 each period if the housewares line is dropped. This is the same answer, of course, as we obtained in our earlier analysis.

Beware of Allocated Fixed Costs

Our conclusion that the housewares line should not be dropped seems to conflict with the data shown earlier in Exhibit 13–2. Recall from the exhibit that the housewares line is showing a loss rather than a profit. Why keep a line that is showing a loss? The explanation for this apparent inconsistency lies at least in part with the common fixed costs that are being allocated to the product lines. As we observed in Chapter 12, one of the great dangers in allocating common fixed costs is that such allocations can make a product line (or other segment of a business) *look* less profitable than it really is. By allocating the common fixed costs among all product lines, the housewares line has been made to *look* as if it were unprofitable, whereas, in fact, dropping the line would result in a decrease in overall company net operating income. This point can be seen clearly if we recast the data in Exhibit 13–2 and eliminate the allocation of the common fixed costs. This recasting of data—using the segmented approach from Chapter 12—is shown in Exhibit 13–4.

Exhibit 13–4 gives us a much different perspective of the housewares line than does Exhibit 13–2. As shown in Exhibit 13–4, the housewares line is covering all of its own traceable fixed costs and is generating a $3,000 segment margin toward covering the common fixed costs of the company. Unless another product line can be found that will generate a greater segment margin than this, the company would be better off keeping the housewares line. By keeping the line, the company's overall net operating income will be higher than if the product line were dropped.

Additionally, we should note that managers may choose to retain an unprofitable product line if the line is necessary to the sale of other products or if it serves as a

Exhibit 13–4
Discount Drug Company
Product Lines—Recast
in Contribution Format
(from Exhibit 13–2)

	Total	Product Line		
		Drugs	**Cosmetics**	**House-wares**
Sales	$250,000	$125,000	$75,000	$50,000
Less variable expenses	105,000	50,000	25,000	30,000
Contribution margin	145,000	75,000	50,000	20,000
Less traceable fixed expenses:				
Salaries	50,000	29,500	12,500	8,000
Advertising	15,000	1,000	7,500	6,500
Depreciation—fixtures	5,000	1,000	2,000	2,000
Insurance	3,000	2,000	500	500
Total	73,000	33,500	22,500	17,000
Product-line segment margin	72,000	$ 41,500	$27,500	$ 3,000*
Less common fixed expenses:				
Utilities	2,000			
Rent	20,000			
General administrative	30,000			
Total	52,000			
Net operating income	$ 20,000			

*If the housewares line is dropped, this $3,000 in segment margin will be lost to the company. In addition, we have seen that the $2,000 depreciation on the fixtures is a sunk cost that cannot be avoided. The sum of these two figures ($3,000 + $2,000 = $5,000) would be the decrease in the company's overall profits if the housewares line were discontinued.

"magnet" to attract customers. Bread, for example, is not an especially profitable line in food stores, but customers expect it to be available, and many would undoubtedly shift their buying elsewhere if a particular store decided to stop carrying it.

The Make or Buy Decision

Objective 4

Prepare a well-organized make or buy analysis.

Vertical integration
The involvement by a company in more than one of the steps from production of basic raw materials to the manufacture and distribution of a finished product.

Make or buy decision
A decision as to whether an item should be produced internally or purchased from an outside supplier.

Many steps may be involved in getting a finished product into the hands of a consumer. First, raw materials may have to be obtained through mining, drilling, growing crops, raising animals, and so forth. Second, these raw materials may have to be processed to remove impurities and to extract the desirable and usable materials. Third, the usable materials may have to undergo some preliminary fabrication so as to be usable in final products. For example, cotton must be made into thread and textiles before being made into clothing. Fourth, the actual manufacturing of the finished product must take place. And finally, the finished product must be distributed to the ultimate consumer. All of these steps taken together are called a *value chain*.

Separate companies may carry out each of the steps in the value chain or a single company may carry out several of the steps. When a company is involved in more than one of these steps in the entire value chain, it is following a policy of **vertical integration.** Vertical integration is very common. Some firms control *all* of the activities in the value chain from producing basic raw materials right up to the final distribution of finished goods. Other firms are content to integrate on a smaller scale by purchasing many of the parts and materials that go into their finished products.

A decision to produce a fabricated part internally, rather than to buy the part externally from a supplier, is called a **make or buy decision.** Actually, any decision relating to vertical integration is a make or buy decision, since the company is deciding whether to meet its own needs internally or to buy externally.

Strategic Aspects of the Make or Buy Decision

Integration provides certain advantages. An integrated firm is less dependent on its suppliers and may be able to ensure a smoother flow of parts and materials for production than a nonintegrated firm. For example, a strike against a major parts supplier can interrupt the operations of a nonintegrated firm for many months, whereas an integrated firm that is producing its own parts might be able to continue operations. Also, many firms feel that they can control quality better by producing their own parts and materials, rather than by relying on the quality control standards of outside suppliers. In addition, the integrated firm realizes profits from the parts and materials that it is "making" rather than "buying," as well as profits from its regular operations.

The advantages of integration are counterbalanced by some advantages of using external suppliers. By pooling demand from a number of firms, a supplier may be able to enjoy economies of scale in research and development and in manufacturing. These economies of scale can result in higher quality and lower costs than would be possible if the firm were to attempt to make the parts on its own. A company must be careful, however, to retain control over activities that are essential to maintaining its competitive position. For example, Hewlett-Packard controls the software for a laser printer it makes in cooperation with Canon Inc. of Japan to prevent Canon from coming out with a competing product. The present trend appears to be toward less vertical integration, with some companies like Sun Microsystems concentrating on hardware and software design and relying on outside supplies for almost everything else in the value chain.[2] These factors suggest that the make or buy decision should be weighed very carefully.

An Example of Make or Buy

To provide an illustration of a make or buy decision, consider Mountain Goat Cycles. The company is now producing the heavy-duty gear shifters used in its most popular line of mountain bikes. The company's Accounting Department reports the following costs of producing the shifter internally:

	Per Unit	8,000 Units
Direct materials	$ 6	$ 48,000
Direct labour	4	32,000
Variable overhead	1	8,000
Supervisor's salary	3	24,000
Depreciation of special equipment	2	16,000
Allocated general overhead	5	40,000
Total cost	$21	$168,000

An outside supplier has offered to sell Mountain Goat Cycles 8,000 shifters a year at a price of only $19 each. Should the company stop producing the shifters internally and start purchasing them from the outside supplier? To approach the decision from a financial point of view, the manager should again focus on the differential costs. As we have seen, the differential costs can be obtained by eliminating those costs that are not avoidable—that is, by eliminating (1) the sunk costs and (2) the future costs that will continue regardless of whether the shifters are produced internally or purchased outside. The costs that remain after making these eliminations are the costs that are avoidable to the company by purchasing outside. If these avoidable costs are less than the outside purchase price, then the company should continue to manufacture its own shifters and reject the outside supplier's offer. That is, the company should purchase outside only if the outside purchase price is less than the costs that can be avoided internally as a result of stopping production of the shifters.

---

2. Ralph E. Drtina, "The Outsourcing Decision," *Management Accounting* (March 1994), pp. 56–62.

Exhibit 13–5   Mountain Goat Cycles Make or Buy Analysis

	Production "Cost" per Unit	Per Unit Differential Costs		Total Differential Costs—8,000 Units	
		Make	Buy	Make	Buy
Direct materials	$ 6	$ 6		$ 48,000	
Direct labour	4	4		32,000	
Variable overhead	1	1		8,000	
Supervisor's salary	3	3		24,000	
Depreciation of special equipment	2	—		—	
Allocated general overhead	5	—		—	
Outside purchase price			$19		$152,000
Total cost	$21	$14	$19	$112,000	$152,000
Difference in favour of continuing to make		$5		$40,000	

Looking at the data on the previous page, note first that depreciation of special equipment is listed as one of the costs of producing the shifters internally. Since the equipment has already been purchased, this depreciation is a sunk cost and is therefore irrelevant. If the equipment could be sold, its salvage value would be relevant. Or if the machine could be used to make other products, this could be relevant as well. However, we will assume that the equipment has no salvage value and that it has no other use except making the heavy-duty gear shifters.

Also note that the company is allocating a portion of its general overhead costs to the shifters. Any portion of this general overhead cost that would actually be eliminated if the gear shifters were purchased rather than made would be relevant in the analysis. However, it is likely that the general overhead costs allocated to the gear shifters are in fact common to all items produced in the factory and would continue unchanged even if the shifters are purchased from the outside. Such allocated common costs are not differential costs (since they do not differ between the make or buy alternatives) and should be eliminated from the analysis along with the sunk costs.

The variable costs of producing the shifters (materials, labour, and variable overhead) are differential costs, since they can be avoided by buying the shifters from the outside supplier. If the supervisor can be discharged and his or her salary avoided by buying the shifters, then it too will be a differential cost and relevant to the decision. Assuming that both the variable costs and the supervisor's salary can be avoided by buying from the outside supplier, then the analysis takes the form shown in Exhibit 13–5.

Since it costs $5 less per unit to continue to make the shifters, Mountain Goat Cycles should reject the outside supplier's offer. However, there is one additional factor that the company may wish to consider before coming to a final decision. This factor is the opportunity cost of the space now being used to produce the shifters.

The Matter of Opportunity Cost

If the space now being used to produce the shifters *would otherwise be idle*, then Mountain Goat Cycles should continue to produce its own shifters and the supplier's offer should be rejected, as stated above. Idle space that has no alternative use has an opportunity cost of zero.

But what if the space now being used to produce shifters could be used for some other purpose? In that case, the space would have an opportunity cost that would have to be considered in assessing the desirability of the supplier's offer. What would this opportunity cost be? It would be the segment margin that could be derived from the best alternative use of the space.

To illustrate, assume that the space now being used to produce shifters could be used to produce a new cross-country bike that would generate a segment margin of $60,000 per year. Under these conditions, Mountain Goat Cycles would be better off to accept the supplier's offer and to use the available space to produce the new product line:

	Make	Buy
Differential cost per unit (see prior example)	$ 14	$ 19
Number of units needed annually	× 8,000	× 8,000
Total annual cost	112,000	152,000
Opportunity cost—segment margin forgone on		
a potential new product line	60,000	
Total cost	$172,000	$152,000
Difference in favour of purchasing from the		
outside supplier		$ 20,000

Opportunity costs are not recorded in accounts of an organization. They do not represent actual dollar outlays. Rather, they represent economic benefits that are *forgone* as a result of pursuing some course of action. The opportunity costs of Mountain Goat Cycles are sufficiently large in this case to make continued production of the shifters very costly from an economic point of view.

Special Orders

Objective 5

Prepare an analysis showing whether a special order should be accepted.

Special order   A one-time order that is not considered part of the company's normal on-going business.

Managers often must evaluate whether a *special order* should be accepted, and if the order is accepted, the price that should be charged. A **special order** is a one-time order that is not considered part of the company's normal ongoing business. To illustrate, Mountain Goat Cycles has just received a request from the Quebec City Police Department to produce 100 specially modified mountain bikes at a price of $179 each. The bikes would be used to patrol some of the more densely populated residential sections of the city. Mountain Goat Cycles can easily modify its City Cruiser model to fit the specifications of the Quebec Police. The normal selling price of the City Cruiser bike is $249, and its unit product cost is $182 as shown below:

Direct materials	$ 86
Direct labour	45
Manufacturing overhead	51
Unit product cost	$182

The variable portion of the above manufacturing overhead is $6 per unit. The order would have no effect on the company's total fixed manufacturing overhead costs.

The modifications to the bikes consist of welded brackets to hold radios, nightsticks, and other gear. These modifications would require $17 in incremental variable costs. In addition, the company would have to pay a graphics design studio $1,200 to design and cut stencils that would be used for spray painting the Quebec Police Department's logo and other identifying marks on the bikes.

This order should have no effect on the company's other sales. The production manager says that she can handle the special order without disrupting any of the regular scheduled production.

What effect would accepting this order have on the company's net operating income?

Only the incremental costs and benefits are relevant. Since the existing fixed manufacturing overhead costs would not be affected by the order, they are not incremental costs and are therefore not relevant. The incremental net operating income can be computed as follows:

	Per Unit	Total 100 Bikes
Incremental revenue	$179	$17,900
Incremental costs:		
Variable costs:		
Direct materials	86	8,600
Direct labour	45	4,500
Variable manufacturing overhead	6	600
Special modifications	17	1,700
Total variable cost	$154	15,400
Fixed cost:		
Purchase of stencils		1,200
Total incremental cost		16,600
Incremental net operating income		$ 1,300

Therefore, even though the price on the special order ($179) is below the normal unit product cost ($182) and the order would require incurring additional costs, the order would result in an increase in net operating income. In general, a special order is profitable as long as the incremental revenue from the special order exceeds the incremental costs of the order. We must note, however, that it is important to make sure that there is indeed idle capacity and that the special order does not cut into normal sales. For example, if the company was operating at capacity, opportunity costs would have to be taken into account as well as the incremental costs that have already been detailed above.

Utilization of a Constrained Resource

Objective 6

Determine the most profitable use of a constrained resource.

Constraint A limitation under which a company must operate, such as limited machine time available or limited raw materials available that restricts the company's ability to satisfy demand.

Managers are routinely faced with the problem of deciding how constrained resources are going to be utilized. A department store, for example, has a limited amount of floor space and therefore cannot stock every product that may be available. A manufacturing firm has a limited number of machine-hours and a limited number of direct labour-hours at its disposal. When a limited resource of some type restricts the company's ability to satisfy demand, the company is said to have a **constraint.** Because of the constrained resource, the company cannot fully satisfy demand, so the manager must decide how the constrained resource should be used. Fixed costs are usually unaffected by such choices, so the manager should select the course of action that will maximize the firm's *total* contribution margin.

Contribution in Relation to a Constrained Resource

To maximize total contribution margin, a firm should not necessarily promote those products that have the highest *unit* contribution margins. Rather, total contribution margin will be maximized by promoting those products or accepting those orders that provide the highest unit contribution margin *in relation to the constrained resource*. To illustrate, Mountain Goat Cycles makes a line of paniers—a saddlebag for bicycles.

There are two models of paniers—a touring model and a mountain model. Cost and revenue data for the two models of paniers are given below:

	Model	
	Mountain Panier	**Touring Panier**
Selling price per unit	$25	$30
Variable cost per unit	10	18
Contribution margin per unit	$15	$12
Contribution margin (CM) ratio	60%	40%

The mountain panier appears to be much more profitable than the touring panier. It has a $15 per unit contribution margin as compared to only $12 per unit for the touring model, and it has a 60% CM ratio as compared to only 40% for the touring model.

But now let us add one more piece of information—the plant that makes the paniers is operating at capacity. Ordinarily this does not mean that every machine and every person in the plant is working at the maximum possible rate. Because machines have different capacities, some machines will be operating at less than 100% of capacity. However, if the plant as a whole cannot produce any more units, some machine or process must be operating at capacity. The machine or process that is limiting overall output is called the **bottleneck**—it is the constraint.

Bottleneck A machine or process that limits total output because it is operating at capacity.

At Mountain Goat Cycles, the bottleneck is a particular stitching machine. The mountain panier requires 2 minutes of stitching time, and each unit of the touring panier requires 1 minute of stitching time. Since this stitching machine already has more work than it can handle, something will have to be cut back. In this situation, which product is more profitable? To answer this question, the manager should look at the *contribution margin per unit of the constrained resource*. This figure is computed by dividing the contribution margin by the amount of the constrained resource a unit of product requires. These calculations are carried out below for the mountain and touring paniers.

	Model	
	Mountain Panier	**Touring Panier**
Contribution margin per unit (above) (a)	$15.00	$12.00
Time on the stitching machine required to produce one unit (b)	2 min.	1 min.
Contribution margin per unit of the constrained resource, (a) ÷ (b)	$7.50/min.	$12.00/min.

It is now easy to decide which product is less profitable and should be deemphasized. Each minute of processing time on the stitching machine that is devoted to the touring panier results in an increase of $12 in contribution margin and profits. The comparable figure for the mountain panier is only $7.50 per minute. Therefore, the touring model should be emphasized. Even though the mountain model has the larger per unit contribution margin and the larger CM ratio, the touring model provides the larger contribution margin in relation to the constrained resource.

To verify that the touring model is indeed the more profitable product, suppose an hour of additional stitching time is available and that there are unfilled orders for both products. The additional hour on the stitching machine could be used to make either 30 mountain paniers (60 minutes ÷ 2 minutes) or 60 touring paniers (60 minutes ÷ 1 minute), with the following consequences:

	Model	
	Mountain Panier	**Touring Panier**
Contribution margin per unit (above) (a)	$ 15	$ 12
Additional units that can be processed in one hour	× 30	× 60
Additional contribution margin	$450	$720

This example clearly shows that looking at unit contribution margins alone is not enough; the contribution margin must be viewed in relation to the amount of the constrained resource each product requires.

Focus on Current Practice

The bottleneck at Ontario Steel is the blanking line. On the blanking line, large rolls of steel up to 60 inches wide are cut into flat sheets. Setting up the blanking line between jobs takes an average of 2.5 hours, and during this time, the blanking line is shut down.

Management estimates the opportunity cost of lost sales at $225 per hour, which is the contribution margin per hour of the blanking line for a typical order. Under these circumstances, a new loading device with an annual fixed cost of $36,000 that would save 720 setup hours per year looked like an excellent investment. The new loading device would have an average cost of only $50 per hour ($36,000 ÷ 720 hours = $50) compared to the $225 per hour the company would generate in added contribution margin.[3] ■

Managing Constraints

Profits can be increased by effectively managing the organization's constraints. One aspect of managing constraints is to decide how to best utilize them. As discussed above, if the constraint is a bottleneck in the production process, the manager should select the product mix that maximizes the total contribution margin. In addition, the manager should take an active role in managing the constraint itself. Management should focus efforts on increasing the efficiency of the bottleneck operation and on increasing its capacity. Such efforts directly increase the output of finished goods and will often pay off in an almost immediate increase in profits.

Relaxing (or elevating) the constraint An action that increases the capacity of a bottleneck.

It is often possible for a manager to effectively increase the capacity of the bottleneck, which is called **relaxing (or elevating) the constraint.** For example, the stitching machine operator could be asked to work overtime. This would result in more available stitching time and hence more finished goods that can be sold. The benefits from relaxing the constraint in such a manner are often enormous and can be easily quantified. The manager should first ask, "What would I do with additional capacity at the bottleneck if it were available?" In the example, if there are unfilled orders for both the touring and mountain paniers, the additional capacity would be used to process more touring paniers, since that would be a better use of the additional capacity. In that situation, the additional capacity would be worth $12 per minute or $720 per hour. This is because adding an hour of capacity would generate an additional $720 of contribution margin if it would be used solely to process more touring paniers. Since overtime pay for the operator is likely to be much less than $720 per hour, running the stitching machine on overtime would be an excellent way to increase the profits of the company while at the same time satisfying customers.

3. Robert J. Campbell, "Steeling Time with ABC or TOC," *Management Accounting* (January 1995), pp. 31–36.

To reinforce this concept, suppose that making touring paniers has already been given top priority and consequently there are only unfilled orders for the mountain panier. How much would it be worth to the company to run the stitching machine overtime in this situation? Since the additional capacity would be used to make the mountain panier, the value of that additional capacity would drop to $7.50 per minute or $450 per hour. Nevertheless, the value of relaxing the constraint would still be quite high.

These calculations indicate that managers should pay great attention to bottleneck operations. If a bottleneck machine breaks down or is ineffectively utilized, the losses to the company can be quite large. In our example, for every minute the stitching machine is down due to breakdowns or setups, the company loses between $7.50 and $12.00. The losses on an hourly basis are between $450 and $720! In contrast, there is no such loss of contribution margin if time is lost on a machine that is not a bottleneck—such machines have excess capacity anyway.

The implications are clear. Managers should focus much of their attention on managing bottlenecks. As we have discussed, managers should emphasize products that most profitably utilize the constrained resource. They should also make sure that products are processed smoothly through the bottlenecks, with minimal lost time due to breakdowns and setups. And they should try to find ways to increase the capacity at the bottlenecks.

The capacity of a bottleneck can be effectively increased in a number of ways, including:

- Working overtime on the bottleneck.
- Subcontracting some of the processing that would be done at the bottleneck.
- Investing in additional machines at the bottleneck.
- Shifting workers from processes that are not bottlenecks to the process that *is* a bottleneck.
- Focusing business process improvement efforts such as TQM and Business Process Reengineering on the bottleneck.
- Reducing defective units. Each defective unit that is processed through the bottleneck and subsequently scrapped takes the place of a good unit that could be sold.

The last three methods of increasing the capacity of the bottleneck are particularly attractive, since they are essentially free and may even yield additional cost savings.

Focus on Current Practice

It is often possible to elevate the constraint at very low cost. Western Textile Products makes pockets, waistbands, and other clothing components. The constraint at the company's branch plant in Greenville, South Carolina, was the slitting machines. These large machines slit huge rolls of textiles into appropriate widths for use on other machines. Management was contemplating adding a second shift to elevate the constraint. However, investigation revealed that the slitting machines were actually being run only one hour in a nine-hour shift. "The other eight hours were required to get materials, load and unload the machine, and do setups. Instead of adding a second shift, a second person was assigned to each machine to fetch materials and do as much of the setting up as possible off-line while the machine was running." This approach resulted in increasing the run time to four hours. If another shift had been added without any improvement in how the machines were being used, the cost would have been much higher and there would have been only a one-hour increase in run time.[4] ∎

---

4. Eric Noreen, Debra Smith, and James T. Mackey, *The Theory of Constraints and Its Implications for Management Accounting* (Croton-on-Hudson, NY: The North River Press, 1995), pp. 84–85.

The Problem of Multiple Constraints

What does a firm do if it has more than one potential constraint? For example, a firm may have limited raw materials, limited direct labour-hours available, limited floor space, and limited advertising dollars to spend on product promotion. How would it proceed to find the right combination of products to produce? The proper combination or "mix" of products can be found by use of a quantitative method known as *linear programming,* which is covered in quantitative methods and operations management courses.

Joint Product Costs and the Contribution Approach

Objective 7

Prepare an analysis showing whether joint products should be sold at the split-off point or processed further.

Joint product costs
Costs that are incurred up to the split-off point in producing joint products.

Joint products Two or more items that are produced from a common input.

Split-off point That point in the manufacturing process where some or all of the joint products can be recognized as individual products.

In some industries, a number of end products are produced from a single raw material input. A grisly, but apt, example is provided by the meat-packing industry. A great variety of end products—bacon, ham, spareribs, pork roasts, and so on—are produced from a single pig. Firms that produce several end products from a common input (e.g., a pig) are faced with the problem of deciding how the cost of that input is going to be divided among the end products. Before we address this problem, it will be helpful to define three terms—joint products, joint product costs, and split-off point.

Two or more products that are produced from a common input are known as **joint products.** The term **joint product costs** is used to describe those manufacturing costs that are incurred in producing joint products up to the split-off point. The **split-off point** is that point in the manufacturing process at which the joint products (bacon, ham, spareribs, and so on) can be recognized as separate products. At that point, some of the joint products will be in final form, ready to be marketed to the consumer. Others will still need further processing on their own before they are in marketable form. These concepts are presented graphically in Exhibit 13–6.

The Pitfalls of Allocation

Joint product costs are really common costs incurred to simultaneously produce a variety of end products. Traditional cost accounting books contain various approaches to allocating these common costs among the different products at the split-off point. A typical approach is to allocate the joint product costs according to the relative sales value of the end products.

Although allocation of joint product costs is needed for some purposes, such as balance sheet inventory valuation, allocations of this kind should be viewed with great

Exhibit 13–6
Joint Products

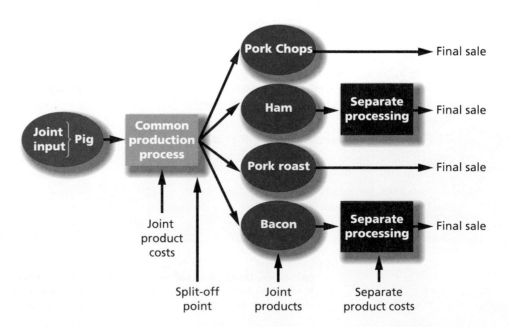

caution *internally* in the decision-making process. Unless a manager proceeds with care, he or she may be led into incorrect decisions as a result of relying on allocated common costs. The Focus on Current Practice box below discusses an actual business situation illustrating an incorrect decision that resulted from using allocated costs.

Focus on Current Practice

A company located on the Gulf of St. Lawrence is a producer of soap products. Its six main soap product lines are produced from common inputs. Joint product costs up to the split-off point constitute the bulk of the production costs for all six product lines. These joint product costs are allocated to the six product lines on the basis of the relative sales value of each line at the split-off point.

The company has a waste product that results from the production of the six main product lines. Until a few years ago, the company loaded the waste onto barges and dumped it into the Gulf of St. Lawrence, since the waste was thought to have no commercial value. The dumping was stopped, however, when the company's research division discovered that with some further processing the waste could be made commercially salable as a fertilizer ingredient. The further processing was initiated at a cost of $175,000 per year. The waste was then sold to fertilizer manufacturers at a total price of $300,000 per year.

The accountants responsible for allocating manufacturing costs included the sales value of

the waste product along with the sales value of the six main product lines in their allocation of the joint product costs at the split-off point. This allocation resulted in the waste product being allocated $150,000 in joint product cost. This $150,000 allocation, when added to the further processing costs of $175,000 for the waste, caused the waste product to show the net loss computed in the table below.

When presented with this analysis, the company's management decided that further processing of the waste was not desirable after all. The company went back to dumping the waste in the Gulf. In addition to being unwise from an economic viewpoint, this dumping also raises questions regarding the company's social responsibility and the environmental impact of its actions.

Sales value of the waste product after further processing	$ 300,000
Less costs assignable to the waste product	325,000
Net loss	$ (25,000)

Sell or Process Further Decisions

Joint product costs are irrelevant in decisions regarding what to do with a product from the split-off point forward. The reason is that by the time one arrives at the split-off point, the joint product costs have already been incurred and therefore are sunk costs. In the case of the soap company (see the accompanying Focus on Current Practice box), the $150,000 in allocated joint costs should not have been permitted to influence what was done with the waste product from the split-off point forward. The analysis should have been as follows:

	Dump in Gulf	Process Further
Sales value	–0–	$300,000
Additional processing costs	–0–	175,000
Contribution margin	–0–	$125,000
Advantage of processing further		$125,000

Sell or process further decision A decision as to whether a joint product should be sold at the split-off point or processed further and sold at a later time in a different form.

Decisions of this type are known as **sell or process further decisions.** It will always be profitable to continue processing a joint product after the split-off point *so long as the incremental revenue from such processing exceeds the incremental processing cost incurred after the split-off point.* Joint product costs that have already been

Exhibit 13–7   Sell or
Process Further Decision

	Product		
	A	**B**	**C**
Sales value at the split-off point	$120,000	$150,000	$60,000
Sales value after further processing	160,000	240,000	90,000
Allocated joint product costs	80,000	100,000	40,000
Cost of further processing	50,000	60,000	10,000
Analysis of sell or process further:			
Sales value after further processing	$160,000	$240,000	$90,000
Sales value at the split-off point	120,000	150,000	60,000
Incremental revenue from further			
processing	40,000	90,000	30,000
Cost of further processing	50,000	60,000	10,000
Profit (loss) from further processing	$(10,000)	$ 30,000	$20,000

incurred up to the split-off point are sunk costs, which are always irrelevant in decisions concerning what to do from the split-off point forward.

To provide a detailed example of a sell or process further decision, assume that three products are derived from a single raw material input. Cost and revenue data relating to the products are presented in Exhibit 13–7 along with an analysis of which products should be sold at the split-off point and which should be processed further. As shown in the exhibit, products B and C should both be processed further; product A should be sold at the split-off point.

Activity-Based Costing and Relevant Costs

As discussed in Chapter 8, activity-based costing can be used to help identify potentially relevant costs for decision-making purposes. Activity-based costing improves the traceability of costs by focusing on the activities caused by a product or other segment. Managers should exercise caution against reading more into this "traceability" than really exists. People have a tendency to assume that if a cost is traceable to a segment, then the cost is automatically an avoidable cost. That is not true. As emphasized in Chapter 8, the costs provided by a well-designed activity-based costing system are only *potentially* relevant. Before making a decision, managers must still decide which of the potentially relevant costs are actually avoidable. Only those costs that are avoidable are relevant and the others should be ignored.

To illustrate, refer again to the data relating to the housewares line in Exhibit 13–4. The $2,000 depreciation on fixtures is a traceable cost of the houseware lines because it relates to activities in that department. We found, however, that the $2,000 is not avoidable if the housewares line is dropped. The key lesson here is that the method used to assign a cost to a product or other segment does not change the basic nature of the cost. A sunk cost such as depreciation of old equipment is still a sunk cost regardless of whether it is traced directly to a particular segment on an activity basis, allocated to all segments on the basis of labour-hours, or treated in some other way in the costing process. Regardless of the method used to assign costs to products or other segments, the manager still must apply the principles discussed in this chapter to determine the costs that are avoidable in each situation.[5]

---

5. For further discussion, see Douglas Sharp and Linda P. Christensen, "A New View of Activity-Based Costing," *Management Accounting* 73, no.7 (September 1991), pp. 32–34; and Maurice L. Hirsch, Jr., and Michael C. Nibbelin, "Incremental, Separable, Sunk, and Common Costs in Activity-Based Costing," *Journal of Cost Management* 6, no. 1 (Spring 1992), pp. 39–47.

Summary

All of the material in this chapter consists of applications of one simple but powerful idea. Only those costs and benefits that differ between alternatives are relevant in a decision. All other costs and benefits are irrelevant and can and should be ignored. In particular, sunk costs are irrelevant as are future costs that do not differ between alternatives.

This simple idea was applied in a variety of situations including decisions that involve replacing equipment, making or buying a component, adding or dropping a product line, processing a joint product further, and using a constrained resource. This list includes only a tiny sample of the possible applications of the relevant cost concept. Indeed, *any* decision involving costs hinges on the proper identification and analysis of the costs that are relevant. We will continue to focus on the concept of relevant costs in the following two chapters where long-run investment decisions are considered.

Review Problem: Relevant Costs

Charter Sports Equipment manufactures round, rectangular, and octagonal trampolines. Data on sales expenses for the past month follow:

| | Total | Trampoline | | |
		Round	Rectangular	Octagonal
Sales	$1,000,000	$ 140,000	$500,000	$360,000
Less variable expenses	410,000	60,000	200,000	150,000
Contribution margin	590,000	80,000	300,000	210,000
Less fixed expenses:				
Advertising—traceable	216,000	41,000	110,000	65,000
Depreciation of special				
equipment	95,000	20,000	40,000	35,000
Line supervisors' salaries	19,000	6,000	7,000	6,000
General factory overhead*	200,000	28,000	100,000	72,000
Total fixed expenses	530,000	95,000	257,000	178,000
Net operating income (loss)	$ 60,000	$(15,000)	$ 43,000	$ 32,000

*A common cost that is allocated on the basis of sales dollars.

Management is concerned about the continued losses shown by the round trampolines and wants a recommendation as to whether or not the line should be discontinued. The special equipment used to produce the trampolines has no resale value. If the round trampoline model is dropped, the two line supervisors assigned to the model would be discharged.

Required

1. Should production and sale of the round trampolines be discontinued? You may assume that the company has no other use for the capacity now being used to produce the round trampolines. Show computations to support your answer.
2. Recast the above data in a format that would be more usable to management in assessing the long-run profitability of the various product lines.

Solution to Review Problem

1. No, production and sale of the round trampolines should not be discontinued. Computations to support this answer follow:

Contribution margin lost if the round trampolines are discontinued		$(80,000)
Less fixed costs that can be avoided:		
Advertising—traceable	$41,000	
Line supervisors' salaries	6,000	47,000
Decrease in net operating income for the company as a whole		$(33,000)

The depreciation of the special equipment represents a sunk cost, and therefore it is not relevant to the decision. The general factory overhead is allocated and will presumably continue regardless of whether or not the round trampolines are discontinued; thus, it also is not relevant to the decision.

Alternative Solution to Question 1

	Keep Round Tramps	Difference: Drop Round Tramps	Net Income Increase or (Decrease)
Sales	$140,000	$ –0–	$(140,000)
Less variable expenses	60,000	–0–	60,000
Contribution margin	80,000	–0–	(80,000)
Less fixed expenses:			
Advertising—traceable	41,000	–0–	41,000
Depreciation of special equipment	20,000	20,000	–0–
Line supervisors' salaries	6,000	–0–	6,000
General factory overhead	28,000	28,000	–0–
Total fixed expenses	95,000	48,000	47,000
Net operating income (loss)	$(15,000)	$(48,000)	$ (33,000)

2. If management wants a clear picture of the profitability of the segments, the general factory overhead should not be allocated. It is a common cost and therefore should be deducted from the total product-line segment margin, as shown in Chapter 12. A more useful income statement format would be as follows:

		Trampoline		
	Total	Round	Rectangular	Octagonal
Sales	$1,000,000	$140,000	$500,000	$360,000
Less variable expenses	410,000	60,000	200,000	150,000
Contribution margin	590,000	80,000	300,000	210,000
Less traceable fixed expenses:				
Advertising—traceable	216,000	41,000	110,000	65,000
Depreciation of special equipment	95,000	20,000	40,000	35,000
Line supervisors' salaries	19,000	6,000	7,000	6,000
Total traceable fixed expenses	330,000	67,000	157,000	106,000
Product-line segment margin	260,000	$ 13,000	$143,000	$104,000
Less common fixed expenses	200,000			
Net operating income (loss)	$ 60,000			

Questions

13–1   What is a *relevant cost?*

13–2   Define the following terms: *incremental cost, opportunity cost,* and *sunk cost.*

13–3   Are variable costs always relevant costs? Explain.

13–4   The book value of a machine (as shown on the balance sheet) is an asset to a company, but this same book value is irrelevant in decision making. Explain why this is so.

13–5 "Sunk costs are easy to spot—they're simply the fixed costs associated with a decision." Do you agree? Explain.

13–6 "Variable costs and differential costs mean the same thing." Do you agree? Explain.

13–7 "All future costs are relevant in decision making." Do you agree? Why?

13–8 Prentice Company is considering dropping one of its product lines. What costs of the product line would be relevant to this decision? Irrelevant?

13–9 "If a product line is generating a loss, then that's pretty good evidence that the product line should be discontinued." Do you agree? Explain.

13–10 What is the danger in allocating common fixed costs among product lines or other segments of an organization?

13–11 How does opportunity cost enter into the make or buy decision?

13–12 Give four examples of possible constraints.

13–13 How will relating product contribution margins to the constrained resource they require help a company ensure that profits will be maximized?

13–14 Define the following terms: *joint products, joint product costs,* and *split-off point.*

13–15 From a decision-making point of view, what pitfalls are there in allocating common costs among joint products?

13–16 What guideline can be used in determining whether a joint product should be sold at the split-off point or processed further?

13–17 Airlines sometimes offer reduced rates during certain times of the week to members of a businessperson's family if they accompany him or her on trips. How does the concept of relevant costs enter into the decision to offer reduced rates of this type?

Exercises

E13–1 Listed below are a number of costs that may be relevant in decisions faced by the management of Svahn, AB, a Swedish manufacturer of sailing yachts:

		Case 1		Case 2	
Item		**Relevant**	**Not Relevant**	**Relevant**	**Not Relevant**
a.	Sales revenue	X			X
b.	Direct materials		X	X	
c.	Direct labour	X		X	
d.	Variable manufacturing overhead	X	X	X	X
e.	Depreciation—Model B100 machine		X		X
f.	Book value—Model B100 machine				
g.	Disposal value—Model B100 machine		X	X	
h.	Market value—Model B300 machine (cost)	X		X	X
i.	Depreciation—Model B300 machine		X		
j.	Fixed manufacturing overhead (general)		X		
k.	Variable selling expense		X		
l.	Fixed selling expense	X			
m.	General administrative overhead	X			

Required   Copy the information above onto your answer sheet and place an X in the appropriate column to indicate whether each item is relevant or not relevant in the following situations (requirement 1 relates to Case 1 above, and requirement 2 relates to Case 2):

1. Management is considering purchasing a Model B300 machine to use in addition to the company's present Model B100 machine. This will increase the company's production and sales. The increase in volume will be large enough to require increases in fixed selling expenses and in general administrative overhead, but not in the fixed manufacturing overhead.

2. Management is instead considering replacing its present Model B100 machine with a new Model B300 machine. The Model B100 machine would be sold. This change will have no effect on production or sales, other than some savings in direct materials costs due to less waste.

E13–2   Bill has just returned from a duck hunting trip. He has brought home eight ducks. Bill's friend, John, disapproves of duck hunting, and to discourage Bill from further hunting, John has presented him with the following cost estimate per duck:

Camper and equipment:

not relevant all but depreciation relevant

    Cost, \$12,000; usable for eight seasons; 10 hunting trips

      per season \$150

Travel expense (pickup truck):

    100 kilometres at \$0.12 per kilometre (gas, oil, and tires—\$0.07 per kilometre:

      depreciation and insurance—\$0.05 per kilometre) 12

R Shotgun shells (two boxes) 20

NR Boat:

    Cost, \$2,320, usable for eight seasons; 10 hunting trips per season 29

NR Hunting licence:

    Cost, \$30 for the season; 10 hunting trips per season 3

NR Money lost playing poker:

    Loss, \$18 (Bill plays poker every weekend) 18

R A fifth of Old Grandad:

    Cost, \$8 (used to ward off the cold) .... <u>8</u>

      Total cost .... <u>\$240</u>

  Cost per duck (\$240 ÷ 8 ducks) .... <u>\$ 30</u>

Required   1. Assuming that the duck hunting trip Bill has just completed is typical, what costs are relevant to a decision as to whether Bill should go duck hunting again this season?

2. Suppose that Bill gets lucky on his next hunting trip and shoots 10 ducks in the amount of time it took him to shoot 8 ducks on his last trip. How much would it have cost him to shoot the last two ducks?

3. Which costs are relevant in a decision of whether Bill should give up hunting? Explain.

E13–3   Thalassines Kataskeves, S.A., of Greece makes marine equipment. The company has been experiencing losses on its bilge pump product line for several years. The most recent quarterly income statement for the bilge pump product line is given below:

THALASSINES KATASKEVES, S.A.
Income Statement—Bilge Pump
For the Quarter Ended March 31

Sales		DR850,000
Less variable expenses:		
Variable manufacturing expenses	DR330,000	
Sales commissions	42,000	
Shipping	18,000	
Total variable expenses		390,000
Contribution margin		460,000
Less fixed expenses:		
Advertising	270,000 X	
Depreciation of equipment (no resale value)	80,000	
General factory overhead	105,000*	
Salary of product-line manager	32,000 X	
Insurance on inventories	8,000	
Purchasing department expenses	45,000†	
Total fixed expenses		540,000
Net loss		DR(80,000)

*Common costs allocated on the basis of machine-hours.

†Common costs allocated on the basis of sales dollars.

    The currency in Greece is the drachma, denoted here by DR. The discontinuance of the bilge pump product line would not affect sales of other product lines and would have no noticeable effect on the company's total general factory overhead or total Purchasing Department expenses.

Required   Would you recommend that the bilge pump product line be discontinued? Support your answer with appropriate computations.

E13–4   Hollings Company sells office furniture in the Rocky Mountain area. As part of its service, it delivers furniture to customers.
    The costs associated with the acquisition and annual operation of a delivery truck are given below:

Insurance	$1,600
Licences	250
Taxes (vehicle)	150
Garage rent for parking (per truck)	1,200
Depreciation ($9,000 ÷ 5 years)	1,800*
Gasoline, oil, tires, and repairs	0.07 per kilometre

*Based on obsolescence rather than on wear and tear.

Required
1. Assume that Hollings Company has purchased one truck and that the truck has been driven 50,000 kilometres during the first year. Compute the average cost per kilometre of owning and operating the truck.
2. At the beginning of the second year, Hollings Company is unsure whether to use the truck or leave it parked in the garage and have all hauling done commercially. (The province requires the payment of vehicle taxes even if the vehicle is not used.) What costs from the previous list are relevant to this decision? Explain.
3. Assume that the company decides to use the truck during the second year. Near year-end an order is received from a customer over 1,000 kilometres away. What costs from the previous list are relevant in a decision between using the truck to make the delivery and having the delivery done commercially? Explain.
4. Occasionally, the company could use two trucks at the same time. For this reason, some thought is being given to purchasing a second truck. The total kilometres driven would be

the same as if only one truck were owned. What costs from the previous list are relevant to a decision over whether to purchase the second truck? Explain.

E13–5 Barlow Company manufactures three products: A, B, and C. The selling price, variable costs, and contribution margin for one unit of each product follow:

	Product		
	A	B	C
Selling price	$180	$270	$240
Less variable expenses:			
Direct materials	24	72	32
Other variable expenses	102	90	148
Total variable expenses	126	162	180
Contribution margin	$ 54	$108	$ 60
Contribution margin ratio	30%	40%	25%

The same raw material is used in all three products. Barlow Company has only 5,000 kilograms of material on hand and will not be able to obtain any more material for several weeks due to a strike in its supplier's plant. Management is trying to decide which product(s) to concentrate on next week in filling its backlog of orders. The material costs $8 per kilogram.

Required
1. Compute the amount of contribution margin that will be obtained per kilogram of material used in each product.
2. Which orders would you recommend that the company work on next week—the orders for product A, product B, or product C? Show computations.
3. A foreign supplier could furnish Barlow with additional amounts of the raw material at a substantial premium over the usual price. If there is unfilled demand for all three products, what is the highest price that Barlow Company should be willing to pay for an additional kilogram of materials?

E13–6 Troy Engines, Ltd., manufactures a variety of engines for use in heavy equipment. The company has always produced all of the necessary parts for its engines, including all of the carburetors. An outside supplier has offered to produce and sell one type of carburetor to Troy Engines, Ltd., for a cost of $35 per unit. To evaluate this offer, Troy Engines, Ltd., has gathered the following information relating to its own cost of producing the carburetor internally:

	Per Unit	15,000 Units per Year
Direct materials	$14	$210,000
Direct labour	10	150,000
Variable manufacturing overhead	3	45,000
Fixed manufacturing overhead, traceable	6*	90,000
Fixed manufacturing overhead, allocated	9	135,000
Total cost	$42	$630,000

*One-third supervisory salaries; two-thirds depreciation of special equipment (no resale value).

Required
1. Assuming that the company has no alternative use for the facilities that are now being used to produce the carburetors, should the outside supplier's offer be accepted? Show all computations.
2. Suppose that if the carburetors were purchased, Troy Engines, Ltd., could use the freed capacity to launch a new product. The segment margin of the new product would be $150,000 per year. Should Troy Engines, Ltd., accept the offer to buy the carburetors for $35 per unit? Show all computations.

E13–7 Waukee Railroad is considering the purchase of a powerful, high-speed wheel grinder to replace a standard wheel grinder that is now in use. Selected information on the two machines is given below:

	Standard Wheel Grinder	High-Speed Wheel Grinder
Original cost new	$20,000	$30,000
Accumulated depreciation to date	6,000	—
Current salvage value	9,000	—
Estimated cost per year to operate	15,000	7,000
Remaining years of useful life	5 years	5 years

Required Prepare a computation covering the five-year period that will show the net advantage or disadvantage of purchasing the high-speed wheel grinder. Use only relevant costs in your analysis.

E13–8 The Regal Cycle Company manufactures three types of bicycles—a dirt bike, a mountain bike, and a racing bike. Data on sales and expenses for the past quarter follow:

	Total	Dirt Bikes	Mountain Bikes	Racing Bikes
Sales	$300,000	$90,000	$150,000	$60,000
Less variable manufacturing and selling expenses	120,000	27,000	60,000	33,000
Contribution margin	180,000	63,000	90,000	27,000
Less fixed expenses:				
Advertising, traceable	30,000	10,000	14,000	6,000
Depreciation of special equipment	23,000	6,000	9,000	8,000
Salaries of product-line managers	35,000	12,000	13,000	10,000
Common allocated costs*	60,000	18,000	30,000	12,000
Total fixed expenses	148,000	46,000	66,000	36,000
Net operating income (loss)	$ 32,000	$17,000	$ 24,000	$ (9,000)

*Allocated on the basis of sales dollars.

Management is concerned about the continued losses shown by the racing bikes and wants a recommendation as to whether or not the line should be discontinued. The special equipment used to produce racing bikes has no resale value and does not wear out.

Required
1. Should production and sale of the racing bikes be discontinued? Show computations to support your answer.
2. Recast the above data in a format that would be more usable to management in assessing the long-run profitability of the various product lines.

E13–9 Han Products manufactures 30,000 units of part S-6 each year for use on its production line. At this level of activity, the cost per unit for part S-6 is as follows:

Direct materials	$ 3.60
Direct labour	10.00
Variable overhead	2.40
Fixed overhead	9.00
Total cost per part	$25.00

An outside supplier has offered to sell 30,000 units of part S-6 each year to Han Products for $21 per part. If Han Products accepts this offer, the facilities now being used to manufacture part S-6 could be rented to another company at an annual rental of $80,000. However, Han Products has determined that two-thirds of the fixed overhead being applied to part S-6 would continue even if part S-6 were purchased from the outside supplier.

Required Prepare computations to show the net dollar advantage or disadvantage of accepting the outside supplier's offer.

E13–10 Dorsey Company manufacturers three products from a common input in a joint processing operation. Joint processing costs up to the split-off point total $350,000 per quarter. The company allocates these costs to the joint products on the basis of their total sales value at the split-off point. Unit selling prices and total output at the split-off point are as follows:

Product	Selling Price	Quarterly Output
A	$16 per kilogram	15,000 kilograms
B	8 per kilogram	20,000 kilograms
C	25 per litre	4,000 litres

Each product can be processed further after the split-off point. Additional processing requires no special facilities. The additional processing costs (per quarter) and unit selling prices after further processing are given below:

Product	Additional Processing Costs	Selling Price
A	$63,000	$20 per kilogram
B	80,000	13 per kilogram
C	36,000	32 per litre

Required Which product or products should be sold at the split-off point and which product or products should be processed further? Show computations.

Problems

P13–11 Relevant Cost Analysis; Book Value Murl Plastics, Inc., purchased a new machine one year ago at a cost of $60,000. Although the machine operates well, the president of Murl Plastics is wondering if the company should replace it with a new electronically operated machine that has just come on the market. The new machine would slash annual operating costs by two-thirds, as shown in the comparative data below:

	Present Machine	Proposed New Machine
Purchase cost new	$60,000	$90,000
Estimated useful life new	6 years	5 years
Annual operating costs	$42,000	$14,000
Annual straight-line depreciation	10,000	18,000
Remaining book value	50,000	—
Salvage value now	10,000	—
Salvage value in 5 years	–0–	–0–

In trying to decide whether to purchase the new machine, the president has prepared the following analysis:

Book value of the old machine	$50,000
Less salvage value	10,000
Net loss from disposal	$40,000

"Even though the new machine looks good," said the president, "we can't get rid of that old machine if it means taking a huge loss on it. We'll have to use the old machine for at least a few more years."

Sales are expected to be $200,000 per year, and selling and administrative expenses are expected to be $126,000 per year, regardless of which machine is used.

Required

1. Prepare a summary income statement covering the next five years, assuming:
   a. That the new machine is not purchased.
   b. That the new machine is purchased.
2. Determine the desirability of purchasing the new machine using only relevant costs in your analysis.

P13–12 Dropping a Flight; Analysis of Operating Policy Profits have been decreasing for several years at Pegasus Airlines. In an effort to improve the company's performance, consideration is being given to dropping several flights that appear to be unprofitable.

A typical income statement for one such flight (flight 482) is given below (per flight):

Ticket revenue (175 seats × 40% occupancy × $200 ticket price)	$14,000	100.0%
Less variable expenses ($15 per person)	1,050	7.5
Contribution margin	12,950	92.5%
Less flight expenses:		
Salaries, flight crew	1,800	
Flight promotion	750	
Depreciation of aircraft	1,550	
Fuel for aircraft	6,800	
Liability insurance	4,200	
Salaries, flight assistants	500	
Baggage loading and flight preparation	1,700	
Overnight costs for flight crew and assistants at destination	300	
Total flight expenses	17,600	
Net operating loss	$ (4,650)	

The following additional information is available about flight 482:

a. Members of the flight crew are paid fixed annual salaries, whereas the flight assistants are paid by the flight.
b. One-third of the liability insurance is a special charge assessed against flight 482 because in the opinion of the insurance company, the destination of the flight is in a "high-risk" area. The remaining two-thirds would be unaffected by a decision to drop flight 482.
c. The baggage loading and flight preparation expense is an allocation of ground crews' salaries and depreciation of ground equipment. Dropping flight 482 would have no effect on the company's total baggage loading and flight preparation expenses.
d. If flight 482 is dropped, Pegasus Airlines has no authorization at present to replace it with another flight.
e. Depreciation of aircraft is due entirely to obsolescence. Depreciation due to wear and tear is negligible.
f. Dropping flight 482 would not allow Pegasus Airlines to reduce the number of aircraft in its fleet or the number of flight crew on its payroll.

Required

1. Prepare an analysis showing what impact dropping flight 482 would have on the airline's profits.
2. The airline's scheduling officer has been criticized because only about 50% of the seats on Pegasus' flights are being filled compared to an average of 60% for the industry. The

scheduling officer has explained that Pegasus' average seat occupancy could be improved considerably by eliminating about 10% of the flights, but that doing so would reduce profits. Explain how this could happen.

P13–13 Relevant Cost Potpourri   Unless otherwise indicated, each of the following parts is independent. In all cases, show computations to support your answer.
1. A merchandising company has two departments, A and B. A recent monthly income statement for the company follows:

	Total	Department A	Department B
		Department	
	Total	**A**	**B**
Sales	$4,000,000	$3,000,000	$1,000,000
Less variable expenses	1,300,000	900,000	400,000
Contribution margin	2,700,000	2,100,000	600,000
Less fixed expenses	2,200,000	1,400,000	800,000
Net operating income (loss)	$ 500,000	$ 700,000	$ (200,000)

A study indicates that $340,000 of the fixed expenses being charged to Department B are sunk costs or allocated costs that will continue even if B is dropped. In addition, the elimination of Department B will result in a 10% decrease in the sales of Department A. If Department B is dropped, what will be the effect on the net operating income of the company as a whole?
2. For many years Futura Company has purchased the starters that it installs in its standard line of farm tractors. Due to a reduction in output of certain of its products, the company has idle capacity that could be used to produce the starters. The chief engineer has recommended against this move, however, pointing out that the cost to produce the starters would be greater than the current $8.40 per unit purchase price:

	Per Unit	Total
Direct materials	$3.10	
Direct labour	2.70	
Supervision	1.50	$60,000
Depreciation	1.00	40,000
Variable manufacturing overhead	0.60	
Rent	0.30	12,000
Total production cost	$9.20	

A supervisor would have to be hired to oversee production of the starters. However, the company has sufficient idle tools and machinery that no new equipment would have to be purchased. The rent charge above is based on space utilized in the plant. The total rent on the plant is $80,000 per period. Depreciation is due to obsolescence rather than wear and tear. Prepare computations to show the dollar advantage or disadvantage per period of making the starters.
3. Wexpro, Inc., produces several products from processing of 1 tonne of clypton, a rare mineral. Material and processing costs total $60,000 per tonne, one-fourth of which is allocated to product X. Seven thousand units of product X are produced from each tonne of clypton. The units can either be sold at the split-off point for $9 each, or processed further at a total cost of $9,500 and then sold for $12 each. Should product X be processed further or sold at the split-off point?
4. Benoit Company produces three products, A, B, and C. Data concerning the three products follows (per unit):

	Product		
	A	**B**	**C**
Selling price	$80	$56	$70
Less variable expenses:			
Direct materials	24	15	9
Other variable expenses	24	27	40
Total variable expenses	48	42	49
Contribution margin	$32	$14	$21
Contribution margin ratio	40%	25%	30%

Demand for the company's products is very strong, with far more orders each month than the company has raw materials available to produce. The same material is used in each product. The material costs $3 per kilogram with a maximum of 5,000 kilograms available each month. Which orders would you advise the company to accept first, those for A, for B, or for C? Which orders second? Third?

5. Delta Company produces a single product. The cost of producing and selling a single unit of this product at the company's normal activity level of 60,000 units per year is:

Direct materials $5.10
Direct labour 3.80
Variable manufacturing overhead 1.00
Fixed manufacturing overhead 4.20
Variable selling and administrative expense 1.50
Fixed selling and administrative expense 2.40

The normal selling price is $21 per unit. The company's capacity is 75,000 units per year. An order has been received from a mail-order house for 15,000 units at a special price of $14 per unit. This order would not affect regular sales. If the order is accepted, by how much will annual profits be increased or decreased? (The order will not change the company's total fixed costs.)

6. Refer to the data in (5) above. Assume the company has 1,000 units of this product left over from last year that are vastly inferior to the current model. The units must be sold through regular channels at reduced prices. What unit cost figure is relevant for establishing a minimum selling price for these units? Explain.

P13–14 Sell or Process Further Decision (Prepared from a situation suggested by Professor John W. Hardy.) Lone Star Meat Packers is a major processor of beef and other meat products located in Sioux City, Iowa. The company has a large amount of T-bone steak on hand, and it is trying to decide whether to sell the T-bone steaks as they are initially cut or to process them further into filet mignon and the New York cut.

If the T-bone steaks are sold as initially cut, the company figures that a 1-pound T-bone steak would yield the following profit:

Selling price ($2.25 per pound) $2.25
Less joint product cost 1.80
Profit per pound $0.45

Instead of being sold as initially cut, the T-bone steaks could be further processed into filet mignon and New York cut steaks. Cutting one side of a T-bone steak provides the filet mignon, and cutting the other side provides the New York cut. One 16-ounce T-bone steak thus cut will yield one 6-ounce filet mignon and one 8-ounce New York cut; the remaining ounces are waste. The cost of processing the T-bone steaks into these cuts is $0.25 per pound. The filet mignon can be sold for $4.00 per pound, and the New York cut can be sold for $2.80 per pound.

Required
1. Determine the profit per pound from further processing the T-bone steaks.
2. Would you recommend that the T-bone steaks be sold as initially cut or processed further? Why?

P13–15 Make or Buy Analysis   "In my opinion, we ought to stop making our own drums and accept that outside supplier's offer," said Wim Niewindt, managing director of Antilles Refining, N.V., of Aruba. "At a price of 18 florins per drum, we would be paying 5 florins less than it costs us to manufacture the drums in our own plant. (The currency in Aruba is the florin, denoted below by fl.) Since we use 60,000 drums a year, that would be an annual cost savings of 300,000 florins." Antilles Refining's present cost to manufacture one drum is given below (based on 60,000 drums per year):

Direct material	fl10.35
Direct labour	6.00
Variable overhead	1.50
Fixed overhead (fl2.80 general company overhead, fl1.60 depreciation and, fl0.75 supervision)	5.15
Total cost per drum	fl23.00

A decision about whether to make or buy the drums is especially important at this time since the equipment being used to make the drums is completely worn out and must be replaced. The choices facing the company are:

Alternative 1: Purchase new equipment and continue to make the drums. The equipment would cost fl810,000; it would have a six-year useful life and no salvage value. The company uses straight-line depreciation.

Alternative 2: Purchase the drums from an outside supplier at fl18 per drum under a six-year contract.

The new equipment would be more efficient than the equipment that Antilles Refining has been using and, according to the manufacturer, would reduce direct labour and variable overhead costs by 30%. The old equipment has no resale value. Supervision cost (fl45,000 per year) and direct materials cost per drum would not be affected by the new equipment. The new equipment's capacity would be 90,000 drums per year. The company has no other use for the space being used to produce the drums.

The company's total general company overhead would be unaffected by this decision.

Required
1. To assist the managing director in making a decision, prepare an analysis showing what the total cost and the cost per drum would be under each of the two alternatives given above. Assume that 60,000 drums are needed each year. Which course of action would you recommend to the managing director?
2. Would your recommendation in (1) above be the same if the company's needs were: (a) 75,000 drums per year or (b) 90,000 drums per year? Show computations to support your answer, with costs presented on both a total and a per unit basis.
3. What other factors would you recommend that the company consider before making a decision?

P13–16 Selected Relevant Cost Questions   Andretti Company has a single product called a Dak. The company normally produces and sells 60,000 Daks each year at a selling price of $32 per unit. The company's unit costs at this level of activity are given below:

Direct materials	$10.00	
Direct labour	4.50	
Variable manufacturing overhead	2.30	
Fixed manufacturing overhead	5.00	($300,000 total)
Variable selling expenses	1.20	
Fixed selling expenses	3.50	($210,000 total)
Total cost per unit	$26.50	

A number of questions relating to the production and sale of Daks follow. Each question is independent.

Required

1. Assume that Andretti Company has sufficient capacity to produce 90,000 Daks each year without any increase in fixed manufacturing overhead costs. The company could increase its sales by 25% above the present 60,000 units each year if it were willing to increase the fixed selling expenses by $80,000. Would the increase fixed expenses be justified?

2. Assume again that Andretti Company has sufficient capacity to produce 90,000 Daks each year. A customer in a foreign market wants to purchase 20,000 Daks. Import duties on the Daks would be $1.70 per unit, and costs for permits and licences would be $9,000. The only selling costs that would be associated with the order would be $3.20 per unit shipping cost. You have been asked by the president to compute the per unit break-even price on this order.

3. The company has 1,000 Daks on hand that have some irregularities and are therefore considered to be "seconds." Due to the irregularities, it will be impossible to sell these units at the normal price through regular distribution channels. What unit cost figure is relevant for setting a minimum selling price?

4. Due to a strike in its supplier's plant, Andretti Company is unable to purchase more material for the production of Daks. The strike is expected to last for two months. Andretti Company has enough material on hand to continue to operate at 30% of normal levels for the two-month period. As an alternative, Andretti could close its plant down entirely for the two months. If the plant were closed, fixed overhead costs would continue at 60% of their normal level during the two-month period; the fixed selling costs would be reduced by 20% while the plant was closed. What would be the dollar advantage or disadvantage of closing the plant for the two-month period?

5. An outside manufacturer has offered to produce Daks for Andretti Company and to ship them directly to Andretti's customers. If Andretti Company accepts this offer, the facilities that it uses to produce Daks would be idle; however, fixed overhead costs would be reduced by 75% of their present level. Since the outside manufacturer would pay for all the costs of shipping, the variable selling costs would be only two-thirds of their present amount. Compute the unit cost figure that is relevant for comparison to whatever quoted price is received from the outside manufacturer.

P13–17 Discontinuance of a Store Superior Markets, Inc., operates three stores in a large metropolitan area. A segmented income statement for the company for the last quarter is given below:

SUPERIOR MARKETS, INC.
Income Statement
For the Quarter Ended September 30

	Total	North Store	South Store	East Store
Sales	$3,000,000	$720,000	$1,200,000	$1,080,000
Cost of goods sold	1,657,200	403,200	660,000	594,000
Gross margin	1,342,800	316,800	540,000	486,000
Operating expenses:				
Selling expenses	817,000	231,400	315,000	270,600
Administrative expenses	383,000	106,000	150,900	126,100
Total expenses	1,200,000	337,400	465,900	396,700
Net operating income (loss)	$ 142,800	$(20,600)	$ 74,100	$ 89,300

The North Store has consistently shown losses over the past two years. For this reason, management is giving consideration to closing the store. The company has retained you to make a recommendation as to whether the store should be closed or kept open. The following additional information is available for your use:

a. The breakdown of the selling and administrative expenses is as follows:

	Total	North Store	South Store	East Store
Selling expenses:				
Sales salaries	$239,000	$ 70,000	$ 89,000	$ 80,000
Direct advertising	187,000	51,000	72,000	64,000
General advertising*	45,000	10,800	18,000	16,200
Store rent	300,000	85,000	120,000	95,000
Depreciation of store fixtures	16,000	4,600	6,000	5,400
Delivery salaries	21,000	7,000	7,000	7,000
Depreciation of delivery				
equipment	9,000	3,000	3,000	3,000
Total selling expenses	$817,000	$231,400	$315,000	$270,600

*Allocated on the basis of sales dollars.

	Total	North Store	South Store	East Store
Administrative expenses:				
Store management salaries	$ 70,000	$ 21,000	$ 30,000	$ 19,000
General office salaries*	50,000	12,000	20,000	18,000
Insurance on fixtures and				
inventory	25,000	7,500	9,000	8,500
Utilities	106,000	31,000	40,000	35,000
Employment taxes	57,000	16,500	21,900	18,600
General office—other*	75,000	18,000	30,000	27,000
Total administrative				
expenses	$383,000	$106,000	$150,900	$126,100

*Allocated on the basis of sales dollars.

b. The lease on the building housing the North Store can be broken with no penalty.
c. The fixtures being used in the North Store would be transferred to the other two stores if the North Store were closed.
d. The general manager of the North Store would be retained and transferred to another position in the company if the North Store were closed. She would be filling a position that would otherwise be filled by hiring a new employee at a salary of $11,000 per quarter. The general manager of the North Store would be retained at her normal salary of $12,000 per quarter. All other employees in the store would be discharged.
e. The company has one delivery crew that serves all three stores. One delivery person could be discharged if the North Store were closed. This person's salary is $4,000 per quarter. The delivery equipment would be distributed to the other stores. The equipment does not wear out through use, but does eventually become obsolete.
f. The company's employment taxes are 15% of salaries.
g. One-third of the insurance in the North Store is on the store's fixtures.
h. The "General office salaries" and "General office—other" relate to the overall management of Superior Markets, Inc. If the North Store were closed, one person in the general office could be discharged because of the decrease in overall workload. This person's salary is $6,000 per quarter.

Required

1. Prepare a schedule showing the change in revenues and expenses and the impact on the company's overall net income that would result if the North Store were closed.
2. Assuming that the store space can't be subleased, what recommendation would you make to the management of Superior Markets, Inc.?
3. Assume that if the North Store were closed, at least one-fourth of its sales would transfer to the East Store, due to strong customer loyalty to Superior Markets. The East Store has ample capacity to handle the increased sales. You may assume that the increased sales in the East Store would yield the same gross margin rate as present sales in that store. What effect would these factors have on your recommendation concerning the North Store? Show all computations to support your answer.

P13–18 Shutdown versus Continue-to-Operate Decision   (Note: This type of decision is similar to that of dropping a product line.)

Birch Company normally produces and sells 30,000 units of RG-6 each month. RG-6 is a small electrical relay used in the automotive industry as a component part in various products. The selling price is $22 per unit, variable costs are $14 per unit, fixed manufacturing overhead costs total $150,000 per month, and fixed selling costs total $30,000 per month.

Employment-contract strikes in the companies that purchase the bulk of the RG-6 units have caused Birch Company's sales to temporarily drop to only 8,000 units per month. Birch Company estimates that the strikes will last for about two months, after which time sales of RG-6 should return to normal. Due to the current low level of sales, however, Birch Company is thinking about closing down its own plant during the two months that the strikes are on. If Birch Company does close down its plant, it is estimated that fixed manufacturing overhead costs can be reduced to $105,000 per month and that fixed selling costs can be reduced by 10%. Start-up costs at the end of the shutdown period would total $8,000. Since Birch Company uses just-in-time (JIT) production methods, no inventories are on hand.

Required
1. Assuming that the strikes continue for two months, as estimated, would you recommend that Birch Company close its own plant? Show computations in good form.
2. At what level of sales (in units) for the two-months period should Birch Company be indifferent between closing the plant or keeping it open? Show computations. (Hint: This is a type of break-even analysis, except that the fixed cost portion of your break-even computation should include only those fixed costs that are relevant [i.e., avoidable] over the two-month period.)

P13–19 Make or Buy Decision   Silven Industries, which manufacturers and sells a highly successful line of summer lotions and insect repellents, has decided to diversify in order to stabilize sales throughout the year. A natural area for the company to consider is the production of winter lotions and creams to prevent dry and chapped skin.

After considerable research, a winter products line has been developed. However, Silven's president has decided to introduce only one of the new products for this coming winter. If the product is a success, further expansion in future years will be initiated.

The product selected (called Chap-Off) is a lip balm that will be sold in a lipstick-type tube. The product will be sold to wholesalers in boxes of 24 tubes for $8 per box. Because of excess capacity, no additional fixed overhead costs will be incurred to produce the product. However, a $90,000 charge for fixed overhead will be absorbed by the product under the company's absorption costing system.

Using the estimated sales and production of 100,000 boxes of Chap-Off, the Accounting Department has developed the following cost per box:

Direct material	$3.60
Direct labour	2.00
Manufacturing overhead	1.40
Total cost	$7.00

The costs above include costs for producing both the lip balm and the tube into which the lip balm is to be placed. As an alternative to making the tubes, Silven has approached a supplier to discuss the possibility of purchasing the tubes for Chap-Off. The purchase price of the empty tubes from the supplier would be $1.35 per box of 24 tubes. If Silven Industries accepts the purchase proposal, it is predicted that direct labour and variable manufacturing overhead costs per box of Chap-Off would be reduced by 10% and that direct materials costs would be reduced by 25%.

Required
1. Should Silven Industries make or buy the tubes? Show calculations to support your answer.
2. What would be the maximum purchase price acceptable to Silven Industries? Support your answer with an appropriate explanation.
3. Instead of sales of 100,000 boxes, revised estimates show sales volume at 120,000 boxes. At this new volume, additional equipment at an annual rental of $40,000 must be acquired to manufacture the tubes. Assuming that the outside supplier will not accept an order for less than 100,000 boxes, should Silven Industries make or buy the tubes? Show computations to support your answer.

4. Refer to the data in (3) above. Assume that the outside supplier will accept an order of any size for the tubes at $1.35 per box. How, if at all, would this change your answer? Show computations.
5. What qualitative factors should Silven Industries consider in determining whether they should make or buy the tubes?

(CMA, heavily adapted)

P13–20 Accept or Reject Special Orders   Polaski Company manufactures and sells a single product called a Ret. Operating at capacity, the company can produce and sell 30,000 Rets per year. Costs associated with this level of production and sales are given below:

	Unit	Total
Direct materials	$15	$ 450,000
Direct labour	8	240,000
Variable manufacturing overhead	3	90,000
Fixed manufacturing overhead	9	270,000
Variable selling expense	4	120,000
Fixed selling expense	6	180,000
Total cost	$45	$1,350,000

The Rets normally sell for $50 each. Fixed manufacturing overhead is constant at $270,000 per year within the range of 25,000 through 30,000 Rets per year.

Required

1. Assume that due to a recession, Polaski Company expects to sell only 25,000 Rets through regular channels next year. A large retail chain has offered to purchase 5,000 Rets if Polaski is willing to accept a 16% discount off the regular price. There would be no sales commissions on this order; thus, variable selling expenses would be slashed by 75%. However, Polaski Company would have to purchase a special machine to engrave the retail chain's name on the 5,000 units. This machine would cost $10,000. Polaski Company has no assurance that the retail chain will purchase additional units any time in the future. Determine the impact on profits next year if this special order is accepted.
2. Refer to the original data. Assume again that Polaski Company expects to sell only 25,000 Rets through regular channels next year. The U.S. Army would like to make a one-time-only purchase of 5,000 Rets. The army would pay a fixed fee of $1.80 per Ret, and in addition it would reimburse Polaski Company for all costs of production (variable and fixed) associated with the units. Since the army would pick up the Rets with its own trucks, there would be no variable selling expenses of any type associated with this order. If Polaski Company accepts the order, by how much will profits be increased or decreased for the year?
3. Assume the same situation as that described in (2) above, except that the company expects to sell 30,000 Rets through regular channels next year. Thus, accepting the U.S. Army's order would require giving up regular sales of 5,000 Rets. If the army's order is accepted, by how much will profits be increased or decreased from what they would be if the 5,000 Rets were sold through regular channels?

P13–21 Utilization of a Constrained Resource   The Walton Toy Company manufactures a line of dolls and a doll dress sewing kit. Demand for the dolls is increasing, and management requests assistance from you in determining an economical sales and production mix for the coming year. The company's Sales Department provides the following information:

Product	Estimated Demand Next Year (units)	Selling Price per Unit
Debbie	50,000	$13.50
Trish	42,000	5.50
Sarah	35,000	21.00
Mike	40,000	10.00
Sewing kit	325,000	8.00

The standard costs for direct materials and direct labour per unit are as follows:

Product	Direct Materials	Direct Labour
Debbie	$4.30	$3.20
Trish	1.10	2.00
Sarah	6.44	5.60
Mike	2.00	4.00
Sewing kit	3.20	1.60

The following additional information is available:

a. The company's plant has a capacity of 130,000 direct labour-hours per year on a single-shift basis. The company's present employees and equipment can produce all five products.

b. The direct labour rate is $8 per hour; this rate is expected to remain unchanged during the coming year.

c. Fixed costs total $520,000 per year. Variable overhead costs are $2 per direct labour-hour.

d. All of the company's nonmanufacturing costs are fixed.

e. The company's present inventory of finished products is negligible and can be ignored.

Required
1. Determine the contribution margin per direct labour-hour expended on each product.
2. Prepare a schedule showing the total direct labour-hours that will be required to produce the units estimated to be sold during the coming year.
3. Examine the data you have computed in (1) and (2) above. Indicate how much of each product should be made so that total production time is equal to the 130,000 hours available.
4. What is the highest price, in terms of a rate per hour, that Walton Toy Company would be willing to pay for additional capacity (that is, for added direct labour time)?
5. Assume again that the company does not want to reduce sales of any product. Identify ways in which the company could obtain the additional output.

(CPA, heavily adapted)

P13–22 Evaluating the Profitability of a Product; Break Even Tracey Douglas is the owner and managing director of Heritage Garden Furniture, Ltd., a South African company that makes museum-quality reproductions of antique outdoor furniture. Ms. Douglas would like advice concerning the advisability of eliminating the model C3 lawnchair. These lawnchairs have been among the company's best-selling products, but they seem to be unprofitable.

A condensed statement of operating income for the company and for the model C3 lawnchair for the quarter ended June 30 follows:

	All Products	Model C3 Lawnchair
Sales	R2,900,000	R300,000
Cost of sales:		
Direct materials	759,000	122,000
Direct labour	680,000	72,000
Fringe benefits (20% of direct labour)	136,000	14,400
Variable manufacturing overhead	28,000	3,600
Building rent and maintenance	30,000	4,000
Depreciation	75,000	19,100
Total cost of sales	1,708,000	235,100
Gross margin	1,192,000	64,900
Selling and administrative expenses:		
Product managers' salaries	75,000	10,000
Sales commissions (5% of sales)	145,000	15,000
Fringe benefits (20% of salaries and commissions)	44,000	5,000
Shipping	120,000	10,000
General administrative expenses	464,000	48,000
Total selling and administrative expenses	848,000	88,000
Net operating income (loss)	R 344,000	R (23,100)

The currency in South Africa is the rand, denoted here by R.

WANG COMPANY—PACIFIC REGION
Statement of Operations
For the Year Ended December 31, 2000

Net sales		$1,800,000
Costs and expenses:		
Advertising fees	$109,400	
Cost of sales (all variable)	920,000	
Freight-out	45,200	
Insurance	20,000	
Salaries and benefits	163,200	
Sales commissions	72,000	
Supplies	24,000	
Travel and entertainment	28,200	
Wages and employee benefits	75,000	
Warehouse depreciation	16,000	
Warehouse operating costs	30,000	1,503,000
Total profit contribution—Pacific Region		$ 297,000

The salaries and benefits consisted of the following items:

Regional vice president	$43,000
Regional marketing manager	35,000
Regional warehouse manager	26,800
Salespeople (one for each of the two territories with each receiving the same salary base)	31,200
Employee benefits (20% of salaries)	27,200
Total salaries and benefits	$ 163,200

The two salespeople each receive the same salary plus a 4% commission on total sales in their territories. Travel and entertainment costs were incurred by the salespeople calling on their customers. Freight-out is a function of the quantity of goods shipped and the distance shipped to customers. Thirty percent of the insurance was expended for protection of the inventory while it was in the regional warehouse; the balance was the cost to insure the warehouse itself. Supplies were used in the warehouse for packing the merchandise that was shipped and total cost fluctuated according to kilograms shipped. Wages relate to the hourly paid employees who fill orders in the warehouse; the total amount of this expense does not change if the annual number of kilograms shipped from the warehouse falls in the range of 550,000 to 650,000. The warehouse operating costs account contained such costs as heat, light, and maintenance.

The following cost analysis and statistics by territory for 2000 were compiled for the regional vice president by the regional warehouse manager an marketing manager:

	Edward	Acadia	Total
Net sales	$800,000	$1,000,000	$1,800,000
Cost of sales	460,000	460,000	920,000
Advertising fees	53,600	55,800	109,400
Travel and entertainment	12,600	15,600	28,200
Freight-out	18,000	27,200	45,200
Units sold	150,000	350,000	500,000
Kilograms shipped	210,000	390,000	600,000
Salesperson kilometres travelled	21,600	38,400	60,000

Required

1. Top management of Wang Company wants the regional operating data to be presented in a more meaningful manner. Provide an outline of a 2000 statement of operations report that would satisfy top management. Identify the contents and main divisions of your statement, but do not include any amounts. Your report should provide the basis for top management to evaluate the performance of the individual territories in the Pacific Region and the overall performance of the region.

2. The Wang Company is planning to introduce a new product line in its manufacturing plant. This line would be automated to a much greater extent, using less labour than the existing production lines. This creates a problem regarding how best to predict and standardize the overhead costs. The suppliers of the automated machinery have provided the following three simple regressions derived from the experience of other companies using similar automated machinery for a similar product line (each regression was based on production data for 36 months of production):

Variable	Coefficient
First Regression:	
Intercept	422,572
Direct labour-hours (independent)	129.43
Total overhead (dependent)	—
Second Regression:	
Intercept	671,102
Machine hours (independent)	23.75
Total overhead (dependent)	—
Third Regression:	
Intercept	379,842
Direct material dollars (independent)	0.29
Total overhead (dependent)	—

Required

a. Which independent variable should the Wang Company use to predict and standardize overhead costs? Fully support your answer.

b. Assuming that an average of 840 direct labour-hours per month are required for the new production line, use the first regression to calculate the amount of total monthly overhead cost.

(SMAC, adapted)

C13–29 Segment Profits   Audain Ltd. produces two products, B and R, in its Cow Bay facility at the unit costs presented below.

	B	R
Expected annual unit sales and production	42,000	41,000
Estimated costs of production:		
Direct materials	$ 3.50	$ 4.30
Direct labour	4.00	2.00
Variable overhead*	1.50	1.00
Fixed overhead*	5.00	3.00
Total production cost	$ 14.00	$ 10.30
Selling expense:		
Variable	0.20	0.20
Fixed†	1.17	0.92
Total selling expense	1.37	1.12
Total cost	$ 15.37	$ 11.42
Selling price	$ 16.50	$ 13.50
Profit per unit	$ 1.13	$ 2.08

*Overhead is charged on the basic of available machine-hours. Total annual overhead is estimated to be $437.000. Fixed overhead is approximately 76.2% of the total of $437,000, at 10,000 machine-hours. Capacity can be extended to 20,000 machine-hours by using another shift or any part thereof.

†Fixed selling expense amounts to $86,860 per year and is allocated for pricing purposes using sales level.

Recently, the sales manager secured a tentative order to supply 70,000 units of N product to a new customer at a price of $17.30. The order is subject to the condition that Audain guarantee to supply the entire 70,000 units.

Estimated costs of producing N are as follows:

	Cost per Unit
Direct materials	$ 4.00
Direct labour	3.50
Variable overhead	3.00
Fixed overhead	4.00
	$14.50

Variable selling expenses are $0.40 per unit and fixed selling expenses are expected to remain unchanged. To produce a single unit of N, 16% of a machine-hour is required.

The plant manager has asked you to go over the figures carefully. He informs you that, if necessary, the required capacity will be made available through refusing orders for the least profitable of the other two subassemblies.

Required

1. Determine what net income would be without the N contract.
2. Assuming that expansion beyond the double shift is not practical and that production of B product can be displaced if necessary, determine the profits if the contract for N is accepted.
3. Audain Ltd. wants to accept the N contract. Assume that the company is contractually committed to provide 42,000 units of B and 41,000 units of R, and the expansion beyond the single shift is not practical. Another firm is willing to produce B for Audain. What is the highest unit price at which B could be contracted out so as to leave Audain with the same net income as that calculated in item 2?
4. Is there a better option for Audain than having B contracted out? Explain.

(SMAC, adapted)

C13–30 Relevant Costs—A Fable[6]   Once upon a time there lived a very thoughtful young accountant who pondered the many mysteries of life like debits and credits and income and value. He had solved some of the greatest mysteries in accounting, but he was still puzzled by the mystery of true and accurate costs.

One day he met a wise old accountant who offered to share with him two truths:

Truth #1:   The true cost of Beetlejuice is $2.
Truth #2:   The true cost of Green Noodles is $12.

The accountant rushed home with these truths, entered them in his linear programming model, and computed the optimal product mix for the two products. Fortunately, the wise old accountant had provided the selling price for the products as well as the constraint equations for their production. The data are shown below.

	Green Noodles	Beetlejuice
Price	$18	$25
Cost	2	12
Margin	$16	$13

Constraints in machine-hours:

---

6. Germain Boer, "The Energy of Youth and the Wisdom of Age: A Fable," *News and News*, Management Accounting Section, vol. 11, no. 2 (American Accounting Association, Fall 1993), pp. 14, 15.

	Capacity			
Dept 1	1	1	≤	120
Dept 2	150	10	≤	7,500
Dept 3	80	20	≤	4,500

The linear programming computation results showed the optimal product mix was 35 units of Green Noodles and 85 units of Beetlejuice, and this provided a total margin of $1,665 as the following tabulation shows.

	Revenue	Cost	Margin	Units	Total Margin
Green Noodles	18	2	16	35	$ 560
Beetlejuice	25	12	13	85	1,105
					$1,665

"Marvelous!" exclaimed the accountant. "At last one of life's greatest mysteries reveals itself." Since he had the true cost for these two products, the accountant decided to test the cost accuracy abilities of some popular cost computation methodologies. Three-letter acronyms were all the rage in costing, so he decided to test the XYZ and the PDQ costing systems to see what answers they would provide.

First he used the PDQ system to estimate the product costs, and it gave a product cost of $8 for Green Noodles and $17 for Beetlejuice. These costs were significantly different from the true costs, but the accountant popped them into the linear programming model anyway. Lo and behold he got the same product mix he computed with the true costs.

The following tabulation shows the apparent margin for these product costs.

Estimate No. 1: PDQ Unit Cost Computation Method

	Revenue	Cost	Margin	Units	Total Margin
Green Noodles	18	8	10	35	$ 350
Beetlejuice	25	17	8	85	680
Apparent margin using PDQ costs					$1,030

"True margin" is the same as the original solution, i.e., $1,665.

The accountant was puzzled that such a large difference between the true unit costs and the PDQ unit costs could still generate the same product mix, so he moved on to try using the XYZ costing method to estimate the cost. This method generated results that were much closer to the true costs: a unit cost of $4 for Green Noodles and a unit cost of $10 for Beetlejuice.

"Aha, this answer appears more accurate than the PDQ system and should give me a product mix just like the true costs since the product costs are so close to the true costs," said the accountant. Alas, these costs generated a product mix that included only Beetlejuice; no Green Noodles entered the solution. The following tabulation shows the results of the XYZ calculation.

Estimate No. 2: XYZ Computation Method

	Revenue	Cost	Margin	Units	Total Margin
Green Noodles	18	4	14	0	$ 0
Beetlejuice	25	10	15	120	1,800
Apparent margin using XYZ costs					$1,800

"True margin" is (120 × $13) = $1,560.

These results really puzzled the young accountant. How could a set of unit costs so close to the true costs give such a different product mix than unit costs that were so far from the true costs? To help understand this enigma, the accountant prepared the following tabulation of product costs and the true margins they generate.

	Unit Cost Estimate		True Cost
	PDQ System	**XYZ System**	**True Cost**
Green Noodles	8	4	2
Beetlejuice	17	10	12
"True margin"	$1,665	$1,560	$1,665

"I always thought that the closer a cost approximated the true cost the more accurate the cost, so why do I get such different answers?" mumbled the young accountant as he checked his calculations again.

Finally, the puzzled young accountant decided he needed help, so he sought out the wise old accountant. "Oh wise accountant," he said, "Why does a cost that is vastly different from the true cost give the correct answer, whereas a cost that is very close to the true cost provides the wrong answer? What makes one cost more accurate than another?"

Required   What might the wise old accountant say?

Group Exercises

GE13–31   What's the Cost?   Nearly 70 years ago, eminent economist J. Maurice Clarke stated that "accountants use different costs because of their differing objectives." The business world has certainly become a lot more complicated since Professor Clarke's insightful comment. Management accountants today are expected to be a lot more conversant and knowledgeable about business operations. They are expected to add value to their company by their ability to bring the right information to bear on a decision. To do that, management accountants must be able to identify, analyze, and help solve problems. They have to operationalize Professor Clarke's statement.

Required
1. What are the different uses for accounting information? That is, for what purposes or functions is cost information used? Try to identify as many uses as you can and then try to group similar or related uses under some common heading, for example, external reporting.
2. Define each of the following cost or revenue concepts and give examples of decisions or situations where the concept would be used.
   a. Sunk cost.
   b. Avoidable cost.
   c. Opportunity cost.
   d. Joint cost.
   e. Contribution margin per unit of constrained resource.

GE13–32   Outsourcing May Be Hazardous to Your Health   Outsourcing, when a company contracts with third parties to produce some of its parts or products, has become commonplace among manufacturers. Thirty years ago, when factories were a lot less complex, factory burden rates of 50% or less of direct labour cost were deemed reasonable. But today, overhead burden rates of 500% of direct labour are common and rates of 1,000% or more are not unusual. As a result, outsourcing has gained widespread acceptance over the past 15 years. Products with high direct labour content are especially susceptible to being outsourced to parts of the world where labour rates are a lot less than they are in the North America.

Required
1. What is the meaning of manufacturing overhead rates of 500% or more of direct labour?
2. What implications do such high burden rates hold for products high in direct labour content?

3. If products with a high direct labour content are outsourced to low-wage areas of less-developed, foreign countries, what impact will that have on the cost structure of the company? Cite specific categories of costs affected by the outsourcing strategy.
4. What happens to the costs of the remaining products when a product is outsourced?
5. Can you think of any drawbacks to outsourcing in a less-developed foreign land or any limitations to a strategy dependent on labour cost savings?
6. Continuing with the line of thinking developed in (1)–(3) above, what happens next?

IE13–33 Information Systems Information systems are designed to provide information of relevance to strategic decisions of management. Computer systems termed Enterprise Resource Planning Systems or ERP are being promoted as a suitable tool to provide this information. Baan, J D Edwards, Oracle, PeopleSoft, and SAP are the dominant systems being promoted to organizations.

Required Using the WWW, locate information about these systems that will permit a description of how they help provide information relevant to decisions and how they compare for a typical organization of your choosing.

Chapter Fourteen

Capital Budgeting Decisions

Business Focus

The superstore concept seems to have really caught on in Canada. Leon's Furniture for example opened a new London, Ontario, superstore in May of 1999 and sales continue to exceed expectations. New openings are expected in Barrie, Ontario; Red Deer, Alberta; Montreal East; Montreal West; Niagara-On-The-Lake/St. Catharines; Kitchener, Ontario; South Edmonton and Quebec City. As well, four completely newly renovated showrooms will open in Weston, Ontario; Laval, Quebec; Edmonton, Alberta; and Burlington, Ontario. A Board of Directors announcement added: "We expect these seven new buildings and four newly renovated showrooms to be completed within the next two and one-half years. Construction in Red Deer and Montreal East is scheduled to begin this fall. This new expansion means a commitment in capital expenditures in excess of $100,000,000.00."

Source: Adapted from CNW release, September 15, 1999.

Learning Objectives

After studying Chapter Fourteen you should be able to:

1 Determine the acceptability of an investment project using the net present value method.

2 Determine the acceptability of an investment project using the internal rate of return method (with interpolation, if needed).

3 Explain how the cost of capital is used as a screening tool.

4 Prepare a net present value analysis of two competing investment projects using either the incremental-cost approach or the total-cost approach.

5 Make a capital budgeting analysis involving automated equipment.

6 Rank investment projects in order of preference using (1) the internal rate of return method and (2) the net present value method with the profitability index.

7 Determine the payback period for an investment.

8 Compute the simple rate of return for an investment.

9 (Appendix 14A) Explain the concept of present value and make present value computations with and without the present value tables.

10 (Appendix 14B) Explain the effect of inflation on capital budgeting decisions.

Capital budgeting The process of planning significant outlays on projects that have long-term implications such as the purchase of new equipment or the introduction of a new product.

The term **capital budgeting** is used to describe

how managers plan significant outlays on projects that have long-term implications such as the purchase of new equipment and the introduction of new products. In a recent fiscal year BCE Inc. had capital expenditures reaching $3.1 billion. Most companies have many more potential projects than can actually be funded. Hence, managers must carefully select those projects that promise the greatest future return. How well managers make these capital budgeting decisions is a critical factor in the long-run profitability of the company.

Capital budgeting involves *investment*—a company must commit funds now in order to receive a return in the future. Investments are not limited to stocks and bonds. Purchase of inventory or equipment is also an investment. For example, Tim Horton's makes an investment when it opens a new restaurant. McCain Food makes an investment when it installs a new computer to handle customer billing. DaimlerChrysler makes an investment when it redesigns a product such as the Jeep Eagle and must retool its production lines. With a combination of public and private funding universities such as UBC, U of T, McGill, and Dalhousie make substantial investments in medical research. All of these investments are characterized by a commitment of funds today in the expectation of receiving a return in the future in the form of additional cash inflows or reduced cash outflows.

Capital Budgeting—Planning Investments

Typical Capital Budgeting Decisions

What types of business decisions require capital budgeting analysis? Virtually any decision that involves an outlay now in order to obtain some return (increase in revenue or reduction in costs) in the future. Typical capital budgeting decisions include:

1. Cost reduction decisions. Should new equipment be purchased to reduce costs?
2. Expansion decisions. Should a new plant, warehouse, or other facility be acquired to increase capacity and sales?
3. Equipment selection decisions. Which of several available machines would be the most cost effective to purchase?
4. Lease or buy decisions. Should new equipment be leased or purchased?
5. Equipment replacement decisions. Should old equipment be replaced now or later?

Screening decision A decision as to whether a proposed investment meets some preset standard of acceptance.

Capital budgeting decisions tend to fall into two broad categories—*screening decisions* and *preference decisions*. **Screening decisions** are those relating to whether a proposed project meets some preset standard of acceptance. For example, a firm may have a policy of accepting projects only if they promise a return of, say, 20% on the investment. The required rate of return is the minimum rate of return a project must yield to be acceptable.

Preference decision A decision as to which of several competing acceptable investment proposals is best.

Preference decisions, by contrast, relate to selecting from among several *competing* courses of action. To illustrate, a firm may be considering five different machines to replace an existing machine on the assembly line. The choice of which machine to purchase is a *preference* decision.

In this chapter, we initially discuss ways of making screening decisions. Preference decisions are discussed toward the end of the chapter.

The Time Value of Money

As stated earlier, business investments commonly promise returns that extend over fairly long periods of time. Therefore, in approaching capital budgeting decisions, it is necessary to employ techniques that recognize *the time value of money.* A dollar today is worth more than a dollar a year from now. The same concept applies in choosing between investment projects. Those projects that promise returns earlier in time are preferable to those that promise returns later in time.

The capital budgeting techniques that recognize the above two characteristics of business investments most fully are those that involve *discounted cash flows.* We will spend most of this chapter illustrating the use of discounted cash flow methods in making capital budgeting decisions. If you are not already familiar with discounting and the use of present value tables, you should read Appendix 14A, The Concept of Present Value, at the end of this chapter before proceeding any further.

Discounted Cash Flows—The Net Present Value Method

Objective 1

Determine the acceptability of an investment project using the net present value method.

There are two approaches to making capital budgeting decisions by means of discounted cash flows. One is the *net present value method,* and the other is the *internal rate of return method* (sometimes called the *time-adjusted rate of return method*). The net present value method is discussed in this section; the internal rate of return method is discussed in the next section.

The Net Present Value Method Illustrated

Net present value The difference between the present value of the cash inflows and the present value of the cash outflows associated with an investment project.

Under the net present value method, the present value of all cash inflows is compared to the present value of all cash outflows that are associated with an investment project. The difference between the present value of these cash flows, called the **net present value,** determines whether or not the project is an acceptable investment. To illustrate, let us assume the following data:

Example A

Harper Company is contemplating the purchase of a machine capable of performing certain operations that are now performed manually. The machine will cost $5,000, and it will last for five years. At the end of the five-year period, the machine will have a zero scrap value. Use of the machine will reduce labour costs by $1,800 per year. Harper Company requires a minimum return of 20% before taxes on all investment projects.[1]

Should the machine be purchased? Harper Company must determine whether a cash investment now of $5,000 can be justified if it will result in an $1,800 reduction in cost each year over the next five years. It may appear that the answer is obvious since the total cost savings is $9,000 (5 × $1,800). However, the company can earn a

---

1. For simplicity, we assume in this chapter and in the next chapter that there is no inflation. The impact of inflation on discounted cash flow analysis is discussed in Appendix 14B to this chapter. Also, in this chapter we ignore income taxes. The impact of income taxes on capital budgeting decisions will be covered in the next chapter.

Exhibit 14–1
Net Present Value Analysis
of a Proposed Project

		Initial cost $5,000		
		Life of the project (years) 5		
		Annual cost savings $1,800		
		Salvage value .... –0–		
		Required rate of return 20%		

Item	Year(s)	Amount of Cash Flow	20% Factor	Present Value of Cash Flows
Annual cost savings	1–5	$ 1,800	2.991*	$ 5,384
Initial investment	Now	(5,000)	1.000	(5,000)
Net present value				$ 384

*From Table 14C–4 in Appendix 14C at the end of this chapter.

20% return by investing its money elsewhere. It is not enough that the cost reductions cover just the original cost of the machine; they must also yield at least a 20% return or the company would be better off investing the money elsewhere.

To determine whether the investment is desirable, it is necessary to discount the stream of annual $1,800 cost savings to its present value and then to compare this discounted present value with the cost of the new machine. Since Harper Company requires a minimum return of 20% on all investment projects, this rate is used in the discounting process. Exhibit 14–1 shows how this analysis is done.

According to the analysis, Harper Company should purchase the new machine. The present value of the cost savings is $5,384, as compared to a present value of only $5,000 for the investment required (cost of the machine). Deducting the present value of the investment required from the present value of the cost savings gives a *net present value* of $384. Whenever the net present value is zero or greater, as in our example, an investment project is acceptable. Whenever the net present value is negative (the present value of the cash outflows exceeds the present value of the cash inflows), an investment project is not acceptable. In sum:

If the Net Present Value Is . . .	Then the Project Is . . .
Positive	Acceptable, since it promises a return greater than the required rate of return.
Zero	Acceptable, since it promises a return equal to the required rate of return.
Negative	Not acceptable, since it promises a return less than the required rate of return.

A full interpretation of the solution would be as follows: The new machine promises more than the required 20% rate of return. This is evident from the positive net present value of $384. Harper Company could spend up to $5,384 for the new machine and still obtain the minimum required 20% rate of return. The net present value of $384, therefore, shows the amount of "cushion" or "margin of error." One way to look at this is that the company could underestimate the cost of the new machine by up to $384, or overestimate the net present value of the future cash savings by up to $384, and the project would still be financially attractive. If the present value of the cost savings were only $5,000 instead of $5,384, the project would still promise the required 20% return.

Emphasis on Cash Flows

In capital budgeting decisions, the focus is on cash flows and not on accounting net income. The reason is that accounting net income is based on accrual concepts that ignore the timing of cash flows into and out of an organization. From a capital budgeting standpoint the timing of cash flows is important, since a dollar received today is more valuable than a dollar received in the future. Therefore, even though the accounting net income figure is useful for many things, it is not used in discounted cash flow analysis. Instead of determining accounting net income, the manager must concentrate on identifying the specific cash flows associated with an investment project.

What kinds of cash flows should the manager look for? Although the specific cash flows will vary from project to project, certain types of cash flows tend to recur as explained in the following paragraphs.

TYPICAL CASH OUTFLOWS   Most projects will have an immediate cash outflow in the form of an initial investment in equipment or other assets. Any salvage value realized from the sale of old equipment can be recognized as a cash inflow or as a reduction in the required investment. In addition, some projects require that a company expand its working capital. **Working capital** is current assets (cash, accounts receivable, and inventory) less current liabilities. When a company takes on a new project, the balances in the current asset accounts will often increase. For example, opening a new Bay's department store would require additional cash in sales registers, increased accounts receivable for new customers, and more inventory to stock the shelves. These additional working capital needs should be treated as part of the initial investment in a project. Also, many projects require periodic outlays for repairs and maintenance and for additional operating costs. These should all be treated as cash outflows for capital budgeting purposes.

> **Working capital**   The excess of current assets over current liabilities.

TYPICAL CASH INFLOWS   On the cash inflow side, a project will normally either increase revenues or reduce costs. Either way, the amount involved should be treated as a cash inflow for capital budgeting purposes. (In regard to this point, notice that so far as cash flows are concerned, a *reduction in costs is equivalent to an increase in revenues*.) Cash inflows are also frequently realized from salvage of equipment when a project is terminated. In addition, upon termination of a project, any working capital that was tied up in the project can be released for use elsewhere and should be treated as a cash inflow. Working capital is released, for example, when a company sells off its inventory or collects its receivables. (If the released working capital is not shown as a cash inflow at the termination of a project, then the project will go on being charged for the use of the funds forever!)

In summary, the following types of cash flows are common in business investment projects:

Cash outflows:

Initial investment (including installation costs).

Increased working capital needs.

Repairs and maintenance.

Incremental operating costs.

Cash inflows:

Incremental revenues.

Reduction in costs.

Salvage value.

Release of working capital.

Recovery of the Original Investment

When computing the present value of a project, depreciation is not deducted for two reasons.

Exhibit 14–2

Carver Dental Clinic—Net Present Value Analysis of X-Ray Attachment

Initial cost				$3,170
Life of the project (years)				4
Annual net cash inflow				$1,000
Salvage value				–0–
Required rate of return				10%

Item	Year(s)	Amount of Cash Flow	10% Factor	Present Value of Cash Flows
Annual net cash inflow	1–4	$ 1,000	3.170*	$ 3,170
Initial investment	Now	(3,170)	1.000	(3,170)
Net present value				$ –0–

*From Table 14C–4 in Appendix 14C.

First, depreciation is not a current cash outflow.[2] As discussed above, discounted cash flow methods of making capital budgeting decisions focus on *cash flows.* Although depreciation is a vital concept in computing net income for financial statements, it is not relevant in an analytical framework that focuses on cash flows.

A second reason for not deducting depreciation is that discounted cash flow methods *automatically* provide for return of the original investment, thereby making a deduction for depreciation unnecessary. To demonstrate this point, let us assume the following data:

Example B

Carver Dental Clinic is considering the purchase of an attachment for its X-ray machine that will cost $3,170. The attachment will be usable for four years, after which time it will have no salvage value. It will increase net cash inflows by $1,000 per year in the X-ray department. The clinic's board of directors has instructed that no investments are to be made unless they have an annual return of at least 10%.

A present value analysis of the desirability of purchasing the X-ray attachment is presented in Exhibit 14–2. Notice that the attachment promises exactly a 10% return on the original investment, since the net present value is zero at a 10% discount rate.

Each annual $1,000 cash inflow arising from use of the attachment is made up of two parts. One part represents a recovery of a portion of the original $3,170 paid for the attachment, and the other part represents a return *on* this investment. The breakdown of each year's $1,000 cash inflow between recover *of* investment and return *on* investment is shown in Exhibit 14–3.

The first year's $1,000 cash inflow consists of a $317 interest return (10%) *on* the $3,170 original investment, plus a $683 return *of* that investment. Since the amount of the unrecovered investment decreases over the four years, the dollar amount of the interest return also decreases. By the end of the fourth year, all $3,170 of the original investment has been recovered.

Simplifying Assumptions

In working with discounted cash flows, at least two simplifying assumptions are usually made.

The first assumption is that all cash flows other than the initial investment occur at the end of a period. This is somewhat unrealistic in that cash flows typically occur

---

2. Although depreciation itself is not a cash outflow, it does have an effect on cash outflows for income taxes. We shall take a look at this effect in the following chapter when we discuss the impact of income taxes on capital budgeting.

Exhibit 14–3   Carver Dental Clinic—Breakdown of Annual Cash Inflows

Year	(1) Investment Outstanding during the Year	(2) Cash Inflow	(3) Return on Investment (1) × 10%	(4) Recovery of Investment during the Year (2) — (3)	(5) Unrecovered Investment at the End of the Year (1) — (4)
1	$3,170	$1,000	$317	$ 683	$2,487
2	2,487	1,000	249	751	1,736
3	1,736	1,000	173	827	909
4	909	1,000	91	909	–0–
Total investment recovered				$3,170	

somewhat uniformly *throughout* a period. The purpose of this assumption is just to simplify computations.

The second assumption is that all cash flows generated by an investment project are immediately reinvested. It is further assumed that the reinvested funds will yield a rate of return equal to the discount rate. Unless these conditions are met, the return computed for the project will not be accurate. To illustrate, we used a discount rate of 10% for the Carver Dental Clinic in Exhibit 14–2. Unless the funds released each period are immediately reinvested at a 10% return, the net present value computed for the X-ray attachment will be misstated.

Choosing a Discount Rate

To use the net present value method, we must choose some rate of return for discounting cash flows to their present value. In Example A we used a 20% rate of return, and in Example B we used a 10% rate of return. These rates were chosen somewhat arbitrarily simply for the sake of illustration.

Cost of capital   The overall cost to an organization of obtaining investment funds, including the cost of both debt sources and equity sources. (Same as *hurdle rate, cutoff rate,* and *required rate of return*.)

The firm's *cost of capital* is usually regarded as the most appropriate choice for the discount rate. The **cost of capital** is the average rate of return the company must pay to its long-term creditors and shareholders for the use of their funds. The mechanics involved in cost of capital computations are covered in finance texts and will not be considered here. The cost of capital is known by various names. It is sometimes called the hurdle rate, the cutoff rate, or the required rate of return.

Most finance specialists would agree that a before-tax cost of capital of 16–20% would be typical for an average industrial corporation. The appropriate after-tax figure would depend on the corporation's tax circumstances, but it would probably average around 10–12%. Among the top Canadian wealth producers, this cost of capital is comparatively high. For example, Barrick Gold Corp's 16.6% cost of capital, and Placer Dome Inc's 17.2% well outpace the 11% average cost of 300 ranked Canadian companies.[3]

An Extended Example of the Net Present Value Method

To conclude our discussion of the net present value method, we present below an extended example of how it is used in analyzing an investment proposal. This example will also help to tie together (and to reinforce) many of the ideas developed thus far.

---

3. "The Financial Post MVA List," *The Financial Post,* June 22/24, 1996, pp. 43–47.

Exhibit 14–4   The Net Present Value Method—An Extended Example

Sales revenues			$200,000
Less cost of goods sold			125,000
Less out-of-pocket costs for salaries, advertising, etc.			35,000
Annual net cash inflows			$ 40,000

Item	Year(s)	Amount of Cash Flows	20% Factor	Present Value of Cash Flows
Purchase of equipment	Now	$ (60,000)	1.000	$ (60,000)
Working capital needed	Now	(100,000)	1.000	(100,000)
Overhaul of equipment	4	(5,000)	0.482*	(2,410)
Annual net cash inflows from sales of the product line	1–5	40,000	2.991†	119,640
Salvage value of the equipment	5	10,000	0.402*	4,020
Working capital released	5	100,000	0.402*	40,200
Net present value				$ 1,450

*From Table 14C–3 in Appendix 14C.

†From Table 14C–4 in Appendix 14C.

Example C

Under a special licensing arrangement, Swinyard Company has an opportunity to market a new product in western Canada for a five-year period. The product would be purchased from the manufacturer, with Swinyard Company responsible for all costs of promotion and distribution. The licensing arrangement could be renewed at the end of the five-year period at the option of the manufacturer. After careful study, Swinyard Company has estimated that the following costs and revenues would be associated with the new product:

Cost of equipment needed	$ 60,000
Working capital needed	100,000
Overhaul of the equipment in four years	5,000
Salvage value of the equipment in five years	10,000
Annual revenues and costs:	
Sales revenues	200,000
Cost of goods sold	125,000
Out-of-pocket operating costs (for salaries, advertising, and other direct costs)	35,000

At the end of the five-year period, the working capital would be released for investment elsewhere if the manufacturer decided not to renew the licensing arrangement. Swinyard Company's discount rate and cost of capital is 20%. Would you recommend that the new product be introduced?

This example involves a variety of cash inflows and cash outflows. The solution is given in Exhibit 14–4.

Notice particularly how the working capital is handled in this exhibit. It is counted as a cash outflow at the beginning of the project and as a cash inflow when it is released at the end of the project. Also notice how the sales revenues, cost of goods sold, and out-of-pocket costs are handled. **Out-of-pocket costs** are actual cash outlays for salaries, advertising, and other operating expenses. Depreciation would not be an out-of-pocket cost, since it involves no current cash outlay.

Since the overall net present value is positive, the new product should be added assuming the company has no better use for the investment funds.

Out-of-pocket costs
Actual cash outlays for salaries, advertising, repairs, and similar costs.

Discounted Cash Flows—The Internal Rate of Return Method

Internal rate of return
The discount rate at which the net present value of an investment project is zero; thus, the internal rate of return represents the interest yield promised by a project over its useful life. This term is synonymous with *time-adjusted rate of return.*

Time-adjusted rate of return   Same as *internal rate of return.*

Yield   A term synonymous with *internal rate of return* and *time-adjusted rate of return.*

The **internal rate of return** (or **time-adjusted rate of return**) can be defined as the interest yield promised by an investment project over its useful life. It is sometimes referred to simply as the **yield** on a project. The internal rate of return is computed by finding the discount rate that equates the present value of a project's cash outflows with the present value of its cash inflows. In other words, the internal rate of return is that discount rate that will cause the net present value of a project to be equal to zero.

The Internal Rate of Return Method Illustrated

To illustrate the internal rate of return method, let us assume the following data:

Example D

Glendale School District is considering the purchase of a large tractor-pulled lawn mower. At present, the lawn is mowed using a small hand-pushed gas mower. The large, tractor-pulled mower will cost $16,950 and will have a useful life of 10 years. It will have only a negligible scrap value, which can be ignored. The tractor-pulled mower would do the job much more quickly than the old mower and would result in a labour savings of $3,000 per year.

To compute the internal rate of return promised by the new mower, we must find the discount rate that will cause the net present value of the project to be zero. How do we do this? The simplest and most direct approach *when the net cash inflow is the same every year* is to divide the investment in the project by the expected net annual cash inflow. This computation will yield a factor from which the internal rate of return can be determined. The formula is as follows:

$$\text{Factor of the internal rate of return} = \frac{\text{Investment required}}{\text{Net annual cash inflow}} \qquad (1)$$

The factor derived from formula (1) is then located in the present value tables to see what rate of return it represents. Using formula (1) and the data for Glendale School District's proposed project, we get:

$$\frac{\text{Investment required}}{\text{Net annual cash inflow}} = \frac{\$16,950}{\$3,000} = 5.650$$

Thus, the discount factor that will equate a series of $3,000 cash inflows with a present investment of $16,950 is 5.650. Now we need to find this factor in Table 14C–4 in Appendix 14C to see what rate of return it represents. We should use the 10-period line in Table 14C–4 since the cash flows for the project continue for 10 years. If we scan along the 10-period line, we find that a factor of 5.650 represents a 12% rate of return. Therefore, the internal rate of return promised by the mower project is 12%. We can verify this by computing the project's net present value using a 12% discount rate. This computation is made in Exhibit 14–5.

Notice from Exhibit 14–5 that using a 12% discount rate equates the present value of the annual cash inflows with the present value of the investment required in the project, leaving a zero net present value. The 12% rate therefore represents the internal rate of return promised by the project.

Salvage Value and Other Cash Flows

The technique just demonstrated works very well if a project's cash flows are identical every year. But what if they are not? For example, what if a project will have some salvage value at the end of its life in addition to the annual cash inflows? Under these

Exhibit 14–5

Evaluation of the Mower
Purchase Using a 12%
Discount Rate

Initial cost	$16,950
Life of the project (years)	10
Annual cost savings	$ 3,000
Salvage value	–0–

Item	Year(s)	Amount of Cash Flow	12% Factor	Present Value of Cash Flows
Annual cost savings	1–10	$ 3,000	5.650*	$ 16,950
Initial investment	Now	(16,950)	1.000	(16,950)
Net present value				$ –0–

*From Table 14C–4 in Appendix 14C.

circumstances, a trial-and-error process is necessary to find the rate of return that will equate the cash inflows with the cash outflows. The trial-and-error process can be carried out by hand, or it can be carried out by means of computer software programs such as spreadsheets that perform the necessary computations in seconds. In short, erratic or uneven cash flows should not prevent a manager from determining a project's internal rate of return.

The Process of Interpolation

Interpolation is used to find rates of return that do not appear in published interest tables. Interest tables are usually printed in terms of whole percentages (10%, 12%, and so forth), whereas projects often have fractional rates of return. To illustrate the process of interpolation, assume the following data:

Investment required	$6,000
Annual cost savings	1,500
Life of the project	10 years

What is the internal rate of return promised by this project? Using formula (1), the appropriate factor is 4.000:

$$\frac{\text{Investment required}}{\text{Net annual cash inflow}} = \frac{\$6,000}{\$1,500} = 4.000$$

Looking at Table 14C–4 in Appendix 14C and scanning along the 10-period line, we find that a factor of 4.000 represents a rate of return somewhere between 20% and 22%. To find the rate we are after, we must interpolate, as follows:

	Present Value Factors	
20% factor	4.192	4.192
True factor	4.000	
22% factor		3.923
Difference	0.192	0.269

$$\text{Internal rate of return} = 20\% + \left(\frac{0.192}{0.269} \times 2\%\right)$$

$$\text{Internal rate of return} = 21.4\%$$

Using the Internal Rate of Return

Once the internal rate of return has been computed, what does the manager do with the information? The internal rate of return is compared to the company's *required rate of*

Required rate of return
The minimum rate of return that an investment project must yield to be acceptable.

return. The **required rate of return** is the minimum rate of return that an investment project must yield to be acceptable. If the internal rate of return is *equal* to or *greater* than the required rate of return, then the project is acceptable. If it is *less* than the required rate of return, then the project is rejected. Quite often, the company's cost of capital is used as the required rate of return. The reasoning is that if a project cannot provide a rate of return at least as great as the cost of the funds invested in it, then it is not profitable.

In the case of the Glendale School District example used earlier, let us assume that the district has set a minimum required rate of return of 15% on all projects. Since the large mower promises a rate of return of only 12%, it does not clear this hurdle and would therefore be rejected as a project.

The Cost of Capital as a Screening Tool

Objective 3

Explain how the cost of capital is used as a screening tool.

As we have seen in preceding examples, the cost of capital often operates as a *screening* device, helping the manager screen out undesirable investment projects. This screening is accomplished in different ways, depending on whether the company is using the internal rate of return method or the net present value method in its capital budgeting analysis.

When the internal rate of return method is used, the cost of capital is used as the *hurdle rate* that a project must clear for acceptance. If the internal rate of return of a project is not great enough to clear the cost of capital hurdle, then the project is ordinarily rejected. We saw the application of this idea in the Glendale School District example, where the hurdle rate was set at 15%.

When the net present value method is used, the cost of capital is the *discount rate* used to compute the net present value of a proposed project. Any project yielding a negative net present value is rejected unless other factors are significant enough to require its acceptance. (This point is discussed further in a following section, Investments in Automated Equipment.)

The use of the cost of capital as a screening tool is summarized in Exhibit 14–6.

Comparison of the Net Present Value and the Internal Rate of Return Methods

The net present value method has several important advantages over the internal rate of return method.

Exhibit 14–6
Capital Budgeting
Screening Decisions

The cost of capital as a screening tool

The net present value method → The cost of capital is used as the discount rate when computing the net present value of a project. Any project with a negative net present value is rejected unless other factors dictate its acceptance.

The internal rate of return method → The cost of capital is *compared* to the internal rate of return promised by a project. Any project whose internal rate of return is less than the cost of capital is rejected unless other factors dictate its acceptance.

First, the net present value method is often simpler to use. As mentioned earlier, the internal rate of return method may require hunting for the discount rate that results in a net present value of zero. This can be a very laborious trial-and-error process, although it can be automated to some degree using a computer spreadsheet.

Second, a key assumption made by the internal rate of return method is questionable. Both methods assume that cash flows generated by a project during its useful life are immediately reinvested elsewhere. However, the two methods make different assumptions concerning the rate of return that is earned on those cash flows. The net present value method assumes the rate of return is the discount rate, whereas the internal rate of return method assumes the rate of return is the internal rate of return on the project. Specifically, if the internal rate of return of the project is high, this assumption may not be realistic. It is generally more realistic to assume that cash inflows can be reinvested at a rate of return equal to the discount rate—particularly if the discount rate is the company's cost of capital or an opportunity rate of return. For example, if the discount rate is the company's cost of capital, this rate of return can be actually realized by paying off the company's creditors and buying back the company's shares with cash flows from the project. In short, when the net present value method and the internal rate of return method do not agree concerning the attractiveness of a project, it is best to go with the net present value method. Of the two methods, it makes the more realistic assumption about the rate of return that can be earned on cash flows from the project.

Expanding the Net Present Value Method

Objective 4

Prepare a net present value analysis of two competing investment projects using either the incremental-cost approach or the total-cost approach.

So far all of our examples have involved only a single investment alternative. We will now expand the net present value method to include two alternatives. In addition, we will integrate the concept of relevant costs into the discounted cash flow analysis.

The net present value method can be used to compare competing investment projects in two ways. One is the *total-cost approach,* and the other is the *incremental-cost approach*. Each approach is illustrated below.

The Total-Cost Approach

The total-cost approach is the most flexible method of making a net present value analysis of competing projects. To illustrate the mechanics of the approach, let us assume the following data:

Example E

Harper Ferry Company provides a ferry service across the Halifax Harbour. One of its ferryboats is in poor condition. This ferry can be renovated at an immediate cost of $20,000. Further repairs and an overhaul of the motor will be needed five years from now at a cost of $8,000. In all, the ferry will be usable for 10 years if this work is done. At the end of 10 years, the ferry will have to be scrapped at a salvage value of approximately $6,000. The scrap value of the ferry right now is $7,000. It will cost $30,000 each year to operate the ferry, and revenues will total $40,000 annually.

As an alternative, Harper Ferry Company can purchase a new ferryboat at a cost of $36,000. The new ferry will have a life of 10 years, but it will require some repairs at the end of 5 years. It is estimated that these repairs will amount to $3,000. At the end of 10 years, it is estimated that the ferry will have a scrap value of $6,000. It will cost $21,000 each year to operate the ferry, and revenues will total $40,000 annually.

Harper Ferry Company requires a return of at least 18% before taxes on all investment projects.

Should the company purchase the new ferry or renovate the old ferry? Exhibit 14–7 gives the solution using the total-cost approach.

Two points should be noted from the exhibit. First, observe that *all* cash inflows and *all* cash outflows are included in the solution under each alternative. No effort has been made to isolate those cash flows that are relevant to the decision and those that are not relevant. The inclusion of all cash flows associated with each alternative gives the approach its name—the *total-cost* approach.

Exhibit 14–9   The Total-Cost Approach (Least-Cost Decision)

Item	Year(s)	Amount of Cash Flows	10% Factor*	Present Value of Cash Flows
Buy the new machine:				
Initial investment	Now	$(25,000)	1.000	$(25,000)†
Salvage of the old machine	Now	3,000	1.000	3,000†
Annual cash operating costs	1–6	(9,000)	4.355	(39,195)
Salvage of the new machine	6	5,000	0.564	2,820
Present value of net cash outflows				(58,375)
Keep the old machine:				
Overhaul needed now	Now	$ (4,000)	1.000	$ (4,000)
Annual cash operating costs	1–6	(15,000)	4.355	(65,325)
Present value of net cash outflows				(69,325)
Net present value in favour of buying the new machine				$ 10,950

*All factors are from Tables 14C–3 and 14C–4 in Appendix 14C.

†These two items could be netted into a single $22,500 incremental-cost figure ($25,000 − $3,000 = $22,000).

Exhibit 14–10   The Incremental-Cost Approach (Least-Cost Decision)

Item	Year(s)	Amount of Cash Flows	10% Factor*	Present Value of Cash Flows
Incremental investment required to purchase the new machine	Now	$(21,000)	1.000	$(21,000)†
Salvage of the old machine	Now	3,000	1.000	3,000†
Savings in annual cash operating costs	1–6	6,000	4.355	26,130
Difference in salvage value in six years	6	5,000	0.564	2,820
Net present value in favour of buying the new machine				$ 10,950

*All factors are from Tables 14C–3 and 14C–4 in Appendix 14C.

†These two items could be netted into a single $18,000 incremental-cost figure ($21,000 − $3,000 = $18,000).

using the incremental-cost approach is presented in Exhibit 14–10. As before, the data in this exhibit represent the differences between the alternatives as shown under the total-cost approach.

Capital Budgeting and Nonprofit Organizations

Capital budgeting concepts can be applied in all types of organizations. Note, for example, the different types of organizations used in the examples in this chapter. These organizations include a dental clinic, a company working under a licensing agreement, a school district, a company operating a ferryboat service, and a manufacturing company. The diversity of these examples shows the range and power of discounted cash flow methods.

One problem faced by *nonprofit* organizations in capital budgeting is determining the proper discount rate. Some nonprofit organizations use the rate of interest paid on special bond issues (such as an issue for street improvements or an issue to build a school) as their discount rate; others use the rate of interest that could be earned by placing money in an endowment fund rather than spending it on capital improvements; and still others use discount rates that are set somewhat arbitrarily by governing boards.

The greatest danger lies in using a discount rate that is too low. Most government agencies, for example, at one time used the interest rate on government bonds as their discount rate. It is now recognized that this rate is too low and has resulted in the acceptance of many projects that should not have been undertaken.[6] The problem has not been resolved in Canada but in the United States, the Office of Management and Budget has specified that federal government units must use a discount rate of at least 10% on all projects.[7] For nonprofit units such as schools and hospitals, it is generally recommended that the discount rate should "approximate the average rate of return on private sector investments."[8]

Investments in Automated Equipment

Objective 5

Make a capital budgeting analysis involving automated equipment.

Future cash flows are often uncertain or difficult to estimate. Investments in automated equipment provide a good example. They tend to be large, and their benefits are often indirect and intangible and therefore hard to quantify.

The cost involved in automating a process is much greater than the cost of purchasing conventional equipment. Single pieces of automated equipment, such as a robot or computerized numerically controlled machine, can cost $1 million or more. A flexible manufacturing system, involving one or more cells, can cost up to $50 million. Even more important, the front-end investment in machinery often constitutes less than half the total cost of automating. The nonhardware costs such as engineering, software development, and implementation of the system can equal or exceed the cost of the equipment itself. Clearly, it is important to realistically estimate such costs before embarking on an automation project.

Focus on Current Practice

Automation can be applied to nonmanufacturing business functions just as successfully as to manufacturing operations. One large Canadian company for example has achieved the following benefits from reengineering and automating its financial function:

- By integrating and automating its processes, the company will eliminate manual rekeying of data, reduce errors, and enhance control through greater data integrity and more timely delivery of financial reports.
- It will introduce new management controls and improve existing controls such as the reporting of daily money market positions.
- As embodied in the new corporate culture, the company will ensure that staff are empowered and gain accountability for tasks.

---

6. See *Federal Capital Budgeting: A Collection of Haphazard Practices*, GAO, P.O. Box 6015, Gaithersburg, MD., PAD-81-19, February 26, 1981
7. Office of Management and Budget Circular No. A-94, March 1972. The U.S. Postal Service is exempted from the 10% rate as are all water resource projects and all lease or buy decisions.
8. Robert N. Anthony and David W. Young, *Management Control in Nonprofit Organizations,* 5th ed. (Homewood, Ill.: Richard D. Irwin, Inc., 1994), p. 445.

- Business units will receive financial market and portfolio information electronically in a timely, relevant fashion, thus improving decision making.
- Integrated data bases will allow for financial risk management and enable the treasury function to integrate financial accounting and management reporting.
- Non-value-added activities will be eliminated, outsourced or transferred to other business units.

- The treasury function will cut total costs by about 55% and reduce its staff by 65%.

Despite encountering difficulties such as turf battles over ownership of processes and financial systems and resistance from employees concerned about their jobs, the company completed the first phase of the project on time and within budget.[9] ∎

Benefits from Automation

The benefits of automation roughly fall into two classes—tangible benefits and intangible benefits.

The tangible benefits are much easier to identify and measure than the intangible benefits. The tangible benefits of automation usually include decreased labour costs and a reduction in defective output. The reduction in defective output results in fewer inspections, and less scrap, waste, and rework. It can also result in less warranty work. General Electric reports, for example, that automating its dishwasher manufacturing plant resulted in a 50% reduction in its service call rate.

The intangible benefits of automated systems generally result from their greater speed, consistency, reliability, and flexibility. These factors permit greater throughput and a greater variety of products, and they enhance product quality. In turn, the greater throughput, variety of products, and higher quality should lead to greater sales and profits, although the precise amount of the increase is very difficult to forecast. Automated processes also allow a company to reduce its inventories, since the company can more quickly respond to shifts in customer demand.

Finally, some managers argue that automation is necessary as a matter of self-preservation. When a company's competition is automating, the company faces the prospect of a loss in market share from attempting to make do with technologically obsolete products and operations. And if a company does not maintain its technical edge, it will lose the ability to catch up with the competition later on. Companies that hold back and do not automate may lose their ability to recognize and then implement the key elements of new technology that provide competitive advantage.

Note that the tangible benefits above represent potential *cost savings,* whereas the intangible benefits represent potential *revenue enhancements.* Generally, it is easier to measure the amount of cost savings associated with an investment project, and that's why items such as reduced direct labour cost always show up in a capital budgeting analysis. But it is harder to measure the impact of a potential revenue enhancement such as greater flexibility or faster market response. As a result, managers may overlook such items when evaluating the benefits from automated equipment. The intangible benefits must be explicitly considered, however, or faulty decisions will follow.

---

9. Adapted from a summary prepared for Industry Canada by Whebco International. "Re-engineering the Financial Function," *CMA Magazine,* October 1995, published by The Society of Management Accountants of Canada.

Focus on Current Practice

The effects of incorporating lost sales in automation decisions can be dramatic. United Architects, a midsized architectural firm, was considering an investment in a computer-aided design and drafting (CADD) system that would produce appealing three-dimensional perspectives to show to clients. The CADD system the firm was considering cost nearly $600,000 and had annual operating costs in the neighbourhood of $100,000. When only the cost savings over the existing means of producing such drawings were considered, the CADD system appeared to be financially unattractive. It had a negative net present value of several hundred thousand dollars. However, professionals at the firm pointed out that several key contracts had been recently lost because competitors had CADD equipment. The drawings produced on competitors' CADD systems looked much more impressive and professional to clients than the drawings produced with United Architects' old equipment. When the estimated lost contribution margins on such projects were included in the cash flow analysis, the project showed a positive net present value in excess of $600,000. Management decided to make the investment.[10] ■

Decision Framework for Intangible Benefits

A fairly simple procedure can be followed when the intangible benefits are uncertain and significant. Suppose, for example, that a company with a 16% cost of capital is considering purchasing automated equipment that would have a 15-year useful life. Also suppose that a discounted cash flow analysis of just the tangible costs and benefits shows a negative net present value of $223,000. Clearly, if the intangible benefits are large enough, they could turn this negative net present value into a positive net present value. In this case, the amount of additional cash flow per year from the intangible benefits that would be needed to make the project financially attractive can be computed as follows:

Net present value (negative) . . . . $(223,000)
Factor for an annuity of 16%
   for 15 periods (from Table 14C–4
   in Appendix 14C) 5.575

$$\frac{\text{Net present value, \$(223,000)}}{\text{Present value factor, 5.575}} = \$40,000$$

Thus, if intangible benefits such as greater flexibility, higher quality of output, and avoidance of capital decay are worth at least $40,000 a year to the company, then the automated equipment should be purchased. If, in the judgment of management, these intangible benefits are *not* worth $40,000 a year, then no purchase should be made.[11]

This technique can be used in other situations in which the future benefits of a current investment are uncertain or intangible. For example, this technique can be used to assess an investment in research on a new type of drug whose market potential is highly uncertain.

---

10. John Y. Lee, "The Service Sector: Investing in New Technology to Stay Alive," *Management Accounting* (June 1991), pp. 45–48.
11. Robert E. Bennett and James A. Hendricks suggest such a procedure in "Justifying the Acquisition of Automated Equipment," *Management Accounting* 69 (July 1987), p. 46.

Preference Decisions—The Ranking of Investment Projects

Objective 6

Rank investment projects in order of preference using (1) the internal rate of return method and (2) the net present value method with the profitability index.

Recall that when considering investment opportunities, managers must make two types of decisions—screening decisions and preference decisions. Screening decisions pertain to whether or not some proposed investment is acceptable. Preference decisions come *after* screening decisions and attempt to answer the following question: "How do the remaining investment proposals, all of which have been screened and provide an acceptable rate of return, rank in terms of preference? That is, which one(s) would be *best* for the firm to accept?"

Preference decisions are more difficult to make than screening decisions because investment funds are usually limited. This often requires that some (perhaps many) otherwise very profitable investment opportunities must be passed up.

Sometimes preference decisions are called ranking decisions, or rationing decisions, because they ration limited investment funds among many competing alternatives, or there may be many alternatives that must be ranked. Either the internal rate of return method or the net present value method can be used in making preference decisions. However, as discussed earlier, if the two methods are in conflict, it is best to use the net present value method, which is more reliable.

Internal Rate of Return Method

When using the internal rate of return method to rank competing investment projects, the preference rule is: *The higher the internal rate of return, the more desirable the project.* An investment project with an internal rate of return of 18% is preferable to another project that promises a return of only 15%. Internal rate of return is widely used to rank projects.

Net Present Value Method

If the net present value method is used to rank projects, the net present value of one project cannot be compared directly to the net present value of another project unless the investments in the projects are of equal size. For example, assume that a company is considering two competing investments, as shown below:

	Investment	
	A	**B**
Investment required	$(80,000)	$(5,000)
Present value of cash inflows	81,000	6,000
Net present value	$ 1,000	$ 1,000

Each project has a net present value of $1,000, but the projects are not equally desirable. The project requiring an investment of only $5,000 is much more desirable when funds are limited than the project requiring an investment of $80,000. To compare the two projects on a valid basis, the present value of the cash inflows should be divided by the investment required. The result is called the **profitability index**. The formula for the profitability index follows:

Profitability index   The ratio of the present value of a project's cash inflows to the investment required.

$$\text{Profitability index} = \frac{\text{Present value of cash inflows}}{\text{Investment required}} \qquad (2)$$

The profitability indexes for the two investments above would be computed as follows:

	Investment	
	A	**B**
Present value of cash inflows (a)	$81,000	$6,000
Investment required (b)	$80,000	$5,000
Profitability index, (a) ÷ (b)	1.01	1.20

When using the profitability index to rank competing investments projects, the preference rule is: *The higher the profitability index, the more desirable the project.* Applying this rule to the two investments above, investment B should be chosen over investment A.

The profitability index is an application of the techniques for utilizing scarce resources discussed in Chapter 13. In this case, the scarce resource is the limited funds available for investment, and the profitability index is similar to the contribution margin per unit of the scarce resource.

A few details should be clarified with respect to the computation of the profitability index. The "Investment required" refers to any cash outflows that occur at the beginning of the project, reduced by any salvage value recovered from the sale of old equipment. The "Investment required" also includes any investment in working capital that the project may need. Finally, we should note that the "Present value of cash inflows" is net of all *out*flows that occur after the project starts.

Comparing the Preference Rules

The profitability index is conceptually superior to the internal rate of return as a method of making preference decisions. This is because the profitability index will always give the correct signal as to the relative desirability of alternatives, even if the alternatives have different lives and different patterns of earnings. By contrast, if lives are unequal, the internal rate of return method can lead the manager to make incorrect decisions.

Assume the following situation:

Parker Company is considering two investment proposals, only one of which can be accepted. Project A requires an investment of $5,000 and will provide a single cash inflow of $6,000 in one year. Therefore, it promises an internal rate of return of 20%. Project B also requires an investment of $5,000. It will provide cash inflows of $1,360 each year for six years. Its internal rate of return is 16%. Which project should be accepted?

Although project A promises an internal rate of return of 20%, as compared to only 16% for project B, project A is not necessarily preferable over project B. It is preferable *only* if the funds released at the end of the year under project A can be reinvested at a high rate of return in some *other* project for the five remaining years. Otherwise, project B, which promises a return of 16% over the *entire* six years, is more desirable.

Let us assume that the company in the example above has an after-tax cost of capital of 12%. The net present value method, with the profitability index, would rank the two proposals as follows:

	Project	
	A	**B**
Present value of cash inflows:		
$6,000 received at the end of one year at 12% factor (factor of 0.893)	$5,358 (a)	
$1,360 received at the end of each year for six years at 12% (factor of 4.111)		$5,591 (a)
Investment required	$5,000 (b)	$5,000 (b)
Profitability index, (a) ÷ (b)	1.07	1.12

The profitability index indicates that project B is more desirable than project A. This is in fact the case if the funds released from project A at the end of one year can be reinvested at only 12% (the cost of capital). Although the computations will not be shown here, in order for project A to be more desirable than project B, the funds released from project A would have to be reinvested at a rate of return *greater* than 14% for the remaining five years.

In short, the internal rate of return method of ranking tends to favour short-term, high-yield projects, whereas the net present value method of ranking (using the profitability index) tends to favour longer-term projects.

The internal rate of return method is problematic. It assumes that funds can be reinvested at a particular project's yield. The problem becomes apparent in the context of MacInnis Company of Kitchener, Ontario. If MacInnis has projects in Cambridge, Guelph, and Waterloo that have IRRs of 20%, 15%, and 10% respectively, it is nonsense to differentiate among the cash flows and assume that a dollar returned from the Waterloo project will earn less than a dollar returned from the Cambridge project. Obviously, a dollar is a dollar regardless of which project it comes from. The net present value method does not suffer from this flaw but assumes that funds can be reinvested at the firm's cost of capital. Because the net present value is conceptually superior, it should be used in ranking projects that are mutually exclusive. However, in choosing among projects that have the same net present values, the IRR should be used to rank them. Projects should then be chosen based on the highest internal rates of return.

Although the NPV method is conceptually superior to the IRR, there are practical reasons for decision makers to choose the latter. Managers typically make project investment decisions within a four- or five-year planning horizon. Faced with this time constraint, projects will be ranked according to their terminal values at the end of the planning horizon. Estimated cash flows after the planning period may be perceived by managers to be too uncertain to rely upon. Projects with larger IRR values will have cash flow patterns with higher short-term terminal values. In summary, although there are problems with the IRR method over the entire life of a project, it will accurately evaluate projects within the planning horizon.

Focus on Current Practice

Several different techniques can be used to take into account uncertainties about future cash flows in capital budgeting. The uncertainties are particularly apparent in the drug business where it costs an average of $359 million and 10 years to bring a new drug through the governmental approval process and to market. And once on the market, 7 out of 10 products fail to return the company's cost of capital.

Merck & Co. manages the financial risks and uncertainties of drug research using a Research Planning Model they have developed. The model, which produces net present value estimates and other key statistics, is based on a wide range of scientific and financial variables—most of which are uncertain. For example, the future selling price of any drug resulting from current research is usually highly uncertain, but managers at Merck & Co. can at least specify a range within which the selling price is likely to fall. The computer is used to draw a value at random, within the permissible range, for each of the variables in the model. The model then computes a net present value. This process is repeated many times, and each time a new value of each of the variables is drawn at random. In this way, Merck is able to produce a probability distribution for the net present value. This can be used, for example, to estimate the probability that the project's net present value will exceed a certain level. "What are the payoffs of all this sophistication? In short, better decisions."[12] ■

12. Nancy A. Nichols, "Scientific Management at Merck: An Interview with CFO Judy Lewent," *Harvard Business Review* (January–February 1994), pp. 89–99.

Other Approaches to Capital Budgeting Decisions

Discounted cash flow methods have gained widespread acceptance as decision-making tools. Other methods of making capital budgeting decisions are also used, however, and are preferred by some managers. In this section, we discuss two such methods known as *payback* and *simple rate of return*. Both methods have been in use for a hundred years or more, but they are now declining in popularity as primary tools for project evaluation.

The Payback Method

Objective 7

Determine the payback period for an investment.

The payback method centres on a span of time known as the *payback period*. The **payback period** can be defined as the length of time that it takes for a project to recoup its initial cost out of the cash receipts that it generates. This period is sometimes referred to as "the time that it takes for an investment to pay for itself." The basic premise of the payback method is that the more quickly the cost of an investment can be recovered, the more desirable is the investment.

Payback period The length of time that it takes for a project to recover its initial cost out of the cash receipts that it generates.

The payback period is expressed in years. *When the net annual cash inflow is the same every year,* the following formula can be used to compute the payback period:

$$\text{Payback period} = \frac{\text{Investment required}}{\text{Net annual cash inflow*}} \qquad (3)$$

*If new equipment is replacing old equipment, this becomes incremental net annual cash inflow.

To illustrate the payback method, assume the following data:

Example G

York Company needs a new milling machine. The company is considering two machines: machine A and machine B. Machine A costs $15,000 and will reduce operating costs by $5,000 per year. Machine B costs only $12,000 but will also reduce operating costs by $5,000 per year.

Required Which machine should be purchased according to the payback method?

$$\text{Machine A payback period} = \frac{\$15,000}{\$5,000} = 3.0 \text{ years}$$

$$\text{Machine B payback period} = \frac{\$12,000}{\$5,000} = 2.4 \text{ years}$$

According to the payback calculations, York Company should purchase machine B, since it has a shorter payback period than machine A.

Evaluation of the Payback Method

The payback method is not a true measure of the profitability of an investment. Rather, it simply tells the manager how many years will be required to recover the original investment. Unfortunately, a shorter payback period does not always mean that one investment is more desirable than another.

To illustrate, consider again the two machines used in the example above. Since machine B has a shorter payback period than machine A, it *appears* that machine B is more desirable than machine A. But if we add one more piece of data, this illusion quickly disappears. Machine A has a projected 10-year life, and machine B has a projected 5-year life. It would take two purchases of machine B to provide the same length of service as would be provided by a single purchase of machine A. Under these circumstances, machine A would be a much better investment than machine B, even though machine B has a shorter payback period. Unfortunately, the payback method has no inherent mechanism for highlighting differences in useful life between investments. Such differences can be very important, and relying on payback alone may result in incorrect decisions.

A further criticism of the payback method is that it does not consider the time value of money. A cash inflow to be received several years in the future is weighed equally with a cash inflow to be received right now. To illustrate, assume that for an investment of $8,000 you can purchase either of the two following streams of cash inflows:

Year	0	1	2	3	4	5	6	7	8
Stream 1		–0–	–0–	–0–	$8,000	$2,000	$2,000	$2,000	$2,000
Stream 2		$2,000	$2,000	$2,000	$2,000	$8,000	–0–	–0–	–0–

Which stream of cash inflows would you prefer to receive in return for your $8,000 investment? Each stream has a payback period of 4.0 years. Therefore, if payback alone were relied on in making the decision, you would be forced to say that the streams are equally desirable. However, from the point of view of the time value of money, stream 2 is much more desirable than stream 1.

On the other hand, under certain conditions the payback method can be very useful. For one thing, it can help identify which investment proposals are in the "ballpark." That is, it can be used as a screening tool to help answer the question, "Should I consider this proposal further?" If a proposal doesn't provide a payback within some specified period, then there may be no need to consider it further. In addition, the payback period is often of great importance to new firms that are "cash poor." When a firm is cash poor, a project with a short payback period but a low rate of return might be preferred over another project with a high rate of return but a long payback period. The reason is that the company may simply need a faster return of its cash investment. And finally, the payback method is sometimes used in industries where products become obsolete very rapidly—such as consumer electronics. Since products may last only a year or two, the payback period on investments must be very short.

Focus on Current Practice

Capital budgeting techniques are widely used in large nonprofit organizations. A survey of universities in the United Kingdom revealed that 41% use the net present value method, 23% use the internal rate of return method, 29% use the payback method, and 11% use the accounting rate of return method. (Some universities use more than one method.) Furthermore, the central Funding Council of the United Kingdom requires that the net present value method be used for projects whose lifespans exceed 20 years.[13] ■

An Extended Example of Payback

As shown by formula (3) given earlier, the payback period is computed by dividing the investment in a project by the net annual cash inflows that the project will generate. If new equipment is replacing old equipment, then any salvage to be received on disposal of the old equipment should be deducted from the cost of the new equipment, and only the *incremental* investment should be used in the payback computation. In addition,

---

13. Paul Cooper, "Management Accounting Practices in Universities," *Management Accounting (U.K.)* (February 1996), pp. 28–30.

Exhibit 14–11
Computation of the
Payback Period

Step 1:	*Compute the net annual cash inflow.* Since the net annual cash inflow is not given, it must be computed before the payback period can be determined:	

Net income (given above) $20,000
Add: Noncash deduction for depreciation 10,000
Net annual cash inflow $30,000

Step 2:	*Compute the payback period.* Using the net annual cash inflow figure from above, the payback period can be determined as follows:	

Cost of the new equipment $80,000
Less salvage value of old equipment 5,000
Investment required $75,000

$$\text{Payback period} = \frac{\text{Investment required}}{\text{Net annual cash inflow}}$$

$$= \frac{\$75,000}{\$30,000} = 2.5 \text{ years}$$

any depreciation deducted in arriving at the project's net income must be added back to obtain the project's expected net annual cash inflow. To illustrate, assume the following data:

Example H

Goodtime Fun Centres, Inc., operates many outlets in the eastern provinces. Some of the vending machines in one of its outlets provide very little revenue, so the company is considering removing the machines and installing equipment to dispense soft ice cream. The equipment would cost $80,000 and have an eight-year useful life. Incremental annual revenues and costs associated with the sale of ice cream would be as follows:

Sales	$150,000
Less cost of ingredients	90,000
Contribution margin	60,000
Less fixed expenses:	
Salaries	27,000
Maintenance	3,000
Depreciation	10,000
Total fixed expenses	40,000
Net income	$ 20,000

The vending machines can be sold for a $5,000 scrap value. The company will not purchase equipment unless it has a payback of three years or less. Should the equipment to dispense ice cream be purchased?

An analysis as to whether the proposed equipment meets the company's payback requirements is given in Exhibit 14–11. Several things should be noted from the data in this exhibit. First, notice that depreciation is added back to net income to obtain the net annual cash inflow from the new equipment. As stated earlier in the chapter, depreciation is not a cash outlay; thus, it must be added back to net income in order to adjust net income to a cash basis. Second, notice in the payback computation that the salvage value from the old machines has been deducted from the cost of the new equipment, and that only the incremental investment has been used in computing the payback period.

Since the proposed equipment has a payback period of less than three years, the company's payback requirement has been met.

Focus on Current Practice

Intel Corporation invests a billion to a billion and a half dollars in plants to fabricate computer processor chips such as the Pentium III. But the fab plants can only be used to make state-of-the-art chips for about two years. By that time, the equipment is obsolete and the plant must be converted to making less complicated chips. Under such conditions of rapid obsolescence, the payback method may be the most appropriate way to evaluate investments. If the project does not pay back within a few years, it may never pay back its initial investment.[14] ■

Payback and Uneven Cash Flows

When the cash flows associated with an investment project change from year to year, the simple payback formula that we outlined earlier is no longer usable, and the computations involved in deriving the payback period can be fairly complex. Consider the following data:

Year	Investment	Cash Inflow
1	$4,000	$1,000
2		–0–
3		2,000
4	2,000	1,000
5		500
6		3,000
7		2,000
8		2,000

What is the payback period on this investment? The answer is 5.5 years, but to obtain this figure it is necessary to track the unrecovered investment year by year. The steps involved in this process are shown in Exhibit 14–12. By the middle of the sixth year, sufficient cash inflows will have been realized to recover the entire investment of $6,000 ($4,000 + $2,000).

The Simple Rate of Return Method

Objective 8

Compute the simple rate of return for an investment.

Simple rate of return
The rate of return computed by dividing a project's annual accounting net income by the initial investment required.

The **simple rate of return** method is another capital budgeting technique that does not involve discounted cash flows. The method is also known as the *accounting rate of return, the unadjusted rate of return,* and *the financial statement method.*

Unlike the other capital budgeting methods that we have discussed, the simple rate of return method does not focus on cash flows. Rather, it focuses on accounting net income. The approach is to estimate the revenues that will be generated by a proposed investment and then to deduct from these revenues all of the projected operating expenses associated with the project. This net income figure is then related to the initial investment in the project, as shown in the following formula:

$$\text{Simple rate of return} = \frac{\overbrace{\text{Incremental revenues} - \text{Incremental expenses, including depreciation}}^{\text{Incremental net income}}}{\text{Initial investment}^*} \qquad (4)$$

*The investment should be reduced by any salvage from the sale of old equipment.

---

14. "Pentium at a Glance," *Forbes ASAP,* February 26, 1996, p. 66.

Exhibit 14–12 Payback and Uneven Cash Flows

Year	(1) Beginning Unrecovered Investment	(2) Additional Investment	(3) Total Unrecovered Investment (1) + (2)	(4) Cash Inflow	(5) Ending Unrecovered Investment (3) − (4)
1	$4,000		$4,000	$1,000	$3,000
2	3,000		3,000	–0–	3,000
3	3,000		3,000	2,000	1,000
4	1,000	$2,000	3,000	1,000	2,000
5	2,000		2,000	500	1,500
6	1,500		1,500	3,000	–0–
7	–0–		–0–	2,000	–0–
8	–0–		–0–	2,000	–0–

Or, if a cost reduction project is involved, formula (4) becomes:

$$\text{Simple rate of return} = \frac{\text{Cost savings} - \text{Depreciation on new equipment}}{\text{Initial investment*}} \qquad (5)$$

*The investment should be reduced by any salvage
from the sale of old equipment.

Example I

Brigham Tea, Inc., is a processor of a nontannic acid tea. The company is contemplating purchasing equipment for an additional processing line. The additional processing line would increase revenues by $90,000 per year. Incremental cash operating expenses would be $40,000 per year. The equipment would cost $180,000 and have a nine-year life. No salvage value is projected.

Required
1. Compute the simple rate of return.
2. Compute the internal rate of return and compare it to the simple rate of return.

Solution
1. By applying the formula for the simple rate of return found in equation (4), we can compute the simple rate of return:

$$\text{Simple rate of return} = \frac{\left[\begin{array}{c}\$90,000 \\ \text{Incremental} \\ \text{revenues}\end{array}\right] - \left[\begin{array}{c}\$40,000 \text{ Cash operating expenses} \\ + \$20,000 \text{ Depreciation}\end{array}\right]}{\$180,000 \text{ Initial investment}}$$

$$= \frac{\$30,000}{\$180,000}$$

$$= 16.7\%$$

2. The rate computed in (1) above, however, is far below the internal rate of return of approximately 24%:

$$\text{Factor of the internal rate of return} = \frac{\$180,000}{\$50,000*} = 3.600$$

*$30,000 net income + $20,000 depreciation = $50,000; or the annual cash inflow can be computed as $90,000 increased revenues − $40,000 cash expenses = $50,000.

By scanning across the nine-year line in Table 14C–4 in Appendix 14C, we can see that the internal rate of return is approximately 24%.

Example J

Midwest Farms, Inc., hires people on a part-time basis to sort eggs. The cost of this hand-sorting process is $30,000 per year. The company is investigating the purchase of an egg-sorting machine that would cost $90,000 and have a 15-year useful life. The machine would have negligible salvage value, and it would cost $10,000 per year to operate and maintain. The egg-sorting equipment currently being used could be sold now for a scrap value of $2,500.

Required   Compute the simple rate of return on the new egg-sorting machine.

Solution   A cost reduction project is involved in this situation. By applying the formula for the simple rate of return found in equation (5), we can compute the simple rate of return as follows:

$$\text{Simple rate of return} = \frac{\$20,000^* \text{ Cost savings} - \$6,000^\dagger \text{ Depreciation on new equipment}}{\$90,000 - \$2,500}$$

$$= 16.0\%$$

*$30,000 − $10,000 = $20,000 cost savings.
†$90,000 ÷ 15 years = $6,000 depreciation.

Criticisms of the Simple Rate of Return

The most damaging criticism of the simple rate of return method is that it does not consider the time value of money. A dollar received 10 years from now is viewed as being just as valuable as a dollar received today. Thus, the manager can be misled if the alternatives being considered have different cash flow patterns. For example, assume that project A has a high simple rate of return but yields the bulk of its cash flows many years from now. Another project, B, has a somewhat lower simple rate of return but yields the bulk of its cash flows over the next few years. Project A has a higher simple rate of return than project B; however, project B might in fact be a much better investment if the time value of money were considered.

Focus on Current Practice

A survey of 133 chief executive officers and chief financial officers of large Canadian companies revealed the following key conclusions:

1. Most of the firms used multiple evaluation criteria to assess capital investments.
2. Discounted cash flow methods were employed by more than 75% of respondents to evaluate projects such as expansion—existing operations, expansion—new operations, foreign operations, and leasing. The use of DCF methods, i.e., NPV, IRR, or both, varies from a low of 23.5% for social expenditures to 66% for replacement projects, and to 84.9% for expansion—new operations. It appears, therefore, that the propensity to use DCF techniques increases with the complexity of the decision.
3. Of the DCF techniques, IRR was used more frequently than NPV.
4. The accounting rate of return (ARR) had a usage rate below 20%. More than 50% use the payback method either alone or in conjunction with other techniques to evaluate various capital budgeting projects. Payback is used most frequently with DCF methods.[15] ∎

15. Vijay M. Jog and Ashwani K. Srivastave, *Capital Budgeting Practices in Canada*, School of Business, Carleton University, Ottawa, 1993.

Postappraisal of Investment Projects

Postappraisal
Following up on a project that has been approved to see if expected results are realized.

Postappraisal of an investment project means a follow-up after the project has been approved to see whether or not expected results are actually realized. This is a key part of the capital budgeting process in that it provides management with an opportunity, over time, to see how realistic the proposals are that are being submitted and approved. It also provides an opportunity to reinforce successful projects as needed, to strengthen or perhaps salvage projects that are encountering difficulty, to terminate unsuccessful projects before losses become too great, and to improve the overall quality of future investment proposals.

Monitoring of capital budgeting projects may also help improve the quality of similar feature investment proposals. Care should be exercised, however, when trying to use past experience as a guide to future decisions because assumptions about the business environment may no longer be valid.

To avoid a liquidity crunch, the firm must respond quickly to significant overruns that require unplanned cash outflows. It may be necessary to arrange additional financing or to amend plans.

Focus on Current Practice

One way of applying the postappraisal process is through a process known as Economic Value Creation (EVC). Economic Value Creation is an increasingly popular concept which serves to provide a framework for valuing corporations, business units and the performance of managers. EVC is an entity's net operating profit after tax (NOPAT) minus a charge for its use of capital. In an earlier chapter we referred to this as residual income. Simply written in equation form,

$$EVC = NOPAT - \left[\begin{array}{c}\text{weighted average}\\\text{cost of capital}\end{array} \times \text{capital}\right]$$

Husky Injection Moulding, Imasco, and Domtar in Canada all use the EVC framework. In 1995, The Society of Management Accountants of Canada (SMAC) sponsored a survey of EVC practice in Canada. The survey was mailed to 942 of the top 1,000 Canadian organizations ranked by profits as reported in the July 1994 issue of the *Report on Business* magazine. The survey results indicated:

- EVC is at an early stage of development among Canadian corporations and different industry sectors are in different stages of EVC development.
- EVC has largely achieved the desired objectives of organizations that have adopted it.

- EVC is primarily used at the corporate or division level.
- The key reasons for adopting EVC relate to goal setting, accountability, performance analysis and compensation.
- The primary reasons for not adopting EVC relate to satisfaction with existing measures, low priority, and insufficient knowledge.

The research concluded that EVC concepts are just now being recognized and understood, and that we can expect increasing interest by Canadian organizations in learning more about and adopting EVC frameworks. Three reasons have been postulated to explain why EVC is increasingly being used by Canadian managers:

1. In contrast to the discounted cash flow or the net present value methods which provide a one time expected value of future investments, EVC allows for an annual measurement of actual (not estimated or forecasted) value creation performance.
2. EVC gains and losses track more closely with shareholder wealth than any traditional earnings or bottom line based measure.
3. EVC aligns desired organizational strategies with appropriate performance measurement and compensation procedures.[16] ■

---

16. Vijay Jog and Howard Armitage, "Economic Value Creation: What Every Management Accountant Should Know," *CMA Management Accounting Magazine* (October 1996), pp. 21–24.

Both firms and accounting bodies are placing increasing importance on the postappraisal process. *Management Accounting Guidelines* has a full section devoted to this process: Guideline No. 1—"Post-Appraisal of Capital Expenditure."[17]

The postappraisal should answer a variety of questions: Was the capital budgeting decision consistent with overall corporate strategy? Did the project meet the specifications that were set out in the appropriation request? Were the original specifications realistically and honestly determined? Were any additional expenditures properly authorized? A proper review may be tedious and time-consuming, and special care should be taken in making assertions about cause and effect. It is often difficult to relate particular costs and revenues to a particular project. This is especially true if there are several projects on-line simultaneously and is absolutely true if there is synergy among the projects.[18] A cost/benefit tradeoff is necessary when deciding how many company sources are to be devoted to the postappraisal.

To ensure objectivity, the postappraisal should be performed by an individual or team that has not been directly involved in the actual project. The postappraisal should not be a witch hunt aimed at placing blame, but should be an accountability process aimed at improving control and a learning process that will improve estimates of future projects.

In performing a postappraisal, the same technique should be used as was used in the original approval process. That is, if a project was approved on a basis of a net present value analysis, then the same procedure should be used in performing the postappraisal. However, the data going into the analysis should be *actual data* as observed in the actual operation of the project, rather than estimated data. This affords management with an opportunity to make a side-by-side comparison to see how well the project has worked out. It also helps assure that estimated data received on future proposals will be carefully prepared, since the persons submitting the data know that their estimates will be given careful scrutiny in the postappraisal process. Actual results that are far out of line with original estimates should be carefully reviewed by management, and corrective action taken as necessary. In accordance with the management by exception principle, those managers responsible for the original estimates should be required to provide a full explanation of any major differences between estimated and actual results.

Summary

Investment decisions should take into account the time value of money since a dollar today is more valuable than a dollar received in the future. The net present value and internal rate of return methods both reflect this fact. In the net present value method, future cash flows are discounted to their present value so that they can be compared on a valid basis with current cash outlays. The difference between the present value of the cash inflows and the present value of the cash outflows is called the project's net present value. If the net present value of the project is negative, the project is rejected. The discount rate in the net present value method is usually a minimum required rate of return such as the company's cost of capital.

The internal rate of return is the rate of return that equates the present value of the cash inflows and the present value of the cash outflows, resulting in a zero net present value. If the internal rate of return is less than the company's minimum required rate of return, the project is rejected.

After rejecting projects whose net present values are negative or whose internal rates of return are less than the minimum required rate of return, the company may still have more projects than can be supported with available funds. The remaining projects can be

---

17. The Society of Management Accountants of Canada, *Management Accountants Handbook* (Hamilton, Ont.: 1984).
18. Synergy occurs when the projects working together generate greater revenue than the sum of the revenues of all projects acting independently.

ranked using either the profitability index or their internal rates of return. The profitability index is computed by dividing the present value of the project's future net cash inflows by the required initial investment.

Some companies prefer to use either payback or the simple rate of return to evaluate investment proposals. The payback period is the number of periods that are required to recover the initial investment in the project. The simple rate of return is determined by dividing a project's accounting net income by the initial investment in the project.

After an investment proposal has been approved, a postappraisal should be performed to see whether expected results are actually being realized. This is a key part of the capital budgeting process, since it tends to strengthen the quality of the estimates going into investment proposals and affords management with an early opportunity to recognize any developing problems or opportunities.

Review Problem 1: Basic Present Value Computations

Each of the following situations is independent. Work out your own solution to each situation, and then check it against the solution provided.

Required

1. John has just reached age 58. In 12 years, he plans to retire. Upon retiring, he would like to take an extended vacation, which he expects will cost at least $4,000. What lump-sum amount must he invest now to have the needed $4,000 at the end of 12 years if the rate of return is:
   a. Eight percent?
   b. Twelve percent?

2. The Morgans would like to send their daughter to an expensive music camp at the end of each of the next five years. The camp costs $1,000 a year. What lump-sum amount would have to be invested now to have the $1,000 at the end of each year if the rate of return is:
   a. Eight percent?
   b. Twelve percent?

3. You have just received an inheritance from a relative. You can invest the money and either receive a $20,000 lump-sum amount at the end of 10 years or receive $1,400 at the end of each year for the next 10 years. If your minimum desired rate of return is 12%, which alternative would you prefer?

Solution to Review Problem 1

1. a. The amount that must be invested now would be the present value of the $4,000, using a discount rate of 8%. From Table 14C–3 in Appendix 14C, the factor for a discount rate of 8% for 12 periods is 0.397. Multiplying this discount factor by the $4,000 needed in 12 years will give the amount of the present investment required: $4,000 × 0.397 = $1,588.

   b. We will proceed as we did in (a) above, but this time we will use a discount rate of 12%. From Table 14C–3 in Appendix 14C, the factor for a discount rate of 12% for 12 periods is 0.257. Multiplying this discount factor by the $4,000 needed in 12 years will give the amount of the present investment required: $4,000 × 0.257 = $1,028.

   Notice that as the discount rate (desired rate of return) increases, the present value decreases.

2. This part differs from (1) above in that we are now dealing with an annuity rather than with a single future sum. The amount that must be invested now will be the present value of the $1,000 needed at the end of each year for five years. Since we are dealing with an annuity, or a series of annual cash flows, we must refer to Table 14C–4 in Appendix 14C for the appropriate discount factor.

   a. From Table 14C–4 in Appendix 14C, the discount factor for 8% for five periods is 3.993. Therefore, the amount that must be invested now to have $1,000 available at the end of each year for five years is $1,000 × 3.993 = $3,993.

   b. From Table 14C–4 in Appendix 14C, the discount factor for 12% for five periods is 3.605. Therefore, the amount that must be invested now to have $1,000 available at the end of each year for five years is $1,000 × 3.605 = $3,605.

Again, notice that as the discount rate (desired rate of return) increases, the present value decreases. At a higher rate of return we can invest less than would have been needed if a lower rate of return were being earned.

3. For this part we will need to refer to both Tables 14C–3 and 14C–4 in Appendix 14C. From Table 14C–3, we will need to find the discount factor for 12% for 10 periods, then apply it to the $20,000 lump sum to be received in 10 years. From Table 14C–4, we will need to find the discount factor for 12% for 10 periods, then apply it to the series of $1,400 payments to be received over the 10-year period. Whichever alternative has the higher present value is the one that should be selected.

$$\$20,000 \times 0.322 = \$6,440$$
$$\$1,400 \times 5.650 = \$7,910$$

Thus, you would prefer to receive the $1,400 per year for 10 years rather than the $20,000 lump sum.

Review Problem 2: Comparison of Capital Budgeting Methods

Lamar Company is studying a project that would have an eight-year life and require a $1,600,000 investment in equipment. At the end of eight years, the project would terminate and the equipment would have no salvage value. The project would provide net income each year as follows:

Sales	$3,000,000
Less variable expenses	1,800,000
Contribution margin	1,200,000
Less fixed expenses:	
Advertising, salaries, and other	
fixed out-of-pocket costs $700,000	
Depreciation 200,000	
Total fixed expenses	900,000
Net income	$ 300,000

The company's discount rate is 18%.

Required

1. Compute the net annual cash inflow from the project.
2. Compute the project's net present value. Is the project acceptable?
3. Compute the project's internal rate of return. Interpolate to one decimal place.
4. Compute the project's payback period. If the company requires a maximum payback of three years, is the project acceptable?
5. Compute the project's simple rate of return.

Solution to Review Problem 2

1. The net annual cash inflow can be computed by deducting the cash expenses from sales:

Sales	$3,000,000
Less variable expenses	1,800,000
Contribution margin	1,200,000
Less advertising, salaries, and	
other fixed out-of-pocket costs	700,000
Net annual cash inflow	$ 500,000

Or it can be computed by adding depreciation back to net income:

Net income	$300,000
Add: Noncash deduction for depreciation	200,000
Net annual cash inflow	$500,000

2. The net present value can be computed as follows:

Item	Year(s)	Amount of Cash Flows	18% Factor	Present Value of Cash Flows
Cost of new equipment	Now	$(1,600,000)	1.000	$(1,600,000)
Net annual cash inflow	1–8	500,000	4.078	2,039,000
Net present value				$ 439,000

Yes, the project is acceptable since it has a positive net present value.

3. The formula for computing the factor of the internal rate of return is:

$$\text{Factor of the internal rate of return} = \frac{\text{Investment required}}{\text{Net annual cash inflow}}$$

$$= \frac{\$1,600,000}{\$500,000} = 3.200$$

Looking in Table 14C–4 in Appendix 14C at the end of the chapter and scanning along the 8-period line, we find that a factor of 3.200 represents a rate of return somewhere between 26% and 28%. To find the rate we are after, we must interpolate as follows:

26% factor	3.241	3.241
True factor	3.200	
28% factor		3.076
Difference	0.041	0.165

$$\text{Internal rate of return} = 26\% + \left(\frac{0.041}{0.165} \times 2\%\right)$$

$$= 26.5\%$$

4. The formula for the payback period is:

$$\text{Payback period} = \frac{\text{Investment required}}{\text{Net annual cash inflow}}$$

$$= \frac{\$1,600,000}{\$500,000}$$

$$= 3.2 \text{ years}$$

No, the project is not acceptable when measured by the payback method. The 3.2 years payback period is greater than the maximum 3 years set by the company.

5. The formula for the simple rate of return is:

$$\text{Simple rate of return} = \frac{\overset{\text{Incremental}}{\text{revenues}} - \overset{\text{Incremental expenses,}}{\text{including depreciation}} = \overset{\text{Net}}{\text{income}}}{\text{Initial investment}}$$

$$= \frac{\$300,000}{\$1,600,000}$$

$$= 18.75\%$$

Appendix 14A: The Concept of Present Value

Objective 9

Explain the concept of present value, and make present value computations with and without present value tables.

The point was made in the main body of the chapter that a manager would rather receive a dollar today than a year from now. There are two reasons why this is true. First, a dollar received today is more valuable than a dollar received a year from now. The dollar received today can be invested immediately, and by the end of the year it will have earned some return, making the total amount in hand at the end of the year *greater* than the investment started with. The person receiving the dollar a year from now will simply have a dollar in hand at that time.

Second, the future involves uncertainty. The longer people have to wait to receive a dollar, the more uncertain it becomes that they will ever get the dollar that they seek. As time passes, conditions change. The changes may be such as to make future payments of the dollar impossible.

Since money has a time value, the manager needs a method of determining whether a cash outlay made now in an investment project can be justified in terms of expected receipts from the project in future years. That is, the manager must have a means of expressing future receipts in present dollar terms so that the future receipts can be compared *on an equivalent basis* with whatever investment is required in the project under consideration. The theory of interest provides managers with the means of making such a comparison.

The Theory of Interest

If a bank pays $105 one year from now in return for a deposit of $100 now, we would say that the bank is paying interest at an annual rate of 5%. The relationships involved in this notion can be expressed in mathematical terms by means of the following equation:

$$F_1 = P(1 + r)$$

where F_1 = the amount to be received in one year, P = the present outlay to be made, and r = the rate of interest involved.

If the present outlay is $100 deposited in a bank savings account that is to earn interest at 5%, then $P = \$100$ and $r = 0.05$. Under these conditions, $F_1 = \$105$, the amount to be received in one year.

Present value The value now of an amount that will be received in some future period.

The $100 present outlay is called the **present value** of the $105 amount to be received in one year. It is also known as the *discounted value* of the future $105 receipt. The $100 figure represents the value in present terms of a receipt of $105 to be received a year from now when the interest rate is 5%.

COMPOUND INTEREST What if the investor leaves his or her money in the bank for a second year? In that case, by the end of the second year the original $100 deposit will have grown to $110.25:

Original deposit	$100.00
Interest for the first year:	
$100 × 0.05	5.00
Amount at the end of the first year	105.00
Interest for the second year:	
$105 × 0.05	5.25
Amount at the end of the second year	$110.25

Notice that the interest for the second year is $5.25, as compared to only $5 for the first year. The reason for the greater interest earned during the second year is that during the second year, interest is being paid *on interest*. That is, the $5 interest earned during the first year has been left in the account and has been added to the original $100 deposit in computing interest for the second year. This concept is known as **compound interest.** The compounding we have done is annual compounding. Interest can be compounded on a semiannual, quarterly, or even more frequent basis. Many savings institutions are now compounding interest on a daily basis. The more frequently compounding is done, the more rapidly the invested balance will grow.

Compound interest The process of paying interest on interest in an investment.

How is the concept of compound interest expressed in equation form? It is expressed by taking equation (5) and adjusting it to state the number of years, n, that a sum is going to be left deposited in the bank:

$$F_n = P(1 + r)^n$$

Exhibit 14A–1 The Relationship between Present Value and Future Value

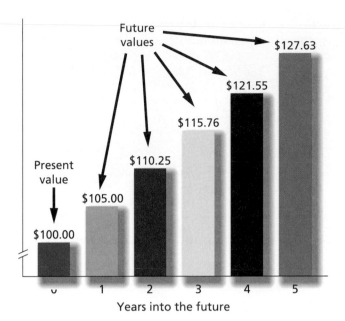

where n = years.

If n = 2 years, then our computation of the value of F in two years will be as follows:

$$F_2 = \$100(1 + 0.05)^2$$
$$F_2 = \$110.25$$

PRESENT VALUE AND FUTURE VALUE Exhibit 14A–1 shows the relationship between present value and future value as expressed in the theory of interest equations. As shown in the exhibit, if $100 is deposited in a bank at 5% interest, it will grow to $127.63 by the end of five years if interest is compounded annually.

Example K

A purchaser promises to pay $96,800 two years from now for a lot of land. This amount includes interest at an annual rate of 10%. What is the selling price of the land today?

As indicated in Table 14C–3 (10% column, down two rows) the present value of $1 is $0.826. The present value of $96,800 is $79,956.80 ($96,800 times .826). A more accurate answer is found by using equation (3) as follows:

$$P = \$96,800(1 + .10)^{-2}$$
$$= \$80,000$$

Example L

A young lady in Vancouver plans to take a vacation trip four years from now. She estimates that she will need $18,000. At an annual interest rate of 16%, compounded quarterly, how much need be deposited in a bank account today to accumulate the required $18,000?

Because interest is compounded quarterly, the interest per period is 4% (the annual rate divided by four quarters). As shown in Table 14C–3, the present value of $1 to be received 16 periods in the future at 4% interest is $0.534. The present value of $18,000 is, therefore, $18,000 times .534 which is $9,612. The calculator solution is $18,000 $\times$ $(1 + 04)^{-16}$, which equals $9,610.35.

Present Value of a Series of Cash Flows (Annuity)

Annuity A series, or stream, of identical cash flows.

The present value of an **annuity** is the percent value of a series of equal payments or receipts discounted at compound interest and made at regular intervals. Stated

Exhibit 14A–2

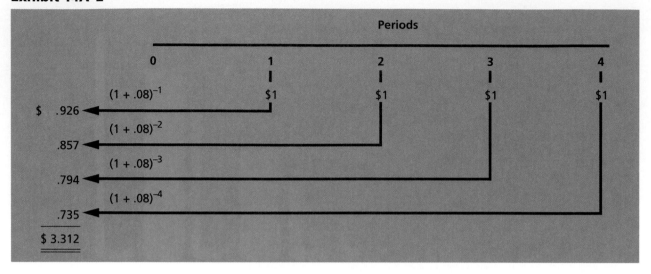

differently, it is the sum that allows the withdrawal of a series of equal amounts at regular intervals if left at compound interest.

The present value of $1 to be received a the end of each of four periods at 8% interest per period is shown graphically in Exhibit 14A–2.

Two points are important in connection with Exhibit 14A–2. First, notice that the farther we go forward in time, the smaller is the present value of the $1 interest receipt. The present value of $1 received a year from now is $0.926, as compared to only $0.735 for the $1 interest payment to be received four periods from now. This point simply underscores the fact that money has a time value.

The second point is that even though the computations involved in Exhibit 14A–2 are accurate, they have involved unnecessary work. The same present value of $3.312 could have been obtained more easily by referring to Table 14C–4 (8% column, down four rows). Table 14C–4 contains the present value of $1 to be received each year over a *series* of years at various interest rates. Table 14C–4 has been derived by simply adding together the factors from Table 14C–3.

The mathematical formula for the present value (P_n) of an annuity of $1 per period compounded at the rate of r for n periods is:

$$P_n = \frac{1 - (1 + r)^{-n}}{r} \text{ or } \frac{1 - (1 + .08)^{-4}}{.08} = \$3.312$$

Example M

What is the present value of a series of six semiannual payments of $2,000 at 8% interest compounded annually? Assume that it is now January 1, 2000, and the first payment is made on June 30, 2000.

The purpose of solving this problem could be to determine (1) the sum that will provide for six semiannual withdrawals of $2,000 if invested at 4% per period (8% divided by two interest periods per year), and (2) the sum that is payable in settlement of a series of obligations of $2,000 that are due at six semiannual intervals and discounted at 4% per period. Using Table 14C–4 (4% column, down six periods) the value 5.242 is found. This present value of an annuity of $1 factor is then multiplied by $2,000 to give $10,484. Alternatively, using the present value of an ordinary annuity (annuity in arrears) formula:

$$P_n = \frac{1 - (1 + .04)^{-6}}{.04} \times \$2,000 = \$10,484.27$$

Example N

How much money would a company be willing to invest in a project that would return $3,000 every three months for three years, and in addition, a lump sum of $20,000 at the end of the third year? The receipts begin three months from now. Interest is 16% per annum.

The $3,000 to be received at the end of each three-month period is an ordinary annuity. The number of interest periods is 12 (4 per year for three years) and the quarterly interest rate is 4% (16%/4 periods). Using Table 14C–4 (4% column, down 12 rows) the value of 9.385 is found. The present value of this annuity is $28,155 (9.385 × $3,000). The present value of the single sum of $20,000 is .625 (Table 14C–3, 4% column, down 12 rows) times $20,000 or $12,500. The present value of the series of receipts and the single lump sum is, therefore, $28,155 plus $12,500, which totals $40,655.

Present Value of an Annuity Due

An annuity due is one in which the payments or receipts occur at the *beginning* of each period. Exhibit 14A–3 compares the present value of an ordinary annuity of $1 for four periods with the present value of an annuity due for $1 for four periods. The interest rate is assumed to be 8%.

Computation of Present Value

An investment can be viewed in two ways. It can be viewed either in terms of its future value or in terms of its present value. We have seen from our computations above that if we know the present value of a sum (such as our $100 deposit), it is a relatively simple task to compute the sum's future value in n years by using equation (6). But what if the tables are reversed, and we know the *future* value of some amount but we do not know its present value?

For example, assume that you are to receive $200 two years from now. You know that the future value of this sum is $200, since this is the amount that you will be receiving in two years. But what is the sum's present value—what is it worth *right now?* The present value of any sum to be received in the future can be computed by turning equation (6) around and solving for P:

$$P = \frac{F_n}{(1 + r)^n}$$

In our example, $F = \$200$ (the amount to be received in the future), $r = 0.05$ (the rate of interest), and $n = 2$ (the number of years in the future that the amount is to be received).

$$P = \frac{\$200}{(1 + 0.05)^2}$$

$$P = \frac{\$200}{1.1025}$$

$$P = \$181.40$$

As shown by the computation above, the present value of a $200 amount to be received two years from now is $181.40 if the interest rate is 5%. In effect, we are saying that $181.40 received *right now* is equivalent to $200 received two years from now if the rate of return is 5%. The $181.40 and the $200 are just two ways of looking at the same item.

The process of finding the present value of a future cash flow, which we have just completed, is called **discounting.** We have *discounted* the $200 to its present value of

Discounting The process of finding the percent value of a future cash flow.

Discount rate The rate of return that is used to find the present value of a future cash flow.

$181.40. The 5% interest figure that we have used to find this present value is called the **discount rate.** Discounting of future sums to their present value is a common practice in business. A knowledge of the present value of a sum to be received in the future can be very useful to the manager, particularly in making capital budgeting decisions.

If you have a power key (y^x) on your calculator, the above calculations are fairly easy. However, some of the present value formulas we will be using are more complex and difficult to use. Fortunately, tables are available in which the calculations have already been done for you. For example, Table 14C–3 in Appendix 14C shows the discounted present value of $1 to be received at various periods in the future at various interest rates. The table indicates that the present value of $1 to be received two periods from now at 5% is 0.907. Since in our example we want to know the present value of $200 rather than just $1, we need to multiply the factor in the table by $200:

$$\$200 \times 0.907 = \$181.40$$

The answer we obtain is the same answer as we obtained earlier using the formula in equation (7).

Note that Part B of Exhibit 14A–3 can be interpreted as an ordinary annuity for $1 for three periods ($0.926 + $0.857 + $0.794) to which we add $1. We can calculate the present value of an annuity due by subtracting one period from n and calculating the present value of an ordinary annuity for $n - 1$ periods. We then add $1 to this annuity factor, which now gives the present value factor of an annuity due of $1.

Exhibit 14A–3

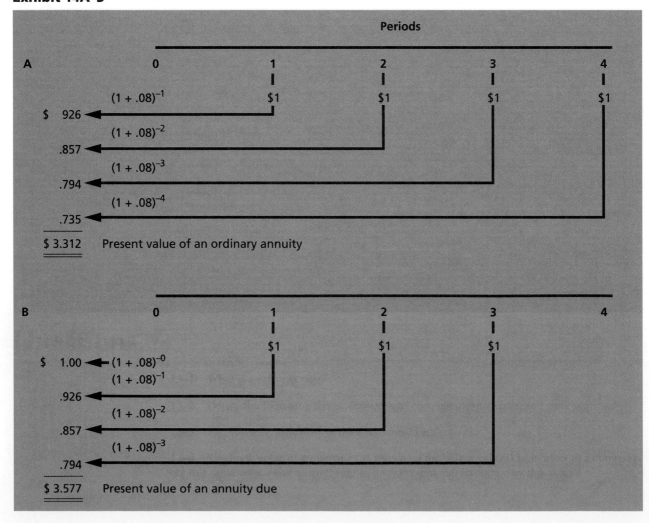

Example O

On February 1, 2000, Vacon Company signed an 18-month lease with Aucoin Leasing Company. The lease payments begin immediately. Calculate the present value of the lease assuming that $2,000 is paid each quarter and that the annual interest rate is 16%.

We can solve this problem by first determining the present value of an ordinary annuity for $n - 1$ period where n is equal to six periods (18 months equals six quarters.)

($000s)

Using Table 14C–4, the present value of an annuity factor for 5 periods ($n - 1$) is 4.452 (4% column, 5 rows down). To this factor we add 1, resulting in an interest factor of 5.452. Next, we multiply the $2,000 payments by 5.452 to arrive at $10,904, the present value of the lease payments. Using the formula approach, the present value of an annuity due is as follows (calculator solution):

$$PV(\text{due}) = \$2,000 \times \left[1 + \frac{(1 - (1 + .04)^{-5}}{.04}\right]$$

$$= \$2,000 \times (1 + 4.4518223)$$
$$= \$2,000 \times 5.4518223$$
$$= \$10,903.65$$

Deferred Annuities

A deferred annuity is one in which the first payment or receipt does not begin until more than one interest period has expired. This is common for capital expenditure decisions that may take several periods to become operational.

Example P

What is the present value on January 1, 2000, of a series of five receipts of $1,000, the first of which is expected to be received on January 1, 2003? The interest rate is 10% per annum.

A graphical representation of the problem is as follows:

($000s)

One way of solving this problem is by the following two-step procedure:

Step 1. Calculate the present value on January 1, 2002, of an ordinary annuity of a series of five receipts of $1,000. This is $1,000 times 3.791 or $3,791.

Step 2. The problem is now translated into a simple present value problem depicted as follows:

The present value on January 1, 2000, can now be computed by discounting the $3,791 back two interest periods.

$$PV\text{January 1, 2000} = \$3,791(1 + .10)^{-2}$$
$$= \$3,133$$

This problem could have also been solved by adding fictitious receipts on January 1, 2001, and on January 1, 2002, and calculating the present value of an ordinary annuity on January 1, 2000, for 7 periods and then subtracting the present value of the receipts that did not occur:

Step 1:

$$\$1,000 \times \frac{(1 - (1 + .10)^{-7})}{.10}$$

$$= \$4,868$$

Step 2:

$$\$4,868 - \left(\frac{\$1,000 \times (1 - (1 + .10)^{-2})}{.10} \right)$$

$$= \$4,868 - \$1,735$$

$$= \$3,133$$

Future Value of an Annuity

Business transactions often involve a series of equal payments spaced evenly apart. As discussed earlier in the chapter, a series of equal payments at regular intervals is known as an annuity. The total that becomes due immediately after the last payment is the amount of an ordinary annuity or an annuity in arrears. If the payments are made or received at the beginning of the first interest period, the annuity is termed an annuity due or an annuity in advance.

The distinction between an ordinary annuity and an annuity due is presented graphically as follows:

Ordinary Annuity

	$1	$1	$1	$1
0	1	2	3	4

Annuity Due

$1	$1	$1	$1	$0
0	1	2	3	4

To illustrate how the future value of an ordinary annuity is determined, assume that $1 is deposited in a savings account at the end of each of four periods at 8% per period.

$1 (no interest)
$1 ⟶ $1(1 + .08)^1
$1 ⟶ $ (1 + .08)^2
$1 ⟶ $ (1 + .08)^3

Thus, the value of an ordinary annuity of $1 due at the end of each period for four periods is:

$$\$1 + \$1 (1 + .08)^1 + \$1(1 + .08)^2 + \$1(1 + .08)^3 =$$
$$\$1 + \quad \$1.08 \quad + \quad \$1.1664 \quad + \quad \$1.2597 \quad = \$4.5061$$

From the preceding illustration it can be seen that the $1 deposited at the end of the first year accumulates interest for a total of three periods, increasing to a value of $1.2597. The deposit at the end of the second year grows to $1.1664, and the $1 deposited at the end of the third period accumulates to $1.08. The $1 deposited at the end of the fourth period has not yet earned any interest. The series of four payments of $1 each period grows to $4.5061 at the end of the fourth period.

This problem can be solved quickly by using a mathematical expression based on a geometric progression. The future value of an annuity in arrears (F_n) compounded at an interest rate (r) for a given number of periods (n) is:

$$F_n = \frac{(1 + r)^n - 1}{r}$$

The value of a series of $1 deposits made at the end of each of four years compounded at 8% annually is

$$F_n = \$1 \times \frac{(1 + .08)^4 - 1}{.08} = \$4.5061$$

The same calculation, rounded at three decimal places, can be determined by referring to Table 14C–2 (8% column, down four rows) and multiplying this factor by the amount of each receipt ($1).

It should be apparent that Tables 14C–1 and 14C–2 are related. We can treat each cash flow of the annuity separately and find the future value of each cash flow (Table 14C–1) and sum them. Alternatively, it is much faster to find the sum of the annuity using Table 14C–2.

To find the future value of an annuity of $1 per period for four periods if each payment is made at the *beginning* of each period (an annuity due), we can modify the formula as follows:

$$F_n \text{ (due)} = \frac{(1 + r)^n - 1}{r} \times (1 + r)$$

$$= \frac{(1 + .08)^4 - 1}{.08} \times (1 + .08)$$

$$= \$4,867$$

The same result can be reached by looking up the interest factor in Table 14C–2 for one additional interest period and then subtracting 1 from this factor (8% column, five rows down, deduct 1 from the factor 5.867 to give 4.867). This problem is illustrated by the following diagram:

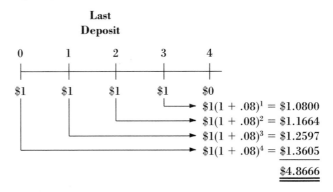

To summarize, the present value tables in Appendix C should be used as follows:

Table 14C–3: This table should be used to find the present value of a single cash flow (such as a single payment or receipt) occurring in the future.

Table 14C–4: This table should be used to find the present value of a series (or stream) of cash flows occurring in the future.

The use of both of these tables is illustrated in various exhibits in the main body of the chapter. *When a present value factor appears in an exhibit, the reader should take the time to trace it back into either Table 14C–3 or Table 14C–4 in order to get acquainted with the tables and how they work.* (Review Problem 1 at the end of this chapter was designed for those readers who would like some practice in present value analysis before attempting other homework exercises and problems.)

Appendix 14B: Inflation and Capital Budgeting

Objective 10

Explain the effect of inflation on capital budgeting decisions.

Doesn't inflation have an impact in a capital budgeting analysis? The answer is a qualified yes in that inflation does have an impact on the *numbers* that are used in a capital budgeting analysis, but it does not have an impact on the *results* of the analysis if certain conditions are satisfied. To show what we mean by this statement, we will use the following data:

Example Q

Martin Company wants to purchase a new machine that costs $36,000. The machine would provide annual cost savings of $20,000, and it would have a three-year life with no salvage value. For each of the next three years, the company expects a 10% inflation rate in the cash flows associated with the new machine. If the company's cost of capital is 23.2%, should the new machine be purchased?

To answer this question, it is important to know how the cost of capital was derived. Ordinarily, it is based on the market rates of return on the company's various sources of financing—both debt and equity. This market rate of return includes expected inflation; the higher the expected rate of inflation, the higher the market rate of return on debt and equity. When the inflationary effect is removed from the market rate of return, the result is called a real rate of return. For example, if the inflation rate of 10% is removed from Martin's cost of capital of 23.2%, the "real cost of capital" is only 12%, as shown in Exhibit 14B–1. (You cannot simply subtract the inflation rate from the market cost of capital to obtain the real cost of capital. The computations are a bit more complex than that.)

Exhibit 14B–1   Capital Budgeting and Inflation

Reconciliation of the Market-Based and Real Costs of Capital

The real cost of capital	12.0%
The inflation factor.	10.0%
The combined effect (12% × 10% = 1.2%) . . .	1.2%
The market-based cost of capital	23.2%

Solution A: Inflation Not Considered

Item	Year(s)	Amount of Cash Flows	12% Factor	Present Value of Cash Flows
Initial investment	Now	$(36,000)	1.000	$(36,000)
Annual cost savings	1–3	20,000	2.402	48,040
Net present value				$ 12,040‡

Solution B: Inflation Considered

Item	Year(s)	Amount of Cash Flows	Price Index Number*	Price-Adjusted Cash Flows	23.2% Factor†	Present Value of Cash Flows
Initial investment	Now	$(36,000)	1.000	$(36,000)	1.000	$(36,000)
Annual cost savings	1	20,000	1.100	22,000	0.812	17,864
	2	20,000	1.210	24,200	0.659	15,948
	3	20,000	1.331	26,620	0.535	14,242
Net present value						$ 12,054‡

*Computation of the price-index numbers, assuming a 10% inflation rate each year: Year 1, $(1.10)^1 = 1.10$; Year 2, $(1.10)^2 = 1.21$; and Year 3, $(1.10)^3 = 1.331$.

†Discount formulas are computed using the formula $1/(1 + r)^n$, where r is the discount factor and n is the number of years. The computations are $1/1.232 = 0.812$ for Year 1; $1/(1.232)^2 = 0.659$ for Year 2; and $1/(1.232)^3 = 0.535$ for Year 3.

‡These amounts are different only because of rounding error.

When performing a net present value analysis, one must be consistent. The market-based cost of capital reflects inflation. Therefore, if a market-based cost of capital is used to discount cash flows, then the cash flows should be adjusted upwards to reflect the effects of inflation in forthcoming periods. Computations for Martin Company under this approach are given in solution B in Exhibit 14B–1.

On the other hand, there is no need to adjust the cash flows upward if the "real cost of capital" is used in the analysis (since the inflationary effects have been taken out of the discount rate). Computations for Martin Company under this approach are given in solution A in Exhibit 14B–1. Note that under solutions A and B that the answer will be the same (within rounding error) regardless of which approach is used, so long as one is consistent and all of the cash flows associated with the project are affected in the same way by inflation.

Several points should be noted about solution B, where the effects of inflation are explicitly taken into account. First, note that the annual cost savings are adjusted for the effects of inflation by multiplying each year's cash savings by a price-index number that reflects a 10% inflation rate. (Observe from the footnotes to the exhibit how the index number is computed for each year.) Second, note that the net present value obtained in solution B, where inflation is explicitly taken into account, is the same, within rounding error, to that obtained in solution A, where the inflation effects are ignored. This result may seem surprising, but it is logical. The reason is that we have adjusted both the cash flows and the discount rate so that they are consistent, and these adjustments cancel each other out across the two solutions.

Throughout the chapter we assume for simplicity that there is no inflation. In that case, the market-based and real costs of capital are the same, and there is no reason to adjust the cash flows for inflation since there is none. When there is inflation, the unadjusted cash flows can be used in the analysis if all of the cash flows are affected identically by inflation and the real cost of capital is used to discount the cash flows. Otherwise, the cash flows should be adjusted for inflation and the market-based cost of capital should be used in the analysis.

Appendix 14C: Future Value and Present Value Tables

Exhibit 14C–1
Future Value of $1;
$F_n = P(1 + r)^n$

Periods	4%	6%	8%	10%	12%	14%	20%
1	1.040	1.060	1.080	1.100	1.120	1.140	1.200
2	1.082	1.124	1.166	1.210	1.254	1.300	1.440
3	1.125	1.191	1.260	1.331	1.405	1.482	1.728
4	1.170	1.263	1.361	1.464	1.574	1.689	2.074
5	1.217	1.338	1.469	1.611	1.762	1.925	2.488
6	1.265	1.419	1.587	1.772	1.974	2.195	2.986
7	1.316	1.504	1.714	1.949	2.211	2.502	3.583
8	1.369	1.594	1.851	2.144	2.476	2.853	4.300
9	1.423	1.690	1.999	2.359	2.773	3.252	5.160
10	1.480	1.791	2.159	2.594	3.106	3.707	6.192
11	1.540	1.898	2.332	2.853	3.479	4.226	7.430
12	1.601	2.012	2.518	3.139	3.896	4.818	8.916
13	1.665	2.133	2.720	3.452	4.364	5.492	10.699
14	1.732	2.261	2.937	3.798	4.887	6.261	12.839
15	1.801	2.397	3.172	4.177	5.474	7.138	15.407
20	2.191	3.207	4.661	6.728	9.646	13.743	38.338
30	3.243	5.744	10.063	17.450	29.960	50.950	237.380
40	4.801	10.286	21.725	45.260	93.051	188.880	1469.800

Exhibit 14C–2
Future Value of an Annuity of $1 in Arrears;

$$F_n = \frac{(1 + r)^n - 1}{r}$$

Periods	4%	6%	8%	10%	12%	14%	20%
1	1.000	1.000	1.000	1.000	1.000	1.000	1.000
2	2.040	2.060	2.080	2.100	2.120	2.140	2.220
3	3.122	3.184	3.246	3.310	3.374	3.440	3.640
4	4.247	4.375	4.506	4.641	4.779	4.921	5.368
5	5.416	5.637	5.867	6.105	6.353	6.610	7.442
6	6.633	6.975	7.336	7.716	8.115	8.536	9.930
7	7.898	8.394	8.923	9.487	10.089	10.730	12.916
8	9.214	9.898	10.637	11.436	12.300	13.233	16.499
9	10.583	11.491	12.488	13.580	14.776	16.085	20.799
10	12.006	13.181	14.487	15.938	17.549	19.337	25.959
11	13.486	14.972	16.646	18.531	20.655	23.045	32.150
12	15.026	16.870	18.977	21.385	24.133	27.271	39.580
13	16.627	18.882	21.495	24.523	28.029	32.089	48.497
14	18.292	21.015	24.215	27.976	32.393	37.581	59.196
15	20.024	23.276	27.152	31.773	37.280	43.842	72.035
20	29.778	36.778	45.762	57.276	75.052	91.025	186.690
30	56.085	79.058	113.283	164.496	241.330	356.790	1181.900
40	95.026	154.762	259.057	442.597	767.090	1342.000	7343.900

Exhibit 14C–3   Present Value of $1; $P = \dfrac{F_n}{(1 + r)^n}$

Period	4%	5%	6%	8%	10%	12%	14%	16%	18%	20%	22%	24%	26%	28%	30%	40%
1	0.962	0.952	0.943	0.926	0.909	0.893	0.877	0.862	0.847	0.833	0.820	0.806	0.794	0.781	0.769	0.714
2	0.925	0.907	0.890	0.857	0.826	0.797	0.769	0.743	0.718	0.694	0.672	0.650	0.630	0.610	0.592	0.510
3	0.889	0.864	0.840	0.794	0.751	0.712	0.675	0.641	0.609	0.579	0.551	0.524	0.500	0.477	0.455	0.364
4	0.855	0.823	0.792	0.735	0.683	0.636	0.592	0.552	0.516	0.482	0.451	0.423	0.397	0.373	0.350	0.260
5	0.822	0.784	0.747	0.681	0.621	0.567	0.519	0.476	0.437	0.402	0.370	0.341	0.315	0.291	0.269	0.186
6	0.790	0.746	0.705	0.630	0.564	0.507	0.456	0.410	0.370	0.335	0.303	0.275	0.250	0.227	0.207	0.133
7	0.760	0.711	0.665	0.583	0.513	0.452	0.400	0.354	0.314	0.279	0.249	0.222	0.198	0.178	0.159	0.095
8	0.731	0.677	0.627	0.540	0.467	0.404	0.351	0.305	0.266	0.233	0.204	0.179	0.157	0.139	0.123	0.068
9	0.703	0.645	0.592	0.500	0.424	0.361	0.308	0.263	0.225	0.194	0.167	0.144	0.125	0.108	0.094	0.048
10	0.676	0.614	0.558	0.463	0.386	0.322	0.270	0.227	0.191	0.162	0.137	0.116	0.099	0.085	0.073	0.035
11	0.650	0.585	0.527	0.429	0.350	0.287	0.237	0.195	0.162	0.135	0.112	0.094	0.079	0.066	0.056	0.025
12	0.625	0.557	0.497	0.397	0.319	0.257	0.208	0.168	0.137	0.112	0.092	0.076	0.062	0.052	0.043	0.018
13	0.601	0.530	0.469	0.368	0.290	0.229	0.182	0.145	0.116	0.093	0.075	0.061	0.050	0.040	0.033	0.013
14	0.577	0.505	0.442	0.340	0.263	0.205	0.160	0.125	0.099	0.078	0.062	0.049	0.039	0.032	0.025	0.009
15	0.555	0.481	0.417	0.315	0.239	0.183	0.140	0.108	0.084	0.065	0.051	0.040	0.031	0.025	0.020	0.006
16	0.534	0.458	0.394	0.292	0.218	0.163	0.123	0.093	0.071	0.054	0.042	0.032	0.025	0.019	0.015	0.005
17	0.513	0.436	0.371	0.270	0.198	0.146	0.108	0.080	0.060	0.045	0.034	0.026	0.020	0.015	0.012	0.003
18	0.494	0.416	0.350	0.250	0.180	0.130	0.095	0.069	0.051	0.038	0.028	0.021	0.016	0.012	0.009	0.002
19	0.475	0.396	0.331	0.232	0.164	0.116	0.083	0.060	0.043	0.031	0.023	0.017	0.012	0.009	0.007	0.002
20	0.456	0.377	0.312	0.215	0.149	0.104	0.073	0.051	0.037	0.026	0.019	0.014	0.010	0.007	0.005	0.001
21	0.439	0.359	0.294	0.199	0.135	0.093	0.064	0.044	0.031	0.022	0.015	0.011	0.008	0.006	0.004	0.001
22	0.422	0.342	0.278	0.184	0.123	0.083	0.056	0.038	0.026	0.018	0.013	0.009	0.006	0.004	0.003	0.001
23	0.406	0.326	0.262	0.170	0.112	0.074	0.049	0.033	0.022	0.015	0.010	0.007	0.005	0.003	0.002	
24	0.390	0.310	0.247	0.158	0.102	0.066	0.043	0.028	0.019	0.013	0.008	0.006	0.004	0.003	0.002	
25	0.375	0.295	0.233	0.146	0.092	0.059	0.038	0.024	0.016	0.010	0.007	0.005	0.003	0.002	0.001	
26	0.361	0.281	0.220	0.135	0.084	0.053	0.033	0.021	0.014	0.009	0.006	0.004	0.002	0.002	0.001	
27	0.347	0.268	0.207	0.125	0.076	0.047	0.029	0.018	0.011	0.007	0.005	0.003	0.002	0.001	0.001	
28	0.333	0.255	0.196	0.116	0.069	0.042	0.026	0.016	0.010	0.006	0.004	0.002	0.002	0.001	0.001	
29	0.321	0.243	0.185	0.107	0.063	0.037	0.022	0.014	0.008	0.005	0.003	0.002	0.001	0.001	0.001	
30	0.308	0.231	0.174	0.099	0.057	0.033	0.020	0.012	0.007	0.004	0.003	0.002	0.001	0.001		
40	0.208	0.142	0.097	0.046	0.022	0.011	0.005	0.003	0.001	0.001						

Exhibit 14C–4 Present Value of an Annuity of $1 in Arrears; $P_n = \dfrac{1}{r}\left[1 - \dfrac{1}{(1+r)^n}\right]$

Period	4%	5%	6%	8%	10%	12%	14%	16%	18%	20%	22%	24%	26%	28%	30%	40%
1	0.962	0.952	0.943	0.926	0.909	0.893	0.877	0.862	0.847	0.833	0.820	0.806	0.794	0.781	0.769	0.714
2	1.886	1.859	1.833	1.783	1.736	1.690	1.647	1.605	1.566	1.528	1.492	1.457	1.424	1.392	1.361	1.224
3	2.775	2.723	2.673	2.577	2.487	2.402	2.322	2.246	2.174	2.106	2.042	1.981	1.923	1.868	1.816	1.589
4	3.630	3.546	3.465	3.312	3.170	3.037	2.914	2.798	2.690	2.589	2.494	2.404	2.320	2.241	2.166	1.879
5	4.452	4.330	4.212	3.993	3.791	3.605	3.433	3.274	3.127	2.991	2.864	2.745	2.635	2.532	2.436	2.035
6	5.242	5.076	4.917	4.623	4.355	4.111	3.889	3.685	3.498	3.326	3.167	3.020	2.885	2.759	2.643	2.168
7	6.002	5.786	5.582	5.206	4.868	4.564	4.288	4.039	3.812	3.605	3.416	3.242	3.083	2.937	2.802	2.263
8	6.733	6.463	6.210	5.747	5.335	4.968	4.639	4.344	4.078	3.837	3.619	3.421	3.241	3.076	2.925	2.331
9	7.435	7.108	6.802	6.247	5.759	5.328	4.946	4.607	4.303	4.031	3.786	3.566	3.366	3.184	3.019	2.379
10	8.111	7.722	7.360	6.710	6.145	5.650	5.216	4.833	4.494	4.192	3.923	3.682	3.465	3.269	3.092	2.414
11	8.760	8.306	7.887	7.139	6.495	5.988	5.453	5.029	4.656	4.327	4.035	3.776	3.544	3.335	3.147	2.438
12	9.385	8.863	8.384	7.536	6.814	6.194	5.660	5.197	4.793	4.439	4.127	3.851	3.606	3.387	3.190	2.456
13	9.986	9.394	8.853	7.904	7.103	6.424	5.842	5.342	4.910	4.533	4.203	3.912	3.656	3.427	3.223	2.468
14	10.563	9.899	9.295	8.244	7.367	6.628	6.002	5.468	5.008	4.611	4.265	3.962	3.695	3.459	3.249	2.477
15	11.118	10.380	9.712	8.559	7.606	6.811	6.142	5.575	5.092	4.675	4.315	4.001	3.726	3.483	3.268	2.484
16	11.652	10.838	10.106	8.851	7.824	6.974	6.265	5.669	5.162	4.730	4.357	4.033	3.751	3.503	3.283	2.489
17	12.166	11.274	10.477	9.122	8.022	7.120	6.373	5.749	5.222	4.775	4.391	4.059	3.771	3.518	3.295	2.492
18	12.659	11.690	10.828	9.372	8.201	7.250	6.467	5.818	5.273	4.812	4.419	4.080	3.786	3.529	3.304	2.494
19	13.134	12.085	11.158	9.604	8.365	7.366	6.550	5.877	5.316	4.844	4.442	4.097	3.799	3.539	3.311	2.496
20	13.590	12.462	11.470	9.818	8.514	7.469	6.623	5.929	5.353	4.870	4.460	4.110	3.808	3.546	3.316	2.497
21	14.029	12.821	11.764	10.017	8.649	7.562	6.687	5.973	5.384	4.891	4.476	4.121	3.816	3.551	3.320	2.498
22	14.451	13.163	12.042	10.201	8.772	7.645	6.743	6.011	5.410	4.909	4.488	4.130	3.822	3.556	3.323	2.498
23	14.857	13.489	12.303	10.371	8.883	7.718	6.792	6.044	5.432	4.925	4.499	4.137	3.827	3.559	3.325	2.499
24	15.247	13.799	12.550	10.529	8.985	7.784	6.835	6.073	5.451	4.937	4.507	4.143	3.831	3.562	3.327	2.499
25	15.622	14.094	12.783	10.675	9.077	7.843	6.873	6.097	5.467	4.948	4.514	4.147	3.834	3.564	3.329	2.499
26	15.983	14.375	13.003	10.810	9.161	7.896	6.906	6.118	5.480	4.956	4.520	4.151	3.837	3.566	3.330	2.500
27	16.330	14.643	13.211	10.935	9.237	7.943	6.935	6.136	5.492	4.964	4.525	4.154	3.839	3.567	3.331	2.500
28	16.663	14.898	13.406	11.051	9.307	7.984	6.961	6.152	5.502	4.970	4.528	4.157	3.840	3.568	3.331	2.500
29	16.984	15.141	13.591	11.158	9.370	8.022	6.983	6.166	5.510	4.975	4.531	4.159	3.841	3.569	3.332	2.500
30	17.292	15.373	13.765	11.258	9.427	8.055	7.003	6.177	5.517	4.979	4.534	4.160	3.842	3.569	3.332	2.500
40	19.793	17.159	15.046	11.925	9.779	8.244	7.105	6.234	5.548	4.997	4.544	4.166	3.846	3.571	3.333	2.500

Questions

14–1 What is the difference between capital budgeting screening decisions and capital budgeting preference decisions?

14–2 What is meant by the term *time value of money?*

14–3 What is meant by the term *discounting?*

14–4 Why can't accounting net income figures be used in the net present value and internal rate of return methods of making capital budgeting decisions?

14–5 Why are discounted cash flow methods of making capital budgeting decisions superior to other methods?

14–6 What is net present value? Can it ever be negative? Explain.

14–7 Identify two simplifying assumptions associated with discounted cash flow methods of making capital budgeting decisions.

14–8 If a firm has to pay interest of 14% on long-term debt, then its cost of capital is 14%. Do you agree? Explain.

14–9   What is meant by an investment project's internal rate of return? How is the internal rate of return computed?

14–10   Explain how the cost of capital serves as a screening tool when dealing with (a) the net present value method and (b) the internal rate of return method.

14–11   As the discount rate increases, the present value of a given future cash flow also increases. Do you agree? Explain.

14–12   Refer to Exhibit 14–4. Is the return on this investment proposal exactly 20%, slightly more than 20%, or slightly less than 20%? Explain.

14–13   Frontier Company is investigating the purchase of a piece of automated equipment, but after considering the savings in labour costs the machine has a negative net present value. If no other cost savings can be identified, should the company reject the equipment? Explain.

14–14   Why are preference decisions sometimes called *rationing* decisions?

14–15   How is the profitability index computed, and what does it measure?

14–16   What is the preference rule for ranking investment projects under the net present value method?

14–17   Can an investment with a profitability index of less than 1.00 be an acceptable investment? Explain.

14–18   What is the preference rule for ranking investment projects using the internal rate of return?

14–19   What is meant by the term *payback period?* How is the payback period determined?

14–20   How can the payback method be useful to the manager?

14–21   What is the major criticism of the payback and simple rate of return methods of making capital budgeting decisions?

Exercises

E14–1   Consider each of the following situations independently. (Ignore income taxes.)

1. In three years, when he is discharged from the Air Force, Steve wants to buy a power boat that will cost $8,000. What lump-sum amount must he invest now to have the $8,000 at the end of three years if he can invest money at:
    a. Ten percent?
    b. Fourteen percent?
2. Annual cash inflows that will arise from two competing investment projects are given below:

	Investment	
Year	**A**	**B**
1	$ 3,000	$12,000
2	6,000	9,000
3	9,000	6,000
4	12,000	3,000
	$30,000	$30,000

Each investment project will require the same investment outlay. You can invest money at an 18% rate of return. Compute the present value of the cash inflows for each investment.

3. Julie has just retired. Her company's retirement program has two options as to how retirement benefits can be received. Under the first option, Julie would receive a lump sum of $150,000 immediately as her full retirement benefit. Under the second option, she would receive $14,000 each year for 20 years plus a lump-sum payment of $60,000 at the end of the 20-year period. If she can invest money at 12%, which option would you recommend that she accept? Use present value analysis.

E14–2 Each of the following parts is independent. (Ignore income taxes.)

1. The Atlantic Medical Clinic can purchase a new computer system that will save $7,000 annually in billing costs. The computer system will last for eight years and have no salvage value. What is the maximum purchase price that the Atlantic Medical Clinic should be willing to pay for the new computer system if the clinic's required rate of return is:
   a. Sixteen percent?
   b. Twenty percent?

2. A Halifax newspaper reported the following story:

   Frank Ormsby of Bedford is the province's newest millionaire. By choosing the six winning numbers on last week's provincial lottery, Mr. Ormsby has won the week's grand prize totalling $1.6 million. The Lottery Commission has indicated that Mr. Ormsby will receive his prize in 20 annual installments of $80,000 each.

   a. If Mr. Ormsby can invest money at a 12% rate of return, what is the present value of his winnings?
   b. Is it correct to say that Mr. Ormsby is the "province's newest millionaire"? Explain your answer.

3. Fraser Company will need a new warehouse in five years. The warehouse will cost $500,000 to build. What lump-sum amount should the company invest now to have the $500,000 available at the end of the five-year period? Assume that the company can invest money at:
   a. Ten percent.
   b. Fourteen percent.

E14–3 Kathy Myers frequently purchases stocks and bonds, but she is uncertain how to determine the rate of return that she is earning. For example, three years ago she paid $13,000 for 200 common shares of Malti Company. She received a $420 cash dividend on the shares at the end of each year for three years. At the end of three years, she sold the shares for $16,000. Kathy would like to earn a return of at least 14% on all of her investments. She is not sure whether the Malti Company shares provided a 14% return and would like some help with the necessary computations.

Required
(ignore income taxes)

Using the net present value method, determine whether or not the Malti Company shares provided a 14% return. Use the general format illustrated in Exhibit 14–4 and round all computations to the nearest whole dollar.

E14–4 Labeau Products, Ltd., of Perth, Australia, has $35,000 to invest. The company is trying to decide between two alternative uses for the funds. The alternatives are:

	Invest in Project X	Invest in Project Y
Investment required	$35,000	$35,000
Annual cash inflows	9,000	—
Single cash inflow at the end of 10 years	—	150,000
Life of the project	10 years	10 years

The company's discount rate is 18%.

Required
(ignore income taxes)

Which alternative would you recommend that the company accept? Show all computations using the net present value approach. Prepare a separate computation for each project.

E14–5 Perot Industries has $100,000 to invest. The company is trying to decide between two alternative uses of the funds. The alternatives are:

	Project	
	A	**B**
Cost of equipment required	$100,000	—
Working capital investment required	—	$100,000
Annual cash inflows	21,000	16,000
Salvage value of equipment in six years	8,000	—
Life of the project	6 years	6 years

The working capital needed for project B will be released at the end of six years for investment elsewhere. Perot Industries' discount rate is 14%.

Required
(ignore income taxes)

Which investment alternative (if either) would you recommend that the company accept? Show all computations using the net present value format. Prepare a separate computation for each project.

E14–6 Complete the following cases (ignore income taxes):

1. Preston Company requires a minimum return of 14% on all investments. The company can purchase a new machine at a cost of $84,900. The new machine would generate cash inflows of $15,000 per year and have a 12-year useful life with no salvage value. Compute the machine's net present value. (Use the format shown in Exhibit 14–1.) Is the machine an acceptable investment? Explain.

2. The Walton *Daily News* is investigating the purchase of a new auxiliary press that has a projected life of 18 years. It is estimated that the new press will save $30,000 per year in cash operating costs. If the new press costs $217,500, what is its internal rate of return? Is the press an acceptable investment if the company's required rate of return is 16%? Explain.

3. Refer to the data above for the Walton *Daily News*. How much would the annual cash inflows (cost savings) have to be for the new press to provide the required 16% rate of return? Round your answer to the nearest whole dollar.

E14–7 Wendell's Doughnut Shoppe is investigating the purchase of a new doughnut-making machine. The new machine would permit the company to reduce the amount of part-time help needed, at a cost savings of $3,800 per year. In addition, the new machine would allow the company to produce one new style of doughnut, resulting in the sale of at least 1,000 dozen more doughnuts each year. The company realizes a contribution margin of $1.20 per dozen doughnuts sold. The new machine would cost $18,600 and have a six-year useful life.

Required
(ignore income taxes)

1. What would be the total annual cash inflows associated with the new machine for capital budgeting purposes?

2. Compute the internal rate of return promised by the new machine. Interpolate, and round your final answer to the nearest tenth of a percent.

3. In addition to the data given above, assume that the machine will have a $9,125 salvage value at the end of six years. Under these conditions, compute the internal rate of return to the nearest *whole* percent. (Hint: You may find it helpful to use the net present value approach; find the discount rate that will cause the net present value to be closest to zero. Use the format shown in Exhibit 14–4.)

E14–8 Henrie's Drapery Service is investigating the purchase of a new machine for cleaning and blocking drapes. The machine would cost $130,400, including freight and installation. Henrie's has estimated that the new machine would increase the company's cash inflows, net of expenses, by $25,000 per year. The machine would have a 10-year useful life and no salvage value.

Required
(ignore income taxes)

1. Compute the machine's internal rate of return.

2. Compute the machine's net present value. Use a discount rate of 14% and the format shown in Exhibit 14–5. Why do you have a zero net present value? If the company's cost of capital is 10%, is this an acceptable investment? Explain.

3. Suppose that the new machine would increase the company's annual cash inflows, net of expenses, by only $22,500 per year. Under these conditions, compute the internal rate of return. Interpolate as needed and round your final answer to the nearest tenth of a percent.

E14–9 Solve the three following present value exercises:

Required
(ignore income taxes)

1. The Cambro Foundation, a nonprofit organization, is planning to invest $104,950 in a project that will last for three years. The project will provide cash inflows as follows:

Year 1	$30,000
Year 2	40,000
Year 3	?

Assuming that the project will yield exactly a 12% rate of return, what is the expected cash inflow for Year 3?

2. Lukow Products is investigating the purchase of a piece of automated equipment that will save $400,000 each year in direct labour and inventory carrying costs. This equipment costs $2,500,000 and is expected to have a 15-year useful life with no salvage value. The company requires a minimum 20% return on all equipment purchases. Management anticipates that this equipment will provide intangible benefits such as greater flexibility, higher quality of output, and experience in automation. What dollar value per year would management have to attach to these intangible benefits to make the equipment an acceptable investment?

3. The Matchless Dating Service has made an investment in video and recording equipment that costs $106,700. The equipment is expected to generate cash inflows of $20,000 per year. How many years will the equipment have to be used to provide the company with a 10% rate of return on its investment?

E14–10 Information on four investment proposals is given below:

	Investment Proposal			
	A	**B**	**C**	**D**
Investment required	$(90,000)	$(100,000)	$(70,000)	$(120,000)
Present value of cash inflows	126,000	90,000	105,000	160,000
Net present value	$ 36,000	$ (10,000)	$ 35,000	$ 40,000
Life of the project	5 years	7 years	6 years	6 years

Required
1. Compute the profitability index for each investment proposal.
2. Rank the proposals in terms of preference.

E14–11 A piece of laboursaving equipment has just come onto the market that Mitsui Electronics, Ltd., could use to reduce costs in one of its plants in Japan. Relevant data relating to the equipment follow (currency is in thousands of yen, denoted by ¥):

Purchase cost of the equipment	¥432,000
Annual cost savings that will be provided by the equipment	¥90,000
Life of the equipment	12 years

Required
(ignore income taxes)

1. Compute the payback period for the equipment. If the company requires a payback period of four years or less, would the equipment be purchased?
2. Compute the simple rate of return on the equipment. Use straight-line depreciation based on the equipment's useful life. Would the equipment be purchased if the company requires a rate of return of at least 14%?

E14–12 Nick's Novelties, Inc., is considering the purchase of electronic pinball machines to place in amusement houses. The machines would cost a total of $300,000, have an eight-year useful life, and have a total salvage value of $20,000. Based on experience with other equipment, the company estimates that annual revenues and expenses associated with the machines would be as follows:

Revenues from use		$200,000
Less operating expenses:		
Commissions to amusement houses . . .	$100,000	
Insurance	7,000	
Depreciation	35,000	
Maintenance	18,000	160,000
Net income		$ 40,000

Required
(ignore income taxes)

1. Assume that Nick's Novelties, Inc., will not purchase new equipment unless it provides a payback period of four years or less. Would the company purchase the pinball machines?
2. Compute the simple rate of return promised by the pinball machines. If the company requires a simple rate of return of at least 12%, will the pinball machines be purchased?

Problems

P14–13 Basic Net Present Value Analysis   Windhoek Mines, Ltd., of Namibia, is contemplating the purchase of equipment to exploit a mineral deposit that is located on land to which the company has mineral rights. An engineering and cost analysis has been made, and it is expected that the following cash flows would be associated with opening and operating a mine in the area:

Cost of new equipment and timbers	R275,000
Working capital required	100,000
Net annual cash receipts	120,000*
Cost to construct new roads in three years	40,000
Salvage value of equipment in four years	65,000

> *Receipts from sales of ore, less out-of-pocket costs for salaries, utilities, insurance, and so forth.

The currency in Namibia is the rand, here denoted by R.

It is estimated that the mineral deposit would be exhausted after four years of mining. At that point, the working capital would be released for reinvestment elsewhere. The company's discount rate is 20%.

Required
(ignore income taxes)

Determine the net present value of the proposed mining project. Should the project be accepted? Explain.

P14–14 Basic Net Present Value Analysis   The Sweetwater Candy Company would like to buy a new machine that would automatically "dip" chocolates. The dipping operation is currently done largely by hand. The machine the company is considering costs $120,000. The manufacturer estimates that the machine would be usable for 12 years but would require the replacement of several key parts at the end of the sixth year. These parts would cost $9,000, including installation. After 12 years, the machine could be sold for about $7,500.

The company estimates that the cost to operate the machine will be only $7,000 per year. The present method of dipping chocolates costs $30,000 per year. In addition to reducing costs, the new machine will increase production by 6,000 boxes of chocolates per year. The company realizes a contribution margin of $1.50 per box. A 20% rate of return is required on all investments.

Required
(ignore income taxes)

1. What are the net annual cash inflows that will be provided by the new dipping machine?
2. Compute the new machine's net present value. Use the incremental cost approach and round all dollar amounts to the nearest whole dollar.

P14–15   Net Present Value Analysis; Automation Decision   "I'm not sure we should lay out $500,000 for that automated welding machine," said Jim Alder, president of the Superior Equipment Company. "That's a lot of money, and it would cost us $80,000 for software and installation, and another $3,000 every month just to maintain the thing. In addition, the manufacturer admits that it would cost $45,000 more at the end of seven years to replace worn-out parts."

"I admit it's a lot of money," said Franci Rogers, the controller. "But you know the turnover problem we've had with the welding crew. This machine would replace six welders at a cost savings of $108,000 per year. And we would save another $6,500 per year in reduced material waste. When you figure that the automated welder would last for 12 years, that adds up to a pile of savings. I'm sure the return would be greater than our 16% required rate of return."

"I'm still not convinced," countered Mr. Alder. "We can only get $12,000 scrap value out of our old welding equipment if we sell it now, and all that new machine will be worth in 12 years is $20,000 for parts. But have your people work up the figures and we'll talk about them at the executive committee meeting tomorrow."

Required
(ignore income taxes)

1. Compute the net annual cost savings promised by the automated welding machine.
2. Using the data from (1) above and other data from the problem, compute the automated welding machine's net present value. (Use the incremental-cost approach.) Would you recommend purchase? Explain.
3. Assume that management can identify several intangible benefits associated with the automated welding machine, including greater flexibility in shifting from one type of product to another, improved quality of output, and faster delivery as a result of reduced throughput time. What dollar value per year would management have to attach to these intangible benefits in order to make the new welding machine an acceptable investment?

P14–16   Preference Ranking of Investment Projects   The management of Revco Products is exploring five different investment opportunities. Information on the five projects under study is given below:

	Project Number				
	1	**2**	**3**	**4**	**5**
Investment required	$(270,000)	$(450,000)	$(400,000)	$(360,000)	$(480,000)
Present value of cash inflows at a 10% discount rate	336,140	522,970	379,760	433,400	567,270
Net present value ...	$ 66,140	$ 72,970	$ (20,240)	$ 73,400	$ 87,270
Life of the project	6 years	3 years	5 years	12 years	6 years
Internal rate of return	18%	19%	8%	14%	16%

The company's required rate of return is 10%; thus, a 10% discount rate has been used in the present value computations above. Limited funds are available for investment, so the company cannot accept all of the available projects.

Required

1. Compute the profitability index for each investment project.
2. Rank the five projects according to preference, in terms of:
    a. Net present value.
    b. Profitability index.
    c. Internal rate of return.
3. Which ranking do you prefer? Why?

P14–17   Simple Rate of Return; Payback   Paul Swanson has an opportunity to acquire a franchise from The Yogurt Place, Inc., to dispense frozen yogurt products under The Yogurt Place name. Mr. Swanson has assembled the following information relating to the franchise:

a. A suitable location in a large shopping mall can be rented for $3,500 per month.
b. Remodelling and necessary equipment would cost $270,000. The equipment would have an estimated 15-year life and an estimated $18,000 salvage value. Straight-line depreciation would be used, and the salvage value would be considered in computing depreciation deductions.
c. Based on similar outlets elsewhere, Mr. Swanson estimates that sales would total $300,000 per year. Ingredients would cost 20% of sales.
d. Operating costs would include $70,000 per year for salaries, $3,500 per year for insurance, and $27,000 per year for utilities. In addition, Mr. Swanson would have to pay a commission to The Yogurt Place, Inc., of 12.5% of sales.

Rather than obtain the franchise, Mr. Swanson could invest his funds in long-term corporate bonds that would yield a 12% annual return.

Required
(ignore income taxes)

1. Prepare an income statement that shows the expected net income each year from the franchise outlet. Use the contribution format.
2. Compute the simple rate of return promised by the outlet. If Mr. Swanson requires a simple rate of return of at least 12%, should he obtain the franchise?
3. Compute the payback period on the outlet. If Mr. Swanson wants a payback of four years or less, should the outlet be opened?

P14–18 Net Present Value Analysis of Securities   Linda Clark received $175,000 from her mother's estate. She placed the funds into the hands of a broker, who purchased the following securities on Linda's behalf:

a. Common shares were purchased at a cost of $95,000. The shares paid no dividends, but they were sold for $160,000 at the end of three years.
b. Preferred shares were purchased at their par value of $30,000. The stock paid a 6% dividend (based on par value) each year for three years. At the end of three years, the shares were sold for $27,000.
c. Bonds were purchased at a cost of $50,000. The bonds paid $3,000 in interest every six months. After three years, the bonds were sold for $52,700. (Note: In discounting a cash flow that occurs semiannually, the procedure is to halve the discount rate and double the number of periods. Use the same procedure in discounting the proceeds from the sale.)

The securities were all sold at the end of three years so that Linda would have funds available to open a new business venture. The broker stated that the investments had earned more than a 16% return, and he gave Linda the following computation to support his statement:

Common shares:	
Gain on sale ($160,000 − $95,000)	$65,000
Preferred shares:	
Dividends paid (6% × $30,000 × 3 years)	5,400
Loss on sale ($27,000 − $30,000)	(3,000)
Bonds:	
Interest paid ($3,000 × 6 periods)	18,000
Gain on sale ($52,700 − $50,000)	2,700
Net gain on all investments	$88,100

$$\frac{\$88,100 \div 3 \text{ years}}{\$175,000} = 16.8\%$$

Required
(ignore income taxes)

1. Using a 16% discount rate, compute the net present value of *each* of the three investments. On which investment(s) did Linda earn a 16% rate of return? (Round computations to the nearest whole dollar.)
2. Considering all three investments together, did Linda earn a 16% rate of return? Explain.
3. Linda wants to use the $239,700 proceeds ($160,000 + $27,000 + $52,700 = $239,700) from sale of the securities to open a retail store under a 12-year franchise contract. What

net annual cash inflow must the store generate for Linda to earn a 14% return over the 12-year period? Round computations to the nearest whole dollar.

P14–19   Net Present Value Analysis of a New Product   Matheson Electronics has just developed a new electronic device which, when mounted on an automobile, will tell the driver how many kilometres the automobile is travelling per litre of gasoline.

The company is anxious to begin production of the new device. To this end, marketing and cost studies have been made to determine probable costs and market potential. These studies have provided the following information:

a.   New equipment would have to be acquired to produce the device. The equipment would cost $315,000 and have a 12-year useful life. After 12 years, it would have a salvage value of about $15,000.

b.   Sales in units over the next 12 years are projected to be as follows:

Year	Sales in Units
1	6,000
2	12,000
3	15,000
4–12	18,000

c.   Production and sales of the device would require working capital of $60,000 to finance accounts receivable, inventories, and day-to-day cash needs. This working capital would be released at the end of the project's life.

d.   The devices would sell for $35 each; variable costs for production, administration, and sales would be $15 per unit.

e.   Fixed costs for salaries, maintenance, property taxes, insurance, and straight-line depreciation on the equipment would total $135,000 per year. (Depreciation is based on cost less salvage value.)

f.   To gain rapid entry into the market, the company would have to advertise heavily. The advertising program would be:

Year	Amount of Yearly Advertising
1–2	$180,000
3	150,000
4–12	120,000

g.   Matheson Electronics' board of directors has specified that all new products must have a return of at least 14% to be acceptable.

**Required
(ignore income taxes)**

1.   Compute the net cash inflow (cash receipts less yearly cash operating expenses) anticipated from sale of the device for each year over the next 12 years.

2.   Using the data computed in (1) above and other data provided in the problem, determine the net present value of the proposed investment. Would you recommend that Matheson accept the device as a new product?

P14–20   Opening a Small Business; Net Present Value   In eight years, Kent Duncan will retire. He has $150,000 to invest, and he is exploring the possibility of opening a self-service auto wash. The auto wash could be managed in the free time he has available from his regular occupation, and it could be closed easily when he retires. After careful study, Mr. Duncan has determined the following:

a.   A building in which an auto wash could be installed is available under an eight-year lease at a cost of $1,700 per month.

b.   Purchase and installation costs of equipment would total $150,000. In eight years the equipment could be sold for about 10% of its original cost.

c.   An investment of an additional $2,000 would be required to cover working capital needs for cleaning supplies, change funds, and so forth. After eight years, this working capital would be released for investment elsewhere.

d. Both an auto wash and a vacuum service would be offered with a wash costing $1.50 and the vacuum costing 25 cents per use.

e. The only variable costs associated with the operation would be 23 cents per wash for water and 10 cents per use of the vacuum for electricity.

f. In addition to rent, monthly costs of operation would be: cleaning, $450; insurance, $75; and maintenance, $500.

g. Gross receipts from the auto wash would be about $1,350 per week. According to the experience of other auto washes, 70% of the customers using the wash would also use the vacuum.

Mr. Duncan will not open the auto wash unless it provides at least a 10% return, since this is the amount that could be earned by simply placing the $150,000 in a high-grade securities.

Required
(ignore income taxes)

1. Assuming that the auto wash will be open 52 weeks a year, compute the expected net annual cash receipts (gross cash receipts less cash disbursements) from its operation. (Do not include the cost of the equipment, the working capital, or the salvage value in these computations.)

2. Would you advise Mr. Duncan to open the car wash? Show computations using the net present value method of investment analysis. Round all dollar figures to the nearest whole dollar.

P14–21 Replacement Decision   Bilboa Freightlines, S.A., of Panama, has a small truck that it uses for intracity deliveries. The truck is in bad repair and must be either overhauled or replaced with a new truck. The company has assembled the following information. (Panama uses the Canadian dollar as its currency):

	Present Truck	New Truck
Purchase cost new	$21,000	$30,000
Remaining book value	11,500	—
Overhaul needed now	7,000	—
Annual cash operating costs	10,000	6,500
Salvage value—now	9,000	—
Salvage value—eight years from now . .	1,000	4,000

If the company keeps and overhauls its present delivery truck, then the truck will be usable for eight more years. If a new truck is purchased, it will be used for eight years, after which it will be traded in on another truck. The new truck would be diesel-operated, resulting in a substantial reduction in annual operating costs, as shown above.

The company computes depreciation on a straight-line basis. All investment projects are evaluated using a 16% discount rate.

Required
(ignore income taxes)

1. Should Bilboa Freightlines keep the old truck or purchase the new one? Use the total-cost approach to net present value in making your decision. Round to the nearest whole dollar.

2. Redo (1) above, this time using the incremental-cost approach.

P14–22 Net Present Value; Automated Equipment; Postaudit   Saxon Products, Inc., is investigating the purchase of a robot for use on the company's assembly line. Selected data relating to the robot are provided below:

Cost of the robot	$1,800,000
Installation and software	900,000
Annual savings in labour costs	?
Annual savings in inventory carrying costs	210,000
Monthly increase in power and maintenance costs	2,500
Salvage value in 10 years	70,000
Useful life	10 years

Engineering studies suggest that use of the robot will result in a savings of 50,000 direct labour-hours each year. The labour rate is $8 per hour. Also, the smoother work flow made possible by the use of automation will allow the company to reduce the amount of inventory on hand by $400,000. This inventory reduction will take place at the end of the first year of operation; the released funds will be available for use elsewhere in the company. Saxon Products requires a 20% return on all purchases of equipment.

Shelly Martins, the controller, has noted that all of Saxon's competitors are automating their plants. She is pessimistic, however, about whether Saxon's management will allow it to automate. In preparing the proposal for the robot, she stated to a colleague, "Let's just hope that reduced labour and inventory costs can justify the purchase of this automated equipment. Otherwise, we'll never get it. You know how the president feels about equipment paying for itself out of reduced costs."

Required
(ignore income taxes)

1. Determine the net *annual* cost savings if the robot is purchased. (Do not include the $400,000 inventory reduction or the salvage value in this computation.)
2. Compute the net present value of the proposed investment in the robot. Based on these data, would you recommend that the robot be purchased? Explain.
3. Assume that the robot is purchased. At the end of the first year, Shelly Martins has found that some items did not work out as planned. Due to unforeseen problems, software and installation costs were $75,000 more than estimated and direct labour has been reduced by only 45,000 hours per year, rather than by 50,000 hours. Assuming that all other cost data were accurate, does it appear that the company made a wise investment? Show computations using the net present value format as in (2) above. (Hint: It might be helpful to place yourself back at the beginning of the first year with the new data.)
4. Upon seeing your analysis in (3) above, Saxon's president stated, "That robot is the worst investment we've ever made. And now we'll be stuck with it for years."
   a. Explain to the president what benefits other than cost savings might accrue from use of the new automated equipment.
   b. Compute for the president the dollar amount of cash inflow that would be needed each year from the benefits in (a) above for the automated equipment to yield a 20% rate of return.

P14–23 Rental Property Decision Raul Martinas, professor of languages at Eastern University, owns a small office building adjacent to the university campus. He acquired the property 10 years ago at a total cost of $530,000—$50,000 for the land and $480,00 for the building. He has just received an offer from a realty company that wants to purchase the property; however, the property has been a good source of income over the years, so Professor Martinas is unsure whether he should keep it or sell it. His alternatives are:

Keep the property. Professor Martinas' accountant has kept careful records of the income realized from the property over the past 10 years. These records indicate the following annual revenues and expenses:

Rental receipts		$140,000
Less building expenses:		
Utilities	$25,000	
Depreciation of building	16,000	
Property taxes and insurance . . .	18,000	
Repairs and maintenance	9,000	
Custodial help and supplies	40,000	108,000
Net income		$ 32,000

Professor Martinas makes a $12,000 mortgage payment each year on the property. The mortgage will be paid off in eight more years. He has been depreciating the building by the straight-line method, assuming a salvage value of $80,000 for the building which he still thinks is an appropriate figure. He feels sure that the building can be rented for another 15 years. He also feels sure that 15 years from now the land will be worth three times what he paid for it.

Sell the property. A realty company has offered to purchase the property by paying $175,000 immediately and $26,500 per year for the next 15 years. Control of the property would go to the realty company immediately. To sell the property, Professor

Martinas would need to pay the mortgage off, which could be done by making a lump-sum payment of $90,000.

Required
(ignore income taxes)

Assume that Professor Martinas requires a 12% rate of return. Would you recommend he keep or sell the property? Show computations using the net present value method and the total-cost approach.

P14–24 Lease or Buy Decision The Riteway Ad Agency provides cars for its sales staff. In the past, the company has always purchased its cars outright from a dealer and then sold the cars after three years' use. The company's present fleet of cars is three years old and will be sold very shortly. To provide a replacement fleet, the company is considering two alternatives:

Alternative 1: The company can purchase the cars outright, as in the past, and sell the cars after three years' use. Ten cars will be needed, which can be purchased at a discounted price of $17,000 each. If this alternative is accepted, the following costs will be incurred on the fleet as a whole:

Annual cost of servicing, taxes, and licensing	$3,000
Repairs, first year	1,500
Repairs, second year	4,000
Repairs, third year	6,000

At the end of three years, the fleet could be sold for one-half of the original purchase price.

Alternative 2: The company can lease the cars under a three-year lease contract. The lease cost would be $55,000 per year (the first payment due at the end of Year 1). As part of this lease cost, the owner would provide all servicing and repairs, license the cars, and pay all the taxes. Riteway would be required to make a $10,000 security deposit at the beginning of the lease period, which would be refunded when the cars were returned to the owner at the end of the lease contract.

Required
(ignore income taxes)

1. Riteway Ad Agency has an 18% cost of capital. Use the total-cost approach to determine the present value of the cash flows associated with each alternative. Round all dollar amounts to the nearest whole dollar. Which alternative should the company accept?
2. Using the data in (1) above and other data as needed, explain why it is often less costly for a company to lease equipment and facilities rather than to buy them.

P14–25 Internal Rate of Return; Sensitivity Analysis "In my opinion, a tanning salon would be a natural addition to our spa and very popular with our customers," said Stacey Winder, manager of the Lifeline Spa. "Our figures show that we could remodel the building next door to our spa and install all of the necessary equipment for $330,000. I have contacted tanning salons in other areas, and I am told that the tanning beds will be usable for about nine years. I am also told that a four-bed salon such as we are planning would generate a cash inflow of about $80,000 per year after all expenses."

"It does sound very appealing," replied Kevin Leblanc, the spa's accountant. "Let me push the numbers around a bit and see what kind of a return the salon would generate."

Required
(ignore income taxes)

1. Compute the internal rate of return promised by the tanning salon. Interpolate to the nearest tenth of a percent.
2. Assume that Ms. Winder will not open the salon unless it promises a return of at least 14%. Compute the amount of annual cash inflow that would provide this return on the $330,000 investment.
3. Although nine years is the average life of tanning salon equipment, Ms. Winder has found that this life can vary substantially. Compute the internal rate of return if the life were (a) 6 years and (b) 12 years rather than 9 years. Interpolate to the nearest tenth of a percent. Is there any information provided by these computations that you would be particularly anxious to show Ms. Winder?
4. Ms. Winder has also found that although $80,000 is an average cash inflow from a four-bed salon, some salons vary as much as 20% from this figure. Compute the internal rate of

return if the annual cash inflows were (a) 20% less and (b) 20% greater than $80,000. Interpolate to the nearest tenth of a percent.

5. Assume that the $330,000 investment is made and that the salon is opened as planned. Because of concerns about the effects of excessive tanning, however, the salon is not able to attract as many customers as planned. Cash inflows are only $50,000 per year, and after eight years the salon equipment is sold to a competitor for $135,440. Compute the internal rate of return (to the nearest whole percent) earned on the investment over the eight-year period. (Hint: A useful way to proceed is to find the discount rate that will cause the net present value to be equal to, or near, zero.)

P14–26 Preference Ranking of Investment Projects   Oxford Company has limited funds available for investment and must ration the funds among five competing projects. Selected information on the five projects follows:

Project	Investment Required	Net Present Value	Life of the Project (years)	Internal Rate of Return (percent)
A	$160,000	$44,323	7	18%
B	135,000	42,000	12	16%
C	100,000	35,035	7	20%
D	175,000	38,136	3	22%
E	150,000	(8,696)	6	8%

The net present values above have been computed using a 10% discount rate. The company wants your assistance in determining which project to accept first, which to accept second, and so forth.

Required
1. Compute the profitability index for each project.
2. In order of preference, rank the five projects in terms of:
    a. Net present value.
    b. Profitability index.
    c. Internal rate of return.
3. Which ranking do you prefer? Why?

P14–27 Simple Rate of Return; Payback   Sharkey's Fun Centre contains a number of electronic games as well as a miniature golf course and various rides located outside the building. Paul Sharkey, the owner, would like to construct a water slide on one portion of his property. Mr. Sharkey has gathered the following information about the slide:

a. Water slide equipment could be purchased and installed at a cost of $330,000. According to the manufacturer, the slide would be usable for 12 years after which it would have no salvage value.

b. Mr. Sharkey would use straight-line depreciation on the slide equipment.

c. To make room for the water slide, several rides would be dismantled and sold. These rides are fully depreciated, but they could be sold for $60,000 to an amusement park in a nearby city.

d. Mr. Sharkey has concluded that about 50,000 more people would use the water slide each year than have been using the rides. The admission price would be $3.60 per person (the same price that the Fun Centre has been charging for the rides).

e. Based on experience at other water slides, Mr. Sharkey estimates that incremental operating expenses each year for the slide would be: salaries, $85,000; insurance, $4,200; utilities, $13,000; and maintenance, $9,800.

Required
(ignore income taxes)
1. Prepare an income statement showing the expected net income each year from the water slide.
2. Compute the simple rate of return expected from the water slide. Based on this computation, would the water slide be constructed if Mr. Sharkey requires a simple rate of return of at least 14% on all investments?

3. Compute the payback period for the water slide. If Mr. Sharkey requires a payback period of five years or less, would the water slide be constructed?

P14–28   Simple Rate of Return; Payback; Internal Rate of Return
Honest John's Used Cars, Inc., has always hired students from the local university to wash the cars on the lot. Honest John is considering the purchase of an automatic car wash that would be used in place of the students. The following information has been gathered by Honest John's accountant to help Honest John make a decision on the purchase:

a.   Payments to students for washing cars total $15,000 per year at present.
b.   The car wash would cost $21,000 installed, and it would have a 10-year useful life. Honest John uses straight-line depreciation on all assets. The car wash would have a negligible salvage value in 10 years.
c.   Annual out-of-pocket costs associated with the car wash would be: wages of students to operate the wash, keep the soap bin full, and so forth, $6,300; utilities, $1,800; and insurance and maintenance, $900.
d.   Honest John now earns a return of 20% on the funds invested in his inventory of used cars. He feels that he would have to earn an equivalent rate on the car wash for the purchase to be attractive.

Required
(ignore income taxes)

1.   Determine the annual savings that would be realized in cash operating costs if the car wash were purchased.
2.   Compute the simple rate of return promised by the car wash. (Hint: Note that this is a cost reduction project.) Will Honest John accept this project if he expects a 20% return?
3.   Compute the payback period on the car wash. Honest John (who has a reputation for being somewhat of a nickel-nurser) will not purchase any equipment unless it has a payback of four years or less. Will he purchase the car wash equipment?
4.   Compute (to the nearest whole percent) the internal rate of return promised by the car wash. Based on this computation, does it appear that the simple rate of return would normally be an accurate guide in investment decisions?

P14–29   Simple Rate of Return; Payback   Westwood Furniture Company is considering the purchase of two different items of equipment, as described below:

Machine A. A compacting machine has just come onto the market that would permit Westwood Furniture Company to compress sawdust into various shelving products. At present the sawdust is disposed of as a waste product. The following information is available on the machine:

a.   The machine would cost $420,000 and would have a 10% salvage value at the end of its 12-year useful life. The company uses straight-line depreciation and considers salvage value in computing depreciation deductions.
b.   The shelving products manufactured from use of the machine would generate revenues of $300,000 per year. Variable manufacturing costs would be 20% of sales.
c.   Fixed expenses associated with the new shelving products would be (per year): advertising, $40,000: salaries, $110,000; utilities, $5,200; and insurance, $800.

Machine B. A second machine has come onto the market that would allow Westwood Furniture Company to automate a sanding process that is now done largely by hand. The following information is available:

a.   The new sanding machine would cost $234,000 and would have no salvage value at the end of its 13-year useful life. The company would use straight-line depreciation on the new machine.
b.   Several old pieces of sanding equipment that are fully depreciated would be disposed of at a scrap value of $9,000.
c.   The new sanding machine would provide substantial annual savings in cash operating costs. It would require an operator at an annual salary of $16,350 and $5,400 in annual maintenance costs. The current, hand-operated sanding procedure costs the company $78,000 per year in total.

Westwood Furniture Company requires a simple rate of return of 15% on all equipment purchases. Also, the company will not purchase equipment unless the equipment has a payback period of 4.0 years or less.

Required
(ignore income taxes)

1. For machine A:
   a. Prepare an income statement showing the expected net income each year from the new shelving products. Use the contribution format.
   b. Compute the simple rate of return.
   c. Compute the payback period.
2. For machine B:
   a. Compute the simple rate of return.
   b. Compute the payback period.
3. According to the company's criteria, which machine, if either, should the company purchase?

P14–30   Simple Rate of Return; Payback; Internal Rate of Return   The Elberta Fruit Farm of Ontario has always hired transient workers to pick its annual cherry crop. Francie Wright, the farm manager, has just received information on a cherry picking machine that is being purchased by many fruit farms. The machine is a motorized device that shakes the cherry tree, causing the cherries to fall onto plastic tarps that funnel the cherries into bins. Ms. Wright has gathered the following information to decide whether a cherry picker would be a profitable investment for the Elberta Fruit Farm:

a. At present, the farm is paying an average of $40,000 per year to transient workers to pick the cherries.
b. The cherry picker would cost $94,500, and it would have an estimated 12-year useful life. The farm uses straight-line depreciation on all assets and considers salvage value in computing depreciation deductions. The estimated salvage value of the cherry picker is $4,500.
c. Annual out-of-pocket costs associated with the cherry picker would be: cost of an operator and an assistant, $14,000; insurance, $200; fuel, $1,800; and a maintenance contract, $3,000.

Required
(ignore income taxes)

1. Determine the annual savings in cash operating costs that would be realized if the cherry picker were purchased.
2. Compute the simple rate of return expected from the cherry picker. (Hint: Note that this is a cost reduction project.) Would the cherry picker be purchased if Elberta Fruit Farm requires a return of 16%?
3. Compute the payback period on the cherry picker. The Elberta Fruit Farm will not purchase equipment unless it has a payback period of five years or less. Would the cherry picker be purchased?
4. Compute (to the nearest whole percent) the internal rate of return promised by the cherry picker. Based on this computation, does it appear that the simple rate of return would normally be an accurate guide in investment decisions?

Cases

C14–31   Lease or Buy Decision   Top-Quality Stores, Inc., owns a nationwide chain of supermarkets. The company is going to open another store soon, and a suitable building site has been located in an attractive and rapidly growing area. In discussing how the company can acquire the desired building and other facilities needed to open the new store, Sam Watkins, the company's vice president in charge of sales, stated, "I know most of our competitors are starting to lease facilities rather than buy, but I just can't see the economics of it. Our development people tell me that we can buy the building site, put a building on it, and get all the store fixtures we need for just $850,000. They also say that property taxes, insurance, and repairs would run $20,000 a year. When you figure that we plan to keep a site for 18 years, that's a total cost of $1,210,000. But then when you realize that the property will be worth at least a half million in 18 years, that's a net cost to us of only $710,000. What would it cost to lease the property?"

has stated that based on the use of game centres elsewhere, Romano's could expect about 26,000 people to use the centre each year and to spend an average of $5 each on the machines. In addition, it is estimated that the snack bar would provide a net cash inflow of $15,000 per year. An investment of $4,000 in working capital would be needed. This working capital investment would be released at the end of the lease term. The snack bar equipment would have a salvage value of about $12,000 in 15 years.

Romano's management is unsure which alternative to select and has asked you to help in making the decision. You have gathered the following information relating to added costs that would be incurred each year under the two alternatives:

	Expand the Pizza Shop	Install the Game Centre
Rent—building space	$18,000	$18,000
Rent—video games	—	30,000
Salaries	54,000	17,000
Utilities	13,200	5,400
Insurance and other	7,800	9,600

Required
(ignore income taxes)

1. Compute the expected net *annual* cash inflow from each alternative (cash receipts from sales and games less related cash expenses). Do *not* include present sales from the pizza shop in the computation.
2. The company requires a rate of return on all of its investments of at least 16%. Compute the net present value of each alternative. Use the total-cost approach and round all dollar amounts to the nearest whole dollar. Which alternative would you recommend?
3. Assume that the company decides to accept alternative 2. At the end of the first year, the company finds that only 21,000 people used the game centre during the year (each person spent $5 on games). Also the snack bar provided a net cash inflow of only $13,000. In light of this information, does it appear that the game centre will provide the company's 16% required rate of return? Show computations to support your answer. (Hint: It might be useful to go back to the beginning of the first year under alternative 2 with the new information.)
4. The sales manager has suggested that an advertising program be initiated to draw another 5,000 people into the game centre each year. Assuming that another 5,000 people can be attracted into the centre and that the snack bar receipts increase to the level originally estimated, how much can be spent on advertising each year and still allow the game centre to provide a 16% rate of return?

Group Exercises

GE14–34 Capital Budgets in Colleges   In recent years, your college or university has probably undertaken a capital budgeting project such as building or renovating a facility. Investigate one of these capital budgeting projects. You will probably need the help of your university's or college's accounting or finance office.

Required

1. Determine the total cost of the project and the source of the funds for the project. Did the money come from provincial funds, gifts, grants, endowments, or the school's general fund?
2. Did the costs of the project stay within budget?
3. What financial criteria were used to evaluate the project?
4. If the net present value method or internal rate of return method was used, review the calculations. Do you agree with the calculations and methods used?
5. If the net present value method was not used to evaluate the project, estimate the project's net present value. If all of the required data are not available, make reasonable estimates for the missing data. What discount rate did you use? Why?
6. Evaluate the capital budgeting procedures that were actually used by your college or university.

GE14–35 Performance Measurement, Capital Budgeting, and Management Compensation Nearly every major decentralized Canadian business uses some measure of profitability or return on investment (ROI) to assess the performance of their divisional managers. Most companies evaluate managers over the short term (quarterly and annually) and tie their bonus compensation to exceeding a target level of profit or ROI for their business unit. This provides top management with a consistent basis for evaluating business unit managers.

It is assumed that there is a high correlation between ROI and the market value of the firm. That is, the underlying assumption is that a high and growing ROI will result in an increase in the common share price and market value of the firm. This is a very important issue since the evaluation and compensation of most managers is determined by using accounting-based measures of performance.

Required

1. Are short-term accounting measures of performance consistent with the long-term interests of customers, employees, and shareholders? Explain and give examples.
2. This chapter indicated that discounted cash flow (DCF) models were best for determining the long-run impact of capital projects on the market value of the firm. The previous chapter indicated that most firms use quarterly and annual accounting measures of performance, like ROI, to evaluate the performance of managers once those assets have been acquired. Discuss the conflicts between short-term accounting-based measures of performance and the DCF models.
3. In an attempt to alleviate some of these conflicts, corporations could evaluate and compensate performance based on improvement in long-term (three to five years) accounting measures of performance like ROI. Evaluate this idea.
4. Historically, companies have used stock options (the right to buy shares at a certain price in the future, usually the price on the date the option was issued) to motivate management to take a long-term viewpoint. What are the advantages and disadvantages of this form of performance evaluation and compensation?
5. Canadian businesses have typically rewarded individual accomplishment rather than broader performance measures that reward team-based results. Evaluate each of these options.

GE14–36 Advanced Manufacturing Technologies and DCF In the 1980s, the use of discounted cash flow (DCF) methods of analysis came under increasing criticism. In particular, DCF methods were found to be deficient when used to evaluate investments in new computer-integrated manufacturing (CIM) technologies. Critics claimed that DCF methods of analysis were biased against investments in CIM technology because DCF analysis did not consider the full range of benefits provided by CIM technology. Kaplan responded to this criticism in Robert Kaplan, "Must CIM Be Justified by Faith Alone," *Harvard Business Review,* March–April 1986, pp. 87–95.

Required

1. Briefly discuss the major technical issues that have led to the misapplication of the DCF analysis.
2. Discuss the more obvious or tangible benefits related to investments in CIM technology.
3. Discuss the less obvious or intangible benefits related to investments in CIM technology.
4. Briefly explain how a capital budgeting analyst might approach quantifying the difficult-to-quantify intangible benefits.

GE14–37 Investing in Wind Power Besides being an environmentally appealing alternative to other methods of generating electrical power, wind turbines can be profitable. The Danish Wind Turbine Manufacturers Association maintains a web site at www.windpower.dk/tour/econ/econ.htm that allows you to compute the net present value of investments in wind-powered turbines.

Required

1. Verify the net present value calculation for the default data that already appear on the screen.
2. Change the real interest rate (i.e., discount rate) to 12%. What happens to the net present value of the wind turbine? What happens to the real rate of return (i.e., the internal rate of return)?
3. Keep the real interest rate set at 12%. How high would the price per kWh (i.e., kilowatt-hour) for electricity have to be to make this an attractive investment?

Capital Budgeting Decisions

Business Focus

During 1998 BCE Mobile Communications Inc. incurred capital expenditures of $392.5 million. There may be significant tax implications relating to capital investment decisions. Companies such as BCE, Magna, and Petro Canada depend on a large staff of accountants and other tax experts to assist with capital budgeting decisions. The cost of complying with income tax regulations is high in many western countries. This fact is strongly driven home in an article that appeared in *Fortune* magazine that referred to the resources that Daimler Chrysler devotes to the task.

According to the article, "Chrysler's chief tax counsel, John Lofredo, has a team of 30 tax pros at his Highland Park, Michigan, headquarters and another 25 at two subsidiaries—typical staffing for a major U.S. corporation . . . He also has two offices full of IRS agents—nine on any given day—camped out at Chrysler, haggling over past and present audits and appeals. Says Lofredo: 'They could end the income tax system today, and I'd still have ten years of work to do just settling up past disputes.' "

Source: Rob Norton, "Our Screwed-Up Tax Code," Fortune, *September 6, 1993, p. 34.*

Learning Objectives

After studying Chapter 15, you should be able to:

1 Compute the after-tax cost of a tax-deductible cash expense and the after-tax benefit from a taxable cash receipt.

2 Explain how capital cost allowance is computed.

3 Compute the tax savings arising from the capital cost allowance tax shield.

4 Compute the after-tax net present value of an investment proposal.

5 (Appendix 15A) Measure risk in assessing capital budgeting projects.

Income Taxes and Capital Budgeting

Objective 1

Compute the after-tax cost of a tax-deductible cash expense and the after-tax benefit from a taxable cash receipt.

In our discussion of capital budgeting in the preceding chapter, the matter of income taxes was omitted for two reasons. First, many organizations have no taxes to pay. Such organizations include not-for-profit schools and hospitals, and governmental units on municipal, provincial, and federal levels. These organizations will always use capital budgeting techniques on a before-tax basis, as illustrated in the preceding chapter. Second, the topic of capital budgeting is somewhat complex, and it is best absorbed in small doses. Now that we have laid a solid groundwork in the concepts of present value and discounting, we can explore the effects of income taxes on capital budgeting decisions with little difficulty.

The Canadian Tax Regulations are enormously complex, and it requires many years of study to master even a portion of the regulations in any depth. We only scratch the surface in this text. To keep the subject within reasonable bounds, we have made many simplifying assumptions about the tax regulations throughout the chapter. The most important of these assumptions are that (1) with the exception of depreciation calculations, taxable income equals net income as computed for financial reports; and (2) the tax rate is a flat percentage of taxable income.[1] The reader should be aware that the actual tax regulations are far more complex than this. However, these and the other simplifications that we make throughout the chapter allow us to cover the most important implications of income taxes for capital budgeting, while suppressing details that are relatively unimportant in understanding the big picture.

The Concept of After-Tax Cost

Businesses, like individuals, must pay income taxes. In the case of businesses, the amount of income tax that must be paid is determined by the company's net taxable income. Tax deductible expenses (tax deductions) decrease the company's net taxable income and hence reduce the taxes the company must pay. For this reason, expenses

No one person can be an expert on the entire Canadian Tax Regulations. Tax lawyers for corporations often end up in tax court wrestling with what the code means in a particular instance.

---

1. Corporations are taxed both federally and provincially. For the year 2000 provincial rates vary from 9.15 to 17%. Rates may be lower on manufacturing income. For example, the rate for manufacturing companies in Newfoundland is 5%. Provincial rates may be further reduced for small businesses. The basic federal rate is 29.12% for nonmanufacturing companies, 22.12% for manufacturing income and 13.12% for eligible small business income. In this chapter we will use combined rates such as 30% and 40% for convenience.

Exhibit 15–1
The Computation of
After-Tax Cost

	Without Training Program	With Training Program
Sales	$850,000	$850,000
Less tax deductible expenses:		
Salaries, insurance, and other	700,000	700,000
New training program		60,000
Total expenses	700,000	760,000
Taxable income	$150,000	$ 90,000
Income taxes (40%)	$ 60,000	$ 36,000

Cost of new training program	$60,000
Less: Reduction in income taxes ($60,000 − $36,000)	24,000
After-tax cost of the new training program	$36,000

After-tax cost The amount of net cash outflow resulting from a tax-deductible cash expense after income tax effects have been considered. The amount is determined by multiplying the tax-deductible cash expense by (1 − Tax rate).

are often stated on an *after-tax* basis. For example, if a company pays rent of $10 million a year but this expense results in a reduction in income taxes of $3 million, the after-tax cost of the rent is $7 million. An expenditure net of its tax effect is known as **after-tax cost.**

To illustrate, assume that a company with a tax rate of 40% is contemplating a training program that costs $60,000. What impact will this have on the company's taxes? To keep matters simple, let's suppose the training program has no immediate effect on sales. How much does the company actually pay for the training program after taking into account the impact of this expense on taxes? The answer is $36,000 as shown in Exhibit 15–1. While the training program costs $60,000 before taxes, it would reduce the company's taxes by $24,000, so its *after-tax* cost would be only $36,000.

The after-tax cost of any tax-deductible cash expense can be determined using the following formula:[2]

$$\text{After-tax cost (net cash outflow)} = (1 - \text{Tax rate}) \times \text{Tax-deductible cash expense} \quad (1)$$

We can verify the accuracy of this formula by applying it to the $60,000 training program expenditure:

$$(1 - 0.40) \times \$60,000 = \$36,000 \text{ after-tax cost of the training program}$$

After-tax benefit The amount of net cash inflow realized from a taxable cash receipt after income tax effects have been considered. The amount is determined by multiplying the taxable cash receipt by (1 − Tax rate).

This formula is very useful since it provides the actual amount of cash a company must pay after taking into consideration tax effects. It is this actual, after-tax, cash outflow that should be used in capital budgeting decisions.

Similar reasoning applies to revenues and other *taxable* cash inflows. Since these cash receipts are taxable, the company must pay out a portion of them in taxes. The **after-tax benefit,** or net cash inflow, realized from a particular cash receipt can be obtained by applying a simple variation of the cash expenditure formula used above:

---

2. This formula assumes that a company is operating at a profit; if it is operating at a loss, the tax situation can be very complex. For simplicity, we assume in all examples, exercises, and problems that the company is operating at a profit.

Exhibit 15–2
The Impact of Capital
Cost allowance on
Tax Payments

	Without CCA Deduction	With CCA Deduction
Sales	$500,000	$500,000
Cash operating expenses	310,000	310,000
Cash flow from operations	190,000	190,000
Capital cost allowance	—	90,000
Taxable income	$190,000	$100,000
Income taxes (40%)	$ 76,000	$ 40,000

$36,000 lower taxes with the capital cost allowance

Cash flow comparison:		
Cash flow from operations (above)	$190,000	$190,000
Income taxes (above)	76,000	40,000
Net cash flow	$114,000	$150,000

$36,000 greater cash flow with the capital cost allowance deduction

$$\frac{\text{After-tax benefit}}{\text{(net cash inflow)}} = (1 - \text{Tax rate}) \times \text{Taxable cash receipt} \qquad (2)$$

We emphasize the term *taxable cash receipts* because not all cash inflows are taxable. For example, the release of working capital at the termination of an investment project would not be a taxable cash inflow, since it simply represents a return of original investment.

Focus on Current Practice

A Working Paper survey study by Brian Erard of the Department of Economics at Carleton University in 1997 shows that the combined federal-provincial income and capital tax compliance burden for the top 500 Canadian nonfinancial corporations in the mid-1990s amounted to $250 million, or about 5% of taxes paid.[3] While this burden is considerable, it is appreciably smaller than recent estimates of the compliance cost for large U.S. corporations whose compliance costs often exceed the income tax liability. ■

Capital Cost Allowance Tax Shield

Depreciation is not a cash flow. For this reason, depreciation was ignored in Chapter 14 in all discounted cash flow computations. However, depreciation does affect the taxes

---

3. B. Erard, "The Income Tax Compliance Burden on Canadian Big Business," *Working Paper 97-2* (Carleton University, Department of Economics, April 1997).

Exhibit 15–3
Tax Adjustments
Required in a Capital
Budgeting Analysis

Item	Treatment
Tax-deductible cash expense*	Multiply by (1 − Tax rate) to get after-tax cost.
Taxable cash receipt*	Multiply by (1 − Tax rate) to get after-tax cash inflow.
CCA deduction	Multiply by the tax rate to get the tax savings from the CCA tax shield.

*Cash expenses can be deducted from the cash receipts and the difference multiplied by (1 − Tax rate). See the example at the top of Exhibit 15–7.

that must be paid and therefore has an indirect effect on the company's cash flows. Customs Canada and Revenue Agency refers to depreciation as capital cost allowance (CCA).

To illustrate the effect of CCA deductions on tax payments, consider a company with annual cash sales of $500,000 and cash operating expenses of $310,000. In addition, the company has a depreciable asset on which the capital cost allowance is $90,000 per year. The tax rate is 40%. As shown in Exhibit 15–2, the CCA deduction reduces the company's taxes by $36,000. In effect, the CCA deduction of $90,000 *shields* $90,000 in revenues from taxation and thereby *reduces* the amount of taxes that the company must pay. Because CCA deductions shield revenues from taxation, they are generally referred to as a **capital cost allowance tax shield.**[4] The reduction in tax payments made possible by the CCA tax shield is equal to the amount of the CCA deduction, multiplied by the tax rate as follows:

Capital cost allowance tax shield A reduction in tax that results from capital cost allowance deductions. The reduction in tax is computed by multiplying the CCA by the tax rate.

$$\text{Tax savings from the CCA tax shield} = \text{Tax rate} \times \text{Capital cost allowance} \qquad (2)$$

We can verify this formula by applying it to the $90,000 depreciation deduction in our example:

$$0.30 \times \$90,000 = \$27,000 \text{ reduction in tax payments}$$

In this chapter, when we estimate after-tax cash flows for capital budgeting decisions, we will include the tax savings provided by the capital cost allowance tax shield.

A summary of the concepts we have introduced so far is given in Exhibit 15–3.

The Capital Cost Allowance System

Objective 2

Explain how capital cost allowance is computed.

Capital cost allowance is Customs Canada and Revenue Agency's counterpart to depreciation. Depreciation is the allocation of the cost of an asset over its useful life. The amount deducted each period for financial statement reporting purposes is based on generally accepted accounting principles (GAAP). Any method that is systemic and rational falls within the bounds of GAAP. Although it is not possible to defend or refute such allocations, the amount deducted should be in proportion to the net revenue contributions expected to be generated by the asset. For income tax purposes, however, depreciation is not an allowable expense. Instead, an allowance commonly referred to as capital cost allowance or CCA is permitted by regulations that accompany the Canadian Income Tax Act.

The income tax regulations group assets into classes and each class is then assigned a maximum capital cost allowance rate for tax reporting purposes. Maximum

---

4. The term *CCA tax shield* may convey the impression that there is something underhanded about capital cost allowances—that companies are getting some sort of special tax break. However, to use the capital cost allowance, a company must have already acquired a depreciable asset—which typically requires a cash outflow. Essentially, the tax regulations requires companies to delay recognizing the cash outflow as an expense until depreciation charges are recorded.

E

capital cost allowance rates are prescribed by the tax regulations for 44 classes or pools of assets. A company has the option of deducting capital cost allowance for each asset class for any amount ranging from zero to the maximum amount prescribed by the act. These prescribed rates are subject to governmental change. Examples of these assets pools and prescribed rates follow:

Asset	Class	Prescribed Rate
Buildings	1	4%
Assets not included in other		
classes	8	20%
Computer equipment	10	30%
Vans, trucks and tractors	10	30%
Passenger automobiles	10.1	Irregular
Small tools, certified films,		
nonsystem software	12	100%
Leasehold improvements	13	Straight line
Rental cars and taxis	16	40%
Excavating equipment	22	30%

Objective 3

Compute the tax savings arising from the capital cost allowance tax shield.

During the early years of an asset's life, CCA generally exceeds what depreciation would be and thus may be an incentive to encourage capital investment. One could also argue that these higher deductions are a partial compensation to taxpayers to help cope with rising inflationary prices of replacement assets. Without entirely removing the incentives, the current legislation now brings CCA rates fairly in line with depreciation for financial reporting purposes. Prescribed CCA rates, however, are and will likely continue to be influenced by a combination of social, economic and political pressures that are not analogous to the determinants of accounting-based depreciation.

Capital cost allowance is calculated essentially by applying the prescribed rate to a declining balance called **undepreciated capital cost (UCC).** Class 13 assets are an exception to the declining balance capital cost allowance write-off pattern. For net additions to each asset during the year, however, only one-half of the prescribed rate is permitted. Under Customs Canada and Revenue Agency's half-year rule only half the normal CCA for most assets is allowed as a tax-deductible expense for the year the asset is put in use. Regardless of when during the year the asset is acquired the half-year rule will apply unless a particular exception is specified by the Tax Act. The act also specifies certain irregular write-off patterns, as in the case with passenger automobiles in Class 10.1. The management accountant may occasionally have to seek the advice of a tax expert to assist in capital budgeting analysis.

An asset becomes eligible for CCA during the year in which it is either put in use or ready for use. This is known as the "put in use" rule. An example illustrating the calculation of CCA for a Class 10 (30%) pool of assets follows:

Undepreciated capital cost (UCC) The remaining book value of an asset class or pool of assets that is available for tax-deductible depreciation (capital cost allowance). The maximum amount of capital cost allowance that can be deducted in a taxation year of a particular CCA class is the UCC multiplied by the CCA rate for that asset class.

UCC, January 1, 2001 (a)		$20,000
Acquisition during the year	$16,000	
Disposal proceeds during the year	6,000	
Thus:		
Acquisitions during the year	$16,000	
Disposals	(6,000)*	
Net additions	$10,000	
One-half of net additions (b)		5,000
UCC for CCA purposes (a + b)		$25,000
CCA at 30%		(7,500)
		$17,500
Add back one-half of net additions ...		5,000
UCC, December 31, 2001		$22,500

*When there is a disposition of assets from the pool, the amount deducted is the lesser of the proceeds or the original capital cost of the asset.

exhibit have already been discussed in connection with Exhibit 15–5. Only a couple of points need elaboration:

1. *Annual cash operating costs.* Because there are no revenues identified with the project, we simply place the cash operating costs on an after-tax basis and discount them as we did in Chapter 14.
2. *Sale of the old press.* The sale of the old press is deducted from the cost of the new press in the computation of the capital cost allowance tax shield. Note that we are making a *net addition* to the asset pool. The CCA half-year rule is applied to the incremental outlay to the asset class. It is the incremental cost of $110,000 ($150,000 minus $40,000) that is relevant in determining this benefit.

Focus on Current Practice

Qualitative factors are important in capital budgeting decisions. Technology assessment cart help hospitals rank the importance of capital requests by providing crucial information both about existing equipment and about new equipment that has been requested. Integrating technology assessment into the capital budgeting process is the best way for hospitals to determine what equipment should be purchased each year: A case study of Hamilton Civic Hospitals (HCH) demonstrates how the capital budgeting process was modified by hiring an independent firm to assess HCH's imaging department's capital needs, By modifying the capital budgeting process, integrating a technology assessment component, and matching technology with need, HCH has created a needs-driven process that has permitted efficient allocation of its limited capital resources to match technology with need.[6] ∎

Focus on Current Practice

As of March 1997, Canada's federal corporate tax revenue as a percentage of GDP was 2.4%. This is comparable to the U.S. (2.5%) and Britain (2.7%). It is lower than Japan (4.1%), but higher than France (1.6%) and Germany (1.1%). On average, Canadian corporations have paid about 36% of their pre-tax profits to government in income and capital taxes over the past three decades, ranging between 32% and 41% since 1965. In this light, why do so many Canadian businesses complain about high tax rates? Because Canadian businesses are required to pay a host of other taxes in addition to income tax and capital gains tax. These include:

- payroll taxes (lower in relation to most major economies but accelerating)
- employment insurance premiums (on the decline)
- CPP (which is expected to increase dramatically in the near future)
- workers' compensation
- in some cases, training
- commercial property taxes (among the highest in the world)
- sales and excise taxes
- indirect taxes such as fuel taxes[7] ∎

---

6. Dave Watts, Donna L. Finneu, and Brian Lovie, "Integrating Technology Assessment into the Capital Budgeting Process," *Healthcare Financial Management* (February 1993), pp. 21–29.
7. Nankivell Neville, "Tax Figures Show That Corporations Are Not Being Let Off Lightly," *The Financial Post*, March 1/3, 1997, p. 23.

Behavioural Considerations

The chapter thus far has emphasized the technical aspects of capital budgeting. The management accountant should also be cognizant of important behavioural considerations. An understanding of the functional and dysfunctional consequences of human input provides deeper insight into the whole capital budgeting process.

Capital budgeting projects require creativity, judgment, and the ability to see ideas through to implementation. The entire capital budgeting process from idea generation to implementation can provide valuable training for managers. There may be nonfinancial reasons for accepting certain projects. Some marginal projects may be accepted because they provide good experience and training benefits.

Estimates of cash flows, discount rates, and salvage values may be affected by the attitudes of individual managers toward risk. Risk-averse managers tend to use more conservative figures in their estimates than those managers who tend to seek risk and take on more venturesome projects.

The micropolitics of the organizations may also affect the capital budgeting process. Key managers may favour their own pet projects. Self-identification with projects may obscure management judgment of when to abandon a particular project. Obtaining truthful estimates may become problematic. Internal politics may also influence how projects are awarded. With only limited company funds available for capital investments, a division with several good investment proposals may be denied acceptance of some proposals for less profitable projects of other divisions. Such sharing of projects may be seen as necessary to maintain harmony and to give the appearance of fairness.

The capital budgeting process itself may create additional pressure on top management. Projects often have to go through several layers of approval before reaching top management. It may be difficult to reject projects already approved by managers at lower levels. On the other hand, some projects rejected at lower levels, and thus never to reach the purview of top management, may actually be acceptable to top management because they help diversify the firm's overall risk.

Projects involving employee safety, environmental or consumer safety or which impact heavily on the firm's social environment may have to be evaluated by nonfinancial criteria. Other projects which cannot be justified on financial grounds may have to be undertaken in order to conform to municipal, provincial, or federal laws.

Unethical behaviour involving nepotism or kickbacks sometimes occur. The management accountant has an ethical responsibility to communicate information fairly and objectively. All relevant information, favourable or unfavourable, should be fully disclosed so as not to bias or undermine the decision-making process. Assumptions regarding cash flows, probabilities, salvage value, etc., should be clearly communicated. The management accountant is expected to act with full integrity and should avoid situations which could prejudice his or her ability to perform capital budgeting analysis in an ethical manner.

Capital budgeting can also be affected by the firm's performance reward system. If too much weight is given to short-term performance measures, there is little incentive for managers to devote time and effort to long-term capital budgeting projects.

In summary, the capital budgeting process involves more factors than first meet the eye. A purely quantitative approach to capital budgeting is not sufficient. Any model developed to solve capital budgeting problems is not broad enough to encompass all decision variables. Important qualitative factors imposed on the process by the political and social environment within the firm may strongly influence capital budgeting decisions. All levels of management should take a broad view, and reward systems within the firm should be flexible enough to encourage the acceptance of projects leading to optimal capital investment decisions.

Summary

Unless a company is a tax-exempt organization, such as a school or a governmental unit, income taxes should be considered in making capital budgeting computations. When income taxes are a factor in a company, tax-deductible cash expenditures must be placed on an after-tax basis by multiplying the expenditure by $(1 - \text{tax rate})$. Only the after-tax amount is used in determining the desirability of an investment proposal. Similarly, taxable cash flows must be placed on an after-tax basis by multiplying the cash inflow by the same formula.

Although capital cost allowances deductions do not involve a present outflow of cash, they are a valid expense for tax purposes and as such affect income tax payments. Capital cost allowances shield income from taxation, resulting in decreased taxes being paid. This shielding of income from taxation is commonly called a capital cost allowance tax shield. The savings in income taxes arising from the CCA tax shield are computed by multiplying the capital cost allowance deduction by the tax rate itself. Since capital cost allowances generally provide the bulk of their tax shield early in the life of an asset, they are superior to a straight-line method from a present value of tax savings point of view.

Review Problem: Capital Budgeting and Taxes

A company is considering two investment projects. Relevant cost and cash inflow information on each project follows:

	Project	
	A	**B**
Investment in passenger bus.....	$70,000	
Investment in working capital ...		$70,000
Net annual cash inflows........	13,500	13,500
Life of the project............	8 years*	8 years

*Useful life of the buses.

The bus will have a $5,000 salvage value in eight years. The capital cost allowance is 30% and the income tax rate is 40%. At the end of eight years, the working capital in project B will be released for use elsewhere.

The company requires an after-tax return of 10% on all investments.

Required
1. Compute the net present value of each investment project.
2. Compute the profitability index for each investment project.

Solution to Review Problem

	Year(s)	Amount	Tax Effect	Cash Flows	Factor	Cash Flows
Investment in passenger buses	Now	$(70,000)	—	$(70,000)	1.000	$(70,000)
Net annual cash inflows	1–8	13,500	1 – 0.40	8,100	5.335	43,214
Present value of CCA tax shield:						

$$PV = \left(\frac{Cdt}{d+k}\right) \times \left(\frac{1+.5k}{1+k}\right) - \left(\frac{S \times d \times t}{d+k}\right) \times (1+k)^{-n}$$

$$= \frac{70,000 \times .3 \times .4}{.3 + .10} \times \frac{1+.05}{1+.10} - \frac{5,000 \times .3 \times .4}{.3 + .10} \times (1+.10)^{-8}$$

$$= (21,000 \times .9545) - (1,500 \times .467)$$

$$= 20,045 - 700 \qquad\qquad\qquad\qquad 19,345$$

Salvage value of the buses	8	5.000	—	5,000	.467	2,335
Net present value						(5,106)

The formula for the profitability index is:

$$\frac{\text{Present value of cash flows}}{\text{Investment required}} = \text{Profitability index}$$

Applying this formula to the data in (1) above, we get:

	Project	
	A	**B**
Present value of cash inflows:		
Net annual cash inflows	$43,214	$43,214
Tax savings from CCA (totals)	19,345	—
Salvage value of the bus	2,335	—
Release of working capital	—	32,690
Total cash inflows (a)	$64,894	$75,904
Investment required (b)	$70,000	$70,000
Profitability index (a) − (b)	0.93	1.08

Note from (1) above that project A has a negative net present value and therefore is not an acceptable investment. This also can be seen in the profitability index computation in that project A has a profitability index of less than 1.00. If a project has a profitability index of less than 1.00, it means that the project is returning less than a dollar of cash inflow for each dollar of investment. By contrast, project B is returning $1.08 of cash inflow for each dollar of investment.

Appendix 15A: Risk and Uncertainty in Capital Budgeting

Objective 5

Measure risk in assessing capital budgeting projects.

The appendix to Chapter 5 introduced probabilities and discussed how a business decision may be influenced by a manager's assessment of the most likely outcomes. The same concepts can also be applied to capital budgeting.

Recall that a probability is a number between 0 and 1 which describes the likelihood that an event will take place. A probability of zero is assigned to an event which has no chance of occurring, while a probability of 1 denotes absolute certainty that an event will occur. An outcome with a 90% chance of occurring is assigned a probability of .9 indicating that it is expected to occur in 9 out of 10 times.

Assume that Lockwood Company in Vancouver is assessing which of two 5-year $12,000 investment projects to undertake. Lockwood uses expected value as its decision criterion. The cost of capital is estimated at 10%.

The analysis in Exhibit 15A–1 shows that the expected returns for both project A and project B are $10,800 per year. The expected return of each project can be thought of as a return of $10,800 by the present value of an annuity factor of 3.791 and subtracting the initial investment of five-year period annuity. The net present value can now be calculated by multiplying the expected $12,000 ($10,800 × 3.791 − $12,000 = $28,943).

A limitation of using expected returns as a benchmark when deciding among competing projects is that it fails to account for the risk preferences of individual managers. A full discussion is beyond the scope of this book, but one should be cognizant that management's attitude toward risk may impact on the selection process. Risk takers may be willing to forgo a project with a high expected return for another project with a lower expected return but with some probability of reaching a higher maximum.

Probable Outcome	Net Cash Flows	Probability	Probable Return
Project A:			
Pessimistic	$ 4,000	.20	$ 800
Most likely	10,000	.60	6,000
Optimistic	20,000	.20	4,000
		1.00	$10,800
Project B:			
Pessimistic	$ –0–	.20	$ –0–
Most likely	11,000	.60	6,600
Optimistic	21,000	.20	4,200
		1.00	$10,800

A Statistical Measure of Risk

Standard deviation   A statistical tool used by the management accountant to determine the amount of variation in a project's actual returns from the project's expected returns.

One way of measuring the risk of capital budgeting projects is to determine the extent to which actual returns deviate from the expected returns by calculating the **standard deviation.** The standard deviation of a project's return is the square root of the sum of the average squared deviations of actual returns from the expected return (EV) of the project. The formula for calculating the standard deviation is as follows:

$$\sigma = \sqrt{\sum_{i=1}^{N}(E_i - \bar{E})^2 P_i}$$

where σ = standard deviation

N = number of possible outcomes

E_i = the value of the ith possible outcome

$\bar{E}$ = the expected returns

P_i = probabilities that the ith outcome will occur

Statisticians have determined that for *normal* probability distributions, 68% of the outcomes are plus or minus one standard deviation from the expected value; 95% are plus or minus two standard deviations; and 99% of all outcomes lie between plus or minus three standard deviations away from the expected value. A normal probability distribution has one-half of the values in the distribution above the expected value and the other one-half below the expected value. Most statistics textbooks illustrate the normal distribution graphically as a bell-shaped curve and also provide tables that give the statistically calculated probabilities that are associated with various deviations from the expected values. Exhibit 15A–2 shows the calculation of the standard deviation of projects A and B for Lockwood Company.

Although projects A and B have equal expected values of $10,800, it is clear from the forgoing analysis that there is more variation in the returns of project B. Standard deviation, a common statistical measure of this variation, is higher for project B than it is for project A.

Coefficient of variation   A relative measure of a project's dispersion calculated as the ratio of a project's standard deviation to its expected value.

Coefficient of Variation

The **coefficient of variation (CV)** is a measure of the relative risk of an investment project. It is calculated by dividing a project's standard deviation by its expected value. For Lockwood Company, the CVs for projects A and B are as follows:

Exhibit 15A–2

Project A	E_i	$\bar{E}$	$(E_i-\bar{E})$	(In thousands of dollars) $(E_i-\bar{E})^2$	P_i	(In thousands of dollars) $(E_i-\bar{E})^2P_i$
Pessimistic	$ 4,000	$10,800	$(6,800)	$46,240	.2	$ 9,248
Most likely	10,000	10,800	(800)	640	.6	384
Optimistic..........	20,000	10,800	9,200	84,640	.2	16,928

Variance = $26,560

Standard deviation = $\sqrt{\text{variance}}$ = $\sqrt{\$26,560,000}$ = $5,154.00

Project B	E_i	$\bar{E}$	$(E_i-\bar{E})$	(In thousands of dollars) $(E_i-\bar{E})^2$	P_i	(In thousands of dollars) $(E_i-\bar{E})^2P_i$
Pessimistic	$ –0–	$10,800	$(10,800)	$166,640	0.20	$23,328
Most likely	11,000	10,800	200	40	0.60	24
Optimistic..........	21,000	10,800	10,200	104,040	0.20	20,808

Variance = $44,160

Standard deviation = $\sqrt{\text{variance}}$ = $\sqrt{\$44,160,000}$ = $6,645.30

$$\text{CV for project A} = \frac{\$5,154}{\$10,800} = .48$$

$$\text{CV for project B} = \frac{\$6,645}{\$10,800} = .62$$

The larger standard deviation is as a percentage of the expected value, the higher the risk is judged to be. Using CV as the decision criterion, project B is clearly riskier than project A. This is consistent with the conclusion reached by using the standard deviation alone. So long as the expected values of the projects are equal, the coefficient of variation does not add any additional information. When the expected values differ, however, the CV is a better measure of risk than the absolute measure that is provided by the standard deviation.

Example

To assist in choosing between two mutually exclusive investment projects (the selection of one precludes the selection of the other), the following information is available for Calgary Equipment Company:

	Project C	Project D
Expected cash returns ($\bar{E}$)	$20,000	$40,000
Standard deviation (SD)	$8,000	$12,000
Coefficient of variation (SD/$\bar{E}$)	.40	.30

On the basis of standard deviation alone the management of Calgary Equipment Company may be tempted to declare project D to be riskier than project C. The absolute measure of risk provided by the standard deviation can lead to an error in the selection process when the expected returns differ between the two projects. Using the coefficient of variation to measure the *relative* risk of projects, it is apparent that project C is riskier than project D.

From the perspective of an individual firm, it may be possible to reduce overall risk by selecting individual projects with returns that vary negatively with the firm's

Correlation   A number ranging from +1 to −1 that is a statistical measure of the degree of association of the returns of one project to those of another.

existing projects. **Correlation** is a statistical technique that measures the relationship of the returns of the project to those of another. A correlation of +1 indicates a perfect positive relationship. This means, for example, that when returns on project X are high, returns on project Y are also high. When returns on project X are low, returns on project Y are low as well. A correlation coefficient of −1 indicates a perfect negative correlation meaning, for example, that when returns are high for project X, they are low for project Y and vice versa. Most correlation coefficients fall somewhere in between +1 and −1. The essential point for the manager to bear in mind is that it may be less risky to select projects with returns that vary inversely with those of existing projects, so that a downturn for one project does not impact negatively on the returns on another project. In other words, by combining projects with returns that correlate negatively with the firm's existing portfolio of projects, the overall variability or risk for the firm may be reduced. In practice, these concepts are very hard to apply. In addition, there is strong theoretical support for choosing projects on their individual merits because the residual owners of the firm (common shareholders) can do their own diversifying by acquiring shares of a variety of companies.

Sensitivity Analysis

Sensitivity analysis   An analysis of the effect that changes in a project's input variables may have on its net present value or internal rate of return.

It is apparent that many estimates are required in the capital budgeting process. Managers may find it useful to prepare a what-if, or sensitivity, analysis to determine how sensitive the net present value or internal rate of return of a project is to changes in these estimates. Although **sensitivity analysis** does not actually quantify risk, it can provide management with useful insights into the effects of changes in such input variables such as cash flow estimates and discount rates. The more the net present value or internal rate of return changes in response to changes in input variables, the riskier the project is perceived to be.

Questions

15–1   What is meant by after-tax cost and how is the concept used in capital budgeting decisions?

15–2   What is a capital cost allowance tax shield and how does it affect capital budgeting decisions?

15–3   The two most widely used depreciation methods are straight line and double-declining balance. Explain why a company might use these methods instead of capital cost allowance for computing depreciation expense in its published financial statements.

15–4   Why do companies generally prefer accelerated methods of capital cost allowance to the straight-line method for income tax reporting?

15–5   Ludlow Company is considering the introduction of a new product line. Would an increase in the income tax rate tend to make the new investment more or less attractive? Explain.

15–6   Assume that an old piece of equipment is sold at a loss. From a capital budgeting point of view, what two cash inflows will be associated with the sale?

15–7   Assume that a new piece of equipment costs $40,000 and that the tax rate is 30%. Should the new piece of equipment be shown in the capital budgeting analysis as a cash outflow of $40,000, or should it be shown as a cash outflow of $28,000 [$40,000 × (1 − 0.30)]? Explain.

15–8   Assume that a company has cash operating expenses of $15,000 and a capital cost allowance of $10,000. Can these two items be added together and treated as one in a capital budgeting analysis, or should they be kept separate? Explain.

15–9   Why might some capital budgeting projects be accepted even when they cannot be justified on a purely financial basis? Could there be some ethical issues involved?

Exercises

E15–1   a.   Neal Company would like to initiate a management development program for its executives. The program would cost $100,000 per year to operate. What would be the after-tax cost of the program if the company's income tax rate is 30%?

b.   Smerk's Department Store has rearranged the merchandise display cases on the first floor of its building, placing fast turnover items near the front door. This rearrangement has caused the company's contribution margin (and taxable income) to increase by $40,000 per month. If the company's income tax rate is 30%, what is the after-tax benefit from this rearrangement of facilities?

c.   Sydney Schoomer, Inc., has just purchased a new electronic score board at a cost of $210,000. The estimated useful life is 15 years and has a $14,000 salvage value. Determine the yearly tax savings from the CCA tax shield. Assume that the income tax rate is 30%, CCA is 30% and cost of capital is 8%.

E15–2   a.   Complete the following table:

	Case 1	Case 2	Case 3	Case 4
Beginning UCC	$60,000	$60,000	$60,000	$60,000
Disposal of assets				
Capital cost	20,000	40,000	70,000	80,000
Proceeds	12,000	78,000	65,000	40,000
Capital gain				
UCC after disposition				
Recapture				
Terminal loss				
UCC for CCA purposes				

b.   Morgan Industries has an opportunity to penetrate a new market by making some modifications to one of its existing products. These modifications would require the purchase of various tools and small items of equipment that would cost $80,000 and have a four-year useful life. The equipment would have a $7,500 salvage value. CCA is 20%.

The modified product would generate before-tax net cash receipts of $35,000 per year. It is estimated that the equipment would require repairs in the third year that would cost $14,000. The company's tax rate is 30%, and its after-tax cost of capital is 12%.

Required   1.   Compute the net present value of the proposed investment in tools and equipment.
2.   Would you recommend that the tools and equipment be purchased? Explain.

E15–3   Dwyer Company is considering two investment projects. Relevant cost and cash flow information on the two projects is given below:

	Project	
	A	B
Investment in heavy trucks	$130,000	
Investment in working capital		$130,000
Net annual cash inflows	25,000	25,000
Life of the project	9 years*	9 years
CCA	30%	

*Useful life of the trucks

The trucks will have a $15,000 salvage value in nine years, and they will be depreciated using the straight-line method for accounting purposes. For accounting purposes at the end of nine years, the working capital will be released for use elsewhere. The company requires an after-tax return of 12% on all investments. The tax rate is 30%.

Required   Compute the net present value of each investment project. Round all dollar amounts to the nearest whole dollar.

E15–4   The Midtown Cafeteria employs five people to operate antiquated dishwashing equipment. The cost of wages for these people and for maintenance of the equipment is $85,000 per year. Management is considering the purchase of a single, highly automated dishwashing machine that would cost $160,000 and have a useful life of 12 years. This machine would require the services of only three people to operate at a cost of $48,000 per year. A maintenance contract on the machine would cost an additional $2,000 per year. New water jets would be needed on the machine in six years at a total cost of $15,000.

   The old equipment is fully depreciated and has no resale value. The new machine will have a salvage value of $9,000 at the end of its 12-year useful life. Management requires a 14% after-tax return on all equipment purchases. The company's tax rate is 30%. CCA is 20%.

Required   1.   Determine the before-tax net annual cost savings that the new dishwashing machine will provide.
   2.   Using the data from (1) above and other data from the exercise, compute the new dishwashing machine's net present value. Round all dollar amounts to the nearest whole dollar. Would you recommend that it be purchased?

Problems

P15–5   Basic Net Present Value Analysis   The Diamond Freight Company has been offered a seven-year contract to haul munitions for the government. Since this contract would represent new business, the company would have to purchase several new heavy-duty trucks at a cost of $350,000 if the contract were accepted. Other data relating to the contract follow:

Net annual cash receipts (before taxes) from the contract	$105,000
Cost of replacing the motors in the trucks in four years	45,000
Salvage value of the trucks at termination of the contract	18,000

With the motors being replaced after four years, the trucks will have a useful life of seven years. To raise money to assist in the purchase of the new trucks, the company will sell several old, fully depreciated trucks for a total selling price of $16,000. The company uses the maximum CCA of 30% and requires a 16% after-tax return on all equipment purchases. The tax rate is 40%.

Required   Compute the net present value of this investment opportunity. Round all dollar amounts to the nearest whole dollar. Would you recommend that the contract be accepted?

P15–6   Straightforward Net Present Value Analysis   The Vancouver Timber Company estimates that the following costs would be associated with the cutting and sale of timber on land to which it has cutting rights:

Investment in equipment needed for cutting and removing the timber	$400,000
Working capital investment needed	75,000
Annual cash receipts, from sale of timber, net of related cash operating costs (before taxes)	88,000
Cost of reseeding the land	60,000

The timber would be exhausted after 10 years of cutting and sales; all reseeding would be done in the 10th year. The equipment would have a useful life of 15 years, but it would be sold for an estimated 20% of its original cost when cutting was completed. The company uses a CCA rate of 30%. The tax rate is 40% and the after-tax cost of captial is 12%. The working capital would be released for use elsewhere at the completion of the project.

Since the timber is difficult to get to and of marginal quality, management is uncertain as to whether it should proceed with the project.

Required

1. Compute the net present value of this investment project. Round all dollar amounts to the nearest whole dollar.
2. Would you recommend that the investment project be undertaken? Explain.
3. What other factors should be considered?

P15–7 Various CCA Methods; Net Present Value Fencik Laboratories has been offered an eight-year contract to provide materials relating to the government's space exploration program. Management has determined that the following costs and revenues would be associated with the contract:

Cost of special equipment	$600,000
Working capital needed	115,000
Annual revenues from the contract	450,000
Annual out-of-pocket costs for materials, salaries, and so forth	280,000
Salvage value of the equipment in eight years	9,000

Although the equipment would have a useful life of nine years, it would have little salvage value remaining at the end of the contract period, as shown above. Fencik's after-tax cost of capital is 14%; its tax rate is 30%. At the end of the contract period, the working capital will be released for use elsewhere.

Required

1. Assume that Fencik Laboratories uses a CCA rate of 20% for tax purposes. Determine the net present value of the proposed contract. Round all dollar amounts to the nearest whole dollar.
2. Assume that Fencik Laboratories uses a CCA rate of 50% to compute CCA deductions. Determine the net present value of the proposed contract. Round all dollar amounts to the nearest whole dollar.
3. How do you explain the difference in rate of return between (1) and (2) above?

P15–8 Net Present Value Analysis The Island Travel Service (ITS) operates out of Sydney, Nova Scotia. ITS has an opportunity to purchase several small charter boats that were recently repossessed by a local bank. Although the boats cost $700,000 new and are only three years old, they can be purchased by ITS for the "bargain basement" price of $430,000, payable $250,000 down and $60,000 each year for three years, without interest.

After some study, ITS's manager, Biff MacNeil has determined that the boats could be operated an average of 250 days per year. Records kept by the previous owner (now in the hands of the bank) indicate that the boats carried an average of 70 tourists per day. Mr. MacNeil is confident that this could be increased to at least 140 tourists per day by dropping the tour price from $18 to $10 per person. The local bank has estimated the following annual expenses associated with the boats:

Salaries for a manager and for boat operators	$160,000
Insurance	9,000
Fuel	72,000
Bank payments*	60,000
Promotion	18,000
Maintenance	4,200
Rent for docking space	10,000
Fees and maritime taxes	6,800
Depreciation per income statement	27,333[†]
Total expenses	$367,333

*For the first three years only.

[†]$430,000 cost − $20,000 estimated salvage value = $410,000 depreciable cost; $410,000 ÷ 15 years = $27,333 per year.

To cover possible damage from docking, ITS would have to make an immediate deposit of $1,800 to the harbour authorities; this deposit would be refundable at the end of the boat's 15-year remaining useful life. In nine years, the boat hulls would require major scraping and resealing at a cost of $35,000.

If the boats are purchased, ITS will use a CCA rate of 30%. ITS's after-tax cost of capital is 10% and the tax rate is 40%.

Required
1. Compute the net cash receipts (before income taxes) each year from operating the boats.
2. Using net present value analysis, determine whether the boats should be purchased. Round all dollar amounts to the nearest whole dollar.

P15–9 Uneven Cash Flows; Net Present Value "All of the engineering studies say that tar sand is excellent for use in road construction," said Holly Edwards, chief engineer for Dieter Mining Company. "With road construction projected to be at peak levels over the next 10 years, now is the time for us to extract and sell the tar sand off of tract 370 in the southern part of the province."

"I'm not so sure," replied Tom Collins, the vice president. "Prices are really soft for tar sand. The best we can hope to get is $7 a tonne, and the accounting people say it will cost us at least $3 a tonne for utilities, supplies, and selling expenses. That doesn't leave much in the way of contribution margin."

"I know we won't get much per tonne," replied Holly, "but our studies show that we have 1,735,000 tonnes of tar sand in the area. I figure we can extract 90,000, 145,000, and 240,000 tonnes the first three years, respectively, and then the remainder evenly over the next seven years. Even at only $7 a tonne, that'll bring a lot of cash flow into the company."

"But you're forgetting that we have other costs, too," said Tom. "Fixed costs for salaries, insurance, and so forth, directly associated with the tar sand project would be $450,000 a year. Besides that, we would have to pay out an additional $250,000 at the end of the project for filling and levelling the land. You know how tough those environmental people can get if things don't look right. And all of this doesn't even consider the $800,000 cost of special equipment that we would need or the $75,000 we would have to put up for working capital to carry inventories and accounts receivable. I'm uneasy about the whole idea."

"You've got to look at the big picture, Tom. You'll get the working capital back in 10 years when the project is completed. In addition, we can write off that equipment and save a bundle in taxes at our 30% tax rate. Besides that, since the equipment would have a 12-year useful life, it would still have some use left when the project was completed. I'm sure we could sell it to someone for at least 5% of its original cost."

"All of that sounds fine, Holly, but I'll still bet the project won't provide the 18% after-tax return we require. Let's give all this to accounting and have them do a present value analysis for us."

Required
1. Compute the before-tax net cash receipts each year from the extraction and sale of the tar sand. (Do not include the cost of filling and levelling the land in this computation.) Assume CCA is 25%.
2. Using the data from (1) above and other data from the problem as needed, prepare a net present value analysis to determine whether the company should purchase the equipment and extract the tar sand. Round all dollar amounts to the nearest whole dollar. You may assume that the company *as a whole* will have a positive taxable income in every year so that a tax benefit would be realized from any operating losses associated with the tar sand project.

P15–10 Various CCA rates; Net Present Value Walter Miller, manufacturing vice president of Atlantic Industries, has been anxious for some time to purchase a piece of high-pressure equipment for use in the company's coal liquefaction research project. The equipment would cost $720,000 and would have an eight-year useful life. It would have a salvage value equal to about 5% of its original cost. In addition to the cost of the equipment, the company would have to increase its working capital by $10,000 to handle the more rapid processing of material by the new equipment.

An analysis that Mr. Miller has just received from his staff indicates that the equipment will not provide the 16% after-tax return required by Atlantic Industries. In making this analysis, Mr. Miller's staff estimated that the equipment would save the company $200,000 per year in its research program as a result of speeding up several key processes. The only significant maintenance work required on the equipment would be the installation of new pressure seals in five years at a cost of $80,000. In doing the analysis, Mr. Miller had instructed his staff to take a CCA rate of 12.5% which is consistent with the straight-line depreciation calculated for accounting purposes. The company's tax rate is 40%.

Upon seeing the analysis done by Mr. Miller's staff, the company's controller has suggested that the analysis be redone using the 25% maximum CCA rate allowed by Revenue Canada rather than the straight-line method. Somewhat irritated by this suggestion, Mr. Miller replied, "You accountants and your fancy bookkeeping methods! What difference does it make what depreciation method we use—we have the same investment, the same cost savings, and the same total depreciation either way. That equipment just doesn't measure up to our rate of return requirements. How you make the bookkeeping entries for depreciation won't change that fact."

Required

1. Compute the net present value of the equipment using the optional straight-line method for computing depreciation as instructed by Mr. Miller.
2. Compute the net present value of the equipment using the maximum CCA rate as suggested by the controller. Round all dollar amounts to the nearest whole dollar.
3. Explain to Mr. Miller how the CCA rate used can affect the rate of return generated by an investment project.

P15–11   A Comparison of Investment Alternatives; Total-Cost Approach

Julia Vanfleet is an assistant professor of mathematics at a Canadian university. She has received a $225,000 inheritance from her father's estate, and she is anxious to invest it between now and the time she retires in 12 years. Professor Vanfleet's position with the university pays a salary of $80,000 per year. Her tax rate is 36% and the business tax rate is 36%. Since the province in which the university is located is experiencing extreme budgetary problems, this salary is expected to remain unchanged in the foreseeable future. Professor Vanfleet is considering two alternatives for investing her inheritance.

Alternative 1. Corporate bonds can be purchased that mature in 12 years and that bear interest at 12.5%. This interest would be taxable and paid annually. Alternative 1 would permit Professor Vanfleet to stay with the university.

Alternative 2. A small retail business is available for sale that can be purchased for $225,000. The following information relates to this alternative:

a. Of the purchase price, $80,000 would be for fixtures and other depreciable items. The remainder would be for the company's working capital (inventory, accounts receivable, and cash). The fixtures and other depreciable items would have a remaining useful life of at least 12 years. At the end of 12 years these depreciable items would have a negligible salvage value; however, the working capital would be recovered (either through sale or liquidation of the business) for reinvestment elsewhere. CCA is 20%.
b. The store building would be leased. At the end of 12 years, if Professor Vanfleet could not find someone to buy the business, it would be necessary to pay $2,500 to the owner of the building to break the lease.
c. Store records indicate that sales have averaged $872,500 per year and out-of-pocket costs (including rent on the building) have averaged $760,000 per year (*not* including income taxes).
d. Since Professor Vanfleet would operate the store herself, it would be necessary for her to leave the university if this alternative were selected.

Required

Advise Professor Vanfleet as to which alternative should be selected. Use the total-cost approach to net present value in your analysis, and a discount rate of 8%. Round all dollar amounts to the nearest whole dollar.

P15–12   Equipment Replacement; Incremental Cost Approach

"That new RAM 8000 is the most sophisticated piece of duplicating equipment available," said Monte Salazar, purchasing agent for Blinko's Copy Service. "The copier it would replace is putting out 5,600,000 pages a year, but the RAM would increase that output by 20%."

"I agree it's a powerful machine," replied Angie Carlson, the operations manager. "But we can only get $110,000 for the copier it would replace and that copier cost us $260,000 just two years ago. I don't think we can justify taking a huge loss on our old equipment every time something new hits the market. Besides, do you realize that the RAM 8000 costs $375,000?"

"Yes, and it's worth every dollar," said Monte. "To prove it, let's have accounting work up an analysis to see if the RAM 8000 meets the 14% after-tax rate of return that we require on new equipment."

In response to Monte's request, accounting has gathered the following information:

a. Both the old copier and the RAM 8000 are eligible for a CCA of 30%.
b. The manufacturer estimates that it would have a $15,000 salvage value at the end of its eight-year useful life. The old copier will be worth nothing in eight years.
c. Blinko's Copy Service pays 1.5 cents per page for paper; the company's customers pay an average of 9 cents per page for copy work.
d. To keep the RAM 8000 operating at peak efficiency, the company would purchase a maintenance contract that would cost $4,000 more per year than its present maintenance contract.
e. The RAM 8000 would need to have the drum and photo plates replaced in five years; the cost would be $30,000.
f. Blinko's Copy Service has a tax rate of 40%.

Required

1. Compute the incremental net annual cash receipts (before taxes) expected from the RAM 8000. (Do not include the cost of the drum and photo plates in this computation.)
2. Use net present value analysis to determine whether the RAM 8000 will provide the company's required rate of return. Use the incremental-cost approach. Round all dollar amounts to the nearest whole dollar.

P15–13   Comparison of Total-Cost and Incremental-Cost Approaches

Reliable Waste Systems provides a solid waste collection service in a large metropolitan area. The company is considering the purchase of several new trucks to replace an equal number of old trucks now in use. The new trucks would cost $650,000, but they would require only one operator per truck (compared to two operators for the trucks now being used), as well as provide other cost savings. A comparision of total annual cash operating costs between the old trucks that would be replaced and the new trucks is provided below:

	Old Trucks	New Trucks
Salaries—operators	$170,000	$ 85,000
Fuel	14,000	9,000
Insurance	6,000	11,000
Maintenance	10,000	5,000
Total annual cash operating costs	$200,000	$110,000

If the new trucks are purchased, the old trucks will be sold to a company in a nearby city for $85,000. These trucks cost $400,000 when they were new, have a current book value of $120,000, and have been used for four years.

If the new trucks are not purchased, the old trucks will be used for seven more years and then sold for an estimated $15,000 scrap value. However, to keep the old trucks operating, extensive repairs will be needed in one year that will cost $170,000. These repairs will be expensed for tax purposes in the year incurred.

The new trucks would have a useful life of seven years. They would have an estimated $60,000 salvage value at the end of their useful life. The company's tax rate is 30%, and its after-tax cost of capital is 12%. The trucks are written off using a 30% CCA.

Required

1. Use the total-cost approach to net present value analysis to determine whether the new trucks should be purchased. Round all dollar amounts to the nearest whole dollar.
2. Repeat the computations in (1) above, this time using the incremental-cost approach to net present value analysis.

P15–14 Ethics and the Manager   The Fore Corporation is an integrated food processing company that has operations in over two dozen countries. Fore's corporate headquarters is in Toronto, and the company's executives frequently travel to visit Fore's foreign and domestic facilities.

Fore has a fleet of aircraft that consists of two business jets with international range and six smaller turboprop aircraft that are used on shorter flights. Company policy is to assign aircraft to trips on the basis of minimizing cost, but the practice is to assign the aircraft based on the organizational rank of the traveller. Fore offers its aircraft for short-term lease or for charter by other organizations whenever Fore itself does not plan to use the aircraft. Fore surveys the market often in order to keep its lease and charter rates competitive.

William Earle, Fore's vice president of finance, has claimed that a third business jet can be justified financially. However, some people in the controller's office have surmised that the real reason for a third business jet was to upgrade the aircraft used by Earle. Presently, the people outranking Earle keep the two business jets busy with the result that Earle usually files in smaller turboprop aircraft.

The third business jet would cost $11 million. A capital expenditure of this magnitude requires a formal proposal with projected cash flows and net present value computations using Fore's minimum required rate of return. If Fore's president and the finance committee of the board of directors approve the proposal, it will be submitted to the full board of directors. The board has final approval on capital expenditures exceeding $5 million and has established a firm policy of rejecting any discretionary proposal that has a negative net present value.

Earle asked Rachel Arnett, assistant corporate controller, to prepare a proposal on a third business jet. Arnett gathered the following data:

- Acquisition cost of the aircraft, including instrumentation and interior furnishing.
- Operating cost of the aircraft for company use.
- Projected avoidable commercial airfare and other avoidable costs from company use of the plane.
- Projected value of executive time saved by using the third business jet.
- Projected contribution margin from incremental lease and charger activity.
- Estimated resale value of the aircraft.
- Estimated income tax effects of the proposal.

When Earle reviewed Arnett's completed proposal and saw the large negative net present value figure, he returned the proposal to Arnett. With a glare, Earle commented, "You must have made an error. The proposal should look better than that."

Feeling some pressure, Arnett went back and checked her computations; she found no errors. However, Earle's message was clear. Arnett discarded her projections and estimates that she believed were reasonable and replaced them with figures that had a remote chance of actually occurring but were more favourable to the proposal. For example, she used first-class airfares to refigure the avoidable commercial airfare costs, even though company policy was to fly coach. She found revising the proposal to be distressing.

The revised proposal still had a negative net present value. Earle's anger was evident as he told Arnett to revise the proposal again, and to start with a $100,000 positive net present value and work backwards to compute supporting estimates and projections.

Required

1. Explain whether Rachel Arnett's revision of the proposal was in violation of the Standards of Ethical Conduct.
2. Was William Earle in violation of the Standards of Ethical Conduct for management accountants by telling Arnett specifically how to revise the proposal? Explain your answer.
3. Identify specific internal controls that Fore Corporation could implement to prevent unethical behaviour on the part of the vice president of finance.

(CMA, adapted)

P15–15 Net Present Value Analysis, Expected Value   Ralph Smith, president of Ralphie Ltd. and chairman of its investment committee, asked the controller for a thorough analysis of the following three investments:

a. A new tool and die machine costing $50,000 has a useful life of three years with an estimated salvage value of $7,000. The existing machine can be sold currently for its book value of $5,000. The new machine would produce savings of $33,000 per year over the three-year period in question. Both machines are class 8 assets with a 20% CCA rate.

b. An in-house telephone system costing $25,000 has an expected useful life of five years before it would require replacement. No salvage value is anticipated at that time. Fixed telephone cost savings of $9,000 per year are expected after installation. In addition, a telephone operator currently working on a part-time basis whose salary amounts to $4,000 per year plus benefits of $800 would be laid off immediately. Severance pay in the amount $700 would be paid at that time. The entire system is in an asset class that has a 30% CCA rate.

c. An advertising billboard mechanism costing $75,000 is expected to generate increased sales. However, the exact amount of the increase is uncertain. The sales manager has summarized his thoughts about possible additional annual sales as follows:

Additional Annual Gross Sales	Probability
$125,000	0.1
145,000	0.2
165,000	0.3
185,000	0.4

The sales manager added that he thought the billboard mechanism would remain effective for a three-year period and, after three years, it would be sold for an estimated value of $6,000. Variable costs amounting to 65% of gross sales are not expected to change for at least five years. The billboard mechanism is in an asset class that has a 35% CCA rate.

Ralphie Ltd. is a going concern and it is anticipated that there will be assets in the appropriate classes at the time any proposed new assets are sold. Ralphie's corporate tax rate of 40% is not expected to change over the period in question. The cost of capital is 16%.

    Smith has asked John Jones, his controller, for a thorough net present value analysis and a recommendation for presentation to the investment committee on how best to place $75,000 in surplus funds which is currently available. He has always asked that such reports be prepared using an appropriate risk-adjusted discount rate giving separate detail on initial investment, salvage of old and new equipment, CCA tax shield effects of investment, as well as salvage, generated savings or income, and any other miscellaneous cash flows.

Required   As John Jones, prepare the analysis and recommendation requested by Ralph Smith.

(SMAC, adapted)

P15–16   **Capital Gain, Net Present Value**   M.S. Computers is considering the viability of erecting a new production facility on a piece of property. The land is presently vacant and can be acquired for the current market value of $700,000. The facility can be erected for $650,000, and equipment worth a further $400,000 needs to be acquired. Capital cost allowance rates on the building and equipment are 10 and 20% respectively. Operating savings from the new facility are expected to be $445,000 per year for the next eight years. M.S. Computers expects to dispose of the property at the end of the eight years for $1.4 million; this amount is solely the anticipated value of the land. The firm's tax rate is 45% and its cost of capital is 14%.

Required   Using the net present value approach, do you believe M.S. Computers should undertake the project? Show all calculations, and state any assumptions necessary.

(CGA, adapted)

P15–17   **Risk and Net Present Value Analysis**   (Appendix 15A) Kentville Ltd. is evaluating two mutually exclusive investment proposals. Tony Atkinson, the firm's chief management accountant, has developed the following estimates for each project. The projects have estimated lifespans of 15 years and the firm's cost of capital is 12%.

| | Probability | Cash Flows | |
		A	B
Investment outlay	1.0	$15,000	$15,000
Net cash inflows	.15	500	2,000
Pessimistic	.70	3,500	3,300
Most likely optimistic ...	.15	4,500	3,900

Required

1. Calculate the net present value of each project for each probability.
2. Calculate the expected net present value for each alternative.
3. Calculate the standard deviation and coefficient of variation for each project.
4. Which project would you recommend? Comment on the risk/return of these two protects.

P15–18   Expected Value; Standard Deviation; Coefficient of Variation

(Appendix 15A) Liu Company of Burnaby, British Columbia, is evaluating the expected returns of two 5-year projects. These projects are not mutually exclusive. The expected returns are expressed in thousands of dollars.

Year	X	Y
20X1	$ 4	$10
20X2	6	6
20X3	7	4
20X4	3	9
20X5	10	6

Required

1. Calculate the expected value for each project.
2. Calculate the standard deviation and coefficient of variation for each project.
3. By observation, does there appear to be any correlation between the returns of the two projects?
4. As a management accountant consulting for Liu Company, suggest how the company may diversify its risk. Support your comments.

Cases

C15–19   Make or Buy Decision; Total-Cost Approach   Jonfran Company

manufactures three different models of paper shredders, including the waste container which serves as the base. While the shredder heads are different for all three models, the waste container is the same. The number of waste containers that Jonfran will need during the next five years is estimated as follows:

Year 1	50,000		Year 4	55,000
Year 2	50,000		Year 5	55,000
Year 3	52,000			

The equipment used to manufacture the waste containers must be replaced because it has broken and cannot be repaired. The new equipment has a list price of $945,000 but will be purchased at a 2% discount. The freight on the equipment would be $11,000, and installation costs would total $22,900. The equipment would be purchased and placed into service in January of Year 1. It would have a five-year useful life. The equipment would have a salvage value of $15,000 at the end of its useful life.

The new equipment would be more efficient than the old equipment and it would slash both direct labour and variable overhead costs in half. However, the new equipment would require the use of a slightly heavier gauge of metal, which would increase direct material costs by 30%. The company uses JIT inventory methods, but the heavier gauge metal is sometimes hard to get so the company would have to keep a small quantity on hand, which would increase working capital needs by $20,000.

The old equipment is fully depreciated and is not included in the fixed overhead. The old equipment can be sold now for $1,500; Jonfran has no alternative use for the manufacturing space at this time, so if the new equipment is not purchased, the old equipment will be left in place.

Rather than replace the old equipment, one of Jonfran's production managers has suggested that the waste containers be purchased. One supplier has quoted a price of $28 per container. This price is $7 less than Jonfran's current manufacturing cost, which is presented below:

Direct materials		$10
Direct labour		8
Variable overhead		6
Fixed overhead:		
Supervision	$2	
Facilities	5	
General	4	11
Total cost per unit		$35

Jonfran uses a plantwide predetermined fixed overhead rate. If the waste containers are purchased outside, the salary and benefits of one supervisor, included in the fixed overhead at $45,000, would be eliminated. No other changes would be made in the other cash and noncash items included in fixed overhead except depreciation on the new equipment.

Jonfran is subject to a 30% tax rate and requires a 14% after-tax return on all equipment purchases.

Required   Using net present value analysis, determine whether the company should purchase the new equipment and make the waste containers or purchase the containers from the outside supplier. Use the total-cost approach and round all dollar amounts to the nearest whole dollar.

(CMA, adapted)

C15–20 **Project Comparison**   At its September 2000 meeting, the board of directors of Transcan Inc., a transport company, received a report from its general manager, Louis Lemieux, concerning modernization of its warehousing system. In his report, Lemieux presented a comparative analysis of the operating expenses of two warehousing systems under consideration for the renovation of one of the company's old warehouses. Transcan's board must decide whether the old warehouse should be sold for $30,000, or be modernized, and if the latter, which system should be chosen to modernize it.

The warehouse has a surface area of 3,600 square metres and a volume of 36,000 cubic metres. The yield on one cubic metre of warehouse space is about $10 per year.

System A uses shelving 10 metres high by 6 metres wide, and is equipped with shelves of variable height. Fork lifts would be used for moving the merchandise. The advantage of this system is its great flexibility, but it requires hiring operators for the fork lifts.

The other system under consideration, system B, uses fork lifts on rails. This system is operated by a remote control computer. Fewer employees are needed to run it than system A.

The following table shows the costs of each system at maximum capacity, which is 20,000 cubic metres. Lemieux thinks that either system would operate at 75% capacity during the first year of operation and at 100% capacity from the second year onward.

System Costs Based on Maximum Capacity of 20,000 Cubic Metres

System A	
Cost of shelving	$ 70,000
Fork lifts (5 at $25,000)	125,000
Salaries—fork lift operators and warehouse workers	165,000

System B	
Cost of shelving	$ 70,000
Rail system and automatic fork lift, including computer	345,000
Salaries—system operators	140,000

Lemieux estimates that, because of anticipated technological change in this area, the interior of the warehouse will have to be refitted in 10 years.

With regard to system A, Lemieux forecasts having to pay out $5,000 per fork lift over the course of the fifth year. These amounts could be expensed in the fifth year or capitalized, at the company's option. It is estimated that, in 10 years' time, the shelving would have a residual value of about $10,000 and the fork lifts could be sold for scrap at $1,000 each.

System B, on the other hand, would require a depreciable cash outlay of $6,000 during the fourth year of operation. Lemieux feels he can sell the shelving for $10,000 in 10 years and the automated system will have a scrap value of only $3,000.

Whichever system is chosen, the warehouse is assumed to have no depreciable value and its residual value in 10 years is also assumed to be nil.

Whereas the forklifts in system A have a maximum CCA rate of 30% using the declining balance method, all the other assets are treated as equipment and have a maximum CCA rate of 20%.

Given the present size and the projected growth of Transcan Inc., it is not believed that the transaction under consideration will cause any of the asset classes to cease to exist.

Last year, when federal government bonds carried 12% interest, Transcan considered a 19% rate of return adequate on a similar project. This year, federal government bonds yield 11%. Transcan's tax rate is 40%.

Required

1. On the basis of the data provided, including the table, and assuming that salaries are the only variable costs, calculate the general break-even point for each of the systems. For accounting purposes, Transcan depreciates its assets on a straight-line basis. For the assets considered here, Transcan used a period of 10 years and took into account the residual values estimated by Lemieux.
2. Calculate the net present value of each modernization project and determine whether Transcan should sell the warehouse, choose system A, or choose system B.
3. Using the results determined in (1) and (2), prepare a short report recommending or rejecting the alternatives. Your answer should show how the general break-even points and net present values determined are useful in making your decision. Be precise.

(CGA, adapted)

C15–21 Product-Line Evaluation   John Able, the general manager of Western Products Inc., is reviewing revenue and cost data for product A, which was added to Western's product line two years ago. These data are as follows:

	2000	**2001**
Units produced and sold	10,000	30,000
Unit selling price	$16.00	$15.00
Unit costs:		
Direct materials	$ 2.40	$ 2.30
Spoilage during fabrication	.28	.24
Direct labour	4.77	4.74
Department overhead—direct	2.44	1.48
—indirect	2.55	.85
Plant overhead*	1.59	1.58
Total plant cost	$14.03	$11.19
General selling and administration†	2.10	1.68
Total unit cost	$16.13	$12.87
Unit profit (loss)	$ (.13)	$ 2.13

*33⅓ percent of direct labour.

†15 percent of total plant cost.

Product A has been fabricated and assembled in one process in one department of the plant at a rate of four units per direct labour hour. All of the direct materials are added during the fabrication process. Variable overhead is a function of direct labour-hours. Safety regulations restrict direct labour to a maximum of 40 hours per day, five days per week. All of Western's products are sold through a salaried sales force such that adding product A to the product line has not affected Western's total selling expense. Indirect department overhead costs, however, were increased by $6,000 annually when the assembly operation for product A was introduced in 2000.

Able has initiated a number of studies concerned with lowering the cost of, and increasing the demand for, product A. The following information, proposals, and recommendations have resulted from these studies.

The purchasing department has located an outside supplier that would deliver the fabricated parts, ready for assembly, to Western's plant at a cost of $6.25 per unit. If Western purchases all of its requirements for fabricated parts from this supplier, the production process could be altered such that product A would be assembled at a rate of six units per direct labour-hour.

The engineering department has proposed that the company invest $800,000 to overhaul the existing general purpose equipment and to purchase new equipment designed to: (1) eliminate the safety regulation restriction on direct labour-hours; (2) eliminate the spoilage of direct materials in fabrication; and (3) reduce overall direct labour costs by 10%. The new equipment would be sold for $50,000 at the end of five years and the old equipment kept for other purposes. All of the equipment concerned is categorized as Class 8 assets for CCA purposes. The Class 8 rate is 20%.

The marketing department has made the following two recommendations designed to increase demand for product A:

a. The first recommendation essentially proposes to increase the annual marketing budget by $25,000 to increase expected demand from 30,000 units to 50,000 units annually.
b. The second recommendation is to increase the annual marketing budget by $25,000 and lower the unit price from $15 to $14. As a result, the marketing department expects, annual demand would be increased from 30,000 to 75,000 units.

The marketing department has carefully pointed out, however, that product A's life cycle will be likely to extend for only another five years with demand dropping off in the last year. The projected demand under each recommendation would be as follows:

Projected Demand for Product A in Units

Year	Recommendation 1	Recommendation 2
2002	50,000	75,000
2003	50,000	75,000
2004	50,000	75,000
2005	50,000	75,000
2006	37,500	37,500
2007	Nil*	Nil*

*Product A will be obsolete in 2007.

Western Products Inc. has a marginal tax rate of 46% and an after-tax cost of capital of 16%.

Required
1. Determine by what amount Western's 2001 net income before tax would have changed if product A had been dropped from the product line at the end of 2000.
2. Identify and evaluate the alternatives open to Able, and recommend a course of action to betaken.

(SMAC, adapted)

C15–22 Make or Buy Decision; Incremental-Cost Approach   Lamb Company manufactures several products, including all of the component parts that go into these products. One unique part, a valve stem, requires specialized tools that are worn out and need to be replaced. Management has decided that the only alternative to replacing these tools is to acquire the valve stem from an outside source. A supplier is willing to provide the valve stem at a unit sales price of $20 if at least 70,000 units are ordered each year.

Lamb Company's average production of valve stems over the past three years has been 80,000 units each year. Expectations are that this volume will remain constant over the next four years. Cost records indicate that unit product costs for the valve stem over the last several years have been as follows:

Direct materials	$ 3.60
Direct labour	3.90
Variable manufacturing overhead	1.50
Fixed manufacturing overhead*	9.00
Unit product cost	$18.00

> *Depreciation of tools (that must now be replaced) accounts for one-third of the fixed overhead. The balance is for other fixed overhead costs of the factory that require cash expenditures.

If the specialized tools are purchased, they will cost $2,500,000 and will have a disposal value of $100,000 at the end of their four-year useful life. Straight-line depreciation would be used for financial reporting purposes, but a CCA rate of 20% would be used for tax purposes. Lamb Company has a 40% tax rate, and management requires a 12% after-tax return on investment.

The sales representative for the manufacturer of the specialized tools has stated, "The new tools will allow direct labour and variable overhead to be reduced by $1.60 per unit." Data from another company using identical tools and experiencing similar operating conditions, except that annual production generally averages 100,000 units, confirms the direct labour and variable overhead cost savings. However, the other company indicates that it experienced an increase in raw material cost due to the higher quality of material that had to be used with the new tools. The other company indicates that its unit product costs have been as follows:

Direct materials	$ 4.50
Direct labour	3.00
Variable manufacturing overhead	0.80
Fixed manufacturing overhead	10.80
Unit product cost	$19.10

Referring to the figures above, Eric Madsen, Lamb's production manager, stated, "These numbers look great until you consider the difference in volume. Even with the reduction in labour and variable overhead cost, I'll bet our total unit cost figure would increase to over $20 with the new tools."

Although the old tools being used by Lamb Company are now fully depreciated, they have a salvage value of $45,000. These tools will be sold if the new tools are purchased; however, if the new tools are not purchased, then the old tools will be retained as standby equipment. Lamb Company's Accounting Department has confirmed that total fixed manufacturing overhead costs, other than depreciation, will not change regardless of the decision made concerning the valve stems. However, Accounting has estimated that working capital needs will increase by $60,000 if the new tools are purchased due to the higher quality of material required in the manufacture of the valve stems.

Required
1. Prepare a net present value analysis that will help Lamb Company's management decide whether the new tools should be purchased. Use the incremental-cost approach and round all dollar amounts to the nearest whole dollar.
2. Identify additional factors that Lamb Company's management should consider before a decision is made about whether to manufacture or buy the valve stems.

(CMA, adapted)

Group Exercises

IE15–23 The Complexity of Canadian Income Taxes   Canadian Income Tax regulations are mind-numbingly complex. As a result Revenue Canada frequently puts out interpretation bulletins to assist corporations and others to comply. Refer to IT-128R—Capital Cost Allowance—Depreciable Property by viewing the web site at http://www.ccra-adrc.gc.ca/E/pub/tp/eit128rw.html

Required   The interpretation bulletin lists six guidelines in determining whether an expenditure is capital in nature because depreciable property was acquired or improved, or whether it is currently deductible because it is in respect of the maintenance or repair of a property. List and briefly explain each of these guidelines.

Visit the Fraser Institute website at
http://www.fraserinstitute.ca/publications/books/capital_gains/section_05.html

The Fraser Institute presents several options relating to the taxation of capital gains in the article, *Unlocking Canadian Capital*.

Required   What is the Fraser Institute's first best solution? What three reasons do they give for taking this position?

Chapter Sixteen

Service Department Costing: An Activity Approach

Business Focus

Saint Mary's University in Halifax, Nova Scotia, has a number of service departments to support the teaching function. Computer services, athletics, library, and physical plant represent the larger ones. The Registrar, admissions, purchasing, art gallery, and the bookstore represent some of the other support service departments. The costs of these service departments are part of the total cost of educating students at St. Mary's University.

Learning Objectives

After studying Chapter 16, you should be able to:

1 Allocate service department costs to other departments using the direct method.

2 Allocate service department costs to other departments using the step method.

3 Allocate service department costs to other departments using the reciprocal method.

4 Allocate variable and fixed service department costs separately at the beginning of a period and at the end of the period.

Operating department
A department or similar unit in an organization within which the central purposes of the organization are carried out.

Service department A department that provides support or assistance to operating departments and that does not engage directly in production or in other operating activities of an organization.

$\mathbf{D}$epartments within an organization can be divided into two broad classes: (1) operating departments and (2) service departments. **Operating departments** include those departments or units where the central purposes of the organization are carried out. Examples of such departments or units would include the Surgery Department at QEII Hospital; the undergraduate and graduate programs at Saint Mary's University; and producing departments such as Milling, Assembly, and Painting in a manufacturing company such as Bombardier.

Service departments, by contrast, do not engage directly in operating activities. Rather, they provide services or assistance to the operating departments. Examples of service departments include Cafeteria, Internal Auditing, Personnel, Cost Accounting, and Purchasing. Although service departments do not engage directly in the operating activities of an organization, the costs that they incur are generally viewed as being part of the cost of the final product or service, the same as are materials, labour, and overhead in a manufacturing company or medications in a hospital.

Chapter 1 stated that most organizations have one or more service departments that provide services for the entire organization. In this chapter, we look more closely at service departments and consider how their costs are allocated to the units they serve for planning, costing, and other purposes. The major question we consider is: How much of a service department's cost is to be allocated to each of the units that it serves? This is an important question, since the amount of service department cost allocated to a particular unit can have a significant impact on the computed cost of the goods or services that the unit is providing and can affect an operating unit's performance evaluation.

Organizationally, managers are placed in charge of departments. For control purposes, costs are often collected by departments to permit the use of responsibility accounting. In Chapter 8, activities served as the basis of classifying costs. This permits an activity focus to cost management rather than the responsibility focus seen with departmental classification. When activities involve more than a single department the specifics of classifications will differ. If activities remain within a single department, then the departmental and activities classifications can yield the same result. If departments involved both operating and support or service groupings then the specifics of this chapter will be needed to allocate properly the costs to the output of the organization.

Focus on Current Practice

A case study of the implementation of an ABC system for a manufacturer of automobile component parts suggests the company's existing departmental structure could be incorporated to advantage within the new ABC system. Because the departments corresponded to the main activities, the departmental structure was used because it was felt that this would create less confusion than an alternative activity centre focus. With some adjustments, 42 centres were specified to accommodate both manufacturing and support departments. The authors suggest that the cost-benefit objectives of the new system were met. [1] ∎

Allocations of Service Department Costs

Allocating service department costs begins with selecting the proper allocation base—the first topic in this section. After completing this discussion, we will move on to consider how to account for services that service departments provide to each other.

---

1. Stephen Bruesewitz and John Talbot, "Implementing ABC in a Complex Organization," *CMA Magazine* (July–August 1997), pp. 16–19.

Exhibit 16–1
Examples of Bases Used
in Allocating Service
Department Costs

Service Department	Bases (cost drivers) Involved
Laundry	Kilograms of laundry
Airport Ground Services	Number of flights
Cafeteria	Number of employees; number of meals
Medical Facilities	Cases handled; number of employees; hours worked
Materials Handling	Hours of service; volume handled
Data Processing	CPU minutes; lines printed; disk storage used; number of personal computers
Custodial Services (building and grounds)	Square metres occupied
Cost Accounting	Labour-hours; clients or patients serviced
Power	KWh used; capacity of machines
Human Resources	Number of employees; employee turnover; training hours
Receiving, Shipping, and Stores	Units handled; number of requisitions; space occupied
Factory Administration	Total labour-hours
Maintenance	Machine-hours

Selecting Allocation Bases

Many companies use a two-stage costing process. In the first stage, costs are assigned to the operating departments; in the second stage, costs are assigned from the operating departments to products and services. We focused on the second stage of this allocation process in Chapter 3 and reserved discussion of first-stage costing procedures to this chapter. On the following pages we discuss the assignment of costs from service departments to operating departments, *which represents the first stage of the two-stage costing process.*

Costs are usually assigned from a service department to other departments using an allocation base, which is some measure of activity. The costs being allocated should be "driven" by the allocation base. Ideally, the total cost of the service department should be proportional to the size of the allocation base. Managers also often argue that the allocation base should reflect as accurately as possible the benefits that the various departments receive from the services that are being provided. For example, most managers would argue that the square metres of building space occupied by each operating department should be used as the allocation base for janitorial services since both the benefits and costs of janitorial services tend to be proportional to the amount of space occupied by a department. Examples of allocation bases for some service departments are listed in Exhibit 16–1. A given service department's costs may be allocated using more than one base. For example, data processing costs may be allocated on the basis of CPU minutes for mainframe computers *and* on the basis of the number of personal computers used in each operating department.

Focus on Current Practice

Companies supplying goods and services to Public Works and Government Services Canada (PWGSC) on a cost plus basis must follow specific rules for inclusion and exclusion of costs. The overhead and other expenses such as selling, general and administrative are accumulated by pools reflecting the organizational and operational structure of the supplier and they in turn are allocated to the contracts using the PWGSC rules. Budgeted costs are often used for interim billings and later adjusted to actual for final billings. Refinements of these rules have been proposed to avoid any distortions caused by volume based output measures of the departmental approach because they may create subsidies for small jobs provided by large volume jobs.[2] ∎

2. Murray A. Best, "ABC for Government Contractors?" *CMA Magazine* (March 1997), pp. 19–22.

Although the previous paragraph explains how to select an allocation base, another critical factor should not be overlooked. The allocations should be clear and straightforward and easily understood by the managers to whom the costs are being allocated.

Interdepartmental Services

Many service departments provide services for each other, as well as for operating departments. The Cafeteria Department, for example, provides food for all employees, including those assigned to other service departments. In turn, the Cafeteria Department may receive services from other service departments, such as from Custodial Services or from Personnel. Services provided between service departments are known as **interdepartmental** or **reciprocal services.**

Three approaches are used to allocate the costs of service departments to other departments. These are known as the *direct method,* the *step method,* and the *reciprocal method.* All three methods are discussed in the following paragraphs.

DIRECT METHOD The **direct method** is the simplest of the three cost allocation methods. It ignores the services provided by a service department to other service departments and allocates all costs directly to operating departments. Even if a service department (such as Personnel) provides a large amount of service to another service department (such as the cafeteria), no allocations are made between the two departments. Rather, all costs are allocated *directly* to the operating departments. Hence the term *direct method.*

To provide an example of the direct method, assume that QEII Hospital has two service departments and two operating departments as shown below:

	Service Department		Operating Department		
	Hospital Administration	**Custodial Services**	**Laboratory**	**Daily Patient Care**	**Total**
Departmental costs before allocation	$360,000	$90,000	$261,000	$689,000	$1,400,000
Employee hours	12,000	6,000	18,000	30,000	66,000
Space occupied— square metres	1,000	20	500	4,500	6,020

In the allocations that follow, Hospital Administration costs will be allocated on the basis of employee-hours and Custodial Services costs will be allocated on the basis of square metres occupied.

The direct method of allocating the hospital's service department costs to the operating departments is shown in Exhibit 16–2. Several things should be carefully noted in this exhibit. First, even though there are employee-hours in both the Hospital Administration Department itself and in the Custodial Services Department, these employee-hours are ignored when allocating service department costs using the direct method. *Under the direct method, any of the allocation base attributable to the service departments themselves is ignored; only the amount of the allocation base attributable to the operating departments is used in the allocation.* Note that the same rule is used when allocating the costs of the Custodial Services Department. Even though the Hospital Administration and Custodial Services departments occupy some space, this is ignored when the Custodial Services costs are allocated. Finally, note that after all allocations have been completed, all of the departmental costs are contained in the two operating departments. These costs will form the basis for preparing overhead rates for purposes of costing products and services produced in the operating departments.

Although the direct method is simple, it is less accurate than the other methods since it ignores interdepartmental services. This can lead to distorted product and service costs. Even so, many organizations use the direct method because of its simplicity.

Interdepartmental services Services provided between service departments. Also see *Reciprocal services.*

Reciprocal services Same as *Interdepartmental services.*

Direct method The allocation of all of a service department's costs directly to operating departments without recognizing services provided to other service departments.

Objective 1

Allocate service department costs to other departments using the direct method.

Exhibit 16–2   Direct Method of Allocation

	Service Department		Operating Department		
	Hospital Administration	Custodial Services	Laboratory	Daily Patient Care	Total
Departmental costs before allocation	$ 360,000	$ 90,000	$261,000	$689,000	$1,400,000
Allocation:					
Hospital Administration costs ($^{18}\!/_{48}$, $^{30}\!/_{48}$)* .	(360,000)		135,000	225,000	
Custodial Services costs ($^{5}\!/_{50}$, $^{45}\!/_{50}$)†		(90,000)	9,000	81,000	
Total costs after allocation	$ –0–	$ –0–	$405,000	$995,000	$1,400,000

*Based on the employee-hours in the two operating departments, which are 18,000 hours + 30,000 hours = 48,000 hours.

†Based on the space occupied by the two operating departments, which is 500 square metres + 4,500 square metres = 5,000 square metres.

Exhibit 16–3
Graphic Illustration—
Step Method

Objective 2

Allocate service department costs to other departments using the step method.

Step method   The allocation of a service department's costs to other service departments, as well as to operating departments, in a sequential manner. The sequence starts with the service department that provides the greatest amount of service to other departments.

STEP METHOD   Unlike the direct method, the **step method** provides for allocation of a service department's costs to other service departments, as well as to operating departments. The step method is sequential. The sequence typically begins with the department that provides the greatest amount of service to other service departments. After its costs have been allocated, the process continues, step by step, ending with the department that provides the least amount of services to other service departments. This step procedure is illustrated in graphic form in Exhibit 16–3, assuming that the Hospital Administration costs are allocated first at QEII Hospital.

Exhibit 16–4 uses the allocations of the QEII Hospital to show the details of the step method. Note the following three key points about these allocations. First, under the Allocation heading in Exhibit 16–4, you see two allocations, or steps. In the step method, the first step allocates the costs of Hospital Administration to another service department (Custodial Services) as well as to the operating departments. The allocation base for Hospital Administration costs now includes the employee-hours for Custodial Services as well as for the operating departments. However, the allocation base still excludes the employee-hours for Hospital Administration itself. *In both the direct and step methods, any amount of the allocation base attributable to the service department whose cost is being allocated is always ignored.* Second, looking again at Exhibit 16–4, note that in the second step under the Allocation heading, the cost of Custodial Services is allocated to the two operating departments, and none of the cost is allocated to Hospital Administration even though Hospital Administration occupies space in the building. *In the step method, any amount of the allocation base that is*

Exhibit 16–4   Step Method of Allocation

	Service Department		Operating Department		
	Hospital Administration	Custodial Services	Laboratory	Daily Patient Care	Total
Departmental costs before allocation	$ 360,000	$ 90,000	$261,000	$ 689,000	$1,400,000
Allocation:					
Hospital Administration costs (6/54, 18/54, 30/54)*	(360,000)	40,000	120,000	200,000	
Custodial Services costs (5/50, 45/50)†		(130,000)	13,000	117,000	
Total costs after allocation	$ –0–	$ –0–	$394,000	$1,006,000	$1,400,000

*Based on the employee-hours in Custodial Services and the two operating departments, which are 6,000 hours + 18,000 hours + 30,000 hours = 54,000 hours.

†As in Exhibit 16–2, this allocation is based on the space occupied by the two operating departments.

Objective 3

Allocate service department costs to other departments using the reciprocal method.

Reciprocal method   A method of allocating service department costs that gives full recognition to interdepartmental services.

attributable to a service department whose cost has already been allocated is ignored. After a service department's costs have been allocated, costs of other service departments are not reallocated back to it. Third, note that the cost of Custodial Services allocated to other departments in the second step ($130,000) in Exhibit 16–4 includes the costs of Hospital Administration that were allocated to Custodial Services in the first step in Exhibit 16–4.

RECIPROCAL METHOD   The **reciprocal method** gives full recognition to interdepartmental services. Under the step method discussed above only partial recognition of interdepartmental services is possible, since the step method always allocates costs forward—never backward. The reciprocal method, by contrast, allocates service department costs in *both* directions. Thus, since Custodial Services in the prior example provides service for Hospital Administration, part of Custodial Services' costs will be allocated *back* to Hospital Administration if the reciprocal method is used. At the same time, part of Hospital Administration's costs will be allocated *forward* to Custodial Services. This type of reciprocal allocation requires the use of simultaneous linear equations.

Focus on Current Practice

Computer software included as part of an overall system for enterprise resource planning or as an add on to such a system can incorporate the routines necessary for overhead allocation either for activity-based costing or departmental overhead allocation. A recent addition to ABC software touted as a major advance is the inclusion of reciprocal allocation. This allows units such as information systems and human resources to incorporate their reciprocal relationships into the cost allocations. This feature is particularly important for banks, insurance companies, and government agencies who tend to have numerous reciprocal situations. The cost of such overhead software is reported to range from $2,000 to $30,000.[3] ∎

To illustrate reciprocal allocation, consider the following illustration in Exhibit 16–5 based on Exhibit 16–2 and the data provided about QE II Hospital.

Note the amount allocated by hospital administration had to be determined outside the schedule before the allocation was made. Similarly the custodial services total

3. Jim Gurowka, "Activity-Based Costing Software—The Market Explodes," *CMA Magazine* (May 1997), pp. 13–19.

Exhibit 16–5   Reciprocal Allocation

Hospital Administration (HA)

$$HA = 360{,}000 + \tfrac{2}{12}\,CS$$

where HA denotes the costs to be allocated; that is, the direct costs plus those allocated from custodial services.

Custodial Services (CS)

$$CS = 90{,}000 + \tfrac{1}{9}\,HA$$

where CS denotes the costs to be allocated; that is, the direct costs plus those allocated from hospital administration.

To solve (1) $-360{,}000 = -HA + \tfrac{2}{12}\,CS$

(2) $-90{,}000 = \tfrac{1}{9}\,HA - CS$

Multiply (2) by 9 (1) $-360{,}000 = -HA + \tfrac{2}{12}\,CS$

(2) $\underline{-810{,}000 = \quad HA - 9\,CS}$

Add (1) and (2) $-1{,}170{,}000 = 0 - 8\,(\tfrac{10}{12})\,CS$

$CS = \$132{,}453$

Substitute in (1) $- 360{,}000 = -HA + \tfrac{2}{12}(132{,}453)$

$HA = \$360{,}000 + \$22{,}076$

$HA = \$382{,}076$

	Service Department		Operating Department		
	Hospital Administration	Custodial Services	Laboratory	Daily Patient Care	Total
Departmental costs before allocation	$ 360,000	$ 90,000	$261,000	$ 689,000	$1,400,000
Allocation:					
Hospital administration costs ($\tfrac{1}{9}$, $\tfrac{3}{9}$, $\tfrac{5}{9}$)	(382,076)	42,453	127,359	212,264	
Custodial services costs ($\tfrac{2}{12}$, $\tfrac{1}{12}$, $\tfrac{9}{12}$)	22,076	(132,453)	11,038	99,339	
Totals	$ 0.0	$ 0.0	$399,397	$1,000,603	$1,400,000

costs of $132,453 include what was charged from administration. These two new amounts include the effect of the reciprocal services each department performed for the other. Once the simultaneous solutions are determined, the allocations proceed like the step method except allocations can go backward rather than proceed in sequence as required by the step method. Once the allocations are completed, totals for the operating departments are checked to ensure that the total overhead of $1.4 million was actually allocated. If more than two service departments exist, the solution procedure to determine the amount to be allocated commonly uses matrix inversion, which is beyond the scope of this book.

The reciprocal method is rarely used in practice for two reasons. First, the computations are relatively complex. Although the complexity issue could be overcome by use of computers, there is no evidence that computers have made the reciprocal method more popular. Second, the step method usually provides results that are a reasonable approximation of the results that the reciprocal method would provide. Thus, companies have little motivation to use the more complex reciprocal method.

REVENUE PRODUCING DEPARTMENTS   To conclude our discussion of allocation methods, it is important to note that even though most service departments are cost centres and therefore generate no revenues, a few service departments such as the cafeteria may charge for the services they perform. If a service department generates revenues, these revenues should be offset against the department's costs, and only the net amount of cost remaining after this offset should be allocated to other departments within the organization. In this manner, the other departments will not be required to bear costs for which the service department has already been reimbursed.

Allocating Costs by Behaviour

Whenever possible, service department costs should be separated into variable and fixed classifications and allocated separately. This approach is necessary to avoid possible inequities in allocation, as well as to provide more useful data for planning and control of departmental operations.

Variable Costs

Variable costs are out-of-pocket costs of providing services that vary in total in proporation to fluctuations in the level of service provided. Food cost in a cafeteria would be a variable cost, for example, and one would expect this cost to vary proportionately with the number of persons using the cafeteria.

As a general rule, variable costs should be charged to consuming departments according to whatever activity causes the incurrence of the costs involved. If, for example, the variable costs of a service department such as maintenance are caused by the number of machine-hours worked in the producing departments, then variable maintenance costs should be allocated to the producing deparments using machine-hours as the allocation basis. By this means, the departments directly responsible for the incurrence of servicing costs are required to bear them in proportion to their actual usage of the service.

Technically, the assigning of variable servicing costs to consuming departments can more accurately be termed *charges* than allocations, since the service department is actually charging the consuming departments at some fixed rate per unit of service provided. In effect, the service department is saying, "I'll charge you X dollars for every unit of my service that you consume. You can consume as much or as little as you desire; the total charge you bear will vary proportionately."

Fixed Costs

The fixed costs of service departments represent the costs of making capacity available for use. These costs should be allocated to consuming departments in *predetermined lump-sum amounts*. By predetermined lump-sum amounts we mean that the total amount charged to each consuming department is determined in advance and, once determined, does not change from period to period. The lump-sum amount charged to a department can be based either on the department's peak-period or long-run average servicing needs. The logic behind lump-sum allocations of this type is as follows:

When a service department is first established, its capacity will be determined by the needs of the departments that it will service. This capacity may reflect the peak-period needs of the other departments, or it may reflect their long-run average or "normal" servicing needs. Depending on how much servicing capacity is provided for, it will be necessary to make a commitment of resources to the servicing unit, which will be reflected in its fixed costs. These fixed costs should be borne by the consuming departments in proportion to the amount of capacity each consuming department requires. That is, if available capacity in the service department has been provided to meet the peak-period needs of consuming departments, then the fixed costs of the service department should be allocated in predetermined lump-sum amounts to consuming departments on this basis. If available capacity has been provided only to meet "normal" or long-run average needs, then the fixed costs should be allocated on this basis.

Once set, allocations should not vary from period to period, since they represent the cost of having a certain level of service capacity available and on line for each consuming department. The fact that a consuming department does not need a peak level or even a "normal" level of servicing every period is immaterial; if it requires such servicing at certain times, then the capacity to deliver it must be available. It is the responsibility of the consuming departments to bear the cost of that availability.

To illustrate this idea, assume that Novak Company has just organized a Maintenance Department to service all machines in the Cutting, Assembly, and Finishing Departments. In determining the capacity of the newly organized Maintenance Department, the various producing departments estimated that they would have the following peak-period needs for maintenance:

Department	Peak-Period Maintenance Needs in Terms of Number of Hours of Maintenance Work Required	Percent of Total Hours
Cutting	900	30%
Assembly	1,800	60%
Finishing	300	10%
	3,000	100%

Therefore, in allocating the Maintenance Department fixed costs to the producing departments, 30% (i.e., 900/3,000 = 30%) should be allocated to the Cutting Department, 60% to the Assembly Department, and 10% to the Finishing Department. These lump-sum allocations *will not change* from period to period unless there is some shift in peak-period servicing needs.

Should Actual or Budgeted Costs Be Allocated?

Should the *actual* or *budgeted* costs of a service department be allocated to operating departments? The answer is that budgeted costs should be allocated. What's wrong with allocating actual costs? Allocating actual costs burdens the operating departments with any inefficiencies in the service department. If actual costs are allocated, then any lack of cost control on the part of the service department is simply buried in a routine allocation to other departments.

Any variance over budgeted costs should be retained in the service department and closed out at year-end against the company's revenues or against cost of goods sold, along with other variances. Operating department managers justifiably complain bitterly if they are forced to absorb service department inefficiencies.

A Summary of Cost Allocation Guidelines

To summarize the material covered in preceding sections, we can note the following three guidelines to remember about allocating service department costs:

1. If possible, the distinction between variable and fixed costs in service departments should be maintained.
2. Variable costs should be allocated at the budgeted rate, according to whatever activity (kilometres driven, direct labour-hours, number of employees) causes the incurrence of the cost.
   a. If the allocations are being made at the beginning of the year, they should be based on the budgeted activity level planned for the consuming departments. The allocation formula would be:

$$\text{Variable cost allocated at the beginning of the period} = \text{Budgeted rate} \times \text{Budgeted activity}$$

   b. If the allocations are being made at the end of the year, they should be based on the actual activity level that has occurred during the year. The allocation formula would be:

$$\text{Variable cost allocated at the end of the period} = \text{Budgeted rate} \times \text{Actual activity}$$

Allocations made at the beginning of the year would be to provide data for computing overhead rates for costing of products and billing of services in the operating departments. Allocations made at the end of the year would be to provide data for comparing actual performance to planned performance.

3. Fixed costs represent the costs of having service capacity available. Where feasible, these costs should be allocated in predetermined lump-sum amounts. The lump-sum amount going to each department should be in proportion to the servicing needs that gave rise to the investment in the service department in the first place. (This might be either peak-period needs for servicing or long-run average needs.) Budgeted fixed costs, rather than actual fixed costs, should always be allocated.

Implementing the Allocation Guidelines

We will now use specific examples to show how to implement the three guidelines given above. First, we focus on the allocation of costs for a single department, and then we will develop a more extended example involving multiple departments.

Objective 4

Allocate variable and fixed service department costs separately at the beginning of a period and at the end of the period.

BASIC ALLOCATION TECHNIQUES   Seaboard Airlines is divided into a Freight Division and a Passenger Division. The company has a single aircraft Maintenance Department that provides servicing to both divisions. Variable servicing costs are budgeted at $10 per flight-hour. The fixed costs of the Maintenance Department are budgeted based on the peak-period demand, which occurs during the Thanksgiving to New Year's holiday period. The airline wants to make sure that none of its aircraft are grounded during this key period due to unavailability of maintenance facilities. Approximately 40% of the maintenance during this period is performed on the Freight Division's equipment, and 60% is performed on the Passenger Division's equipment. These figures and the budgeted flight-hours for the coming year appear below:

	Percent of Peak Period Capacity Required	Budgeted Flight-Hours
Freight Division	40%	9,000
Passenger Division ...	60%	15,000
Total	100%	24,000

Given these data, the amount of cost that would be allocated to each division from the aircraft Maintenance Department at the beginning of the coming year would be as follows:

		Division	
	Budgeted activity	Freight	Passenger
Variable cost allocation:			
$10 × 9,000 flight-hours	....	$ 90,000	
$10 × 15,000 flight-hours	....		$150,000
Fixed cost allocation:			
40% × $750,000	....	300,000	
60% × $750,000	....		450,000
Total cost allocated	....	$390,000	$600,000

Budgeted variable rate

Peak-period capacity required

Budgeted fixed cost

As explained earlier, these allocated costs would be included in the flexible budgets of the respective divisions and included in the computation of divisional overhead rates.

At the end of the year, Seaboard Airlines' management may want to make a second allocation, this time based on actual activity, in order to compare actual performance for the year against planned performance. To illustrate, year-end records show that actual costs in the aircraft Maintenance Department for the year were variable costs, $260,000; and fixed costs, $780,000. One division logged more flight-hours during the year than planned, and the other division logged fewer flight-hours than planned, as shown below:

	Flight-Hours	
	Budgeted (see above)	Actual
Freight Division	9,000	8,000
Passenger Division	15,000	17,000
Total flight-hours	24,000	25,000

The amount of actual service department cost charged to each division for the year would be as follows:

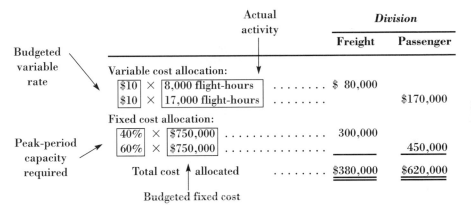

Notice that variable servicing cost is charged to the operating divisions based on the budgeted rate ($10 per hour) and the *actual activity* for the year. In contrast, the charges for fixed costs are exactly the same as they were at the beginning of the year. Also note that the two operating divisions are *not* charged for the actual costs of the service department, which may be influenced by inefficiency in the service department and be beyond the control of the managers of the operating divisions. Instead, the service department is held responsible for the unallocated actual costs as shown below:

	Variable	Fixed
Total actual costs incurred	$260,000	$780,000
Costs allocated (above)	250,000*	750,000
Spending variance—not allocated . . .	$ 10,000	$ 30,000

*$10 per flight-hour × 25,000 actual flight-hours = $250,000

These variances will be closed out against the company's overall revenues for the year, along with any other variances that may occur.

Effect of Allocations on Operating Departments

Once allocations have been completed, what do the operating departments do with the allocated service department costs? The allocations are typically included in performance evaluations of the operating departments and also included in determining their profitability.

In addition, if the operating departments are responsible for developing overhead rates for costing of products or services, then the allocated costs are combined with the

Exhibit 16–6 Effect of Allocations on Products and Services

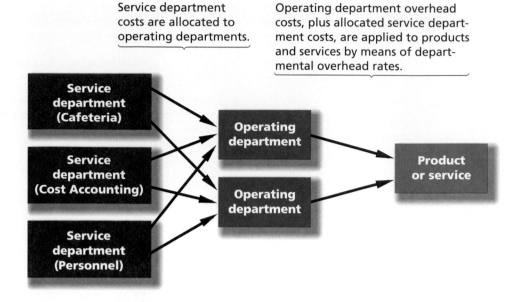

First Stage
Service department costs are allocated to operating departments.

Second Stage
Operating department overhead costs, plus allocated service department costs, are applied to products and services by means of departmental overhead rates.

other costs of the operating departments, and the total is used as a basis for rate computations. This rate development process is illustrated in Exhibit 16–6.

The flexible budget serves as the means for combining allocated service department costs with operating department costs and for computing overhead rates. An example is presented in Exhibit 16–7. Note from the exhibit that both variable and fixed service department costs have been allocated to Superior Company's Milling Department and are included on the latter's flexible budget. Since allocated service department costs become an integral part of the flexible budget, they are automatically included in overhead rate computations, as shown at the bottom of the exhibit.

An Extended Example

Proctor Company has three service departments—Building Maintenance, Cafeteria, and Inspection. The company also has two operating departments—Shaping and Assembly. The service departments provide services to each other, as well as to the operating departments. Types of costs in the service departments and bases for allocation are given below:

Department	Type of Cost	Base for Allocation
Building Maintenance	Fixed costs	Square metres occupied
Cafeteria	Variable costs	Number of employees
	Fixed costs	10% to Inspection, 40% to Shaping, and 50% to Assembly
Inspection	Variable costs	Direct labour-hours
	Fixed costs	70% to Shaping and 30% to Assembly

Proctor Company allocates service department costs by the step method in the following order:

1. Building Maintenance.
2. Cafeteria.
3. Inspection.

Assume the following budgeted cost and operating data for the year:

Exhibit 16–7
Flexible Budget
Containing Allocated
Service Department
Costs

SUPERIOR COMPANY
Flexible Budget—Milling Department

Budgeted direct labour-hours 50,000

Overhead Costs	Cost Formula (per direct labour-hour)	Direct labour-Hours 40,000	50,000	60,000
Variable overhead costs:				
Indirect labour	$1.45	$ 58,000	$ 72,500	$ 87,000
Indirect material	0.90	36,000	45,000	54,000
Utilities	0.10	4,000	5,000	6,000
Allocation—Cafeteria	0.15	6,000	7,500	9,000
Total variable overhead cost	$2.60	104,000	130,000	156,000
Fixed overhead costs:				
Depreciation		85,000	85,000	85,000
Supervisory salaries		110,000	110,000	110,000
Property taxes		9,000	9,000	9,000
Allocation—Cafeteria		21,000	21,000	21,000
Allocation—Human Resources		45,000	45,000	45,000
Total fixed overhead cost		270,000	270,000	270,000
Total overhead cost		$374,000	$400,000	$426,000

$$\text{Predetermined overhead rate} = \frac{\$400,000}{50,000 \text{ DLH}} = \$8 \text{ per direct labour-hour}$$

Department	Variable Cost	Fixed Cost
Building Maintenance	—	$130,000
Cafeteria	$200 per employee	250,000
Inspection	$0.06 per direct labour-hour	548,000

Department	Number of Employees	Direct Labour-Hours	Square Metres of Space Occupied
Building Maintenance	6*	—	300
Cafeteria	9*	—	400
Inspection	30	—	100
Shaping	190	300,000	800
Assembly	250	500,000	1,300
Total	485	800,000	2,900

*Although there are employees in both of these service departments, under the step method, costs are only allocated *forward*—never backward. For this reason, the costs of the Cafeteria Department will be allocated *forward* on the basis of the number of employees in the Inspection, Shaping, and Assembly departments.

In addition to the service department costs listed above, the company's Shaping Department has budgeted $1,340,000 in overhead costs, and its Assembly Department has budgeted $1,846,000 in overhead costs.

Cost allocations from the service departments to the operating departments are as shown in Exhibit 16–8. In the first panel of Exhibit 16–8, the variable costs of the service department sent are allocated to the various departments using the step method and

Exhibit 16–8

THE PROCTOR COMPANY
Beginning-of-Year Cost Allocations for Purposes of Preparing Predetermined Overhead Rates

	Building Maintenance	Cafeteria	Inspection	Shaping	Assembly
Variable costs to be allocated	$ –0–	$ 94,000	$ 42,000	$ —	$ —
Cafeteria allocation at $200 per employee:					
30 employees × $200	—	(6,000)	6,000	—	—
190 employees × $200	—	(38,000)	—	38,000	—
250 employees × $200	—	(50,000)	—	—	50,000
Inspection allocation at $0.06 per direct labour-hour:					
300,000 DLH × $0.06	—	—	(18,000)	18,000	—
500,000 DLH × $0.06	—	—	(30,000)	—	30,000
Total	–0–	–0–	–0–	56,000	80,000
Fixed costs to be allocated	130,000	250,000	548,000		
Building Maintenance allocation at $50 per square metre:*					
400 square metres × $50	(20,000)	20,000	—	—	—
100 square metres × $50	(5,000)	—	5,000	—	—
800 square metres × $50	(40,000)	—	—	40,000	—
1,300 square metres × $50	(65,000)	—	—	—	65,000
Cafeteria allocation:†					
10% × $270,000	—	(27,000)	27,000	—	—
40% × $270,000	—	(108,000)	—	108,000	—
50% × $270,000	—	(135,000)	—	—	135,000
Inspection allocation: ‡					
70% × $580,000	—	—	(406,000)	406,000	—
30% × $580,000	—	—	(174,000)	—	174,000
Total	–0–	–0–	–0–	554,000	374,000
Total allocated costs	$ –0–	$ –0–	$ –0–	610,000	454,000
Other flexible budget costs at the planned activity level				1,340,000	1,846,000
Total overhead costs				$1,950,000	$2,300,000(a)
Budgeted direct labour-hours				300,000	500,000(b)
Predetermined overhead rate, (a) ÷ (b)				$ 6.50	$ 4.60

*Square metres of space .... 2,900 square metres
 Less Building Maintenance space .... 300 square metres
 Net space for allocation .... 2,600 square metres

$$\frac{\text{Building Maintenance fixed costs, \$130,000}}{\text{Net space for allocation, 2,600 square metres}} = \$50 \text{ per square metre}$$

†Cafeteria fixed costs $250,000
 Allocated from Building Maintenance 20,000
 Total cost to be allocated $270,000

 Allocation percentages are given in the problem.

‡Inspection fixed costs $548,000
 Allocated from Building Maintenance 5,000
 Allocated from Cafeteria 27,000
 Total cost to be allocated $580,000

 Allocation percentages are given in the problem.

budgeted rates and budgeted activity. For example, the variable cost of the Cafeteria Department is $200 per employee, so the Inspection Department, with 30 employees, is allocated $6,000 of this variable cost. In the second panel of Exhibit 16–8, the fixed costs of the service departments are allocated. Building Maintenance is allocated first using square metres occupied by each of the other departments as the allocation base. Then the fixed costs of the Cafeteria and Inspection departments are allocated based on the given percentages. After both the variable and fixed service department costs have been allocated, the predetermined overhead rates for the two operating departments are computed toward the bottom of the exhibit.

Some Cautions in Allocating Service Department Costs

Pitfalls in Allocating Fixed Costs

Rather than allocate fixed costs in predetermined lump-sum amounts, some firms allocate them by use of a *variable* allocation base that fluctuates from period to period. This practice can distort decisions and create serious inequities between departments. The inequities will arise from the fact that the fixed costs allocated to one department will be heavily influenced by what happens in *other* departments or segments of the organization.

To illustrate, assume that Kolby Products has an auto service centre that provides maintenance work on the fleet of autos used in the company's two sales territories. The auto service centre costs are all fixed. Contrary to good practice, the company allocates these fixed costs to the sales territories on the basis of actual kilometres driven (a variable base). Selected cost data for the last two years follow:

	Year 1	Year 2
Auto service centre costs (all fixed)	$120,000 (a)	$120,000 (a)
Western sales territory—kilometres driven ...	1,500,000	1,500,000
Eastern sales territory—kilometres driven ...	1,500,000	900,000
Total kilometres driven	3,000,000 (b)	2,400,000 (b)
Allocation rate per kilometre, (a) ÷ (b)	$0.04	$0.05

Notice that the Western sales territory maintained an activity level of 1,500,000 kilometres driven in both years. On the other hand, the Eastern sales territory allowed its activity to drop off from 1,500,000 kilometres in Year 1 to only 900,000 kilometres in Year 2. The auto service centre costs that would have been allocated to the two sales territories over the two-year span using actual kilometres driven as the allocation base are as follows:

Year 1:
    Western sales territory: 1,500,000 kilometres at $0.04 ..... $ 60,000
    Eastern sales territory: 1,500,000 kilometres at $0.04   60,000
       Total cost allocated $120,000

Year 2:
    Western sales territory: 1,500,000 kilometres at $0.05 ..... $ 75,000
    Eastern sales territory: 900,000 kilometres at $0.05   45,000
       Total cost allocated $120,000

In Year 1, the two sales territories share the service department costs equally. In Year 2, however, the bulk of the service department costs are allocated to the Western sales territory. This is not because of any increase in activity in the Western sales territory; rather, it is because of the *decrease* in activity in the Eastern sales territory. Even though the Western sales territory maintained the same level of activity in both years, the use of a variable allocation base has caused it to be penalized with a heavier cost allocation in Year 2 because of what has happened in *another* part of the company.

This kind of inequity is almost inevitable when a variable allocation base is used to allocate fixed costs. The manager of the Western sales territory undoubtedly will be upset about the inequity forced on his territory, but he will feel powerless to do anything about it. The result will be a loss of confidence in the system and considerable ill feeling.

Beware of Sales Dollars as an Allocation Base

Over the years, sales dollars have been a favourite allocation base for service department costs. One reason is that a sales dollars base is simple, straightforward, and easy to work with. Another reason is that people tend to view sales dollars as a measure of well-being, or "ability to pay," and, hence, as a measure of how readily costs can be absorbed from other parts of the organization.

Unfortunately, sales dollars are often a very poor allocation base, for the reason that sales dollars vary from period to period, whereas the costs being allocated are often largely *fixed* in nature. As discussed earlier, if a variable base is used to allocate fixed costs, inequities can result between departments, since the costs being allocated to one department will depend in large part on what happens in *other* departments. For example, a letup in sales effort in one department will shift allocated costs off that department and onto other, more productive departments. In effect, the departments putting forth the best sales efforts are penalized in the form of higher allocations, simply because of inefficiencies elsewhere that are beyond their control. The result is often bitterness and resentment on the part of the managers of the better departments.

Consider the following situation encountered by one of the authors:

A large men's clothing store has one service department and three sales departments—Suits, Shoes, and Accessories. The Service Department's costs total $60,000 per period and are allocated to the three sales departments according to sales dollars. A recent period showed the following allocation:

	Department			
	Suits	**Shoes**	**Accessories**	**Total**
Sales by department	$260,000	$40,000	$100,000	$400,000
Percentage of total sales	65%	10%	25%	100%
Allocation of service department costs, based on percentage of total sales	$ 39,000	$ 6,000	$ 15,000	$ 60,000

In a following period, the manager of the Suits Department launched a very successful program to expand sales by $100,000 in his department. Sales in the other two departments remained unchanged. Total service department costs also remained unchanged, but the allocation of these costs changed substantially, as shown below:

	Department			
	Suits	**Shoes**	**Accessories**	**Total**
Sales by department	$360,000	$40,000	$100,000	$500,000
Percentage of total sales	72%	8%	20%	100%
Allocation of service department costs, based on percentage of total sales	$ 43,200	$ 4,800	$ 12,000	$ 60,000
Increase (or decrease) from prior allocation	4,200	(1,200)	(3,000)	—

The manager of the Suits Department complained that as a result of his successful effort to expand sales in his department, he was being forced to carry a larger share of the service department costs. On the other hand, the managers of the departments that showed no improvement in sales were relieved of a portion of the costs that they had been carrying. Yet there had been no change in the amount of services provided for any department.

The manager of the Suits Department viewed the increased service department cost allocation to his department as a penalty for his outstanding performance, and he wondered whether his efforts had really been worthwhile after all in the eyes of top management.

Sales dollars should be used as an allocation base only in those cases where there is a direct causal relationship between sales dollars and the service department costs being allocated. In those situations where service department costs are fixed, they should be allocated according to the three guidelines discussed earlier in the chapter.

No Distinction Made between Fixed and Variable Costs

Unfortunately, many companies do not distinguish between fixed and variable costs in their service department allocations. An example of such an allocation was given earlier in Exhibit 16–4, where we first illustrated the step method.

Should All Costs Be Allocated?

As a general rule, any service department costs that are incurred as a result of specific services provided to operating departments should be allocated back to these departments and used to compute overhead rates and to measure performance and profitability. The only time when this general rule is not followed is in those situations where, in the view of the management, allocation would result in an undesirable behavioural response from people in the operating departments. This is particularly a problem when, in violation of the principles stated earlier, fixed costs are allocated to operating units on the basis of their actual usage of a service. For example, in periods when departments are under pressure to cut costs, they may be reluctant to use the services of systems design analysts and internal consultants because of the charges that would be involved.

To avoid discouraging use of a service that is beneficial to the entire organization, some firms do not charge for the service at all. These managers feel that by making such services a free commodity, departments will be more inclined to take full advantage of their benefits.

Retainer fee approach
A method of allocating service department costs in which other departments are charged a flat amount each period regardless of usage of the service involved.

Other firms take a somewhat different approach. They agree that charging according to usage may discourage utilization of such services as systems design, but they argue that such services should not be free. Instead of providing free services, these firms take what is sometimes called a **retainer fee approach.** This is essentially the predetermined lump-sum approach discussed above for fixed costs. Each department is charged a flat amount each year, regardless of how much or how little of the service it utilizes. If a department knows it is going to be charged a certain amount for systems design services, *regardless of usage*, then it is more likely to use the service.

Focus on Current Practice

It can be unwise for a service department to offer free services to other departments, as shown by the following experience:

[A hospital] established a policy of allowing its employees to eat all they wanted in the cafeteria, free of charge. The administration believed that the hospital's cost of providing this employee benefit would be low because the kitchen facilities were a fixed cost.

However, the hospital's food services costs shot up. An investigation revealed that the employees were wasting large amounts of food. Some were taking several entrees, tasting them, and throwing the rest away.

When the policy was changed and the employees were charged a token amount—about a third of a comparable meal elsewhere—the wasting of food declined dramatically. In fact, the decrease in the Food Service Department's costs were greater than the revenue generated by the nominal charge.[4] ■

---

4. Leon B. Hoshower and Robert P. Crum, "Controlling Service Center Costs," *Management Accounting* 69, no. 5 (November 1987), p. 44. Used by permission.

Summary

Service departments are organized to provide some needed service in a single, centralized place, rather than to have all units within the organization provide the service for themselves. Although service departments do not engage directly in production or other operating activities, the costs that they incur are vital to the overall success of an organization and therefore are properly included as part of the cost of its products and services.

Service department costs are charged to operating departments by an allocation process. In turn, the operating departments include the allocated costs within their flexible budgets, from which overhead rates are computed for purposes of costing of products or services.

Variable and fixed service department costs should be allocated separately. The variable costs should be allocated according to whatever activity causes their incurrence. The fixed costs should be allocated in predetermined lump-sum amounts according to either the peak-period or the long-run average servicing needs of the consuming departments. Budgeted costs, rather than actual costs, should always be allocated to avoid the passing on of inefficiency between departments. Any variances between budgeted and actual service department costs should be kept within the service departments for analysis purposes, then written off against revenues or against cost of goods sold, along with other variances.

Review Problem: Direct and Step Methods

Kovac Printing Company has three service departments and two operating departments. Selected data for the five departments relating to the most recent period follow:

	Service Department			Operating Department		
	Train-ing	Jani-torial	Mainte-nance	Offset Printing	Lithog-raphy	Total
Overhead costs	$360,000	$210,000	$96,000	$400,000	$534,000	$1,600,000
Number of employees	120	70	280	630	420	1,520
Square metres of space occupied	1,000	2,000	4,000	8,000	20,000	35,000
Hours of press time	—	—	—	30,000	60,000	90,000

The company allocates service department costs in the following order and using the bases indicated: Training (number of employees), Janitorial (space occupied), and Maintenance (hours of press time). The company makes no distinction between variable and fixed service department costs.

Required
1. Use the direct method to allocate service department costs to the operating departments.
2. Use the step method to allocate service department costs to the operating departments.

Solution to Review Problem
1. Under the direct method, service department costs are allocated directly to the operating departments. Supporting computations for these allocations follow:

	Allocation Bases					
	Training		Janitorial		Maintenance	
Offset Printing data ...	630 employees	3/5	8,000 square metres	2/7	30,000 hours	1/3
Lithography data	420 employees	2/5	20,000 square metres	5/7	60,000 hours	2/3
Total	1,050 employees	5/5	28,000 square metres	7/7	90,000 hours	3/3

Given these allocation rates, the allocations to the operating departments would be as follows:

	Service Department			Operating Department		
	Train-ing	Jani-torial	Mainte-nance	Offset Printing	Lithog-raphy	Total
Overhead costs	$ 360,000	$ 210,000	$ 96,000	$400,000	$534,000	$1,600,000
Allocation:						
Training						
(3/5; 2/5)	(360,000)			216,000	144,000	
Janitorial						
(2/7; 5/7)		(210,000)		60,000	150,000	
Maintenance						
(1/3; 2/3)			(96,000)	32,000	64,000	
Total overhead cost after allocations	$ –0–	$ –0–	$ –0–	$708,000	$892,000	$1,600,000

2. Under the step method, services rendered between service departments are recognized when costs are allocated to other departments. Starting with the training service department, supporting computations for these allocations follow:

	Allocation Bases					
	Training		Janitorial		Maintenance	
Janitorial data	70 employees	5%	—		—	
Maintenance data ...	280 employees	20%	4,000 square metres	1/8	—	
Offset Printing data ..	630 employees	45%	8,000 square metres	2/8	30,000 hours	1/3
Lithography data	420 employees	30%	20,000 square metres	5/8	60,000 hours	2/3
Total	1,400 employees	100%	32,000 square metres	8/8	90,000 hours	3/3

Given these allocation rates, the allocations to the various departments would be as follows:

	Service Department			Operating Department		
	Train-ing	Jani-torial	Mainte-nance	Offset Printing	Lithog-raphy	Total
Overhead costs	$ 360,000	$ 210,000	$ 96,000	$400,000	$534,000	$1,600,000
Allocation:						
Training						
(5%; 20%; 45%; 30%)*	(360,000)	18,000	72,000	162,000	108,000	
Janitorial						
(1/8; 2/8; 5/8)		(228,000)	28,500	57,000	142,500	
Maintenance						
(1/3; 2/3)			(196,500)	65,500	131,000	
Total overhead cost after allocations	$ –0–	$ –0–	$ –0–	$684,500	$915,500	$1,600,000

*Allocation rates can be shown either in percentages, in fractions, or as a dollar rate per unit of activity. Both percentages and fractions are shown in this problem for sake of illustration. *It is better to use fractions if percentages would result in odd decimals.*

Questions

16–1   What is the difference between a service department and an operating department? Give several examples of service departments.

16–2   How are service department costs assigned to products and services?

16–3   What are interdepartmental service costs? How are such costs allocated to other departments under the step method?

16–4   How are service department costs allocated to other departments under the direct method?

16–5   If a service department generates revenues, how do these revenues enter into the allocation of the department's costs to other departments?

16–6   What guidelines should govern the allocation of fixed service department costs to other departments? The allocation of variable service department costs?

16–7   "A variable base should never be used in allocating fixed service department costs to operating departments." Explain.

16–8   Why might it be desirable not to allocate some service department costs to operating departments?

16–9   In what way are service department costs similar to costs such as lubricants, utilities, and factory supervision?

16–10   "Products and services can be costed equally well with or without allocations of service department costs." Do you agree? Why or why not?

16–11   What criteria are relevant to the selection of allocation bases for service department costs?

16–12   What is the purpose of the retainer fee approach to cost allocation?

16–13   How does the reciprocal method allocate interdepartmental services? How does the approach differ from the step method?

16–14   When is it proper to pass on variances from budget in a service department to departments using the services?

16–15   Why are arbitrary allocations a practice that should be avoided whenever possible?

16–16   When are arbitrary allocations necessary?

Exercises

E16–1   The Ferre Publishing Company has three service departments and two operating departments. Selected data from a recent period on the five departments follow:

| | Service Department | | | Operating Department | | |
	A	B	C	1	2	Total
Overhead costs	$140,000	$105,000	$48,000	$275,000	$430,000	$998,000
Number of employees	60	35	140	315	210	760
Square metres of space occupied	1,500	1,000	2,000	4,000	10,000	18,500
Hours of press time	—	—	—	30,000	60,000	90,000

The company allocates service department costs by the step method in the following order: A (number of employees), B (space occupied), and C (hours of press time). The company makes no distinction between variable and fixed service department costs.

Required   Using the step method, allocate the service department costs to the operating departments.

E16–2   Refer to the data for the Ferre Publishing Company in E16–1. Assume that the company allocates service department costs by the direct method, rather than by the step method.

Required   Assuming that the company uses the direct method, how much overhead cost would be allocated to each operating department?

E16–3   Hannibal Steel Company has a Transport Services Department that provides trucks to haul ore from the company's mine to its two steel mills—the Northern Plant and the Southern Plant. Budgeted costs for the Transport Services Department total $350,000 per year, consisting of $0.25 per tonne variable cost and $300,000 fixed cost. The level of fixed cost is determined by peak-period requirements. During the peak period, the Northern Plant requires 70% of the Transport Services Department's capacity and the Southern Plant requires 30%.

During the coming year, 120,000 tonnes of ore are budgeted to be hauled for the Northern Plant and 60,000 tonnes of ore for the Southern Plant.

Required   Compute the amount of Transport Services Department cost that should be allocated to each plant at the beginning of the year for purposes of computing predetermined overhead rates. (The company allocates variable and fixed costs separately.)

E16–4   Refer to the data in E16–3. Assume that it is now the end of the year. During the year, the Transport Services Department actually hauled the following amounts of ore for the two plants: Northern Plant, 130,000 tonnes; Southern Plant, 50,000 tonnes. The Transport Services Department incurred $364,000 in cost during the year, of which $54,000 was variable cost and $310,000 was fixed cost.

Management wants end-of-year service department cost allocations in order to compare actual performance to planned performance.

Required   1. Determine how much of the $54,000 in variable cost should be allocated to each plant.
2. Determine how much of the $310,000 in fixed cost should be allocated to each plant.
3. Should any of the $364,000 in the Transport Services Department cost not be allocated to the plants? Explain.

E16–5   Konig Enterprises, Ltd., owns and operates three restaurants in Vancouver, B.C. The company allocates its fixed administrative expenses to the three restaurants on the basis of sales dollars. During 1998, the fixed administrative expenses totalled $2,000,000. These expenses were allocated as follows:

| | *Restaurant* | | | |
	Rick's Harbourside	Imperial Garden	Ginger Wok	Total
Total sales—1998	$16,000,000	$15,000,000	$9,000,000	$40,000,000
Percentage of total sales	40%	37.5%	22.5%	100%
Allocation (based on the above percentages)	$ 800,000	$ 750,000	$ 450,000	$ 2,000,000

During 1999, the following year, the Imperial Garden restaurant increased its sales by two-thirds. The sales levels in the other two restaurants remained unchanged. As a result of the Imperial Garden's sales increase, the company's 1999 sales data were as follows:

| | *Restaurant* | | | |
	Rick's Harbourside	Imperial Garden	Ginger Wok	Total
Total sales—1999	$16,000,000	$25,000,000	$9,000,000	$50,000,000
Percentage of total sales	32%	50%	18%	100%

Fixed administrative expenses remained unchanged at $2,000,000 during 1999.

Required
1. Using sales dollars as an allocation base, show the allocation of the fixed administrative expenses among the three restaurants for 1999.
2. Compare your allocation from (1) above to the allocation for 1998. As the manager of the Imperial Garden, how would you feel about the allocation that has been charged to you for 1999?
3. Comment on the usefulness of sales dollars as an allocation base.

E16–6 Westlake Hospital has a Radiology Department that provides X-ray services to the hospital's three operating departments. The variable costs of the Radiology Department are allocated to the operating departments on the basis of the number of X-rays provided for each department. Budgeted and actual data relating to the cost of X-rays taken last year are given below:

	Variable Costs	
	Budgeted	**Actual**
Radiology Department	$18 per X-ray	$20 per X-ray

The budgeted and actual number of X-rays provided for each operating department last year follow:

	Pediatrics	**OB Care**	**General Hospital**
Budgeted number of X-rays	7,000	4,500	12,000
Actual number of X-rays taken ...	6,000	3,000	15,000

Required Determine the amount of Radiology Department variable cost that should have been allocated to each of the three operating departments at the end of last year for purposes of comparing actual performance to planned performance.

E16–7 Refer to Westlake Hospital in E16–6. In addition to the Radiology Department, the hospital also has a Janitorial Services Department that provides services to all other departments in the hospital. The fixed costs of the two service departments are allocated on the following bases:

Department	Basis for Allocation
Janitorial Services	Square metres of space occupied:
	Radiology Department .... 600 square metres
	Pediatrics .... 3,000 square metres
	OB Care .... 2,400 square metres
	General Hospital .... 9,000 square metres
Radiology	Long-run average X-ray needs per year:
	Pediatrics .... 9,000 X-rays
	OB Care .... 6,000 X-rays
	General Hospital .... 15,000 X-rays

Budgeted and actual fixed costs in the two service departments for the year follow:

	Janitorial Services	**Radiology**
Budgeted fixed costs	$375,000	$590,000
Actual fixed costs	381,000	600,000

Required
1. Show the allocation of the fixed costs of the two service departments at the beginning of the year for purposes of computing overhead rates in the operating departments. The hospital uses the step method of allocation.
2. Show the allocation of the fixed costs of the two service departments at the end of the year for purposes of comparing actual performance to planned performance.

E16–8   Refer to the data concerning Westlake Hospital in E16–6 and E16–7.

Required
1. Using the data, allocate the service departments to the operating departments using the reciprocal method.
2. Would the managers of the two service departments care which method was used to allocate? The operating department managers?

Problems

P16–9   Various Allocation Methods   Sharp Motor Company has an Auto Division and a Truck Division. The company has a cafeteria that serves the employees of both divisions. The costs of operating the cafeteria are budgeted at $40,000 per month plus $3 per meal served. The company pays all the cost of the meals.

The fixed costs of the cafeteria are determined by peak-period requirements. The Auto Division is responsible for 65% of the peak-period requirements, and the Truck Division is responsible for the other 35%.

For June, the Auto Division has estimated that it will need 35,000 meals served, and the Truck Division has estimated that it will need 20,000 meals served.

Required
1. At the beginning of June, how much cafeteria cost should be allocated to each division for flexible budget planning purposes?
2. Assume that it is now the end of June. Cost records in the cafeteria show that actual fixed costs for the month totalled $42,000 and that actual meal costs totalled $128,000. Due to unexpected layoffs of employees during the month, only 20,000 meals were served to the Auto Division. Another 20,000 meals were served to the Truck Division, as planned. How much of the actual cafeteria costs for the month should be allocated to each division? (Management uses these end-of-month allocations to compare actual performance with planned performance.)
3. Refer to the data in (2) above. Assume that the company follows the practice of allocating *all* cafeteria costs to the divisions in proportion to the number of meals served to each division during the month. On this basis, how much cost would be allocated to each division for June?
4. What criticisms can you make of the allocation method used in (3) above?
5. If managers of operating departments know that fixed service costs are going to be allocated on the basis of peak-period requirements, what will be their probable strategy as they report their estimate of peak-period requirements to the company's budget committee? As a member of top management, what would you do to neutralize any such strategies?

P16–10   Cost Allocation in a Hospital; Step Method   Woodbury Hospital has three service departments and three operating departments. Estimated cost and operating data for all departments in the hospital for the forthcoming quarter are presented in the table below:

	Service Department			Operating Department			
	Housekeeping Services	Food Services	Admin. Services	Labor-atory	Radiology	General Hospital	Total
Variable costs	$ —	$193,860	$158,840	$243,600	$304,800	$ 74,500	$ 975,600
Fixed costs	87,000	107,200	90,180	162,300	215,700	401,300	1,063,680
Total cost	$87,000	$301,060	$249,020	$405,900	$520,500	$475,800	$2,039,280
Meals served	—	—	800	2,000	1,000	68,000	71,800
Percentage of peak-period needs—Food Services	—	—	0.8%	2.4%	1.6%	95.2%	100%
Square metres of space	500	1,300	650	1,000	750	10,800	15,000
Files processed	—	—	—	14,000	7,000	25,000	46,000
Percentage of peak-period needs—Admin. Services	—	—	—	30%	20%	50%	100%

The costs of the service department are allocated by the step method using the bases and in the order shown in the following table:

Service Department	Costs Incurred	Bases for Allocation
Housekeeping Services	Fixed	Square metres of space
Food Services	Variable	Meals served
	Fixed	Peak-period needs—Food Services
Administrative Services	Variable	Files processed
	Fixed	Peak-period needs—Admin. Services

All billing in the hospital is done through Laboratory, Radiology, or General Hospital. The hospital's administrator wants the costs of the three service departments allocated to these three billing centres.

Required   Prepare the cost allocation desired by the hospital administrator. (Use the step method.) Include under each billing centre the direct costs of the centre, as well as the costs allocated from the service departments.

P16–11   Beginning- and End-of-Year Allocations   Tasman Products, Ltd., of Australia has a Maintenance Department that services the equipment in the company's Forming Department and Assembly Department. The cost of this servicing is allocated to the operating departments on the basis of machine-hours. Cost and other data relating to the Maintenance Department and to the other two departments for the most recent year are presented below. (The currency in Australia is the Australian dollar.)

Data for the Maintenance Department follow:

	Budget	Actual
Variable costs for lubricants	$ 96,000*	$110,000
Fixed costs for salaries and other	150,000	153,000

   *Budgeted at $0.40 per machine-hour.

Data for the Forming and Assembly departments follow:

	Machine-Hours		
	Percentage of Peak-Period Capacity Required	Budget	Actual
Forming Department	70%	160,000	190,000
Assembly Department	30%	80,000	70,000
Total	100%	240,000	260,000

The company allocates variable and fixed costs separately. The level of fixed costs in the Maintenance Department is determined by peak-period requirements.

Required   1. Assume that it is the beginning of the year. An allocation of Maintenance Department cost must be made to the operating departments to assist in computing predetermined overhead rates. How much of the budgeted Maintenance Department cost above would be allocated to each department?

2. Assume that it is now the end of the year. Management would like data to assist in comparing actual performance against planned performance in the Maintenance Department and in the other departments.

   a. How much of the actual Maintenance Department costs above should be allocated to the Forming Department and to the Assembly Department? Show all computations.

   b. Is there any portion of the actual Maintenance Department costs that should not be allocated to the other departments? If all costs would be allocated, explain why; if a portion would not be allocated, compute the amount and explain why it would not be allocated.

P16–12 Equity in Allocations; Computer Centre "These allocations don't make any sense at all," said Bob Cosic, manager of National Airlines' Freight Division. "We used the computer less during the second quarter than we did during the first quarter, yet we were allocated more cost. Is that fair? In fact, we picked up the lion's share of the computer's cost during the second quarter, even though we're a lot smaller than the Domestic Passenger Division."

National Airlines established a Computer Centre to service its three operating divisions. The company allocates the cost of the centre to the divisions on the basis of the number of pages of printout for invoices, tickets, and so forth, provided each quarter. Allocations for the first two quarters to which Mr. Cosic was referring are given below:

			Division	
			Passenger	
	Total	Freight	Domestic	Overseas
First quarter actual results:				
Pages of printout	300,000	90,000	180,000	30,000
Percentage of total	100%	30%	60%	10%
Computer cost allocated	$172,000	$51,600	$103,200	$17,200
Second quarter actual results:				
Pages of printout	200,000	80,000	70,000	50,000
Percentage of total	100%	40%	35%	25%
Computer cost allocated	$168,000	$67,200	$ 58,800	$42,000

"Now don't get upset, Bob," replied Colleen Rogers, the controller. "Those allocations are fair. As you can see, your division received the largest share of the computer's output during the second quarter and therefore it has been allocated the largest share of cost. Although use of the Computer Centre was off somewhat during the second quarter, keep in mind that most of the centre's costs are fixed and therefore continue regardless of how much the computer is used. Also, remember that we built enough capacity into the Computer Centre to handle the divisions' peak-period needs, and that cost has to be absorbed by someone. The fairest way to handle it is to charge according to usage from quarter to quarter. When you use the computer more, you get charged more; it's as simple as that."

"That's just the point," replied Cosic. "I didn't use the computer more, I used it less. So why am I charged more?"

The Freight Division requires 30% of the Computer Centre's capacity during peak periods; the Domestic Passenger Division, 50%; and the Overseas Passenger Division, 20%. The peak period occurs in the fourth quarter of the year.

Required
1. Is there any merit to Mr. Cosic's complaint? Explain.
2. Using the high-low method, determine the cost formula for the Computer Centre in terms of a variable rate per page and total fixed cost each quarter.
3. Reallocate the Computer Centre costs for the first and second quarters in accordance with the cost allocation principles discussed in the chapter. Allocate the variable and fixed costs separately.

P16–13 Multiple Departments; Step Method; Predetermined Overhead Rates Bombay Castings, Ltd., has two producing departments, Fabrication and Finishing, and three service departments. The service departments and the bases on which their costs are allocated to using departments are listed below:

Department	Cost	Allocation Bases
Building and Grounds	Fixed	Square metres occupied
Administration	Variable	Number of employees
	Fixed	Employees at full capacity
Equipment Maintenance	Variable	Machine-hours
	Fixed	40% to Fabrication
		60% to Finishing

Indian currency is denominated in rupees, denoted here by R.

Service department costs are allocated to using departments by the step method in the order shown. The company has developed the cost and operating data given in the following table for purposes of preparing overhead rates in the two producing departments:

	Building and Grounds	Adminis-tration	Equip-ment Mainte-nance	Fabrication	Finishing	Total
Variable costs	R –0–	R22,200	R16,900	R146,000	R320,000	R 505,100
Fixed costs	88,200	60,000	24,000	420,000	490,000	1,082,200
Total cost	R88,200	R82,200	R40,900	R566,000	R810,000	R1,587,300
Budgeted employees	6	4	30	450	630	1,120
Employees at full capacity	8	4	45	570	885	1,512
Square metres of space occupied	60	50	140	1,200	1,550	3,000
Budgeted machine-hours	—	—	—	70,000	105,000	175,000

Required
1. Show the allocation of service department costs to producing departments for purposes of preparing overhead rates in Fabrication and Finishing.
2. Assuming that overhead rates are set on the basis of machine-hours, compute the overhead rate for each producing department.
3. Assume the following *actual* data for the year for the Administration Department:

Actual variable costs	R23,800
Actual employees for the year:	
Building and Grounds	6
Administration	4
Equipment Maintenance	32
Fabrication	460
Finishing	625
	1,127

Compute the amount of end-of-year Administration Department variable cost that should be allocated to each department. (Management uses these end-of-year allocations to compare actual performance to planned performance.)

P16–14 Cost Allocation in a Resort; Step Method   The Bayview Resort has three operating units—the Convention Centre, Food Services, and Guest Lodging—through which all billing is done. These three operating units are supported by three service units—General Administration, Cost Accounting, and Laundry. The costs of the service units are allocated by the step method using the bases and in the order shown below:

General Administration:
 Fixed costs—allocated 10% to Cost Accounting, 4% to the Laundry, 30% to the Convention Centre, 16% to Food Services, and 40% to Guest Lodging.

Cost Accounting:
 Variable costs—allocated on the basis of the number of items processed each period.
 Fixed costs—allocated on the basis of peak-period requirements.

Laundry:
 Variable costs—allocated on the basis of the number of kilograms of laundry processed each period.
 Fixed costs—allocated on the basis of peak-period requirements.

Cost and operating data for all units in the resort for a recent quarter are given in the following table:

	Service Unit			Operating Unit			
	General Adminis-tration	Cost Ac-counting	Laundry	Conven-tion Centre	Food Services	Guest Lodging	Total
Variable costs	$ –0–	$ 70,000	$143,000	$ –0–	$ 52,000	$ 24,000	$ 289,000
Fixed costs	200,000	110,000	65,900	95,000	375,000	486,000	1,331,900
Total overhead cost	$200,000	$180,000	$208,900	$95,000	$427,000	$510,000	$1,620,900
Kilograms of laundry processed	—	—	—	20,000	15,000	210,000	245,000
Percentage of peak-period requirements—Laundry	—	—	—	10%	6%	84%	100%
Number of items processed	1,000	—	800	1,200	3,000	9,000	15,000
Percentage of peak-period requirements—Cost Accounting	—*	—	7%	13%	20%	60%	100%

*General administration is excluded from the computation of peak-period requirements due to the order in which the service unit costs are allocated.

Since all billing is done through the Convention Centre, Food Services, and Guest Lodging, the resort's general manager wants the costs of the three service units allocated to these three billing centres.

Required Prepare the cost allocation desired by the resort's general manager. Include under each billing centre the direct costs of the centre, as well as the costs allocated from the service units.

P16–15 Direct and Reciprocal Methods At the beginning of this year, a group of lawyers and accountants in Calgary decided to join efforts in providing one-stop legal and accounting consulting services to industry and the government. The group established a consulting company, rented office space, and hired both professional and clerical staff.

Following several initial organizational meetings, the partners decided to divide the operation into three parts: the consulting department, the legal department, and the accounting department.

The consulting department dealt directly with the clients, providing two somewhat distinct services, accounting consulting (AC) and legal consulting (LC). In its first full month of operations, this department recorded its own identifiable costs as $20,000, 30% attributed to accounting consultations and 70% to legal work. Billings to clients amounted to $30,000 and $20,500 for accounting and legal consultations, respectively. This department made use of the other two departments' services in preparing work for the external clients.

The accounting and legal departments provided professional services for each other and for the consulting department on the basis of time according to the following schedule:

	Accounting Department	Legal Department	Consulting AC	Consulting LC
Accounting services	—	20%	60%	20%
Legal services	50%	—	10	40

The accounting department incurred $8,000 in costs in the first month and the legal department incurred $10,000. Neither department directly bills external clients.

Having completed the first month's activity, the partners are ready to evaluate the performance of the group and of the individual areas. The managing partner is concerned that his organizational structure may be a major determinant of success and has asked you, as an outside consultant, to prepare some performance information for him.

Required 1. Prepare an income statement for each consulting branch separately under each of the following allocation approaches:
  a. Direct
  b. Reciprocal

2. Prepare a brief memorandum to the managing partner on the performance of the group and the individual areas. In your memorandum, comment on the usefulness of standard costing for this service organization.

(SMAC, adapted)

Cases

C16–16 Step Method versus Direct Method   "This is really an odd situation," said Jim Carter, general manager of Highland Publishing Company. "We get most of the jobs we bid on that require a lot of press time in the Printing Department, yet profits on those jobs are never as high as they ought to be. On the other hand, we lose most of the jobs we bid on that require a lot of time in the Binding Department. I would be inclined to think that the problem is with our overhead rates, but we're already computing separate overhead rates for each department like the trade journals advise. So what else could be wrong?"

Highland Publishing Company is a large organization that offers a variety of printing and binding work. The Printing and Binding departments are supported by three service departments. The costs of these service departments are allocated to other departments in the order listed below. (For each service department, use the allocation base that provides the best measure of service provided, as discussed in the chapter.)

Department	Total Labour-Hours	Square Metres of Space Occupied	Number of Employees	Machine-Hours	Direct Labour-Hours
Personnel	20,000	400	10	—	—
Custodial Services	30,000	600	15	—	—
Maintenance	50,000	2,000	25	—	—
Printing	90,000	8,000	40	150,000	60,000
Binding	260,000	4,000	120	30,000	175,000
	450,000	15,000	210	180,000	235,000

Budgeted overhead costs in each department for the current year are shown below (no distinction is made between variable and fixed costs):

Personnel	$ 360,000
Custodial Services	141,000
Maintenance	201,000
Printing	525,000
Binding	373,500
Total budgeted cost	$1,600,500

Because of its simplicity, the company has always used the direct method to allocate service department costs to the two operating departments.

Required
1. Using the step method, allocate the service department costs to the other departments. Then compute predetermined overhead rates for the current year using a machine-hours basis in the Printing Department and a direct labour-hours basis in the Binding Department.
2. Repeat (1) above, this time using the direct method. Again compute predetermined overhead rates in the Printing and Binding departments.
3. Assume that during the current year the company bids on a job that requires machine and labour time as follows:

	Machine-Hours	Direct Labour-Hours
Printing Department	15,400	900
Binding Department	800	2,000
Total hours	16,200	2,900

a. Determine the amount of overhead cost that would be assigned to the job if the company used the overhead rates developed in (1) above. Then determine the amount of overhead cost that would be assigned to the job if the company used the overhead rates developed in (2) above.

b. Explain to Mr. Carter, the general manager, why the step method would provide a better basis for computing predetermined overhead rates than the direct method.

C16–17 Direct Method; Plantwide versus Departmental Overhead Rates Hobart Products manufactures a complete line of fiberglass attaché cases and suitcases. Hobart has three manufacturing departments—Molding, Component, and Assembly—and two service departments—Power and Maintenance.

The sides of the cases are manufactured in the Molding Department. The frames, hinges, locks, and so forth, are manufactured in the Component Department. The cases are completed in the Assembly Department. Varying amounts of materials, time, and effort are required for each of the various cases. The Power Department and Maintenance Department provide services to the manufacturing departments.

Hobart has always used a plantwide overhead rate. Direct labour-hours are used to assign the overhead to products. The overhead rate is computed by dividing the company's total estimated overhead cost by the total estimated direct labour-hours to be worked in the three manufacturing departments.

Whit Portlock, manager of Cost Accounting, has recommended that the company use departmental overhead rates rather than a single, plantwide rate. Planned operating costs and expected levels of activity for the coming year have been developed by Mr. Portlock and are presented below:

	Service Department	
	Power	Maintenance
Departmental activity measures:		
Estimated usage in the coming year	80,000 KWh	12,500 hours*
Departmental costs:		
Materials and supplies	$ 500,000	$ 25,000
Variable labour	140,000	–0–
Fixed overhead	1,200,000	375,000
Total service department cost	$1,840,000	$400,000

*Hours of maintenance time.

	Manufacturing Department		
	Molding	Component	Assembly
Departmental activity measures:			
Direct labour-hours	50,000	200,000	150,000
Machine-hours	87,500	12,500	–0–
Departmental costs:			
Raw materials	$1,630,000	$3,000,000	$ 25,000
Direct labour	350,000	2,000,000	1,300,000
Variable overhead	210,500	1,000,000	1,650,000
Fixed overhead	1,750,000	620,000	749,500
Total departmental cost	$3,940,500	$6,620,000	$3,724,500

	Manufacturing Department		
	Molding	**Component**	**Assembly**
Use of service departments:			
Maintenance:			
Estimated usage in hours of maintenance time for the coming year	9,000	2,500	1,000
Percentage of peak-period Maintenance Department capacity required	70%	20%	10%
Power:			
Estimated usage in kilowatt-hours for the coming year	36,000	32,000	12,000
Percentage of peak-period Power Department capacity required	50%	35%	15%

Required

1. Assume that the company will use a single, plantwide overhead rate for the coming year, the same as in the past. Compute the plantwide rate that would be used.

2. Assume that Whit Portlock has been asked to develop departmental overhead rates for the three manufacturing departments for comparison with the plantwide rate. In order to develop these rates, do the following:

   a. Using the direct method, allocate the service department costs to the manufacturing departments. In each case, allocate the variable and fixed costs separately.

   b. Compute overhead rates for the three manufactuing departments for the coming year. In computing the rates, use a machine-hours basis in the Molding Department and a direct labour-hours basis in the other two departments.

3. Assume that Hobart Products has one small attaché case that has the following annual requirements for machine time and direct labour time in the various departments:

	Machine-Hours	Direct Labour-Hours
Molding Department	3,000	1,000
Component Department	800	2,500
Assembly Department	—	4,000
Total hours	3,800	7,500

   a. Compute the amount of overhead cost that would be allocated to this attaché case if a plantwide overhead rate is used. Repeat the computation, this time assuming that departmental overhead rates are used.

   b. Hobart Products bases its selling prices on its computed costs—adding a percentage markup. Management is concerned because this attaché case is priced well below competing products of competitors. On the other hand, certain other of Hobart's products are priced well above the prices of competitors with the result that profits in the company are deteriorating because of declining sales. Looking at the computations in (a) above, what effect is the use of a plantwide rate having on the costing of products and therefore on selling prices?

4. What additional steps could Hobart Products take to improve its overhead costing?

(CMA, adapted)

C16–18 Comprehensive   St. Mary's College, founded under the Provincial Colleges and Universities Act, is a no profit organization involved in the delivery of educational programs. St. Mary's is multi-faceted. Its activities are separated into four categories: academic programs, federal government programs, profit centres, and support services. (See Exhibit 16–9 for a macro-version of its organizational chart.)

Exhibit 16–9   St. Mary's College Organization Chart

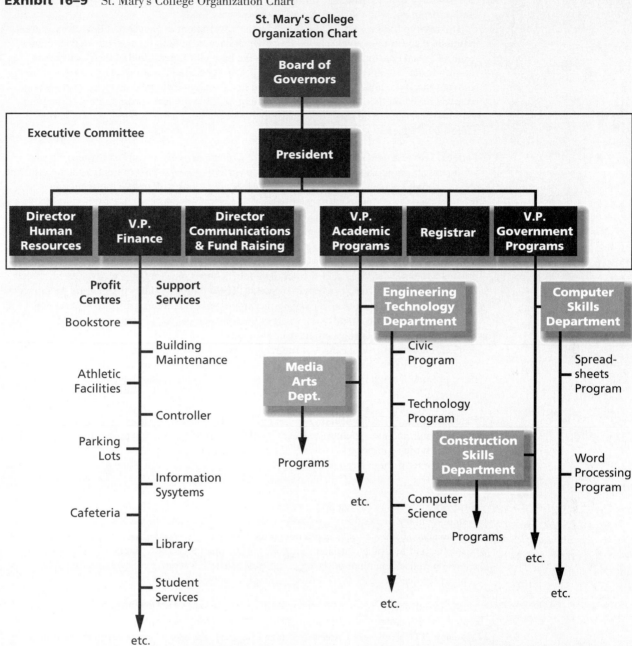

Academic Programs   St. Mary's College delivers post-secondary academic educational programs on a trimester basis. These trimesters run from September to December, January to April and May to August. This activity accounts for 70% of the college's operations and is funded by the provincial government. These funds are provided by the government at the beginning of every trimester and are based on a formula, with an allowance for inflation and overhead, applied to student enrollment for the same trimester two years previous. For example, if the enrollment for the September to December trimester in 1998 was 750 students, the inflation/overhead-adjusted funding received for September to December 1999 is based on 750 students even if the actual enrollment is 800 students or 700 students. In addition to the government funds, the college charges a government-regulated student fee to each student.

This funding formula allows the college, in planning for the academic programs being offered in a particular trimester, to know how much revenue it will receive. If the college has a cash shortage in any particular trimester due to increased enrollment, it can use its reserve fund or it can apply to the government for emergency funds.

The reserve fund is closely monitored by the government to ensure that the reserves are maintained at a certain level. The reserves which have been built up over the years are the result of actual enrollments being lower than the base enrollment used in the government funding formula. For example, if actual enrollment for September to December 1999 is 650 students and if the college conducts its affairs in a fiscally responsible manner, excess funds received based on the 1998 trimester enrollment of 750 would be added to the reserve fund. These reserves are to be used for expansion, replacement of capital assets, or as a buffer against hard times.

Federal Government Programs   St. Mary's College delivers, on an "as required" basis, adult skills training and apprenticeship programs for the federal government. This government service activity accounts for 20% of the college's operations and, unlike the academic programs, does not run on a trimester basis. The federal government directly, and indirectly through local Industry Training Committees, purchases these programs from the college. The purchase price is a per diem rate per student enrolled in the program. For example, if the federal government directly purchases a computer skills training program from the college for 50 students for a period of four weeks (20 days) at $55 per day per student, the total purchase price is $55,000. Calculation of the per diem rate is based on a target of recovering all direct costs plus 8% of direct costs to cover overhead. The duration of the skills training programs can vary from 4 to 52 weeks. The apprenticeship programs can run from 2 to 4 years and require the students to attend classes part of the time and gain work experience through co-op placement with local businesses the rest of the time.

Negotiations for purchasing and running all federal government programs are conducted in November and December and are finalized in March. Courses commence in April. Some of these programs could have a small surplus and some a small deficit, but overall they achieve their target.

Profit Centres   The bookstore, athletic facilities, cafeteria and parking lots are operated as profit centres and are synchronized with the delivery of the academic programs. These profit centre activities comprise 5% of the college's operations. The profits generated by the profit centres are used for expansion or to purchase capital assets for any of the college's activities at the discretion of the college executive committee. The pricing policy is full cost plus 30%.

Support Services   The support services include administration, finance, information systems, library, student services, human resources, communications and building maintenance. These services operate regardless of the time frames and funding patterns of the academic and federal government programs. They operate as individual cost centres for control purposes, but their costs are completely allocated to other college activities. The support services account for 5% of the college's operations.

Budgets and Reports   Under the terms of the Colleges and Universities Act, each year the college is obligated to provide audited financial statements and an annual report to the Ministry of Colleges and Universities as at March 31, the end of the government's fiscal year. Each December, the managers of the profit centres, support services departments, academic programs departments and federal government programs departments prepare their area's overall budget for the upcoming April to March year. No budgets are prepared for individual programs operating within the various departments. For example, the manager of the Engineering Technology Department will prepare the budget for his whole department after some discussion with the individual program heads. The managers then go through a negotiation process with the college's executive committee and the department/profit centre budgets are finalized in February.

For control purposes during the year, the managers are provided with monthly accounting reports. (See Exhibit 16–10 for an example.) Although individual program data is not provided, department managers are informally aware of what is going on in the programs. At the end of the year, comparative accounting statements are prepared for each profit centre/department for evaluation purposes. (See Exhibit 16–11 for an example of a year-end profit centre report.)

Exhibit 16–10

Engineering Technology Department
Accounting Report
For the Period April 1 to April 30, 1999

	Current Month Actual	Year to Date Actual	Annual Budget
Salaries and benefits:			
Full-time faculty	$ 65,408	$ 65,408	$ 780,000
Part-time faculty	–0–	–0–	45,000
Administrative staff	18,400	18,400	216,000
Support staff	9,317	9,317	120,000
	93,125	93,125	1,161,000
Instructional materials	32,000	32,000	35,000
Equipment rental	200	200	2,400
Supplies	421	421	2,000
Meetings and seminars	–0–	–0–	2,000
Overhead*	150	150	10,000
Printing and publications	65	65	1,000
Honorariums	–0–	–0–	10,000
Total operating costs	$125,961	$125,961	$1,223,400

*Overhead represents both direct departmental overhead and the support services costs. The support services costs are allocated at the end of the year.

Executive Committee Meeting, March 31, 2000

President: I presume all those present have had an opportunity to review the preliminary set of financial statements. This is the second year in a row that we are showing a deficit in the operating fund. Fortunately, we still have enough in the reserve fund to cover this deficit, but how are we going to explain continuous deficits to the board of governors? More importantly, what are we going to do for the future since the pie and our slice of it are shrinking? Are we spending more than we get? If so, how are we going to control spending? Remember, nowhere is it stated that we cannot run certain types of operations at a profit.

Vice President, Finance: I have been with the college for only six months and, as I see it, the issue is not the deficit, but rather whether the college is achieving its mission and objectives of providing and promoting high-quality education in the most economic, effective, and efficient manner possible. We have been concentrating on getting information for financial audits and external reports, while the more important aspect of regularly using information for management planning and control has been nonexistent.

Vice President, Academic Programs: I have to agree. The monthly reports my department managers get make no sense to them. More often than not, these reports are neatly filed away for review at a later date. The accounting reports we receive provide no insights as to how a program is doing financially or whether it is achieving its goal of providing students with the skills and education that will make them competitive and marketable in the workplace. If I want to find out how a program is doing, I have to call the registrar's office for enrollment information and the student placement office for information as to how many graduates of the program were successful in obtaining employment.

Vice President, Government Programs: While reviewing the accounting records of one of my departments, I noticed that a major purchase of computer equipment was included in the expenses. Correct me if I am wrong, but isn't this a capital item? Expensing this item has put that department in a deficit position.

Vice President, Finance: The issues raised and problems confronting us arise from a basic flaw in our information system. Accounting records and budget information are being prepared and maintained solely for the purpose of satisfying the legal requirement of audited financial statements at the end of the year. According to the manager of information systems, the present information system is inflexible and not integrated. The

Exhibit 16–11

Bookstore
Statement of Revenues and Expenses
For the Year Ended March 31, 1998

	2000	1999
Sales revenue	$5,750,000	$6,145,000
Cost of sales	4,515,000	4,620,000
	1,235,000	1,525,000
Operating expenses	520,000	525,000
Net profit	$ 715,000	$1,000,000

In 1999, the standard mark-up was reduced with the hope of increasing
sales volume. In 1998 and prior years, the bookstore maintained a markup
of 30% on full cost. The bookstore accounts for 25% of the revenue generated by the profit centres.

main computer system is geared only to the financial reporting and audit function. Other
information is recorded on individual department's personal computers. My counterpart
at DEF College told me that they have installed a computerized information system that
serves both management and financial audit requirements. I have arranged to meet with
him together with our controller and manager of information systems.

The Registrar: We need a computerized student information system that will eliminate
duplication and errors that occur in the current system of recording student enrollments.
At present, the registrar's office records student enrollments in its own computer system
which is not connected to the accounting system. Then enrollment data has to be
manually input separately into the accounting system. This has led to discrepancies and
errors.

Director, Communications and Fund Raising: We need to go through all this and come up
with a plan that enables us to function in a fiscally responsible manner while at the same
time not forgetting our main objective. It appears that programs are not being reviewed
for their effectiveness and program heads are not being held accountable for the efficient
running of their programs. Department managers are preparing budgets without senior
management guidance or input. There does not seem to be any uniformity or consistency
throughout the college in the preparation of budgets.

President: I have been concerned about the accounting reports that are sent to me every
month. I receive every department's report and I do not have the time to go through them
all. What I require is one report that will enable me to see total college activities.

Furthermore, these reports are of a purely financial nature. This is well and good, but
we are a nonprofit organization whose success is also evaluated based on nonmonetary
factors such as the quality of our services, and the need for the services we offer.

One opportunity has arisen for the college. I recently met with the board of directors
of GHI Motors Company. They would like us to run a mechanics training program for
their employees and they have offered to donate to the college the building, equipment
and services of an administrator that we would need to run the program. The building
could be built on the currently unused grounds by the northeast student parking lot. The
duration of a training session would be 20 days. The company wants 11 such sessions in
the course of a year. Each session would be attended by at least 40 employees.

The company is willing to pay the college a per diem rate per student, adjusted for
inflation each year. I would like to know how much the per diem rate per student should
be if we are to cover the additional costs to the college of this program. I am also looking
into the possibility of running this program as a profit centre. What is the maximum per
diem rate per student we could charge given our pricing policy? Here is a breakdown of
the projected annual costs to run this program (see Exhibit 16–12). Since this is the first
time the college has received such a donation, some clarification as to the
accounting/financial treatment of the donation and its impact on the college is essential.

I'd like you, Mary (Vice President, Finance), to analyze all of the concerns raised at
today's meeting and make recommendations for next Thursday's meeting.

Exhibit 16–12

> **GHI Motor Company**
> **Projected Annual Costs**
> **Mechanics Training Program**
>
> Salaries and benefits:
>
> | | |
> |---|---|
> | Full-time faculty . . . . | $200,000 |
> | Part-time faculty . . . . | 50,000 |
> | Administrative staff* . . . . | 100,000 |
> | Support staff . . . . | 40,000 |
> | | 390,000 |
> | Instructional materials . . . . | 36,000 |
> | Supplies . . . . | 12,000 |
> | Utilities and building maintenance . . . . | 11,000 |
> | Equipment maintenance . . . . | 8,000 |
> | Overhead† . . . . | 11,000 |
> | Total operating costs . . . . | $468,000 |
>
> *Includes administrator's salary of $75,000 to be paid by GHI Motor Company.
>
> †Overhead represents direct program overhead plus $10,000 of allocated support services costs.

Required   Assume the role of Mary Wise, Vice President, Finance, and prepare the requested report for Peter Smith, President of St. Mary's College.

(SMAC, adapted)

Group Exercises

GE16–19   Understanding the Cost of Complexity   Service departments (or production support departments in the case of a manufacturer) make up a large and growing part of the cost structure of most businesses. This is as true in hospitals, financial institutions, universities, and other service industries as it is in manufacturing. The overall costs of service departments are high and rising. In many manufacturing firms, production support department costs can average 40% or more of total manufacturing costs. Yet, in reality, very little is known about the source or behaviour of these discretionary fixed costs. If you don't know where these costs came from and you do not have a good understanding of how the costs behave, it is going to be very difficult to control and reduce these costs.

In an effort to reduce costs, many companies think all they have to do is reduce head count, a demoralizing and debilitating experience not only for those who lose their jobs, but also for those who remain employed. One sure sign of problems with this head-count-reduction approach is that more than half of firms refill these positions within a year after eliminating them.

Required   1. Choose an industry with which you are somewhat familiar (or know someone who is familiar with the industry) and list seven or eight major production support or service departments in the factory or other facility in this industry. What is the output of each of these support or service departments?

2. Assume a relatively uncomplicated factory (facility) where just a single, standard product (or service) is mass produced. Describe the activity or work being done in each of the service areas of this focused firm.

3. Now assume a more complicated operation for another factory located close by where a wide range of products are made or services are offered—some are standard products/ services while others are made to order, some are high-volume products/services while others are low volume, and some are fairly complex products/services while others are

relatively simple. Describe the activity or work being done in the various service functions for this full-service firm.

4. Which factory or facility has higher production support costs? Why?
5. Explain the relationship between the range of products produced and the size of the support departments. When does the output of each of these support departments increase? When does the cost of each of these support departments increase?
6. Most firms are under increasing pressure to reduce costs. How would you go about bringing the overall level of service department costs down?

GE16–20   Complexity and Cost Drivers in the Purchasing Function

Have several different groups contact the purchasing departments of a number of local manufacturers (one per group), a chain of grocery or retail stores, and at least one large hospital (or, if you can find a purchasing manager willing to speak to your class, that could be almost as effective). Indicate that your management accounting class is studying the purchasing function and would like to interview someone who has an in-depth knowlege of all the department's activities. The interviews should be designed to help you understand how complex purchasing has become—how many employees work in purchasing, what are their major activities, how many different parts (or items) does the company purchase, how many purchase orders are prepared during a year, how many vendors does the company deal with, how many shipments are received, what is the average size of a purchase order, how many purchase orders are for less than $500, and so forth. Once the interview is completed, organize the information in a form that can be reported to the rest of the class in an understandable fashion.

The purchasing representative may not know all of this information, especially if his or her company has not undergone a study in preparation for reducing the cost of the procurement process. That's OK. The objective here is to gain an understanding of all the complexities involved and their impact on cost.

GE16–21   Reengineering Purchasing

Each group should take the information developed from GE16–20 above and begin to consider how to reduce the cost of the purchasing function while maintaining (or even improving) the quality and service level of the various activities performed. It may be helpful to speak with someone who has either reengineered his or her company's purchasing function or is applying continuous improvement techniques to reduce the time spent on low-value activities.

It would be even better if one of these individuals could speak to the class about his or her experiences in redesigning the purchasing function.

Required

1. Who are the customers of purchasing and accounts payable and what are their requirements?
2. With the help of your instructor and starting with the preparation of a materials requisition, map out or document the process flow. Identify as many steps or tasks in the entire procurement/accounts payable process as you can.
3. Prepare a process flowchart or workflow diagram (with boxes and circles) for each step in the process. This provides a good visual reference of the order as it moves through the entire procurement cycle.
4. Determine whether each step or task is value-added (VA) or non-value-added (NVA). To determine whether a step is VA or NVA, ask if eliminating that step or task would in any way cause customer satisfaction to decline.

GE16–22   Necessity Is the Mother of Invention

In an effort to reduce spending in areas where the value added is low, many companies are attempting to reduce or eliminate the "paper chase" so endemic to the purchasing and accounts payable process. Corporate management is putting pressure on purchasing and finance to cut costs of processing transactions by anywhere from 35% to 90%.

Many companies have found that purchases of less than $2,500 make up the majority of purchase orders. On average, more than half of all purchases are for less than $500. A phenomenon often observed in business—called Pareto's Law—holds forth here too: 80% of the purchases account for only 20% of the dollar volume. Most of these are for so-called MRO purchases (maintenance, repairs, and operations) for things like office supplies, replacement machine parts, machine lubrication, and other relatively low-cost items incidental to production. It can cost a company anywhere from $15 to $150 to process a purchase order (PO) and another $100 to manage the purchase. No company can afford to spend this much to process a PO of $500 or less. By some estimates, the cost to process a PO is far more costly than this once you consider the requestor's time, purchasing's time, receiving's time, accounts payable's time, and the treasury office's time, not to mention the supplier's time.

Required If you have answered (4) of GE16–21 above, you have completed all the steps preliminary to improving or reengineering the purchasing of MRO items. How could you significantly reduce the cost of processing MRO items? Think boldly and identify all activities that can be either reduced or eliminated altogether.

GE 16–23 **Allocation of Space Costs**[5]

John, the owner of John's Place, a family restaurant, wants to make a few extra dollars by selling special peanuts from a display rack on his bar. The rack costs $50 and each bag of peanuts costs $0.25. John expects to sell each bag for $0.50. If John can sell 100 bags a week, he will cover the cost of the rack in two weeks and the rest will be profit.

John is visited by his accountant. The accountant notices the new rack of peanuts and asks John about how he proposes to account for the cost of the peanuts. John provides the accountant with the details. The accountant suggests after a few calculations that the peanuts should be charged $2,500 in yearly rent. John can't believe it! That would be $48 per week. At that rate the profit on his 100 bags would be used up in space cost.

Required How should the space costs of businesses be allocated to products? Contact a local business to determine their view on the subject.

---

5. This case was suggested by Dr. Frank Doherty of Saint Mary's University.

Chapter Seventeen

"How Well Am I Doing?" Financial Statement Analysis

Business Focus

Rick Burrock, the managing director of an accounting firm based in Mississauga, advises his small business clients to keep a tight rein on credit extended to customers. "You need to convey to your customers, right from the beginning, that you will work very hard to satisfy them and that in return, you expect to be paid on time. Start by investigating all new customers. A credit report helps, but with a business customer you can find out even more by requesting financial statements . . . Using the balance sheet, divide current assets by current liabilities to calculate the current ratio. If a company's current ratio is below 1.00, it will be paying out more than it expects to collect; you may want to reconsider doing business with that company or insist on stricter credit terms."

Source: Jill Andresky Fraser, "Hands on Collections: Get Paid Promptly," Inc., *November 1996, p. 87.*

Learning Objectives

After studying Chapter 17, you should be able to:

1 Explain the need for and limitations of financial statement analysis.

2 Prepare financial statements in comparative form and explain how such statements are used.

3 Place the balance sheet and the income statement in common-size form and properly interpret the results.

4 Identify the ratios used to measure the well-being of the common shareholder and state each ratio's formula and interpretation.

5 Explain what is meant by the term *financial leverage* and show how financial leverage is measured.

6 Identify the ratios used to measure the well-being of the short-term creditor and state each ratio's formula and interpretation.

7 Identify the ratios used to measure the well-being of the long-term creditor and state each ratio's formula and interpretation.

All financial statements are essentially historical documents. They tell what *has happened* during a particular period of time. However, most users of financial statements are concerned about what *will happen* in the future. Shareholders are concerned with future earnings and dividends. Creditors are concerned with the company's future ability to repay its debts. Managers are concerned with the company's ability to finance future expansion. Despite the fact that financial statements are historical documents, they can still provide valuable information bearing on all of these concerns.

Financial statement analysis involves careful selection of data from financial statements for the primary purpose of forecasting the financial health of the company. This is accomplished by examining trends in key financial data, comparing financial data across companies, and analyzing key financial ratios. In this chapter, we consider some of the more important ratios and other analytical tools that analysts use in attempting to predict the future course of events in business organizations.

Managers are also vitally concerned with the financial ratios discussed in this chapter. First, the ratios provide indicators of how well the company and its business units are performing. Some of these ratios would ordinarily be used in a balanced scorecard approach as discussed in Chapter 10. The specific ratios selected depend on the company's strategy. For example, a company that wants to emphasize responsiveness to customers may closely monitor the inventory turnover ratio discussed later in this chapter. Second, since managers must report to shareholders and may wish to raise funds from external sources, managers must pay attention to the financial ratios used by external investors to evaluate the company's investment potential and creditworthiness.

Need for and Limitations of Financial Statement Analysis

Objective 1

Explain the need for and limitations of financial statement analysis.

The Internal Use of Ratios

From the perspective of top management, ratio analysis can serve as a useful tool for performance evaluation, analysis of threats, constraints, and opportunities, and for strategic planning.

As was discussed in Chapter 12, ratios such as ROI combined with other measures can aid in evaluating the performance of individual unit managers. Further, ratios such as the current ratio and debt ratio can be calculated to determine whether managers are operating in accordance with contractual agreements regarding restrictions such as minimum working capital requirements and borrowing limitations.

Ratios can be helpful in formulating policy and in developing an ongoing organizational plan. A deeper awareness of the total business environment is essential for long-term growth and survival. Key business ratios of competitors, customers, and suppliers can be calculated to provide input data for marketing strategy. Indeed, regular monitoring of competitors may help to predict competitors' reactions to pricing and production decisions. Key ratios of customers can prove valuable in assessing their ability to honour purchase commitments. Ratios of suppliers can provide signals on their ability to meet deadlines and other contractual provisions. In summary, ratios of competitors, customers, and suppliers can be of great potential value in the competitive struggle for business survival and growth.

Benchmarking

Financial statements are not only historical documents but also essentially static documents. They speak only of the events of a single period of time. However, statement users are concerned about more than just the present; they are also concerned about the *trend* of events over time. For this reason, financial statement analysis directed toward a single period is of limited usefulness. The results of financial statement analysis for a particular period are of value only when viewed in *comparison* with the results of other periods (intrafirm analysis) and, in some cases, with the results of other firms (interfirm analysis). It is only through comparison that one can gain insight into trends and make intelligent judgements as to their significance.

Benchmarking The process of measuring a firm against the most successful firms in the industry.

Ratios of other firms in the same industry can serve as standards by which to make comparisons. Industry ratios are available from a number of sources such as Dun & Bradstreet, which provides statistics on the median, upper quartile, and lower quartile for 14 key ratios. (See Exhibit 17–10 at the end of this chapter for a list of sources.) Rather than industry averages, the ratios of the most successful firms may be chosen as standards of comparison. This is known as **benchmarking,** a process of continuously measuring a firm against the best firms in the industry. In today's increasingly competitive international environment, successful firms set benchmarks based on the highest industry standards. The most successful companies emphasize the highest standards in terms of cost efficiency, quality products and services, and customer focus. Once benchmarks are chosen a manager can make individual comparisons. Depending on the direction and extent of any deviation from a ratio's benchmark, a judgment is made as to whether a particular ratio is good, bad, or satisfactory. Plans should then be put in place by management to address any weak spots while maintaining strengths. This requires looking beyond ratios and seeking out detailed information on what best practices successful firms use. It is not always easy to obtain sensitive information from competitors but much can be learned by visiting both competing and noncompeting firms and by keeping up to date with recent industry and trade publications and talking with knowledgeable industry experts, discriminating customers, and discerning suppliers.

Industry benchmarks should be interpreted with caution. For example, structural or technological change in an industry can cause a benchmark to become outdated and limit its usefulness. Used properly, benchmarks should lead both production and service firms to continuous quality improvements. The aim is to be the best in all value-added activities in terms of lower costs, better quality, and greater customer satisfaction. This may necessitate major changes to value chain activities and the elimination of non-value-added activities. Such major changes are referred to as reengineering and may involve 30% or more of a firm's activities. At the least, however, there should be ongoing incremental improvement.

Ratios should be interpreted in the context of management's chosen competitive strategy. If the chosen strategy is high turnover/low profit margin, benchmarks should reflect performance of companies with a similar strategic focus and may not be comparable to firms that employ a lower turnover/high profit margin strategy. For example, a successful company with a low turnover/high profit margin strategy would react with less concern to ratios reflecting lower cost control. This is because it can recover its cost through the relatively higher prices it charges for its goods or services. Customers are willing to pay more because of real or perceived differences in the firm's product or services. On the other hand, a company with a high turnover/low profit margin strategy would be unable to pass these costs on to customers. Such companies are no-frill operations that attempt to keep costs as low as possible. Successful companies using this strategy are profitable as a consequence of their high sales volume. Even a small change in unit cost will make a relatively large impact on total cost because many units are affected. High cost for a firm following this strategy translates into lower profits and may severely threaten a firm's ability to compete.

Although financial statement analysis is a highly useful tool, it has two limitations that we must mention before proceeding any further. These two limitations involve the comparability of financial data between companies and the need to look beyond ratios.

Comparison of Financial Data

Comparisons of one company with another can provide valuable clues about the financial health of an organization. Unfortunately, differences in accounting methods between companies sometimes make it difficult to compare the companies' financial data. For example, if one firm values its inventories by the FIFO method and another firm by the average cost method, then direct comparisons of financial data such as inventory valuations and cost of goods sold between the two firms may be misleading. Sometimes enough data is presented in footnotes to the financial statements to restate data to a comparable basis. Otherwise, the analyst should keep in mind the lack of comparability of the data before drawing any definite conclusions. Nevertheless, even with this limitation in mind, comparisons of key ratios with other companies and with industry averages often suggest avenues for further investigation.

The Need to Look beyond Ratios

An inexperienced analyst may assume that ratios are sufficient in themselves as a basis for judgments about the future. Nothing could be further from the truth. Conclusions based on ratio analysis must be regarded as tentative in nature. Ratios should not be viewed as an end, but rather they should be viewed as a *starting point,* as indicators of what to pursue in greater depth. They raise many questions, but they rarely answer any questions by themselves.

In addition to ratios, other sources of data should be analyzed in order to make judgments about the future of an organization. The analyst should look, for example, at industry trends, technological changes, changes in consumer tastes, changes in broad economic factors, and changes within the firm itself. A recent change in a key management position, for example, might provide a basis for optimism about the future, even though the past performance of the firm (as shown by its ratios) may have been mediocre.

Statements in Comparative and Common-Size Form

Few figures appearing on financial statements have much significance standing by themselves. It is the relationship of one figure to another and the amount and direction of change over time that are important in financial statement analysis. How does the analyst key in on significant relationships? How does the analyst dig out the important trends and changes in a company? Three analytical techniques are widely used:

1. Dollar and percentage changes on statements.
2. Common-size statements.
3. Ratios.

The first and second techniques are discussed in this section; the third technique is discussed in the next section. To illustrate these analytical techniques, we analyze the financial statements of Brickey Electronics, a producer of computer and television components.

Objective 2

Prepare financial statements in comparative form and explain how such statements are used.

Dollar and Percentage Changes on Statements

A good place to begin in financial statement analysis is to put statements in comparative form. This consists of little more than putting two or more years' data side by side. Statements cast in comparative form underscore movements and trends and may give the analyst valuable clues as to what to expect.

Examples of financial statements placed in comparative form are given in Exhibits 17–1 and 17–2. These statements of Brickey Electronics reveal the firm has been experiencing substantial growth. The data on these statements are used as a basis for discussion throughout the remainder of the chapter.

Horizontal analysis A side-by-side comparison of two or more years' financial statements.

Trend analysis Same as horizontal analysis.

HORIZONTAL ANALYSIS   Comparison of two or more years' financial data is known as **horizontal analysis** or **trend analysis.** Horizontal analysis is facilitated by showing changes between years in both dollar *and* percentage form, as has been done in Exhibits 17–1 and 17–2. Showing changes in dollar form helps the analyst focus on key factors that have affected profitability or financial position. For example, observe in Exhibit 17–2 that sales for 1999 were up $4 million over 1998, but that this increase in sales was more than negated by a $4.5 million increase in cost of goods sold.

Showing changes between years in percentage form helps the analyst to gain *perspective* and to gain a feel for the *significance* of the changes that are taking place. A $1 million increase in sales is much more significant if the prior year's sales were $2 million than if the prior year's sales were $20 million. In the first situation, the increase would be 50%—undoubtedly a significant increase for any firm. In the second situation, the increase would be only 5%—perhaps just a reflection of normal growth.

Trend percentages The expression of several years' financial data in percentage form in terms of a base year.

TREND PERCENTAGES   Horizontal analysis of financial statements can also be carried out by computing *trend percentages.* **Trend percentages** state several years' financial data in terms of a base year. The base year equals 100%, with all other years stated as some percentage of this base. To illustrate, consider Compaq Computer Corporation which vies with IBM and Dell Computer for the number one position in personal computer sales. Compaq enjoyed tremendous growth in the early to mid-1990s, as evidenced by the following data:

	1996	1995	1994	1993	1992	1991	1990	1989
Sales (millions) ..	$18,109	$14,775	$10,866	$7,191	$4,000	$3,271	$3,599	$2,876
Net income (millions)	1,313	789	867	462	213	131	455	333

By simply looking at these data, one can see that sales increased in nearly every year since 1989. But how rapidly have sales been increasing and have the increases in net income kept pace with the increases in sales? By looking at the raw data alone, it is difficult to answer these questions. The increases in sales and the increases in net

Exhibit 17–1

BRICKEY ELECTRONICS
Comparative Balance Sheet
December 31, 1999, and 1998
(dollars in thousands)

	1999	1998	Increase (Decrease) Amount	Percent
Assets				
Current assets:				
Cash	$ 1,200	$ 2,350	$(1,150)	(48.9)%*
Accounts receivable, net	6,000	4,000	2,000	50.0%
Inventory	8,000	10,000	(2,000)	(20.0)%
Prepaid expenses	300	120	180	150.0%
Total current assets	15,500	16,470	(970)	(5.9)%
Property and equipment:				
Land	4,000	4,000	–0–	–0–%
Buildings and equipment, net	12,000	8,500	3,500	41.2%
Total property and equipment	16,000	12,500	3,500	28.0%
Total assets	$31,500	$28,970	$ 2,530	8.7%
Liabilities and Shareholders' Equity				
Current liabilities:				
Accounts payable	$ 5,800	$ 4,000	$ 1,800	45.0%
Accrued payables	900	400	500	125.0%
Notes payable, short term	300	600	(300)	(50.0)%
Total current liabilities	7,000	5,000	2,000	40.0%
Long-term liabilities:				
Bonds payable, 8%	7,500	8,000	(500)	(6.3)%
Total liabilities	14,500	13,000	1,500	11.5%
Shareholders' equity:				
Preferred shares, $6 no par, $100 liquidation value	2,000	2,000	–0–	–0–%
Common shares, 500 no par	7,000	7,000	–0–	–0–%
Total paid-in capital	9,000	9,000	–0–	–0–%
Retained earnings	8,000	6,970	1,030	14.8%
Total shareholders' equity	17,000	15,970	1,030	6.4%
Total liabilities and shareholders' equity	$31,500	$28,970	$ 2,530	8.7%

*Since we are measuring the amount of change between 1998 and 1999, the dollar amounts for 1998 become the base figures for expressing these changes in percentage form. For example, Cash decreased by $1,150 between 1998 and 1999. This decrease expressed in percentage form is computed as follows: $1,150 ÷ $2,350 = 48.9%. Other percentage figures in this exhibit and Exhibit 17–2 are computed in the same way.

income can be put into better perspective by stating them in terms of trend percentages, with 1989 as the base year. These percentages (all rounded) are given below:

	1996	1995	1994	1993	1992	1991	1990	1989
Sales (millions)*	630%	513%	378%	250%	139%	114%	125%	100%
Net income (millions)	394%	237%	260%	139%	64%	39%	137%	100%

*For 1990, $3,599 ÷ $2,876 = 125%; for 1991, $3,271 ÷ $2,876 = 114%; and so forth.

Exhibit 17–2

BRICKEY ELECTRONICS
Comparative Income Statement and Reconciliation
of Retained Earnings
For the Years Ended December 31, 1999, and 1998
(dollars in thousands)

	1999	1998	Increase (Decrease) Amount	Increase (Decrease) Percent
Sales	$52,000	$48,000	$4,000	8.3%
Cost of goods sold	36,000	31,500	4,500	14.3%
Gross margin	16,000	16,500	(500)	(3.0)%
Operating expenses:				
Selling expenses	7,000	6,500	500	7.7%
Administrative expenses	5,860	6,100	(240)	(3.9)%
Total operating expenses	12,860	12,600	260	2.1%
Net operating income	3,140	3,900	(760)	(19.5)%
Interest expense	640	700	(60)	(8.6)%
Net income before taxes	2,500	3,200	(700)	(21.9)%
Less income taxes (30%)	750	960	(210)	(21.9)%
Net income	1,750	2,240	$ (490)	(21.9)%
Dividends to preferred shareholders, $6 per share (see Exhibit 17–1)	120	120		
Net income remaining for common shareholders	1,630	2,120		
Dividends to common shareholders, $1.20 per share	600	600		
Net income added to retained earnings	1,030	1,520		
Retained earnings, beginning of year	6,970	5,450		
Retained earnings, end of year	$ 8,000	$ 6,970		

The trend analysis is particularly striking when the data are plotted as in Exhibit 17–3. Compaq's sales growth has been impressive and even spectacular since 1992, but the growth in net income has been more sporadic. The roller-coaster-like performance of net income is likely due to a combination of intense competitive pressures, rapid technological change in the personal computer industry, general trends in the economy, and strategic decisions made by management. As explained in *The Wall Street Journal:*

> [In 1992], Compaq jettisoned its strategy of charging premium prices, after experiencing slumping sales and plummeting earnings in 1991. Under its new chief executive officer . . . the company initiated a price war, slashed its costs to offset plunging margins and broadened its product line. Sales have been surging ever since.[1]

---

1. Jim Carlton, "Compaq PCs Outsold IBM and Apple World-Wide during the First Quarter," *The Wall Street Journal,* Wednesday, May 25, 1994, p. A3.

Exhibit 17–3
COMPAQ COMPUTER
CORPORATION
Trend Analysis of Sales
and Net Income

Common-Size Statements

Common-size statements
A statement that shows
the items appearing on it
in percentage form as well
as in dollar form. On the
income statement, the percentages are based on
total sales revenue; on the
balance sheet, the percentages are based on total
assets.

Vertical analysis The
presentation of a com-
pany's financial state-
ments in common-size
form.

Key changes and trends can also be highlighted by the use of *common-size statements*. A **common-size statement** is one that shows the items appearing on it in percentage form as well as in dollar form. Each item is stated as a percentage of some total of which that item is a part. The preparation of common-size statements is known as **vertical analysis.**

Common-size statements are particularly useful when comparing data from different companies. For example, in a recent year, Wendy's net income was about $110 million, whereas McDonald's was $1,427 million. This comparison is somewhat misleading because of the dramatically different sizes of the two companies. To put this in better perspective, the net income figures can be expressed as a percentage of the sales revenues of each company. Since Wendy's sales revenues were $1,746 million and McDonald's were $9,794 million, Wendy's net income as a percentage of sales was about 6.3% and McDonald's was about 14.6%. While the comparison still favours McDonald's, the contrast between the two companies has been placed on a more comparable basis.

THE BALANCE SHEET   One application of the vertical analysis idea is to state the separate assets of a company as percentages of total assets. A common-size statement of this type is shown in Exhibit 17–4 for Brickey Electronics.

Notice from Exhibit 17–4 that placing all assets in common-size form clearly shows the relative importance of the current assets as compared to the noncurrent assets. It also shows that significant changes have taken place in the *composition* of the current assets over the last year. Notice, for example, that the receivables have increased in relative importance and that both cash and inventory have declined in relative importance. Judging from the sharp increase in receivables, the deterioration in the cash position may be a result of inability to collect from customers.

Exhibit 17–4

	BRICKEY ELECTRONICS Common-Size Comparative Balance Sheet December 31, 1999, and 1998 (dollars in thousands)			
			Common-Size Percentages	
	1999	1998	1999	1998
Assets				
Current assets:				
Cash	$ 1,200	$ 2,350	3.8%*	8.1%
Accounts receivable, net	6,000	4,000	19.0%	13.8%
Inventory	8,000	10,000	25.4%	34.5%
Prepaid expenses	300	120	1.0%	0.4%
Total current assets	15,500	16,470	49.2%	56.9%
Property and equipment:				
Land	4,000	4,000	12.7%	13.8%
Buildings and equipment, net	12,000	8,500	38.1%	29.3%
Total property and equipment	16,000	12,500	50.8%	43.1%
Total assets	$31,500	$28,970	100.0%	100.0%
Liabilities and Shareholders' Equity				
Current liabilities:				
Accounts payable	$ 5,800	$ 4,000	18.4%	13.8%
Accrued payables	900	400	2.8%	1.4%
Notes payable, short term	300	600	1.0%	2.1%
Total current liabilities	7,000	5,000	22.2%	17.3%
Long-term liabilities:				
Bonds payable, 8%	7,500	8,000	23.8%	27.6%
Total liabilities	14,500	13,000	46.0%	44.9%
Shareholders' equity:				
Preferred shares, $6 no par,				
$100 liquidation value	2,000	2,000	6.4%	6.9%
Common shares, 500 no par	7,000	7,000	22.2%	24.2%
Total paid-in capital	9,000	9,000	28.6%	31.1%
Retained earnings	8,000	6,970	25.4%	24.0%
Total shareholders' equity	17,000	15,970	54.0%	55.1%
Total liabilities and				
shareholders' equity	$31,500	$28,970	100.0%	100.0%

*Each asset account on a common-size statement is expressed in terms of total assets, and each liability and equity account is expressed in terms of total liabilities and shareholders' equity. For example, the percentage figure above for Cash in 1999 is computed as follows: $1,200 ÷ $31,500 = 3.8%.

THE INCOME STATEMENT   Another application of the vertical analysis idea is to place all items on the income statement in percentage form in terms of sales. A common-size statement of this type is shown in Exhibit 17–5.

By placing all items on the income statement in common size in terms of sales, it is possible to see at a glance how each dollar of sales is distributed among the various costs, expenses, and profits. And by placing successive years' statements side by side, it is easy to spot interesting trends. For example, as shown in Exhibit 17–5, the

Exhibit 17–5

BRICKEY ELECTRONICS
Common-Size Comparative Income Statement
For the Years Ended December 31, 1999, and 1998
(dollars in thousands)

	1999	1998	Common-Size Percentages 1999	Common-Size Percentages 1998
Sales	$52,000	$48,000	100.0%	100.0%
Cost of goods sold	36,000	31,500	69.2%	65.6%
Gross margin	16,000	16,500	30.8%	34.4%
Operating expenses:				
Selling expenses	7,000	6,500	13.5%	13.5%
Administrative expenses	5,860	6,100	11.3%	12.7%
Total operating expenses	12,860	12,600	24.7%	26.2%
Net operating income	3,140	3,900	6.0%	8.1%
Interest expense	640	700	1.2%	1.5%
Net income before taxes	2,500	3,200	4.8%	6.7%
Income taxes (30%)	750	960	1.4%	2.0%
Net income	$ 1,750	$ 2,240	3.4%	4.7%

*Note that the percentage figures for each year are expressed in terms of total sales for the year. For example, the percentage figure for cost of goods sold in 1999 is computed as follows: $36,000 ÷ $52,000 = 69.2%

cost of goods sold as a percentage of sales increased from 65.6% in 1998 to 69.2% in 1999. Or looking at this from a different viewpoint, the *gross margin percentage* declined from 34.4% in 1998 to 30.8% in 1999. Managers and investment analysts often pay close attention to the gross margin percentage since it is considered a broad gauge of profitability. The **gross margin percentage** is computed as follows:

Gross margin percent-age   A broad gauge of profitability, calculated by dividing sales into the gross margin.

$$\text{Gross margin percentage} = \frac{\text{Gross margin}}{\text{Sales}}$$

The gross margin percentage tends to be more stable for retailing companies than for other service companies and for manufacturers since the cost of goods sold in retailing excludes fixed costs. When fixed costs are included in the cost of goods sold figure, the gross margin percentage tends to increase and decrease with sales volume. With increases in sales volume, the fixed costs are spread across more units and the gross margin percentage improves.

While a higher gross margin percentage is generally considered to be better than a lower gross margin percentage, there are exceptions. Some companies purposely choose a strategy emphasizing low prices (and hence low gross margins). An increasing gross margin in such a company might be a sign that the company's strategy is not being effectively implemented.

Common-size statements are also very helpful in pointing out efficiencies and inefficiencies that might otherwise go unnoticed. To illustrate, in 1999, Brickey Electronics' selling expenses increased by $500,000 over 1998. A glance at the common-size income statement shows, however, that on a relative basis, selling expenses were no higher in 1999 than in 1998. In each year they represented 13.5% of sales.

Ratio Analysis—The Common Shareholder

Earnings per share Net income available for common shareholders divided by the average number of common shares outstanding during the year

A number of financial ratios are used to assess how well the company is doing from the standpoint of the shareholders. These ratios naturally focus on net income, dividends, and shareholders' equities.

Earnings per Share

An investor buys a share in the hope of realizing a return in the form of either dividends or future increases in the value of the share. Since earnings form the basis for dividend payments, as well as the basis for future increases in the value of shares, investors are always interested in a company's reported *earnings per share*. Probably no single statistic is more widely quoted or relied on by investors than earnings per share, although it has some inherent limitations, as discussed below.

Earnings per share is computed by dividing net income available for common shareholders by the average number of common shares outstanding during the year. "Net income available for common shareholders" is net income less dividends paid to the owners of the company's preferred shares.[2]

$$\text{Earnings per share} = \frac{\text{Net income} - \text{Preferred dividends}}{\text{Average number of common shares outstanding}}$$

Using the data in Exhibits 17–1 and 17–2, we see that the earnings per share for Brickey Electronics for 1999 would be computed as follows:

$$\frac{\$1,750,000 - \$120,000}{(500,000 \text{ shares} + 500,000 \text{ shares})/2} = \$3.26 \tag{1}$$

Note that the denominator in the earnings per share formula uses the weighted average number of common shares outstanding for the year. Using a weighted average is appropriate because it recognizes that common shareholders may contribute varying amounts of capital for varying amounts of time. A weighted average number of shares reflects earnings per share during the period and is not a measure of entitlement to earnings at period-end. Assume that a company began operations on January 2, 2000, by issuing 10,000 common shares, and on October 1, 2000, an additional 10,000 shares were issued. The company obviously has 20,000 shares outstanding at year-end. However, the weighted average number of shares outstanding for the year is calculated as follows:

$$
\begin{array}{rcl}
10,000 \text{ shares} \times 9 \text{ months} &=& 90,000 \text{ share months} \\
20,000 \text{ shares} \times \dfrac{3}{12} \text{ months} &=& \underline{60,000} \text{ share months} \\
&& 150,000 \text{ share months}
\end{array}
$$

The 10,000 shares issued on January 2 were outstanding for nine months before any new shares were issued. On October 1 another 10,000 shares were issued, bringing the total outstanding to 20,000 for the last three months of the year. The weighted average can now be determined by dividing the number of share months (150,000) by the number of months in a year (12) to give a weighted average of 12,500 shares.

---

2. Another complication can arise when a company has issued securities such as executive stock options or warrants that can be converted into common shares. If these conversions were to take place, the same earnings would have to be distributed among a greater number of common shares. Therefore, a supplemental earnings per share figure, called diluted earnings per share, may have to be computed.

Two complications can arise in connection with the computation of earnings per share. The first arises whenever an extraordinary gain or loss appears as part of net income. The second arises whenever a company has convertible securities on its balance sheet. These complications are discussed in the following paragraphs.

Extraordinary Items and Earnings per Share

Extraordinary items are items which result from transactions or events that have all of the following characteristics:

1. They are not expected to occur frequently over several years.
2. They do not typify the normal business activities of the entity.
3. They do not depend primarily on the decisions of management or determinations by management or owners.

If a company has extraordinary gains or losses appearing as part of net income, *two* earnings per share figures must be computed—one showing the earnings per share resulting from *normal* operations and one showing the earnings per share impact of the *extraordinary* items. This approach to computing earnings per share accomplishes three things. First, it helps statement users to recognize extraordinary items for what they are—unusual events that probably will not recur. Second, it eliminates the distorting influence of the extraordinary items from the basic earnings per share figure. And third, it helps statement users to properly assess the *trend of normal* earnings per share over time. Since one would not expect the extraordinary or unusual items to be repeated year after year, they should be given less weight in judging earnings performance than is given to profits resulting from normal operations.

In addition to reporting extraordinary items separately, the accountant also reports them *net of their tax effect*. This means that whatever impact the unusual item has on income taxes is *deducted from* the unusual item on the income statement. Only the net, after-tax gain or loss is used in earnings per share computations.

To illustrate these ideas, let us assume that Amata Company has suffered a fire loss of $6,000 and that management is wondering how the loss should be reported on the company's income statement. The correct and incorrect approaches to reporting the loss are shown in Exhibit 17–6.

As shown under the Correct Approach in the exhibit, the $6,000 loss is reduced to only $4,200 after tax effects are taken into consideration. The reasoning behind this computation is as follows: The fire loss is fully deductible for tax purposes. Therefore, this deduction will reduce the firm's taxable income by $6,000. If taxable income is $6,000 lower, then income taxes will be $1,800 *less* (30% × $6,000) than they *otherwise* would have been. In other words, the fire loss of $6,000 saves the company $1,800 in taxes that otherwise would have been paid. The $1,800 savings in taxes is deducted from the loss that caused it, leaving a net loss of only $4,200. This same $4,200 figure could have been obtained by multiplying the original loss by the formula (1 − Tax rate): [$6,000 × (1 − 0.30) = $4,200].

This same procedure is used in reporting extraordinary gains. The only difference is that extraordinary gains *increase* taxes; thus, any tax resulting from a gain must be deducted from it, with only the net gain reported on the income statement.

To continue our illustration, assume that the company in Exhibit 17–6 has 2,000 common shares outstanding. Earnings per share would be reported as follows:

Earnings per share on common stock:
On net income before extraordinary item ($7,000 ÷ 2,000 shares) . . . . $ 3.50
On extraordinary item, net of tax ($4,200 ÷ 2,000 shares) . . . . (2.10)

Net earnings per share . . . . $ 1.40

Exhibit 17–6

Reporting Extraordinary Items Net of Their Tax Effects

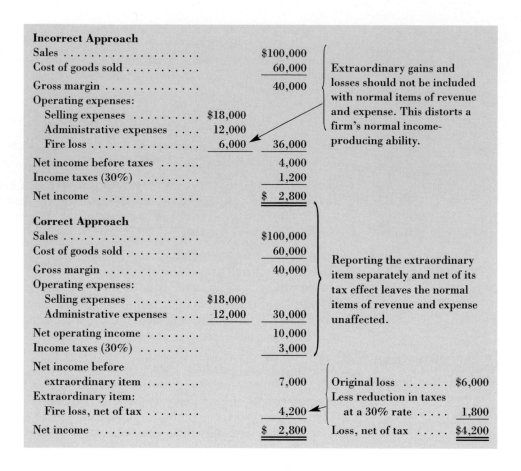

Incorrect Approach		
Sales		$100,000
Cost of goods sold		60,000
Gross margin		40,000
Operating expenses:		
Selling expenses	$18,000	
Administrative expenses	12,000	
Fire loss	6,000	36,000
Net income before taxes		4,000
Income taxes (30%)		1,200
Net income		$ 2,800

Extraordinary gains and losses should not be included with normal items of revenue and expense. This distorts a firm's normal income-producing ability.

Correct Approach		
Sales		$100,000
Cost of goods sold		60,000
Gross margin		40,000
Operating expenses:		
Selling expenses	$18,000	
Administrative expenses	12,000	30,000
Net operating income		10,000
Income taxes (30%)		3,000
Net income before extraordinary item		7,000
Extraordinary item:		
Fire loss, net of tax		4,200
Net income		$ 2,800

Reporting the extraordinary item separately and net of its tax effect leaves the normal items of revenue and expense unaffected.

Original loss		$6,000
Less reduction in taxes at a 30% rate		1,800
Loss, net of tax		$4,200

In summary, clearly segregating extraordinary items as we have done above is necessary to avoid misunderstanding a company's normal income-producing ability. Reporting *only* the flat $1.40 per share figure would be misleading and perhaps cause investors to regard the company less favourably than they should.

Fully Diluted Earnings per Share

A problem sometimes arises in trying to determine the number of common shares to use in computing earnings per share. Until recent years, the distinctions between common shares, preferred shares, and debt were quite clear. However, these distinctions have become murkier due to a growing tendency to issue convertible securities of various types. Rather than simply issuing common shares, firms today often issue preferred stock or bonds that carry a **conversion feature** allowing the purchaser to convert the preferred shares or bonds into common shares at some future time.

When convertible securities are present in the financial structure of a firm, the question arises as to whether these securities should be retained in their unconverted form or treated as common shares in computing earnings per share. The generally accepted position is that convertible securities should be treated *both* in their present and prospective forms. This requires the presentation of *two* earnings per share figures, one showing earnings per share assuming no conversion into common shares and the other showing full conversion into common shares. The latter figure is known as the **fully diluted earnings per share.**

To illustrate the computation of a company's fully diluted earnings per share, let us assume that the preferred shares of Brickey Electronics in Exhibit 17–1 is convertible into common on the basis of five shares of common for each share of preferred. Since 20,000 shares of preferred are outstanding, conversion would require issuing an

Conversion feature A preferred stock or bond feature that allows the purchaser to convert preferred shares or bonds into common shares at some future time.

Fully diluted earnings per share An earnings per share figure showing full conversion into common shares.

additional 100,000 shares of common stock. Earnings per share on a fully diluted basis would be computed as follows:

$$\frac{\text{Net income}}{\text{(Weighted average number of common shares outstanding + potential shares issued on convertible securities)}} = \frac{\text{Fully diluted}}{\text{earnings per share}}$$

$$\frac{\text{Net income}}{\text{(500,000 shares outstanding + 100,000 converted shares)}}$$

$$= \frac{\$1,750,000}{600,000 \text{ shares}} = \$2.92 \quad (2)$$

In comparing equation (2) with equation (1) on page 848 we can note that the earnings per share figure has dropped by 34 cents. Although the impact of full dilution is relatively small in this case, it can be very significant in situations where large amounts of convertible securities are present.

Earnings per Share and Profitability

Earnings per share can be a misleading measure of profitability. To illustrate, assume that Simyar Company has 100,000 shares outstanding over a three-year period. Simyar Company has total assets for 2000 of $1 million and it is company policy to pay out 50% of its after-tax income as dividends. Note from the following data that earnings per share increased each period. This increase may be misinterpreted as improved operating performance when in fact it is totally attributable to Simyar Company reinvesting 50% of its earnings. Return on investment has actually remained at 10%. For this illustration, it is assumed that ROI is calculated on total assets at the beginning of the year.

Year	Assets	Earnings Available for Common Shareholders	Return on Investment	Earnings per Share
2001	$1,000,000	$100,000	10%	$1.0000
2002	1,050,000	105,000	10%	1.0500
2003	1,102,500	110,250	10%	1.1025

Price-Earnings Ratio

Price earnings ratio
An index of whether a share is relatively cheap or relatively expensive in relation to current earnings.

The relationship between the market price of a share and the share's current earnings per share is often quoted in terms of a **price-earnings ratio.** If we assume that the current market price for Brickey Electronics' shares is $40 each, the company's price-earnings ratio would be computed as follows:

$$\text{Price-earnings ratio} = \frac{\text{Market price per share}}{\text{Earnings per share}}$$

$$\frac{\$40}{\$3.26} = 12.3$$

The price-earnings ratio is 12.3; that is, the shares are selling for about 12.3 times current earnings.

The price-earnings ratio is widely used by investors as a general guideline in gauging share values. A high price-earnings ratio means that investors are willing to pay a premium for the company's shares—presumably because the company is expected to have higher than average future earnings growth. Conversely, if investors believe a company's future earnings growth prospects are limited, the company's price-earnings ratio would be relatively low.

Dividend Payout and Yield Ratios

Investors hold shares in a company because they anticipate an attractive return. The return sought is not always dividends. Many investors prefer not to receive dividends. Instead, they prefer to have the company retain all earnings and reinvest them internally in order to support growth. The shares of companies that adopt this approach, loosely termed *growth shares,* often enjoy rapid upward movement in market price. Other investors prefer to have a dependable, current source of income through regular dividend payments. Such investors seek out shares with consistent dividend records and payout ratios.

Dividend payout ratio
An index showing whether a company pays out most of its earnings in dividends or reinvests the earnings internally.

THE DIVIDEND PAYOUT RATIO   The **dividend payout ratio** gauges the portion of current earnings being paid out in dividends. Investors who seek growth in market price would like this ratio to be small, whereas investors who seek dividends prefer it to be large. This ratio is computed by relating dividends per share to earnings per share for common stock:

$$\text{Dividend payout ratio} = \frac{\text{Dividends per share}}{\text{Earnings per share}}$$

For Brickey Electronics, the dividend payout ratio for 1999 is computed as follows:

$$\frac{\$1.20 \text{ (see Exhibit 17–2)}}{\$3.26} = 36.8\%$$

There is no such thing as a "right" payout ratio, even though it should be noted that the ratio tends to be similar for companies within a particular industry. Industries with ample opportunities for growth at high rates of return on assets tend to have low payout ratios, whereas payout ratios tend to be high in industries with limited reinvestment opportunities.

Dividend yield ratio
Shows the return in terms of cash dividends being provided by a share.

THE DIVIDEND YIELD RATIO   The **dividend yield ratio** is obtained by dividing the current dividends per share by the current market price per share:

$$\text{Dividend yield ratio} = \frac{\text{Dividends per share}}{\text{Market price per share}}$$

The market price for Brickey Electronics' shares is $40 each so the dividend yield is computed as follows:

$$\frac{\$1.20}{\$40} = 3.0\%$$

The dividend yield ratio measures the rate of return (in the form of cash dividends only) that would be earned by an investor who buys the common stock at the current market price. A low dividend yield ratio is neither bad nor good by itself. As discussed above, a company may pay out very little dividends because it has ample opportunities for reinvesting funds within the company at high rates of return.

Return on Total Assets

Managers have both *financing* and *operating* responsibilities. Financing responsibilities relate to how one *obtains* the funds needed to provide for the assets in an organization. Operating responsibilities relate to how one *uses* the assets once they have been obtained. Both are vital to a well-managed firm. However, care must be taken not to confuse or mix the two when assessing the performance of a manager. That is, whether funds have been obtained from creditors or from shareholders should not be allowed to influence one's assessment of *how well* the assets have been employed since being received by the firm.

Return on total assets
Measure of how well assets have been employed by management.

The **return on total assets** is a measure of operating performance that shows how well assets have been employed. It is defined as follows:

$$\text{Return on total assets} = \frac{\text{Net income} + [\text{Interest expense} \times (1 - \text{Tax Rate})]}{\text{Average total assets}}$$

Adding interest expense back to net income results in an adjusted earnings figure that shows what earnings would have been if the assets had been acquired solely by selling shares. With this adjustment, the return on total assets can be compared for companies with differing amounts of debt or over time for a single company that has changed its mix of debt and equity. Thus, the measurement of how well the assets have been employed is not influenced by how the assets were financed. Notice that the interest expense is placed on an after-tax basis by multiplying it by the factor (1 − Tax rate).

The return on total assets for Brickey Electronics for 1999 would be computed as follows (from Exhibits 17–1 and 17–2):

Net income	$ 1,750,000
Add back interest expense: $640,000 × (1 − 0.30)	448,000
Total	$ 2,198,000 (a)
Assets, beginning of year	$28,970,000
Assets, end of year	31,500,000
Total	$60,470,000
Average total assets: $60,470,000 ÷ 2	$30,235,000 (b)
Return on total assets, (a) ÷ (b)	7.3%

Brickey Electronics has earned a return of 7.3% on average assets employed over the last year.

Return on common shareholders' equity
When compared to the return on total assets, measures the extent to which financial leverage is working for or against common shareholders.

Return on Common Shareholders' Equity

One of the primary reasons for operating a corporation is to generate income for the benefit of the common shareholders. One measure of a company's success in this regards is the **return on common shareholders' equity**, which divides the net income remaining for common shareholders by the average common shareholders' equity for the year. The formula is as follows:

$$\frac{\text{Return on common}}{\text{shareholders' equity}} = \frac{\text{Net income} - \text{Preferred dividends}}{\text{Average common shareholders' equity}}$$

$$\text{where} \quad \frac{\text{Average common}}{\text{shareholders' equity}} = \frac{\text{Average total shareholders' equity}}{- \text{Average preferred shares}}$$

For Brickey Electronics, the return on common shareholders' equity is 11.3% for 1999 as shown below:

Net income	$ 1,750,000
Deduct preferred dividends	120,000
Net income remaining for common shareholders	$ 1,630,000 (a)
Average shareholders' equity	$16,485,000*
Deduct average preferred shares	2,000,000†
Average common shareholders' equity	$14,485,000 (b)
Return on common shareholders' equity, (a) ÷ (b)	11.3%

*$15,970,000 + $17,000,000 = $32,970,000; $32,970,000 ÷ 2 = $16,485,000.

†$2,000,000 + $2,000,000 = $4,000,000; $4,000,000 ÷ 2 = $2,000,000.

Objective 5

Explain what is meant by the term *financial leverage* and show how financial leverage is measured.

Financial leverage
Acquiring assets with funds that have been obtained from creditors or from preferred shareholders at a fixed rate of return.

Positive financial leverage A situation in which the fixed return to a company's creditors and preferred shareholders is less than the return on total assets. In this situation, the return on common shareholders' equity will be *greater* than the return on total assets.

Negative financial leverage A situation in which the fixed return to a company's creditors and preferred shareholders is greater than the return on total assets. In this situation, the return on common shareholders' equity will be *less* than the return on total assets.

Compare the return on common shareholders' equity above (11.3%) with the return on total assets computed in the preceding section (7.3%). Why is the return on common shareholders' equity so much higher? The answer lies in the principle of *financial leverage*. Financial leverage is discussed in the following paragraphs.

Financial Leverage

Financial leverage (often called *leverage* for short) involves acquiring assets with funds that have been obtained from creditors or from preferred shareholders at a fixed rate of return. If the assets in which the funds are invested are able to earn a rate of return *greater* than the fixed rate of return required by the funds' suppliers, then we have **positive financial leverage** and the common shareholders benefit.

For example, suppose that ATV is able to earn an after-tax return of 12% on its broadcasting assets. If the company can borrow from creditors at a 10% interest rate in order to expand its assets, then the common shareholders can benefit from positive leverage. The borrowed funds invested in the business will earn an after-tax return of 12%, but the after-tax interest cost of the borrowed funds will be only 7% [10% interest rate × (1 − 0.30) = 7%]. The difference will go to the common shareholders.

We can see this concept in operation in the case of Brickey Electronics. Notice from Exhibit 17–1 that the company's bonds payable bear a fixed interest rate of 8%. The after-tax interest cost of these bonds is only 5.6% [8% interest rate × (1 − 0.30) = 5.6%]. The company's assets are generating an after-tax return of 7.3%, as we computed earlier. Since this return on assets is greater than the after-tax interest cost of the bonds, leverage is positive, and the difference accrues to the benefit of the common shareholders. This explains in part why the return on common shareholders' equity (11.3%) is greater than the return on total assets (7.3%).

Unfortunately, leverage is a two-edged sword. If assets are unable to earn a high enough rate to cover the interest costs of debt, or to cover the preferred dividend due to the preferred shareholders, *then the common shareholder suffers*. Under these circumstances, we have **negative financial leverage.**

THE IMPACT OF INCOME TAXES Debt and preferred shares are not equally efficient in generating positive leverage. The reason is that interest on debt is tax deductible, whereas preferred dividends are not. This usually makes debt a much more effective source of positive leverage than preferred shares.

To illustrate this point, suppose that the Hotel Corporation of America is considering three ways of financing a $100 million expansion of its chain of hotels:

1. $100 million from an issue of common shares.
2. $50 million from an issue of common shares, and $50 million from an issue of preferred shares bearing a dividend rate of 8%.
3. $50 million from an issue of common shares, and $50 million from an issue of bonds bearing an interest rate of 8%.

Assuming that the Hotel Corporation of America can earn an additional $15 million each year before interest and taxes as a result of the expansion, the operating results under each of the three alternatives are shown in Exhibit 17–7.

If the entire $100 million is raised from an issue of common shares, then the return to the common shareholders will be only 10.5%, as shown under alternative 1 in the exhibit. If half of the funds are raised from an issue of preferred shares, then the return to the common shareholders increases to 13%, due to the positive effects of leverage. However, if half of the funds are raised from an issue of bonds, then the return to the common shareholders jumps to 15.4%, as shown under alternative 3. Thus, long-term debt is much more efficient in generating positive leverage than is preferred shares. The reason is that the interest expense on long-term debt is tax deductible, whereas the dividends on preferred shares are not.

THE DESIRABILITY OF LEVERAGE   Because of leverage, having some debt in the capital structure can substantially benefit the common shareholder. For this reason, most companies today try to maintain a level of debt that is considered to be normal within the industry. Many companies, such as commercial banks and other financial institutions, rely heavily on leverage to provide an attractive return on their common shares.

Book Value per Share

Book value per share
Measures the amount that would be distributed to holders of common shares if all assets were sold at their balance sheet carrying amounts and if all creditors were paid off.

Another statistic frequently used in attempting to assess the well-being of the common shareholder is book value per share. The **book value per share** measures the amount that would be distributed to holders of each common share if all assets were sold at their balance sheet carrying amounts (i.e., book values) and if all creditors were paid

Exhibit 17–7   Leverage from Preferred Shares and Long-Term Debt

	Alternatives: $100,000,000 Issue of Securities		
	Alternative 1: $100,000,000 Common Shares	Alternative 2: $50,000,000 Common Shares; $50,000,000 Preferred Shares	Alternative 3: $50,000,000 Common Shares; $50,000,000 Bonds
Earnings before interest and taxes	$ 15,000,000	$15,000,000	$15,000,000
Deduct interest expense (8% × $50,000,000)	—	—	4,000,000
Net income before taxes	15,000,000	15,000,000	11,000,000
Deduct income taxes (30%)	4,500,000	4,500,000	3,300,000
Net income	10,500,000	10,500,000	7,700,000
Deduct preferred dividends (8% × $50,000,000)	—	4,000,000	—
Net income remaining for common (a)	$ 10,500,000	$ 6,500,000	$ 7,700,000
Common shareholders' equity (b)	$100,000,000	$50,000,000	$50,000,000
Return on common shareholders' equity (a) ÷ (b)	10.5%	13.0%	15.4%

off. Thus, book value per share is based entirely on historical costs. The formula for computing it is as follows:

$$\text{Book value per share} = \frac{\text{Common shareholders' equity (Total shareholders' equity} - \text{Preferred shares)}}{\text{Number of common shares outstanding}}$$

Total shareholders' equity (see Exhibit 17–1) ..	$17,000,000
Deduct preferred shares (see Exhibit 17–1)	2,000,000
Common shareholders' equity	$15,000,000

The book value per share of Brickey Electronics' common shares is computed as follows:

$$\frac{\$15,000,000}{500,000 \text{ shares}} = \$30$$

If this book value is compared with the $40 market value of Brickey Electronics shares, then the shares appear to be somewhat overpriced. However, as we discussed earlier, market prices reflect expectations about future earnings and dividends, whereas book value largely reflects the results of events that occurred in the past. Ordinarily, the market value of a share exceeds its book value. For example, in a recent year, Microsoft's common shares often traded at over 4 times their book value, and Coca-Cola's market value was over 17 times its book value.

Ratio Analysis—The Short-Term Creditor

Objective 6

Identify the ratios used to measure the well-being of the short-term creditor and state each ratio's formula and interpretation.

Short-term creditors, such as suppliers, want to be repaid on time. Therefore, they focus on the company's cash flows and on its working capital since these are the company's primary sources of cash in the short run.

Working Capital

Working capital
Measures the company's ability to repay current liabilities using only current assets.

The excess of current assets over current liabilities is known as **working capital.** The working capital for Brickey Electronics is computed below:

Working capital = Current assets − Current liabilities

	1999	1998
Current assets	$15,500,000	$16,470,000
Current liabilities	7,000,000	5,000,000
Working capital	$ 8,500,000	$11,470,000

The amount of working capital available to a firm is of considerable interest to short-term creditors, *since it represents assets financed from long-term capital sources that do not require near-term repayment.* Therefore, the greater the working capital, the greater is the cushion of protection available to short-term creditors and the greater is the assurance that short-term debts will be paid when due.

Although it is always comforting to short-term creditors to see a large working capital balance, a large balance by itself is no assurance that debts will be paid when due. Rather than being a sign of strength, a large working capital balance may simply mean that obsolete inventory is being accumulated. Therefore, to put the working capital figure into proper perspective, it must be supplemented with other analytical work. The following four ratios (the current ratio, the acid-test ratio, the accounts receivable turnover, and the inventory turnover) should all be used in connection with an analysis of working capital.

Current Ratio

Current ratio Test of short-term debt-paying ability.

The elements involved in the computation of working capital are frequently expressed in ratio form. A company's current assets divided by its current liabilities is known as the **current ratio:**

$$\text{Current ratio} = \frac{\text{Current assets}}{\text{Current liabilities}}$$

For Brickey Electronics, the current ratios for 1998 and 1999 would be computed as follows:

1999	1998
$\dfrac{\$15,500,000}{\$7,000,000} = 2.21 \text{ to } 1$	$\dfrac{\$16,470,000}{\$5,000,000} = 3.29 \text{ to } 1$

Although widely regarded as a measure of short-term debt-paying ability, the current ratio must be interpreted with great care. A *declining* ratio, as above, might be a sign of a deteriorating financial condition. On the other hand, it might be the result of eliminating obsolete inventories or other stagnant current assets. An *improving* ratio might be the result of an unwise stockpiling of inventory, or it might indicate an improving financial situation. In short, the current ratio is useful, but tricky to interpret. To avoid a blunder, the analyst must take a hard look at the individual assets and liabilities involved.

The general rule of thumb calls for a current ratio of 2 to 1. This rule is subject to many exceptions, depending on the industry and the firm involved. Some industries can operate quite successfully on a current ratio of slightly over 1 to 1. The adequacy of a current ratio depends heavily on the *composition* of the assets involved. For example, as we see in the table below, both Worthington Corporation and Greystone, Inc., have current ratios of 2 to 1. However, they are not in comparable financial condition. Greystone is likely to have difficulty meeting its current financial obligations, since almost all of its current assets consist of inventory rather than more liquid assets such as cash and accounts receivable.

	Worthington Corporation	Greystone, Inc.
Current assets:		
Cash	$ 25,000	$ 2,000
Accounts receivable, net	60,000	8,000
Inventory	85,000	160,000
Prepaid expenses	5,000	5,000
Total current assets	$175,000	$175,000 (a)
Current liabilities	$ 87,500	$ 87,500 (b)
Current ratio, (a) ÷ (b)	2 to 1	2 to 1

Acid-Test (Quick) Ratio

Acid-test (quick) ratio
Test of short-term debt-paying ability without having to rely on inventory.

The **acid-test (quick) ratio** is a much more rigorous test of a company's ability to meet its short-term debts. Inventories and prepaid expenses are excluded from total current assets, leaving only the more liquid (or "quick") assets to be divided by current liabilities.

$$\text{Acid-test ratio} = \frac{\text{Cash} + \text{Marketable securities} + \text{Current receivables*}}{\text{Current liabilities}}$$

*Current receivables include both accounts receivable and any short-term notes receivable.

The acid-test ratio is designed to measure how well a company can meet its obligations without having to liquidate or depend too heavily on its inventory. Since inventory may be difficult to sell in times of economic stress, it is generally felt that to be properly protected, each dollar of liabilities should be backed by at least $1 of quick assets. Thus, an acid-test ratio of 1 to 1 is broadly viewed as being adequate in many firms.

The acid-test ratios for Brickey Electronics for 1998 and 1999 are computed below:

	1999	1998
Cash (see Exhibit 17–1)	$1,200,000	$2,350,000
Accounts receivable (see Exhibit 17–1)	6,000,000	4,000,000
Total quick assets	$7,200,000	$6,350,000 (a)
Current liabilities (see Exhibit 17–1)	$7,000,000	$5,000,000 (b)
Acid-test ratio, (a) ÷ (b)	1.03 to 1	1.27 to 1

Although Brickey Electronics has an acid-test ratio for 1999 that is within the acceptable range, an analyst might be concerned about several disquieting trends revealed in the company's balance sheet. Notice in Exhibit 17–1 that short-term debts are rising, while the cash position seems to be deteriorating. Perhaps the weakened cash position is a result of the greatly expanded volume of accounts receivable. One wonders why the accounts receivable have been allowed to increase so rapidly in so brief a time.

In short, as with the current ratio, the acid-test ratio should be interpreted with one eye on its basic components.

Accounts Receivable Turnover

Accounts receivable turnover A rough measure of how many times a company's accounts receivable have been turned into cash during the year.

The **accounts receivable turnover** is a rough measure of how many times a company's accounts receivable have been turned into cash during the year. It is frequently used in conjunction with an analysis of working capital, since a smooth flow from accounts receivable into cash is an important indicator of the "quality" of a company's working capital and is critical to its ability to operate. The accounts receivable turnover is computed by dividing sales on account (i.e., credit sales) by the average accounts receivable balance for the year.

$$\text{Accounts receivable turnover} = \frac{\text{Sales on account}}{\text{Average accounts receivable balance}}$$

Assuming that all sales for the year were on account, the accounts receivable turnover for Brickey Electronics for 1999 would be computed as follows:

$$\frac{\text{Sales on account}}{\text{Average accounts receivable balance}} = \frac{\$52,000,000}{\$5,000,000*} = 10.4 \text{ times}$$

*$4,000,000 + $6,000,000 = $10,000,000; $10,000,000 ÷ 2 = $5,000,000 average.

Average collection period Measure of the average number of days taken to collect an account receivable.

The turnover figure can then be divided into 365 to determine the average number of days being taken to collect an account (known as the **average collection period**).

$$\text{Average collection period} = \frac{365 \text{ days}}{\text{Accounts receivable turnover}}$$

The average collection period for Brickey Electronics for 1999 is computed as follows:

$$\frac{365}{10.4 \text{ times}} = 35 \text{ days}$$

This simply means that on average it takes 35 days to collect on a credit sale. Whether the average of 35 days taken to collect an account is good or bad depends on the credit terms Brickey Electronics is offering its customers. If the credit terms are 30 days, than a 35-day average collection period would usually be viewed as very good. Most customers will tend to withhold payment for as long as the credit terms will allow and may even go over a few days. This factor, added to ever-present problems with a few slow-paying customers, can cause the average collection period to exceed normal credit terms by a week or so and should not cause great alarm.

On the other hand, if the company's credit terms are 10 days, then a 35-day average collection period is worrisome. The long collection period may result from many old unpaid accounts of doubtful collectability, or it may be a result of poor day-to-day credit management. The firm may be making sales with inadequate credit checks on customers, or perhaps no follow-ups are being made on slow accounts.

Inventory Turnover

Inventory turnover ratio Measure of how many times a company's inventory has been sold during the year.

The **inventory turnover ratio** measures how many times a company's inventory has been sold and replaced during the year. It is computed by dividing the cost of goods sold by the average level of inventory on hand:

$$\text{Inventory turnover} = \frac{\text{Cost of goods sold}}{\text{Average inventory balance}}$$

The average inventory figure is the average of the beginning and ending inventory figures. Since Brickey Electronics has a beginning inventory of $10,000,000 and an ending inventory of $8,000,000, its average inventory for the year would be $9,000,000. The company's inventory turnover for 1999 would be computed as follows:

$$\frac{\text{Cost of goods sold}}{\text{Average inventory balance}} = \frac{\$36,000,000}{\$9,000,000} = 4 \text{ times}$$

Average sale period Measure of the average number of days taken to sell the inventory one time.

The number of days being taken to sell the entire inventory one time (called the **average sale period**) can be computed by dividing 365 by the inventory turnover figure:

$$\text{Average sale period} = \frac{365 \text{ days}}{\text{Inventory turnover}}$$

$$\frac{365}{4 \text{ times}} = 91\tfrac{1}{4} \text{ days}$$

The average sale period varies from industry to industry. Grocery stores tend to turn their inventory over very quickly, perhaps as often as every 12 to 15 days. On the other hand, jewellery stores tend to turn their inventory over very slowly, perhaps only a couple of times each year.

If a firm has a turnover that is much slower than the average for its industry, then it may have obsolete goods on hand, or its inventory may be needlessly high. Excessive inventories tie up funds that could be used elsewhere in operations. Managers sometimes argue that they must buy in very large quantities to take advantage of the best discounts being offered. But these discounts must be carefully weighed against the added costs of insurance, taxes, financing, and risks of obsolescence and deterioration that result from carrying added inventories.

Inventory turnover has been increasing in recent years as companies have adopted just-in-time (JIT) methods. Under JIT, inventories are purposely kept low, and thus a company utilizing JIT methods may have a very high inventory turnover as compared to other companies. Indeed, one of the goals of JIT is to increase inventory turnover by systematically reducing the amount of inventory on hand.

Cash Flow Ratios

In analyzing the firm's short-term liquidity risk, the manager may find it useful to refer to the statement of cash flows in conjunction with a firm's balance sheet and income statement to compute various ratios. The ratio of cash flow from operations (CFO) to current liabilities can provide valuable clues to management on how best to finance business operations. This ratio is an indicator of the amount of cash the firm has derived from operations after meeting current debt and working capital obligations. In calculating this ratio it is best to use cash flow from continuing operations so as not to be misled by unusual or nonrecurring items. A ratio of .40 or more is considered good for a manufacturing or retailing firm.

In addition to short-term ratio analysis, a manager may also find it useful to do a trend analysis comparing net income over several periods with cash flow from operations. To reduce the effect of noncash items, such as depreciation and accruals of revenue and expenses, one could use the following ratio:

$$\frac{\text{CFO before interest and taxes}}{\text{Operating income before interest, taxes and depreciation}}$$

Any evidence of the CFO and operating income not moving in parallel could signal trouble and the cause should be investigated in time to take corrective action.

Other cash flow ratios may also be of interest. In assessing the quality of earnings, for example, insight can be gained by dividing cash flow from operations by sales. A high ratio signals high-quality earnings. Cash flow from operations is used in lieu of operating income because the latter is more subject to judgment regarding cost allocation and revenue recognition. Another indicator of quality of earnings is cash flow from operations divided by operating income. Because of noncash expenses such as depreciation and noncash revenues such as credit sales or the recognition of previously deferred revenue, a substantial difference may exist between CFO and operating income.

In addition to assessing quality of earnings, CFO can also be used to compute other ratios of interest to management. A manager may be interested, for example, in determining the firm's ability to make capital expenditures from internally generated funds. A helpful ratio is CFO divided by capital asset acquisitions. Dividends are usually deducted from CFO under the assumption that current dividends will not be cut.

$$\frac{\text{CFO} - \text{Dividends}}{\text{Cash paid for capital assets}}$$

Although it is likely that a firm will seek long-run sources of financing for major acquisitions, CFO has information content. CFO can be interpreted as an indicator of the firm's ability to service debt. However, this ratio does have limitations as do cash flow ratios generally. Because managers often have considerable discretion regarding capital asset decisions, the CFO to capital expenditures ratio can be easily manipulated. One should look for trends and seek explanations for changes in these trends.

Caution should be exercised in the use and interpretation of all cash flow ratios. Cash flow ratios, for example, should not be interpreted as a measure of the firm's ability to distribute cash. This is because cash flow ratios do not include some critical information that has future cash flow effects. Cash flow ratios, for example, do not include provision for asset replacement or for contingencies. When used in conjunction with other ratios, however, cash flow ratios may provide useful insights for managerial decisions.

Ratio Analysis—The Long-Term Creditor

Objective 7

Identify the ratios used to measure the well-being of the long-term creditor and state each ratio's formula and interpretation.

The position of long-term creditors differs from that of short-term creditors in that they are concerned with both the near-term *and* the long-term ability of a firm to meet its commitments. They are concerned with the near term since the interest they are entitled to is normally paid on a current basis. They are concerned with the long term since they want to be fully repaid on schedule.

Since the long-term creditor is usually faced with greater risks than the short-term creditor, firms are often required to agree to various restrictive covenants, or rules, for the long-term creditor's protection. Examples of such restrictive covenants include the maintenance of minimum working capital levels and restrictions on payment of dividends to common shareholders. Although these restrictive covenants are in widespread use, they must be viewed as a poor second to adequate future *earnings* from the point of view of assessing protection and safety. Creditors do not want to go to court to collect their claims; they would much prefer staking the safety of their claims for interest and eventual repayment of principal on an orderly and consistent flow of funds from operations.

Times Interest Earned Ratio

Times interest earned ratio Measure of the company's ability to make interest payments.

The most common measure of the ability of a firm's operations to provide protection to the long-term creditor is the **times interest earned ratio.** It is computed by dividing earnings *before* interest expense and income taxes (i.e., net operating income) by the yearly interest charges that must be met:

$$\text{Times interest earned} = \frac{\text{Earnings before interest expense and income taxes (EBIT)}}{\text{Interest expense}}$$

For Brickey Electronics, the times interest earned ratio for 1999 would be computed as follows:

$$\frac{\$3,140,000}{\$640,000} = 4.9 \text{ times}$$

Earnings before income taxes must be used in the computation, since interest expense deductions come *before* income taxes are computed. Creditors have first claim on earnings. Only those earnings remaining after all interest charges have been provided for are subject to income taxes.

Generally, earnings are viewed as adequate to protect long-term creditors if the times interest earned ratio is 2 or more. Before making a final judgment, however, it would be necessary to look at a firm's long-run *trend* of earnings and evaluate how vulnerable the firm is to cyclical changes in the economy.

Debt-to-Equity Ratio

Long-term creditors are also concerned with keeping a reasonable balance between the portion of assets provided by creditors and the portion of assets provided by the shareholders of a firm. This balance is measured by the **debt-to-equity ratio:**

Debt-to-equity ratio
Measure of the amount of assets being provided by creditors for each dollar of assets being provided by the shareholders.

$$\text{Debt-to-equity ratio} = \frac{\text{Total liabilities}}{\text{Shareholders' equity}}$$

	1999	1998
Total liabilities	$14,500,000	$13,000,000 (a)
Shareholders' equity	17,000,000	15,970,000 (b)
Debt-to-equity ratio, (a) ÷ (b)	0.85 to 1	0.81 to 1

The debt-to-equity ratio indicates the amount of assets being provided by creditors for each dollar of assets being provided by the owners of a company. In 1998, creditors of Brickey Electronics were providing 81 cents of assets for each $1 of assets being provided by shareholders; the figure increased only slightly to 85 cents by 1999.

Creditors would like the debt-to-equity ratio to be relatively low. The lower the ratio, the greater the amount of assets being provided by the owners of a company and the greater is the buffer of protection to creditors. By contrast, common shareholders would like the ratio to be relatively high, since through leverage, common shareholders can benefit from the assets being provided by creditors.

In most industries, norms have developed over the years that serve as guides to firms in their decisions as to the "right" amount of debt to include in the capital structure. Different industries face different risks. For this reason, the level of debt that is appropriate for firms in one industry is not necessarily a guide to the level of debt that is appropriate for firms in a different industry.

Monitoring Productivity

The importance of productivity has taken on a heightened awareness among Canadian business firms. In the manufacturing sector, Canadian firms have not kept pace with U.S. and Japanese competitors. To help reverse this trend, management must be alert to new production techniques that result in long-term productivity gains and must make use of measurement methods that help the firm assess its relative position. Long-term productivity gains can result from the early adoption of more efficient production techniques. The development and application of knowledge and new ideas are the primary drivers of productivity. Improved productivity may manifest itself in savings in material, labour, capital and energy costs. Productivity benefits could also include improved quality or more variety, faster cycle time, faster and more efficient production runs and better customer service.

To management, improving productivity can mean obtaining higher profitability and greater assurance of survival in an ever more competitive business environment. The management accountant can play an important role in the assessment of a firm's productivity.

Productivity can be determined as a ratio of some measure of output to some measure of input. Outputs can be expressed in physical units or by dollar values corresponding to the firm's objectives. Inputs consist of materials, labour, overhead, and capital. Corporate annual reports typically provide physical data useful for measuring a company's productivity.

Numerous methods can be used to measure productivity. They range from sophisticated computer models that perform sensitivity analysis on productivity (profitability) as any or all of the elements of the input mix are changed, to the simple utilization of financial data readily available from the firm's existing accounting system. Both performance and productivity of invested capital can be measured by calculating financial ratios that help to relate production inputs to production outputs.

One measurement ratio useful in assessing productivity is the return on investment formula calculated in Chapter 12 as follows:

$$\text{ROI} = \frac{\text{Net operating income}}{\text{Sales}} \times \frac{\text{Sales}}{\text{Average operating assets}} = \frac{\text{Net operating income}}{\text{Average operating assets}}$$

Other financial ratios which may help assess productivity include such ratios as manufacturing cost to sales, selling cost to sales, and administrative cost to sales. More detailed productivity analysis can be extended, for example, to analyze the individual components of manufacturing cost. Separate ratios can be computed for raw materials, labour, and manufacturing overhead as percentages of the market value of production (manufacturing cost times the ratio of sales to cost of sales).

Other partial measures of productivity can be computed by expressing components of the balance sheet as percentages of sales. The lower the investment for a given level of sales, the more productive is the business in the utilization of its resources. For example, taking the ratio of capital assets to sales, the higher the sales that can be generated for each dollar invested in capital assets, the greater is the productivity of the firm's fixed assets.

Focus on Current Practice

Key business leaders believe the commitment to quality is essential to Canadian competitiveness. With the recent removal of tariff protection Canadian business is forced to compete with world standards in terms of cost, quality, and engineering and administrative capability. Companies such as IBM Canada have developed key principles that are critical for success in the new global competitive business environment. One such principle is benchmarking. IBM measures itself against American Express for billing, Imperial Oil for planning and benchmarks its telemarketing against Land's End. Other key principles are customer focus and a commitment to total quality management and continuous improvement. At IBM Canada management believes that strong leadership and communication from senior management is essential to putting these principles into practice and making real improvements in productivity. ■

The management accountant should be cautious, however, in interpreting productivity ratios. The interrelationships among the various measures of productivity and their ultimate effect on the firm's profitability must be clearly understood. For example, labour may be decreasing as a percentage of manufacturing cost as a result of the purchase of higher-quality raw materials. Careful analysis may reveal that increased productivity of labour was more than offset by the increased cost of the raw materials.

Nevertheless, partial productivity ratios can provide information on how output is affected by a given input factor, and changes in these ratios can serve as a signal for investigation that might otherwise go unnoticed.

Productivity analysis is as important to service industries as it is to manufacturing firms. Measures such as the number of customers served per day or the number of transactions completed per week for a given staff complement are examples of productivity measures for service industries.

In spite of the fact that productivity can be measured for any input factor, labour-hours have been the most commonly used input in measuring productivity. Productivity measures derived from labour no doubt can be useful to management in assessing learning curve effects and the motivational level of employees. However, as firms face stiffer competition both nationally and internationally, it seems prudent for management to assess the interrelationships among several productivity measures. This is especially true in the new manufacturing environment where costs are mostly fixed. Even the direct labour that remains can be interpreted as fixed in the sense that employee skills are essential to a firm's success. The amount invested in training and development may be a critical performance measure in this environment in assessing current position and as an indicator of future productivity. Since workers need multiple skills in the high-tech environment, a measure such as percent cross-trained could be a revealing statistic in monitoring productivity. Other useful measures could include number of defects, percentage passing first inspection, work in process turnover, scrap as a percentage of output, and percentage of on-time shipments. What is measured and reported should be determined by the measure's relationship to the firm's operating and strategic goals. For example, if a major objective of a company is to increase market share, measures of delivery and quality improvements may provide useful strategic information. By using **productivity ratios** and new performance indicators to help understand key interrelationships, management may be able to more quickly adopt cost-reducing innovations that lead to improvements in total productivity and to increased long-term profitability.

Productivity ratios
Ratios that measure output in relation to some measure of input, such as direct labour-charges.

Ratios and Profit Planning

Profit planning and the projection of budgeted financial statements were discussed in Chapter 9. Ratios can be linked to the budgeting process to help project financial statement account balances as well as to assist in estimating cash flows. In addition, using ratios in the forecasting process allows a complete articulation of the balance sheet, income statement, and statement of changes in financial position.

To illustrate, consider the accounts receivable turnover. Recalling that the accounts receivable turnover is equal to sales on account divided by accounts receivable, a simple manipulation of the formula solves for accounts receivable. Note that because we are projecting for the *end* of 1999, we are not using *average* accounts receivable in the turnover formula.

$$\text{Accounts receivable turnover} = \frac{\text{Sales on account}}{\text{Accounts receivable}}$$

$$\text{Accounts receivable} = \frac{\text{Sales on account}}{\text{Accounts receivable turnover}}$$

Budgeted accounts receivable can, therefore, be estimated by dividing projected sales on account by the accounts receivable turnover. For example, if projected sales for 1999 for Brickey Electronics, from Exhibit 17–2, is $52,000 and if the accounts receivable turnover is forecasted to be 8.67, then estimated accounts receivable for 1999 is $6,000 ($52,000/8.67 rounded).

Similarly, inventory for 1999 can be projected by manipulating the inventory turnover formula. Recall that:

$$\text{Inventory turnover} = \frac{\text{Cost of goods sold}}{\text{Inventory}}$$

Then:

$$\text{Inventory} = \frac{\text{Cost of goods sold}}{\text{Inventory turnover}}$$

If the cost of goods sold is estimated at 69% of sales and the inventory turnover is expected to be 4.5, then inventory is projected to be 7,973 [($52,000 $\times$ 0.69)/4.5].

Accounts payable can be projected by linking budgeted purchases to a new ratio called the accounts payable turnover.

$$\text{Accounts payable turnover} = \frac{\text{Purchases on account}}{\text{Accounts payable}}$$

Therefore:

$$\text{Accounts payable} = \frac{\text{Purchases on account}}{\text{Accounts payable turnover}}$$

However, because purchases on account is not disclosed, it too must be estimated. A convenient way to project purchases is through the algebraic manipulation of the cost of goods sold (CGS) formula.

$$\text{Beginning inventory} + \text{Purchases} - \text{Ending inventory} = \text{CGS}$$

Therefore:

$$
\begin{aligned}
\text{Purchases} &= \text{CGS} - \text{Beginning inventory} + \text{Ending inventory} \\
&= \$35,880 - \$10,000 + \$7,973 \\
&= \$33,853
\end{aligned}
$$

If 5.8 times is the accounts payable turnover, then accounts payable is projected to equal $5,837 ($33,853/5.8).

A full integration of the sales forecast for 1999 is presented in Exhibit 17–8, which incorporates the following additional assumptions. Prepaid expenses are projected to be $300 at December 31, 1999. The Land account balance is expected not to change, and buildings and equipment are forecasted at $12,000 net of depreciation. The expected balance of accrued payables is $900; $500 will be used to retire bonds and $300 to pay short-term notes. Where amounts in Exhibit 17–8 differ with corresponding items in Exhibits 17–1 and 17–2, it is a result of rounding.

Exhibit 17–8

Estimated Income Statement*

Sales revenue (given)	$52,000
Cost of goods sold	35,880
Gross margin on sales	16,120
Operating expenses:	
Selling expenses (13.5%)	7,000
Administrative expenses (11.2%)	5,860
Total operating expenses	12,860
Net operating income	3,260
Interest expense (1.2%)	640
Net income before taxes	2,620
Income tax (30%)	786
Net income	$ 1,834

Estimated Statement of Changes in Financial Position

Operating activities:	
Net income	$ 1,834
Increase in accounts receivable (52,000/8.67 − 4,000)	(1,998)
Decrease in inventory (35,880/4.5 − 10,000)	2,027
Increase in prepaid expenses (given)	(180)
Depreciation expense (given)	1,500
Increase in accounts payable (33,853/5.8 − 4,000)	1,837
Increase in accrued payable (900 given − 400)	500
Cash flow from operations	5,520
Financing activities:	
Retired bonds (given)	(500)
Retired short-term notes	(300)
Paid dividends (given)	(600)
Investing activities:	
Purchased equipment (given)	(5,000)
Net change in cash and cash equivalents	(880)
Cash balance 1998	2,350
Balance of cash and cash equivalents	$ 1,470

Estimated Balance Sheet, December 31, 1999

Assets

Current Assets:	
Cash and cash equivalents	$ 1,470
Accounts receivable (52,000 ÷ 8.67)	5,998
Inventory (35,880 ÷ 4.5)	7,973
Prepaid expenses	300
Total	15,741
Capital assets:	
Land	4,000
Buildings and equipment, net	12,000
Total assets	$31,741

Liabilities

Current liabilities:	
Accounts payable (33,853 ÷ 5.8)	$5,837
Accrued payables (given)	900
Notes payable, short-term	300
Total	7,037
Long-term liabilities:	
Bonds payable, 8% (8,000 − 500)	7,500
Total	14,537

Exhibit 17–8
(*concluded*)

Shareholders' Equity	
Preferred shares, $100 liquidation value $6 no par	2,000
Common shares 500 no par	7,000
Total contributed capital	9,000
Retained earnings (6,970 + 1,834 − 600 given)	8,204
Total shareholders' equity	17,204
Total liabilities and shareholders' equity	$31,741

*Assumes depreciation of $1,500 is included in selling and administrative expenses.

Summary of Ratios and Sources of Comparative Ratio Data

Exhibit 17–9 contains a summary of the ratios discussed in this chapter. The formula for each ratio and a summary comment on each ratio's significance are included in the exhibit.

Exhibit 17–10 contains a listing of published sources that provide comparative ratio data organized by industry. These sources are used extensively by managers, investors, and analysts in doing comparative analyses and in attempting to assess the well-being of companies. The World Wide Web also contains a wealth of financial and other data. A search engine such as Alta Vista, Yahoo, or Excite can be used to track down information on individual companies. Many companies have their own web sites on which they post their latest financial reports and news of interest to potential investors. The Sedar and *EDGAR* databases listed in Exhibit 17–10 is a particularly rich source of data. They contain copies of all reports filed by companies with the agencies since about 1995—including U.S. annual reports filed as form 10-K.

Summary

The data contained in financial statements represent a quantitative summary of a firm's operations and activities. Someone who is skillful at analyzing these statements can learn much about a company's strengths, weaknesses, emerging problems, operating efficiency, profitability, and so forth.

Many techniques are available to analyze financial statements and to assess the direction and importance of trends and changes. In this chapter, we have discussed three such analytical techniques—dollar and percentage changes in statements, common-size statements, and ratio analysis. Refer to Exhibit 17–9 for a detailed listing of the ratios. This listing also contains a brief statement as to the significance of each ratio.

Exhibit 17–9   Summary of Ratios

Ratio	Formula	Significance
Gross margin percentage	Gross margin ÷ Sales	A broad measure of profitability
Earnings per share (of common shares)	(Net income − Preferred dividends) ÷ Average number of common shares outstanding	Tends to have an effect on the market price per share, as reflected in the price-earnings ratio
Price-earnings ratio	Market price per share ÷ Earnings per share	An index of whether a share is relatively cheap or relatively expensive in relation to current earnings
Dividend payout ratio	Dividends per share ÷ Earnings per share	An index showing whether a company pays out most of its earnings in dividends or reinvests the earnings internally
Dividend yield ratio	Dividends per share ÷ Market price per share	Shows the return in terms of cash dividends being provided by a share
Return on total assets	{Net income + [Interest expense × (1 − Tax rate)]} ÷ Average total assets	Measure of how well assets have been employed by management
Return on common shareholders' equity	(Net income − Preferred dividends) ÷ Average common shareholders' equity (Average total shareholders' equity − Average preferred shares)	When compared to the return on total assets, measures the extent to which financial leverage is working for or against common shareholders
Book value per share	Common shareholders' equity (Total shareholders' equity − Preferred shares) ÷ Number of common shares outstanding	Measures the amount that would be distributed to holders of common shares if all assets were sold at their balance sheet carrying amounts and if all creditors were paid off
Working capital	Current assets − Current liabilities	Measures the company's ability to repay current liabilities using only current assets.
Current ratio	Current assets ÷ Current liabilities	Test of short-term debt-paying ability
Acid-test (quick) ratio	(Cash + Marketable securities + Current receivables) ÷ Current liabilities	Test of short-term debt-paying ability without having to rely on inventory
Accounts receivable turnover	Sales on account ÷ Average accounts receivable balance	A rough measure of how many times a company's accounts receivable have been turned into cash during the year
Average collection period (age of receivables)	365 days ÷ Accounts receivable turnover	Measure of the average number of days taken to collect an account receivable
Inventory turnover	Cost of goods sold ÷ Average inventory balance	Measure of how many times a company's inventory has been sold during the year
Average sale period (turnover in days)	365 days ÷ Inventory turnover	Measure of the average number of days taken to sell the inventory one time
Times interest earned	Earnings before interest expense and income taxes ÷ Interest expense	Measure of the company's ability to make interest payments
Debt-to-equity ratio	Total liabilities ÷ Shareholders' equity	Measure of the amount of assets being provided by creditors for each dollar of assets being provided by the shareholders

Exhibit 17–10
Published Sources of
Financial Ratios

Source	Content
Canadian Statistics	
Dun & Bradstreet's Canadian Key Directory	Business profile on top 3% of Canadian companies.
Dun & Bradstreet's Key Business Ratios	Ratio analysis of top 3% of Canadian companies.
Financial Post's Corporation Service	Individual companies' financial statements.
Financial Post's Dividend Record	Record of dividends.
Financial Post's "500"	Largest 500 companies, by sales, in Canada.
Financial Post's "Surveys of . . ."	Performance of industry sectors.
Moody's Handbook of Common Stock	Canadian companies on the New York Stock Exchange, dividend and share performance.
Moody's Bond Record	Performance of corporate, convertible, government, and municipal bonds.
Moody's Dividend Record	List of dividends.
Toronto Stock Exchange *TSE Review*	Stock market activity of the Toronto Stock Exchange.
Blue Book of Canadian Business	Survey of individual companies.
Federal Corporation Index	Annual reports of private companies.
Bank of Canada *Annual Report*	Canada's balance of payments, bank operations.
Bank of Canada *Review*	Monetary, banking, and other financial statistics.
Other	
Consumer and Corporate Affairs *Annual Report*	Funding of consumer groups, patents, trademarks.
Consumer and Corporate Affairs *Canada Corporations Bulletin*	Statistical data on Canadian corporations.
Finance Canada Economic Review	Reviews of economic developments in Canada, main economic indicators.
Industry Trade and Commerce *Small Business in Canada*	Statistical profile of the small business sector.
Insurance Canada *List of Securities*	Market value of all securities owned by Canadian insurance companies.
http://www.Sedar.com	Financial statements of companies listed by the Ontario Securities Commission.
http://www.ic.gc.ca/	Industry Canada interfirm comparisons.
U.S.	
EDGAR, Securities and Exchange Commission. Web site that is updated continuously. http://www.sec.gov/edaux/formlynx.htm or http://www.freeedgar.com	An exhaustive database accessible on the World Wide Web that contains reports filed by companies with the SEC. These reports can be downloaded.
Annual Statement Studies. Robert Morris Associates. Published annually.	A widely used publication that contains common-size statements and financial ratios on individual companies. The companies are arranged by industry.

Exhibit 17–10
(*concluded*)

Source	Content
Moody's Industrial Manual and *Moody's Bank and Finance Manual.* Published annually.	An exhaustive source that contains financial ratios on all companies listed on the New York Stock Exchange, the American Stock Exchange, and regional American exchanges.
Key Business Ratios. Dun & Bradstreet. Published annually.	Fourteen commonly used financial ratios are computed for over 800 major industry groupings.
Standard & Poor's Industry Survey. Standard & Poor's. Published annually.	Various statistics, including some financial ratios, are provided by industry and on leading companies within each industry grouping.

Review Problem: Selected Ratios and Financial Leverage

Starbucks Coffee Company is the leading retailer and roaster of specialty coffee in North America with over 1,000 stores offering freshly brewed coffee, pastries, and coffee beans. Data from recent financial statements are given below:

STARBUCKS COFFEE COMPANY
Comparative Balance Sheet
(dollars in thousands)

	End of Year	Beginning of Year
Assets		
Current assets:		
Cash	$126,215	$ 20,944
Marketable securities	103,221	41,507
Accounts receivable	17,621	9,852
Inventories	83,370	123,657
Other current assets	9,114	9,390
Total current assets	339,541	205,350
Property and equipment, net	369,477	244,728
Other assets	17,595	18,100
Total assets	$726,613	$468,178
Liabilities and Shareholders' Equity		
Current liabilities:		
Accounts payable	$ 38,064	$ 28,668
Short-term bank loans	16,241	13,138
Accrued payables	18,005	13,436
Other current liabilities	28,881	15,804
Total current liabilities	101,091	71,046
Long-term liabilities:		
Bonds payable	165,020	80,398
Other long-term liabilities	8,842	4,503
Total liabilities	274,953	155,947

Shareholders' equity:

		Current Year	Prior Year
Preferred stock		–0–	–0–
Common shares		361,309	265,679
Retained earnings		90,315	46,552
Total shareholders' equity		451,660	312,231
Total liabilities and shareholders' equity		$726,613	$468,178

Note: The effective interest rate on the bonds payable was about 5%.

STARBUCKS COFFEE COMPANY
Comparative Income Statement
(dollars in thousands)

	Current Year	Prior Year
Revenue	$696,481	$465,213
Cost of goods sold	335,800	211,279
Gross margin	360,681	253,934
Operating expenses:		
Store operating expenses	210,693	148,757
Other operating expenses	19,787	13,932
Depreciation and amortization	35,950	22,486
General and administrative expenses	37,258	28,643
Total operating expenses	303,688	213,818
Net operating income	56,993	40,116
Gain on sale of investment	9,218	–0–
Plus interest income	11,029	6,792
Less interest expense	8,739	3,765
Net income before taxes	68,501	43,143
Less income taxes (about 38.5%)	26,373	17,041
Net income	$ 42,128	$ 26,102

Required   For the current year:

1. Compute the return on total assets.
2. Compute the return on common shareholders' equity.
3. Is Starbucks' financial leverage positive or negative? Explain.
4. Compute the current ratio.
5. Compute the acid-test (quick) ratio.
6. Compute the inventory turnover.
7. Compute the average sale period.
8. Compute the debt-to-equity ratio.

1. Return on total assets:

Solution to Review Problem

$$\text{Return on total assets} = \frac{\text{Net income} + [\text{Interest expense} \times (1 - \text{Tax rate})]}{\text{Average total assets}}$$

$$\frac{\$42,128 + [\$8,739 \times (1 - 0.385)]}{(\$726,613 + \$468,178)/2} = 8.0\% \text{ (rounded)}$$

2. Return on common shareholders' equity:

$$\text{Return on common shareholders' equity} = \frac{\text{Net income} - \text{Preferred dividends}}{\text{Average common shareholders' equity}}$$

$$\frac{\$42,128 - \$0}{(\$451,660 + \$312,231)/2} = 11.0\% \text{ (rounded)}$$

3. The company has positive financial leverage, since the return on common shareholders' equity (11%) is greater than the return on total assets (8%). The positive financial leverage was obtained from current liabilities and the bonds payable. The interest rate on the bonds is substantially less than the return on total assets.
4. Current ratio:

$$\text{Current ratio} = \frac{\text{Current assets}}{\text{Current liabilities}}$$

$$\frac{\$339,541}{\$101,091} = 3.36 \text{ (rounded)}$$

5. Acid-test (quick) ratio:

$$\text{Acid-test ratio} = \frac{\text{Cash} + \text{Marketable securities} + \text{Current receivables}}{\text{Current liabilities}}$$

$$\frac{\$126,215 + \$103,221 + \$17,261}{\$101,091} = 2.44 \text{ (rounded)}$$

This acid-test ratio is quite high and provides Starbucks with the ability to fund rapid expansion.

6. Inventory turnover:

$$\text{Inventory turnover} = \frac{\text{Cost of goods sold}}{\text{Average inventory balance}}$$

$$\frac{\$335,800}{(\$83,370 + \$123,657)/2} = 3.24 \text{ (rounded)}$$

7. Average sale period:

$$\text{Average sale period} = \frac{365 \text{ days}}{\text{Inventory turnover}}$$

$$\frac{365 \text{ days}}{3.24} = 113 \text{ days (rounded)}$$

8. Debt-to-equity ratio:

$$\text{Debt-to-equity ratio} = \frac{\text{Total liabilities}}{\text{Shareholders' equity}}$$

$$\frac{\$274,953}{\$451,660} = 0.61 \text{ (rounded)}$$

Questions

17–1   What three basic analytical techniques are used in financial statement analysis?

17–2   Distinguish between horizontal and vertical analysis of financial statement data.

17–3   What is the basic purpose for examining trends in a company's financial ratios and other data? What other kinds of comparisons might an analyst make?

17–4   Why does the financial analyst compute financial ratios rather than simply studying raw financial data? What dangers are there in the use of ratios?

17–5   Assume that two companies in the same industry have equal earnings. Why might these companies have different price-earnings ratios? If a company has a price-earnings ratio of 20 and reports earnings per share for the current year of $4, at what price would you expect to find the share selling on the market?

17–6   Armcor, Inc., is in a rapidly growing technological industry. Would you expect the company to have a high or low dividend payout ratio?

17–7   Distinguish between a manager's *financing* and *operating* responsibilities. Which of these responsibilities is the return on total assets ratio designed to measure?

17–8   What is meant by the dividend yield on a common share investment?

17–9   What is meant by the term *financial leverage?*

17–10   The president of a medium-size plastics company was recently quoted in a business journal as stating, "We haven't had a dollar of interest-paying debt in over 10 years. Not many companies can say that." As a shareholder in this firm, how would you feel about its policy of not taking on interest-paying debt?

17–11   Why is it more difficult to obtain positive financial leverage from preferred shares than from long-term debt?

17–12   If a share's market value exceeds its book value, then the share is overpriced. Do you agree? Explain.

17–13   Weaver Company experiences a great deal of seasonal variation in its business activities. The company's high point in business activity is in June; its low point is in January. During which month would you expect the current ratio to be highest?

17–14   A company seeking a line of credit at a bank was turned down. Among other things, the bank stated that the company's 2 to 1 current ratio was not adequate. Give reasons why a 2 to 1 current ratio might not be adequate.

17–15   If you were a long-term creditor of a firm, would you be more interested in the firm's long-term or short-term debt-paying ability? Why?

17–16   A young university student once complained to one of the authors, "The reason that corporations are such big spenders is that Revenue Canada always picks up part of the tab." What did he mean by this statement?

17–17   What pitfalls are involved in computing earnings per share? How can these pitfalls be avoided?

17–18   What is meant by reporting an extraordinary item on the income statement net of its tax effect? Give an example of both an extraordinary gain and an extraordinary loss net of its tax effect. Assume a tax rate of 30%.

17–19   "Earnings per share this year is higher than last year. Profitability is definitely improving." Comment.

17–20   How can cash flow ratios be used to access earnings quality? Explain.

Exercises

E17–1   Rotorua Products, Ltd., of New Zealand markets agricultural products for the burgeoning Asian consumer market. The company's current assets, current liabilities, and sales have been reported as follows over the last five years (Year 5 is the most recent year):

	Year 5	Year 4	Year 3	Year 2	Year 1
Sales	$NZ2,250,000	$NZ2,160,000	$NZ2,070,000	$NZ1,980,000	$NZ1,800,000
Cash	$NZ 30,000	$NZ 40,000	$NZ 48,000	$NZ 65,000	$NZ 50,000
Accounts receivable, net	570,000	510,000	405,000	345,000	300,000
Inventory	750,000	720,000	690,000	660,000	600,000
Total current assets	$NZ1,350,000	$NZ1,270,000	$NZ1,143,000	$NZ1,070,000	$NZ 950,000
Current liabilities	$NZ 640,000	$NZ 580,000	$NZ 520,000	$NZ 440,000	$NZ 400,000

$NZ stands for New Zealand dollars.

Required

1. Express all of the asset, liability, and sales data in trend percentages. (Show percentages for each item.) Use Year 1 as the base year and carry computations to one decimal place.
2. Comment on the results of your analysis.

E17–2   A comparative income statement is given below for McKenzie Sales, Ltd., of Toronto:

McKENZIE SALES, LTD.
Comparative Income Statement
For the Years Ended June 30, 1999, and 1998

	1999	1998
Sales	$8,000,000	$6,000,000
Less cost of goods sold	4,984,000	3,516,000
Gross margin	3,016,000	2,484,000
Less operating expenses:		
Selling expenses	1,480,000	1,092,000
Administrative expenses	712,000	618,000
Total expenses	2,192,000	1,710,000
Net operating income	824,000	774,000
Less interest expense	96,000	84,000
Net income before taxes	$ 728,000	$ 690,000

Members of the company's board of directors are surprised to see that net income increased by only $38,000 when sales increased by two million dollars.

Required

1. Express each year's income statement in common-size percentages. Carry computations to one decimal place.
2. Comment briefly on the changes between the two years.

E17–3   The financial statements for Castile Products, Inc., are given below:

CASTILE PRODUCTS, INC.
Balance Sheet
December 31

Assets

Current assets:

Cash	$ 6,500
Accounts receivable, net	35,000
Merchandise inventory	70,000
Prepaid expenses	3,500
Total current assets	115,000
Property and equipment, net	185,000
Total assets	$300,000

Liabilities and Shareholders' Equity

Liabilities:

Current liabilities		$ 50,000
Bonds payable, 10%		80,000
Total liabilities		130,000
Shareholders' equity:		
Common shares, 6000 no par	$ 30,000	
Retained earnings	140,000	
Total shareholders' equity		170,000
Total liabilities and equity		$300,000

CASTILE PRODUCTS, INC.
Income Statement
For the Year Ended December 31

Sales	$420,000
Less cost of goods sold	292,500
Gross margin	127,500
Less operating expenses	89,500
Net operating income	38,000
Interest expense	8,000
Net income before taxes	30,000
Income taxes (30%)	9,000
Net income	$ 21,000

Account balances at the beginning of the year were: accounts receivable, $25,000; and inventory, $60,000. All sales were on account.

Required   Compute financial ratios as follows:

1. Gross margin percentage. 30.4 %
2. Current ratio. (Industry average: 2.5 to 1.) 2.3 to 1
3. Acid-test (quick) ratio. (Industry average: 1.3 to 1.) .83 to 1
4. Debt-to-equity ratio. .76 to 1
5. Accounts receivable turnover in days. (Terms: 2/10, n/30.) 30.4 days
6. Inventory turnover in days. (Industry average: 64 days.) 86.9
7. Times interest earned. 4.75 times   4.8 times
8. Book value per share. (Market price: $42.)

E17–4   Refer to the financial statements for Castile Products, Inc., in E17–3. In addition to the data in these statements, assume that Castile Products, Inc., paid dividends of $2.10 per share during the year. Also assume that the company's common share had a market price of $42 at the end of the year and there was no change in the number of outstanding common shares during the year.

Required   Compute financial ratios as follows:

1. Earnings per share.
2. Dividend payout ratio.
3. Dividend yield ratio.
4. Price-earnings ratio. (Industry average: 10.)

E17–5   Refer to the financial statements for Castile Products, Inc., in E17–3. Assets at the beginning of the year totalled $280,000, and the shareholders' equity totalled $161,600.

Required   Compute the following:

1. Return on total assets.
2. Return on common shareholders' equity.
3. Was financial leverage positive or negative for the year? Explain.

E17–6   Selected financial data from the June 30 year-end statements of Safford Company are given below:

Total assets	$3,600,000
Long-term debt (12% interest rate)	500,000
Preferred shares, $8 no par, 9,000 share	9,000,000
Total shareholders' equity	2,400,000
Interest paid on long-term debt	60,000
Net income	280,000

Total assets at the beginning of the year were $3,000,000; total shareholders' equity was $2,200,000. There has been no change in the preferred shares during the year. The company's tax rate is 30%.

Required
1. Compute the return on total assets.
2. Compute the return on common shareholders' equity.
3. Is financial leverage positive or negative? Explain.

E17–7   Norsk Optronics, ALS, of Bergen, Norway, had a current ratio of 2.5 to 1 on June 30 of the current year. On that date, the company's assets were:

Cash		Kr	90,000
Accounts receivable	Kr300,000		
Less allowance for doubtful accounts	40,000		260,000
Inventory			490,000
Prepaid expenses			10,000
Plant and equipment, net			800,000
Total assets			Kr1,650,000

The Norwegian currency is the krone, denoted here by the symbol Kr.

Required
1. What was the company's working capital on June 30?
2. What was the company's acid-test (quick) ratio on June 30?
3. The company paid an account payable of Kr40,000 immediately after June 30.
   a. What effect did this transaction have on working capital? Show computations.
   b. What effect did this transaction have on the current ratio? Show computations.

E17–8   Emerson Ltd. produces custom furniture for commercial establishments. Because of competition, productivity is a key factor in pricing bids. To evaluate upcoming projects, Emerson wishes to analyze the productivity effects of using partially assembled materials. Material costs are $10 per metre while labour is $18 per hour. Two alterations for an average unit of output are:

	Material	Labour
Option 1	20 m	30 hrs
Option 2	80 m	18 hrs

Required

1. Compute the productivity of each option for production of two countertops.
2. Compute the relative costs of each option for producing the two countertops.
3. Which option is the most economical? What lesson is evident from the analysis?

Problems

P17–9 Effects of Transactions on Working Capital, Current Ratio, and Acid-Test (Quick) Ratio   Denna Company's working capital accounts at the beginning of the year are given below:

Cash	$ 50,000
Marketable Securities	30,000
Accounts Receivable, net	200,000
Inventory	210,000
Prepaid Expenses	10,000
Accounts Payable	150,000
Notes Due within One Year	30,000
Accrued Liabilities	20,000

During the year, Denna Company completed the following transactions:

x. Paid a cash dividend previously declared, $12,000.
a. Issued additional common shares for cash, $100,000.
b. Sold inventory costing $50,000 for $80,000, on account.
c. Wrote off uncollectible accounts in the amount of $10,000. The company uses the allowance method of accounting for bad debts.
d. Declared a cash dividend, $15,000.
e. Paid accounts payable, $50,000.
f. Borrowed cash on a short-term note with the bank, $35,000.
g. Sold inventory costing $15,000 for $10,000 cash.
h. Purchased inventory on account, $60,000.
i. Paid off all short-term notes due, $30,000.
j. Purchased equipment for cash, $15,000.
k. Sold marketable securities costing $18,000 for cash, $15,000.
l. Collected cash on accounts receivable, $80,000.

Required

1. Compute the following amounts and ratios as of the beginning of the year:
   a. Working capital.
   b. Current ratio.
   c. Acid-test (quick) ratio.
2. Indicate the effect of each of the transactions given above on working capital, the current ratio, and the acid-test (quick) ratio. Give the effect in terms of increase, decrease, or none. Item (x) is given below as an example of the format to use:

		The Effect on	
Transaction	**Working Capital**	**Current Ratio**	**Acid-Test Ratio**
(x) Paid a cash dividend previously declared	None	Increase	Increase

P17–10   Ratio Analysis and Common-Size Statements   Paul Sabin organized Sabin Electronics 10 years ago in order to produce and sell several electronic devices on which he had secured patents. Although the company has been fairly profitable, it is now experiencing a severe cash shortage. For this reason, it is requesting a $500,000 long-term loan from Gulf Credit Union, $100,000 of which will be used to bolster the Cash account and $400,000 of which will be used to modernize certain key items of equipment. The company's financial statements for the two most recent years follow:

SABIN ELECTRONICS
Comparative Balance Sheet

	This Year	Last Year
Assets		
Current assets:		
Cash	$ 70,000	$ 150,000
Marketable securities	—	18,000
Accounts receivable, net	480,000	300,000
Inventory	950,000	600,000
Prepaid expenses	20,000	22,000
Total current assets	1,520,000	1,090,000
Plant and equipment, net	1,480,000	1,370,000
Total assets	$3,000,000	$2,460,000
Liabilities and Shareholders' Equity		
Liabilities:		
Current liabilities	$ 800,000	$ 430,000
Bonds payable, 12%	600,000	600,000
Total liabilities	1,400,000	1,030,000
Shareholders' equity:		
Preferred shares, 10,000, $2 no par	250,000	250,000
Common shares, 5,000 no par	500,000	500,000
Retained earnings	850,000	680,000
Total shareholders' equity	1,600,000	1,430,000
Total liabilities and equity	$3,000,000	$2,460,000

SABIN ELECTRONICS
Comparative Income Statement

	This Year	Last Year
Sales	$5,000,000	$4,350,000
Less cost of goods sold	3,875,000	3,450,000
Gross margin	1,125,000	900,000
Less operating expenses	653,000	548,000
Net operating income	472,000	352,000
Less interest expense	72,000	72,000
Net income before taxes	400,000	280,000
Less income taxes (30%)	120,000	84,000
Net income	280,000	196,000
Dividends paid:		
Preferred dividends	20,000	20,000
Common dividends	90,000	75,000
Total dividends paid	110,000	95,000
Net income retained	170,000	101,000
Retained earnings, beginning of year	680,000	579,000
Retained earnings, end of year	$ 850,000	$ 680,000

During the past year, the company introduced several new product lines and raised the selling prices on a number of old product lines in order to improve its profit margin. The company also hired a new sales manager, who has expanded sales into several new territories. Sales terms are 2/10, n/30. All sales are on account. Assume that the following ratios are typical of firms in the electronics industry:

Current ratio	2.5 to 1
Acid-test (quick) ratio	1.3 to 1
Average age of receivables	18 days
Inventory turnover in days	60 days
Debt-to-equity ratio	0.90 to 1
Times interest earned	6.0 times
Return on total assets	13%
Price-earnings ratio	12

Required

1. To assist the Gulf Credit Union in making a decision about the loan, compute the following ratios for both this year and last year:
   a. The amount of working capital.
   b. The current ratio.
   c. The acid-test (quick) ratio.
   d. The average age of receivables. (The accounts receivable at the beginning of last year totalled $250,000.)
   e. The inventory turnover in days. (The inventory at the beginning of last year totalled $500,000.)
   f. The debt-to-equity ratio.
   g. The number of times interest was earned.
2. For both this year and last year:
   a. Present the balance sheet in common-size format.
   b. Present the income statement in common-size format down through net income.
3. Comment on the results of your analysis in (1) and (2) above and make a recommendation as to whether or not the loan should be approved.

P17–11   Investor Ratios; Recommendation on Share Purchase   Refer to the financial statements and other data in P17–10. Assume that you are an account executive for a large brokerage house and that one of your clients has asked for a recommendation about the possible purchase of Sabin Electronics' shares. You are not acquainted with the shares and for this reason wish to do certain analytical work before making a recommendation.

Required

1. You decide first to assess the well-being of the common shareholders. For both this year and last year, compute:
   a. The earnings per share. There has been no change in preferred or common shares over the last two years.
   b. The dividend yield ratio for common. The company's shares are currently selling for $40 per share; last year they sold for $36 per share.
   c. The dividend payout ratio for common.
   d. The price-earnings ratio. How do investors regard Sabin Electronics as compared to other firms in the industry? Explain.
   e. The book value per share of common. Does the difference between market value and book value suggest that the shares are overpriced? Explain.
2. You decide next to assess the company's rate of return. Compute the following for both this year and last year:
   a. The return on total assets. (Total assets at the beginning of last year were $2,300,000.)
   b. The return on common equity. (Shareholders' equity at the beginning of last year was $1,329,000.)
   c. Is the company's financial leverage positive or negative? Explain.
3. Would you recommend that your client purchase shares of Sabin Electronics' shares? Explain.

P17–12 Comprehensive Problem on Ratio Analysis   You have just been hired as a loan officer at Slippery Rock Bank. Your supervisor has given you a file containing a request from Lydex Company, a manufacturer of safety helmets, for a $3,000,000, five-year loan. Financial statement data on the company for the last two years follow:

LYDEX COMPANY
Comparative Balance Sheet

	This Year	Last Year
Assets		
Current assets:		
Cash	$ 960,000	$ 1,260,000
Marketable securities	–0–	300,000
Accounts receivable, net	2,700,000	1,800,000
Inventory	3,900,000	2,400,000
Prepaid expenses	240,000	180,000
Total current assets	7,800,000	5,940,000
Plant and equipment, net	9,300,000	8,940,000
Total assets	$17,100,000	$14,880,000
Liabilities and Shareholders' Equity		
Liabilities:		
Current liabilities	$ 3,900,000	$ 2,760,000
Note payable, 10%	3,600,000	3,000,000
Total liabilities	7,500,000	5,760,000
Shareholders' equity:		
Preferred shares, 60,000, $2.40 no par	1,800,000	1,800,000
Common shares, 75,000 no par	6,000,000	6,000,000
Retained earnings	1,800,000	1,320,000
Total shareholders' equity	9,600,000	9,120,000
Total liabilities and shareholders' equity	$17,100,000	$14,880,000

LYDEX COMPANY
Comparative Income Statement

	This Year	Last Year
Sales (all on account)	$15,750,000	$12,480,000
Less cost of goods sold	12,600,000	9,900,000
Gross margin	3,150,000	2,580,000
Less operating expenses	1,590,000	1,560,000
Net operating income	1,560,000	1,020,000
Less interest expense	360,000	300,000
Net income before taxes	1,200,000	720,000
Less income taxes (30%)	360,000	216,000
Net income	840,000	504,000
Dividends paid:		
Preferred dividends	144,000	144,000
Common dividends	216,000	108,000
Total dividends paid	360,000	252,000
Net income retained	480,000	252,000
Retained earnings, beginning of year	1,320,000	1,068,000
Retained earnings, end of year	$ 1,800,000	$ 1,320,000

Helen McGuire, who just a year ago was appointed president of Lydex Company, argues that although the company has had a "spotty" record in the past, it has "turned the corner," as evidenced by a 25% jump in sales and by a greatly improved earnings picture between last year and this year. McGuire also points out that investors generally have recognized the improving situation at Lydex, as shown by the increase in market value of the company's common shares, which is currently selling for $72 per share (up from $40 per share last year). McGuire feels that with her leadership and with the modernized equipment that the $3,000,000 loan will permit the company to buy, profits will be even stronger in the future. McGuire has a reputation in the industry for being a good manager who runs a "tight" ship.

Not wanting to botch your first assignment, you decide to generate all the information that you can about the company. You determine that the following ratios are typical of firms in Lydex Company's industry:

Current ratio	2.3 to 1
Acid-test (quick) ratio	1.2 to 1
Average age of receivables	30 days
Inventory turnover	60 days
Return on assets	9.5%
Debt-to-equity ratio	0.65 to 1
Times interest earned	5.7
Price-earnings ratio	10

Required

1. You decide first to assess the rate of return that the company is generating. Compute the following for both this year and last year:
   a. The return on total assets. (Total assets at the beginning of last year were $12,960,000.)
   b. The return on common equity. (Shareholders' equity at the beginning of last year totalled $9,048,000. There has been no change in preferred or common shares over the last two years.)
   c. Is the company's financial leverage positive or negative? Explain.
2. You decide next to assess the well-being of the common shareholders. For both this year and last year, compute:
   a. The earnings per share.
   b. The dividend yield ratio for common.
   c. The dividend payout ratio for common.
   d. The price-earnings ratio. How do investors regard Lydex Company as compared to other firms in the industry? Explain.
   e. The book value per share of common. Does the difference between market value per share and book value per share suggest that the shares at their current price are a bargain? Explain.
   f. The gross margin percentage.
3. You decide, finally, to assess creditor ratios to determine both short-term and long-term debt-paying ability. For both this year and last year, compute:
   a. Working capital.
   b. The current ratio.
   c. The acid-test ratio.
   d. The average age of receivables. (The accounts receivable at the beginning of last year totalled $1,560,000.)
   e. The inventory turnover. (The inventory at the beginning of last year totalled $1,920,000.) Also compute the number of days required to turn the inventory one time (use a 365-day year).
   f. The debt-to-equity ratio.
   g. The number of times interest was earned.
4. Evaluate the data computed in (1) to (3) above, and using any additional data provided in the problem, make a recommendation to your supervisor as to whether the loan should be approved.

P17–13 Common-Size Financial Statements Refer to the financial statement data for Lydex Company given in P17–12.

Required   For both this year and last year:

1. Present the balance sheet in common-size format.
2. Present the income statement in common-size format down through net income.
3. Comment on the results of your analysis.

P17–14   Interpretation of Completed Ratios   Paul Ward is interested in the shares of Pecunious Products, Inc. Before purchasing the shares, Mr. Ward would like to learn as much as possible about the company. However, all he has to go on is the current year's (Year 3) annual report, which contains no comparative data other than the summary of ratios given below:

	Year 3	Year 2	Year 1
Sales trend	128.0	115.0	100.0
Current ratio	2.5:1	2.3:1	2.2:1
Acid-test (quick) ratio	0.8:1	0.9:1	1.1:1
Accounts receivable turnover	9.4 times	10.6 times	12.5 times
Inventory turnover	6.5 times	7.2 times	8.0 times
Dividend yield	7.1%	6.5%	5.8%
Dividend payout ratio	40%	50%	60%
Return on total assets	12.5%	11.0%	9.5%
Return on common equity	14.0%	10.0%	7.8%
Dividends paid per share*	$1.50	$1.50	$1.50

*There have been no changes in common shares outstanding over the three-year period.

Mr. Ward would like answers to a number of questions about the trend of events in Pecunious Products, Inc., over the last three years. His questions are:

a. Is it becoming easier for the company to pay its bills as they come due? *harder*
b. Are customers paying their accounts at least as fast now as they were in Year 1? *longer*
c. Is the total of the accounts receivable increasing, decreasing, or remaining constant?
d. Is the level of inventory increasing, decreasing, or remaining constant?
e. Is the market price of the company's shares going up or down?
f. Is the amount of the earnings per share increasing or decreasing?
g. Is the price-earning ratio going up or down?
h. Is the company employing financial leverage to the advantage of the common shareholders?

[handwritten notes in left margin: increase turnover is lower – Sales increase increasing – turnover lower – sales increase]

Required   Answer each of Mr. Ward's questions using the data given above. In each case, explain how you arrived at your answer.

P17–15   Effects of Transactions on Various Financial Ratios   In the right-hand column below, certain financial ratios are listed. To the left of each ratio is a business transaction or event relating to the operating activities of Delta Company.

Business Transaction or Event	Ratio
1. The company declared a cash dividend.	Current ratio
2. The company sold inventory on account at cost.	Acid-test (quick) ratio
3. The company issued bonds with an interest rate of 8%. The company's return on assets is 10%.	Return on common shareholders' equity
4. The company's net income decreased by 10% between last year and this year. Long-term debt remained unchanged.	Times interest earned
5. A previously declared cash dividend was paid.	Current ratio
6. The market price of the company's common shares dropped from 24½ to 20. The dividend paid per share remained unchanged.	Dividend payout ratio

7.	Obsolete inventory totalling $100,000 was written off as a loss.	Inventory turnover ratio
8.	The company sold inventory for cash at a profit.	Debt-to-equity ratio
9.	Changed customer credit terms from 2/10, n/30 to 2/15, n/30 to comply with a change in industry practice.	Accounts receivable turnover ratio
10.	Issued a common share dividend on common shares.	Book value per share
11.	The market price of the company's common shares increased from 24½ to 30.	Book value per share
12.	The company paid $40,000 on accounts payable.	Working capital
13.	Issued a common share dividend to common shareholders.	Earnings per share
14.	Paid accounts payable.	Debt-to-equity ratio
15.	Purchased inventory on open account.	Acid-test (quick) ratio
16.	Wrote off an uncollectible account against the Allowance for Bad Debts.	Current ratio
17.	The market price of the company's common shares increased from 24½ to 30. Earnings per share remained unchanged.	Price-earnings ratio
18.	The market price of the company's common shares increased from 24½ to 30. The dividend paid per share remained unchanged.	Dividend yield ratio

Required Indicate the effect that each business transaction or event would have on the ratio listed opposite to it. State the effect in terms of increase, decrease, or no effect on the ratio involved, and give the reason for your choice of answer. In all cases, assume that the current assets exceed the current liabilities both before and after the event or transaction. Use the following format for your answers:

Effect on Ratio	**Reason for Increase, Decrease, or No Effect**

1.

Etc.

P17–16 Comprehensive Problem   Part 1   Investor Ratios (P17–17 and P17–18 delve more deeply into the data presented below. Each problem is independent.) Empire Labs, Inc., was organized several years ago to produce and market several new "miracle drugs." The company is small but growing, and you are considering the purchase of some of its common shares as an investment. The following data on the company are available for the past two years:

EMPIRE LABS, INC.
Comparative Income Statement
For the Years Ended December 31

	This Year	Last Year
Sales	$20,000,000	$15,000,000
Less cost of goods sold	13,000,000	9,000,000
Gross margin	7,000,000	6,000,000
Less operating expenses	5,260,000	4,560,000
Net operating income	1,740,000	1,440,000
Less interest expense	240,000	240,000
Net income before taxes	1,500,000	1,200,000
Less income taxes (30%)	450,000	360,000
Net income	$ 1,050,000	$ 840,000

EMPIRE LABS, INC.
Comparative Retained Earnings Statement
For the Years Ended December 31

	This Year	Last Year
Retained earnings, January 1	$2,400,000	$1,960,000
Add net income (above)	1,050,000	840,000
Total	3,450,000	2,800,000
Deduct cash dividends paid:		
Preferred dividends	120,000	120,000
Common dividends	360,000	280,000
Total dividends paid	480,000	400,000
Retained earnings, December 31	$2,970,000	$2,400,000

EMPIRE LABS, INC.
Comparative Balance Sheet
December 31

	This Year	Last Year
Assets		
Current assets:		
Cash	$ 200,000	$ 400,000
Accounts receivable, net	1,500,000	800,000
Inventory	3,000,000	1,200,000
Prepaid expenses	100,000	100,000
Total current assets	4,800,000	2,500,000
Plant and equipment, net	5,170,000	5,400,000
Total assets	$9,970,000	$7,900,000
Liabilities and Shareholders' Equity		
Liabilities:		
Current liabilities	$2,500,000	$1,000,000
Bonds payable, 12%	2,000,000	2,000,000
Total liabilities	4,500,000	3,000,000
Shareholders' equity:		
Preferred shares, 150,000, $0.80 no par	1,500,000	1,500,000
Common shares, 200,000 no par	1,000,000	1,000,000
Retained earnings	2,970,000	2,400,000
Total shareholders' equity	5,470,000	4,900,000
Total liabilities and shareholders' equity	$9,970,000	$7,900,000

After some research, you have determined that the following ratios are typical of firms in the pharmaceutical industry:

Dividend yield ratio	3%
Dividend payout ratio	40%
Price-earnings ratio	16
Return on total assets	13.5%
Return on common equity	20%

The company's common shares are currently selling for $60 per share. Last year the shares sold for $45 per share.

There has been no change in the preferred or common shares outstanding over the last three years.

Required

1. In analyzing the company, you decide first to compute the earnings per share and related ratios. For both last year and this year, compute:
   a. The earnings per share.
   b. The dividend yield ratio.
   c. The dividend payout ratio.
   d. The price-earnings ratio.
   e. The book value per share of common.
   f. The gross margin percentage.
2. You decide next to determine the rate of return that the company is generating. For both last year and this year, compute:
   a. The return on total assets. (Total assets were $6,500,000 at the beginning of last year.)
   b. The return on common shareholders' equity. (Common shareholders' equity was $2,900,000 at the beginning of last year.)
   c. Is financial leverage positive or negative? Explain.
3. Based on your work in (1) and (2) above, do the company's common shares seem to be an attractive investment? Explain.

P17–17 Comprehensive Problem   Part 2   Creditor Ratios   Refer to the data in P17–16. Although Empire Labs, Inc., has been very profitable since it was organized several years ago, the company is beginning to experience some difficulty in paying its bills as they come due. Management has approached National Bank requesting a two-year, $500,000 loan to bolster the cash account.

National Bank has assigned you to evaluate the loan request. You have gathered the following data relating to firms in the pharmaceutical industry:

Current ratio	2.4 to 1
Acid-test (quick) ratio	1.2 to 1
Average age of receivables	16 days
Inventory turnover in days	40 days
Time interest earned	7 times
Debt-to-equity ratio	0.70 to 1

The following additional information is available on Empire Labs, Inc.:

a. All sales are on account.
b. At the beginning of last year, the accounts receivable balance was $600,000 and the inventory balance was $1,000,000.

Required

1. Compute the following amounts and ratios for both last year and this year:
   a. The working capital.
   b. The current ratio.
   c. The acid-test ratio.
   d. The accounts receivable turnover in days.
   e. The inventory turnover in days.
   f. The times interest earned.
   g. The debt-to-equity ratio.
2. Comment on the results of your analysis in (1) above.
3. Would you recommend that the loan be approved? Explain.

P17–18 Comprehensive Problem   Part 3   Common-Size Statements
Refer to the data in P17–16. The president of Empire Labs, Inc., is deeply concerned. Sales increased by $5 million from last year to this year, yet the company's net income increased by only a small amount. Also, the company's operating expenses went up this year, even though a major effort was launched during the year to cut costs.

Required

1. For both last year and this year, prepare the income statement and the balance sheet in common-size format. Round computations to one decimal place.
2. From your work in (1) above, explain to the president why the increase in profits was so small this year. Were any benefits realized from the company's cost-cutting efforts? Explain.

P17–19   Incomplete Statements; Analysis of Ratios   Incomplete financial statements for Pepper Industries follow:

PEPPER INDUSTRIES
Balance Sheet
March 31

Current assets:
Cash	$?
Accounts receivable, net	?
Inventory	?
Total current assets	?
Plant and equipment, net	?
Total assets	$?

Liabilities:
Current liabilities	$ 320,000
Bonds payable, 10%	?
Total liabilities	?

Shareholders' equity:
Common shares, 140,000 no par,$5 per share	?
Retained earnings	?
Total shareholders' equity	?
Total liabilities and shareholders' equity	$?

PEPPER INDUSTRIES
Income Statement
For the Year Ended March 31

Sales	$4,200,000
Less cost of goods sold	?
Gross margin	?
Less operating expenses	?
Net operating income	?
Less interest expense	80,000
Net income before taxes	?
Less income taxes (30%)	?
Net income	$?

The following additional information is available about the company:

a.   All sales during the year were on account.

b.   There was no change in the number of common shares outstanding during the year. The common shares have a stated value of $5 each.

c.   The interest expense on the income statement relates to the bonds payable; the amount of bonds outstanding did not change during the year.

d.   Selected balances at the *beginning* of the current fiscal year were:

Accounts receivable	$ 270,000
Inventory	360,000
Total assets	1,800,000

e.   Selected financial ratios computed from the statements above for the current year are:

Earnings per share	$2.30
Debt-to-equity ratio	0.875 to 1
Accounts receivable turnover	14.0 times
Current ratio	2.75 to 1
Return on total assets	18.0%
Times interest earned	6.75 times
Acid-test (quick) ratio	1.25 to 1
Inventory turnover	6.5 times

Required   Compute the missing amounts on the company's financial statements. (Hint: What's the difference between the acid-test ratio and the current ratio?)

P17–20   Ethics and the Manager   Venice InLine, Inc., was founded by Russ Perez to produce a specialized in-line skate he had designed for doing aerial tricks. Up to this point, Russ has financed the company from his own savings and from retained profits. However, Russ now faces a cash crisis. In the year just ended, an acute shortage of high-impact roller bearings had developed just as the company was beginning production for the Christmas season. Russ had been assured by the suppliers that the roller bearings would be delivered in time to make Christmas shipments, but the suppliers had been unable to fully deliver on this promise. As a consequence, Venice InLine had large inventories of unfinished skates at the end of the year and had been unable to fill all of the orders that had come in from retailers for the Christmas season. Consequently, sales were below expectations for the year, and Russ does not have enough cash to pay his creditors.

Well before the accounts payable were to become due, Russ visited a local bank and inquired about obtaining a loan. The loan officer at the bank assured Russ that there should not be any problem getting a loan to pay off his accounts payable—providing that on his most recent financial statements the current ratio was above 2.0, the acid-test ratio was above 1.0, and net operating income was at least four times the interest on the proposed loan. Russ promised to return later with a copy of his financial statements.

Russ would like to apply for an $80,000 six-month loan bearing an interest rate of 10% per year.

The unaudited financial reports of the company appear below:

VENICE INLINE, INC.
Comparative Balance Sheet
As of December 31
(dollars in thousands)

	This Year	Last Year
Assets		
Current assets:		
Cash	$ 70	$150
Accounts receivable, net	50	40
Inventory	160	100
Prepaid expenses	10	12
Total current assets	290	302
Property and equipment	270	180
Total assets	$560	$482
Liabilities and Shareholders' Equity		
Current liabilities:		
Accounts payable	$154	$ 90
Accrued payables	10	10
Total current liabilities	164	100
Long-term liabilities	—	—
Total liabilities	164	100
Shareholders' equity:		
Common shares	100	100
Retained earnings	296	282
Total shareholders' equity	396	382
Total liabilities and shareholders' equity	$560	$482

VENICE INLINE, INC.
Income Statement
For the Year Ended December 31
(dollars in thousands)

	This Year
Sales (all on account)	$420
Cost of goods sold	290
Gross margin	130
Operating expenses:	
Selling expenses	42
Administrative expenses	68
Total operating expenses	110
Net operating income	20
Interest expense	—
Net income before taxes	20
Less income taxes (30%)	6
Net income	$ 14

Required

1. Based on the above unaudited financial statements and the statement made by the loan officer, would the company qualify for the loan?
2. Last year Russ purchased and installed new, more efficient equipment to replace an older plastic injection molding machine. Russ had originally planned to sell the old machine but found that it is still needed whenever the plastic injection molding process is a bottleneck. When Russ discussed his cash flow problems with his brother-in-law, he suggested to Russ that the old machine be sold or at least reclassified as inventory on the balance sheet since it could be readily sold. At present, the machine is carried in the Property and Equipment account and could be sold for its net book value of $45,000. The bank does not require audited financial statements. What advice would you give to Russ concerning the machine?

P17–21   Effect of Leverage on the Return on Common Equity   Several investors are in the process of organizing a new company. The investors believe that $1,000,000 will be needed to finance the new company's operations, and they are considering three methods of raising this amount of money.

Method A: All $1,000,000 can be obtained through issue of common shares.
Method B: $500,000 can be obtained through issue of common shares and the other $500,000 can be obtained through issue of $8 (8% × $100) no par preferred shares.
Method C: $500,000 can be obtained through issue of common shares, and the other $500,000 can be obtained through issue of bonds carrying an interest rate of 8%.

The investors organizing the new company are confident that it can earn $170,000 each year before interest and taxes. The tax rate will be 30%.

Required

1. Assuming that the investors are correct in their earnings estimate, compute the net income that would go to the common shareholders under each of the three financing methods listed above.
2. Using the income data computed in (1) above, compute the return on common equity under each of the three methods.
3. Why do methods B and C provide a greater return on common equity than does method A? Why does method C provide a greater return on common equity than method B?

P17–22   Forecast Financial Statements: Computer Spreadsheet   Koberg
Company has just prepared the comparative annual financial statements for 2000 given below:

KOBERG COMPANY
Income Statement
For the Years Ended
December 31, 2000, 1999

	2000	1999
Sales revenue	$100,000	$95,000
Cost of goods sold		46,000
Gross margin		49,000
Expenses (including $3,000 interest expense each year)		33,000
Pretax income		16,000
Income tax on operations (22%)		3,520
Net income		$12,480

KOBERG COMPANY
Balance Sheet
At December 31, 2000, 1999

	2000	1999
Assets		
Cash		$20,000
Accounts receivable (net)		30,000
Inventory		40,000
Capital assets (net)		100,000
Total assets		$190,000
Liabilities		
Accounts payable		$50,000
Income tax payable		1,000
Note payable, long-term		25,000
Shareholders' Equity		
Capital stock		80,000
Retained earnings		34,000
Total liabilities and shareholders' equity		$190,000

Additional information: Depreciation expense was $20,000 in 2000; no long-term notes payable were paid during 2000; $1,500 of income tax was unpaid at the end of 2000; $12,000 was paid in dividends during 2000; $10,000 was spent for additions to capital assets during 2000; $46,000 was in inventory, January 1, 1999.

Required   Using a computer spreadsheet, prepare forecasts of the 2000 income statement, Statement of Cash Flows, and December 31, 2000 balance sheet. (Hint: Use 1999 turnovers as estimates for 2000.)

P17–23 Productivity Analysis   Corel Construction wants to assess whether it should invest in equipment so that it can save on labour and material costs associated with its construction of custom built executive houses. To provide the basis for comparison, Corel analyzed a recent house that it built in terms of options it has under construction.

	Existing	Proposed
Contract price	$350,000	$350,000
Input quantities/costs		
Material	$140,000	$120,000
Labour hours	6,000	4,500
Labour rate	$18/hr	$20/hr
Overhead	$80,000	$110,000

Hourly wage rates include all employee benefit. Overhead costs increased because of the use of new computer analysis and inventory procedures and new mechanized equipment.

Required   1. How much gain occurs from the new overhead?
2. What is the value added per dollar of input cost? Comment.

Group Exercises

GE17–24 What Information Do the Experts Use?   Who better to consult than the experienced professionals whose job it is to ferret out information about a company's value or creditworthiness?

Required   1. Have students volunteer to contact an experienced securities analyst from a local brokerage firm and a credit analyst from a local financial institution and invite them to speak to the class about what sources of information they use and how they use that information in making informed decisions about companies. It would be helpful if the class prepared a set of questions far enough in advance of their scheduled presentation that the guest speakers had time to think about the questions and prepare any relevant materials.
2. Capital markets appear to adjust very rapidly to new information about a company, an industry, or general economic conditions—both domestic and international. For this to happen, there must be nearly continuous communication and exchange of information between financial analysts, companies, and investors/credit grantors. Ask the guest analysts to explain this information exchange process and the flow of information between the different groups.
3. As sophisticated as this information system is, sometimes professional analysts and investors get "fooled." How does this happen? What can be done to minimize this problem?

GE17–25 Has GE Conquered the Business Cycle?   *The Wall Street Journal* alleges that General Electric, the industrial and financial-services conglomerate, manages its earnings to smooth out the high earnings years and to fill in the low earnings years. The end result of this smoothing is that the company is able to report steady earnings growth year after year.

   Practitioners of earnings management can use a variety of manoeuvres to show a steady upward trend in earnings. These manoeuvres include timing gains and losses to smooth out earnings and timing the acquisitions of other companies so as to use their earnings to cover blips in the acquiring company's own earnings. Source: Randall Smith, Steven Lipin, and Amal Kumar Naj, "How General Electric Damps Fluctuations in Its Annual Earnings," *The Wall Street Journal,* November 3, 1994, pp. A1, A11.

Required
1. Why would companies "manage earnings"?
2. Are there any risks of having business decisions (e.g., the acquisition of another business) influenced by the decision's impact on the reported profits of the company?
3. Do you see any ethical issues involved in managing earnings? Explain.
4. How would investors and financial analysts view the financial statements of companies that are known to manage earnings?

GE17–26 Striving for Quality on the Earnings Statement How successful a company has been over a period of time usually involves some assessment of the firm's earnings. When evaluating profits, investors should consider the quality and sources of the company's earnings as well as their amount. In other words, the source of earnings is as important a consideration as the size of earnings.

For this series of questions, students will need the financial statements of a firm. The financial statements of BCE Inc., Paragon Entertainment, Alcan, Seagram Co. Ltd., Royal Bank of Canada, George Weston Ltd., and Canadian Airlines are just a few that might prove helpful for answering the following questions:

Required
1. What products or services is this business selling? With this in mind, discuss the differences between operating profits and the bottom line—profits after all revenues and expenses.
2. Do you think a dollar of earnings coming from operations is any more or less valuable than a dollar of earnings generated from some other source below operating profits (e.g., one-time gains from selling assets or one-time write-offs for charges related to closing a plant)? Explain.

IE17–27 Comparing Financial Ratios Sears, Roebuck and Co. has its web home page at www.sears.com. The company's recent annual reports can be accessed from this web site.

Required
1. Compute the following financial ratios for Sears for the two most recent years and indicate whether each ratio has improved or deteriorated.
   a. Return on total assets.
   b. Current ratio.
   c. Acid-test (quick) ratio.
   d. Inventory turnover.
   e. Average sale period.
   f. Times interest earned.
   g. Debt-to-equity ratio.
2. Based on your analysis above, can you conclude anything about the performance of Sears over the past year?

Appendix A

Pricing Products and Services

Learning Objectives

After studying this appendix, you should be able to:

1. Compute the profit-maximizing price of a product or service using the price elasticity of demand and variable cost.
2. Compute the selling price of a product using the absorption costing approach.
3. Compute the markup percentage under the absorption costing approach.
4. Compute the target cost for a new product or service.
5. Compute and use the billing rates used in time and material pricing.

Introduction

Markup The difference between the selling price of a product or service and its cost. The markup is usually expressed as a percentage of cost.

Cost-plus pricing A pricing method in which a predetermined markup is applied to a cost base to determine the target selling price.

Some businesses have no pricing problems. They make a product that is in competition with other, identical products for which a market price already exists. Customers will not pay more than this price, and there is no reason for any company to charge less. Under these circumstances, the company simply charges the prevailing market price. Markets for basic raw materials such as farm products and minerals follow this pattern.

In this appendix, we are concerned with the more common situation in which a company is faced with the problem of setting its own prices. Clearly, the pricing decision can be critical. If the price is set too high, customers will avoid purchasing the company's products. If the price is set too low, the company's costs may not be covered.

The usual approach in pricing is to *mark up* cost.[1] A product's **markup** is the difference between its selling price and its cost. The markup is usually expressed as a percentage of cost. This approach is called **cost-plus pricing** because the predetermined markup percentage is applied to the cost base to determine a target selling price.

> Selling price = Cost + (Markup percentage × Cost)

For example, if a company uses a markup of 50%, it adds 50% to the costs of its products to determine the selling price. If a product costs $10, then it would charge $15 for the product.

---

1. There are some legal restrictions on prices. Competition laws prohibit "predatory" prices, which are generally interpreted by the courts to mean a price below average variable cost. "Price discrimination"— charging different prices to customers in the same market for the same product or service—is also prohibited by the law.

There are two key issues when the cost-plus approach to pricing is used. First, what cost should be used? Second, how should the markup be determined? Several alternative approaches are considered in this appendix, starting with the approach generally favoured by economists.

The Economists' Approach to Pricing

Objective 1

Compute the profit-maximizing price of a product or service using the price elasticity of demand and variable cost.

Price elasticity of demand A measure of the degree to which the volume of unit sales for a product or service is affected by a change in price.

If a company raises the price of a product, unit sales ordinarily fall. Because of this, pricing is a delicate balancing act in which the benefits of higher revenues per unit are traded off against the lower volume that results from charging higher prices. The sensitivity of unit sales to changes in price is called the *price elasticity of demand*.

Elasticity of Demand

A product's price elasticity should be a key element in setting its price. The **price elasticity of demand** measures the degree to which the volume of unit sales for a product or service is affected by a change in price. Demand for a product is said to be *inelastic* if a change in price has little effect on the number of units sold. The demand for designer perfumes sold by trained personnel at cosmetic counters in department stores is relatively inelastic. Lowering prices on these luxury goods has little effect on sales volume; factors other than price are more important in generating sales. On the other hand, demand for a product is said to be *elastic* if a change in price has a substantial effect on the volume of units sold. An example of a product whose demand is elastic is gasoline. If a gas station raises its price for gasoline, there will usually be a substantial drop in volume as customers seek lower prices elsewhere.

Price elasticity is very important in determining prices. Managers should set higher markups over cost when customers are relatively insensitive to price (i.e., demand is inelastic) and lower markups when customers are relatively sensitive to price (i.e., demand is elastic). This principle is followed in department stores. Merchandise sold in the bargain basement has a much lower markup than merchandise sold elsewhere in the store because customers who shop in the bargain basement are much more sensitive to price (i.e., demand is elastic).

The price elasticity of demand for a product or service, ϵ_d, can be estimated using the following formula.[2,3]

$$\epsilon_d = \frac{\ln(1 + \% \text{ change in quantity sold})}{\ln(1 + \% \text{ change in price})}$$

For example, suppose that the managers of Nature's Garden believe that every 10% increase in the selling price of their apple-almond shampoo would result in a 15% decrease in the number of bottles of shampoo sold.[4] The price elasticity of demand for this product would be computed as follows:

$$\epsilon_d = \frac{\ln(1 + (-0.15))}{\ln(1 + (0.10))} = \frac{\ln(0.85)}{\ln(1.10)} = -1.71$$

---

2. The term "ln( )" is the natural log function. You can compute the natural log of any number using the LN or ln$x$ key on your calculator. For example, $\ln(0.85) = -0.1625$.
3. This formula assumes that the price elasticity of demand is constant. This occurs when the relation between the selling price, p, and the unit sales, q, can be expressed in the following form: $\ln(q) = a + \epsilon_d \ln(p)$. Even if this is not precisely true, the formula provides a useful way to estimate a product's real price elasticity.
4. The estimated change in unit sales should take into account competitors' responses to a price change.

For comparison purposes, the managers of Nature's Garden believe that another product, strawberry glycerin soap, would experience a 20% drop in unit sales if its price were increased by 10%. (Purchasers of this product are more sensitive to price than the purchasers of the apple-almond shampoo.) The price elasticity of demand for the strawberry glycerin soap is:

$$\epsilon_d = \frac{\ln(1 + (-0.20))}{\ln(1 + (0.10))} = \frac{\ln(0.80)}{\ln(1.10)} = -2.34$$

Both of these products, like other normal products, have a price elasticity that is less than -1. Note also that the price elasticity of demand for the strawberry glycerin soap is larger (in absolute value) than the price elasticity of demand for the apple-almond shampoo. The more sensitive customers are to price, the larger (in absolute value) is the price elasticity of demand. In other words, a larger (in absolute value) price elasticity of demand indicates a product whose demand is more elastic.

In the next subsection, the price elasticity of demand will be used to compute the selling price that maximizes the profits of the company.

The Profit-Maximizing Price

Under certain conditions, it can be shown that the profit-maximizing price can be determined by marking up *variable cost* using the following formula:[5]

$$\text{Profit-maximizing markup on variable cost} = \left(\frac{\epsilon_d}{1 + \epsilon_d}\right) - 1$$

Using the above markup is equivalent to setting the selling price using the formula:

$$\text{Profit-maximizing price} = \left(\frac{\epsilon_d}{1 + \epsilon_d}\right) \text{Variable cost per unit}$$

The profit-maximizing prices for the two Nature's Garden products are computed below using these formulas:

	Apple-Almond Shampoo	Strawberry Glycerin Soap
Price elasticity of demand (ϵ_d)	-1.71	-2.34
Profit-maximizing markup on variable cost (a)	$\left(\frac{-1.71}{-1.71+1}\right) - 1$	$\left(\frac{-2.34}{-2.34+1}\right) - 1$
	$=2.41 - 1 = 1.41$ or 141%	$= 1.75 - 1 = 0.75$ or 75%
Variable cost per unit—given (b)	$2.00	$0.40
Markup, (a) $\times$ (b)	2.82	0.30
Profit-maximizing price	$\underline{\underline{\$4.82}}$	$\underline{\underline{\$0.70}}$

---

5. The formula assumes that (a) the price elasticity of demand is constant; (b) Total cost = Total fixed cost + Variable cost per unit $\times$ q; and (c) the price of the product has no effect on the sales or costs of any other product. The formula can be derived using calculus.

Exhibit A-1 The Optimal Markup on Variable Cost as a Function of the Sensitivity of Unit Sales to Price

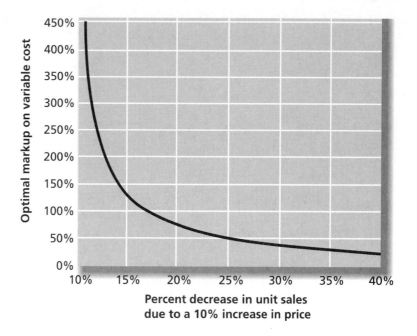

Note that the 75% markup for the strawberry glycerin soap is lower than the 141% markup for the apple-almond shampoo. The reason for this is that purchasers of strawberry glycerin soap are more sensitive to price than the purchasers of apple-almond shampoo. This could be because strawberry glycerin soap is a relatively common product with close substitutes available in nearly every grocery store.

Exhibit A–1 shows how the profit-maximizing markup is affected by how sensitive unit sales are to price. For example, if a 10% increase in price leads to a 20% decrease in unit sales, then the optimal markup on variable cost according to the exhibit is 75%—the figure computed above for the strawberry glycerin soap. Note that the optimal markup drops as unit sales become more sensitive to price.

Caution is advised when using these formulas to establish a selling price. The assumptions underlying the formulas are probably not completely true, and the estimate of the percentage change in unit sales that would result from a given percentage change in price is likely to be inexact. Nevertheless, the formulas can provide valuable clues regarding whether prices should be increased or decreased. Suppose, for example, that the strawberry glycerin soap is currently being sold for $0.60 per bar. The formula indicates that the profit-maximizing price is $0.70 per bar. Rather than increasing the price by $0.10, it would be prudent to increase the price by a more modest amount to observe what happens to unit sales and to profits.

The formula for the profit-maximizing price also conveys a very important lesson. The optimal selling price should depend on two factors—the variable cost per unit and how sensitive unit sales are to changes in price. In particular, fixed costs play no role in setting the optimal price. If the total fixed costs are the same whether the company charges $0.60 or $0.70, they cannot be relevant in the decision of which price to charge for the soap. Fixed costs are relevant when deciding whether to offer a product but are not relevant when deciding how much to charge for the product.

Incidentally, we can directly verify that an increase in selling price for the strawberry glycerin soap from the current price of $0.60 per bar is warranted, based just on the forecast that a 10% increase in selling price would lead to a 20% decrease in unit sales. Suppose, for example, that Nature's Garden is currently selling 200,000 bars of the soap per year at the price of $0.60 a bar. If the change in price has no effect on the company's fixed costs or on other products, the effect on profits of increasing the price by 10% can be computed as follows:

	Present Price	Higher Price
Selling price	$0.60	$0.60 + (0.10 × $0.60) = $0.66
Unit sales	200,000	200,000 − (0.20 × 200,000) = 160,000
Sales	$120,000	$105,600
Variable cost	80,000	64,000
Contribution margin	$ 40,000	$ 41,600

Despite the apparent optimality of prices based on marking up variable costs according to the price elasticity of demand, surveys consistently reveal that most managers approach the pricing problem from a completely different perspective.[6] They prefer to mark up some version of full, not variable, costs, and the markup is based on desired profits rather than on factors related to demand.

The Absorption Costing Approach to Cost-Plus Pricing

Objective 2

Compute the selling price of a product using the absorption costing approach.

The absorption costing approach to cost-plus pricing differs from the economists' approach both in what costs are marked up and in how the markup is determined. Under the absorption approach to cost-plus pricing, the cost base is the absorption costing unit product cost as defined in Chapters 2, 3, and 4 rather than variable cost.

Setting a Target Selling Price Using the Absorption Costing Approach

To illustrate, let us assume that the management of Ritter Company wants to set the selling price on a product that has just undergone some design modifications. The Accounting Department has provided cost estimates for the redesigned product as shown below:

	Per Unit	Total
Direct materials	$6	
Direct labour	4	
Variable manufacturing overhead	3	
Fixed manufacturing overhead	—	$70,000
Variable selling, general, and administrative expenses . . .	2	
Fixed selling, general, and administrative expenses	—	60,000

---

6. One study found that 83% of the 504 large manufacturing companies surveyed used some form of full cost (either absorption cost or absorption cost plus selling, general, and administrative expenses) as a basis for pricing. The remaining 17% used only variable costs as a basis for pricing decisions. See V. Govindarajan and Robert N. Anthony, "How Firms Use Cost Data in Pricing Decisions," *Management Accounting* (July 1983), pp. 30–36. A more recent, but less extensive, survey by Eunsup Shim and Ephraim F. Sudit, "How Manufacturers Price Products," *Management Accounting* (February 1995), pp. 37–39, found similar results.

On the other hand, a survey of small-company executives summarized in *Inc.* (November 1996), p. 84, revealed that only 41% set prices based on cost. The others charge what they think customers are willing to pay or what the market demands.

Exhibit A–2
Price Quotation
Sheet—Absorption Basis
(10,000 Units)

Direct materials	$ 6
Direct labour	4
Variable manufacturing overhead	3
Fixed manufacturing overhead (based on 10,000 units)	7
Unit product cost	20
Markup to cover selling, general, and administrative expenses and desired profit—50% of unit manufacturing cost	10
Target selling price	$30

The first step in the absorption costing approach to cost-plus pricing is to compute the unit product cost. For Ritter Company, this amounts to $20 per unit at a volume of 10,000 units, as computed below:

Direct materials	$ 6
Direct labour	4
Variable manufacturing overhead	3
Fixed manufacturing overhead ($70,000 ÷ 10,000 units)	7
Unit product cost	$20

Ritter Company has a general policy of marking up unit product costs by 50%. A price quotation sheet for the company prepared using the absorption approach is presented in Exhibit A-2. Note that selling, general, and administrative (SG&A) costs are not included in the cost base. Instead, the markup is supposed to cover these expenses. Let us see how some companies compute these markup percentages.

Determining the Markup Percentage

Objective 3

Compute the markup percentage under the absorption costing approach.

How did Ritter Company arrive at its markup percentage of 50%? This figure could be a widely used rule of thumb in the industry or just a company tradition that seems to work. The markup percentage may also be the result of an explicit computation. As we have discussed, the markup over cost ideally should be largely determined by market conditions. However, a popular approach is to at least start with a markup based on cost and desired profit. The reasoning goes like this. The markup must be large enough to cover SG&A expenses and provide an adequate return on investment (ROI). Given the forecasted unit sales, the markup can be computed as follows:

$$\text{Markup percentage on absorption cost} = \frac{\left(\begin{array}{c}\text{Required ROI}\\ \times \text{ Investment}\end{array}\right) + \text{SG\&A expenses}}{\text{Unit sales} \times \text{Unit product cost}}$$

To show how the formula above is applied, assume Ritter Company must invest $100,000 to produce and market 10,000 units of the product each year. The $100,000 investment covers purchase of equipment and funds needed to carry inventories and accounts receivable. If Ritter Company requires a 20% ROI, then the markup for the product would be determined as follows:

$$\text{Markup percentage on absorption cost} = \frac{(20\% \times \$100,000) + (\$2 \times 10,000 + \$60,000)}{10,000 \times \$20}$$

$$\text{Markup percentage on absorption cost} = \frac{(\$20,000) + (\$80,000)}{\$200,000} = 50\%$$

Exhibit A–3 Income
Statement and ROI
Analysis—Ritter Company
Actual Unit Sales
= 10,000 Units; Selling
Price = $30

Direct materials	$ 6
Direct labour	4
Variable manufacturing overhead	3
Fixed manufacturing overhead ($70,000 ÷ 10,000 units)	7
Unit product cost	$20

RITTER COMPANY
Absorption Costing Income Statement

Sales ($30 × 10,000 units)	$300,000
Less cost of goods sold ($20 × 10,000 units)	200,000
Gross margin	100,000
Less selling, general, and administration expenses ($2 × 10,000 units +$60,000)	80,000
Net operating income	$ 20,000

ROI

$$ROI = \frac{Net\ operating\ income}{Average\ operating\ assets}$$

$$= \frac{\$20,000}{\$100,000}$$

$$= 20\%$$

As shown earlier, this markup of 50% leads to a target selling price of $30 for Ritter Company. As shown in Exhibit A–3, *if the company actually sells 10,000 units* of the product at this price, the company's ROI on this product will indeed be 20%. If it turns out that more than 10,000 units are sold at this price, the ROI will be greater than 20%. If less than 10,000 units are sold, the ROI will be less than 20%. *The required ROI will be attained only if the forecasted unit sales volume is attained.*

Problems with the Absorption Costing Approach

Using the absorption costing approach, the pricing problem looks deceptively simple. All you have to do is compute your unit product cost, decide how much profit you want, and then set your price. It appears that you can ignore demand and arrive at a price that will safely yield whatever profit you want. However, as noted above, the absorption costing approach relies on a forecast of unit sales. Neither the markup nor the unit product cost can be computed without such a forecast.

The absorption costing approach essentially assumes that customers *need* the forecasted unit sales and will pay whatever price the company decides to charge. However, customers have a choice. If the price is too high, they can buy from a competitor or they may choose not to buy at all. Suppose, for example, that when Ritter Company sets its price at $30, it sells only 7,000 units rather than the 10,000 units forecasted. As shown in Exhibit A–4, the company would then have a loss of $25,000 on the product instead of a profit of $20,000.[7] Some managers believe that the absorption

---

7. When there is only one product and it is inherently profitable, it is always possible to at least break even using the absorption costing approach. This is not true when there is more than one product and the company has common fixed costs. It may be *impossible* to break even using an absorption costing approach when there is more than one product—even when it would be possible to make substantial profits using the economists' approach to pricing. For details, see Eric Noreen and David Burgstahler, "Full Cost Pricing and the Illusion of Satisficing," *Journal of Management Accounting Research* 9 (1997).

Exhibit A–4 Income Statement and ROI Analysis—Ritter Company Actual Unit Sales = 7,000 Units; Selling Price = $30

Direct materials	$ 6
Direct labour	4
Variable manufacturing overhead	3
Fixed manufacturing overhead ($70,000 ÷ 7,000 units)	10
Unit product cost	$23

RITTER COMPANY
Absorption Costing Income Statement

Sales ($30 × 7,000 units)	$210,000
Less cost of goods sold ($23 × 7,000 units)	161,000
Gross margin	49,000
Less selling, general, and administration expenses ($2 × 7,000 units + $60,000)	74,000
Net operating income	$ (25,000)

ROI

$$\text{ROI} = \frac{\text{Net operating income}}{\text{Average operating assets}}$$

$$= \frac{-\$25,000}{\$100,000}$$

$$= -25\%$$

costing approach to pricing is safe. This is an illusion. The absorption costing approach is safe only as long as customers choose to buy at least as many units as managers forecasted they would buy.

Focus on Current Practice

Rather than focusing on costs—which can be dangerous if forecasted unit volume does not materialize—many managers focus on customer value when making pricing decisions.

The ticket-services manager of a North American Opera Company, Jimmy Hanson, faced a difficult decision. After a financially unsuccessful season, he knew he had to do something about the opera company's pricing policy. Friday and Saturday performances were routinely sold out, and demand for the best seats far exceeded supply. Meanwhile, tickets for midweek performances were often left unsold. "Hanson also knew that not all seats were equal, even in the sought-after orchestra section. So the ticket manager and his staff sat in every one of the opera house's 2,200 seats and gave each a value according to the view and the acoustics. . . . In the end, the opera raised prices for its most coveted seats by as much as 50% but also dropped the prices of some 600 seats. The gamble paid off in a 9% revenue increase during the next season."[8] ■

Target Costing

Objective 4

Compute the target cost for a new product or service.

Our discussion thus far has presumed that a product has already been developed, has been costed, and is ready to be marketed as soon as a price is set. In many cases, the sequence of events is just the reverse. That is, the company will already *know* what

---

8. Susan Greco, "Are Your Prices Right?" *Inc.* (January 1997), p. 88.

price should be charged, and the problem will be to *develop* a product that can be marketed profitably at the desired price. Even in this situation, where the normal sequence of events is reversed, cost is still a crucial factor. The company's approach will be to employ *target costing*. **Target costing** is the process of determining the maximum allowable cost for a new product and then developing a prototype that can be profitably made for that maximum target cost figure. Many companies use target costing, including Compaq, Culp, DaimlerChrysler, Ford, ITT Automotive, NEC, Nissan, Sharp, Texas Instruments, and Toyota.

Target costing The process of determining the maximum allowable cost for a new product and then developing a prototype that can be profitably manufactured and distributed for that maximum target cost figure.

The target cost for a product is computed by starting with the product's anticipated selling price and then deducting the desired profit, as follows:

Target cost = Anticipated selling price − Desired profit

The product development team is given the responsibility of designing the product so that it can be made for no more than the target cost.

Focus on Current Practice

Target costing is widely used in Japan. In the automobile industry, the target cost for a new model is decomposed into target costs for each of the elements of the car—down to a target cost for each of the individual parts. The designers draft a trial blueprint, and a check is made to see if the estimated cost of the car is within reasonable distance of the target cost. If not, design changes are made, and a new trial blueprint is drawn up. This process continues until there is sufficient confidence in the design to make a prototype car according to the trial blueprint. If there is still a gap between the target cost and estimated cost, the design of the car will be further modified.

After repeating this process a number of times, the final blueprint is drawn up and turned over to the production department. In the first several months of production, the target costs will ordinarily not be achieved due to problems in getting a new model into production. However, after that initial period, target costs are compared to actual costs and discrepancies between the two are investigated with the aim of eliminating the discrepancies and achieving target costs.[9] ■

Reasons for Using Target Costing

The target costing approach was developed in recognition of two important characteristics of markets and costs. The first is that many companies have less control over price than they would like to think. The market (i.e., supply and demand) really determines prices, and a company that attempts to ignore this does so at its peril. Therefore, the anticipated market price is taken as a given in target costing. The second observation is that most of the cost of a product is determined in the design stage. Once a product has been designed and has gone into production, not much can be done to significantly reduce its cost. Most of the opportunities to reduce cost come from designing the product so that it is simple to make, uses inexpensive parts, and is robust and reliable. If the company has little control over market price and little control over cost once the prod-

---

9. Yasuhiro Monden and Kazuki Hamada, "Target Costing and Kaizen Costing in Japanese Automobile Companies," *Journal of Management Accounting Research* 3 (Fall 1991), pp. 16–34.

uct has gone into production, then it follows that the major opportunities for affecting profit come in the design stage where valuable features that customers are willing to pay for can be added and where most of the costs are really determined. So that is where the effort is concentrated—in designing and developing the product. The difference between target costing and other approaches to product development is profound. Instead of designing the product and then finding out how much it costs, the target cost is set first and then the product is designed so that the target cost is attained.

An Example of Target Costing

To provide a simple numerical example of target costing, assume the following situation: Handy Appliance Company feels that there is a market niche for a hand mixer with certain new features. Surveying the features and prices of hand mixers already on the market, the Marketing Department believes that a price of $30 would be about right for the new mixer. At that price, Marketing estimates that 40,000 of the new mixers could be sold annually. To design, develop, and produce these new mixers, an investment of $2,000,000 would be required. The company desires a 15% ROI. Given these data, the target cost to manufacture, sell, distribute, and service one mixer is $22.50 as shown below.

Projected sales (40,000 mixers × $30)	$1,200,000
Less desired profit (15% × $2,000,000)	300,000
Target cost for 40,000 mixers	$ 900,000
Target cost per mixer ($900,000 ÷ 40,000 mixers)	$22.50

This $22.50 target cost would be broken down into target costs for the various functions: manufacturing, marketing, distribution, after-sales service, and so on. Each functional area would be responsible for keeping its actual costs within target.

Service Companies—Time and Material Pricing

Time and material pricing A pricing method, often used in service firms, in which two pricing rates are established— one based on direct labour time and the other based on direct materials used.

Some companies—particularly in service industries—use a variation on cost-plus pricing called **time and material pricing.** Under this method, two pricing rates are established—one based on direct labour time and the other based on the cost of direct material used. This pricing method is widely used in repair shops, in printing shops, and by many professionals such as physicians and dentists. The time and material rates are usually market-determined. In other words, the rates are determined by the interplay of supply and demand and by competitive conditions in the industry. However, some companies set the rates using a process similar to the process followed in the absorption costing approach to cost-plus pricing. In this case, the rates include allowances for selling, general, and administrative expenses; for other direct and indirect costs; and for a desired profit. This section will show how the rates might be set using the cost-plus approach.

Time Component

The time component is typically expressed as a rate per hour of labour. The rate is computed by adding together three elements: (1) the direct costs of the employee, including salary and fringe benefits; (2) a pro rata allowance for selling, general, and administrative expenses of the organization; and (3) an allowance for a desired profit per hour of employee time. In some organizations (such as a repair shop), the same hourly rate will be charged regardless of which employee actually works on the job; in other organizations, the rate may vary by employee. For example, in a public accounting firm, the rate charged for a new assistant accountant's time will generally be less than the rate charged for an experienced senior accountant or for a partner.

Material Component

Material loading charge A markup applied to the cost of materials that is designed to cover the costs of ordering, handling, and carrying materials in inventory and to provide for some profit.

The material component is determined by adding a **material loading charge** to the invoice price of any materials used on the job. The material loading charge is designed to cover the costs of ordering, handling, and carrying materials in inventory, plus a profit margin on the materials themselves.

An Example of Time and Material Pricing

To provide a numerical example of time and material pricing, assume the following data:

The Quality Auto Shop uses time and material pricing for all of its repair work. The following costs have been budgeted for the coming year:

	Repairs	Parts
Mechanics' wages	$300,000	$ —
Service manager—salary	40,000	—
Parts manager—salary	—	36,000
Clerical assistant—salary	18,000	15,000
Retirement and insurance—		
16% of salaries and wages	57,280	8,160
Supplies	720	540
Utilities	36,000	20,800
Property taxes	8,400	1,900
Depreciation	91,600	37,600
Invoice cost of parts used	—	400,000
Total budgeted cost	$552,000	$520,000

The company expects to bill customers for 24,000 hours of repair time. A profit of $7 per hour of repair time is considered to be feasible, given the competitive conditions in the market. For parts, the competitive markup on the invoice cost of parts used is 15%.

Exhibit A–5 shows the computation of the billing rate and the material loading charge to be used over the next year. Note that the billing rate, or time component, is $30 per hour of repair time and the material loading charge is 45% of the invoice cost of parts used. Using these rates, a repair job that requires 4.5 hours of mechanics time and $200 in parts would be billed as follows:

Labour time: 4.5 hours × $30		$135
Parts used:		
Invoice cost	$200	
Material loading charge: 45% × $200	90	290
Total price of the job		$425

Rather than using labour-hours as the basis for computing the time rate, a machine shop, a printing shop, or a similar organization might use machine-hours.

This method of setting prices is a variation of the absorption costing approach. As such, it is not surprising that it suffers from the same problem. Customers may not be willing to pay the rates that have been computed. If actual business is less than the forecasted 24,000 hours and $400,000 worth of parts, the profit objectives will not be met and the company may not even break even.

Exhibit A–5 Time and Material Pricing

	Time Component: Repairs		Parts: Material Loading Charge	
	Total	Per Hour*	Total	Percent†
Cost of mechanics' time:				
Mechanics' wages	$300,000			
Retirement and insurance (16% of wages)	48,000			
Total cost	348,000	$14.50		
For repairs—other cost of repair service. For parts—costs of ordering, handling, and storing parts:				
Repairs service manager—salary	40,000		$ —	
Parts manager—salary	—		36,000	
Clerical assistant—salary	18,000		15,000	
Retirement and insurance (16% of salaries)	9,280		8,160	
Supplies	720		540	
Utilities	36,000		20,800	
Property taxes	8,400		1,900	
Depreciation	91,600		37,600	
Total cost	204,000	8.50	120,000	30%
Desired profit:				
24,000 hours × $7	168,000	7.00	—	
15% × $400,000	—		60,000	15%
Total amount to be billed	$720,000	$30.00	$180,000	45%

*Based on 24,000 hours.

†Based on $400,000 invoice cost of parts. The charge for ordering, handling, and storing parts, for example, is computed as follows:
$120,000 cost ÷ $400,000 invoice cost = 30%.

Pricing and "The Law"

Canadian legislation forbids certain forms of price discrimination. Price discrimination is illegal in Canada, however, only if different prices are charged for goods of like quality and quantity. Price fixing is also illegal in Canada. A manufacturer may suggest a list price but it cannot be mandated. According to the Federal Bureau of Competition Policy for the period covering 1985 to 1989 there were 15 companies and two individuals convicted of bid-rigging offences in Canada. In contrast to other countries, it is rare in Canada for individuals to be charged in such cases. However, it is individuals who ultimately commit these offences, and unless these individuals are held personally responsible, such criminal actions may be difficult to deter. Other illegal acts include false or misleading advertising, agreements not to bid on contracts that are not revealed to customers, and pyramid selling. Pyramid selling is the process of paying a fee to participate in selling and receiving the right to charge others for the right to sell. A recent investigation of the major oil in Canada by the federal Competition Bureau looking for evidence of pricing fixing and intimidation of retailers was in response to complaints about price changes.[10]

International restrictions relating to pricing exist in the form of the antidumping laws. These laws prohibit the sale of products below cost in international markets.

---

10. The Canadian Press, "Watch Dog Probes Oil Giants," *The Mail Star/The Chronicle-Herald,* July 23, 1999, pp. B1 and B4. Other examples include three foreign-owned companies that were fined millions for fixing prices of citric acid in Canada as noted by Alan Toulin, "Two Firms Fined Total of $6.7 M for Price-Fixing Scheme," *The Financial Post,* October 22, 1998, p. 10.

Again, cost is interpreted as full cost, including fully allocated fixed costs. Such laws are designed to protect a domestic manufacturer in its home market in those instances where it is in direct competition with a foreign supplier.

Summary

Pricing involves a delicate balancing act. Higher prices result in more revenue per unit sold but drive down unit sales. Exactly where to set prices to maximize profit is a difficult problem, but, in general, the markup over cost should be highest for those products where customers are least sensitive to price. The demand for such products is said to be price inelastic.

Managers often rely on cost-plus formulas to set target prices. In the absorption costing approach, the cost base is absorption costing unit product cost and the markup is computed to cover both nonmanufacturing costs and to provide an adequate return on investment. However, costs will not be covered and there will not be an adequate return on investment unless the unit sales forecast used in the cost-plus formula is accurate. If applying the cost-plus formula results in a price that is too high, the unit sales forecast will not be attained.

Some companies take a different approach to pricing. Instead of starting with costs and then determining prices, they start with prices and then determine allowable costs. Companies that use target costing estimate what a new product's market price is likely to be based on its anticipated features and prices of products already on the market. They subtract desired profit from the estimated market price to arrive at the product's target cost. The design and development team is then given the responsibility of ensuring that the actual cost of the new product does not exceed the target cost.

Questions

A–1   What is meant by cost-plus pricing?

A–2   What does the price elasticity of demand measure? What is meant by inelastic demand? What is meant by elastic demand?

A–3   According to the economists' approach to setting prices, the profit-maximizing price should depend on what two factors?

A–4   Which product should have a larger markup over variable cost, a product whose demand is elastic or a product whose demand is inelastic?

A–5   When the absorption costing approach to cost-plus pricing is used, what is the markup supposed to cover?

A–6   What assumption does the absorption costing approach make about how consumers react to prices?

A–7   Discuss the following statement: "Full cost can be viewed as a floor of protection. If a firm always sets its prices above full cost, it will never have to worry about operating at a loss."

A–8   What is target costing? How do target costs enter into the pricing decision?

A–9   What is time and material pricing?

Exercises

EA–1 Maria Lorenzi owns an ice cream stand that she operates during the summer months in Lake Louise. Her store caters primarily to tourists passing through town on their way to Lake Louise and Banff.

Maria is unsure of how she should price her ice cream cones and has experimented with two prices in successive weeks during the busy August season. The number of people who entered the store was roughly the same in the two weeks. During the first week, she priced the cones at $1.89 and 1,500 cones were sold. During the second week, she priced the cones at $1.49 and 2,340 cones were sold. The variable cost of a cone is $0.43 and consists solely of the costs of the ice cream and of the cone itself. The fixed expenses of the ice cream stand are $675 per week.

Required
1. Did Maria make more money selling the cones for $1.89 or for $1.49?
2. Estimate the price elasticity of demand for the ice cream cones.
3. Estimate the profit-maximizing price for ice cream cones.

EA–2 Martin Company is considering the introduction of a new product. To determine a target selling price, the company has gathered the following information:

Number of units to be produced and sold each year	14,000
Unit product cost	$ 25
Projected annual selling, general, and administrative expenses	50,000
Estimated investment required by the company	750,000
Desired return on investment (ROI)	12%

Required The company uses the absorption costing approach to cost-plus pricing.

1. Compute the markup the company will have to use to achieve the desired ROI.
2. Compute the target selling price per unit.

EA–3 Shimada Products Corporation of Japan is anxious to enter the electronic calculator market. Management believes that in order to be competitive in world markets, the electronic calculator that the company is developing cannot be priced at more than $15. Shimada requires a minimum return of 12% on all investments. An investment of $5,000,000 would be required to acquire the equipment needed to produce the 300,000 calculators that management believes can be sold each year at the $15 price.

Required Compute the target cost of one calculator.

EA–4 The Reliable TV Repair Shop had budgeted the following costs for next year:

Repair technicians:	
Wages	$120,000
Fringe benefits	30,000
Selling, administrative, and other costs of the repairs operation	
per year	90,000
Materials:	
Costs of ordering, handling, and storing parts	20% of invoice cost

In total, the company expects 10,000 hours of repair time it can bill to customers. According to competitive conditions, the company believes it should aim for a profit of $6 per hour of repair time. The competitive markup on materials is 40% of invoice cost. The company uses time and material pricing.

Required
1. Compute the time rate and the material loading charge that would be used to bill jobs.
2. One of the company's repair technicians has just completed a repair job that required 2.5 hours of time and $80 in parts (invoice cost). Compute the amount that would be billed for the job.

Problems

PA–5 Economists' Approach to Pricing The postal service of St. Vincent, an island in the West Indies, obtains a significant portion of its revenues from sales of special souvenir sheets to stamp collectors. The souvenir sheets usually contain several high-value St. Vincent stamps depicting a common theme, such as the life of the Queen. The souvenir sheets are designed and printed for the postal service by Imperial Printing, a stamp agency service company in the United Kingdom. The souvenir sheets cost the postal service $0.80 each. (The currency in St. Vincent is the East Caribbean dollar.) St. Vincent has been selling these souvenir sheets for $7.00 each and ordinarily sells about 100,000 units. To test the market, the postal service recently priced a new souvenir sheet at $8.00 and sales dropped to 85,000 units.

Required
1. Does the postal service of St. Vincent make more money selling souvenir sheets for $7.00 each or $8.00 each?
2. Estimate the price elasticity of demand for the souvenir sheets.
3. Estimate the profit-maximizing price for souvenir sheets.
4. If Imperial Printing increases the price it charges to the St. Vincent postal service for souvenir sheets to $1.00 each, how much should the St. Vincent postal service charge its customers for the souvenir sheets?

PA–6 Standard Costs; Markup Computations; Pricing Decisions
Wilderness Products, Inc., has designed a self-inflating sleeping pad for use by backpackers and campers. The following information is available about the new product:

a. An investment of $1,350,000 will be necessary to carry inventories and accounts receivable and to purchase some new equipment needed in the manufacturing process. The company requires a 24% return on investment for new products.
b. A standard cost card has been prepared for the sleeping pad, as shown below:

	Standard Quantity or Hours	Standard Price or Rate	Standard Cost
Direct materials	4.0 metres	$ 2.70 per metre	$10.80
Direct labour	2.4 hours	8.00 per hour	19.20
Manufacturing overhead ($\frac{1}{5}$ variable)	2.4 hours	12.50 per hour	30.00
Total standard cost per pad ..			$60.00

c. The only variable selling, general, and administrative expenses on the pads will be $9 per pad sales commission. Fixed selling, general, and administrative expenses will be (per year):

Salaries	$ 82,000
Warehouse rent	50,000
Advertising and other	600,000
Total	$732,000

d. Since the company manufactures many products, it is felt that no more than 38,400 hours of direct labour time per year can be devoted to production of the new sleeping pads.
e. Manufacturing overhead costs are allocated to products on the basis of direct labour-hours.

Required
1. Assume that the company uses the absorption approach to cost-plus pricing.
   a. Compute the markup that the company needs on the pads to achieve a 24% return on investment (ROI) if it sells all of the pads it can produce.
   b. Using the markup you have computed, prepare a price quotation sheet for a single sleeping pad.
   c. Assume that the company is able to sell all of the pads that it can produce. Prepare an income statement for the first year of activity and compute the company's ROI for the year on the pads.

2. After marketing the sleeping pads for several years, the company is experiencing a falloff in demand due to an economic recession. A large retail outlet will make a bulk purchase of pads if its label is sewn in and if an acceptable price can be worked out. What is the absolute minimum price that would be acceptable for this special order?

PA–7 Target Costing   National Restaurant Supply, Inc., sells restaurant equipment and supplies throughout most of North America. Management of the company is considering adding a machine that makes sorbet to its line of ice cream making machines. Management is preparing to enter into negotiations with the Swedish manufacturer of the sorbet machine concerning the price at which the machine would be sold to National Restaurant Supply.

Management of National Restaurant Supply believes the sorbet machine can be sold to its customers in Canada for $4,950. At that price, annual sales of the sorbet machine should be 100 units. If the sorbet machine is added to National Restaurant Supply's product lines, the company will have to invest $600,000 in inventories and special warehouse fixtures. The variable cost of selling the sorbet machines would be $650 per machine.

Required

1. If National Restaurant Supply requires a 15% return on investment (ROI), what is the maximum amount the company would be willing to pay the Swedish manufacturer for the sorbet machines?
2. The manager who is flying to Sweden to negotiate the purchase price of the machines would like to know how the purchase price of the machines would affect National Restaurant Supply's ROI. Construct a chart that shows National Restaurant Supply's ROI as a function of the purchase price of the sorbet machine. Put the purchase price on the X-axis and the resulting ROI on the Y-axis. Plot the ROI for purchase prices between $3,000 and $4,000 per machine.
3. After many hours of negotiations, management has concluded that the Swedish manufacturer is unwilling to sell the sorbet machine at a low enough price so that National Restaurant Supply is able to earn its 15% required ROI. Apart from simply giving up on the idea of adding the sorbet machine to National Restaurant Supply's product lines, what could management do?

PA–8 Time and Material Pricing   City Appliance, Inc., operates an appliance service business with a fleet of trucks dispatched by radio in response to calls from customers. The company's profit margin has dropped steadily over the last two years, and management is concerned that pricing rates for time and material may be out of date. According to industry trade magazines, the company should be earning $8.50 per hour of repair service time, and a profit of 10% of the invoice cost of parts used. The company maintains a large parts inventory in order to give prompt repair service to customers.

Costs associated with repair work and with the parts inventory over the past year are provided below:

	Repairs	Parts
Repair service manager—salary	$ 25,000	$ —
Parts manager—salary	—	20,000
Repair technicians—wages	180,000	—
Office assistant—salary	9,000	3,000
Depreciation—trucks and equipment	15,400	—
Depreciation—buildings and fixtures	6,000	17,500
Retirement benefits (15% of salaries and wages)	32,100	3,450
Health insurance (5% of salaries and wages)	10,700	1,150
Utilities	2,600	12,000
Truck operating costs	36,000	—
Property taxes	900	3,400
Liability and fire insurance	1,500	1,900
Supplies	800	600
Invoice cost of parts used	—	210,000
Total cost	$320,000	$273,000

During the past year, customers were billed for 20,000 hours of repair time.

Required
1. Using the data above, compute the following:
   a. The rate that would be charged per hour of repair service time using time and material pricing.
   b. The material loading charge that would be used in billing jobs. The material loading charge should be expressed as a percentage of the invoice cost of parts.
2. Assume that the company adopts the rates that you have computed in (1) above. What would be the total price charged on a repair that requires 1½ hours of service time and $108 in parts?
3. During the past year, the company billed repair service time at $20 per hour and added a material loading charge of 45% to parts. If the company adopts the rates that you have computed in (1) above, would you expect the company's profits to improve? Explain.

PA–9 Missing Data; Markup Computations: Return on Investment (ROI); Pricing   North Seas Products, Inc., has designed a new surfboard to replace its old surfboard line which it expects to work better in the surf off Nova Scotia. Because of the unique design of the new surfboard, the company anticipates that it will be able to sell all the boards that it can produce. On this basis, the following incomplete budgeted income statement for the first year of activity is available:

Sales (? boards at ? per board)	$?
Less cost of goods sold (? boards at ? per board)	1,600,000
Gross margin	?
Less selling, general, and administrative expenses	1,130,000
Net income	$?

Additional information on the new surfboard is given below:

a. An investment of $1,500,000 will be necessary to carry inventories and accounts receivable and to purchase some new equipment needed in the manufacturing process. The company requires an 18% return on investment for all products.

b. A partially completed standard cost card for the new surfboard follows:

	Standard Quantity or Hours	Standard Price or Rate	Standard Cost
Direct materials	6 board feet	$4.50 per board foot	$27
Direct labour	2 hours	? per hour	?
Manufacturing overhead	?	? per hour	?
Total standard cost per surfboard			$?

c. The company will employ 20 workers in the manufacture of the new surfboards. Each will work a 40-hour week, 50 weeks a year.

d. Other information relating to production and costs follows:

Variable manufacturing overhead cost (per board)	$ 5
Variable selling cost (per board)	10
Fixed manufacturing overhead cost (total)	600,000
Fixed selling, general, and administrative cost (total)	?
Number of boards produced and sold (per year)	?

e. Overhead costs are allocated to production on the basis of direct labour-hours.

Required
1. Complete the standard cost card for a single surfboard.
2. Assume that the company uses the absorption costing approach to cost-plus pricing.
   a. Compute the markup that the company needs on the surfboards to achieve an 18% ROI.
   b. Using the markup you have computed, prepare a price quotation sheet for a single surfboard.
   c. Assume, as stated, that the company is able to sell all of the surfboards that it can produce. Complete the income statement for the first year of activity, and then compute the company's ROI for the year.

3. Assuming that direct labour is a variable cost, how many units would the company have to sell at the price you computed in (2) above to achieve the 18% ROI? How many units would have to be sold to just break even without achieving the 18% ROI?

PA–10 Economists' Approach to Pricing; Absorption Costing Approach to Cost-Plus Pricing Software Solutions, Inc., was started by two young software engineers to market SpamBlocker, a software application they had written that screens incoming e-mail messages and eliminates unsolicited mass mailings. Sales of the software have been good at 50,000 units a month, but the company has been losing money as shown on next page:

Sales (50,000 units × $25 per unit)	$1,250,000
Variable cost (50,000 units × $6 per unit)	300,000
Contribution margin	950,000
Fixed expenses	960,000
Net operating income (loss)	$ (10,000)

The company's only variable cost is the $6 fee it pays to another company to reproduce the software on floppy diskettes, print manuals, and package the result in an attractive box for sale to consumers. Monthly fixed selling, general, and administrative expenses total $960,000

The company's marketing manager has been arguing for some time that the software is priced too high. She estimates that every 5% decrease in price will yield an 8% increase in unit sales. The marketing manager would like your help in preparing a presentation to the company's owners concerning the pricing issue.

Required

1. To help the marketing manager prepare for her presentation, she has asked you to fill in the blanks in the following table. The selling prices in the table were computed by successively decreasing the selling price by 5%. The estimated unit sales were computed by successively increasing the unit sales by 8%. For example, $23.75 is 5% less than $25.00 and 54,000 units is 8% more than 50,000 units.

Selling Price	Estimated Unit Sales	Sales	Variable Cost	Fixed Expenses	Net Operating Income
$25.00	50,000	$1,250,000	$300,000	$960,000	$(10,000)
$23.75	54,000	$1,282,500	$324,000	$960,000	$ (1,500)
$22.56	58,320	?	?	?	?
$21.43	62,986	?	?	?	?
$20.36	68,025	?	?	?	?
$19.34	73,467	?	?	?	?
$18.37	79,344	?	?	?	?
$17.45	85,692	?	?	?	?
$16.58	92,547	?	?	?	?
$15.75	99.951	?	?	?	?

2. Using the data from the table, construct a chart that shows the net operating income as a function of the selling price. Put the selling price on the X-axis and the net operating income on the Y-axis. Using the chart, determine the approximate selling price at which net operating income is maximized.

3. Compute the price elasticity of demand for the SpamBlocker software. Based on this calculation, what is the profit-maximizing price?

4. The owners have invested $400,000 in the company and feel that they should be earning at least 10% on these funds. If the absorption costing approach to pricing were used, what would be the target selling price based on the current sales of 50,000 units? What do you think would happen to the net operating income of the company if this price were charged?

5. If the owners of the company are dissatisfied with the net operating income and return on investment at the selling price you computed in (3) above, should they increase the selling price? Explain.

Group Exercises

GEA–11   What's the Relationship between Costs and Prices?   Consider two restaurants in the same general area of town. One restaurant is an up-scale dining establishment offering a wide variety of appetizers, soups, entrées, and desserts. The other restaurant is a franchise of a national fast-food chain.

1. What role do costs play in arriving at prices?
2. What are the variable and fixed costs?
3. How are prices determined at these two different establishments?
4. Are the products of both restaurants quality products?
5. What is the product at each restaurant?

Appendix B
Cost of Quality

Learning Objectives

After studying this appendix, you should be able to:

1. Identify the four types of quality costs.
2. Understand the organization, content, and uses of a quality cost report.

Introduction

Companies that develop a reputation for low-quality products generally lose market share and face declining profits. It does not do much good to have a product with a high-quality design that is made with high-quality materials if the product falls apart on the first use. One very important aspect of quality is the absence of defects. Defective products result in high warranty costs, but more importantly, they result in dissatisfied customers. People who are dissatisfied with a product are unlikely to buy the product again. They are also likely to tell others about their bad experiences. One study found that "[c]ustomers who have bad experiences tell approximately 11 people about it."[1] This is the worst possible sort of advertising. To prevent such problems, companies have been expending a great deal of effort to reduce defects. The objective is to have high *quality of conformance*.

Quality of Conformance

Objective 1

Identify the four types of quality costs.

Quality of conformance The degree to which a product or service meets or exceeds its design specifications and is free of defects or other problems that mar its appearance or degrade its performance.

A product that meets or exceeds its design specifications and is free of defects that mar its appearance or degrade its performance is said to have high **quality of conformance**. Note that if an economy car is free of defects, it can have a quality of conformance that is just as high as a defect-free luxury car. The purchasers of economy cars cannot expect their cars to be as opulently equipped as luxury cars, but they can and do expect them to be free of defects.

Preventing, detecting, and dealing with defects cause costs that are called *quality costs* or the *cost of quality*. The use of the term *quality cost* is confusing to some people. It does not refer to costs such as using a higher-grade leather to make a wallet or using 14K gold instead of gold-plating in jewellery. Instead, the term **quality cost** refers to all of the costs that are incurred to prevent defects or that are incurred as a result of defects occurring.

---

1. Christopher W. L. Hart, James L. Heskett, and W. Earl Sasser, Jr., "The Profitable Art of Service Recovery," *Harvard Business Review* (July–August 1990), p. 153.

Exhibit B–1 Typical
Quality Costs

Prevention Costs	*Internal Failure Costs*
Systems development	Net cost of scrap
Quality engineering	Net cost of spoilage
Quality training	Rework labour and overhead
Quality circles	Reinspection of reworked products
Statistical process control activities	Retesting of reworked products
Supervision of prevention activities	Downtime caused by quality problems
Quality data gathering, analysis, and reporting	Disposal of defective products
Quality improvement projects	Analysis of the cause of defects in production
Technical support provided to suppliers	Re-entering data because of keying errors
Audits of the effectiveness of the quality system	Debugging software errors
	External Failure Costs
Appraisal Costs	Cost of field servicing and handling complaints
Test and inspection of incoming materials	Warranty repairs and replacements
Test and inspection of in-process goods	Repairs and replacements beyond the warranty period
Final product testing and inspection	Product recalls
Supplies used in testing and inspection	Liability arising from defective products
Supervision of testing and inspection activities	Returns and allowances arising from quality problems
Depreciation of test equipment	Lost sales arising from a reputation for poor quality
Maintenance of test equipment	
Plant utilities in the inspection area	
Field testing and appraisal at customer site	

Quality cost Costs that are incurred to prevent defective products from falling into the hands of customers or that are incurred as a result of defective units.

Prevention costs Costs that are incurred to keep defects from occurring.

Quality circles Small groups of employees that meet on a regular basis to discuss ways of improving quality.

Statistical process control A charting technique used to monitor the quality of work being done in a workstation for the purpose of immediately correcting any problems.

Quality costs can be broken down into four broad groups. Two of these groups—known as *prevention costs* and *appraisal costs*—are incurred in an effort to keep defective products from falling into the hands of customers. The other two groups of costs—known as *internal failure costs* and *external failure costs*—are incurred because defects are produced despite efforts to prevent them. Examples of specific costs involved in each of these four groups are given in Exhibit B–1.

Several things should be noted about the quality costs shown in the exhibit. First, note that quality costs do not relate to just manufacturing; rather, they relate to all the activities in a company from initial research and development (R&D) through customer service. Second, note that the number of costs associated with quality is very large; therefore, total quality cost can be quite high unless management gives this area special attention. Finally, note how different the costs are in the four groupings. We will now look at each of these groupings more closely.

Prevention Costs

The most effective way to minimize quality costs while maintaining high-quality output is to avoid having quality problems arise in the first place. This is the purpose of **prevention costs**; such costs relate to any activity that reduces the number of defects in products or services. Companies have learned that it is much less costly to prevent a problem from ever happening than it is to find and correct the problem after it has occurred.

Note from Exhibit B–1 that prevention costs include activities relating to quality circles and statistical process control. **Quality circles** consist of small groups of employees that meet on a regular basis to discuss ways to improve the quality of output. Both management and workers are included in these circles. Quality circles are widely used and can be found in manufacturing companies, utilities, health care organizations, banks, and many other organizations.

Statistical process control is a technique that is used to detect whether a process is in or out of control. An out-of-control process results in defective units and may be caused by a miscalibrated machine or some other factor. In statistical process control, workers use charts to monitor the quality of units that pass through their workstations. Using these charts, workers can quickly spot processes that are out of control and that are creating defects. Problems can be immediately corrected and further defects prevented rather than waiting for an inspector to catch the defects later.

Note also from the list of prevention costs in Exhibit B–1 that some companies provide technical support to their suppliers as a way of preventing defects. Particularly in just-in-time (JIT) systems, such support to suppliers is vital. In a JIT system, parts are delivered from suppliers just in time and in just the correct quantity to fill customer orders. There are no stockpiles of parts. If a defective part is received from a supplier, the part cannot be used and the order for the ultimate customer cannot be filled on time. Hence, every part received from a supplier must be free of defects. Consequently, companies that use JIT often require that their suppliers use sophisticated quality control programs such as statistical process control and that their suppliers certify that they will deliver parts and materials that are free of defects.

Appraisal Costs

Appraisal costs Costs that are incurred to identify defective products before the products are shipped to customers.

Any defective parts and products should be caught as early as possible. **Appraisal costs**, which are sometimes called *inspection costs*, are incurred to identify defective products *before* the products are shipped to customers. Unfortunately, performing appraisal activities doesn't keep defects from happening again, and most managers now realize that maintaining an army of inspectors is a costly (and ineffective) approach to quality control.

Professor John K. Shank of Dartmouth College has aptly stated, "The old-style approach was to say, 'We've got great quality. We have 40 quality control inspectors in the factory.' Then somebody realized that if you need 40 inspectors, it must be a lousy factory. So now the trick is to run a factory without any quality control inspectors; each employee is his or her own quality control person."[2]

Employees in both manufacturing and service functions are increasingly being asked to be responsible for their own quality control. This approach, along with designing products to be easy to manufacture properly, allows quality to be built into products rather than relying on inspection to get the defects out.

Internal Failure Costs

Internal failure costs Costs that are incurred as a result of identifying defective products before they are shipped to customers.

Failure costs are incurred when a product fails to conform to its design specifications. Failure costs can be either internal or external. **Internal failure costs** result from identification of defects during the appraisal process. Such costs include scrap, rejected products, reworking of defective units, and downtime caused by quality problems. It is crucial that defects be discovered before a product is shipped to customers. Of course, the more effective a company's appraisal activities, the greater the chance of catching defects internally and the greater the level of internal failure costs (as compared to external failure costs). Unfortunately, appraisal activities focus on symptoms rather than on causes and they do nothing to reduce the number of defective items. However, appraisal activities do bring defects to the attention of management, which may lead to efforts to increase prevention activities so that the defects do not happen.

External Failure Costs

External failure costs Costs that are incurred when a product or service that is defective is delivered to a customer.

External failure costs result when a defective product is delivered to a customer. As shown in Exhibit B–1, external failure costs include warranty repairs and replacements, product recalls, liability arising from legal action against a company, and lost sales arising from a reputation for poor quality. Such costs can devastate profits.

---

2. Robert W. Casey, "The Changing World of the CEO," *PPM World* 24, no. 2 (1990), p. 31.

Exhibit B–2 Effect of Quality Costs on Quality of Conformance

In the past, some managers have taken the attitude, "Let's go ahead and ship everything to customers, and we'll take care of any problems under the warranty." This attitude generally results in high external failure costs, customer ill will, and declining market share and profits.

The automotive industry has had some spectacular external failure situations. One example is a recent U.S. case against Ford where it was suggested that to save $4 per unit, an ignition device was mounted in a high heat area over the engine. The heat on the device was supposed to cause vehicles to stall and in turn resulted in 15 million replacements and a $43 billion U.S. lawsuit.[3]

Distribution of Quality Costs

We stated earlier that a company's total quality cost is likely to be very high unless management gives this area special attention. Studies show that quality costs for U.S. companies range between 10% and 20% of total sales, whereas experts say that these costs should be more in the 2% to 4% range. How does a company reduce its total quality cost? The answer lies in how the quality costs are distributed. Refer to the graph in Exhibit B–2, which shows total quality costs as a function of the quality of conformance.

The graph shows that when the quality of conformance is low, total quality cost is high and that most of this cost consists of costs of internal and external failure. A low quality of conformance means that a high percentage of units are defective and hence the company must incur high failure costs. However, as a company spends more and more on prevention and appraisal, the percentage of defective units drops (the percentage of defect-free units increases). This results in lower costs of internal and external failure. Ordinarily, total quality cost drops rapidly as the quality of conformance increases. Thus, a company can reduce its total quality cost by focusing its efforts on prevention and appraisal. The cost savings from reduced defects usually swamp the costs of the additional prevention and appraisal efforts.

---

3. Associated Press, "Ford Hid Stall Defect, Lawyer Says," *The Chronicle-Herald/Mail Star,* May 19, 1999, p. B6.

The graph in Exhibit B–2 has been drawn so that the total quality cost is minimized when the quality of conformance is less than 100%. However, some experts and managers contend that the total quality cost is not minimized until the quality of conformance is 100% and there are no defects. Indeed, many companies have found that the total quality costs seem to keep dropping even when the quality of conformance approaches 100% and defect rates get as low as 1 in a million units. Others argue that eventually total quality cost increases as the quality of conformance increases. However, in most companies this does not seem to happen until the quality of conformance is very close to 100% and defect rates are very close to zero.

As a company's quality program becomes more refined and as its failure costs begin to fall, prevention activities usually become more effective than appraisal activities. Appraisal can only find defects, whereas prevention can eliminate them. The best way to prevent defects from happening is to design processes that reduce the likelihood of defects and to continually monitor processes using statistical process control methods.

Quality Cost Reports

Objective 2

Understand the organization, content, and uses of a quality cost report.

Quality cost report A report that details prevention costs, appraisal costs, and the costs of internal and external failures.

As an initial step in quality improvement programs, companies often construct a *quality cost report* that provides an estimate of the financial consequences of the company's current level of defects. A **quality cost report** details the prevention costs, appraisal costs, and costs of internal and external failures that arise from the company's current level of defective products and services. Managers are often shocked by the magnitude of these costs. A typical quality cost report is shown in Exhibit B–3.

Several things should be noted from the data in the exhibit. First, note that Ventura Company's quality costs are poorly distributed in both years, with most of the costs being traceable to either internal failure or external failure. The external failure costs are particularly high in Year 1 in comparison to other costs.

Second, note that the company increased its spending on prevention and appraisal activities in Year 2. As a result, internal failure costs go up in that year (from $2 million in Year 1 to $3 million in Year 2), but external failure costs drop sharply (from $5.15 million in Year 1 to only $2 million in Year 2). Because of the increase in appraisal activity in Year 2, more defects are being caught inside the company before they are shipped to customers. This results in more cost for scrap, rework, and so forth, but saves huge amounts in warranty repairs, warranty replacements, and other external failure costs.

Third, note that as a result of greater emphasis on prevention and appraisal, *total* quality cost has decreased in Year 2. As continued emphasis is placed on prevention and appraisal in future years, total quality cost should continue to decrease. That is, future increases in prevention and appraisal costs should be more than offset by decreases in failure costs. Moreover, appraisal costs should also decrease as more effort is placed into prevention.

Quality Cost Reports in Graphic Form

As a supplement to the quality cost report shown in Exhibit B–3, companies frequently prepare quality cost information in graphic form. Graphic presentations include pie charts, bar graphs, trend lines, and so forth. The data for Ventura Company from Exhibit B–3 are presented in bar graph form in Exhibit B–4.

The first bar graph in Exhibit B–4 is scaled in terms of dollars of quality cost, and the second is scaled in terms of quality cost as a percentage of sales. In both graphs, the data are "stacked" upward. That is, appraisal costs are stacked on top of prevention costs, internal failure costs are stacked on top of the sum of prevention costs plus appraisal costs, and so forth. The percentage figures in the second graph show that total quality cost equals 18% of sales in Year 1 and 15% of sales in Year 2, the same as reported earlier in Exhibit B–3.

Exhibit B–3   Quality Cost Report

VENTURA COMPANY
Quality Cost Report
For Years 1 and 2

	Year 2		Year 1	
	Amount	Percent*	Amount	Percent*
Prevention costs:				
Systems development	$ 400,000	0.80%	$ 270,000	0.54%
Quality training	210,000	0.42%	130,000	0.26%
Supervision of prevention activities	70,000	0.14%	40,000	0.08%
Quality improvement projects	320,000	0.64%	210,000	0.42%
Total	1,000,000	2.00%	650,000	1.30%
Appraisal costs:				
Inspection	600,000	1.20%	560,000	1.12%
Reliability testing	580,000	1.16%	420,000	0.84%
Supervision of testing and inspection	120,000	0.24%	80,000	0.16%
Depreciation of test equipment	200,000	0.40%	140,000	0.28%
Total	1,500,000	3.00%	1,200,000	2.40%
Internal failure costs:				
Net cost of scrap	900,000	1.80%	750,000	1.50%
Rework labour and overhead	1,430,000	2.86%	810,000	1.62%
Downtime due to defects in quality	170,000	0.34%	100,000	0.20%
Disposal of defective products	500,000	1.00%	340,000	0.68%
Total	3,000,000	6.00%	2,000,000	4.00%
External failure costs:				
Warranty repairs	400,000	0.80%	900,000	1.80%
Warranty replacements	870,000	1.74%	2,300,000	4.60%
Allowances	130,000	0.26%	630,000	1.26%
Cost of field servicing	600,000	1.20%	1,320,000	2.64%
Total	2,000,000	4.00%	5,150,000	10.30%
Total quality cost	$7,500,000	15.00%	$9,000,000	18.00%

*As a percentage of total sales. We assume that in each year sales totalled $50,000,000.

Data in graphic form help managers to see trends more clearly and to see the magnitude of the various costs in relation to each other. Such graphs are easily prepared using computer graphics packages.

Uses of Quality Cost Information

The information provided by a quality cost report is used by managers in several ways. First, quality cost information helps managers see the financial significance of defects. Managers usually are not aware of the magnitude of their quality costs because these costs cut across departmental lines and are not normally tracked and accumulated by the cost system. Thus, when first presented with a quality cost report, managers often are surprised by the amount of cost attributable to poor quality.

Second, quality cost information helps managers identify the relative importance of the quality problems faced by the firm. For example, the quality cost report may show that scrap is a major quality problem or that the company is incurring huge warranty costs. With this information, managers have a better idea of where to focus efforts.

Exhibit B–4 Quality Cost Reports in Graphic Form

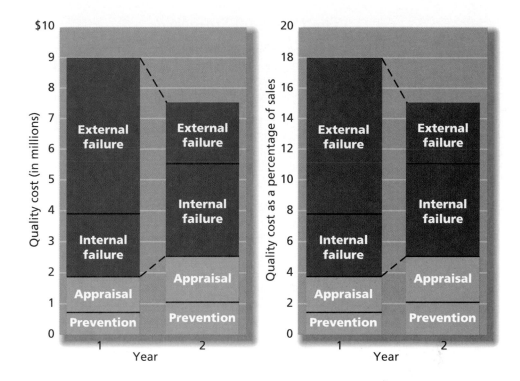

Third, quality cost information helps managers see whether their quality costs are poorly distributed. In general, quality costs should be distributed more toward prevention and appraisal activities and less toward failures.

Counterbalancing these uses, three limitations of quality cost information should be recognized. First, simply measuring and reporting quality costs does not solve quality problems. Problems can be solved only by taking action. Second, results usually lag behind quality improvement programs. Initially, total quality cost may even increase as quality control systems are designed and installed. Decreases in these costs may not begin to occur until the quality program has been in effect for a year or more. And third, the most important quality cost, lost sales arising from customer ill will, is usually omitted from the quality cost report because it is difficult to estimate.

Typically, during the initial years of a quality improvement program, the benefits of compiling a quality cost report outweigh the costs and limitations of the reports. As managers gain experience in balancing prevention and appraisal activities, the need for quality cost reports often diminishes.

International Aspects of Quality

Many of the tools used in quality management today were developed in Japan after World War II. In statistical process control, Japanese companies borrowed heavily from the work of W. Edwards Deming. However, Japanese companies are largely responsible for quality circles, JIT, the idea that quality is everyone's responsibility, and the emphasis on prevention rather than on inspection.

In the 1980s, quality re-emerged as a pivotal factor in the market. Many companies now find that it is impossible to effectively compete without a very strong quality program in place. This is particularly true of companies that wish to compete in the European market.

The ISO 9000 Standards

ISO 9000 standards
Quality control require-
ments issued by the
International Standards
Organization that relate to
products sold in European
countries.

The International Standards Organization (ISO), based in Geneva, Switzerland, has established quality control guidelines known as the **ISO 9000 standards**. Many companies and organizations in Europe will buy only from ISO 9000 standard-certified suppliers. This means that the suppliers must demonstrate to a certifying agency that:

1. A quality control system is in use, and the system clearly defines an expected level of quality.
2. The system is fully operational and is backed up with detailed documentation of quality control procedures.
3. The intended level of quality is being achieved on a sustained, consistent basis.

The key to receiving certification under the ISO 9000 standards is documentation. It is one thing for a company to say that it has a quality control system in operation, but it is quite a different thing to be able to document the steps in that system. Under ISO 9000, this documentation must be so detailed and precise that if all the employees in a company were suddenly replaced, the new employees could use the documentation to make the product exactly as it was made by the old employees. Even companies with good quality control systems find that it takes up to two years of painstaking work to develop this detailed documentation. But companies often find that compiling this documentation results in improvements in their quality systems.

The ISO 9000 standards have become an international measure of quality. Although the standards were developed to control the quality of goods sold in European countries, they have become widely accepted elsewhere as well. Companies in North America that export to Europe often expect their own suppliers to comply with the ISO 9000 standards, since these exporters must document the quality of the materials going into their products as part of their own ISO 9000 certification.

The ISO program for certification of quality management programs is not limited to manufacturing companies. The American Institute of Certified Public Accountants was the first professional membership organization in the United States to win recognition under an ISO certification program.[4]

Suggestions by business consultants are that approximately 4000 ISO registered companies in Canada can use their ISO registration for purposes of analyzing the management capabilities as well as strengthening their marketing efforts.[5]

Summary

Defects cause costs, which can be classified into prevention costs, appraisal costs, internal failure costs, and external failure costs. Prevention costs are incurred to keep defects from happening. Appraisal costs are incurred to ensure that defective products, once made, are not shipped to customers. Internal failure costs are incurred as a consequence of detecting defective products before they are shipped to customers. External failure costs are the consequences (in terms of repairs, servicing, and lost future business) of delivering defective products to customers. Most experts agree that management effort should be focused on preventing defects. Small investments in prevention can lead to dramatic reductions in appraisal costs and costs of internal and external failure.

Quality costs are summarized on a quality cost report. This report shows the type of quality costs being incurred and their significance and trends. The report helps managers understand the importance of quality costs, spot problem areas, and assess the way in which the quality costs are distributed.

---

4. *The CPA Letter* (May 1998), p.1.
5. Victor Kellner, "Marketing with ISO 9000—More Than Meets the Eye," *KPMG Business Advisor* (Spring 1998).

Questions

B–1   Costs associated with the quality of conformance can be broken down into four broad groups. What are these four groups and how do they differ?

B–2   In their efforts to reduce the total cost of quality, should companies generally focus on decreasing prevention costs and appraisal costs?

B–3   What is probably the most effective way to reduce a company's total quality costs?

B–4   What are the main uses of quality cost reports?

B–5   Why are managers often unaware of the magnitude of quality costs?

Exercises

EB–1   Listed below are a number of costs that are incurred in connection with a company's quality control system.

a. Product testing.
b. Product recalls.
c. Rework labour and overhead.
d. Quality circles.
e. Downtime caused by defects.
f. Cost of field servicing.
g. Inspection of goods.
h. Quality engineering.
i. Warranty repairs.
j. Statistical process control.
k. Net cost of scrap.
l. Depreciation of test equipment.
m. Returns and allowances arising from poor quality.
n. Disposal of defective products.
o. Technical support to suppliers.
p. Systems development.
q. Warranty replacements.
r. Field testing at customer site.
s. Product design.

Required
1. Classify each of the costs above into one of the following categories: prevention cost, appraisal cost, internal failure cost, or external failure cost.
2. Which of the costs in (1) above are incurred in an effort to keep poor quality of conformance from occurring? Which of the costs in (1) above are incurred because poor quality of conformance has occurred?

EB–2   Listed below are a number of terms relating to quality management:

Appraisal costs	Quality circles
Quality cost report	Prevention costs
Quality of conformance	External failure costs
Internal failure costs	Quality costs

Required   Choose the term or terms that most appropriately complete the following statements. The terms can be used more than once. (A fill-in blank can hold more than one word.)

1. A product that has a high rate of defects is said to have a low _____.
2. All of the costs associated with preventing and dealing with defects once they occur are known as _____.
3. In many companies, small groups of employees, known as _____, meet on a regular basis to discuss ways to improve quality.
4. A company incurs _____ and _____ in an effort to keep defects from occurring.
5. A company incurs _____ and _____ because defects have occurred.
6. Of the four groups of costs associated with quality of conformance, _____ are generally the most damaging to a company.
7. Inspection, testing, and other costs incurred to keep defective products from being shipped to customers are known as _____.

8. _____ are incurred in an effort to eliminate poor product design, defective manufacturing practices, and the providing of substandard service.

9. The costs relating to defects, rejected products, and downtime caused by quality problems are known as _____.

10. When a product that is defective in some way is delivered to a customer, _____ are incurred.

11. Over time a company's total quality costs should decrease if it redistributes its quality costs by placing its greatest emphasis on _____ and _____.

12. One way to ensure that management is aware of the costs associated with quality is to summarize such costs on a _____.

Problems

PB-3 Quality Cost Report   In response to intensive foreign competition, the management of Florex Company has attempted over the past year to improve the quality of its products. A statistical process control system has been installed and other steps have been taken to decrease the amount of warranty and other field costs, which have been trending upward over the past several years. Costs relating to quality and quality control over the last two years are given below:

	This Year	Last Year
Inspection	$ 900,000	$ 750,000
Quality engineering	570,000	420,000
Depreciation of test equipment ...	240,000	210,000
Rework labour	1,500,000	1,050,000
Statistical process control	180,000	—
Cost of field servicing	900,000	1,200,000
Supplies used in testing	60,000	30,000
Systems development	750,000	480,000
Warranty repairs	1,050,000	3,600,000
Net cost of scrap	1,125,000	630,000
Product testing	1,200,000	810,000
Product recalls	750,000	2,100,000
Disposal of defective products ...	975,000	720,000

Sales have been flat over the past few years, at $75,000,000 per year. A great deal of money has been spent in the effort to upgrade quality, and management is anxious to see whether or not the effort has been effective.

Required

1. Prepare a quality cost report that contains data for both this year and last year. Carry percentage computations to two decimal places.

2. Prepare a bar graph showing the distribution of the various quality costs by category.

3. Prepare a written evaluation to accompany the reports you have prepared in (1) and (2) above. This evaluation should discuss the distribution of quality costs in the company, changes in this distribution that you see taking place, the reasons for changes in costs in the various categories, and any other information that would be of value to management.

PB-4   Quality Cost Report   "Maybe the emphasis we've placed on upgrading our quality control system will pay off in the long run, but it doesn't seem to be helping us much right now," said Renee Penretti, president of Halogen Products. "I thought improved quality would give a real boost to sales, but sales have remained flat at $50,000,000 for the last two years."

Halogen Products has seen its market share decline in recent years due to increased foreign competition. An intensive effort to strengthen the quality control system was initiated at the beginning of the current year in the hope that better quality would strengthen the company's competitive position and also reduce warranty and servicing costs. Costs relating to quality and quality control over the last two years are given below:

	This Year	Last Year
Product testing	$ 800,000	$ 490,000
Rework labour	1,000,000	700,000
Systems development	530,000	320,000
Warranty repairs	700,000	2,100,000
Net cost of scrap	620,000	430,000
Supplies used in testing	30,000	20,000
Field servicing	600,000	900,000
Quality engineering	400,000	280,000
Warranty replacements	90,000	300,000
Inspection	600,000	380,000
Product recalls	410,000	1,700,000
Statistical process control	370,000	—
Disposal of defective products ...	380,000	270,000
Depreciation of testing equipment .	170,000	110,000

Required

1. Prepare a quality cost report that contains data for both years. Carry percentage computations to two decimal places.
2. Prepare a bar graph showing the distribution of the various quality costs by category.
3. Prepare a written evaluation to accompany the reports you have prepared in (1) and (2) above. This evaluation should discuss the distribution of quality costs in the company, changes in this distribution that you detect have taken place over the last year, and any other information you believe would be useful to management.

PB–5 Analyzing a Quality Cost Report   Mercury, Inc., produces pagers at its plant in Ottawa. In recent years, the company's market share has been eroded by stiff competition from overseas competitors. Price and product quality are the two key areas in which companies compete in this market.

A year ago, the company's pagers had been ranked low in product quality in a consumer survey. Shocked by this result. Jorge Gomez, Mercury's president, initiated a crash effort to improve product quality. Gomez set up a task force to implement a formal quality improvement program. Included on this task force were representatives from the Engineering, Marketing, Customer Service, Production, and Accounting departments. The broad representation was needed because Gomez believed that this was a companywide program and that all employees should share the responsibility for its success.

After the first meeting of the task force, Holly Elsoe, manager of the Marketing Department, asked John Tran, production manager, what he thought of the proposed program. Tran replied, "I have reservations. Quality is too abstract to be attaching costs to it and then to be holding you and me responsible for cost improvements. I like to work with goals that I can see and count! I'm nervous about having my annual bonus based on a decrease in quality costs; there are too many variables that we have no control over."

Mercury's quality improvement program has now been in operation for one year. The company's most recent quality cost report is shown below.

MERCURY, INC.
Quality Cost Report
(in thousands)

	This Year	Last Year
Prevention costs:		
Machine maintenance	$ 120	$ 70
Training suppliers	10	—
Quality circles	20	—
Total	150	70
Appraisal costs:		
Incoming inspection	40	20
Final testing	90	80
Total	130	100
Internal failure costs:		
Rework	130	50
Scrap	70	40
Total	200	90
External failure costs:		
Warranty repairs	30	90
Customer returns	80	320
Total	110	410
Total quality cost	$ 590	$ 670
Total production cost	$4,800	$4,200

As they were reviewing the report, Elsoe asked Tran what he now thought of the quality improvement program. Tran replied. "I'm relieved that the new quality improvement program hasn't hurt our bonuses, but the program has increased the workload in the Production Department. It is true that customer returns are way down, but the pagers that were returned by customers to retail outlets were rarely sent back to us for rework."

Required

1. Expand the company's quality cost report by showing the costs in both years as percentages of both total production cost and total quality cost. Carry all computations to one decimal place. By analyzing the report, determine if Mercury, Inc.'s quality improvement program has been successful. *List specific evidence to support your answer.*
2. Do you expect the improvement program as it progresses to continue to increase the workload in the Production Department?
3. Jorge Gomez believed that the quality improvement program was essential and that Mercury, Inc., could no longer afford to ignore the importance of product quality. Discuss how Mercury, Inc., could measure the cost of *not* implementing the quality improvement program.

(CMA, adapted)

Group Exercises

GEB–6 TQM and COQ Total quality management, or TQM, was to North American companies competing in the nineties what it was for Japanese firms throughout the seventies and eighties. The concept of cost of quality (COQ) gives quality a bottom-line discipline that is at the core of many well-managed quality improvement programs (QIP). With a focus on satisfying the customer, those who view quality as a marathon race stand a greater chance of improving market share than do those who view quality as the latest project with a start date and a completion date.

Required

1. Surveys have shown that when financial managers are asked to estimate the total cost of quality (prior to implementing a QIP), half or more estimate that COQ is less than 5% of sales revenue. The reality is that actual COQ is typically 10% to 20% of sales, and in some cases it has exceeded 60% of sales. Why do you think there is such a large gap between the perception and the reality of the quality problem?

2. Why do you think the cost of poor quality reached such an epidemic level before companies were motivated to do something about the problem?

3. What function(s) does COQ reporting play in a quality improvement program?

4. For most companies starting a QIP, investments in prevention and appraisal usually result in major cost savings in other areas. Explain this phenomenon.

5. The traditional view of quality is that the total costs of prevention and appraisal plus internal and external failure costs are minimized at a point somewhere above zero defects. Additional investments in prevention beyond this point would result in savings that are less than the additional investment in prevention. An alternative view of quality is that the total costs of the four categories of quality are minimized at zero defects. Additional investments in prevention will always result in larger reductions in appraisal and failure costs. With the zero defects model, the search for quality improvements is continuous. Explain these two viewpoints.

Company Index

Subject Index